HTML5 AND CSS

Seventh Edition

COMPREHENSIVE

HTML5 AND CSS

Seventh Edition

COMPREHENSIVE

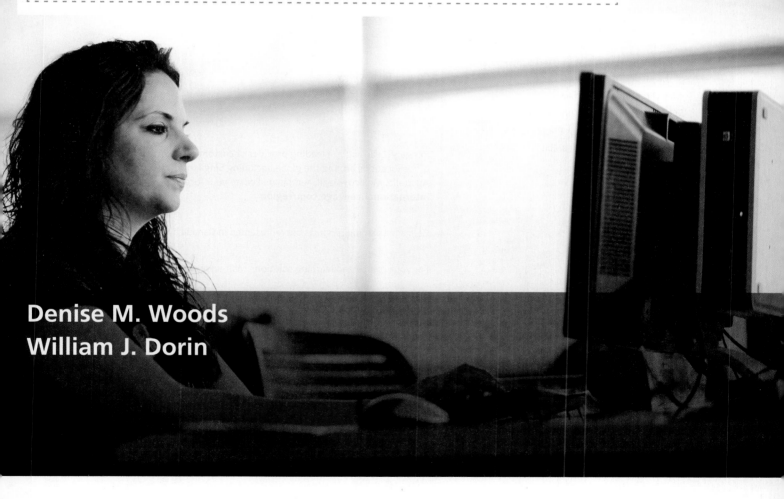

Denise M. Woods
William J. Dorin

COURSE TECHNOLOGY
CENGAGE Learning

Australia • Brazil • Japan • Korea • Mexico • Singapore • Spain • United Kingdom • United States

HTML5 and CSS
Comprehensive, Seventh Edition
Denise M. Woods, William J. Dorin

Vice President, Publisher: Nicole Pinard
Executive Editor: Kathleen McMahon
Product Manager: Nada Jovanovic
Associate Product Manager: Caitlin Womersley
Editorial Assistant: Angela Giannopoulos
Director of Marketing: Elisa Roberts
Associate Marketing Manager: Adrienne Fung
Print Buyer: Julio Esperas
Director of Production: Patty Stephan
Content Project Manager: Jennifer Feltri-George
Development Editor: Karen Stevens
Proofreader: Andrea Schein
Indexer: Michael Brackney
QA Manuscript Reviewers: Jeff Schwartz and Danielle Shaw
Art Director: Marissa Falco
Cover Designer: Lisa Kuhn, Curio Press, LLC
Cover Photo: Tom Kates Photography
Compositor: PreMediaGlobal

For product information and technology assistance, contact us at
Cengage Learning Customer & Sales Support, 1-800-354-9706
For permission to use material from this text or product,
submit all requests online at **cengage.com/permissions**
Further permissions questions can be emailed to
permissionrequest@cengage.com

Library of Congress Control Number: 2012935297

ISBN-13: 978-1-1335-2614-8

ISBN-10: 1-1335-2614-4

Course Technology
20 Channel Center Street
Boston, MA 02210
USA

Cengage Learning is a leading provider of customized learning solutions with office locations around the globe, including Singapore, the United Kingdom, Australia, Mexico, Brazil, and Japan. Locate your local office at: **international.cengage.com/region**

Cengage Learning products are represented in Canada by Nelson Education, Ltd.

For your course and learning solutions, visit **www.cengage.com**

To learn more about Course Technology, visit **www.cengage.com/coursetechnology**

Purchase any of our products at your local collage bookstore or at our preferred online store at **www.CengageBrain.com**

Printed in the United States of America
3 4 5 6 16 15 14

HTML5 AND CSS
Seventh Edition
COMPREHENSIVE

Contents

Preface xiv

HTML5 and CSS

CHAPTER ONE
Introduction to HTML, XHTML, and CSS

Objectives	**HTML 1**
Introduction	**HTML 2**
What Is the Internet?	**HTML 2**
What Is the World Wide Web?	**HTML 3**
Web Servers	HTML 4
Web Site Types and Purposes	HTML 5
Web Browsers	HTML 7
What Is Hypertext Markup Language?	**HTML 8**
HTML Elements	HTML 9
Useful HTML Practices	HTML 10
HTML Versions	HTML 11
Cascading Style Sheets	HTML 11
Document Object Model (DOM)	HTML 12
Extensible Hypertext Markup Language (XHTML)	HTML 12
Tools for Creating HTML Documents	**HTML 13**
Web Development Life Cycle	**HTML 15**
Web Site Planning	HTML 16
Web Site Analysis	HTML 16
Web Site Design and Development	HTML 17
Web Site Testing	HTML 22
Web Site Implementation and Maintenance	HTML 24
Be an Observant Web User	**HTML 25**
Chapter Summary	**HTML 25**
Learn It Online	**HTML 26**
Apply Your Knowledge	**HTML 26**
Extend Your Knowledge	**HTML 27**
Make It Right	**HTML 28**
In the Lab	**HTML 29**
Cases and Places	**HTML 32**

CHAPTER TWO
Creating and Editing a Web Page Using Inline Styles

Objectives	**HTML 33**
Introduction	**HTML 34**
Project — Rock Climbing Fun Web Page	**HTML 34**
Overview	HTML 34
Elements of a Web Page	**HTML 37**
Browser Window Elements	HTML 37
Text Elements	HTML 38
Image Elements	HTML 38
Hyperlink Elements	HTML 38
Defining Web Page Structure	**HTML 39**
Defining the HTML Document	HTML 39
To Start Notepad++	HTML 40
To Enable Word Wrap in Notepad++	HTML 42
To Define the Web Page Structure Using HTML Tags	HTML 42
Formatting the Web Page	HTML 45
Entering Web Page Content	**HTML 46**
To Enter a Paragraph of Text	HTML 48
To Enter a Heading	HTML 49
Using Lists to Present Content	HTML 49
To Create an Unordered List	HTML 51
More About List Formats	HTML 51
Adding a Footer	HTML 53
To Add a Footer	HTML 53
Saving and Organizing HTML Files	**HTML 54**
To Save an HTML File	HTML 55
Using a Browser to View a Web Page	**HTML 58**
To Start a Browser	HTML 58
To View a Web Page in a Browser	HTML 59
To Activate Notepad++	HTML 60
Improving the Appearance of Your Web Page	**HTML 60**
Using Style Sheets	HTML 61
Using Web Page Divisions	HTML 63

Types of Web Page Images HTML 64
Image Attributes HTML 65
Other Visual Enhancements HTML 67
To Add Color to a Web Page Heading HTML 69
To Change the Bulleted List Style HTML 70
To Add a Horizontal Rule HTML 70
To Change the Footer Style HTML 71
To Refresh the View in a Browser HTML 72
Validating and Viewing HTML Code HTML 72
To Validate HTML Code HTML 73
To View HTML Source Code for a Web Page HTML 76
To Print a Web Page and an HTML File HTML 77
Chapter Summary HTML 79
Learn It Online HTML 79
Apply Your Knowledge HTML 80
Extend Your Knowledge HTML 81
Make It Right HTML 82
In the Lab HTML 83
Cases and Places HTML 86

CHAPTER THREE
Creating Web Pages with Links, Images, and Embedded Style Sheets
Objectives HTML 87
Introduction HTML 88
Project — Underwater Tours by Eloise Web Site HTML 88
Overview HTML 89
Using Links on a Web Page HTML 91
Linking to Another Web Page Within the Same Web Site HTML 93
Linking to a Web Page in Another Web Site HTML 94
Linking Within a Web Page HTML 96
Linking to an E-mail Address HTML 96
Creating a Home Page HTML 97
To Start Notepad++ HTML 98
To Add a Banner Image HTML 100
To Add Paragraphs of Text HTML 102
Adding a Text Link to Another Web Page Within the Same Web Site HTML 103
To Add a Text Link to Another Web Page Within the Same Web Site HTML 104
Adding an E-mail Link HTML 105
To Add an E-mail Link HTML 105
Adding Other Information to an E-mail Link HTML 106
To Add a Text Link to a Web Page in Another Web Site HTML 107
Using Absolute and Relative Paths HTML 107
Adding Interest and Focus with Styles HTML 110
Adding Interest and Focus with HTML Tags HTML 110
Style Sheet Precedence Review HTML 112
Using Embedded Style Sheets HTML 112
To Add Embedded Style Sheet Statements HTML 115
To Add an Inline Style for Color HTML 117
To Save an HTML File HTML 117
Validating the HTML, Viewing the Web Page, and Testing Links HTML 117
To Validate HTML Code HTML 118
To Print an HTML File HTML 119
To Test Links on a Web Page HTML 121
To Print a Web Page HTML 123
Editing the Second Web Page HTML 123
To Open an HTML File HTML 125
Working with Classes in Style Statements HTML 126
Adding an Image with Wrapped Text HTML 128
Using Thumbnail Images HTML 130
To Wrap Text Around Images Using CSS Classes HTML 132
To Clear Text Wrapping HTML 134
Adding Links Within a Web Page HTML 135
To Set Link Targets HTML 136
To Add Links to Link Targets Within a Web Page HTML 137
To Add Links to a Target at the Top of the Page HTML 138
To Copy and Paste HTML Code HTML 138
To Add an Image Link to a Web Page HTML 139
To View and Test a Web Page HTML 141
Chapter Summary HTML 142
Learn It Online HTML 142
Apply Your Knowledge HTML 143
Extend Your Knowledge HTML 144
Make It Right HTML 146
In the Lab HTML 147
Cases and Places HTML 152

CHAPTER FOUR
Creating Tables in a Web Site Using an External Style Sheet
Objectives HTML 155
Introduction HTML 156
Project — Oceanside Hotel and Sports Club Web Site HTML 156
Overview HTML 158
Planning and Designing a Multipage Web Site HTML 159
Creating Web Pages with Tables HTML 159
Table Elements HTML 161
Adding Style to Table Elements HTML 162
Table Borders, Headers, Captions, and Rules HTML 163

Determining the Need for, Planning, and Coding a Table HTML 164
Determining If a Table Is Needed HTML 164
Planning the Table HTML 165
Coding the Table HTML 166
Table Tag Attributes HTML 167
Creating a Home Page with Banner Logo and Borderless Navigation Table HTML 169
To Insert, Center, and Style an Image with a Box-Shadow HTML 172
Using a Table to Create a Horizontal Navigation Bar HTML 174
To Create a Horizontal Menu Bar with Image Links HTML 175
Viewing the Web Page and Testing Links HTML 178
External Style Sheets HTML 179
Adding an External Style Sheet HTML 181
To Create an External Style Sheet HTML 182
Examining the External Style Sheet HTML 184
Linking to the External Style Sheet HTML 187
To Link to an External Style Sheet HTML 187
Validating and Printing the HTML, Viewing the Web Page, and Testing Links HTML 188
Creating a Second Web Page HTML 190
Adding a Table with Borders HTML 193
To Create a Table with Borders and Insert Text HTML 194
Adding a Link, Border Spacing, Padding, and Row Color HTML 198
To Add Border Spacing, Padding, and Row Color to a Table HTML 200
Adding a Caption and Spanning Rows HTML 201
To Add a Table Caption HTML 204
To Create the Headings That Span Rows HTML 204
To Add the Bolder Class to Data Cells HTML 206
Chapter Summary HTML 208
Learn It Online HTML 208
Apply Your Knowledge HTML 209
Extend Your Knowledge HTML 210
Make It Right HTML 211
In the Lab HTML 212
Cases and Places HTML 217

SPECIAL FEATURE 1
Attracting Visitors to Your Web Site
Objectives HTML 219
Introduction HTML 220
Project — Attracting Visitors HTML 220
Overview HTML 220
Adding Keywords HTML 222
To Open the File HTML 223
Meta Names HTML 223
To Add Keywords HTML 224
To Add a Description HTML 225
Determining a Domain Name HTML 226
Check Domain Name Availability HTML 226
Finding a Web Hosting Site HTML 227
Publishing Your Web Site HTML 227
Marketing Your Web Site HTML 228
Registering with Search Engines HTML 228
To Register Your Web Site with Search Engines HTML 229
Feature Summary HTML 230
In the Lab HTML 230

CHAPTER FIVE
Creating an Image Map
Objectives HTML 233
Introduction HTML 234
Project — Lake Tahanna Tourism HTML 234
Overview HTML 236
Introduction to Image Maps HTML 237
Using Image Maps HTML 237
Server-Side vs. Client-Side Image Maps HTML 242
Creating an Image Map HTML 243
Selecting Images HTML 243
Sketching the Borders of Hotspots HTML 244
Mapping Image Coordinates HTML 246
Coding the Map HTML 248
Using Paint to Locate X- and Y-Coordinates HTML 249
To Start Paint HTML 249
The Paint Window HTML 250
To Open an Image File in Paint HTML 251
Locating X- and Y-Coordinates of an Image HTML 251
To Locate X- and Y-Coordinates of an Image HTML 252
Other Software Tools HTML 254
Creating the Home Page HTML 255
Inserting an Image to Use as an Image Map HTML 257
To Insert an Image to Use as an Image Map HTML 258
Inserting Special Characters HTML 260
To Insert a Special Character HTML 261
Coding the Image Map Using HTML Tags and Attributes HTML 263
To Create an Image Map HTML 264
Viewing the Web Page and Testing Links HTML 265
Creating an External Style Sheet HTML 268
To Create an External Style Sheet HTML 268
Chapter Summary HTML 271
Learn It Online HTML 272
Apply Your Knowledge HTML 272
Extend Your Knowledge HTML 274
Make It Right HTML 275
In the Lab HTML 276
Cases and Places HTML 280

CHAPTER SIX
Creating a Form on a Web Page

Objectives **HTML 283**
Introduction **HTML 284**
Project — Creating Forms on a Web Page **HTML 284**
Overview HTML 286
Web Page Forms **HTML 287**
Input Controls HTML 287
HTML Tags Used to Create Forms HTML 291
Attributes of HTML Tags Used to Create Forms HTML 291
Creating a Form on a Web Page **HTML 292**
Creating a Form and Identifying the Form Process HTML 293
To Create a Form and Identify the Form Process HTML 294
To Change the Text Message HTML 295
Adding Text Boxes HTML 296
To Add Text Boxes HTML 296
Adding Check Boxes HTML 297
To Add Check Boxes HTML 298
Adding Radio Buttons HTML 298
To Add Radio Buttons HTML 299
Adding a Selection Menu HTML 299
To Add a Selection Menu HTML 300
Adding a Textarea Box HTML 303
To Add a Textarea Box HTML 303
Adding Submit and Reset Buttons HTML 304
To Add Submit and Reset Buttons HTML 305
Organizing a Form Using Form Groupings **HTML 306**
To Add Fieldset Controls to Create Form Groupings HTML 307
Adding an Embedded Style Sheet HTML 308
Chapter Summary **HTML 314**
Learn It Online **HTML 314**
Apply Your Knowledge **HTML 315**
Extend Your Knowledge **HTML 316**
Make It Right **HTML 317**
In the Lab **HTML 318**
Cases and Places **HTML 321**

CHAPTER SEVEN
Using Advanced Cascading Style Sheets

Objectives **HTML 323**
Introduction **HTML 324**
Project — Using Advanced Cascading Style Sheets **HTML 324**
Overview HTML 326
Using Style Sheets **HTML 327**
Style Sheet Precedence Review HTML 330
Adding Style Sheets to the Jared Adam's Adventure Travel Site **HTML 330**
Adding a Navigation Bar with an Embedded Style Sheet **HTML 332**
Setting the Body Style and Link Style, and Adding a Drop-down Menu HTML 333
To Add an Embedded Style Sheet HTML 340
Adding Pop-up Images with an External Style Sheet **HTML 342**
Structuring the Web Page HTML 343
Creating a Pop-up Image Using Cascading Style Sheets HTML 343
To Create an External Style Sheet HTML 345
Linking to an External Style Sheet HTML 346
To Link to an External Style Sheet HTML 346
Creating an External Style Sheet for Printing **HTML 348**
Understanding the Page Box Model HTML 348
To Create an External Style Sheet for Printing HTML 348
Chapter Summary **HTML 351**
Learn It Online **HTML 351**
Apply Your Knowledge **HTML 352**
Extend Your Knowledge **HTML 353**
Make It Right **HTML 354**
In the Lab **HTML 355**
Cases and Places **HTML 358**

CHAPTER EIGHT
Adding Multimedia Content to Web Pages

Objectives **HTML 361**
Introduction **HTML 362**
Project — Adding Multimedia to an English Literature Class Web Site **HTML 362**
Overview HTML 362
Using Multimedia **HTML 364**
Creating or Finding Multimedia Files HTML 366
Embedded vs. External Multimedia HTML 366
Media Players and Plug-Ins HTML 367
HTML5 and Multimedia HTML 368
Audio and Video File Formats HTML 368
Adding an Audio File to a Web Page **HTML 369**
New HTML5 Multimedia Tags HTML 370
The Object Tag HTML 370
Object Tag Parameters HTML 372
The HMTL5 <audio> Tag HTML 373
To Add an Audio Clip to a Web Page HTML 376
To Validate and View a Web Page Using ActiveX Controls HTML 377
Adding a Video Clip to a Web Page **HTML 380**
The HTML5 <video> Tag HTML 381
Using the <video> Tag HTML 381
To Add a Video Clip to a Web Page HTML 383

Chapter Summary **HTML 385**
Learn It Online **HTML 386**
Apply Your Knowledge **HTML 386**
Extend Your Knowledge **HTML 387**
Make It Right **HTML 388**
In the Lab **HTML 389**
Cases and Places **HTML 392**

SPECIAL FEATURE 2
Converting Frames on Your Web Site

Objectives **HTML 393**
Introduction **HTML 394**
Project — Converting Frames **HTML 394**
Overview HTML 394
The Frame Definition File **HTML 396**
To View a Web Site with Frames HTML 398
Frame Layouts **HTML 399**
Determining a Conversion Strategy **HTML 401**
To Copy HTML Code for a Navigation Bar HTML 402
To Paste Code into the Home Page and Edit the Code HTML 403
To Copy and Paste Code into the Schedule and Contact Web Pages HTML 404
Feature Summary **HTML 405**
In the Lab **HTML 406**

CHAPTER NINE
Integrating JavaScript and HTML5

Objectives **HTML 409**
Introduction **HTML 410**
Project — Midwest Bridal Expo Web Page **HTML 410**
Overview HTML 410
JavaScript **HTML 412**
User-Defined Functions HTML 414
To Enter a <div> Tag Container HTML 416
Writing User-Defined Functions HTML 416
Inserting <script> Tags in the <head> Section HTML 417
To Enter the Start <script> and Comment Tags HTML 418
Using JavaScript Variables HTML 418
Extracting the Current System Date HTML 420
To Extract the Current System Date Using the Date() Object HTML 423
Calculating the Number of Days Until a Future Event HTML 424
To Calculate the Number of Days to a Future Date HTML 425
Displaying Text and Variable Values to a Web Page with innerHTML HTML 426
To Display Text and Variable Values to a Web Page Using innerHTML HTML 427
Changing the Color of the Browser Scroll Bar HTML 428
To Enter the User-Defined Function to Change the Browser Scroll Bar Color HTML 428
Using the selectedIndex Property and the Location Object to Link to a New URL HTML 429
To Enter the User-Defined Function to Link to a New URL Using the Drop-Down Menu HTML 431
Displaying the Date the Document Was Last Modified HTML 432
To Include the Date Last Modified and a Copyright Message in a Text String HTML 433
Completing the JavaScript Section HTML 433
To Enter the End Comment and End </script> Tags HTML 434
Calling JavaScript Functions Using Event Handlers **HTML 435**
To Associate User-Defined Functions with the OnLoad Event HTML 435
To Associate a User-Defined Function with the OnChange Event HTML 436
Chapter Summary **HTML 439**
Learn It Online **HTML 440**
Apply Your Knowledge **HTML 440**
Extend Your Knowledge **HTML 442**
Make It Right **HTML 444**
In the Lab **HTML 446**
Cases and Places **HTML 451**

CHAPTER TEN
Creating Pop-Up Windows, Adding Scrolling Messages, and Validating Forms

Objectives **HTML 453**
Introduction **HTML 454**
Project — Shoreline State Bank Loan Calculator **HTML 454**
Overview HTML 456
Inserting a Scrolling Message on a Web Page **HTML 457**
To Create a Form Text Field to Display a Scrolling Message HTML 458
Creating the scrollingMsg() User-Defined Function HTML 459
To Create the scrollingMsg() User-Defined Function HTML 460
To Enter the Code to Increment the Position Locator Variable HTML 461

To Enter an if Statement HTML 463
To Add the setTimeout() Method to Create a Recursive Call HTML 464
Adding an Onload Event Handler HTML 465
To Enter the onLoad Event Handler to Call the scrollingMsg() Function HTML 466
Adding a Loan Calculator with Validation HTML 468
Validating Forms Using Nested if...else Statements HTML 469
Using Built-In Functions to Validate Data HTML 471
To Add the validSalesAmt() Function with Nested if...else Statements to Validate Form Data HTML 474
To Enter the onBlur Event Handler to Call the validSalesAmt() Function HTML 475
Validating the Interest Rate and the Number of Years for the Loan HTML 475
To Enter the CalcLoanAmt() User-Defined Function HTML 476
To Enter an onClick Event Handler to Call the CalcLoanAmt() Function HTML 477
Adding the Monthly Payment Calculation HTML 479
To Enter Code to Call the monthlyPmt() Function HTML 479
To Create the monthlyPmt() Function HTML 481
Formatting the Monthly Payment Output as Currency HTML 482
To Enter the dollarFormat() Function HTML 484
To Enter an if...else Statement and while Loop to Extract the Dollar Portion of the Output and Insert Commas HTML 486
To Reconstruct the Formatted Output and Return the Formatted Value HTML 487
To Pass the Monthly Payment Value to the dollarFormat() Function HTML 487
Adding a Pop-Up Window HTML 488
To Enter the popUpNotice() Function to Open a Pop-Up Window HTML 490
To Add the Event Handler to Call the popUpNotice() Function HTML 490
Adding Copyright and the Date Last Modified HTML 491
To Display the Date Last Modified Using the substring() Method HTML 492
Chapter Summary HTML 494
Learn It Online HTML 494
Apply Your Knowledge HTML 495
Extend Your Knowledge HTML 496
Make It Right HTML 498
In the Lab HTML 499
Cases and Places HTML 505

CHAPTER ELEVEN
Using DOM to Enhance Web Pages

Objectives HTML 507
Introduction HTML 508
Project — The Hickory Oaks Forest Preserve Web Site HTML 508
Overview HTML 510
The Document Object Model (DOM) HTML 510
Creating the Navigation Bar HTML 512
To Create an HTML Table to Contain the Navigation Bar HTML 513
Creating the JavaScript User-Defined Functions for the Image Rollovers HTML 514
To Create User-Defined Functions for Image Rollovers HTML 516
To Enter Mouse Event Handlers to Invoke User-Defined Functions HTML 516
To Save and Test the Hickory Oaks Forest Preserve Web Page Navigation Bar HTML 517
Creating the User-Defined Function Random Number Generator HTML 519
To Enter a Random Number Generator User-Defined Function HTML 521
To Enter Code to Show Copyright Information and Date Last Modified HTML 521
To Enter onLoad Event Handlers in the <body> Tag HTML 522
Creating a Slide Show on the Nature Center Web Page HTML 524
Creating and Placing an Image Object HTML 525
To Create an Image Object HTML 525
Creating the Slide Show User-Defined Function HTML 526
To Create a User-Defined Function to Add a Slide Show HTML 527
Adding a Floating Image to the Gift Shop Web Page HTML 529
Entering the floatingImage(), stopFloat(), and restartFloat()Functions HTML 531
To Enter the floatingImage() Function HTML 531
To Enter the stopFloat() Function HTML 532
To Enter the restartFloat() Function HTML 532
To Enter the coupon() Function HTML 533
To Enter an Embedded Style Sheet to Format the Floating Image HTML 534
Entering an Image Object for the Floating Image Using the <div> and <img> Tags HTML 534
To Enter <div> and <img> Tags for the Floating Image HTML 535
To Add an OnLoad Event Handler to Call the floatingImage() Function HTML 535

Creating Pop-up Captions on the Trails Web Page **HTML 537**
Creating the popupCaption() User-Defined Function HTML 538
To Enter the popupCaption() Function HTML 540
Adding an Embedded Style Sheet Using id and Class Properties HTML 540
To Enter Cascading Style Sheet id and Class Selectors for the Pop-up Captions HTML 543
To Add Links and Event Handlers to Call the popupCaption() Function HTML 543
Entering the <div> Tags Containing Pop-up Caption Text HTML 545
To Enter <div> Tags Containing Pop-up Caption Text HTML 545
Chapter Summary **HTML 547**
Learn It Online **HTML 548**
Apply Your Knowledge **HTML 548**
Extend Your Knowledge **HTML 550**
Make It Right **HTML 552**
In the Lab **HTML 553**
Cases and Places **HTML 560**

CHAPTER TWELVE
Creating and Using XML Documents

Objectives **HTML 561**
Introduction **HTML 562**
Project — Creating an XML Document **HTML 562**
Overview HTML 564
XML vs. HTML5 **HTML 564**
Designing XML Documents **HTML 565**
XML Standards HTML 565
Syntax Rules HTML 566
Creating a Well-Formed XML Document **HTML 568**
To Start Notepad++ and Create a New XML Schema Document HTML 570
Creating an XML Schema Definition HTML 570
To Enter the Code for the Prolog, Root, Annotation, and Documentation Elements HTML 573
Defining the Parent Element HTML 574
To Enter Code for the <products> Element HTML 574
Defining and Inserting the Child Elements HTML 575
To Enter Code for the <complexType> Element HTML 575
To Enter Code for the Child Group Elements HTML 576
To Save and Validate an XML Schema Definition File HTML 577
Creating the Prolog in an XML Document HTML 578
To Create a New XML Document and Enter the Prolog Code HTML 579
Creating the Document Instance in an XML Document HTML 580
To Start Entering a Document Instance in an XML Document HTML 580
To Finish Entering a Document Instance in an XML Document HTML 581
To Correct a Tag Error and Retest an XML Document HTML 584
To Validate XML and XSD Files HTML 585
Formatting an XML Document Using an XSL Style Sheet **HTML 587**
Creating an XSL Style Sheet HTML 588
To Start Creating an XSL Style Sheet HTML 589
To Enter HTML Code to Display the Banner and Header Text in a Web Page HTML 590
Using XSL Style Sheet Tags HTML 590
To Add XSL Style Sheet Tags HTML 591
Linking an XSL Style Sheet to an XML Document HTML 593
To Link an XSL Style Sheet to an XML Document HTML 594
To Save and Test an XML Document Formatted Using an XSL Style Sheet HTML 594
Using an HTML Table with Paging to Display XML Data **HTML 595**
To Enter Code to Link an XML Document with an HTML Web Page HTML 597
Adding Navigation Controls HTML 597
To Enter Code to Add Navigation Buttons HTML 597
To Enter <table> Table Header and Row Tags HTML 598
To Enter <tr> Tags and Attribute Values to Bind XML Elements to a Table HTML 600
To Save the HTML File and Test the Web Page HTML 601
Using JavaScript to Search an XML Document and Display Results on a Web Page **HTML 602**
To Enter Code to Bind an XML Document with an HTML Web Page HTML 603
To Enter Code for the <input> and <button> Elements HTML 603
To Enter an HTML <div> Tag Container HTML 604
Creating the JavaScript User-defined Functions, findItem() and keyPressed() HTML 605
To Enter Code for the findItem() User-defined Function HTML 605
Searching the Recordset Values and Outputting Results HTML 606
To Enter Code to Search the Recordset Values and Build the Output String HTML 607
To Enter Code to Complete the findItem() Function HTML 608

To Enter Code for the keyPressed() Function HTML 608
To Enter Code for the clearField() Function HTML 609
To Save and Test the HTML Document in the Browser HTML 610
To Verify the Links on the Calumet Restaurant Supply Home Page HTML 611
Chapter Summary HTML 612
Learn It Online HTML 613
Apply Your Knowledge HTML 613
Extend Your Knowledge HTML 615
Make It Right HTML 617
In the Lab HTML 619
Cases and Places HTML 624

Appendices

APPENDIX A
HTML Quick Reference
HTML Coding Standards APP 1
HTML Tags and Attributes APP 2

APPENDIX B
Browser-Safe Color Palette
Browser-Safe Colors APP 15

APPENDIX C
Accessibility Standards and the Web
Making the Web Accessible APP 17
Section 508 Guidelines Examples APP 17
WAI Guidelines APP 20

APPENDIX D
CSS Properties and Values
CSS Concepts and Terminology APP 25
CSS Properties APP 27
Acceptable Units of Measure APP 27
Animation Properties APP 28
Background and Color Properties APP 28
Border Properties APP 29
Box Properties APP 30
Classification Properties APP 31
Color Properties APP 31
Content for Paged Media Properties APP 32
Dimension Properties APP 32
Flexible Box Properties APP 33
Font Properties APP 33
Generated Content Properties APP 34
Grid Properties APP 35
Hyperlink Properties APP 35
Linebox Properties APP 35
List Properties APP 36
Margin and Padding Properties APP 37
Marquee Properties APP 37
Multicolumn Properties APP 37
Paged Media Properties APP 38
Positioning Properties APP 38
Print Properties APP 40
Ruby Properties APP 41
Speech Properties APP 41
Table Properties APP 42
Text Properties APP 42
2D/3D Transform Properties APP 44
Transition Properties APP 44
User-Interface Properties APP 45

APPENDIX E
Publishing Web Pages to a Web Server
Choosing a Web Host APP 47
Uploading Files to the Host APP 47

APPENDIX F
Symbols and Characters Quick Reference
Using Symbols and Special Characters APP 49

APPENDIX G
JavaScript Quick Reference
JavaScript Introduction APP 51
Why Use JavaScript? APP 52
Reserved Words APP 52
Data Types APP 53
Variable Names APP 53
Literals APP 54
Escape Sequences in Strings APP 54
Operators APP 55
Operator Types APP 55
Order of Precedence APP 56
JavaScript Statements APP 57
Event Handlers APP 58
Objects APP 60
Date Object APP 61
Document Object APP 62

Assigning Color to an Object APP 63
Form Object APP 63
History Object APP 64
Image Object APP 64
JSON Object APP 64
Math Object APP 65
Location Object APP 66
Navigator Object APP 66
Window and Frame Objects APP 67
Number Object APP 68
Function Object APP 69
Screen Object APP 69
Boolean Object APP 70
Array Object APP 70
String Object APP 71
Regular Expression APP 72
Global Functions APP 72

APPENDIX H
XML Quick Reference
What Is XML? APP 73
Well-Formed and Valid XML Documents APP 73
XML Processing Instructions APP 74
XML Element and Attribute Rules APP 74
XML Schema Definition (XSD) APP 75
Simple Types APP 77
Complex Types APP 79
XSL Style Sheets APP 79
Document Type Definition (DTD) APP 80
Attribute List Declarations APP 82
Entity Declarations APP 83
Unparsed Entities and Notation Declarations APP 84

Index IND 1

Preface

The Shelly Cashman Series® offers the finest textbooks in computer education. We are proud that our previous HTML books have been so well received. With each new edition of our HTML books, we have made significant improvements based on the comments made by instructors and students. The *HTML5 and CSS, Seventh Edition* books continue with the innovation, quality, and reliability you have come to expect from the Shelly Cashman Series.

For this text, the Shelly Cashman Series development team carefully reviewed its pedagogy and analyzed its effectiveness in teaching today's student. Students today read less, but need to retain more. They need not only to be able to perform skills, but to retain those skills and know how to apply them to different settings. Today's students need to be continually engaged and challenged to retain what they're learning.

With this HTML book, we continue our commitment to focusing on the user and how they learn best.

Objectives of This Textbook

HTML5 and CSS: Comprehensive, Seventh Edition is intended for use in a three-unit course that presents an in-depth coverage of HTML and basic Web design techniques. No experience with Web page development or computer programming is required. Specific objectives of this book are as follows:

- To teach the fundamentals of developing Web pages using a comprehensive Web development life cycle
- To acquaint students with the HTML and CSS languages and creating Web pages suitable for course work, professional purposes, and personal use
- To expose students to common Web page formats and functions
- To promote curiosity and independent exploration of World Wide Web resources
- To develop an exercise-oriented approach that allows students to learn by example
- To encourage independent study and help those who are learning how to create Web pages in a distance education environment
- To acquaint students with the XHTML guidelines
- To illustrate how to create dynamic Web pages and add functionality using JavaScript and the Document Object Model (DOM)
- To show the benefits of XML

The Shelly Cashman Approach

A Proven Pedagogy with an Emphasis on Project Planning
Each chapter presents a practical problem to be solved, within a project planning framework. The project orientation is strengthened by the use of Plan Ahead boxes that encourage critical thinking about how to proceed at various points in the project. Step-by-step instructions with supporting screens guide students through the steps. Instructional steps are supported by the Q&A, Experimental Step, and BTW features.

A Visually Engaging Book that Maintains Student Interest
The step-by-step tasks, with supporting figures, provide a rich visual experience for the student. Call-outs on the screens that present both explanatory and navigational information provide students with information they need when they need to know it.

Supporting Reference Materials (Appendices)
The appendices provide additional information about HTML5 and CSS topics, with appendices such as the HTML Quick Reference, Browser-Safe Color Palette, Accessibility Standards and the Web, CSS Properties and Values, and Publishing Web Pages to a Web Server.

Integration of the World Wide Web
The World Wide Web is integrated into the HTML5 and CSS learning experience by (1) BTW annotations; and (2) the Learn It Online section for each chapter.

End-of-Chapter Student Activities
Extensive end-of-chapter activities provide a variety of reinforcement opportunities for students where they can apply and expand their skills through individual and group work.

Online Companion

The Online Companion includes Learn It Online exercises for each chapter, as well as @Source links, Your Turn links, and Q&As. To access these course materials, please visit **www.cengagebrain.com**. At the CengageBrain.com home page, search for *HTML5 and CSS 7th Edition* using the search box at the top of the page. This will take you to the product page for this book. On the product page, click the Access Now button below the Study Tools heading.

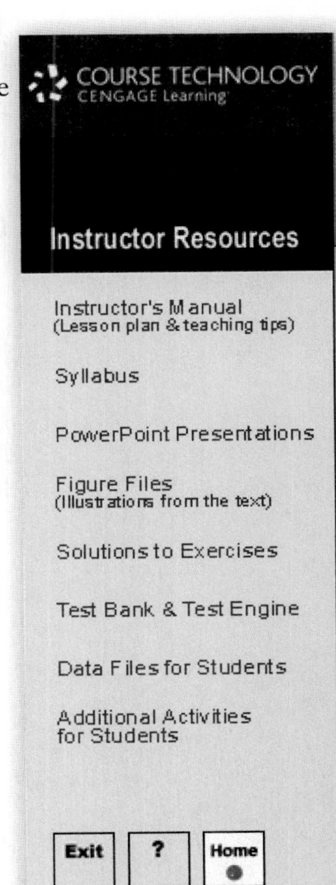

Instructor Resources

The Instructor Resources include both teaching and testing aids and can be accessed via CD-ROM or at login.cengage.com.

Instructor's Manual Includes lecture notes summarizing the chapter sections, figures and boxed elements found in every chapter, teacher tips, classroom activities, lab activities, and quick quizzes in Microsoft Word files.

Syllabus Easily customizable sample syllabi that cover policies, assignments, exams, and other course information.

Figure Files Illustrations for every figure in the textbook in electronic form.

PowerPoint Presentations A multimedia lecture presentation system that provides slides for each chapter. Presentations are based on chapter objectives.

Solutions to Exercises Includes solutions for all end-of-chapter and chapter reinforcement exercises.

Test Bank & Test Engine Test Banks include 112 questions for every chapter, featuring objective-based and critical thinking question types, and including page number references. Also included is the test engine, ExamView, the ultimate tool for your objective-based testing needs.

Data Files for Students Includes all the files that are required by students to complete the exercises.

Additional Activities for Students Consists of Chapter Reinforcement Exercises, which are true/false, multiple-choice, and short answer questions that help students gain confidence in the material learned.

SAM: Skills Assessment Manager

SAM 2010 is designed to help bring students from the classroom to the real world. It allows students to train on and test important computer skills in an active, hands-on environment. SAM's easy-to-use system includes powerful interactive exams, training, and projects on the most commonly used Microsoft Office applications. SAM simulates the Microsoft Office 2010 application environment, allowing students to demonstrate their knowledge and think through the skills by performing real-world tasks such as bolding word text or setting up slide transitions. Add in live-in-the-application projects, and students are on their way to truly learning and applying skills to business-centric documents. Designed to be used with the Shelly Cashman Series, SAM includes handy page references so that students can print helpful study guides that match the Shelly Cashman textbooks used in class. For instructors, SAM also includes robust scheduling and reporting features.

WebTUTOR™

Content for Online Learning

Course Technology has partnered with the leading distance learning solution providers and class-management platforms today. To access this material, Instructors will visit our password-protected instructor resources available at login.cengage.com. Instructor resources include the following: additional case projects, sample syllabi, PowerPoint presentations per chapter, and more. For additional information or for an instructor username and password, please contact your sales representative. For students to access this material, they must have purchased a WebTutor PIN-code specific to this title and your campus platform. The resources for students may include (based on instructor preferences), but are not limited to: topic review, review questions and practice tests.

course|notes™
quick reference guide

CourseNotes

Course Technology's CourseNotes are six-panel quick reference cards that reinforce the most important concepts and features of a software application in a visual and user-friendly format. CourseNotes serve as a great reference tool for students, both during and after the course. CourseNotes are available for Adobe Dreamweaver CS5, Web 2.0: Recharged, Buyer's Guide: Tips for Purchasing a New Computer, Best Practices in Social Networking, Hot Topics in Technology and many more. Visit **www.cengagebrain.com** to learn more!

Guided Tours

Add excitement and interactivity to your classroom with "*A Guided Tour*" product line. Play one of the brief mini-movies to spice up your lecture and spark classroom discussion. Or, assign a movie for homework and ask students to complete the correlated assignment that accompanies each topic. "*A Guided Tour*" product line takes the prep-work out of providing your students with information on new technologies and software applications and helps keep students engaged with content relevant to their lives; all in under an hour!

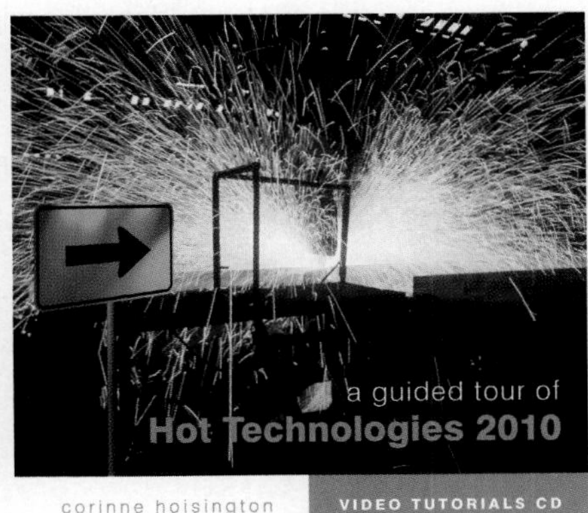

About Our Covers

The Shelly Cashman Series is continually updating our approach and content to reflect the way today's students learn and experience new technology. This focus on student success is reflected on our covers, which feature real students from Bryant University using the Shelly Cashman Series in their courses, and reflect the varied ages and backgrounds of the students learning with our books. When you use the Shelly Cashman Series, you can be assured that you are learning computer skills using the most effective courseware available.

Textbook Walk-Through

The Shelly Cashman Series Pedagogy: Project-Based — Step-by-Step — Variety of Assessments

Plan Ahead boxes prepare students to create successful projects by encouraging them to think strategically about what they are trying to accomplish before they begin working.

Plan Ahead

General Project Guidelines

When creating a Web page, the actions you perform and decisions you make will affect the appearance and characteristics of the finished page. As you create a Web page, such as the project shown in Figure 2–1 on the previous page, you should follow these general guidelines:

1. **Complete Web page planning.** Before developing a Web page, you must know the purpose of the Web site, identify the users of the site and their computing environments, and decide who owns the information on the Web page.
2. **Analyze the need for the Web page.** In the analysis phase of the Web development life cycle, you should analyze what content to include on the Web page. In this phase, you determine the tasks and the information that the users need. Refer to Table 1–4 on page HTML 15 in Chapter 1 for information on the phases of the Web development life cycle.
3. **Choose the content for the Web page.** Once you have completed the analysis, you need to determine what content to include on the Web page. Follow the *less is more* principle. The less text, the more likely the Web page will be read. Use as few words as possible to make a point.
4. **Determine the file naming convention that you will use for this Web page.** Before you start creating and saving files, you should decide on a standard way of naming your files. Should you use the .htm or .html extension? As explained later in the chapter, you use the .htm extension when the host Web server only allows short file names. You use .html when the host Web server allows long file names. What name should you give your file to indicate the file's content or purpose? For instance, naming a Web page page1.html does not describe what that Web page is; a more descriptive name is helpful in development of the Web site.
5. **Determine where to save the Web page.** You can store a Web page permanently, or **save** it, on a variety of storage media, including a hard disk, USB flash drive, CD, or DVD. Your instructor or the company for whom you are developing the Web page may have specific storage media requirements.
6. **Determine what folder structure to use on your storage device.** Once you have determined the storage media to use, you should also determine folder location, structure, and names on which to save the Web page. This should be done before you start to save any of your files.

...ormat various elements of the Web page. The overall appearance of a ...cantly affects its ability to communicate clearly. Examples of how you ...ppearance, or **format**, of the Web page include adding an image, color ... horizontal rules.

...graphical images. Eye-catching graphical images help convey the Web ...ssage and add visual interest. Graphics can be used to show a product, ... benefit, or visually convey a message that is not expressed easily ...

...to position and how to format the graphical images. The position and ...aphical images should grab the attention of viewers and draw them ... Web page.

...ge for W3C compliance. An important part of Web development ...re that your Web page follows standards. The World Wide Web ...C) has an online validator that allows you to test your Web page and ...ny errors.

...more specific details concerning the above guidelines are presented ... in the chapter. The chapter will also identify the actions performed ...egarding these guidelines during the creation of the Web page shown

Step-by-step instructions now provide a context beyond the point-and-click. Each step provides information on why students are performing each task, or what will occur as a result.

HTML Chapter 2

To Save an HTML File

You have entered a lot of text while creating this project and do not want to risk losing the work you have done so far. Also, to view HTML in a browser, you must save the file. The following steps show how to save an HTML file.

1

- With a USB flash drive connected to one of the computer's USB ports, click File on the Notepad++ menu bar (Figure 2–17).

File menu

Save As command

File menu options

recently opened files display in this section

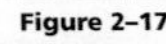

Figure 2–17

2

- Click Save As on the File menu to display the Save As dialog box (Figure 2–18).

Q&A

Do I have to save to a USB flash drive?

No. You can save to any device or folder. A folder is a specific location on a storage medium. Use the same process, but select your device or folder.

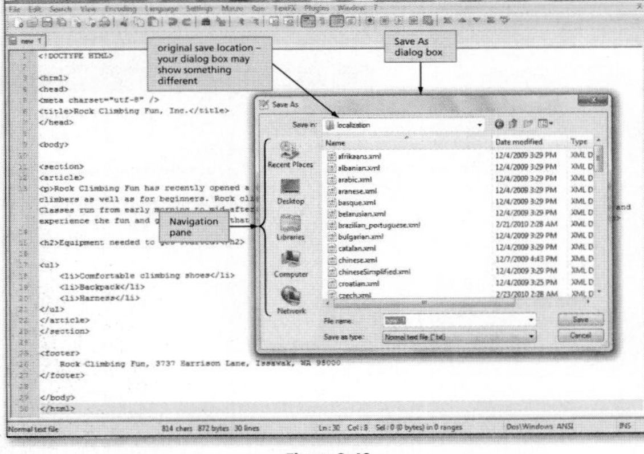

Figure 2–18

Textbook Walk-Through

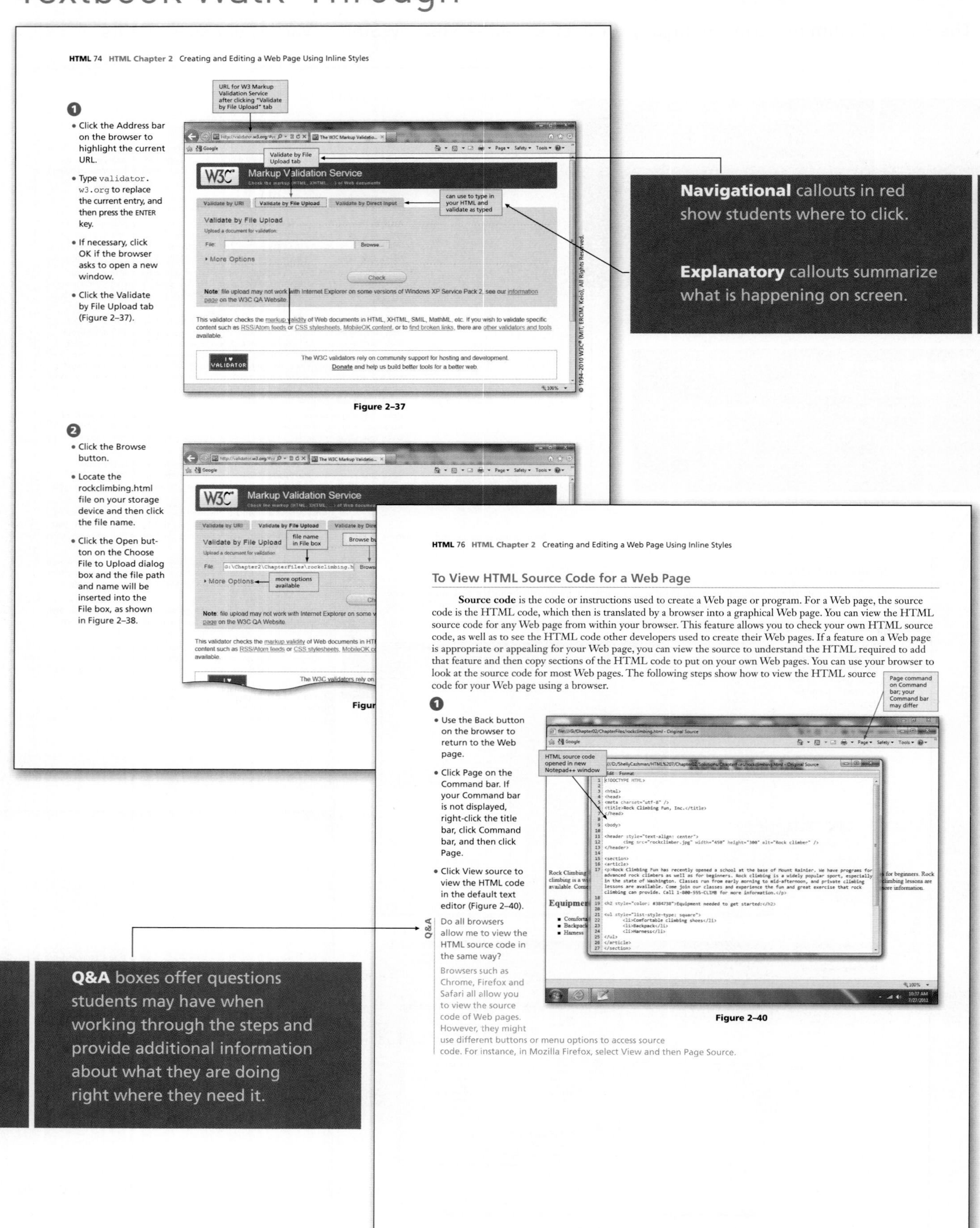

HTML 74 HTML Chapter 2 Creating and Editing a Web Page Using Inline Styles

1
- Click the Address bar on the browser to highlight the current URL.
- Type `validator.w3.org` to replace the current entry, and then press the ENTER key.
- If necessary, click OK if the browser asks to open a new window.
- Click the Validate by File Upload tab (Figure 2–37).

Figure 2–37

2
- Click the Browse button.
- Locate the rockclimbing.html file on your storage device and then click the file name.
- Click the Open button on the Choose File to Upload dialog box and the file path and name will be inserted into the File box, as shown in Figure 2–38.

Figure 2–38

Navigational callouts in red show students where to click.

Explanatory callouts summarize what is happening on screen.

HTML 76 HTML Chapter 2 Creating and Editing a Web Page Using Inline Styles

To View HTML Source Code for a Web Page

Source code is the code or instructions used to create a Web page or program. For a Web page, the source code is the HTML code, which then is translated by a browser into a graphical Web page. You can view the HTML source code for any Web page from within your browser. This feature allows you to check your own HTML source code, as well as to see the HTML code other developers used to create their Web pages. If a feature on a Web page is appropriate or appealing for your Web page, you can view the source to understand the HTML required to add that feature and then copy sections of the HTML code to put on your own Web pages. You can use your browser to look at the source code for most Web pages. The following steps show how to view the HTML source code for your Web page using a browser.

1
- Use the Back button on the browser to return to the Web page.
- Click Page on the Command bar. If your Command bar is not displayed, right-click the title bar, click Command bar, and then click Page.
- Click View source to view the HTML code in the default text editor (Figure 2–40).

Figure 2–40

Q&A Do all browsers allow me to view the HTML source code in the same way?
Browsers such as Chrome, Firefox and Safari all allow you to view the source code of Web pages. However, they might use different buttons or menu options to access source code. For instance, in Mozilla Firefox, select View and then Page Source.

Q&A boxes offer questions students may have when working through the steps and provide additional information about what they are doing right where they need it.

To Refresh the View in a Browser

As you continue developing the HTML file in Notepad++, it is a good idea to view the file in your browser as you make modifications. Clicking the Refresh button when viewing the modified Web page in the browser, ensures that the latest version of the Web page is displayed. The following step shows how to refresh the view of a Web page in a browser in order to view the modified Web page.

1

- Click the Internet Explorer button on the taskbar to display the rockclimbing.html Web page.
- Click the Refresh button on the Address bar to display the modified Web page (Figure 2–35).

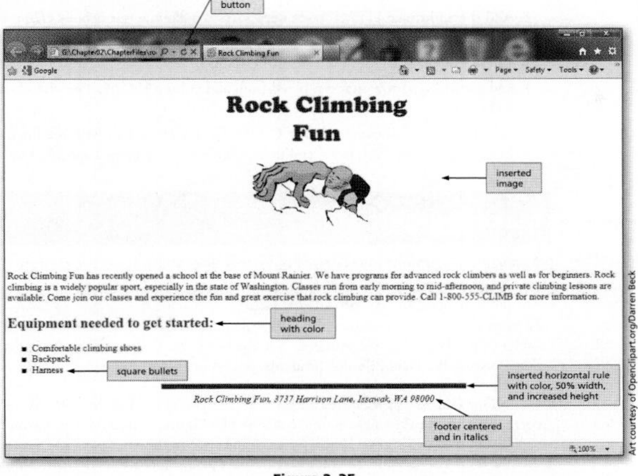

Figure 2–35

Other Ways
1. In Internet Explorer, press F5 to refresh

Other Ways boxes that follow many of the step sequences explain the other ways to complete the task presented.

Validating and Viewing HT

BTW **HTML and HTML5 Tags** The Web has excellent sources that list HTML5 tags. For more information about HTML and HTML5, search for "HTML tags" or "HTML5 tags" in a search engine.

In Chapter 1, you read about validating your H available on the Web that can be used to assure This should always be a part of your Web page this book is the W3C Markup Validation Servi the markup validity of Web documents in HTM markup languages. The validator looks at the D of HTML or XHTML you are using, and then version. In this chapter, the project uses the H

If validation detects an error in your HTM found while checking this document as HTML5 2–36a on the next page). The Result line shows t scroll down the page or click the Jump To: Valida each error.

It is important to note that one error can </h2> tag on line 19 in the rockclimbing.html f Figure 2–36b shows that in this case, one initial be used within the <h2> tag on line 19) resulted

6. Save the revised HTML file in the Chapter02\Apply folder using the file name apply2-1solution.html.
7. Validate your HTML code at validator.w3.org.
8. Enter g:\Chapter02\Apply\apply2-1solution.html (or the path where your data file is stored) as the URL to view the revised Web page in your browser.
9. Print the Web page.
10. Submit the revised HTML file and Web page in the format specified by your instructor.

Extend Your Knowledge

Extend the skills you learned in this chapter and experiment with new skills.

Creating a Definition List

Instructions: Start Notepad++. Open the file, extend2-1.html from the Chapter02\Extend folder of the Data Files for Students. See the inside back cover of this book for instructions on downloading the Data Files for Students, or contact your instructor for information about accessing the required files. This sample Web page contains all of the text for the Web page. You will add the necessary tags to make this a definition list with terms that are bold, as shown in Figure 2–45.

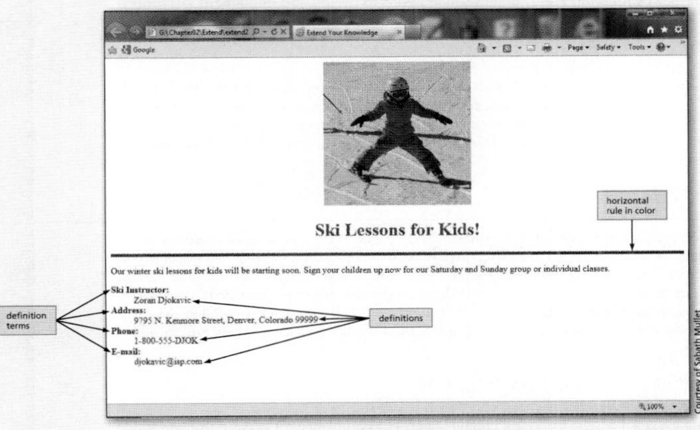

Figure 2–45

Perform the following tasks:

1. Using the text given in the file extend2-1.html, make changes to the HTML code to change the Web page from a single line of text to a definition list by following the definition list code shown in Table 2–6 on page HTML 52.

Continued >

Extend Your Knowledge projects at the end of each chapter allow students to extend and expand on the skills learned within the chapter. Students use critical thinking to experiment with new skills to complete each project.

Textbook Walk-Through

STUDENT ASSIGNMENTS

Extend Your Knowledge *continued*

2. Add the additional HTML code necessary to make the terms bold. (*Hint:* Review the font-weight property with a value of bold.)
3. Add the image skier.jpg. Find the dimensions of the image by reviewing the image properties.
4. Add a horizontal rule that is 5 pixels high and color #414565. The <h1> heading is also color #414565.
5. Save the revised document in the Chapter02\Extend folder with the file name extend2-1solution.html, validate the Web page, and then submit it in the format specified by your instructor.

Make It Right

Analyze a document and correct all errors and/or improve the design.

Correcting the Star of India Web Page

Instructions: Start Notepad++. Open the file makeitright2-1.html from the Chapter02\MakeItRight folder of the Data Files for Students. See the inside back cover of this book for instructions on downloading the Data Files for Students, or contact your instructor for information about accessing the required files.

The data file is a modified version of what you see in Figure 2–46. Make the necessary corrections to the Web page to make it look like Figure 2–46. Add a background color to the Web page using color #515c7a. (*Hint:* Use an inline style in the <body> tag.) Format the heading to use the Heading 1 style with the color black. Add a paragraph of text in white and four circle bullets also in white. (*Hint:* Use the color property in the heading, paragraph, and bullet tags.) Save the file in the Chapter02\MakeItRight folder as makeitright2-1solution.html, validate the Web page, and then submit it in the format specified by your instructor. Be prepared to discuss the four questions posed in the bullet list.

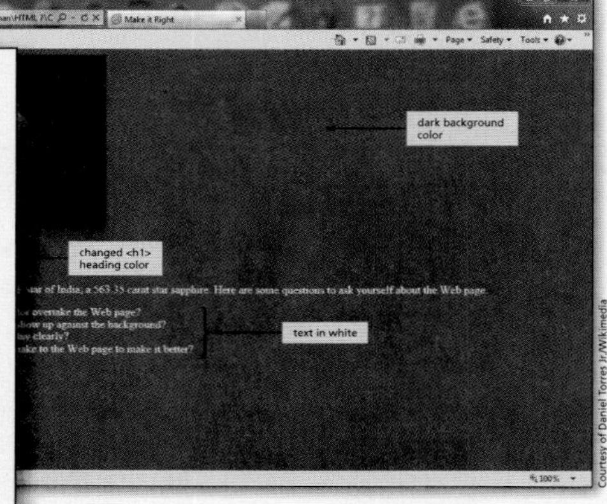

Figure 2–46

Make It Right projects call on students to analyze a file, discover errors in it, and fix them using the skills they learned in the chapter.

STUDENT ASSIGNMENTS

In the Lab *continued*

3. Insert the image file piggybank.png, stored in the Chapter02\IntheLab folder. You can find the dimensions of an image by clicking on the image using Windows Explorer. You can also right-click the image, click Properties, and then click the Details tab to find out the image's dimensions, or open it in a graphics program. Note that the bullets used for the list are square in shape.
4. Save the HTML file in the Chapter02\IntheLab folder using the file name lab2-3solution.html.
5. Enter g:\Chapter02\IntheLab\lab2-3solution.html (or the path where your data file is stored) as the URL to view the Web page in your browser.
6. Print the Web page from your browser.
7. Submit the revised HTML file and Web page in the format specified by your instructor.

Cases and Places

Apply your creative thinking and problem-solving skills to design and implement a solution.

1: Research HTML5 Structural Tags

Academic

There are many Web sites dedicated to HTML5. Search the Web to find sites that have training modules for HTML5. Discover training specifically targeting the new structural elements discussed in the chapter. How do these new tags differ from the <div> tag? Are there situations in which the <div> tag is a better option? Write a brief report. Identify the URLs for the training Web sites and share them with your fellow students in class.

2: Create a Personal Web Page

Personal

Your class instructor wants to post all of the students' Web pages on the school server to show what his or her students are interested in. Create a Web page of personal information, listing items such as your school major, jobs that you have had in the past, and your hobbies and interests. To make your personal Web page more visually interesting, search the Web for images that reflect your interests. (Remember that if the image is copyrighted, you cannot use it on a personal Web page unless you follow the guidelines provided with the image.) Insert an image or two onto the Web page to help explain who you are.

3: Investigate Methods for Working with Images

Professional

You are creating a new Web site for a local photographer. The photographer has asked that you determine methods to help his Web site load quickly despite having so many large images. To this end, find information on using thumbnail images. Review other photography Web sites and create a list of suggestions for loading large images. Additionally, search the Web for information on adding useful, descriptive alt attributes for images. Write a brief synopsis explaining the information that you found in your research.

Found within the Cases & Places exercises, the **Personal** exercises call on students to create an open-ended project that relates to their personal lives.

HTML5 AND CSS

Seventh Edition

COMPREHENSIVE

1 Introduction to HTML, XHTML, and CSS

Objectives

You will have mastered the material in this chapter when you can:

- Describe the Internet and its associated key terms
- Describe the World Wide Web and its associated key terms
- Describe the types and purposes of Web sites
- Discuss Web browsers and identify their purpose
- Define the Hypertext Markup Language (HTML) and HTML5 standards used for Web development
- Discuss the use of Cascading Style Sheets (CSS) in Web development
- Define the Document Object Model (DOM) and describe its relationship to HTML
- Define Extensible Hypertext Markup Language (XHTML) and describe its relationship to HTML
- Identify tools used to create HTML documents
- Describe the five phases of the Web development life cycle
- Describe the different methods of Web site design and the purpose of each Web site structure
- Discuss the importance of testing throughout the Web development life cycle
- Explain the importance of being an observant Web user

1 Introduction to HTML, XHTML, and CSS

Introduction

Before diving into the details of creating Web pages with HTML5 and CSS, it is useful to look at how these technologies relate to the development of the Internet and the World Wide Web. The Internet began with the connection of computers and computer networks. This connectivity has had a huge impact on our daily lives. Today, millions of people worldwide have access to the Internet, the world's largest network. Billions of Web pages, providing information on any subject you can imagine, are currently available on the World Wide Web. People use the Internet to search for information, to communicate with others around the world, and to seek entertainment. Students register for classes, pay tuition, and find out final grades via this computer network. Stores and individuals sell their products using computer connectivity, and most industries rely on the Internet and the World Wide Web for business transactions.

Hypertext Markup Language (HTML) and more recently HTML5 and Cascading Style Sheets (CSS) allow the World Wide Web to exist. In order to utilize these technologies effectively, you need to understand the main concepts behind the Internet and HTML. In this chapter, you learn some basics about the Internet, the World Wide Web, intranets, and extranets. You are introduced to Web browsers, definitions of HTML and associated key terms, the five phases of the Web development life cycle, and the tasks that are involved in each phase.

What Is the Internet?

Most people today have had exposure to the Internet at school, in their homes, at their jobs, or at their local library. The **Internet** is a worldwide collection of computers and computer networks that links billions of computers used by businesses, government, educational institutions, organizations, and individuals using modems, phone lines, television cables, satellite links, fiber-optic connections, and other communications devices and media (Figure 1–1).

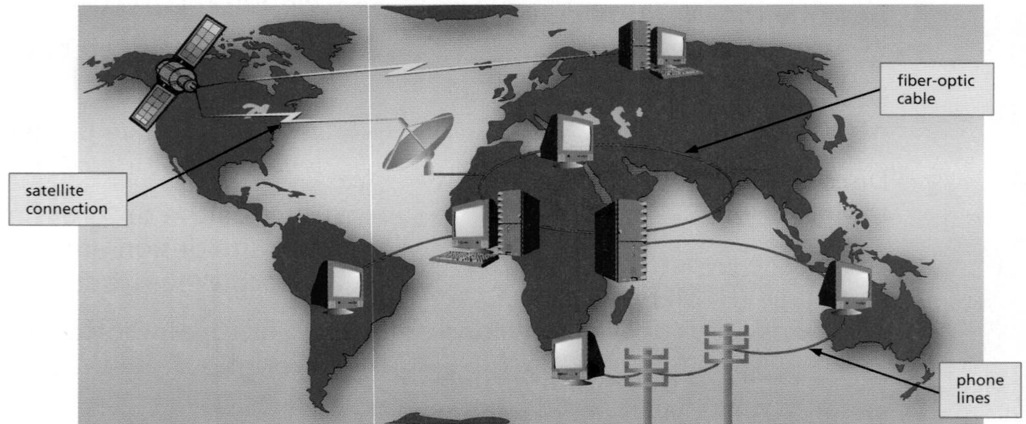

Figure 1–1 The Internet is a worldwide collection of computer networks.

The Internet was developed in the 1960s by the Department of Defense Advanced Research Projects Agency (ARPA). ARPANET (as the Internet was originally called) had only four nodes on it and sent its first message in 1969. Today's Internet has millions of nodes on thousands of networks. A **network** is a collection of two or more computers that are connected to share resources and information. Today, high-, medium-, and low-speed data lines connect networks. These data lines allow data (including text, graphical images, and audio and video data) to move from one computer to another. The **Internet backbone** is a collection of high-speed data lines that connect major computer systems located around the world. An **Internet service provider (ISP)** is a company that has a permanent connection to the Internet backbone. ISPs utilize high- or medium-speed data lines to allow individuals and companies to connect to the backbone for access to the Internet. An Internet connection at home generally is a DSL or cable data line that connects to an ISP.

Millions of people in most countries around the world connect to the Internet using computers in their homes, offices, schools, and public locations such as libraries. In fact, the Internet was designed to be a place in which people could share information or collaborate. Users with computers connected to the Internet can access a variety of services, including e-mail, social networking, and the World Wide Web where they can find a variety of information at many different types of Web sites (Figure 1–2).

Figure 1–2 The Internet makes available a variety of services such as the World Wide Web.

What Is the World Wide Web?

Many people use the terms "Internet" and "World Wide Web" interchangeably, but that is not accurate. The Internet is the infrastructure, the physical networks of computers. The **World Wide Web**, also called the **Web**, is the part of the Internet that supports

BTW

Internet and WWW History
The World Wide Web Consortium (W3C or w3.org), the de facto organization that governs HTML, provides a particularly rich history of the Internet and the World Wide Web. Search on "Internet history" or "WWW history" in your browser for many additional sources.

multimedia and consists of a collection of linked documents. To support multimedia, the Web relies on the **Hypertext Transfer Protocol** (**HTTP**), which is a set of rules for exchanging text, graphic, sound, video, and other multimedia files. The linked documents, or pages of information, on the Web are known as **Web pages**. Because the Web supports text, graphics, sound, and video, a Web page can include any of these multimedia elements. The Web is ever-changing and consists of billions of Web pages. Because of the ease of creating Web pages, more are being added all the time.

A **Web site** is a related collection of Web pages that is created and maintained by an individual, company, educational institution, or other organization. For example, as shown in Figure 1–3, many organizations, such as the U.S. Department of Labor, publish and maintain Web sites. Each Web site contains a **home page**, which is the first document users see when they access the Web site. The home page often serves as an index or table of contents to other documents and files displayed on the site.

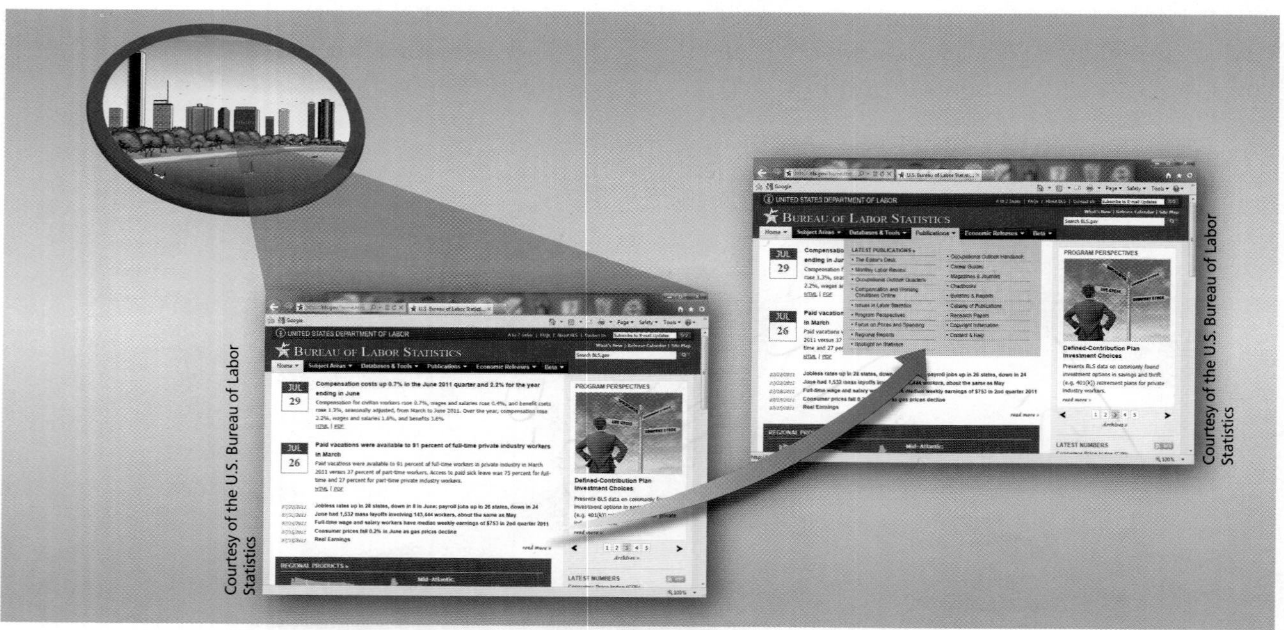

Figure 1–3 A Web site is a related collection of Web pages that is created and maintained by an individual, company, educational institution, or other organization.

Web Servers

Web pages are stored on a **Web server**, or **host**, which is a computer that stores and sends (serves) requested Web pages and other files. Any computer that has Web server software installed and is connected to the Internet can act as a Web server. Every Web site is stored on, and runs from, one or more Web servers. A large Web site may be spread over several servers in different geographic locations.

In order to make the Web pages that you have developed available to your audience, you have to publish those pages. **Publishing** is copying the Web pages and associated files such as graphics and audio to a Web server. Once a Web page is published, anyone who has access to the Internet can view it, regardless of where the Web server is located. For example, although the U.S. Department of Labor Web site is stored on a Web server somewhere in the United States, it is available for viewing by anyone in the world. Once a Web page is published, it can be read by almost any computer: whether you use the Mac, Windows, or Linux operating system, with a variety of computer hardware, you have access to billions of published Web pages.

Web Site Types and Purposes

The three general types of Web sites are Internet, intranet, and extranet. Table 1–1 lists characteristics of each of these three types of Web sites.

An **Internet site**, also known as a **Web site**, is a site generally available to the public. Individuals, groups, companies, and educational institutions use Web sites for a variety of purposes. Intranets and extranets also use Internet technology, but access is limited to specified groups. An **intranet** is a private network that uses Internet technologies to share company information among employees. An intranet is contained within a company or organization's network, which makes it private and only available to those who need access. Policy and procedure manuals usually are found on an intranet. Other documents such as employee directories, company newsletters, product catalogs, and training manuals often are distributed through an intranet.

An **extranet** is a private network that uses Internet technologies to share business information with select corporate partners or key customers. Companies and organizations can use an extranet to share product manuals, training modules, inventory status, and order information. An extranet also might allow retailers to purchase inventory directly from their suppliers or to pay bills online.

Companies use Web sites to advertise or sell their products and services worldwide, as well as to provide technical and product support for their customers. Many company Web sites also support **electronic commerce (e-commerce)**, which is the buying and selling of goods and services on the Internet. Using e-commerce technologies, these Web sites allow customers to browse product catalogs, comparison shop, and order products online. Figure 1–4 shows Cengage.com, which is a company that sells and distributes

BTW

Intranets and Extranets
There are many Web sites that discuss ideas for intranets and extranets. Many companies are already using these technologies and share their "best practice" techniques. Many Web sites provide valuable information on building and maintaining an intranet or extranet, along with additional resources.

BTW

E-Commerce
Today, e-commerce is a standard part of doing business. E-commerce technologies, however, continue to change, offering new applications and potential uses.

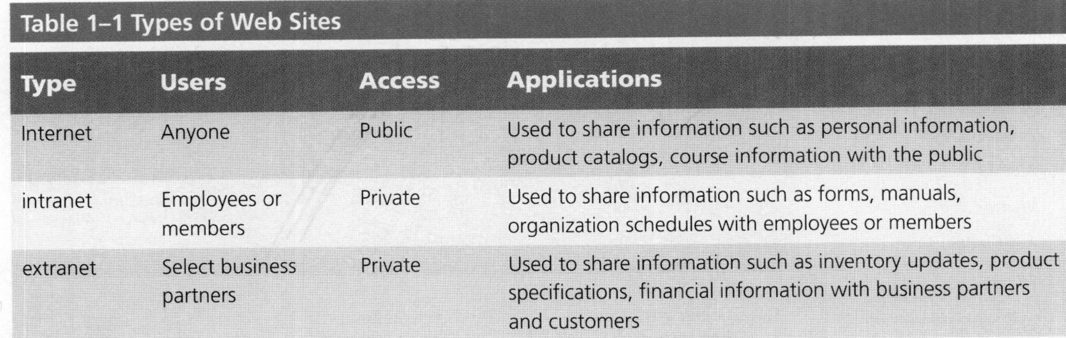

Table 1–1 Types of Web Sites

Type	Users	Access	Applications
Internet	Anyone	Public	Used to share information such as personal information, product catalogs, course information with the public
intranet	Employees or members	Private	Used to share information such as forms, manuals, organization schedules with employees or members
extranet	Select business partners	Private	Used to share information such as inventory updates, product specifications, financial information with business partners and customers

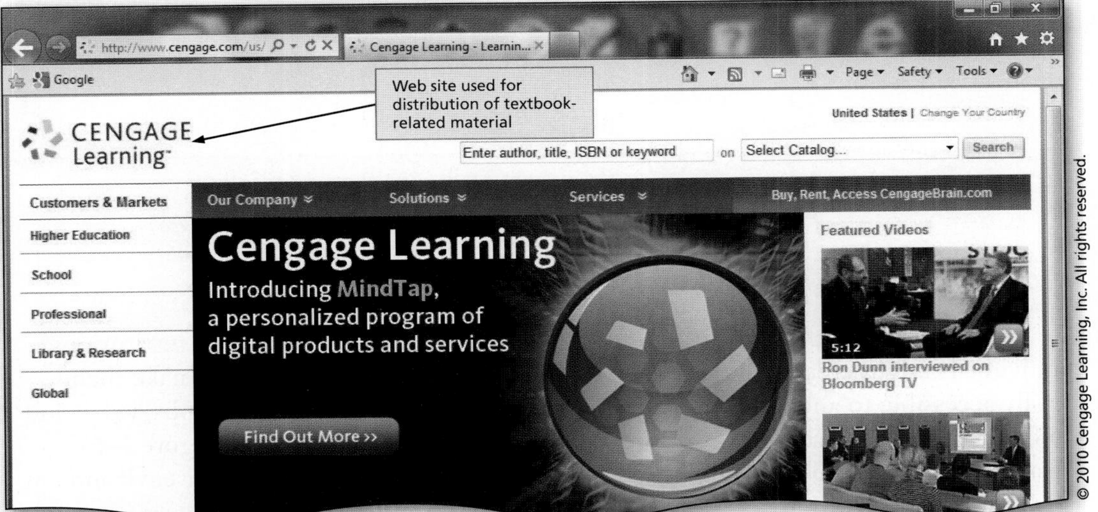

Figure 1–4 Cengage.com is a Web site that provides online educational material.

textbook-related materials online. Many company Web sites also provide job postings and announcements, a frequently asked questions (FAQs) section, customer feedback links to solicit comments from their customers, and searchable technical support databases.

Colleges, universities, and other schools use Web sites to distribute information about areas of study, provide course information, or register students for classes online. Instructors use their Web sites to issue announcements, post questions on reading material, list contact information, and provide easy access to lecture notes and slides. Many instructors today use the course management software adopted by their respective schools to upload course content. Using a standard course management product across a university makes it easier for students to find information related to their various courses. Many course management tools allow instructors to write their own Web content for courses. With many systems, instructors can use Web pages to provide further information for their students within the structure of the course management tool provided by the school. In addition to keeping in contact with current students via the Web, universities also provide a variety of Web site functionality to a variety of visitors as shown in Figure 1–5.

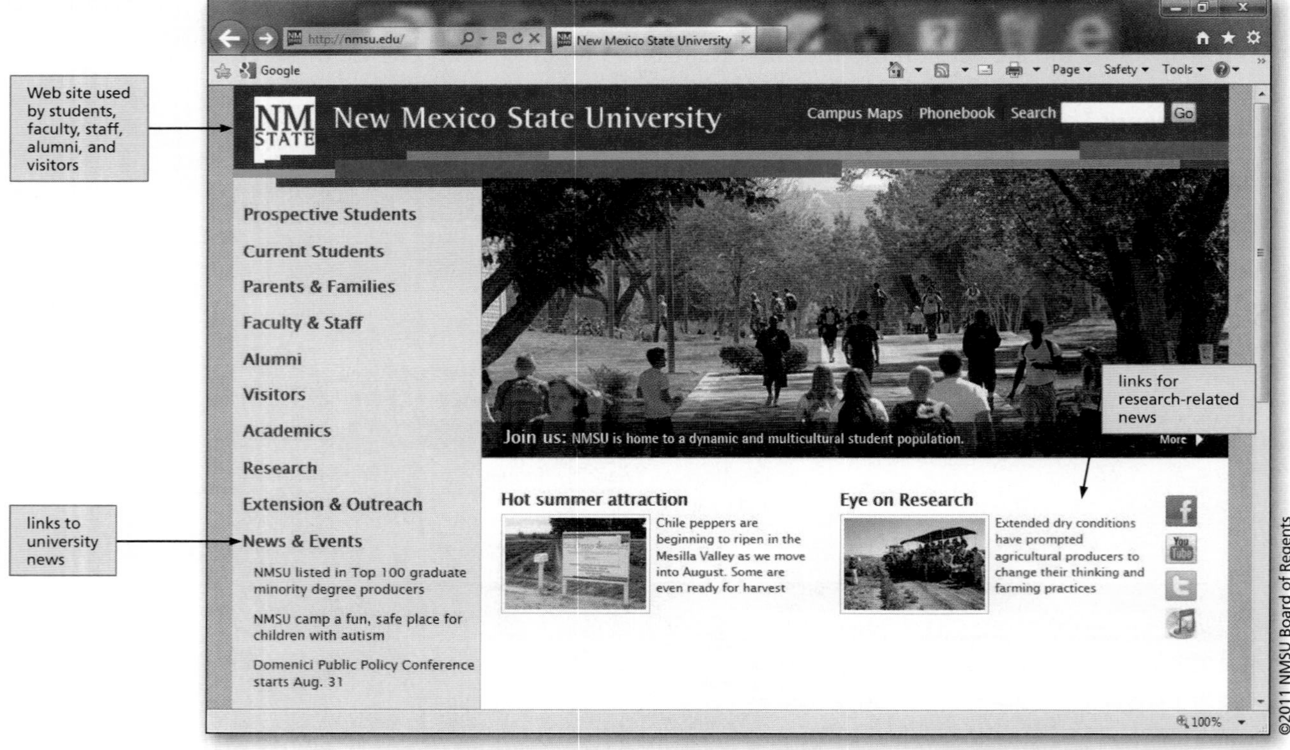

Figure 1–5 University Web sites are varied.

In addition to the use of the Internet by companies and educational institutions, individuals might create personal Web sites that include their résumés to make them easily accessible to any interested employers. Families can share photographs, video and audio clips, stories, schedules, or other information through Web sites (Figure 1–6). Many individual Web sites allow password protection, which makes a safer environment for sharing information.

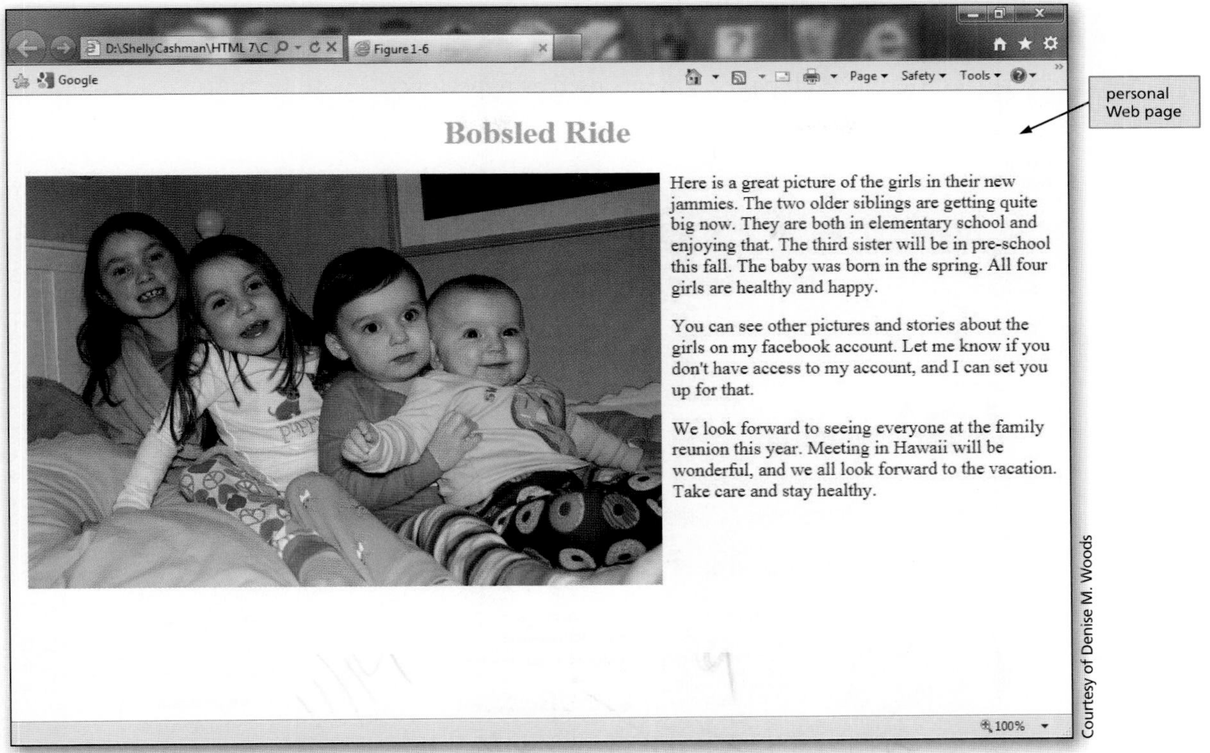

Figure 1–6 Personal Web page used to communicate with family and friends.

Web Browsers

To display a Web page on any type of Web site, a computer needs to have a Web browser installed. A **Web browser**, also called a **browser**, is a program that interprets and displays Web pages and enables you to view and interact with a Web page. Microsoft Internet Explorer, Mozilla Firefox, Google Chrome, and Apple Safari are popular browsers today. Browsers provide a variety of features, including the capability to locate Web pages, to link forward and backward among Web pages, to add a favorite or bookmark a Web page, and to choose security settings.

To locate a Web page using a browser, you type the Web page's Uniform Resource Locator (URL) in the browser's Address or Location bar. A **Uniform Resource Locator (URL)** is the address of a document or other file accessible on the Internet. An example of a URL on the Web is:

http://www.cengagebrain.com/shop/index.html

The URL indicates to the browser to use the HTTP communications protocol to locate the index.html Web page in the shop folder on the cengagebrain.com Web server. Web page URLs can be found in a wide range of places, including school catalogs, business cards, product packaging, and advertisements.

Hyperlinks are an essential part of the World Wide Web. A **hyperlink**, also called a **link**, is an element used to connect one Web page to another Web page on the same server or to Web pages on different Web servers located anywhere in the world. Clicking a hyperlink allows you to move quickly from one Web page to another, and the user does not have to be concerned about where the Web pages reside. You can also click hyperlinks to move to a different section of the same Web page.

With hyperlinks, a Web site user does not necessarily have to view information in a linear way. Instead, he or she can click the available hyperlinks to view the information in a variety of ways, as described later in this chapter. Many different Web page elements, including text, graphics, and animations, can serve as hyperlinks. Figure 1–7 shows examples of several different Web page elements used as hyperlinks.

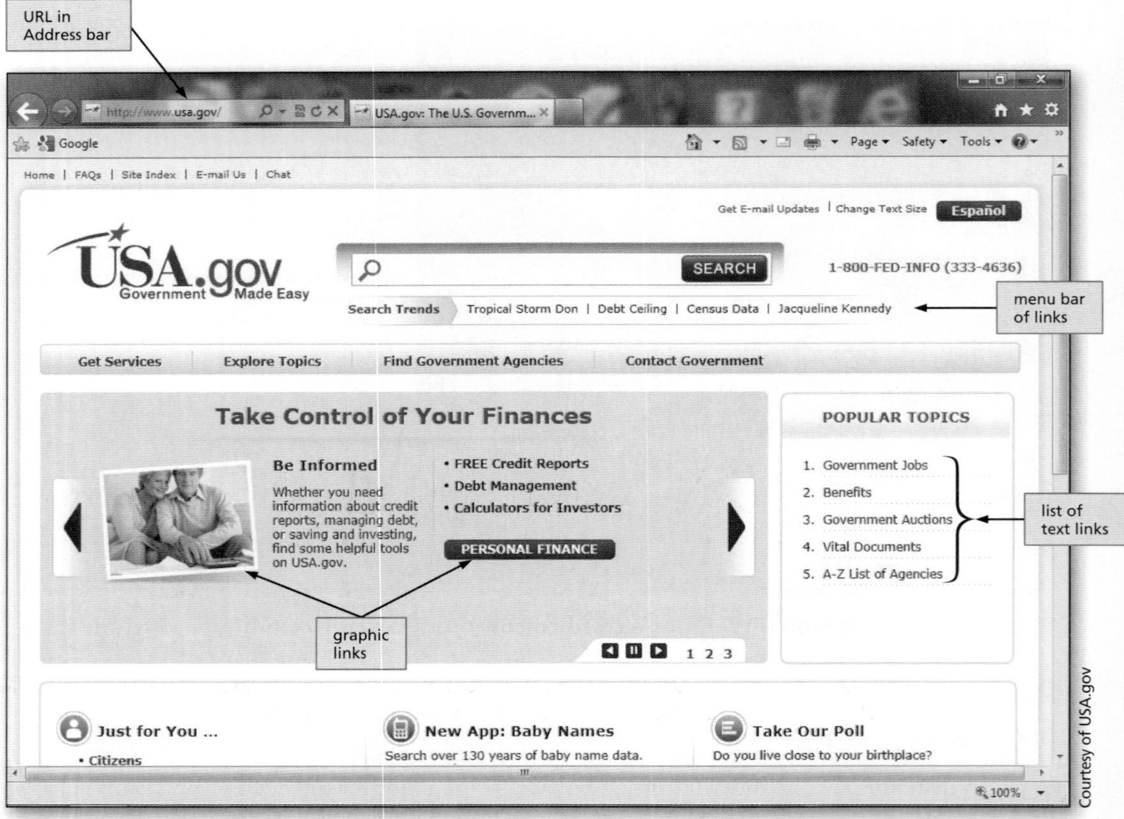

Figure 1–7 A Web page can use several different Web page elements as hyperlinks.

What Is Hypertext Markup Language?

Web pages are created using **Hypertext Markup Language** (**HTML**), which is an authoring language used to create documents for the World Wide Web. HTML uses a set of special instructions called **tags** or **markup** to define the structure and layout of a Web document and specify how the page is displayed in a browser.

A Web page is a file that contains both text and HTML tags. HTML tags mark the text to define how it should appear when viewed in a browser. HTML includes hundreds of tags used to format Web pages and create hyperlinks to other documents or Web pages. For instance, the HTML tags <p> and </p> are used to indicate a new paragraph with a blank line above it, <table> and </table> are used to indicate the start and end of a table, and <hr /> is used to display a horizontal rule across the page. Figure 1–8a shows the HTML tags needed to create the Web page shown in Figure 1–8b. You can also enhance HTML tags by using attributes, as shown in Figure 1–8a. **Attributes** define additional characteristics such as font weight or style for the HTML tag.

HTML is **platform independent**, meaning you can create, or code, an HTML file on one type of computer and then use a browser on another type of computer to view that file as a Web page. The page looks the same regardless of what platform you are using. One of the greatest benefits of Web technology is that the same Web page can be viewed on many different types of digital hardware, including mobile devices like smartphones.

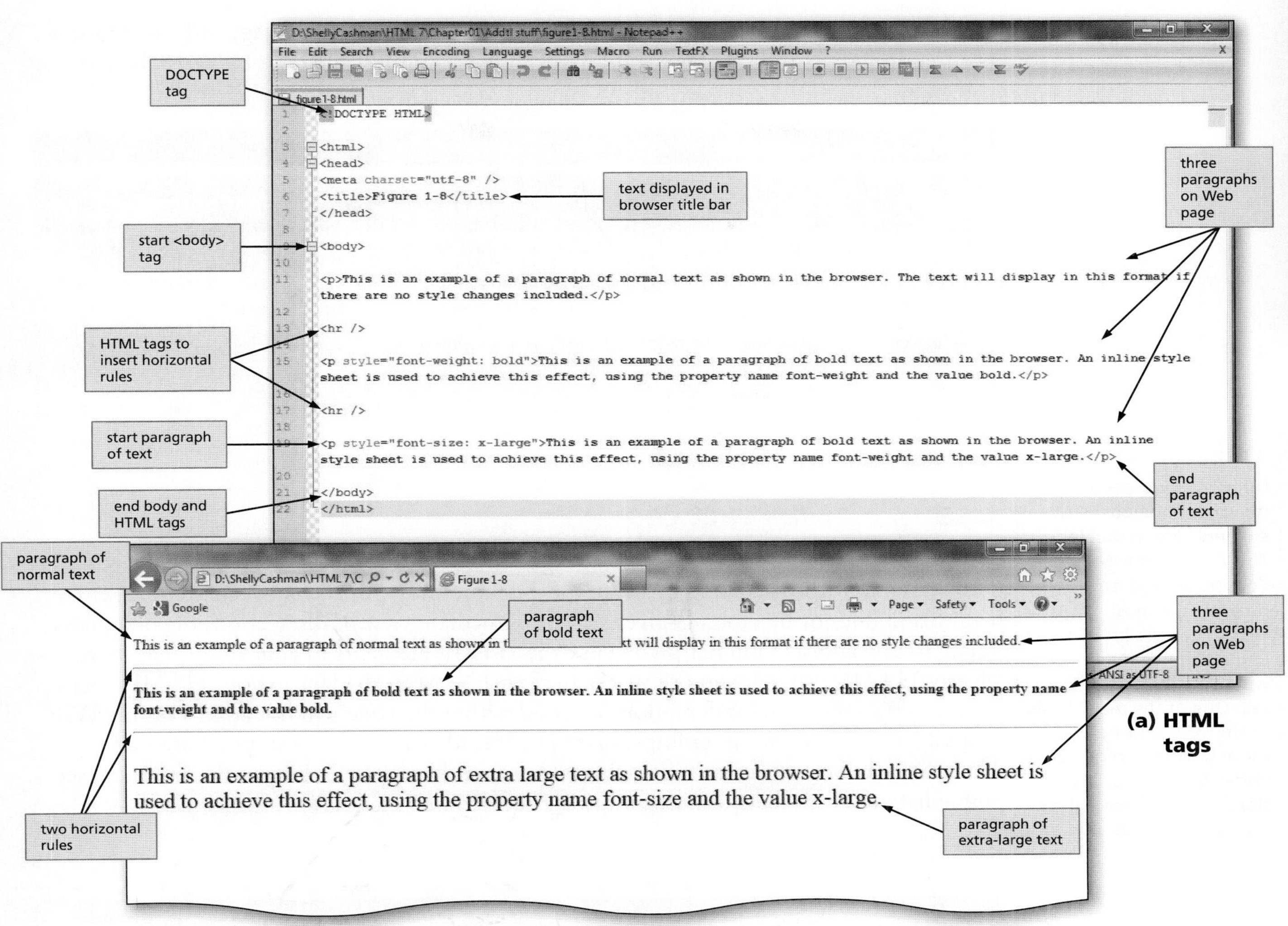

(b) Resulting Web page

Figure 1–8 A Web page is a file that contains both text and HTML tags.

HTML Elements

HTML combines tags and descriptive attributes that define how a document should appear in a Web browser. HTML elements include headings, paragraphs, hyperlinks, lists, images, and more. HTML element syntax is as follows:

- HTML elements begin with a **start tag / opening tag**
- HTML elements finish with an **end tag / closing tag**
- The **element content** is everything inserted between the start and end tags
- Some HTML elements have **empty content** (e.g., <br /> or <hr />)
- Empty elements are **closed in the start tag** (use space-/ to close as in <br />)
- Most HTML elements can have **attributes**

For example, to specify a paragraph of text on a Web page, you would enter the following HTML code:

```
<p>This is a paragraph of text.</p>
```

where <p> is the start or opening tag, </p> is the end or closing tag, and the content is situated between those tags. Table 1–2 shows examples of some HTML elements.

Table 1–2 HTML Elements

Element	Purpose	Code and Content
Title	Indicates title to appear on the title bar in the browser	<title>This is the title text.</title>
Anchor	Creates a link to a Web page named default.html	<a href="default.html">This is text for a link.</a>
Line break	Inserts a line break before the next element (without a blank line); there is no content or closing tag; use space-/ as closing tag	

BTW

HTML Elements
Numerous sources of information about HTML elements are available. The World Wide Web Consortium (w3.org) provides the most comprehensive list of tags and attributes together with examples of their use. One of the main goals of the W3C is to help those building Web sites understand and utilize standards that make the Web accessible to all.

Useful HTML Practices

When creating an HTML file, it is good coding practice to separate sections of the HTML code with spaces and by using the Tab key. Adding space between sections, either with blank lines or by tabbing, gives you an immediate view of the sections of code that relate to one another and helps you view the HTML elements in your document more clearly. HTML browsers ignore spaces that exist between the tags in your HTML document, so the spaces and indentations inserted within the code will not appear on the Web page. Figure 1–9 shows an example of an HTML file with code sections separated by blank lines and code section indentations. Another developer looking at this code can see immediately where the specific sections are located in the code.

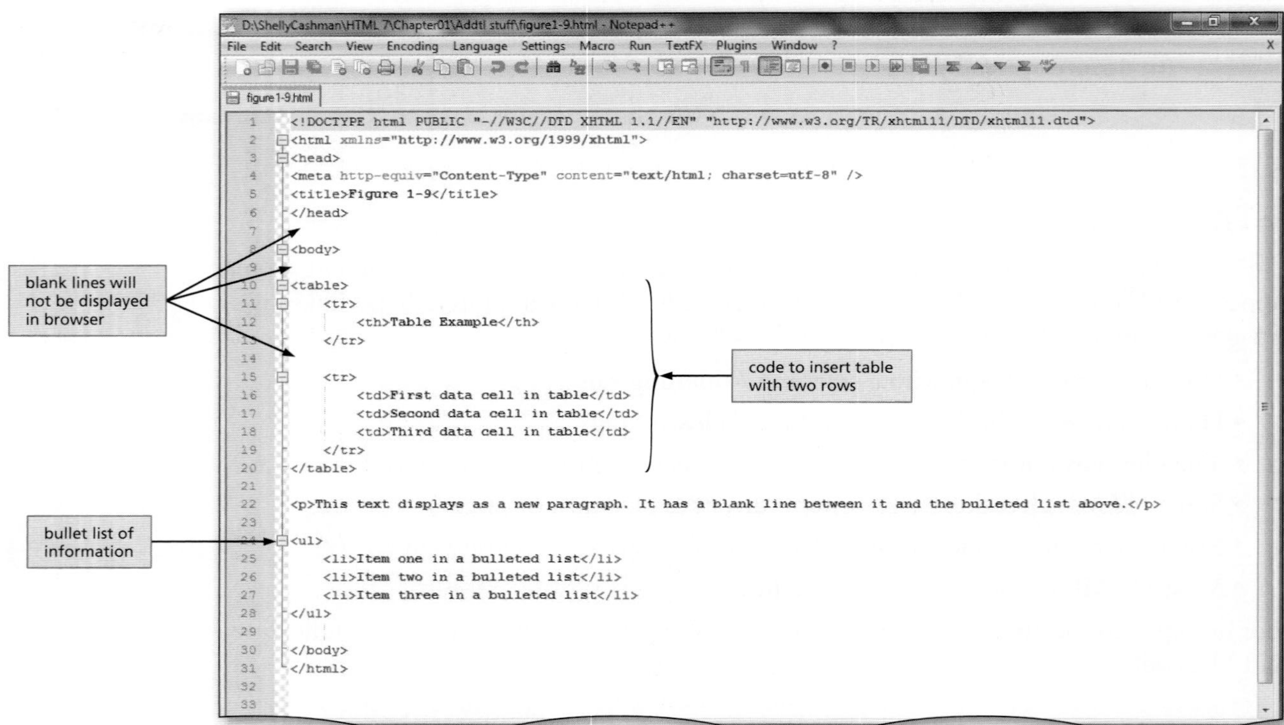

Figure 1–9 Adding spaces to HTML code separates sections to make reading easier.

HTML Versions

HTML has gone through several versions, each of which expands the capabilities of the authoring language. To ensure that browsers can interpret each new version of HTML, the World Wide Web Consortium (W3C) maintains HTML standards, or specifications, which are publicly available on its Web site. HTML5 is the newest version of HTML. HTML5 provides a more flexible approach to Web development. For instance, with HTML5, you can combine lowercase, uppercase, or mixed-case lettering in your tags and attributes. Despite the HTML5 flexibility, this book will adhere to good coding practices that would make it easy to convert to XHTML standards if they should one day override HTML5. The coding practices to which the book adheres are: using all lowercase tags and attributes, enclosing all attribute values in quotation marks, closing all tags, and nesting tags properly (see Table 1–3 on page HTML 13). Although HTML5 has become very popular with Web developers, it is still being developed by the World Wide Web Consortium. The challenge for Web developers, therefore, is to know which new tags and attributes are supported by which browser. This book utilizes HTML5 tags and attributes that are currently supported by Internet Explorer. Additionally, we combine HTML 4.01 tags and attributes with HTML5 to create all of the Web pages in the book. Despite the popularity of HTML5 and HTML 4.01, most browsers continue to support HTML versions 3.2 and 2.0. As described later in this chapter, it is important to verify that Web pages are displayed as intended in a variety of browsers during the testing phase of development.

Cascading Style Sheets

This book has taken a new direction by eliminating deprecated tags and attributes. **Deprecated** tags and attributes are tags and attributes that are being phased out and therefore no longer recommended in the latest W3C standard. Deprecated tags are still used in many Web pages, however, so it is good to know their purpose from a maintenance standpoint. In Appendix A, deprecated tags and attributes are highlighted with an asterisk. In an effort to eliminate deprecated HTML tags, the projects utilize Cascading Style Sheets (CSS) to alter the style (or look) of a Web page. Although HTML allows Web developers to make changes to the structure, design, and content of a Web page, it is limited in its ability to define the appearance, or style, across one or more Web pages. **Cascading Style Sheets** (**CSS**) allow you to specify styles for various Web page elements. A **style** is a rule that defines the appearance of a Web page element. A **style sheet** is a series of rules that defines the style for a Web page or an entire Web site. With a style sheet, you can alter the appearance of a Web page or pages by changing characteristics such as font family, font size, margins, and link specifications, as well as visual elements such as colors and borders. CSS is not used to add any content to your Web site; it just makes your content look more stylish.

With CSS you can specify the style for an element within a single Web page or throughout an entire Web site. For example, if you want all text paragraphs on a Web page to be indented by five spaces, you can use a style sheet to handle the indenting, rather than coding each paragraph with an indentation. And, if you decided you wanted to change the indent to three spaces, you would change just one style sheet line rather than changing the coding for each paragraph. So you can see that using CSS saves a lot of time and makes it much easier to make style changes.

CSS is not HTML; it is a separate language used to enhance the display capabilities of HTML. The World Wide Web Consortium, the same organization that defines HTML standards, defines the specifications for CSS. This book will provide information about CSS3, the newest version of CSS that is currently being developed. We address the new features that CSS3 brings to the world of Web development. Be forewarned that this is a moving target and

BTW

CSS, DOM, and XHTML
The w3.org Web site has an extensive amount of information and tutorials about Cascading Style Sheets (CSS), Document Object Model (DOM), and Extensible HTML (XHTML). The standards suggested in the W3C Web site are the ones that most Web developers follow.

not all browsers support the latest selector syntax provided by CSS3. Appendix A at the back of this book and available online provides a list of HTML tags and corresponding attributes that will allow you to alter the Web page elements as needed, and Appendix D has complete information on the properties and values associated with different CSS elements.

Document Object Model (DOM)

HTML can be used with other Web technologies to provide additional Web page functionality. For example, the term **Document Object Model** (**DOM**) describes a combination of HTML tags, CSS, and a scripting language such as JavaScript. DOM allows JavaScript and other languages to manipulate the structure of the underlying document to create interactive, animated Web pages. This is a model in which the Web page (or document) contains objects (elements, links, etc.) that can be manipulated. DOM allows a Web developer to add, delete, or change an element or attribute. Web pages enhanced with DOM can be more responsive to visitor interaction than basic HTML Web pages. Not all interactive Web pages require DOM, but if you have a need for extensive interactivity, then this might be a model to consider. CSS, JavaScript, and DOM are covered in later chapters in the Comprehensive (12-chapter) version of this book.

Extensible Hypertext Markup Language (XHTML)

As you have learned, HTML uses tags to describe how a document should appear in a Web browser, or the Web page format. HTML is used to display data, whereas **Extensible Markup Language** (**XML**) is designed to transport and store data. XML provides a set of rules that are used to encode documents in machine-readable form. XML is not a replacement for HTML, but it is a software- and hardware-independent tool that is used to carry information. Chapter 12 discusses XML in depth and is used to teach XML specifics to students. **Extensible Hypertext Markup Language** (**XHTML**) is a reformulation of HTML formatting so it conforms to XML structure and content rules. By combining HTML and XML, XHTML combines the display features of HTML and the stricter coding standards required by XML.

As mentioned previously, the projects in this book utilize some of the new tags and attributes introduced with HTML5. The XHTML standards do not apply to HTML5, but we will adhere to the XHTML coding practices as per Table 1–3 because these practices create a uniformity of coding styles. Applying the XHTML coding practices together with any new HTML5 tags or attributes will not cause a problem when you validate your code as long as you use the HTML5 <!DOCTYPE> statement:

```
<!DOCTYPE HTML>
<html>
```

at the start of your Web page.

An important step in Web development is to check that your Web pages are compliant with HTML5 standards as defined by W3C. You will validate your Web pages starting in Chapter 2, using the new HTML5 <!DOCTYPE> statement noted above, and continue that process throughout the book. Most Web pages already developed do not validate. However, it is best that you begin your Web development training using the standards recommended by W3C.

Table 1–3 lists some of the coding rules that Web developers should follow to ensure that their HTML code conforms to XHTML standards when using a combination of HTML 4.01 and HTML5 tags and attributes. All of the projects in this book follow XHTML standards (except for the <!DOCTYPE>) and adhere to the rules outlined in Table 1–3. The specifics of each rule are explained in detail when used in a project.

Table 1–3 XHTML Coding Practices

Practice	Invalid Example	Valid Example
All tags and attributes must be written in lowercase	<TABLE WIDTH="100%">	<table width="100%">
All attribute values must be enclosed by single or double quotation marks	<table width=100%>	<table width="100%">
All tags must be closed, including tags such as img, hr, and br, which do not have end tags, but which must be closed as a matter of practice	 <hr> <p>This is another paragraph	 <hr /> <p>This is another paragraph</p>
All elements must be nested properly	<p><strong>This is a bold paragraph</p></strong>	<p><strong>This is a bold paragraph</strong></p>

Tools for Creating HTML Documents

You can create Web pages using HTML with a simple text editor, such as Notepad++, Notepad, TextPad, or TextEdit. A **text editor** is a program that allows a user to enter, change, save, and print text, such as HTML. Text editors do not have many advanced features, but they do allow you to develop HTML documents easily. For instance, if you want to insert the DOCTYPE tags into the Web page file, type the necessary text into any of the text editors, as shown in Figure 1–10a and Figure 1–10b on the next page. Although Notepad (Figure 1–10b) is an adequate text editor for Web development, note its differences from Notepad++. Notepad++ is a more robust text editor that uses color schemes for HTML code as it is entered.

You can also create Web pages using an HTML text editor, such as EditPlus or BBEdit (Mac OS). An **HTML text editor** is a program that provides basic text-editing functions, as well as more advanced features such as color-coding for various HTML tags, menus to insert HTML tags, and spell checkers. An **HTML object editor**, such as EiffelStudio object editor, provides the additional functionality of an outline editor that allows you to expand and collapse HTML objects and properties, edit parameters, and view graphics attached to the expanded objects.

Many popular software applications also provide features that enable you to develop Web pages easily. Microsoft Word, Excel, and PowerPoint, for example, have a Save as Web Page option that converts a document into an HTML file by automatically adding HTML tags to the document. Using Microsoft Access, you can create a Web page that allows you to view data in a database. Adobe Acrobat also has an export feature that creates HTML files. Each of these applications also allows you to add hyperlinks, drop-down boxes, option buttons, or scrolling text to the Web page.

These advanced Web features make it simple to save any document, spreadsheet, database, or presentation to display as a Web page. Corporate policy and procedures manuals and PowerPoint presentations, for example, can be easily saved as Web pages and published to the company's intranet. Extranet users can be given access to Web pages that allow them to view or update information stored in a database.

You can also create Web pages using a WYSIWYG editor such as Adobe Dreamweaver, Amaya, or CoffeeCup HTML Editor. A **WYSIWYG editor** is a program that provides a graphical user interface that allows a developer to preview the Web page during its development. WYSIWYG (pronounced wizzy-wig) is an acronym for What You See Is What You Get. A WYSIWYG editor creates the HTML code for you as you

BTW

Free HTML WYSIWYG Editors
There are a number of popular WYSIWYG editors that are being used by many novice Web developers to create well-designed, interactive Web sites. You can find these by searching for "WYSIWYG HTML editor" in most search engines.

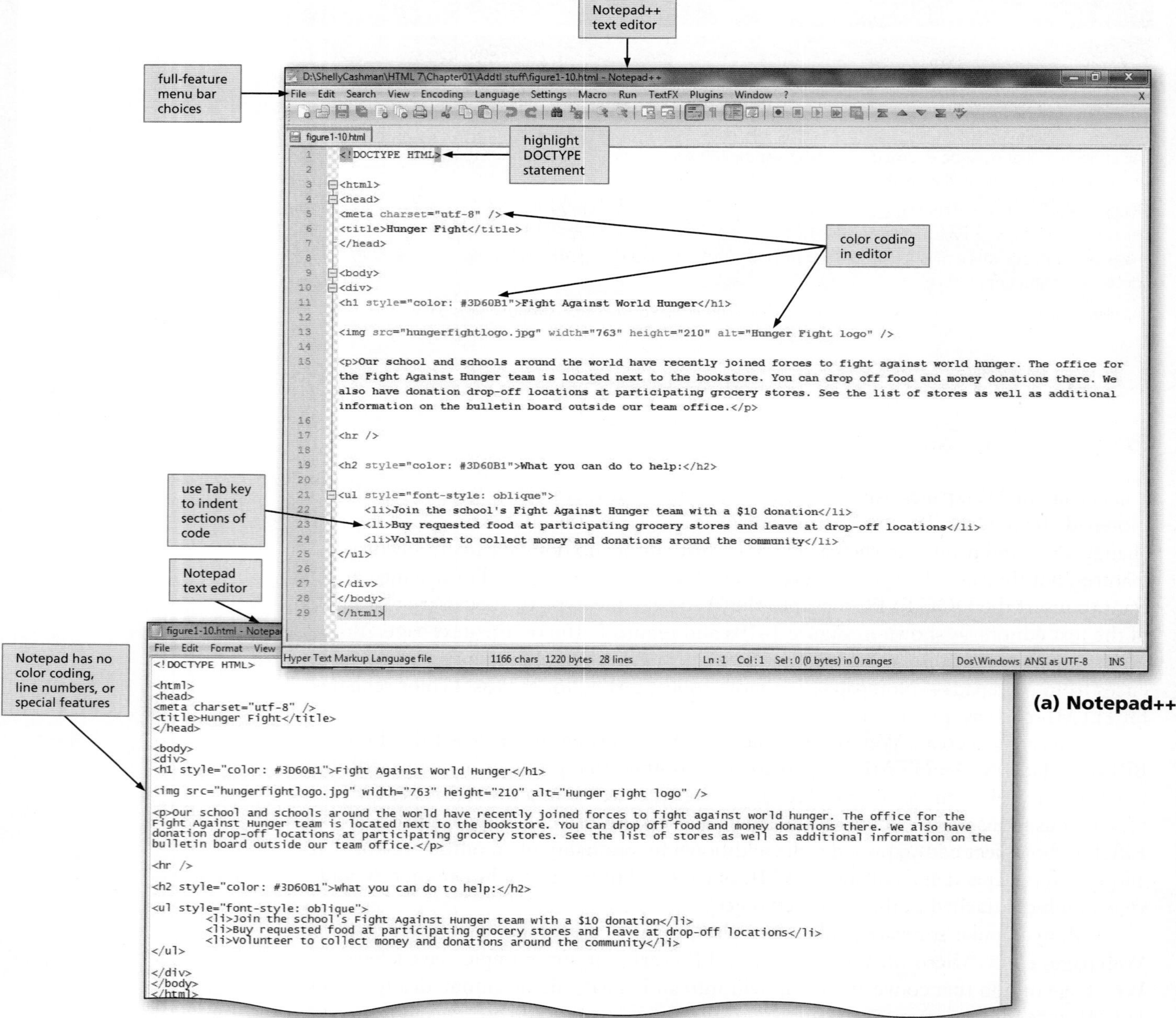

(a) Notepad++

(b) Notepad

Figure 1–10 With text editors such as Notepad++ or Notepad, you can type HTML tags directly in the files.

add elements to the Web page, which means that you do not have to enter HTML tags directly. The main problem with WYSIWYG editors is that they often create "puffed-up" HTML code (HTML tags with many lines of unnecessary additional code surrounding them).

Regardless of which type of program you use to create Web pages, it is important to understand the specifics of HTML so you can make changes outside of the editor. For instance, you may be able to create a Web page with Dreamweaver, but if you want to make some minor changes, it is very helpful to know the HTML tags themselves. It is also important to understand the Web development life cycle so the Web pages in your Web site are consistent and complete.

Web Development Life Cycle

For years, university and college information technology courses have stressed the importance of following the Systems Development Life Cycle when designing and implementing new software to ensure consistency and completeness. The Web development process should follow a similar cycle. Comprehensive planning and analysis ensure that developers will provide what the users want. If you start to code your Web pages without thorough planning and analysis, you run the risk of missing pertinent information. It is much less expensive to make corrections to a Web site in the early phases of project development than it is to alter Web pages that are completed.

The Web development life cycle outlined in this section is one that can be utilized for any type or size of Web development project. The **Web development life cycle** is a process that can be used for developing Web pages at any level of complexity. The Web development life cycle includes the following phases: planning, analysis, design and development, testing, and implementation and maintenance. Table 1–4 lists several questions that should be asked during each phase in the Web development life cycle. Throughout this book, you will follow this systematic cycle as you develop your Web pages.

Table 1–4 Web Development Phases and Questions

Web Development Phase	Questions to Ask
Planning	• What is the purpose of this Web site? • Who will use this Web site? • What are the users' computing environments? • Who owns and authors the information on the Web site? • Who decides if/where the information goes on the Web site?
Analysis	• What tasks do the users need to perform? • What information is useful to the users? • What process considerations must be made?
Design and Development	• How many Web pages will be included in the Web site? • How will the Web pages be organized? • What type of Web site structure is appropriate for the content? • How can I best present the content for ease of use? • What file naming convention will be employed for this Web site? • What folder structure will be used for the Web page files? • How do I apply standards throughout the development process? • What forms of multimedia contribute positively to the Web site? • How can accessibility issues be addressed without limiting usability? • Will there be an international audience?
Testing	• Do the Web pages pass the World Wide Web Consortium (W3C) validation process as HTML5 compliant? • Is the Web site content correct? • Does the Web site function correctly? • Are users able to find the information they need to complete desired tasks? • Is navigation clear and easy to use?
Implementation and Maintenance	• How is the Web site published? • How can users be attracted to visit and revisit the Web site? • How is the Web site updated? • Who is responsible for content updates? • Who is responsible for structure updates? • How will users be notified about updates to the Web site? • Will the Web site be monitored?

Web Site Planning

Web site planning, which is the first phase of the Web development life cycle, involves identifying the goals or purpose of the Web site. The first step in the Web site planning phase is to answer the question "What is the purpose of this Web site?" As you have learned, individuals and groups design and publish Web sites for a variety of purposes. Individuals develop Web sites to share their hobbies, to post résumés, or just to share ideas on personal interests. Organizations create Web sites to keep members informed of upcoming events or to recruit new members. Businesses create Web sites to advertise and sell products or to give their customers 24-hour online support. Instructors publish Web sites, or add information to their courses using the school's online course management software, to inform students of course policies, assignments, and due dates, as well as course requirements. Until you can adequately identify the intended purpose of the Web site, you should not proceed with the Web development project.

In addition to understanding the Web site's purpose, you should also understand who will use the Web site and the computing environments of most of the users. Knowing the makeup of your target audience — including age, gender, general demographic background, and level of computer literacy — will help you design a Web site appropriate for the target users. Understanding users' computing environments will determine what types of Web technologies to use. For example, if most users have low-speed Internet connections, you would not want to create pages with large graphics or multimedia elements.

A final aspect to the Web site planning phase is to identify the content owners and authors. To determine this, you need to ask the questions:

- Who owns and authors the information on the Web site?
- Who decides if/where the information goes on the Web site?

Once you have identified who will provide and authorize the Web site content, you can include those individuals in all aspects of the Web development project.

Web Site Analysis

During the analysis phase, you make decisions about the Web site content and functionality. To help define the appropriate Web site content and functionality, you should first identify the tasks that users need to perform. Answering that question allows you to define necessary content to facilitate those tasks and determine useful information for the users. Extraneous content that does not serve any purpose should be eliminated from the Web site.

In the analysis phase, it is also important to consider the processes required to support Web site features. For example, if you determine that users should be able to order products through the Web site, then you also need to define the processes or actions to be taken each time an order is submitted. For instance, after an order is submitted, how will that order be processed throughout the back-office business applications such as inventory control and accounts payable? Will users receive e-mail confirmations with details about their orders? The analysis phase is one of the more important phases in the Web development life cycle. Clearly understanding and defining the desired content and functionality of the Web site will direct the type of Web site that you design and reduce changes during Web site development.

Web Site Design and Development

After determining the purpose of the Web site and defining the content and functionality, you need to consider the Web site's design. Some key considerations in Web site design are defining how to organize Web page content, selecting the appropriate Web site structure, determining how to use multimedia, addressing accessibility issues, and designing pages for an international audience. One of the most important aspects of Web site design is determining the best way to provide navigation on the Web site. If users cannot easily find the information that they are seeking, they will not return to your Web site.

Many ways to organize a Web page exist, just as many ways to organize a report or paper exist. Table 1–5 lists some organizational standards for creating a Web page that is easy to read and navigate.

BTW

Accessibility Standards
Creating a Web site that is accessible to all users allows your Web site to reach the widest audience. Further, under Section 508 law, any Web site or technology used by a U.S. federal agency must be usable by people with disabilities. See Appendix C for Section 508 guidelines.

Table 1–5 Web Page Organizational Standards

Element	Organizational Standard	Reason
Titles	Use simple titles that clearly explain the purpose of the page	Titles help users understand the purpose of the page; a good title explains the page in the search engine results lists
Headings	Use headings to separate main topics	Headings make a Web page easier to read; simple headlines clearly explain the purpose of the page
Horizontal Rules	Insert horizontal rules to separate main topics	Horizontal rules provide graphical elements to break up Web page content
Paragraphs	Use paragraphs to help divide large amounts of text	Paragraphs provide shorter, more readable sections of text
Lists	Utilize bulleted or numbered lists when appropriate	Lists provide organized, easy-to-read text that readers can scan
Page Length	Maintain suitable Web page lengths	Web users do not always scroll to view information on longer pages; appropriate page lengths increase the likelihood that users will view key information
Information	Emphasize the most important information by placing it at the top of a Web page	Web users are quick to peruse a page; placing critical information at the top of the page increases the likelihood that users will view key information
Other	Incorporate a contact e-mail address; include the date of the last modification	E-mail addresses and dates give users a way to contact a Web site developer with questions; the date last modified helps users determine the timeliness of the site information

Web sites can use several different types of structures, including linear, hierarchical, and webbed. Each structure links, or connects, the Web pages in a different way to define how users navigate the site and view the Web pages. You should select a structure for the Web site based on how users will navigate the site and view the Web site content.

A **linear** Web site structure connects Web pages in a straight line, as shown in Figure 1–11 on the next page. A linear Web site structure is appropriate if the information on the Web pages should be read in a specific order. For example, if the information on the first Web page, Module 1, is necessary for understanding information on the second Web page, Module 2, you should use a linear structure. Each page would have links from one Web page to the next, as well as a link back to the previous Web page. There are many cases in which Web pages need to be read one after the other, such as in the case of training material in which Module 1 needs to be completed before Module 2 can be attempted.

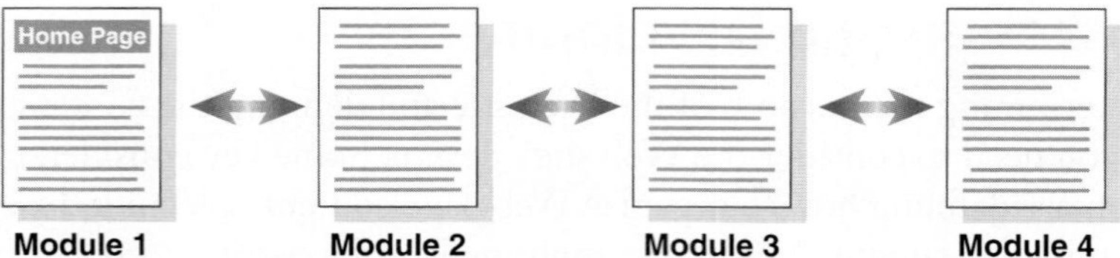

Figure 1–11 Linear Web site structure.

A variation of a linear Web site structure includes the addition of a link to the home page of the Web site, as shown in Figure 1–12. For some Web sites, moving from one

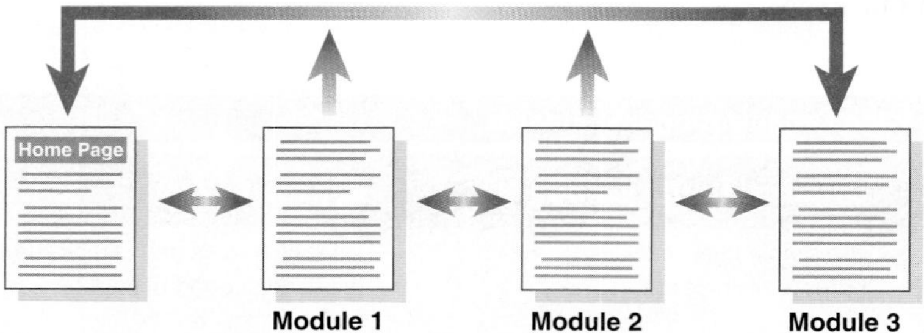

Figure 1–12 Linear Web site structure with links to home page.

module to the next module is still important, but you also want to provide users with easy access to the home page at any time. In this case, you would still provide links from the module Web pages to the previous and next module, but each Web page would also have a link back to the home page. In this way, the user does not have to click the previous link multiple times in order to get back to the home page.

> **BTW**
> **User Interface Design**
> The user interface design is an important aspect of a Web site. If a site is designed poorly, users may not be able to find the desired information or complete a task, which makes the Web site ineffective.

A **hierarchical** Web site structure connects Web pages in a treelike structure, as shown in Figure 1–13. A hierarchical Web site structure works well on a site with a main

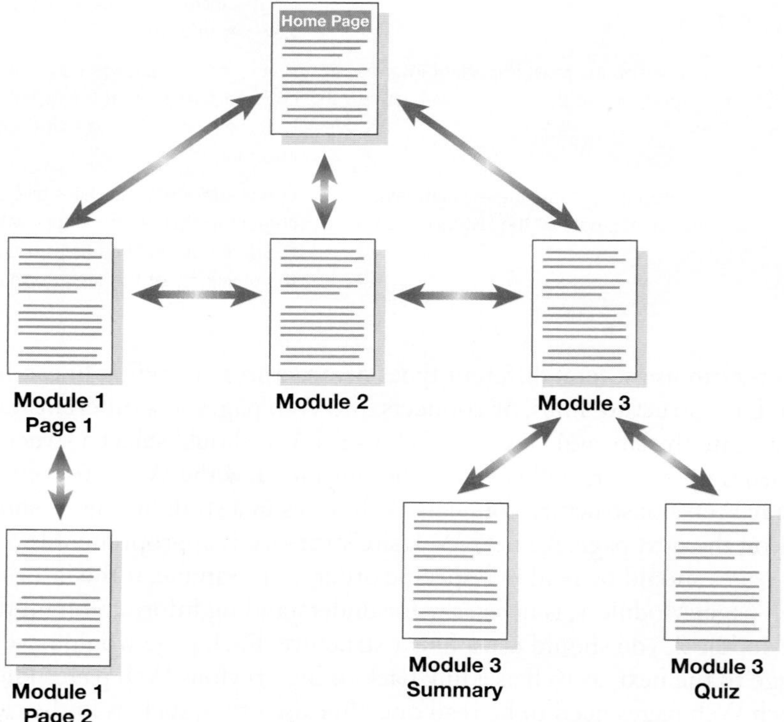

Figure 1–13 Hierarchical Web site structure.

index or table of contents page that links to all other Web pages. With this structure, the main index page would display general information, and secondary pages would include more detailed information. Notice how logically the information in Figure 1–13 is organized. A Web page visitor can easily go from the home page to any of the three modules. In addition, the visitor can easily get to the Module 3 Quiz by way of the Module 3 link. One of the inherent problems with this structure, though, is the inability to move easily from one section of pages to another. As an example, to move from Module 1 Page 2 to the Module 3 Summary, the visitor would have to use the Back button to get to the Home Page and then click the Module 3 link. This is moderately annoying for a site with two Web pages, but think what it would be like if Module 1 had 100 Web pages!

To circumvent the problems with the hierarchical model, you can use a webbed model. A **webbed** Web site structure has no set organization, as shown in Figure 1–14. A webbed Web site structure works best on sites with information that does not need to be read in a specific order and with many navigation options. The World Wide Web uses a webbed structure, so users can navigate among Web pages in any order they choose. Notice how the Web site visitor can more easily move between modules or module summaries with this structure. With this model, you most often provide a link to the Home Page from each page, resulting in an additional arrow going from each individual Web page back to the home page (which is difficult to depict in these small figures). Many Web sites today utilize a graphical image (usually the company or institutional logo) in the top-left corner of each Web page as a link to the home page. You will use that technique later in the book.

Most Web sites are a combination of the linear, hierarchical, and webbed structures. Some information on the Web site might be organized hierarchically from an index page, other information might be accessible from all areas of the site, and still other information might be organized linearly to be read in a specific order. Using a combination of the three structures is appropriate if it helps users navigate the site easily. The key is to get the right information to the users in the most efficient way possible.

Regardless of the structure or structures that you use, you should balance the narrowness and depth of the Web site. A **broad Web site** is one in which the home page

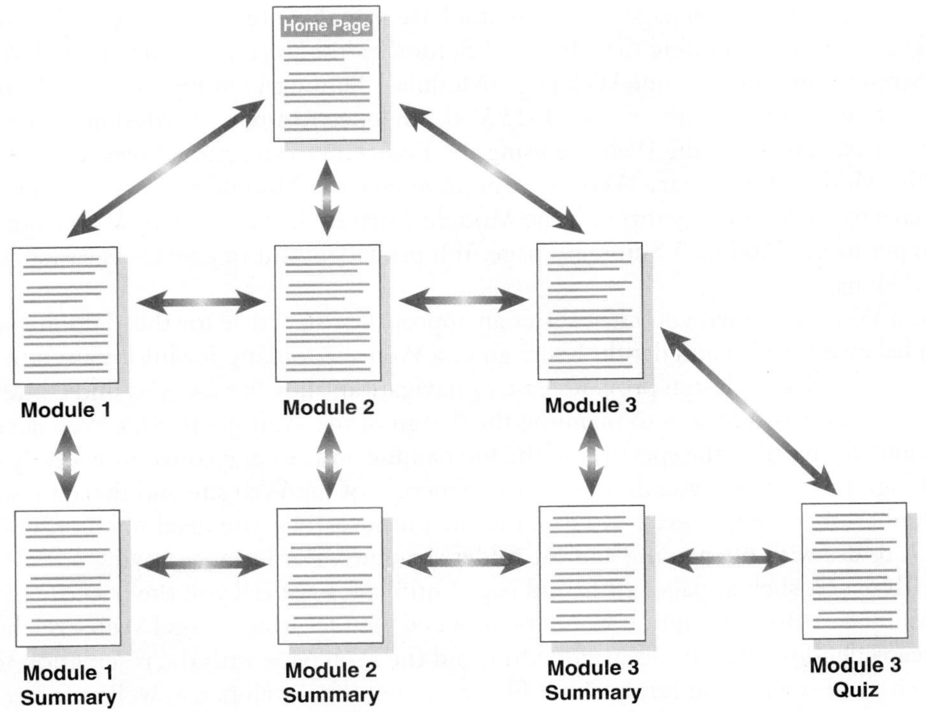

Figure 1–14 Webbed Web site structure.

is the main index page, and all other Web pages are linked individually to the home page (Figure 1–15). By making the other Web pages accessible only through the home page, a broad Web site forces the user to return to the home page to move from one Web page to another. The structure makes navigation time-consuming and limiting for users. A better structure would present a user with navigation alternatives that allow for direct movement between Web pages.

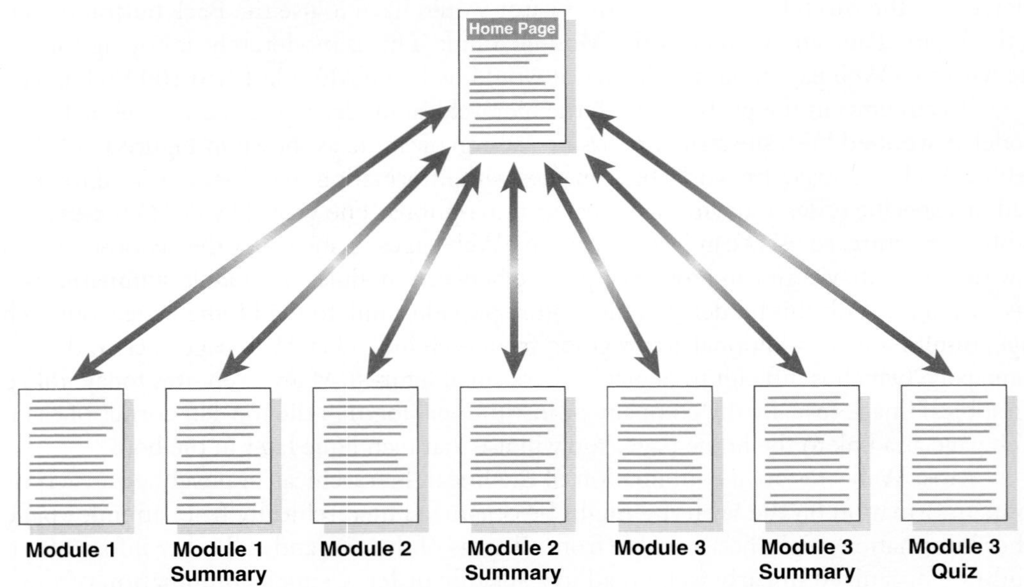

Figure 1–15 Broad Web site.

A **deep Web site** is one that has many levels of pages, requiring the user to click many times to reach a particular Web page (Figure 1–16). By requiring a visitor to move through several Web pages before reaching the desired page, a deep Web site forces a user to spend time viewing interim pages that may not have useful content. As an example, note the difference between finding the Module 3 Summary in Figure 1–13 on page HTML 18 as compared to finding the same Web page (Module 3 Summary) in Figure 1–16. Assume that the user went through the Figure 1–13 Web site once to study the Module 3 material. When the user returns to the Web site using the Figure 1–16 structure, however, to review the Module 3 Summary Web page and then take the Module 3 Quiz, the user would have to go completely through the Module 3 material, Web page by Web page, in order to get to the Module 3 Summary page. You probably want to give users easier access to that Web page.

As a Web developer, you must select an appropriate structure for the Web site and work to balance breadth and depth. Users go to a Web site looking for information to complete a task. Good design provides ease of navigation, allowing users to find content quickly and easily. In addition to planning the design of the Web site itself, a Web developer should always plan the specifics of the file naming and storage conventions early on in the design phase. Once you determine the structure of the Web site and the approximate number of pages necessary to fulfill the site purpose, then you need to identify what standards to use with file naming and the folder structure. For instance, saving your Web pages with names such as page1.html and page2.html does not tell you the purpose of those Web pages. A better option would be to name the Oceanside Hotel Web site's home page oceansidehome.html or oceanside.html, and the Web page with the reservation form could be named reservation.html. Those file names tell the developer, as well as future developers maintaining the Web site, the purpose of those Web pages.

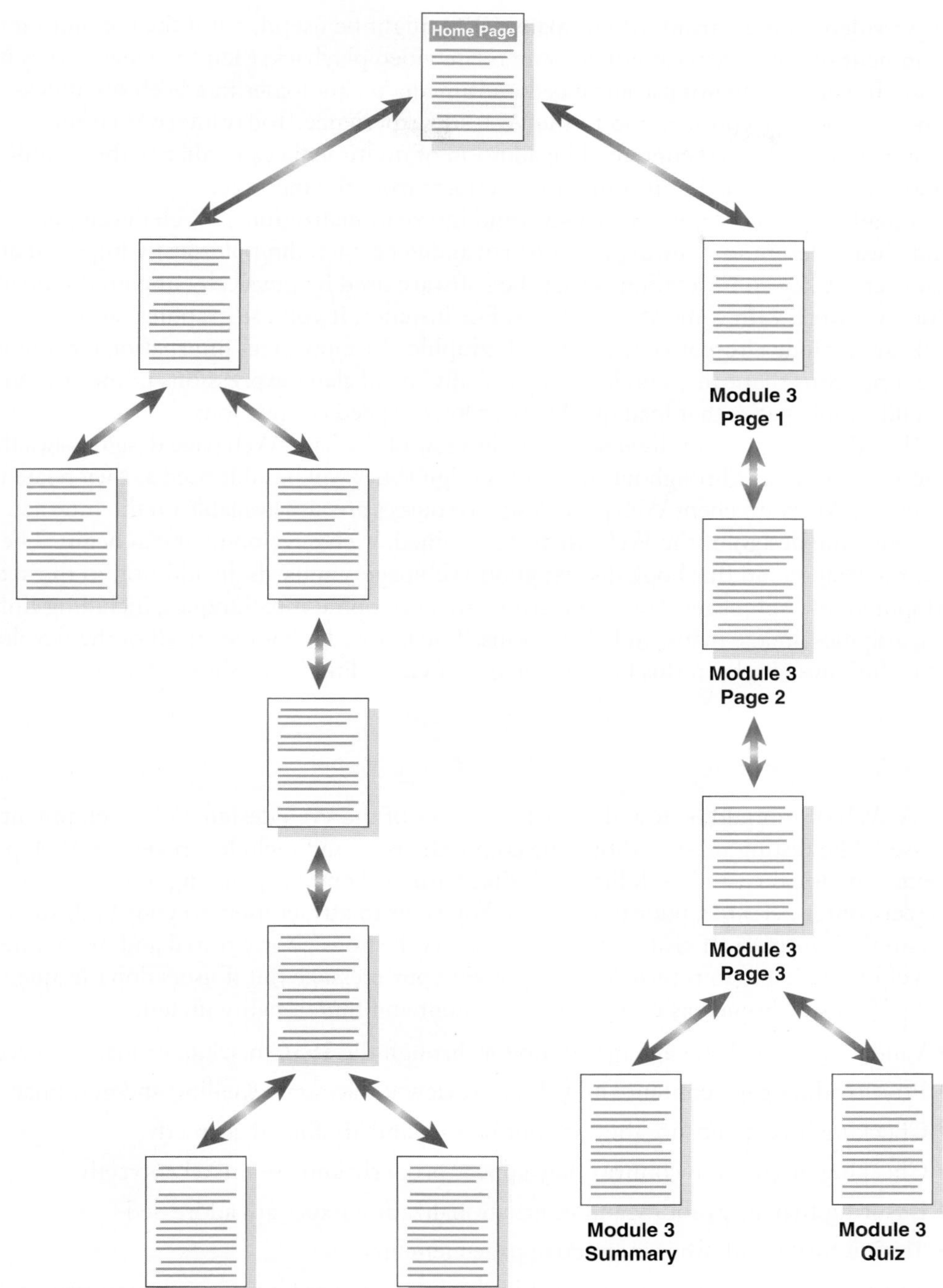

Figure 1–16 Deep Web site.

The same principle applies to the folder structure that you use in your Web development. The projects in this book have so few Web page files and graphic files that all content (Web pages and graphics) is stored together in one folder. With a large Web site, however, you may want to put the Web page files in a separate folder from the graphics files. Larger, more complex Web sites might also require a folder just to store video or audio clips. Where you store the files will affect how you access those files in your HTML code. Determining a good folder structure in the planning phase of the Web development life cycle is important. You'll learn more about effective folder structures in Chapter 3.

During the design and development phase, you should also consider what, if any, types of multimedia could contribute positively to the Web site experience. For instance,

BTW

Web Page Structure

There are many resources available on the Web that further discuss Web site structures. In addition to general design information, there are a number of tools available for sale or free download that can help you design your Web sites. Enter the phrase "Web site structure" into a search engine to find many valuable design sources.

adding a video message from the company CEO might be useful, but if the computing environment of your users cannot accommodate video playback, then the video serves no purpose. In general, do not use advanced multimedia technologies in a Web site unless they make a positive contribution to the Web site experience. Today, more Web sites are using audio and video content. The addition of multimedia can enhance the overall purpose of the Web site, but it sometimes detracts from the message.

Finally, consider accessibility issues and internationalization. A Web developer should always design for viewing by a diverse audience, including physically impaired and global users. A key consideration is that the software used by physically impaired individuals does not work with some Web features. For instance, if you use graphics on the Web site, always include alternative text for each graphic. To support an international audience, use generic icons that can be understood globally, avoid slang expressions in the content, and build simple pages that load quickly over lower-speed connections.

The design issues just discussed are only a few of the basic Web page design issues that you need to consider. Throughout this book, design issues will be addressed as they relate to each project. Many excellent Web page design resources are also available on the Internet.

Once the design of the Web site is determined, Web development can begin. The rest of the chapters in this book discuss good Web page standards, in addition to the actual development of Web pages. You will learn many development techniques, including links, tables, graphics, image maps, and Web forms. The umbrella that covers all of the development techniques taught in this book is the use of Cascading Style Sheets (CSS).

BTW

Web Site Testing
Testing should be done on all pages in a Web site. You should also test the links within the Web page, to other Web pages in the Web site, and to external Web sites. Testing is an important part of Web development and assures that your Web pages work as intended.

Web Site Testing

A Web site should be tested at various stages of the Web design and development processes. The testing process should be comprehensive and include a review of Web page content, functionality, and usability. Web sites with broken links, missing graphics, and incorrect content create a poor impression. You want to attract users to your Web site and maintain their interest. If visitors find that your Web site is poorly tested and maintained, they will be less likely to return. You cannot get your message out if users don't frequently visit the Web site. Some basic steps to test content and functionality include:

- Validating each Web page by running it through the W3C markup validation service
- Proofreading page content and titles to review for accurate spelling and grammar
- Checking links to ensure they are not broken and are linked correctly
- Checking graphics to confirm they appear properly and are linked correctly
- Ensuring that accessibility and internationalization issues are addressed
- Testing forms and other interactive page elements
- Testing pages to make sure they load quickly, even over lower-speed connections
- Printing each page to check how printed pages look

Usability is the measure of how well a product, such as a Web site, allows a user to accomplish his or her goals. **Usability testing** is a method by which users of a Web site or other product are asked to perform certain tasks in an effort to measure the product's ease-of-use and the user's perception of the experience. Usability testing for a Web site should focus on three key aspects: content, navigation, and presentation.

Usability testing can be conducted in several ways; one effective way is to directly observe users interfacing with (or using) the Web site. As you observe users, you can track the links they click and record their actions and comments. You can even ask the users to explain what tasks they were trying to accomplish while navigating the site. The information gained by observing users can be invaluable in helping identify potential problem areas in the Web site. For example, if you observe that users have difficulty finding the

Web page that lists store locations and hours of operation, you may want to clarify the link descriptions or make the links more prominent on the home page.

Another way to conduct usability testing is to give users a specific task to complete (such as finding a product price list) and then observe how they navigate the site to complete the task. If possible, ask them to explain why they selected certain links. Both of these observation methods are extremely valuable, but require access to users.

Usability testing can also be completed using a questionnaire or survey. When writing a questionnaire or survey, be sure to write open-ended questions that can give you valuable information. For instance, asking the yes/no question "Is the Web site visually appealing?" will not gather useful information. If you change that question to use a scaled response, such as, "Rate the visual appeal of this Web site, using a scale of 1 for low and 5 for high," you can get more valuable input from the users. Make sure, however, that the scale itself is clear and understandable to the users. If you intend that a selection of 1 equates to a "low" rating, but the users think a 1 means "high," then your survey results are questionable. A usability testing questionnaire should always include space for users to write additional explanatory comments.

Figure 1–17 shows some examples of types of questions and organization that you might include in a Web site usability testing questionnaire.

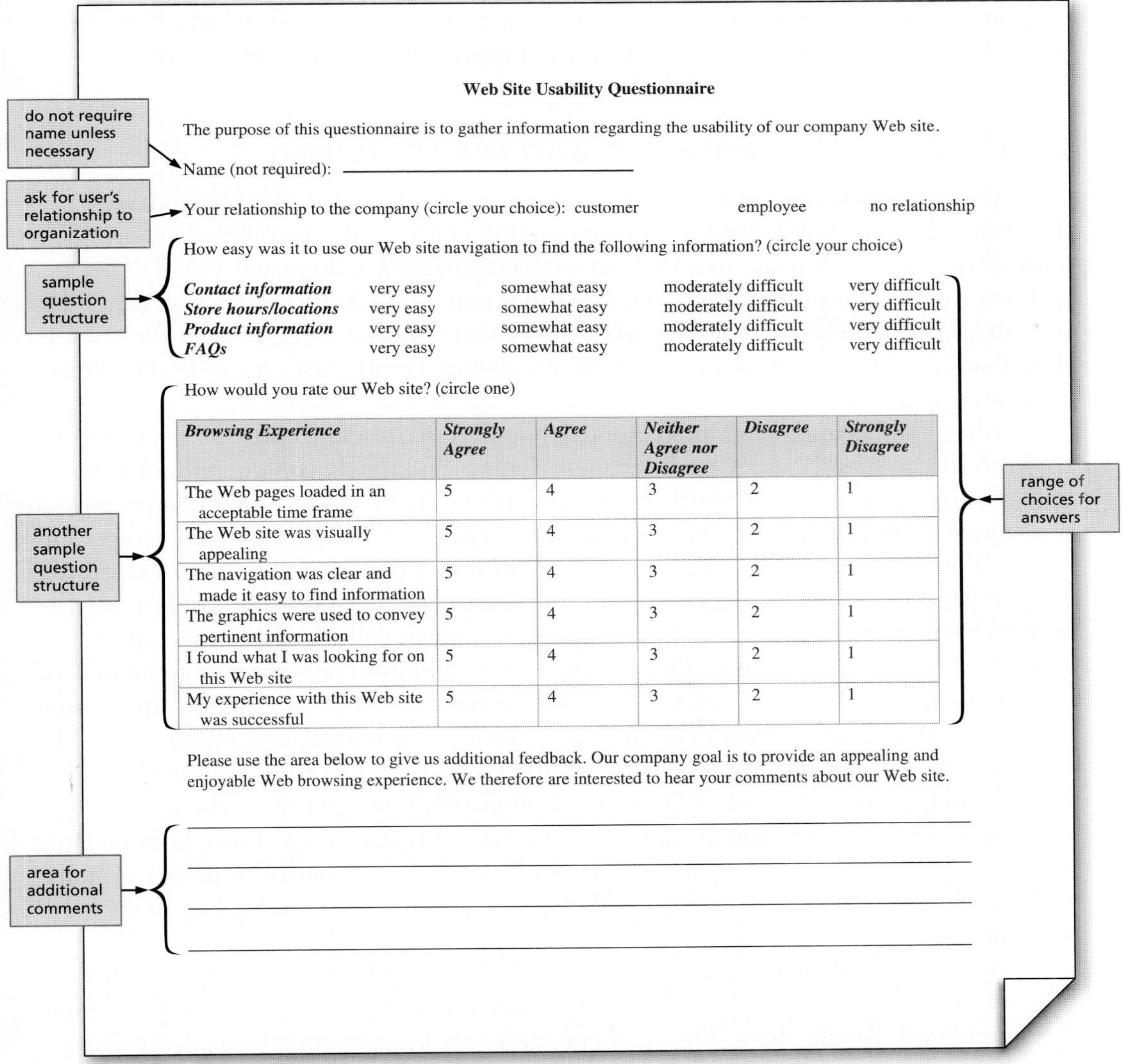

Web Site Usability Questionnaire

The purpose of this questionnaire is to gather information regarding the usability of our company Web site.

Name (not required): ____________________

Your relationship to the company (circle your choice): customer employee no relationship

How easy was it to use our Web site navigation to find the following information? (circle your choice)

Contact information	very easy	somewhat easy	moderately difficult	very difficult
Store hours/locations	very easy	somewhat easy	moderately difficult	very difficult
Product information	very easy	somewhat easy	moderately difficult	very difficult
FAQs	very easy	somewhat easy	moderately difficult	very difficult

How would you rate our Web site? (circle one)

Browsing Experience	***Strongly Agree***	***Agree***	***Neither Agree nor Disagree***	***Disagree***	***Strongly Disagree***
The Web pages loaded in an acceptable time frame	5	4	3	2	1
The Web site was visually appealing	5	4	3	2	1
The navigation was clear and made it easy to find information	5	4	3	2	1
The graphics were used to convey pertinent information	5	4	3	2	1
I found what I was looking for on this Web site	5	4	3	2	1
My experience with this Web site was successful	5	4	3	2	1

Please use the area below to give us additional feedback. Our company goal is to provide an appealing and enjoyable Web browsing experience. We therefore are interested to hear your comments about our Web site.

Figure 1–17 Web site usability testing questionnaire.

In addition to content, functionality, and usability testing, there are other types of testing. For a newly implemented or maintained Web site, two other types of tests should be conducted: compatibility testing and stress testing. **Compatibility testing** is done to verify that the Web site works with a variety of browsers and browser versions. Initially, test using the browsers that your audience is most likely to use. Different browsers display some aspects of Web pages differently, so it is important to test Web pages in several different browsers to verify they appear correctly in each browser. If you have used technologies that are not supported by older browsers or that require plug-ins, consider changing the content or providing alternative Web pages for viewing in older browsers. If your audience uses both PC and Macintosh computers, you need to test the Web pages using browsers on both platforms. You may also want to test the Web pages in several versions of the same browser (usually the two most recent versions), in the event users have not yet upgraded.

Stress testing determines what happens on your Web site when greater numbers of users access the site. A Web site with 100 users accessing it simultaneously may be fine. When thousands of users use the Web site at once, it may operate at an unacceptably slow speed. Stress testing verifies that a Web site runs at an acceptable speed with many users. There are many cases in which companies did not effectively stress test their Web sites. The results of this lack of testing have been disastrous, with Web sites locking up when too many users tried to access the same Web site function. Especially in the case of Web sites used for e-commerce, it is imperative for the Web site to stay online. A crashed or locked-up Web site will not sell products or services, and the company stands to lose a lot of money.

Web Site Implementation and Maintenance

Once Web site testing is complete and any required changes have been made, the Web site can be implemented. Implementation of a Web site involves the actual publishing of the Web pages to a Web server. Many HTML editors and WYSIWYG editors provide publishing capabilities. You can also use FTP software, such as WS_FTP or CuteFTP, to publish your Web pages to a Web server. After you publish a Web site, you should test the Web pages again to confirm no obvious errors exist such as broken links or missing graphics.

After a site is tested and implemented, you need to develop a process to maintain the Web site; users will undoubtedly request changes and timely content will require updates. You need to ensure, however, that updates to the Web site do not compromise the site's integrity and consistency. For example, if you have several different people updating various Web pages on a large Web site, you might find it difficult to maintain a consistent look on pages across the Web site. You should plan to update your Web site on a regular basis to keep content up-to-date. This could mean hourly, daily, weekly, or less often, depending on the site's purpose. Do not allow your content to become stale, outdated, or include broken links to Web pages that no longer exist. As a user looking for information related to a specific topic, how likely are you to believe the information found on a Web site that says "Last update on December 10, 1998" comes from a reliable source?

To help manage the task of Web site maintenance, first determine who is responsible for updates to content, structure, functionality, and so on. Then, limit update responsibilities to specific users. Be sure the implementation is controlled by one or more Web developers who can verify that the Web pages are tested thoroughly before they are published.

As updates and changes are made to a Web site, consider notifying users with a graphic banner or a "What's New" announcement, explaining any new features and how the features will benefit them. This technique not only keeps users informed, but also encourages them to come back to the Web site to see what is new.

Finally, Web site monitoring is another key aspect of maintaining a Web site. Usually, the Web servers that host Web sites keep logs of information about Web site usage. A **log** is the file that lists all of the Web pages that have been requested from the Web site. Web site logs are an invaluable source of information for a Web developer. Obtaining and analyzing the logs allow you to determine such things as the number of visitors, browser types and versions, connection speeds, pages most commonly requested, and usage patterns. With this information, you can design a Web site that is effective for your targeted audience, providing visitors with a rich and rewarding experience.

Be an Observant Web User

As you embark on this course, and perhaps start your Web development career, one useful practice is to be an observant Web user. Most of us use the Web several times a day (or more often) to complete our daily tasks. As a Web developer, you should review the Web pages that you access with an eye on functionality and design. As described in the first In the Lab exercise at the end of the chapter, you can bookmark Web sites you think are effective and ineffective, good and bad, and use them as references for your own Web development efforts. Watch for trends on the Web as you search for information or make online purchases. For example, blinking text and patterned backgrounds used to be very popular on the Web, but now other design techniques have taken over. Being an observant Web user can help you become a more effective Web developer.

BTW

Quick Reference
For a list of HTML tags and their associated attributes, see the HTML Quick Reference (Appendix A) at the back of this book, or visit the HTML Quick Reference on the Book Companion Site Web page for this book at www.cengagebrain.com.

Chapter Summary

In this chapter, you have learned about the Internet, the World Wide Web, and associated technologies, including Web servers and Web browsers. You learned the essential role of HTML in creating Web pages and reviewed tools used to create HTML documents. You also learned that most Web development projects follow a five-phase life cycle. The items listed below include all the new concepts you have learned in this chapter.

1. Describe the Internet (HTML 2)
2. Describe the World Wide Web (HTML 3)
3. Define Web servers (HTML 4)
4. Describe the Internet, intranets, and extranets (HTML 5)
5. Discuss Web browsers (HTML 7)
6. Define Hypertext Markup Language (HTML 8)
7. Describe HTML elements (HTML 9)
8. List useful HTML practices (HTML 10)
9. Explain HTML versions (HTML 11)
10. Describe Cascading Style Sheets (HTML 11)
11. Define the Document Object Model (HTML 12)
12. Define Extensible Hypertext Markup Language (XHTML) (HTML 12)
13. Describe tools for creating HTML documents (HTML 13)
14. Discuss the Web development life cycle (HTML 15)
15. Describe steps in the Web development planning phase (HTML 16)
16. Explain the Web development analysis phase (HTML 16)
17. Discuss Web design and development (HTML 17)
18. Describe various Web site structures (HTML 17)
19. Discuss the importance of Web site testing, including usability testing, compatibility testing, and stress testing (HTML 22)
20. Discuss Web site implementation and maintenance (HTML 24)
21. Explain the importance of being an observant Web user (HTML 25)

Learn It Online

Test your knowledge of chapter content and key terms.

Instructions: To complete the following exercises, please visit www.cengagebrain.com. At the CengageBrain.com home page, search for *HTML5 and CSS 7th Edition* using the search box at the top of the page. This will take you to the product page for this book. On the product page, click the Access Now button below the Study Tools heading. On the Book Companion Site Web page, select chapter 1, and then click the link for the desired exercise.

Chapter Reinforcement TF, MC, and SA

A series of true/false, multiple choice, and short answer questions that test your knowledge of the chapter content.

Flash Cards

An interactive learning environment where you identify chapter key terms associated with displayed definitions.

Practice Test

A series of multiple choice questions that test your knowledge of chapter content and key terms.

Who Wants to Be a Computer Genius?

An interactive game that challenges your knowledge of chapter content in the style of a television quiz show.

Wheel of Terms

An interactive game that challenges your knowledge of chapter key terms in the style of the television show *Wheel of Fortune*.

Crossword Puzzle Challenge

A crossword puzzle that challenges your knowledge of key terms presented in the chapter.

Apply Your Knowledge

Reinforce the skills and apply the concepts you learned in this chapter.

Understanding Web Page Structures

Instructions: Figure 1–18 shows the Web site of OnGuardOnline.gov. As you learned in this chapter, three common Web site structures include linear, hierarchical, and webbed. Based on that information, determine the structure used in the OnGuardOnline.gov Web site. Review other similar Web sites and determine which Web site design features are beneficial to a user. Incorporate those ideas into a new Web site design for OnGuardOnline.gov. Use paper to sketch the new Web site design for the OnGuardOnline.gov Web site.

Perform the following tasks:

1. Start your browser. Open the OnGuardOnline.gov Web site in your browser. Print the home page by clicking Print on the File menu or by clicking the Print icon.
2. Explore the OnGuardOnline.gov Web site, determine the structure that the Web site utilizes (linear, hierarchical, or webbed), and then write that on the printout.
3. Find two other government Web sites. Print the home pages for each of those sites. Navigate these Web sites to identify any design features that are beneficial to a user.
4. Using ideas from the government Web sites that you found in Step 3, sketch a new Web site structure and design for the OnGuardOnline.gov site on paper.
5. Submit your answers in the format specified by your instructor.

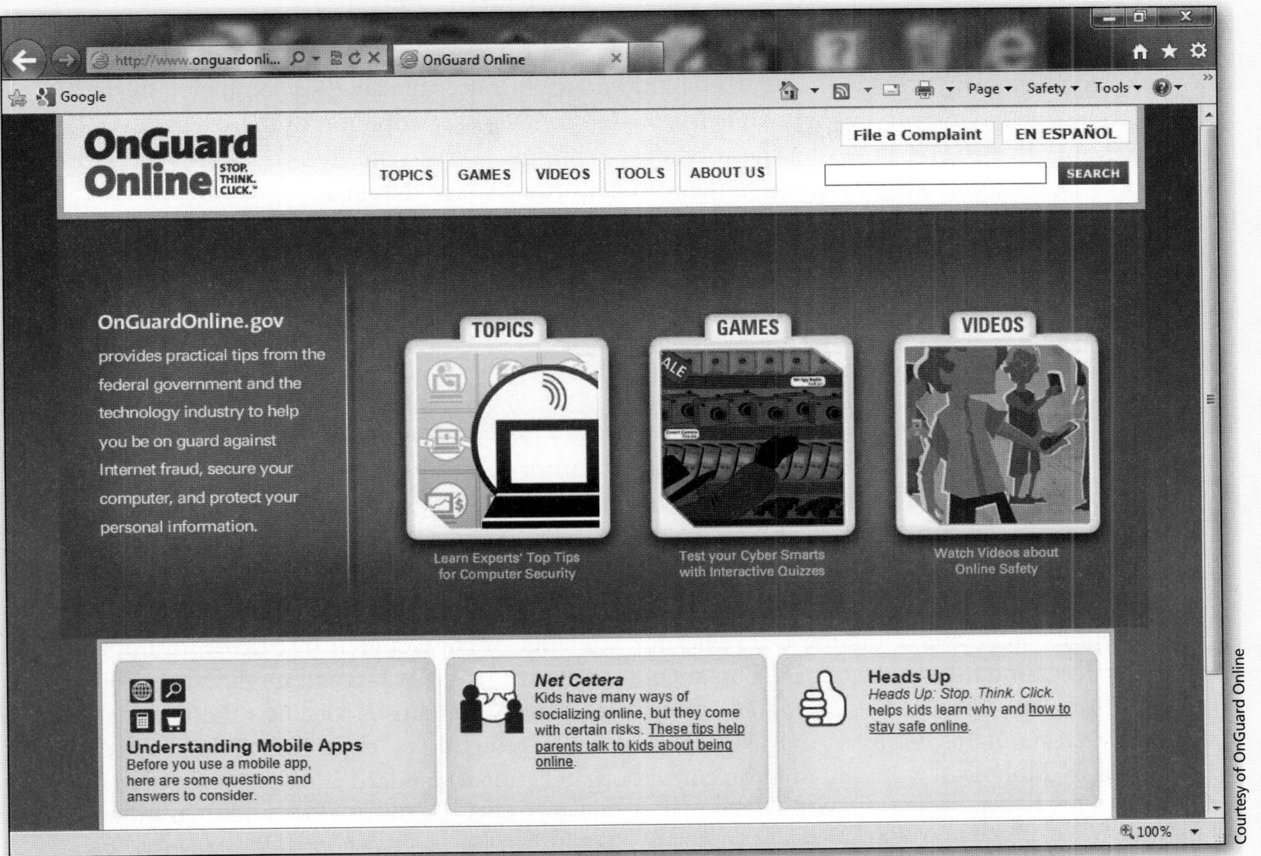

Courtesy of OnGuard Online

Figure 1–18

Extend Your Knowledge

Extend the skills you learned in this chapter and experiment with new skills.

Evaluating a User Survey

Instructions: Start your word-processing program. Open the document extend1-1.docx from the Chapter01\Extend folder of the Data Files for Students. See the inside back cover of this book for instructions on downloading the Data Files for Students, or contact your instructor for information about accessing the required files. This sample Web site survey shows various questions that could be asked in gathering feedback on Web site usability. It is important to assess the usability of your Web site, as mentioned in the chapter.

You will evaluate the user survey and modify the questions or add new questions that apply to the Web site that you have chosen. Then you will ask five people to take your survey.

Perform the following tasks:

1. Determine if the survey questions would provide you with valuable information about a Web site. Why or why not?
2. Identify what you can do to improve the Web site survey. Using a word processor, type your analysis into a new file, and save the file as extend1-1solution.docx.
3. Once you have analyzed the questions in the original survey, make changes to the user survey by following some of the guidelines provided in Figure 1–17 on page HTML 23. Type your new

Continued >

Extend Your Knowledge *continued*

survey questions into the new extend1-1solution.docx file after the analysis completed in step 2. Add questions to the survey that will help you determine a user's opinion of the selected Web site. Remember that the purpose of using surveys is to improve a Web site. Your questions therefore have to provide you with information that can help you achieve that goal.

4. After you have completed these steps, submit the extend1-1solution.docx file in the format specified by your instructor.

Make It Right

Analyze a document and correct all errors and/or improve the design.

Correcting the Web Site Type Table

Instructions: Start your word-processing program. Open the file makeitright1-1.docx from the Chapter01\MakeItRight folder of the Data Files for Students. See the inside back cover of this book for instructions on downloading the Data Files for Students, or contact your instructor for information about accessing the required files. The document, shown in Table 1–6, is a modified version of Table 1–5 (on page HTML 17). The table, which intentionally contains errors, lists the Web page organizational standards discussed in this chapter. Without referring to Table 1–5, make the necessary corrections to Table 1–6 by identifying the correct organizational standard and reason for each of the seven elements listed. Save the revised document as makeitright1-1solution.docx and then submit it in the form specified by your instructor.

Table 1–6 Web Page Organizational Standards

Element	Organizational Standard	Reason
Titles	Use these to separate main topics	These provide graphical elements to break up Web page content
Headings	Use simple ones that clearly explain the purpose of the page	These provide shorter, more-readable sections of text
Horizontal Rules	Utilize these in bulleted or numbered format when appropriate	Web users do not always scroll to view information on longer pages; appropriate page lengths increase the likelihood that users will view key information
Paragraphs	Maintain suitable Web page lengths	Web users are quick to peruse a page; placing critical information at the top of the page increases the likelihood that users will view key information
Lists	Insert these graphical elements to separate main topics	These provide organized, easy-to-read text that readers can scan
Page Length	Use these to help divide large amounts of text	Titles help users understand the purpose of the page; a good title explains the page in the search engine results lists
Information	Emphasize the most important information by placing it at the top of a Web page	These make a Web page easier to read; simple headlines clearly explain the purpose of the page

In the Lab

Design and/or create a document using the guidelines, concepts, and skills presented in this chapter. Labs are listed in order of increasing difficulty.

Lab 1: Evaluating Web Sites

Problem: In this chapter, you learned the importance of being an observant Web user, which can help you become a more effective Web developer. To further develop that concept, find and then discuss "good" and "bad" ("effective" and "ineffective") Web sites. Start your browser and your word-processing program. Open the file lab1-1.docx from the Chapter01\IntheLab folder of the Data Files for Students. See the inside back cover of this book for instructions for downloading the Data Files for Students, or contact your instructor for information on accessing the required files for this book.

Instructions: Perform the following steps using your browser and the file listed.

1. Browse the Internet and find one "good" (i.e., effective) and one "bad" (i.e., ineffective) Web site. Determine, based on your own opinion, what is "good" and what is "bad" in these Web sites. You will identify the specific reason for your opinion in Step 2 below.
2. Using the lab1-1.docx file, rate the usability of the good and bad Web sites that you selected. Be sure to add additional comments in the survey to specifically identify your positive or negative feelings about the Web site. Save the documents using the file names lab1-1goodsolution.docx and lab1-1badsolution.docx.
3. Team up with one other student and discuss your survey results while reviewing the Web sites that you selected. Also review your student partner's Web sites and surveys.
4. Open the word-processing document named lab1-1comparison.docx and note any differences of opinion in your survey results and the opinion of your student partner. Make sure to include the URLs of the four Web sites that you and your partner reviewed in this new document. Save the document using the file name lab1-1comparison.docx.
5. Submit your own solutions (lab1-1goodsolution.docx and lab1-1badsolution.docx) and the team document (lab1-1comparison.docx) in the format specified by your instructor.

In the Lab

Lab 2: Designing a Web Site for a Flower Shop

Problem: Your neighborhood flower shop wants you to design a Web site that will give visitors access to a full range of information. To do this, you must complete the planning and analysis phases by answering such questions as:

- What tasks do flower shop visitors want to complete on the Web site?
- What tasks will the flower shop owner want to complete on the Web site?
- What types of information should be included?
- Who will provide information on the Web site content?

Interview several friends or relatives who have visited flower shops in the past and determine the answers to these questions. Based on that information, you will draw a sketch of a design for the home page of the flower shop's Web site, such as the design shown in Figure 1–19 on the next page.

Continued >

STUDENT ASSIGNMENTS

In the Lab *continued*

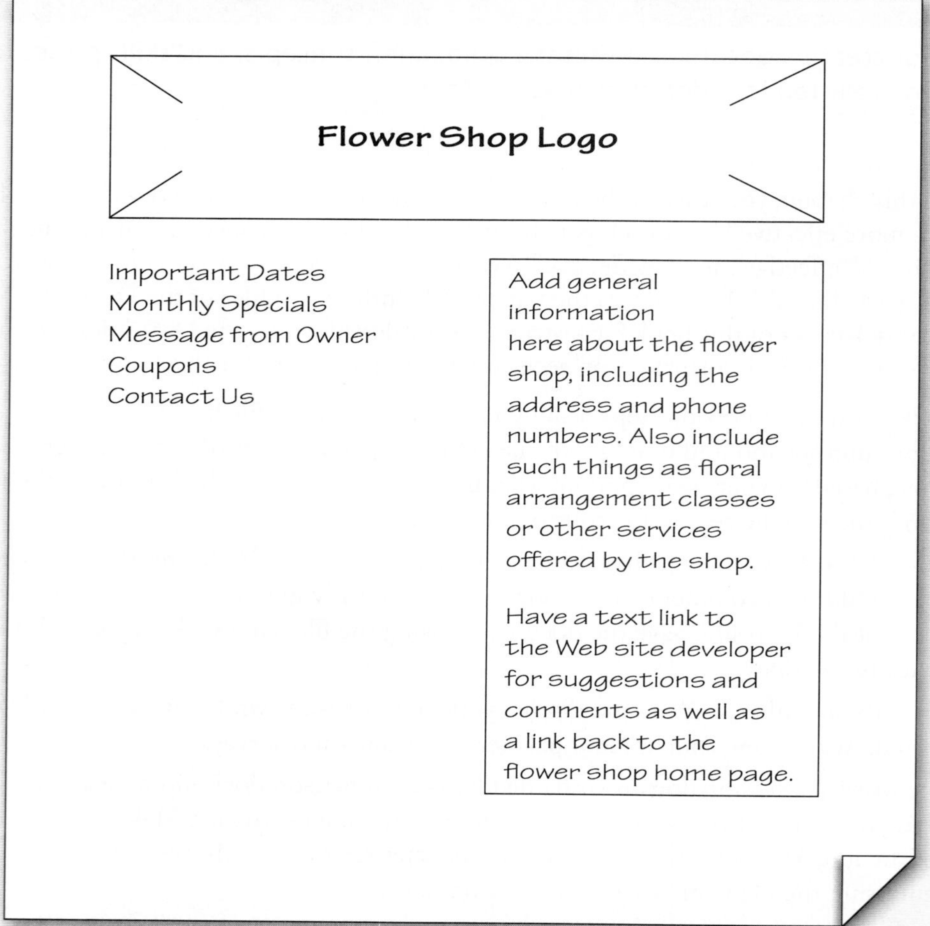

Figure 1–19

Instructions: Perform the following tasks using your word-processing program and paper.

1. Review the questions in the planning and analysis phases of the Web development life cycle, as shown in Table 1–4 on page HTML 15.
2. Assess the value of those questions listed in the table. Add other questions that you think are relevant to the planning and analysis of a flower shop Web site.
3. Start your word-processing program. If necessary, open a new document. Enter the questions you will use for planning and analysis. Save the document using the file name lab1-2solution.docx. Print the document.
4. Using the questions that you developed, interview friends and family who have visited flower shops to determine what information should be included in the Web site, who will provide the information, and so on.
5. After gathering the required information, sketch a design for the home page of the Web site on paper.
6. Share your design sketch with the people who you interviewed to get their opinions on your design.

7. Redraw the design on paper, making any changes based on the input from the friends and relatives with whom you have worked.
8. Write Original Design on the first design sketch.
9. Write Second Design on the second design sketch.
10. Submit your solution (lab1-2solution.docx) in the format specified by your instructor.

In the Lab

Lab 3: Asking Planning Phase Questions: Internet, Intranet, and Extranet Designs

Problem: Three different types of Web sites were discussed in this chapter — Internet, intranet, and extranet. Each type of Web site is designed for a different target audience. Think of a retail business that you frequently visit and how that business might use an Internet, intranet, and extranet site. The Planning phase questions found in Table 1–4 on page HTML 15 have been reproduced in Table 1–7. Determine the answers to these questions and enter your ideas in the table. If there are questions that are difficult/impossible to answer directly (for example, What are users' computing environments?), list ways that you can find the answers to those questions.

Instructions: Start your word-processing program. Open the file lab1-3.docx from the Chapter01\IntheLab folder of the Data Files for Students. See the inside back cover of this book for instructions for downloading the Data Files for Students, or contact your instructor for information on accessing the required files. Perform the following tasks using your word-processing program.

1. Enter the type of business in the first row of the table. Determine the answers to the first question for all three types of Web sites and then enter the answers in the appropriate table cells. If the business you chose has no reason to maintain one of the three types of Web sites (Internet, intranet, or extranet), thoroughly identify in your answer why they would not need it.
2. Continue answering the other four questions.
3. Save the file using the file name lab1-3solution.docx and then submit it in the format specified by your instructor.

Table 1–7 Planning Phase Questions

Type Of Business			
Planning Question	**Internet**	**Intranet**	**Extranet**
What is the purpose of this Web site?			
Who will use this Web site?			
What are users' computing environments?			
Who owns and authors the information on the Web site?			
Who decides if/where the information goes on the Web site?			

Cases and Places

Apply your creative thinking and problem-solving skills to design and implement a solution.

Note: To complete these assignments, you may be required to use the Data Files for Students. See the inside back cover of this book for instructions on downloading the Data Files for Students, or contact your instructor for information about accessing the required files.

1: Create a Usability Survey

Academic

Your school recently updated its Web site. The school administration has selected a team to develop a usability survey or questionnaire that you can give to a group of users (including students, parents, and teachers) to evaluate the new Web site. What types of information do you hope to gain by distributing this survey or questionnaire? How can you convey information on the survey or questionnaire so it clearly identifies what you are asking? Create a usability survey using your word-processing program. Give the survey or questionnaire to at least five people, including at least one from each group identified above. Allow participants to complete the survey or questionnaire and then look at the results. If possible, ask the users what they thought the various questions conveyed. Is that what you wanted to convey? If not, think of clearer, more relevant questions and redistribute the survey to another group of participants.

2: Learn More About HTML5

Personal

This chapter introduced the use of HTML5 in Web development. You will utilize HTML5 throughout this book, so it is important that you become familiar with it. Visit the W3Schools Web site (w3schools.com) to learn more about HTML5. Find three other sources of information about HTML5 on other Web sites. Using a word-processing program, create a document that briefly describes the Web sites that you found and an explanation about how you could utilize these three Web sites for Web development.

3: Learn More About Web Access Issues

Professional

Your company wants to offer online courses to employees. Several employees have physical challenges, and it is imperative that the online courses be accessible to everyone. Your manager has asked you to learn more about accessibility guidelines to determine what changes are needed to make the company's online courses accessible to those with physical challenges. Research accessibility issues on the Web and determine what needs should be considered to satisfy accessibility requirements. Make sure to visit the w3.org Web site. Consider the following questions when doing your research: What types of physical challenges do you have to consider when developing Web pages? What recommendations do the Web sites make for accessibility? Why is this important to you as a Web developer?

2 Creating and Editing a Web Page Using Inline Styles

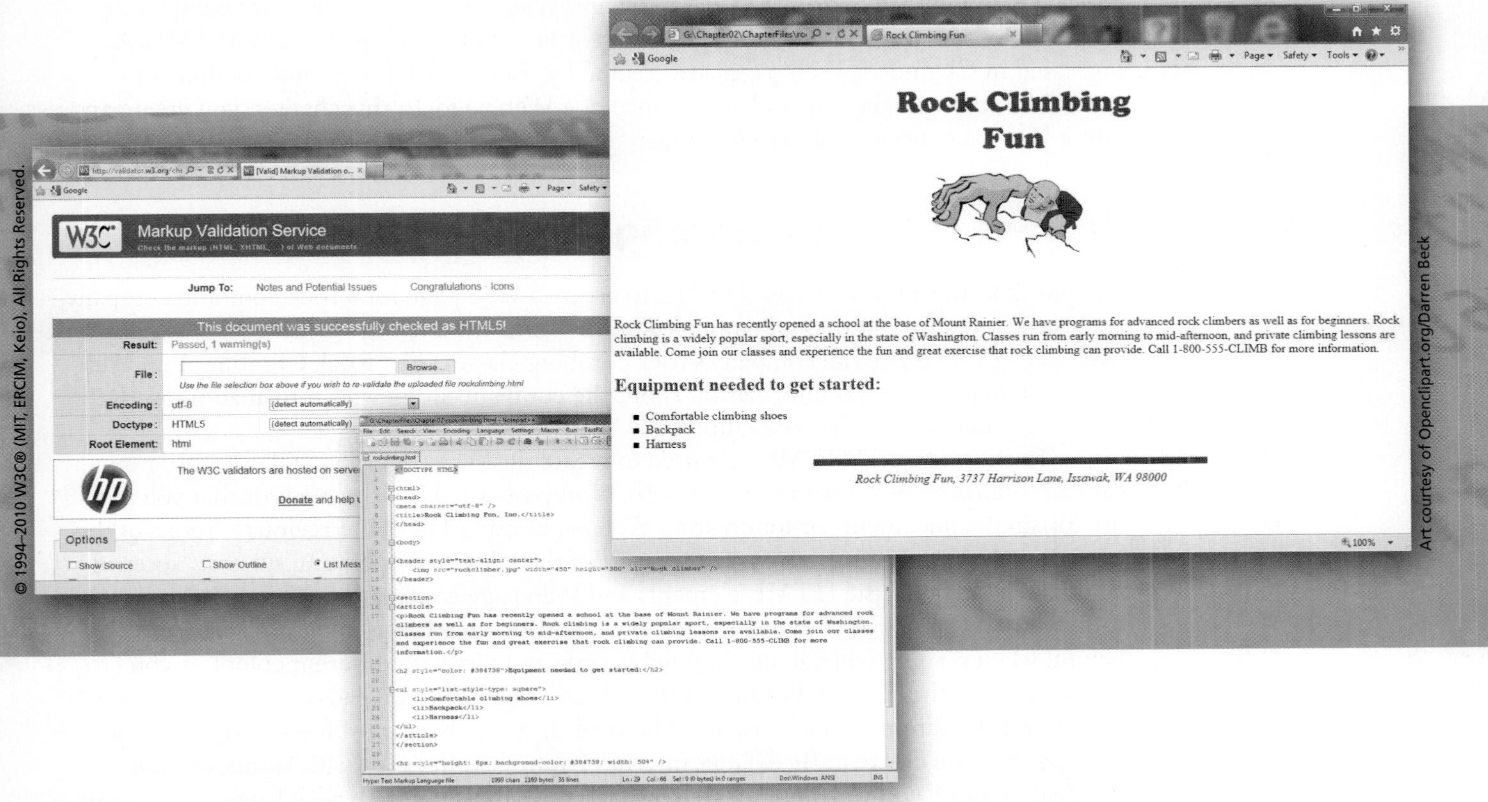

Objectives

You will have mastered the material in this chapter when you can:

- Identify elements of a Web page
- Start Notepad++ and describe the Notepad++ window
- Enable word wrap in Notepad++
- Enter HTML tags
- Enter a centered heading and a paragraph of text
- Create an unordered, ordered, or definition list
- Save an HTML file
- Use a browser to view a Web page
- Activate Notepad++
- Identify Web page image types and attributes
- Add an image, change the color of headings on a Web page, change a bulleted list style, and add a horizontal rule using inline styles
- View the HTML source code in a browser
- Print a Web page and an HTML file
- Quit Notepad++ and a browser

2 Creating and Editing a Web Page Using Inline Styles

Introduction

With an understanding of the Web development life cycle, you should have a good idea about the importance of proper Web site planning, analysis, and design. After completing these phases, the next phase is the actual development of a Web page using HTML. As discussed in Chapter 1, Web pages are created by using HTML tags and attributes to define the structure, layout, and appearance of a Web page. In this chapter, you create and edit a Web page using basic HTML tags.

Project — Rock Climbing Fun Web Page

Chapter 2 illustrates how to use HTML to create a Web page for a rock climbing company, as shown in Figure 2–1a. As an employee of the company, one of your tasks is to develop a Web page to advertise the company's rock climbing classes. The Rock Climbing Fun Web page will include general information about the company along with information on the equipment needed to start rock climbing.

To enter text and HTML tags used to create the Web page, you will use a program called Notepad++, as shown in Figure 2–1b. **Notepad++** is a basic text editor that you can use for simple documents or for creating Web pages using HTML. Previous editions of this book used Notepad, a text editor that is a part of the Windows operating system. Notepad worked well to enter the HTML elements and Web page content, but Notepad++ is a more sophisticated text editor with more features. Notepad++ has line numbering, which is very helpful when reading code. It also highlights code and text with different colors, as you will see later in the chapter. Because of this added versatility, Notepad++ is the chosen text editor for this edition. You will use the Microsoft Internet Explorer browser to view your Web page as you create it. By default, Internet Explorer is installed with Windows, and Notepad++ can be downloaded for free on the Web. If you do not have Notepad++ on your computer, you can download it from the notepad-plus-plus.org Web site. If you do not have Internet Explorer available on your computer, another browser program will work.

Overview

As you read this chapter, you will learn how to create the Web page shown in Figure 2–1 by performing these general tasks:

- Enter HTML code into the Notepad++ window.
- Save the file as an HTML file.
- Enter basic HTML tags and add text to the file.
- Organize the text by adding headings and creating a bulleted list.
- Enhance the Web page's appearance with an image and inline styles.
- View the Web page and HTML code in your browser.
- Validate the Web page.
- Print the Web page.

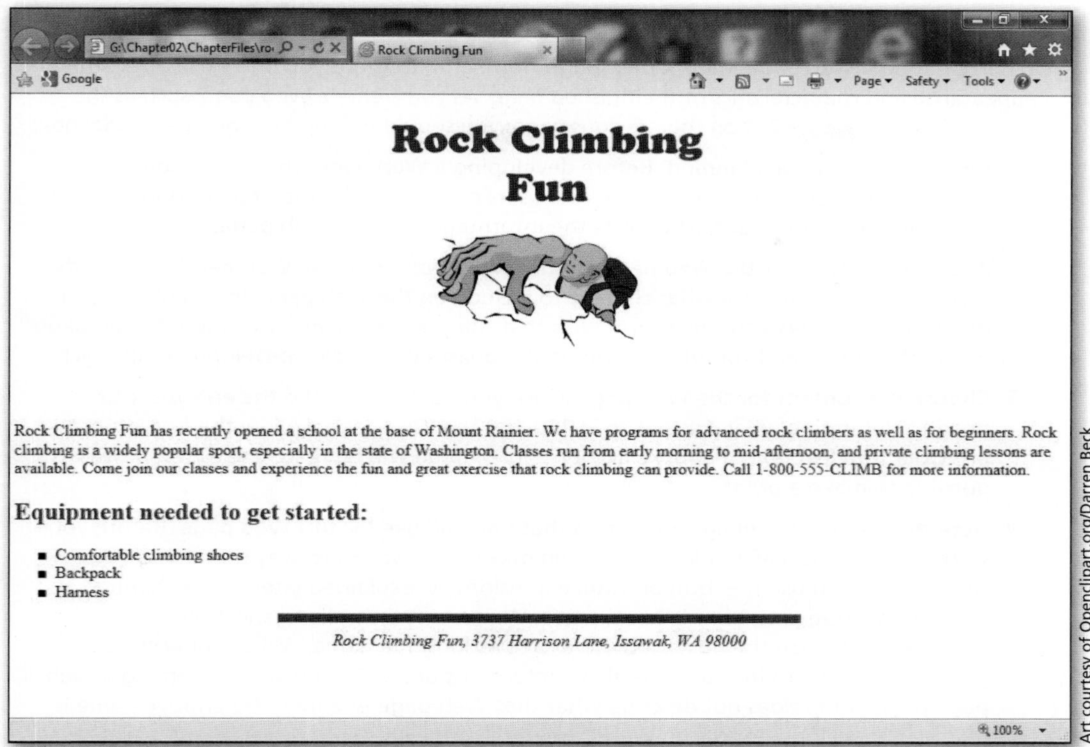

Art courtesy of Openclipart.org/Darren Beck

(a) Rock Climbing Fun Web page.

G:\ChapterFiles\Chapter02\rockclimbing.html - Notepad++

File Edit Search View Encoding Language Settings Macro Run TextFX Plugins Window ?

rockclimbing.html

```
<!DOCTYPE HTML>

<html>
<head>
<meta charset="utf-8" />
<title>Rock Climbing Fun, Inc.</title>
</head>

<body>

<header style="text-align: center">
    <img src="rockclimber.jpg" width="450" height="300" alt="Rock climber" />
</header>

<section>
<article>
<p>Rock Climbing Fun has recently opened a school at the base of Mount Rainier. We have programs for advanced rock climbers as well as for beginners. Rock climbing is a widely popular sport, especially in the state of Washington. Classes run from early morning to mid-afternoon, and private climbing lessons are available. Come join our classes and experience the fun and great exercise that rock climbing can provide. Call 1-800-555-CLIMB for more information.</p>

<h2 style="color: #384738">Equipment needed to get started:</h2>

<ul style="list-style-type: square">
    <li>Comfortable climbing shoes</li>
    <li>Backpack</li>
    <li>Harness</li>
</ul>
</article>
</section>

<hr style="height: 8px; background-color: #384738; width: 50%" />

<footer style="text-align: center; font-style: italic">
    Rock Climbing Fun, 3737 Harrison Lane, Issawak, WA 98000
</footer>

</body>
</html>
```

Hyper Text Markup Language file | 1099 chars 1169 bytes 36 lines | Ln : 36 Col : 8 Sel : 0 (0 bytes) in 0 ranges | Dos\Windows ANSI | INS

(b) HTML code used to create the Web page.

Figure 2–1

Plan Ahead

General Project Guidelines

When creating a Web page, the actions you perform and decisions you make will affect the appearance and characteristics of the finished page. As you create a Web page, such as the project shown in Figure 2–1 on the previous page, you should follow these general guidelines:

1. **Complete Web page planning.** Before developing a Web page, you must know the purpose of the Web site, identify the users of the site and their computing environments, and decide who owns the information on the Web page.
2. **Analyze the need for the Web page.** In the analysis phase of the Web development life cycle, you should analyze what content to include on the Web page. In this phase, you determine the tasks and the information that the users need. Refer to Table 1–4 on page HTML 15 in Chapter 1 for information on the phases of the Web development life cycle.
3. **Choose the content for the Web page.** Once you have completed the analysis, you need to determine what content to include on the Web page. Follow the *less is more* principle. The less text, the more likely the Web page will be read. Use as few words as possible to make a point.
4. **Determine the file naming convention that you will use for this Web page.** Before you start creating and saving files, you should decide on a standard way of naming your files. Should you use the .htm or .html extension? As explained later in the chapter, you use the .htm extension when the host Web server only allows short file names. You use .html when the host Web server allows long file names. What name should you give your file to indicate the file's content or purpose? For instance, naming a Web page page1.html does not describe what that Web page is; a more descriptive name is helpful in development of the Web site.
5. **Determine where to save the Web page.** You can store a Web page permanently, or **save** it, on a variety of storage media, including a hard disk, USB flash drive, CD, or DVD. Your instructor or the company for whom you are developing the Web page may have specific storage media requirements.
6. **Determine what folder structure to use on your storage device.** Once you have determined the storage media to use, you should also determine folder location, structure, and names on which to save the Web page. This should be done before you start to save any of your files.
7. **Identify how to format various elements of the Web page.** The overall appearance of a Web page significantly affects its ability to communicate clearly. Examples of how you can modify the appearance, or **format**, of the Web page include adding an image, color to headings, and horizontal rules.
8. **Find appropriate graphical images.** Eye-catching graphical images help convey the Web page's overall message and add visual interest. Graphics can be used to show a product, service, result, or benefit, or visually convey a message that is not expressed easily with words.
9. **Establish where to position and how to format the graphical images.** The position and format of the graphical images should grab the attention of viewers and draw them into reading the Web page.
10. **Test the Web page for W3C compliance.** An important part of Web development is testing to assure that your Web page follows standards. The World Wide Web Consortium (W3C) has an online validator that allows you to test your Web page and clearly explains any errors.

When necessary, more specific details concerning the above guidelines are presented at appropriate points in the chapter. The chapter will also identify the actions performed and decisions made regarding these guidelines during the creation of the Web page shown in Figure 2–1a.

Elements of a Web Page

Today, many people — individuals, students, teachers, business executives, Web developers, and others — are developing Web pages for personal or professional reasons. Each person has his or her own style and the resulting Web pages are as diverse as the people who create them. Most Web pages, however, include several basic features, or elements, as shown in Figure 2–2.

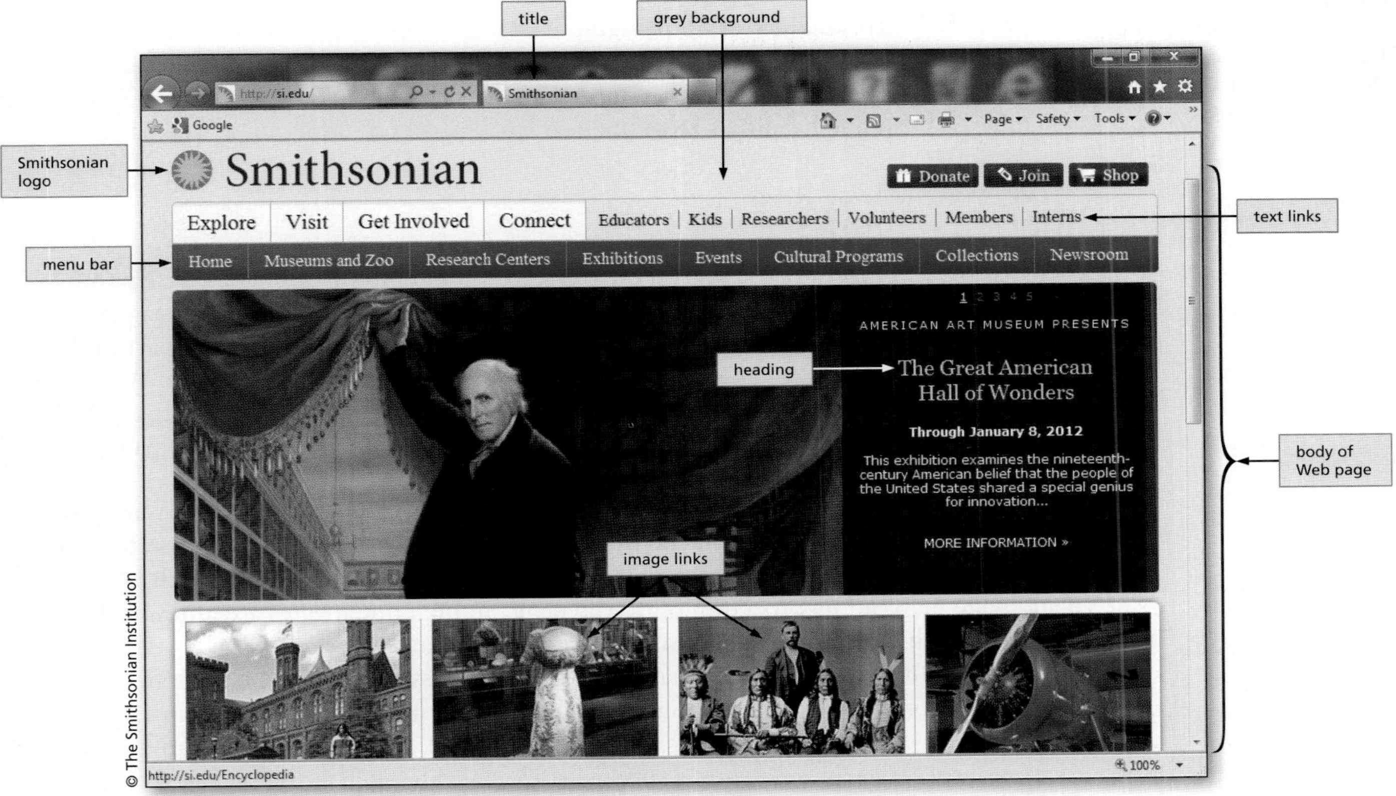

Figure 2–2 Elements of a Web page.

Browser Window Elements

The **title** of a Web page is the text that appears on the title bar and taskbar of the browser window when the Web page appears. The title is also the name assigned to the page if a user adds the page to the browser's list of **favorites**, or **bookmarks**. Because of its importance, you should always include a title on your Web page. The title, which usually is the first element you see, should identify the subject or purpose of the page. The title should be concise, yet descriptive, and briefly explain the page's content or purpose to the visitor.

The **body** of the Web page contains the information that is displayed in the browser window. The body can include text, graphics, and other elements. The Web page displays anything that is contained within the <body> (start body) and </body> (end body) tags. The **background** of a Web page is a solid color, a picture, or a graphic against which the other elements on the Web page appear. When choosing your background, be sure it does not overpower the information on the Web page. As you surf the Web, watch for background colors or images that do not allow the content of the Web page to show through. This is certainly a "what not to do" guideline for Web developers.

BTW

Favorites and Bookmarks
Internet Explorer, Google Chrome, and Mozilla Firefox have a feature that allows you to add Web pages to a list so you can quickly access them in the future. Internet Explorer refers to these as Favorites, while Chrome and Firefox calls them Bookmarks. Web developers need to make sure that they include a descriptive title on their Web pages because that is the title that is shown in the bookmark or favorite.

BTW

HTML Resources
The Web has many wonderful sources of information on HTML and Web page development. One of the better sources is the HTML Goodies Web site, which has primers and tutorials on a variety of topics as well as free downloads and discussion areas. To learn more about this Web site, search for the term "HTML Goodies" in a search engine.

Text Elements

Normal text is the default text format used for the main content of a Web page. Normal text can be used in a standard paragraph or formatted to appear as: bold, italic, or underlined; in different colors; and so on. You can also use inline styles to alter the format of the text, an approach used throughout this book. Normal text can also be used in a series of text items called a **list**. Typically, lists are bulleted or numbered. Various attributes of lists can be altered. For example, you might want to have square bullets rather than the default round bullets, or to have your list text in italic or bold.

Headings are used to set off paragraphs of text or different sections of a page. Headings are a larger font size than normal text and are often bold or italic or a different color than normal text. Heading sizes run from 1 (the largest) to 6 (the smallest). You generally go from one heading size to the next smallest when setting up a Web page.

Image Elements

Web pages typically use several different types of graphics, or images, such as an icon, bullet, line, photo, illustration, or other picture. An image used in a Web page is also called an **inline image**, which means that the image or graphic file is not part of the HTML file. Instead, the Web browser merges the separate graphic file into the Web page as it is displayed in the browser window. The HTML file contains <img> tags that tell the browser which graphic file to request from the server, where to insert it on the page, and how to display it.

Web pages typically use several different types of inline images. An **image map** is a special type of inline image in which you define one or more areas as hotspots. A **hotspot** is an area of an image that activates a function when selected. For example, each hotspot in an image map can link to a different Web page. Some inline images are **animated**, meaning they include motion and can change in appearance.

Horizontal rules are lines that are displayed across a Web page to separate different sections of the page. Although the appearance of a horizontal rule can vary, many Web pages use an inline image as a horizontal rule. Alternatively, you can use the horizontal rule tag (<hr />) to add a simple horizontal rule, such as the one used in this chapter project.

Hyperlink Elements

One of the more important elements of a Web page is a hyperlink, or link. A **link** is text, an image, or another Web page element that you click to instruct the browser to go to a location in a file or to request a file from a server. On the Web, links are the primary way to navigate between Web pages and among Web sites. Links point not only to Web pages, but also to graphics, sound, video, program files, e-mail addresses, and parts of the same Web page. Text links, also called hypertext links, are the most commonly used hyperlinks. For example, the text "Volunteers" in Figure 2–2 on the previous page links to opportunities for volunteer service. When text identifies a hyperlink, it usually appears as underlined text, in a color different from the rest of the Web page text. Image links are also very common. For example, there are two image links identified in Figure 2–2. Clicking either of those image links sends (or links) the user to another Web page that contains further information about those items. A corporate or organizational logo, such as the Smithsonian logo, often serves as an image link to the home page or corporate information.

Defining Web Page Structure

To create an HTML document, you use a text editor to enter information about the structure of the Web page, the content of the Web page, and instructions for how that content should be displayed. This book uses the Notepad++ text editor to enter the HTML elements and content for all projects and exercises.

Before you begin entering the content for this project, you must start by entering tags that define the overall structure of the Web page. You do this by inserting a <!DOCTYPE> tag and five tags (<html>, <head>, <meta />, <title>, and <body>) together with the closing tags (</html>, </head>, </title>, and </body>). These tags define the structure of a standard Web page and divide the HTML file into its basic sections: header information and the body of the page that contains text and graphics.

The **<!DOCTYPE>** tag is used to tell the browser which HTML or XHTML version and type the document uses. Throughout this book, we will utilize the HTML5 <!DOCTYPE> tag. In addition to that tag, the World Wide Web Consortium (W3C) supports three document types for other versions of HTML or XHTML: strict, transitional, and frameset. The **strict** document type is specified when you want to prohibit the use of deprecated tags. **Deprecated tags** are tags that the W3C has earmarked for eventual removal from their specifications, because those tags have been replaced with newer, more functional tags, attributes, or CSS properties. The **transitional** document type allows the use of deprecated tags. The **frameset** document type, which is used to support frames on a Web page, also allows the use of deprecated tags although the frame tags have been eliminated by HTML5. The <!DOCTYPE> tag includes a URL that references a Document Type Definition found on the w3.org Web site. Although this book does not use deprecated tags, the projects do use HTML5, which does not require a URL reference to a Document Type Definition.

BTW

The <!DOCTYPE> Tag
The w3schools.com Web site provides additional information about the <!DOCTYPE> tag used for the HTML5 or XHTML strict, transitional, and frameset document types. To learn more about the <!DOCTYPE> tag, visit the W3C Web site at w3.org. It provides a wealth of information on this and other HTML tags.

Defining the HTML Document

The first set of tags beyond the <!DOCTYPE> tag, **<html>** and **</html>**, indicates the start and end of an HTML document. This set of tags contains all of the content of the Web page, the tags that format that content, and the tags that define the different parts of the document. Software tools, such as browsers, use these tags to determine where the HTML code in a file begins and ends.

The Head The next set of tags, **<head>** and **</head>**, contains the Web page title and other document header information. One of the tags inserted into the <head> </head> container is the meta tag. The **<meta />** tag has several functions. In this chapter, it is used to declare the character encoding UTF-8. The **Unicode Transformation Format** (**UTF**) is a compressed format that allows computers to display and manipulate text. When the browser encounters this meta tag, it will display the Web page properly, based on the particular UTF-8 encoding embedded in the tag. UTF-8 is the preferred encoding standard for Web pages, e-mail, and other applications. The encoding chosen is also important when validating the Web page. The meta tag has other purposes that are described in subsequent chapters of the book. The <title> tag is another tag inserted into the <head> </head> container. The **<title>** and **</title>** tags indicate the title of the Web page, which appears on the browser title bar and taskbar when the Web page is displayed in the browser window. The title is also the name given to the page when a user adds the page to a favorites or bookmarks list.

The Body The final set of tags, **<body>** and **</body>**, contains the main content of the Web page. All text, images, links, and other content are contained within this final set of tags. Table 2–1 on the next page lists the functions of the tags described so far, as well as other tags that you will use in this chapter.

Table 2–1 Basic HTML Tags and Their Functions

HTML Tag	Function
<!DOCTYPE>	Indicates the version and type of HTML used; may include a URL reference to a DTD
<html> </html>	Indicates the start and end of an HTML document
<head> </head>	Indicates the start and end of a section of the document used for the title and other document header information
<meta />	Indicates hidden information about the Web page
<title> </title>	Indicates the start and end of the title. The title does not appear in the body of the Web page, but appears on the title bar of the browser.
<body> </body>	Indicates the start and end of the body of the Web page
<h*n*> </h*n*>	Indicates the start and end of the text section called a heading; sizes range from <h1> through <h6>. See Figure 2–9a on page HTML 47 for heading size samples.
<p> </p>	Indicates the start and end of a new paragraph; inserts a blank line above the new paragraph
<ul> </ul>	Indicates the start and end of an unordered (bulleted) list
<li> </li>	Indicates that the item that follows the tag is an item within a list
<hr />	Inserts a horizontal rule
 	Inserts a line break at the point where the tag appears

BTW **WordPad**
WordPad is a text editor included with Windows that you can also use to create HTML files. To start WordPad, click the Start button on the taskbar, click All Programs in the Start menu, click Accessories in the All Programs submenu, and then click WordPad in the Accessories folder. WordPad Help provides tips on how to use the product.

BTW **Notepad++ Help**
Notepad++ has a wealth of help information available. There is Notepad++ Help internal to the program as well as help facilities online.

Most HTML start tags, such as <html>, <head>, <title>, and <body>, have corresponding end tags, </html>, </head>, </title>, and </body>. Note that, for tags that do not have end tags, such as <meta />, <hr />, and <br />, the tag is closed using a space followed by a forward slash.

To Start Notepad++

With the planning, analysis, and design of the Web page complete, you can begin developing the Web page by entering the HTML code and Web page content using a text editor.

The following steps, which assume Windows 7 is running and Notepad++ is installed, start Notepad++ based on a typical installation. You may need to ask your instructor how to download, install, and start Notepad++ for your computer.

1

- Click the Start button on the Windows taskbar to display the Start menu.
- Click All Programs at the bottom of the left pane on the Start menu to display the All Programs list.
- Click the Notepad++ folder in the All Programs list (Figure 2–3).

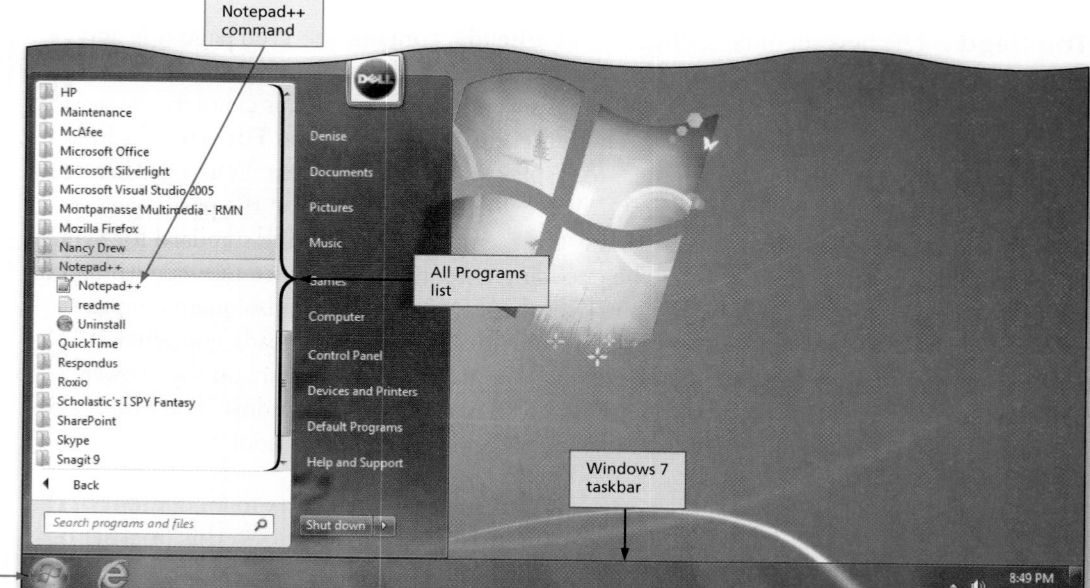

Figure 2–3

2

- Click Notepad++ in the list to display a blank Notepad++ window (Figure 2–4).
- If the Notepad++ window is not maximized, click the Maximize button on the Notepad++ title bar to maximize it. Note that by default, Notepad++ starts with the most recently used file open, so your Notepad++ screen may not look like Figure 2–4. To close all open files, click File and then click Close All.

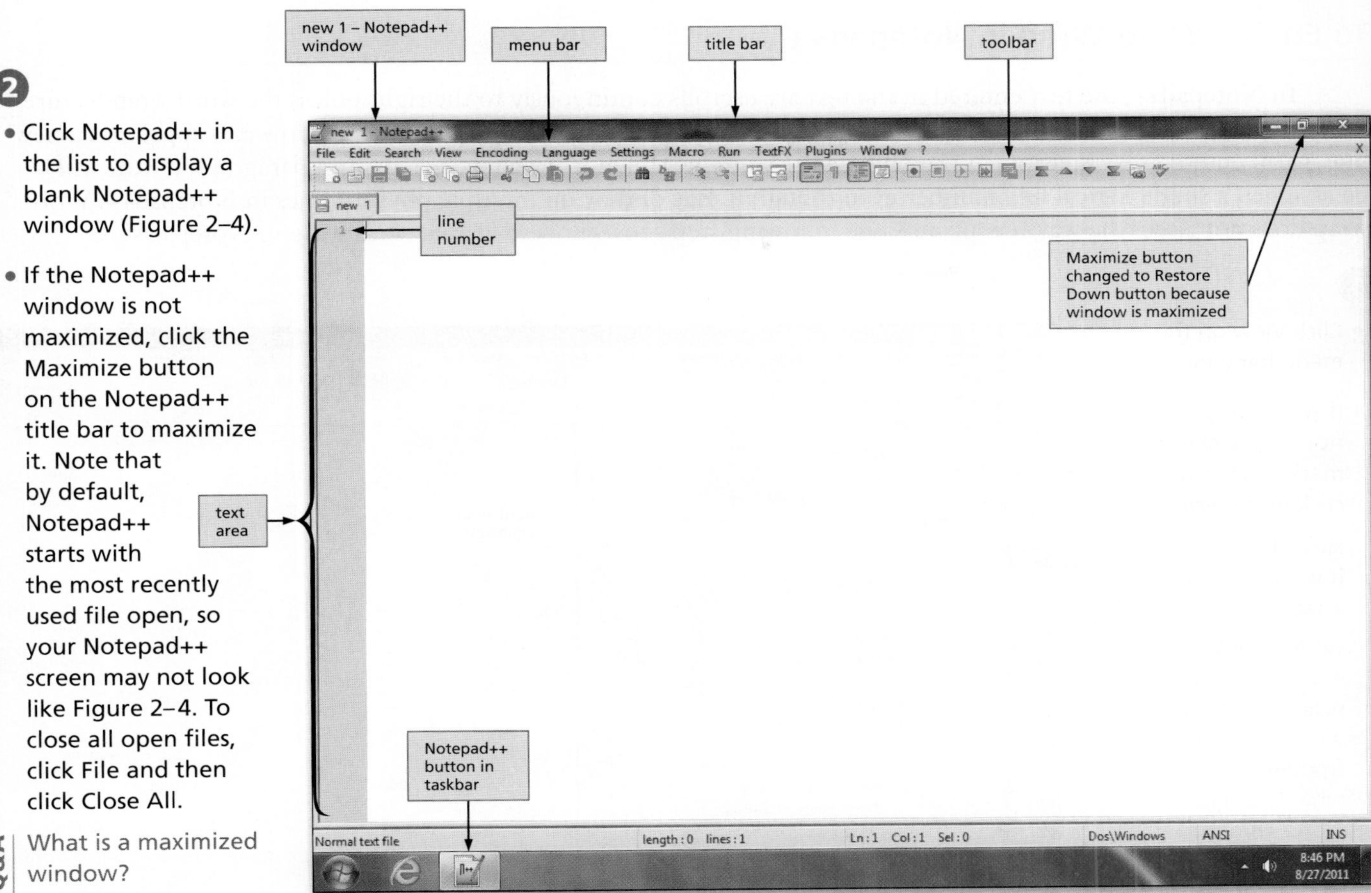

Figure 2–4

Q&A What is a maximized window?

A maximized window fills the entire screen. When you maximize a window, the Maximize button changes to a Restore Down button.

Q&A How can I add Notepad++ to my Start menu or the taskbar?

To add Notepad++ to the Start menu or taskbar, complete Step 1 above, right-click Notepad++, and then click Pin to Start Menu or Pin to Taskbar.

Other Ways

1. Double-click Notepad++ icon on desktop, if one is present
2. Click Notepad++ on Start menu, if it is present

To Enable Word Wrap in Notepad++

In Notepad++, the text entered in the text area scrolls continuously to the right unless the word wrap feature is enabled, or turned on. **Word wrap** causes text lines to break at the right edge of the window and appear on a new line, so all entered text is visible in the Notepad++ window. When word wrap is enabled, a paragraph of text will be assigned a single logical line number even though it may display on multiple physical lines in Notepad++. Word wrap does not affect the way text prints. The following step shows how to enable word wrap in Notepad++.

1

- Click View on the menu bar (Figure 2–5).
- If word wrap does not have a check mark next to it, click word wrap.

Q&A How do I know if word wrap is enabled?

When word wrap is enabled, a check mark precedes the word wrap command on the View menu, and when you type, your words remain on the screen.

Q&A What happens to the text if word wrap is not enabled?

The text of a paragraph would appear all on one line in Notepad++ and scroll off the screen, though the Web page would still be displayed correctly in the browser. For readability in Notepad++, you should enable word wrap.

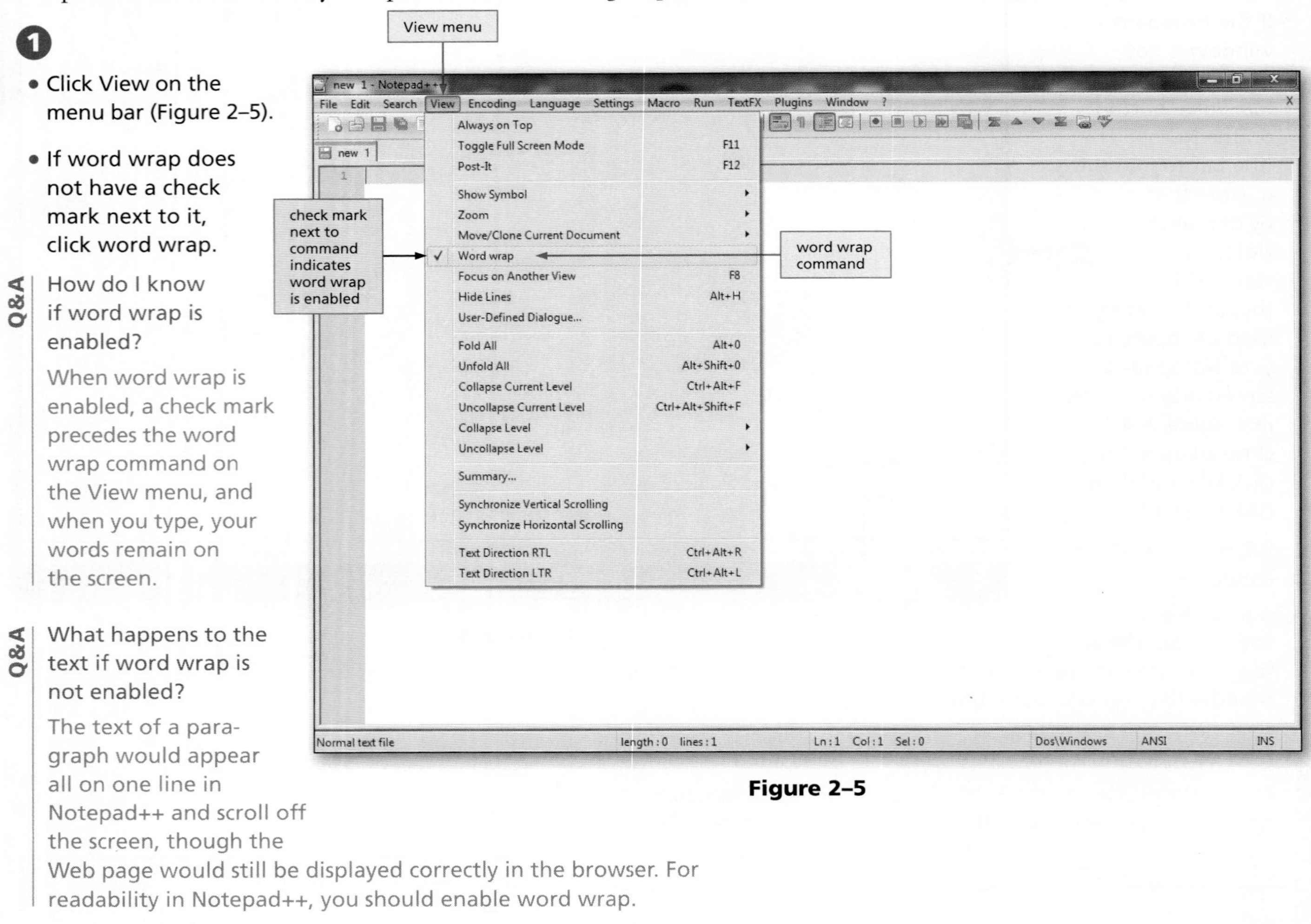

Figure 2–5

To Define the Web Page Structure Using HTML Tags

The first task is to enter the initial tags that define the Web page structure. Table 2–2 contains the HTML tags and text used to create the Web page shown in Figure 2–1a on page HTML 35. In this chapter and throughout this book, where large segments of HTML code or text are to be entered, you will find this code or text in tables with line number references, rather than within the steps. The steps will direct you to enter the text shown in the tables.

Table 2–2 Initial HTML Tags

Line	HTML Tag and Text
1	`<!DOCTYPE HTML>`
2	
3	`<html>`
4	`<head>`
5	`<meta charset="utf-8" />`
6	`<title>Rock Climbing Fun</title>`
7	`</head>`

The following steps illustrate how to enter the initial tags that define the structure of the Web page.

1

- Enter the HTML code shown in Table 2–2 (Figure 2–6). Press ENTER at the end of each line. If you make an error as you are typing, use the BACKSPACE key to delete all the characters back to and including the incorrect characters, and then continue typing.
- Press the ENTER key to start the next line of code, leaving one blank line after the </head> tag.
- Compare what you typed to Figure 2–6. If you notice errors, use your mouse pointer or arrow keys to move the insertion point to the right of each error and use the BACKSPACE key to correct the error.

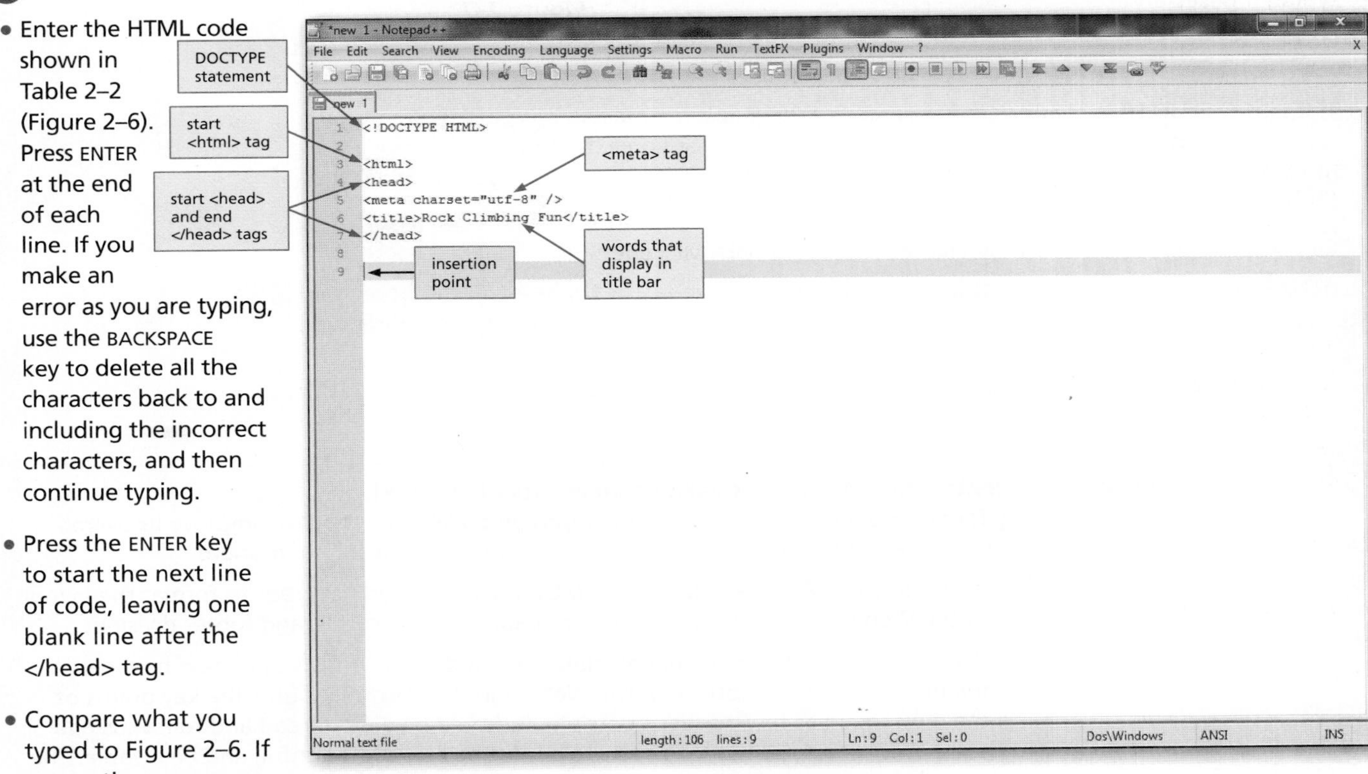

Figure 2–6

- On line 9, type `<body>` and then press the ENTER key twice.
- Type `</body>` and then press the ENTER key.
- Type `</html>` as the end tag (Figure 2–7).
- Compare what you typed to Figure 2–7 and correct errors in your typing if necessary.

```
1  <!DOCTYPE HTML>
2
3  <html>
4  <head>
5  <meta charset="utf-8" />
6  <title>Rock Climbing Fun</title>
7  </head>
8
9  <body>
10
11 </body>
12 </html>
```


Figure 2–7

Q&A Do I have to type the initial HTML tags for every Web page that I develop?

The same initial HTML tags are used in many other chapters. To avoid retyping these tags, you can save the code that you just typed, and give it a new file name, something like structure.html or template.html. If you save this file at the root level of your folders, you will have easy access to it for other chapters.

Q&A Can I use either uppercase or lowercase letters for my HTML code?

HTML5 allows tags to be entered in upper-, lower-, or mixed-case. However, in this book, the project directions follow the guidelines presented in Table 1–3 on page HTML 13 in Chapter 1.

Plan Ahead

Identify how to format various elements of the text.

By formatting the characters and paragraphs on a Web page, you can improve its overall appearance. On a Web page, consider the following formatting suggestions.

- **Determine the Web page layout.** HTML5 has introduced new tags to format the layout of the Web page. The tags include the head, section, articles, and footer divisions.
- **Use default text size when appropriate.** The body text consists of all text between the heading and the bottom of the Web page. This text highlights the key points of the message in as few words as possible. It should be easy to read and follow. While emphasizing the positive, the body text must be realistic, truthful, and believable. The default font size and style are appropriate to use for the body of text.
- **Effectively utilize headings.** The main heading is generally the first line of text on the Web page. It conveys the purpose of the Web page, such as identifying the company name. In this project, the company name is part of the image that is used at the top of the page, so a heading size 1 is not needed. Heading size standards should be followed, as shown in Figure 2–9 on page HTML 47. The main heading should be size 1, and subtopics or subheadings should be size 2. For the Web site in this chapter, you start with heading size 2 because the main heading is part of the image. That heading identifies the equipment needed. It is generally not a good idea to jump from one heading size to a heading two sizes smaller. For instance, if your main heading is size 1, then the next heading down should be heading size 2, not heading size 4.
- **Highlight key points with a bulleted list.** A **bullet** is a dot or other symbol positioned at the beginning of a list item. The bulleted list contains specific information that is more clearly identified by a list versus a paragraph of text.

Formatting the Web Page

In HTML 4.01, <div> </div> tags were introduced to separate sections within a Web page. This works well, and we utilize the <div> tag throughout the book. HTML5 has introduced new semantic elements to help Web developers structure the layout of a Web page. These tags are **semantic** in that the name of the tag reflects the purpose of the tag. For instance, the new <footer> tag is used to display content at the bottom (or footer) of the Web page. The <aside> tag is used to add content that is **tangential** or a side issue to the main Web page content. These new HTML5 tags, including <article>, <aside>, <footer>, <header>, <nav>, and <section>, are used for layout in the Web page projects in this book. Although the <div> tags, together with an id attribute (see Figure 2-8a), achieve the same results in layout, the future of Web development includes the new HTML5 layout tags. Figure 2-8b shows the new structural elements provided in HTML5 and how they help structure a Web page. Note that the <nav> (navigation) tag can also be used across the top of the page under the header depending on the Web page design.

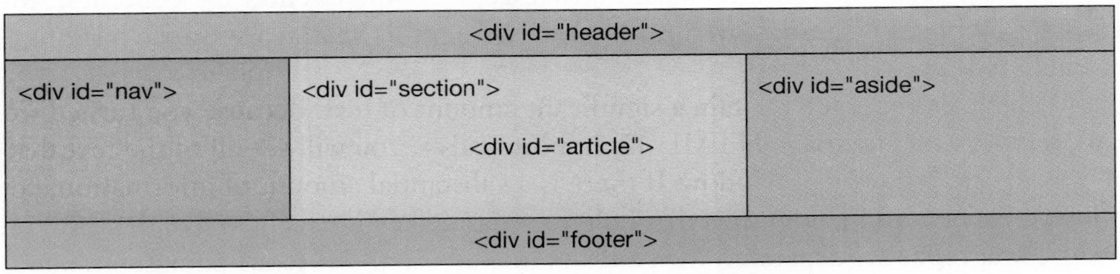

(a) Structural elements with HTML 4.01 tags

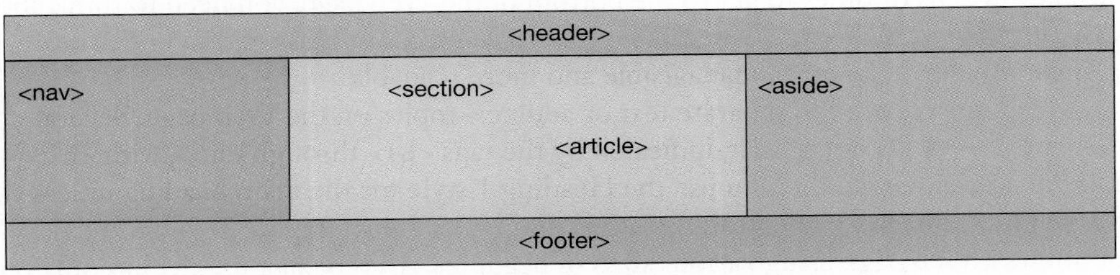

(b) Structural elements with new HTML5 tags

Figure 2–8

The header section is the top area of a Web page and is generally used for company logos, main heading text, or navigation. The <nav> tag identifies a section of the Web page that can alternately be used for navigation. The <section> tag is used as a generic document or application section. A section can be used to incorporate Web page content together with heading tags (i.e., h1 through h6). Articles are inserted within sections, adding to the content. An <aside> tag is used to represent content that is slightly related to the rest of the page, such as comments, biography, or background information. The footer is generally used for company information. Table 2–3 on the next page describes the purpose for each of these new tags. The project in this chapter contains a header, a footer, and one section that contains one article.

Table 2–3 HTML5 Structural Elements

Element	Purpose
Header	Information placed at the top of the Web page, such as logos or main headings
Navigation	Navigation structure that links to other parts of the Web page, Web site, or external to the Web site
Section	Major content area on the Web page
Article	Content that represents an independent piece of information
Aside	Content that is tangential or slightly related to the main topic of the Web page
Footer	Content placed at the bottom of the Web page, such as copyright or contact information

Entering Web Page Content

Once you have established the Web page structure, it is time to enter the content of the Web page, including headings, an informational paragraph of text, a subtopic heading, and a bulleted list.

Web pages generally contain a significant amount of text. Because you turned word wrap on (Figure 2–5 on page HTML 42) in Notepad++, you will see all of the text that you type in one Notepad++ window. If there is a substantial amount of information, you can break the text into paragraphs that help to separate key ideas and make the text easier to read. Paragraphs are separated with a blank line by using <p> (start paragraph) and </p> (end paragraph) tags. Putting too much text on one Web page is not a good choice. Your audience can get lost in large amounts of text. If you find that you have to press the Page Down key dozens of times to get to the bottom of the Web page, you need to think about restructuring your Web page. You can split up large pieces of information under more headings, which will be more manageable and more readable.

Headings are used to separate text or add new topics on the Web page. Several styles and sizes of headings exist, indicated by the tags <h1> through <h6>, with <h1> being the largest. Generally, you use the Heading 1 style for the main heading unless you use a graphical image for the heading (as we do in later steps). Figure 2–9a on the next page shows a Web page using various sizes of headings. A Web page usually has only one main heading; therefore, the HTML file for that Web page usually has only one set of <h1> </h1> tags. One method of maintaining a consistent look on a Web page is to use the same heading size for headings at the same topic level (Figure 2–9b). The header image that is inserted later in the chapter takes the place of the Main heading at the top of the Web page in Figure 2–9b. The complete Web page will therefore not have any <h1> headings. Notice that the paragraphs of text and the bulleted lists are all separated by size 2 headings in Figure 2–9b. This separation indicates that the text (i.e., two paragraphs plus one bulleted list) is all at the same level of importance on the Web page.

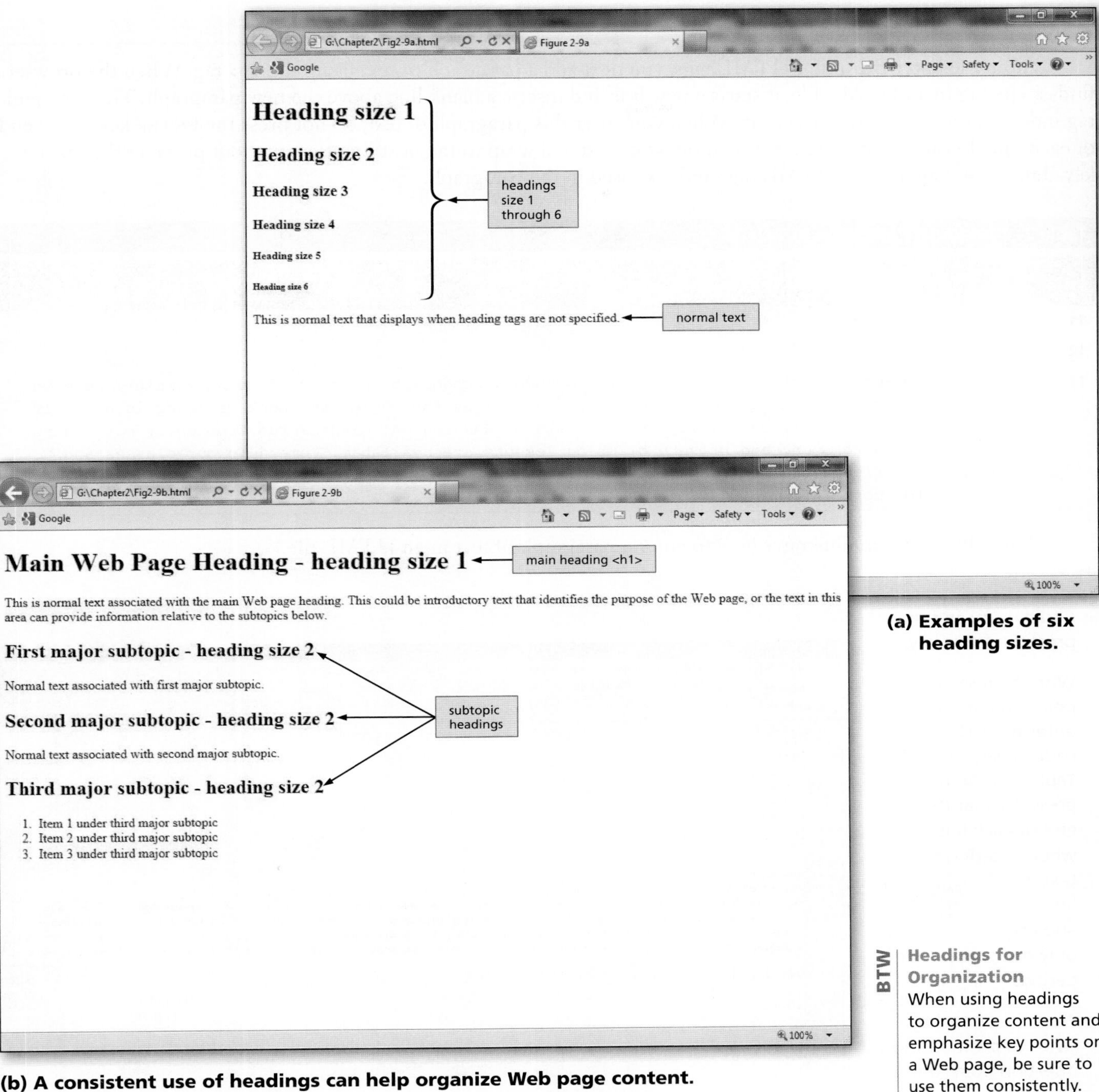

(a) Examples of six heading sizes.

(b) A consistent use of headings can help organize Web page content.

Figure 2–9

Sometimes text on a Web page is easier for users to read and understand when it is formatted as a list, instead of as a paragraph. HTML provides several types of lists, but the most popular are unordered (bulleted) and ordered (numbered) lists. During the design phase of the Web development life cycle, you decide on the most effective way to structure the Web content and format the text on the Web page. Your main goal is to give Web page visitors an effective way to find the information that they need. If users cannot easily find what they need, they will not revisit your Web site.

BTW

Headings for Organization

When using headings to organize content and emphasize key points on a Web page, be sure to use them consistently. That is, if you use a heading 2 (<h2>) style for a specific level of text, you always should use a heading 2 style to break up information at that level. Also, do not skip levels of headings in your document. For example, do not start with a heading 1 (<h1>) style and then use a heading 3 (<h3>) style.

To Enter a Paragraph of Text

After you enter the initial HTML tags, you next add a paragraph of text using the <p> tag. When the browser finds a <p> tag in an HTML file, it starts a new line and inserts a blank line above the new paragraph. The </p> end tag indicates the end of the paragraph. When you enter this paragraph of text, do not press the ENTER key at the end of each line. Because word wrap is turned on, your text will wrap to the next line even without pressing the ENTER key. Table 2–4 contains the HTML tags and text used in the paragraph.

Table 2–4 Adding a Paragraph of Text

Line	HTML Tag and Text
11	`<section>`
12	`<article>`
13	`<p>Rock Climbing Fun has recently opened a school at the base of Mount Rainier. We have programs for advanced rock climbers as well as for beginners. Rock climbing is a widely popular sport, especially in the state of Washington. Classes run from early morning to mid-afternoon, and private climbing lessons are available. Come join our classes and experience the fun and great exercise that rock climbing can provide. Call 1-800-555-CLIMB for more information.</p>`

The following step illustrates how to enter a paragraph of text in an HTML file.

1

- Click line 10 and then press the ENTER key.
- With the insertion point on line 11, enter the HTML code, as shown in Table 2–4. Do not press ENTER at the end of each line when entering the text in line 13 and use only one space after periods.
- Press the ENTER key twice to position the insertion point on line 15 (Figure 2–10).

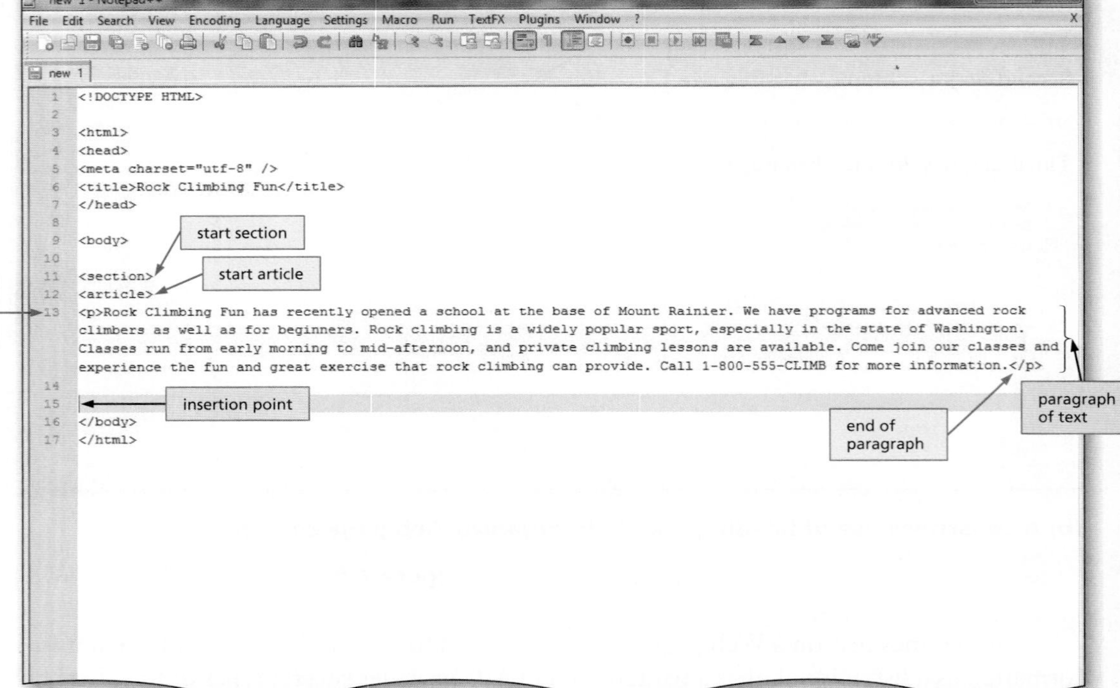

Figure 2–10

Q&A Why do you not press the ENTER key after each line of code in line 13 in Table 2–4?

Because you turned on word wrap right after you started Notepad++, the text that you enter as the paragraph will automatically wrap to the next line. The text goes to the end of the Notepad++ window and then wraps. If you had not turned on word wrap, your text would continue scrolling to the right as you type, and text to the left would scroll off the screen. With word wrap on, all text remains visible in the Notepad++ window.

To Enter a Heading

The heading, Equipment needed to get started, is the heading that separates the paragraph of text from the bulleted list. You use an <h2> heading because it is not really the main heading of the Web page. You insert an image as the main heading later in the chapter. The following step illustrates how to enter a heading on the Web page.

- With the insertion point on line 15, type `<h2>Equipment needed to get started:</h2>` in the text area, and then press the ENTER key twice (Figure 2–11).

h2 heading on line 15

```
*new 1 - Notepad++
File Edit Search View Encoding Language Settings Macro Run TextFX Plugins Window ?
new 1
1  <!DOCTYPE HTML>
2
3  <html>
4  <head>
5  <meta charset="utf-8" />
6  <title>Rock Climbing Fun</title>
7  </head>
8
9  <body>
10
11 <section>
12 <article>
13 <p>Rock Climbing Fun has recently opened a school at the base of Mount Rainier. We have programs for advanced rock
   climbers as well as for beginners. Rock climbing is a widely popular sport, especially in the state of Washington.
   Classes run from early morning to mid-afternoon, and private climbing lessons are available. Come join our classes and
   experience the fun and great exercise that rock climbing can provide. Call 1-800-555-CLIMB for more information.</p>
14
15 <h2>Equipment needed to get started:</h2>
16
17
18 </body>
19 </html>
Normal text file    length : 670   lines : 19    Ln : 17   Col : 1   Sel : 0    Dos\Windows   ANSI   INS
```

Figure 2–11

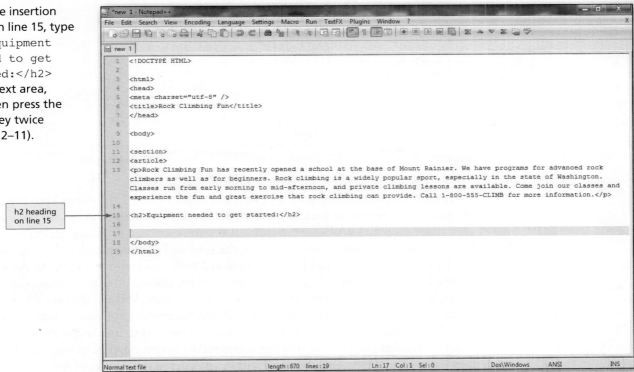

Using Lists to Present Content

Lists structure text into an itemized format. Typically, lists are bulleted (unordered) or numbered (ordered). An **unordered list**, which also is called a **bulleted list**, formats information using small images called bullets. Figure 2–12 shows Web page text formatted as unordered, or bulleted, lists and the HTML code used to create the lists.

An **ordered list**, which also is called a **numbered list**, formats information in a series using numbers or letters. An ordered list works well to organize items where

BTW

List Styles
It is sometimes helpful to structure the text of a Web page in a list. There are several list options that you can use. The Web page purpose determines which would be more effective. See the section on List Styles in Appendix D for style options that can be used with lists.

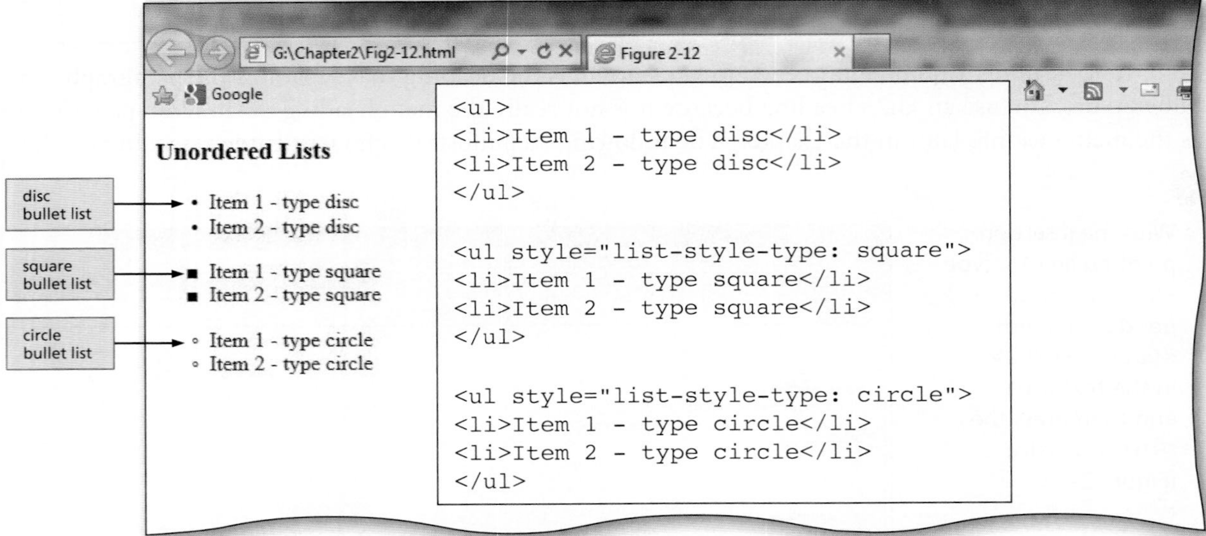

Figure 2–12

order must be emphasized, such as a series of steps. Figure 2–13 shows Web page text formatted as ordered, or numbered, lists and the HTML tags used to create the lists.

The **<ul>** and **</ul>** tags must be at the start and end of an unordered or bulleted list. The **<ol>** and **</ol>** tags are used at the start and end of an ordered or numbered list. Unordered and ordered lists have optional bullet and number types. As shown in Figure 2–12, an unordered list can use one of three different bullet options: disc, square, or circle. If no type is identified, the default, disc, is used. You can also use an image as a bullet as is shown in a later chapter. An ordered list can use numbers, letters, or Roman numerals, as shown in Figure 2–13. The default option is to use Arabic numbers, such as 1, 2, and 3. After the <ul> or <ol> tag is entered to define the type of list, the **<li>** and **</li>** tags are used to define each list item within an ordered or unordered list.

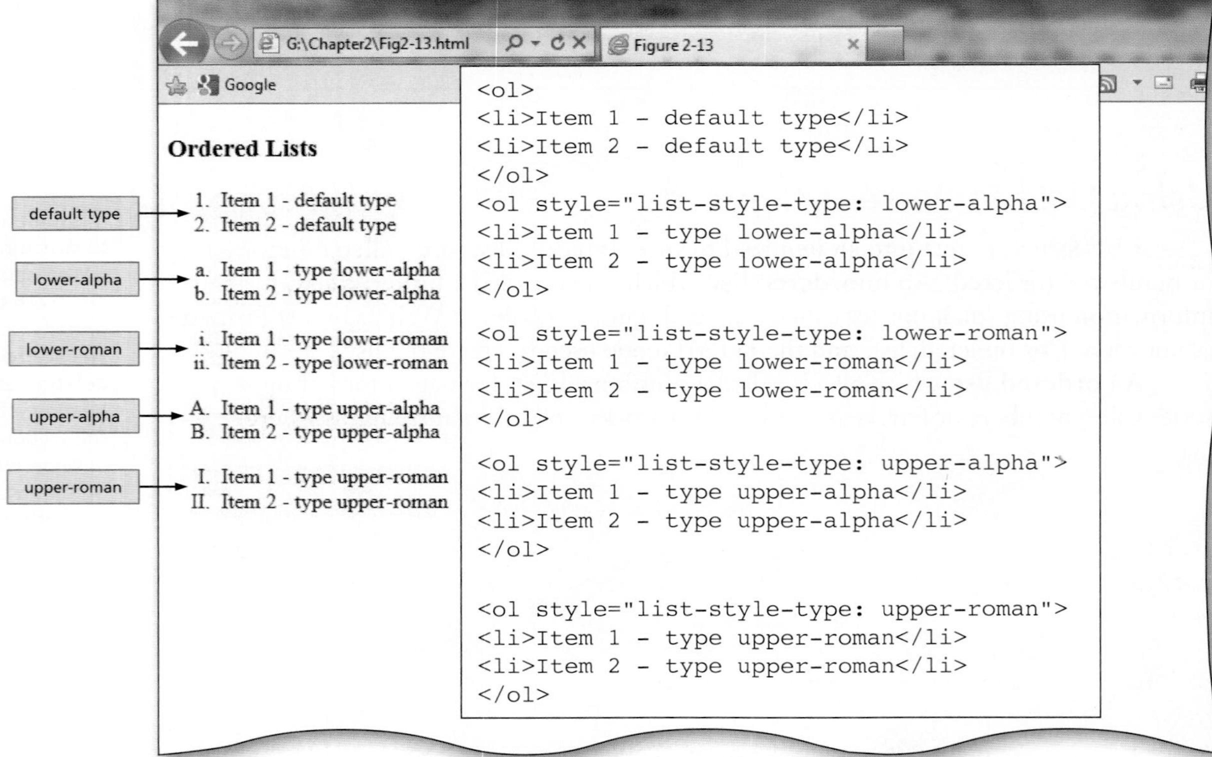

Figure 2–13

To Create an Unordered List

To highlight what Web site visitors will need for equipment when taking a class with Rock Climbing Fun you will create a bulleted (unordered) list using the HTML tags and text shown in Table 2–5. Remember that each list item must start with <li> and end with </li>.

Table 2–5 Adding an Unordered List

Line	HTML Tag and Text
17	`<ul>`
18	`<li>Comfortable climbing shoes</li>`
19	`<li>Backpack</li>`
20	`<li>Harness</li>`
21	`</ul>`
22	`</article>`
23	`</section>`

The following step illustrates how to create an unordered, or bulleted, list using the default bullet style.

1

- With the insertion point on line 17, enter the HTML code, as shown in Table 2–5. When you type the text on line 18, make sure to press the TAB key at the start of the line (also on lines 19 and 20 if they are not automatically indented). Press ENTER at the end of each line.

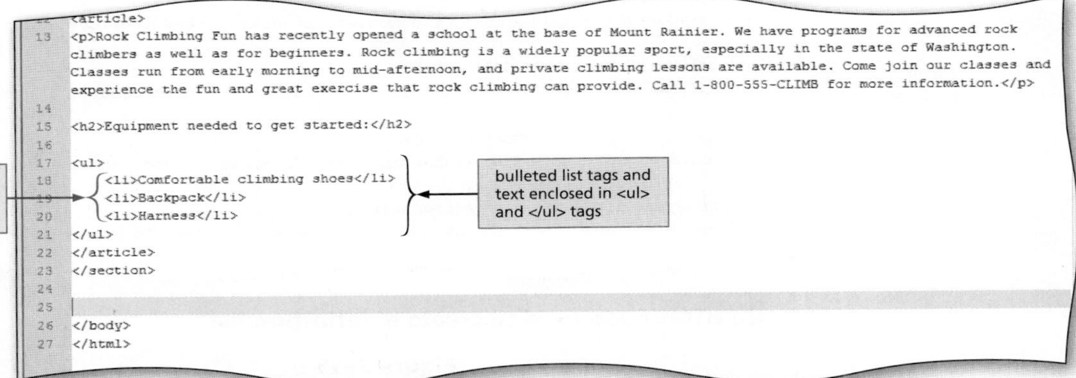

Figure 2–14

- On line 23, press the ENTER key twice, positioning the cursor on line 25 and leaving a blank line on 24 (Figure 2–14).

Q&A Why do you press the TAB key at the start of the lines with the <li> (list item) code?

Using the TAB key (to indent) when you enter list items helps format the text so that you can easily see that this text is different from the paragraph of text. Indenting text helps the Web developer see that certain segments of code are related to each other.

More About List Formats

If you use the <ul> or <ol> start tags without attributes, you will get the default bullet (disc) or number style (Arabic numerals). To change the bullet or number type, the **list-style-type** property is entered within the <ol> or <ul> tags. To create a list with square bullets, you would type the line

```
<ul style="list-style-type: square">
```

as the inline style (CSS) code. You can find other list-style properties and values in Appendix D.

In addition to ordered and unordered lists, there is a third kind of list, called a **definition list**, which offsets information in a dictionary-like style. Although they are used less often than unordered or ordered lists, definition lists are useful to create a glossary-like list of terms and definitions, as shown in Figure 2–15a. Figure 2–15b shows the HTML code used to create the definition list.

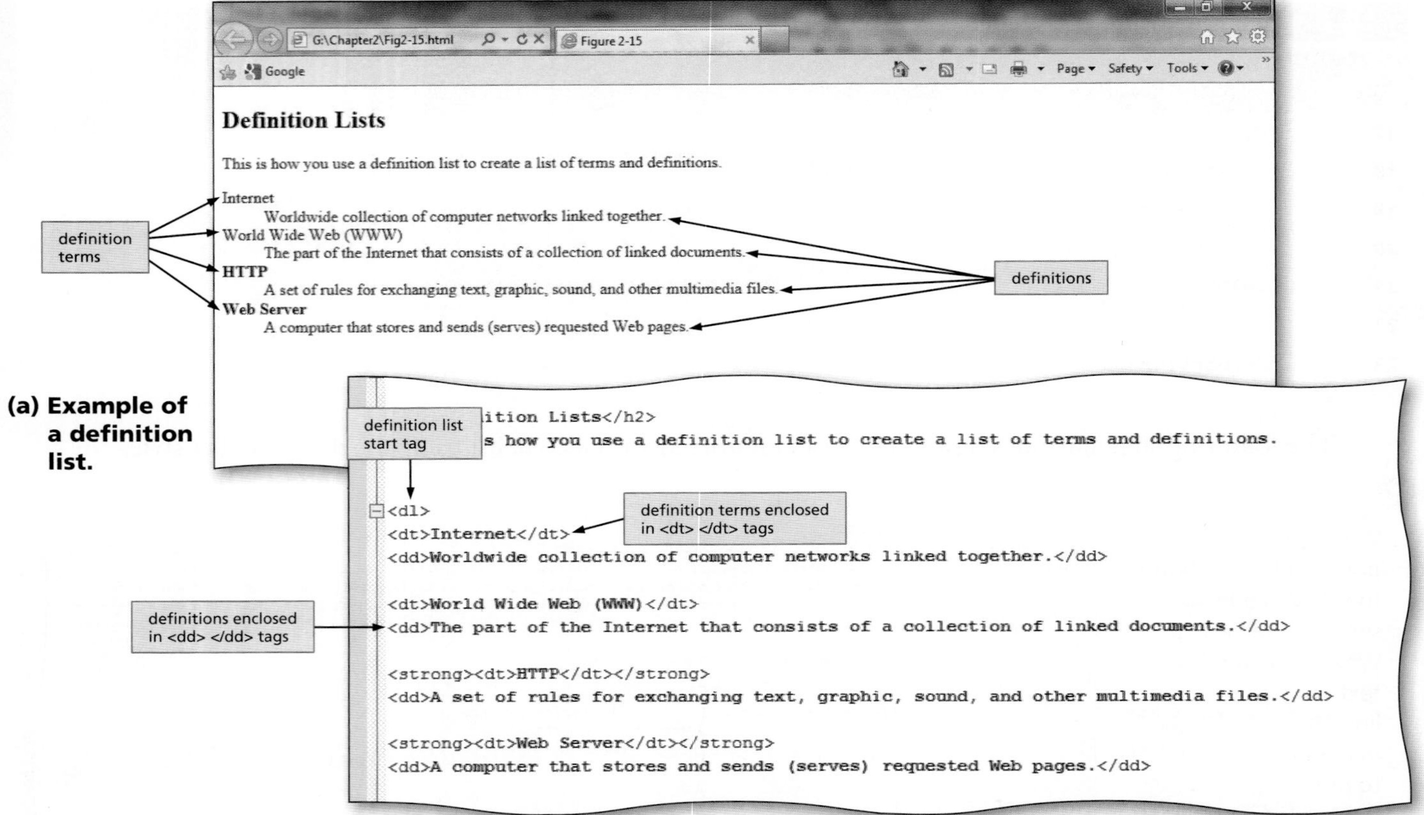

(a) Example of a definition list.

(b) HTML code used to create a definition list.

Figure 2–15

The syntax for definition lists is not as straightforward as the <ul>, <ol>, or <li> structure that is used in the unordered and ordered list styles. With definition lists, you use the **<dl>** and **</dl>** tags to start and end the list. A **<dt>** tag indicates a term, and a **<dd>** tag identifies the definition of that term by offsetting the definition from the term. Table 2–6 lists definition list tags and their purposes.

Table 2–6 Definition List Tags and Purposes

Definition List Tags	Purpose
<dl> </dl>	Start and end a definition list
<dt> </dt>	Identify a term
<dd> </dd>	Identify the definition of the term directly above

As shown in Figure 2–15, by default, the definition term is left-aligned on the line and the definition for each term is indented so it is easily distinguishable as the definition for the term above it. In order to more clearly identify the definition term, you may want to make the term bold, as shown in the last two definitions (HTTP and Web Server) in Figure 2–15. You could do this by wrapping the term inside a <strong></strong>

container. That gives the term a strong emphasis, so text is usually displayed as bold text. The following code would do that for the HTTP definition term.

```
<strong><dt>HTTP</dt></strong>
```

Adding a Footer

As mentioned earlier in the chapter, HTML5 introduced several new structural elements that help to enhance the layout of a Web page. One of these new elements, the footer, is inserted in the next section of the chapter. The footer tag is used to position text toward the bottom of a Web page. Content placed there generally has to do with the company's address, copyright, or contact information.

To Add a Footer

It is important for Web site visitors to be able to contact the company. In the next step, you enter company contact information onto the Web page by inserting a tag in the HTML file using the tags and text shown in Table 2–7.

Table 2–7 Adding a Footer

Line	HTML Tag and Text
25	<footer>
26	Rock Climbing Fun, 3737 Harrison Lane, Issawak, WA 98000
27	</footer>

- With the insertion point on line 25, enter the HTML code, as shown in Table 2–7. Press ENTER at the end of each line (Figure 2–16).

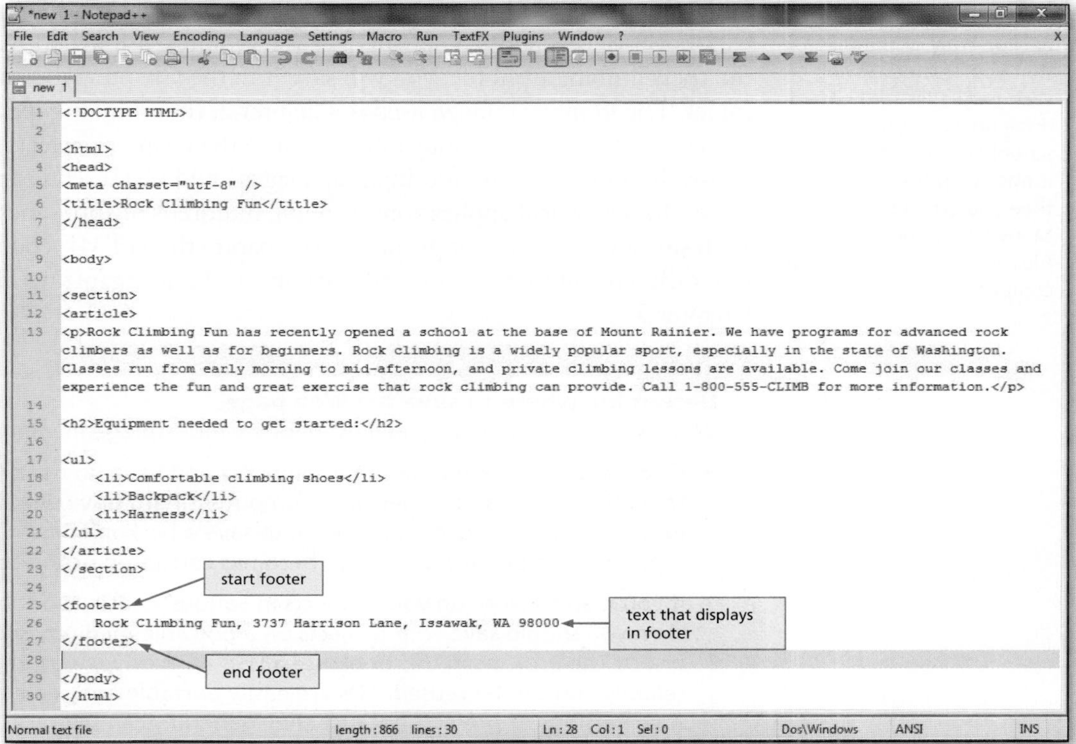

Figure 2–16

BTW **HTML File Names**
HTML files have an extension of .html or .htm. The home page of a Web site is often called index.html, index.htm, default.html, or default.htm. Check with your Web hosting service provider to find out which name they use.

BTW **Saving Your Work**
It is a good idea to save your HTML file periodically as you are working to avoid the risk of losing your work completed thus far. You should get into the habit of saving your file after any large addition of information (i.e., a paragraph or image). You might also want to save the file after typing in several HTML tags that would be difficult to re-do.

BTW **Storing Your Files**
Many schools provide students with space on a Web server to store their Web pages. However, saving your Web pages to another medium (e.g., a USB flash drive) assures that you have a backup copy of the files that you created. Saving Web page files to the hard drive on a computer in a school lab runs the risk of it not being there the next time you are in that lab. Many schools delete all files at the start-up of each computer.

Saving and Organizing HTML Files

Before you can see how your HTML file looks in a Web browser, you must save it. It is also important to save your HTML file for the following reasons:

- The document in memory will be lost if the computer is turned off or you lose electrical power while the text editor is open.
- If you run out of time before completing your project, you may finish your document at a future time without starting over.

To save your file, you use the Notepad++ File, Save command. When you save a file, you give your file a name and follow that with the file extension. As mentioned earlier in the book, file names should always make sense relative to their purpose. For instance, naming a file page1 does not indicate the purpose of that file. Naming the file rockclimbing immediately identifies that this file has something to do with that topic. The Web page files in this book are always named with all lowercase letters and with no spaces. This is a standard that is followed throughout the book.

HTML files must end with an extension of **.htm** or **.html**. Many older Web page servers can only display pages with the .htm extension, or short file names (i.e., file names that are only up to eight characters in length). HTML files with an extension of .html can be viewed on Web servers running an operating system that allows long file names (i.e., file names that can be up to 255 characters in length). Almost all current operating systems allow long file names, including Windows 7, Windows Vista, Windows XP, Windows Server 2003/2008, Windows 2000, Mac OS X, and Linux. For Web servers that run an operating system that does not accept long file names, you need the .htm extension. In this book, all files are saved using the .html extension.

You will use a very simple folder structure with all the projects in this book. It is therefore important to organize your files in folders so that all files for a project or end-of-chapter exercise, including HTML code and graphical images, are saved in the same folder. If you correctly downloaded the files from the Data Files for Students (see the inside back cover of this book), you will have the required file structure. When you initially save the rockclimbing.html file, you will save it in the ChapterFiles subfolder of the Chapter02 folder. The graphical image used in Chapter 2, rockclimbing.jpg, will be stored in that same folder — Chapter02\ChapterFiles. Because the chapter projects in this book are relatively simple and use few images, images and HTML code are stored in the same folder. In real-world applications, though, hundreds or thousands of files might exist in a Web site, and it is more appropriate to separate the HTML code and graphical images into different subfolders. You will learn more about organizing HTML files and folders in Chapter 3.

Plan Ahead

Determine where to save the Web page.
When saving a Web page, you must decide which storage medium to use.

- If you always work on the same computer and have no need to transport your projects to a different location, then your computer's hard drive will suffice as a storage location. It is a good idea, however, to save a backup copy of your projects on a separate medium in case the file becomes corrupted or the computer's hard disk fails.
- If you plan to work on your projects in various locations or on multiple computers, then you should save your projects on a portable medium, such as a USB flash drive or CD. The projects in this book use a USB flash drive, which saves files quickly and reliably and can be reused. CDs are easily portable and serve as good backups for the final versions of projects because they generally can save files only one time.

The above are general guidelines about saving your files. Your instructor may give you specific instructions for saving your work that differ from the steps that follow.

To Save an HTML File

You have entered a lot of text while creating this project and do not want to risk losing the work you have done so far. Also, to view HTML in a browser, you must save the file. The following steps show how to save an HTML file.

1

- With a USB flash drive connected to one of the computer's USB ports, click File on the Notepad++ menu bar (Figure 2–17).

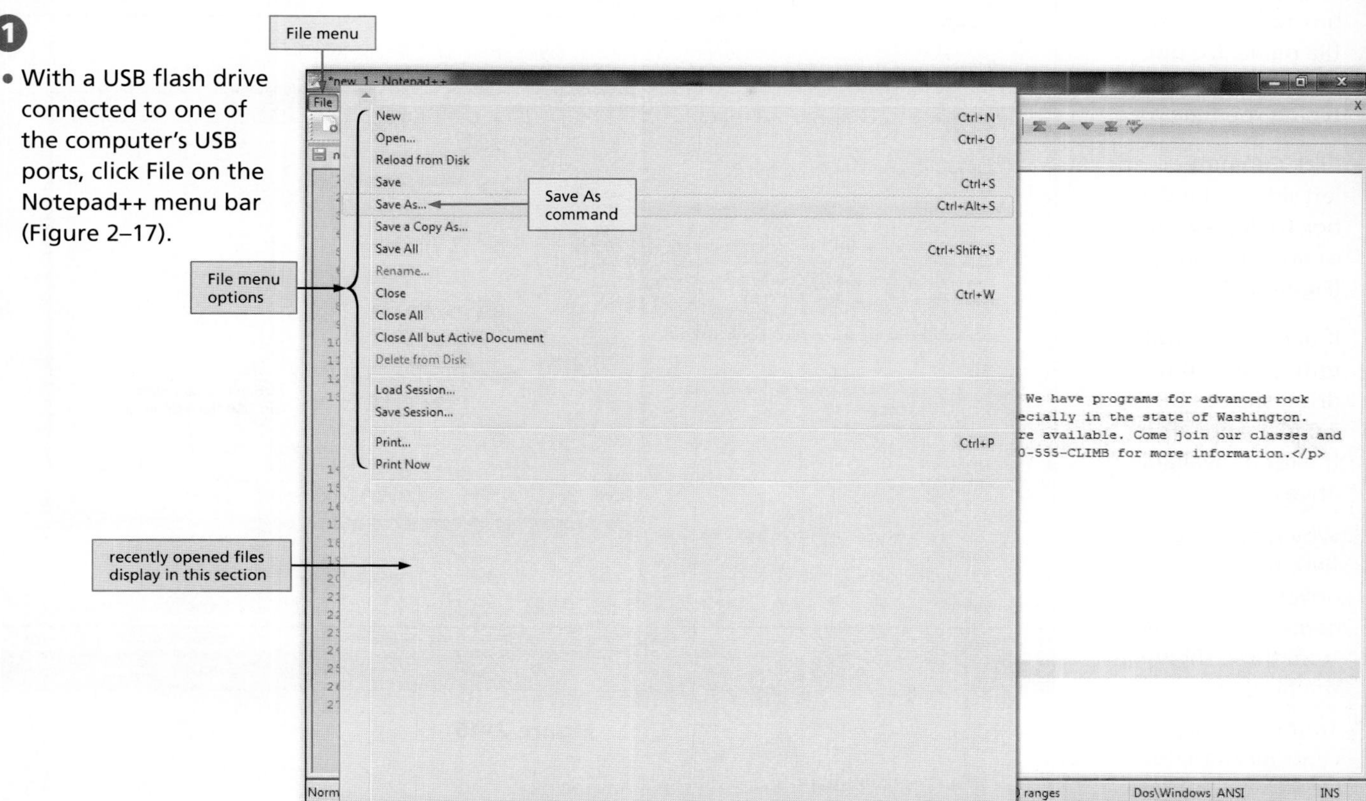

Figure 2–17

2

- Click Save As on the File menu to display the Save As dialog box (Figure 2–18).

Q&A Do I have to save to a USB flash drive?

No. You can save to any device or folder. A folder is a specific location on a storage medium. Use the same process, but select your device or folder.

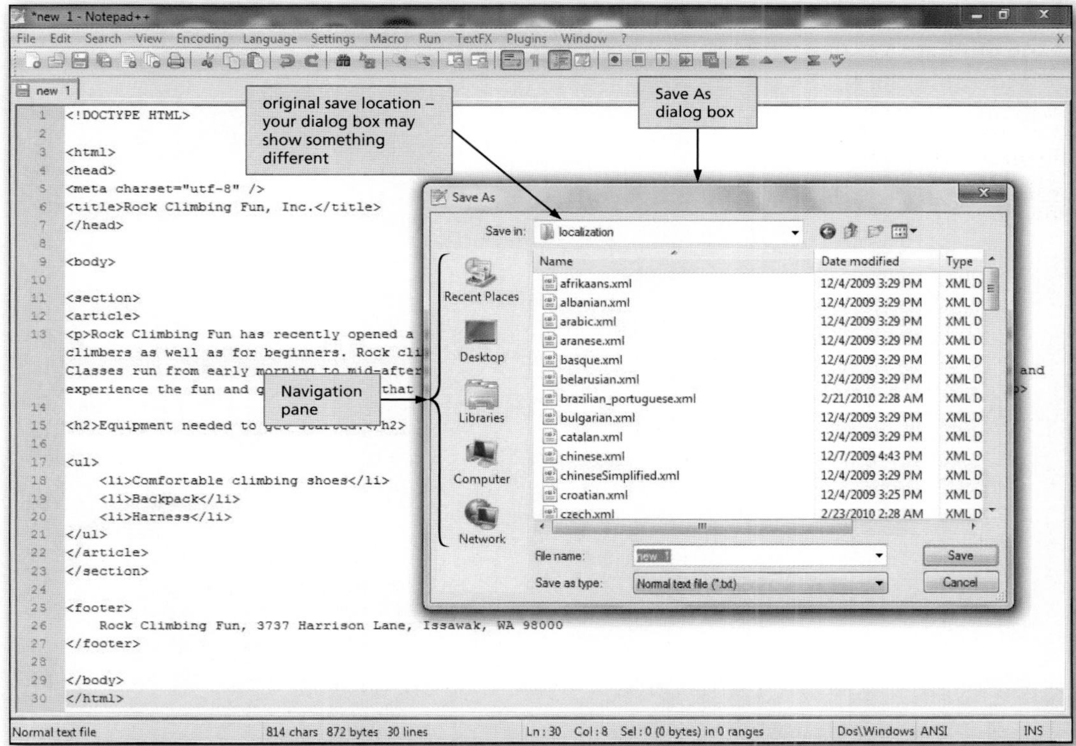

Figure 2–18

- Type `rockclimbing.html` in the File name text box to change the file name. Do not press ENTER after typing the file name.
- Click Computer in the left side of the dialog box to display a list of available drives (Figure 2–19).
- If necessary, scroll until your USB flash drive, such as UDISK 2.0 (G:), appears in the list of available drives.

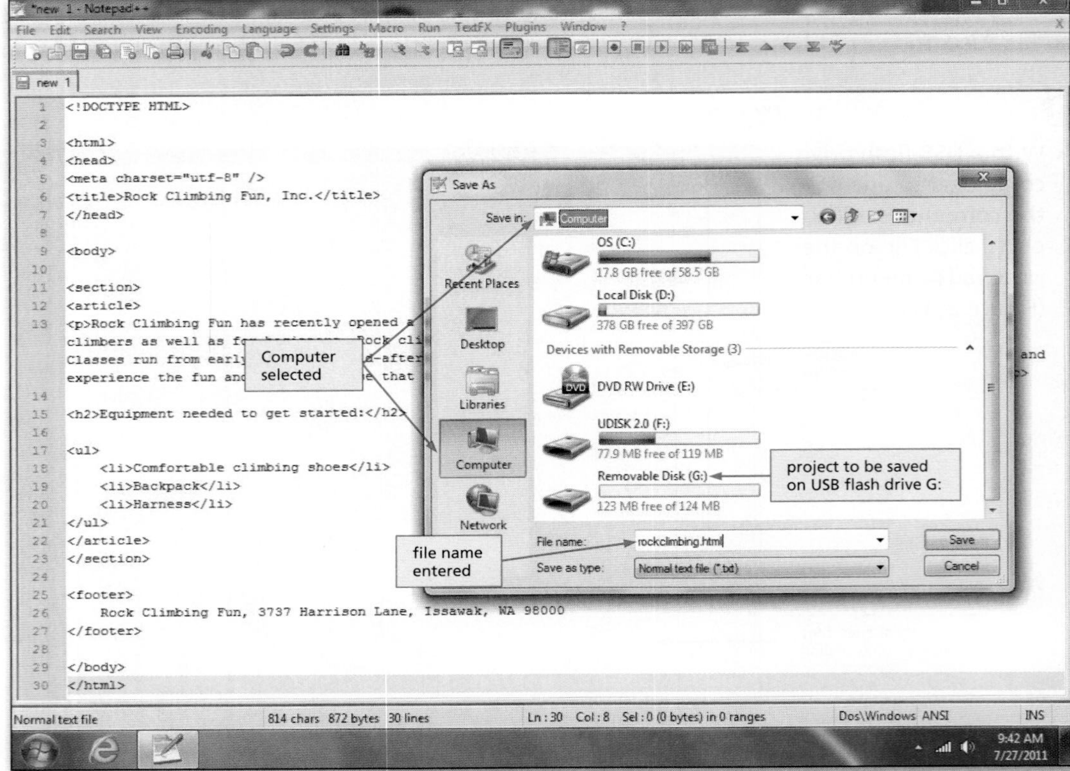

Figure 2–19

Q&A Why is my list of files, folders, and drives arranged and named differently from those shown in the figure?

Your computer's configuration determines how the list of files and folders is displayed and how drives are named.

Q&A How do I know the drive and folder in which my file will be saved?

Notepad++ displays a list of available drives and folders. You then select the drive and/or folder into which you want to save the file.

4

- Double-click UDISK 2.0 (G:) (or your storage device) in the Computer list to select the USB flash drive, drive G in this case, as the new save location.

Q&A What if my USB flash drive has a different name or letter?

It is likely that your USB flash drive will have a different name and drive letter and be connected to a different port. Verify that the device in your Computer list is correct.

- If necessary, open the Chapter02\ChapterFiles folder (Figure 2–20).

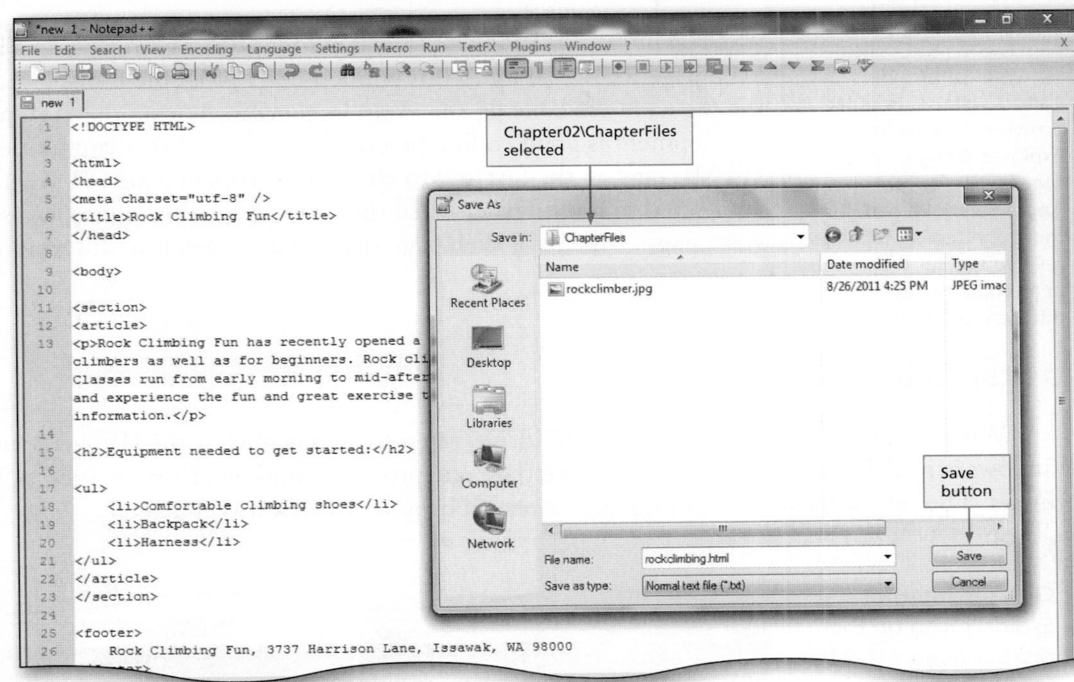

Figure 2–20

Q&A What if my USB flash drive does not have a folder named Chapter02\ChapterFiles?

If you followed the steps to download the chapter files from the Data Files for Students, you should have a folder named Chapter02\ChapterFiles. If you do not, check with your instructor.

5

- Click the Save button in the Save As dialog box to save the file on the USB flash drive with the name rockclimbing.html (Figure 2–21).

Q&A Is my file only on the USB drive now?

No, although the HTML file is saved on a USB drive, it also remains in memory and is displayed on the screen (Figure 2–21). Notepad++ displays the new file name on the title bar and on the document tab.

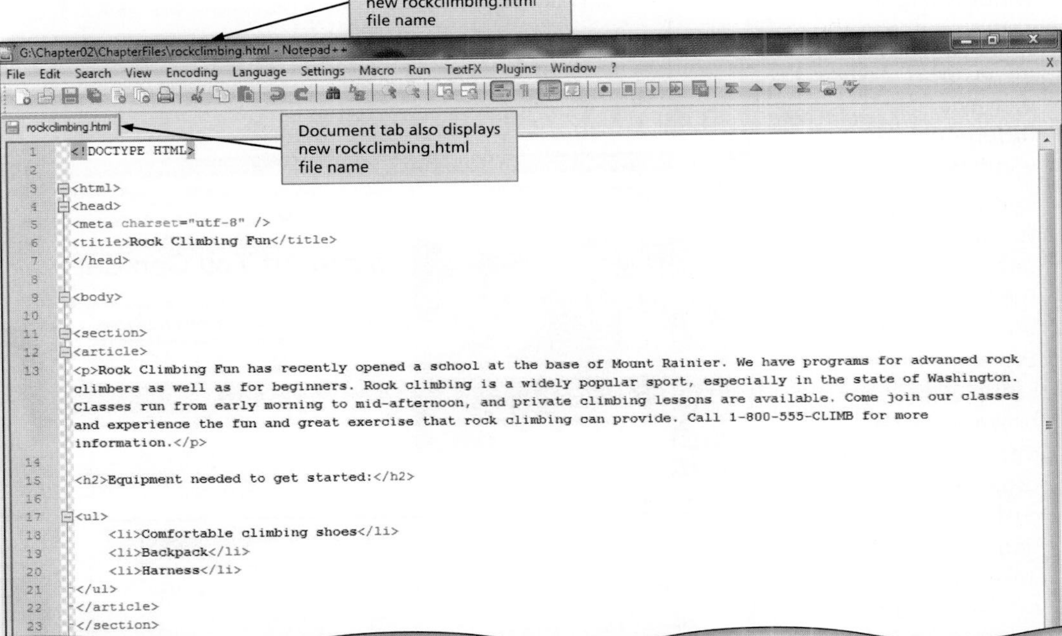

Figure 2–21

Other Ways

1. Press CTRL+ALT+S, type file name, click Computer, select drive or folder, click Save button

BTW

Developing Web Pages for Multiple Browsers
When developing Web pages, you must consider the types of browsers visitors will use. Popular browsers include Internet Explorer, Google Chrome, Mozilla Firefox, and Apple Safari. Part of thorough testing includes reviewing your Web pages in multiple versions of different browsers.

Using a Browser to View a Web Page

After saving the HTML file, you should view the Web page in a browser to see what the Web page looks like up to this point. The HTML file is displayed in the browser as if the file were available on the Web. In general, viewing the Web page periodically during development is good coding practice, because it allows you to see the effect of various HTML tags on the text and to check for errors in your HTML file. If your computer is connected to the Internet when the browser window opens, it displays a **home page**, or **start page**, which is a Web page that appears each time Internet Explorer starts.

To Start a Browser

With the HTML file saved on the USB drive, the next step is to view the Web page using a browser. Because Windows is **multitasking**, you can have more than one program running at a time, such as Notepad++ and your browser. The following steps illustrate how to start a browser to view a Web page.

1

- Click the Internet Explorer icon on the taskbar (Figure 2–22).

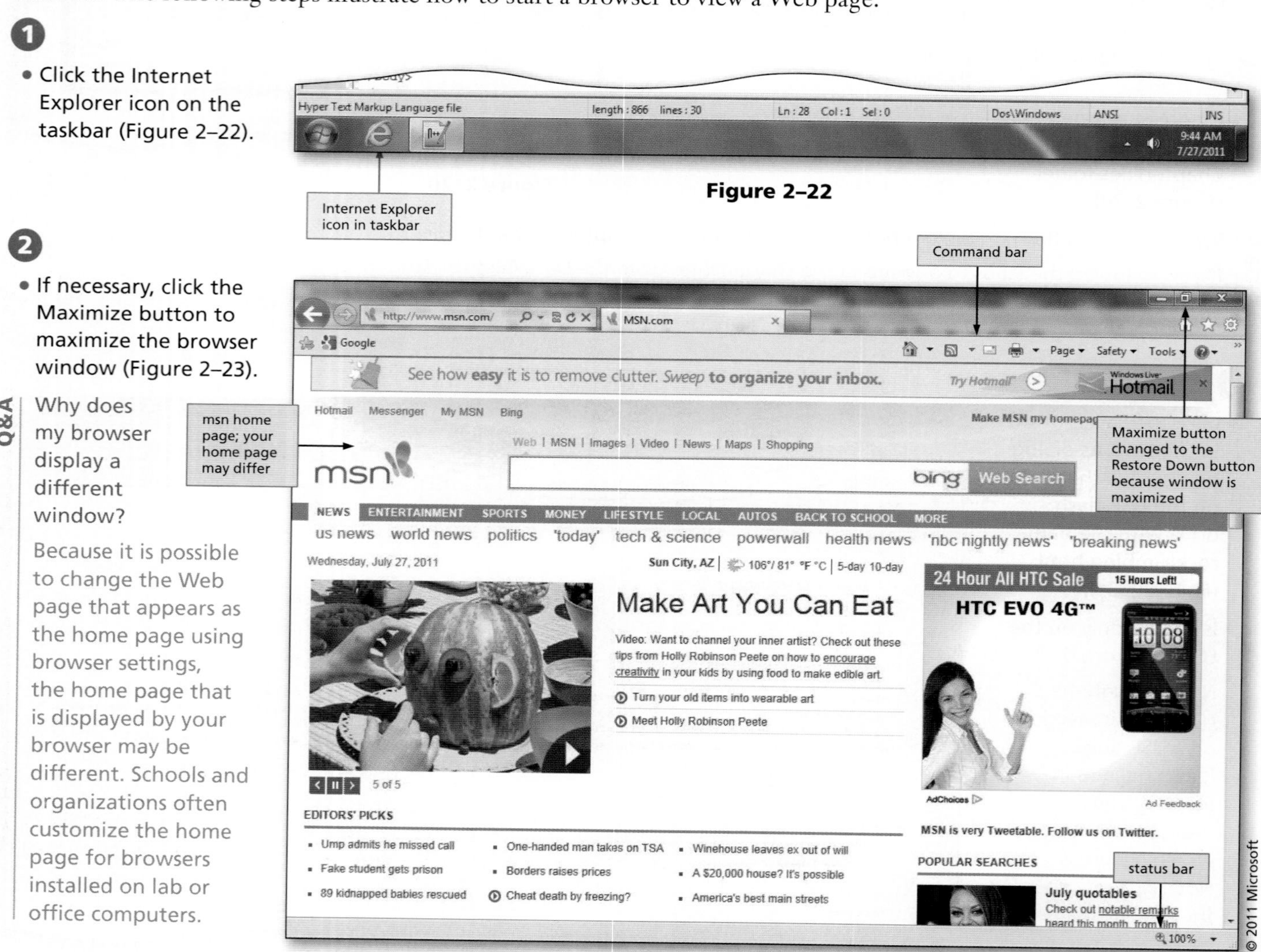

Figure 2–22

2

- If necessary, click the Maximize button to maximize the browser window (Figure 2–23).

Q&A

Why does my browser display a different window?

Because it is possible to change the Web page that appears as the home page using browser settings, the home page that is displayed by your browser may be different. Schools and organizations often customize the home page for browsers installed on lab or office computers.

Figure 2–23

Other Ways

1. Click Start, click All Programs, click Internet Explorer
2. Double-click Internet Explorer icon on desktop, if one is present

To View a Web Page in a Browser

A browser allows you to open a Web file located on your computer and have full browsing capabilities, as if the Web page were stored on a Web server and made available on the Web. The following steps use this technique to view the HTML file, rockclimbing.html, in a browser.

1

- Click the Address bar to select the URL.
- Type `g:\Chapter02\ChapterFiles\rockclimbing.html` to enter the path of the HTML file in the Address bar (Figure 2–24).

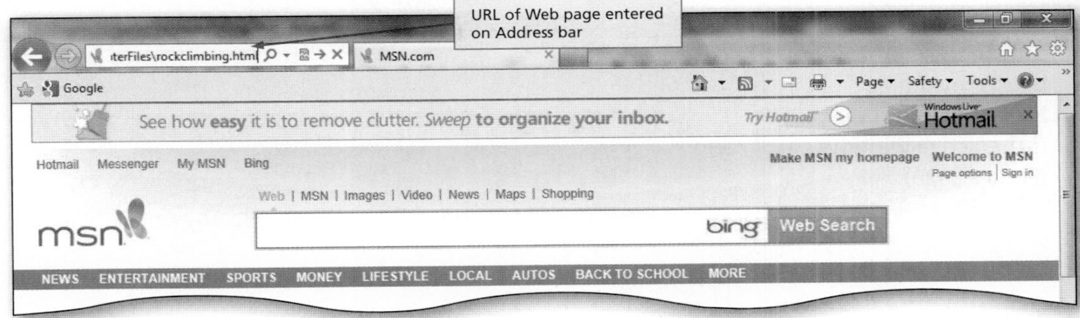

Figure 2–24

Q&A What if my file is in a different location?

You can type in the path to your file in the Address bar or browse to your file, as shown in Other Ways.

2

- Press the ENTER key to display the rockclimbing.html page as if it were available on the Web (Figure 2–25).

Q&A What if my page is not displayed correctly?

Check your rockclimbing.html file carefully against Figure 2–26 on the next page to make sure you have not made any typing errors or left anything out. Correct the errors, resave the file, and try again by refreshing the Web page in the browser.

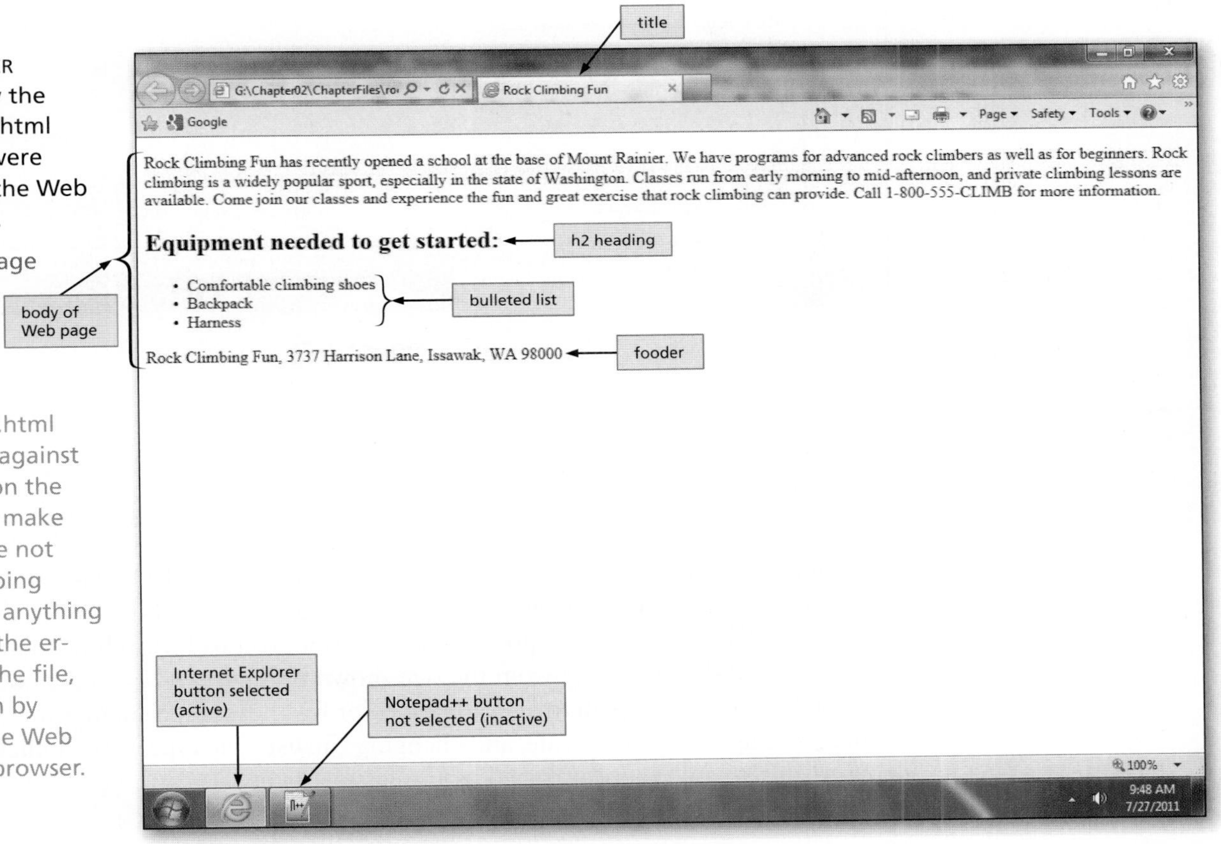

title

body of Web page

h2 heading

bulleted list

fooder

Internet Explorer button selected (active)

Notepad++ button not selected (inactive)

Figure 2–25

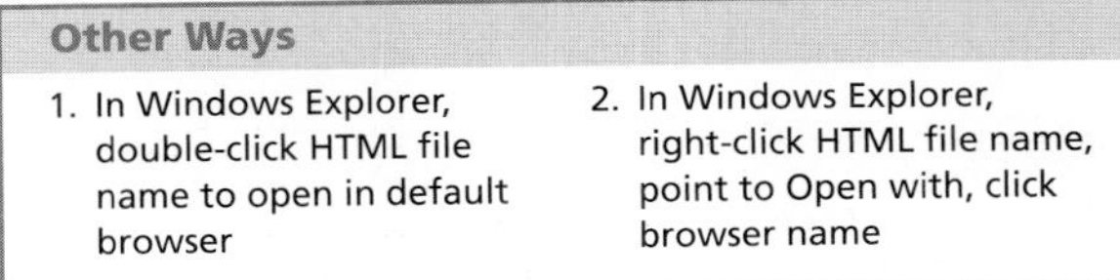

Other Ways

1. In Windows Explorer, double-click HTML file name to open in default browser
2. In Windows Explorer, right-click HTML file name, point to Open with, click browser name

To Activate Notepad++

After viewing the Web page, you can modify it by adding additional tags or text to the HTML file. To continue editing, you first must return to the Notepad++ window. The following step illustrates how to activate Notepad++.

- Click the Notepad++ button on the taskbar to maximize Notepad++ and make it the active window (Figure 2–26).

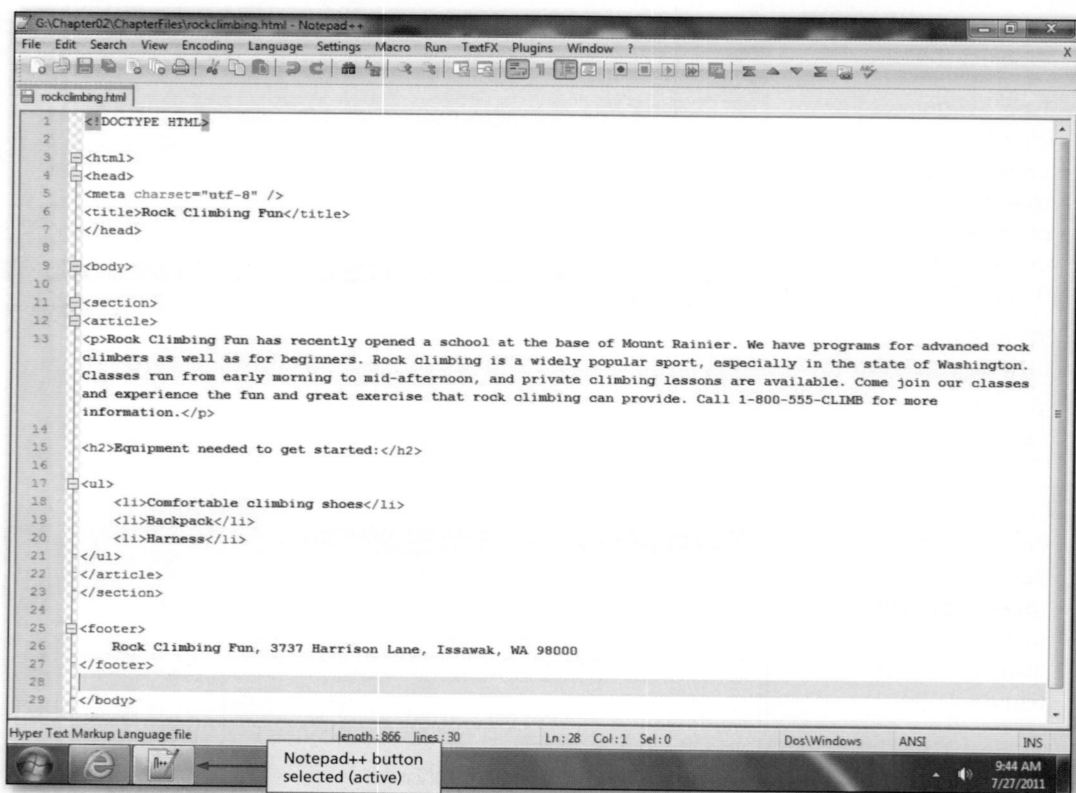

Figure 2–26

Improving the Appearance of Your Web Page

One goal in Web page development is to create a Web page that is visually appealing and maintains the interest of the visitors. The Web page developed thus far in the chapter is functional, but lacks visual appeal. In this section, you will learn how to improve the appearance of the Web page from the one shown in Figure 2–27a to the one shown in Figure 2–27b by adding an image, adding color to a heading, changing the style of the footer, adding a horizontal rule, and changing the list style type of the bulleted list. Many of these tasks can be accomplished by using style sheets.

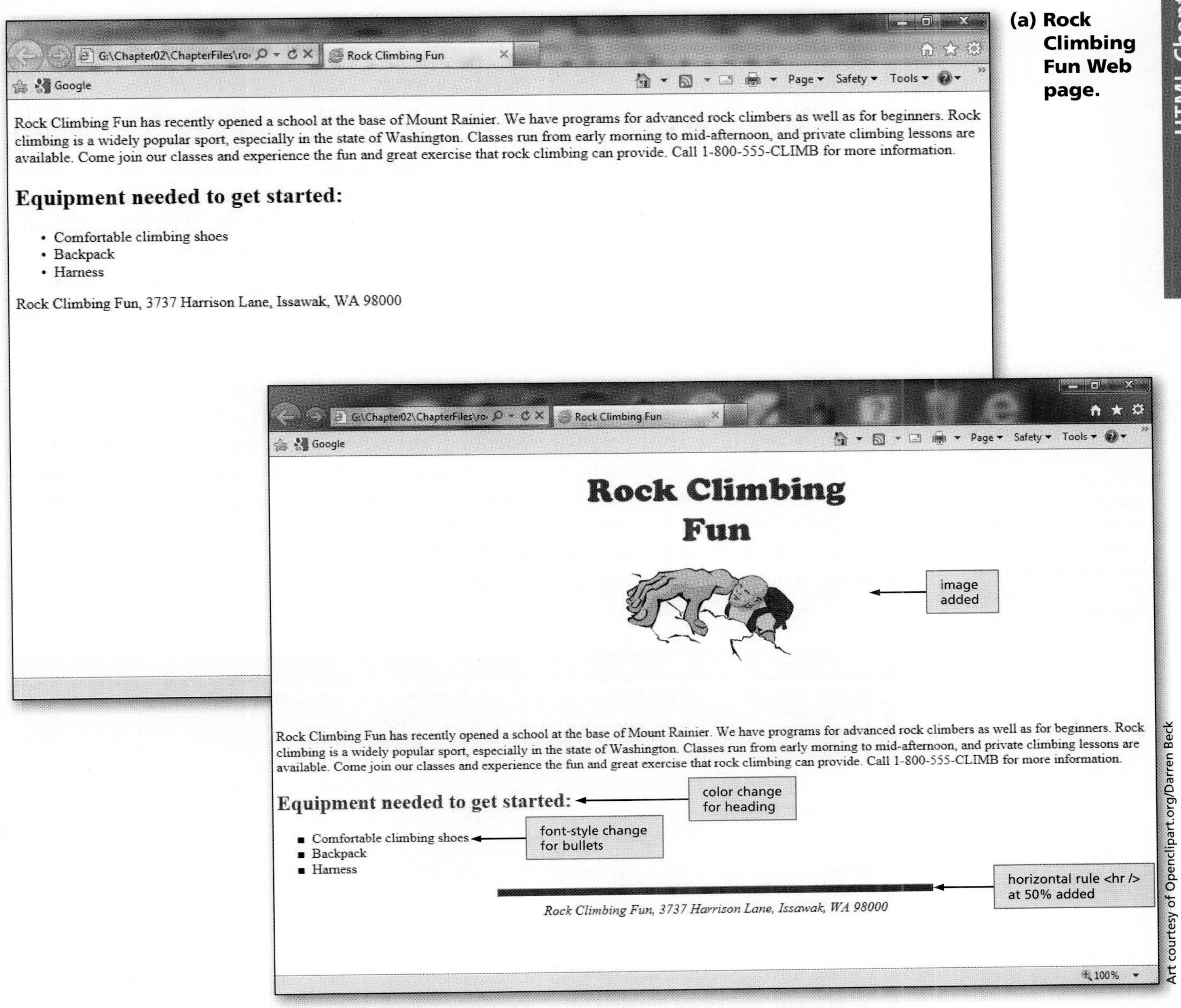

(a) Rock Climbing Fun Web page.

(b) Rock Climbing Fun Web page formatted to improve appearance.

Figure 2–27

Art courtesy of Openclipart.org/Darren Beck

Using Style Sheets

Although HTML allows Web developers to make changes to the structure, design, and content of a Web page, HTML is limited in its ability to define the appearance, or style, across one or more Web pages. As a result, style sheets were created.

As a review, a **style** is a rule that defines the appearance of an element on a Web page. A **Cascading Style Sheet (CSS)** is a series of rules that defines the style for a Web page or an entire Web site. With a style sheet, you can alter the appearance of a Web page or pages by changing characteristics such as font family, font size, margins, and link specifications.

The latest version of CSS is CSS3. As with HTML5, CSS3 is still in a working draft status at the World Wide Web Consortium (W3C). CSS3 adds many new style features, including column-based layouts, rounded borders, and enhanced text effects. For full CSS3 styles, visit w3.org. We will utilize some of the new styles in later chapters.

CSS supports three types of style sheets: inline, embedded (or internal), and external (or linked). With an **inline style**, you add a style to an individual HTML tag, such as a heading or paragraph. The style changes that specific tag, but does not affect other tags in the document. With an **embedded style sheet**, or **internal style sheet**, you add the style sheet within the <head> tags of the HTML document to define the style for an entire Web page. With an **external style sheet**, or **linked style sheet**, you create a text file that contains all of the styles you want to apply, and save the text file with the file extension .css. You then add a link to this external style sheet on any Web page in the Web site. External style sheets give you the most flexibility and are ideal to apply the same formats to all of the Web pages in a Web site. External style sheets also make it easy to change formats quickly across Web pages. You will use inline styles in this chapter's project to enhance the styles of the heading (change the color) and the bulleted list (change the font style).

BTW

Inline Styles
Using an inline style is helpful when you want to alter the appearance (or style) of a single HTML element. Appendix D contains the Cascading Style Sheet Properties and Values supported by most browsers. The inline styles used in this chapter can be found in the appendix. For more information on CSS, look at w3.org.

Style Sheet Precedence As shown in Table 2–8, the three style sheets supported by CSS control the appearance of a Web page at different levels. Each type of style sheet also has a different level of precedence or priority in relationship to the others. An external style sheet, for example, is used to define styles for multiple pages in a Web site. An embedded style sheet is used to change the style of one Web page, and overrides or takes precedence over any styles defined in an external style sheet. An inline style is used to control the style within an individual HTML tag and takes precedence over the styles defined in both embedded and external style sheets.

Table 2–8 Style Sheet Precedence

Type	Level and Precedence
Inline	• To change the style within an individual HTML tag • Overrides embedded and external style sheets
Embedded	• To change the style of one Web page • Overrides external style sheets
External	• To change the style of multiple pages in a Web site

Because style sheets have different levels of precedence, all three types of style sheets can be used on a single Web page. For example, you may want some elements of a Web page to match the other Web pages in the Web site, but you also may want to vary the look of certain sections of that Web page. You can do this by using the three types of style sheets.

Style Statement Format No matter what type of style sheet you use, you must use a **style statement** to define the style. The following code shows an example of a style statement used in an inline style:

```
<h1 style="font-family: Garamond; font-color: navy">
```

A style statement is made up of a selector and a declaration. The part of the style statement that identifies the page elements is called the **selector**. In this example, the selector is h1 (header size 1). The part of the style statement that identifies how the element(s) should appear is called the **declaration**. In this example, the declaration is everything between the quotation marks: the font-family and font-color properties and their values (Garamond and navy, respectively). A declaration includes at least one type of style, or **property**, to apply to the selected element. Examples of properties include color, text-indent, border-width, and font-style. For each property, the declaration includes a related **value**, which specifies the display parameters for that specific property.

Each property accepts specific values, based on the styles that property can define. The property, font-color, for example, can accept the value, navy, but cannot accept the value, 10%, because that is not a valid color value. In the next section of this chapter, you will change the heading color to the color #384738 for the h2 heading. Using an inline style in this case is appropriate because there is only one heading to change on the Web page. If you had many headings to change, an embedded or external style sheet would be more appropriate. This will be discussed in later chapters.

Inline Styles An inline style is used to define the style of an individual HTML tag. For example, to change the style of a horizontal rule, you could add an inline style with the <hr /> (horizontal rule) tag as the selector and a declaration that defines new height, width, and background-color styles, as shown here:

```
<hr style="height: 8px; background-color: #384738; width: 50%" />
```

Because inline styles take precedence over the other types of style sheets and affect the style for individual HTML tags, they are helpful when one section or one element of a Web page needs to have a style different from the rest of the Web page. In this chapter's project, an inline style is used to change the color of the <h2> heading, the bullet list type, the footer, and the horizontal rule styles on the Web page.

Now that you understand how style sheets and inline styles function, it is time to think about adding an image to enhance the appearance of your Web page.

Using Web Page Divisions

It can be helpful to break up your Web page into divisions (or sections), which allows you to apply styles to different Web page elements. Throughout this book, you sometimes use the start <div> and end </div> division tags as a container in which to insert images. You also use the new HTML5 layout elements to help structure your Web page into sections. As mentioned earlier, these new semantic elements are useful because the name of the tag actually reflects the purpose of the tag. For example, the <header> tag is used to display text at the top (or the header) of the Web page. Utilizing structural and division tags allows you to add styles such as centering your image or adding background color to your images.

Plan Ahead

Find appropriate graphical images.
To use graphical images, also called graphics, on a Web page, the image must be stored digitally in a file. Files containing graphical images are available from a variety of sources:

- Some Web sites offer images that are free and are not subject to copyright; these images are considered to be in the **public domain**. Other Web sites offer images that require permission from the copyright owner or a fee for use.
- You can take a picture with a digital camera and **download** it, which is the process of copying the digital picture from the camera to your computer.
- With a scanner, you can convert a printed picture, drawing, or diagram to a digital file.

If you receive a picture from a source other than yourself, do not use the file until you are certain it does not contain a virus. A **virus** is a computer program that can damage files and programs on your computer. Use an antivirus program to verify that any files you use are virus free.

(continued)

Plan Ahead

(continued)

Establish where to position and how to format the graphical image. The content, size, shape, position, and format of a graphic should capture the interest of viewers, enticing them to stop and read the Web page. Often, the graphic is the center of attraction and visually the largest element on a page. If you use colors in the graphical image, be sure they are part of the Web page's color scheme.

Identify the width and height of the image. The width and height (measured in pixels) of an image should always be identified in the <img> tag. These dimensions are used by the browser to determine the size to display the image.

Provide alternate text for the image. Text describing the image, known as alternate text, should always be used for each image. This text is especially useful to users with visual impairments who use a screen reader, which translates information on a computer screen into audio output. The length of the alternate text should be reasonable.

Types of Web Page Images

Images are used in many ways to enhance the look of a Web page and make it more interesting and colorful. Images can be used to add background color, to help organize a Web page, to help clarify a point being made in the text, or to serve as links to other Web pages. Images are often also used to break up Web page sections (such as with a horizontal rule) or as directional elements that allow a visitor to navigate a Web site.

BTW

Images
Images on Web pages are viewed in a variety of environments, including on computers with slow connctions to the Internet. Optimizing your images is important to increase the speed of download for all of your Web page visitors. Search the Web for more information on image optimization.

Web pages use three types of files as images: GIF, JPEG, and PNG (Table 2–9). **Graphics Interchange Format (GIF)** files have an extension of .gif. A graphic image saved as a GIF (pronounced *jiff* or *giff*) uses compression techniques, called LZW compression, to make it smaller for download on the Web. Standard (or noninterlaced) GIF images are displayed one line at a time when loading. Interlaced GIF images load all at once, starting with a blurry look and becoming sharper as they load. Using interlaced GIFs for large images is a good technique, because a Web page visitor can see a blurred outline of the image as it loads.

A second type of image file is **Portable Network Graphics (PNG)**, which has a .png extension. The PNG (pronounced *ping*) format is also a lossless compressed file format that supports multiple colors and resolutions. The PNG format is a patent-free alternative to the GIF format. Most newer browsers support PNG images.

Finally, **Joint Photographic Experts Group (JPEG)** files have an extension of .jpg, .jpe, or .jpeg. A JPEG (pronounced *JAY-peg*) is a graphic image saved using a lossy compression technique that discards some data during the compression process and is best suited for images with smooth variations of tone and color. JPEG files are often used for more complex images, such as photographs, because the JPEG file format supports more colors and resolutions than the other file types.

Table 2–9 Image Types and Uses

Image Type	Use
Graphics Interchange Format (GIF)	• Use for images with few colors (<256) • Allows for transparent backgrounds
Portable Network Graphics (PNG)	• Newest format for images • Use for all types of images • Allows for variation in transparency
Joint Photographic Experts Group (JPEG)	• Use for images with many colors (>256), such as photographs

If an image is not in one of these formats, you can use a paint or graphics-editing program to convert an image to a .gif, .jpg, or .png format. Some paint programs even allow you to save a standard GIF image as interlaced. A number of paint and graphics-editing programs, such Adobe Photoshop and Corel Paint Shop Pro, are available in the marketplace today.

Image Attributes

You can enhance HTML tags by using attributes. **Attributes** define additional characteristics for the HTML tag. For instance, you should use the width and height attributes for all <img> tags. Table 2–10 lists the attributes that can be used with the <img> tag. In this chapter, the src and alt attributes are used in the <img> tag. Image attributes will be explained in detail, because they are used in later chapters.

BTW

Overusing Images
Be cautious about overusing images on a Web page. Using too many images may give your Web page a cluttered look or distract the visitor from the purpose of the Web page. An image should have a purpose, such as to convey content, visually organize a page, provide a hyperlink, or serve another function.

Table 2–10 Image Attributes

Attribute	Function
alt	• Alternative text to display when an image is being loaded • Especially useful for screen readers, which translate information on a computer screen into audio output • Should be a brief representation of the purpose of the image • Generally should stick to 50 characters or fewer
height	• Defines the height of the image, measured in pixels • Improves loading time
src	• Defines the URL of the image to be loaded
width	• Defines the width of the image, measured in pixels • Improves loading time

To Add an Image

In the early days when the Web was used mostly by researchers needing to share information with each other, having purely functional, text-only Web pages was the norm. Today, Web page visitors are used to a more graphically oriented world, and have come to expect Web pages to use images that provide visual interest. The following step illustrates how to add an image to a Web page by entering an <img> tag in the HTML file using the tags and text shown in Table 2–11.

Table 2–11 Adding an Image

Line	HTML Tag and Text
11	`<header style="text-align: center">`
12	`  <img src="rockclimber.jpg" width="450" height="300" alt="Rock climber" />`
13	`</header>`

- Click the blank line 10 and then press the ENTER key.
- With the insertion point on line 11, enter the HTML code, as shown in Table 2–11. Press ENTER at the end of each line (Figure 2–28).

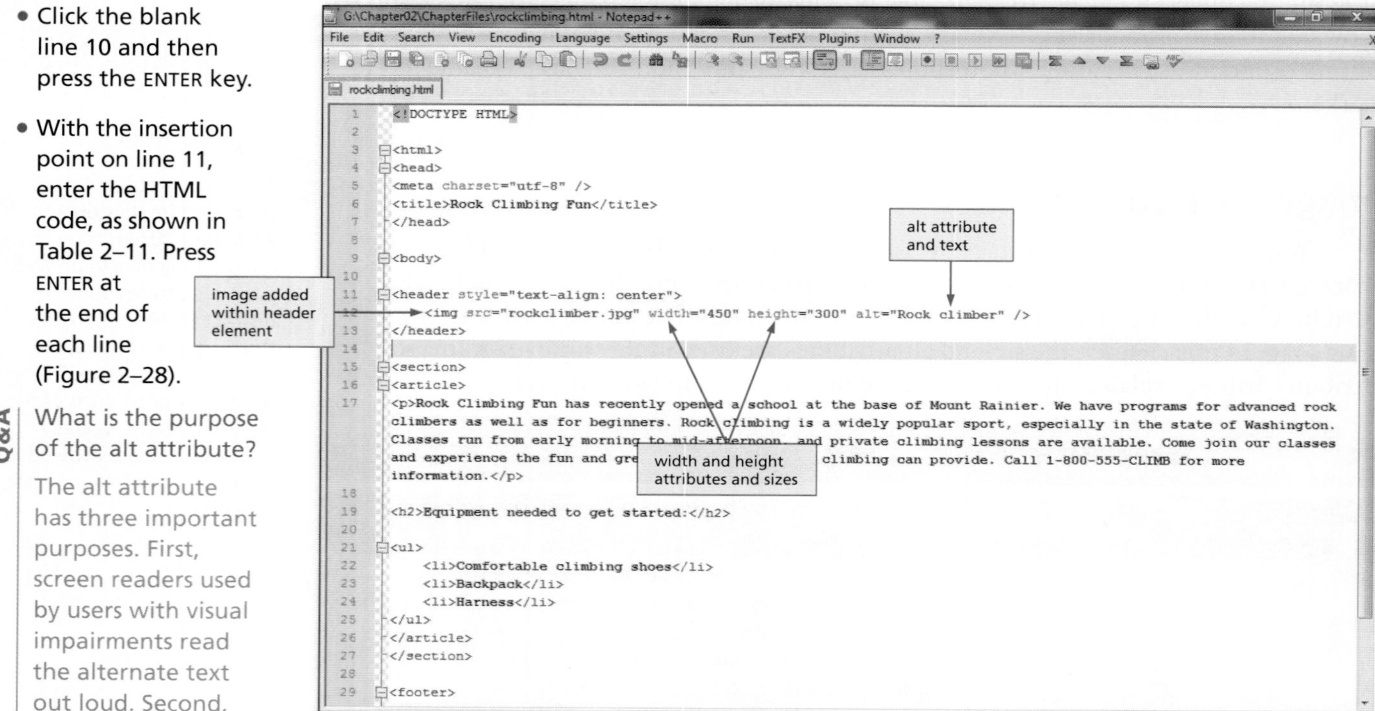

Figure 2–28

Q&A

What is the purpose of the alt attribute?

The alt attribute has three important purposes. First, screen readers used by users with visual impairments read the alternate text out loud. Second, the alternate text is displayed while the image is being loaded. Finally, the alt tag is required for compliance to good programming standards.

Q&A

What is the purpose of the inline style used in the <header> tag?

You use the style="text-align: center" statement to center the header on the Web page.

Plan Ahead

Make other visual enhancements.
In addition to images, there are several ways to add visual interest.

Add color to headings. Web developers often use colors to call attention to elements on a Web page. The color selected should coordinate with the images selected for the page. It should also allow the Web page text to be read easily. Some colors, such as dark colors, may not be appropriate because the default black text cannot be displayed effectively on a dark background. When changing the color of an element such as a heading, it is usually best to apply the same style to all headings on the Web page for consistency.

Change the list style type of a bulleted list. It is sometimes aesthetically pleasing to change the style of the bullet in a bulleted list. When you want to call attention to the information, you might also want to italicize or bold the bullet text.

Insert a horizontal rule. It is useful to use a horizontal rule to break up text on a Web page. A horizontal rule is used as a divider for a page to separate text sections.

Alter the footer style. A footer contains content, such as contact information, that does not have to be strongly highlighted. Changes can be made to that tag to make its style different from the other content on the page.

Other Visual Enhancements

One way to help capture a Web page visitor's attention is to use color. Many colors are available for use as a Web page background, text, border, or link. Figure 2–29 shows colors often used on Web pages, with the corresponding six-digit number codes. The six-digit number codes, known as **hexadecimal** codes, can be used to specify a color for a background, text, or links. The heading on the Rock Climbing Fun Web page is currently black (the default color). You will spruce up the Web page by adding color to the heading and the horizontal rule using inline styles.

> **BTW**
> **Colors**
> Figure 2–29 does not list all possible Web colors. Many other colors are available that you can use for Web page backgrounds or text fonts. For more information about colors, see Appendix B or search the Web for browser colors.

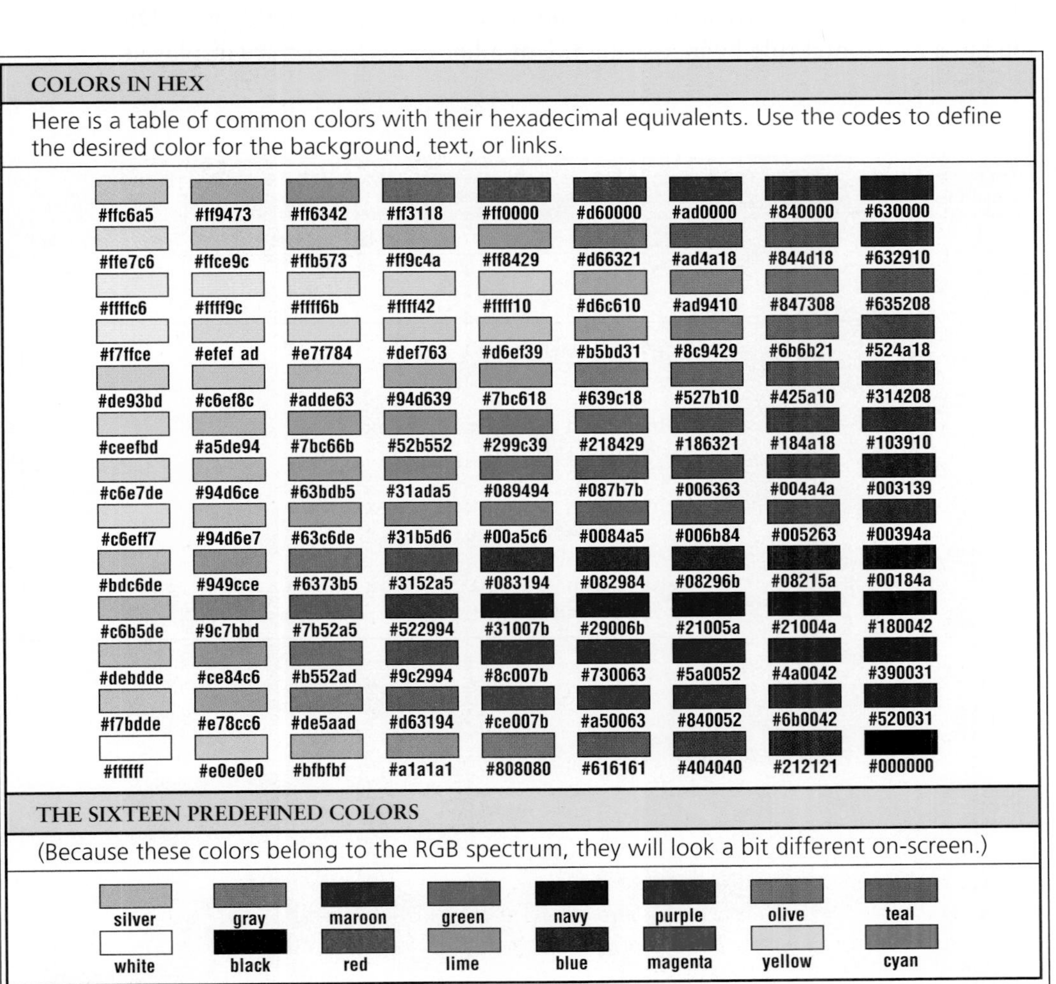

COLORS IN HEX

Here is a table of common colors with their hexadecimal equivalents. Use the codes to define the desired color for the background, text, or links.

#ffc6a5	#ff9473	#ff6342	#ff3118	#ff0000	#d60000	#ad0000	#840000	#630000
#ffe7c6	#ffce9c	#ffb573	#ff9c4a	#ff8429	#d66321	#ad4a18	#844d18	#632910
#ffffc6	#ffff9c	#ffff6b	#ffff42	#ffff10	#d6c610	#ad9410	#847308	#635208
#f7ffce	#efef ad	#e7f784	#def763	#d6ef39	#b5bd31	#8c9429	#6b6b21	#524a18
#de93bd	#c6ef8c	#adde63	#94d639	#7bc618	#639c18	#527b10	#425a10	#314208
#ceefbd	#a5de94	#7bc66b	#52b552	#299c39	#218429	#186321	#184a18	#103910
#c6e7de	#94d6ce	#63bdb5	#31ada5	#089494	#087b7b	#006363	#004a4a	#003139
#c6eff7	#94d6e7	#63c6de	#31b5d6	#00a5c6	#0084a5	#006b84	#005263	#00394a
#bdc6de	#949cce	#6373b5	#3152a5	#083194	#082984	#08296b	#08215a	#00184a
#c6b5de	#9c7bbd	#7b52a5	#522994	#31007b	#29006b	#21005a	#21004a	#180042
#debdde	#ce84c6	#b552ad	#9c2994	#8c007b	#730063	#5a0052	#4a0042	#390031
#f7bdde	#e78cc6	#de5aad	#d63194	#ce007b	#a50063	#840052	#6b0042	#520031
#ffffff	#e0e0e0	#bfbfbf	#a1a1a1	#808080	#616161	#404040	#212121	#000000

THE SIXTEEN PREDEFINED COLORS

(Because these colors belong to the RGB spectrum, they will look a bit different on-screen.)

silver	gray	maroon	green	navy	purple	olive	teal
white	black	red	lime	blue	magenta	yellow	cyan

Figure 2–29

The color codes and names shown in Figure 2–29 can be used for background, text, border, and link colors. The color property is used in the <h2> tag to specify the color for the heading. The color #384738 will be used for the heading because it is one of the colors found in the graphical image inserted in the steps above.

Another way to visually enhance the Web page is to change the style of some of the text. This calls attention to that particular text on the Web page. In this section, you will change the text in the footer to an italic style using an inline style. This change helps call attention to that tangential content.

> **BTW**
> **Browser-safe Colors**
> Web developers used to have to make sure that they used browser-safe colors (Appendix B). The trend for monitors today is to display "true color", which means that any of 16 million colors can be displayed on the monitor. Few people use 8-bit monitors anymore, so you generally do not have to limit yourself to browser-safe colors.

Finally, you will add a horizontal rule and an inline style to further enhance this Web page. As discussed earlier in the chapter, horizontal rules are lines that act as dividers on a Web page to provide a visual separation of sections on the page. You can use an inline image to add a horizontal rule, or you can use the horizontal rule tag (<hr />) to add a simple horizontal rule, as shown in the following steps. To make the horizontal rule more apparent, you will give it a height of 8 pixels and color the background the same color as the <h2> heading. You will also set the width of the horizontal rule to 50% of the Web page. You do all three of those changes to the horizontal rule using an inline style. Figure 2–30 shows examples of a variety of horizontal rules and the HTML code used to add them. The default horizontal rule is shown in the first rule on the page. Dimension is added to a horizontal rule by increasing the number of pixels that are displayed.

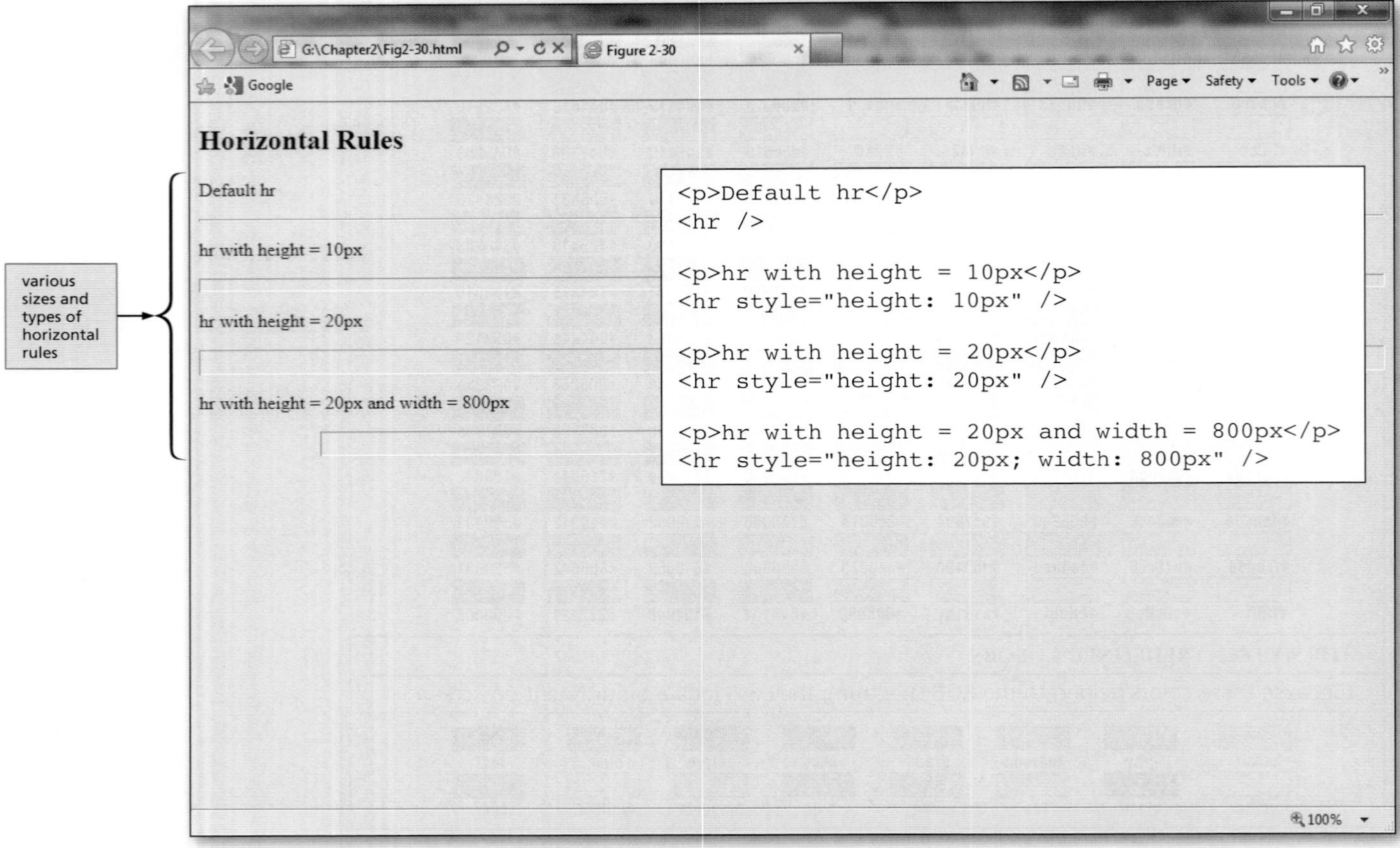

Figure 2–30

To Add Color to a Web Page Heading

To change the color of a heading on a Web page, the color property must be added in the <h2> tag of the HTML file. The **color** property lets you change the color of various elements on the Web page. The following step shows how to add a color using the color property in an inline style.

1

- Click after the "2" but before the closing bracket in <h2> on line 19 and then press the SPACEBAR.
- Type `style="color: #384738"` as the color code for the heading (Figure 2–31).

Q&A

Can I use any hexadecimal code or color name to change colors of headings?

Although you may use any of the hexadecimal codes or color names available, you have to make sure that the color is appropriate for the headings of your Web page. You do not want a heading that is too light in color or otherwise diminishes the headings.

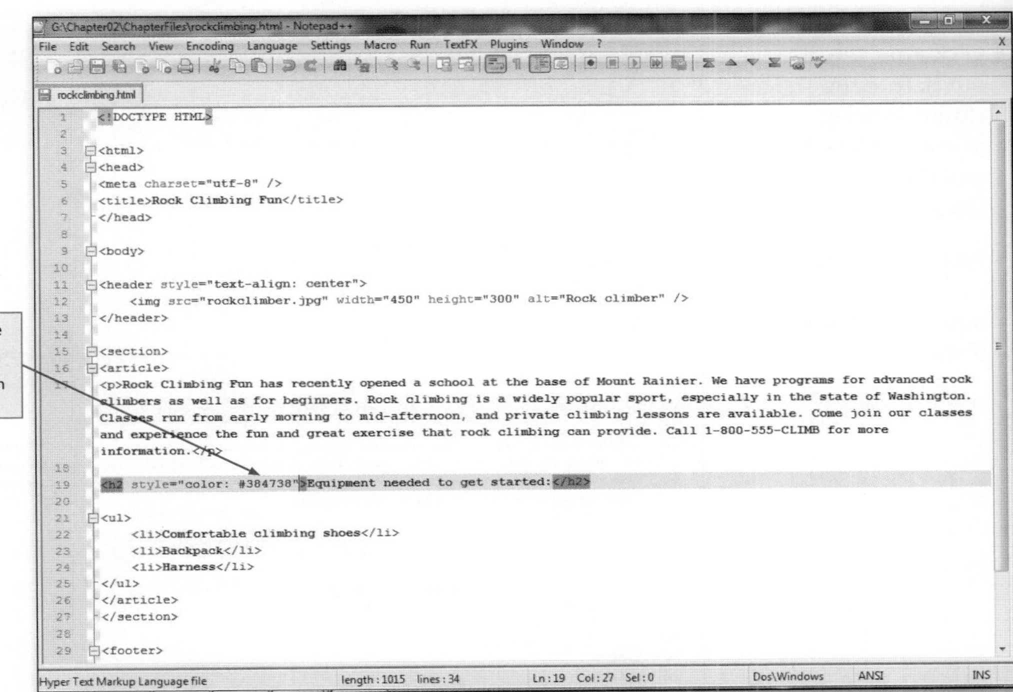


```
<!DOCTYPE HTML>

<html>
<head>
<meta charset="utf-8" />
<title>Rock Climbing Fun</title>
</head>

<body>

<header style="text-align: center">
    <img src="rockclimber.jpg" width="450" height="300" alt="Rock climber" />
</header>

<section>
<article>
<p>Rock Climbing Fun has recently opened a school at the base of Mount Rainier. We have programs for advanced rock climbers as well as for beginners. Rock climbing is a widely popular sport, especially in the state of Washington. Classes run from early morning to mid-afternoon, and private climbing lessons are available. Come join our classes and experience the fun and great exercise that rock climbing can provide. Call 1-800-555-CLIMB for more information.</p>

<h2 style="color: #384738">Equipment needed to get started:</h2>

<ul>
    <li>Comfortable climbing shoes</li>
    <li>Backpack</li>
    <li>Harness</li>
</ul>
</article>
</section>

<footer>
```

Figure 2–31

To Change the Bulleted List Style

To change the style of the bulleted list, you again use an inline style with the list-style-type property. The list-style-type property lets you change the style of the bullet type from the default disc to other options. There are several values for the list-style-type, as shown in Appendix D. The following step shows how to change the list-style-type property using an inline style.

- Click after the "l" but before the closing bracket in <ul> on line 21 and then press the SPACEBAR.
- Type `style="list-style-type: square"` as the code (Figure 2–32).

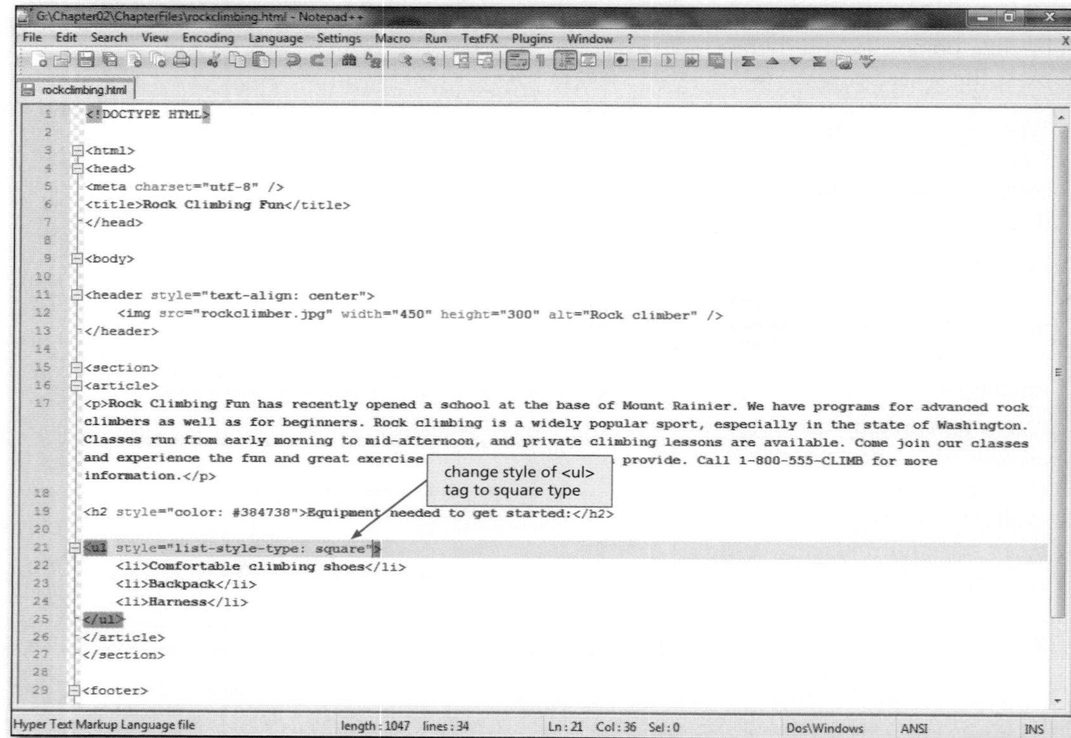

Figure 2–32

To Add a Horizontal Rule

You next insert a horizontal rule to separate the top part of the Web page from the footer area. You also give the horizontal rule more height (8 pixels) than the default, change the background color to match the heading, and make the width 50%. The following step illustrates how to add a horizontal rule to a Web page.

1

- Click the blank line 28 and then press the ENTER key.
- Type `<hr style="height: 8px; background-color: #384738; width: 50%" />` and then press the ENTER key (Figure 2–33).

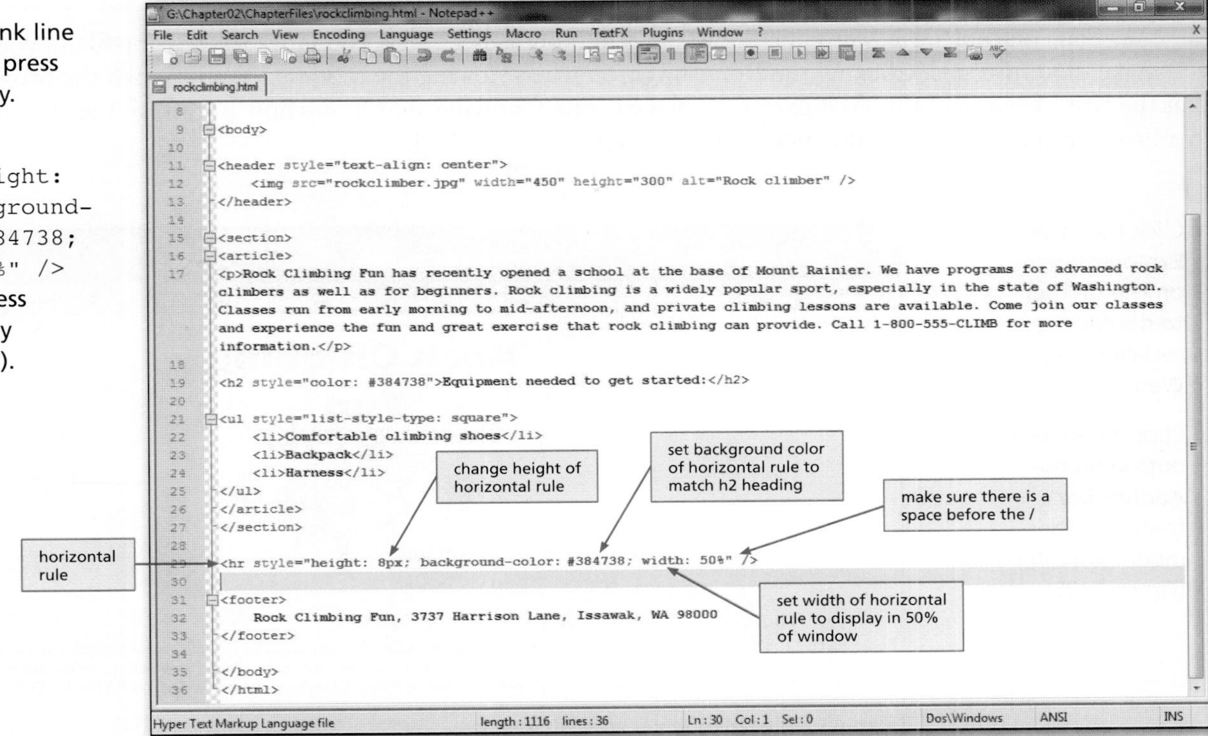

Figure 2–33

To Change the Footer Style

To change the style of the footer element, you again use an inline style with the font-style property. In this step, you center the footer across the Web page and change the font style to italic. Footer information is not generally intended to be the highlight of the Web page, so making the footer content italic is appropriate. The following steps show how to center and change the text using an inline style.

1

- Click after the "r" but before the closing bracket in <footer> on line 31 and then press the SPACEBAR.
- Type `style="text-align: center; font-style: italic"` as the code (Figure 2–34).

2

- Click File on the menu bar and then click Save.

```
15  <section>
16  <article>
17  <p>Rock Climbing Fun has recently opened a school at the base of Mount Rainier. We have programs for advanced rock
    climbers as well as for beginners. Rock climbing is a widely popular sport, especially in the state of Washington.
    Classes run from early morning to mid-afternoon, and private climbing lessons are available. Come join our classes
    and experience the fun and great exercise that rock climbing can provide. Call 1-800-555-CLIMB for more
    information.</p>
18
19  <h2 style="color: #384738">Equipment needed to get started:</h2>
20
21  <ul style="list-style-type: square">
22      <li>Comfortable climbing shoes</li>
23      <li>Backpack</li>
24      <li>Harness</li>
25  </ul>
26  </article>
27  </section>
28
29  <hr style="height: 8px; background-color: #384738; width: 50%" />
30
31  <footer style="text-align: center; font-style: italic">
32      Rock Climbing Fun, 3737 Harrison Lane, Issawak, WA 98000
33  </footer>
34
35  </body>
```

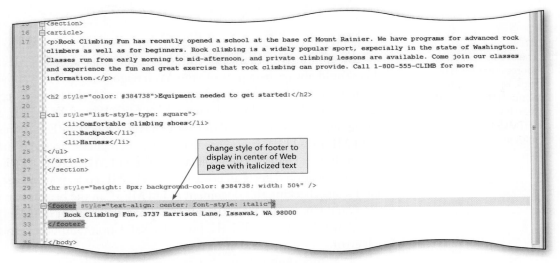

change style of footer to display in center of Web page with italicized text

Figure 2–34

To Refresh the View in a Browser

As you continue developing the HTML file in Notepad++, it is a good idea to view the file in your browser as you make modifications. Clicking the Refresh button when viewing the modified Web page in the browser, ensures that the latest version of the Web page is displayed. The following step shows how to refresh the view of a Web page in a browser in order to view the modified Web page.

1

- Click the Internet Explorer button on the taskbar to display the rockclimbing.html Web page.
- Click the Refresh button on the Address bar to display the modified Web page (Figure 2–35).

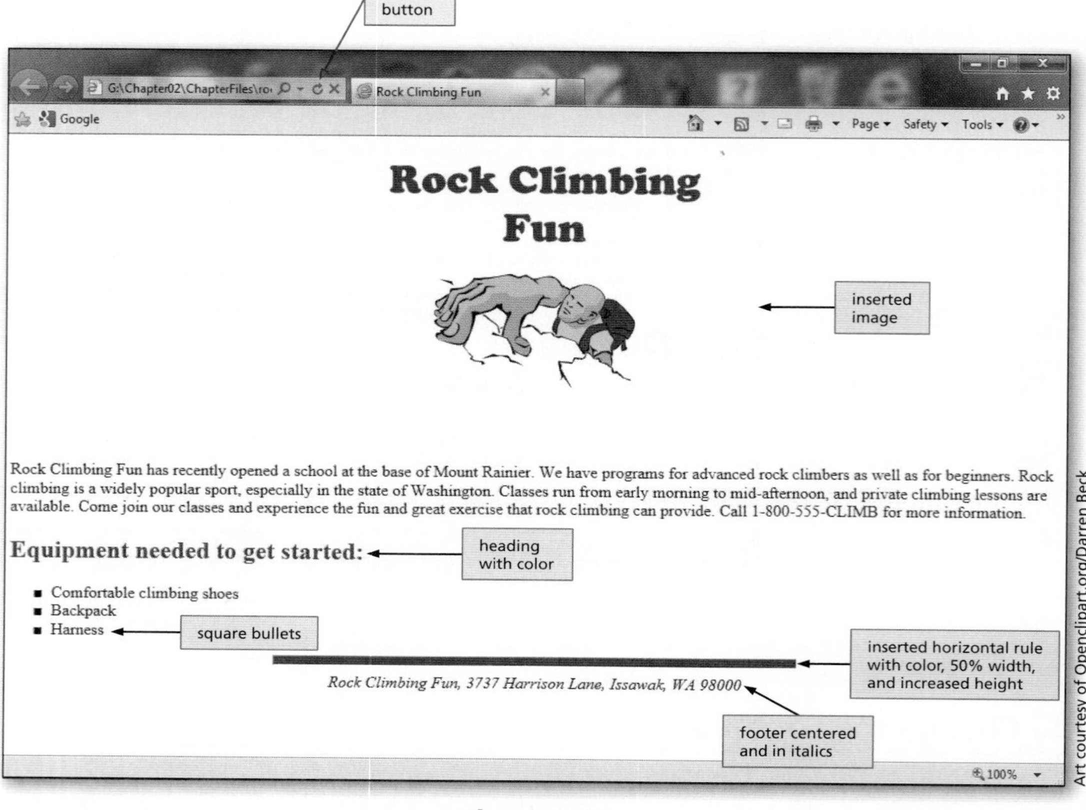

Figure 2–35

Other Ways

1. In Internet Explorer, press F5 to refresh

Validating and Viewing HTML Code

BTW

HTML and HTML5 Tags
The Web has excellent sources that list HTML5 tags. For more information about HTML and HTML5, search for "HTML tags" or "HTML5 tags" in a search engine.

In Chapter 1, you read about validating your HTML code. Many validation services are available on the Web that can be used to assure that your HTML code follows standards. This should always be a part of your Web page testing. The validation service used in this book is the W3C Markup Validation Service (validator.w3.org). This validator checks the markup validity of Web documents in HTML and XHTML, along with some other markup languages. The validator looks at the DOCTYPE statement to see which version of HTML or XHTML you are using, and then checks to see if the code is valid for that version. In this chapter, the project uses the HTML5 DOCTYPE.

If validation detects an error in your HTML code, you will see the warning "Errors found while checking this document as HTML5!" in the header bar, which is in red (Figure 2–36a on the next page). The Result line shows the number of errors that you have. You can scroll down the page or click the Jump To: Validation Output link to see detailed comments on each error.

It is important to note that one error can result in more errors. As an example, the </h2> tag on line 19 in the rockclimbing.html file was removed to show code with an error. Figure 2–36b shows that in this case, one initial error (that the <ul> tag on line 21 cannot be used within the <h2> tag on line 19) resulted in a total of three errors and one warning.

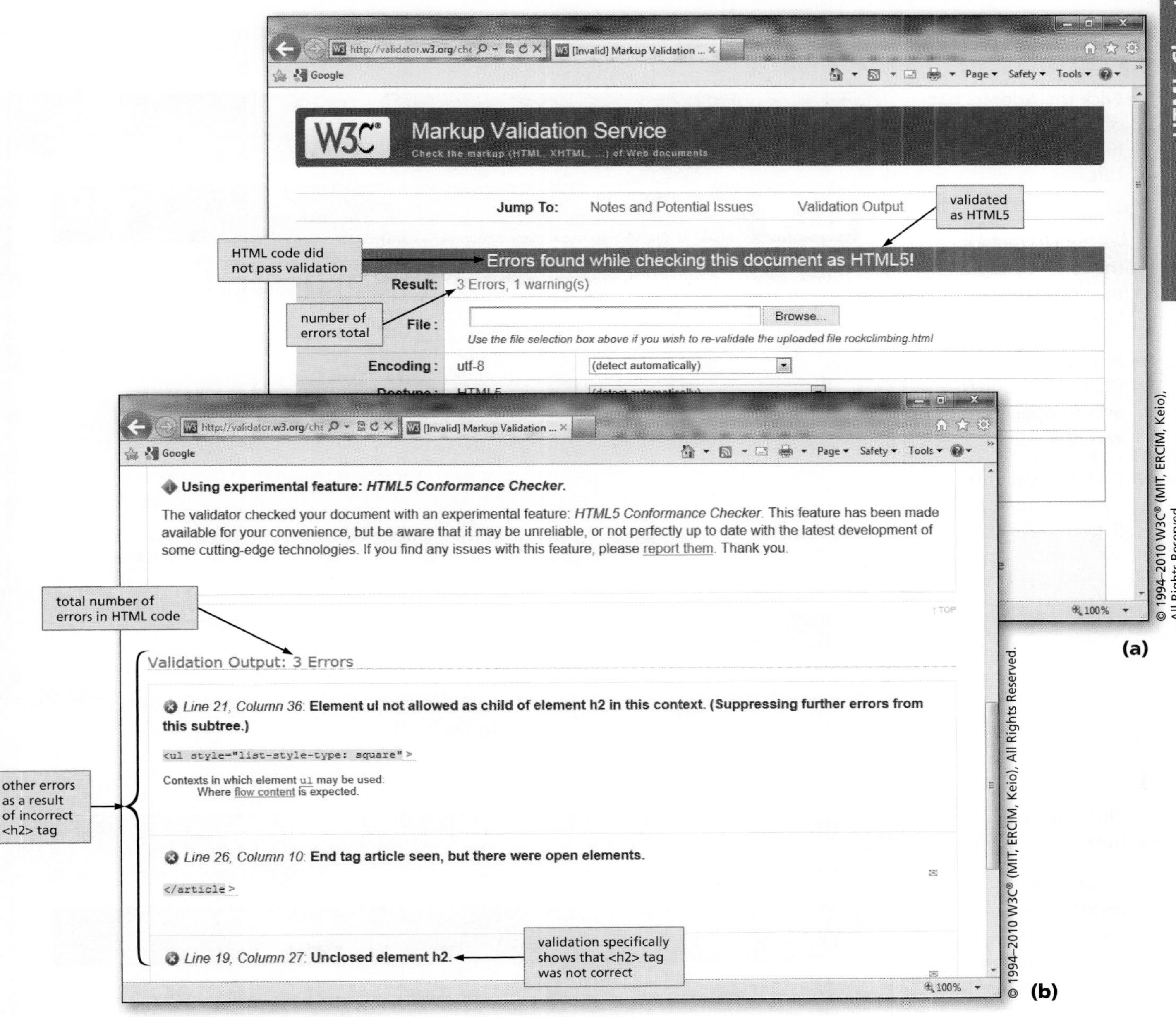

Figure 2–36

To Validate HTML Code

Now that you have added all the basic elements to your Web page and enhanced it with images, color, italics, and rules, you need to validate your code. The current validation process for HTML5 returns not just errors, but informational warnings, as shown in Figure 2–39a on page HTML 75. Although the validator says the code "was successfully checked as HTML5" it also displays a warning for the code. Figure 2–39b explains that warning, which says that the HTML5 Conformance Checker used for validation on HTML5 code is experiemental. As mentioned earlier in the chapter, HTML5 is still experimental as are associated support features, and this warning is just telling you that. The warning is fine though, so your code has passed the validation process. The following steps illustrate how to validate your HTML code using the W3 validator.

1

- Click the Address bar on the browser to highlight the current URL.
- Type `validator.w3.org` to replace the current entry, and then press the ENTER key.
- If necessary, click OK if the browser asks to open a new window.
- Click the Validate by File Upload tab (Figure 2–37).

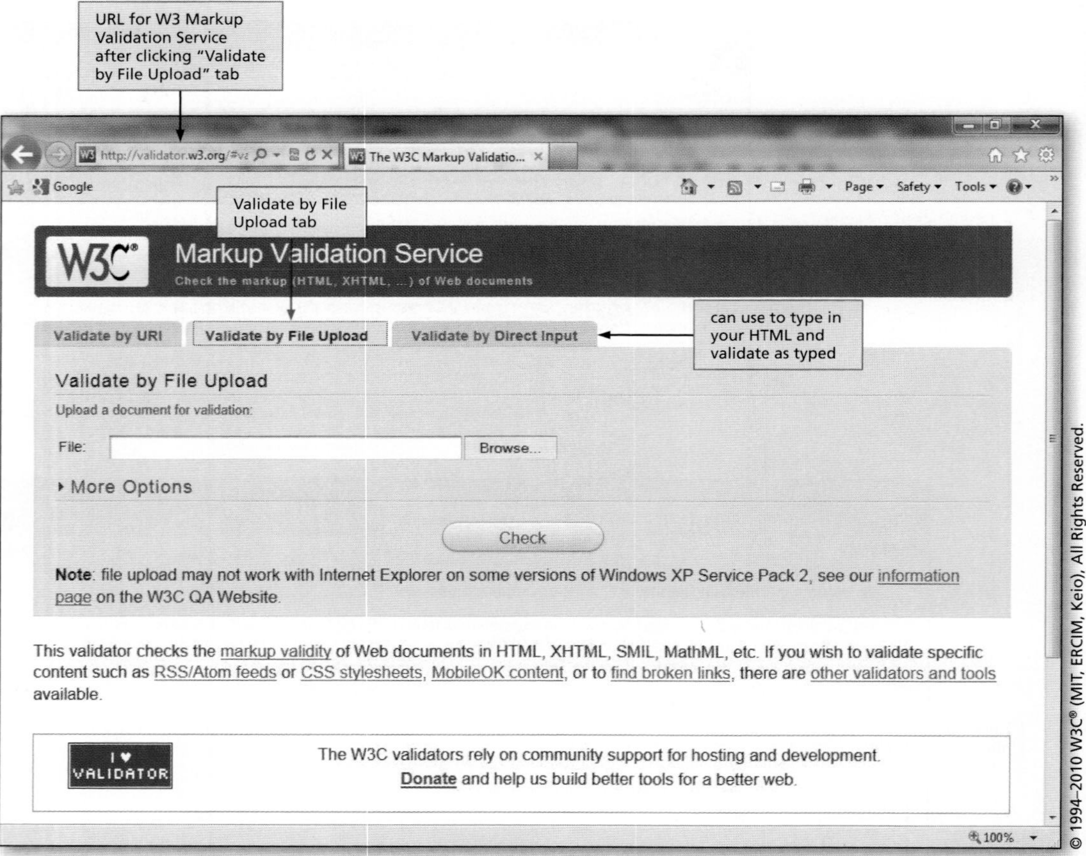

Figure 2–37

2

- Click the Browse button.
- Locate the rockclimbing.html file on your storage device and then click the file name.
- Click the Open button on the Choose File to Upload dialog box and the file path and name will be inserted into the File box, as shown in Figure 2–38.

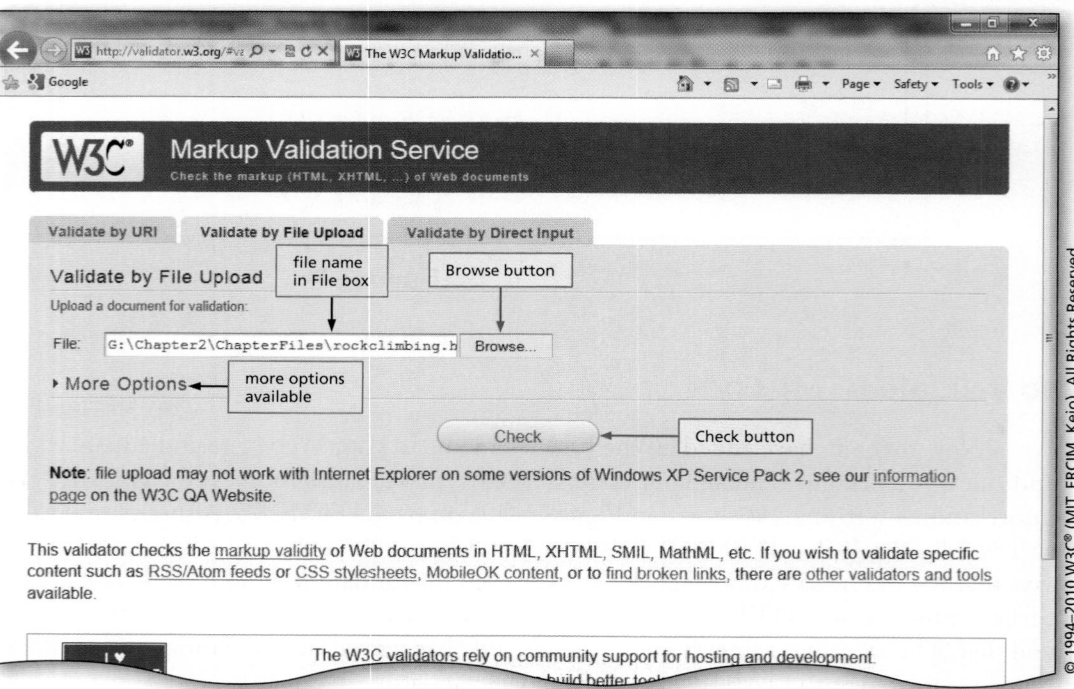

Figure 2–38

3

- Click the Check button. The resulting validation should be displayed, as shown in Figure 2–39a and 2–39b.
- Return to the Rock Climbing Fun Web page, either by clicking the Back button on your browser or by clicking the Internet Explorer button in the taskbar.

Q&A How do I know if my HTML code is valid?

The notification header will be green, and in the Result area, you should see the word "Passed."

Q&A What can I do if my HTML code is not validated?

If your code has errors, edit your HTML file to correct the errors. The Markup Validation Service report lists what is wrong with your code. Once you make the necessary changes and save the file, you can use the Browse button to open the corrected HTML file, then scroll down and click the Revalidate button to validate the changed code.

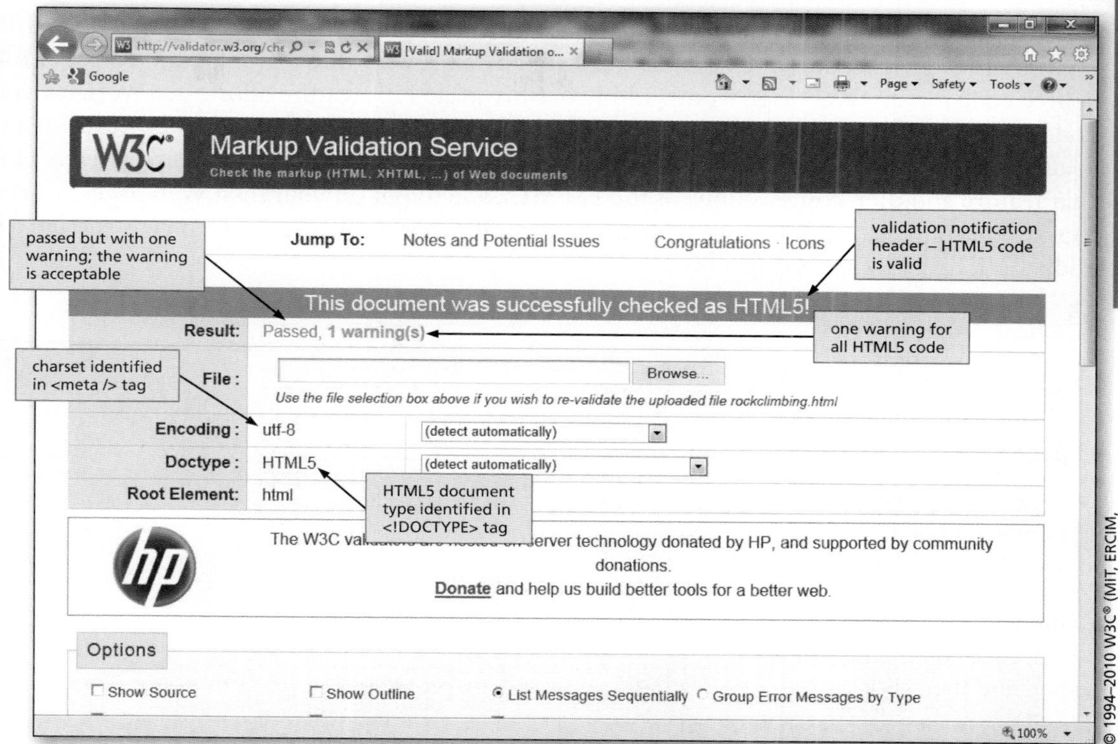

(a)

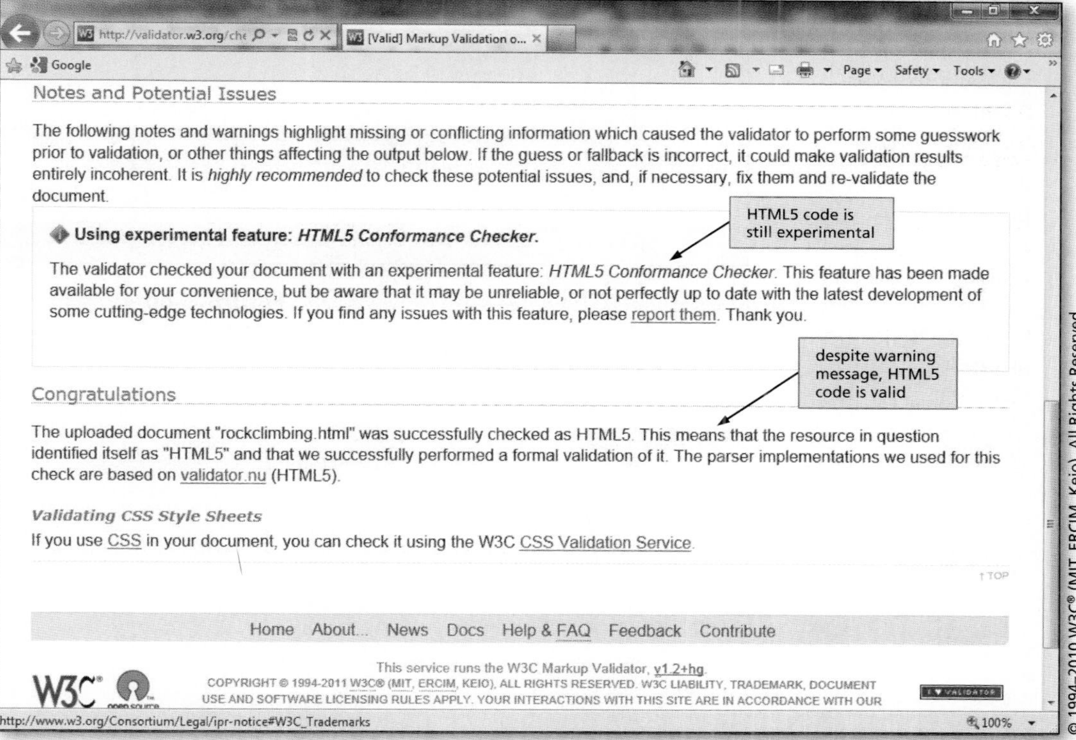

(b)

Figure 2–39

To View HTML Source Code for a Web Page

Source code is the code or instructions used to create a Web page or program. For a Web page, the source code is the HTML code, which then is translated by a browser into a graphical Web page. You can view the HTML source code for any Web page from within your browser. This feature allows you to check your own HTML source code, as well as to see the HTML code other developers used to create their Web pages. If a feature on a Web page is appropriate or appealing for your Web page, you can view the source to understand the HTML required to add that feature and then copy sections of the HTML code to put on your own Web pages. You can use your browser to look at the source code for most Web pages. The following steps show how to view the HTML source code for your Web page using a browser.

1

- Use the Back button on the browser to return to the Web page.
- Click Page on the Command bar. If your Command bar is not displayed, right-click the title bar, click Command bar, and then click Page.
- Click View source to view the HTML code in the default text editor (Figure 2–40).

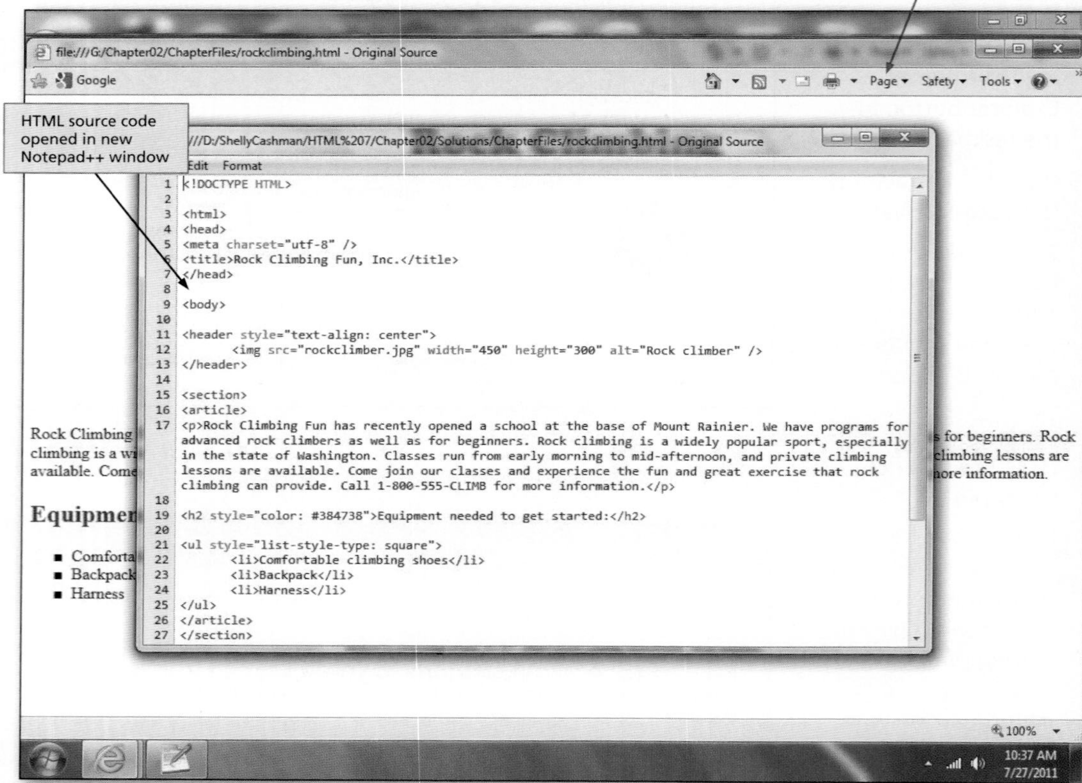

Figure 2–40

Q&A Do all browsers allow me to view the HTML source code in the same way?

Browsers such as Chrome, Firefox and Safari all allow you to view the source code of Web pages. However, they might use different buttons or menu options to access source code. For instance, in Mozilla Firefox, select View and then Page Source.

- Click the Close button on the text editor menu bar to close the active text editor window (Figure 2–41).

Q&A What is the default text editor?

It is likely to be Notepad for Internet Explorer, but could be Notepad++ or another editor depending on your browser setup.

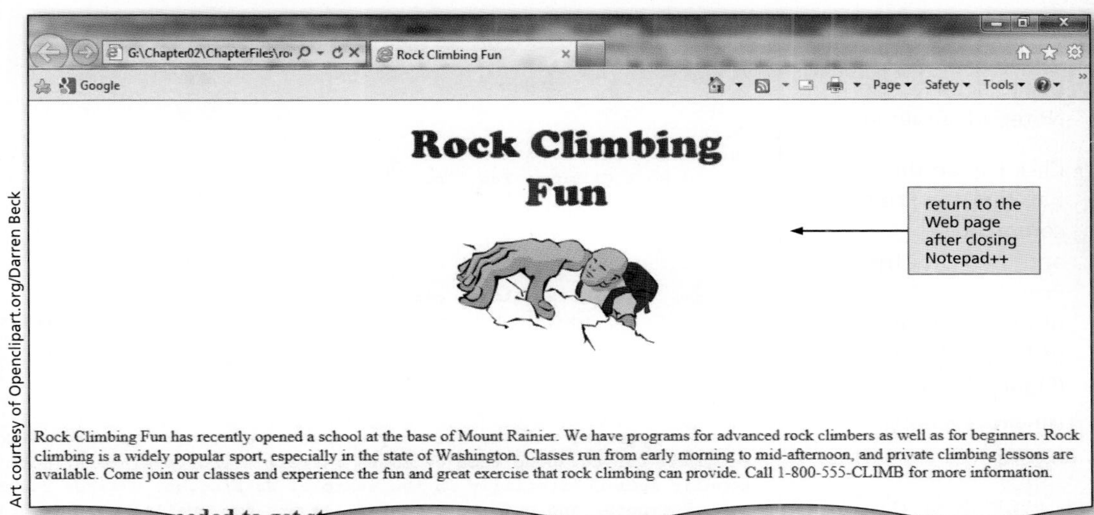

Figure 2–41

To Print a Web Page and an HTML File

After you have created the HTML file and saved it, you might want to print a copy of the HTML code and the resulting Web page. A printed version of a file, Web page, or other document is called a **hard copy** or **printout**. Printed copies of HTML files and Web pages can be kept for reference or to distribute. The following steps show how to print a Web page and its corresponding HTML file.

- Ready the printer according to the printer instructions.
- With the Rock Climbing Fun Web page open in the browser window, click the Print icon on the Command bar.
- When the Print dialog box appears, click the Print button.
- When the printer stops printing the Web page, retrieve the printout (Figure 2–42).

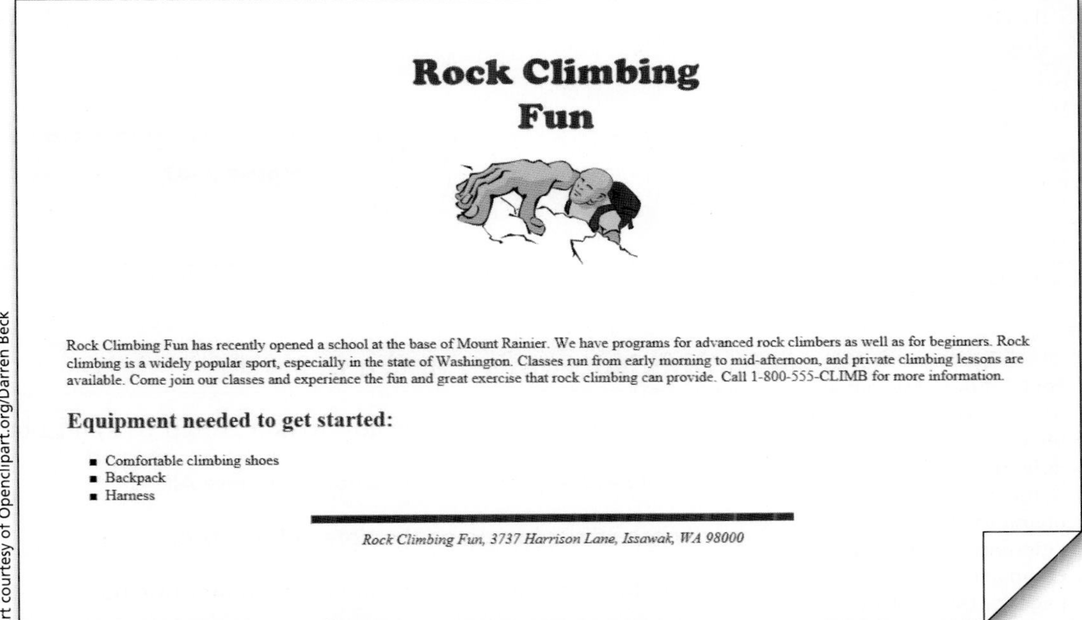

Figure 2–42

Q&A Are there other ways to print a Web page?

Pressing CTRL+P opens the Print dialog box, where you can select print options. You can also use the Print option in the File menu on the menu bar.

2

- Click the Notepad++ button on the taskbar to activate the Notepad++ window.
- Click File on the menu bar, click the Print command, and then click the Print button to print a hard copy of the HTML code (Figure 2–43).

Q&A

Why do I need a printout of the HTML code?

Having a hard-copy printout is an invaluable tool for beginning developers. A printed copy can help you immediately see the relationship between the HTML tags and the Web page that you view in the browser.

```
<!DOCTYPE HTML>

<html>
<head>
<meta charset="utf-8" />
<title>Rock Climbing Fun, Inc.</title>
</head>

<body>

<header style="text-align: center">
    <img src="rockclimber.jpg" width="450" height="300" alt="Rock climber" />
</header>

<section>
<article>
<p>Rock Climbing Fun has recently opened a school at the base of Mount Rainier. We have
programs for advanced rock climbers as well as for beginners. Rock climbing is a widely
popular sport, especially in the state of Washington. Classes run from early morning to
mid-afternoon, and private climbing lessons are available. Come join our classes and
experience the fun and great exercise that rock climbing can provide. Call
1-800-555-CLIMB for more information.</p>

<h2 style="color: #384738">Equipment needed to get started:</h2>

<ul style="list-style-type: square">
    <li>Comfortable climbing shoes</li>
    <li>Backpack</li>
    <li>Harness</li>
</ul>
</article>
</section>

<hr style="height: 8px; background-color: #384738; width: 50%" />

<footer style="text-align: center; font-style: italic">
    Rock Climbing Fun, 3737 Harrison Lane, Issawak, WA 98000
</footer>

</body>
</html>
```

Figure 2–43

BTW

Quick Reference
For a list of HTML tags and their associated attributes, see the HTML Quick Reference (Appendix A) at the back of this book, or visit the HTML Quick Reference on the Book Companion Site Web page for this book at www.cengagebrain.com. For a list of CSS properties and values, see Appendix D.

To Quit Notepad++ and a Browser

The following steps show how to quit Notepad++ and a browser.

1. In Notepad++, click the File menu, then Close All.
2. Click the Close button on the Notepad++ title bar.
3. Click the Close button on the Internet Explorer title bar.

Chapter Summary

In this chapter, you have learned how to identify the elements of a Web page, define the Web page structure, and enter Web page content using a text editor. You enhanced the appearance of your Web page using inline styles, saved and validated your code, and viewed your Web page and source code in a browser. The items listed below include all the new HTML skills you have learned in this chapter.

1. Start Notepad++ (HTML 40)
2. Enable word wrap in Notepad++ (HTML 42)
3. Define the Web Page Structure Using HTML Tags (HTML 42)
4. Enter a Paragraph of Text (HTML 48)
5. Enter a Heading (HTML 49)
6. Create an Unordered List (HTML 51)
7. Add a Footer (HTML 53)
8. Save an HTML File (HTML 55)
9. Start a Browser (HTML 58)
10. View a Web Page in a Browser (HTML 59)
11. Activate Notepad++ (HTML 60)
12. Add an Image (HTML 65)
13. Add Color to a Web Page Heading (HTML 69)
14. Change the Bulleted List Style (HTML 70)
15. Add a Horizontal Rule (HTML 70)
16. Change the Footer Style (HTML 71)
17. Refresh the View in a Browser (HTML 72)
18. Validate HTML Code (HTML 73)
19. View HTML Source Code for a Web Page (HTML 76)
20. Print a Web Page and an HTML File (HTML 77)

Learn It Online

Test your knowledge of chapter content and key terms.

Instructions: To complete the following exercises, please visit www.cengagebrain.com. At the CengageBrain.com home page, search for *HTML5 and CSS 7th Edition* using the search box at the top of the page. This will take you to the product page for this book. On the product page, click the Access Now button below the Study Tools heading. On the Book Companion Site Web page, select Chapter 2, and then click the link for the desired exercise.

Chapter Reinforcement TF, MC, and SA

A series of true/false, multiple choice, and short answer questions that test your knowledge of the chapter content.

Flash Cards

An interactive learning environment where you identify chapter key terms associated with displayed definitions.

Practice Test

A series of multiple choice questions that test your knowledge of chapter content and key terms.

Who Wants To Be a Computer Genius?

An interactive game that challenges your knowledge of chapter content in the style of a television quiz show.

Wheel of Terms

An interactive game that challenges your knowledge of chapter key terms in the style of the television show, *Wheel of Fortune*.

Crossword Puzzle Challenge

A crossword puzzle that challenges your knowledge of key terms presented in the chapter.

STUDENT ASSIGNMENTS

Apply Your Knowledge

Reinforce the skills and apply the concepts you learned in this chapter.

Editing the Apply Your Knowledge Web Page

Instructions: Start Notepad++. Open the file apply2-1.html from the Chapter02\Apply folder of the Data Files for Students. See the inside back cover of this book for instructions for downloading the Data Files for Students, or contact your instructor for information about accessing the required files for this book.

The apply2-1.html file is a partially completed HTML file that you will use for this exercise. Figure 2–44 shows the Apply Your Knowledge Web page as it should be displayed in a browser after the additional HTML tags and attributes are added.

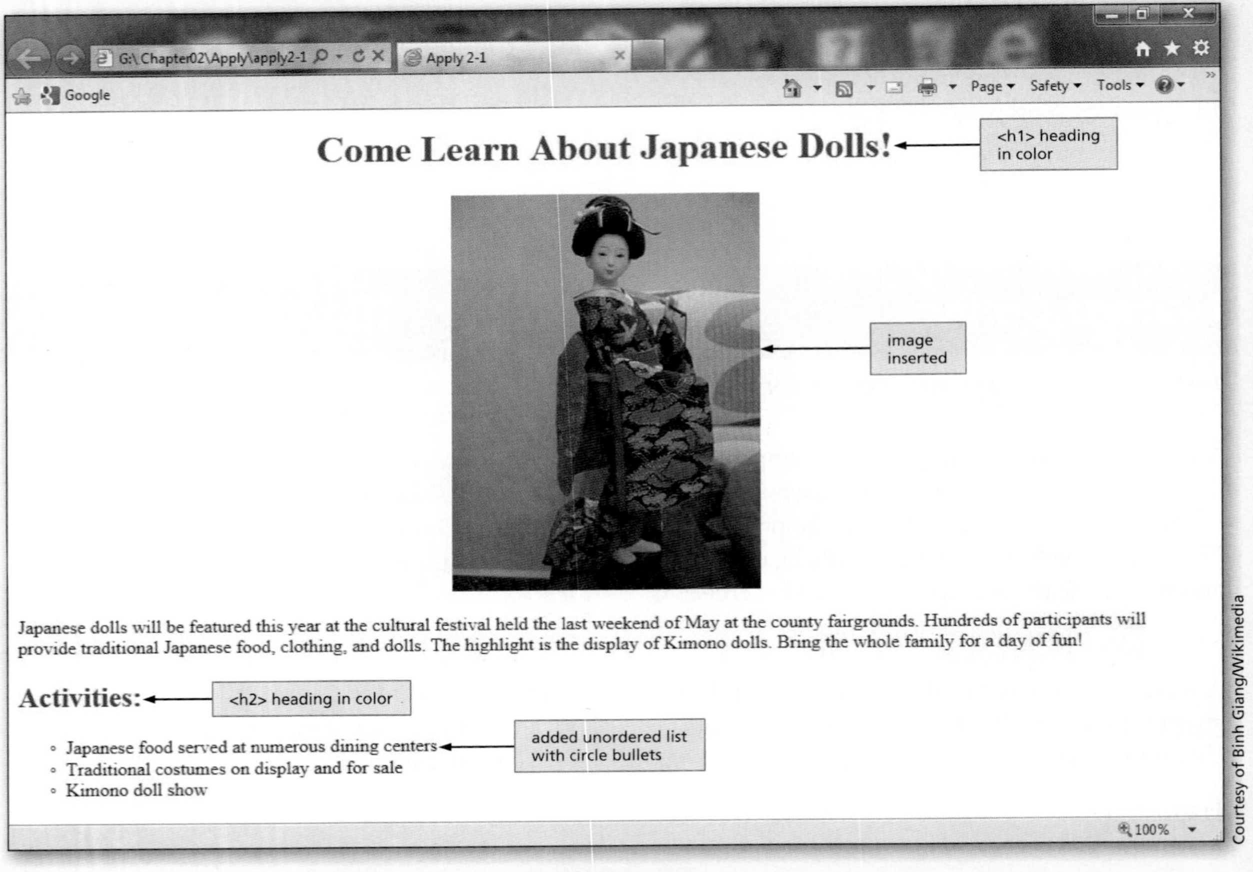

Courtesy of Binh Giang/Wikimedia

Figure 2–44

Perform the following tasks:

1. Enter g:\Chapter02\Apply\apply2-1.html as the URL to view the Web page in your browser.
2. Examine the HTML file and its appearance in the browser.
3. Using Notepad++, change the HTML code to make the Web page look similar to the one shown in Figure 2–44. Both headings are the color #910603. (*Hint:* Use the style="color: #910603" property and value.)
4. Add the image kimono_doll.jpg (in the Chapter02\Apply folder) to the Web page. It has a width of 260 pixels and a height of 346 pixels. (*Hint:* Include the image in a <header> </header> container and remember to use the alt attribute.)
5. Make the bulleted list using bullet type "circle" as shown in Figure 2–44.

6. Save the revised HTML file in the Chapter02\Apply folder using the file name apply2-1solution.html.
7. Validate your HTML code at validator.w3.org.
8. Enter g:\Chapter02\Apply\apply2-1solution.html (or the path where your data file is stored) as the URL to view the revised Web page in your browser.
9. Print the Web page.
10. Submit the revised HTML file and Web page in the format specified by your instructor.

Extend Your Knowledge

Extend the skills you learned in this chapter and experiment with new skills.

Creating a Definition List

Instructions: Start Notepad++. Open the file, extend2-1.html from the Chapter02\Extend folder of the Data Files for Students. See the inside back cover of this book for instructions on downloading the Data Files for Students, or contact your instructor for information about accessing the required files. This sample Web page contains all of the text for the Web page. You will add the necessary tags to make this a definition list with terms that are bold, as shown in Figure 2–45.

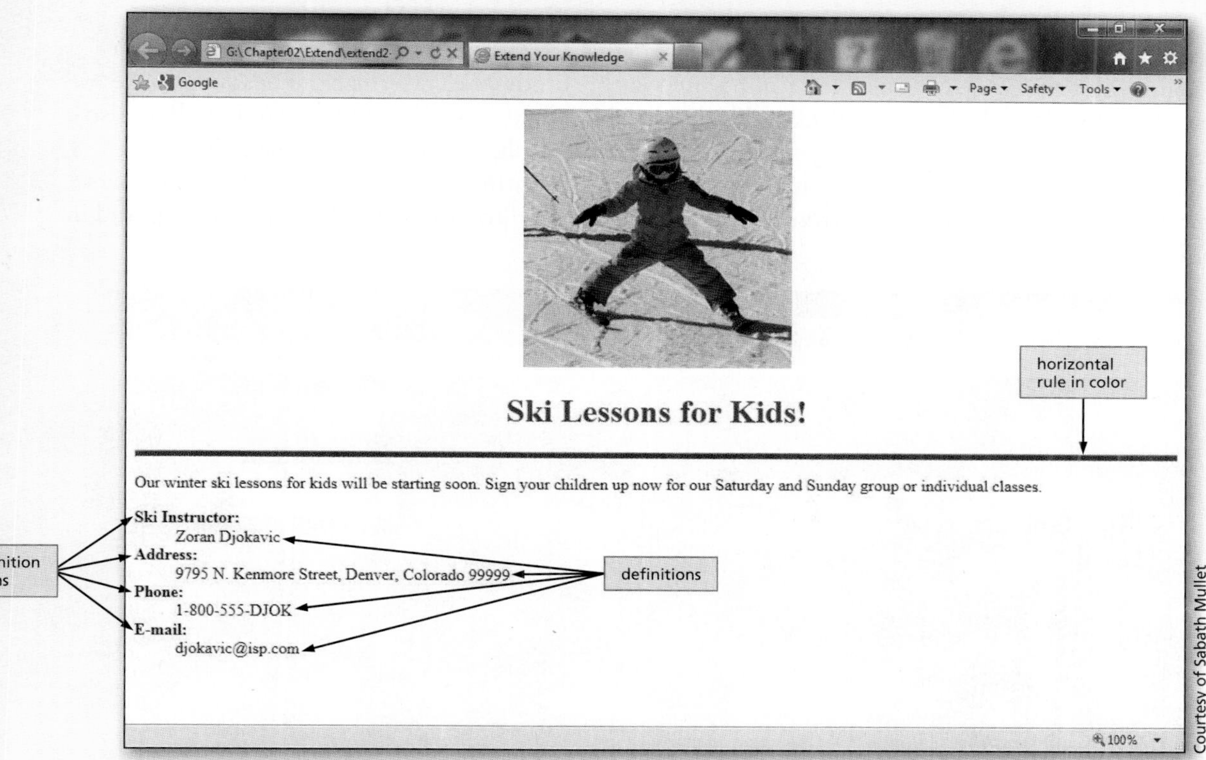

Figure 2–45

Perform the following tasks:

1. Using the text given in the file extend2-1.html, make changes to the HTML code to change the Web page from a single line of text to a definition list by following the definition list code shown in Table 2–6 on page HTML 52.

Continued >

Extend Your Knowledge *continued*

2. Add the additional HTML code necessary to make the terms bold. (*Hint:* Review the font-weight property with a value of bold.)
3. Add the image skier.jpg. Find the dimensions of the image by reviewing the image properties.
4. Add a horizontal rule that is 5 pixels high and color #414565. The <h1> heading is also color #414565.
5. Save the revised document in the Chapter02\Extend folder with the file name extend2-1solution.html, validate the Web page, and then submit it in the format specified by your instructor.

Make It Right

Analyze a document and correct all errors and/or improve the design.

Correcting the Star of India Web Page

Instructions: Start Notepad++. Open the file makeitright2-1.html from the Chapter02\MakeItRight folder of the Data Files for Students. See the inside back cover of this book for instructions on downloading the Data Files for Students, or contact your instructor for information about accessing the required files.

The data file is a modified version of what you see in Figure 2–46. Make the necessary corrections to the Web page to make it look like Figure 2–46. Add a background color to the Web page using color #515c7a. (*Hint:* Use an inline style in the <body> tag.) Format the heading to use the Heading 1 style with the color black. Add a paragraph of text in white and four circle bullets also in white. (*Hint:* Use the color property in the heading, paragraph, and bullet tags.) Save the file in the Chapter02\MakeItRight folder as makeitright2-1solution.html, validate the Web page, and then submit it in the format specified by your instructor. Be prepared to discuss the four questions posed in the bullet list.

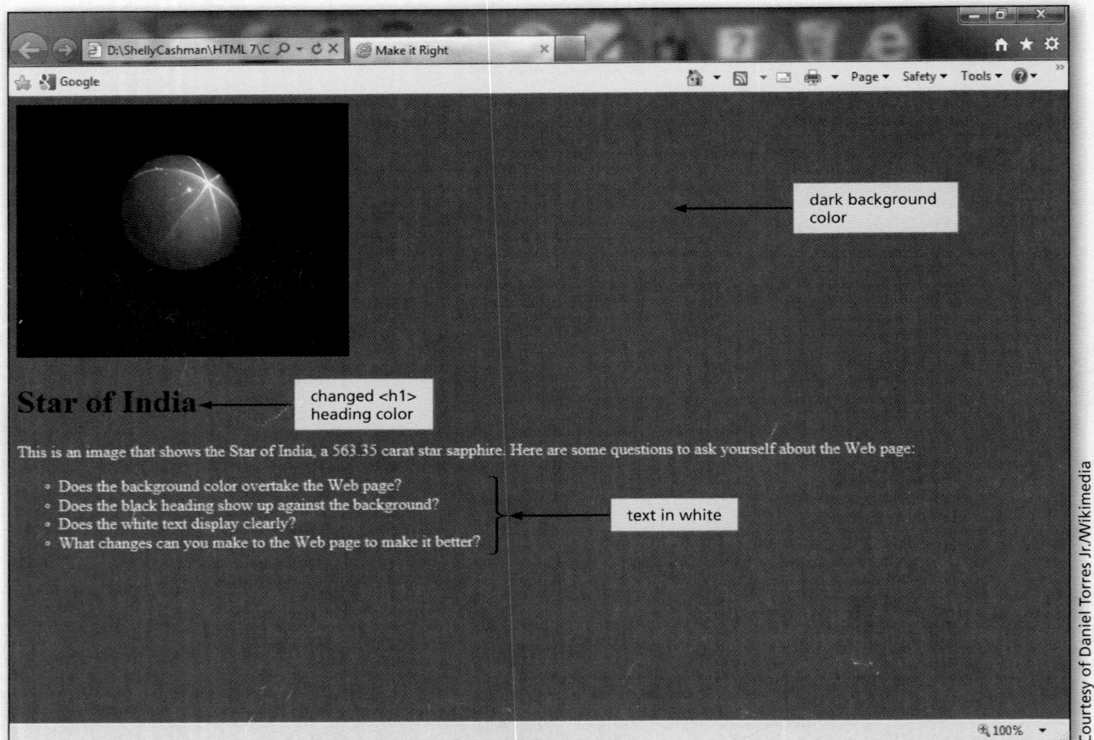

Figure 2–46

In the Lab

Lab 1: Creating an Informational Web Page

Problem: You enjoy volunteering and decide to prepare a Web page announcement, such as the one shown in Figure 2–47, to promote the latest food drive.

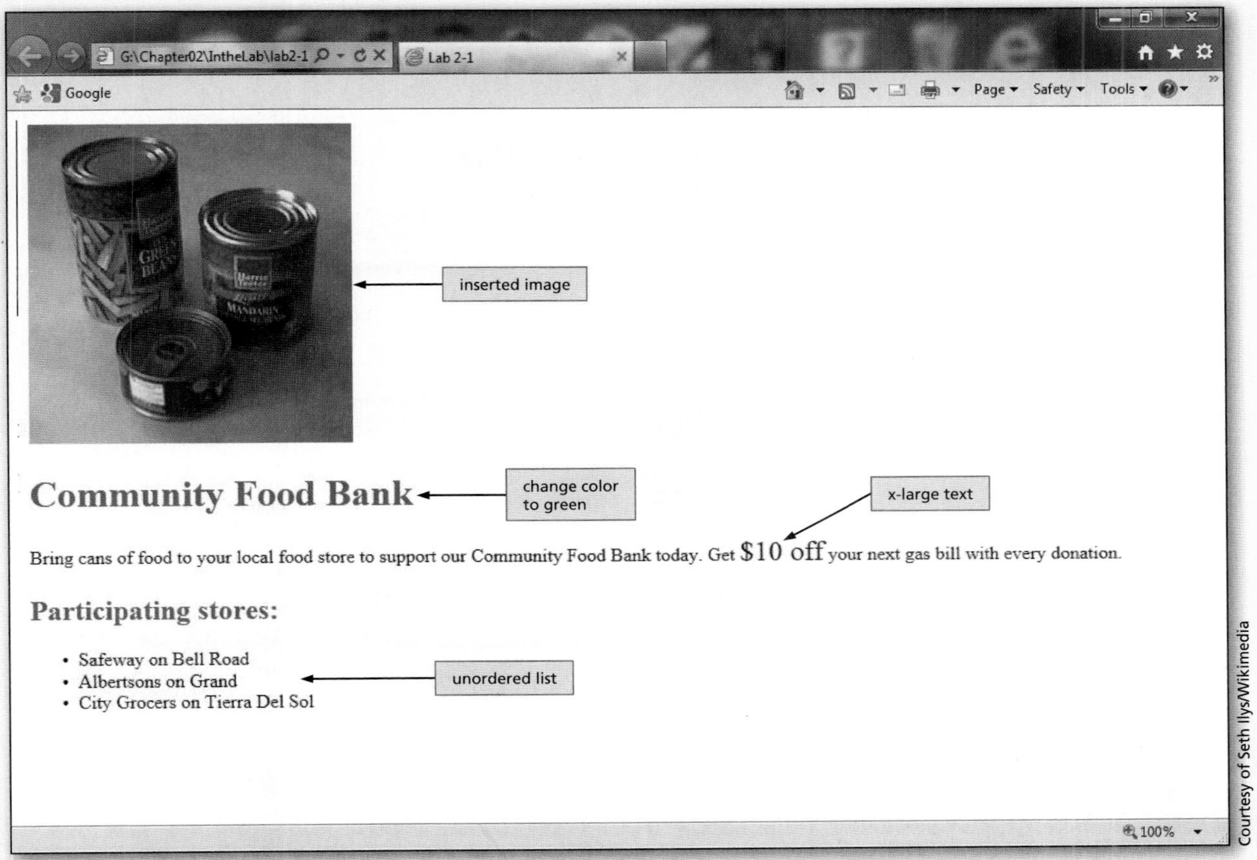

Courtesy of Seth Ilys/Wikimedia

Figure 2–47

Instructions: Perform the following steps:

1. Create a new HTML file in Notepad++ with the title Lab 2-1 within the <title> </title> tags.
2. Add the donations.jpg image file, which has a width of 272 and a height of 277. Place the image on the left side of the Web page. Use the color green for both headings.
3. Add the paragraph of text, as shown in Figure 2–47. Make the words "$10 off" x-large style of font. (*Hint:* Review the <span> HTML tag in Appendix A.)
4. Create one bulleted list with the information shown.
5. Save the file in the Chapter02\IntheLab folder using the file name lab2-1solution.html.
6. Print the lab2-1solution.html file.
7. Enter g:\Chapter02\IntheLab\lab2-1solution.html (or the path where your data file is stored) as the URL to view the Web page in your browser.
8. Print the Web page.
9. Submit the revised HTML file and Web page in the format specified by your instructor.

STUDENT ASSIGNMENTS

In the Lab

Lab 2: Creating a Healthy Living Web Page

Problem: You work for the Healthy Living Commission in your city. You would like to create a Web page showing two great ideas for healthy living, as shown in Figure 2–48.

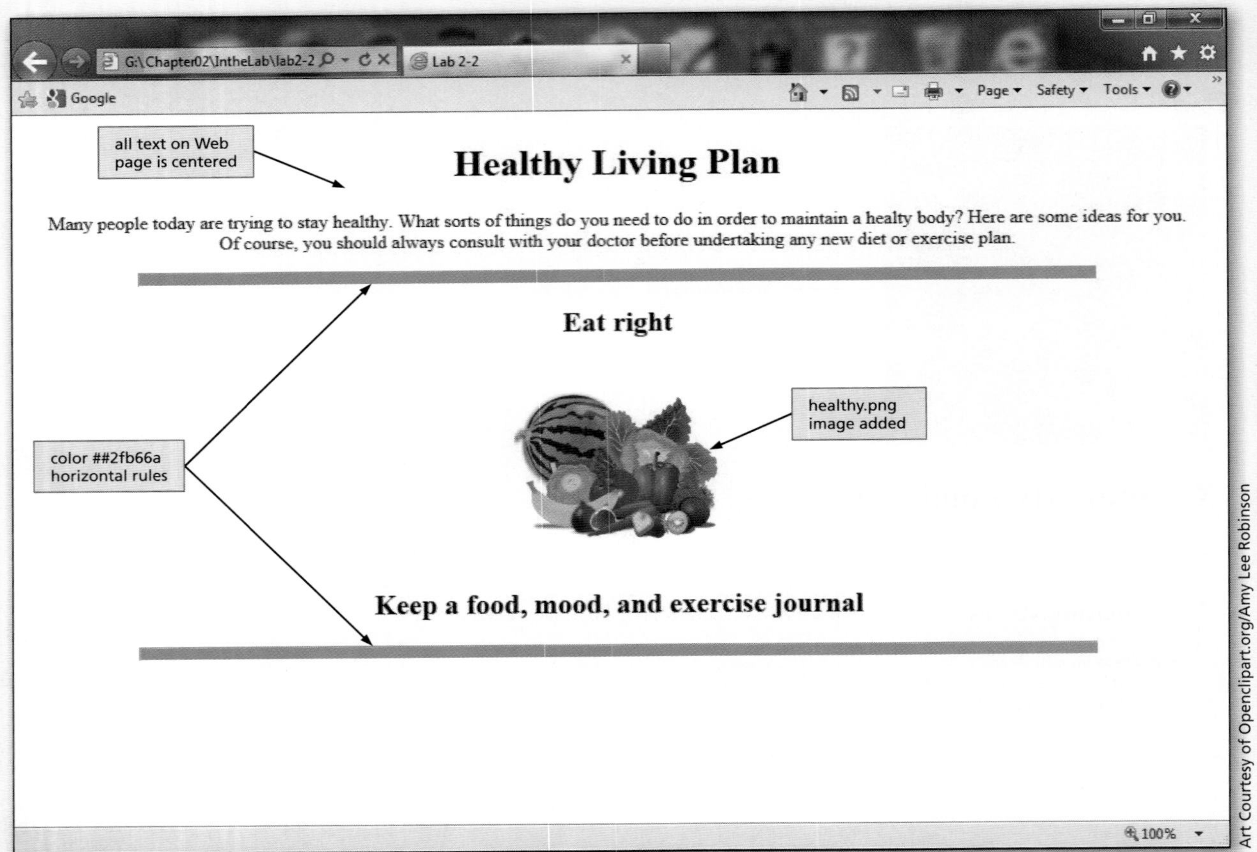

Art Courtesy of Openclipart.org/Amy Lee Robinson

Figure 2–48

Instructions: Perform the following steps:

1. Create a new HTML file in Notepad++ with the title, Lab 2-2, within the <title> </title> tags. For the initial HTML tags, you can use the structure.html file if you created one at the start of this chapter's project, otherwise type the initial tags.
2. Begin the body section by adding an <h1> heading, Healthy Living Plan. Format the heading to use the heading 1 style center-aligned on the Web page. (*Hint:* See the text-align property in Appendix D to center the heading.)
3. Add the centered paragraph of text shown in Figure 2–47. Make sure the fourth sentence displays on the next line with no blank line in between. (*Hint:* Use the <br /> tag.)
4. Add a horizontal rule with a height of 10 pixels, a width of 80%, and a background color of #2fb66a.
5. Add a centered heading, as shown, using the heading 2 style.
6. Add the healthy.png image. Find the height and width properties for that image and include them together with alternate text.

7. Add another <h2> heading and horizontal rule.
8. Save the file in the Chapter02\IntheLab folder as lab2-2 solution.html.
9. Print the lab2-2.html file.
10. Enter g:\Chapter02\IntheLab\lab2-2solution.html (or the path where your data file is stored) as the URL to view the Web page in your browser.
11. Print the Web page.
12. Submit the revised HTML file and Web page in the format specified by your instructor.

In the Lab

Lab 3: Composing a Personal Web Page

Problem: Your friends are concerned that they aren't able to save money. They have asked you for help, since you seem to always have money saved for a rainy day. You decide to compose a Web page with some advice for them. You plan to use a paragraph of text, an image and a bulleted list, as shown in Figure 2–49. The text and bullets in the figure should be replaced with your own money-saving experience and tips.

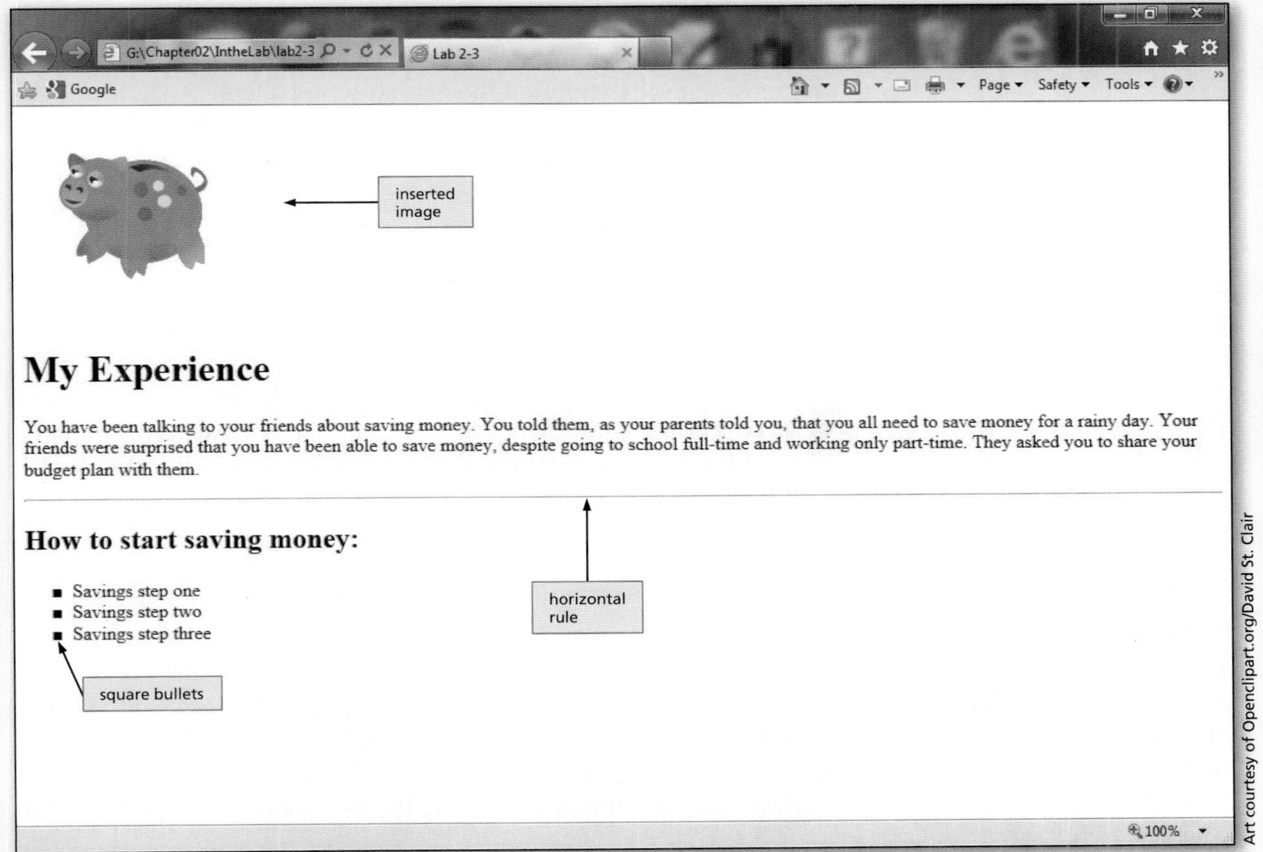

Art courtesy of Openclipart.org/David St. Clair

Figure 2–49

Instructions: Perform the following steps:

1. Create a new HTML file with the title Lab 2-3 within the <title> </title> tags.
2. Include a short paragraph of information and a bulleted list, using a format similar to the one shown in Figure 2–49, to provide information about your money-saving experience.

Continued >

In the Lab *continued*

3. Insert the image file piggybank.png, stored in the Chapter02\IntheLab folder. You can find the dimensions of an image by clicking on the image using Windows Explorer. You can also right-click the image, click Properties, and then click the Details tab to find out the image's dimensions, or open it in a graphics program. Note that the bullets used for the list are square in shape.
4. Save the HTML file in the Chapter02\IntheLab folder using the file name lab2-3solution.html.
5. Enter g:\Chapter02\IntheLab\lab2-3solution.html (or the path where your data file is stored) as the URL to view the Web page in your browser.
6. Print the Web page from your browser.
7. Submit the revised HTML file and Web page in the format specified by your instructor.

Cases and Places

Apply your creative thinking and problem-solving skills to design and implement a solution.

1: Research HTML5 Structural Tags

Academic

There are many Web sites dedicated to HTML5. Search the Web to find sites that have training modules for HTML5. Discover training specifically targeting the new structural elements discussed in the chapter. How do these new tags differ from the <div> tag? Are there situations in which the <div> tag is a better option? Write a brief report. Identify the URLs for the training Web sites and share them with your fellow students in class.

2: Create a Personal Web Page

Personal

Your class instructor wants to post all of the students' Web pages on the school server to show what his or her students are interested in. Create a Web page of personal information, listing items such as your school major, jobs that you have had in the past, and your hobbies and interests. To make your personal Web page more visually interesting, search the Web for images that reflect your interests. (Remember that if the image is copyrighted, you cannot use it on a personal Web page unless you follow the guidelines provided with the image.) Insert an image or two onto the Web page to help explain who you are.

3: Investigate Methods for Working with Images

Professional

You are creating a new Web site for a local photographer. The photographer has asked that you determine methods to help his Web site load quickly despite having so many large images. To this end, find information on using thumbnail images. Review other photography Web sites and create a list of suggestions for loading large images. Additionally, search the Web for information on adding useful, descriptive alt attributes for images. Write a brief synopsis explaining the information that you found in your research.

3 Creating Web Pages with Links, Images, and Embedded Style Sheets

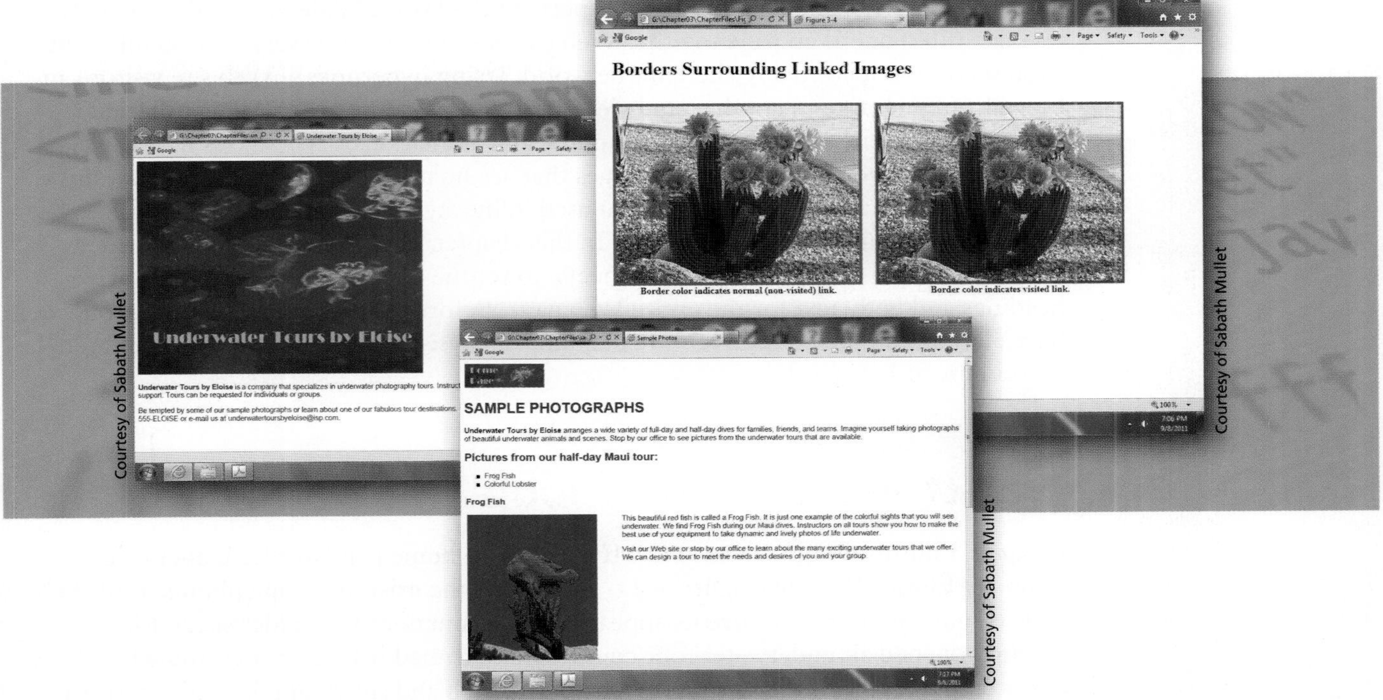

Courtesy of Sabath Mullet

Courtesy of Sabath Mullet

Courtesy of Sabath Mullet

Objectives

You will have mastered the material in this chapter when you can:

- Describe linking terms and definitions
- Create a home page and enhance a Web page using images
- Change body and heading format using embedded (internal) style sheets
- Align and add color to text using embedded and inline styles
- Add a text link to a Web page in the same Web site
- Add an e-mail link
- Add a text link to a Web page on another Web site
- Use absolute and relative paths
- Save, validate, and view an HTML file and test the links
- Use style classes to add an image with wrapped text
- Add links to targets within a Web page
- Use an inline style to change the default bullet list type to square bullets
- Copy and paste HTML code
- Add an image link to a Web page in the same Web site

3 Creating Web Pages with Links, Images, and Embedded Style Sheets

Introduction

One of the most useful and important aspects of the World Wide Web is the ability to connect (link) one Web page to other Web pages — on the same server or on different Web servers — located anywhere in the world. Using hyperlinks, a Web site visitor can move from one page to another, and view information in any order. Many different Web page elements, including text, graphics, and animations, can serve as hyperlinks. In this chapter, you will create Web pages that are linked together using both text links and image links. In the last chapter, you used inline styles to change the appearance of individual elements or HTML tags. In this chapter, you will also use embedded style sheets (also called internal style sheets) to set the appearance of elements such as headings and body text for the entire Web page. Before starting on this project, you would have already completed the Web site planning, analysis, and design phases of the Web Development Life Cycle.

Project — Underwater Tours by Eloise Web Site

Chapter 3 illustrates how to use HTML to create a home page for the Underwater Tours by Eloise Web site (Figure 3–1a) and to edit the existing samplephotos.html Web page (Figure 3–1b) to improve its appearance and function. Your older sister, Eloise, recently opened an underwater tour company and named it Underwater Tours by Eloise. She would like to advertise her company on the Web and show sample pictures of sea creatures. She knows that you have studied Web development in college and asks you to develop two Web pages that are linked together: a home page and a Web page with the sample pictures. During your analysis, you determined that there are four basic types of links to use. The first type is a link from one Web page to another in the same Web site. The second type is a link to a Web page on a different Web site. The third type is an e-mail link. The fourth type is a link within one Web page. You plan to utilize all four of these types of links for your sister's Web site.

The Underwater Tours by Eloise home page (Figure 3–1a) includes a logo image, headings, an e-mail link, and a text link to a Web page on another Web site. This page also includes a link to the samplephotos.html Web page. The Sample Photographs Web page (Figure 3–1b) contains two images with text wrapped around them and internal links that allow visitors to move easily from section to section within the Web page. The Web page also has an image link back to the Underwater Tours by Eloise's home page.

(b) Sample Photographs Web page.

(a) Underwater Tours by Eloise home page.

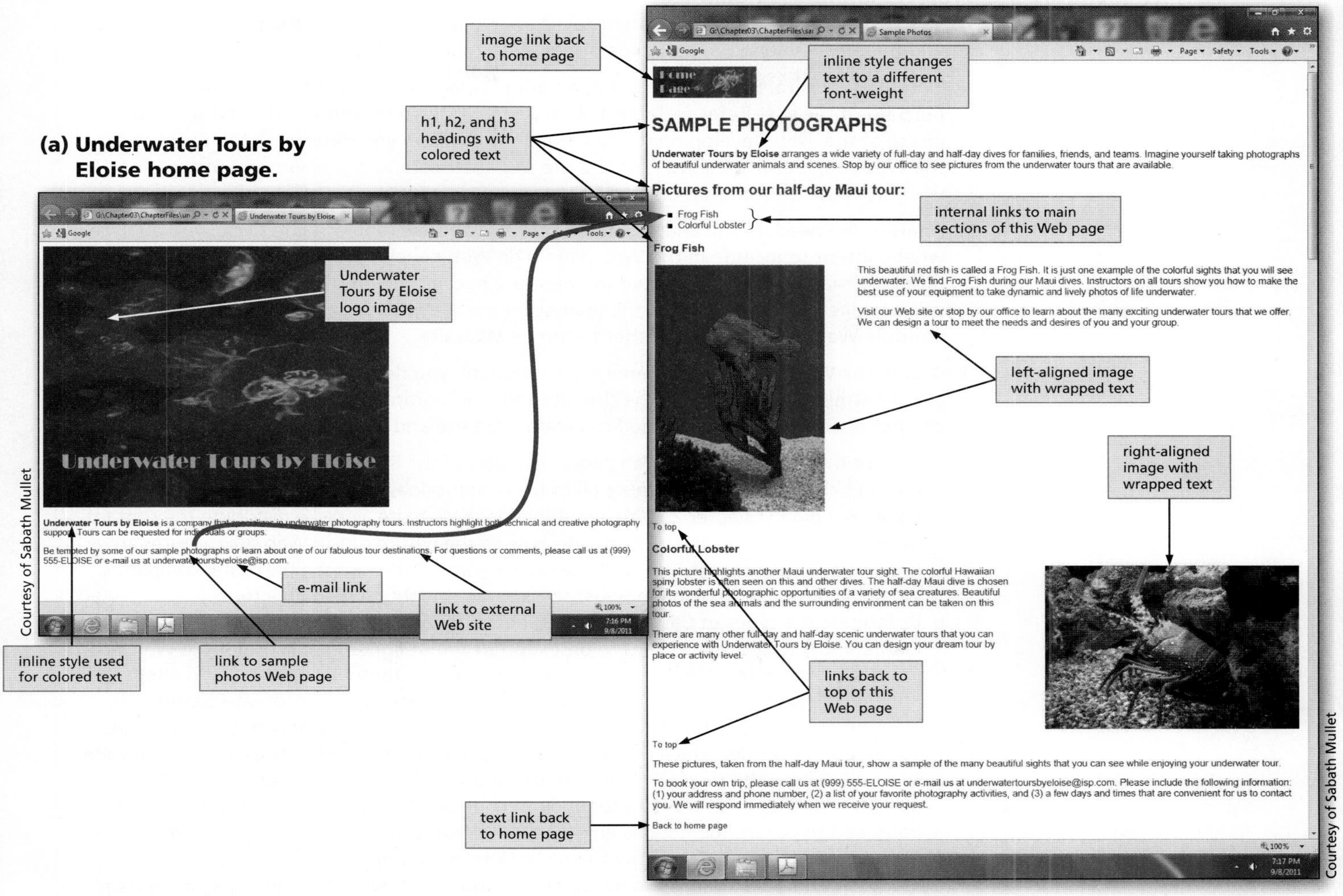

Figure 3–1

Overview

As you read this chapter, you will learn how to create the Web page shown in Figure 3–1 by performing these general tasks:

- Use embedded style sheets, inline styles, and classes to change the format of text, links, images, and headings.
- Use an inline style to create a bulleted list with a square bullet style.
- Add a link to another Web page in the same Web site.
- Add a link to an external Web site.
- Add an e-mail link.
- Add targets and links within the same Web page.

Plan Ahead

Project Planning Guidelines

As you create Web pages, such as the project shown in Figure 3–1 on the previous page, you should follow these general guidelines:

1. **Plan the Web site**. Before developing a multiple-page Web site, you must plan the purpose of the site. Refer to Table 1–4 on page HTML 15 for information on the planning phase of the Web Development Life Cycle. In this phase, you determine the purpose of the Web site, identify the users of the site and their computing environments, and decide who owns the information on the Web page.

2. **Analyze the need**. In the analysis phase of the Web Development Life Cycle, you analyze what content to include in the Web page. The Web development project in Chapter 3 is different than the one completed in Chapter 2 because it contains two Web pages that will be linked together. Part of the analysis phase then includes determining how the multiple Web pages work together to form a Web site.

3. **Design the Web site.** Once the analysis is complete, you design the Web site. In this phase, you determine the content of the site, both text and graphics. Design steps specific to this chapter also include determining links within the site and to external Web sites.

   a. **Choose the content for the Web pages**. This part of the life cycle also differs from the previous chapter's project because all of the content does not have to appear on one Web page, as it did in Chapter 2. With a multiple-page Web site, you can distribute the content as needed throughout the Web site. Because of the nature of this Web site, pictures are a large part of the content. The Web site owner wants to show a sample of her company's work. Pictures help to highlight what sea creatures might be seen on a tour.

   b. **Determine the types of Cascading Style Sheets (CSS) that you will use**. You already learned how to use inline styles to best support the design and purpose of the Web site. In this chapter, you utilize both inline and embedded (internal) style sheets to alter the appearance (or style) of various Web page elements. You also incorporate classes with your embedded style sheets to further control the style of elements on the Web page. You need to consider which of these options is best suited for the styles of your Web site.

   c. **Determine how the pages will link to one another**. This Web site consists of a **home page** (the first page in a Web site) and a secondary Web page to which you will link. You need to determine how to link (e.g., with text or a graphic) from the home page to the secondary page and how to link back to the home page.

   d. **Establish what other links are necessary**. In addition to links between the home page and secondary Web page, you need an e-mail link. It is standard for Web developers to provide an e-mail link on the home page of a Web site for visitor comments or questions. Additionally, the secondary Web page (samplephotos.html) is a long page that requires visitors to scroll down for navigation. Because of its length, it is important to provide easy and quick ways to navigate the Web page. You do this using links within the Web page.

4. **Develop the Web page(s) and insert all links**. Once the analysis and design is complete, the Web developer creates the Web page(s) using HTML and CSS. Good Web development standard practices should be followed in this step. Examples of good practices include utilizing the proper initial HTML tags, as shown in the previous chapter, and always identifying alt text with images.

5. **Test all Web pages within the Web site**. An important part of Web development is testing to assure that you are following the standards outlined in the previous chapter. For the projects in this book, you will use the World Wide Web Consortium (W3C) validator that allows you to test your Web pages and clearly explains any errors it finds. When testing, you should check all content for accuracy. Also, all links (external, internal, and page to page within the same Web site) should be tested.

When necessary, more specific details concerning the above guidelines are presented at appropriate points in the chapter. The chapter will also identify the actions performed and decisions made regarding these guidelines during the creation of the Web page shown in Figure 3–1.

Using Links on a Web Page

As you have learned, many different Web page elements, including text, images, and animations, can serve as links. Text and images are the elements most widely used as links. Figure 3–2 shows examples of text and image links.

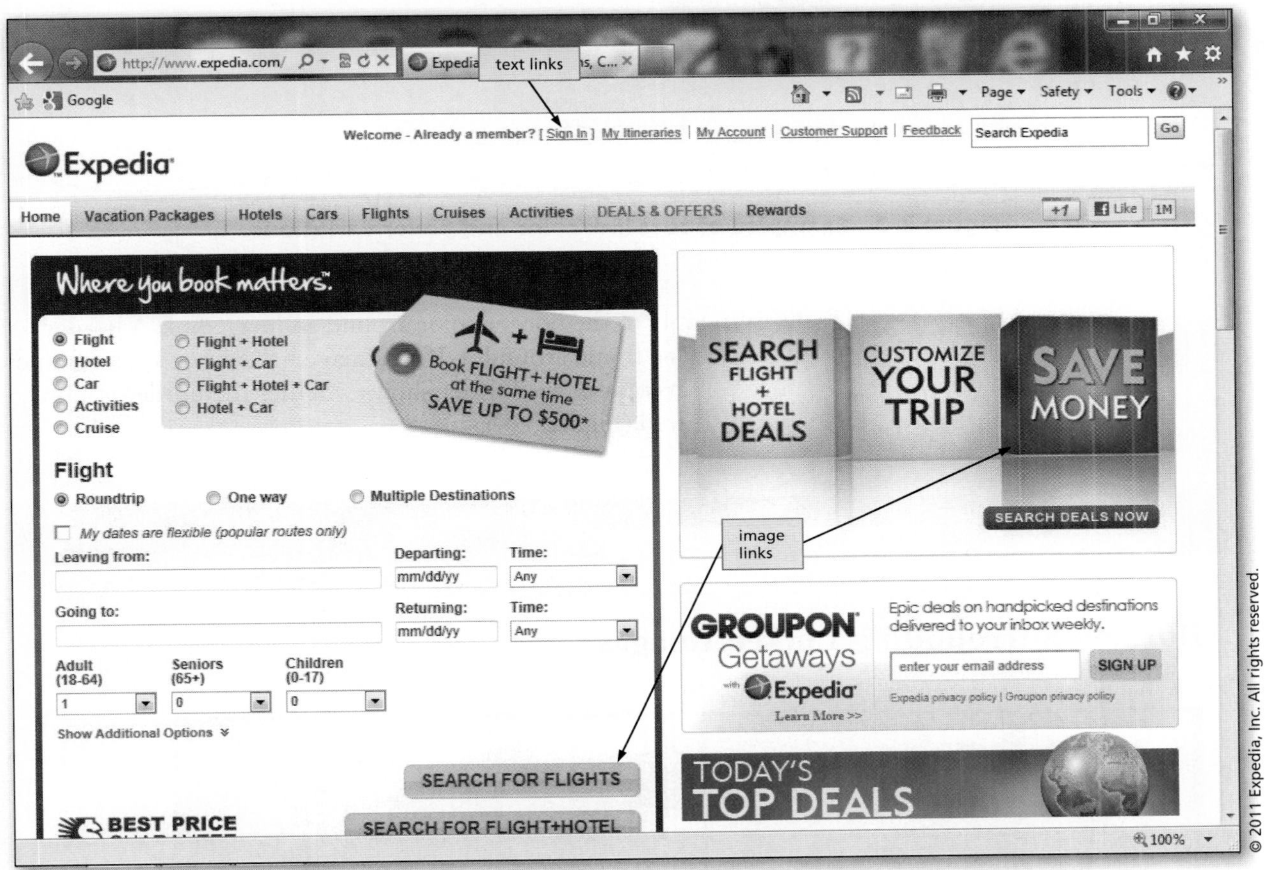

Figure 3–2 Text and image links on a Web page.

When using text links on a Web page, use descriptive text as the clickable word or phrase. For example, the phrase "Click here" does not explain the purpose of the link to the visitor. By contrast, the phrase "SAVE MONEY" (in Figure 3–2) indicates that the link connects to a Web page with discounted airline tickets.

When a link is identified with text, it often appears as underlined text, in a color different from the main Web page text. Unless otherwise changed in the anchor <a> or <body> tags, the browser settings define the colors of text links throughout a Web page. For example, with Internet Explorer, the default color for a normal link that has not been clicked (or visited) is blue, a visited link is purple, and an active link (a link just clicked by a user) varies in color. Figure 3–3 on the next page shows examples of text links in normal and visited states. Generally, moving the mouse pointer over a link causes the mouse pointer to change to a pointing hand. This change notifies the user that a link is available from that text or image.

BTW

Link Help
Many Web sites provide help for new HTML5 developers. For more information about links, search for keywords such as "HTML5 Tutorials" or "HTML5 Help" in any good search engine.

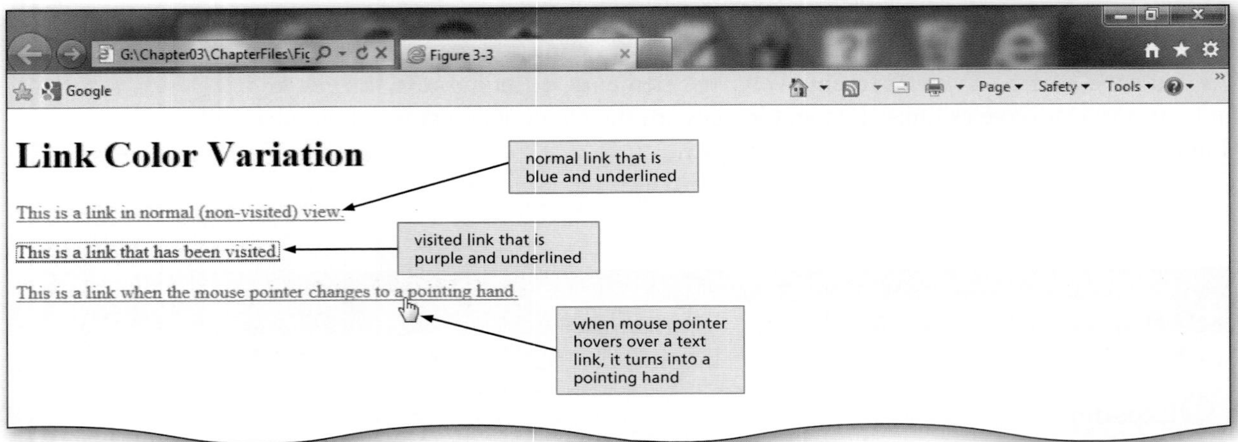

Figure 3–3 Examples of text link color and hover variations.

The same color defaults apply to the border color around an image link. A border makes the image appear as if it has a frame around it. If the image has no border, no frame will appear around the image. The color of the border shows whether the border is a link, and whether the link has been visited (Figure 3–4).

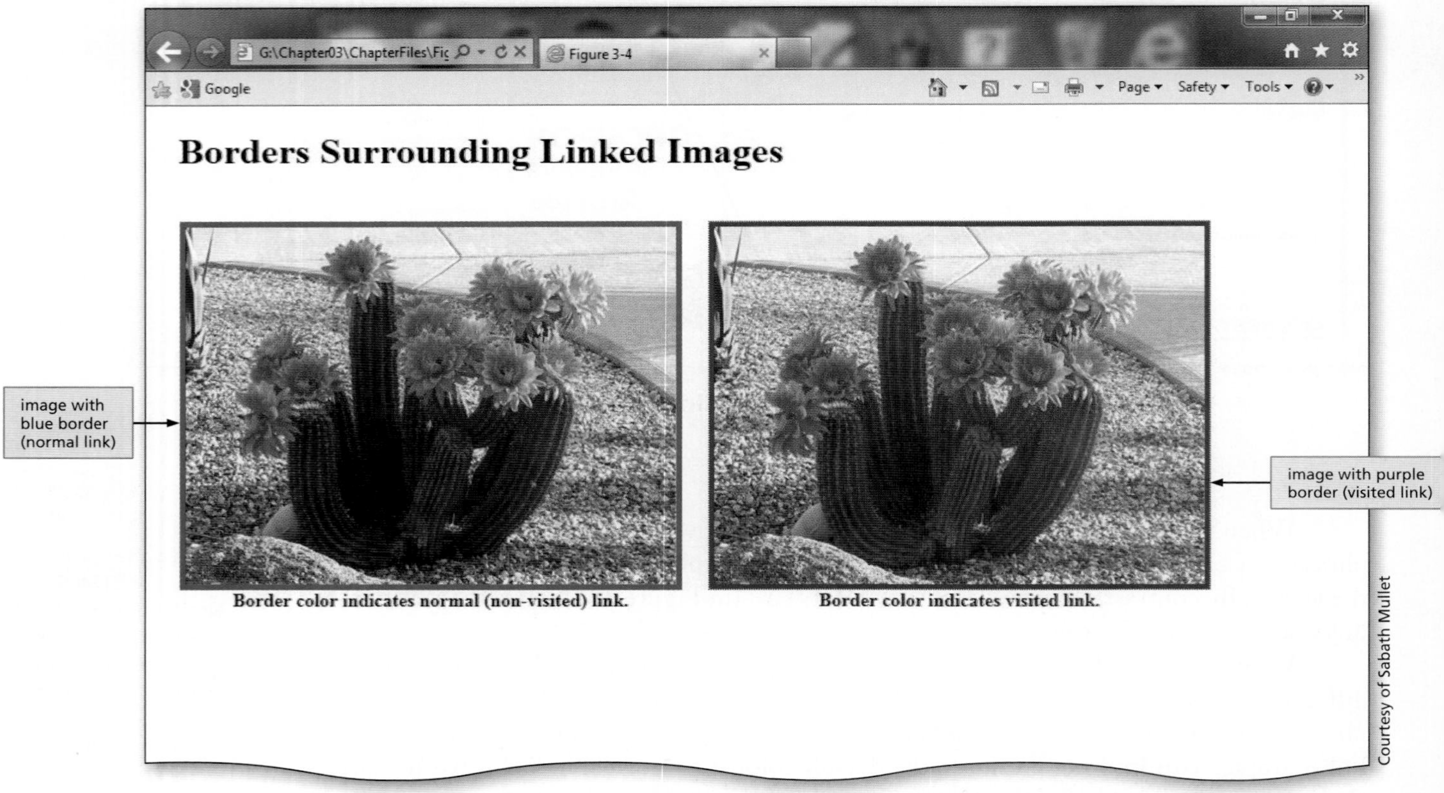

Borders Surrounding Linked Images

image with blue border (normal link)

image with purple border (visited link)

Border color indicates normal (non-visited) link.

Border color indicates visited link.

Courtesy of Sabath Mullet

Figure 3–4 Normal and visited link colors.

The <a> tag also is called the **anchor tag** because it is used to create anchors for links to another page in the same Web site, to a Web page in an external Web site, within the same Web page, and for e-mail links. This is the tag that you will use throughout the project for the four types of links inserted in the Web pages.

If you want to change the color of text links or image link borders to override the browser defaults, you can designate those changes in the anchor <a> or <body> elements using an embedded or external style sheet, or by using an inline style. Recall that you use an inline style to change the appearance (or style) of a single element. An embedded (or internal) style sheet is used to change the styles of similar elements in one Web page. Finally, an external style sheet is contained in a separate .css document and is used to change the style in an entire Web site. (You will use an external style sheet in the next chapter.) To use an embedded or external style sheet in the anchor element to change normal, visited, and active link colors from the default, you would use the following format:

```
a     {color: black;}
```

where color is a designated color name, such as black, or a hexadecimal color code. To make the same change with an inline style, the tag format is:

```
<a style="color: black">
```

Links, by default, are underlined to indicate that they are links. You can disable the underlining of a link with the text-decoration property within the anchor tag. The **text-decoration property** allows text to be "decorated" with one of five values: underline, overline, line-through, blink, or none. This property can be used in a variety of tags including the anchor tag.

In the design phase you should carefully consider the benefits and disadvantages of any style change, especially to a default style. Be sure that users are still able to immediately see that specific text is used as a link before turning off link underlines or changing the default link color. If you determine that you can effectively turn the underline off on a link (as you do for the image link that you create later in this chapter), you can change the text-decoration attribute to none. To do this with an embedded or external style, you would enter the following code:

```
a     {text-decoration: none;}
```

To change text-decoration to none with an inline style, enter:

```
<a style="text-decoration: none">
```

BTW

Link Colors
You can change the link colors in popular browsers. In Internet Explorer, click the Tools button on the Command bar, click Internet Options, General tab, and the Colors button under Appearance. In Mozilla Firefox, click the Tools menu, Options, Content tab, and the Colors button under Fonts & Colors. In both browsers, you change colors by selecting a color from a color palette.

Linking to Another Web Page Within the Same Web Site

Web pages often include links to connect one Web page to another page within the same Web site. For example, a visitor can click a link on the home page of a Web site (Figure 3–5a on the next page) to connect and view another Web page on the same Web site (Figure 3–5b). The Web pages created in this project include links to other pages in the same Web site: (1) the Underwater Tours by Eloise home page includes a text link to the Sample Photographs Web page; and (2) the Sample Photographs Web page includes both text and image links back to the Underwater Tours by Eloise home page. To link the words "sample photographs" on the underwatertours.html home page to the samplephotos.html Web page, you need the following HTML code:

```
<a href="samplephotos.html">sample photographs</a>
```

The href in the anchor <a> tag indicates that when the words "sample photographs" are clicked, the visitor links to the samplephotos.html Web page. You end the link with the </a> tag. If you did not add the </a> tag, then all text after the words "sample photographs" would be linked.

BTW

Links on a Web Page
An anchor tag also allows visitors to move within a single Web page. Use the id attribute to allow movement from one area to another on the same page. This linking technique is useful, particularly on long pages. An index of links can also provide easy access to various areas within the Web page.

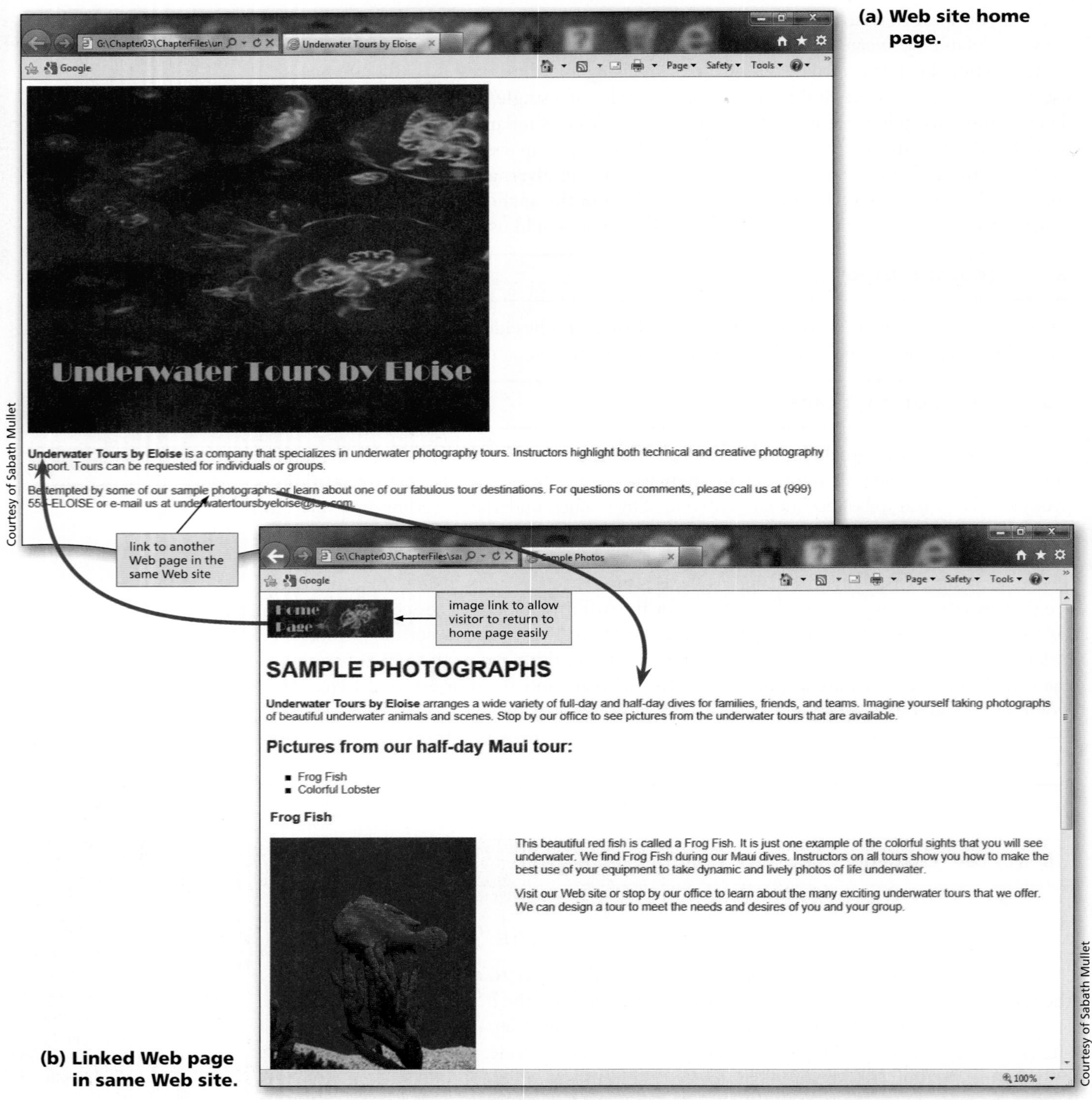

Figure 3–5

Linking to a Web Page in Another Web Site

One of the most powerful features of Web development is the ability to link to Web pages outside of your Web site. Web developers use these links to connect their Web pages to other Web pages with information on the same topic. The links are what give the Web its value as an interconnected resource and provide its “webbiness.” In this project, the home page (Figure 3–6a) includes a link to a page on another Web site where the visitor can find additional information about Hawaii’s national parks (Figure 3–6b). To link the words "one of our fabulous tour destinations" on the underwatertours.html home page to an external Web site, you need the following HTML code:

```
<a href="http://www.nps.gov/state/hi/index.htm">one of our
fabulous tour destinations</a>
```

Notice that the code is basically the same as that used to link to a Web page within the same Web site. However, you have to add the complete URL (http://www.nps.gov/state/hi/index.htm) when you link to an external Web site.

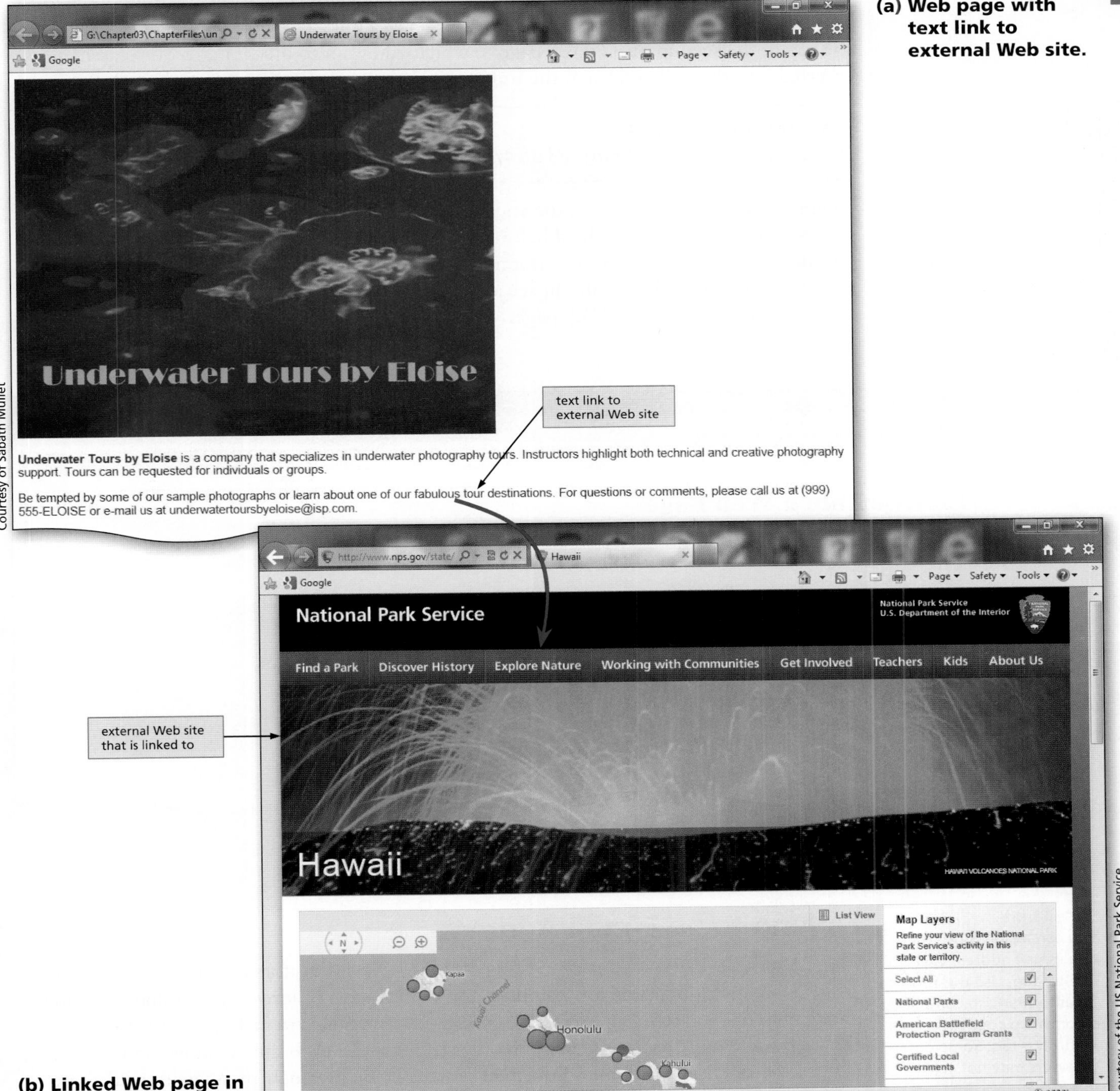

(a) Web page with text link to external Web site.

(b) Linked Web page in external Web site.

Figure 3–6

Linking Within a Web Page

Links within a Web page allow visitors to move quickly from one section of the Web page to another. This is especially important in Web pages that are long and require a visitor to scroll down to see all of the content. Many Web pages contain a list of links like a menu or table of contents at the top of the page, with links to sections within the Web page (Figure 3–7). In this project, the Sample Photographs Web page includes links from the top section of the Web page to other sections within the page, as well as links back to the top of the Web page. There are two steps to link within a Web page. First, you have to set a target using a name that makes sense to the purpose of the link. Then, you create a link to that target using the name given. The following HTML code shows an example of a target named fish and then the use of that target as a link. The first statement is inserted at the top of the section of the Web page to which you want to link. The second statement is inserted into the bulleted list at the top of the Web page where you want the link to appear.

```
<a id="fish"></a>
<a href="#fish">Frog Fish</a>
```

Again, notice that you also use the anchor <a> tag for this type of link. However, with this inner-page link, you insert the # before the target id to indicate that you want to link to a specific section of the Web page, not necessarily the top of the page. Sometimes when you are browsing the Web, you might see a # used in a link address. That generally links you to a specific section of the Web page.

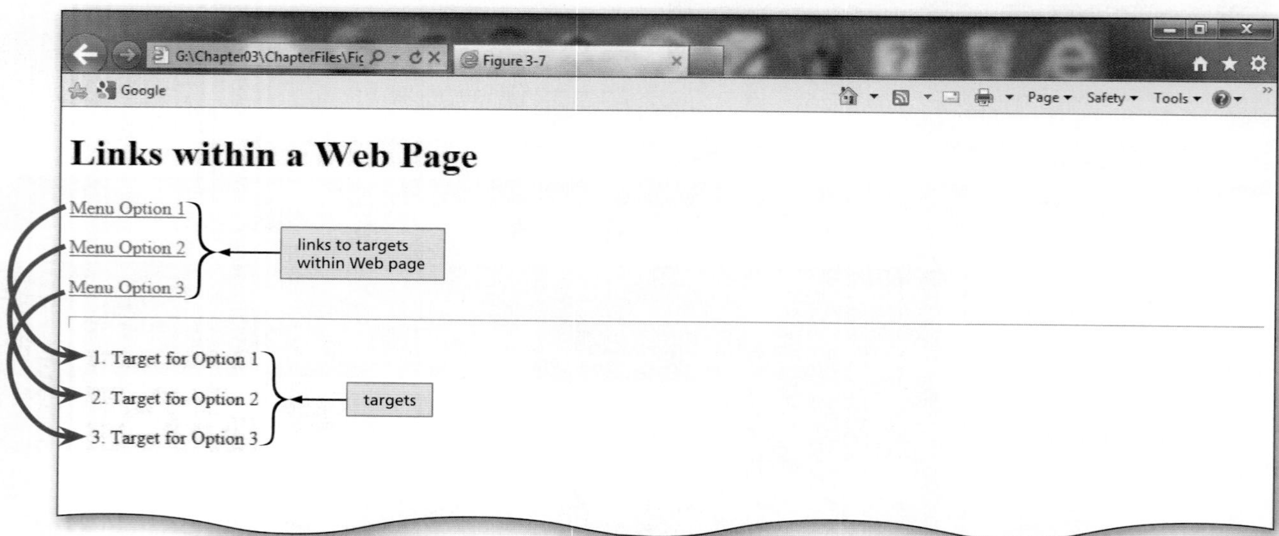

Figure 3–7 Web page with internal links.

> **BTW**
> **E-mail Links**
> You can assign more than one e-mail address to a mailto: tag. Use the form "mailto:first@isp.com, second@isp.com" in the <a href=> tag. Some older browsers may not support this tag.

Linking to an E-mail Address

A well-designed Web page always provides a way for visitors to contact the person at the company responsible for maintaining the Web site or addressing customer questions and comments. An easy way to provide contact information is to include an e-mail link on the Web site's home page, as well as on other pages in the Web site. As shown in Figure 3–8, when a visitor clicks the **e-mail link**, it automatically opens a new message in the default e-mail program and inserts the appropriate contact e-mail address in the To field. Visitors then can type and send an e-mail to request additional information, comment on the

Web site, or notify the company of a problem with its Web site. (*Note*: If your browser is not configured to send e-mail, the e-mail link will not work.) The following HTML code shows an example of how to link the words underwatertoursbyeloise@isp.com to an e-mail link.

```
<a href="mailto:underwatertoursbyeloise@isp.com">
underwatertoursbyeloise@isp.com</a>
```

You again use the anchor <a> tag for this type of link. In the href attribute, though, you use the mailto:*e-mail address* as the value. It may seem strange to have the e-mail address underwatertoursbyeloise@isp.com twice in this code. The first occurrence of the e-mail address is for the link itself. The second occurrence of underwatertoursbyeloise@isp.com is used for the words on the Web page that you use as the link.

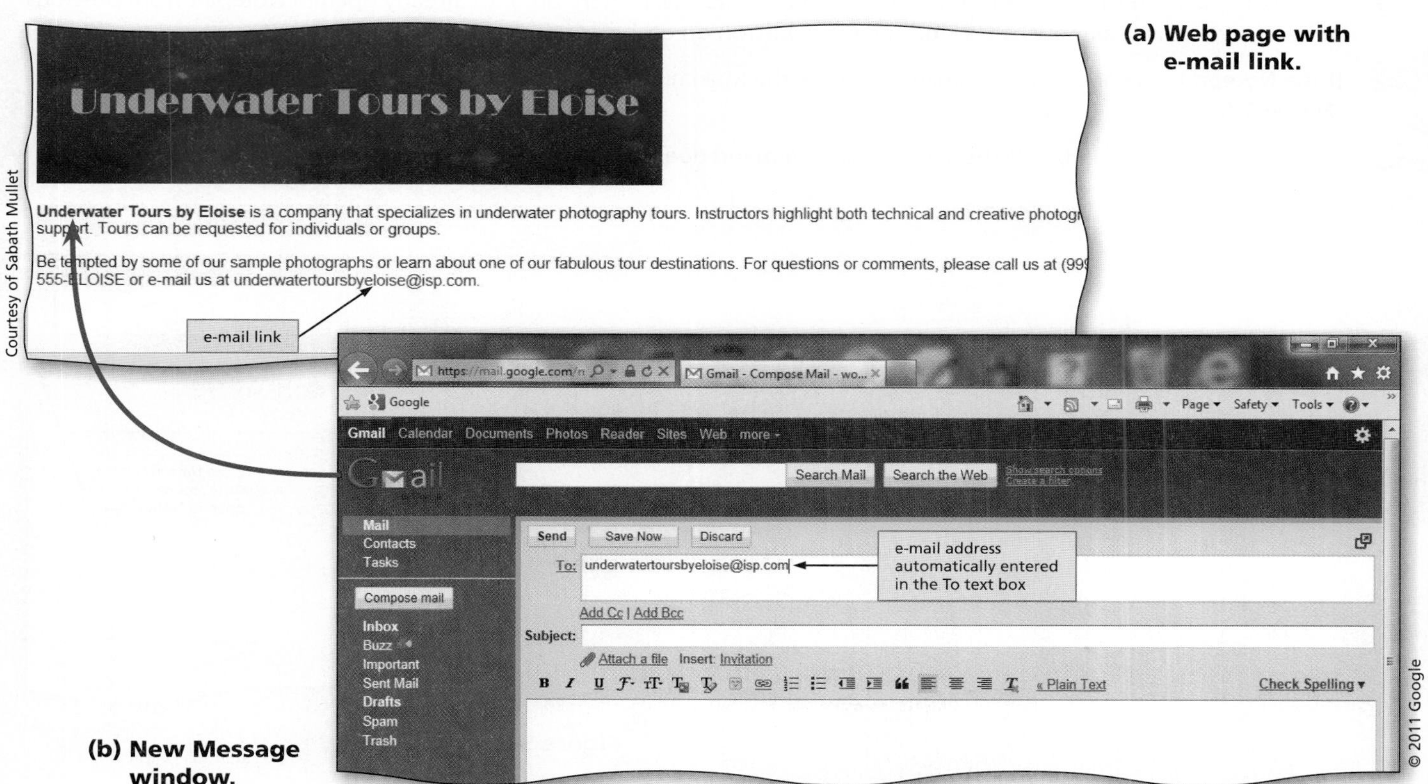

(a) Web page with e-mail link.

(b) New Message window.

Figure 3–8

Creating a Home Page

The first Web page developed in this chapter is the home page of the Underwater Tours by Eloise Web site. A home page is the main page of a Web site, which visitors to a Web site will generally view first. A Web site home page should identify the purpose of the Web site by briefly stating what content, services, or features it provides. The home page also should indicate clearly what links the visitor should click to move from one page on the site to another. A Web developer should design the Web site in such a way that the links from one Web page to another are apparent and the navigation is clear. The Web site home page most often includes an e-mail link, so visitors can easily find contact information for the individual or organization. Many Web sites now include an additional e-mail link to the Web development team. Users can utilize this e-mail link to notify the Web developers of any problems with the Web site or to comment on the site.

You begin creating the home page by starting Notepad++ and entering the initial HTML tags. Then you add an image, heading, text, and an unordered list to your home page. Finally, you add text and e-mail links, and then test the links.

To Start Notepad++

The following steps, which assume Windows 7 is running, start Notepad++ based on a typical installation. You may need to ask your instructor how to start Notepad++ for your computer.

1. Click the Start button on the Windows taskbar to display the Start menu.
2. Click All Programs at the bottom of the left pane on the Start menu to display the All Programs list.
3. Click Notepad++ in the All Programs list to open the Notepad++ folder.
4. Click Notepad++ in the list to display the Notepad++ window. If there are files already open in Notepad from previous projects, close them all now by clicking the Close button on each open file.
5. If the Notepad++ window is not maximized, click the Maximize button on the Notepad++ title bar to maximize it (Figure 3–9).
6. Click View on the menu bar. If the Word wrap command does not have a check mark next to it, click Word wrap.

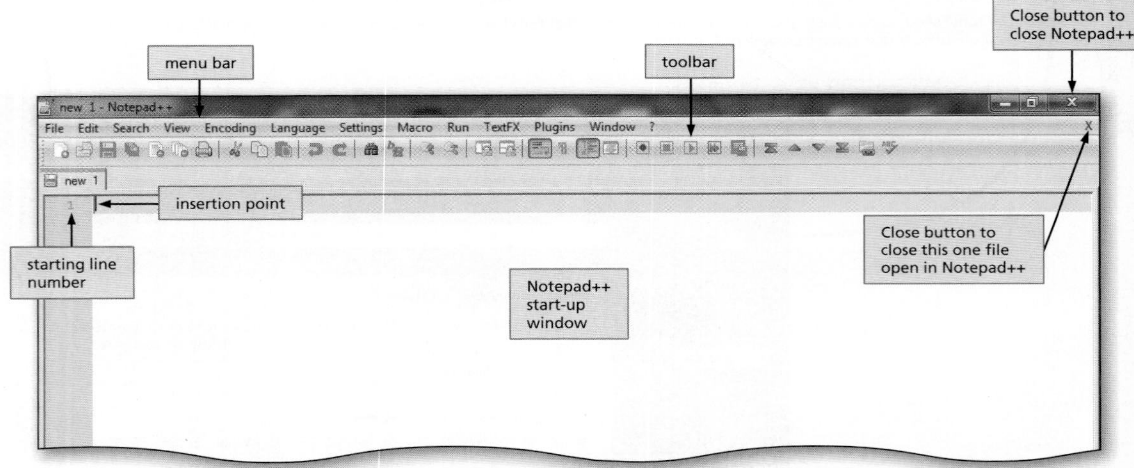

Figure 3–9

To Enter Initial HTML Tags to Define the Web Page Structure

Just as you did in Chapter 2, you start your file with the initial HTML tags that define the structure of the Web page. Table 3–1 contains the tags and text for this task.

> **BTW** **Copy Initial Structure**
> Remember that you can type in the initial HTML tags and save that code in a file called structure.html, which you can then open and use as the basis for all HTML files. This eliminates the need for you to type this same code at the beginning of every HTML file. Just remember to save structure.html with a new name as soon as you open it.

Table 3–1 Initial HTML Tags

Line	HTML Tag and Text
1	`<!DOCTYPE HTML>`
2	
3	`<html>`
4	`<head>`
5	`<meta charset="utf-8" />`

Table 3–1 Initial HTML Tags (continued)

Line	HTML Tag and Text
6	<title>Underwater Tours by Eloise</title>
7	</head>
8	
9	<body>
10	
11	</body>
12	</html>

The following steps illustrate how to enter the initial tags that define the structure of the Web page.

1. Enter the HTML code shown in Table 3–1. Press ENTER at the end of each line. If you make an error as you are typing, use the BACKSPACE key to delete all the characters back to and including the incorrect characters, then continue typing.

2. Position the insertion point on the blank line between the <body> and </body> tags (line 10) and press the ENTER key (Figure 3–10).

3. Compare what you typed to Figure 3–10. If you notice errors, use your mouse pointer or arrow keys to move the insertion point to the right of each error and use the BACKSPACE key to correct the error.

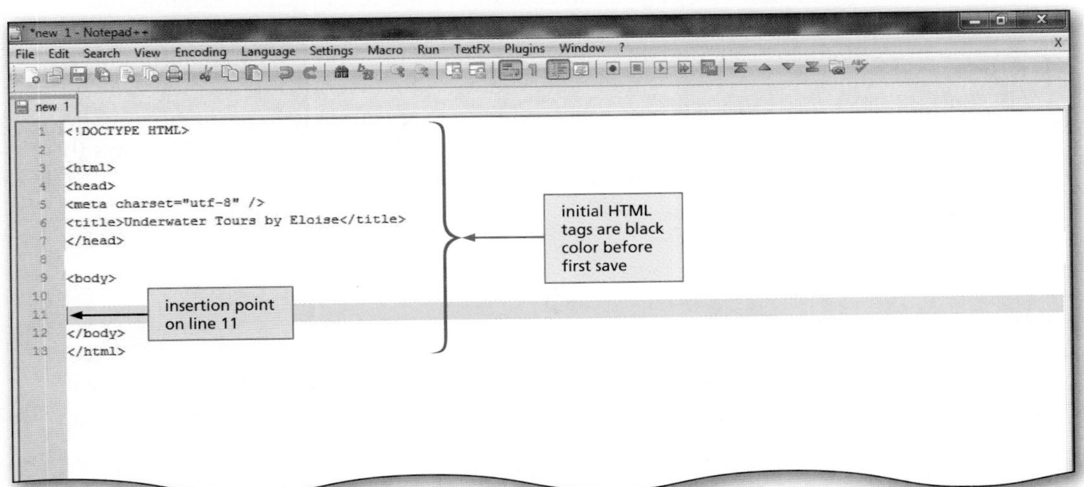

Figure 3–10

To Save an HTML File

With the initial HTML code for the Underwater Tours by Eloise home page entered, you should save the file. Saving the file frequently ensures you won't lose your work. Saving a file in Notepad++ also adds color to code that can help you identify different elements more easily. The following step illustrates how to save an HTML file in Notepad++.

1. With a USB flash drive connected to one of the computer's USB ports, click File on the Notepad++ menu bar and then click Save.
2. Type `underwatertours.html` in the File name text box (do not press ENTER).
3. Click Computer in the left pane of the Save As dialog box to display a list of available drives.
4. If necessary, scroll until UDISK 2.0 (G:) or the name of your storage device is displayed in the list of available drives.
5. Open the Chapter03\ChapterFiles folder.
6. Click the Save button in the Save As dialog box to save the file on the USB flash drive in the Chapter03\ChapterFiles folder with the name underwatertours.html.

Plan Ahead

Identify how to format various elements of the text.
Before inserting the graphical and color elements on a Web page, you should plan how you want to format them. By effectively utilizing graphics and color, you can call attention to important topics on the Web page without overpowering it. Consider the following formatting suggestions.

- **Effectively utilize graphics.** An important part of Web development is the use of graphics to call attention to a Web page. Generally, companies utilize the same logo on their Web site as they use on print material associated with the company, such as business cards and letterheads. Using the same graphical image on all marketing materials, including the Web site, is a good way to provide a consistent visual and brand message to customers.
- **Utilize headings that connect to the graphics.** In many cases, companies use a logo image as the main heading on their home page, as opposed to using an <h1> heading. It is sometimes good to coordinate the color of the headings and graphics contained on the Web page to the logo. This can bring attention to the company logo image, and it makes the Web page look cohesive with coordinating colors. Heading size standards should generally be followed from h1 (the largest) to h6 (the smallest). In this project, though, you use the company logo image as your main heading, so you have no h1 heading. Figure 3–1b on page HTML 89 shows the use of h1 and h2 headings in appropriate precedence.

To Add a Banner Image

The Underwater Tours by Eloise home page includes a logo image to provide visual appeal, catch the visitor's interest, and promote the company's brand. The following steps illustrate how to add an image to a Web page using the <header></header> container. Table 3–2 contains the code for adding the logo image.

Table 3–2 HTML Code for Adding a Banner Image

Line	HTML Tag and Text
11	`<header>`
12	`<img src="underwaterlogo.jpg" width="581" height="450" alt="Underwater Tours logo" />`
13	`</header>`

1

- With the insertion point on line 11, enter the HTML code shown in Table 3–2, pressing ENTER at the end of each line. Make sure to indent the second line of code by using the TAB key. This separates the start and end <header> tags from the <img> tag, highlighting the image insertion. Press the ENTER key twice at the end of line 13 to position the insertion point on line 15 (Figure 3–11).

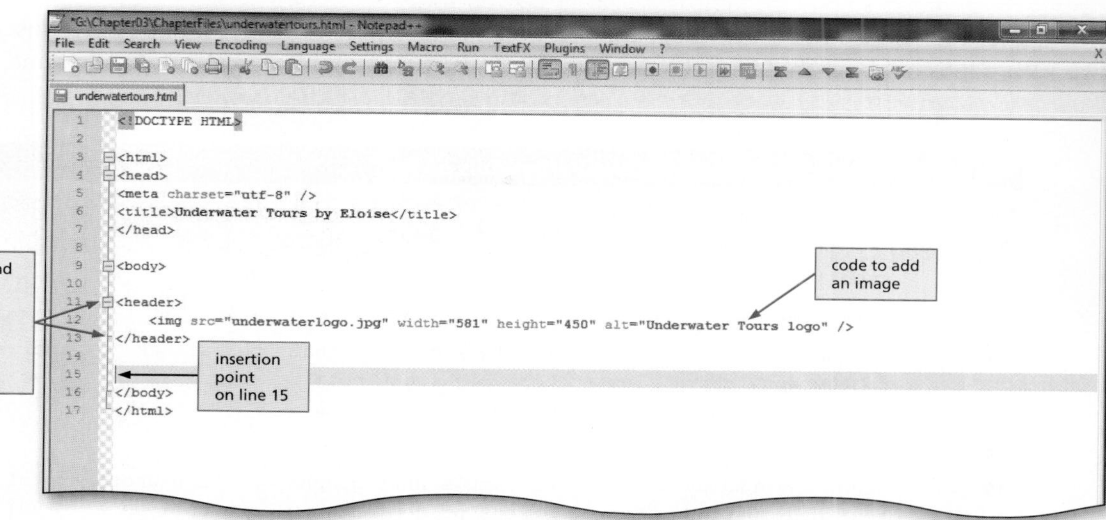

Figure 3–11

Q&A

Why should I include the width, height, and alt attributes?

Adding width and height attributes can improve page loading time because the browser does not have to figure the width and height before loading the image. Avoid using the height and width attributes to resize an image when possible. Use graphic editing software to resize it and save it with a different filename. The height and width attributes as used in the img tag should reflect the actual image size. The alt attribute provides information about the purpose of the image for assistive technology such as screen readers.

Plan Ahead

Identify how to format text elements of the home page.

You should always make a plan before inserting the text elements of a Web page. By formatting the characters and paragraphs on a Web page, you can improve its overall appearance. Effectively formatting the text also makes the message or purpose of the Web page clearer to the users. On a Web page, consider the following formatting suggestions.

- **Use default text size when appropriate**. The body text consists of all text between the heading and the bottom of the Web page. This text is the main content of the Web page and should be used to highlight the key points of your message. You can vary your content by utilizing both paragraphs of text and lists.
- **Determine what text formatting to use**. In a long Web page, it may help to vary your text as a way to break information up between headings. Using bold, color, or italicized text sparingly gives the Web page a more interesting look. Make sure not to overdo the formatting of text because you can make the page look cluttered. It is more difficult to find the content for which you are searching in a cluttered Web page.
- **Determine what style sheets to use**. Consider using style sheets to vary the format of text elements. If the text varies across paragraphs, an inline style is good to use. If you want all of the text in the Web page to be the same, an embedded style sheet is appropriate. If the text is common across more than one Web page, an external style sheet (discussed in the next chapter) should be used.
- **Determine other information suitable for the home page**. Other information that is suitable for a home page includes: the company address (often found in the logo), a phone number, and an e-mail link.

To Add Paragraphs of Text

After the underwater tours image for the Underwater Tours by Eloise home page is inserted, you need to add two paragraphs of text introducing Underwater Tours by Eloise. Table 3–3 shows the tags and text to enter.

Table 3–3 HTML Code for Adding Two Paragraphs of Text

Line	HTML Tag and Text
15	<section>
16	<article>
17	<p>Underwater Tours by Eloise is a company that specializes in underwater photography tours. Instructors highlight both technical and creative photography support. Tours can be requested for individuals or groups.</p>
18	
19	<p>Be tempted by some of our sample photographs or learn about one of our fabulous tour destinations. For questions or comments, please call us at (999) 555-ELOISE or e-mail us at underwatertoursbyeloise@isp.com.</p>
20	</article>
21	</section>

1. With the insertion point on line 15, enter the HTML code shown in Table 3–3. Press ENTER twice after the </p> tag on line 17 and once after the </section> tag on line 21. After entering the closing </article> and </section> tags, the insertion point is on line 22 (Figure 3–12).

Q&A

Do I have to end all paragraphs of text with the </p> tag?

A Web page without </p> tags would display in the browser correctly. This Web page would not pass validation using the W3C Markup Validation Service, however. One missed </p> tag will result in many errors during validation.

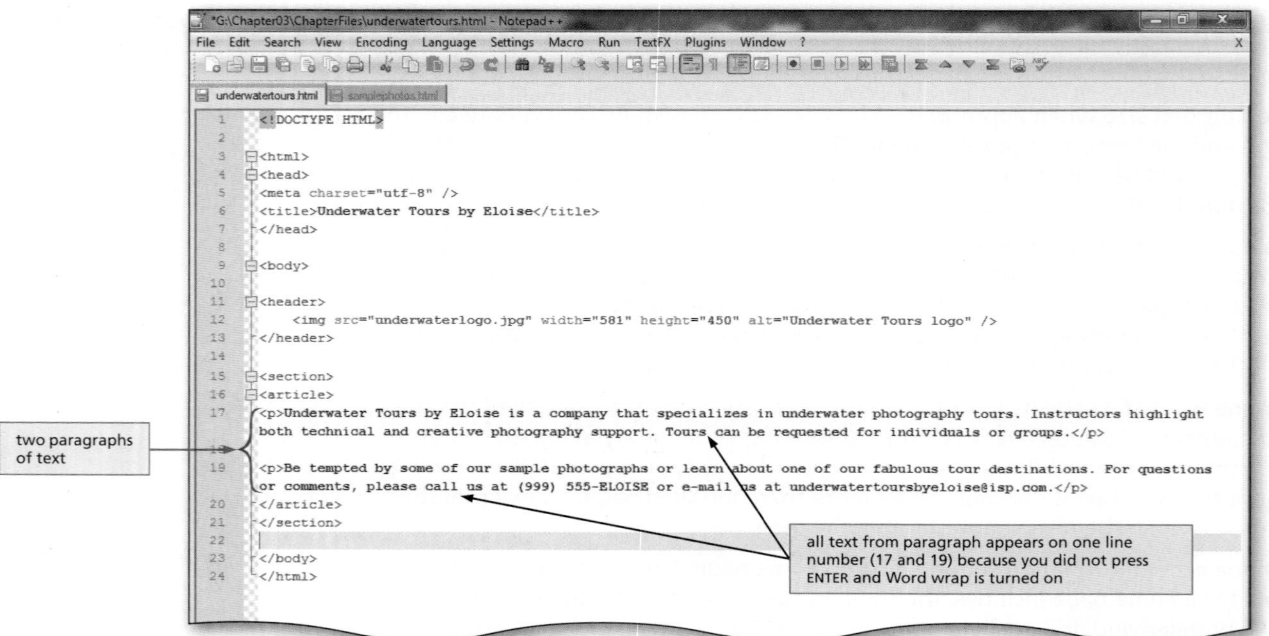

Figure 3–12

Plan Ahead

Plan how and where to use the four types of links.

- **Identify how to link from the home page to another page in the same Web site.** Linking to another Web page in the same Web site is often done with text links. When determining what words to use, make sure that the text links are clear and easy to understand. Using a phrase such as "click here" is not one that clearly identifies where the link will go. Choosing words such as "sample photographs" tells the Web site visitor to click that link if they want to see sample photographs.
- **Use an e-mail link on the home page.** A good standard practice is to include an e-mail link on the home page. Again, using words such as "click here" are not as effective as using a company's actual e-mail address (underwatertoursbyeloise@isp.com in this case) as the e-mail link text.
- **Determine external links for the home page.** Visitors to a Web site might want additional information on a topic, so a link can also be included on the home page (or any other Web page in the Web site). Linking to an external Web site (i.e., one that is outside of the boundaries of the current Web site) is appropriate to provide additional information. Again, it is important to select words or phrases that make sense for that link.
- **Use internal links on long Web pages.** Another good standard practice is to include links within a Web page when the page is long (i.e., when you have to use the scroll bar or press the PAGE DOWN key several times to get to the end of the Web page). Internal links help visitors navigate more easily within long Web pages. Also consider using links to help the visitor easily return back to the top of a long Web page.

Adding a Text Link to Another Web Page Within the Same Web Site

For the purpose of this Web site, the <a> and </a> tags are used to create links on a Web page. As mentioned earlier, the <a> (anchor) tag is used to create anchors for the links. The anchor tag can also be used to specify the base language of the target URL or to specify the media type of the link. The href attribute stands for a hyperlink reference. This is a reference (an address) to a resource on the Web. Hyperlinks can point to any resource on the Web, including an HTML page, an image, a sound file, or a video. The basic form of the tag used to create a link is:

```
<a href="URL">linktext</a>
```

where *linktext* is the clickable word or phrase that is displayed on the Web page and the value for href (hypertext reference) is the name or URL of the linked page or file. Table 3–4 shows some of the <a> tag attributes and their functions.

BTW

Other Links
You also can create links to other locations on the Internet (that is, non-http) such as FTP sites, and newsgroups. To link to an FTP site, type ftp:// URL rather than http:// URL as used in this project. For a newsgroup, type news:newsgroup name, and for any particular article within the newsgroup, type news:article name as the entry.

Table 3–4 <a> Tag Attributes and Functions

Attribute	Function
href	Specifies the URL of the linked page or file.
id	Defines a name (or id) for the current anchor so it may be the target or destination of another link. Each anchor on a Web page must use a unique id.
rel	Specifies the relationship between the current document and the linked document. The value of the rel attribute is a link type, such as prev, next, author, or license. For example, the Web page chapter3.html might include the tag <a rel="next" href="chapter4.html"> to indicate a link to the Web page for the next chapter, chapter4.html.

Table 3–4 <a> Tag Attributes and Functions (continued)

Attribute	Function
type	Specifies the content type (also known as media types or MIME types) of the linked page or file to help a browser determine if it can handle the resource type. Examples of content types include text/html, image/jpeg, video/quicktime, application/java, text/css, and text/javascript.

Before creating a link, be sure you know the URL or name of the file to be linked and the text that will serve as the clickable word or phrase. The words should be descriptive and tell the Web page visitor the purpose of the link. For the Underwater Tours by Eloise home page, the text link is a phrase in a paragraph at the bottom of the Web page.

To Add a Text Link to Another Web Page Within the Same Web Site

The Underwater Tours by Eloise home page includes a text link to the Sample Photographs Web page, which is part of the same Web site. The following step illustrates how to add a text link to another Web page within the same Web site.

- Click immediately to the left of the s in the word sample on line 19.
- Type `<a href="samplephotos.html">` to start the link, setting the Web page samplephotos.html as the linked Web page.
- Click immediately to the right of the s in photographs on line 19. Type `</a>` to close the link (Figure 3–13).

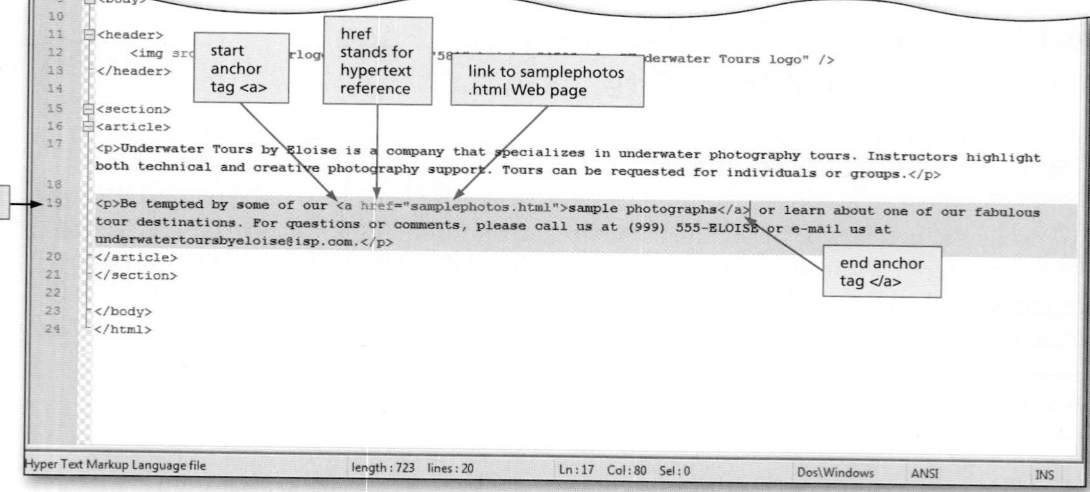
start anchor tag <a>
href stands for hypertext reference
link to samplephotos .html Web page
line 19
end anchor tag </a>
<p>Be tempted by some of our <a href="samplephotos.html">sample photographs</a> or learn about one of our fabulous tour destinations. For questions or comments, please call us at (999) 555-ELOISE or e-mail us at underwatertoursbyeloise@isp.com.</p>
Hyper Text Markup Language file
length : 723 lines : 20
Ln : 17 Col : 80 Sel : 0
Dos\Windows
ANSI
INS

Figure 3–13

Q&A

What is the href attribute for?

The href stands for "hypertext reference" and precedes the URL of the destination Web page.

Q&A

How will I know if my text is a link when it is displayed in the browser?

In the browser, the mouse pointer turns into a pointing finger where there is a link. Also, as the default, text used as a link will be blue and underlined. You can change the color and style of a link, and you do that later in the chapter.

Q&A

What happens if I forget to insert the </a> tag on a link?

A text link without the </a> tag will not display correctly in the browser. If you forget to use the </a> tag to end this text link, all of the text beyond the <a href=""> tag will serve as that link. In this example, all of the text that follows the s in sample will link to the samplephotos.html Web page, which is certainly not what you want.

Adding an E-mail Link

BTW

E-mail Links
E-mail Links may not work in a lab setting because there may not be an e-mail client installed on the school servers. You therefore may not be able to test this link.

Adding an e-mail link is similar to adding a text link, but instead of using a URL as the href attribute value, the href attribute value for an e-mail link uses the form:

```
<a href="mailto:address@email.com">linktext</a>
```

where the href attribute value uses the word mailto to indicate it is an e-mail link, followed by a colon and the e-mail address to which to send the e-mail message. When the browser recognizes a **mailto** URL in a clicked link, it automatically opens a new message in the default e-mail program and inserts the appropriate contact e-mail address in the To field. The clickable text used for an e-mail link typically is the e-mail address used in the e-mail link. The Web page should also provide some information before the link, so visitors know the purpose of the e-mail link.

To Add an E-mail Link

The Underwater Tours by Eloise home page includes an e-mail link so customers can contact Underwater Tours by Eloise for additional information or to comment on the Web page. The <a> and </a> tags used to create a text link to a Web page are also used to create an e-mail link. The following step shows how to add an e-mail link to a Web page.

- Click immediately to the left of the u in the beginning of underwatertours-byeloise@isp.com on line 19. Type `<a href="mailto:underwatertours-byeloise@isp.com">` as the start of the e-mail link. This will link to the e-mail address underwater-toursbyelo-ise@isp.com when the link is clicked.
- Click immediately after the m in isp.com and before the period in the e-mail address text on line 19.
- Type `</a>` to end the e-mail link, as shown in Figure 3–14.

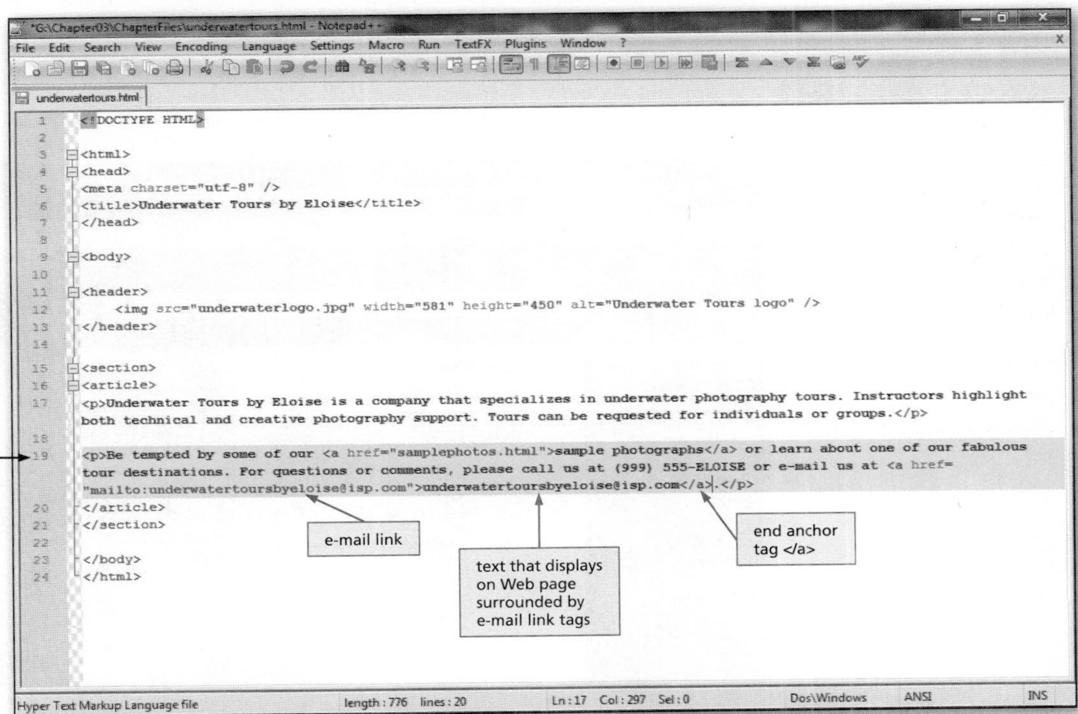

Figure 3–14

Q&A

I see two occurrences of underwatertoursbyeloise@isp.com on line 19. Why do I need two?

The first occurrence of underwatertoursbyeloise@isp.com (the one within the link <a> tag following the mailto:) is the destination of the link. The second occurrence of the e-mail address is the text link itself that will be displayed in the browser.

Adding Other Information to an E-mail Link

Sometimes, you need to add a subject to the e-mail message. This technique can be very helpful when more than one e-mail link is positioned on a Web page, and each link has a different purpose. For instance, one e-mail might be used for general questions, whereas another link might be used for specific information. You can also include a carbon-copy (cc) address. For instance, to include a subject in the above mailto:, you would use the form:

```
<a href="mailto:underwatertoursbyeloise@isp.com?subject=Maui
tours">
```

Sometimes, you need to add a message in the body of the e-mail in addition to the subject. This technique can be very helpful when more than one e-mail link is positioned on a Web page, and each link has a different purpose. For instance, one e-mail might be used for general questions, whereas another link might be used for specific information. Using the subject and body attributes can be helpful for this scenario. Notice that the two attributes (subject and body) are separated by an ampersand in the following form:

```
<a href="mailto:underwatertoursbyeloise@isp.com?subject=Maui
tours&body=Do you have half-day group tours?">
```

Figure 3–15 shows how the subject "Maui tours" and the message text "Do you have half-day group tours?" would appear in an e-mail program.

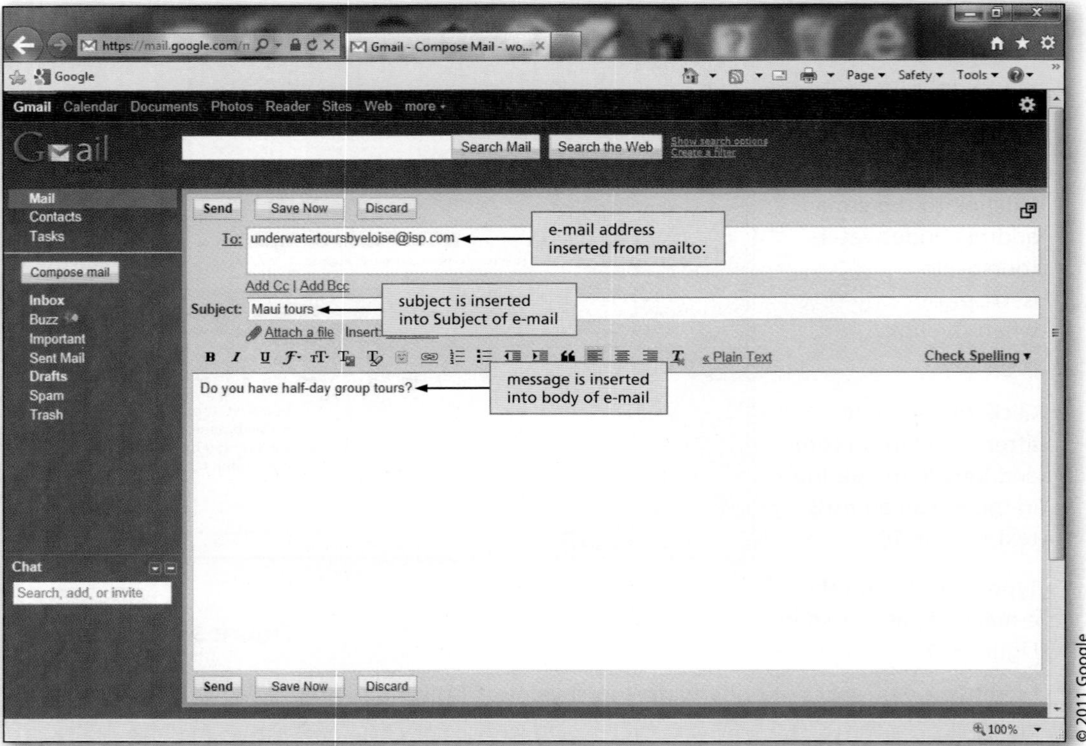

Figure 3–15

To Add a Text Link to a Web Page in Another Web Site

The <a> and </a> tags used to create a text link to a Web page within the same Web site are also used to create a link to a Web page in another Web site. The following step illustrates how to add a text link on the Underwater Tours by Eloise Web page to an external Web page that describes Hawaii's national parks.

1

- Click immediately to the left of the o in the word, one, on line 19 and type `<a href="http://www.nps.gov/state/hi/index.htm">` to add the URL for the external Web site when clicked.

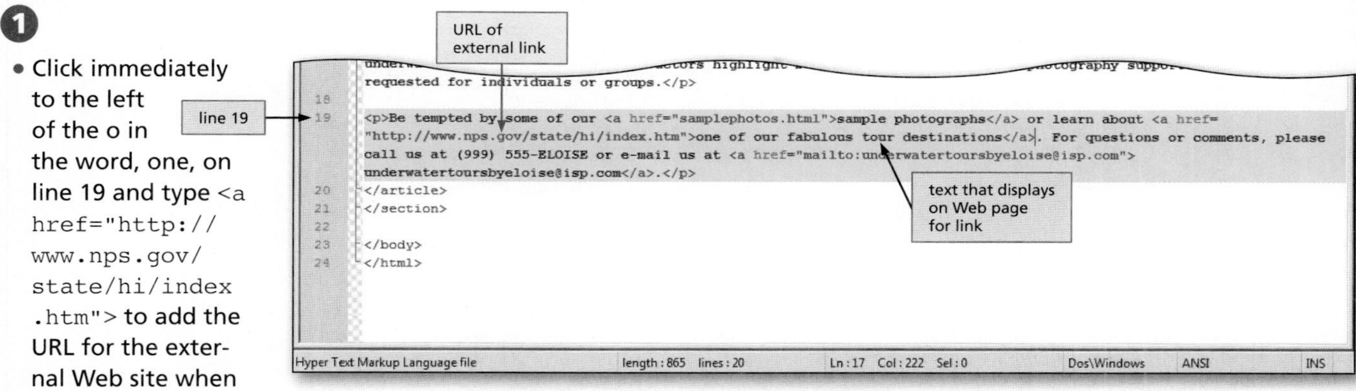

Figure 3–16

- Click immediately to the right of the last letter s in destinations on line 19 and type `</a>` to end the tag, as shown in Figure 3–16.

Q&A

When I type in the URL in the Address box of my browser, I never type in the http:// part of the URL. Why do I have to add the http:// in the link? I did not need the http:// for the sample photographs link.

Although you do not need to type the http:// into the URL on the browser, you always must include this as part of the href when creating external links. The Sample Photographs Web page is stored in the same folder as the home page from which you are linking. You therefore do not need to include any information other than the name of the Web page file. See the discussion on absolute and relative paths below for more information.

Q&A

When I link to the external Web page (www.nps.gov), I have to use the Back button on the browser to return to my home page. Is that the only way to get back?

Yes. You have to use the Back button to return to the home page because this is an external Web site. There is no way to provide a link back to your home page from an external Web site. In later chapters, you will learn how to open a new window for external.

Using Absolute and Relative Paths

At this point, it is appropriate to revisit the overall concept of how the files are organized and saved. As noted in the last chapter, the projects in this book use a very simple folder structure. In this book, the graphical images are stored in the same folder as the HTML files, for example, in the Chapter03\ChapterFiles folder. For most real-world applications, however, it would be more appropriate to separate the HTML code and the graphical images into different folders. Figure 3–17 on the next page shows an example of a more complex file structure that could be used for this book.

To understand how to use this sort of folder structure, you need to identify the folder location, or path, to the files. A **path** describes the location (folder or external Web site) where the files can be found, beginning with the UDISK G:\ drive (or another drive on your computer). This beginning location is also known as the **root** location. You can use either an absolute or relative path when identifying the location of the files. An **absolute path** specifies the exact address for the file to which you are linking or displaying a graphic. You can think of an absolute path as the complete address of

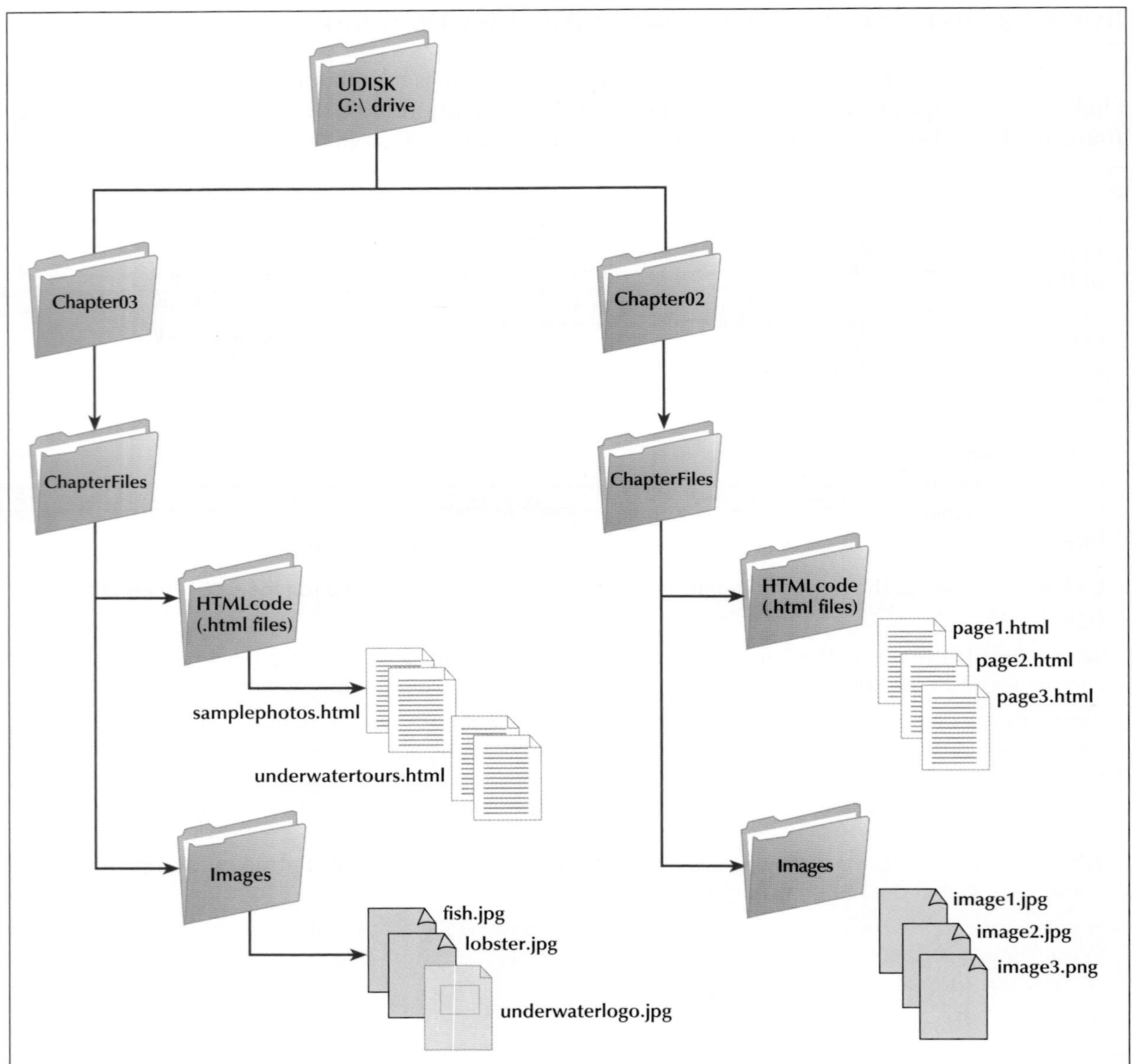

Figure 3–17

a house, including the house number, street name, city, state, and zip. In order to use that absolute address, you would have to give the entire path (or address) to a person who wants to get to that particular house. When you are referencing a Web page from a server outside of the server on which your Web pages reside, you have to use an absolute path. In this chapter, you use the absolute path to the National Park Service Web site for Hawaii. This is because that Web page is located outside of the server (or storage media) on which the Web pages created in the chapter reside. Your link statement for this external Web site is:

```
<a href="http://www.nps.gov/state/hi/index.htm">one of our
fabulous tour destinations</a>
```

Although absolute paths indicate the specific addresses of files, they can be cumbersome. For instance, if you use absolute paths for specific addressing of external Web pages, and those Web pages are moved to a different folder or different Web server, then all of the absolute paths would have to be changed. In the example above, if the home page for href="http://www.nps.gov/state/hi/index.htm" moved to a new Web server, your link would not work and would therefore have to be changed.

Relative paths specify the location of a file, relative to the location of the file that is currently in use. This is analogous to telling someone your house is located four doors down from the only gas station on that street. Your address in this case is relative to the beginning point, the gas station. Because your user has a beginning point (the gas station), you can describe the ending address (the house) relative to the beginning. A relative path allows you to move up the folder structure. So in the example shown in Figure 3–17, to display the image underwaterlogo.jpg (stored in the Images subfolder) from the Web page underwatertours.html (stored in the HTMLcode subfolder) within the Chapter03\ChapterFiles folder, you would use the following relative path structure:

```
\Images\underwaterlogo.jpg
```

Looking at Figure 3–17, you would store the image underwaterlogo.jpg in the Images subfolder and store the Web page itself, the underwatertours.html file, in the HTMLcode subfolder. If you moved the image to the HTMLcode subfolder and viewed the underwatertours.html file, the image underwaterlogo.jpg would not appear because it is not in the original folder.

Another example is storing one file at the root level and one in a subfolder. If you stored the underwatertours.html file in the HTMLcode subfolder, but stored the image underwaterlogo.jpg in the ChapterFiles folder, you would use the following relative path structure, in which the two dots (..) indicate one directory level up:

```
..\underwaterlogo.jpg
```

To display the underwatertours.html file with the underwaterlogo.jpg image, you would use the following relative path when identifying the image:

```
<img src="underwaterlogo.jpg" width="581" height="450"
alt="Underwater Tours logo" />
```

Another example is the relative addressing that you use in this chapter to link to the second Web page from the home page, and vice versa. The HTML code to link from the home page, underwatertours.html, to the second Web page is:

```
<a href="samplephotos.html">sample photographs</a>
```

and to go from the samplephotos.html Web page back to the home page, the HTML code is:

```
<a href="underwatertours.html">home page</a>
```

You currently have one folder ChapterFiles in the Chapter03 folder. Because HTML code and images are all in the same folder, your HTML code to access those images would look like this:

```
<img src="fish.jpg" width="259" height="387" alt="Frog fish" />
<img src="lobster.jpg" width="387" height="259" alt="Lobster" />
```

It is better to use relative paths for flexibility whenever feasible. If the root folder (i.e., the "highest" folder in the hierarchy) must change for some reason, you do not have to change all addressing if you used relative paths.

Adding Interest and Focus with Styles

In Chapter 2, you learned how to vary the size of headings with the <h1> through <h6> tags. Any text on a Web page, including headings, can be formatted with a different color or style to make it stand out by using style properties. Table 3–5 lists some properties that can be used to enhance standard text on a Web page using styles. Remember that CSS and inline styles are the preferred technique to alter the style of the content on a Web page.

BTW

Font Properties
Refer to Appendix D for a more complete list of CSS font properties and values. You can also set font characteristics with the HTML <font> tag (see Appendix A), but this tag has been removed from the HTML5 specification.

Table 3–5 Font Properties and Values

Property	Function
color	• Changes the font color • Values include six-digit (hexadecimal) color codes, color names, or RGB values
font-family	• Changes the font face or type • Values include fonts, such as Verdana or Arial; text appears using the default font if the font face is not specified
font-size	• Changes the font size • Value can be an actual numeric size, a percentage, or values such as large, medium, small, etc.
font-style	• Changes the style of a font • Values include normal, italic, and oblique
font-weight	• Changes the weight of a font • Values include normal, bold, bolder, and lighter

Figure 3–18 shows how several of these attributes affect the appearance of text.

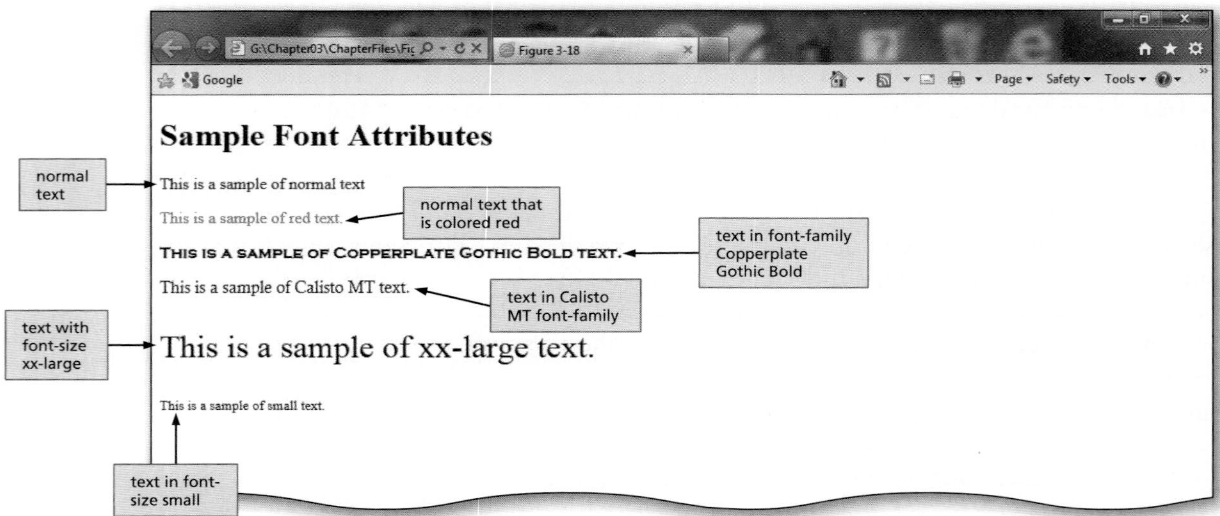

Figure 3–18 Examples of various fonts.

Adding Interest and Focus with HTML Tags

There is another way to format text in addition to the inline styles used in Chapter 2. Web pages that use the HTML5 DOCTYPE statement allow the use of deprecated tags, as explained in Chapter 2. These Web pages validate the HTML elements and attributes, including deprecated elements, successfully. Text can also be formatted using the formatting tags in HTML. In Chapter 2, you changed the font-style of some text on the Web page using an inline style. Instead of using an inline style, you could have used the HTML bold tags (<b> </b>) that make text bold. HTML provides a number of tags that can be used to format text, several of which are listed in Table 3–6.

Table 3–6 Text Formatting Tags

HTML Tag	Function
<b> </b>	Physical style tag that displays text as bold
<blockquote> </blockquote>	Designates a long quotation; indents margins on sections of text
<em> </em>	Logical style tag that displays text with emphasis (usually appears as italicized)
<i> </i>	Physical style tag that displays text as italicized
<pre> </pre>	Sets enclosed text as preformatted material, meaning it preserves spaces and line breaks; often used for text in column format in another document pasted into HTML code
<small> </small>	Decreases the font-size in comparison to the surrounding text
<strong> </strong>	Logical style tag that displays text with strong emphasis (usually appears as bold)
	Displays text as subscript (below normal text)
	Displays text as superscript (above normal text)

BTW

Deprecated and Non supported Tags
A deprecated element or attribute is one that has been outdated. Deprecated elements may become obsolete in the future, but most browsers continue to support deprecated elements for backward compatibility. You can still use deprecated tags with an HTML5 document type as used in this book. There are many tags and attributes not supported by HTML5, as noted in Appendx A.

Figure 3–19 shows a sample Web page with some HTML text format tags. These tags fall into two categories: logical style tags and physical style tags. **Logical style tags** allow a browser to interpret the tag based on browser settings, relative to other text on a Web page. The <h2> heading tag, for example, is a logical style that indicates the heading text should be larger than regular text but smaller than text formatted using an <h1> heading tag. The <strong> tag is another logical style, which indicates that text should have a strong emphasis, and which most browsers interpret as displaying the text in bold font. **Physical style tags** specify a particular font change that is interpreted strictly by all browsers. For example, to ensure that text appears as bold font, you would enclose it between a start <b> and end </b> tag. The <strong> tag is a better fit because it does not dictate how the browser displays the text. In practice, the <strong> and <b> tags usually have the same result when the Web page is displayed.

BTW

Logical versus Physical Tags
For more information about the differences between logical and physical tags, search the Web for the keywords "HTML logical tags" or "HTML physical tags."

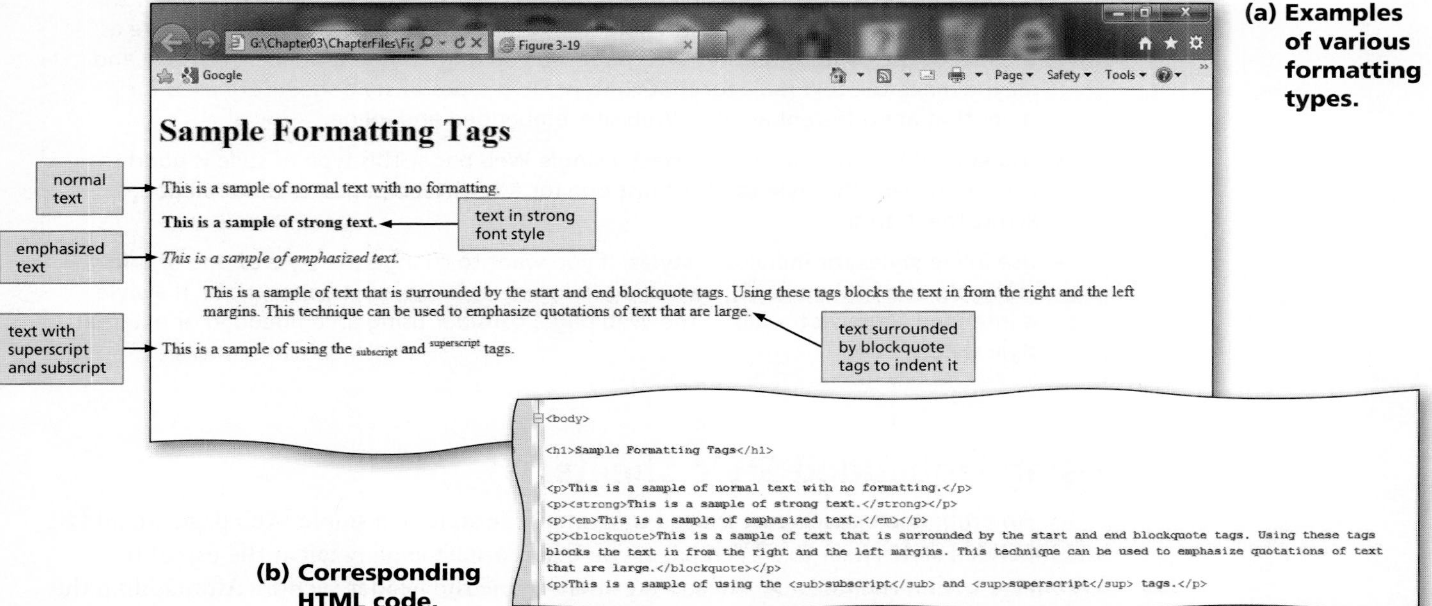

(a) Examples of various formatting types.

(b) Corresponding HTML code.

Figure 3–19

BTW

Types of Styles
Remember that an inline style changes the style of an individual element; an embedded style sheet changes the style of an entire Web page; and an external style sheet changes the style in multiple Web pages in the same Web site. If you want to change the style of a single element, use an inline style.

Style Sheet Precedence Review

In Chapter 2, you learned how to insert an inline style. The project in this chapter uses an inline style and also introduces you to embedded style sheets. You will learn about the third and final form of style, external style sheets, in Chapter 4. It will be helpful at this point to review the information from Chapter 2 on the precedence of styles (see Table 2-6 on page HTML 53). An inline style is used to control the style within an individual HTML tag and takes precedence over both embedded and external style sheets. An embedded sheet is used to change the style of an element over one Web page, but overrides or takes precedence over any styles defined in an external style sheet. An external style sheet is a separate document with a .css extension that is used to define styles for multiple pages in a Web site.

Because styles have different levels of precedence, all three types of styles can be used on a single Web page. For example, in this part of the chapter, you define body, anchor, and heading styles with embedded style sheets that are used for both the underwatertours.html file and the samplephotos.html file. You also insert a few inline styles on each Web page. Because of the precedence rules, the inline styles take precedence over the embedded style sheets. For instance, if you use an embedded style sheet to make all paragraphs Garamond font-family in normal text type and size 12, you can override that font-family, style, and size for a specific paragraph with an inline style within that paragraph's <p> tag. Maybe there is a paragraph that you want to highlight, so you make it bold with an inline style. Or maybe there is a paragraph that you want to downplay, and you make it smaller and italic with an inline style. It is important to determine how and when to use the various styles in the design phase of Web development.

Plan Ahead

Identify which level of style or style sheet to use.
Because of precedence rules, it is generally better to look at the broadest level style first. In this chapter project, you use inline and embedded style sheets, with embedded being the broader level. In other words, an embedded style sheet is used for the entire Web page, and an inline style is used in a particular HTML tag. In Chapter 4, you will add an external style sheet (the broadest level) to your chapter project.

- **Identify what styles need to be different than the standards used across the Web site**. Sometimes you need to vary a style in order to call attention to the content or pull attention away from it. Many Web sites have a legal statement on the bottom of the home page. That is not necessarily something that needs to be the same font-size as the rest of the content on that Web page. So you may choose a smaller font-size and maybe make the text italic for that content. Two types of style sheets are used for styles that are different across a Web site: embedded and inline.
- **Use embedded style sheets to affect a single Web page**. This type of style is good to use if you want the style to affect just one (or a few) Web pages, and not all pages across the Web site.
- **Use inline styles for individual styles**. If you want to change the style of one or a few elements of one Web page, then using inline styles is the most appropriate. If a style is intended for most (or all) of the Web page, consider using an embedded or external style sheet.

Using Embedded Style Sheets

An embedded style sheet is used to control the style of a single Web page. To add an embedded style sheet to a Web page, you insert a start <style> tag at the top of the Web page within the <head> </head> tags that define the header section. After adding the desired style statements, you end the embedded style sheet by adding an end </style> tag.

The following code shows an example of an embedded style sheet to set the h1 heading to the Garamond font-family, point size 32. This code would be added between the <head> and </head> tags within <style> </style> tags:

```
<style type="text/css">
<!--
h1 {font-family: Garamond;
   font-size: 32pt;}
-->
</style>
```

In this embedded style, you identify the code as a style sheet by using the "text/css" type. You should also use comment tags in your embedded (internal) style sheet. The comment tags are positioned just after the start style <style> and just before the end style </style> tags. The <!-- is used to start a comment, and the --> code is used to end the comment. These comment lines tell the browser to ignore whatever is between the comment lines if the browser cannot interpret the code between. So if your Web page user has a browser that is not current, it may not be able to interpret embedded style sheets. An older browser would see the start of the comment <!-- and disregard anything between that line and the end of the comment -->. Enclosing your style sheet within comment lines is a good Web development technique. The h1 (header size 1) element is the **selector**, and the remainder of the code is the **declaration**. The declaration sets the values for two different properties. The first property-value statement sets the h1 font-family to Garamond. The second property-value statement sets the font size to 32 point. The style statement is enclosed in curly brackets and each property-value statement ends with a semicolon. This statement tells the browser to display all h1 headers in 32-point Garamond font. You could use this embedded style sheet to easily change all h1 headings, in lieu of making the same change with an inline style in each individual heading tag.

The various types of Cascading Style Sheets allow you to control many different property values for various elements on a Web page. Table 3–7 lists six main properties and related options that are used in CSS. A complete list of properties and property values that can be used in CSS is included in Appendix D.

BTW

HTML/CSS Terminology
In HTML, a *tag* is a special instruction to the browser to specify how the Web page is displayed. Many tags have attributes that help to further modify what is displayed. In CSS, a style *statement* is made up of a selector and a declaration. The part of the style statement that identifies the page element(s) is called the *selector*. The part of the style statement that identifies how the element(s) should appear is called the *declaration*. A declaration includes at least one type of style, or property, to apply to the selected element.

Table 3–7 CSS Properties and Options

Property Name	Options That Can Be Controlled
background	• color • image • position
border	• color • style • width
font	• family • size • style • variant • weight
list	• image • position • type

Table 3–7 CSS Properties and Options (continued)

Property Name	Options That Can Be Controlled
margin	• length • percentage
text	• alignment • color • decoration • indentation • spacing • white space

BTW

Specifying Alternative Fonts

If a Web page font is not available on users' computers, you can create a list of fonts and the browser will determine the font to use. For example, if the Web page uses a Geneva font, but Arial or Helvetica would also work well, you create a comma-separated list of acceptable fonts, using <font face="geneva, arial, helvetica"> *your text*</font> as the code. If a Web page uses a font that Web page visitors do not have on their computers, the Web page appears using a default font (usually Times New Roman).

The following code shows an example of an embedded style sheet that you will use in the chapter project:

```
<style type="text/css">
<!--
body            {font-family: Arial, Verdana, Garamond;
                font-size: 11pt;}
h1, h2, h3      {color: #020390;}
a               {text-decoration: none;
                color: #020390;}
a:hover         {background: #020390;
                color: #01d3ff;}
-->
</style>
```

This embedded style sheet defines four elements on the page: body, headings, links, and the link-hover property. The first style statement uses the **body** selector to specify that all text on the Web page should be one of the font families: Arial, Verdana, or Garamond, in 11-point size. Computers do not always have every font-family installed, so Web developers usually specify multiple font-families. If the first font-family is not available, then the next takes effect. If none of the named font-families are installed, the computer's default font is used. Separate the font-families by commas.

The second style statement defines values for the h1, h2, and h3 properties. The value #020390 will give all h1, h2, and h3 headings on this Web page the color dark blue. On the home page, there are no headings, but there are headings on the second Web page, and later in the chapter you will use this same embedded style sheet for that Web page, which has h1, h2, and h3 headings.

The third style statement defines one property of the link element. The selector **a** is used to indicate the link element. The property-value statement text-decoration: none; color: #020390; changes the appearance of links from the default underlined, blue color text. The default style for text links is underlined text. In order to eliminate that underline, you can set text-decoration to none. There are several values for text-decoration, including: none, underline, overline, and line-through. Also as a default, linked text is blue before being visited. With the inline style, you can change that color. Because the style statement uses **a** as the selector, it changes all link states (normal, visited, active) to these property values. You can also define a unique style for normal, visited, and active links by creating three separate style statements with **a:link**, **a:visited**, and **a:active** as the selectors.

The last style statement uses the **a:hover** selector to define the style of a link when the mouse pointer points to, or **hovers** over, a link. In this statement, you use a pseudo-class (hover) to have more control over the anchor (link) element. A **pseudo-class** is attached to a selector with a colon to specify a state or relation to the selector to give the Web developer more control over that selector. The format to use with a pseudo-class is entered in the form:

```
selector:pseudo-class {property: value;}
```

with a colon between the selector and the pseudo-class. There are four pseudo-classes that can be used when applied to the anchor or link selector:

- link, for an unvisited link
- visited, for a link to a page that has already been visited
- active, for a link when it gains focus (for example, when it is clicked)
- hover, for a link when the cursor is held over it.

The hover statement tells the browser to display light blue (color #01d3ff) link text on a dark blue (#020390) background when the mouse hovers over the link as shown in Figure 3–20. Adding a link-hover style significantly changes the look of the links and adds a dimension of interactivity to the Web page.

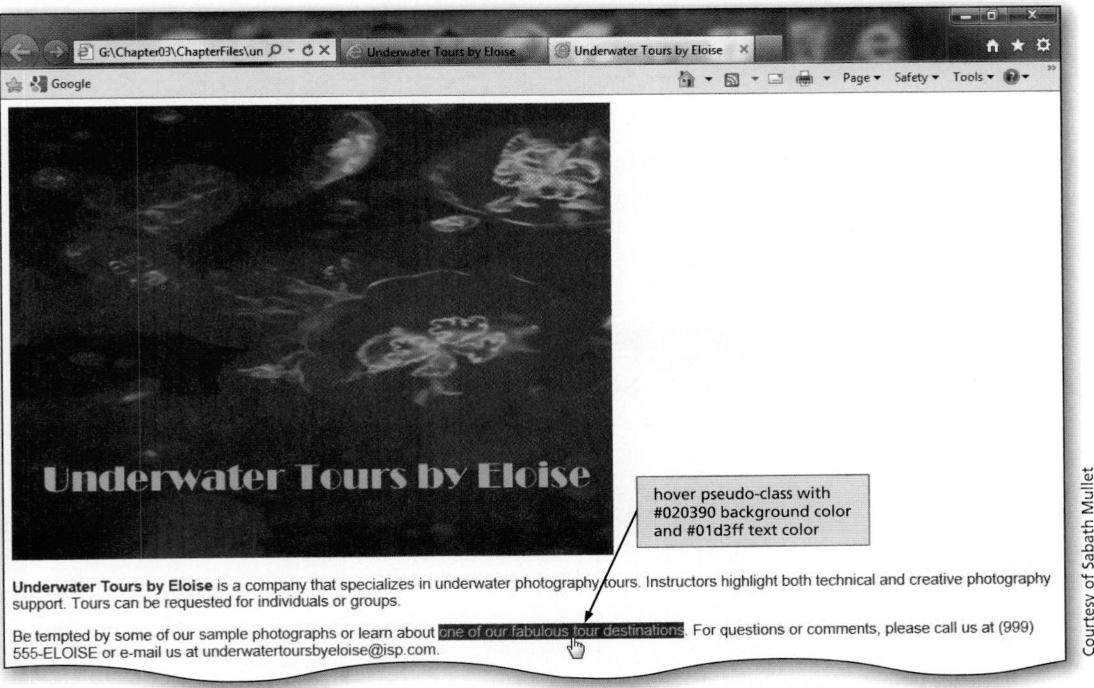
Underwater Tours by Eloise
hover pseudo-class with #020390 background color and #01d3ff text color
Underwater Tours by Eloise is a company that specializes in underwater photography tours. Instructors highlight both technical and creative photography support. Tours can be requested for individuals or groups.
Be tempted by some of our sample photographs or learn about one of our fabulous tour destinations. For questions or comments, please call us at (999) 555-ELOISE or e-mail us at underwatertoursbyeloise@isp.com.
Courtesy of Sabath Mullet

Figure 3–20 Completed home page with hover effect.

As mentioned earlier, the <!-- and --> code used in the embedded style sheet (just after the start style <style> and just before the end style </style> tags) are comment lines. These comment lines tell the browser to ignore whatever is between the comment lines if the browser cannot interpret the code between.

Recall that embedded style sheets have the second-highest level of precedence of the three types of styles. Although an inline style overrides the properties of an embedded style sheet, the embedded style sheet takes precedence over an external style sheet.

To Add Embedded Style Sheet Statements

Table 3–8 on the next page shows the CSS code for an embedded style sheet to specify the font-family and font-size for the body text on the underwatertours.html Web page.

Table 3–8 CSS Code for an Embedded Style Sheet

Line	CSS Selectors and Declarations
7	<style type="text/css">
8	`<!--`
9	
10	`body     {font-family: Arial, Verdana, Garamond;`
11	`         font-size: 11pt;}`
12	
13	`h1, h2, h3     {color: #020390;}`
14	
15	`a        {text-decoration: none;`
16	`         color: #020390;}`
17	
18	`a:hover {background: #020390;`
19	`         color: #01d3ff;}`
20	
21	`-->`
22	`</style>`

The following step shows how to enter the embedded style sheet code to change h1, h2, and h3 headings to blue, change all links to blue with no text-decoration, and change the color of the link hover to a dark blue background with light blue text to provide visual impact.

1

- Click immediately to the right of the > in </title> on line 6 and press the ENTER key.
- Type the code in Table 3–8 but do not press the ENTER key at the end of line 22 (Figure 3–21).

Q&A What other styles can I use on my Web pages?

Appendix D lists available CSS properties and values. You can also search the Web for examples of how CSS are used for Web development. Finally, be an active Web page visitor and review the source code on Web pages with styles that you think are particularly effective or ineffective.

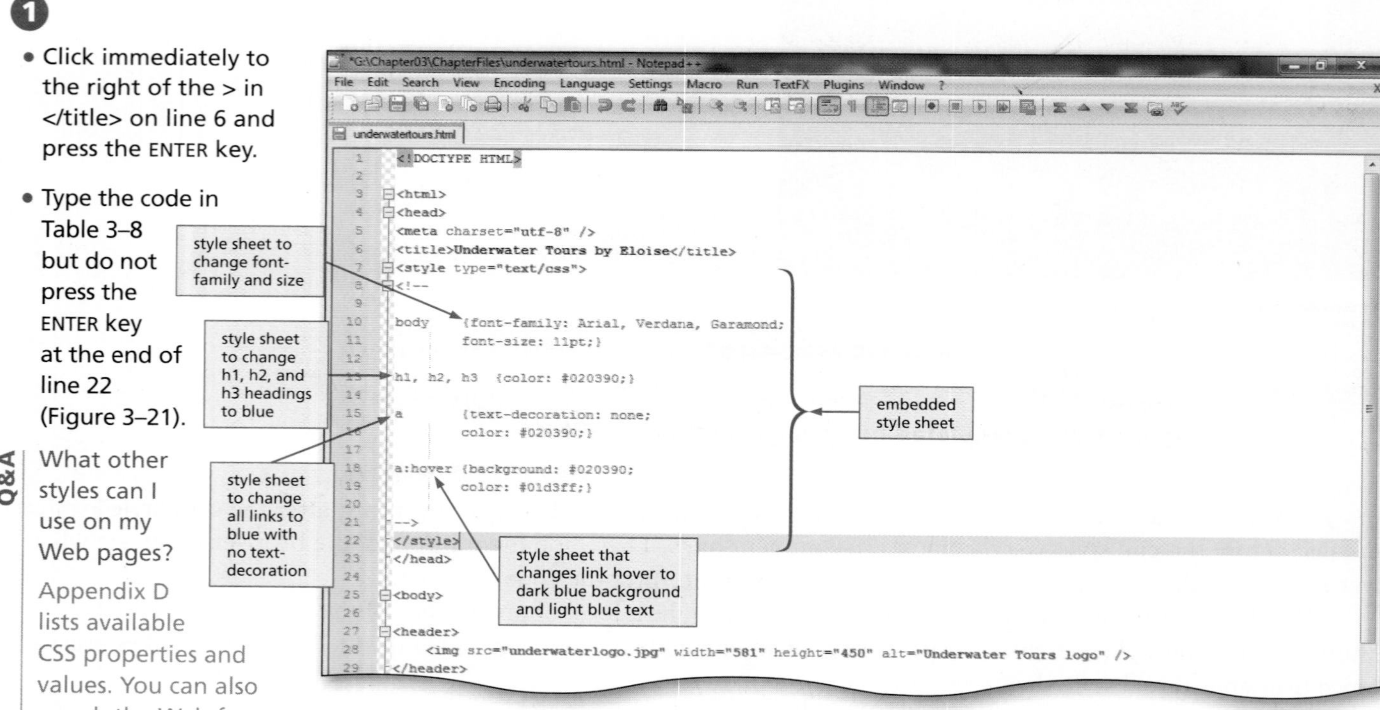

Figure 3–21

To Add an Inline Style for Color

The following step shows how to enter an inline style to add a blue color (#020390) in a bold font-weight to provide visual impact and call attention to the company name, Underwater Tours by Eloise. With this inline style, you use the <span> </span> tags. The **<span> </span>** tags create a container into which a user can add an inline style. The <span> tag provides a finer level of control for styles than the <div> </div> tags, which define block-level structure or division in the HTML document. The <span> tag tells the browser to apply the chosen styles to whatever is within the <span></span> container.

1

- With the insertion point right after the > in <p> on line 33, type `<span style="color: #020390; font-weight: bold">` (Figure 3–22).
- With the insertion point right after the last e in Eloise on line 33, type `</span>` (Figure 3–22).

Q&A What other font-weights could I have used?

The font-weights are normal, bold, bolder, and lighter. Additionally, you can add values of 100–900 in which 400 is the same as normal, and 700 is the same as bold. If you don't specify a font-weight, normal is the default.

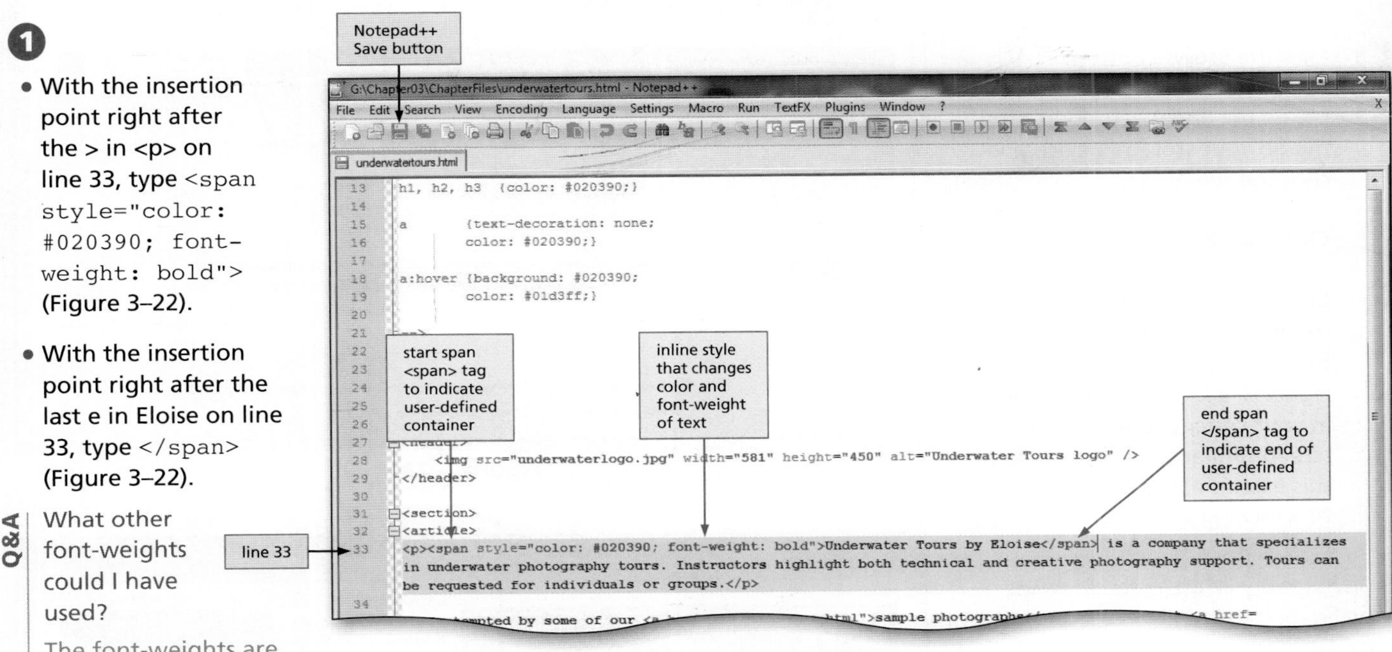

Figure 3–22

Q&A What different colors can I use for text?

There are a variety of colors that you can use for headings, text, and backgrounds. You can name the color by color name or hexadecimal code. See Figure 2–27 on page HTML 64 for examples.

To Save an HTML File

With the HTML code for the Underwater Tours by Eloise home page complete, you should save the changes to the file. The following step shows how to save an HTML file that has been previously saved.

1 Click the Save button on the Notepad++ toolbar to save the most recent version of underwatertours.html on the same storage device and in the same folder as the last time you saved it.

Validating the HTML, Viewing the Web Page, and Testing Links

After you save the HTML file for the Underwater Tours by Eloise home page, it should be validated to ensure that it meets current HTML5 standards and viewed in a browser to confirm the Web page is displayed as desired. It is also important to test the two links in the Underwater Tours by Eloise home page to verify that they function as expected.

To Validate HTML Code

1. Open Internet Explorer.
2. Navigate to the Web site validator.w3.org.
3. Click the Validate by File Upload tab.
4. Click the Browse button.
5. Locate the underwatertours.html file on your storage device and click the file name.
6. Click the Open button.
7. Click the Check button. A successful validation should be displayed, as shown in Figure 3–23. If you have errors in your code, you may see a screen similar to Figure 3–24. In this example, the errors relate to a missing </p> tag.

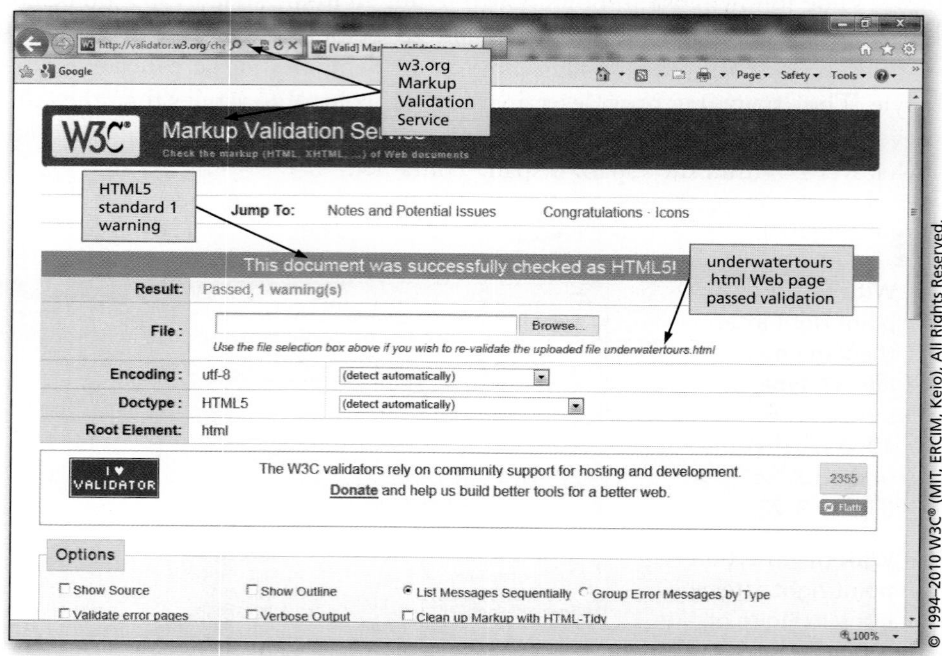

Figure 3–23

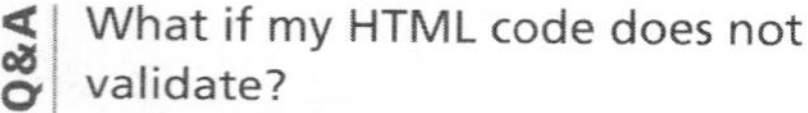

Q&A What if my HTML code does not validate?

If your code has errors, you should edit your HTML file to correct the errors. The Markup Validation Service report lists clearly what is wrong with your code. Once you make the necessary changes and save the file, you can again use the Browse button to open the corrected HTML file. You then use the Revalidate button to validate the changed code.

Q&A Why is there a warning noted on the validation screen, but it still says that it passed HTML5 validation?

As you learned in Chapter 2, all HTML5 files result in a warning in validation because HTML5 is still under development.

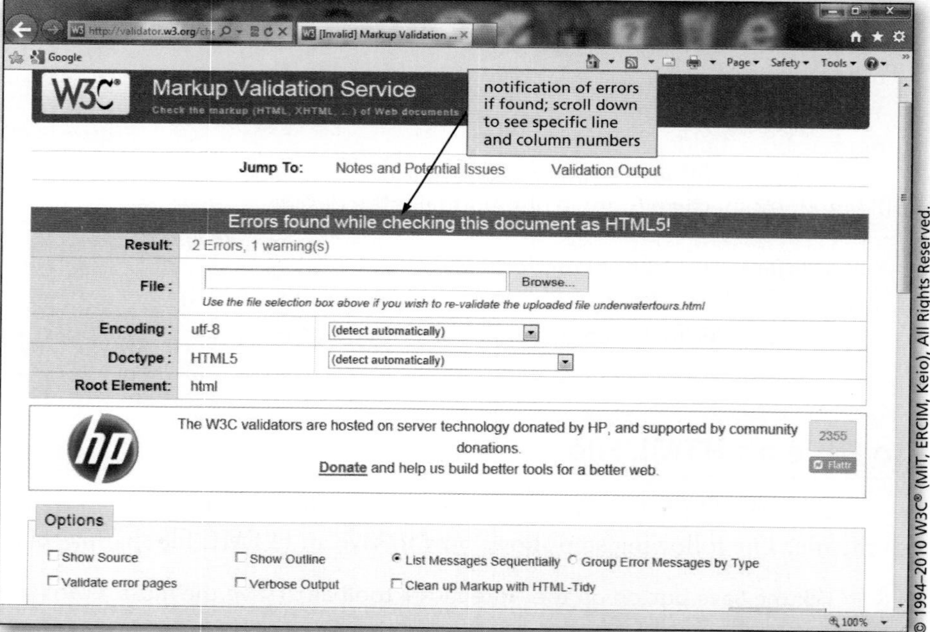

Figure 3–24

BTW

Common Validation Errors

Common validation errors include not spelling tags, selectors, or attributes correctly; using uppercase letters (except for DOCTYPE); and not nesting tags correctly. A single coding error can cause many lines of errors during validation. For instance, Figure 3-24 shows a Web page that has two errors.

To Print an HTML File

After your HTML code has passed validation, it's a good idea to make a hard copy printout of it to have a record of that file.

1. Click the Notepad++ button on the taskbar to activate the Notepad++ window.
2. Click File on the menu bar, click Print, and then click the Print button to print a hard copy of the HTML code (Figure 3–25).

```
<!DOCTYPE HTML>

<html>
<head>
<meta charset="utf-8" />
<title>Underwater Tours by Eloise</title>
<style type="text/css">
<!--

body    {font-family: Arial, Verdana, Garamond;
        font-size: 11pt;}

h1, h2, h3  {color: #020390;}

a       {text-decoration: none;
        color: #020390;}

a:hover {background: #020390;
        color: #01d3ff;}

-->
</style>
</head>

<body>

<header>
    <img src="underwaterlogo.jpg" width="581" height="450" alt="Underwater Tours logo" />
</header>

<section>
<article>
<p><span style="color: #020390; font-weight: bold">Underwater Tours by Eloise</span> is
a company that specializes in underwater photography tours. Instructors highlight both
technical and creative photography support. Tours can be requested for individuals or
groups.</p>

<p>Be tempted by some of our <a href="samplephotos.html">sample photographs</a> or
learn about <a href="http://www.nps.gov/state/hi/index.htm">one of our fabulous tour
destinations</a>. For questions or comments, please call us at (999) 555-ELOISE or
e-mail us at <a href="mailto:underwatertoursbyeloise@isp.com">
underwatertoursbyeloise@isp.com</a>.</p>
</article>
</section>

</body>
</html>
```

-1-

Figure 3–25

To View a Web Page

The following steps illustrate how to view the HTML file in a browser.

1. Open Internet Explorer.
2. In Internet Explorer, click the Address bar to select the URL in the Address bar.
3. Type `G:\Chapter03\ChapterFiles\underwatertours.html` (or the specific path to your file) to display the new URL in the Address bar and then press the ENTER key (Figure 3–26).

Q&A What if my page does not display correctly?

Check your underwatertours.html code carefully in Notepad++ to make sure you have not made any typing errors or left anything out. Correct the errors, save the changes, and try again.

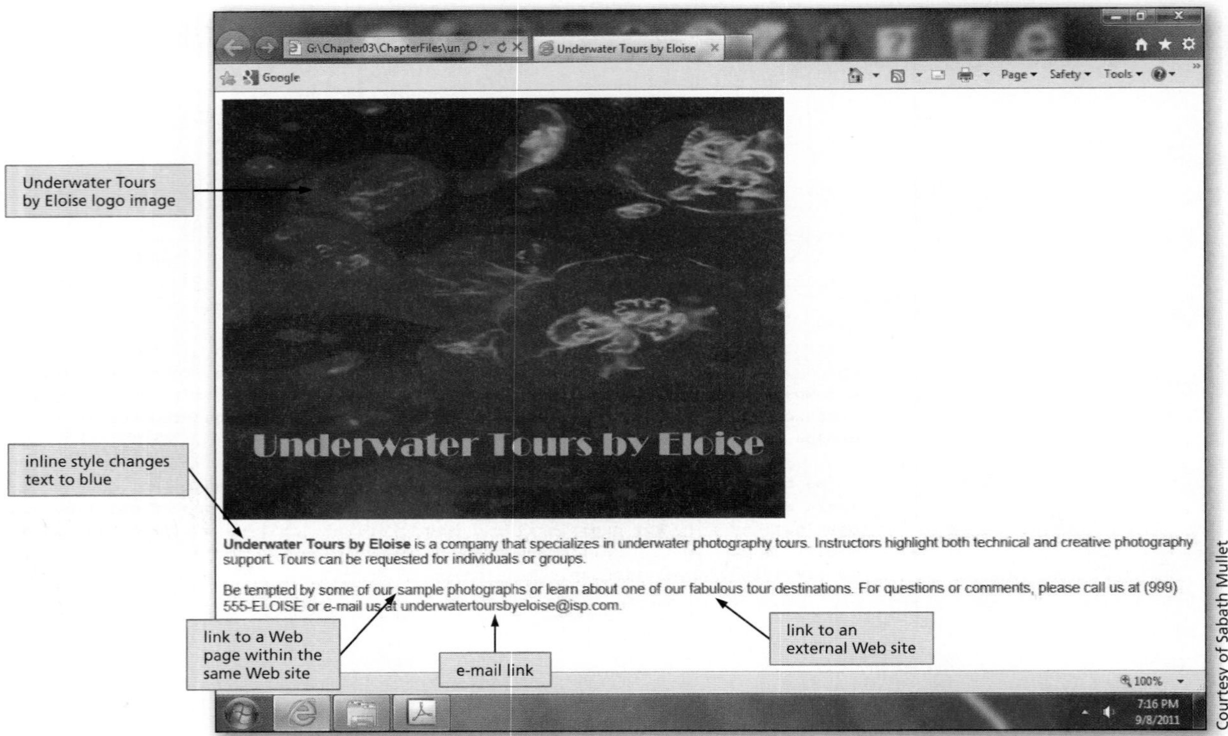

Underwater Tours by Eloise logo image
inline style changes text to blue
link to a Web page within the same Web site
e-mail link
link to an external Web site
Underwater Tours by Eloise
Underwater Tours by Eloise is a company that specializes in underwater photography tours. Instructors highlight both technical and creative photography support. Tours can be requested for individuals or groups.
Be tempted by some of our sample photographs or learn about one of our fabulous tour destinations. For questions or comments, please call us at (999) 555-ELOISE or e-mail us at underwatertoursbyeloise@isp.com.
Courtesy of Sabath Mullet

Figure 3–26

Plan Ahead

Test your Web page.

- **Determine what you need to test.** It is important to have a test plan when you test your Web pages. Planning what to test assures that all functionality of the Web page is tested. You should specifically test the display of the Web page itself on multiple browsers and test that all of the links on the Web page work correctly.
- **Test the Web page as displayed in multiple browsers.** Certainly the first part of testing is to verify that your Web page is displayed in each browser as intended. Ask yourself the following questions: (1) Are the images all displayed where they should be? (2) Is the text presented as intended? (3) Are the links displayed as intended?
- **Test the links.** In your testing plan, you need to address all of the links that you have inserted into the Web page. It is especially important to test external links, that is, those over which you have no control. If you need to link outside of the Web pages that you developed, then periodically test the links to make sure they are still valid.
- **Have a test plan.** A test plan can be as simple as a matrix that includes three columns of information. The first column contains information about all of the links on the Web page. The second column contains information about the intended results of those links. The third column is the one that you complete during testing. If a link tests as it should, you can note that by putting a check mark in the third column. If a link test result is not as it should be, you can note in the third column what the result is. Using a technique such as this makes it easier to do thorough testing. When you know what the results of the test should be, it helps you verify valid links. This is an excellent technique to use when there are different people developing and testing the Web pages. The matrix will notify the developers of the test results clearly.

BTW

Web Page Testing
An important part of Web page development is testing Web page links. For more information about link testing, search the Web for keywords such as "HTML testing" or look at the World Wide Web Consortium (w3.org) Web site.

To Test Links on a Web Page

The following steps show how to test the links in the Underwater Tours by Eloise home page to verify that they work correctly. (Note that you might not be able to test the e-mail link if your browser is not configured to work with an e-mail client.)

- With the Underwater Tours by Eloise home page displayed in the browser, point to the e-mail link, underwatertoursbyeloise@isp.com and then click the link to open the default e-mail program with the address underwatertoursbyeloise@isp.com in the To: text box, as shown in Figure 3–27.
- Click the Close button in the Compose Mail window. If a dialog box asks if you want to save changes, click No.

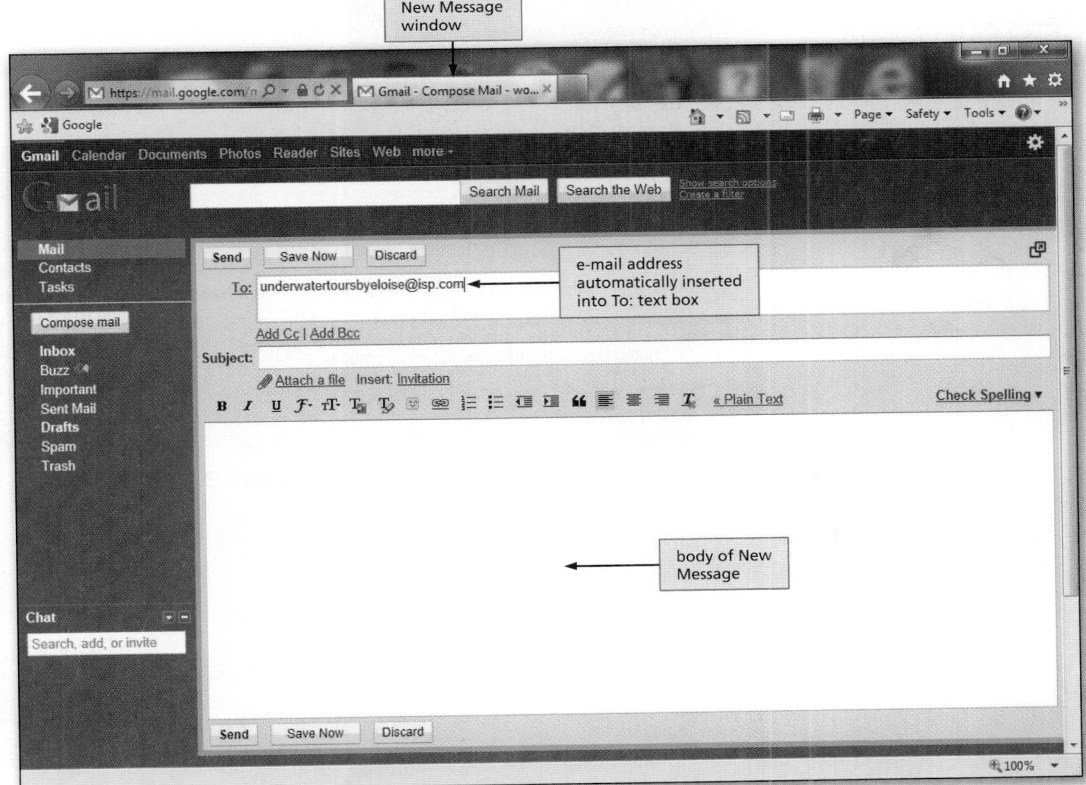

Figure 3–27

2

- Click the 'one of our fabulous tour destinations' link to test the external link on the Web page. Use the Back button to return to the Underwater Tours by Eloise home page.
- With the USB flash drive in drive G, point to the sample photographs link and click the link. The secondary Web page, samplephotos .html, is displayed (Figure 3–28), although it is not completed.

Q&A

My e-mail does not work when I click the link. Why does that happen?

You may not have an e-mail client installed on your computer or your school's servers. You therefore may not be able to test this e-mail link.

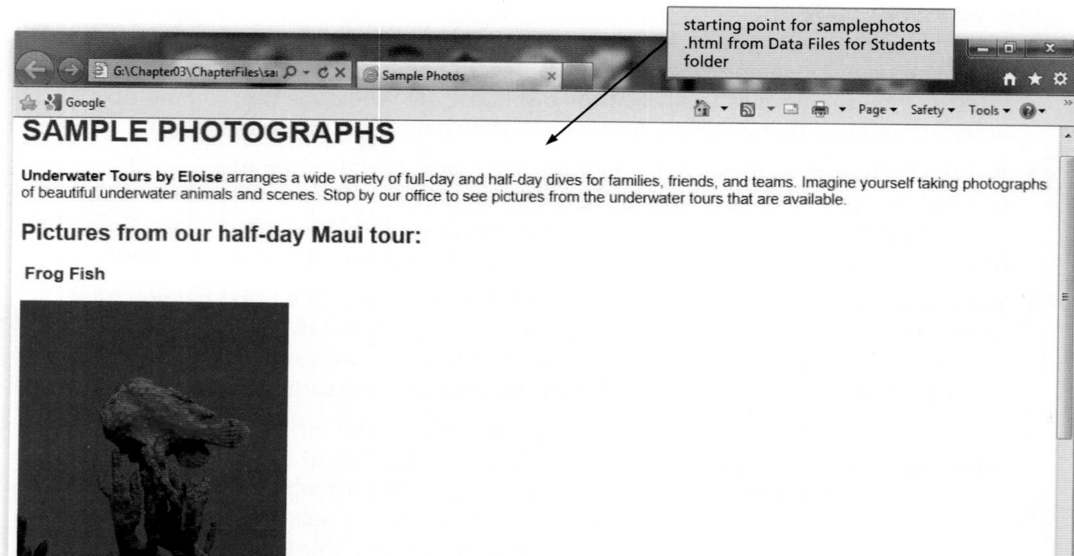

starting point for samplephotos .html from Data Files for Students folder
G:\Chapter03\ChapterFiles\sa
Sample Photos
Google
Page ▾ Safety ▾ Tools ▾
SAMPLE PHOTOGRAPHS
Underwater Tours by Eloise arranges a wide variety of full-day and half-day dives for families, friends, and teams. Imagine yourself taking photographs of beautiful underwater animals and scenes. Stop by our office to see pictures from the underwater tours that are available.
Pictures from our half-day Maui tour:
Frog Fish
This beautiful red fish is called a Frog Fish. It is just one example of the colorful sights that you will see underwater. We find Frog Fish during our Maui dives. Instructors on all tours show you how to make the best use of your equipment to
Visit our Web site or stop by our office to learn about the many exciting underwater tours that we offer. We can design a tour to meet the needs and desires of you and your group.
Colorful Lobster

Courtesy of Sabath Mullet

Figure 3–28

To Print a Web Page

Print the Web page for future reference.

1. Click the Back button on the Standard toolbar to return to the Underwater Tours by Eloise home page.
2. Click the Print button on the Command bar.
3. Once the Underwater Tours by Eloise home page is printed (Figure 3–29), click the sample photographs link to return to that Web page.

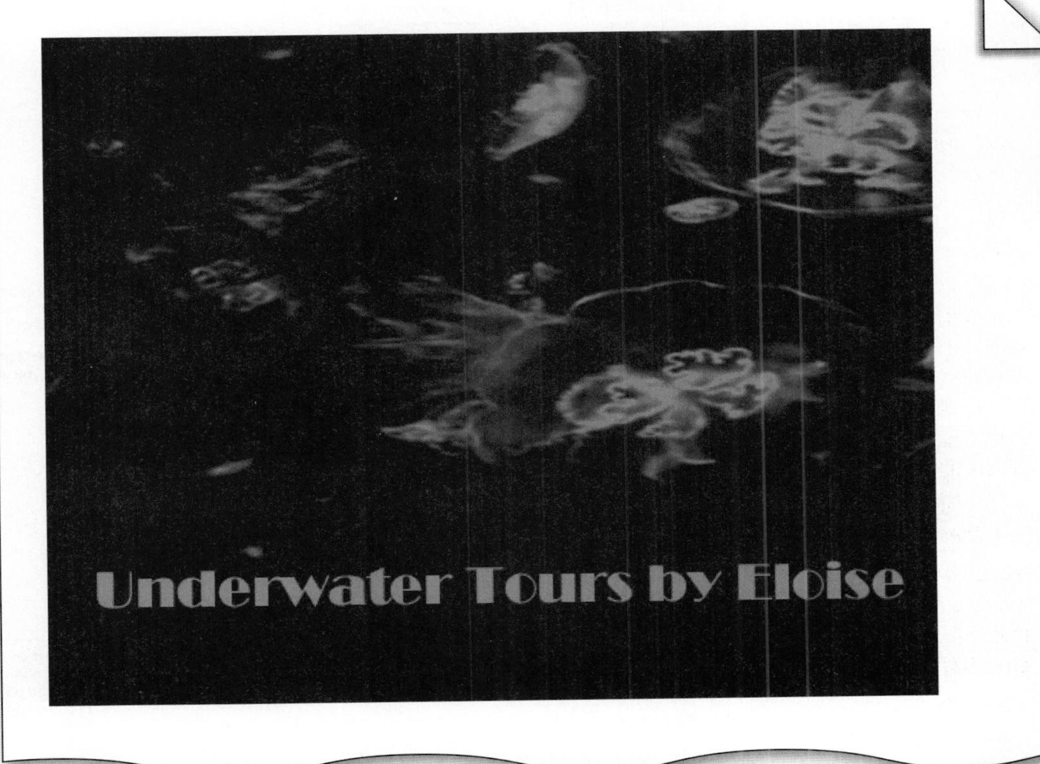

Courtesy of Sabath Mullet

Figure 3–29

Editing the Second Web Page

With the home page complete, the next step is to enhance the Sample Photographs Web page. For this part of the project, you will download an existing Web page file and edit the HTML code to create the Web page shown in Figure 3–30 on the next page. You will insert a class id in both image tags that set text to wrap around the images. You also will add two additional types of links: links within the same Web page and an image link to a Web page in the same Web site.

As you have learned, the <a> tag used to create a link must specify the page, file, or location to which it links. In the case of a link within a Web page, the <a> tag specifies a **target**, or named location, in the same file. Before adding the links and targets in the Sample Photographs Web page, you need to add an unordered (bulleted) list that uses the square list style type as the bullets. This list contains two items — Frog Fish and Colorful Lobster — and must be added to the page. The list items will serve as the links that are directed to the heading at the top of each major section of the Sample Photographs Web page. When clicked, these links will move the Web page visitor to the targets, which are named fish and lobster, respectively.

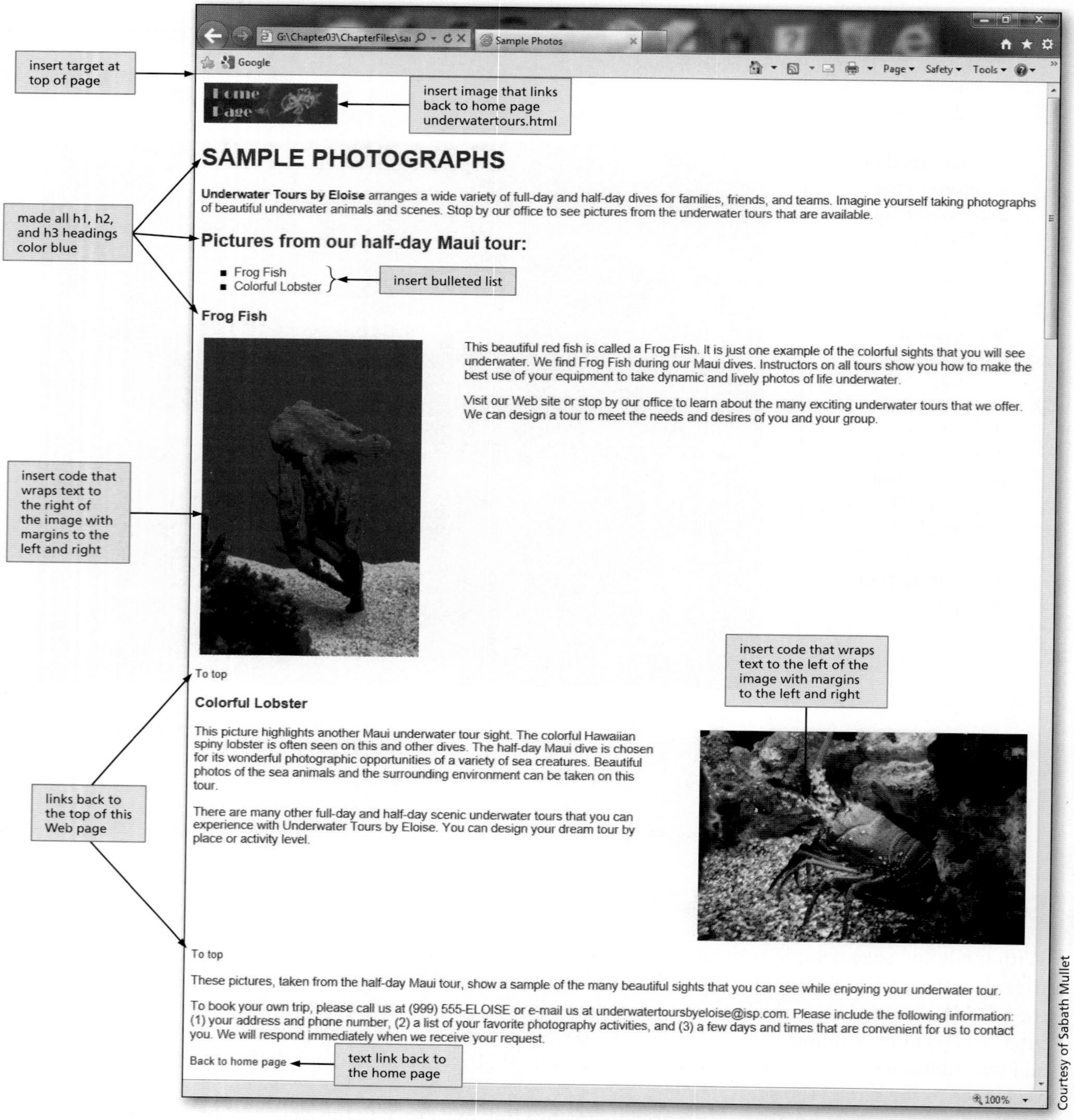

insert target at top of page

insert image that links back to home page underwatertours.html

made all h1, h2, and h3 headings color blue

insert bulleted list

insert code that wraps text to the right of the image with margins to the left and right

insert code that wraps text to the left of the image with margins to the left and right

links back to the top of this Web page

text link back to the home page

SAMPLE PHOTOGRAPHS

Underwater Tours by Eloise arranges a wide variety of full-day and half-day dives for families, friends, and teams. Imagine yourself taking photographs of beautiful underwater animals and scenes. Stop by our office to see pictures from the underwater tours that are available.

Pictures from our half-day Maui tour:

- Frog Fish
- Colorful Lobster

Frog Fish

This beautiful red fish is called a Frog Fish. It is just one example of the colorful sights that you will see underwater. We find Frog Fish during our Maui dives. Instructors on all tours show you how to make the best use of your equipment to take dynamic and lively photos of life underwater.

Visit our Web site or stop by our office to learn about the many exciting underwater tours that we offer. We can design a tour to meet the needs and desires of you and your group.

To top

Colorful Lobster

This picture highlights another Maui underwater tour sight. The colorful Hawaiian spiny lobster is often seen on this and other dives. The half-day Maui dive is chosen for its wonderful photographic opportunities of a variety of sea creatures. Beautiful photos of the sea animals and the surrounding environment can be taken on this tour.

There are many other full-day and half-day scenic underwater tours that you can experience with Underwater Tours by Eloise. You can design your dream tour by place or activity level.

To top

These pictures, taken from the half-day Maui tour, show a sample of the many beautiful sights that you can see while enjoying your underwater tour.

To book your own trip, please call us at (999) 555-ELOISE or e-mail us at underwatertoursbyeloise@isp.com. Please include the following information: (1) your address and phone number, (2) a list of your favorite photography activities, and (3) a few days and times that are convenient for us to contact you. We will respond immediately when we receive your request.

Back to home page

Courtesy of Sabath Mullet

Figure 3–30

> **BTW**
> **Web Page Improvement**
> Web page development is an ongoing process. In Web page development, you create a Web page, view it in a browser, and then look for ways to improve the appearance of the page.

Because this Web page is so long, it is a good design practice to provide users with a quick way to move back to the top of the Web page without scrolling back. For this purpose, the Web page includes two text links named To top. These links are located just below the Frog Fish and Colorful Lobster sections. When clicked, any To top link takes the Web page visitor back to the top of the page.

To complete the Sample Photographs Web page, you will create an image link, so users can click the back to home page link to return to the Underwater Tours by Eloise home page. There is already a text link inserted at the bottom of the Web page that can be used to return to the home page. It is always important to provide a link back to the home page from subsequent Web pages. Your visitors should not have to use the Back button on the browser to return to the home page.

To Open an HTML File

The following steps illustrate how to open the samplephotos.html file in Notepad++.

1. Click the Notepad++ button on the taskbar.
2. With a USB flash drive connected to one of the computer's USB ports, click File on the menu bar and then click Open.
3. Click Computer in the navigation pane to display a list of available drives.
4. If necessary, scroll until UDISK 2.0 (G:) is displayed in the list of available drives.
5. If necessary, navigate to the USB drive (G:). Click the Chapter03 folder, and then click the ChapterFiles folder in the list of available folders.
6. Click samplephotos.html in the list of files.
7. Click the Open button in the Open dialog box to display the HTML code for the samplephotos.html Web page, as shown in Figure 3–31.

Q&A

If I open another file in Notepad++, will I lose the underwatertours.html file?

The last saved version of underwatertours.html will still be on the USB drive, even though another HTML file is open in Notepad++. Additionally, even after you open the new file in Notepad++ the other file (underwatertours.html) remains open in another tab in Notepad++. That is one of the benefits of Notepad++; you can have more than one file open at the same time.

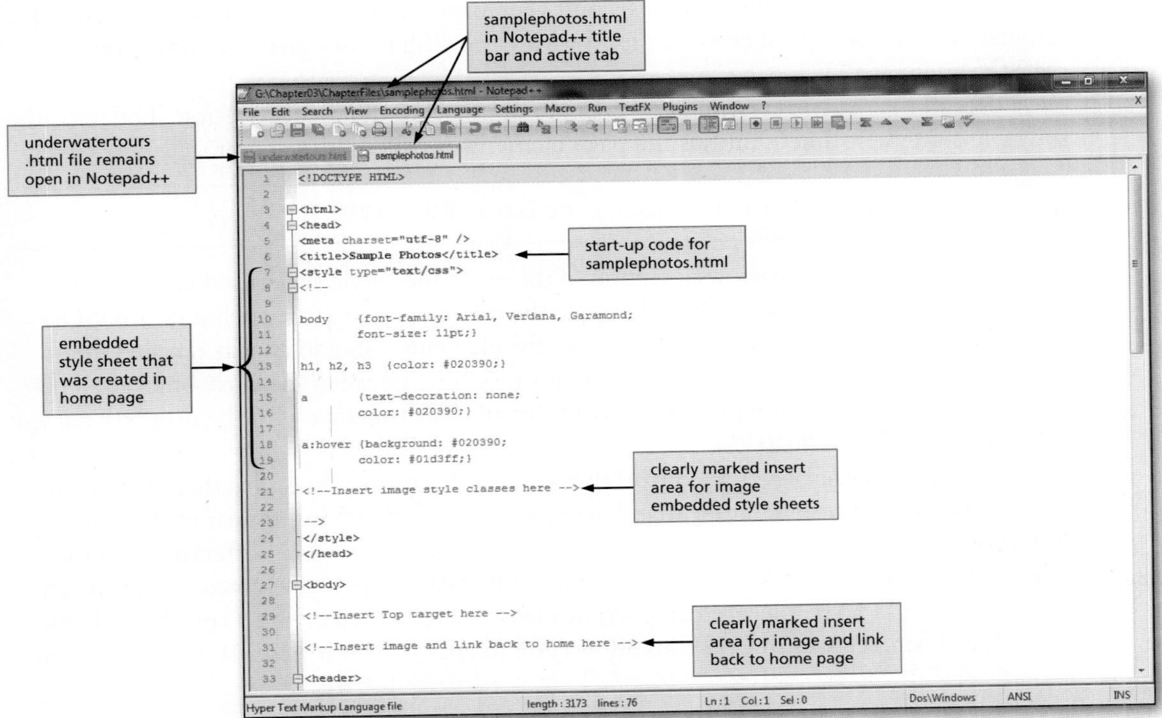

Figure 3–31

Plan Ahead

- **Determine what graphic images will be used and how to format them.** They say that a picture is worth a thousand words. In Web development, it sometimes makes your message clearer and more attractive if you use pictures. In the planning stage, you have to consider which pictures will help (and not hinder) your content. You also have to decide how to align the text relative to the pictures. Sometimes it makes sense to put the text above or below the picture. It might also be appropriate to wrap the text around the picture. You need to determine all of these specifics before you create the Web page.
- **Identify what links are needed on a long Web page.** When you have an especially long Web page (one in which the visitor has to use the PAGE DOWN key), you should provide links within the Web page for easier navigation. You need to decide where it makes sense to put page breaks. Often it is best to put a link to major topics within the Web page. Make sure that the Web page visitor can easily move to those areas by providing links close to the top of the Web page.
- **Use links back to the top of the page.** Another good technique for long Web pages is to allow visitors to link back to the top of the Web page easily from several places on the page. Providing links back to the top of a long Web page makes browsing more enjoyable.
- **Create a link back to the home page.** If possible, you should always provide a link from secondary Web pages back to the home page. Your visitors should not have to use the Back button on the browser to get back to the home page of the Web site. A common Web development practice is to use a company logo (often a smaller version) to navigate back to the home page. Again, the purpose of this image link as well as other links mentioned here is to make your Web site easy to navigate.

Working with Classes in Style Statements

Notice that the samplephotos.html file contains the same embedded style sheet that you created in the underwatertours.html file earlier in this chapter. For the second Web page, you will add one additional element (img) to the embedded style sheet. In order to utilize the image element as needed on the second Web page (samplephotos.html), you need to understand the concept of classes as used with CSS. CSS classes give you more control over the style on a Web page.

Recall that a style statement is made up of a selector and a declaration. The part of the style statement that identifies the page elements is called the selector.

```
a     {text-decoration: none; color: #020390;}
```

The example above shows a section of the embedded style sheet used in the samplephotos.html Web page. The selector in the example is the a (the anchor or link). The part of the style statement that identifies how the element(s) should appear is called the declaration. In this example, the declaration is everything between the curly brackets. This includes the text-decoration property and a value of none together with the property named color and the value of #030290.

There is another level of control that you can have over the styles that display on a Web page. For example, rather than having all paragraphs of text appear in the same style, you might want the style of the first paragraph on a page to be different from the other paragraphs of text. To gain more control for these purposes, you can define specific elements of an HTML file as a category, or **class**. You can then create a specific style for each class. Using classes in CSS thus allows you to apply styles to HTML tags selectively.

Using a class, for example, you could apply one style to a beginning paragraph and a different style to a closing paragraph on the same Web page.

Defining and using classes in CSS is a two-step process. First, any elements that belong to the class are marked by adding the tag:

```
class="classname"
```

where *classname* is the identifier or name of the class.

Any word can be used as a class name, as long as it does not contain spaces. In general, however, you should use descriptive names that illustrate the purpose of a class (for example, beginning, legallanguage, or copyrighttext), rather than names that describe the appearance of the class (for example, bluetext, largeritalic, or boldsmallarial). Using names that describe the purpose makes the code easier to read and more flexible. For this chapter, you will use the class names align-left and align-right in the img element. This immediately tells someone reviewing the code that the styles defined by those classes are used to align images either left or right.

After you have named the classes, you can use the class names in a selector and define a specific style for the class. For example, within the <style> and comment tags in an embedded or internal style sheet, you enter a style statement in the format:

```
p.beginning {color: red;
             font-size: 20pt;}
```

where the p indicates that the class applies to a specific category of the paragraph tag and beginning is the class name. The tag and the class name are separated by a period. Together, the tag and the class name make up the selector for the style statement. The declaration then lists the property-value statements that should be applied to elements in the class.

For instance, if you want to display the beginning paragraph text in a 20-point red font, you would add a style statement like the one shown in the sample code in Figure 3–32 on the next page and then use the tag, <p class="beginning">, to apply the style defined by the declaration associated with the p.beginning selector. If the paragraph <p> tag is used without the class name, the paragraph appears in the default format or other format as defined by a style. To use this class name in an HTML tag, you would type:

```
<p class="beginning">
```

as the code.

In addition to the style for the beginning paragraphs, Figure 3–32a shows an example of HTML code with classes defined for and applied to the middle and end paragraphs. Figure 3–32b shows how the resulting Web page appears in the browser.

You can add as many classes to your Web pages as you need. This is a very useful Web development technique that allows flexibility and variety in a Web page. One drawback is that classes can be defined for use only in embedded or external style sheets. Because the purpose of using classes is to format a group of elements, not individual elements, classes do not work in inline styles.

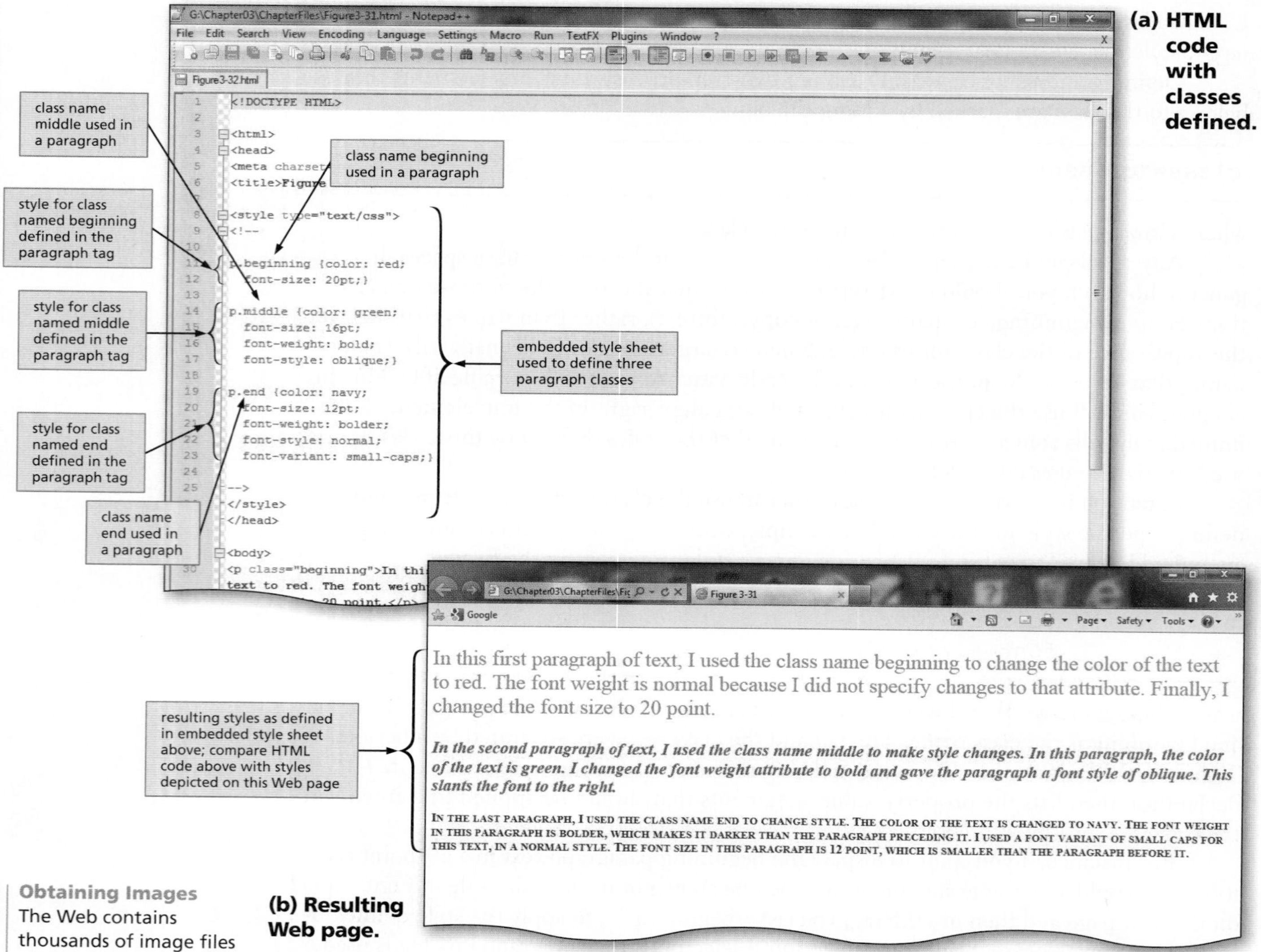

G:\Chapter03\ChapterFiles\Figure3-31.html - Notepad++

File Edit Search View Encoding Language Settings Macro Run TextFX Plugins Window ?

Figure3-32.html

```
<!DOCTYPE HTML>

<html>
<head>
<meta charset
<title>Figure

<style type="text/css">
<!--

p.beginning {color: red;
  font-size: 20pt;}

p.middle {color: green;
  font-size: 16pt;
  font-weight: bold;
  font-style: oblique;}

p.end {color: navy;
  font-size: 12pt;
  font-weight: bolder;
  font-style: normal;
  font-variant: small-caps;}

-->
</style>
</head>

<body>
<p class="beginning">In thi
text to red. The font weigh
20 point.</p>
```

class name middle used in a paragraph

class name beginning used in a paragraph

style for class named beginning defined in the paragraph tag

style for class named middle defined in the paragraph tag

embedded style sheet used to define three paragraph classes

style for class named end defined in the paragraph tag

class name end used in a paragraph

(a) HTML code with classes defined.

G:\Chapter03\ChapterFiles\Fic Figure 3-31

Google

Page ▾ Safety ▾ Tools ▾

In this first paragraph of text, I used the class name beginning to change the color of the text to red. The font weight is normal because I did not specify changes to that attribute. Finally, I changed the font size to 20 point.

In the second paragraph of text, I used the class name middle to make style changes. In this paragraph, the color of the text is green. I changed the font weight attribute to bold and gave the paragraph a font style of oblique. This slants the font to the right.

IN THE LAST PARAGRAPH, I USED THE CLASS NAME END TO CHANGE STYLE. THE COLOR OF THE TEXT IS CHANGED TO NAVY. THE FONT WEIGHT IN THIS PARAGRAPH IS BOLDER, WHICH MAKES IT DARKER THAN THE PARAGRAPH PRECEDING IT. I USED A FONT VARIANT OF SMALL CAPS FOR THIS TEXT, IN A NORMAL STYLE. THE FONT SIZE IN THIS PARAGRAPH IS 12 POINT, WHICH IS SMALLER THAN THE PARAGRAPH BEFORE IT.

resulting styles as defined in embedded style sheet above; compare HTML code above with styles depicted on this Web page

(b) Resulting Web page.

Figure 3–32

> **BTW**
> **Obtaining Images**
> The Web contains thousands of image files that can be downloaded for free and used for noncommercial purposes. Search for "free images" to find images. If you find a graphic you want to use, right-click the image, click Save picture as on the shortcut menu, and then save the image to your computer. Many applications come with clip art that can be used on Web pages. Other types of digital images, such as images scanned by a scanner or pictures taken with a digital camera, can also be included on a Web page. You can also create images using a paint or image-editing program. Regardless of where you get the images, always follow copyright rules and regulations.

Adding an Image with Wrapped Text

As shown in Appendix A, the <img> tag has many attributes, including attributes to specify height, width, and alternative text.

Alignment is also a key consideration when inserting an image. Alignment can give an image and the surrounding text completely different looks. Figure 3–33 shows two images, the first of which is left-aligned and wraps any text to the right of the image. In this chapter, you use an embedded style sheet to align (float) the image to the left or right and wrap the text to the right or left of the positioned image. You will also add some space (margins) around the image so that it is separated from the text. To accomplish these tasks, you use the float and margin properties.

The float property indicates in which direction (in this case left and right) to display (or float) an element being inserted on a Web page. **Floating** an element like an image allows the element to move to the side indicated in the float statement. As a result of that repositioning (floating), the other elements, like text, are moved up and allowed to wrap next to the floated element. When you first open the samplephotos.html file in Internet Explorer (Figure 3–28 on page HTML 122), both images are left-aligned. Notice that the text is aligned beneath each image, leaving a lot of white space to the right of the images. The text does not surround the images in Figure 3–28, as it does in Figure 3–30 on page HTML 124. You achieve this text wrap by applying the float property to the image. In addition to floating the element, you should also provide some space around the image. The margin-left and margin-right properties indicate how many pixels of space to put around each element. In this case, you will have five pixels of space around the right and left of each image. Figure 3–33 shows examples of images with margin spacing.

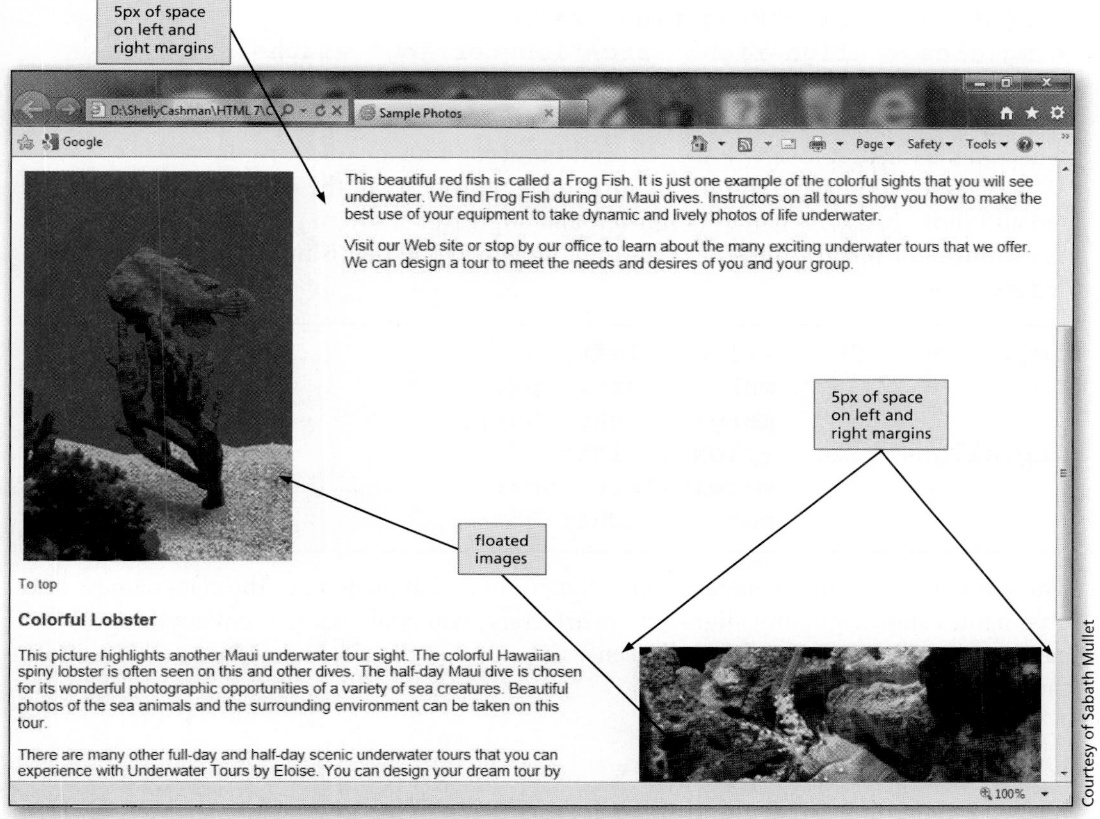

Figure 3–33 Left- and right-aligned images.

There are several ways to align text around images using styles. You can do this with an inline style (HTML code shown below) or with an embedded style sheet. The format of the HTML code to add the left- and right-aligned images with an inline style is:

```
<img style="float: left; margin-left: 5px; margin-right:
5px" src="fish.jpg" width="259" height="387" alt="Frog fish" />
<img style="float: right; margin-left: 5px; margin-right:
5px" src="lobster.jpg" width="387" height="259" alt="Lobster"
align="right" />
```

where the float property tells the browser on which side to float the image element, and the margin properties tell the browser how much space (5 pixels) to add around the image. Using an inline style is a perfectly acceptable way to float an image element, wrap the text, and add margins of space around the image, but there may be a more efficient way to do it.

If you have numerous images to float on the page, it is better to use classes in an embedded style sheet than to use inline styles.

This project uses an embedded style sheet with a two-step approach. First, you will insert the class names align-left and align-right into the image <img> tags that will use the classes. Then, you will add those class names (align-left and align-right) to an image <img> element in the embedded style sheet. To use this two-step approach, first you will add the HTML code for the left-align and right-align class names in the <img> tag itself within the Web page content:

```
<img class="align-left" src="fish.jpg" width="259"
height="387" alt="Frog fish" />
<img class="align-right" src="lobster.jpg" width="387"
height="259" alt="Lobster" />
```

which aligns the first image to the left, and the second image to the right.

Second, you have to insert the img (image) property in the embedded style sheet and add those two class names (align-left and align-right) where you define the style that you will use for images. This involves the following code that is inserted into the embedded style sheet:

```
img.align-left     {float: left;
                    margin-left: 5px;
                    margin-right: 5px;}
img.align-right    {float: right;
                    margin-left: 5px;
                    margin-right: 5px;}
```

where img is the property element and align-right and align-left are the class names. The class names align-right and align-left are arbitrary; you could name them anything. When naming classes, use names that make sense. Notice that the class names are separated from the element img with a period.

Using Thumbnail Images

BTW

Thumbnail Size

The size of a thumbnail varies depending on the clarity of the image and its purpose. Generally a 100–150 pixel height and 100–150 pixel width is an appropriate size. If you need the visitor to see more of the image even in the small size, then a larger thumbnail is fine. If a thumbnail is easily distinguishable at a very small size (100 x 100), then that size is appropriate. Also, you should never resize an image using the height and width attributes in the HTML code. You should resize the image in an editing program and save it with a new file name.

Many Web developers use thumbnail images to improve page loading time. A **thumbnail image** is a smaller version of the image itself. The thumbnail is used as a link that, when clicked, will load the full-sized image. Figure 3–34a shows an example of a thumbnail image. When the image is clicked, the browser loads the full-sized image (Figure 3–34b). Loading images can take a long time, depending on the size and the complexity of the image. Using a thumbnail image gives a visitor the opportunity to decide whether to view the full-sized image.

To create a thumbnail version of an image, the image can be resized to a smaller size in a paint or image-editing program and then saved with a different file name. The thumbnail image then is added to a Web page as an image link to the larger version of the image. The HTML code to add a thumbnail image that links to a larger image takes the form:

```
<a href="largeimage.gif"><img src="thumbnail.gif" /></a>
```

where largeimage.gif is the name of the full-sized image and thumbnail.gif is the name of the smaller version of the image. In the case of this simple thumbnail example, a visitor clicks the thumbnail image to view the larger image, but there is no "return" button or link on the full-sized image Web page for the user to return to the original Web page.

In this case, the visitor would have to use the Back button on the browser's toolbar to return to the original Web page displaying the thumbnail image. For most Web development projects, however, you always want to provide a link for visitors and not force them to use the Back button.

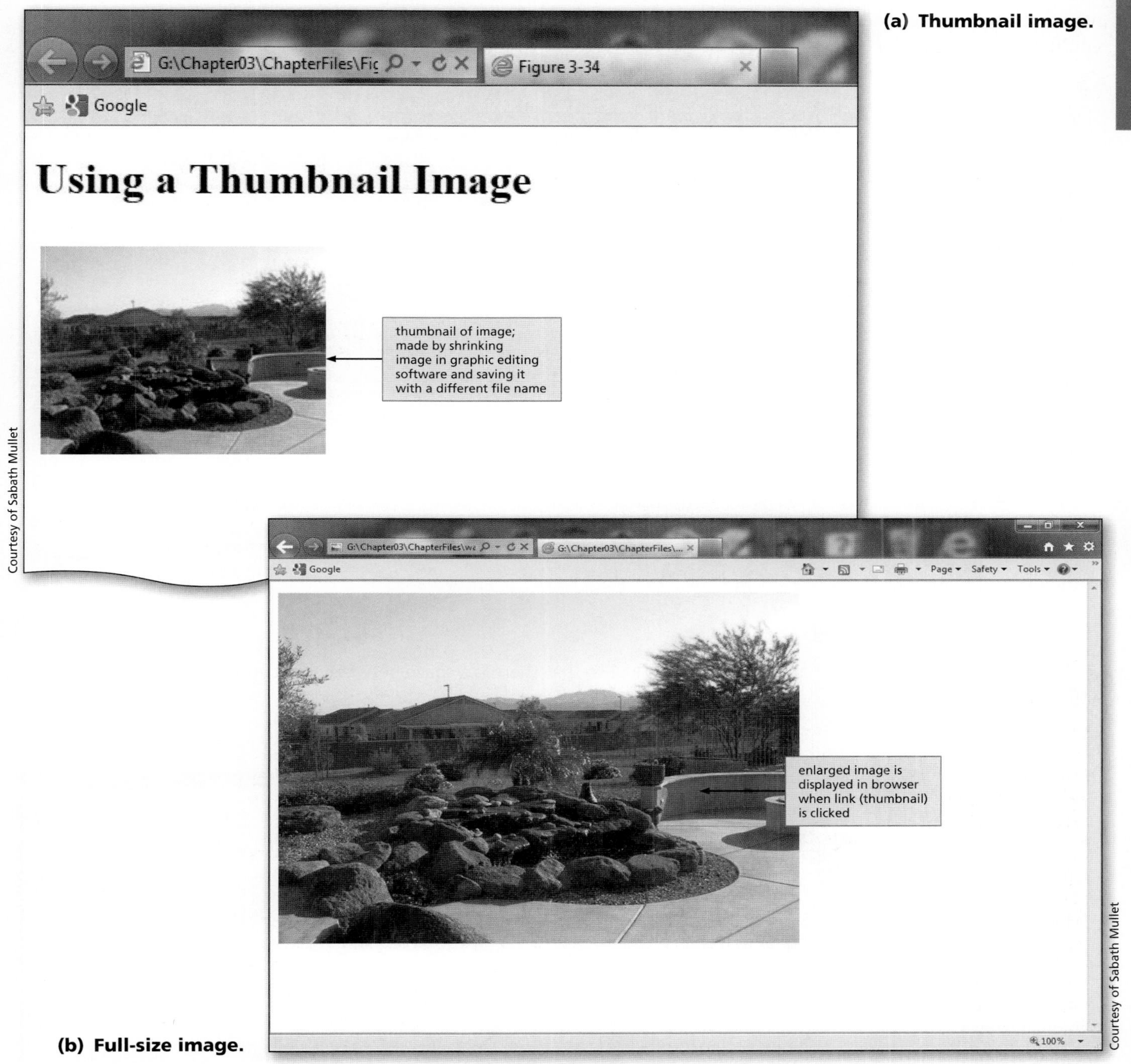

(a) Thumbnail image.

(b) Full-size image.

Figure 3–34

To Wrap Text Around Images Using CSS Classes

Now you will use an embedded style sheet to wrap the text around the two images on the samplephotos.html Web page. Remember that an embedded style sheet affects only the Web page into which it is embedded. The embedded style sheet is placed within the <head> </head> container at the top of the Web page file.

The following steps show you how to insert left- and right-aligned images with wrapped text by adding class names to the img tags and then defining the classes within the embedded style sheets. Table 3–9 shows the code you'll need to define the classes in Step 3.

- With the samplephotos.html file displayed in Notepad++, click immediately to the left of the s in src on line 45 to begin adding the class name to the first <img> tag.
- Type `class="align-left"` and press the SPACEBAR so that there is a space between what you just typed and src.
- Click immediately to the left of the s in src on line 57, to begin adding the class name to the second <img> tag.
- Type `class="align-right"` and press the SPACEBAR so that there is a space between what you just typed and src (Figure 3–35).

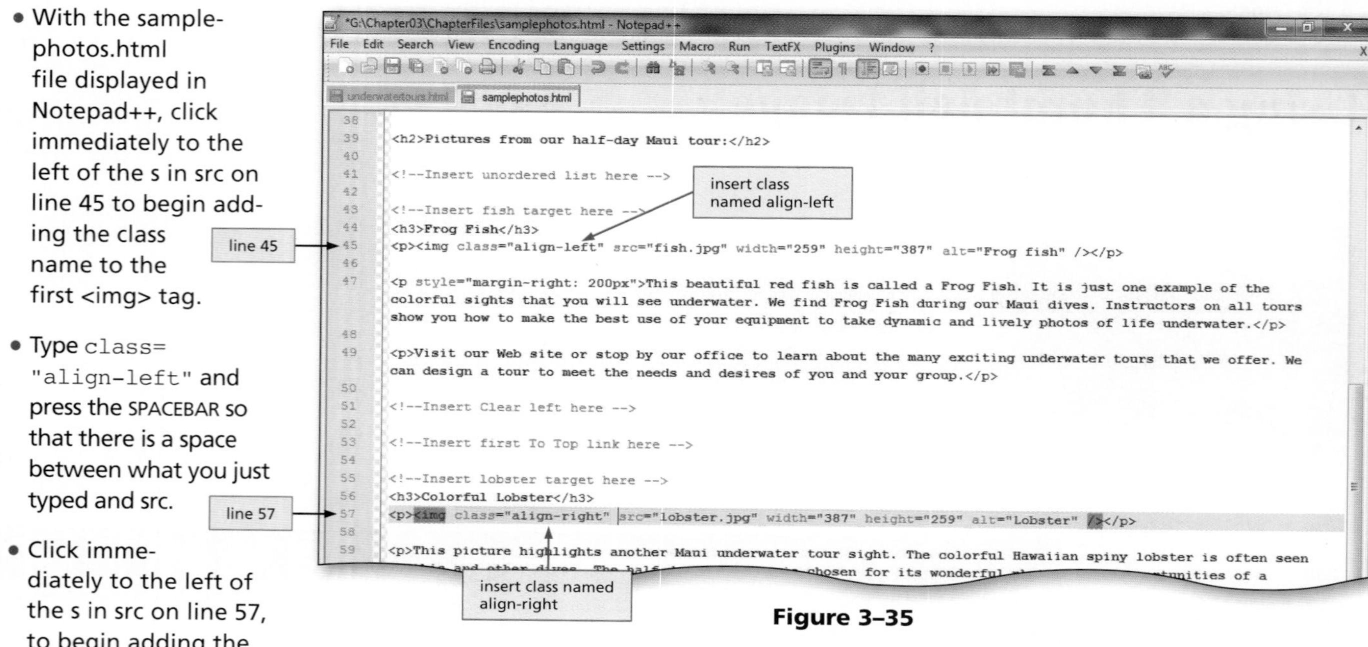

Figure 3–35

- Highlight the line <! Insert image style classes here --> on line 21, as shown in Figure 3–36, to begin adding image classes.

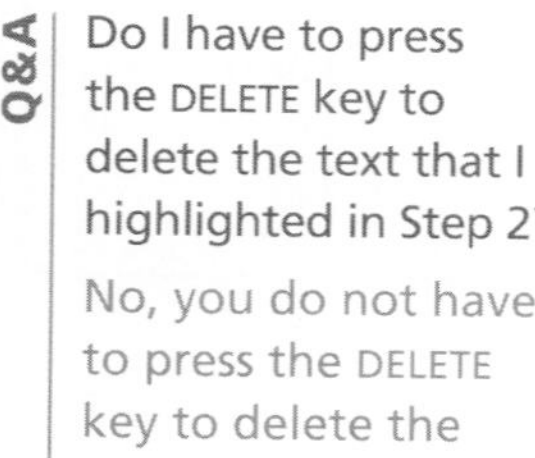

Q&A Do I have to press the DELETE key to delete the text that I highlighted in Step 2?

No, you do not have to press the DELETE key to delete the text on line 21. As long as the text is highlighted, the text is automatically deleted as soon as you start typing the HTML code in Step 3.

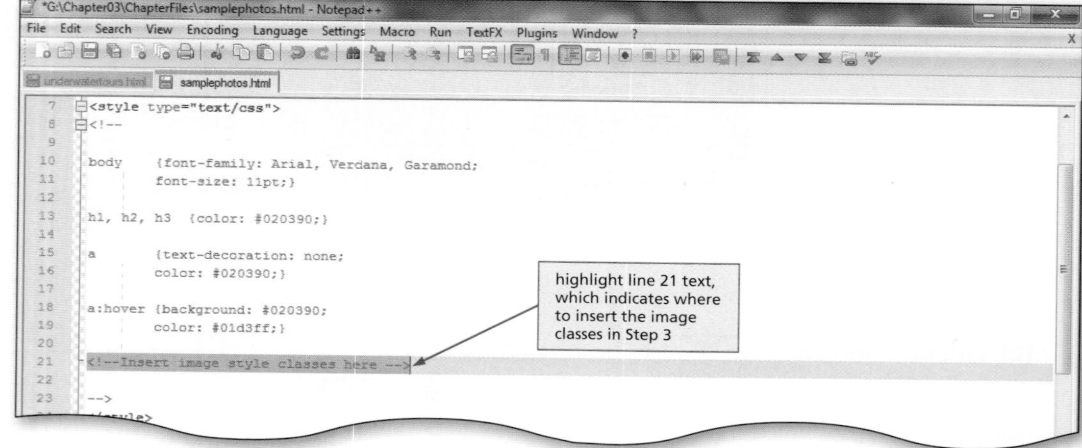

Figure 3–36

Table 3–9 CSS Code to Insert Class Definitions in Embedded Style Sheets

Line	CSS Selectors and Declarations	
21	`img.align-left`	`{float: left;`
22		`margin-left: 5px;`
23		`margin-right: 5px;}`
24		
25	`img.align-right`	`{float: right;`
26		`margin-left: 5px;`
27		`margin-right: 5px;}`

3

- Type the HTML code in Table 3–9 but do not press the ENTER key at the end of line 27. This HTML code inserts the embedded style sheets that will be used by the align-left and align-right class names inserted in the previous step. This will align the images left or right on the Web page, with text wrapped to the right or left and with five pixels of horizontal space around the image (Figure 3–37).

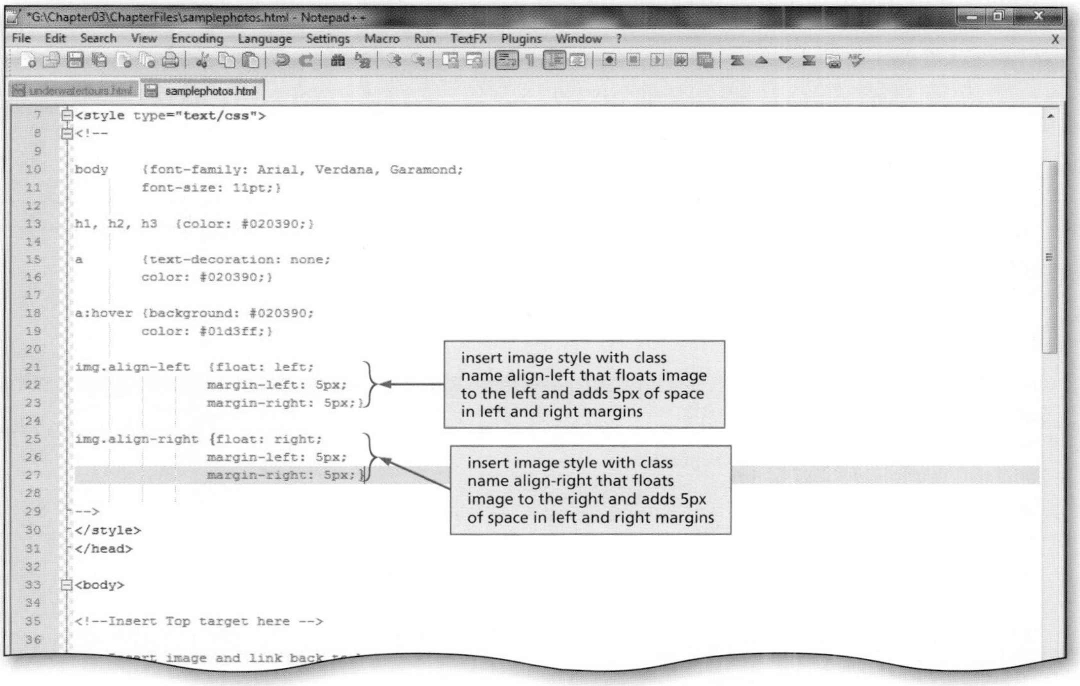

insert image style with class name align-left that floats image to the left and adds 5px of space in left and right margins

insert image style with class name align-right that floats image to the right and adds 5px of space in left and right margins

Figure 3–37

Q&A What does the float property do?

The float property allows you to position elements (in this case photographs) on the Web page.

Q&A Why do we need margin-left and margin-right properties?

These properties add five pixels (in this case) of space around the left and right sides of the image that is being inserted. If those are not entered, then the text aligns itself right next to the image. Allowing a bit of space between these two elements makes the image and text neater.

To Clear Text Wrapping

After specifying an image alignment and defining how text wraps, you must enter a break (<br />) tag to stop the text wrapping. You use the <br style="clear: left" />" and the <br style="clear: right" /> tags to reset the margins after you used code to wrap text around an image. If you did not insert this code to clear the wrapping, then all text would continue to wrap. For instance, without the <br style="clear: left" /> code inserted below, the following text (Colorful Lobster and the paragraphs beyond it) would continue just after the paragraphs about the Frog Fish. The following steps show how to enter code to clear the text wrapping.

- Highlight the line <Insert Clear left here --> on line 57, and then type `<br style="clear: left" />` as the tag (Figure 3–38).

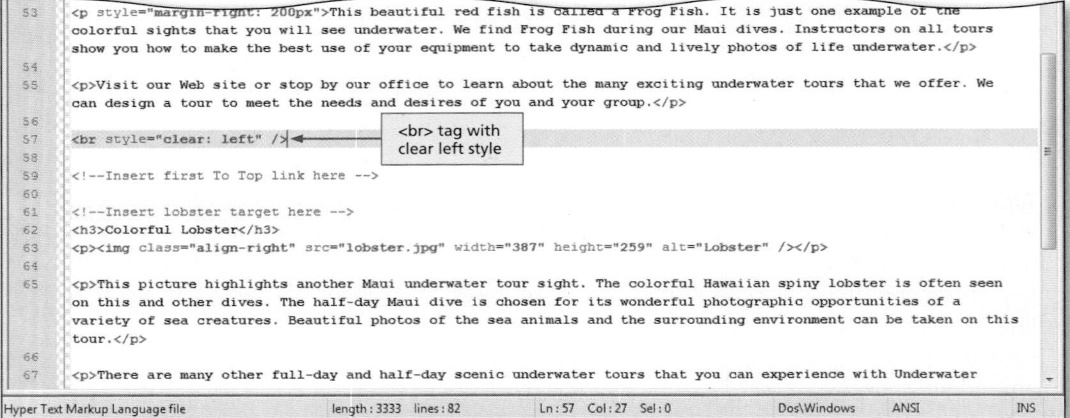

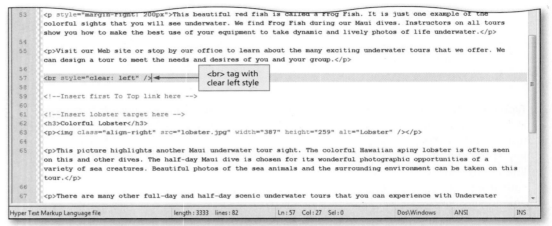

Figure 3–38

- Highlight the line <!--Insert Clear right here --> on line 69, and then type `<br style="clear: right" />` as the tag to clear the text wrapping for both left- and right-aligned images, as displayed in Figure 3–39.

Q&A What happens if you do not use the <br style="clear: direction" /> tag?

Your text following the wrapped image will not be displayed as you intended. The following text will continue to wrap beyond the end of the text and image combination.

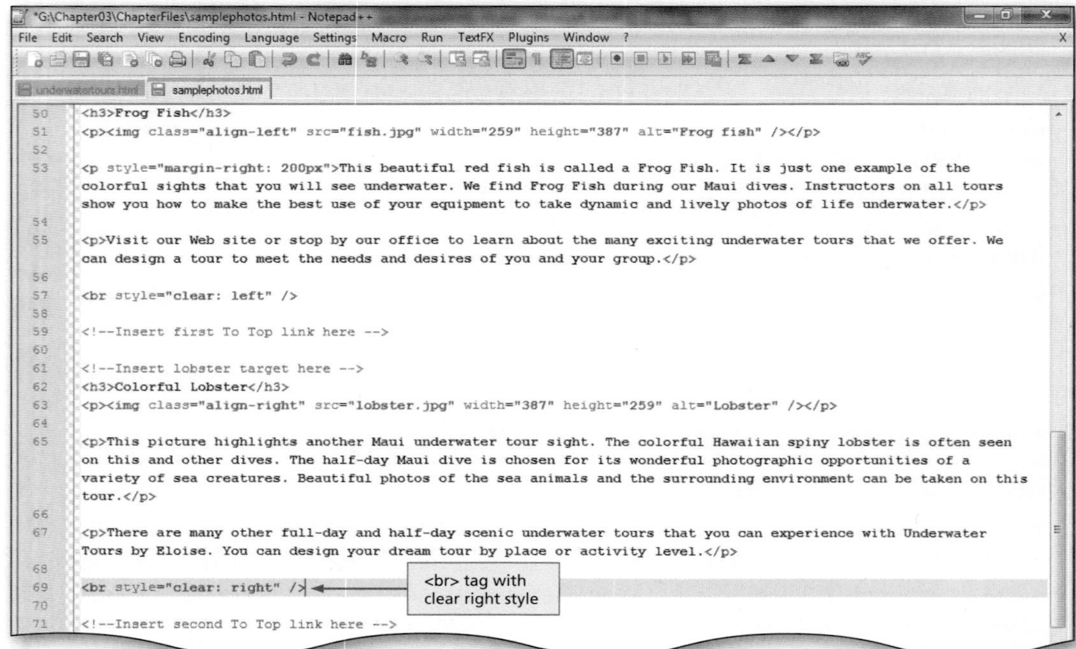

Figure 3–39

Q&A Is there one tag to clear all alignments?

Yes. The <br style="clear: both" /> tag clears all text alignments.

Adding Links Within a Web Page

The final links to be added in this project are links within the Sample Photographs Web page and a link back to the Underwater Tours by Eloise home page. Because the Sample Photographs Web page is quite long, it would be easier for visitors to have a menu or list at the top of the Web page that facilitates immediate movement to another section. Figure 3–40 shows how clicking the text link Frog Fish in the bulleted list near the top of the page links to the Frog Fish section in another part of the Web page. When the mouse pointer is moved over the words Frog Fish and is clicked, the browser repositions, or links, the page to the target named fish. Notice when the mouse hovers over the link, the link changes to a dark blue background with light blue text. That is because of the a:hover styles that are embedded on this Web page.

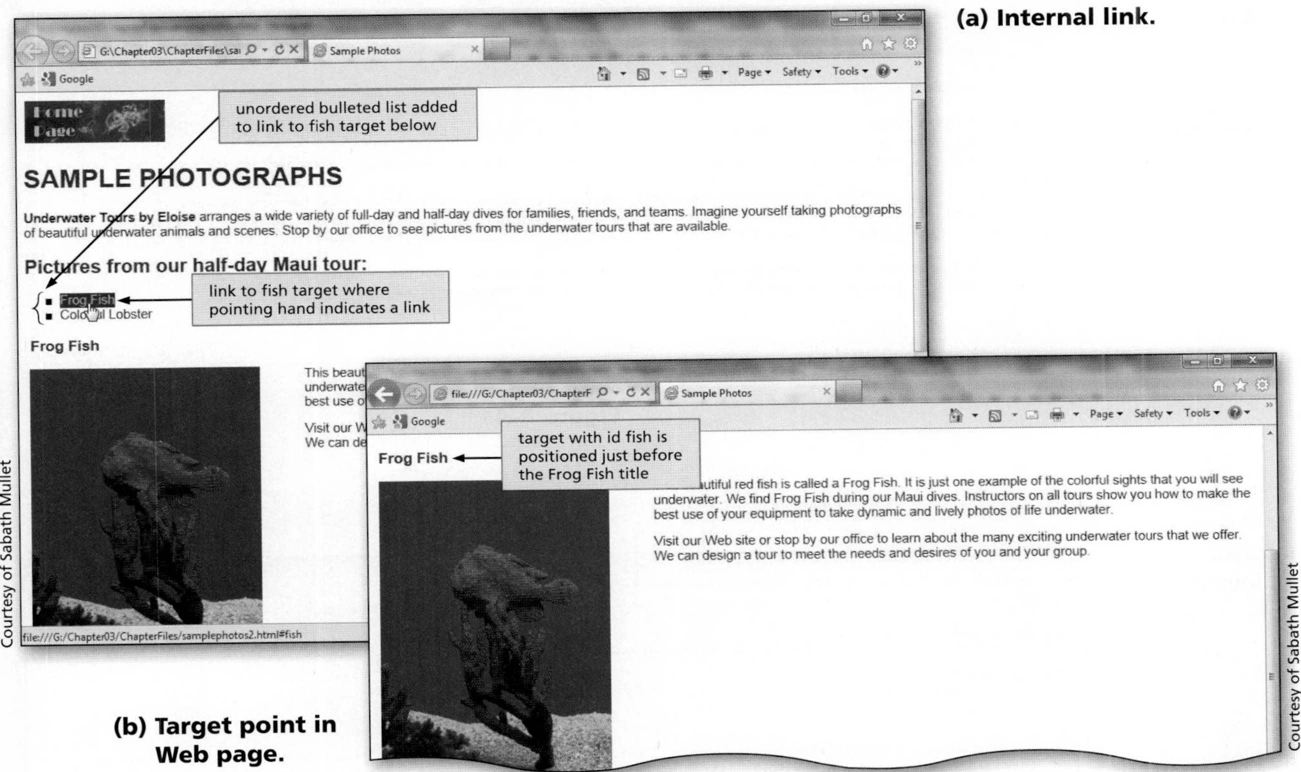

(a) Internal link.

(b) Target point in Web page.

Figure 3–40

To create links within the same Web page, the targets for the links must first be created. Link targets are created using the <a> tag with the id attribute, using the form:

```
<a id="targetname"></a>
```

where targetname is a unique name for a link target within that Web page. Notice that the tag uses the id attribute, rather than the href attribute, and that no text is included between the start <a> and end </a> tag, because the target is not intended to appear on the Web page as a clickable link. Instead, the link target is intended to mark a specific area of the Web page, to which a link can be directed.

Links to targets are created using the <a> tag with the href attribute, using the form:

```
<a href="#targetname">
```

where targetname is the name of a link target in that Web page. Notice that the tag uses the href attribute, followed by the pound sign (#) and the target name enclosed in quotation marks.

To Set Link Targets

The next step is to set link targets to the Frog Fish and Colorful Lobster sections of the Web page. The following steps show how to set the two link targets in the Sample Photographs Web page.

- Highlight the line <!-- Insert fish target here --> on line 49.
- Type `<a id="fish"></a>` to create a link target named fish (Figure 3–41).

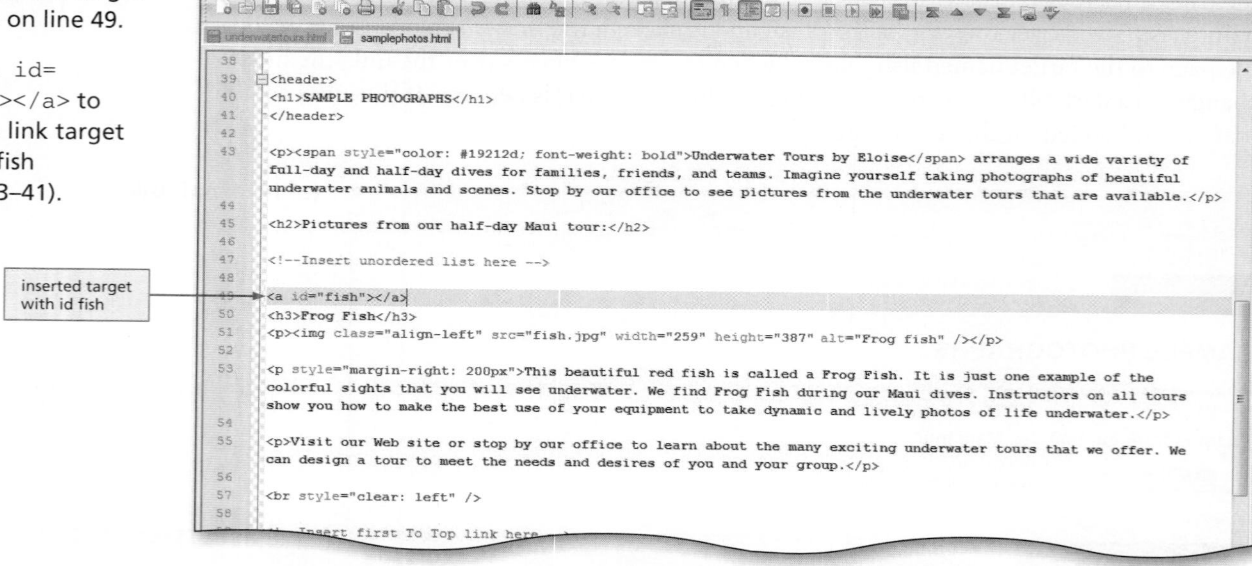

Figure 3–41

- Highlight the line <!--Insert lobster target here --> on line 61.
- Type `<a id="lobster"></a>` to create a link target named lobster (Figure 3–42).

Q&A There is nothing between the start anchor and end anchor tags for these targets. Will they work?

These targets are just placeholders, so they do not need any words or phrases; they only need a target name, as shown in the anchor tag.

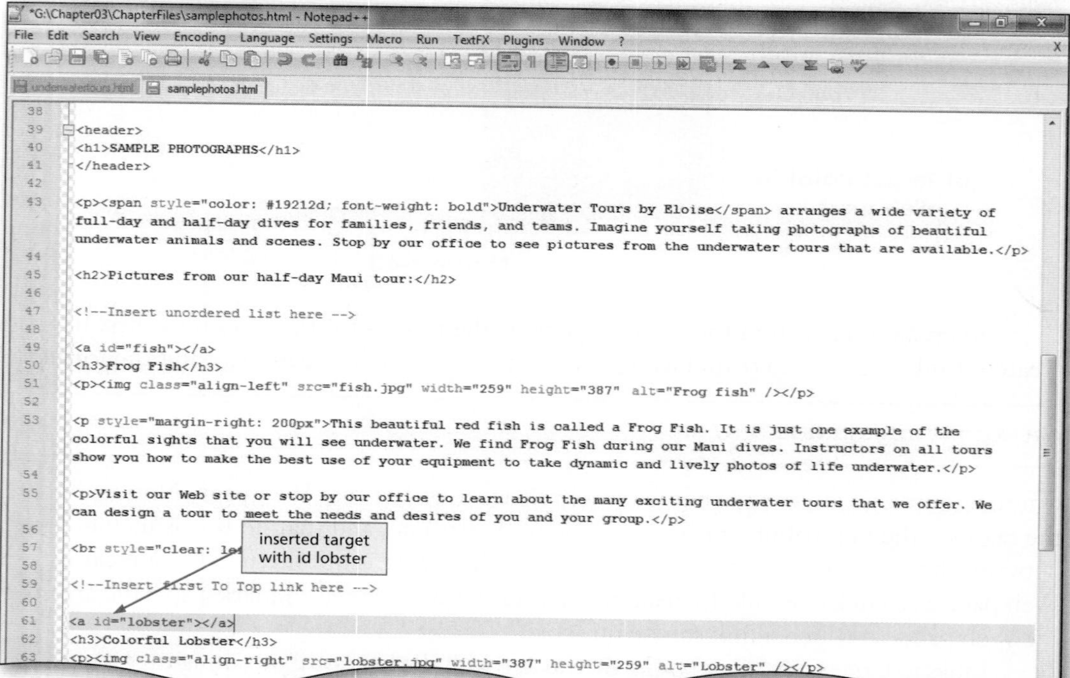

Figure 3–42

To Add Links to Link Targets Within a Web Page

The next step is to add link targets using the code shown in Table 3–10.

Table 3–10 HTML Code to Insert Bulleted List with Links to Link Targets

Line	HTML Tag and Text
47	`<ul style="list-style-type: square">`
48	`    <li><a href="#fish">Frog Fish</a></li>`
49	`    <li><a href="#lobster">Colorful Lobster</a></li>`
50	`</ul>`

The following step shows how to add the code to create an unordered (bulleted) list and then to use the list items as links to link targets within the Web page.

- Highlight the line <!--Insert unordered list here --> on line 47.
- Type the HTML code in Table 3–10 but do not press the ENTER key at the end of line 50.
  This HTML code inserts the bulleted list that provides links to the two targets (fish and lobster) inserted above.

Q&A

Do I have to use a bulleted list for the links?

No, you can use any text for the links to the targets created in the step above. The bulleted list makes the links easy to see and keeps the links in one area of the Web page.

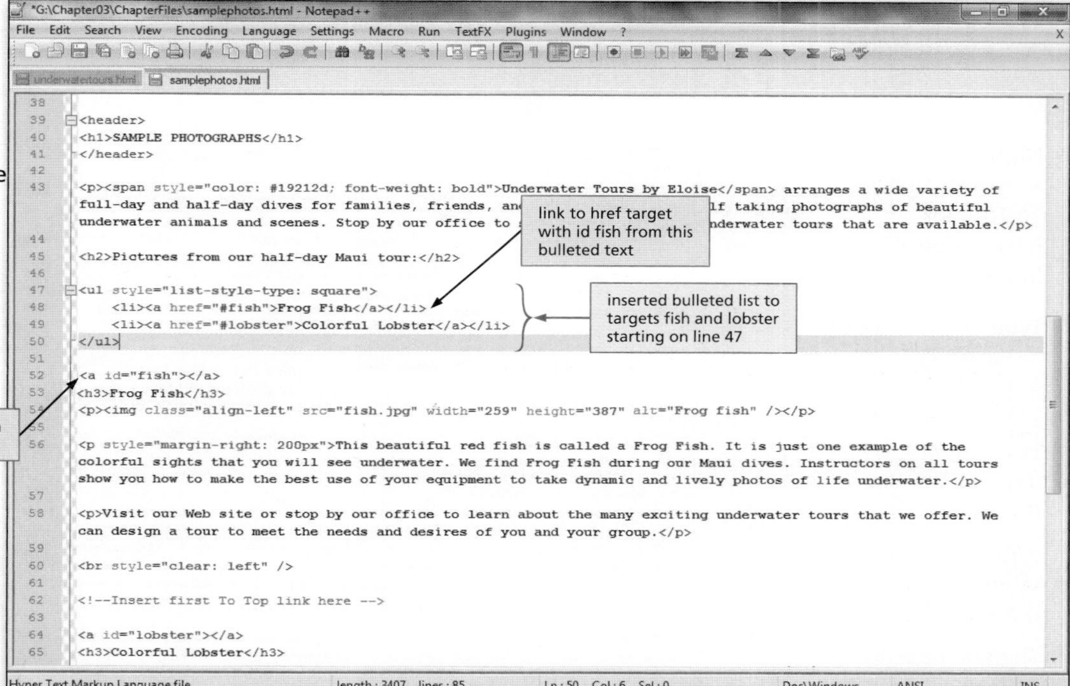

Figure 3–43

To Add Links to a Target at the Top of the Page

In this step, you add two To top links to provide a quick way to move back to the top of the Web page. To make these links, you first set the target at the top of the page, and then create the links to that target. You will also use an inline style to make the link text smaller than the regular font-size. The following steps illustrate how to add links to a target at the top of the page.

- Highlight the line <!--Insert Top target here --> on line 35.
- Type `<a id="top"></a>` as the tag that will create a target at the top of the Web page named top (Figure 3–44).

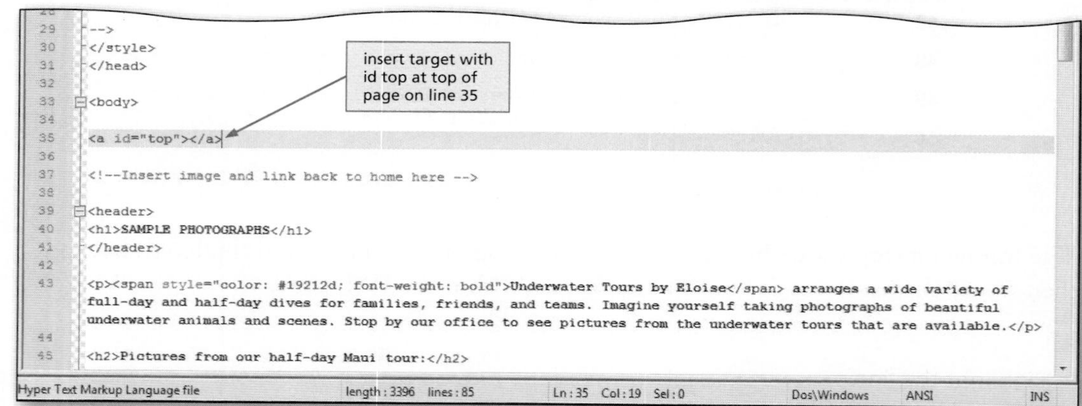

Figure 3–44

2

- Highlight the line <!--Insert first To Top link here --> on line 62.
- Type `<p><a href="#top"><span style="font-size: small">To top</span></a></p>` as the tag (Figure 3–45).

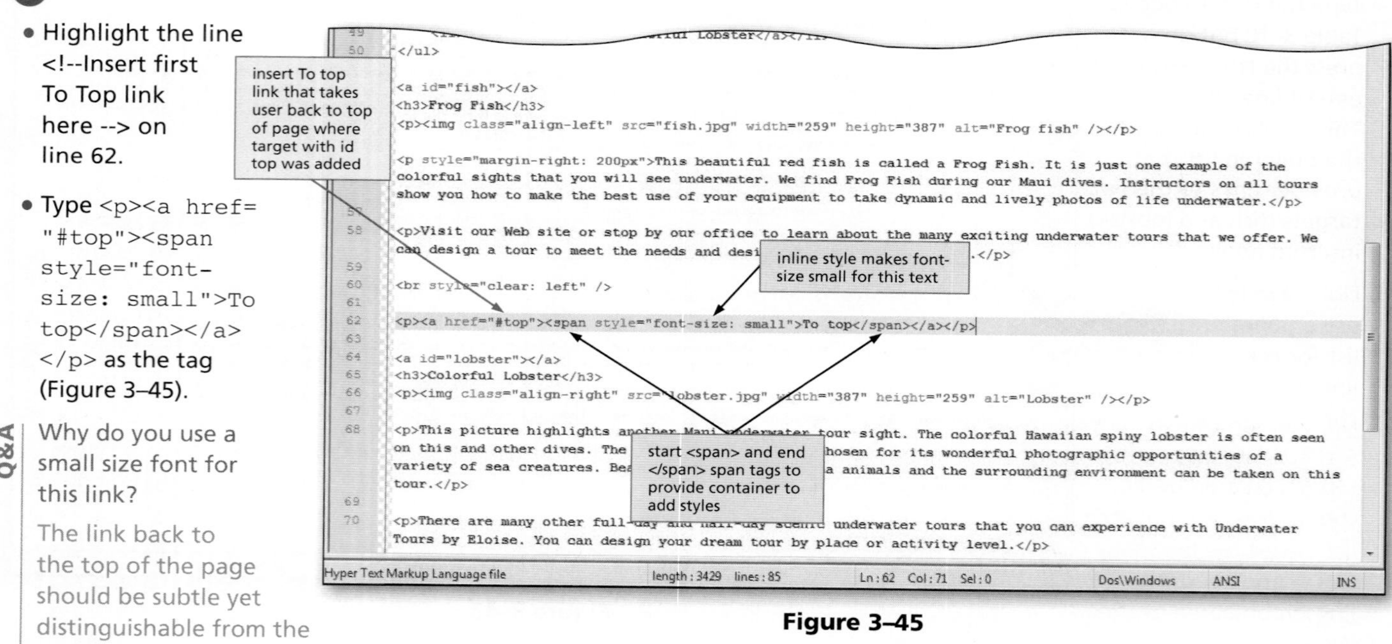

Figure 3–45

Q&A

Why do you use a small size font for this link?

The link back to the top of the page should be subtle yet distinguishable from the other text on the page. Notice that the text link at the very bottom of the Web page to return to the home page is the same small size.

To Copy and Paste HTML Code

The copy and paste feature can be very useful for entering the same code in different places. The following step shows how to copy and paste the link code to another line in the HTML code.

- Highlight the HTML code `<p><a href="#top"><span style="font-size: small">To top</span></a></p>` on line 62.
- Click Edit on the menu bar and then click Copy.
- Highlight the line <!--Insert second To top link here --> on line 74 to position the pointer.
- Click Edit on the menu bar and then click Paste to paste the HTML code that you copied into line 74 (Figure 3–46).

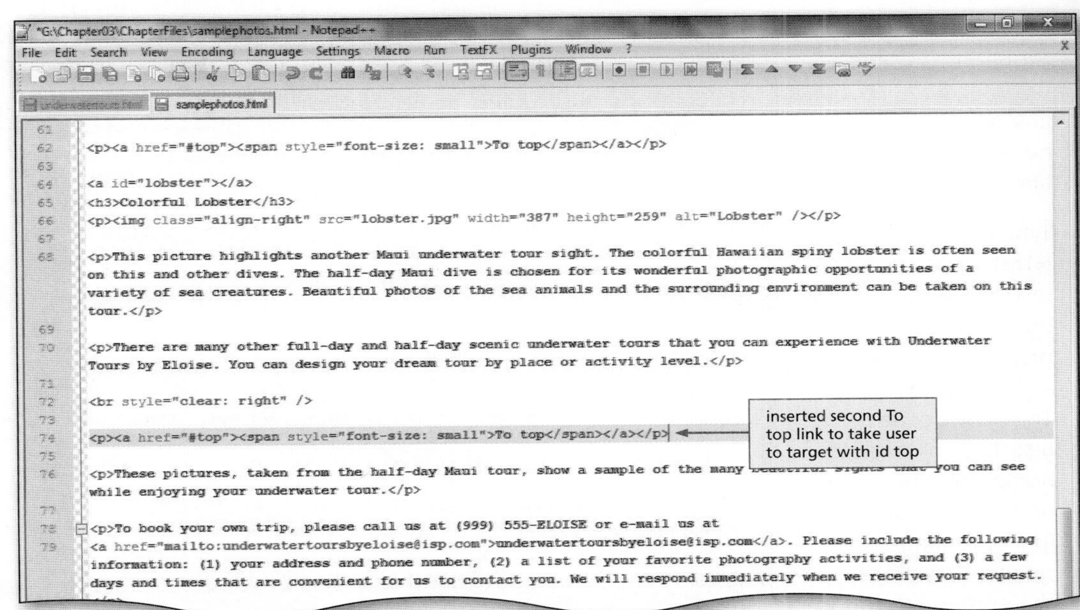
*G:\Chapter03\ChapterFiles\samplephotos.html - Notepad++
File Edit Search View Encoding Language Settings Macro Run TextFX Plugins Window ?
samplephotos.html
<a href="#top">To top</a>
<a id="lobster"></a>
<h3>Colorful Lobster</h3>
<img class="align-right" src="lobster.jpg" width="387" height="259" alt="Lobster" />
This picture highlights another Maui underwater tour sight. The colorful Hawaiian spiny lobster is often seen on this and other dives. The half-day Maui dive is chosen for its wonderful photographic opportunities of a variety of sea creatures. Beautiful photos of the sea animals and the surrounding environment can be taken on this tour.
There are many other full-day and half-day scenic underwater tours that you can experience with Underwater Tours by Eloise. You can design your dream tour by place or activity level.
<br style="clear: right" />
<a href="#top">To top</a>
inserted second To top link to take user to target with id top
These pictures, taken from the half-day Maui tour, show a sample of the many you can see while enjoying your underwater tour.
To book your own trip, please call us at (999) 555-ELOISE or e-mail us at
<a href="mailto:underwatertoursbyeloise@isp.com">underwatertoursbyeloise@isp.com</a>. Please include the following information: (1) your address and phone number, (2) a list of your favorite photography activities, and (3) a few days and times that are convenient for us to contact you. We will respond immediately when we receive your request.

Figure 3–46

To Add an Image Link to a Web Page

The last step is to add an image link from the Sample Photographs Web page back to the Underwater Tours by Eloise home page. The style for links that you set with an embedded style sheet earlier set the link background color to dark blue and the text to light blue. For an image link, however, this would not be appropriate. To override the embedded style sheet for just this one instance, you will use an inline style to set a background-color that is transparent with text-decoration of none (no underline). Remember that according to the style precedence rules, an inline style takes precedence over an embedded style sheet. These two styles in the <a> tag (background-color: transparent; text-decoration: none) together with the border-color: transparent style in the <img> tag ensure that no border appears around the image and there is no line under the link image. Remember that the <div> </div> tags create a container that defines logical divisions in your Web page. The <div> tag is similar to a paragraph tag, but it allows you to divide the page into larger sections and to define the style of whole sections within your Web page. You could define a section of your page and give that section a different style from the surrounding text. When you use the <div> </div> tags, you are able to design a layout that uses CSS properties. You use the <div> </div> tags in this case to insert the image that will be used as a link on the Web page. Table 3–11 shows the code used to insert the image link.

Table 3–11 HTML Code to Insert Image Link to Home

Line	HTML Tag and Text
37	`<div>`
38	`<a href="underwatertours.html" style="background-color: transparent; text-decoration: none">`
39	`<img style="border-color: transparent" src="underwaterlogosm.jpg" width="158" height="49" alt="Back to home page" /></a>`
40	`</div>`

The following step shows how to create an image link at the top of the Sample Photographs Web page.

- Highlight the line <!--Insert image and link back to home here --> on line 37.
- Type the HTML code in Table 3–11 but do not press the ENTER key at the end of line 40. This HTML code inserts a link back to home from the image underwaterlogosm.jpg. This image is a smaller version of the underwaterlogo.jpg image that you used on the home page (Figure 3–47).

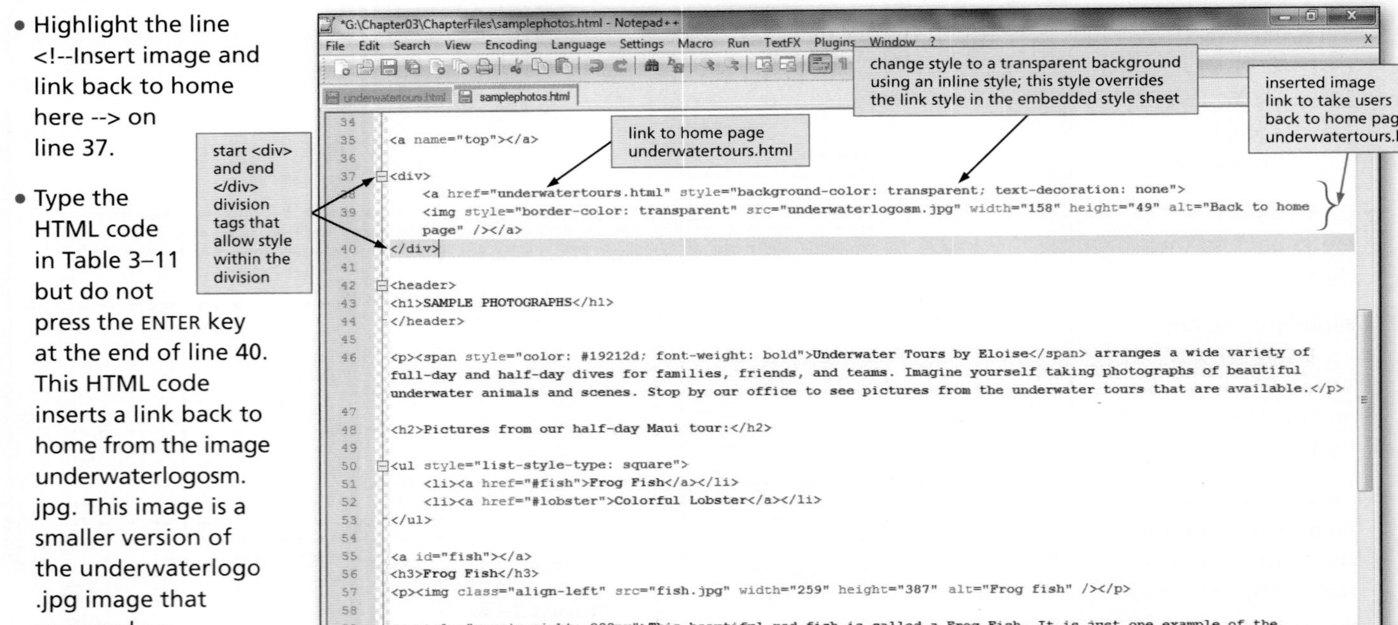

Figure 3–47

To Save, Validate, and Print the HTML File

With the HTML code for the Sample Photographs Web page complete, the HTML file should be saved, the Web page should be validated at w3.org, and a copy of the file should be printed as a reference.

1. Click File on the menu bar, and then click Save to save the HTML file as samplephotos.html.
2. Open a new browser window and go to validator.w3.org.
3. Click the Validate by File Upload tab, browse to the samplephotos.html Web page, and then click Open.
4. Click the Check button to determine if the Web page is valid. If the file is not valid, make corrections, re-save, and revalidate.
5. Click the Notepad++ button on the taskbar to display the samplephotos.html code. Click File on the menu bar, click Print, and then click the Print button in the Print dialog box to print the HTML code.

To View and Test a Web Page

With the HTML code validated and saved, you should view the Web page and test the links.

1. Click the Internet Explorer button on the taskbar to view the samplephotos.html page in your browser.

2. Click the Refresh button in the Address bar to display the changes made to the Web page, which should now look like Figure 3–1b on page HTML 89.

3. Verify that all internal links work correctly. Click the two links in the bulleted list at the top of the Web page. Then scroll down and click each To top link to check its function. Finally, verify that the image link to the home page works.

Q&A

How can I tell if internal links are working when the link and target are displayed in the same browser window?

To see movement to a target within a page, you might need to restore down and resize the browser window so that the target is not visible, then click the link.

To Print a Web Page

1. Click the Print button on the Command bar to print the Web page (Figure 3–48).

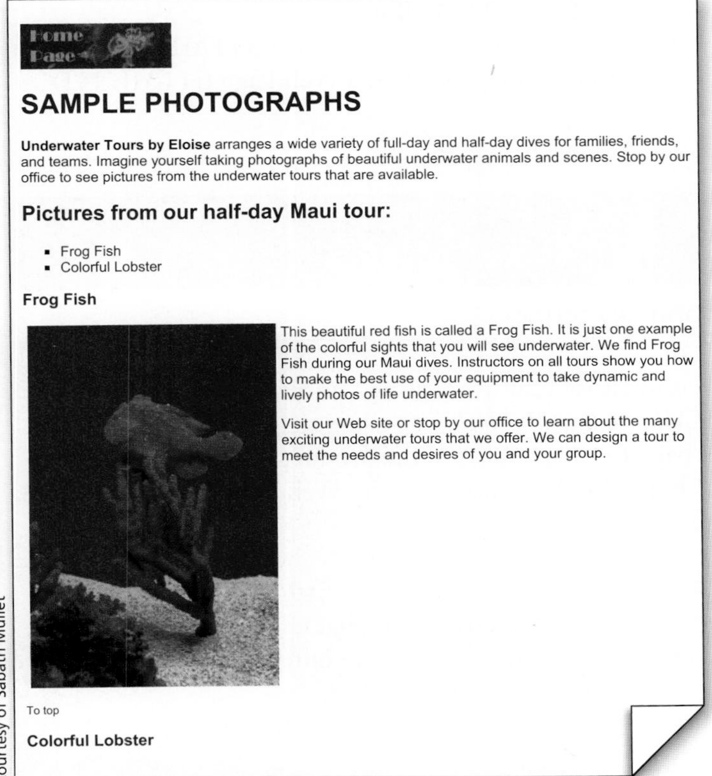

Home Page

SAMPLE PHOTOGRAPHS

Underwater Tours by Eloise arranges a wide variety of full-day and half-day dives for families, friends, and teams. Imagine yourself taking photographs of beautiful underwater animals and scenes. Stop by our office to see pictures from the underwater tours that are available.

Pictures from our half-day Maui tour:

- Frog Fish
- Colorful Lobster

Frog Fish

This beautiful red fish is called a Frog Fish. It is just one example of the colorful sights that you will see underwater. We find Frog Fish during our Maui dives. Instructors on all tours show you how to make the best use of your equipment to take dynamic and lively photos of life underwater.

Visit our Web site or stop by our office to learn about the many exciting underwater tours that we offer. We can design a tour to meet the needs and desires of you and your group.

To top

Colorful Lobster

Courtesy of Sabath Mullet

Figure 3–48

BTW

Quick Reference
For a list of HTML tags and their associated attributes, see the HTML Quick Reference (Appendix A) at the back of this book, or visit the HTML Quick Reference on the Book Companion Site Web page for this book at cengagebrain.com. For a list of CSS properties and values, see Appendix D.

To Quit Notepad++ and a Browser

1. In Notepad++, click the File menu, then Close All.
2. Click the Close button on the Notepad++ title bar.
3. Click the Close button on all open browser windows.

Chapter Summary

In this chapter, you have learned how to develop a two-page Web site with links, images, and formatted text. You learned how to use inline and embedded style sheets and style classes to format elements in each Web page. The items listed below include all the new HTML and CSS skills you have learned in this chapter.

1. Add a Banner Image (HTML 102)
2. Add a Text Link to Another Web Page Within the Same Web Site (HTML 106)
3. Add an E-mail Link (HTML 107)
4. Add a Text Link to a Web Page in Another Web Site (HTML 109)
5. Add Embedded Style Sheet Statements (HTML 117)
6. Add an Inline Style for Color (HTML 119)
7. Test Links on a Web Page (HTML 123)
8. Wrap Text Around Images Using CSS Classes (HTML 134)
9. Clear Text Wrapping (HTML 136)
10. Set Link Targets (HTML 138)
11. Add Links to Link Targets Within a Web Page (HTML 139)
12. Add Links to a Target at the Top of the Page (HTML 140)
13. Copy and Paste HTML Code (HTML 140)
14. Add an Image Link to a Web Page (HTML 141)

Learn It Online

Test your knowledge of chapter content and key terms.

Instructions: To complete the following exercises, please visit `www.cengagebrain.com`. At the CengageBrain.com home page, search for *HTML5 and CSS 7th Edition* using the search box at the top of the page. This will take you to the product page for this book. On the product page, click the Access Now button below the Study Tools heading. On the Book Companion Site Web page, select Chapter 3, and then click the link for the desired exercise.

Chapter Reinforcement TF, MC, and SA

A series of true/false, multiple choice, and short answer questions that test your knowledge of the chapter content.

Flash Cards

An interactive learning environment where you identify chapter key terms associated with displayed definitions.

Practice Test

A series of multiple choice questions that test your knowledge of chapter content and key terms.

Who Wants To Be a Computer Genius?

An interactive game that challenges your knowledge of chapter content in the style of a television quiz show.

Wheel of Terms

An interactive game that challenges your knowledge of chapter key terms in the style of the television show, *Wheel of Fortune*.

Crossword Puzzle Challenge

A crossword puzzle that challenges your knowledge of key terms presented in the chapter.

Apply Your Knowledge

Reinforce the skills and apply the concepts you learned in this chapter.

Adding Text Formatting to a Web Page Using Inline Styles

Instructions: Start Notepad++. Open the file apply3-1.html from the Chapter03\Apply folder of the Data Files for Students. See the inside back cover of this book for instructions on downloading the Data Files for Students, or contact your instructor for information about accessing the required files. The apply3-1.html file is a partially completed HTML file that you will use for this exercise. Figure 3–49 shows the Apply Your Knowledge Web page as it should be displayed in a browser after the additional HTML tags and attributes are added.

Perform the following tasks:

1. Enter G:\Chapter03\Apply\apply3-1.html as the URL to view the Web page in your browser.
2. Examine the HTML file in Notepad++ and its appearance in the browser.
3. In Notepad++, change the HTML code to make the Web page look similar to the one shown in Figure 3–49.

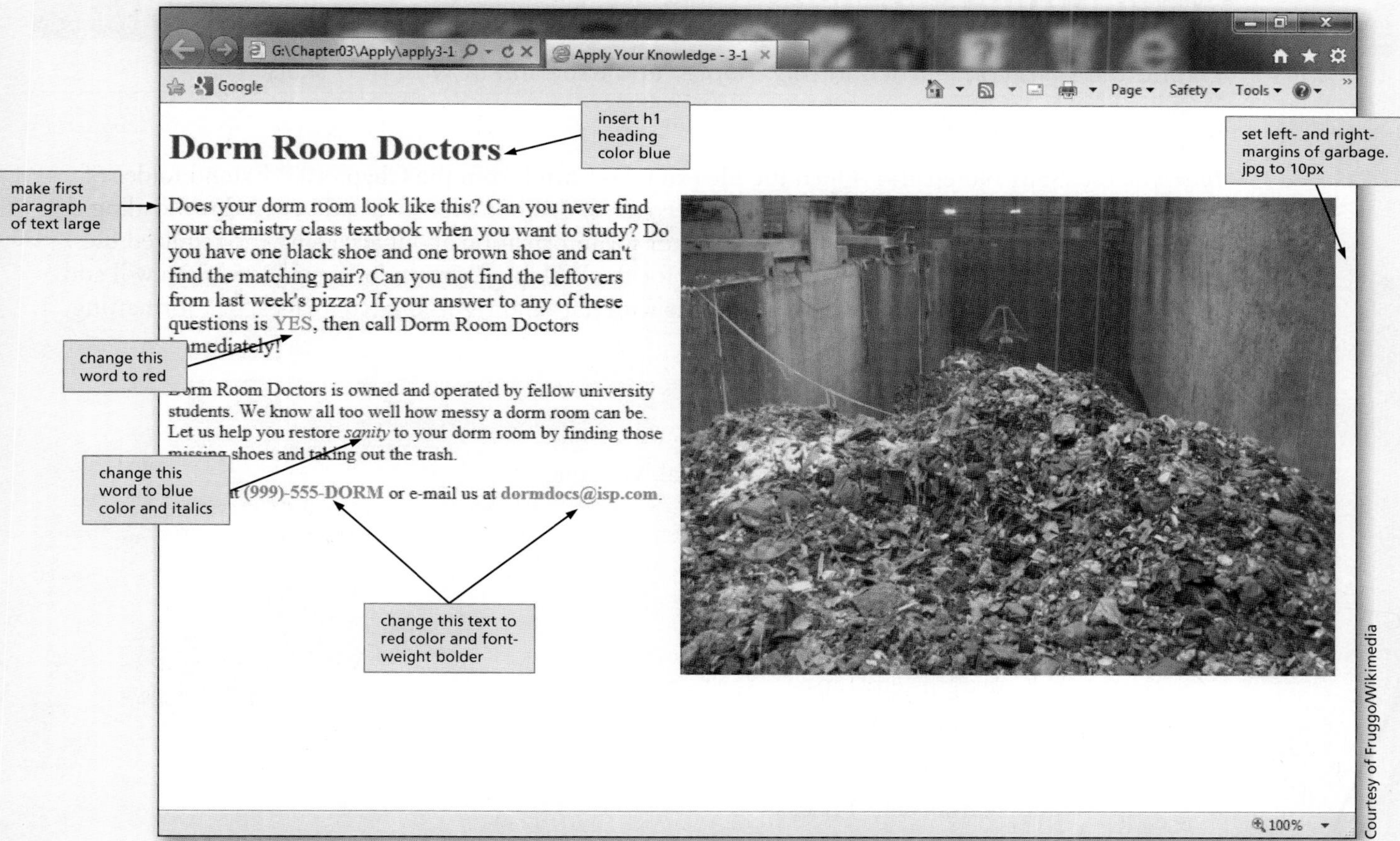

Figure 3–49

Continued >

Apply Your Knowledge *continued*

4. Use an inline style to create the h1 heading, Dorm Room Doctors, and make it blue.
5. Using the <div></div> container, right-align the image garbage.jpg (width=560, height=420). Give the image right- and left-margins of 10 pixels. (*Hint:* Make sure to use the alt attribute.)
6. Make the first paragraph a large font. Color the word YES red in that paragraph. (*Hint:* Use the <span> tag.)
7. The second paragraph should be normal font, but make the word sanity blue and italic.
8. In the third paragraph, make the phone number and e-mail address red and in a bolder font-weight.
9. Save the revised HTML file in the Chapter03\Apply folder using the file name apply3-1solution.html.
10. Validate your code.
11. Print the revised HTML file.
12. Enter G:\Chapter03\Apply\apply3-1solution.html as the URL to view the revised Web page in your browser.
13. Print the Web page.
14. Submit the revised HTML file and Web page in the format specified by your instructor.

STUDENT ASSIGNMENTS

Extend Your Knowledge

Extend the skills you learned in this chapter and experiment with new skills.

Creating Targets and Links

Instructions: Start Notepad++. Open the file extend3-1.html from the Chapter03\Extend folder of the Data Files for Students. See the inside back cover of this book for instructions on downloading the Data Files for Students, or contact your instructor for information about accessing the required files. This sample HTML file contains all of the text for the Web page shown in Figure 3–50. You will add the necessary tags to make this Web page appear with left- and right-aligned images, text formatting, and links, as shown in Figure 3–50.

Perform the following tasks:

1. Insert the following embedded styles:

```
body          {font-family: Garamond, Arial, Verdana;
               font-size: 12pt;}
h1, h2        {color: red;
               font-variant: small-caps;}
.align-right  {float: right;
               margin-left: 15px;
               margin-right: 15px;}
.align-left   {float: left;
               margin-left: 15px;
               margin-right: 15px;}
a             {text-decoration: underline;
               color: red;}
a:hover       {background: red;
               color: white;}
```

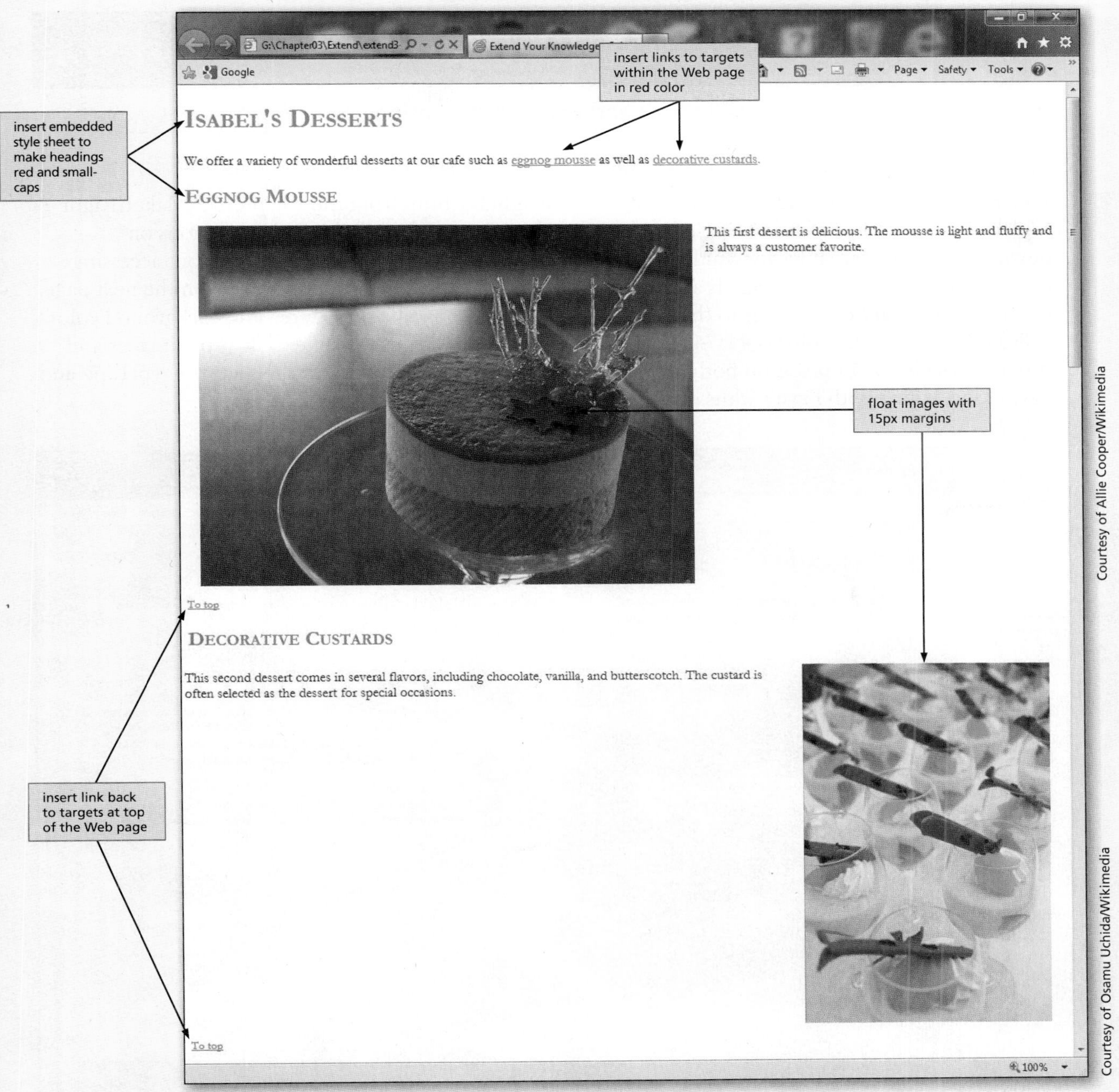

Figure 3–50

2. Make sure to use inline styles for all other styles. Add code to align the first picture on the left and the second picture on the right, with margins of 15px. (*Hint:* Remember to clear alignment for both images.)
3. Add the HTML code to create three targets (one at the top of the Web page, one near the first h2 heading, and the last near the second h2 heading). Create links from the first paragraph to the heading for each dessert. Also create two link(s) back to the top with font-size small, as shown in Figure 3–50.
4. Validate your HTML code and test all links.
5. Save the revised document as extend3-1solution.html and submit it in the format specified by your instructor.

Make It Right

Analyze a document; correct all errors and improve the design.

Correcting the Egypt Vacation Web Page

Instructions: Start Notepad++. Open the file makeitright3-1.html from the Chapter03\MakeItRight folder of the Data Files for Students. See the inside back cover of this book for instructions on downloading the Data Files for Students, or contact your instructor for information about accessing the required files. The Web page is a modified version of what you see in Figure 3–51 on the next page. Make the necessary corrections to the Web page to make it look like the figure. The background color is #e5aa64, and the h1 color is #4a7493 for this Web page. Use an inline style to float the images and provide margins of 15 pixels on both right and left sides. The Web page uses the images egypt1.jpg and egypt2.jpg, which both have widths and heights of 512 and 384.

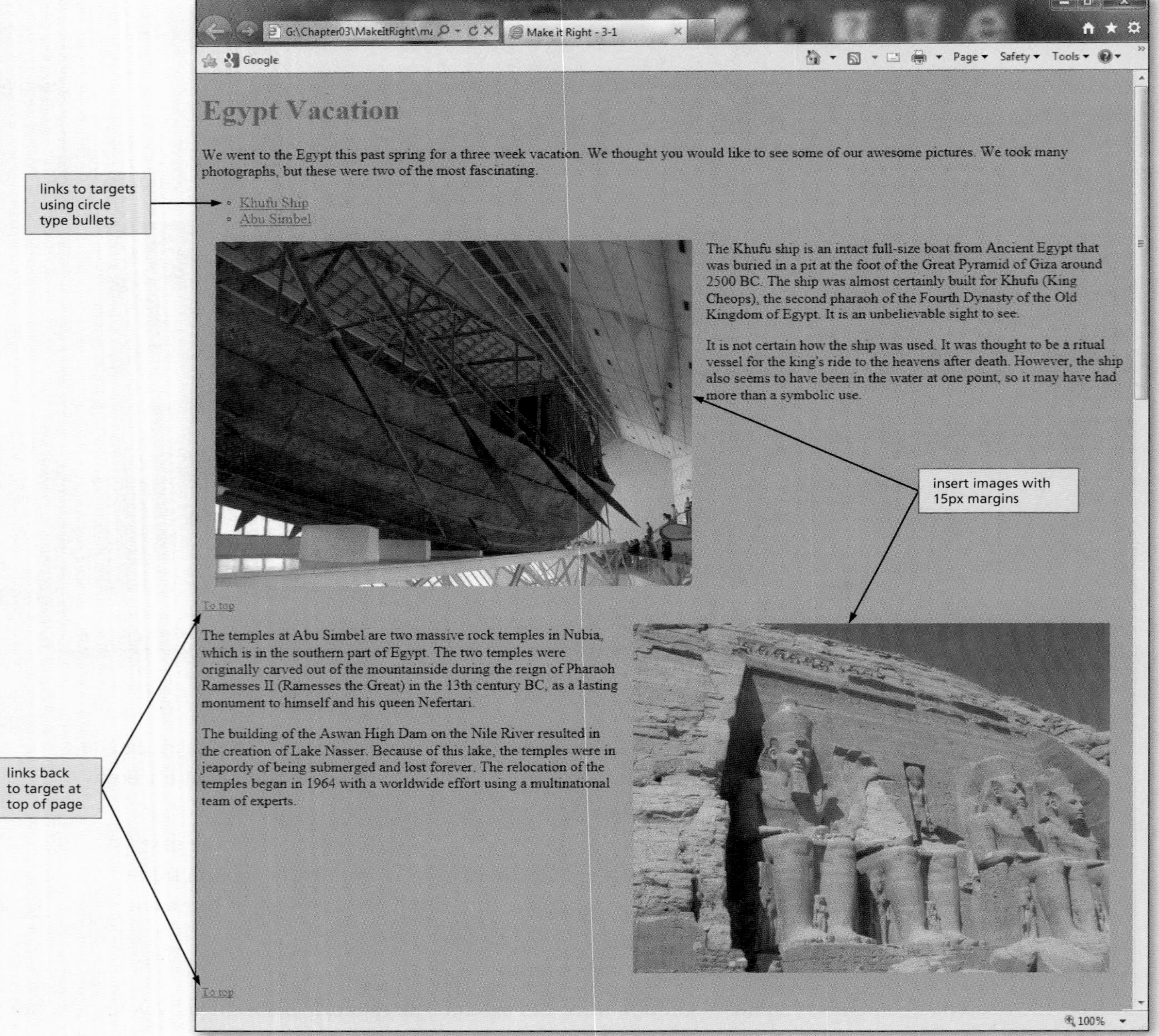

Figure 3–51

In the Lab

Lab 1: Creating a Web Page with Links

Problem: Your instructor wants you to create a Web page demonstrating your knowledge of link targets. You have been asked to create a Web page to demonstrate this technique, similar to the one shown in Figure 3–52. Use inline styles for all styles in the Web page.

Instructions: Perform the following steps:

1. Start Notepad++ and create a new HTML file with the title, Lab 3-1, in the head section.
2. Begin the body section by adding the image recycle.png and aligning it to the left. Use the margin-left and -right with values of 10 pixels.
3. Add the heading Help the Earth - Recycle. Format the heading to use the Heading 1 style, left-aligned, italic, with the font color black.
4. Add an unordered list with the three list items, as shown in Figure 3–52. These three items will be used to link to the three sections of text below them.

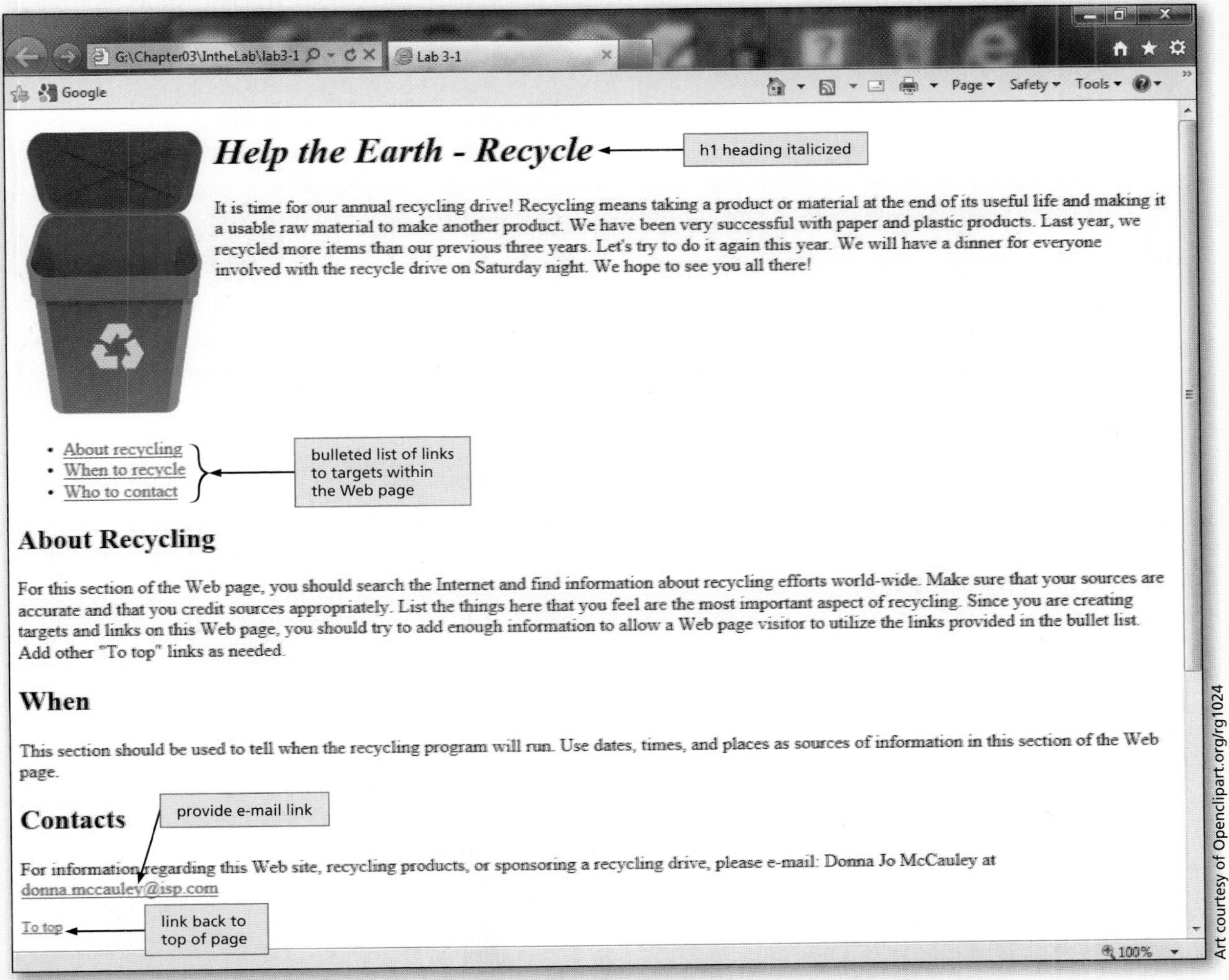

Figure 3–52

Continued >

In the Lab *continued*

5. Add a Heading 2 style heading, About Recycling, and set a link target named about. Type a paragraph of text based on your research of the topic, as shown in Figure 3–52.
6. Add a Heading 2 style heading, When, and set a link target named when. Type a paragraph based on your research of the topic, as shown in Figure 3–52.
7. Add a Heading 2 style heading, Contacts, and set a link target named contact. Type the paragraph, as shown in Figure 3–52.
8. Create a link target at the top of the page named top.
9. Create a To top link at the bottom of the page, as shown in Figure 3–52. Set the link to direct to the top target at the top of the page.
10. Create links from the bulleted list to the three targets.
11. Create an e-mail link, as shown in Figure 3–52.
12. Save the HTML file in the Chapter03\IntheLab folder using the file name lab3-1solution.html.
13. Validate the lab-3-1solution.html file.
14. Print the lab3-1solution.html file.
15. Enter the URL `G:\Chapter03\IntheLab\lab3-1solution.html` to view the Web page in your browser.
16. Print the Web page.
17. Submit the HTML file and Web page in the format specified by your instructor.

In the Lab

Lab 2: Creating a Web Page with Links

Problem: Your instructor wants you to create a Web page demonstrating your knowledge of link targets. You have been asked to create a Web page to demonstrate this technique, similar to the one shown in Figure 3–53.

Instructions: Perform the following steps:

1. Start Notepad++ and create a new HTML file with the title, Lab 3-2, in the head section.
2. Begin the body section by adding an h1 heading that is left-aligned.
3. Add the following code into an embedded style. Notice that all text links have the same background color as the h1 heading at the top of the Web page. This is because of the code that you put in the embedded style, as follows:

```
body              {font-family: Arial, Verdana, Garamond;
                  font-size: 11pt;}
h1, h2, h3        {color: #19212d;}
a                 {color: black;}
a:hover           {background: #19212d;
                  color: white;}
img.align-right   {float: right;
                  margin-left: 5px;
                  margin-right: 5px;}
img.align-left    {float: left;
                  margin-left: 5px;
                  margin-right: 5px;}
```

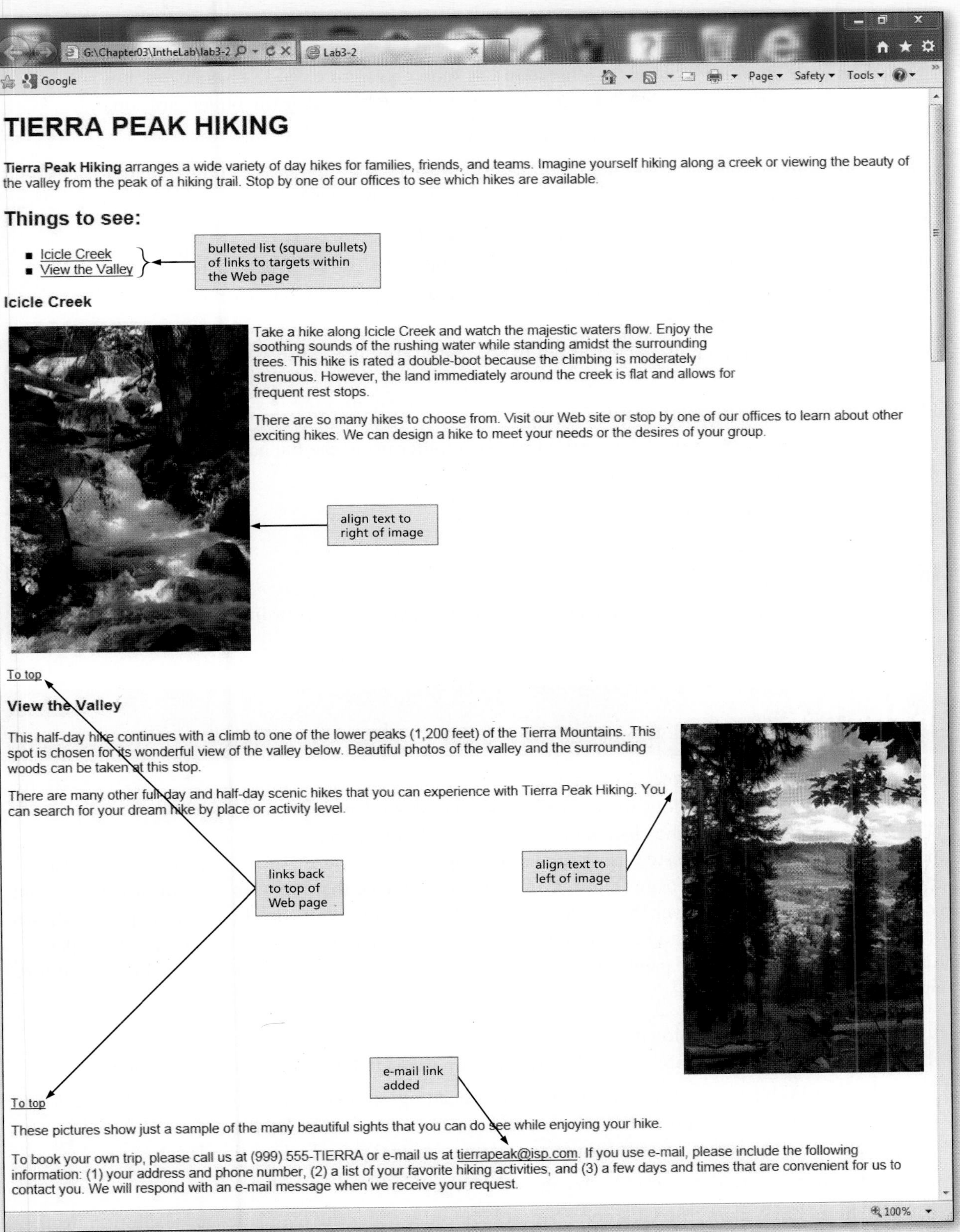

Figure 3–53

Continued >

In the Lab *continued*

4. Add an unordered list with the two list items, as shown in Figure 3–53. These two items will be used to link to the two sections of text below them. (*Hint:* Note that the bullets are square.)
5. Add one h1 heading, one h2 heading, and two h3 headings.
6. Add an inline style sheet changing the first three words of the first paragraph to be color #19212d and font-weight of bold. (*Hint:* Use the <span></span> container.)
7. Add the two images provided (creek.jpg and valley.jpg).
8. Create a link target at the top of the page named top.
9. Add two To top links, one after each section, as shown in Figure 3–53. Set the link to direct to the top target at the top of the page.
10. Create links from the bulleted list to the two targets. (*Hint:* Remember to insert a unique id for both targets.)
11. Create an e-mail link, as shown in Figure 3–53.
12. Save the HTML file in the Chapter03\IntheLab folder using the file name lab3-2solution.html.
13. Validate the lab3-2solution.html file.
14. Print the lab3-2solution.html file.
15. View the Web page in your browser.
16. Print the Web page.
17. Submit the HTML file and Web page in the format specified by your instructor.

In the Lab

Lab 3: Creating Two Linked Web Pages

Problem: Your Communications instructor has asked each student in the class to create a two-page Web site to help students in the class get to know more about the subject area in which you are majoring in school. She suggested using the basic template shown in Figures 3–54a and 3–54b as a starting point. The first Web page (Figure 3–54a) is a home page that includes basic information about your major. Really try to answer the questions listed (for example, why you chose this major), as shown on the Web page. If you can, add an image related to your chosen field somewhere on the Web page. Add a link to the second Web page. The second Web page (Figure 3–54b) includes a paragraph of text and numbered lists with links.

Instructions: Perform the following steps:

1. Start Notepad++ and create a new HTML file with the title Lab 3-3 in the head section.
2. In the first Web page, include a Heading style 1 heading, similar to the one shown in Figure 3–54a, and a short paragraph of text. Experiment and use any color for the heading (navy is shown). (*Hint:* Review the text-align: center property and value in Appendix D and online.)
3. Create a text link to the second Web page, lab3-3specifics.html.
4. Save the HTML file in the Chapter03\IntheLab folder using the file name lab3-3solution.html. Validate the lab3-3solution.html file. Print the lab3-3solution.html file.
5. Start a new HTML file with the title Lab 3-3 Specifics in the head section.

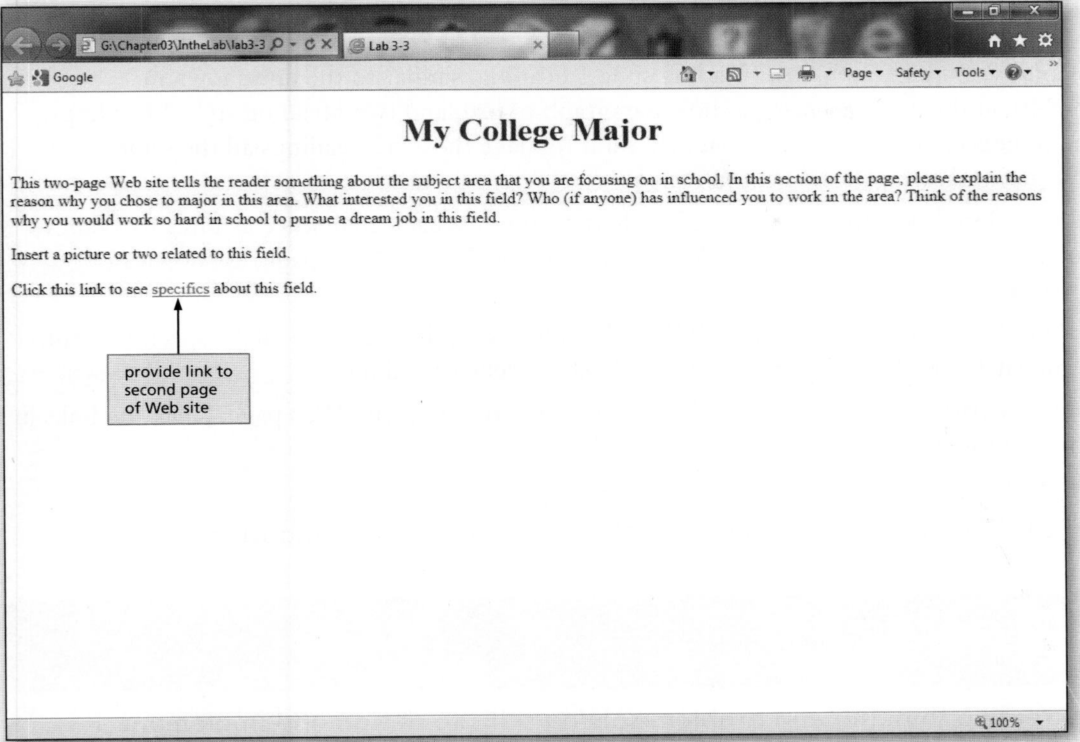

(a) First Web page.

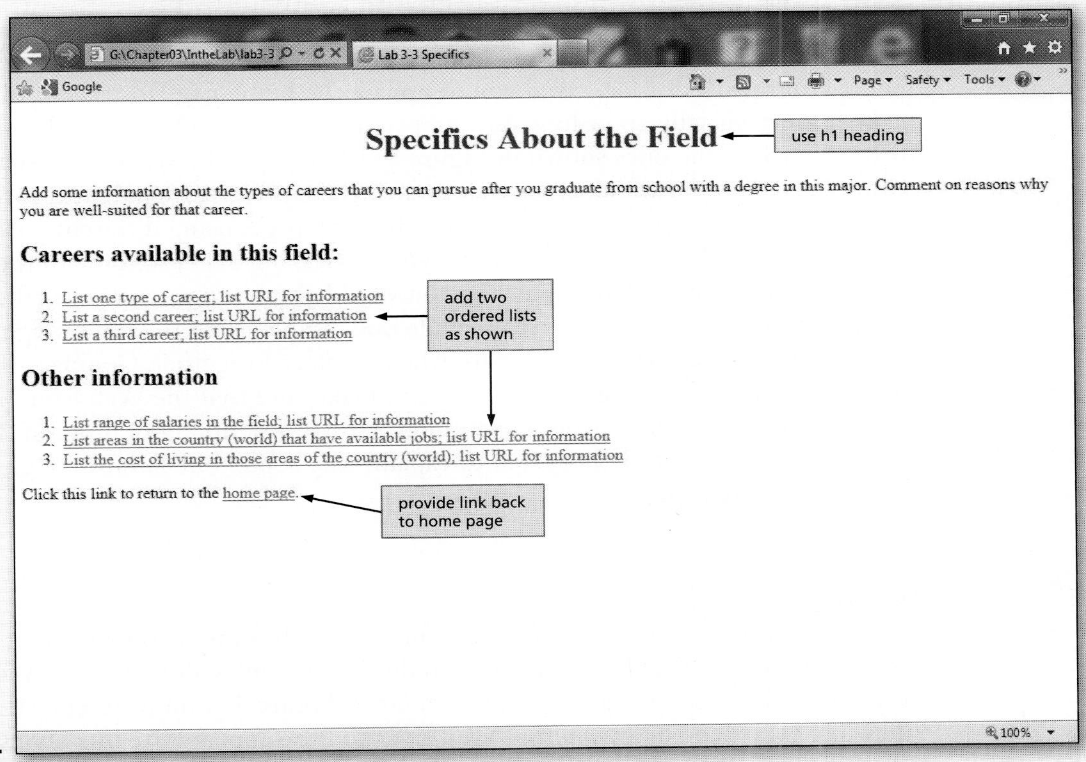

(b) Second Web page.

Figure 3–54

Continued >

In the Lab *continued*

6. In the second Web page, include a Heading style 1 heading, similar to the one shown in Figure 3–54b on the previous page, a short paragraph of text, and two Heading style 2 headings. From the standpoint of consistency, you may want to make those h2 headings all the same color. (*Hint:* Use an inline style sheet sheet for this.)
7. Create two ordered (numbered) lists with at least two items each that serve as links to Web pages on another (external) Web site. Add a link back to the first Web page, as shown in Figure 3–54b.
8. Save the HTML file in the Chapter03\IntheLab folder using the file name lab3-3specifics.html. Validate the lab3-3specifics.html file. Print the lab3-3specifics.html file.
9. View the home page in your browser. Click the text link to the second Web page. Click the links in the lists to test them.
10. Print the Web pages.
11. Submit the HTML files and Web pages in the format specified by your instructor.

Cases and Places

Apply your creative thinking and problem-solving skills to design and implement a solution.

1: Create a Web Page with Text Formatting

Academic

You recently got a work-study position developing Web pages for your academic department at school. Your professor has asked you to update the home page for the department's Web site to make it more visually appealing. As a first step, you plan to create a Web page with sample text formats, such as the ones shown in Figure 3–19 on page HTML 111, to share with your professor and get her input on which types of formatting she prefers. Include text formatted as bold, italic, underlined, superscript, and subscript on the Web page, using different colors and sizes for each type of text. Use CSS styles for most of your styles, but also use some of the text formatting tags shown in the chapter. Determine why you would choose to use one over the other (i.e., styles versus formatting tags). Be sure to include one sample using the font-weight bold style and one using bolder to see how they compare when displayed together. Compare those to using <bold> or <strong> as formatting tags. Be creative and make sure that the Web page looks good but that the new styles do not distract from the content. Utilize a sampling of different font-families on the Web page to show contrast. Be prepared to explain why some font-families (e.g., a curvy script style) might not be appropriate.

2: Create a Web Page with Text Links and Define Link Colors

Personal

You are starting a small business to provide you with some income while in school. You have asked a friend to design your logo, and you would like the link colors on your Web page to match the colors you chose. Create a Web page similar to Figure 3–3 on page HTML 92, with three text links to a Web page in an external Web site. Add the appropriate link styles to define the link colors to match your logo. Also, explain why you might not want to change the colors of the links from the standard blue and violet but show ways that you can accommodate different colors and not confuse users.

3: Create a Prototype Web Site with Five Pages

Professional

Your manager at Uptown Enterprises has asked you to create a simple five-page prototype of the Web pages in the new Entertainment section for the online magazine CityStuff. The home page should include headings and brief paragraphs of text for Arts, Music, Movies, and Dining. Within each paragraph of text is a link to one of the four detailed Web pages for each section (for example, the Arts link should connect to the Arts Web page). The home page also includes an e-mail link at the bottom of the page. Add a To top link that connects to a target at the top of the page. The four detailed Web pages should include links to external Web sites of interest and a link back to the home page. If possible, also find appropriate images to use as a background or in the Web page, and set text to wrap around the images. Remember to use CSS. Determine during the design phase whether it would be better to use inline or embedded style sheets or both for this Web site.

4 Creating Tables in a Web Site Using an External Style Sheet

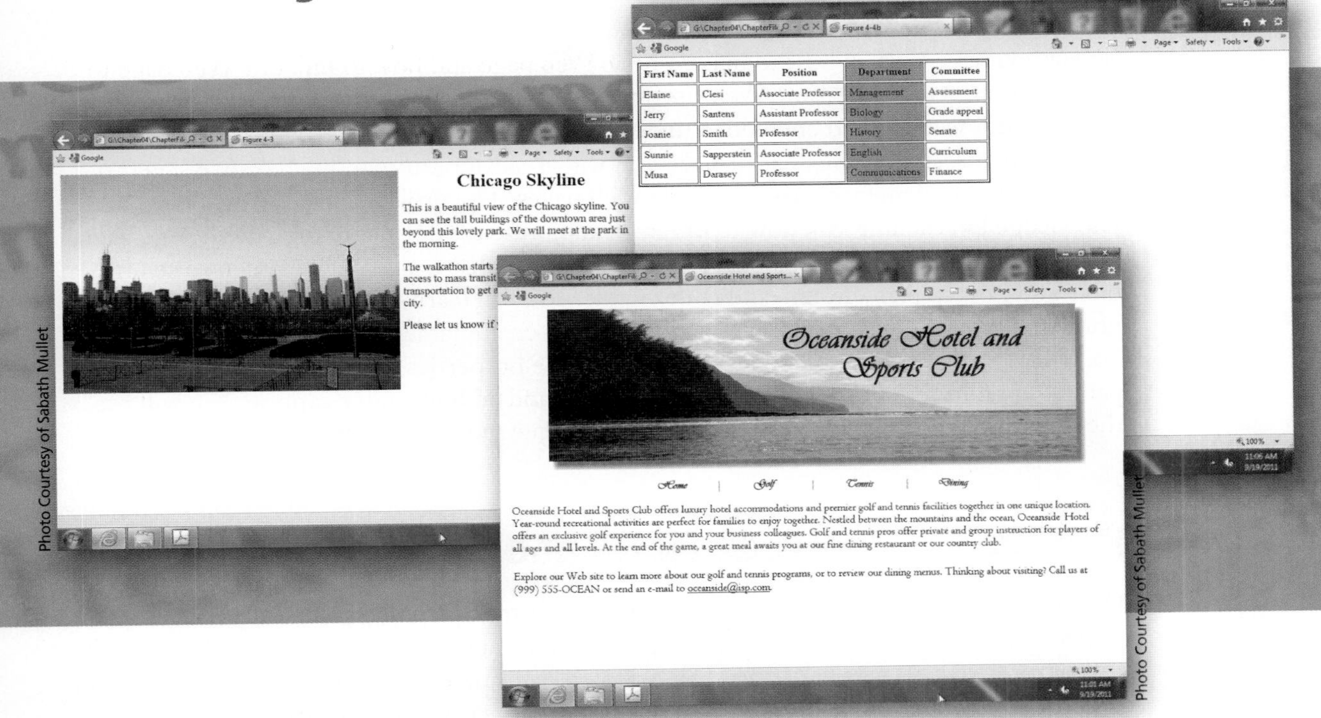

Photo Courtesy of Sabath Mullet

Photo Courtesy of Sabath Mullet

Objectives

You will have mastered the material in this chapter when you can:

- Define table elements
- Describe the steps used to plan, design, and code a table
- Create a borderless table for a horizontal navigation bar with text links
- Create an external style sheet to define styles across a Web site
- Utilize classes to give you more control over styles
- Link an external style sheet to Web pages where you want its styles applied
- Create a table with borders and insert text
- Use the box-shadow property to alter the appearance of an image
- Alter the spacing between and within cells using the border spacing and padding properties
- Utilize inline styles to alter the style of individual elements on a Web page
- Add background color to rows and cells
- Insert a caption below a table
- Create headings that span rows using the rowspan attribute

4 Creating Tables in a Web Site Using an External Style Sheet

Introduction

So far, you have learned how to make a basic Web page and how to link one Web page to another, both within the same Web site and external to the Web site. You also learned how to create inline styles and embedded (internal) style sheets to alter the appearance of Web page elements. In this chapter's project, you will create an external (linked) style sheet to set the style for elements across multiple Web pages. The project adds to your HTML knowledge by teaching you how to organize and present information on a Web page using tables with rows and columns. In this chapter, you will learn about the elements used in a table and how to plan, design, and code a table. You will learn how to use a table to create a horizontal navigation bar with image links, and to create tables to organize text and images. You will enhance the Web site by manipulating the properties and attributes of tables and paragraphs, altering borders, colors, and spacing, and adding a table caption. You will use the new CSS3 box-shadow property to give a unique look to the banner image.

Project — Oceanside Hotel and Sports Club Web Site

Having a reliable Web site makes it easier for a company's customers to find the establishment, provides a way to communicate the company's brand, and allows the company to provide additional services. As advertising director for Oceanside Hotel and Sports Club, you want to enhance Oceanside's Web site to increase the hotel's exposure to current and new customers and to incorporate ideas gathered from customer feedback surveys. The new site will allow customers to browse through tables of information that outline the golf, tennis, and dining options offered by the hotel and sports club.

As shown in Figure 4–1a, the Oceanside Hotel and Sports Club home page includes a company logo banner and a borderless table that contains a navigation bar under the logo. The borderless table gives users easy access to all pages in the Web site. This table is available on every Web page in the Web site. The Golf, Tennis, and Dining Web pages (Figures 4–1b, 4–1c, and 4–1d) each include the company logo banner and the same borderless table at the top, as well as one table with borders that displays the contents of that particular Web page. In this project, you will create the oceanside.html and golf.html Web pages. You will edit the tennis.html Web page (Figure 4–1c) to add border spacing and padding properties, thereby adjusting the spacing between cells. The dining.html Web page file (Figure 4–1d) is also edited to add a caption with information about the table and to use the rowspan attribute to create headings that span several rows.

As you read through this chapter and work on the project, you will learn how to plan, design, and code tables to create a user-friendly Web site. You also will learn to format tables and to combine table features to make the pages more readable. In addition, you will learn to create a navigation bar with image links.

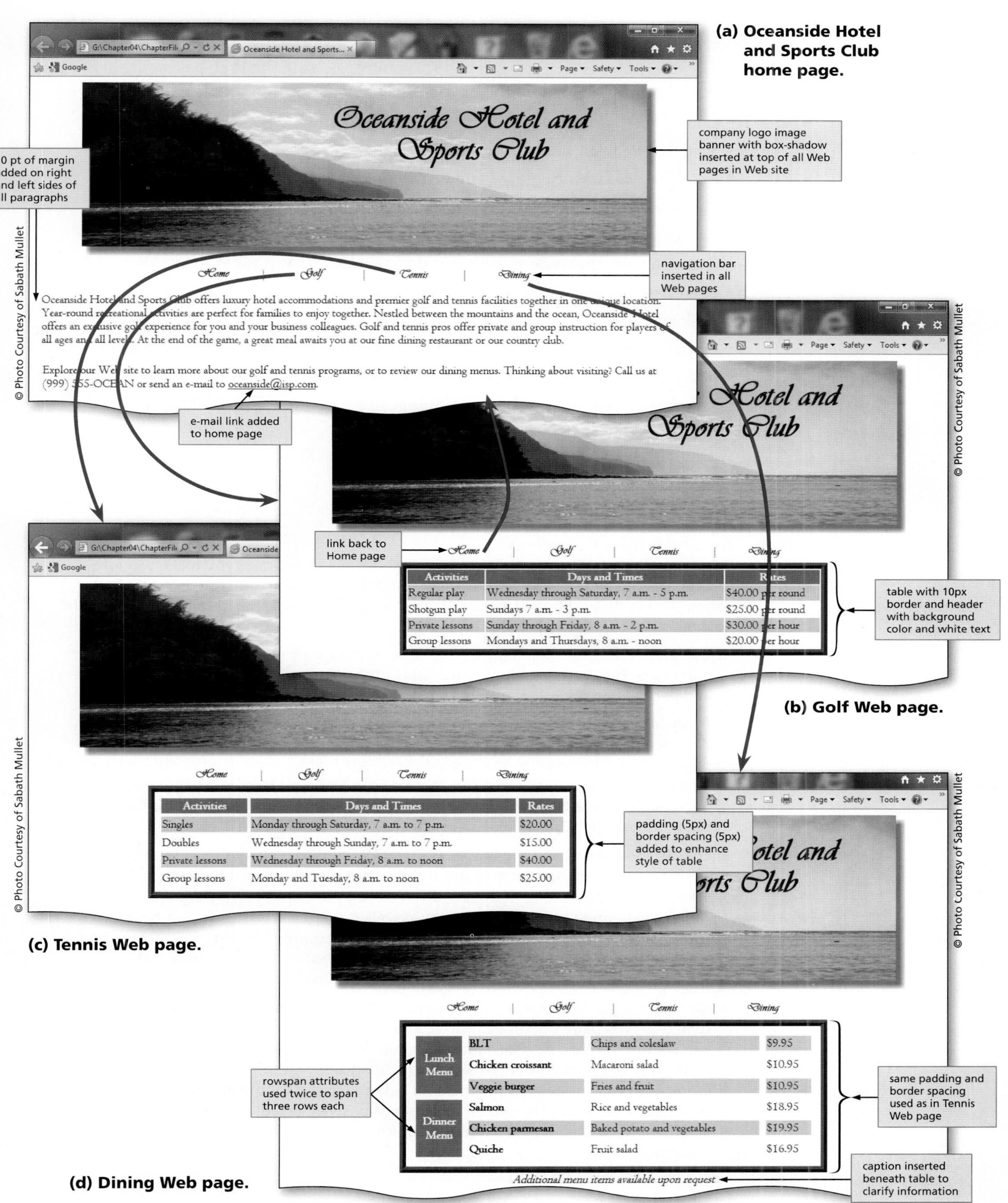

(a) Oceanside Hotel and Sports Club home page.
Oceanside Hotel and Sports Club
company logo image banner with box-shadow inserted at top of all Web pages in Web site
10 pt of margin added on right and left sides of all paragraphs
Home | Golf | Tennis | Dining
navigation bar inserted in all Web pages
Oceanside Hotel and Sports Club offers luxury hotel accommodations and premier golf and tennis facilities together in one unique location. Year-round recreational activities are perfect for families to enjoy together. Nestled between the mountains and the ocean, Oceanside Hotel offers an exclusive golf experience for you and your business colleagues. Golf and tennis pros offer private and group instruction for players of all ages and all levels. At the end of the game, a great meal awaits you at our fine dining restaurant or our country club.
Explore our Web site to learn more about our golf and tennis programs, or to review our dining menus. Thinking about visiting? Call us at (999) 555-OCEAN or send an e-mail to oceanside@isp.com.
e-mail link added to home page
© Photo Courtesy of Sabath Mullet
link back to Home page
Activities | Days and Times | Rates
Regular play | Wednesday through Saturday, 7 a.m. - 5 p.m. | $40.00 per round
Shotgun play | Sundays 7 a.m. - 3 p.m. | $25.00 per round
Private lessons | Sunday through Friday, 8 a.m. - 2 p.m. | $30.00 per hour
Group lessons | Mondays and Thursdays, 8 a.m. - noon | $20.00 per hour
table with 10px border and header with background color and white text
(b) Golf Web page.
Activities | Days and Times | Rates
Singles | Monday through Saturday, 7 a.m. to 7 p.m. | $20.00
Doubles | Wednesday through Sunday, 7 a.m. to 7 p.m. | $15.00
Private lessons | Wednesday through Friday, 8 a.m. to noon | $40.00
Group lessons | Monday and Tuesday, 8 a.m. to noon | $25.00
padding (5px) and border spacing (5px) added to enhance style of table
(c) Tennis Web page.
Lunch Menu | BLT | Chips and coleslaw | $9.95
Chicken croissant | Macaroni salad | $10.95
Veggie burger | Fries and fruit | $10.95
Dinner Menu | Salmon | Rice and vegetables | $18.95
Chicken parmesan | Baked potato and vegetables | $19.95
Quiche | Fruit salad | $16.95
Additional menu items available upon request
rowspan attributes used twice to span three rows each
same padding and border spacing used as in Tennis Web page
caption inserted beneath table to clarify information
(d) Dining Web page.

Figure 4–1

Overview

As you read this chapter, you will learn how to create the Web pages shown in Figures 4–1a through 4–1d on the previous page by performing these general tasks:

- Enter HTML code into the Notepad++ window.
- Save the file as an HTML file.
- Enter basic HTML tags and add text to the file.
- Add a horizontal navigation bar with image links.
- Create a table with borders to display information in an organized manner.
- Create an external style sheet to set the style for all Web pages in the Web site.
- Use classes to give more control over the styles used.
- Link an external style sheet to Web pages.
- Utilize inline styles to alter the style of individual elements on the Web page.
- Add HTML tags that enhance a table with padding and border spacing.
- Enhance a Web table with rowspanning.
- Add a caption to a table.
- Print the HTML code and Web pages

Plan Ahead

General Project Guidelines

When creating a Web page, the actions you perform and decisions you make will affect the appearance and characteristics (the styles) of the finished page. As you create Web pages, such as those shown in Figures 4–1a through 4–1d, you should follow these general guidelines:

1. **Complete Web page planning.** Before developing a Web page, you must know the purpose of the Web site, identify the users of the site and their computing environments, and decide who owns the information on the Web page.
2. **Analyze the content and organization of the Web page**. In the analysis phase of the Web development life cycle, you should analyze what content to include on the Web page and how to organize that information. In this phase, you need to determine what information you want to convey so that you can highlight that information on the Web page using different techniques. Refer to Table 1–4 on page HTML 15 for information on the phases of the Web development life cycle.
3. **Choose the content and organization for the Web page**. Once you have completed the analysis, you need to determine specifically what content to include on the Web page. With tables, you are able to display the Web page content in a very organized manner. Tables can be used to display text only, as well as graphical images or combinations of text and images. Some text is better highlighted by using different colors for column or row headings. Other information is displayed more effectively with row- and column-spanning techniques. This should all be determined before coding the Web pages.
4. **Identify how to format various elements of the Web page**. The overall appearance or style of a Web page significantly affects its ability to communicate clearly. Additionally, you want to provide easy navigation for your Web site visitors. Adding images and color helps to communicate your message and adding a navigation bar with links to the other Web pages within the Web site makes it easy to navigate the Web site. Determine what style sheets to use for the overall appearance or style, including external, embedded, and inline style sheets. Also determine which formatting tag attributes need to be implemented.

(continued)

Plan Ahead

5. **Determine where to save the Web page.** You can store a Web page permanently, or save it on a variety of storage media, including a hard disk, USB flash drive, CD, or DVD. You can also indicate a specific location on the storage media for saving the Web page. Recognize the appropriate absolute and relative addressing that you will need as determined by your analysis.
6. **Create the Web page and links.** After analyzing and designing the Web site, you need to develop the individual Web pages. It is important to maintain a consistent look throughout the Web site. Use graphics and links consistently so that your Web site visitor does not become confused.
7. **Test all Web pages within the Web site.** An important part of Web development is testing to assure that you are following XHTML standards. This book uses the World Wide Web Consortium (W3C) validator that allows you to test your Web page and clearly explains any errors you have. Additionally, you should check all content for accuracy and test all links.

When necessary, more specific details concerning the above guidelines are presented at appropriate points in the chapter. The chapter will also identify the actions performed and decisions made regarding these guidelines during the creation of the Web pages shown in Figures 4–1a through 4–1d on page HTML 155.

Planning and Designing a Multipage Web Site

The Web site that you create in this chapter consists of four Web pages: oceanside.html, golf.html, tennis.html, and dining.html. With a multipage Web site, you need to design the overall look of the Web site itself, as well as the individual Web pages. You will use both formatting tag attributes and style sheets to create the overall appearance (or style) of the Web site. An **external style sheet** is used to define styles for multiple pages in a Web site. With external (linked) style sheets, you create the style sheet first in a separate file saved with a .css extension. You then link this style sheet into any Web page in which you want to use it.

In Chapters 2 and 3, you learned how to insert inline and embedded (internal) style sheets into your Web pages. Recall that inline style sheets are used to change the style of an individual HTML tag. An embedded style sheet is inserted between the <head> and </head> tags of a single Web page within the style container (<style> and </style>). Embedded (or internal) style sheets are used to change the style for elements on an entire Web page. For the project in this chapter, where you have a multipage Web site, you will learn how to create an external, or linked, style sheet.

Creating Web Pages with Tables

Tables allow you to organize information on a Web page using HTML tags. Tables are useful when you want to arrange text and images into rows and columns in order to make the information straightforward and clear to the Web page visitor. You can use tables to create Web pages with newspaper-type columns of text or structured lists of information. Tables can be complex, with text or images spanning rows and columns, background colors in cells, and borders (Figure 4–2a on the next page). Tables can also be simple, with a basic grid format and no color (Figure 4–2b). The purpose of the table helps to define what formatting is appropriate.

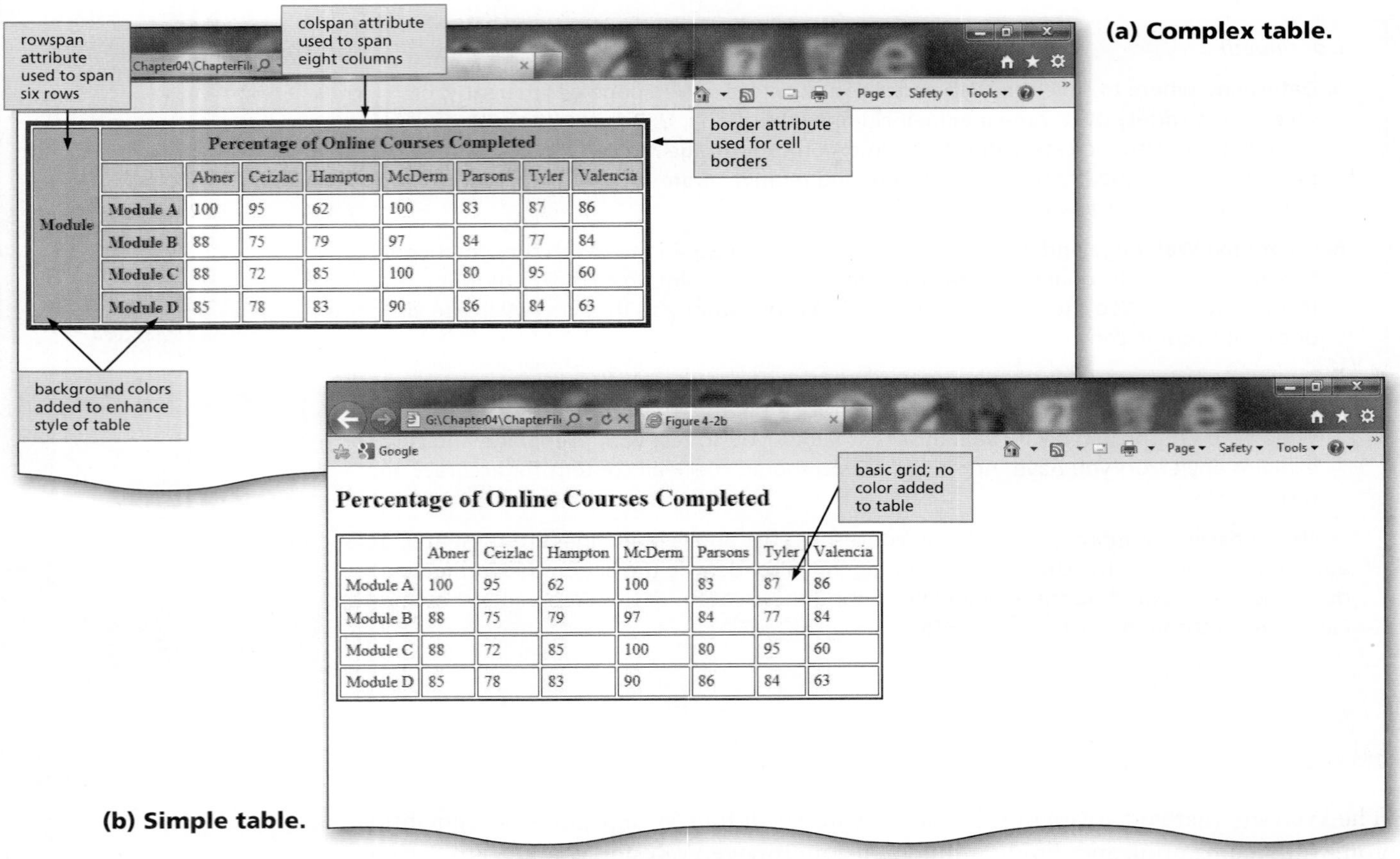

rowspan attribute used to span six rows

colspan attribute used to span eight columns

border attribute used for cell borders

background colors added to enhance style of table

(a) Complex table.

Percentage of Online Courses Completed								
Module		Abner	Ceizlac	Hampton	McDerm	Parsons	Tyler	Valencia
	Module A	100	95	62	100	83	87	86
	Module B	88	75	79	97	84	77	84
	Module C	88	72	85	100	80	95	60
	Module D	85	78	83	90	86	84	63

basic grid; no color added to table

Percentage of Online Courses Completed

	Abner	Ceizlac	Hampton	McDerm	Parsons	Tyler	Valencia
Module A	100	95	62	100	83	87	86
Module B	88	75	79	97	84	77	84
Module C	88	72	85	100	80	95	60
Module D	85	78	83	90	86	84	63

(b) Simple table.

Figure 4–2

In Chapter 3, you learned how to wrap text around an image. You can also use tables to position text and images, such as the one shown in Figure 4–3; this is a borderless table used to position text to the right of the image. One advantage of using a table to position text and images instead of just wrapping the text around the image is that you have greater control over the placement of the text and image. However, CSS is the preferred method for structuring Web sites; tables are often found in legacy (i.e., older) Web sites.

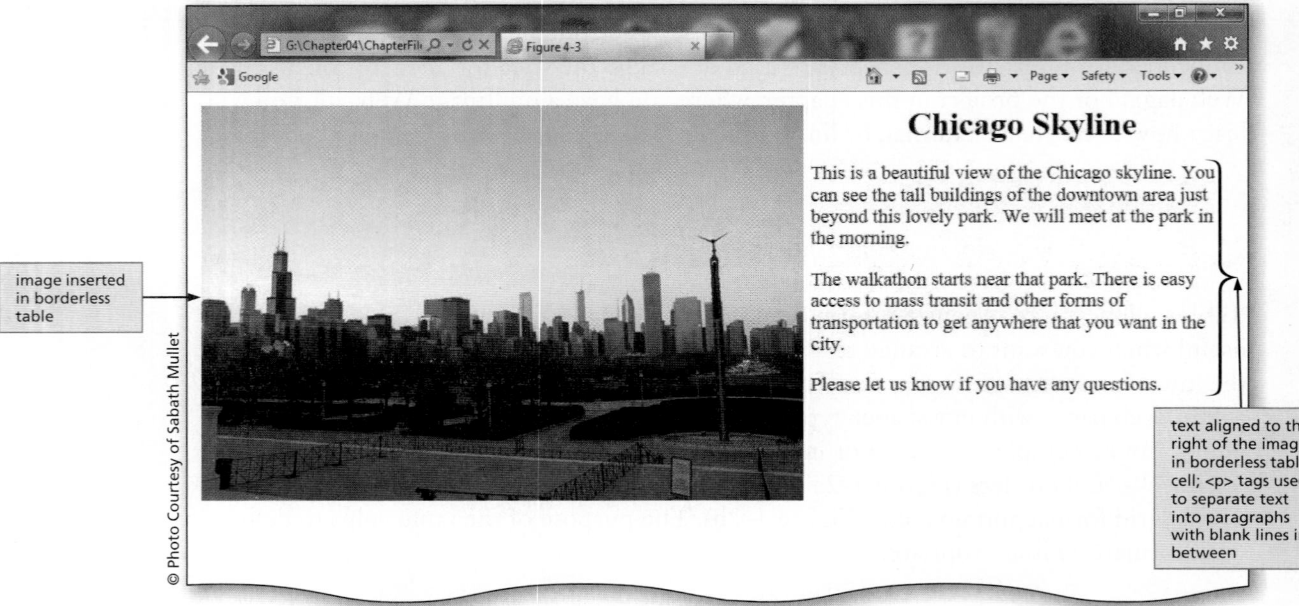

Figure 4–3 Image and text positioned in table.

Table Elements

Tables consist of rows, columns, and cells, much like spreadsheets. A **row** is a horizontal line of information. A **column** is a vertical line of information. A **cell** is the intersection of a row and a column. Figure 4–4 shows examples of these three elements. In Figure 4–4a, the fifth row in the table has a green background. In Figure 4–4b, the fourth column has a blue background. In Figure 4–4c, the cell at the intersection of column 2 and row 6 has an orange background.

As shown in Figure 4–4c, a cell can be one of two types: a heading cell or a data cell. A **heading cell** displays text as bold and center-aligned. A **data cell** displays normal text that is left-aligned.

Understanding the row, column, and cell elements is important as you create a table using HTML. Properties and attributes are set relative to these table elements. For example, you can set attributes for an entire row of information, for a single cell, or for one or more cells within a row. Appendix A lists all attributes not supported by HTML5, indicated by a double asterisk (**). Review that appendix for more information.

BTW

Tables
Tables are useful for a variety of purposes. They can store information in tabular form or create a layout on a Web page.

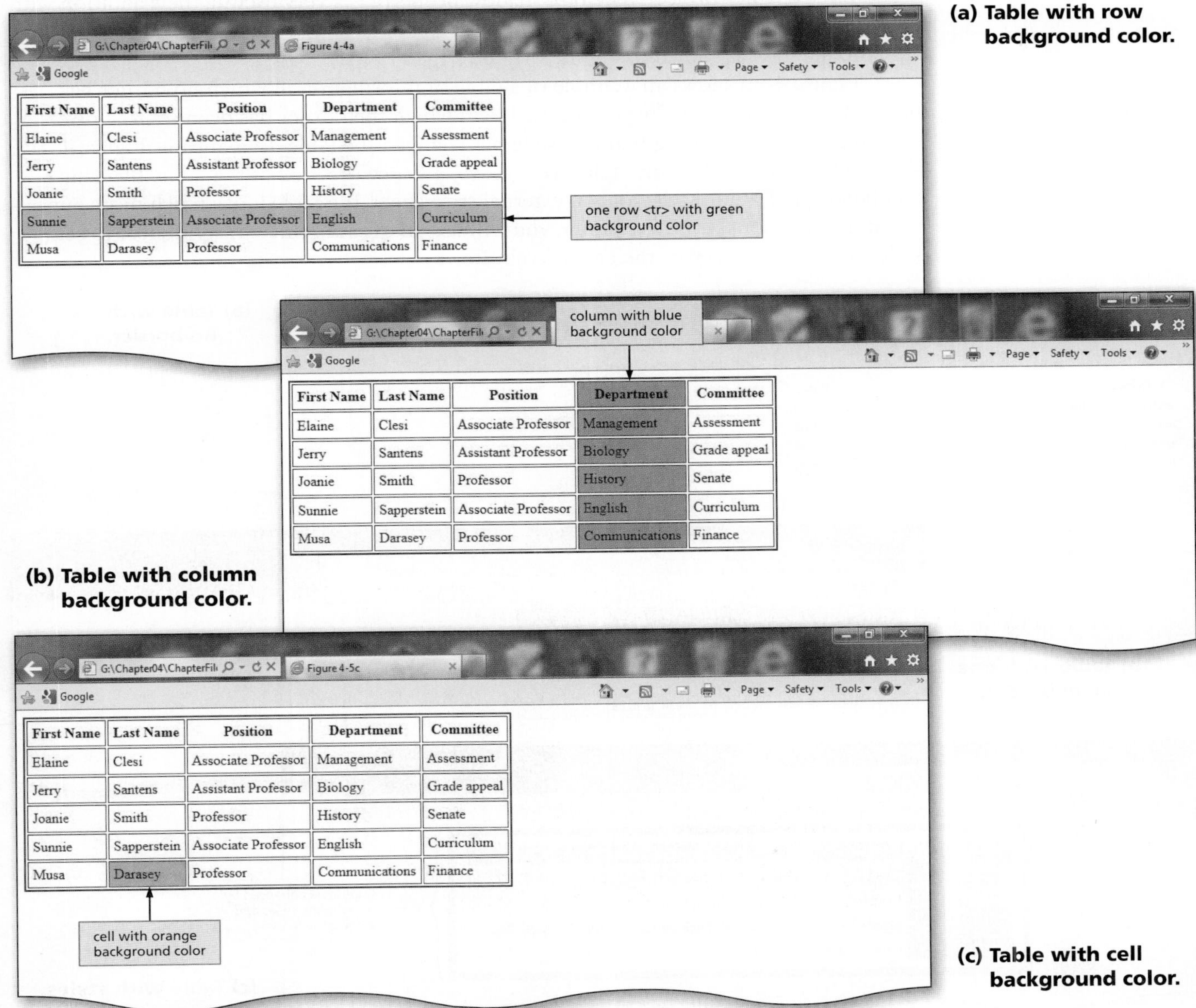

(a) Table with row background color.

(b) Table with column background color.

(c) Table with cell background color.

Figure 4–4

BTW

Table Elements
Many Web sources discuss how to use and code tables, giving numerous examples and tips. For more information about HTML table parts, search the Web for key terms such as "HTML Table Elements" or "HTML Table Properties".

Adding Style to Table Elements

As discussed earlier, there are many ways to set the style (or appearance) of a Web page element. You can use formatting tag attributes (e.g., setting the border in the <table> tag or setting colspan in the <td> or <th> tag) to set the appearance or style. You can also use inline, embedded, or external (linked) style sheets to set the style. During the design phase of the Web development life cycle, you will determine how to set the styles for the elements on your Web pages.

HTML5 established a major change in how tables are formatted. All <table> tag attributes (as indicated in Appendix A) have been eliminated in HTML5 except for the border attribute. In this book, you will utilize the new tags and properties available in HTML5 when formatting tables. For instance, instead of using the cellspacing attribute, which is not supported in HTML5, to increase the space between cells, you will use the border-spacing property in an inline style. If you used the cellspacing attribute in your HTML code and tried to validate the file using an HTML5 DOCTYPE, you would get an error that said, "The cellspacing attribute on the table element is obsolete. Use CSS instead." In this book we do not use any attributes that are unsupported in HTML5.

In addition, you will use a new CSS3 property to add a style to the banner image used in this chapter project. The box-shadow property is a very exciting new addition with CSS3 and can be used in a variety of ways. For this Web site, it gives the banner image a very unique look as shown in Figure 4–1a on page HTML 155.

Figure 4–5a shows an example of a table of information in which no border has been added. In Figure 4–5b, you see a table in which the border has been set to 1 pixel. As you can see, just adding that one style has changed the table dramatically. Figure 4–5c shows a table in which many styles were set to enhance the look of the table. By using a combination of inline styles and an external style sheet, the table looks much more appealing and professional. In this chapter, you will use an external (linked) style sheet to set styles for the tables across the entire Web site.

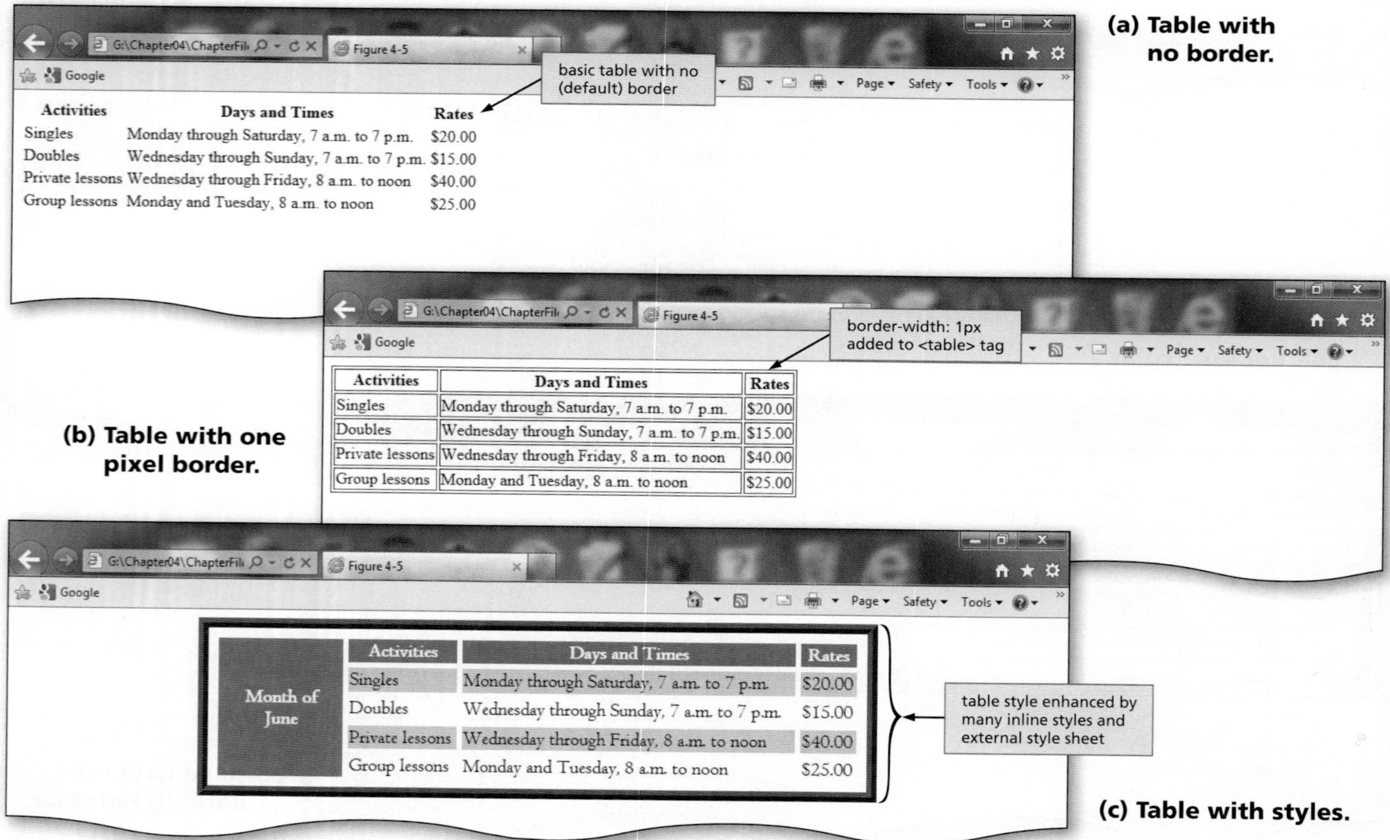

Figure 4–5

Table Borders, Headers, Captions, and Rules

Tables not only contain columns and rows, but they also include features such as table borders, table headers, and table captions (Figure 4–6). A **table border** is the line that encloses the perimeter of the table. A **table header** is the same as a heading cell — it is any cell with bold, centered text that indicates the purpose of the row or column. A header row is used to identify the meaning of the numbers in each column, and headings that span columns and rows are used to provide additional information. Headers also are used by nonvisual browsers to identify table content. See the guidelines in Appendix C for specific information about making your Web pages accessible to those with disabilities. A **table caption** is descriptive text located above or below the table that further describes the purpose of the table.

Tables can use these features individually or in combination. The purpose for the table dictates which of these features are used. For example, the table shown in Figure 4–6 lists columns of numbers. A header row is used to identify the meaning of the numbers in each column, and headings that span columns and rows are used to provide additional information. Finally, the table caption explains that each number is based on thousands (that is, the 10 listed in the table represents 10,000).

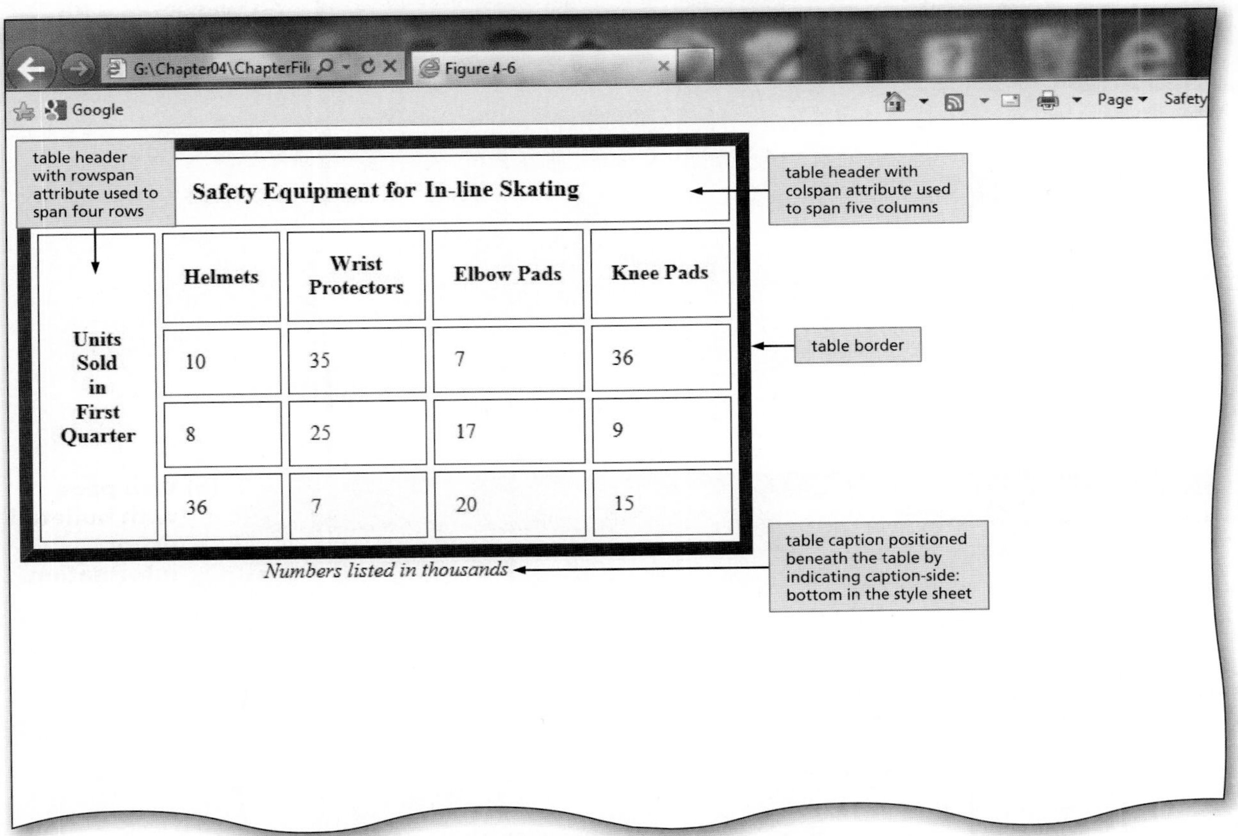

Figure 4–6 Table headers, border, and caption.

Determining the Need for, Planning, and Coding a Table

Creating tables for a Web page is a three-step process: (1) determining if a table is needed, (2) planning the table, and (3) coding the table. Each of these steps is discussed in detail in the following sections.

Determining if a Table Is Needed

First, you must determine whether a table is necessary. Not all Web pages require the use of tables. A general rule is that a table should be used when it will help organize information or Web page elements in such a way that it is easier for the Web page visitor to read. Tables generally are useful on a Web page if the Web page needs to display a structured, organized list of information or includes text and images that must be positioned in a very specific manner. Figures 4–7a and 4–7b show examples of information displayed as text in both a table and a bulleted list. To present this information, a table (Figure 4–7a) would be the better choice. The bulleted list (Figure 4–7b) might give the Web page an acceptable look, but the table presents the information more clearly.

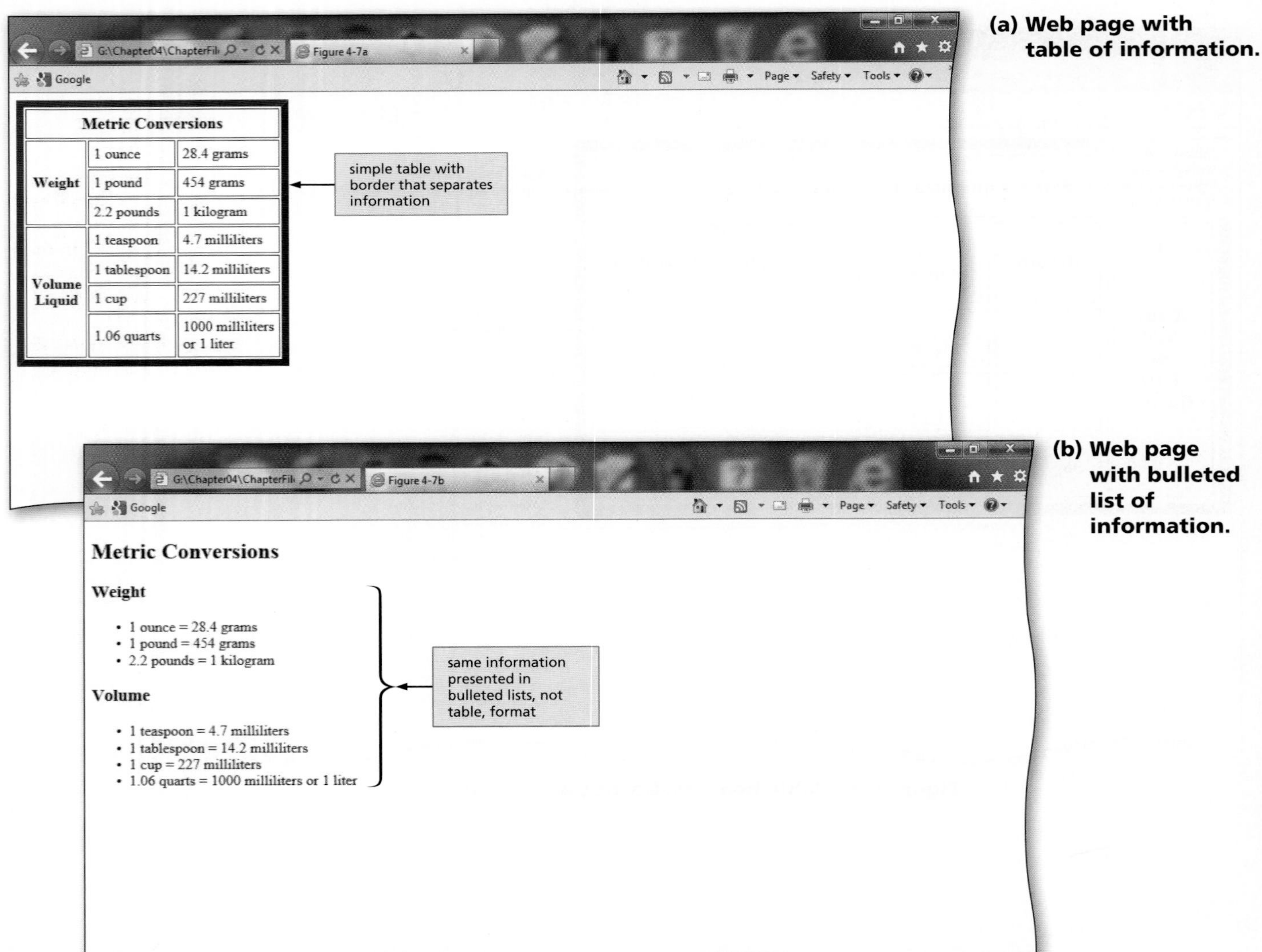

Figure 4–7

Planning the Table

To create effective tables, you must plan how the information will appear in the table and then create a good design. Before writing any HTML code, sketch the table on paper. After the table is sketched on paper, it is easier to see how many rows and columns to create, if the table will include headings, and if any of the headings span rows or columns. Conceptualizing the table on paper first saves time when you try to determine which HTML table tags to use to create the table.

For example, to create a simple table that lists the times run by various cross-country team members, you might sketch the table shown in Figure 4–8a. If runners participate in two different race lengths, such as 5K and 10K, that information can be included in a table designed as shown in Figure 4–8b. If the table needs to include different race dates for each race length, that information can be included in a table such as the one shown in Figure 4–8c. Finally, to make the table easier for the Web page visitor to understand, the table should include headings that span rows and columns. For instance, in Figure 4–8b, the headings 5K and 10K each span two columns of data. Because column spanning is used, you can easily see which runners ran in the 5K or 10K races. In Figure 4–8c, because of row spanning, you can easily tell what date each race was run. Design issues such as these should be considered in the planning stage before any HTML code is entered. Figure 4–9, on the next page, shows how the table might look after it is coded. You will use a variety of style sheets together with formatting tag attributes to create the tables for the project in this chapter.

NAME1	NAME2	NAME3	NAME4
TIME	TIME	TIME	TIME

(a) Simple table.

5K		10K	
NAME1	NAME2	NAME3	NAME4
TIME	TIME	TIME	TIME

(b) Column spanning added.

		5K		10K	
		NAME1	NAME2	NAME3	NAME4
Meet Dates	MAY 5	TIME	TIME	TIME	TIME
	MAY 12	TIME	TIME	TIME	TIME
	MAY 19	TIME	TIME	TIME	TIME
	MAY 26	TIME	TIME	TIME	TIME

(c) Row spanning added.

Figure 4–8

BTW

Table Tutorial
Table tutorials are available through online sources. Tutorials take you step-by-step through the table creation process. Search the Web for the phrase HTML Table Tutorial to find excellent sources of information.

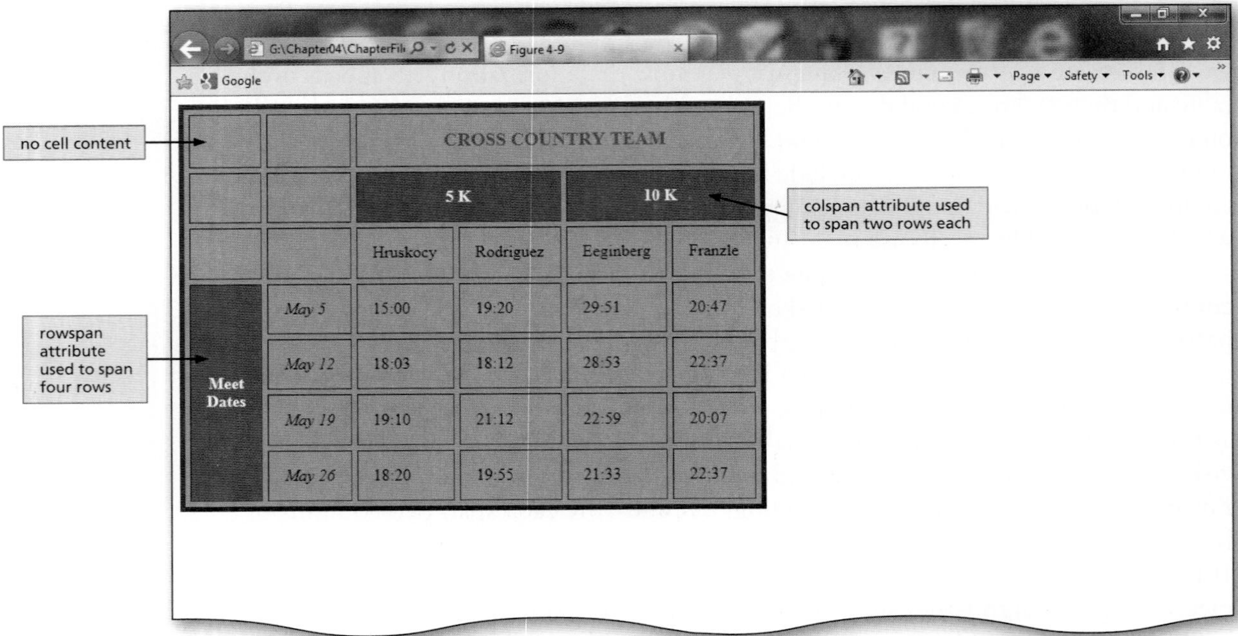

Figure 4–9 Table with row and column spanning.

Coding the Table

After you have completed the table design, you can begin coding the table using HTML tags. Table 4–1 shows the four main HTML tags used to create a table. Some of the tags have attributes, which are discussed later in this chapter.

Table 4–1 HTML Table Tags

Tag	Function
<table> </table>	• Indicates the start and end of a table • All other table tags are inserted within these tags
<tr> </tr>	• Indicates the start and end of a table row • Rows consist of heading or data cells
<th> </th>	• Indicates the start and end of a table heading (also called a heading cell) • Table headings default to bold text and center-alignment
<td> </td>	• Indicates the start and end of a data cell in a table • Data cells default to normal text and left-alignment

Figure 4–10a shows an example of these tags used in an HTML file, and Figure 4–10b shows the resulting Web page. As shown in Figure 4–10b, the table has four rows (a table header and three rows of data cells) and two columns. The rows are indicated in the HTML file in Figure 4–10a by the start **<tr>** tags and the end **</tr>** tags. For this simple table, the number of columns in the table is determined based on the number of cells within each row. As shown in Figure 4–10b, each row has two cells, which results in a table with two columns. (Later in this chapter, you will learn how to indicate the number of columns within the <table> tag.)

As shown in the HTML in Figure 4–10a, the first row includes table heading cells, as indicated by the start **<th>** tag and end **</th>** tag. In the second, third, and fourth rows, the cells contain data, indicated by the start **<td>** tag and end **</td>** tag. In the resulting table, as shown in Figure 4–10b, the table header in row 1 appears as bold and centered text. The text in the data cells in rows 2 through 4 is left-aligned and normal text. The

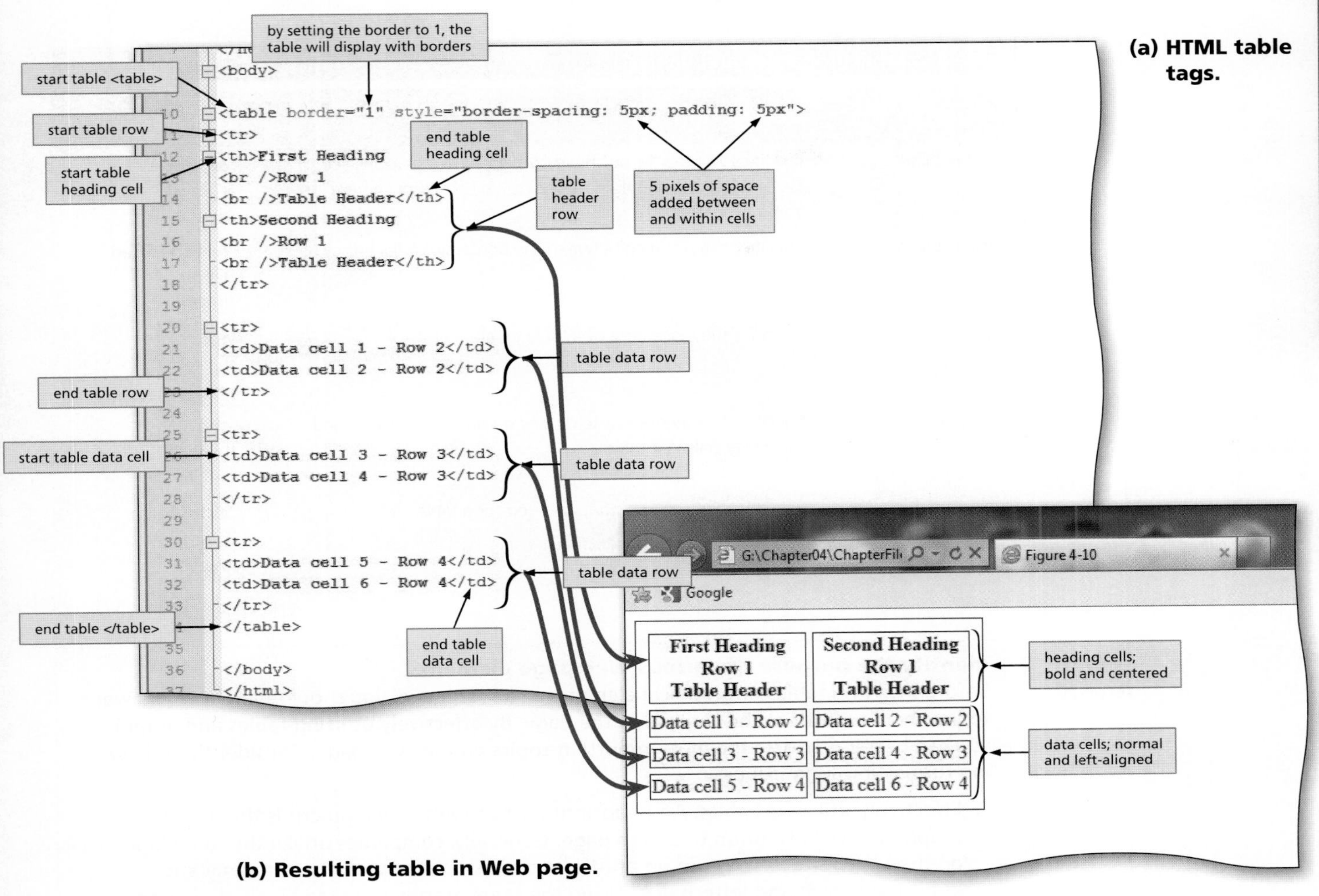

(a) HTML table tags.

(b) Resulting table in Web page.

Figure 4–10

table in Figure 4–10b has a border, and using inline styles, the border-spacing and padding was set to 5 pixels each to highlight further differences between the cells. You will learn about border-spacing and padding styles later in the chapter.

Table Tag Attributes

Prior to HTML5, the four table tags had many attributes that could be used to format tables. These attributes are all shown in Appendix A. However, HTML5 does not support most of those attributes, and it is recommended that you use Cascading Style Sheets to style tables in a Web page. With HTML5:

- the <table> tag only allows the use of the border attribute
- the <tr> tag has no attributes still in use
- the <th> and <td> tags still allow use of the rowspan, colspan, and headers attributes

Table 4–2 lists the CSS properties and values that can be used to style tables. You use the border-spacing property in this chapter project to create more space between borders in the table. Many other styles are added to style the tables in the Web site in this chapter by using a combination of HTML5 supported attributes along with inline styles and an external style sheet.

BTW

Table Borders
Table borders can be used to frame an image. You can insert a single image into a one-row, one-column table. Using a border gives the image a 3-D appearance, making the image appear to have a frame around it. The border attribute can have a value of "1" or " " only. You can also use CSS border properties to define borders.

Table 4–2 Table Properties and Values

Property	Description	Values
border-collapse	Specifies whether or not table borders should be collapsed, i.e., if table cells should have their own border, or share a common border	**separate** collapse inherit
border-spacing	Specifies the distance between the borders of adjacent cells	**not specified** length inherit
caption-side	Specifies the placement of a table caption	**top** bottom inherit
empty-cells	Specifies whether or not to display borders and background on empty cells in a table	**show** hide inherit
table-layout	Sets the layout algorithm to be used for a table	**auto** fixed inherit

Plan Ahead

Identify the purpose of various Web page elements.

Before inserting tables or graphical elements in a Web page, you should plan how you want to use them to present the content of the page. By effectively utilizing tables and graphics, you can better organize the most important topics on the Web page. Consider the following formatting suggestions:

- **Effectively utilize graphics.** An important part of Web development is the use of graphics to call attention to a Web page. Generally, companies utilize the same logo on their Web site as they use on print material associated with the company, such as business cards and letterheads. Using the same graphical image on all marketing materials, including the Web site, is a good way to provide a consistent visual image and brand message to customers. Colorful company logos can also add an attention-grabbing element to a Web page.
- **Format tables to present Web page content.** Sometimes it is better to have no border around the table, while other times borders enhance the look of the table, depending on the content and purpose of the table. For example, when creating a table containing image links, you may not want a border to break up the images. In other cases, you may want only separators (e.g., pipe symbols) between the links to visually organize them for the viewer. In this chapter, you will use both bordered and borderless tables. Another consideration is where to place the table (left-, right-, or center-aligned).
- **Identify what links are needed**. Each Web page in a multipage Web site should have a link back to the home page of the Web site. Web developers often use the company logo to link back to the home page. In this project, the logo is also the central image of the Web pages. Because of that, a better option might be to provide a link called Home that visitors can use to return to the home page. Each Web page should include links to the other pages on the Web site. Putting these links in a table at the top of each Web page helps visitors navigate easily, and providing the navigation bar across all Web pages in the Web site is also important for consistency. Again, the purpose of providing links is to make it easy to navigate the Web site.

Creating a Home Page with Banner Logo and Borderless Navigation Table

The first Web page developed in this chapter's project is the home page of the Oceanside Hotel and Sports Club Web site. As you have learned, the home page is the main page of a Web site and is what Web site visitors generally view first. Visitors then click links to move from the home page to the other Web pages in the site. The Oceanside Hotel and Sports Club home page includes the company logo as a banner image and a borderless table that contains a navigation bar with four image links. Three of the links allow the user to navigate to other pages: the Golf Web page, the Tennis Web page, and the Dining Web page. The navigation bar also includes a link to return to the Home page. In addition to these links, the home page also provides an e-mail link, so visitors can contact Oceanside Hotel and Sports Club easily.

To Start Notepad++

The first step in creating the Oceanside Hotel and Sports Club Web site is to start Notepad++ and ensure that word wrap is enabled. The following steps, which assume Windows 7 is running, start Notepad++ based on a typical installation. You may need to ask your instructor how to start Notepad++ for your computer.

1. Click the Start button on the Windows taskbar to display the Start menu.
2. Click All Programs at the bottom of the left pane on the Start menu to display the All Programs list.
3. Click Notepad++ in the All Programs list to expand the folder.
4. Click Notepad++ in the expanded list to start the Notepad++ program.
5. If the Notepad++ window is not maximized, click the Maximize button on the Notepad++ title bar to maximize it.
6. Click View on the menu bar and verify that the Word wrap command has a check mark next to it. If it does not, click Word wrap.

To Enter Initial HTML Tags to Define the Web Page Structure

Just as you did in Chapters 2 and 3, you start your file with the initial HTML tags that define the structure of the Web page. Table 4–3 contains the tags and text for this task.

Table 4–3 Initial HTML Tags

Line	HTML Tag and Text
1	<!DOCTYPE HTML>
2	
3	<html>
4	<head>
5	<meta charset="utf-8" />
6	<title>Oceanside Hotel and Sports Club</title>
7	</head>
8	

Table 4–3 Initial HTML Tags (continued)

Line	HTML Tag and Text
9	<body>
10	
11	</body>
12	</html>

The following steps illustrate how to enter the initial tags that define the structure of the Web page.

1. Enter the HTML code shown in Table 4–3. Press ENTER at the end of each line.
2. Position the insertion point on the blank line between the <body> and </body> tags (line 10) and press the ENTER key to position the insertion point on line 11 (Figure 4–11).
3. Compare your screen with Figure 4–11 and correct any errors.

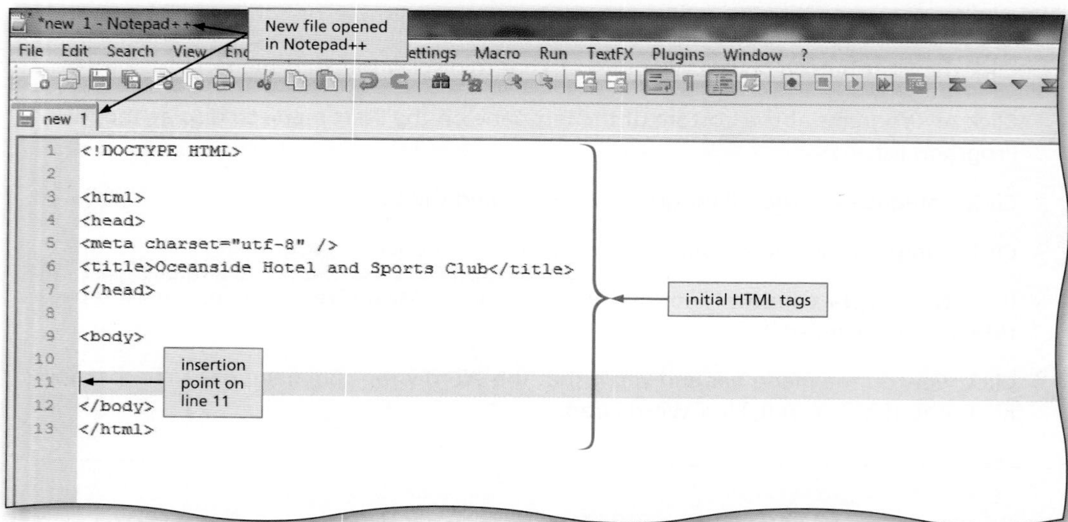

Figure 4–11

To Save an HTML File

With the initial HTML code for the Oceanside Hotel and Sports Club home page entered, you should save the file. Saving the file frequently ensures you won't lose your work. Saving a file in Notepad++ also adds color to code that can help you identify different elements more easily. The following steps save an HTML file in Notepad++.

1. Click File on the menu bar, click Save, and then type `oceanside.html` in the File name text box (do not press ENTER).
2. Navigate to storage device and folder (Chapter04\ChapterFiles) where you save your Data Files and then click the Save button in the Save As dialog box to save the file.

Using the Box-Shadow Property

A new property with CSS3 is the box-shadow (see Border Properties in Appendix D). The box-shadow property allows designers to easily implement multiple drop shadows (outer or inner) on box elements, specifying values for color, size, blur, and offset to a <div> element. Table 4–4 lists the values that can be used with the box-shadow property.

Table 4–4 Box-Shadow Property

Value	Description
h-shadow	Required. The position of the horizontal shadow. Negative values are allowed. If positive, shadow will be on the right of the box; if negative, shadow is on the left of the box.
v-shadow	Required. The position of the vertical shadow. Negative values are allowed. If negative, shadow will be above the box; if positive, shadow is below the box.
blur	Optional. The blur distance. If set to 0 (zero), shadow will be sharp; the higher the number, the more blurred it will be.
spread	Optional. The size of shadow.
color	Optional. The color of the shadow.
insert	Optional. Changes the shadow from an outer shadow (outset) to an inner shadow.

You can use the box-shadow property to give an image a shadow. You can use an inline style within the <img> tag to set a box-shadow around the oceanside.jpg banner image as shown in Figure 4-12a on the next page. The following inline style is added to the <img> tag:

```
<img src="oceansidelogo.jpg" style="box-shadow: 10px 10px 12px
#888888" />
```

(Note: All of the <img> tags shown in this section would also include the height, width, and alt attributes for the image as per good coding standards. They are not shown here for clarity.) In the box-shadow property, the horizontal and vertical shadows are both set to 10 pixels as shown in Figure 4–12a. The blur value is set to 12 pixels, and the shadow color is set to gray (#888888). Figure 4–12b shows an example of the same code except that the horizontal and vertical shadows are set to –10 pixels each as shown below.

```
<img src="oceansidelogo.jpg" style="box-shadow: -10px -10px
12px #888888" />
```

Finally, you can also layer shadows by using multiple box-shadow values separated by a comma. When more than one shadow is specified, the shadows are layered front to back. The following code offers an example of how the box-shadow property can be customized for a unique effect as shown in Figure 4–12c.

```
<img src="oceansidelogo.jpg" style="box-shadow: 20px 20px 12px
darkgreen, -20px -20px 12px darkblue" />
```

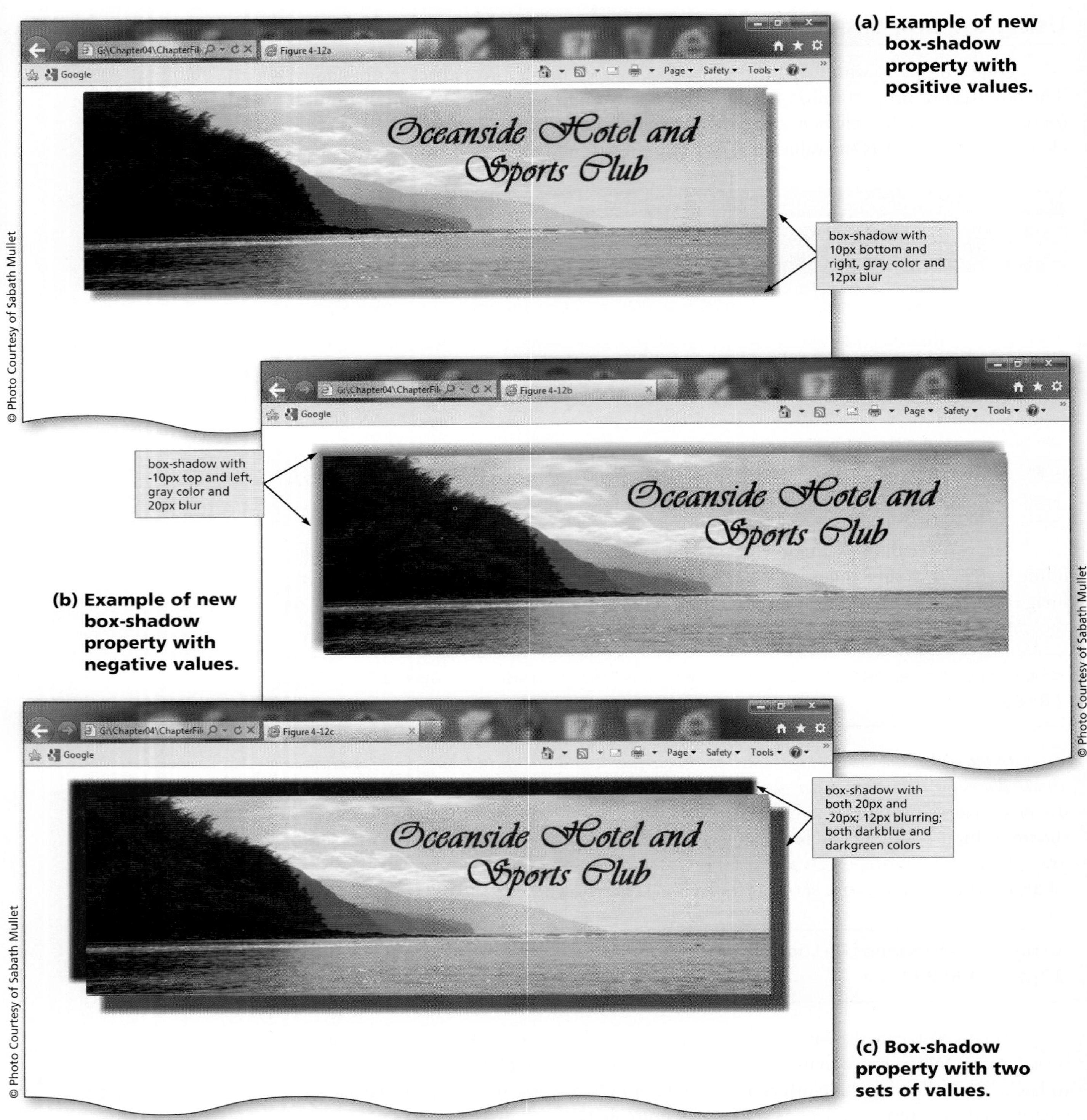

Figure 4–12

To Insert, Center, and Style an Image with a Box-Shadow

The first task for the Oceanside Hotel and Sports Club home page is to insert the company logo banner, oceansidelogo.jpg. As stated earlier in the book, the company logo is generally used in all communication that represents the company, including on the Web site, on business cards, and on company letterheads. Table 4–5 contains the HTML code to add the centered logo banner image.

Table 4–5 HTML Code for Adding and Centering an Image

Line	HTML Tag and Text
11	`<div style="text-align: center">`
12	`<img src="oceansidelogo.jpg" width="866" height="259" alt="Oceanside logo" style="box-shadow: 10px 10px 12px #888888" />`
13	`</div>`

The following step shows how to add a centered banner image.

1

- With the insertion point on line 11, enter the HTML code shown in Table 4–5, pressing ENTER at the end of each line. Make sure to indent the second line of code by using the TAB key. This separates the start and end <div> tag from the <img> tag, highlighting the image insertion. Press the ENTER key twice at the end of line 13 to position the insertion point on line 15 (Figure 4–13).

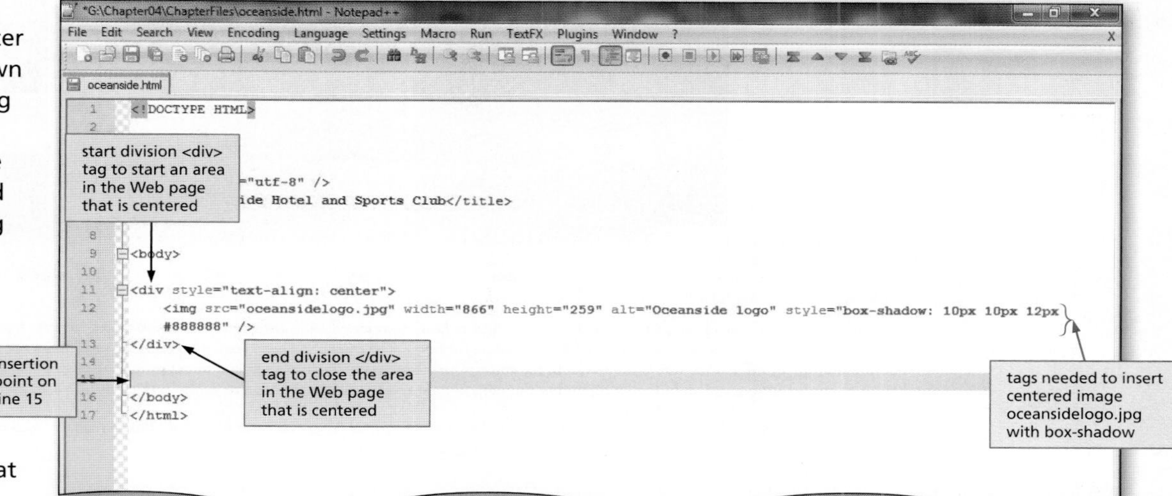

Figure 4–13

Q&A When I pressed ENTER at the end of line 12, Notepad++ indented line 13 also. How do I remove the indent?

You have to press the left arrow key or Backspace to get back to the left margin before you insert the </div> tag.

Q&A How can I determine the height and width of an image?

There are several ways to determine the height and width of an image. The first way is to click on the image in Windows Explorer; the height and width display in the status bar. Another way is to right-click the image in Windows Explorer, select Properties, and display the Details tab. A third way is to open the image in a paint or image-editing program and view the dimensions in the status bar or via a command in the program. Although you can adjust the width and height by using the width and height attributes in the <img> tag, doing so might cause the image to look distorted on the Web page.

Using a Table to Create a Horizontal Navigation Bar

The Web site created in this project consists of four Web pages. Visitors should be able to move easily from one Web page to any of the other three Web pages. Providing a navigation bar prominently across the top of the Web page (Figure 4–14) gives the visitor ready access to navigation links. You will create a table to hold the navigation bar links.

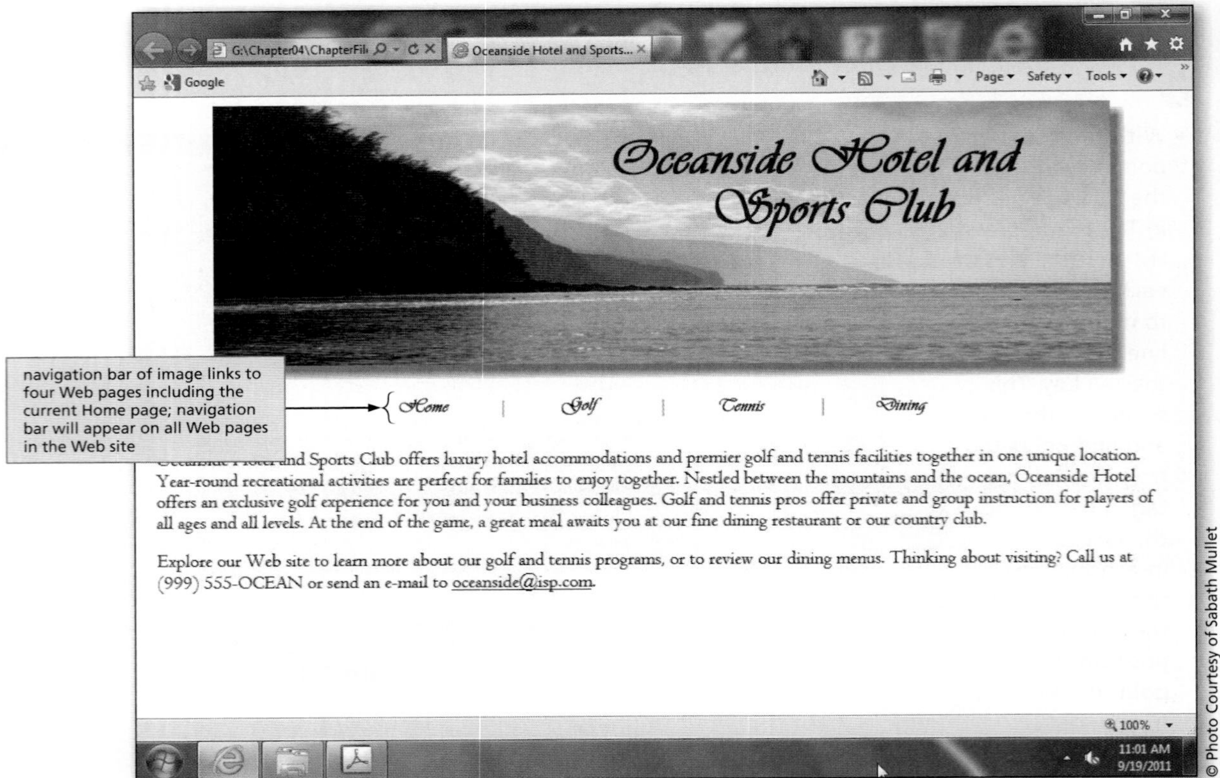

Figure 4–14

BTW

Navigation
Studies have been conducted to assess the best location on a Web page to place navigation bars and lists. The research results are varied, with indications that navigation options on the top, side, and bottom of a Web page show slight differences in visitor usability. The most important aspect of Web page navigation is to make the options easy enough to locate so visitors do not have to search for them.

All of the styles for this and other tables are set in the external style sheet that you will create in the next section of this chapter. The horizontal navigation bar table is borderless (the border-style is set to "none"), and has one row and seven columns (each of the four link options is in a column, as is each of the three dividers). To better align the navigation bar with the Oceanside Hotel and Sports Club logo, the table is set to 60% of the window's width, so that it is not as wide as the logo. The navigation bar has four links — Home, Golf, Tennis, and Dining — that link to the Web pages oceanside.html, golf.html, tennis.html, and dining.html, respectively. Each link has its own image file, including home.gif, golf.gif, tennis.gif, and dining.gif. Each link image is inserted in a single column (cell). The | (pipe) symbol is included in a column between each of the four links to separate them visually. Although you could have used plain text for these links, using images allows you to create a consistent visitor experience across all browsers, regardless of whether a visitor has the Vivaldi font installed. The link images were created using a simple paint program. All four images are equal in size and utilize the same font family (Vivaldi) as shown in the logo.

The width of each column (cell) in the table is specified as a class in the external style sheet, which will be linked to the home page and all other Web pages in this Web site later in the chapter. (If you do not define the width for these cells, the width defaults to the size of the word, image, or symbol in the cell.) The menuicon and menupipe classes need to be inserted in the navigation bar in order to adopt the styles as defined in the external style sheet. The class menuicon will be used to set each of the cells in which there are images to 23% of the width of the table. The menupipe class will be used to set each of the cells in which there are pipe symbols to 1% of the size of the table. When you specify sizes in percentages, it is generally best not to set the width to 100% as it will fill the entire width of the browser window.

Just as you did in Chapter 3, you will add the class names to your Web pages before you create the classes, in this case, in the external style sheet. All navigation bar styles are controlled with the external style sheet. If you didn't use an external style sheet, you would have to type each style into each navigation bar on each Web page in the Web site. The advantage of using an external (linked) style sheet is that if you need to make a change across the entire Web site, you make that change only once — in the external style sheet. The change then takes effect in every Web page into which the external (linked) style sheet has been linked. Using an external style sheet, you will create the .css file once and link it with one line of code into each Web page.

To Create a Horizontal Menu Bar with Image Links

Table 4–6 shows the HTML code for the horizontal navigation bar table.

Table 4–6 HTML Code to Insert a Menu Bar

<table>
<tr><th>Line</th><th>HTML Tag and Text</th></tr>
<tr><td>15</td><td>
<table class="menu" style="border-style: none"></td></tr>
<tr><td>16</td><td><tr></td></tr>
<tr><td>17</td><td><td class="menuicon"><a href="oceanside.html"><img src="home.gif" width="50" height="21" alt="Home" /></a></td></td></tr>
<tr><td>18</td><td><td class="menupipe">|</td></td></tr>
<tr><td>19</td><td><td class="menuicon"><a href="golf.html"><img src="golf.gif" width="50" height="21" alt="Golf" /></a></td></td></tr>
<tr><td>20</td><td><td class="menupipe">|</td></td></tr>
<tr><td>21</td><td><td class="menuicon"><a href="tennis.html"><img src="tennis.gif" width="50" height="21" alt="Tennis" /></a></td></td></tr>
<tr><td>22</td><td><td class="menupipe">|</td></td></tr>
<tr><td>23</td><td><td class="menuicon"><a href="dining.html"><img src="dining.gif" width="50" height="21" alt="Dining" /></a></td></td></tr>
<tr><td>24</td><td></tr></td></tr>
<tr><td>25</td><td></table></td></tr>
</table>

The following step shows how to create a table that contains image links to four pages on the Web site, separated by pipe symbols. The pipe symbol is usually found above the ENTER key; it is inserted when you press Shift and the \ (backslash) key.

1

- With the insertion point on line 15, enter the HTML code, as shown in Table 4–6, pressing ENTER after each line. Use the TAB key to indent the code, as shown in the table. Press the ENTER key once more after line 26 (Figure 4–15) to position the insertion point on line 27.

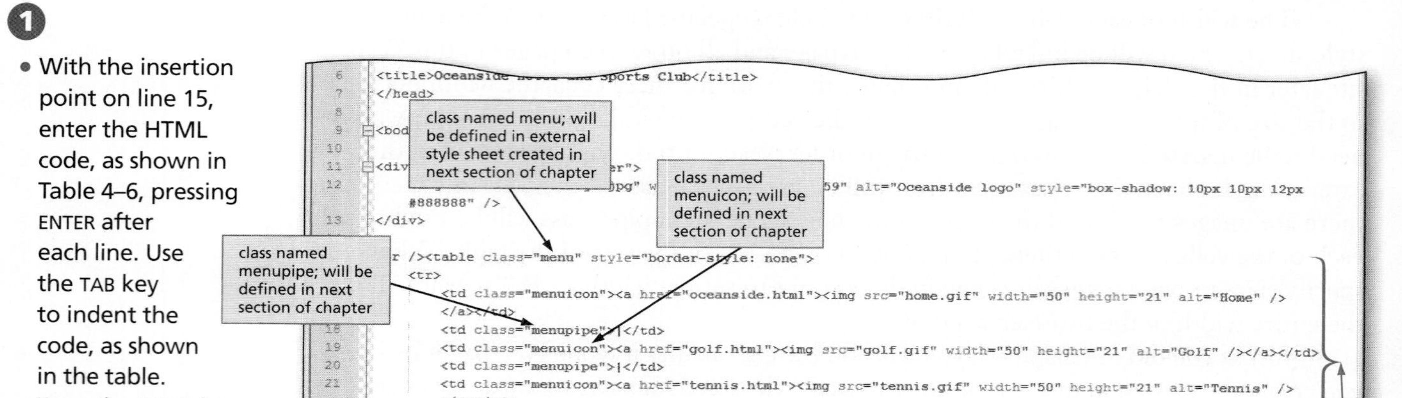

Figure 4–15

Q&A

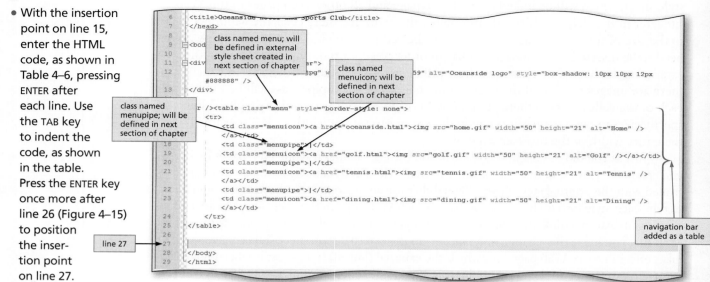

Why indent my code with the TAB key?

Indenting is a good way to organize your code so sections are recognizable. You can immediately see what lines of code are related to a single row in the table, as contained within the indented <tr> </tr> tags. This is helpful when you have many rows in the table, as in the dining.html file, which you will encounter later in the chapter.

To Add Paragraphs of Text

Next, two paragraphs of text must be added to the Web page. The text is displayed beneath the navigation bar of links that you just inserted. You will use a paragraph <p> tag to insert a blank line between the navigation bar and the text. Table 4–7 contains the code to add the paragraphs of text. In line 29, you will enter an inline style in the <span> tag to set the link text-decoration to underline. Although links appear as underlined text by default, you will set text-decoration to none for all links when you create the external style sheet in the next section. The inline style inserted on line 29 overrides that external style sheet link style and sets just this e-mail link to be underlined.

Table 4–7 HTML Code to Add Paragraphs of Text

Line	HTML Tag and Text
27	`<p>Oceanside Hotel and Sports Club offers luxury hotel accommodations and premiere golf and tennis facilities together in one unique location. Year-round recreational activities are perfect for families to enjoy together. Nestled between the mountains and the ocean, Oceanside Hotel offers an exclusive golf experience for you and your business colleagues. Golf and tennis pros offer private and group instruction for players of all ages and all levels. At the end of the game, a great meal awaits you at our fine dining restaurant or our country club.</p>`
28	
29	`<p>Explore our Web site to learn more about our golf and tennis programs, or to review our dining menus. Thinking about visiting? Call us at (999) 555-OCEAN or send an e-mail to <a href="mailto:oceanside@isp.com"><span style="text-decoration: underline">oceanside@isp.com</span></a>.</p>`

The following step illustrates how to add paragraphs of text.

1. With the insertion point on line 27, enter the HTML code, as shown in Table 4–7, to insert the paragraphs of text, pressing the ENTER key after each line, including line 29 (Figure 4–16).

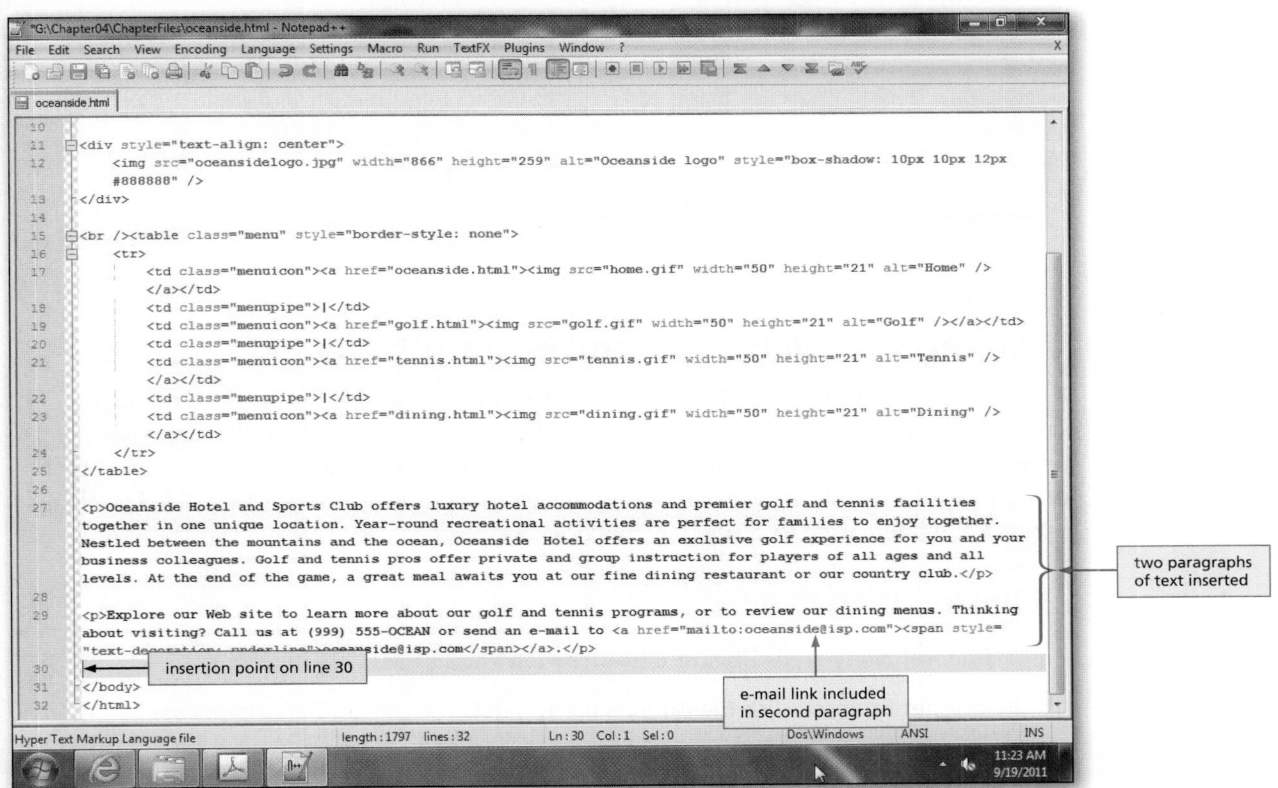

Figure 4–16

To Save the HTML File

With the HTML code for the Oceanside Hotel and Sports Club home page complete, you should resave the file. The following step shows how to save an HTML file that has been previously saved.

1. Click the Save icon on the Notepad++ toolbar to save the most recent version of oceanside.html on the same storage device and in the same folder as the last time you saved it (Figure 4–17).

Save icon

oceanside.html filename inserted

```
<div style="text-align: center">
    <img src="oceansidelogo.jpg" width="866" height="259" alt="Oceanside logo" style="box-shadow: 10px 10px 12px
    #888888" />
</div>

<br /><table class="menu" style="border-style: none">
    <tr>
        <td class="menuicon"><a href="oceanside.html"><img src="home.gif" width="50" height="21" alt="Home" />
        </a></td>
        <td class="menupipe">|</td>
        <td class="menuicon"><a href="golf.html"><img src="golf.gif" width="50" height="21" alt="Golf" /></a></td>
        <td class="menupipe">|</td>
        <td class="menuicon"><a href="tennis.html"><img src="tennis.gif" width="50" height="21" alt="Tennis" />
        </a></td>
        <td class="menupipe">|</td>
        <td class="menuicon"><a href="dining.html"><img src="dining.gif" width="50" height="21" alt="Dining" />
        </a></td>
    </tr>
```

Figure 4–17

Viewing the Web Page and Testing Links

After you save the HTML file for the Oceanside Hotel and Sports Club home page, it should be viewed in a browser to confirm the Web page appears as desired. You do not validate or print the Web page yet because you still have one statement (the link to the external style sheet) to add to the file. It is also important to test the four links on the Oceanside Hotel and Sports Club home page to verify they function as expected.

To View a Web Page

The following steps illustrate how to view the HTML file in a browser.

1. In Internet Explorer, click the Address bar to select the URL on the Address bar.
2. Type `G:\Chapter04\ChapterFiles\oceanside.html` or the location of your file on the Address bar of your browser and press ENTER to display the Web page (Figure 4–18).

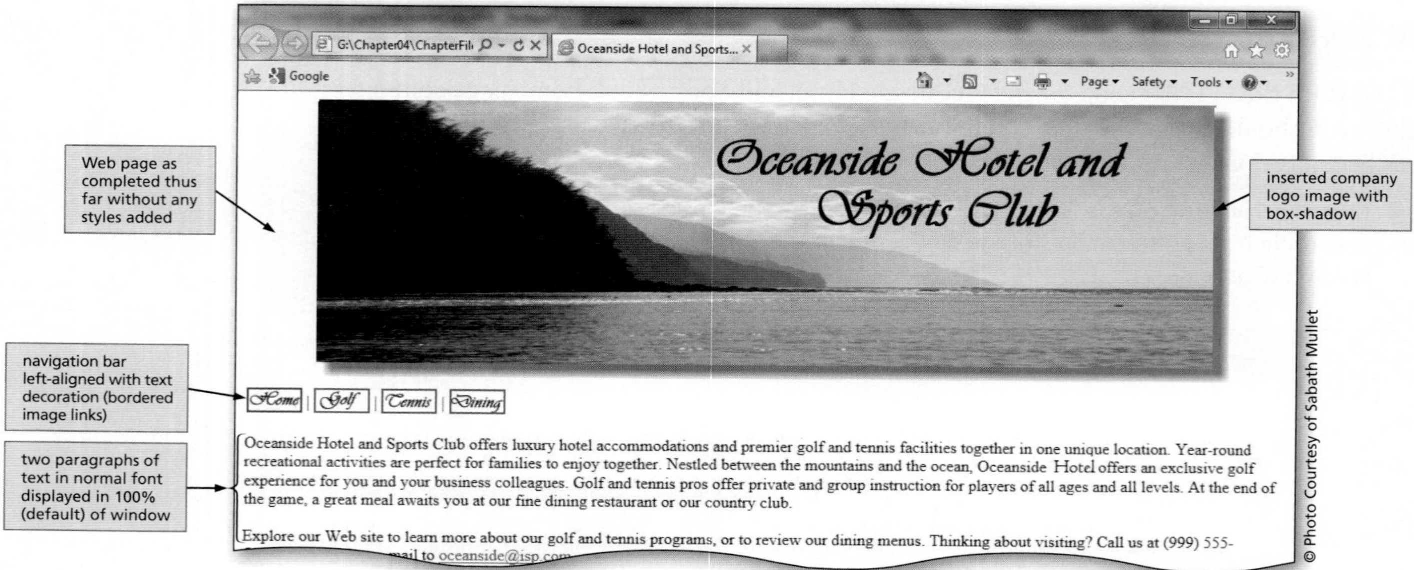

Figure 4–18

To Test Links on a Web Page

The following steps show how to test the links on the Oceanside Hotel and Sports Club home page to verify that they work correctly.

1. With the Oceanside Hotel and Sports Club's home page displayed in the browser, point to the e-mail link, oceanside@isp.com and click the link to open the default e-mail program with the address oceanside@isp.com in the To: text box.
2. Click the Close button in the new message window. If a dialog box asks if you want to save changes, click No.
3. With the USB flash drive in drive G, click the Tennis link from the home page just created. Click Home to return to the home page from the Tennis page. Next, click the Dining link from the Home page. Click Home to return to the home page from the Dining page. The link for the Golf page will not work because that Web page is not yet created; you will create it later in this chapter. The links work on the Tennis and Dining Web pages as those pages were supplied in the Data Files with the navigation already coded.

External Style Sheets

External style sheets are the most comprehensive type of style sheet and can be used to control the consistency and look of many Web pages within a Web site. Adding an external style sheet to a Web page involves a two-step process of creating an external style sheet and then linking this style sheet to the desired Web pages. The most beneficial feature of the external style sheet is that you can easily change the style (appearance) of all Web pages into which the style sheet is linked just by changing the external style sheet. For instance, the font-family and font-size for all four Web pages in this chapter's project are set in the external style sheet. If the owners of the Web site decide that they do not like the look (or style) of that font-family or font-size, you only have to make the change in one file — the external style sheet. Compare that process to having the font-family and font-size inserted into every single Web page in a Web site either with embedded style sheets or (worst case) inline styles. To make a change to all font-family and font-size styles, you would have to change those in every single place that the styles reside. External (linked) style sheets are the most efficient and powerful way to change styles for an entire Web site.

An external style sheet is a text file that contains the selectors and declarations for the styles you want to apply across the Web site. The sample code that follows shows an example of an external style sheet used to set table, paragraph, image, and link formatting. Note the use of classes (e.g., menu, menuicon, menupipe) in this external style sheet that provides a finer level of control within a table used for navigation.

```
body          {font-family: Centaur, "Century Gothic", Arial;
                        font-size: 14pt;}
p                       {margin-left: 10pt;
                        margin-right: 10pt;}
a                       {text-decoration: none;
                        color: black;}
img                     {border-color: transparent;}
```

BTW

Classes
Note that the classes are named with a period (.) after the element is defined. Thus, the table .menu statement identifies a class named menu that will be used with the table elements.

```
table       {width: 65%;
            margin-left:auto;
            margin-right:auto;
            border-color: #545859;
            border-style: ridge;
            border-width: 10px;}
            .menu    {text-align: center;
                     width: 60%;}
            .menuicon  {width: 23%;}
            .menupipe  {width: 1%;}
th          {color: white;
            background-color: #757775;}
tr.stripe   {background-color: #d8d8ce;}
td.bolder   {font-weight: bold;}
caption     {caption-side: bottom;
            font-style: italic;}
```

The format of the external style sheet is very similar to the format of an embedded style sheet. An external style sheet, however, does not need <style> </style> tags to start and end the style sheet; it only needs the style statements.

To create an external style sheet, enter all of the style statements in a text file using Notepad++ or another text editor, and then save the text file with a .css (for Cascading Style Sheets) extension. The code shown above, for example, can be saved with the filename stylesch4.css and then linked onto multiple Web pages.

Remember that the <head> tag is used for a variety of purposes. The information contained within the <head> </head> container of your HTML document provides information to browsers and search engines but is not displayed on the Web page itself. The following tags can be used within the <head> </head> container: <base>, <link>, <meta>, <script>, <style>, and <title>. For each Web page to which you want to apply the styles in an external style sheet, a <link /> tag similar to the sample code below must be inserted within the <head> </head> tags of the Web page:

```
<link rel="stylesheet" type="text/css" href="stylesch4.css" />
```

The <link /> tag indicates that the style sheet stylesch4.css should be applied to this Web page. The property-value statement rel="stylesheet" defines the relationship of the linked document (that is, it defines it as a style sheet). The property-value statement type="text/css" indicates the content and language used in the linked document. The property-value statement href="stylesch4.css" indicates the name and location of the linked style sheet, stylesch4.css. To apply this style sheet to other pages in the Web site, you would insert the same <link /> tag between the <head> </head> tags of each Web page.

Plan Ahead

Determine what type of style sheets or other formatting to use in your Web pages.

- **Determine which styles will be common across the Web pages in the Web site.** Web sites should strive for a consistent experience across all pages. For instance, if tables are used, the style of the tables should be common or consistent throughout the Web site. A font-family style is also something that is generally common across all Web pages in a Web site. Consider using external (or linked) style sheets for styles that will encompass all Web pages in a multipage Web site. Because it is a four-page Web site, the project in this chapter is a perfect application for external (or linked) style sheets. You will use an external style sheet in this project to set styles for the body, paragraphs, links, images, and tables. *(Note: Although it is important to maintain consistency across a Web site, the three tables created in the Web pages in this project will all be different, so that you will learn different table techniques.)*
- **Identify elements that need to differ from the style used across the Web site**.
  - Consider using embedded style sheets for Web pages in which the styles apply only to one particular Web page. You can use embedded style sheets when you want elements within one Web page to look similar to one another. In the projects in this chapter, however, you do not use embedded style sheets.
  - Consider using inline styles for any style that is unique for a single element, such as when you want one word or paragraph on one Web page to look different than all others. In this project, you will use inline styles to align images and vary some text.

Adding an External Style Sheet

The next step is to create an external style sheet (.css file) and link it to the Web pages where it will be used. The external (linked) style sheet will set the style for body text, paragraphs, links, images, and table format.

Because the font-family and font-size style is used for all text on all Web pages, you can put that style in the body element, identified on the external style sheet as body. All links (identified using the a tag in the external style sheet) will be black through all states (normal, visited, and active) and use no text decoration (i.e., the text links will not be underlined). Note that you overrode this style on the home page by adding an inline style to the e-mail address link. Your inline style adds underlining to the e-mail link. Most of the tables will have a 65% width relative to the window. The exception is the navigation bar table that you created earlier, which will be slightly smaller (60% width). Finally, you will use classes, as discussed in Chapter 3, to have more control over particular elements of the tables in the Web site. You will use a class named menu for the navigation bar links. You also want to separate the navigation bar table cells with pipe symbols. To do that, you will use classes named menuicon and menupipe to specify the width of each of those cells. Note that the classes are named with a period (.) after the element is defined. Thus, the table.menu statement identifies a class named menu that will be used with the table elements.

BTW

Adding Comments
If your instructor wants you to add your name to the CSS code file, you can do that by adding your name within a comment line. Use /* and */ to surround the added information (e.g., your name), marking it as a comment.

Plan Ahead

Create and link an external style sheet.
The external style sheet is the most powerful style sheet and has the lowest precedence. You can easily create a common look across a Web site by creating an external (.css) style sheet and linking it to all Web pages.

- **Create the .css file**. The first step is to create the external style sheet itself. This file, which contains all of the style statements that you want, has to be saved with a filename extension of .css. Make sure to store this file in the same folder as the other Web pages.
- **Link the external style sheet onto the Web pages**. The second step is to link the external style sheet (.css file) onto the Web pages where you want the styles to be applied. The link statement is placed between the <head> and </head> tags.

To Create an External Style Sheet

Table 4–8 shows the style statements for an external style sheet for the Oceanside Hotel and Sports Club Web site. To create an external style sheet, you will open a new text file and enter the CSS code for the style statements that define the Web page style. After coding the style statements, you will save the file with the file extension .css to identify it as a CSS file.

Table 4–8 Code for an External Style Sheet

CSS Properties and Values

```
body    {font-family: Centaur, "Century Gothic", Arial;
        font-size: 14 pt;}

p       {margin-left: 10pt;
        margin-right: 10pt;}

a       {text-decoration: none;
        color: black;}

img     {border-color: transparent;}

table   {width: 65%;
        margin-left: auto;
        margin-right: auto;
        border-color: #545859;
        border-style: ridge;
        border-width: 10px;}

   .menu    {text-align: center;
            width: 60%;}

   .menuicon {width: 23%;}

   .menupipe {width: 1%;}

th      {color: white;
        background-color: #757775;}

tr.stripe {background-color: #d8d8ce;}

td.bolder {font-weight: bold;}

caption    {caption-side: bottom;
           font-style: italic;}
```

The following steps illustrate how to create, save, and validate an external style sheet. You must use a different w3.org validation service to validate a .css file. You will use jigsaw.w3.org/css-validator/#validate_by_upload for the .css file type. The validation result page looks very similar to the ones you saw in the HTML validation process.

1

- If necessary, click the Notepad++ button on the taskbar to display oceanside.html. Click File on the navigation bar and then click New.
- Enter the CSS code, as shown in Table 4–8, using the TAB key to align text, as shown (Figure 4–19).

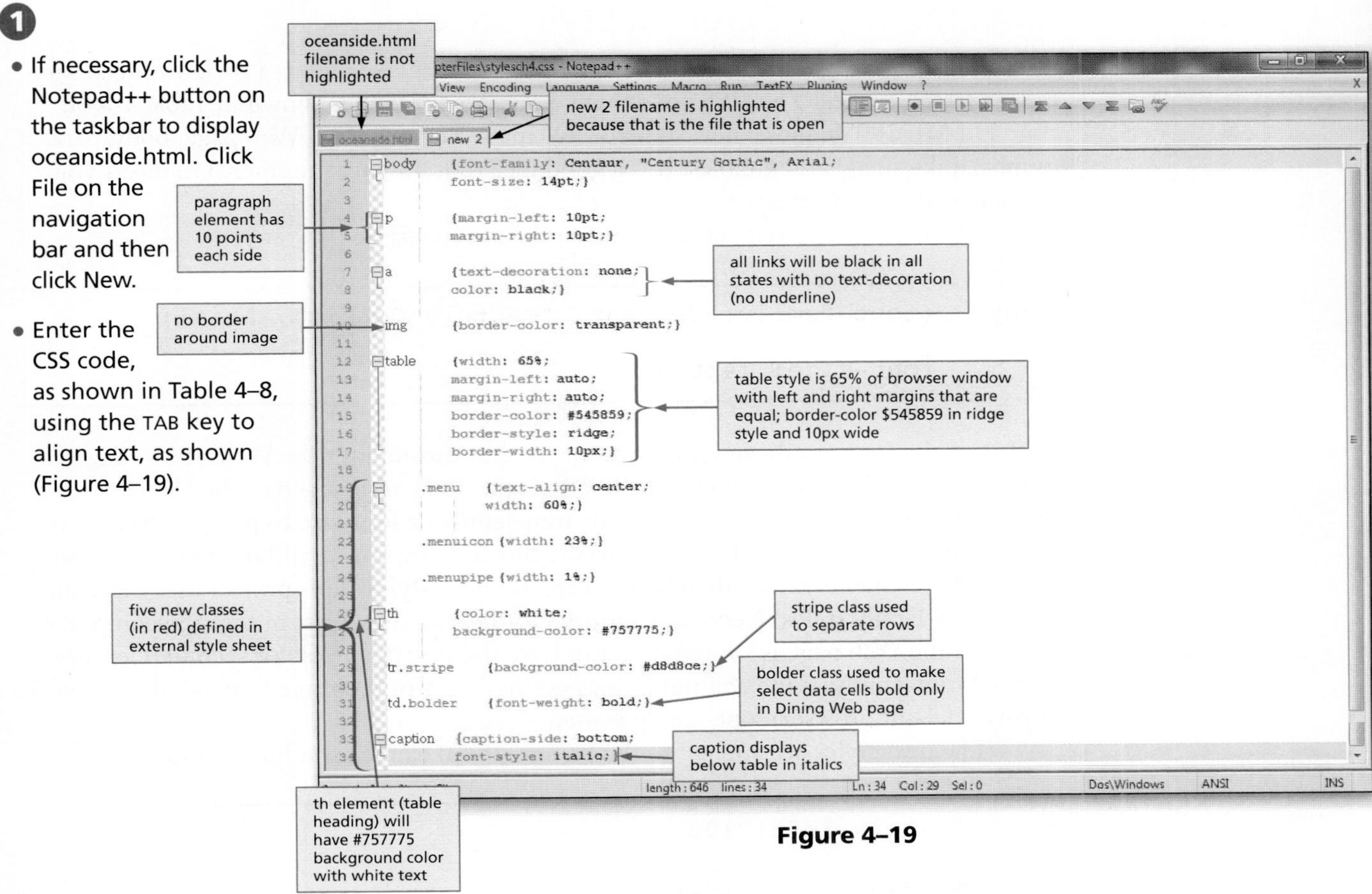

Figure 4–19

2

- With the USB drive plugged into your computer, click File on the menu bar and then click Save As. Type `stylesch4.css` in the File name text box. If necessary, navigate to the G:\Chapter04\ChapterFiles folder. Click the Save button in the Save As dialog box to save the file as stylesch4.css.
- Open Internet Explorer and navigate to jigsaw.w3.org/css-validator/#validate_by_upload.
- Validate the stylesch4.css file.
- Return to the stylesch4.css Notepad++ file and print a hard copy of the style sheet (Figure 4–20).

```
body {font-family: Centaur, "Century Gothic", Arial;
      font-size: 14pt;}

p     {margin-left: 10pt;
      margin-right: 10pt;}

a     {text-decoration: none;
      color: black;}

img   {border-color: transparent;}

table {width: 65%;
      margin-left: auto;
      margin-right: auto;
      border-color: #545859;
      border-style: ridge;
      border-width: 10px;}

    .menu   {text-align: center;
            width: 60%;}

    .menuicon {width: 23%;}

    .menupipe {width: 1%;}

th    {color: white;
      background-color: #757775;}
```

Figure 4–20

Examining the External Style Sheet

Because the CSS code for the external style sheet is complex, a review is necessary to learn what it does. The CSS code that you entered, which is shown in Table 4-8 on page HTML 180 defines a new style for five main elements on a Web page: body, paragraphs, links, images, and tables. It is a good idea (but not a requirement) to insert your styles in order in the external style sheet.

The first style statement on lines 1 and 2 is entered as:

```
body   {font-family: Centaur, "Century Gothic", Arial;
       font-size: 14pt;}
```

to change the font-family and font-size for the text throughout the Web site. You use the body element because you want these styles to apply to text across the Web site (Figure 4-19). If you wanted to apply one font-family or font-size to paragraphs of text and another font-family and font-size to the text in links, you would use the paragraph (p) and link (a) elements rather than body to create those styles. This project uses three different font-family styles (Centaur, Century Gothic, and Arial) just in case the computer on which the Web page is viewed does not have the first (Centaur) or second (Century Gothic) font-family. If the computer does not have any of the three font-families, then the normal (default browser) font-family is used.

The next styles are applied to the paragraph (p) element on lines 4 and 5:

```
p     {margin-left: 10pt;
      margin-right: 10pt;}
```

With this style, you are adding right and left margins that are 10 points wide. This pulls the paragraph text in 10 points both from the left and right. To see what that style statement does to the look of the home page for this Web site, look at Figure 4–18 on page HTML 176 compared to Figure 4–1a on page HTML 155.

Lines 7 and 8 define the styles for all links by using the link (a) element:

```
a     {text-decoration: none;
      color: black;}
```

BTW Colors
To find the exact color, you can open the logo in a graphic image editing program and use one of the tools (such as the eye dropper tool) to click on the logo itself. If you then look at the color box, you should see the six-digit hexadecimal code for that color.

This statement sets links to have no text-decoration (no underlines) and makes all link states (normal, visited, and active) black in color. With a text-decoration setting of none, the browser will not display lines under any links. Setting the link color to black throughout eliminates the blue and purple (normal and visited) link colors that you would normally have. The next statement, on line 10 in the external style sheet, sets the border color of the image tag to transparent. With that setting, no border will display around any images.

```
img   {border-color: transparent;}
```

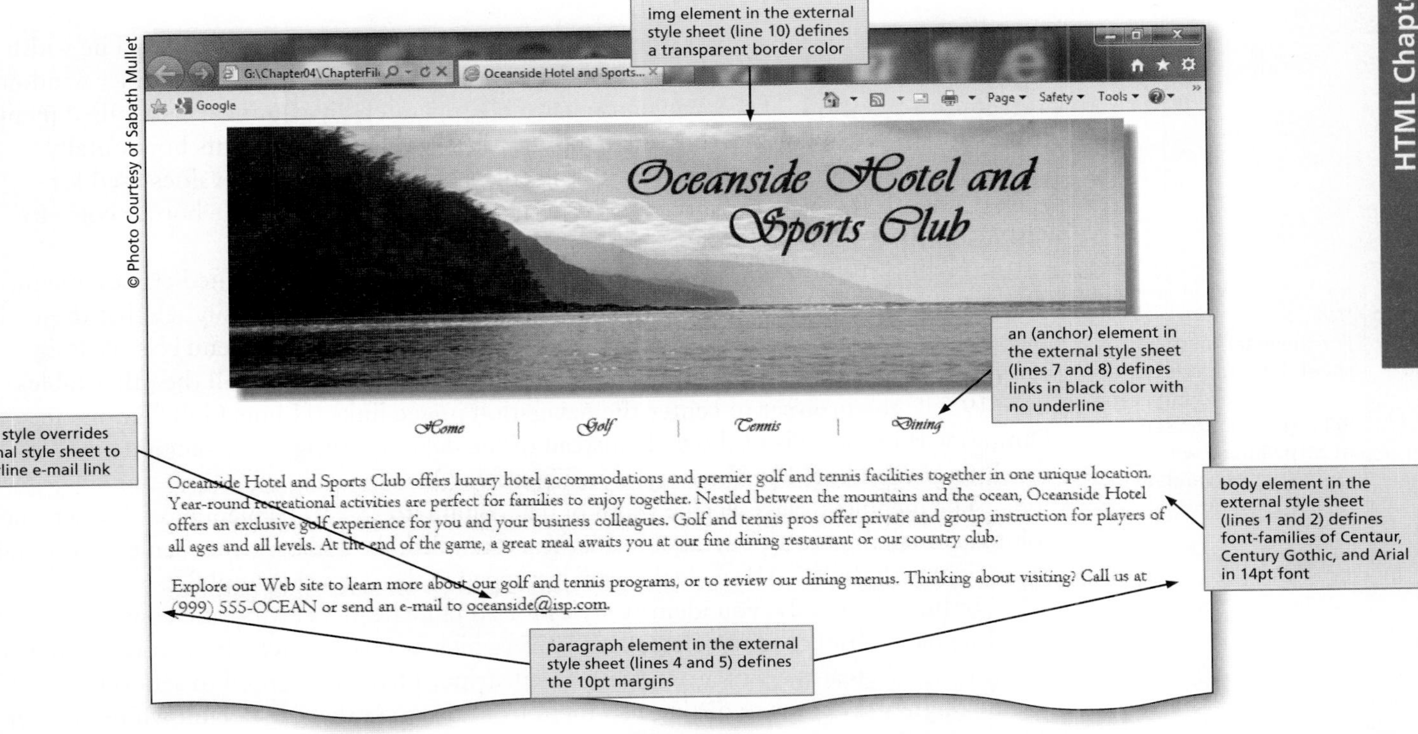

Figure 4–21

In this external style sheet, all table-related styles are inserted together from lines 12 through 34:

```
table               {width: 65%;
                    margin-left: auto;
                    margin-right: auto;
                    border-color: #545859;
                    border-style: ridge;
                    border-width: 10px;}
    .menu           {text-align: center;
                    width: 60%;}
    .menuicon       {width: 23%;}
    .menupipe       {width: 1%;}
th                  {color: white;
                    background-color: #757775;}
tr.stripe           {background-color: #d8d8ce;}
td.bolder           {font-weight: bold;}
caption             {caption-side: bottom;
                    font-style: italic;}
```

Lines 12 through 17 identify the general style for all tables on the Web pages. The width of all tables (with the exception of the navigation bar) will be 65% of the browser window. You control the width of the navigation bar table separately by naming a class called menu (remember this can be any arbitrary name). The margin: auto statements horizontally center the element table with respect to the edges of the window. The values used for each side are equal because of the auto designator. You also set the table border color to #545859, with a ridge style and a width of 10 pixels.

On lines 19 through 24, beneath the table element, are three named classes: menu, menuicon, and menupipe. Those lines are indented so that you can easily see that these classes are related to the table element. On line 20, the width of the menu class is designated to be 60% of the browser window, instead of the 65% width of all the other tables. Line 19 tells the browser to center the navigation image links (Home, Golf, Tennis, and Dining) within the cells of the table instead of the default setting of left-alignment. See the differences created by these styles in Figure 4–22.

The menuicon class sets the width of that column to 23%. The menupipe class sets the column containing the pipe symbol to 1%. You can utilize these classes (menu, menuicon, and menupipe) with the HTML code that you just typed in the oceanside.html file.

In lines 26 and 27, you identify styles for all table headers (<th>) and rows (<tr>). You designate a background color of #757775 (which is a dark gray) with text color that is white. Line 29 creates a table row class named stripe. That will be used to set every other row to a light gray color to distinguish them from the rows that are default white in color (Figure 4–22). Line 31 creates a table data cell named bolder that is used in the Dining Web page as shown in Figure 4-1d on page HTML 155.

BTW

External Style Sheet Validator

For the external style sheet, be sure to use the CSS validator found at the w3.org validation service at http://jigsaw.w3.org/css-validator/#validate_by_upload.

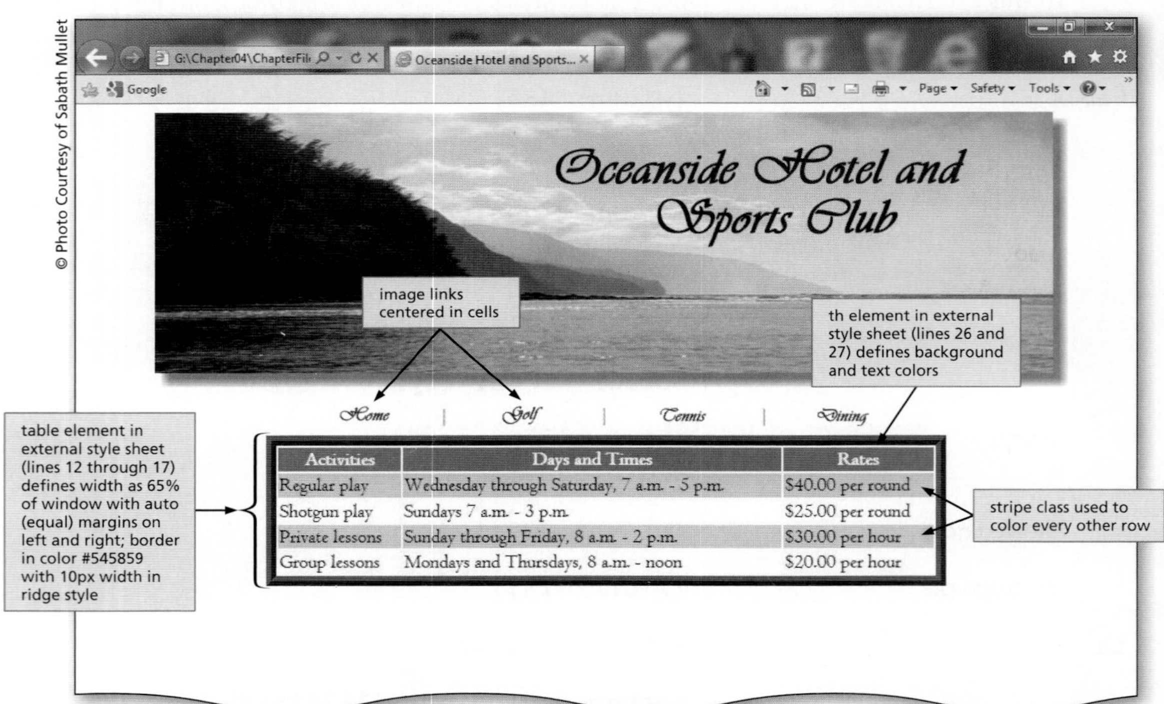

Figure 4–22

The final section of CSS code, lines 33 and 34, defines the styles to be applied to table captions. You want all captions to be aligned beneath the table and italicized.

Linking to the External Style Sheet

Four Web pages in the Oceanside Hotel and Sports Club Web site require the same style: oceanside.html, golf.html, tennis.html, and dining.html. Linking the external style sheet to each of these Web pages gives them the same styles for margins, paragraph text, links, images, and tables.

To link to the external style sheet, a <link /> tag must be inserted onto each of these four Web pages. The <link /> tag used to link an external style sheet is added within the <head> </head> tags of the Web page HTML code. The general format of the <link /> tag is:

```
<link rel="stylesheet" type="text/css" href="stylesch4.css" />
```

where rel="stylesheet" establishes that the linked document is a style sheet, type="text/css" indicates that the CSS language is used in the text file containing the style sheet, and href="stylesch4.css" provides the name and location (URL) of the linked style sheet. To link a style sheet to a Web page, the <link /> tag must use "stylesheet" as the value for the rel property and text/css as the value for the type property. The URL used as the value for the href property varies, based on the name and location of the file used as the external style sheet. The URL used here indicates that the external style sheet, stylesch4.css, is located in the main or root directory of the Web site.

To Link to an External Style Sheet

After creating and saving the external style sheet, .css file, you use a <link /> tag to link the external style sheet to any Web pages to which you want to apply the style. Notice that the link tag is one of those (like the <img /> tag) that does not have a separate end tag (e.g., <body> and </body>). You therefore should use the / after a space and before the > in the tag to indicate the end of the tag.

The following step illustrates how to add a link to an external style sheet using a <link /> tag:

- Click the oceanside .html tab in Notepad++ to make it the active window.
- With the oceanside .html file open, click the end of line 6 after the > and press the ENTER key twice. Your insertion point should be positioned on line 8.
- Type `<link rel="stylesheet" type="text/css" href="stylesch4.css" />` as the HTML code and then press the ENTER key, as shown in Figure 4–23.
- Click the Save button on the Notepad++ toolbar.

```
1  <!DOCTYPE HTML>
2
3  <html>
4  <head>
5  <meta charset="utf-8" />
6  <title>Oceanside Hotel and Sports Club</title>
7
8  <link rel="stylesheet" type="text/css" href="stylesch4.css" />
9
10 </head>
11
12 <body>
13
14 <div style="text-align: center">
15     <img src="oceansidelogo.jpg" width="866" height="259" alt="Oceanside logo" style="box-shadow: 10px 10px 12px
       #888888" />
16 </div>
17
18 <br /><table class="menu" style="border-style: none">
19     <tr>
20         <td class="menuicon"><a href="oceanside.html"><img src="home.gif" width="50" height="21" alt="Home" />
           </a></td>
21         <td class="menupipe">|</td>
22         <td class="menuicon"><a href="golf.html"><img src="golf.gif" width="50" height="21" alt="Golf" /></a></td>
23         <td class="menupipe">|</td>
24         <td class="menuicon"><a href="tennis.html"><img src="tennis.gif" width="50" height="21" alt="Tennis" />
           </a></td>
25         <td class="menupipe">|</td>
26         <td class="menuicon"><a href="dining.html"><img src="dining.gif" width="50" height="21" alt="Dining" />
           </a></td>
27     </tr>
28 </table>
```

link to external style sheet; because of this one line of code, all styles defined in stylesch4.css external style sheet will take effect on the Web page

Figure 4–23

Q&A Is that all it takes to use an external style sheet — to insert that link statement?

Yes, that is all you need to do to use the styles identified in the external style sheet. The styles specified in the external style sheet will apply to that page, unless an embedded or inline style sheet takes precedence. Also remember that if you want to change a style, you just change it in the external (linked) style sheet itself. It automatically takes effect in any Web page that is linked to the external style sheet. (Remember to click the Refresh button if that Web page is already open in the browser.)

Q&A Will the table styles from the stylesch4.css file take effect for all tables within the Web site?

As long as you insert the style sheet link statement onto the Web page, then the table styles will take effect. Remember that you can override those styles with either an embedded or an inline style sheet. You would do this if there is a table that you want to vary from all other tables in the Web site.

Q&A Why is an external style sheet sometimes called a linked style sheet?

The style sheet that you created above is external to (as opposed to inline or embedded in) the Web page in which it is used. That's why it is called an external style sheet. The external style sheet is used by linking it into a Web page. It is called linked because you use a <link /> tag to insert it.

Validating and Printing the HTML, Viewing the Web Page, and Testing Links

After you save the HTML file for the Oceanside Hotel and Sports Club home page, it should be validated to ensure that it meets the current standards applied throughout this text and viewed in a browser to confirm the Web page displays as desired. It is also important to test the links in the Oceanside Hotel and Sports Club home page to verify that they function as expected.

To Validate a Web Page

The following steps illustrate how to validate an HTML file:

1. Open Internet Explorer and navigate to the Web site validator.w3.org.
2. Click the Validate by File Upload tab.
3. Click the Browse button.
4. Locate the oceanside.html file on your storage device, click the filename, and then click the Open button in the Choose File to Upload dialog box and the filename will be inserted into the File box.
5. Click the Check button.

Q&A What if my HTML code does not pass the validation process?

If your file does not pass validation, make changes to the file to correct your errors. You should then revalidate the file.

To Print an HTML File

After your HTML code has passed validation, it is a good idea to make a hard copy printout of it.

1. Click the Notepad++ button on the taskbar to activate the Notepad++ window.
2. Click File on the menu bar, click the Print command, and then click the Print button to print a hard copy of the HTML code (Figure 4–24).

```
<!DOCTYPE HTML>

<html>
<head>
<meta charset="utf-8" />
<title>Oceanside Hotel and Sports Club</title>

<link rel="stylesheet" type="text/css" href="stylesch4.css" />

</head>

<body>

<div style="text-align: center">
    <img src="oceansidelogo.jpg" width="866" height="259" alt="Oceanside logo" style=
    "box-shadow: 10px 10px 12px #888888" />
</div>

<br /><table class="menu" style="border-style: none">
    <tr>
        <td class="menuicon"><a href="oceanside.html"><img src="home.gif" width="50"
        height="21" alt="Home" /></a></td>
        <td class="menupipe">|</td>
        <td class="menuicon"><a href="golf.html"><img src="golf.gif" width="50" height=
        "21" alt="Golf" /></a></td>
        <td class="menupipe">|</td>
        <td class="menuicon"><a href="tennis.html"><img src="tennis.gif" width="50"
        height="21" alt="Tennis" /></a></td>
        <td class="menupipe">|</td>
        <td class="menuicon"><a href="dining.html"><img src="dining.gif" width="50"
        height="21" alt="Dining" /></a></td>
    </tr>
</table>

<p>Oceanside Hotel and Sports Club offers luxury hotel accommodations and premier golf
and tennis facilities together in one unique location. Year-round recreational
activities are perfect for families to enjoy together. Nestled between the mountains
and the ocean, Oceanside Hotel offers an exclusive golf experience for you and your
business colleagues. Golf and tennis pros offer private and group instruction for
players of all ages and all levels. At the end of the game, a great meal awaits you at
our fine dining restaurant or our country club.</p>

<p>Explore our Web site to learn more about our golf and tennis programs, or to review
our dining menus. Thinking about visiting? Call us at (999) 555-OCEAN or send an e-mail
to <a href="mailto:oceanside@isp.com"><span style="text-decoration: underline">
oceanside@isp.com</span></a>.</p>

</body>
</html>
```

Figure 4–24

To View, Test, and Print a Web Page

1. Click the Internet Explorer button on the Windows taskbar to activate Internet Explorer.
2. In Internet Explorer, click the Address bar to select the URL in the Address bar.
3. Type `G:\Chapter04\ChapterFiles\oceanside.html` (or the specific path to your file) to display the new URL in the Address bar and then press the ENTER key.
4. Click the Tennis link and then click the Back button. Click the Dining link and then click the Back button.

Q&A Why isn't the Tennis Web page formatted with the styles in the external style sheet?
In order for the external style sheet to take effect, you have to insert the <link> statement into the HTML code in the Tennis file.

5. Click the Print button on the Internet Explorer Command bar to print the Web page (Figure 4–25).

Figure 4–25

Creating a Second Web Page

You have created the Oceanside Hotel and Sports Club home page with a horizontal navigation bar of image links for easy navigation to other pages in the site and an external style sheet. Now it is time to create one of those linked pages — the Golf page (Figure 4–26 on the next page). Like the home page, the Golf page includes the logo image and a horizontal navigation bar of text links. Having the Oceanside Hotel and Sports Club logo and the horizontal navigation bar at the top of each page provides consistency throughout the Web site. The navigation bar lists the four Web pages — Home, Golf, Tennis, and Dining — with a | (pipe) symbol between links. Beneath the navigation bar is a table listing the golf options that are available at Oceanside Hotel and Sports Club.

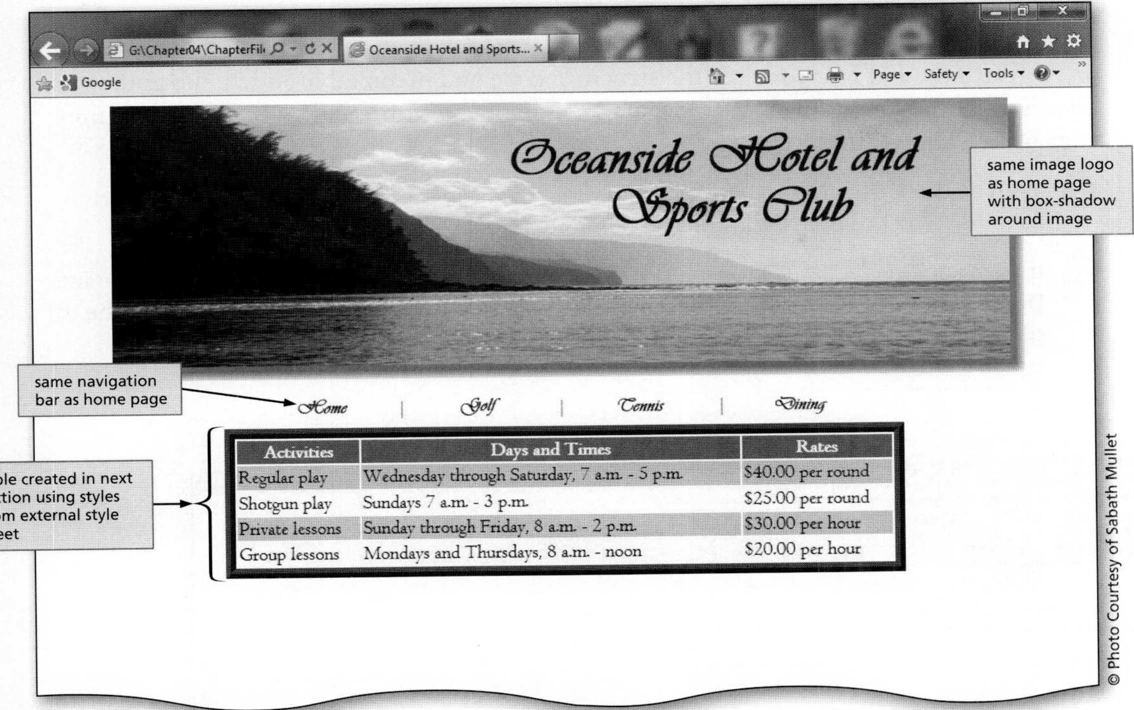

Figure 4–26

The first step in creating the Golf Web page is to add the HTML tags to define the Web page structure, the Oceanside Hotel and Sports Club logo banner image, and the horizontal navigation bar. Because the logo banner image and navigation bar are the same as on the home page, you can copy and paste HTML code from the Home page and then edit it for the Golf page. You would copy/paste this code because you have already tested it by opening the oceanside.html file in the browser, and you know the code works. Rather than retyping the code, and possibly getting errors, a copy/paste will assure that it is correct.

To Copy and Paste HTML Code to a New File

The following steps show how to copy the HTML tags to define the Web page structure and the horizontal menu table from the HTML file, oceanside.html, to a new HTML file.

1. If necessary, click the Notepad++ button on the taskbar and click the oceanside.html tab to make it the active window.
2. Click immediately to the left of the < in the <!DOCTYPE> html tag on line 1.
3. Drag through the </table> tag on line 28 to highlight lines 1 through 28.
4. Press CTRL+C to copy the selected lines to the Clipboard.
5. Click File on the Notepad++ menu bar and then click New.
6. Press CTRL+V to paste the contents from the Clipboard into a new file. Press the ENTER key twice to position the insertion point on line 30.
7. After the words Oceanside Hotel and Sports Club in the <title> on line 6, add ~ Golf (using the tilde ~ character).

To Save an HTML File

With the HTML code for the structure code and menu table added, the golf.html file should be saved. For this Web page, the end body </body> and end HTML </html> tags will be added later.

1. With a USB drive plugged into the computer, click File on the menu bar and then click Save As. Type `golf.html` in the File name text box.
2. If necessary, click USB (G:) (or the drive where you store your data files) in the Save in list. Double-click the Chapter04 folder and then double-click the ChapterFiles folder in the list of available folders. Click the Save button in the Save As dialog box (Figure 4–27).

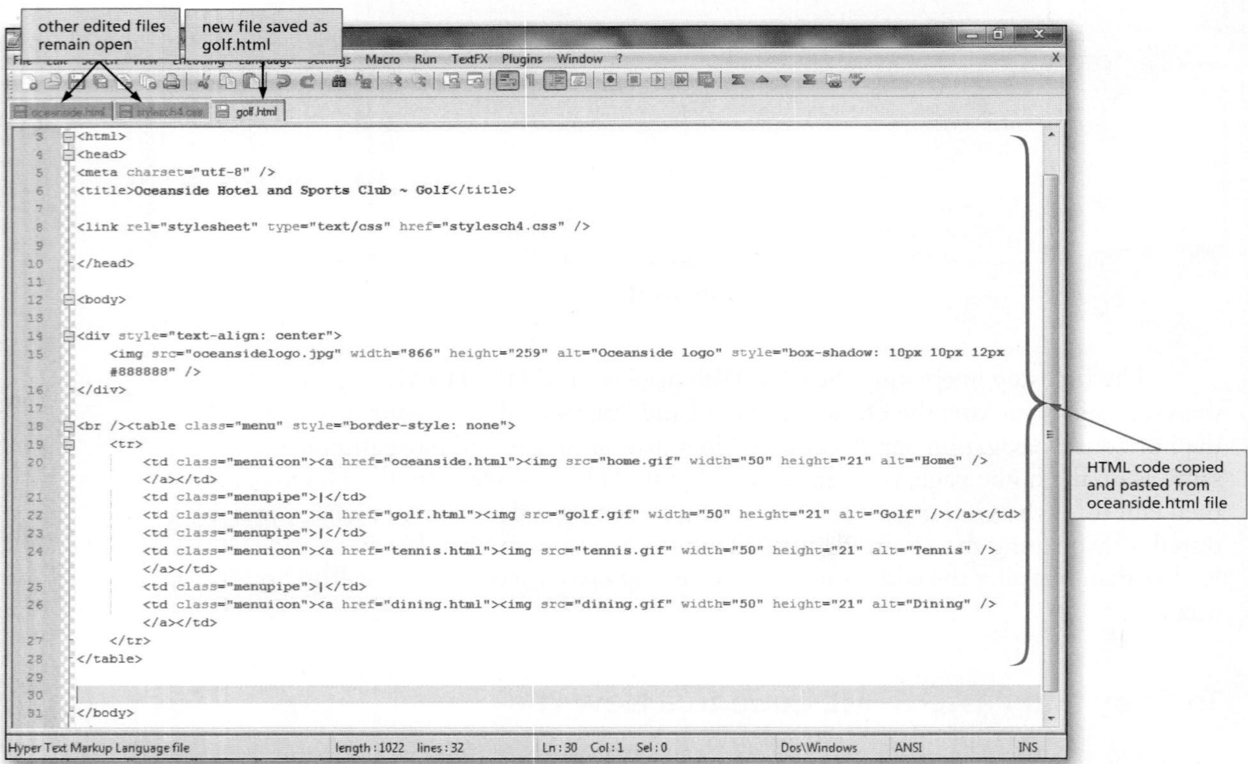

Figure 4–27

Plan Ahead

Determine what styles are needed for the second Web page.
Prior to adding more code to the Golf Web page, think through what styles you have defined and determine if there is anything in this Web page that needs to differ from the external style sheet. Any differences can be inserted as a formatting attribute, an inline style, or as an embedded style sheet that will override the styles defined in the external style sheet.

- **Review the table formatting in the external style sheet to see if it is appropriate for this page.** Borderless tables are often appropriate when the tables are used to position text and image elements. In other instances, such as when a table is used to structure columns and rows of information, borders are appropriate.
- **Identify any other styles that may need to be applied to tables on this page.** It is important to make your tables clear enough that users can easily identify the information that they need. You may want to start with the basic table format and add options as necessary.

Adding a Table with Borders

The borderless table style defined in the stylesch4.css external style sheet works well for the horizontal navigation bar that appears on every page. However, the borderless format would be less effective in presenting the three columns and five rows of information about available golf options at Oceanside Hotel and Sports Club. Figure 4–28a shows this information in a table with borders. Figure 4–28b shows the same information in a table without borders and with a distinct background color in every other row. As shown in this figure, using a table with borders makes the information on the Golf Web page easier to read and provides a frame that gives the table a three-dimensional appearance.

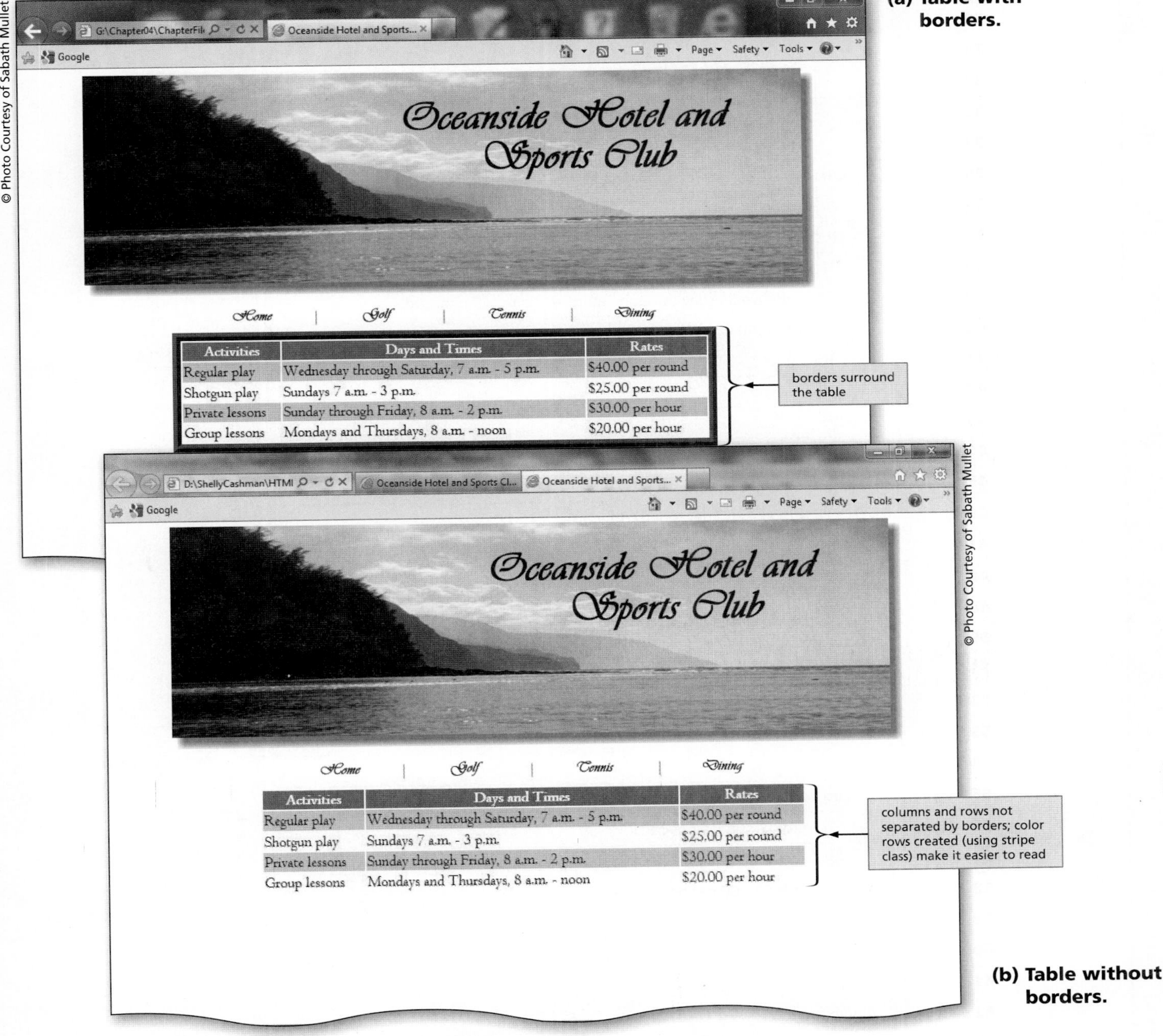

Figure 4–28

To Create a Table with Borders and Insert Text

Creating the table shown in Figure 4–28a involves first creating a table with three columns and five rows. The first row of the table is for column headings; the other rows are for data. As you have learned, table heading cells <th> differ from data cells <td> in their appearance. Text in a heading cell appears as bold and centered, while text in a data cell appears as normal and left-aligned. In the external style sheet stylesch4.css that you created in an earlier section of the project, you gave table header cells a background color of #757775 and white text. Table 4–9 contains the HTML tags and text used to create the table of golf options on the Golf Web page.

Table 4–9 HTML Code to Create a Table

HTML Tag and Text

```
<table>
   <tr>
      <th>Activities</th>
      <th>Days and Times</th>
      <th>Rates</th>
   </tr>

   <tr class="stripe">
      <td>Regular play</td>
      <td>Wednesday through Saturday, 7 a.m. - 5 p.m.</td>
      <td>$40.00 per round</td>
   </tr>

   <tr>
      <td>Shotgun play</td>
      <td>Sundays 7 a.m. - 3 p.m.</td>
      <td>$25.00 per round</td>
   </tr>

   <tr class="stripe">
      <td>Private lessons</td>
      <td>Sunday through Friday, 8 a.m. - 2 p.m.</td>
      <td>$30.00 per hour</td>
   </tr>

   <tr>
      <td>Group lessons</td>
      <td>Mondays and Thursdays, 8 a.m. - noon</td>
      <td>$20.00 per hour</td>
   </tr>
</table>

</body>
</html>
```

The following step illustrates how to create a table with borders and insert text into heading and data cells.

1

- With the insertion point on line 30, enter the HTML code for the Golf table, as shown in Table 4–9, using TAB to create indents, and pressing ENTER after each line except the last line (line 63) (Figure 4–29).

Q&A Are there other attributes that can be used in the <table>, <tr>, <th>, and <td> tags?

Most table attributes are no longer supported by HTML5. You can still change the style of tables by using Cascading Style Sheets as is done in this chapter project.

Q&A Why are we using a white font color for the headings?

Because the background color is so dark (#757775), you could not easily read the heading if it was the default color of black. Changing the font color to white on a dark background color makes it easier to read.

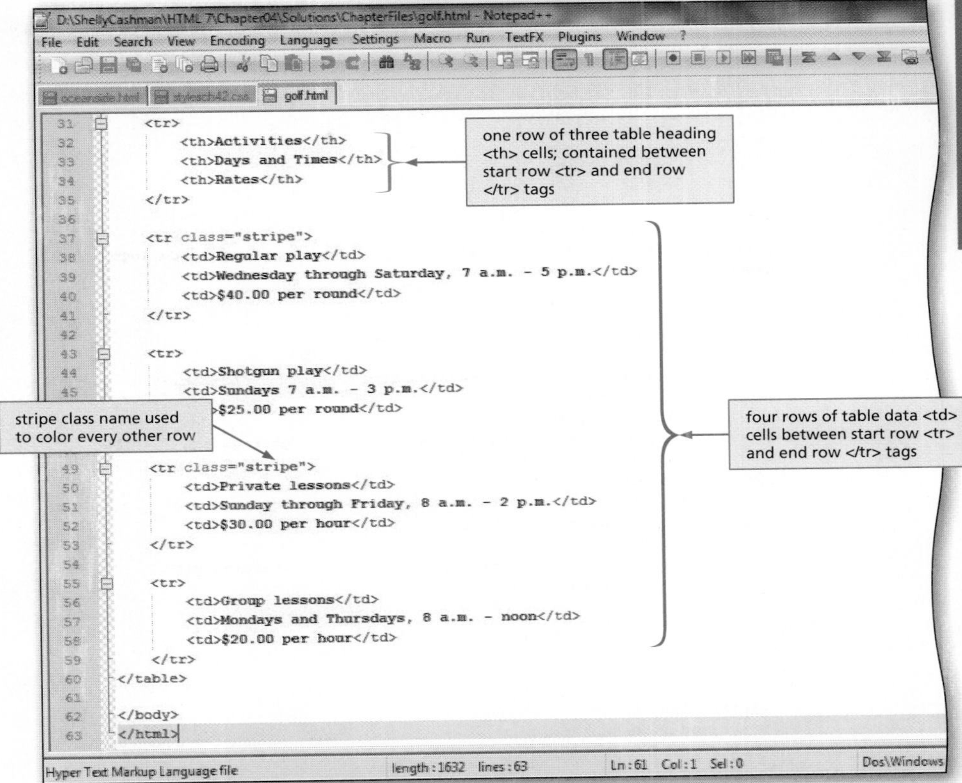

Figure 4–29

To Save, Validate, View, and Print the Web Page

After adding the remaining HTML code, perform the following steps to save, validate, view, and print the Golf Web page.

1. In Notepad++, save the golf.html file.
2. Click the Internet Explorer button on the taskbar.
3. Use the W3C validator service to validate the golf.html Web page.
4. Return to Notepad++ and print the golf.html Notepad++ file (Figure 4–30).
5. Return to the Oceanside's home page, click the Golf link to show the most recent file, and then print the Web page, as shown in Figure 4–31 on the next page.

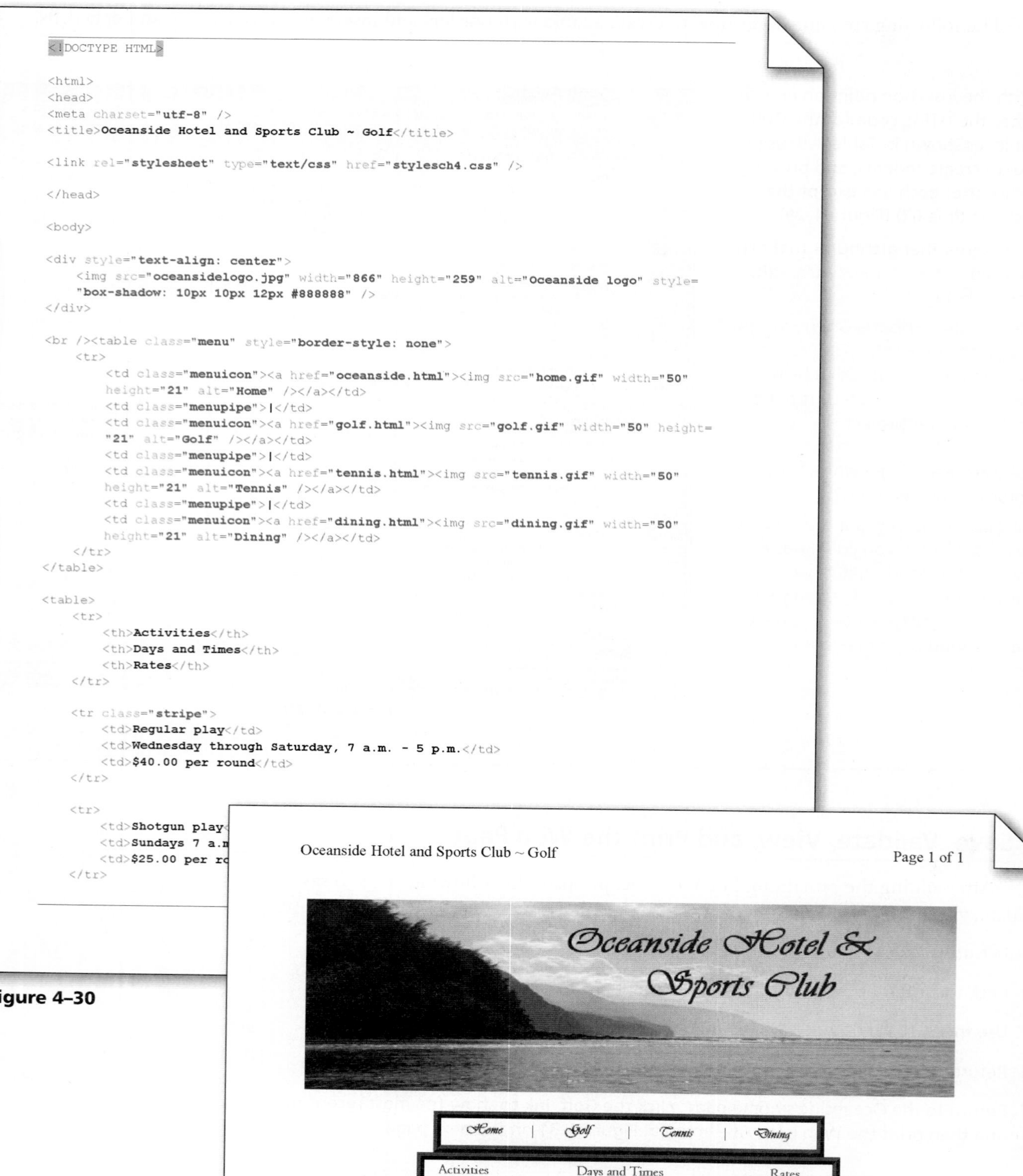

```
<!DOCTYPE HTML>

<html>
<head>
<meta charset="utf-8" />
<title>Oceanside Hotel and Sports Club ~ Golf</title>

<link rel="stylesheet" type="text/css" href="stylesch4.css" />

</head>

<body>

<div style="text-align: center">
    <img src="oceansidelogo.jpg" width="866" height="259" alt="Oceanside logo" style=
    "box-shadow: 10px 10px 12px #888888" />
</div>

<br /><table class="menu" style="border-style: none">
    <tr>
        <td class="menuicon"><a href="oceanside.html"><img src="home.gif" width="50"
        height="21" alt="Home" /></a></td>
        <td class="menupipe">|</td>
        <td class="menuicon"><a href="golf.html"><img src="golf.gif" width="50" height=
        "21" alt="Golf" /></a></td>
        <td class="menupipe">|</td>
        <td class="menuicon"><a href="tennis.html"><img src="tennis.gif" width="50"
        height="21" alt="Tennis" /></a></td>
        <td class="menupipe">|</td>
        <td class="menuicon"><a href="dining.html"><img src="dining.gif" width="50"
        height="21" alt="Dining" /></a></td>
    </tr>
</table>

<table>
    <tr>
        <th>Activities</th>
        <th>Days and Times</th>
        <th>Rates</th>
    </tr>

    <tr class="stripe">
        <td>Regular play</td>
        <td>Wednesday through Saturday, 7 a.m. - 5 p.m.</td>
        <td>$40.00 per round</td>
    </tr>

    <tr>
        <td>Shotgun play
        <td>Sundays 7 a.m
        <td>$25.00 per ro
    </tr>
```

Figure 4–30

Activities	Days and Times	Rates
Regular play	Wednesday through Saturday, 7 a.m. - 5 p.m.	$40.00 per round
Shotgun play	Sundays 7 a.m. - 3 p.m.	$25.00 per round
Private lessons	Sunday through Friday, 8 a.m. - 2 p.m.	$30.00 per hour
Group lessons	Mondays and Thursdays, 8 a.m. - noon	$20.00 per hour

Figure 4–31

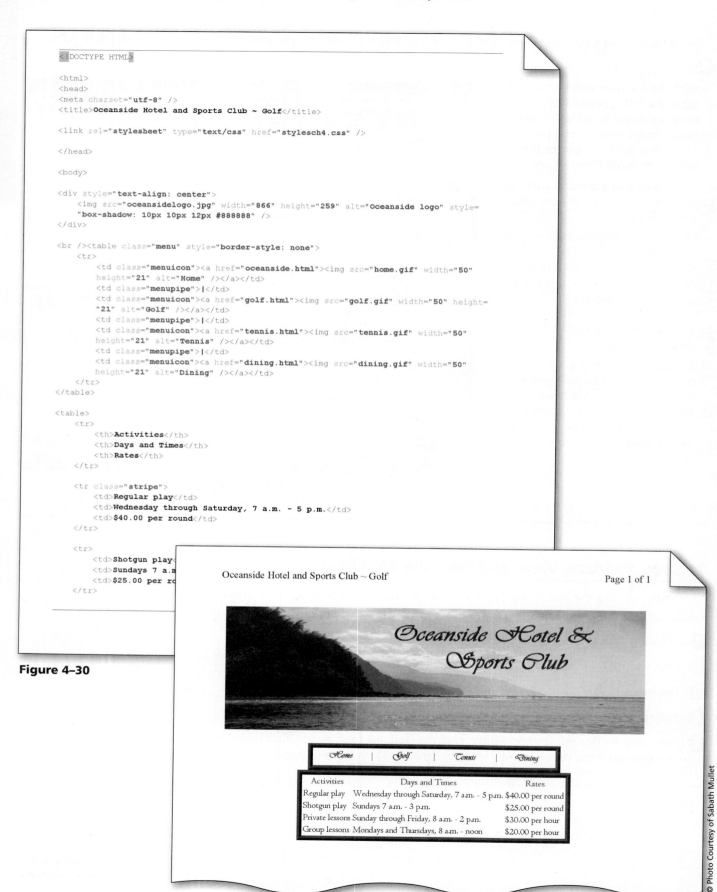

To Test Links on a Web Page

After confirming that the Web page appears as desired, the four links on the horizontal navigation bar should be tested to verify that they function as expected. The following steps show how to test the links on the golf.html Web page. Compare Figure 4–32a (the starting Web page) to Figure 4–32b (the ending Web page after the HTML code is entered in the next section).

1. Click the Home link to change to the Oceanside Hotel and Sports Club home page.
2. Click the Golf link to return to the golf.html Web page.
3. Click the Dining link.
4. Click the Tennis link (Figure 4–32a).

Q&A Why aren't the Dining and Tennis Web pages formatted with the styles in the external style sheet?

In order for the external style sheet to take effect, you have to insert the <link> statement into the HTML code in the Dining and Tennis files.

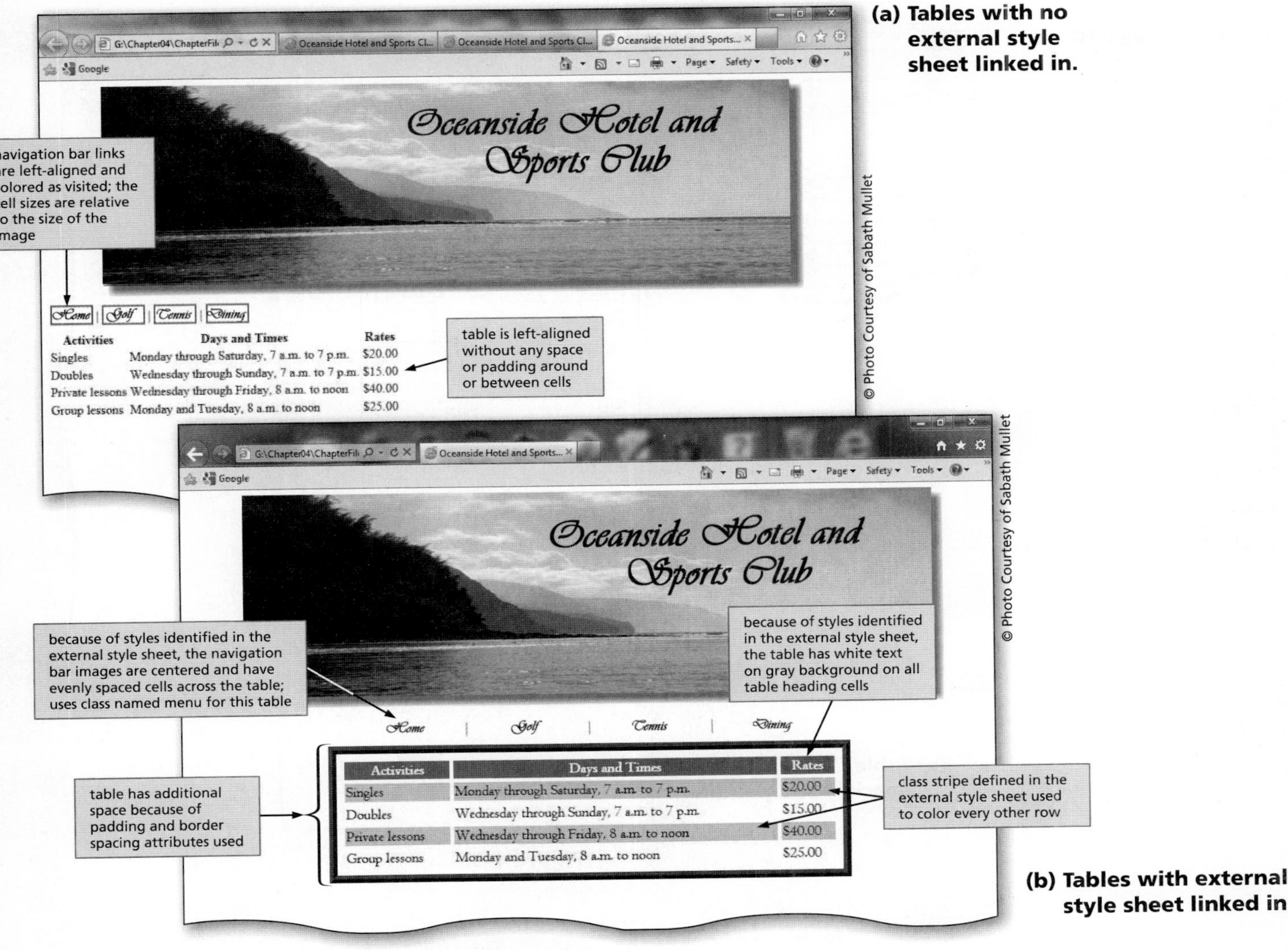
Oceanside Hotel and Sports Club
navigation bar links are left-aligned and colored as visited; the cell sizes are relative to the size of the image
Home | Golf | Tennis | Dining
Activities | Days and Times | Rates
Singles | Monday through Saturday, 7 a.m. to 7 p.m. | $20.00
Doubles | Wednesday through Sunday, 7 a.m. to 7 p.m. | $15.00
Private lessons | Wednesday through Friday, 8 a.m. to noon | $40.00
Group lessons | Monday and Tuesday, 8 a.m. to noon | $25.00
table is left-aligned without any space or padding around or between cells
© Photo Courtesy of Sabath Mullet
because of styles identified in the external style sheet, the navigation bar images are centered and have evenly spaced cells across the table; uses class named menu for this table
because of styles identified in the external style sheet, the table has white text on gray background on all table heading cells
table has additional space because of padding and border spacing attributes used
class stripe defined in the external style sheet used to color every other row

(a) Tables with no external style sheet linked in.

(b) Tables with external style sheet linked in.

Figure 4–32

Adding a Link, Border Spacing, Padding, and Row Color

The table of information on the Golf Web page did not use any additional spacing or padding styles. The size of each data cell, therefore, automatically was set to the minimum size needed for the text inserted in the data cell. The tennis.html Web page, however, should be modified to use border spacing and padding by adding an inline style to the <table> tag. **Border spacing** specifies the distance between the borders of adjacent cells in a table. (See Table Properties in Appendix D for more information about border spacing.) Additional spacing makes the borders around each cell look thicker (see the thickness of the borders in Figure 4–33b versus Figure 4–33a). **Padding** is shorthand to set the top, right, bottom, and left padding around an element (see Margin and Padding Properties in Appendix D for more information). In other words, if you add padding, you give more space around the content within that cell. Figures 4–33a and 4–33b illustrate how adding an inline style with border spacing and padding in the <table> tag can affect a table's appearance. Adding the class, stripe, to certain rows also helps to differentiate one row from another using color and gives the table a unique style.

(a) Tables without border spacing and padding.

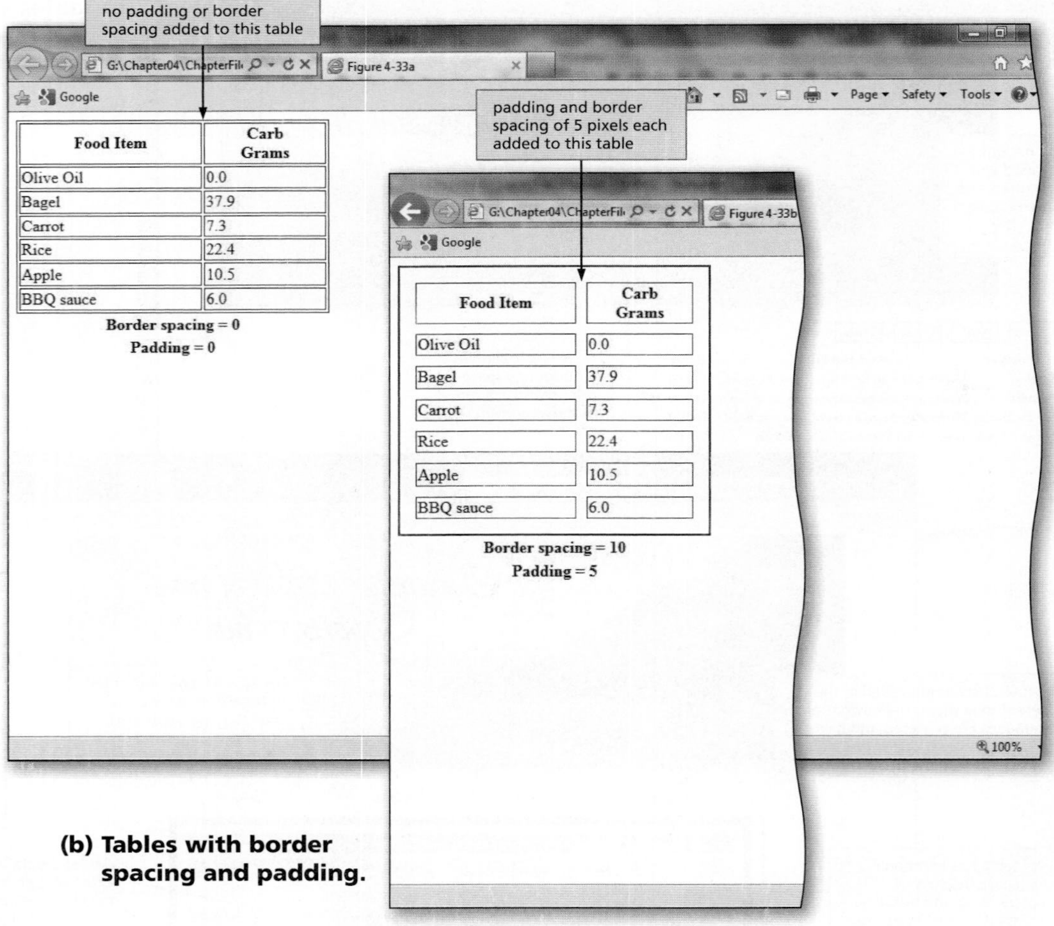

(b) Tables with border spacing and padding.

Figure 4–33

Plan Ahead

- **Determine if you need to use padding, border spacing, or both.** The first thing you should consider is if you need these spacing properties at all. If your content is getting across to the users without any modification to the spacing, then maybe you do not need to do this. Look again at the golf.html Web page. The information there is completely readable, and there is no padding or border spacing.
- **Determine what type of spacing to use.** If you decide that you do need to insert space within or around the cells of data, then you should next consider how much space to provide within the table. Border spacing is the distance between the borders of adjacent cells. Padding sets the top, right, bottom, and left padding around an element. Both properties serve the purpose of making the table of information easier to read. No rule of thumb says how much padding or border spacing should be used. Try various values to see the effect on the table.
- **Determine whether to use color in the table.** Color can be used to separate or highlight information in a table. The row colors used in this Web page help viewers differentiate rows from one another.

To Open an HTML File

In the following step, you will activate Notepad++ and open the tennis.html Web page file.

1. Switch to Notepad++ and open tennis.html, located in the Chapter04\ChapterFiles folder (Figure 4–34).

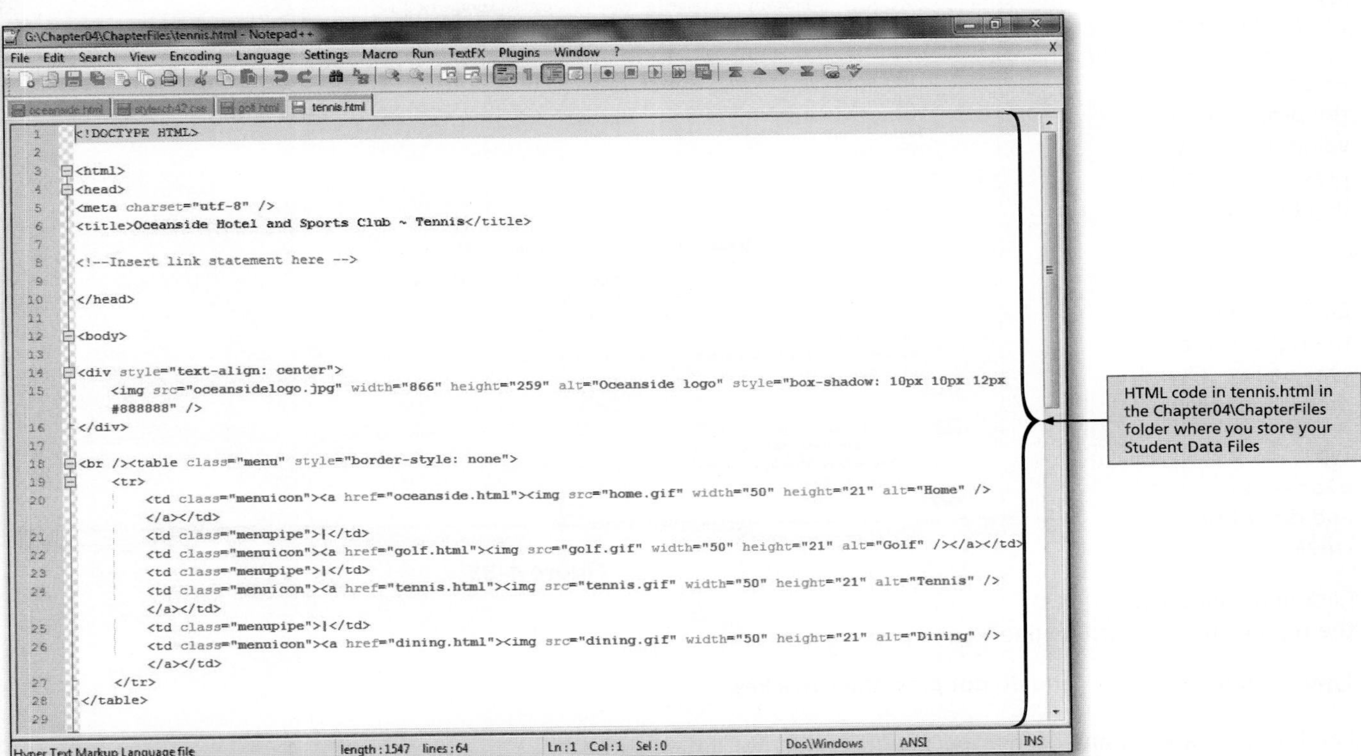

Figure 4–34

To Link to an External Style Sheet

The first thing you need to do in this Web page is link to the external style sheet that contains the overall styles you want this Web page to have.

1. Highlight the phrase <!--Insert link statement here --> on line 8.
2. Type `<link rel="stylesheet" type="text/css" href="stylesch4.css" />` to enter the link to the external style sheet. Do not press the ENTER key.

Q&A Remind me, what does this link statement do?

This statement links this Web page to the external style sheet that you created earlier. You need this link to the external (or linked) style sheet in order to apply those styles to the Web page.

To Add Border Spacing, Padding, and Row Color to a Table

With the tennis.html file open, the HTML code to add border spacing, padding, and row color can be added. The following step shows how to add border spacing, padding, and decorative color stripes to a table.

1

- Click immediately to the right of the e in the <table> tag on line 30 and then press the SPACEBAR.
- Type `style="border-spacing: 5px; padding: 5px"` as the properties and values but do not press the ENTER key (Figure 4–35).

2

- Click immediately to the right of the r in <tr> on line 37 and press the spacebar.
- Type `class="stripe"` and do not press the ENTER key.

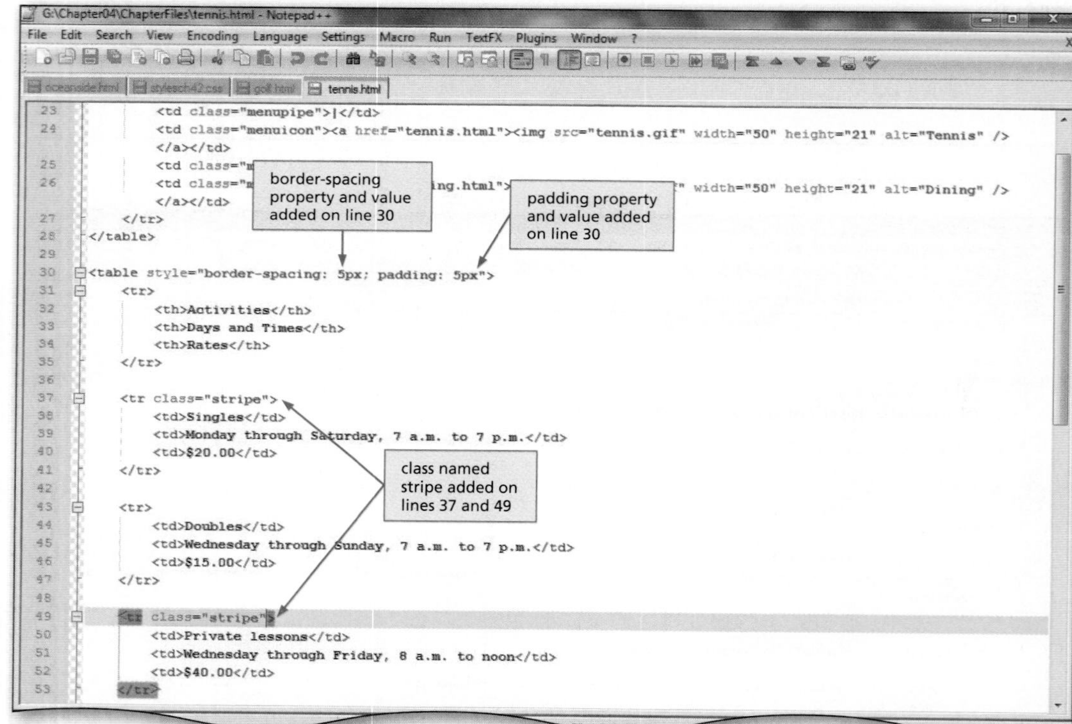

Figure 4–35

- Click immediately to the right of the r in <tr> on line 49 and press the spacebar.
- Type `class="stripe"` and do not press the ENTER key.

Q&A Can I set the padding and border spacing differently for different cells?

With the flexibility of inline styles, you can adjust the border spacing and padding at the table header or table data cell level.

To Save, Validate, Print, and View the HTML File and Print the Web Page

1. With the USB drive plugged into your computer, click File on the menu bar and then click Save to save the tennis.html file.
2. Display the Oceanside Hotel and Sports Club's ~ Tennis page in Internet Explorer.
3. Validate the Web page using the W3C validator service.
4. Return to the Oceanside Hotel and Sports Club's ~ Tennis page, refresh the Web page, and then print it.
5. Return to Notepad++ and print the file.

Adding a Caption and Spanning Rows

If you need to add information to a table that does not fit into the table data cells, a caption can be a good option. For example, look at the dining.html Web page in Figure 4–1d on page HTML 155. The caption indicates that additional menu items are available upon request. That "additional menu items" information does not fit into either the heading or data cells for the table. It is also not appropriate to have that information as an h1 or h2 heading. Putting that information in a caption is a perfect solution. The <caption> tag defines a table caption. The <caption> tag must be inserted immediately after the <table> tag and only one caption may be specified per table. By default, the caption will be centered above the table. In this project, you previously inserted the caption-side property in the external style sheet to align the caption at the bottom of (beneath) the table.

When you want to merge several cells into one, you can use row or column spanning. You can span rows or columns anywhere in a table. Generally, row and column spanning is used to create headings in tables. The **rowspan attribute** of the <th> or <td> tag sets a number of rows spanned by a cell. Although the chapter project uses only row spanning, you can also span columns. The **colspan attribute** of the <th> or <td> tag sets a number of columns spanned by a cell. Figure 4–9 on page HTML 164 shows examples of both column and row spanning. Notice that both the 5K and 10K headings span (or go across) two columns each. The heading Meet Dates spans (or goes across) four rows of information.

Figure 4–36, on the next page, shows what the dining.html Web page looks like at the start of the process. All of the table content is present, but there is no row or column spanning. You decide during the design phase that this table would benefit from row spanning, but that column spanning is unnecessary. You will enter the HTML code to complete the row spanning. In Figure 4–37, on the next page, the heading Lunch Menu is an example of row spanning. In this case, this heading spans three rows. In the same figure, the words Dinner Menu also span three rows of information.

The "stripe" class is already added to every other row to give the table a unique style. In addition, in this section of the project, you will insert the <td> class "bolder" (line 31 in the stylech4.css file) to make the text in certain cells bolder than the surrounding text. This helps to highlight the name of the main dish in every row, as shown in Figure 4-37. You could have added individual inline styles specifying the bold font weight to each data cell that you wanted to make bolder, but using a class in the external style sheet allows you to apply that same font weight in other tables, if it is appropriate.

BTW

Row and Column Spanning
Creating headings that span rows and columns defines tables more clearly. Many Web sites contain information about row and column spanning. For more information about row and column spanning, search the Web.

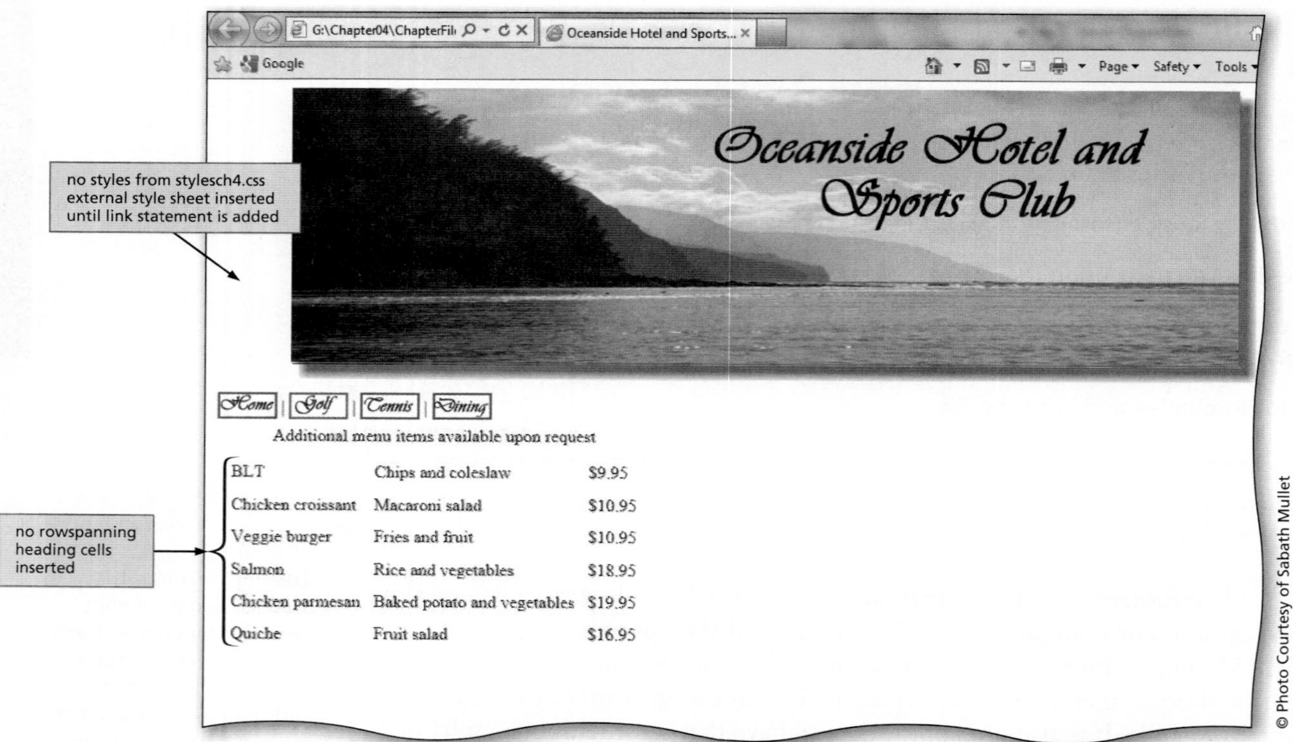

Figure 4–36 Dining Web page before enhancements.

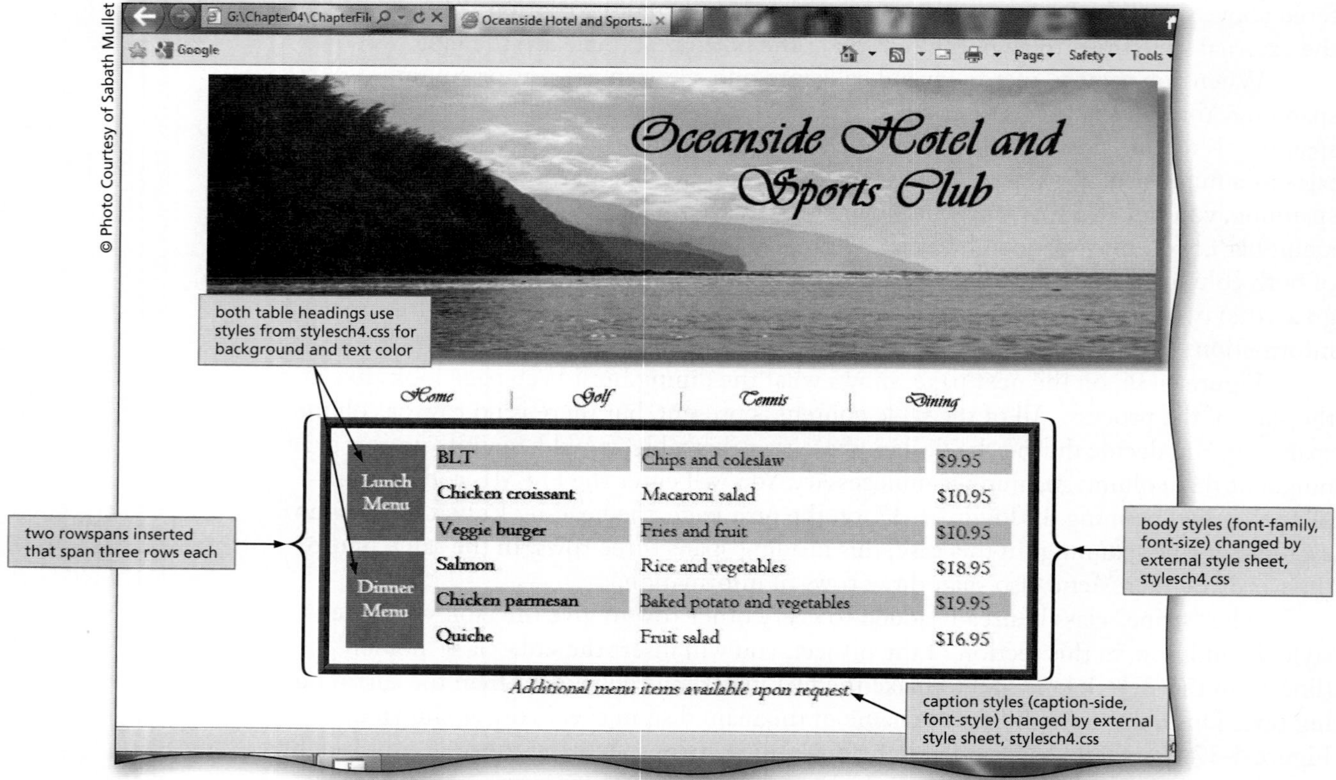

Figure 4–37 Dining Web page after enhancements.

The first step when deciding to span rows or columns is to sketch the table design on a piece of paper, as shown in Figure 4–38. Again, for this Web page, it was determined that column spanning was unnecessary. The table organizes menu items by lunch and dinner and thus should have rowspanning for those two row headings.

<table>
<tr><td rowspan="3">Lunch Menu</td><td>BLT</td><td>Chips and coleslaw</td><td>$9.95</td></tr>
<tr><td>Chicken croissant</td><td>Macaroni salad</td><td>$10.95</td></tr>
<tr><td>Veggie burger</td><td>Fries and fruit</td><td>$10.95</td></tr>
<tr><td rowspan="3">Dinner Menu</td><td>Salmon</td><td>Rice and vegetables</td><td>$18.95</td></tr>
<tr><td>Chicken parmesan</td><td>Baked potatoes and vegetables</td><td>$19.95</td></tr>
<tr><td>Quiche</td><td>Fruit salad</td><td>$16.95</td></tr>
</table>

Figure 4–38

After defining the main sections of the table, you must determine how many rows each heading should span. In this project, the headings, Lunch Menu and Dinner Menu, should span three rows. In the following steps, you will open the file dining.html, link the external style sheet stylesch4.css, and add rowspan attributes to create table headings that span rows.

Plan Ahead

- **Determine if a caption is needed**. A caption can help clarify the table's purpose. For some tables, such as the table used to position images and the tables used to create navigation bars, captions are not appropriate. Tables used to structure columns and rows of information, such as the dining table, can benefit from having a caption to clarify or add information about the contents of the table. The caption tag must be inserted directly after the <table> tag.
- **Determine whether to use row and column spanning**. The purpose of the table determines whether you need to add row or column spanning. If the content is broken into logical segments of information, you may also need to include row or column spanning in order to make the content clear. If you decide to add row or column spanning, it is best to sketch your ideas on paper first. This could help you understand more clearly what tags you need to use where.
- **Determine if different colors are needed for backgrounds**. You can help visitors more easily read a table full of information by varying the background colors effectively. If you use the same color background for the same level (or type) of information, it can help visually organize the information. Again, you may have to use a light font color if the background color is very dark.

To Open an HTML File

1. Switch to Notepad++ and open dining.html, located in the Chapter04\ChapterFiles folder.

To Link the External Style Sheet

The first thing you need to do in this Web page is link to the external style sheet that contains the styles that you want for this Web page.

1. Highlight the text <!--Insert link statement here --> on line 8.
2. Type `<link rel="stylesheet" type="text/css" href="stylesch4.css" />` to enter the link to the external style sheet. Do not press the ENTER key.

To Add a Table Caption

Captions are added to tables using the <caption> </caption> tags to enclose the caption text. The formatting to make the caption italic and align it at the bottom of the table is included in the external style sheet (stylesch4.css) that is now linked to this page. The following step shows how to add a caption below the menu table.

- Highlight the text <!--Insert caption statement here --> on line 32.
- Type `<caption> Additional menu items available upon request </caption>` as the tag to add the italic caption below the table (Figure 4–39).

Experiment

- By default, captions are aligned at the top (above) a table. You changed the style of the caption in the external style sheet to align the caption on the bottom. To see what the caption would look like at the top of the table, insert an inline style sheet in the <caption> tag and use the caption-side property to align the caption at the top. (Hint: You could also remove lines 33 and 34 in the stylesch4.css file.)

```
8   <link rel="stylesheet" type="text/css" href="stylesch4.css" />
9
10  </head>
11
12  <body>
13
14  <div style="text-align: center">
15      <img src="oceansidelogo.jpg" width="866" height="259" alt="Oceanside logo" style="box-shadow: 10px 10px 12px
        #888888" />
16  </div>
17
18  <br /><table class="menu" style="border-style: none">
19      <tr>
20          <td class="menuicon"><a href="oceanside.html"><img src="home.gif" width="50" height="21" alt="Home" />
            </a></td>
21          <td class="menupipe">|</td>
22          <td class="menuicon"><a href="golf.html"><img src="golf.gif" width="50" height="21" alt="Golf" /></a></td>
23          <td class="menupipe">|</td>
24          <td class="menuicon"><a href="tennis.html"><img src="tennis.gif" width="50" height="21" alt="Tennis" />
            </a></td>
25          <td class="menupipe">|</td>
26          <td class="menuicon"><a href="dining.h                       "50" height="21" alt="Dining" />
            </a></td>
27      </tr>
28  </table>
29
30  <table style="border-spacing: 10px; padding: 5px">
31
32  <caption>Additional menu items available upon request</caption>
33
34      <tr class="stripe">
35  <!--Insert first rowspan heading here -->
36          <td>BLT</td>
```

inserted link statement to stylesch4.css, the external style sheet with all styles defined

caption element inserted into Web page; styles for caption will be taken from the stylesch4.css, the external style sheet

next step to insert HTML code here on line 35

Figure 4–39

To Create the Headings That Span Rows

The following steps illustrate how to enter HTML code to create two headings that each span three rows:

1

- Highlight <!--Insert first rowspan heading here --> on line 35.
- Press the TAB key twice and then type `<th rowspan="3">Lunch` and then press the ENTER key; the next line is automatically indented to the same level.
- Type `<br />Menu` and then press the ENTER key.
- Type `</th>` as the HTML code but do not press the ENTER key (Figure 4–40).

Q&A What is the purpose of the <br /> tag in the steps above?

The <br /> tag moves the word Menu to a second line so that the first column is not too much wider than the other columns in the table.

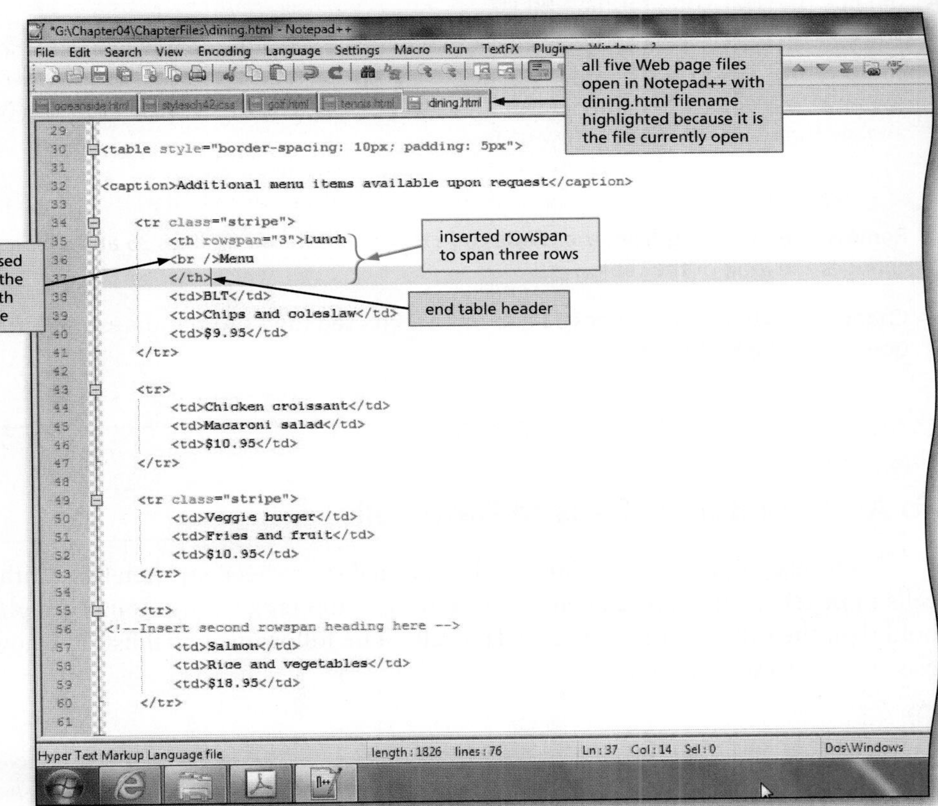

Figure 4–40

2

- Highlight <!--Insert second rowspan heading here --> on line 56.
- Press the TAB key twice and then type `<th rowspan="3">Dinner` and then press the ENTER key.
- Type `<br />Menu` and then press the ENTER key.
- Type `</th>` as the HTML code but do not press the ENTER key (Figure 4–41).

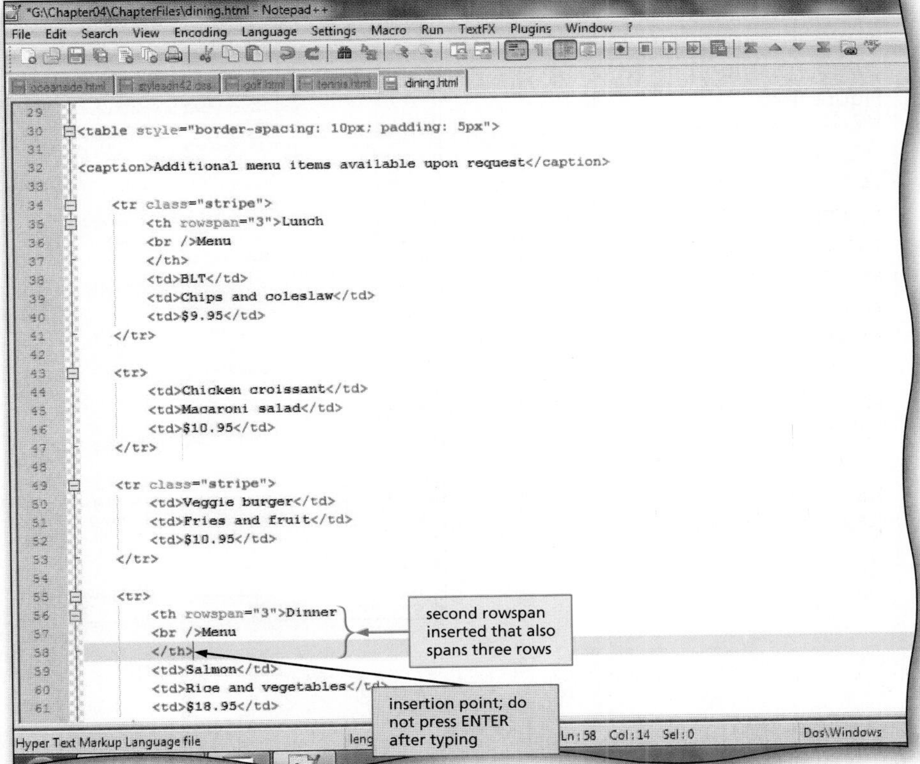

Figure 4–41

Q&A Why isn't there an extra pair of <tr> </tr> tags between the rowspan title (Lunch Menu) and the line of HTML code for data (BLT)?

The words Lunch Menu and BLT are on the same row (row 1) that is being spanned. Row 2 contains the line with Chicken croissant; row 3 is the line with Veggie burger. Therefore, the rowspan value is set to 3. The text that spans the rows (Lunch Menu and Dinner Menu) is always aligned with the first row of text.

Experiment

- Remove the <br /> tag from the HTML code that you entered on lines 36 and 57. See how this changes the look of the table.
- Change the <br /> tag on lines 36 and 57 to a <p> tag (don't forget the </p>). See what that does to the look of the table.

To Add the Bolder Class to Data Cells

The class bolder was defined in the external style sheet, stylesch4.css. Although we want the text in the data cells to be left-justified (the default option of the <td> tag), we also want to highlight that text by making it more bold than the other text in the table data cells. The following step illustrates how to enter HTML code to insert the class bolder to six data cells.

- Click just after the d in <td> on line 38.
- Type `class="bolder"` and do not press the ENTER key.
- Repeat these steps for lines 44, 50, 59, 65, and 71 as shown in Figure 4–42.

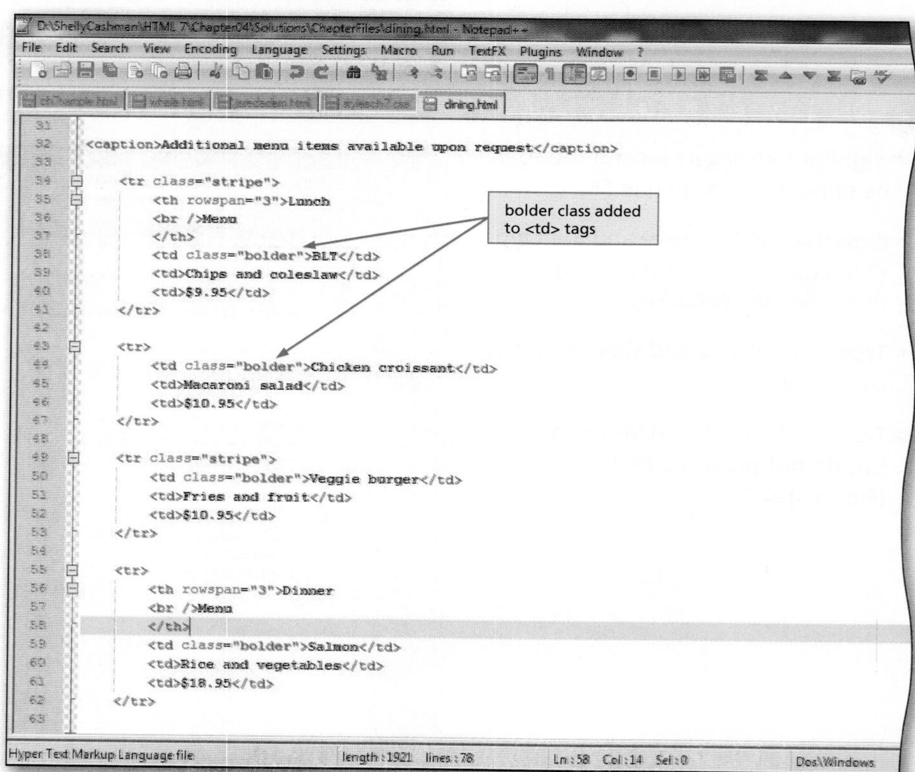

Figure 4–42

To Save, Validate, and Print the HTML File

1. With the USB drive plugged into your computer, click the Save icon on the Notepad++ toolbar to save the dining.html file.
2. Validate the HTML file using the validator.w3.org Web page.
3. Print the Notepad++ file.

To View and Print the Web Page

1. Click the Internet Explorer button on the taskbar.
2. Click the Dining link on the navigation bar to display the Dining Web page.
3. Print the Web page with rowspan attributes entered (Figure 4–43).

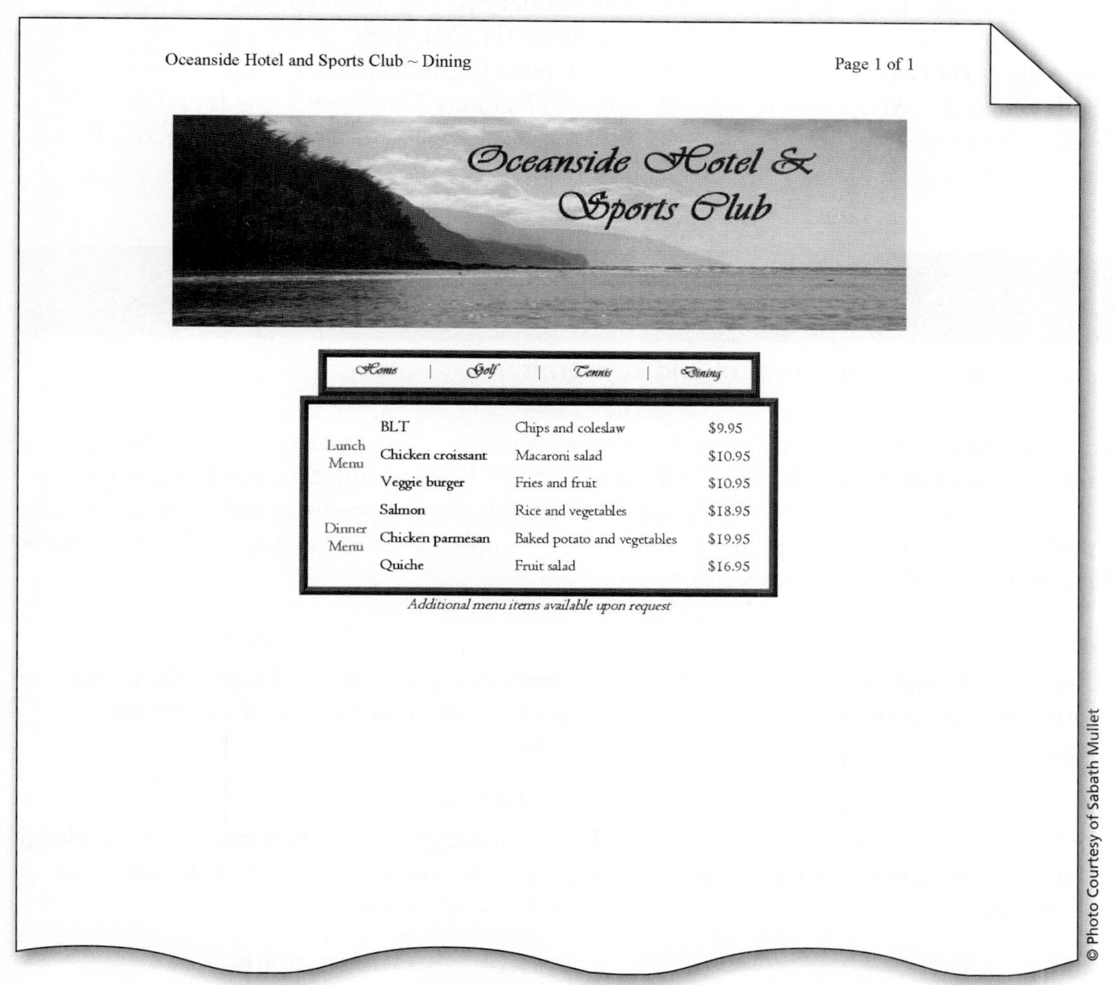

Oceanside Hotel and Sports Club ~ Dining
Page 1 of 1
Oceanside Hotel & Sports Club
Home | Golf | Tennis | Dining
Lunch Menu
BLT
Chips and coleslaw
$9.95
Chicken croissant
Macaroni salad
$10.95
Veggie burger
Fries and fruit
$10.95
Dinner Menu
Salmon
Rice and vegetables
$18.95
Chicken parmesan
Baked potato and vegetables
$19.95
Quiche
Fruit salad
$16.95
Additional menu items available upon request
© Photo Courtesy of Sabath Mullet

Figure 4–43

To Quit Notepad++ and a Browser

1. In Notepad++, click the File menu, then Close All.
2. Click the Close button on the Notepad++ title bar.
3. Click the Close button on the browser title bar. If necessary, click the Close all tabs button.

Chapter Summary

In this chapter, you learned how to create and link an external style sheet. You learned about about table elements, and the necessary steps to plan, design, and code a table in HTML. You also learned to enhance a table with background color, border spacing, padding, a caption, classes, and headers that span rows. The items listed below include all the new HTML skills you learned in this chapter.

1. Insert, Center, and Style an Image with a Box-Shadow (HTML 170)
2. Create a Horizontal Menu Bar with Image Links (HTML 173)
3. Create an External Style Sheet (HTML 180)
4. Link to an External Style Sheet (HTML 185)
5. Copy and Paste HTML Code to a New File (HTML 189)
6. Create a Table with Borders and Insert Text (HTML 192)
7. Add Border Spacing, Padding, and Row Color to a Table (HTML 198)
8. Add a Table Caption (HTML 202)
9. Create Headings That Span Rows (HTML 202)
10. Add the Bolder Class to Data Cells (HTML 204)

Learn It Online

Test your knowledge of chapter content and key terms.

Instructions: To complete the following exercises, please visit `www.cengagebrain.com`. At the CengageBrain.com home page, search for *HTML5 and CSS 7th Edition* using the search box at the top of the page. This will take you to the product page for this book. On the product page, click the Access Now button below the Study Tools heading. On the Book Companion Site Web page, select Chapter 4, and then click the link for the desired exercise.

Chapter Reinforcement TF, MC, and SA

A series of true/false, multiple choice, and short answer questions that test your knowledge of the chapter content.

Flash Cards

An interactive learning environment where you identify chapter key terms associated with displayed definitions.

Practice Test

A series of multiple choice questions that test your knowledge of chapter content and key terms.

Who Wants To Be a Computer Genius?

An interactive game that challenges your knowledge of chapter content in the style of a television quiz show.

Wheel of Terms

An interactive game that challenges your knowledge of chapter key terms in the style of the television show, *Wheel of Fortune*.

Crossword Puzzle Challenge

A crossword puzzle that challenges your knowledge of key terms presented in the chapter.

Apply Your Knowledge

Reinforce the skills and apply the concepts you learned in this chapter.

Editing a Table on a Web Page

Instructions: Start Notepad++. Open the file apply4-1.html from the Chapter04\Apply folder of the Data Files for Students. See the inside back cover of this book for instructions on downloading the Data Files for Students, or contact your instructor for information about accessing the required files.

The apply4-1.html file is a partially completed HTML file that you will use for this exercise. Figure 4–44 shows the Apply Your Knowledge Web page as it should display in a browser after the additional HTML tags, attributes, and styles are added.

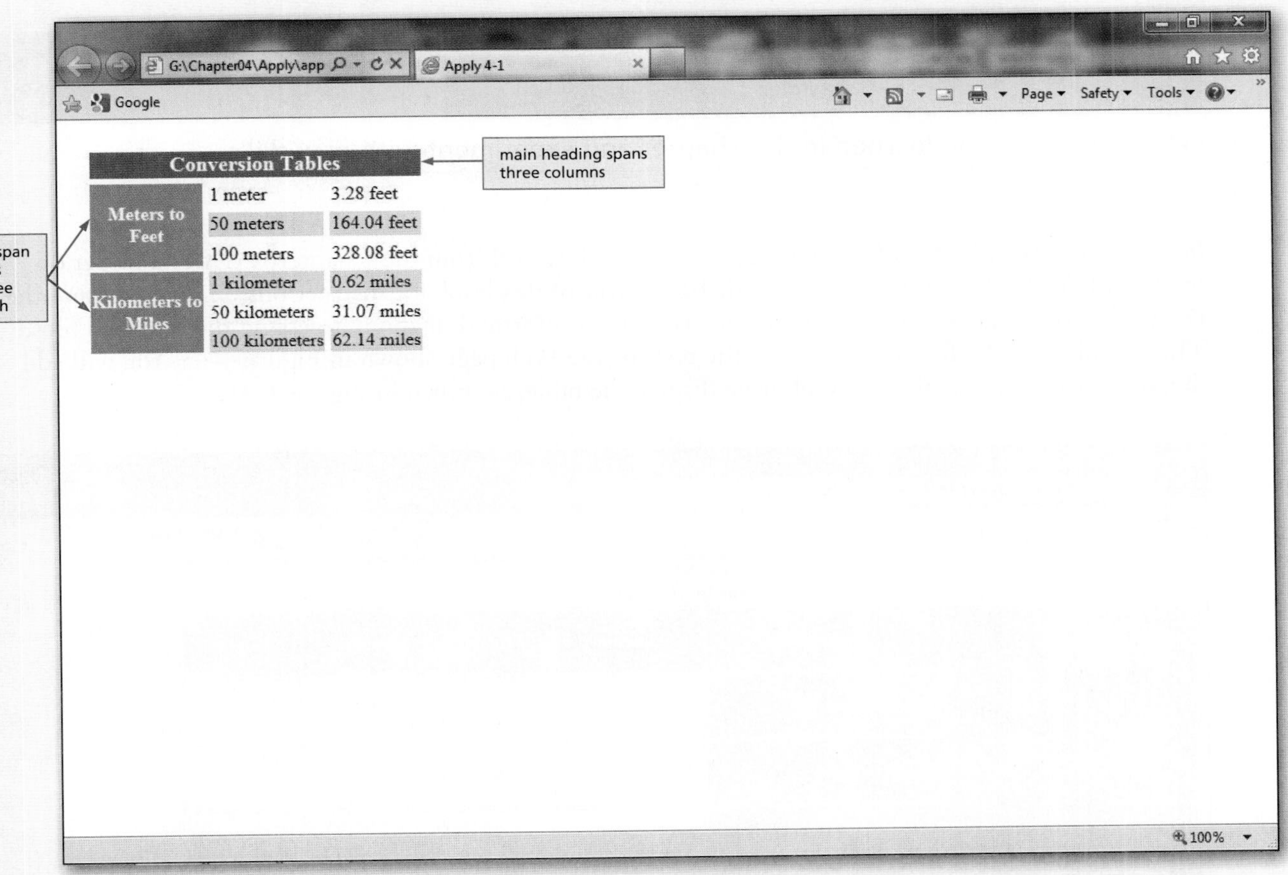

Figure 4–44

Perform the following tasks:

1. Enter the URL G:\Chapter04\Apply\apply4-1.html to view the Web page in your browser.
2. Examine the HTML file and its appearance as a Web page in the browser.
3. Add a border width of 10, border spacing of 5, and padding of 15 in an inline style to the table.
4. Add any HTML code necessary for additional features shown on the Web page in Figure 4–44. Your changes should include a colspan heading that spans three columns of information and two rowspan headings that span three rows each. The main heading is font-size large.

Continued >

Apply Your Knowledge *continued*

5. Colors used for the headings are colspan - #bc4676; first and second rowspan - #87aaae (experiment with the colors if you wish). The background color of the striped rows is #ddecef. All text in those colored cells is white.
6. Save the revised file in the Chapter04\Apply folder using the filename apply4-1solution.html.
7. Validate the code using the W3C validator service.
8. Print the revised HTML file.
9. Enter the URL G:\Chapter04\Apply\apply4-1solution.html to view the Web page in your browser.
10. Print the Web page.
11. Submit the revised HTML file and Web page in the format specified by your instructor.

Extend Your Knowledge

Extend the skills you learned in this chapter and experiment with new skills.

Creating a Table with Rules

Instructions: Start Notepad++. Open the file extend4-1.html from the Chapter04\Extend folder of the Data Files for Students. See the inside back cover of this book for instructions on downloading the Data Files for Students, or contact your instructor for information about accessing the required files. This sample HTML file contains all of the text for the Web page shown in Figure 4–45. You will add the necessary tags to make this Web page display the table, as shown in Figure 4–45.

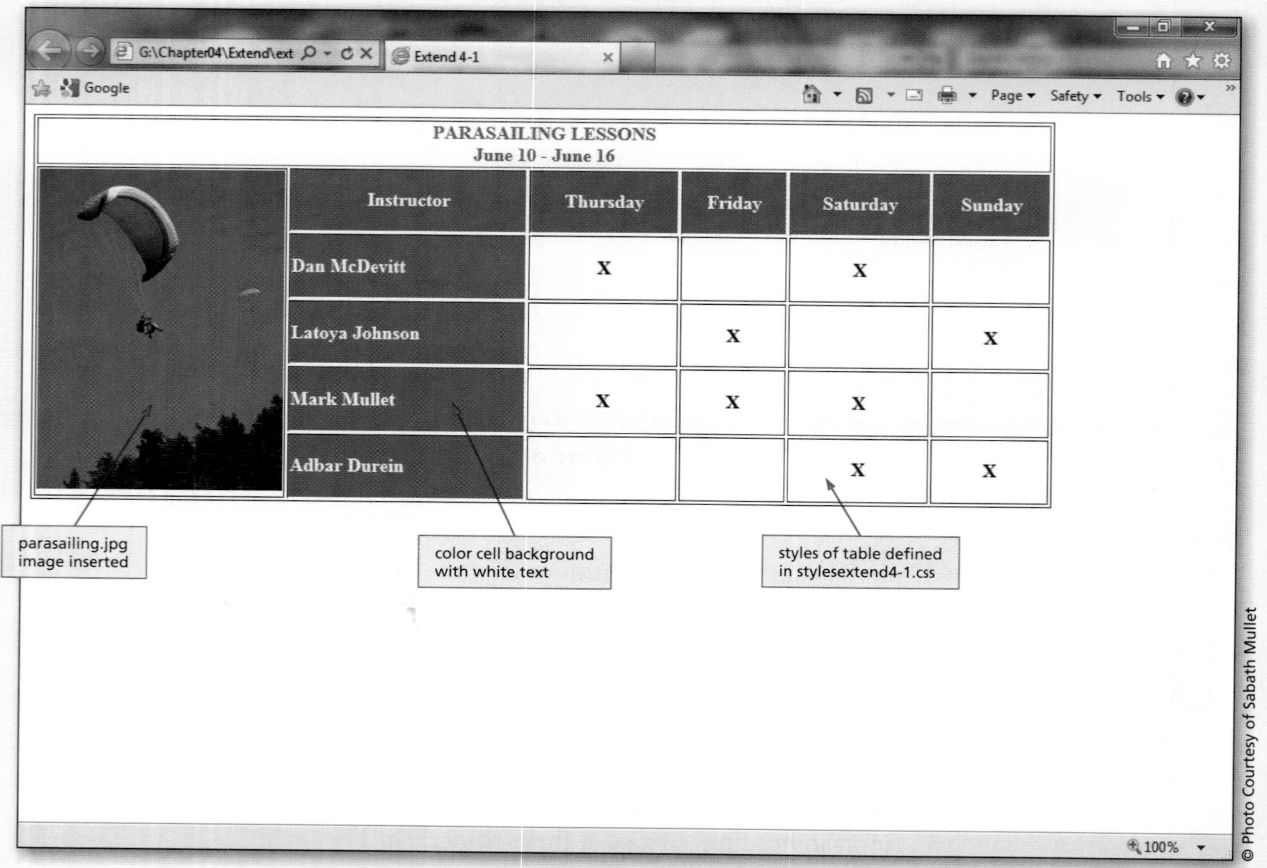

Figure 4–45

Perform the following tasks:

1. Add HTML code to align the table on the left of the Web page. Give the table a border of 1 with padding of 15 pixels. Add a heading spanning six columns in color #4174ab.
2. Insert the image parasailing.jpg in to a new table header cell that spans five rows. Determine the width and height of the image using methods discussed in the chapter.
3. Create an external style sheet that contains the following styles and save it as stylesextend4-1.css. Validate the CSS code.
4. Link stylesextend4-1.css into the Web page extend4-1solution.html.

```
table              {text-align: center;}
.twentyfive        {width: 25%;}
.twelve            {width: 12%;}
th.blue            {background-color: #4174ab;
                   color: white;}
td.instructors     {font-weight: bold;
                   text-align: left;
                   color: white;
                   background-color: #4174ab;}
```

5. Add the class, twentyfive, to the first two columns (image and instructors). Add the classes, twelve and blue, in the next four columns (days of week). (Hint: Separate multiple class names with a comma.)
6. Add the class, instructors, to the table cells that contain the instructor names.
7. Save the revised document as extend4-1solution.html and validate the code using the W3C validator service.
8. Resave extend4-1solution.html. Print the revised HTML file and Web page and submit them in the format specified by your instructor.

Make It Right

Analyze a document and correct all errors and/or improve the design.

Correcting the Golf Course Tournament Schedule

Instructions: Start your browser. Open the file makeitright4-1.html from the Chapter04\MakeItRight folder of the Data Files for Students. See the inside back cover of this book for instructions on downloading the Data Files for Students, or contact your instructor for information about accessing the required files. The Web page is a modified version of what you see in Figure 4–46 on the next page. Make the necessary corrections to the Web page to make it look like Figure 4–46, using inline styles for all styles. The Web page should include the six columns of information with a main heading that spans all six columns. The second row contains the image golfcourse.png in the first cell. The second row also has a line break between the person's first and last name. (*Hint:* Use the <br /> tag.) Move the caption to the bottom in italics. Make every other row of the table color #9ecc39. Save the file as makeitright4-1solution.html and validate the code. Submit the files in the format requested by your instructor.

Continued >

Make It Right *continued*

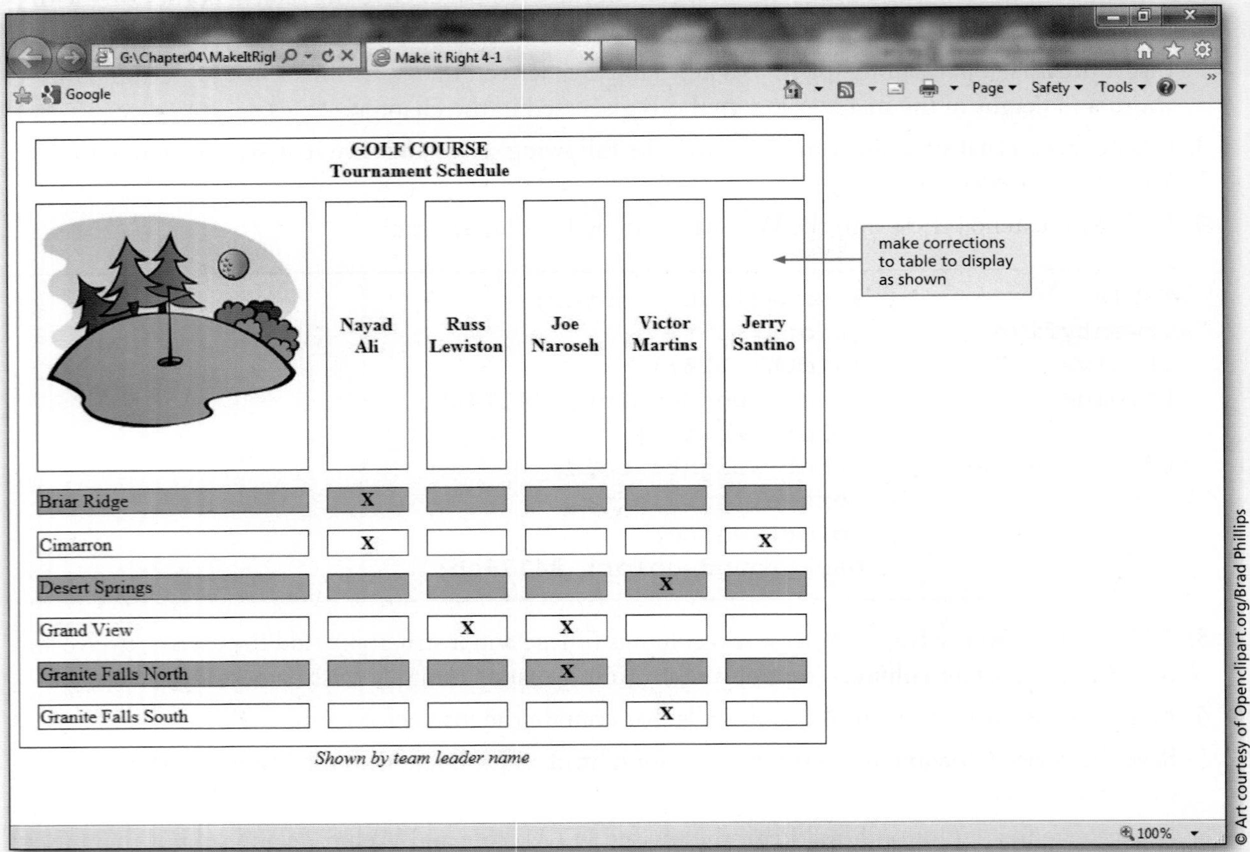

Figure 4–46

In the Lab

Lab 1: Creating a Table with Multiple Images

Problem: The owners of Beautiful Backyards want to review the potential for the use of tables on their company home page. You have been asked to create a Web page that shows the two images and how tables can be used to display them and the associated text, as shown in Figure 4–47.

Instructions: Perform the following steps:

1. Start a new HTML file with the title Lab 4-1 in the main heading section.
2. The heading <h1> should be color #00934a.
3. Insert the text shown in the top lines of the Web page using a font size of large.
4. Add a centered borderless table with two columns and two rows and padding of 15.

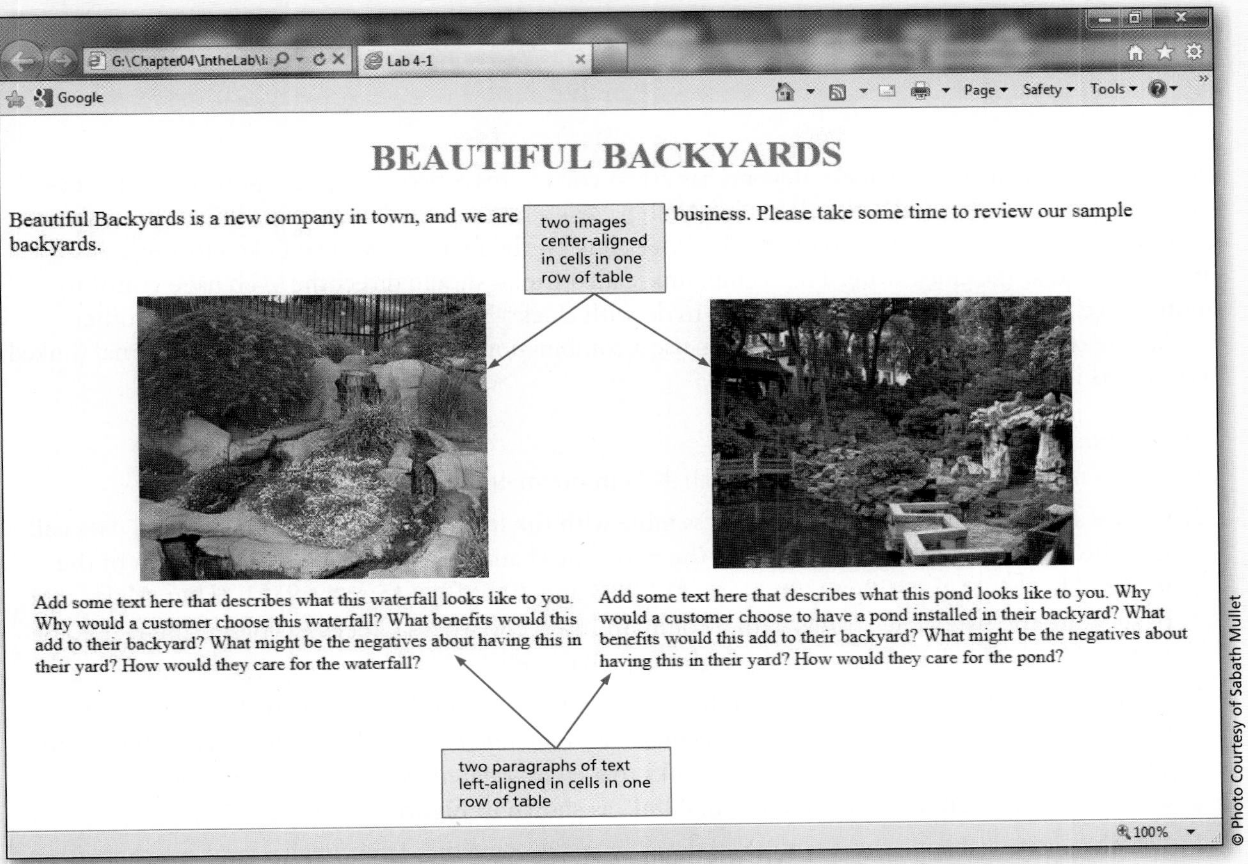

Figure 4–47

5. Insert the image largewaterfall.jpg in the first column of the first row. (*Hint:* You can use the techniques discussed in this chapter to determine the width and height of each image.)
6. Add the second image pond.jpg to that same row in a second column.
7. Start a new row and add a paragraph of text for each of the images.
8. Save the HTML file in the Chapter04\IntheLab folder using the filename lab4-1solution.html.
9. Validate the Web page using the W3C validator service.
10. Print the lab4-1solution.html file.
11. Open the lab4-1solution.html file in your browser to view it as a Web page.
12. Print the Web page.
13. Submit the revised HTML file and Web page in the format specified by your instructor.

In the Lab

Lab 2: Creating Two Linked Pages

Problem: Your manager at Clocks Beyond has asked you to create two Web pages, similar to the ones shown in Figures 4–48a and 4–48b. The first Web page is a home page that presents information about Clocks Beyond, together with two links. The Prices link on the first page will be linked to a price list of items found at the clock store. The second link, called Links, should direct the Web page visitor to another Web page of your choosing that has to do with clocks. You may select a museum or another similar site of your choosing. For this project, use a combination of inline style sheets and external (linked) style sheets in order to accomplish the tasks.

Instructions: Perform the following steps:

1. Start a new HTML file with the title Lab 4-2a in the main heading section.
2. Create a one-row, two-column borderless table with the image clock.jpg in the left-hand data cell. Use the box-shadow property to create the two-tone shadow around the top and bottom of the image. The values are: -20px -20px 15px #122973 and 20px 20px 15px #9a9391. (*Hint:* Make sure to separate the two value strings with a comma.) Insert the words Clocks Beyond using text color #122973 and font size xx-large in the right-hand data cell.
3. Create a second one-row, two-column borderless table with border-spacing of 10 pixels. In the first column, use the background color #eddaa7 and include two text links: Prices (which links to lab4-2bsolution.html) and Links (which links to a clock-related Web site of your choosing). In the second column, add the text and an e-mail link, as shown in Figure 4–48a.
4. Create an external style sheet with the following styles. Save it as lab4-2styles.css. Link this external style sheet into the Web page.

```
body       {font-family: Arial, Verdana, Garamond;
           font-size: 11pt;}
a          {text-decoration: none;
           color: #122973;}
table      {width: 65%;
           margin-left: auto;
           margin-right: auto;}
.menu      {text-align: left;
           width: 20%;}
.content   {width: 80%;}
```

5. Save the HTML file using the filename lab4-2asolution.html in the Chapter04\IntheLab folder. Validate the file using the W3C validator service. Print the HTML file.
6. Start a new HTML file with the title Lab 4-2b in the main heading section. Link the external style sheet lab4-2styles.css into the file.
7. Create a five-row, two-column table with a border of 1, padding of 15 pixels, and border-spacing of 5 pixels.
8. Span the first heading across both columns, as shown in Figure 4–48b, using a text color of #122973, a background color of #eddaa7, and font size large.
9. Enter the headings, Item and Price, along with the additional information, in the appropriate table cells, as shown in Figure 4–48b. Make sure to include a link (font size small and center-aligned) back to the home page.

10. Save the HTML file in the Chapter04\IntheLab folder using the filename lab4-2bsolution.html. Validate the HTML and CSS files using the W3C validator services. Print the HTML file.
11. Open the file lab4-2asolution.html in your browser and test that Prices links to the lab4-2bsolution.html Web page and that the link, Back to home, links to lab2-4asolution.html.
12. Print both Web pages.
13. Submit the HTML files, .css file, and Web pages in the format specified by your instructor.

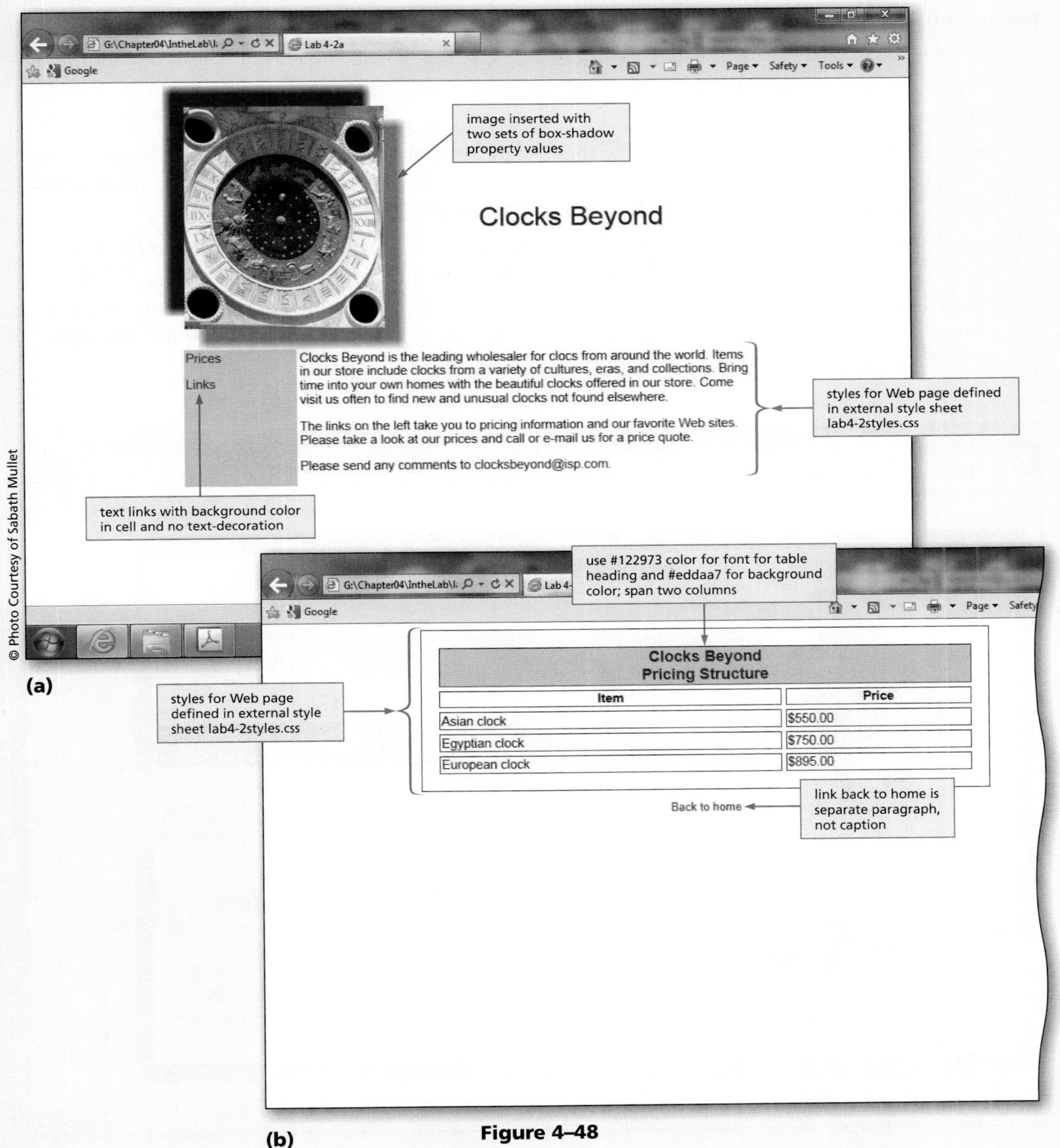

Figure 4–48

In the Lab

Lab 3: Creating Schedules

Problem: You want to create a Web page and an external style sheet that lists your piano practice and volunteer schedule, similar to the one shown in Figure 4–49. The Web page will use a table with images that span several rows and columns to organize the information.

Instructions: Perform the following steps:

1. Start a new HTML file with the title Lab 4-3 in the main heading section.
2. In the Web page, create a bordered table that displays in 90% of the browser, as shown in Figure 4–49.
3. Insert an inline style into the <table> tag that assigns the border a color of #194a70, a border width of 20 pixels, and a border style of groove. Give the table a rounded-edge look by using the border-radius property (see Appendix D). The radius should be 25 pixels.
4. Include the headings and data cells as shown, with valid information (i.e., real days and times as per a normal schedule of activities) in the data cells. The main headings (Piano Practice Schedule and Kid Camp Schedule) should be center-aligned across three columns and have a line height of 30 pixels. The data, other than the main headings, will have an indent of 10 pixels when the style sheet is coded and attached.

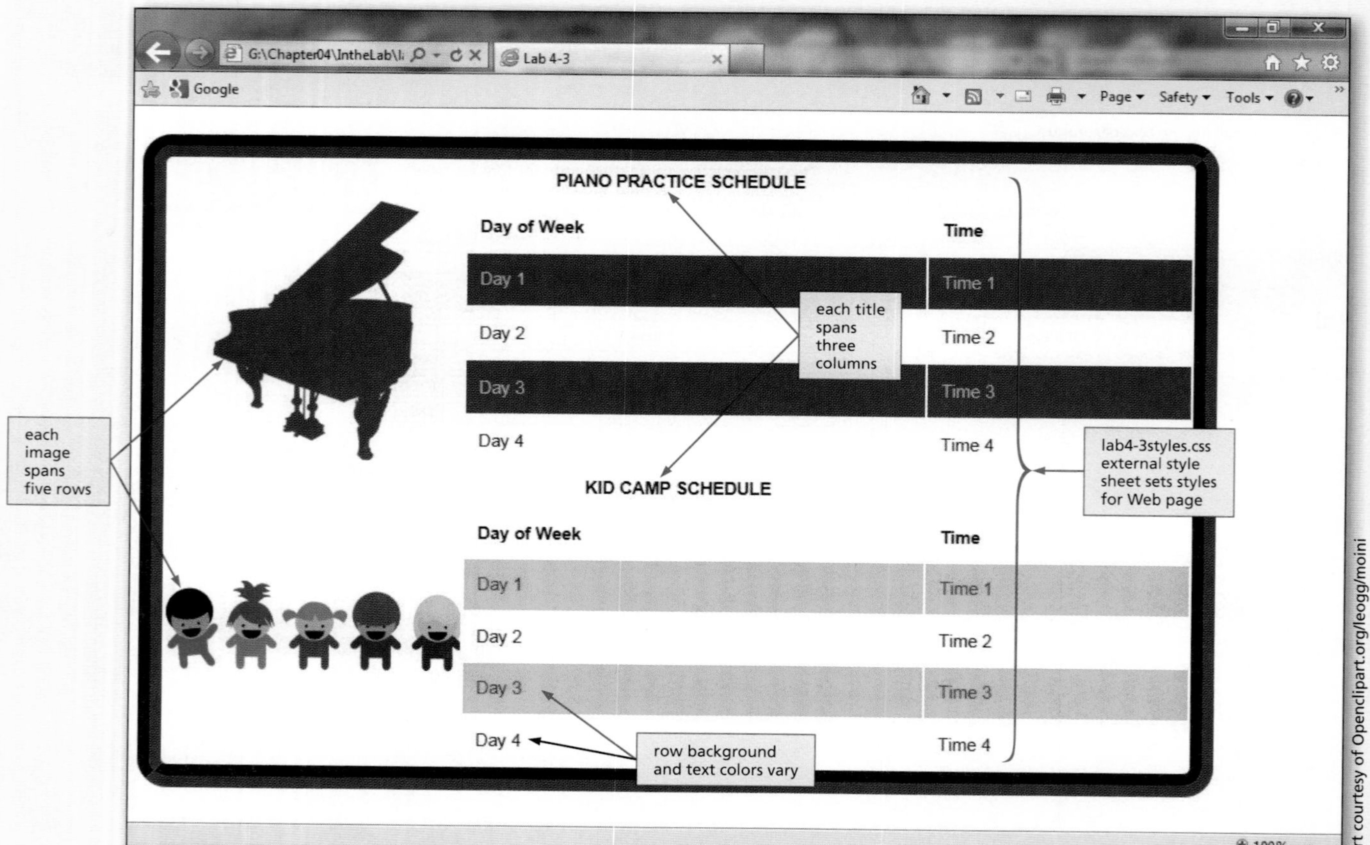

Art courtesy of Openclipart.org/leogg/moini

Figure 4–49

5. Add two images, piano.png and kids.png, with all appropriate image attributes, each spanning five rows.
6. The external style sheet should contain the following styles and be saved as lab4-3styles.css:

```
body         {font-family: Arial, Verdana, Garamond;
             font-size: 11 pt;}
th.subtitle  {text-align: left; text-indent: 10px;}
td           {text-indent: 10px;}
```

   (*Hint:* The <th> element aligns text left. Where would you use that class named subtitle?)
7. Link lab4-3styles.css to the HTML file, and save the HTML file as lab4-3solution.html.
8. Validate the HTML and CSS files using the W3C validator services.
9. Print the HTML and CSS files.
10. Print the Web page from your browser.
11. Submit the HTML file, .css file, and Web page in the format specified by your instructor.

Cases and Places

Apply your creative thinking and problem-solving skills to design and implement a solution.

1: Finding Tables on the Web

Academic

The Dean of your school wants to update the Web pages for the school's Web site. She has asked your help in doing this and wants to see a proposal. You think that tables would provide the perfect format for displaying the various academic programs available in your school, potential class schedules, and a calendar of events. Browse the Web to find examples of tables used for information such as what is needed on your school's Web site. Print those pages so that you have concrete examples to show the Dean. Prepare a document that explains to the Dean how you would use such tables for your school's particular needs. Try using a storyboard (a series of illustrations or images, displayed in sequence, that visually depicts your ideas). Sketch a Web page design (see Figure 4–8 on page HTML 163 and Figure 4–38 on page HTML 201) that incorporates tables for your purpose.

2: Creating a Time Schedule

Personal

Your computer club wants you to create a table that lists meeting, open lab, and lab class times for the computer labs. Sketch a basic table format to use for this purpose and ask a few friends (or classmates) what they think. Once you have determined a good design for the Web page, begin to code the table needed. As you begin to build the Web page, you should start thinking about other table properties that could make the Web pages look even better. Create a Web page with a basic five-row, two-column table with a border. Review additional properties listed in Appendix D that can be used with tables. Find information on those properties on other Web sites, including the W3C Web site (w3.org). Modify the basic table on your Web page to incorporate at least four of these properties.

Continued >

Cases and Places *continued*

3: Creating a Gift Shop Web Site

Professional

Your design team at Webber Design has been asked to create a proposal that explains the value of using Cascading Style Sheets to an existing customer. Select a Web site with which you are familiar. Verify which of the three types of style sheets the Web site uses. Develop a graphic of the Web site hierarchy. Determine how the three types of style sheets could possibly be used differently in this Web site and develop an outline explaining how they could enhance pages or sections of the site, add style consistency, or make the site easier to maintain. Write a proposal to the owners of the Web site that describes the features you could add with style sheets and the benefits of doing so, relative to the formatting techniques currently used in the Web site. Use ideas as discussed in the chapter to emphasize the other benefits of style sheets. Write the proposal in the form of a bid, giving time estimates and costs associated with the development effort. Include your hierarchy chart and style sheet outline as appendices to the proposal.

Special Feature 1

Attracting Visitors to Your Web Site

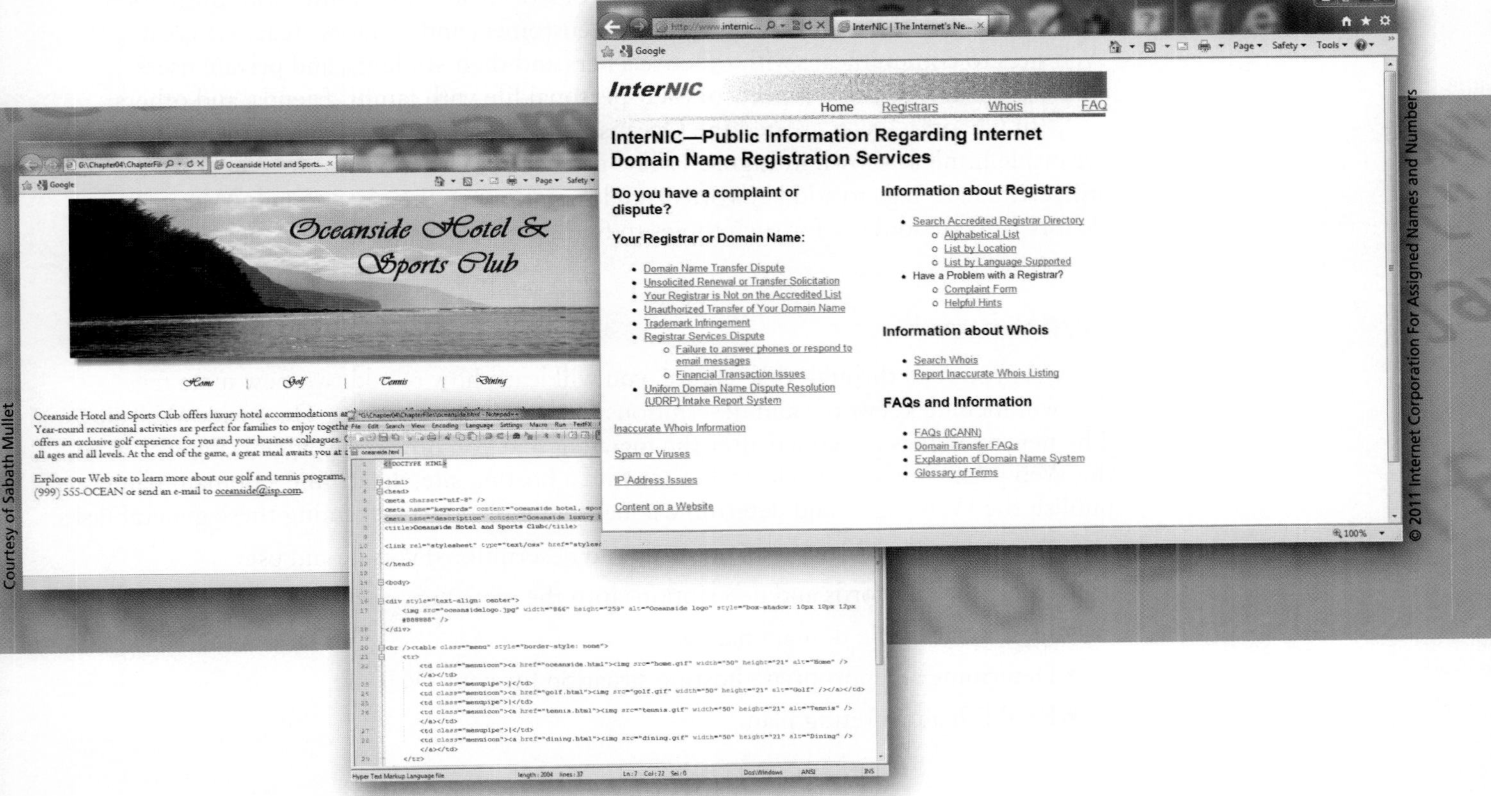

Objectives

You will have mastered the material in this special feature when you can:

- Add keywords and descriptions to your Web pages
- Find appropriate Web site servers
- Determine the availability of a domain name
- Discuss Web page publishing options
- Develop a marketing plan to get the word out about your Web site

Introduction

In Chapter 4, you developed the Oceanside Hotel and Sports Club Web site, which consisted of four Web pages. In this special feature, you will learn how to fine-tune that Web site to make sure that it will attract visitors. A Web site is a passive marketing tool; it serves no purpose if no one knows that it is there. It is not enough to just develop a Web site. You also have to make modifications to the Web pages to ensure that they will attract visitors.

Project — Attracting Visitors

Web sites have become an important means of worldwide communication. Businesses utilize Web sites to communicate with their customers and vendors. Teachers create Web sites to communicate with other teachers and their students, and private users create Web sites to share aspects of their personal life with family, friends, and others.

In Chapter 4, you created the Oceanside Hotel and Sports Club home page, oceanside.html, as shown in Figure 1. The project in this feature shows you how to utilize <meta /> tags to add keywords and descriptions to this page to help Web site visitors who are looking for such topics to find your Web page.

Overview

As you read through this feature, you will learn how to add two new meta tags that will include keywords and descriptions to attract visitors to the Oceanside Web site. The new meta tags are added after the meta tag that you previously added (Figure 1a) to the Web page. You will also learn how to find a hosting site, determine a domain name, publish the Web pages, and determine a marketing plan by performing these general tasks:

- Decide what meta names (keywords and descriptions) you should use.
- Insert the keywords and descriptions into the meta tags.
- Identify available domain names.
- Determine an appropriate hosting situation for your Web site.
- Establish a marketing plan.

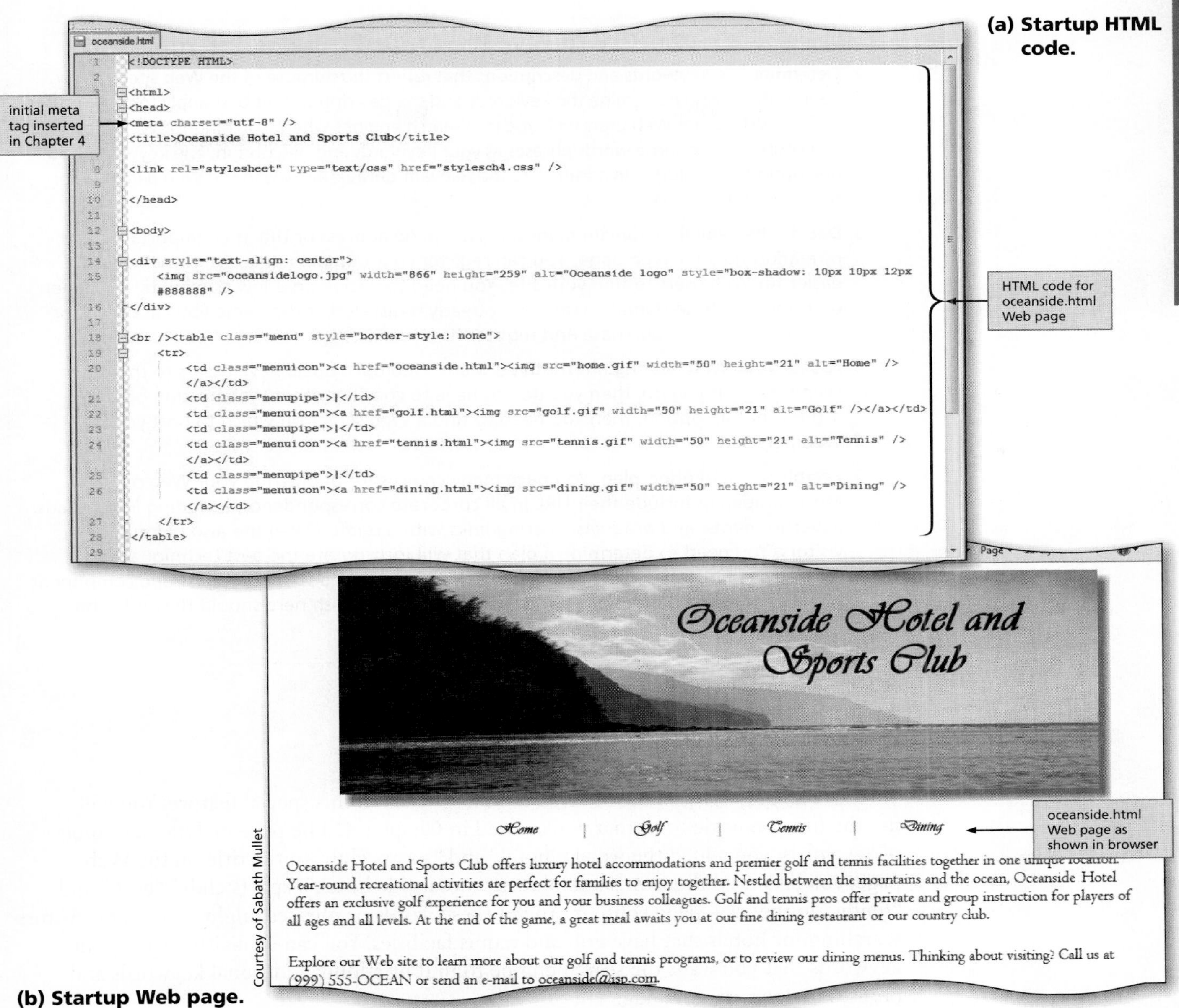

(a) Startup HTML code.

(b) Startup Web page.

Figure 1

Plan Ahead

General Project Guidelines

In the Oceanside Hotel and Sports Club home page in Chapter 4, you added a title, Oceanside Hotel and Sports Club that included the keywords "hotel" and "sports club" in it. The words "hotel" and "sports club" identify the main subject matter for the Web site, but while your topic is clear, more must be done to your Web site. Once your Web page is complete, you need to publish it and attract visitors. There are several ways to attract visitors, which you will accomplish in the following project. In preparation for this project, you should follow these general guidelines:

1. **Identify the meta names you should use.** There are different meta names that you can use within the <meta /> tag, including keywords and description. In this step, you will determine whether to use keywords or description or to use both keywords and description in different meta tags.

(continued)

Plan Ahead

(continued)

2. **Determine the keywords and descriptions that reflect the purpose of the Web site.** Review your Web site and determine the keywords and the description that best apply to the Web site. Consider what Web users will type into search engines when searching for Web sites like yours and use those words/phrases as your keywords and description. The keywords and description are included in addition to the relevant phrases already in the Web page title or body content.
3. **Decide the available domain names.** A Web page address or URL is an important part of marketing your Web page. You can register your domain name, which will make it easier for Web users to find your site. You need to decide on a few possibilities and then determine if those domain names are already registered. If the name you choose is not registered, you can purchase and register it.
4. **Assess your Web hosting alternatives.** Many Web developers have access to their own Web servers. If you do, then you do not have to consider other Web hosting options. If this is not an option, then you need to find a Web server on which to host your Web pages.
5. **Establish a marketing plan.** You have many choices for publicizing your Web pages. Most companies include their URL in all corporate correspondence, including letterheads, advertisements, and products. Sharing links with a related Web site also helps get visitors. You need to determine a plan that will incorporate the best techniques to effectively publicize your Web pages. Keep in mind that a Web site is just one component of a corporate marketing plan. The plan that you establish here should flow into the larger marketing plan.

Adding Keywords

You have already created the HTML file that is used in this special feature. You will use the file oceanside.html that you created in Chapter 4. The page includes a number of keywords: you added the words "hotel" and "sports club" to the title on the Web page; you also used the words and phrases "oceanside hotel," "sports club," "golf," and "tennis" in the Web page content. Any of these words or phrases might be used by visitors searching for hotels that have golf and tennis facilities. You can explicitly identify the keywords that you want the search engine to find by adding additional keywords and phrases to your <meta /> tag.

As with other projects, you use Notepad++ to enhance this file by adding keywords and descriptions. To include additional information in your Web page, you will follow these general steps:

1. Open the oceanside.html file in Notepad++.
2. Add the keywords and description to new <meta /> tags.
3. Save and validate the file.

To Open the File

For this project, you will add keywords and a description to the oceanside.html Web page already created. The following steps show you how to add keywords.

1. Start Notepad++.
2. Open the oceanside.html file in the Chapter04\ChapterFiles folder that you stored on the G:\ drive (Figure 2). If necessary, enable Word wrap in Notepad++.

Q&A What if I did not create the oceanside.html file from Chapter 4?

Your instructor should have a copy of the oceanside.html file.

Other Ways

1. Right-click the filename oceanside.html in Windows Explorer, click Edit with Notepad++

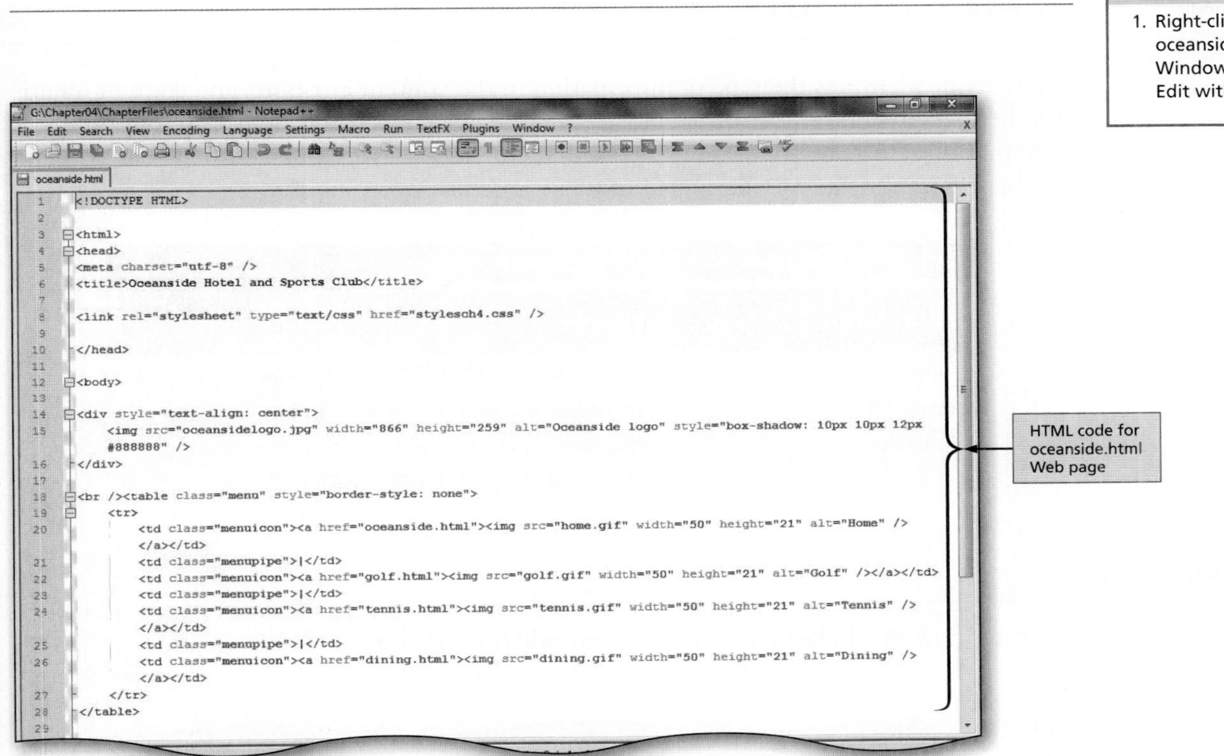

Figure 2

Meta Names

The meta tag derives from the word, metadata, which is data (or information) about data. You already included one meta tag in the initial HTML code that you inserted into every Web page created thus far. The

```
<meta charset="utf-8" />
```

line has been included in all Web pages throughout the book. As mentioned earlier, this statement declares the character-encoding as UTF-8. The Unicode Transformation Format (UTF) is a compressed format that allows computers to display and manipulate text. When the browser encounters this meta tag, it will display the Web page properly, based on the particular UTF-8 encoding embedded in the tag. UTF-8 is the preferred encoding standard for Web pages, e-mail, and other applications.

The meta tag also allows you to specify the keywords, description, and author for the Web page through the use of the name and content attributes. Some of the more frequently

> **BTW**
> **SEO**
> SEO is an acronym for search engine optimization. SEO is the process of improving the amount of traffic that you get on your Web site by improving the ranking of your site in search engine results. Optimizing a Web site involves editing the content and HTML in the Web page to increase its relevance to specific keywords and to remove barriers to the page indexing functions of search engines. To find more information, search for SEO on the Internet.

used meta name values are listed in Table 1. In this project, you will use two of those meta name values: description and keywords. The keywords are used by some search engines to find your Web pages. Other search engines use the keywords included in the content of your Web pages. The best plan includes putting keywords in both places. The description, on the other hand, is what some search engines add next to your Web page URL to describe the content of the Web page. Visitors often look at that description to determine whether they want to click that particular link (or URL) from the list of URLs in the search engine results. The format that is used for each name and content attribute pair is:

```
<meta name="keywords" content="oceanside hotel, sports club,
golf, tennis" />
<meta name="description" content="Oceanside luxury hotel, golf,
tennis for family."
```

where name identifies the type of information in the content attribute, and content identifies the specific phrases or words that you want to appear as metadata. It is important to note that these two attributes must be used in conjunction with one another—the content attribute cannot be defined if the name attribute is not.

Table 1 Meta Names and Their Functions

Meta Name	Function
author	Supplies the name of the document author
description	Provides a description of the document
keywords	Provides a list of keywords that a user might type in a search engine to search for the document

To Add Keywords

The following step illustrates how to add keywords to the oceanside.html Web page:

- Click after the > at the end of line 5 and press the ENTER key to position the insertion point on line 6.
- Type `<meta name="keywords" content="oceanside hotel, sports club, golf, tennis"/>` and then press the ENTER key (Figure 3).

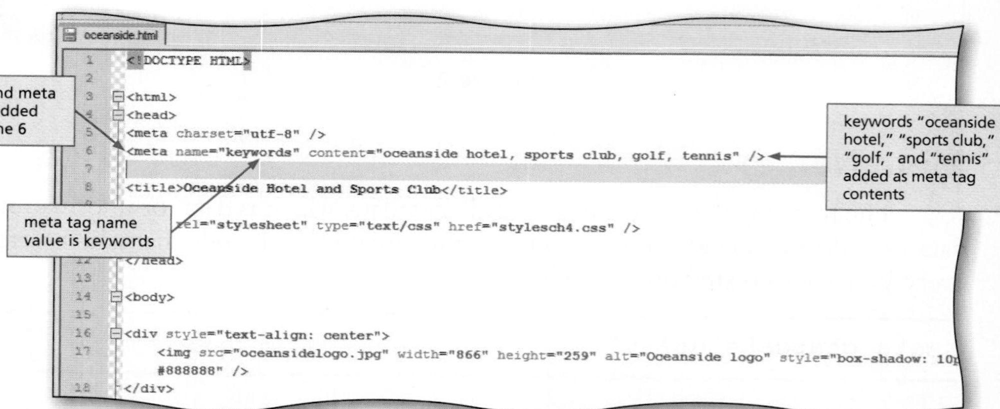

Figure 3

To Add a Description

The following step illustrates how to add a meta tag description to your Web page.

1

- If necessary, position the insertion point on line 7.
- Type `<meta name="description" content="Oceanside luxury hotel, golf, tennis for family."/>` but do not press the ENTER key (Figure 4).

```
1   <!DOCTYPE HTML>
2
3   <html>
4   <head>
5   <meta charset="utf-8" />
6   <meta name="keywords" content="oceanside hotel, sports club, golf, tennis" />
7   <meta name="description" content="Oceanside luxury hotel, golf, tennis for family." />
8   <title>Oceanside Hotel and Sports Club</title>
9
10  <link rel="stylesheet" type="text/css" href="stylesch4.css" />
11
12  </head>
13
14  <body>
15
```

third meta tag added on line 7

description content added

meta tag name value is description

Figure 4

Q&A Is there a difference between keywords and description?

Yes. Search engines use keywords to find your Web pages, while descriptions are displayed next to their respective Web page URLs in a search results list.

Q&A If I have relevant keywords in the content of my Web page, why should I add other words to the <meta /> tags?

It always helps to have keywords identified in both places for those search engines that rely on the meta tag for keywords versus those that rank results by analyzing the page content.

To Save, Validate, and Print a Document

You are finished entering the meta tags. As with all Web development projects, you now need to save, validate, and print the file.

1. In Notepad++, click the Save icon on the toolbar to save the file with the new meta tags.
2. Validate the file using the w3.org validation service.
3. Once the file is successfully validated, print the file (Figure 5).
4. Close Notepad++.

```
<!DOCTYPE HTML>

<html>
<head>
<meta charset="utf-8" />
<meta name="keywords" content="oceanside hotel, sports club" />
<meta name="description" content="Oceanside luxury hotel, golf, tennis for family."  />
<title>Oceanside Hotel and Sports Club</title>

<link rel="stylesheet" type="text/css" href="stylesch4.css" />

</head>

<body>

<div style="text-align: center">
    <img src="oceansidelogo.jpg" width="866" height="259" alt="Oceanside logo" style=
    "box-shadow: 10px 10px 12px #888888" />
</div>

<br /><table class="menu" style="border-style: none">
    <tr>
        <td class="menuicon"><a href="oceanside.html"><img src="home.gif" width="50"
        height="21" alt="Home" /></a></td>
        <td class="menupipe">|</td>
        <td class="menuicon"><a href="golf.html"><img src="golf.gif" width="50" height=
        "21" alt="Golf" /></a></td>
        <td class="menupipe">|</td>
        <td class="menuicon"><a href="tennis.html"><img src="tennis.gif" width="50"
        height="21" alt="Tennis" /></a></td>
        <td class="menupipe">|</td>
        <td class="menuicon"><a href="dining.html"><img src="dining.gif" width="50"
        height="21" alt="Dining" /></a></td>
    </tr>
</table>
```

Figure 5

Determining a Domain Name

A **domain name** is the server name portion of a URL. You can use the domain name of the server on which you publish your Web pages together with a path to your specific pages for your Web page address. However, this Web page address option can result in a URL that is long, hard to remember, and not representative of your Web site or business. You can register your own domain name on the Internet for minimal cost per year. A unique domain name can make it easier for visitors to find your Web pages. In the case of the oceanside.html file, you could register a unique domain name for your Oceanside Hotel and Sports Club Web site, if you can find a name that is both suitable and available.

To determine if the domain name you are considering is available, you can start your search at InterNIC. InterNIC is a registered service mark of the U.S. Department of Commerce. The InterNIC Web site (www.internic.net) is operated by the Internet Corporation for Assigned Names and Numbers (ICANN) to provide information to the public regarding Internet domain name registration services. ICANN is responsible for managing and coordinating the Domain Name System (DNS) to ensure that every Internet address is unique, and that all users of the Internet can find all valid addresses.

> **BTW**
> **InterNIC**
> InterNIC contains trusted public information regarding Internet domain name registration services. The InterNIC Web site has a FAQ section, information about domain name registrars, as well as links for domain name disputes.

Check Domain Name Availability

In order to check to see if a domain name is available, complete the following steps:

1

- Type `http://www.internic.net` into the address bar of the browser and press ENTER, as shown in Figure 6.
- Review the FAQ section of the Web site to better understand the domain naming process.
- Click the Whois link to see what domain names have previously been registered for oceansidehotel. Type `oceansidehotel.com` into the text box provided on the Whois Web page and click the Submit button to see if the domain name has been registered. Next, type `oceanside-hotel.net` into the text box and view that result. Finally, try oceansidehotel.org and view the results.

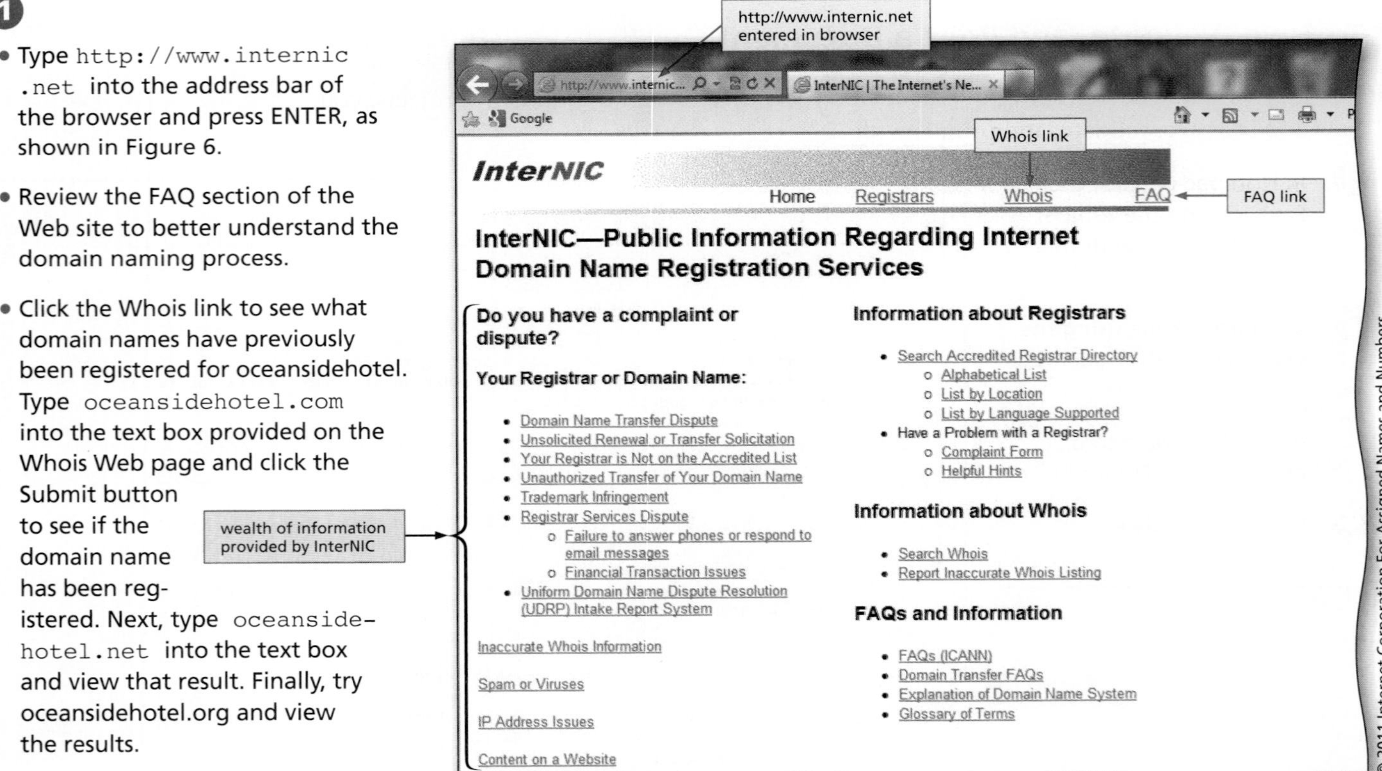

Figure 6

Finding a Web Hosting Site

The next step in the Web development process is to publish your Web pages so that visitors can see them. In order to publish your Web site, you need hosting services. There are many options available for Web hosting. You will need access to a Web server onto which you can upload all of the Web pages in your Web site.

One option is to use the ISP that you use to connect to the Internet. ISPs sometimes provide space for their clients to host a Web site. If you registered your own domain name, you can have your ISP set up a virtual domain, or shared Web hosting, on their server with your new domain name. Your ISP's server may be set up to allocate hosting services and bandwidth to more than one Web site by using a virtual domain. In other words, although you register the domain name oceansidehotel.com, your ISP would host it on its own Web server. Virtual Web hosting is a less expensive option because you do not have to pay for a dedicated server to host just your Web site. You can check with your ISP for details. A second option is to use a company that charges for Web site hosting. There are thousands of companies that provide Web hosting services. Most charge a monthly fee, but some offer free Web hosting in exchange for advertising on your Web site. A final option is for you to set up your own Web server. You would have to know enough about the technology to set it up and keep it running.

BTW

Web Site Hosting
There are a variety of Web site hosting options available today. To search for Web hosting services, use different search engines to find different alternatives. Make sure to use the checklist shown on this page to assess the hosting services and fees.

Whether you choose to utilize your ISP to host your Web site, to use a Web hosting service, or to set up your own Web server, you need to consider the following:

- What is the total cost? Compare monthly or annual costs; the highest cost may not always provide the best service.
- How much space is available to you? You need to assess your current needs (i.e., file sizes, sizes of graphics) and also your future needs (i.e., how much more information you will create).
- How fast is the connection speed? The speed of the connection to the Internet is important to efficiently serve your visitors.
- How much total bandwidth transfer is available? The number and size of Web pages in your Web site together with the number and size of graphical images is important to consider.
- Is technical support provided? You may occasionally need help, especially in the beginning.
- Are tracking services provided? Many hosting companies allow you to see how visitors utilize your Web site by viewing a tracking log.

After you have selected a Web hosting service, you need to transfer your files to that server.

Publishing Your Web Site

Once you have determined a Web hosting strategy, the next step is to publish your Web pages so that visitors can see them. **Publishing** your Web site means transferring your files to the Web server. There are many options available for file transfers. You could use a File Transfer Protocol (FTP) program such as WS_FTP for Windows (Figure 7 on the next page) or Fetch for Mac (for more information about FTP programs, see Appendix E). In addition, many Web page editors also provide publishing functionality. Once your Web pages are published, the last step is to market their location to attract visitors.

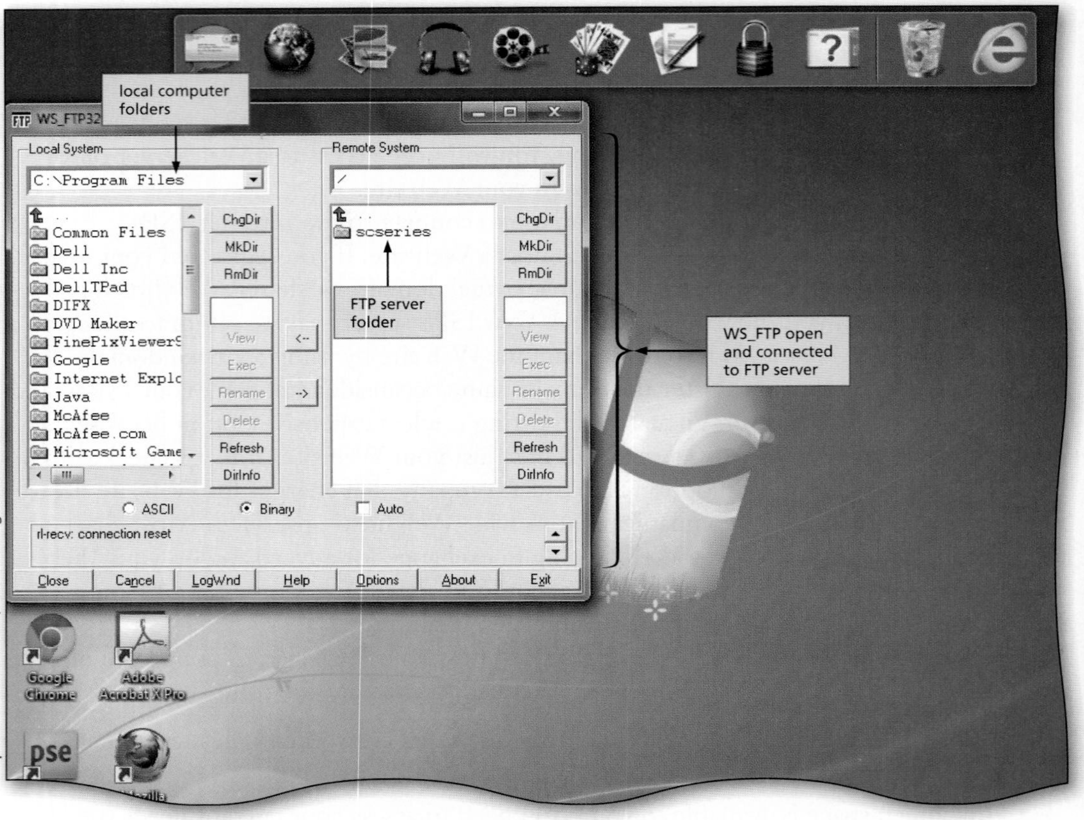

Figure 7

Marketing Your Web Site

Now that your Web pages are published, you need to get the word out to potential Web site visitors. You need to determine a comprehensive marketing plan. It serves no purpose for you to publish a Web site if no one visits it. There are several ways to start a marketing campaign:

- Put your URL on your business cards, company brochures, stationery, and e-mail signature.
- Advertise your URL in newsletters and print articles.
- Tell people verbally about your Web site.
- Find and get listed on targeted directories and search engines specific to your industry.
- Buy banner ads.
- Negotiate reciprocal links in which you agree to link to a Web site if they agree to link to your Web site.
- Utilize newsgroups specific to your industry.

> **BTW** **Search Engines**
> Both Google and Yahoo! contain information about optimizing your Web sites. Review their Webmaster guidelines and resources for great ideas on registering with their search engines.

Registering with Search Engines

You are finished entering the meta tags, publishing, and marketing your Web site. The next step is to register your Web site with the two most popular search engines, Google and Yahoo! It is also a good idea to register your site with search engines that specialize in subject matter related to your Web site.

To Register Your Web Site with Search Engines

The next steps show you how to register your Web pages with the Google and Yahoo! search engines. Note that both Google and Yahoo! search engines require or recommend that you register with their site before you can submit a Web site to the search engine.

- In Internet Explorer, type `http://www.google.com/addurl.html` in the address bar and press the ENTER key (Figure 8).
- Click the Learn more link. Some of the worthwhile links on that page are: Google Basics and Webmaster FAQ. These links provide excellent starting points. This page also contains articles and links to other valuable resources, including tools and contacts for Webmasters.

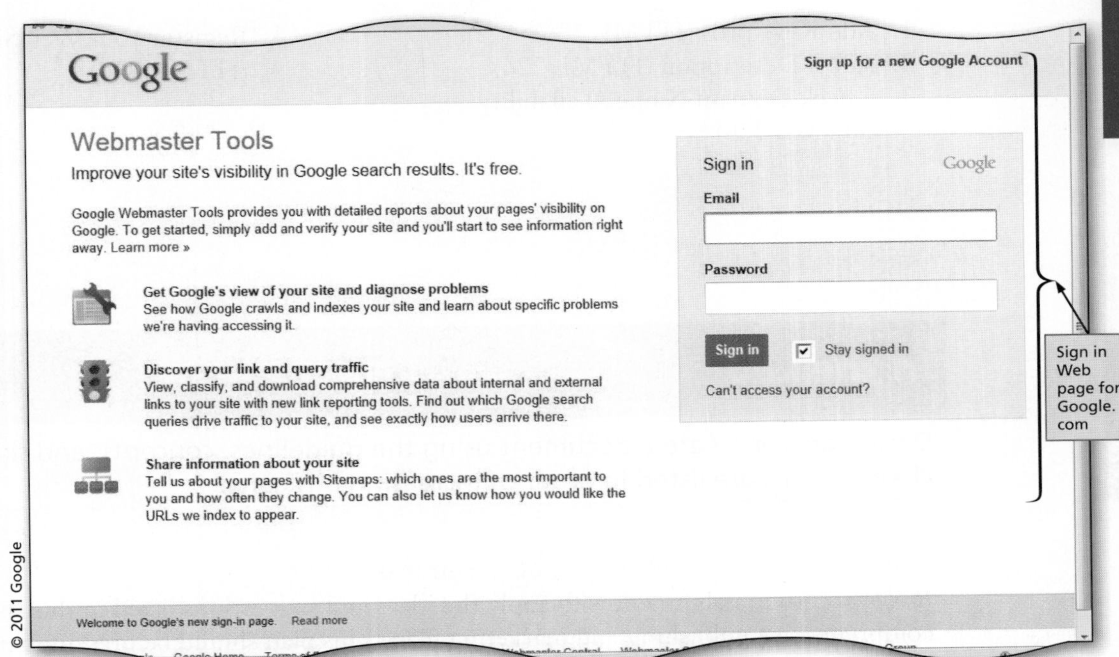

Figure 8

- For the Yahoo! registration, type `http://search.yahoo.com/info/submit.html` in the address bar and press the ENTER key (Figure 9).
- Follow the directions to add your URL.
- Close the browser.

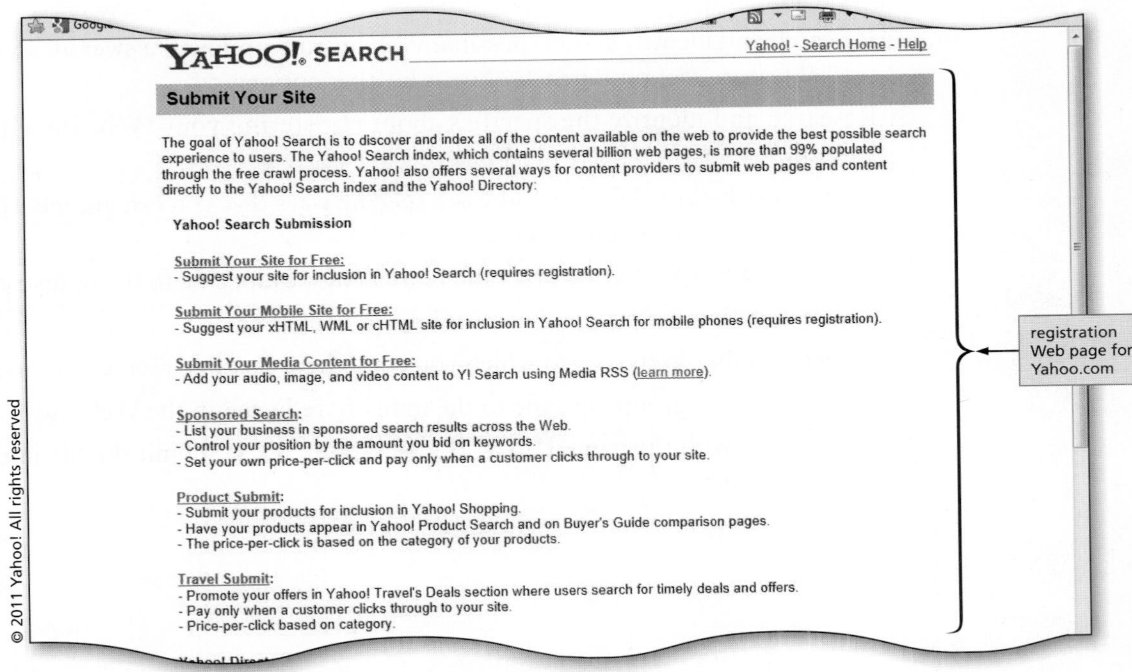

Figure 9

Feature Summary

In this feature, you have learned how to insert keywords and description meta tags into your Web page. You also learned about domain names, what questions to ask of a potential a Web host, how to publish your Web page, ways to market your Web site, and how to register your site with search engines. The items listed below include all the new skills you have learned in this feature.

1. Add Keywords (HTML 226)
2. Add a Description (HTML 226)
3. Check Domain Name Availability (HTML 228)
4. Register Your Web Site with Search Engines (HTML 230)

In the Lab

Design and/or create a document using the guidelines, concepts, and skills presented in this chapter. Labs are listed in order of increasing difficulty.

Lab 1: Creating a Publishing and Marketing Plan

Problem: Your assignment is to apply the ideas and suggestions listed in this special feature to write a comprehensive publishing and marketing plan. This plan should be presented in a Word file that can be submitted to your instructor.

Instructions:

1. Determine a domain name that is available to use for your Oceanside Hotel and Sports Club Web site.
2. Research and identify several possible Web hosting options. Answer all six questions covered in this special feature section for each of your hosting options.
3. Research and identify the specifics about registering your Web site with both Google and Yahoo!.
4. Write a marketing plan that addresses specific ways that you can get the word out about your Web site. Specific plans should include:
   a. Locating targeted directories and search engines specific to the industry reflected in the Web site
   b. Investigating the pros and cons of buying banner ads
   c. Determining Web sites to which you could have possible reciprocal links
   d. Finding newsgroups specific to the industry reflected in the Web site
5. Save the file with the name Lab SF1-1 Marketing.docx. Submit the file in the format specified by your instructor.

In the Lab

Lab 2: Attracting Visitors to Another Web Site

Problem: In this assignment, you will assess another Web site to complete the same basic steps as taken in this feature to improve the site's visibility on the Internet.

Instructions:

1. Select a Web site that is of interest to you and open the site's home page.
2. Review the meta tags (if any) that are used on the home page. (*Hint:* View the page source to review those tags.) Determine how you can utilize additional meta tags for this Web page. What keywords and descriptions would be good to use? What keywords and descriptions do other related Web sites use?
3. Write a marketing plan that addresses specific ways that you can get the word out about this Web site. Specific plans should include:
   a. Locating targeted directories and search engines specific to the industry reflected in the Web site
   b. Determining Web sites to which you could have possible reciprocal links
   c. Finding newsgroups specific to the industry reflected in the Web site
4. Save the file with the name Lab SF1-2 Marketing.docx. Submit the file in the format specified by your instructor.

5 Creating an Image Map

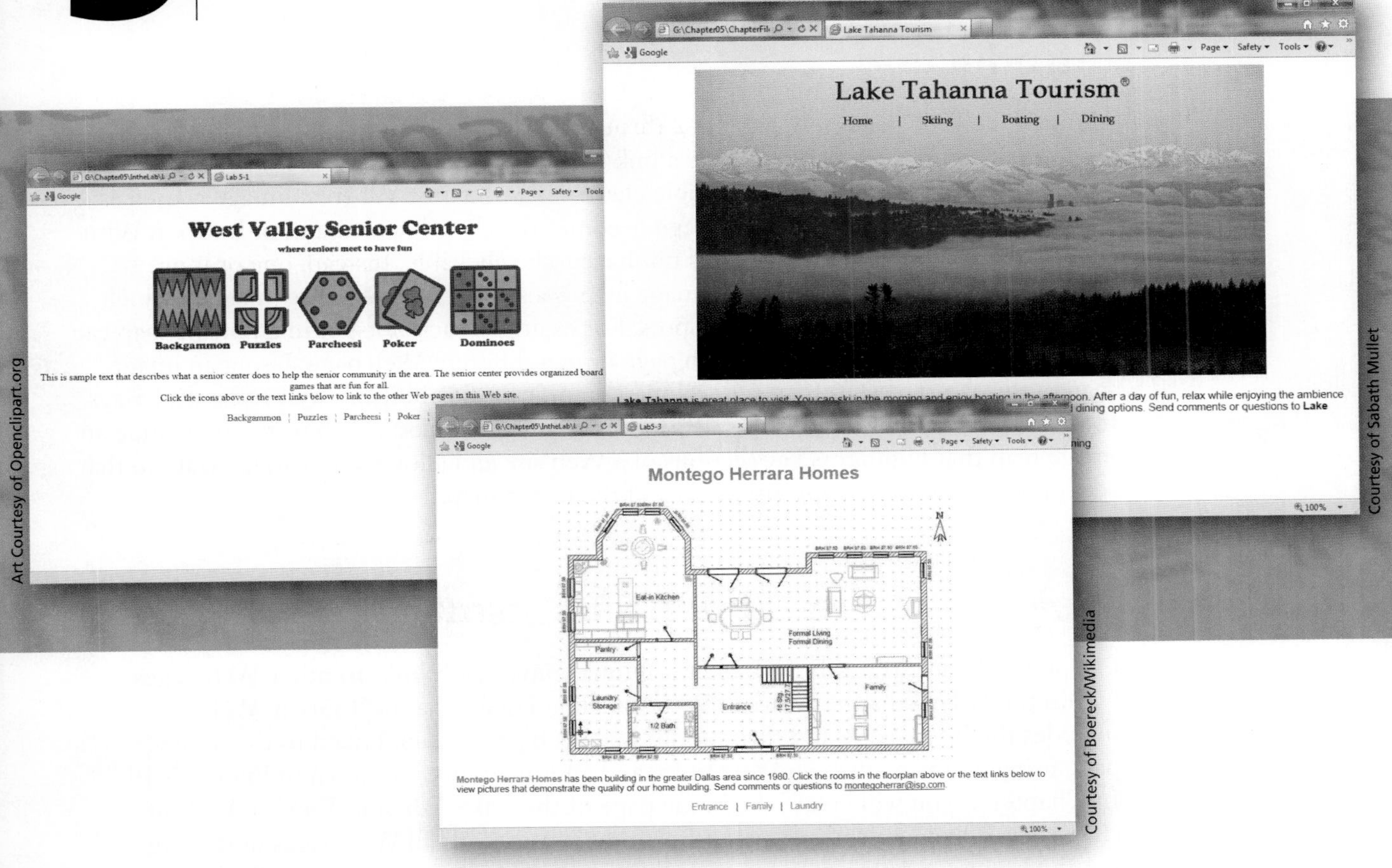

Art Courtesy of Openclipart.org

Courtesy of Sabath Mullet

Courtesy of Boereck/Wikimedia

Objectives

You will have mastered the material in this chapter when you can:

- Define terms relating to image mapping
- List the differences between server-side and client-side image maps
- Name the two components of an image map and describe the steps to implement an image map
- Distinguish between appropriate and inappropriate images for mapping
- Sketch hotspots on an image
- Describe how the x- and y-coordinates relate to vertical and horizontal alignment
- Open an image in Paint and use Paint to locate the image map coordinates
- Create a home page
- Create a navigation bar of text links
- Insert an image onto a Web page that is used as an image map and use the usemap attribute to define an image map
- Insert special characters into a Web page
- Use the <map> </map> tags to start and end a map
- Use the <area> tag to indicate the shape, coordinates, and URL for a mapped area
- Create an external style sheet for styles used across the Web site

5 Creating an Image Map

Introduction

Many of the Web pages in Chapters 2 through 4 used the <img> tag to add images. In Chapter 3, an image was also used as a link back to the home page, by using the <a> </a> tags to define the image as the clickable element for the link. When an image is used as a link, as in Chapter 3, the entire image becomes the clickable element, or hotspot. With an image map, the entire image does not have to be clickable. Instead, one or more specific areas serve as hotspots. An image map is a special type of inline image in which you define one or more areas as hotspots. For example, each hotspot in an image map can link to another part of the same Web page or to a different Web page. Using an image map in this way gives Web page developers significant flexibility, as well as creative ways to include navigation options. Instead of using only text links, a Web page can include an image map that highlights key sections of a Web site and allows a user to navigate to that section by clicking the appropriate area of the image map.

Project — Lake Tahanna Tourism

Chapter 5 demonstrates how to create an image map with links to other Web pages within the Lake Tahanna Tourism Web site. The Lake Tahanna Tourism Web site includes the home page and three additional Web pages, each linked to the home page using an image map and text links, and an e-mail link, as shown in Figure 5–1. In Chapter 5, you will create the home page of the Lake Tahanna Tourism Web site (Figure 5–1a) and an external style sheet that is used with all Web pages in the site. On the home page, you will include a link to the tahanna@isp.com e-mail address that opens an e-mail program. The Web pages shown in Figures 5–1b, 5–1c, and 5–1d are included in the Data Files for Students. Two images, tahanna.jpg and tahannasm.jpg, are also included in the Data Files for Students. The first image, tahanna.jpg, is shown in Figure 5–1a. All linked Web pages use the smaller image tahannasm.jpg, as shown in Figures 5–1b, 5–1c, and 5–1d. Even though the second image is smaller, the text links are in the same position. (See the inside back cover of this book for instructions on downloading the Data Files for Students, or contact your instructor for information about accessing the required files.) HTML tags are used to create the image map that supports the four clickable areas in the image. One feature of the Web is its support for graphics, so Web visitors expect to view many images on the Web pages that they visit. Images make Web pages more exciting and interesting to view and, in the case of image maps, provide a creative navigational tool.

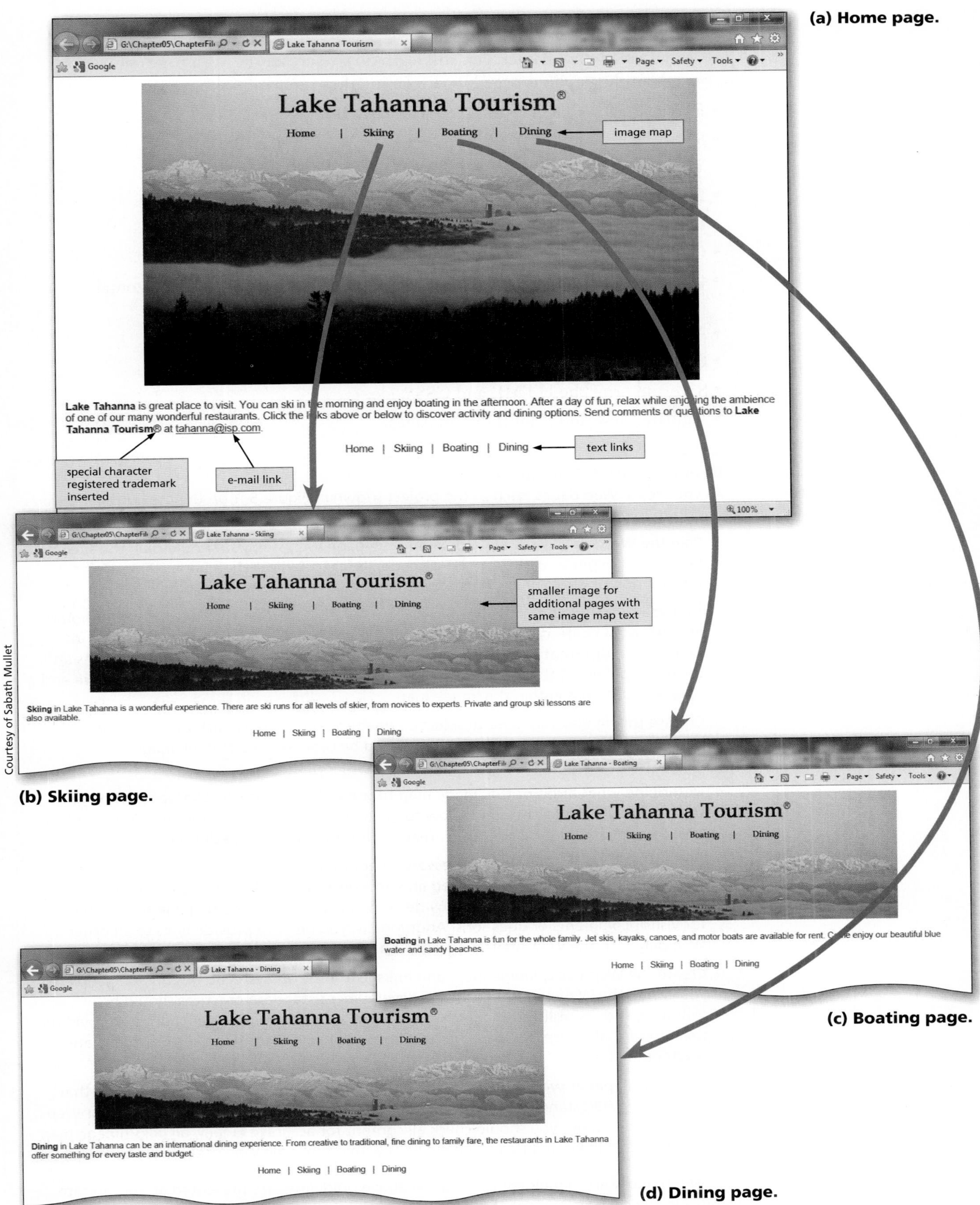

(a) Home page.
Lake Tahanna Tourism®
Home | Skiing | Boating | Dining
image map
Lake Tahanna is great place to visit. You can ski in the morning and enjoy boating in the afternoon. After a day of fun, relax while enjoying the ambience of one of our many wonderful restaurants. Click the links above or below to discover activity and dining options. Send comments or questions to Lake Tahanna Tourism® at tahanna@isp.com.
Home | Skiing | Boating | Dining
text links
special character registered trademark inserted
e-mail link
smaller image for additional pages with same image map text
Skiing in Lake Tahanna is a wonderful experience. There are ski runs for all levels of skier, from novices to experts. Private and group ski lessons are also available.
Boating in Lake Tahanna is fun for the whole family. Jet skis, kayaks, canoes, and motor boats are available for rent. Come enjoy our beautiful blue water and sandy beaches.
Dining in Lake Tahanna can be an international dining experience. From creative to traditional, fine dining to family fare, the restaurants in Lake Tahanna offer something for every taste and budget.
Courtesy of Sabath Mullet
(b) Skiing page.
(c) Boating page.
(d) Dining page.

Figure 5–1

Overview

As you read this chapter, you will learn how to create the Web pages shown in Figure 5–1 on the previous page by performing these general tasks:

- Enter HTML code into the Notepad++ window.
- Save the file as an HTML file.
- View an image in Microsoft Paint to see image map coordinates.
- Enter basic HTML tags and add text to the file.
- Insert an image to be used as an image map.
- Create an image map by mapping hotspots on the image.
- Create links to the other Web pages and to the home page with a horizontal navigation bar.
- Add special characters to the home page.
- Create an external style sheet and insert the link into the home page.
- Save and print the HTML and CSS code.
- Validate, view, and print the Web pages.

Plan Ahead

General Project Guidelines

As you create Web pages, such as the project shown in Figure 5–1 on the previous page, you should follow these general guidelines:

1. **Plan the Web site.** As always with a multiple-page Web site, you should plan the site before you begin to write your HTML code. Refer to Table 1–4 on page HTML 15 for information on the planning phase of the Web Development Life Cycle.
2. **Analyze the need.** In the analysis phase of the Web Development Life Cycle, you should analyze what content to include on the Web page. The Web development project in Chapter 5 is different from the one completed in other chapters because it contains an image map. Part of the analysis phase then includes determining what image to use and where to put links within the image map.
3. **Choose the image.** You need to select an image that has areas, such as the four words (Home, Skiing, Boating, and Dining), that can be used as links. Not all images are conducive to image mapping, as described in the chapter.
4. **Determine what areas of the image map to use as links.** Once an appropriate image is selected, you need to determine how to divide up the image map for links. You want to make sure that your hotspot (link) areas do not spill over into each other.
5. **Establish what other links are necessary.** In addition to links between the home page and secondary Web pages, you need an e-mail link on this Web site. It is a general standard for Web developers to provide an e-mail link on the home page of a Web site for visitor comments or questions. Additionally, you need to provide links to all other Web pages on the Web site (skiing.html, boating.html, and dining.html).
6. **Create the Web page, image map, and links.** Once the analysis and design are complete, you create the Web pages. Good Web development standard practices should be followed, such as utilizing the initial HTML tags as shown in previous chapters, providing text links for all hotspots in the image map, and always identifying alt text (alternate text) for images.
7. **Test all Web pages within the Web site.** It is important to test your pages to assure that they follow W3C standards. In this book, you use the W3C validator to validate your Web pages. Additionally, you should check all content for accuracy. Finally, all links (image map hotspots, text links, and page-to-page links within the same Web site) should be tested.

When necessary, details concerning the above guidelines are presented at appropriate points in the chapter. The chapter will also identify the actions performed and decisions made regarding these guidelines during the creation of the Web pages shown in Figure 5–1.

Introduction to Image Maps

In this chapter, you will use an image map to create four clickable areas within a single image: a link to the home page, a link to the Skiing page, a link to the Boating page, and a link to the Dining page. All four of the clickable areas have a rectangular shape. Figure 5–2 shows the four rectangular clickable areas, each of which encloses a specific area. A Web page visitor clicking one of the rectangular-shaped clickable areas will link to one of the associated Web pages (Home, Skiing, Boating, or Dining).

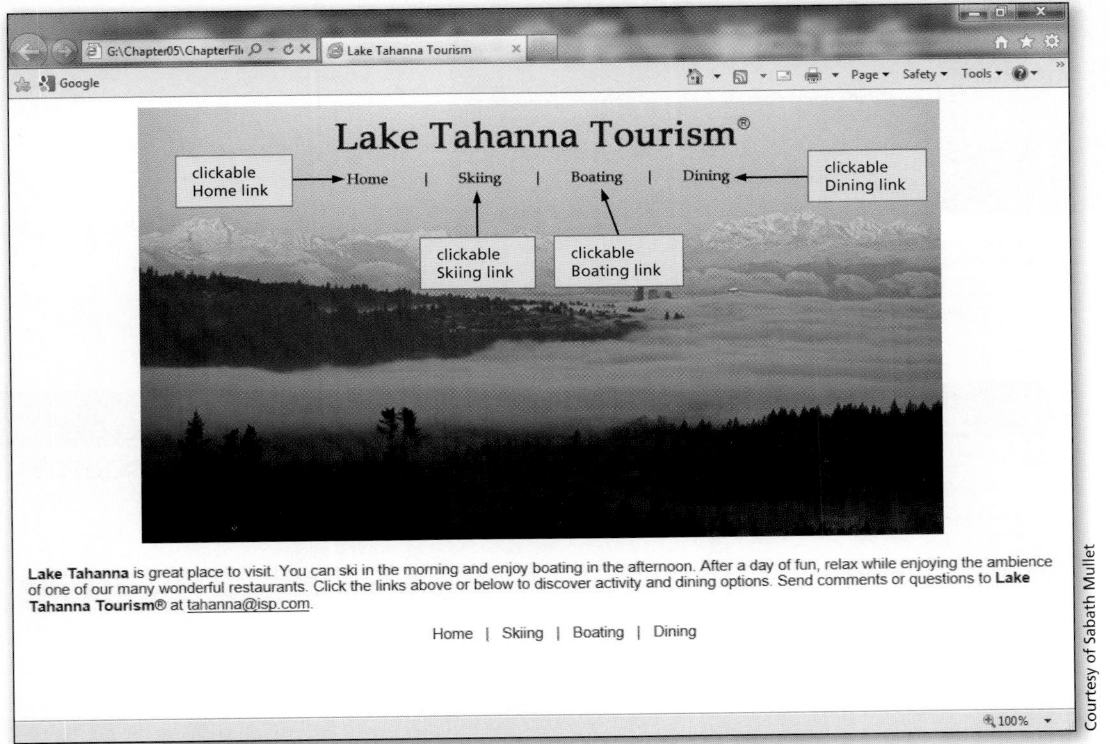

Courtesy of Sabath Mullet

Figure 5–2 Clickable areas on menu image.

Using Image Maps

One of the risks in using image maps to provide navigational elements is that if the image does not load, a user will not have the ability to navigate to other linked Web pages. Another potential issue is that using a large image for an image map can increase the amount of time required for pages to download over lower-speed connections. To avoid such performance issues, some people turn off the viewing of images when they browse Web pages, electing to display only text in their browsers. These users, and users of text-based browsers, will also not be able to navigate a Web page that relies on an image map. For these reasons, a Web page that uses an image map for navigation should also include text links to the URLs, as shown in Figure 5–3a on the next page. Using text links in conjunction with the image map ensures that if the image does not download or a Web page visitor has images turned off, as shown in Figure 5–3b, a user still can navigate to other Web pages using the text links.

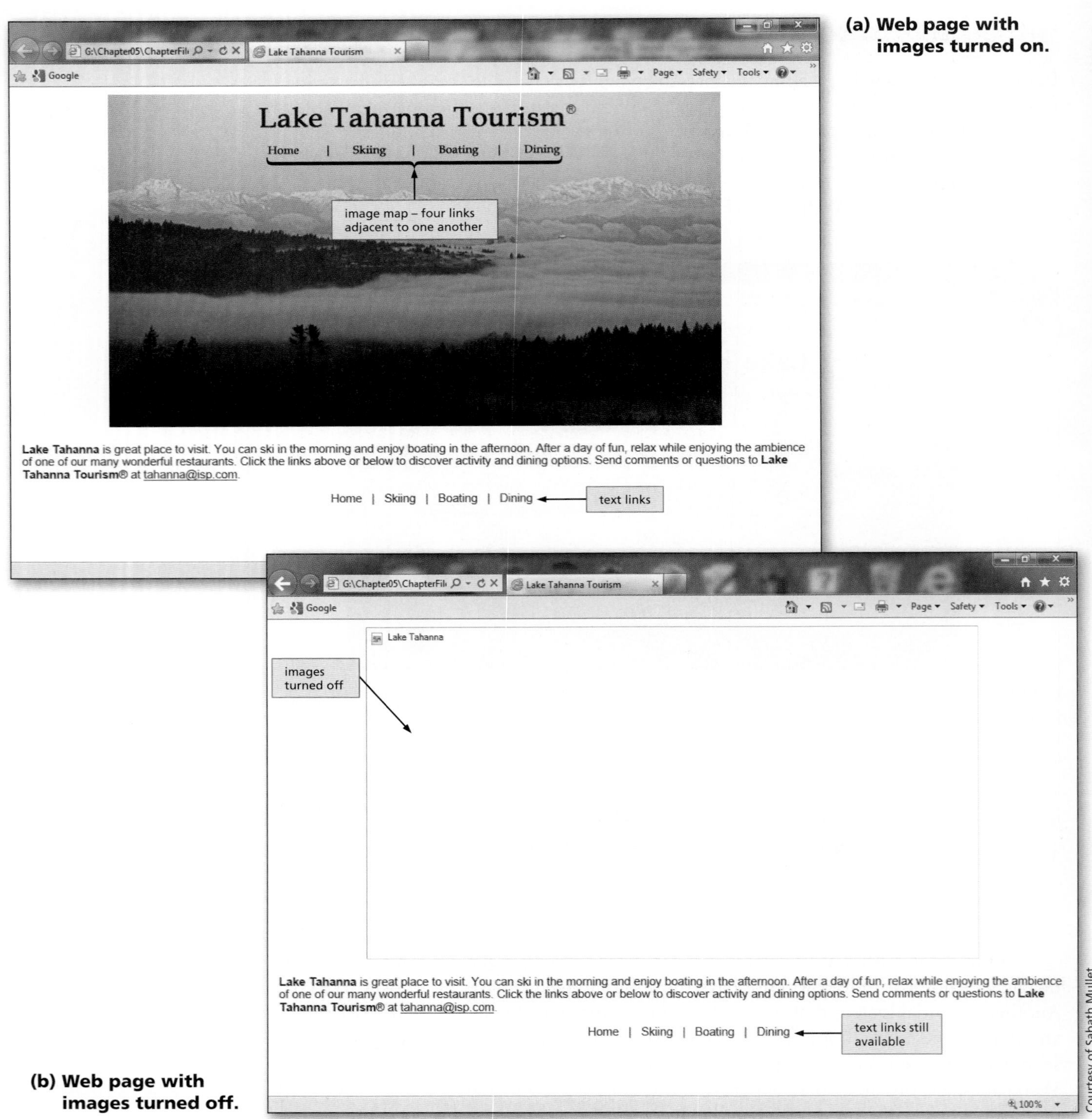

(a) Web page with images turned on.

(b) Web page with images turned off.

Figure 5–3

Image maps can enhance the functionality and appeal of Web pages in many ways. For example, an image map can be used as an **image map button bar**, which is a navigation bar that uses graphical images, as shown in Figure 5–4 and in one of the end-of-chapter projects. This makes the navigation bar a more attractive feature of the Web page.

Figure 5–4 Image map navigation bar.

Image maps are also utilized to divide a geographical map into hotspots, as shown in Figure 5–5. A Web page visitor can click a geographical area on the map and be linked to additional information about that location.

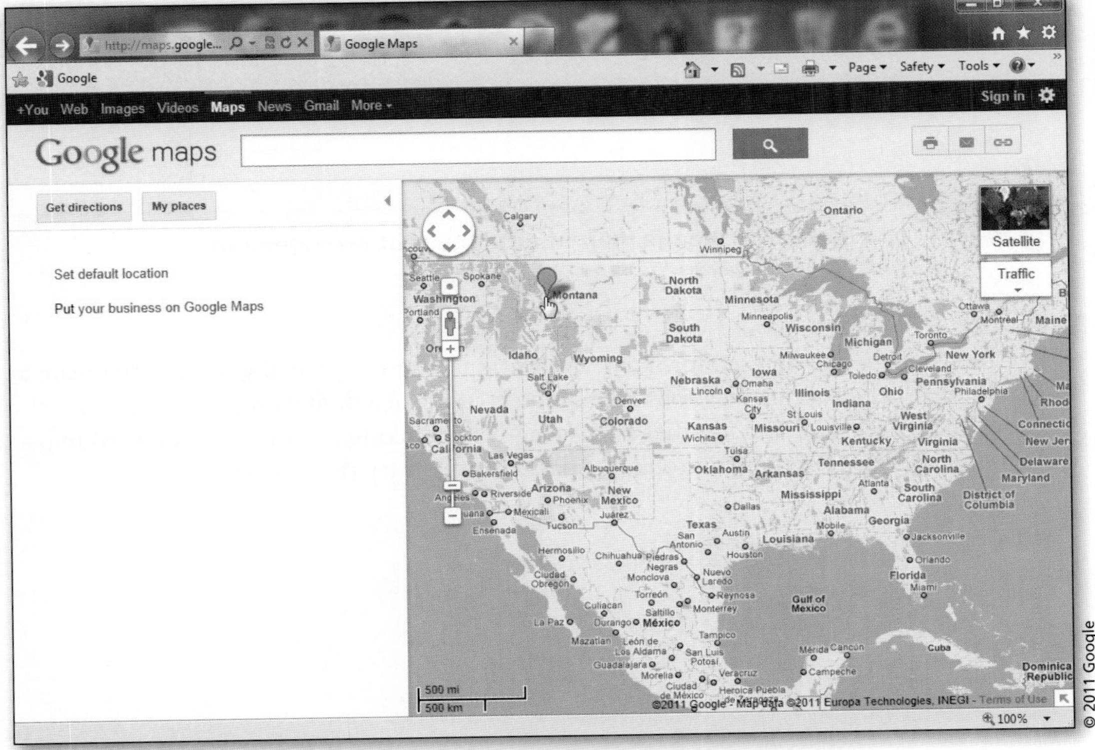

Figure 5–5 Image map on Web page with map.

An airline company may use an image map to show the seating chart of one of their planes (Figure 5–6). You could develop an application that links from the airplane ticket purchase Web page to the seating chart image map and allow customers to select their seats. This map shows how the various airplane seats are arranged, which helps customers understand the general layout of the airplane.

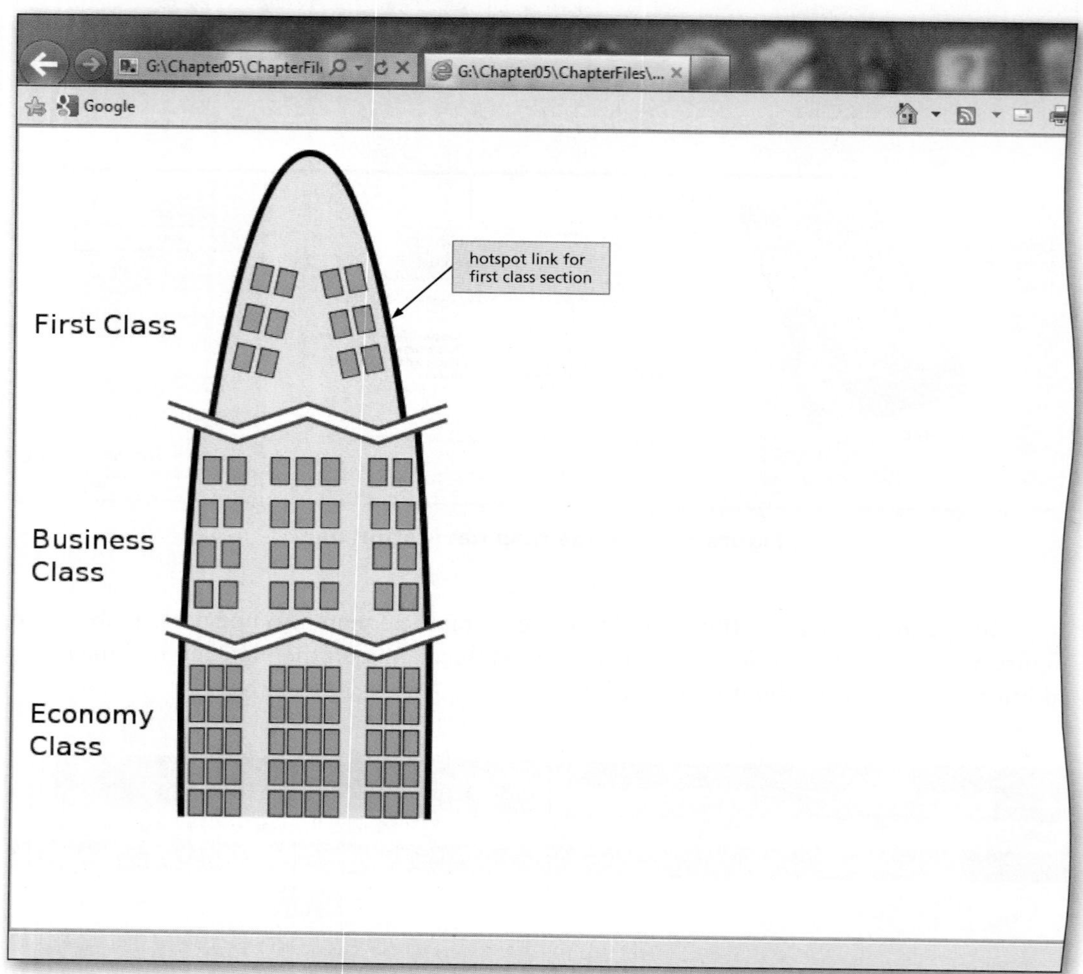

Figure 5–6 Image map of airplane seat arrangement.

> **BTW**
> **Image Maps**
> Image maps are used frequently for Web site navigation. Many online HTML sources address the purposes of image maps and give suggestions for their use. Use any good search engine to find more information on image maps.

Image maps can be used for many applications. For instance, if you want to create a Web site that depicts your vacation travels, you could take a digital picture of your travel souvenirs (Figure 5–7a) and use that as an image map, linking personal souvenirs to photographs (Figure 5–7b) that you took in a particular country that you visited.

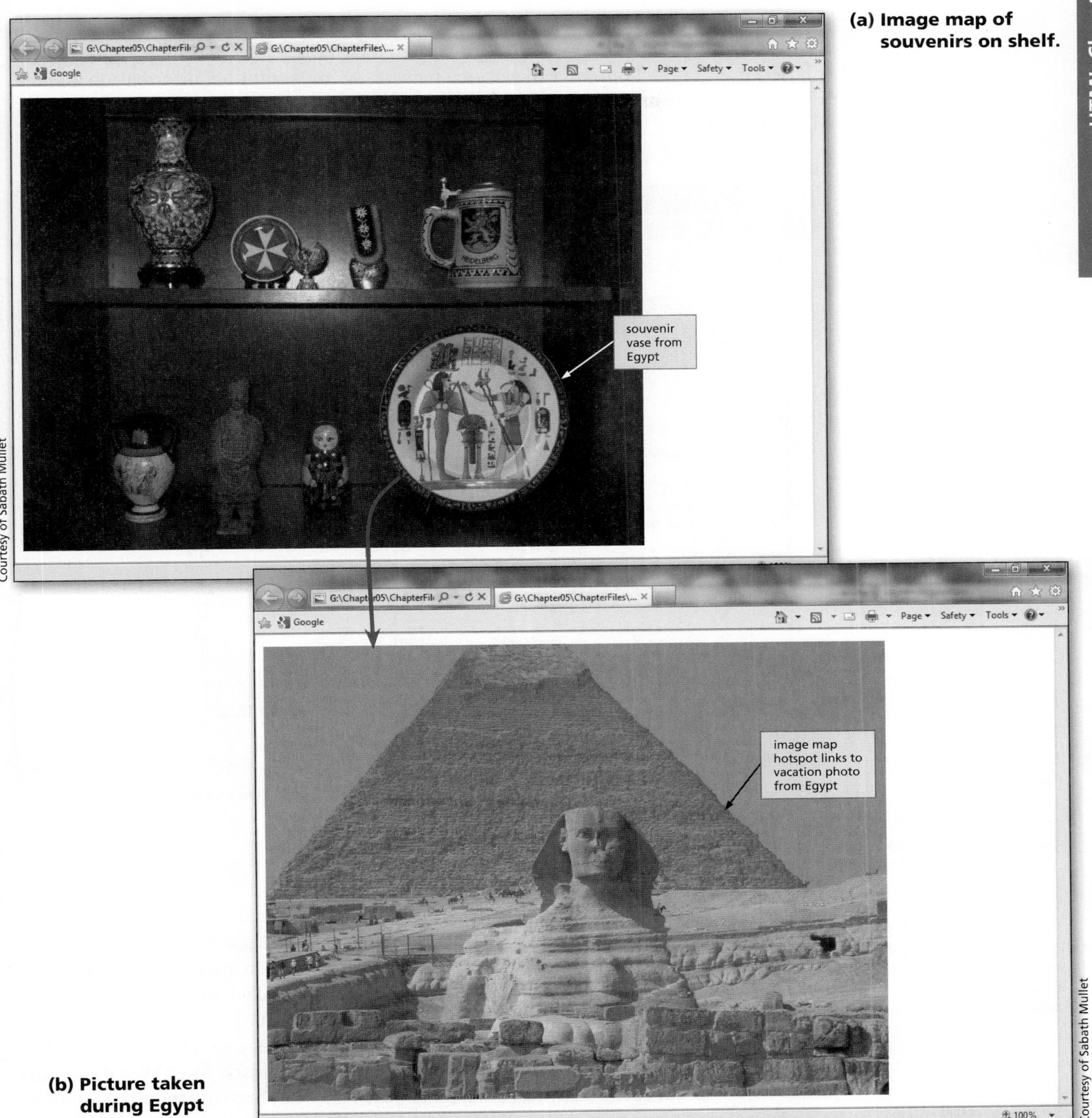

(a) Image map of souvenirs on shelf.

(b) Picture taken during Egypt vacation.

Figure 5–7

There are real estate applications in which an image map of the house floor plan is used (Figure 5–8). This map allows a potential customer to click a hotspot of a particular room in the house in order to see pictures or get additional information about that room. Using an image map like this gives people the opportunity to view houses for sale online.

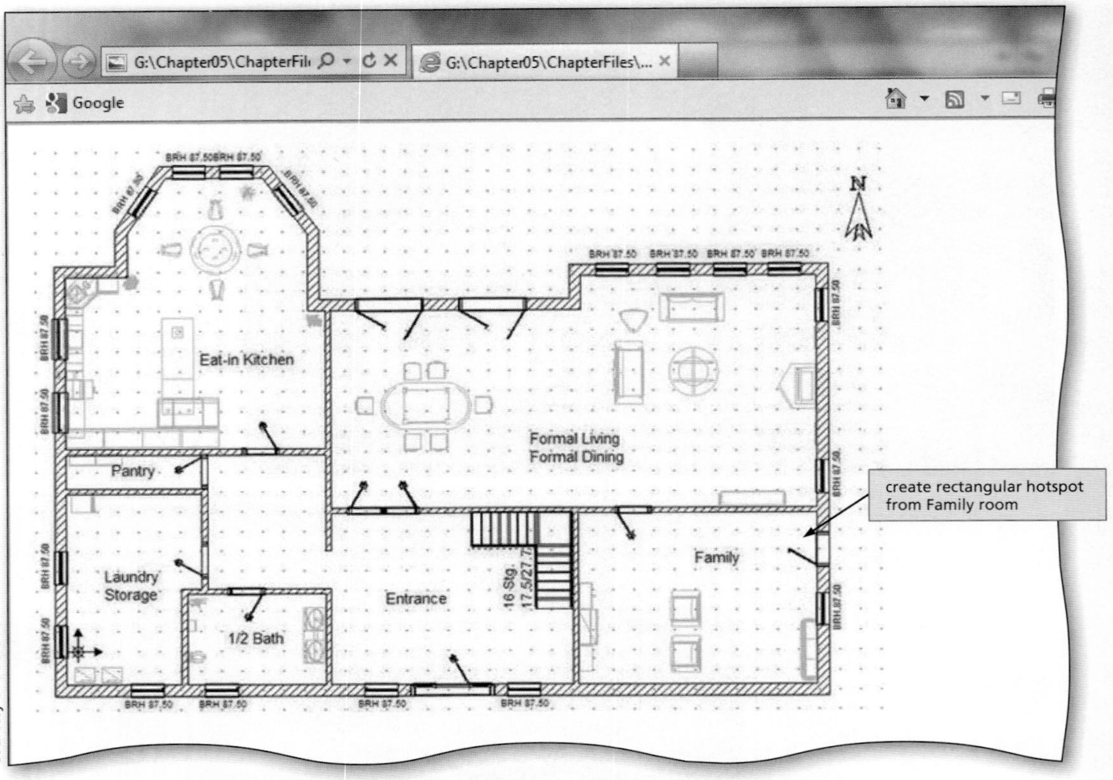

create rectangular hotspot from Family room

Courtesy of Boereck/Wikimedia

Figure 5–8 Floor plan can be used as image map.

BTW
Server-Side vs. Client-Side Image Maps
There are Web sites that provide information about server-side versus client-side image maps. To see an example of how image maps can be used for Web pages and which type is more efficient, use a search engine to search for the terms "server-side image maps" and "client-side image maps."

BTW
Server-Side Image Maps
When a hotspot on an image map is clicked, a special image map program that is stored on the Web server is run. In addition, the browser also sends the x- and y-coordinates to the Web server for the position of the link on the image map. Most, if not all, browsers support server-side image maps.

Server-Side vs. Client-Side Image Maps

Two types of image maps exist: server-side and client-side. In a **server-side image map**, the image is displayed by the client (browser) and implemented by a program that runs on the Web server. When a Web page visitor clicks a link on a server-side image map, the browser sends the x- and y-coordinates of the mouse click to the Web server, which interprets them and then links the visitor to the correct Web page based on those coordinates. Thus, with a server-side image map, the Web server does all the work.

With a **client-side image map**, the browser does all the work. Most Web developers prefer to work with client-side image mapping, which does not have to send the x- and y-coordinates of the mouse click to the Web server to be interpreted. Instead, the coordinates are included in the HTML file along with the URL to which the hotspot will link. When a visitor to a Web page clicks within a client-side image map, the browser processes the data without interaction with the Web server.

Server-side image maps have disadvantages. They require additional software in order to run on a Web server. This requires that the server administrator maintain and update the server software on a regular basis. Also, an image map available on a particular Web site's server must be registered to the server before it can be used. Although this process is simple, it must be done. Further, all changes to that registered image map must be coordinated on the Web server, which does not allow for quick updates. Client-side image maps help reduce the load on the Web server, generally download faster, and provide a faster response when a user clicks a link. In this chapter's project, you will create a client-side image map with four links on the home page of the Lake Tahanna Tourism Web site. You will learn more about client- and server-side image maps later in the chapter.

Plan Ahead

Understand the image map process.

Before inserting the graphical and color elements on a Web page, you should plan how you want to format them. By effectively utilizing graphics and color, you can call attention to important topics on the Web page without overpowering it. Creating a client-side image map for a Web page is a four-step process:

1. **Select an image to use as an image map.** Not all images are appropriate for good image mapping. Besides causing difficulty to the Web developer to find the points to plot, nondistinct areas make it difficult for visitors to see where one link might end and another begins. When choosing an image to map, choose wisely.
2. **Sketch in the hotspots on the image.** It is sometimes good to print a copy of the image and draw the hotspot areas on top of the paper image. You can then take that hard copy and review it while working with the image in the image editing software. When sketching (either on paper or in the software), determine what shapes (i.e., circle, rectangle, or polygon) make sense for the specific area that you want to link. Based on this determination, start the next step of plotting those areas on the image.
3. **Map the image coordinates for each hotspot**. This chapter explains what x- and y-coordinates you need to provide for every linkable area. One thing to consider is making sure that the linkable areas do not run over one another. This overrun ends up confusing your Web site visitors because they think they will link to one area, and the coordinates take them somewhere else.
4. **Create the HTML code for the image map**. Writing HTML code for an image map is different from anything that you have done thus far in the book. When you create an image map, you first insert the image itself and then identify the name of the map that you use later in the HTML code. Further down in the code, you actually use that name and identify the map areas that form the boundaries around the hotspot.

Creating an Image Map

An image map consists of two components: an image and a map definition that defines the hotspots and the URLs to which they link.

Selecting Images

Not all images are appropriate candidates for image mapping. An appropriate image, and a good choice for an image map, is one that has obvious visual sections. The map of Italy image shown in Figure 5–9a on the next page, for example, has distinct, easy-to-see sections, which serve as ideal hotspots. A user could easily select an individual area on the map to link to more information about each region. The image of Italy in Figure 5–9b, however, would not be a good choice because the boundaries of the regions are indistinct.

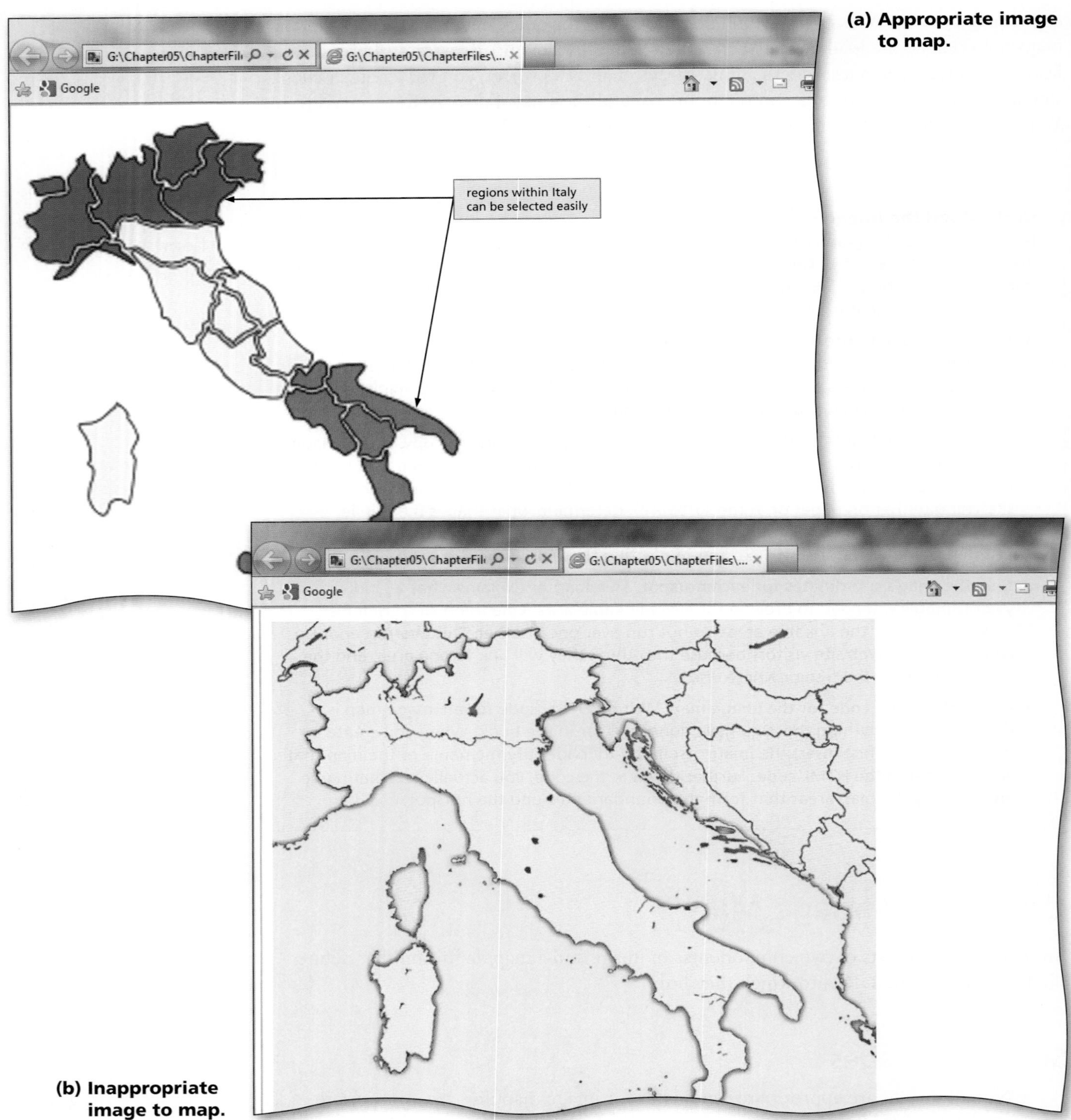

(a) Appropriate image to map.

(b) Inappropriate image to map.

Figure 5–9

Sketching the Borders of Hotspots

After an appropriate image is selected for the image map, the next step is to sketch the hotspots (clickable areas) within the image. Figure 5–10 shows an example of an image map with the borders of the hotspots sketched on the image. The map of Italy is used, with two regions (Sardinia and Sicily) defined as hotspots. The image map thus will include a hotspot for the two regions, each of which can link to a different Web page.

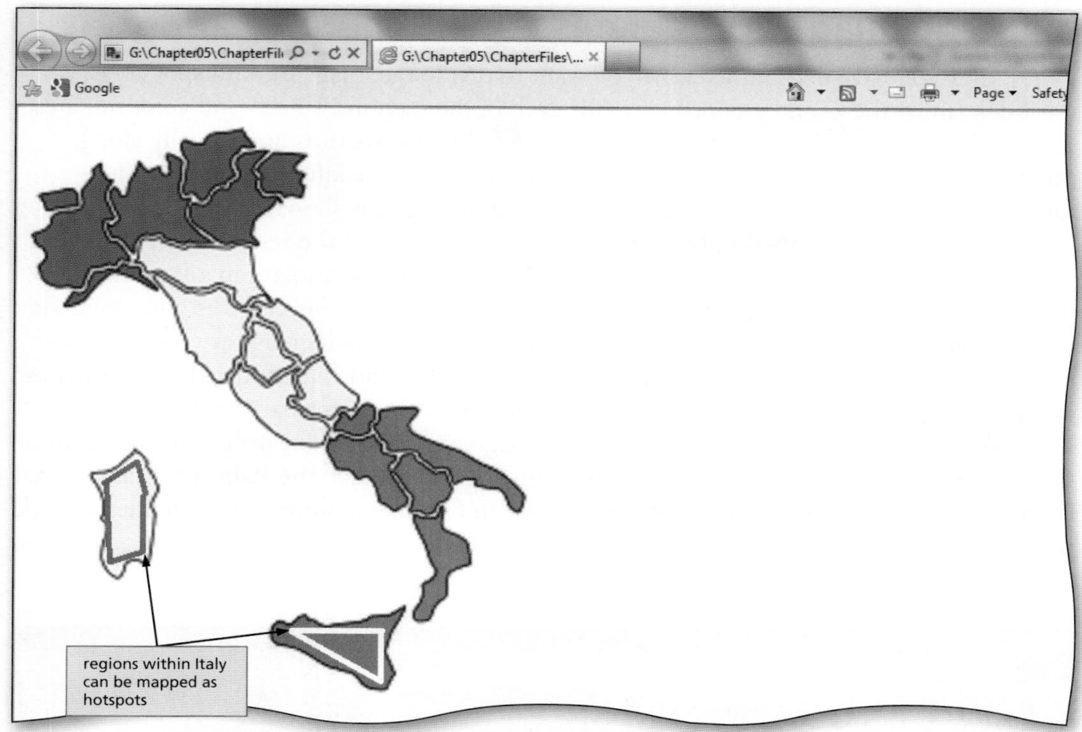

Figure 5–10 Sketched areas for image map hotspots.

Figure 5–11 shows an enlarged version of the text in the Lake Tahanna Tourism image that will be used as a navigation bar in this project. It is made larger in this screenshot so that it is easier to show how you can sketch hotspots on this particular image. This image, tahanna.jpg, is used as the image map in this chapter, and is shown here with the hotspots sketched in. The image is included in the Data Files for Students. For the chapter project, you use the four words (Home, Skiing, Boating, and Dining) as your image map links. You surround the four words with rectangular shapes using image map tags. These four rectangular shapes are defined as hotspots, which will link to the Web pages that contain information about each option. The process of mapping the image coordinates for each hotspot is based on this initial sketch. The four words used in this navigation bar are easily recognizable. When sketching a hotspot, you have to be careful to provide enough space around the words but not overflow from one word to the next, which would confuse the user, as shown in Figure 5–11.

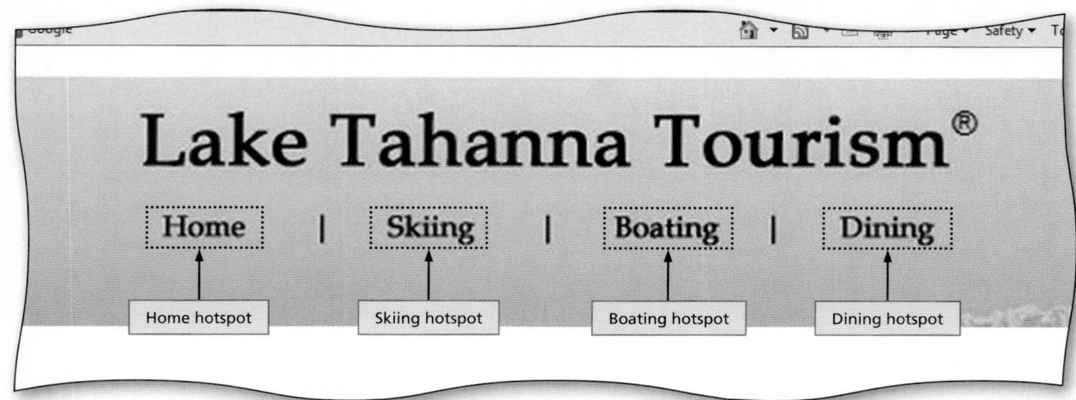

Figure 5–11 Sketched rectangular areas to be used as hotspots.

Mapping Image Coordinates

After you have determined how you want to divide the image into hotspot areas, you must determine the x- and y-coordinates for each of the sections. The x- and y-coordinates are based on a position relative to the x- and y-axes. The **x-axis** runs horizontally along the base of the image, while the **y-axis** runs vertically along the left of the image. The top-left corner of an image thus is the coordinate point (0,0), as shown in Figure 5–12. The first number of a **coordinate pair** is the x-coordinate, and the second number is the y-coordinate. Figure 5–12 shows the starting (0,0) x- and y-coordinates in a Paint window that contains the image tahanna.jpg. The y-coordinate numbers increase as you move the mouse pointer down the image, and the x-coordinate numbers increase as you move the mouse pointer to the right on the image. As you move the mouse pointer, the coordinates of its position as it relates to the image are displayed on the status bar.

You can use a simple or a sophisticated image editing or paint program to determine the x- and y-coordinates of various image points. In this project, the Paint program is used to find the x- and y-coordinates that you will use in the map definition that divides a single image into several areas.

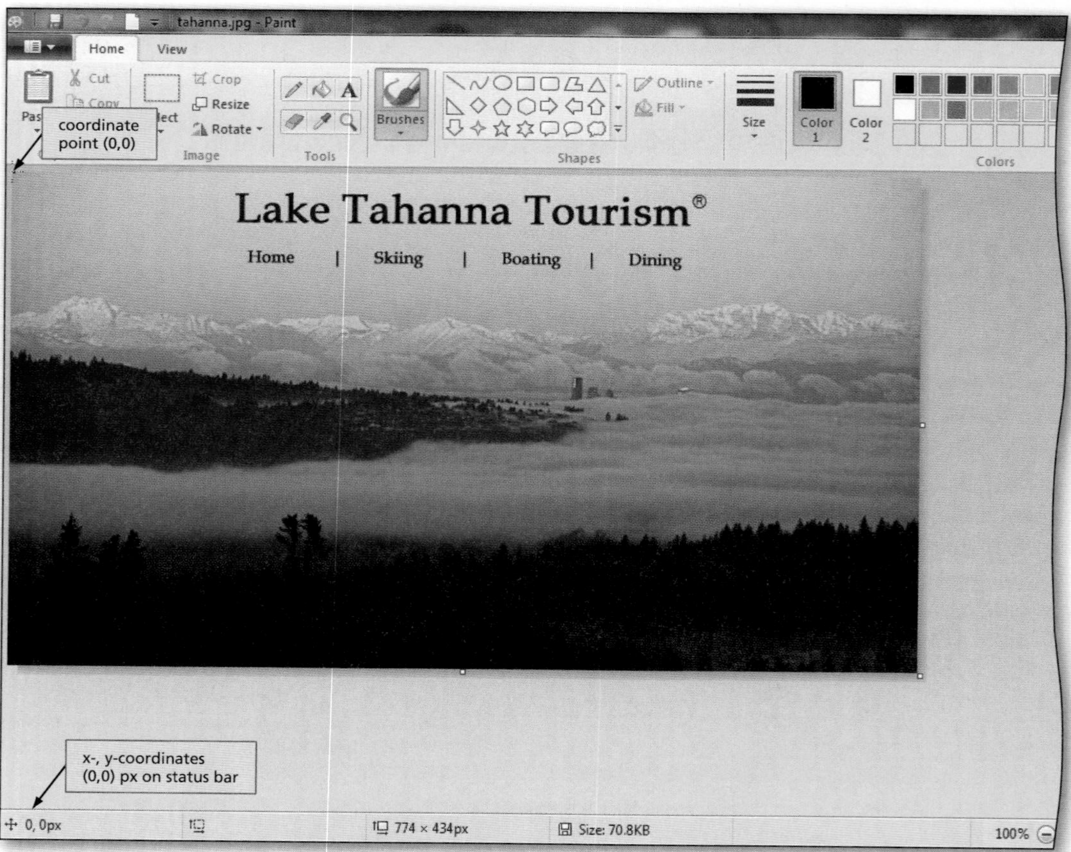

Figure 5–12

Map areas can use one of three shapes: rectangle, circle, or polygon. These shapes are shown in Figure 5–13. To define a map area of an image, you must determine the x- and y-coordinates for that shape and then insert the coordinates for the various map shapes in the HTML code.

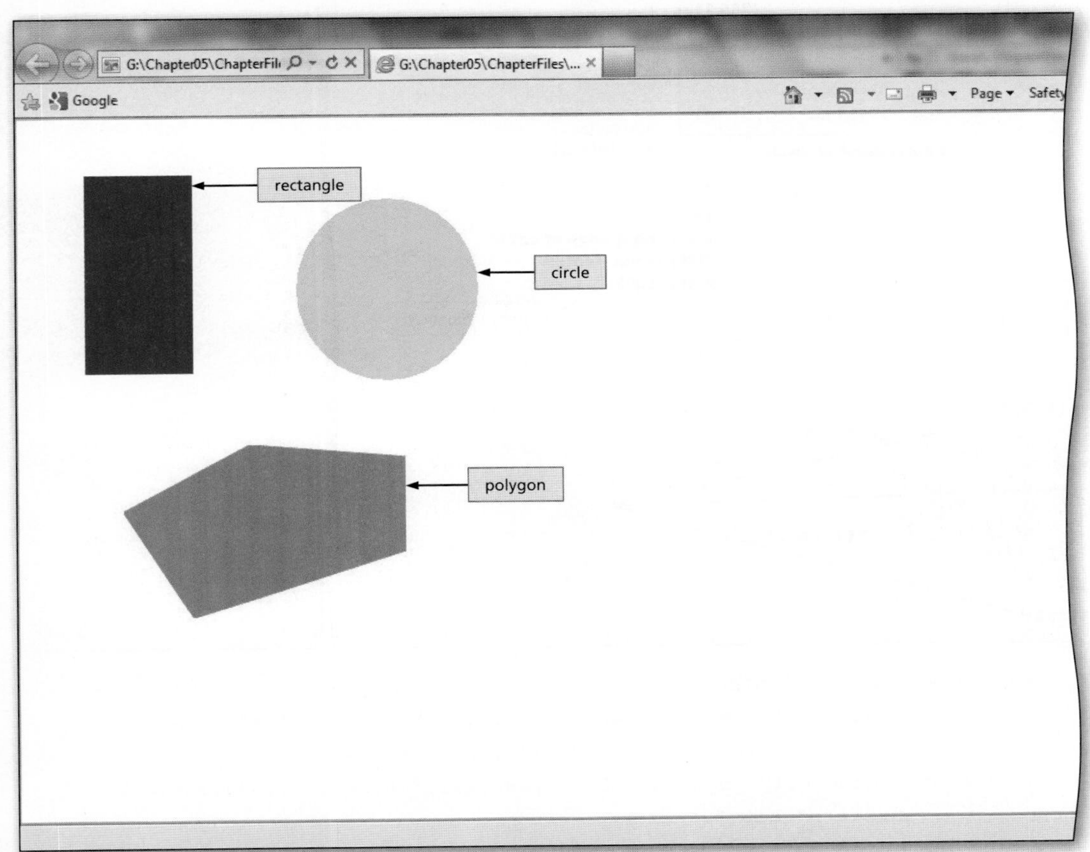

Figure 5–13

For a rectangular map area, you use the coordinates of the top-left and the bottom-right corners. For example, as shown in Figure 5–14a on the next page, the rectangle's x- and y-coordinates are (46,35) for the top-left corner and (137,208) for the bottom-right corner. You use "rect" as the value for the shape attribute for rectangles. For a circular map area, you use the center point and the radius as the coordinates. The x- and y-coordinates of the center point of the circle in Figure 5–14a are (308,113). If the mouse pointer is moved along the y-axis (113) to the border of the circle, the x-axis is 380. The radius can be calculated by subtracting the x-axis value of the center point (308) from the x-axis value of the circle's right border (380), which gives a radius of 72 (380 − 308). For circles, you use "circle" as the value for the shape attribute. For a polygonal map area, you must use the coordinates for each corner of the shape. For example, in Figure 5–14a, the polygon has five corners with the coordinates (78,309), (183,251), (316,262), (317,344), and (136,402). For polygonal shapes, you use "poly" as the value for the shape attribute. Figure 5–14b shows how you would use those x- and y-coordinates in the map statements needed to define these three shapes as clickable areas.

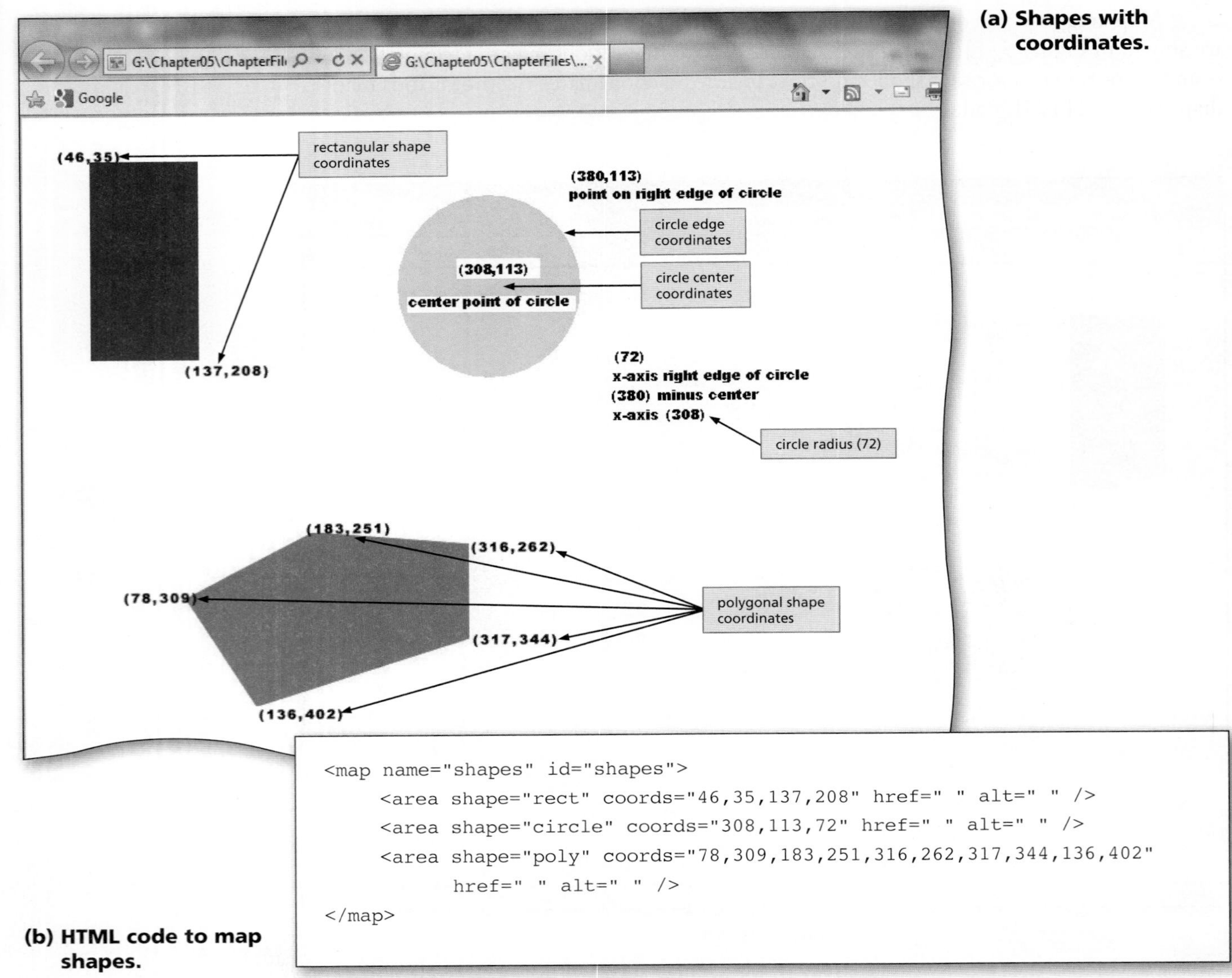


```
<map name="shapes" id="shapes">
    <area shape="rect" coords="46,35,137,208" href=" " alt=" " />
    <area shape="circle" coords="308,113,72" href=" " alt=" " />
    <area shape="poly" coords="78,309,183,251,316,262,317,344,136,402"
          href=" " alt=" " />
</map>
```

Figure 5–14

In the Lake Tahanna Tourism image (tahanna.jpg), the image map will use four rectangular shapes for the four hotspots, as sketched in Figure 5–11 on page HTML 245. Clickable areas are mapped in rectangular shapes enclosing the following areas: Home, Skiing, Boating, and Dining.

Coding the Map

The final step in creating an image map is writing the HTML code for the map. To create a client-side image map, the tags <map> </map> and <area> are used. The map start tag (**<map>**) and map end tag (**</map>**) create the client-side image map. The **<area>** tag defines the specific areas of the map and the links and anchors for those areas. The x- and y-coordinates for each map area are inserted into the <area> tag with the **coords** attribute, within quotation marks and separated by commas. The HTML tags, attributes, and values needed to code the map are discussed later in this chapter.

Plan Ahead

Working with the image.
In order to determine the x- and y-coordinates for image map points, you need to open the image in the chosen software tool.

- **Select a software tool.** Computers running the Windows operating system already have an image editing tool available, Paint. This chapter shows you how to work with your image within Paint. For other suggested editing software products, see Table 5–2 on page HTML 240.
- **Edit the image.** It is sometimes necessary to alter the image before using it on the Web page (you may want to resize it or reposition it). Paint also gives you the image dimensions (i.e., width and height) you need for the <img> tag.
- **Make other changes to the image**. In Paint, you can make other changes to the image such as flipping the image horizontally or vertically, or altering the colors of the image. Other graphic editing software options provide a variety of tools to alter an image slightly or significantly.

Using Paint to Locate X- and Y-Coordinates

As you have learned, you can use a simple or a sophisticated image editing or paint program to determine the x- and y-coordinates of various points on an image. In this chapter, the Paint program is used to find the x- and y-coordinates used in the map definition that divides a single image into several areas.

To Start Paint

The following steps start Paint.

- Click the Start button on the taskbar.
- Click All Programs on the Start menu, click Accessories on the All Programs submenu, and then point to Paint on the Accessories submenu (Figure 5–15).
- Click Paint.

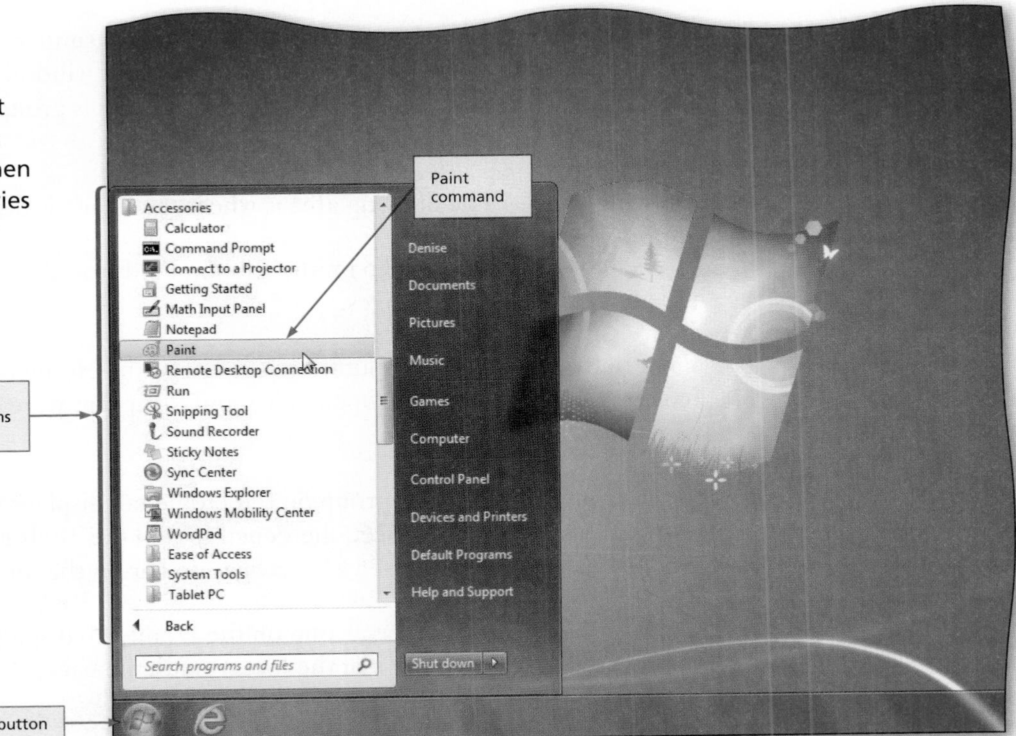

Figure 5–15

2

- If necessary, click the Maximize button on the right side of the title bar to maximize the window (Figure 5–16).

Q&A Do all computers running Windows include Paint?

Yes, Paint should be included with all Windows operating systems.

Q&A How can I find out more about using Paint?

The Paint Help utility is quite good. You can search for information using its Search option or Index. Paint Help gives step-by-step instructions for many tasks.

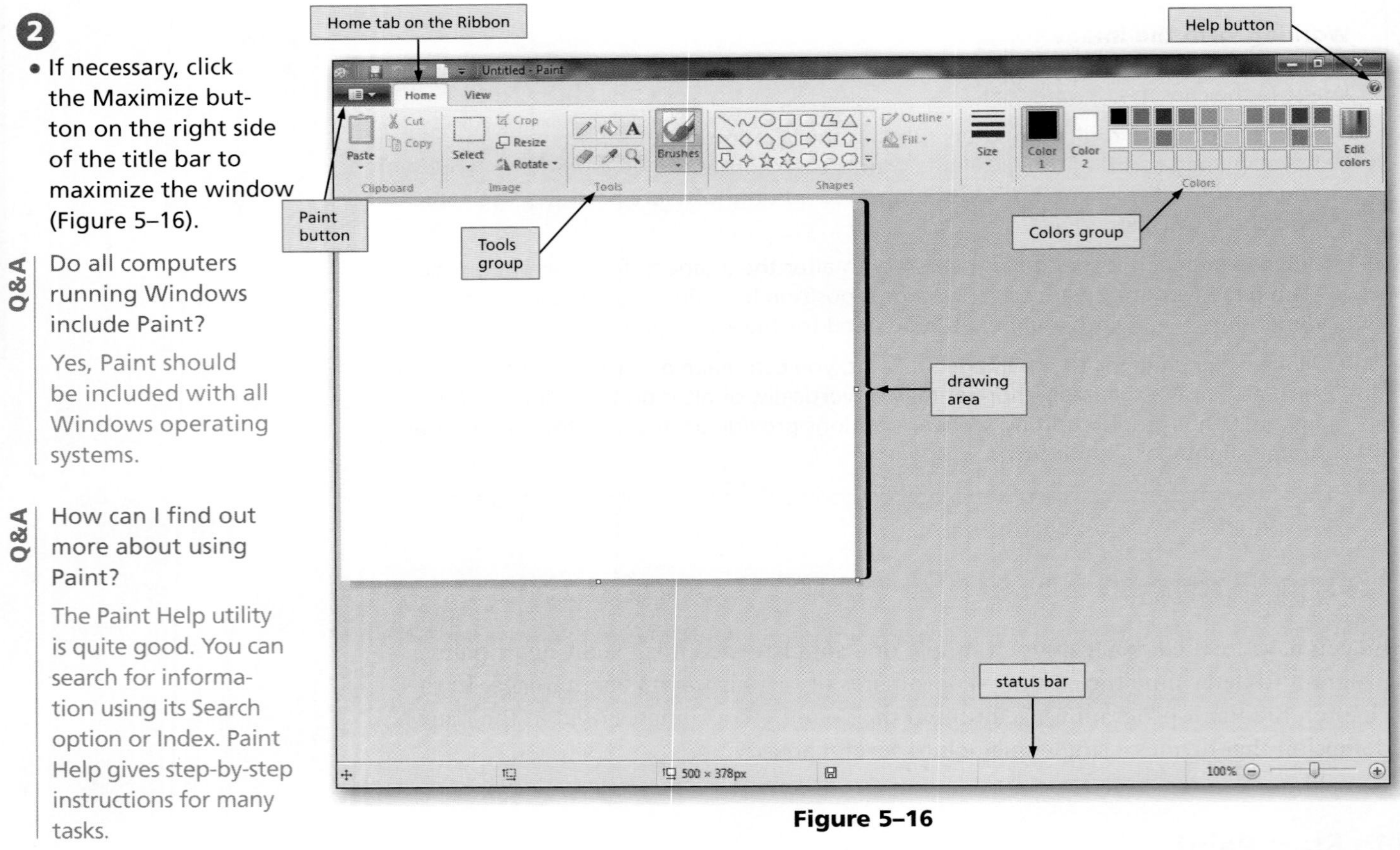

Figure 5–16

The Paint Window

The Paint window contains several elements similar to the document windows in other applications. The main elements of the Paint window are the drawing area, the Home tab on the Ribbon, the Paint button, the Tools group, the Colors group, and the status bar, as shown in Figure 5–16.

Drawing area — The drawing area is where the image is displayed.

Home tab — The Home tab on the Ribbon holds tools and commands most frequently used to create and edit images.

Paint button — The Paint button to the left of the Home tab contains a drop-down arrow to access functions such as Open, Save, and Print that were on the File menu in earlier versions of Windows.

Tools group — The Tools group on the Home tab displays tools that are used to edit or draw an image. In this project, the Pencil tool in the Tools group is used to find the x- and y-coordinates of the text used as a navigation bar on the image.

Colors group — The Colors group on the Home tab displays a palette of colors that can be used to set the colors of the foreground, the background, or other elements in a drawing.

Status bar —The status bar displays the coordinates of the center of the mouse pointer at its current position on the image.

To Open an Image File in Paint

The image file (tahanna.jpg) used for the image map in this chapter is stored in the Data Files for Students. This image is a picture of Lake Tahanna that includes four words (from left to right) that are used for the following navigation functions: Home, Skiing, Boating, and Dining. The following step opens an image file in Paint.

1

- With a USB drive plugged into your computer, click the Paint button and then click Open.
- Navigate to where you store your Data Files, double-click the Chapter05 folder, and then double-click the ChapterFiles folder in the list of available folders.
- Click the tahanna.jpg image, and then click the Open button in the Open dialog box to display the image that will be used for image mapping in this chapter, as shown in Figure 5–17.

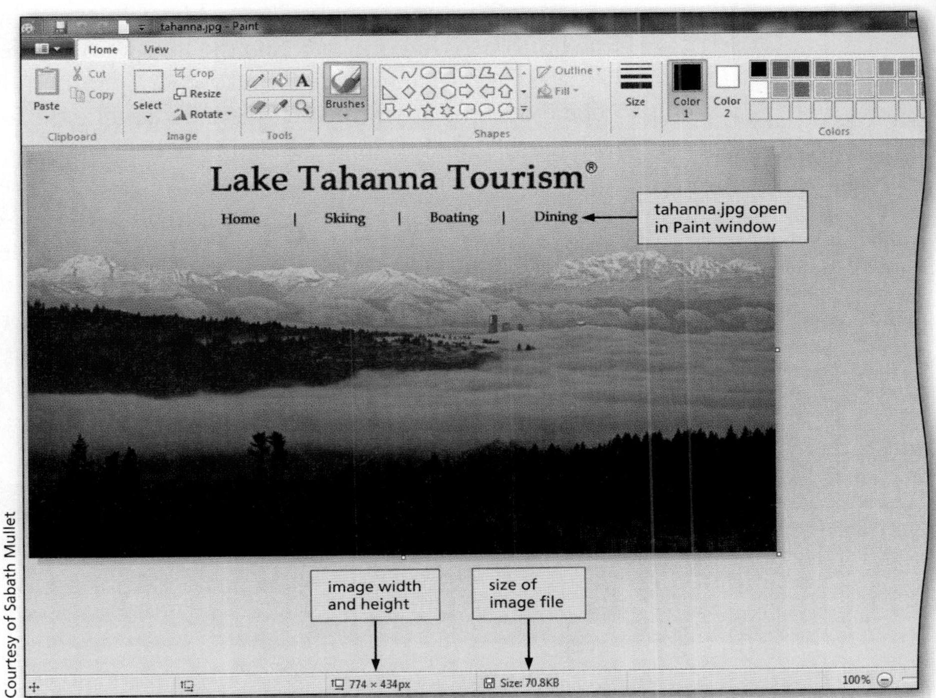

Figure 5–17

Locating X- and Y-Coordinates of an Image

The next step is to locate the x- and y-coordinates of the areas that should be mapped on the image. As shown in Figure 5–18, the image map should include four clickable rectangular areas that will link to other Web pages. For each of the four linkable map areas, the top-left corner x- and y-coordinate pair must be determined first. You then identify the x- and y-coordinates of the bottom-right corner.

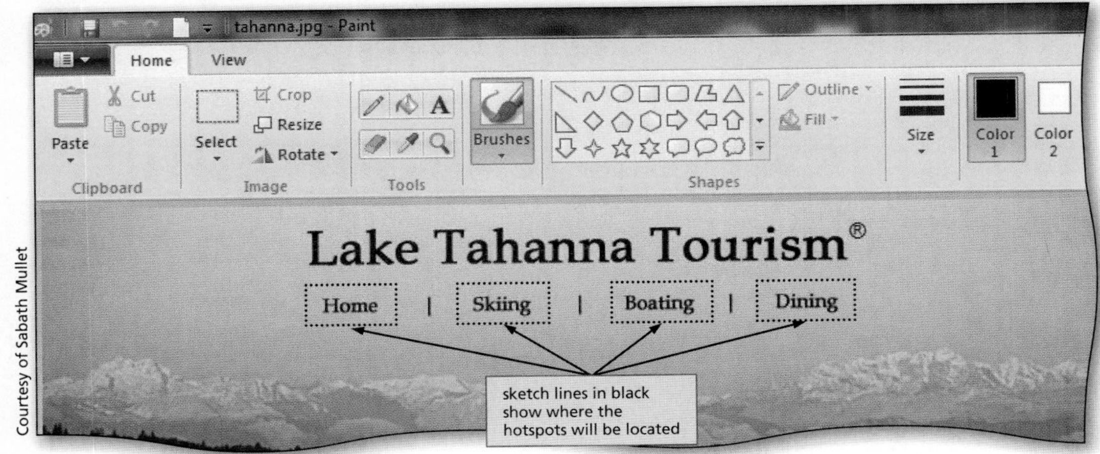

Figure 5–18

As you have learned, the x- and y-coordinates begin with (0,0) in the top-left corner of the image, as shown in Figure 5–12 on page HTML 246. As stated previously, moving the mouse pointer to the right (horizontally) increases the x-coordinate, and moving the mouse pointer down (vertically) increases the y-coordinate. Because the four clickable areas in the navigation bar image sketched in black on the tahanna.jpg image are rectangular, the map definition must include the x- and y-coordinate of the top-left and bottom-right corners of each rectangular shape. Those four numbers (x, y of the top-left corner + x, y of the bottom-right corner) define the hotspot of the rectangular shape.

Table 5–1 shows the x- and y-coordinates for the four rectangular-shaped map areas. The rectangles are formed closely surrounding the four words that will be used for links (Home, Skiing, Boating, and Dining). Notice in Table 5–1 that the y-coordinate (63 and 82) is the same for all four words. That means that your rectangles will be the same vertically across the navigation links. The first number is the x-coordinate, and the second number is the y-coordinate. For example, the Home rectangle consists of two pairs of x- and y-coordinates. One point is in the top-left corner of the word Home, and the other is in the bottom-right corner of the word. The first x-coordinate (in the top-left corner of the word Home) is 195 and the first y-coordinate is 63 at the top-left corner of the word Home. You then locate a point on the bottom-right corner of the word, Home. These x- and y-coordinates are used in the <area> tag to create the map definition for the image map.

Table 5–1 X- and Y-Coordinates

Location	Coordinates
Home	195,63,247,82
Skiing	305,63,354,82
Boating	413,63,470,82
Dining	521,63,574,82

To Locate X- and Y-Coordinates of an Image

The following steps locate the x- and y-coordinates of the boundary points of each clickable rectangular area by moving the mouse pointer to the various points to see the x- and y-coordinates of those points. Although you do not need to record the coordinates for this project, you generally would do that. In this case though, you will compare the coordinates with those shown in Table 5–1, which lists the exact coordinates used in the <area> tags for this project.

- If necessary, click the Pencil button in the Tools group (Figure 5–19).

Figure 5–19

2

- Move the mouse pointer to the top-left corner of the word Home in the image and note the x- and y-coordinates for that point, as indicated in the status bar. Move the mouse until the coordinates read (195,63) (Figure 5–20a). (Do not click the mouse button.)
- Move the mouse pointer to the bottom-right corner of the word Home. The coordinates should read (247,82) (your coordinates may differ slightly), as indicated on the status bar (Figure 5–20b). (Do not click the mouse button.) The four coordinates to be used for this rectangular hotspot are 195,63,247,82, as shown in Table 5–1.
- Move the mouse pointer to the top-left and bottom-right corners of the four other words that are used as hotspots for navigation (Skiing, Boating, and Dining) in the image. Locate the corresponding x- and y-coordinates in Table 5–1.

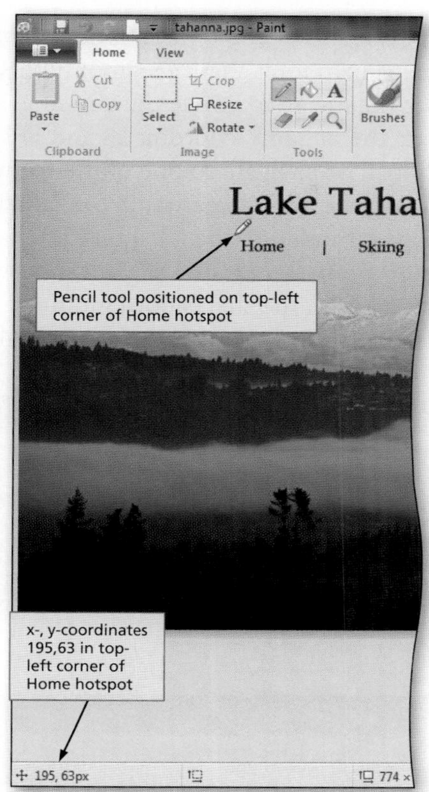

(a) Getting top-left coordinates.

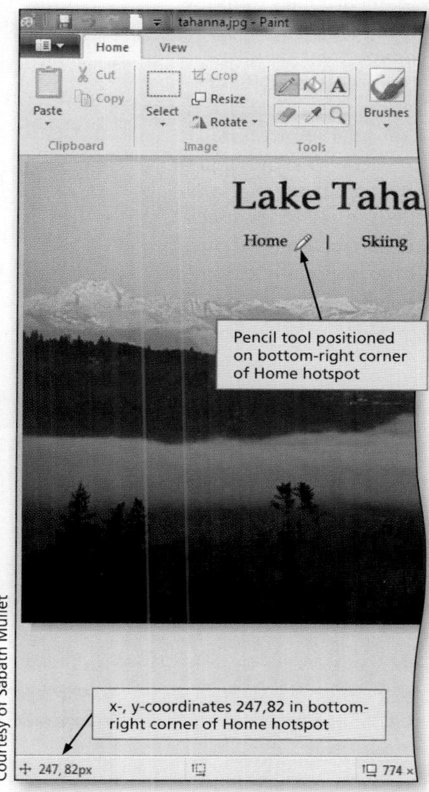

(b) Getting bottom-right corner coordinates.

Courtesy of Sabath Mullet

Figure 5–20

- After you have finished, click the Close button on the right side of the title bar. If prompted, do not save any changes to the file.

Q&A

I am not sure of the purpose of this exercise because the coordinates are already given to us for the project. Why am I doing these steps using Paint?

For the purpose of the project, the coordinates are given. The normal image mapping process, however, consists of: finding an appropriate image, sketching out where you think the boundaries will be, and finding the coordinates on your own using a software tool that shows that information. The purpose of this exercise is to become familiar with using Paint to find the coordinates.

Experiment

- Play with the Image and Colors groups on the Home tab. They give you many options to alter the image. Make sure to save the file with a different filename so that the image file included in the Data Files for Students folder remains untouched.

BTW **Graphics Software**
Many graphics tools are available for advanced image creation and maintenance. One of the more popular tools is Adobe Photoshop. Photoshop allows you to create images that can be used as image maps or to crop sections out of existing images.

Other Software Tools

Although Paint allows you to identify the coordinates for a map area manually, there are dedicated image map tools that can simplify this process (see Table 5–2). These tools allow you to click the image to define the clickable areas of the image map and then automatically generate the x- and y-coordinates and HTML code needed for the image map. If possible, download or navigate to one of the software tools listed in Table 5–2 and use that software to map the clickable areas in the tahanna.jpg image. As further practice, open the file shapecoord.gif found in the Chapter05\ChapterFiles folder of the Data Files for Students in Paint (Figure 5–21) and use your mouse pointer to identify the coordinates to map the clickable areas in the shapecoord.gif image. You could also experiment with using one or more of the tools in Table 5–2 to map clickable areas in the image.

Table 5–2 Image Map Software Tools

Tool	Platform
Mapedit	Windows, UNIX, Mac OS
CoffeeCup Image Mapper	Windows
Image Map Tool	Online (image-maps.com)

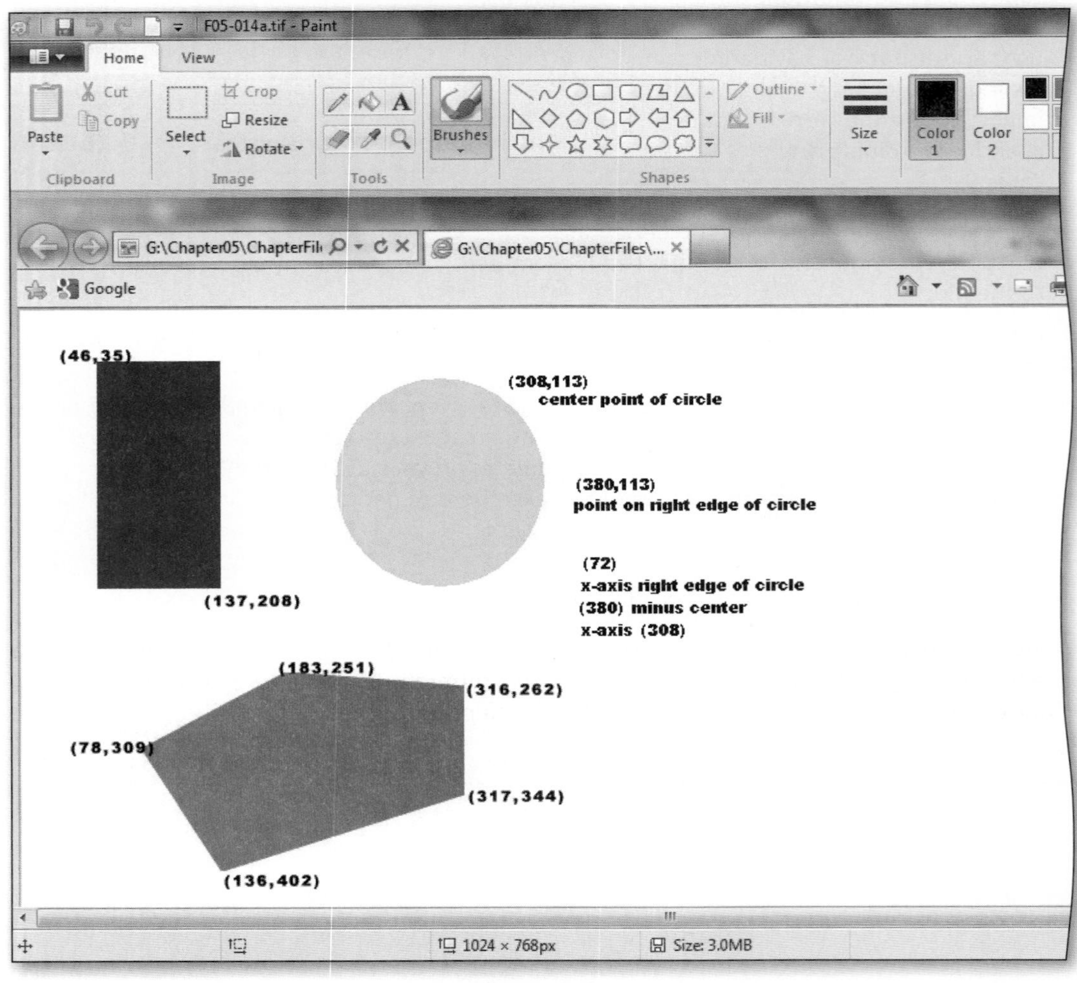

Figure 5–21

Plan Ahead

Starting the home page.
Just as with the other projects in previous chapters, you need to review good Web development standards before you start a new Web page.

- **Use the required HTML structure tags.** You will validate your Web pages for this project, so make sure that you use the HTML tags needed to make the page HTML5 compliant. This includes using the <meta> tag and a DOCTYPE statement.
- **Copy what you can.** In earlier chapters, you copied HTML code from one completed page to another to make it easier. You should do the same in this project. Once a Web page is validated, you know that the initial HTML tags are correct. It makes sense then to copy/paste those lines of code to the next Web page file. If you are utilizing the same navigation bar throughout a Web site, it also makes sense to copy that code from one Web page to another.

Creating the Home Page

Before the image map can be added to the home page of the Lake Tahanna Tourism Web site, the home page must be created. The home page includes a logo image and paragraphs of text, which includes an e-mail link. At the bottom of the home page, a horizontal list of text links is inserted. The text links allow the Web page visitor to navigate to the home page and to the skiing, boating, and dining Web pages.

To Start Notepad++

1. Click the Start button on the Windows taskbar to display the Start menu.
2. Click All Programs at the bottom of the left pane on the Start menu to display the All Programs list.
3. Click the Notepad++ folder in the All Programs list.
4. Click the Notepad++ icon in the list to display the Notepad++ window. Maximize the Notepad++ window if necessary.
5. Click View on the menu bar. If the word wrap command does not have a check mark next to it, click word wrap.

To Enter Initial HTML Tags to Define the Web Page Structure

To create the home page, you will start Notepad++ and enter the initial HTML tags to define the overall structure of the Web page, as shown in Table 5–3 on the next page. Notice that line 8 is the link statement that links the external style sheet named stylesch5.css to the Web page. You will create the external style sheet later in this project.

Table 5–3 HTML Code to Define Web Page Structure

Line	HTML Tag and Text
1	`<!DOCTYPE HTML>`
2	
3	`<html>`
4	`<head>`
5	`<meta charset="utf-8" />`
6	`<title>Lake Tahanna Tourism</title>`
7	
8	`<link rel="stylesheet" type="text/css" href="stylesch5.css" />`
9	
10	`</head>`
11	
12	`<body>`
13	
14	
15	`</body>`
16	`</html>`

1. Enter the HTML code shown in Table 5–3. Press ENTER at the end of each line.
2. Position the insertion point on the blank line 14 and compare what you typed to Figure 5–22. Correct any errors if necessary.

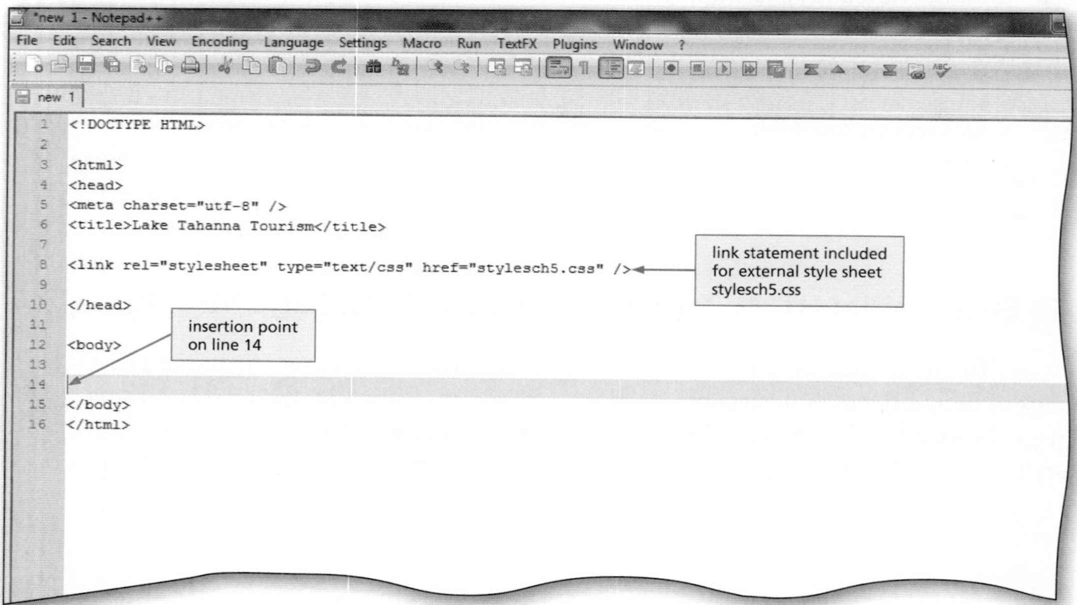

Figure 5–22

To Save an HTML File

With the initial HTML code for the Lake Tahanna Tourism home page entered, you should save the file. Saving the file frequently ensures you won't lose your work. Saving a file in Notepad++ also adds color to code that can help you identify different elements more easily.

1. Click File on the menu bar, click Save, and then type `tahanna.html` in the File name text box (do not press ENTER).
2. Navigate to the storage device and folder (Chapter05\ChapterFiles) where you save your Data Files and then click the Save button in the Save As dialog box to save the file.

Inserting an Image to Use as an Image Map

The next step in creating the home page is to add the image that will be used as the image map. The image, tahanna.jpg, is stored in the Data Files for Students. This image consists of four words (Home, Skiing, Boating, Dining) that are used as navigation, separated by vertical lines, and placed upon a photo of the Lake Tahanna region.

Table 5–4 shows the attributes associated with the <img> tag. The usemap attribute, a client-side image map, is what you use in this project. A client-side image map is an image map that is run by the browser (the client) rather than by a CGI script on the Web server. You provide all the information required to run the map, the image, and the hotspot coordinates in your HTML document. The map's functions are provided on the client's side, rather than on the server's side. When a visitor clicks a hotspot on the image map, the browser opens the corresponding URL.

A server-side image map uses CGI scripts to make the map work. The ismap attribute tells the browser to send the coordinates of the user mouse click directly to an associated map file on the server. If you look in Appendix C, Accessibility Standards and the Web, you will see that there is a reason to use client-side image maps instead of server-side image maps from a usability standpoint. The guideline in §1194.22(f) states, "Client-side image maps shall be provided instead of server-side image maps except where the regions cannot be defined with an available geometric shape." Also, the WCAG 2.0 Guidelines address this issue in guideline 1.4.5 where it says, "If the technologies being used can achieve the visual presentation, text is used to convey information rather than images of text."

Table 5–4 Tag Attributes Used to Create Image Maps

Tag	Attribute	Function
<img>	usemap ismap	• Indicates the URL of a client-side image map • Indicates a server-side image map

BTW

Image Width and Height
As you have learned in earlier projects, specifying the width and height attributes helps improve page loading time. By identifying these attributes in the HTML code, the browser does not have to determine the width and height of the image.

The Lake Tahanna Tourism home page will use a client-side image map. The HTML code to add the image thus will use attributes of the <img> tag — src, width, height, alt, and usemap — as follows:

```
<img src="tahanna.jpg" width="774" height="434" alt="Lake
        Tahanna" usemap="#menubar" />
```

where the src attribute identifies the image, the width and height attributes define the image size, and the alt attribute defines the text a screen reader will play.

The usemap attribute indicates to the browser which client-side image map will be used for that image. The client-side image map is placed within the <map> tag and defines the x- and y-coordinates of the areas on the image being used for the image map. When adding the image to use as an image map, the value of the usemap attribute — in this case, usemap="#menubar" — indicates that the browser should use the image map named menubar as its image map source.

To Insert an Image to Use as an Image Map

The following step inserts an image to use for the image map.

1

- If necessary, click line 14.
- Type `<div style="text-align: center">` and then press the ENTER key.
- Press the TAB key once and type `<img src="tahanna.jpg" width="774" height="434" alt="Lake Tahanna" usemap="#menubar"/>` and then press the ENTER key.

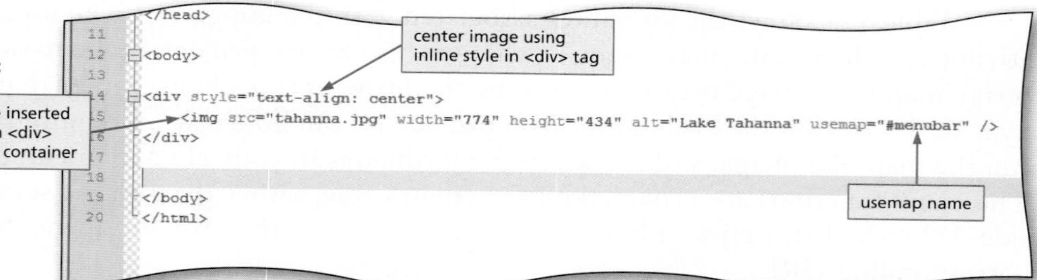

Figure 5–23

- Press SHIFT+TAB to move back to the left margin, type `</div>`, and then press the ENTER key twice (Figure 5–23).

Q&A

I do not understand the purpose of the usemap attribute. Can you explain it?

The usemap attribute specifies an image as a client-side image map and associates the map element's id with the image. The <map> tag that will be inserted at the end of this Web page contains the coordinates of the image map. The usemap value (i.e., #menubar) tells the browser that this is an image map, and that it needs to look at the <map> tag id with that name (menubar) for the mapping coordinates.

Q&A

If I want to speed up the download of a large image, can I change the dimensions of the image using the width and height attributes to make it smaller?

Although you can do this, you should not. Making a change to an image with these attributes still forces the browser to download the entire image and then display it as you indicate in the width and height attributes. If you want to speed up the download by making the image smaller, you should use image editing software (such as Paint) to change the dimensions and then save the image. In Paint, use the Resize button in the Image group on the Home tab.

To Add a Paragraph of Text

Now you will add a paragraph of text for the home page. You will use a class named "boldword" twice in the paragraph. This class is defined later in the chapter in the external style sheet.The HTML code for this text is shown in Table 5–5.

Table 5–5 HTML Code for a Header and Paragraphs

Line	HTML Tag and Text
18	`<p><span class="boldword">Lake Tahanna</span> is a great place to visit. You can ski in the morning and enjoy boating in the afternoon. After a day of fun, relax while enjoying the ambience of one of our many wonderful restaurants. Click the links above or below to discover activity and dining options. Send comments or questions to <span class="boldword">Lake Tahanna Tourism</span> at <a href="mailto:tahanna@isp.com"><span style="text-decoration: underline">tahanna@isp.com</span></a>.</p>`

The following step enters the tags for the heading and paragraphs of text.

1 Enter the HTML code shown in Table 5–5 and then press the ENTER key twice (Figure 5–24).

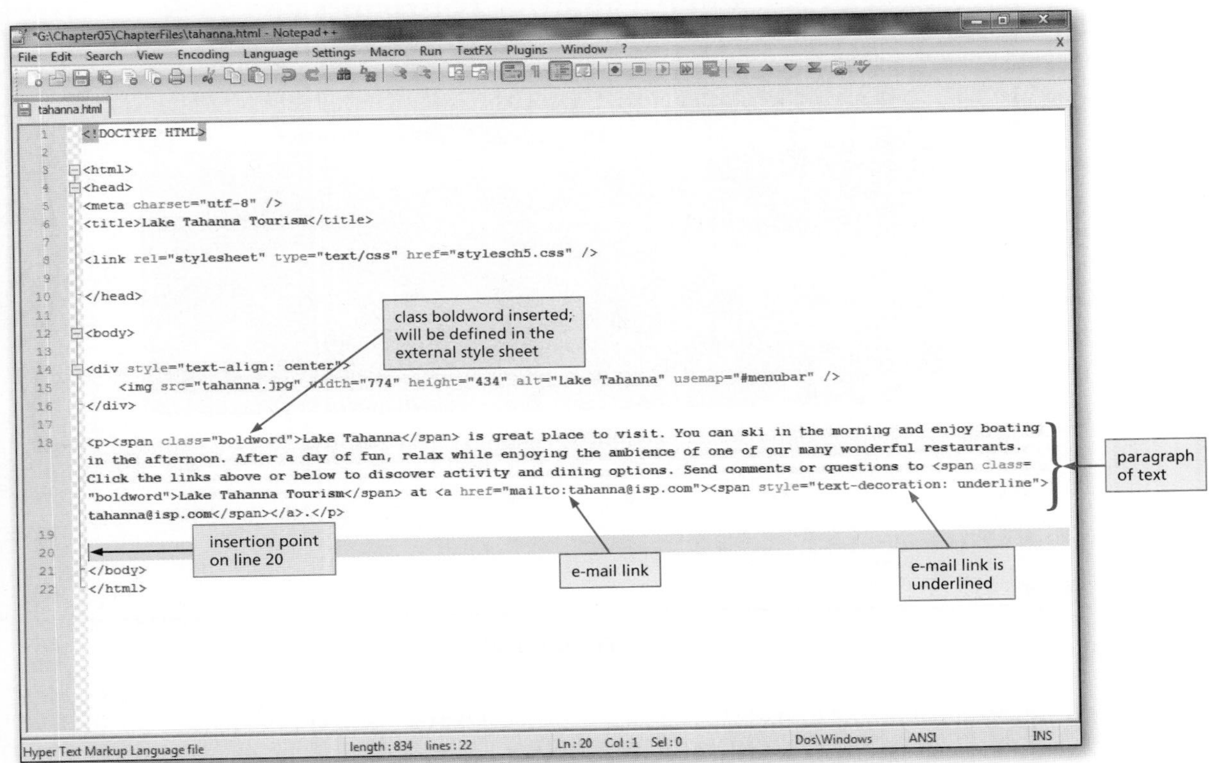

Figure 5–24

> **BTW**
> **Using Special Characters**
> Some characters are reserved in HTML. If you want the browser to actually display these characters, you must insert the character entities in the HTML source. For example, you cannot use the greater than or less than signs within your text because the browser could mistake them for markup. You therefore use the special characters > (greater than) and < (less than) to display those characters.

Inserting Special Characters

The next step in creating the home page is to add the registered trademark symbol, as shown in Figure 5–25. The registered trademark symbol (®) is a special character, many of which are listed in Appendix F. To display the registered trademark symbol, you use the following entity: ® as the code. In HTML, **character entity references** are code snippets that are interpreted by Web browsers to display special characters. These predefined character entities enhance the content on the Web pages that you create. A registered trademark symbol is a distinctive indicator used by an individual, a business organization, or another type of legal entity to identify that the products or services with which the trademark appears originate from a unique source. This symbol indicates that the trademark has been federally registered. This symbol differs from the ™ (trademark) symbol in that the ™ symbol is one in which the individual or business either has a pending federal trademark application, or they are simply claiming the rights to the mark. The entity for the ™ symbol is ™ as found in Appendix F.

In this project, you will insert the ® entity on line 18 within the paragraph of text that you just entered. You will insert the registered trademark symbol after the </span> tag because there is no reason to have the symbol be a different color font in bold.

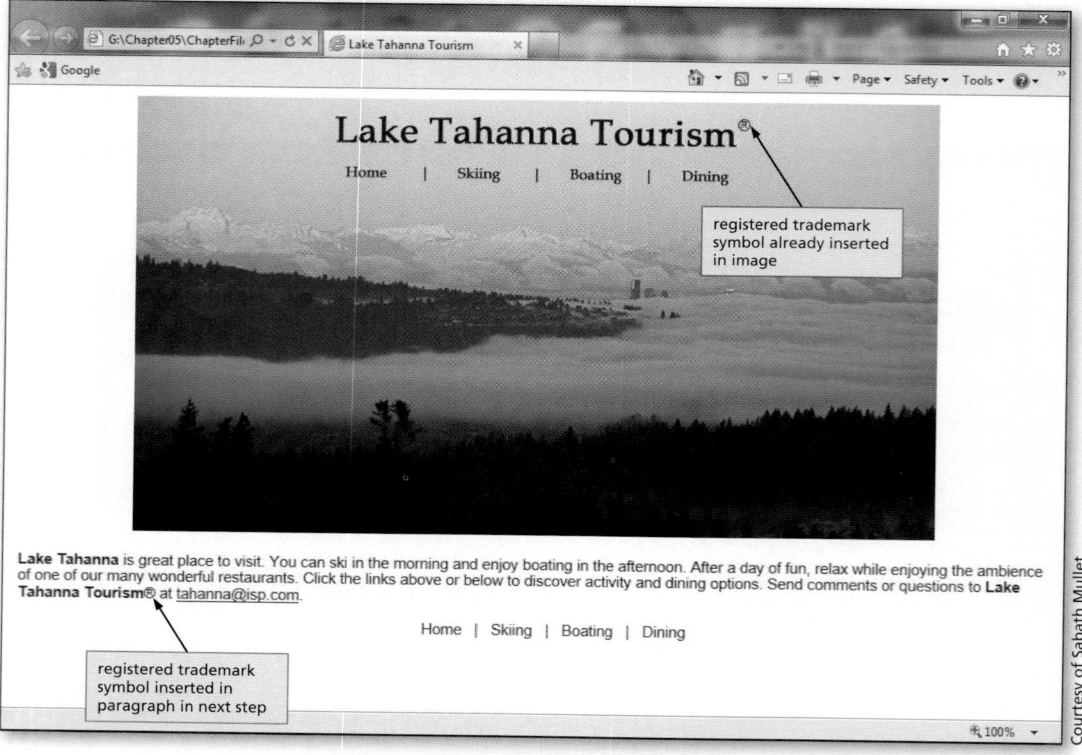

Courtesy of Sabath Mullet

Figure 5–25

You will use one other special character on this Web page. In the next section of code, you will insert a nonbreaking space to separate the navigation bar at the bottom of the Web page. The nonbreaking space ( ) is a common character entity used in HTML. Browsers will always truncate spaces in HTML pages. If you include 10 spaces in a row in your HTML file, the browser will remove 9 of them before displaying the page. To add spaces to your text, you use the   character entity. The   special character is used in this project to add space that separates the menu items.

The horizontal menu bar shown in Figure 5–26b is created using an unordered bulleted list. You have created several unordered bulleted lists in projects throughout the book so far. In each case, your bulleted list displays as shown in Figure 5–26a. Certainly, that is not an attractive look for this Web page. In later steps, you will convert this unordered bullet list to display horizontally (inline) by using statements inserted into the external style sheet.

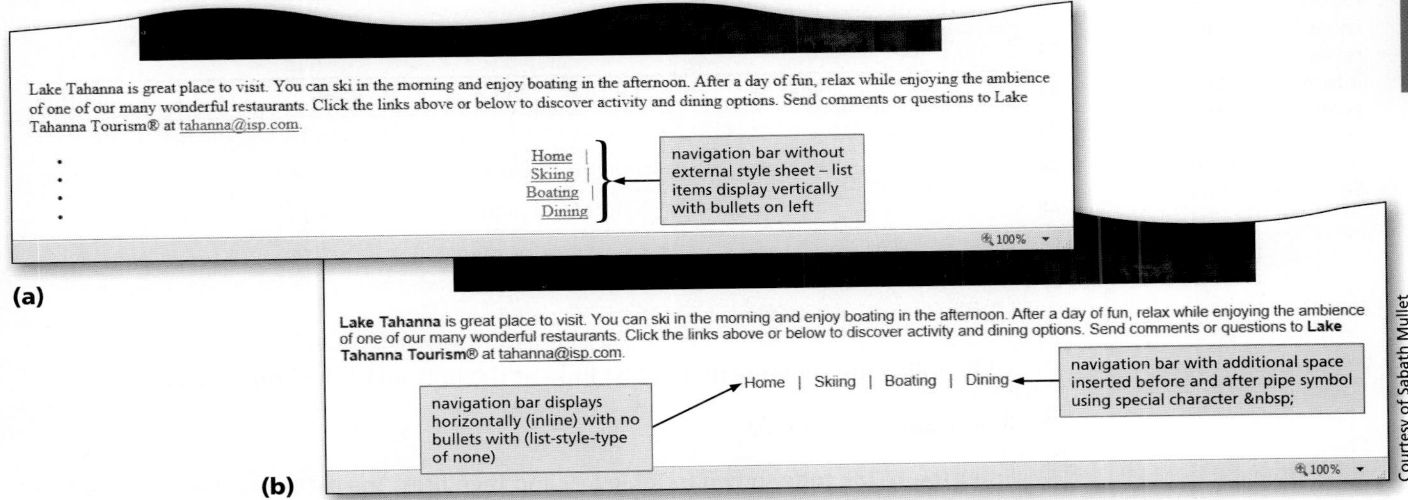

Figure 5–26

To Insert a Special Character

The following step inserts a registered trademark symbol.

- Position the insertion point to the right of the > in the second </span> tag on line 18 and type `®` and then press the SPACE bar as shown in Figure 5–27.

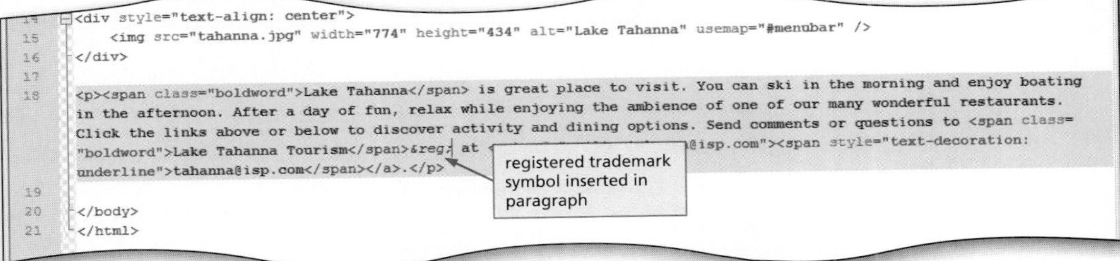

Figure 5–27

To Create a Horizontal Navigation Bar with Text Links

The next step is to create a horizontal navigation bar of text links at the bottom of the page that mirror the image map links. As previously discussed, it is important that a Web page include text links to all URLs in the image map, in the event the image does not download, a user is using a screen reader, or a user's browser is set to not display images. In Figure 5–27, you can see that there are three pipe symbols (|) inserted between the menu bar text items. The pipe symbols help to separate the text to make it easy for users to select a menu item. In addition to those pipe symbols, you use another special character entity, the nonbreaking space, between the menu options, using the character entity .

BTW

Text Links
It is very important to use text links on all Web pages in addition to using an image map for navigation. You want to give your Web site visitors access to all Web pages in the Web site. Text links should provide that access.

BTW

Accessibility
Developers should follow accessibility guidelines when developing Web pages. It is important that the Web page content is understandable and navigable. The W3C gives some good suggestions for Web site accessibility issues that should be reviewed. For more information about accessibility, visit the W3C Web site, or refer to Appendix C, Accessibility Standards and the Web.

Table 5–6 shows the HTML code used to create the horizontal navigation bar. As shown in lines 20 through 27, the HTML code adds the navigation bar to the bottom of the Web page beneath the paragraph of text.

Table 5–6 HTML Code for Creating a Horizontal Navigation Bar

Line	HTML Tag and Text
20	`<div style="text-align: center">`
21	`<ul>`
22	`<li class="navlist"><a href="tahanna.html">Home</a>   |  `
23	`<li class="navlist"><a href="skiing.html">Skiing</a>   |  `
24	`<li class="navlist"><a href="boating.html">Boating</a>   |  `
25	`<li class="navlist"><a href="dining.html">Dining</a>`
26	`</ul>`
27	`</div>`

The following steps create the text links at the bottom of the home page.

1. If necessary, click line 20.
2. Enter the HTML code shown in Table 5–6 and then press the ENTER key twice (Figure 5–28).

Q&A

I notice that we use a horizontal navigation bar for many projects in the book. Are there other ways to display a navigation bar?

The horizontal navigation bar is used because it makes sense aesthetically in these projects, but there are many other ways to display navigation items. A great idea is to review other navigation bar options on the Internet and view the HTML source. You can get a lot of ideas by looking at the Web pages and source code from other Web developers. Remember that the whole point of the navigation bar is to provide easy navigation for your Web site visitors.

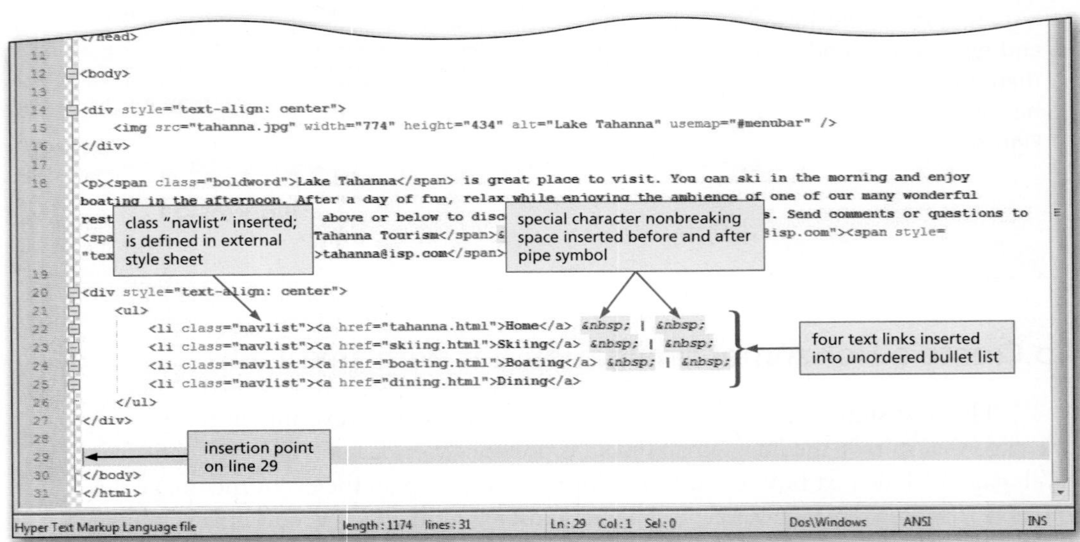

Figure 5–28

Plan Ahead

Creating an image map.

This is the final step in the four-step process of image mapping. The HTML code is very specific about what is required for image mapping. It only takes one coordinate that is not correct or one shape that is wrong for the image map not to work as intended.

- **Use the <map> tag.** The <map> tag identifies the name and ID for the image map. It is important that the name is spelled correctly, and that the same name is used in the usemap attribute in the <img> tag.
- **Use the <area> tag.** The <area> tag is also very important in image mapping. You identify the area shape and the x- and y-coordinates in this tag. Again, if even one number is typed incorrectly, it can make the image map nearly unusable.

Coding the Image Map Using HTML Tags and Attributes

Thus far, the chapter has addressed three of the four steps in creating an image map: the tahanna.jpg image to use as an image map has been selected and added to the home page; the hotspots have been sketched on the tahanna.jpg image; and Paint was used to locate the x- and y-coordinates for each map area on the image that serves as a hotspot. With these steps completed, the final step is to code the image map using HTML. Table 5–7 shows the two HTML tags used to create an image map, along with several key attributes of each.

Table 5–7 Tags and Tag Attributes Used to Create Image Maps

Tag	Attribute	Function
<map> </map>		• Creates a client-side image map
	name	• Defines the map's name
<area>		• Defines clickable areas within a <map> element, as well as links and anchors
	shape	• Indicates the shape of the map area; possible values are rect, poly, and circle
	coords	• Indicates the x- and y-coordinates of the points bounding the map area
	href	• Indicates the link (URL) used for a map area
	alt	• Indicates the alternate text for the image

The start <map> tag and end </map> tag define the section of code that includes the client-side image map. The <area> tag is used to define the clickable areas on the image map. An example of the <area> tag is:

```
<area shape="rect" coords="305,63,354,82" href="skiing.html"
           alt="Skiing" />
```

where the shape attribute with the rect value defines the clickable map area as a rectangle. Other possible values for the shape attribute are poly (polygon) and circle (circle). The alt attribute defines alternate text for the image. The coords attribute indicates the pairs of x- and y-coordinates that identify the boundaries of the clickable area. In a rectangle, you next have to determine the coordinates of the top-left and bottom-right corners. The href attribute designates the URL of the link. In this example, a Web page visitor can click anywhere within the rectangles surrounding the four words on the image (Home, Skiing, Boating, and Dining). For instance, the rectangle with top-left x- and y-coordinates 305,63 and bottom-right x- and y-coordinates 354,82 will link to the Web page skiing.html.

To insert the <area> tag for the circle, rectangle, and polygon shapes, such as those shown in Figure 5–14 on page HTML 248, the HTML code would be as follows:

```
<area shape="circle" coords="308,113,72" href="circle.html">
<area shape="rect" coords="46,35,137,208" href="rect.html">
<area shape="poly" coords="78,309,183,251,316,262,317,344,
          136,402" href="poly.html">
```

To Create an Image Map

For the image map on the Lake Tahanna Tourism home page, four clickable areas are created: Home, Skiing, Boating, and Dining. All four clickable areas are rectangular in shape. Table 5–8 shows the HTML code used to create the image map for the tahanna.jpg image on the home page. Line 29 defines the name of the image map as menubar, which is the name referenced in the usemap attribute of the <img> tag that added the tahanna.jpg image. Lines 29 through 32 define the four rectangular map areas for the image map, based on the x- and y-coordinates listed in Table 5–1 on page HTML 252. Each rectangular map area links to one of the four other Web pages on the Web site.

Table 5–8 HTML Code for Creating an Image Map

Line	HTML Tag and Text
29	<map name="menubar" id="menubar">
30	<area shape="rect" coords="195,63,247,82" href="tahanna.html" alt="Home" />
31	<area shape="rect" coords="305,63,354,82" href="skiing.html" alt="Skiing" />
32	<area shape="rect" coords="413,63,470,82" href="boating.html" alt="Boating" />
33	<area shape="rect" coords="521,63,574,82" href="dining.html" alt="Dining" />
34	</map>

The following step enters the HTML code to create the image map for the tahanna.jpg image.

1

- If necessary, click line 29.
- Enter the HTML code shown in Table 5–8 and press the ENTER key once on line 34 (Figure 5–29).

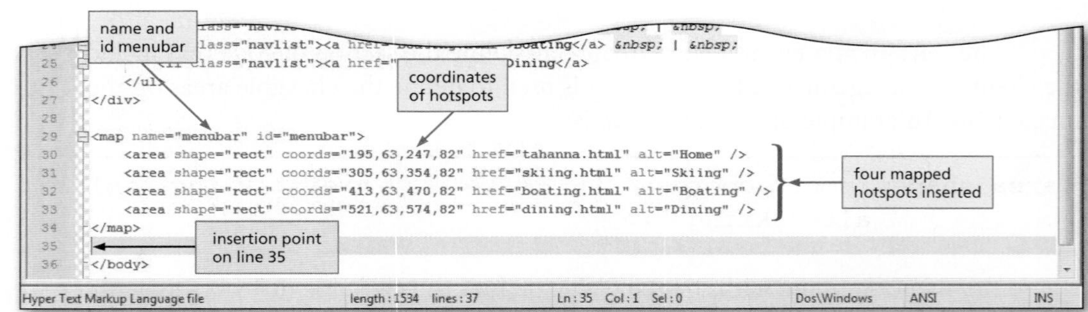

Figure 5–29

Q&A For this project, I am using all rectangular shapes. Could I have used other shapes for these four clickable areas?

For these navigation links, there really is no other shape that could be used. You may think to use a polygon shape for the links, for instance, but that would make the clickable areas confusing to the user.

Q&A Could I have used other x- and y-coordinates for this image map?

Yes. This is a very subjective part of image mapping. You need to select the points in the boundaries that make sense to you. Just make sure that the points will also make sense to your Web page visitors. Also, take care not to overlap the points or you will end up with false results.

To Save the HTML File

With the HTML code for the Lake Tahanna Tourism home page complete, you should save the file.

1. Click the Save button on the Notepad++ toolbar to save the most recent version of tahanna.html on the same storage device and in the same folder as the last time you saved it.

To Validate a Web Page

1. Open Internet Explorer, navigate to the Web site `validator.w3.org`, and then click the Validate by File Upload tab.
2. Click the Browse button.
3. Locate the tahanna.html file on your storage device, click the filename, and then click the Open button in the Choose File to Upload dialog box.
4. Click the Check button to validate the file.

Viewing the Web Page and Testing Links

After you save the HTML file for the Lake Tahanna Tourism home page, it should be viewed in a browser to confirm the Web page appears as desired. It is also important to test the links on the Lake Tahanna Tourism home page to verify they function as expected. Note that the image on the subsequent Web pages is a smaller version of the image on the home page (Figure 5–30). This gives the Web developer more room to add content to the additional Web pages.

To View a Web Page

1. In Internet Explorer, click the Address bar to select the URL on the Address bar.
2. Type `G:\Chapter05\ChapterFiles\tahanna.html` on the Address bar of your browser and press ENTER to display the Web page (Figure 5–30 on the next page).

Q&A

Why do the Skiing, Boating, and Dining links work?

These links work because the files skiing.html, boating.html, and dining.html are stored in the Chapter05\ChapterFiles folder of the Data Files for Students.

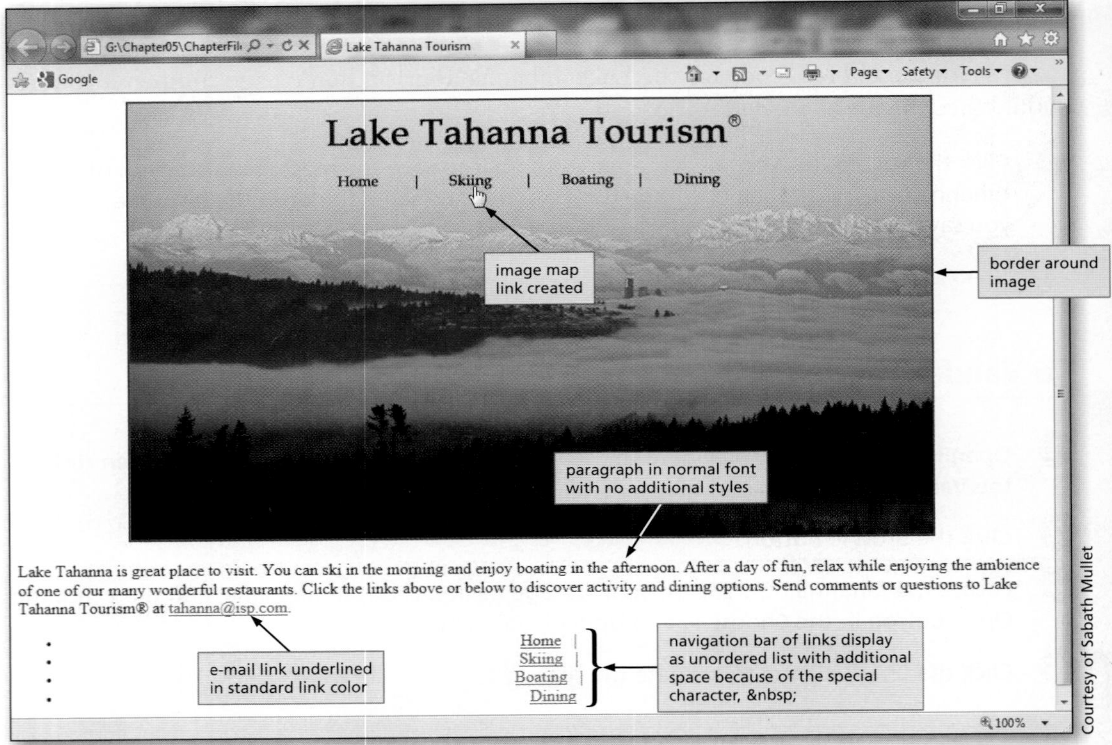

Figure 5–30

> **BTW**
> **Testing**
> Especially with image maps, it is important to test the Web page thoroughly in the browser. If one incorrect number is typed as an x- or y-coordinate, the entire image map can be wrong as a result. Make sure that the clickable area is exactly where you want it to be by testing your Web pages.

To Test Links on a Web Page

1. With the USB flash drive in drive G, click the Skiing link from the home page just created. Click back to the Home page from there, using either the image map or the text link. Next, click the other links to test the additional Web pages provided in the Data Files for Students (boating.html and dining.html). Test the links back to the Home page from those Web pages.

To Print an HTML File

After your HTML code has passed validation, it is a good idea to make a hard copy printout of it.

1. Click the Notepad++ button on the taskbar to activate the Notepad++ window.
2. Click the Print Now button on the toolbar to print a hard copy of the HTML code (Figure 5–31).

```
<!DOCTYPE HTML>

<html>
<head>
<meta charset="utf-8" />
<title>Lake Tahanna Tourism</title>

<link rel="stylesheet" type="text/css" href="stylesch5.css" />

</head>

<body>

<div style="text-align: center">
    <img src="tahanna.jpg" width="774" height="434" alt="Lake Tahanna" usemap="#menubar"
     />
</div>

<p><span class="boldword">Lake Tahanna</span> is great place to visit. You can ski in
the morning and enjoy boating in the afternoon. After a day of fun, relax while
enjoying the ambience of one of our many wonderful restaurants. Click the links above
or below to discover activity and dining options. Send comments or questions to <span
class="boldword">Lake Tahanna Tourism</span>&reg; at <a href="mailto:tahanna@isp.com"
><span style="text-decoration: underline">tahanna@isp.com</span></a>.</p>

<div style="text-align: center">
    <ul>
        <li class="navlist"><a href="tahanna.html">Home</a>   |  
        <li class="navlist"><a href="skiing.html">Skiing</a>   |  
        <li class="navlist"><a href="boating.html">Boating</a>   |  
        <li class="navlist"><a href="dining.html">Dining</a>
    </ul>
</div>

<map name="menubar" id="menubar">
    <area shape="rect" coords="195,63,247,82" href="tahanna.html" alt="Home" />
    <area shape="rect" coords="305,63,354,82" href="skiing.html" alt="Skiing" />
    <area shape="rect" coords="413,63,470,82" href="boating.html" alt="Boating" />
    <area shape="rect" coords="521,63,574,82" href="dining.html" alt="Dining" />
</map>

</body>
</html>
```

Figure 5–31

Plan Ahead

Planning an external style sheet.

The home page is complete, but some style details are lacking. It is important to maintain a consistent look across a Web site. By creating an external style sheet, you can maintain that consistent look with great style.

- **Determine what styles you want to use.** As you have seen, there are many styles that you can use to enhance your Web site (see Appendix D). Some that you can utilize in this Web site are:
  - Font family – maintaining a consistent font family is very important because the style of font is what you see the most across a Web site.
  - Font size – for the same reason as above, you should maintain consistency in font size; there are exceptions to this, especially in titles on the Web page.
  - Margins – it is helpful to utilize margins to help define the structure of a Web page.
  - Borders around links – you do not always want to see borders around images that you use as links; setting the border to zero is sometimes better style.
  - Determine if you need to add any classes. If there is code that will be repeated across Web pages, you should add a class to the external style sheet and use the class name in the HTML files. If you want to make a change across a Web site (such as font color), it is much easier to do that one time in an external style sheet rather than changing it multiple times in many Web pages.

Creating an External Style Sheet

With the home page complete, the next step is to create an external style sheet that is linked to all pages in the Web site. You already added the link statement into the HTML code in the tahanna.html file on line 8. This statement tells the browser to link to the external (linked) style sheet named stylesch5.css. If there is no stylesch5.css file available, as is the case at this time, then the styles used are the default styles, as shown in Figure 5–32a. Once you create the stylesch5.css external style sheet, your Web page looks like that shown in Figure 5–32b.

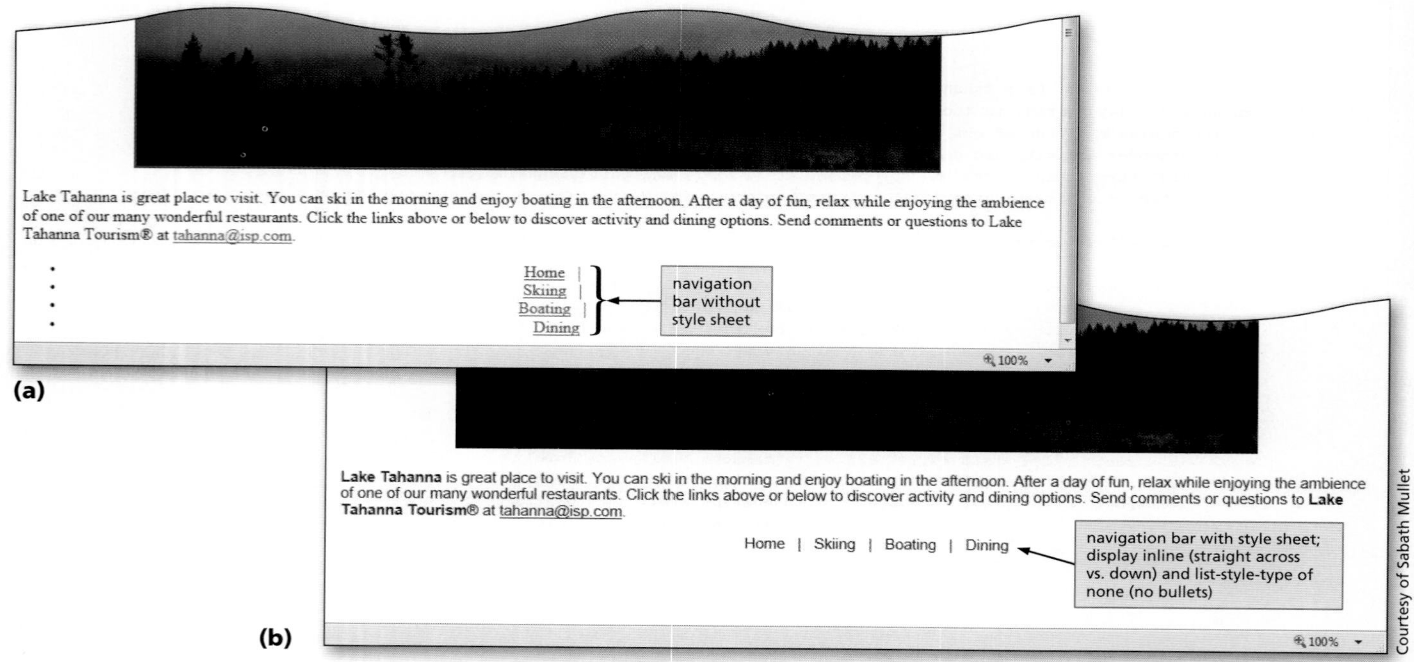

Figure 5–32

To create an external style sheet, you first have to start a new file in Notepad++. Remember from Chapter 4 that an external style sheet does not need the initial HTML DOCTYPE tags that you use for all Web pages. The external style sheet contains only the code for the various styles that you want to use across a Web site.

To Create an External Style Sheet

Table 5–9 contains the CSS code for the external style sheet that is used in all Web pages. Lines 1 and 2 define the font-family and font-size for the Web page. Lines 4 and 5 set the right and left margins to 5 points. That will give 5 points of space from the edge of the Web page to the start of the text in a paragraph. Lines 7 and 8 create a paragraph class named “boldword” that will be used to format text with a navy blue color and a bolder font-weight. Line 10 puts a transparent border around all images so that there is no border. Lines 12 and 13 create a list class named navlist (navigation list) that is used to display each list item inline (horizontally) without a bullet type. This is a good technique to use for navigation menus. Lines 15 through 19 are styles that you have used in past projects. In these lines, you set the style of a link color with no text-decoration (no underline). You also use the pseudoclass hover to set the background and text color for hovered links.

Table 5–9 Code for External Style Sheet

CSS Properties and Values	
`body`	`{font-family: Arial, Centaur, "Century Gothic";`
	`font-size: 11pt;}`
`p`	`{margin-left: 5pt;`
	`margin-right: 5pt;}`
`.boldword`	`{color: #030a24;`
	`font-weight: bolder;}`
`img`	`{border-color: transparent;}`
`li.navlist`	`{display: inline;`
	`list-style-type: none;}`
`a`	`{text-decoration: none;`
	`color: #030a24;}`
`a:hover`	`{background: #030a24;`
	`color: #d0a4bb;}`

The following step creates an external style sheet.

1

- If necessary, click the Notepad++ button on the taskbar.
- Click the New button on the toolbar.
- Enter the HTML code shown in Table 5–9 (Figure 5–33).

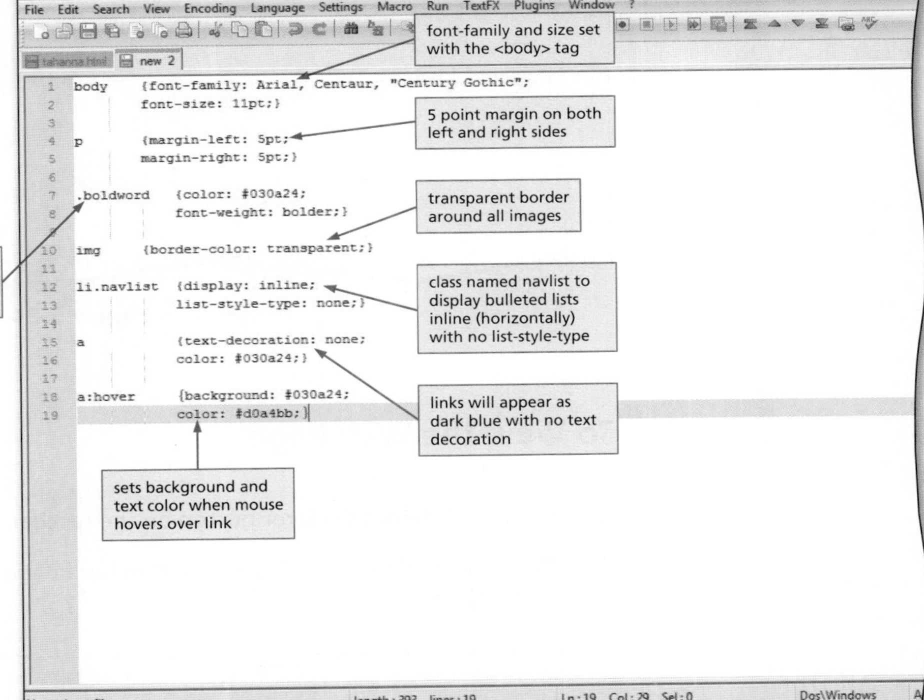

Figure 5–33

To Save and Print the CSS File

1. With a USB drive plugged into your computer, click File on the menu bar and then click Save As. Type `stylesch5.css` in the File name text box.
2. If necessary, click UDISK (G:) or your storage device in the Save in list. Click the Chapter05 folder and then double-click the ChapterFiles folder in the list of available folders. Click the Save button in the Save As dialog box.
3. Click File on the menu bar and then click Print Now toolbar (Figure 5–34).

```
body{font-family: Arial, Centaur, "Century Gothic";
        font-size: 11pt;}

p       {margin-left: 5pt;
        margin-right: 5pt;}

.boldword     {color: #030a24;
              font-weight: bolder;}

img     {border-color: transparent;}

li.navlist    {display: inline;
              list-style-type: none;}

a             {text-decoration: none;
              color: #030a24;}

a:hover       {background: #030a24;
              color: #d0a4bb;}
```

Figure 5–34

To View the Web Page

1. Click the Internet Explorer button on the taskbar.
2. Click the Skiing area on the navigation bar image map to display the Skiing Web page, as shown in Figure 5–35.

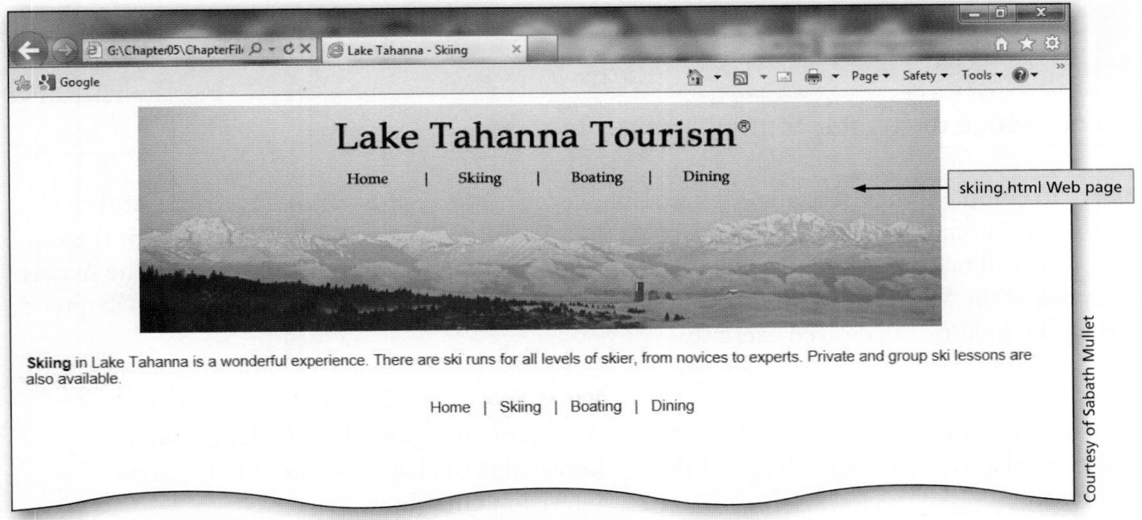

Figure 5–35

To Test and Print the Web Page

1. Click the Home link (either text or from the image map) on the Skiing Web page.
2. Click the Print button on the Command bar to print the Web page. If the Command bar is not visible, right-click the toolbar and click Command bar on the shortcut menu.
3. Test the links, both those in the image map and those in the text navigation bar. If any of the links do not work correctly, return to Notepad++ to modify the HTML code, save the changes, and then retest the links in the browser.

To Quit Notepad++ and a Browser

1. In Notepad++, click the File menu, then Close All.
2. Click the Close button on the Notepad++ title bar.
3. Click the Close button on the browser title bar. If necessary, click the Close all tabs button.

Chapter Summary

In this chapter, you have learned how to develop a Web site that utilizes image mapping from the home page to create three clickable areas. The items listed below include all the new HTML skills you have learned in this chapter.

1. Start Paint (HTML 249)
2. Open an Image File in Paint (HTML 251)
3. Locate X- and Y-Coordinates of an Image (HTML 252)
4. Insert an Image to Use as an Image Map (HTML 258)
5. Insert a Special Character (HTML 261)
6. Create an Image Map (HTML 264)
7. Create an External Style Sheet (HTML 268)

BTW **Quick Reference**
For a list of special characters, see the Symbols and Characters Quick Reference (Appendix F) at the back of this book or visit the Book Companion Site Web page for this book at www.cengagebrain.com.

Learn It Online

Test your knowledge of chapter content and key terms.

Instructions: To complete the following exercises, please visit `www.cengagebrain.com`. At the CengageBrain.com home page, search for *HTML5 and CSS 7th Edition* using the search box at the top of the page. This will take you to the product page for this book. On the product page, click the Access Now button below the Study Tools heading. On the Book Companion Site Web page, select Chapter 5, and then click the link for the desired exercise.

Chapter Reinforcement TF, MC, and SA
A series of true/false, multiple choice, and short answer questions that test your knowledge of the chapter content.

Flash Cards
An interactive learning environment where you identify chapter key terms associated with displayed definitions.

Practice Test
A series of multiple choice questions that test your knowledge of chapter content and key terms.

Who Wants To Be a Computer Genius?
An interactive game that challenges your knowledge of chapter content in the style of a television quiz show.

Wheel of Terms
An interactive game that challenges your knowledge of chapter key terms in the style of the television show, *Wheel of Fortune*.

Crossword Puzzle Challenge
A crossword puzzle that challenges your knowledge of key terms presented in the chapter.

Apply Your Knowledge

Reinforce the skills and apply the concepts you learned in this chapter.

Adding an Image Map to a Web Page
Instructions: You decide to use your image mapping skills to create a Web page that describes the population of a city throughout the years. You plan to create a Web page similar to the one shown in Figure 5–36, with the file barchart.png as an image map that links to a sample Web page upon which you can add information on the various reasons for the population increase. The exercise calls for you to only use the bars at 10,000 and above. As a bonus exercise, create hotspots using the other bars (under 10,000). See the inside back cover of this book for instructions on downloading the Data Files for Students, or contact your instructor for information about accessing the required files.

Perform the following steps:

1. Using Paint, open the file barchart.png from the Chapter05\Apply folder of the Data Files for Students.
2. Each area on the bar chart image is a rectangular area. You need to only use the four bars on the right (10,000 and above) for your image map. Use good judgment when planning the shapes of your image map, ensuring that no clickable areas overlap from one rectangular shape into another and that each shape makes sense for its respective area. Using Paint, estimate the x- and y-coordinates necessary to create four clickable areas on the barchart.png image. Write down these coordinates for later use.

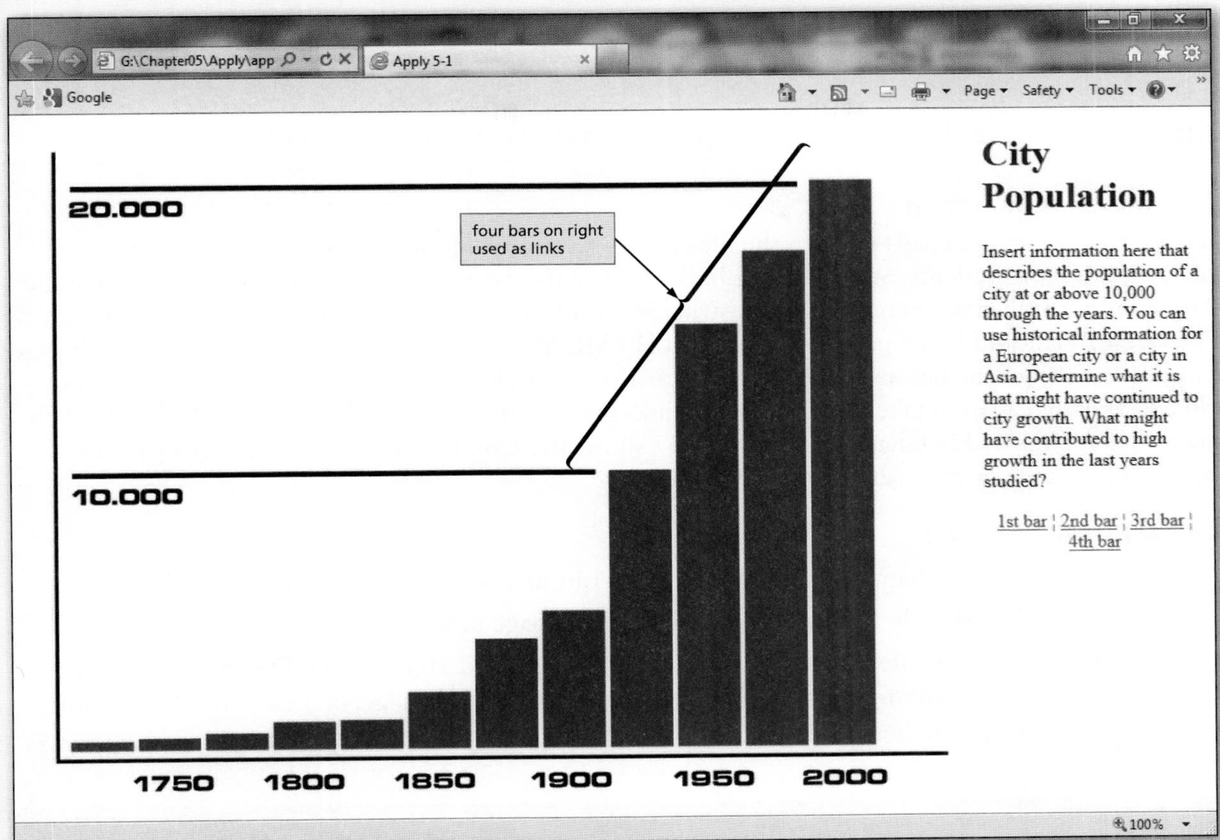

Figure 5–36

3. Using Notepad++, create a new HTML file with the title Apply 5-1 in the title section. Add the heading (using an h1 heading and the color #000064) and text, as shown in Figure 5–36. Use the ¦ special character (broken vertical bar) to separate the text links.
4. Use Paint to determine the dimensions of the image for the <img> tag. Align the image so that it is to the left of the text.
5. Use the usemap attribute usemap="#chart" in the <img> tag.
6. Enter the <map> </map> tags required to create the image map named chart.
7. Enter the <area> tags required to define four clickable areas on the image barchart.png. Use the x- and y-coordinates determined in Step 2 and set the href attribute to link to the sample.html file from the Data Files for Students or create your own secondary Web pages.
8. Save the HTML file in the Chapter05\Apply folder using the filename apply5-1solution.html Validate the Web page(s) using W3C. Print the HTML file.
9. Open the file apply5-1solution.html in your browser and test the image map and text links to the sample.html Web page provided. As a bonus, link to other Web pages of your choosing.
10. Print the main Web page.
11. Submit the completed files in the format specified by your instructor.

STUDENT ASSIGNMENTS

Extend Your Knowledge

Extend the skills you learned in this chapter and experiment with new skills.

Creating an Image Map

Instructions: Start Notepad++. Open the file extend5-1.html from the Chapter05\Extend folder of the Data Files for Students. See the inside back cover of this book for instructions on downloading the Data Files for Students, or contact your instructor for information about accessing the required files. The extend5-1.html file is a partially completed HTML file that needs to be completed. The Web page is a continuation of the oceanside.html project that you completed in Chapter 4. In this project, you will add an image map to take the place of the links inserted in Chapter 4. You can use the linked Web pages that you created in Chapter 4. Figure 5–37 shows the Extend Your Knowledge Web page as it should appear in your browser after it is completed.

Perform the following tasks:

1. Enter the URL G:\Chapter05\Extend\extend5-1.html to view the Web page in your browser.
2. Examine the HTML file and its appearance as a Web page in the browser.
3. Using Paint, open the file menubar.jpg from the Chapter05\Extend folder. Determine the x- and y-coordinates necessary to create six clickable areas on the map image, one each for Home, Golf, Tennis, Dining, Room Service, and Salon. Use rectangle shapes for the six areas.

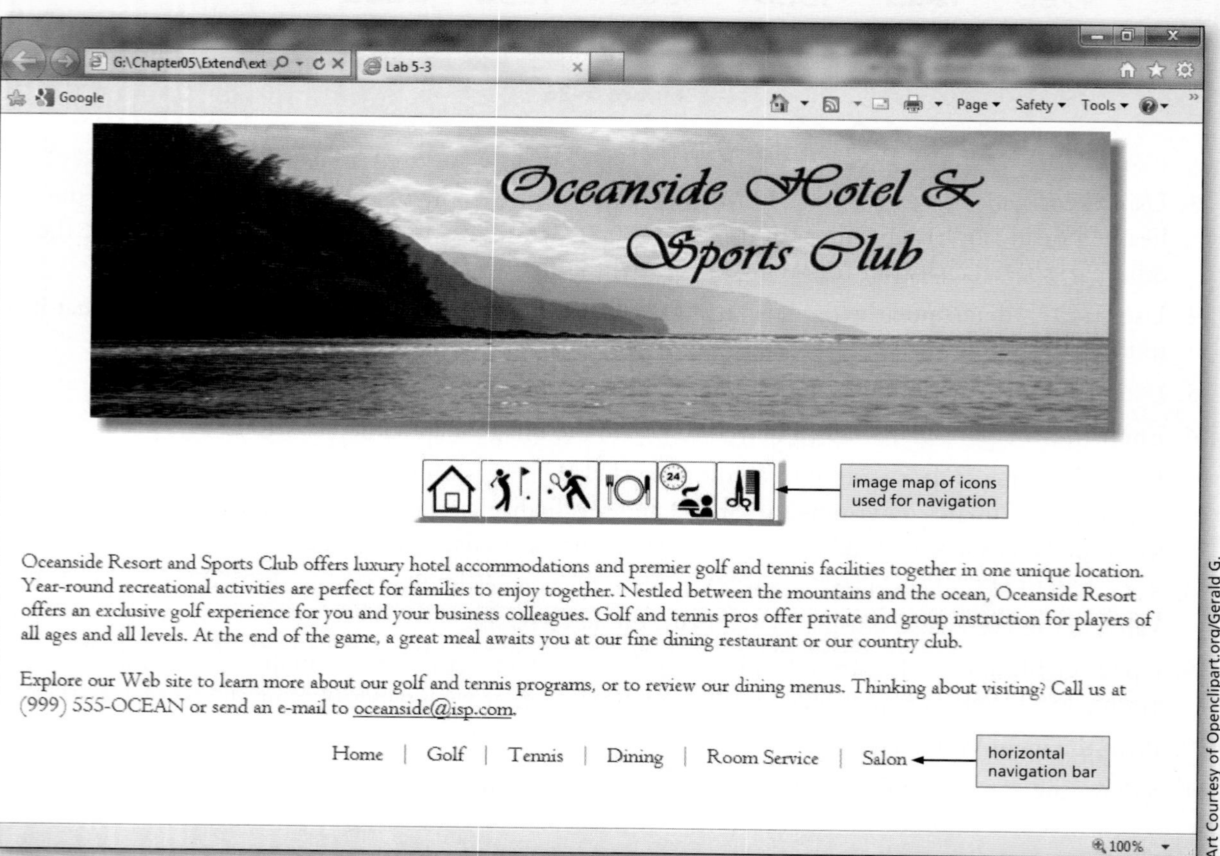

Figure 5–37

4. Add HTML code to the extend5-1.html file to create an image map that links each clickable area on the map image to an external Web page of your choice. If you created the Web pages for this site in Chapter 4, you can copy those and the external style sheet created in Chapter 4 over to the Chapter 5 folder. It might be best to rename them (e.g., golfch5.html) to separate them from the original pages. You will also create a Salon or Room Service Web page.
5. Add the code to include a horizontal navigation bar at the bottom of the Web page, similar to what you created in this chapter. Edit the external style sheet from Chapter 4 to add the styles needed for the menu bar at the bottom of the Web page.
6. Use the provided file, futurech5.html, to create one of the two new Web pages (Room Service or Salon). Include a table of relevant information on that page.
7. Save the revised file in the Chapter05\Extend folder using the filename extend5-1solution.html. Save the external style sheet as extend5-1styles.css.
8. Validate the Web pages to assure that you are in compliance with current standards.
9. Test the links completely.
10. Print the revised HTML home page file. If requested, also print any additional Web pages that you created.
11. Enter the URL G:\Chapter05\Extend\extend5-1solution.html to view the Web page in your browser.
12. Print the Web page.
13. Submit the completed files in the format specified by your instructor.

Make It Right

Analyze a document and correct all errors and/or improve the design.

Correcting the Travel Agency Web Page

Instructions: Start Notepad++. Open the file makeitright5-1.html from the Chapter05\MakeItRight folder of the Data Files for Students. See the inside back cover of this book for instructions on downloading the Data Files for Students, or contact your instructor for information about accessing the required files. The Web page is a modified version of what you see in Figure 5–38 on the next page. Make the necessary corrections to the Web page to make it look like the figure. The Web page uses the image ctmenu.jpg for the image map and should have links from four hotspots. The Web page also uses the image ctdivider.jpg for the divider between items in the text navigation bar at the bottom of the Web page. Add five text links at the bottom of the Web page using Table 5–10 for the coordinates and the filenames of the images that should be displayed when a link is clicked. Be sure to include alt text. Submit the completed HTML file(s) and Web page(s) in the format specified by your instructor.

Table 5–10 Image Map Coordinates, URLs, and Text Links

Text Link	Image Map Coordinates	Filename
Near the wall	346,152,493,179	wall.jpg
Indian corn	346,202,493,234	corn.jpg
On the farm	346,253,493,284	farm.jpg
By the lake	346,303,493,334	lake.jpg

Continued >

Make It Right *continued*

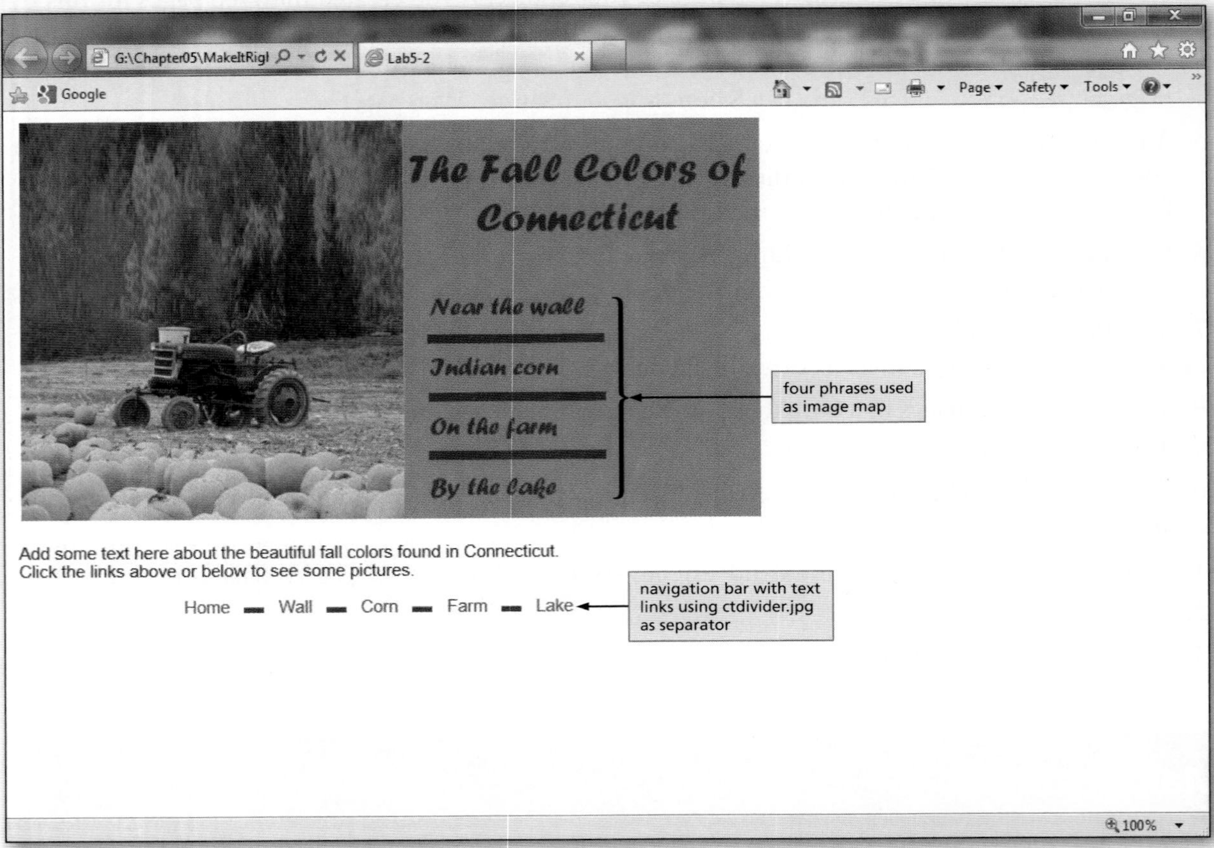

Figure 5–38

In the Lab

Lab 1: Creating a Web Page for a Senior Center

Problem: You are very involved in volunteer work at your local senior center. You decide to create a Web page similar to the Web page in Figure 5–39, with the file seniorlogo.png as an image map that links to five Web pages of your choosing. The Web page sample.html is provided as a temporary page to which you can link.

Instructions: Perform the following steps:

1. Using Paint, open the file seniorlogo.png from the Chapter05\IntheLab folder.
2. Determine the x- and y-coordinates necessary to create three rectangular clickable areas and two polygonal areas (for Parcheesi and Poker) on the graphical image. (*Hint:* For the polygonal shapes, note the coordinates of each point, as discussed in the chapter.) Write down these coordinates for later use.
3. Using Notepad++, create a new HTML file with the title Lab 5-1 in the title section. Add the text links, as shown in Figure 5–39.
4. Insert the image seniorlogo.png. Use the usemap attribute usemap="#menubar" in the <img> tag.
5. Enter the <map> </map> tags required to create the image map named menubar.

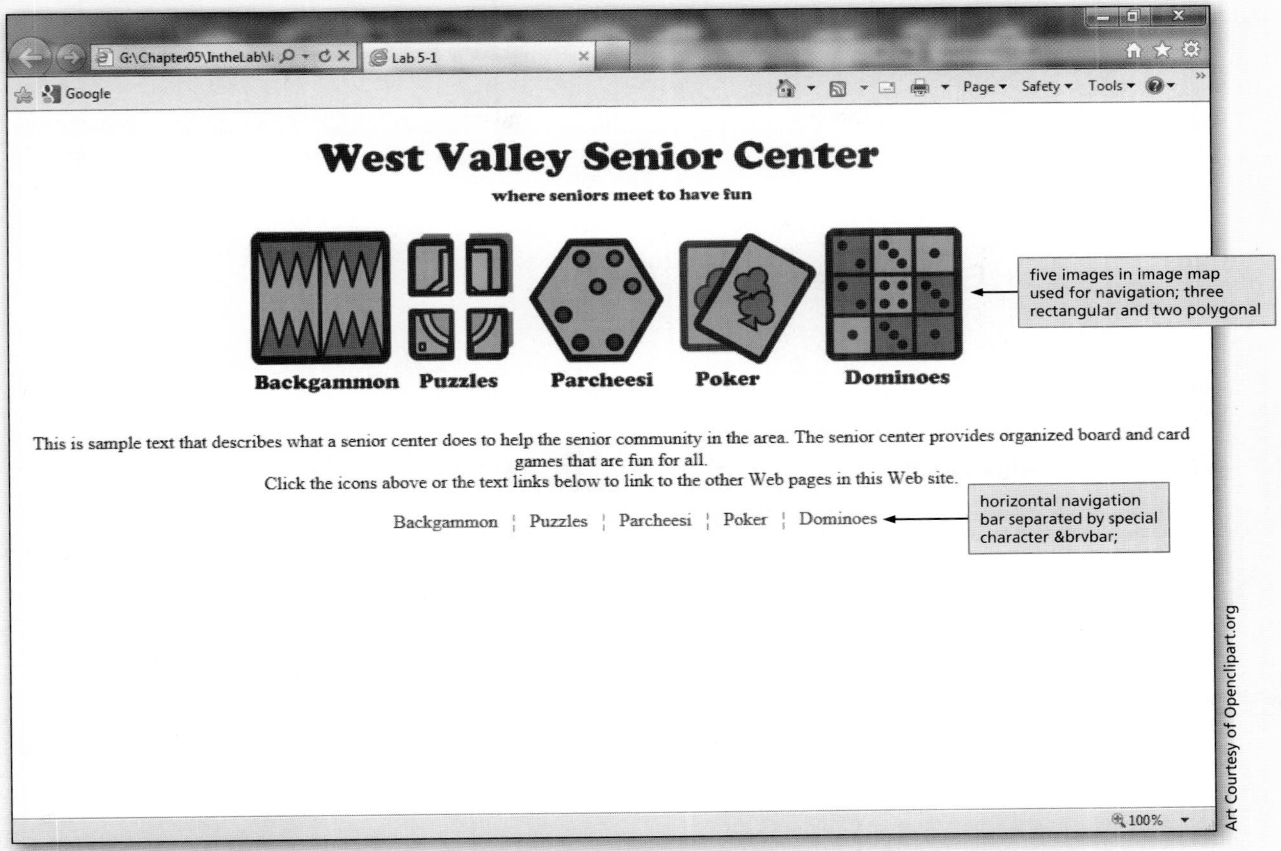

Figure 5–39

6. Enter the <area> tags required to define three rectangular and two polygonal clickable areas on the seniorlogo.png image. Use the x- and y-coordinates determined in Step 2 and set the href attribute to display the sample.html Web page provided in the Data Files for Students.
7. Add a navigation bar of text links at the bottom of the Web page. Include the special character ¦ in between the text links to display the broken vertical bar.
8. Save the HTML file in the Chapter05\IntheLab folder using the filename lab5-1solution.html. Validate the Web page using W3C. Print the HTML file.
9. Open the file lab5-1solution.html in your browser and test the image map and text links to verify they link to the sample Web page.
10. Print the Web page.
11. Submit the completed HTML files and Web pages in the format specified by your instructor.

In the Lab

Lab 2: Mapping a Horizontal Navigation Bar

Problem: You are learning how to utilize a button bar on a Web page as seen in many Web sites. Use your image mapping skills to create a Web page that has four circular links. You plan to create a Web page similar to the one shown in Figure 5–40, with the file bluebuttons.jpg as an image map that links to the sample.html Web page.

Continued >

In the Lab *continued*

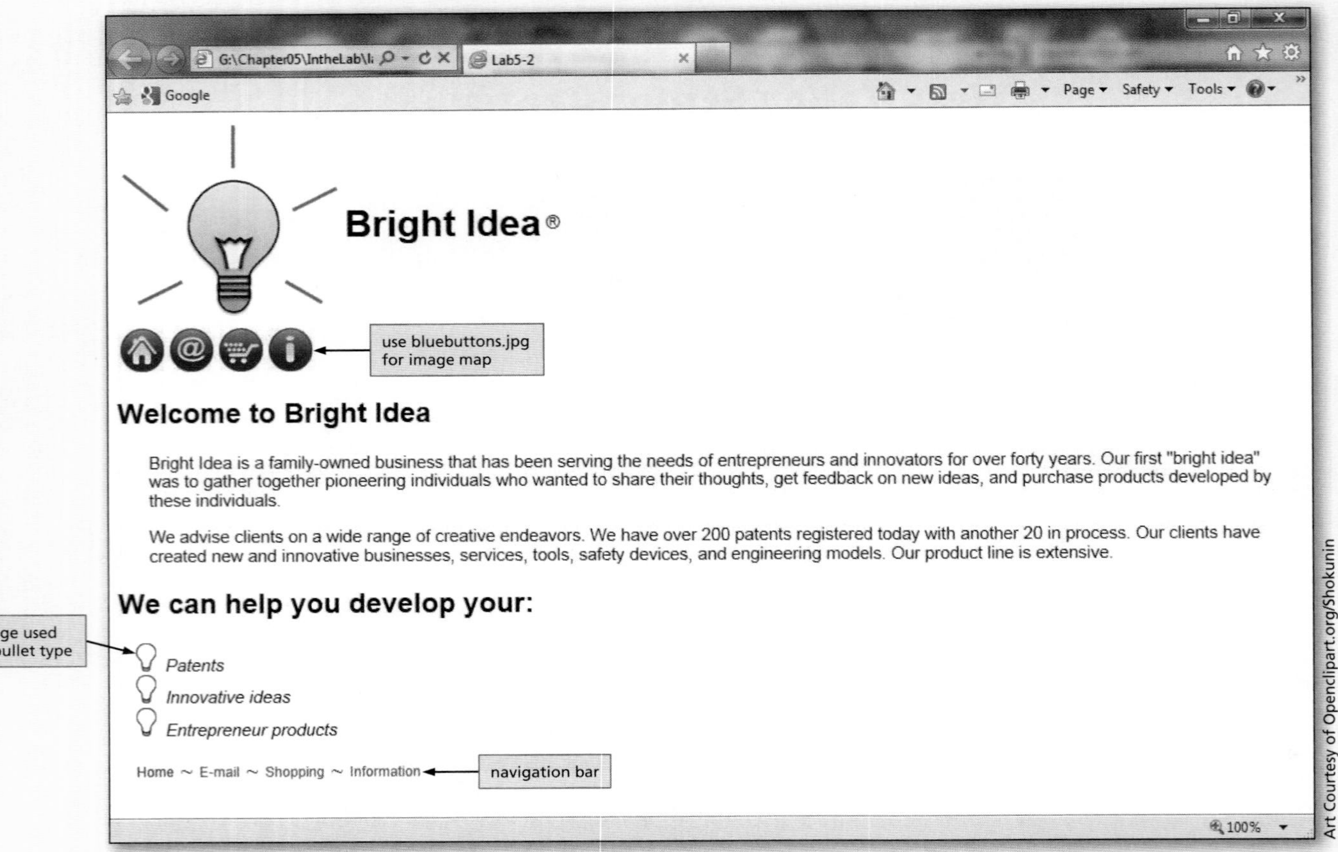

Figure 5–40

Instructions: Perform the following steps:

1. Using Paint, open the file bluebuttons.jpg from the Chapter05\IntheLab folder.
2. Each area on the image is a circular shape. Use good judgment when planning the shapes of your image map, ensuring that no clickable areas overlap from one circular shape into another and that each shape makes sense for its respective area. Using Paint, estimate the x- and y-coordinates necessary to create four circular clickable areas on the bluebuttons.jpg image. (*Hint:* For a circular shape, find the coordinates of the center of the circle, then one point on the edge of the circle. Determine the radius, as discussed in the chapter.)
3. Using Notepad++, create a new HTML file with the title Lab 5-2 in the title section. Add a link to the external style sheet lab5-2styles.css that is included in the Data Files. Add the headings (one h1 and two h2 headings) and text as shown in Figure 5–40.
4. Begin the body section by adding a one-row, three-data-cell table. The first cell contains the brightidealogo.png image; the second cell contains an <h1> heading as shown in Figure 5–40. Include the special character (see Appendix F) for the registered trademark in the third data cell.
5. Within a <div></div> container, insert the image bluebuttons.jpg that is used for the image map. Use the usemap attribute usemap="#menubar" in the <img> tag. Enter the required <map> </map> tags to create the image map named menubar.
6. Insert a bulleted list and use the image bulbsm.png as the bullet type. (*Hint:* Use the list-style-image and include a URL for the image.) The bullet text should have font-size of 11 point and font-style of italic.

7. Enter the <area> tags required to define four circular clickable areas on the image bluebuttons.jpg. Use the x- and y-coordinates determined in Step 2 and set the href attributes to link to the home page, the e-mail link, and two links to the sample.html Web page.
8. Create the navigation bar shown at the bottom of the Web page.
9. Save the HTML file in the Chapter05\IntheLab folder using the filename lab5-2solution.html. Validate the Web page(s) using W3C. Print the HTML file.
10. Open the file lab5-2solution.html in your browser and test the image map and text links.
11. Print the main Web page.
12. Submit the completed HTML files and Web pages in the format specified by your instructor.

In the Lab

Lab 3: Creating a Home Builder's Web Site

Problem: You are trying to help your Uncle Montego increase the reach of his home building business. To help him show people the quality of the construction, you will create a Web site with a home page similar to Figure 5–41.

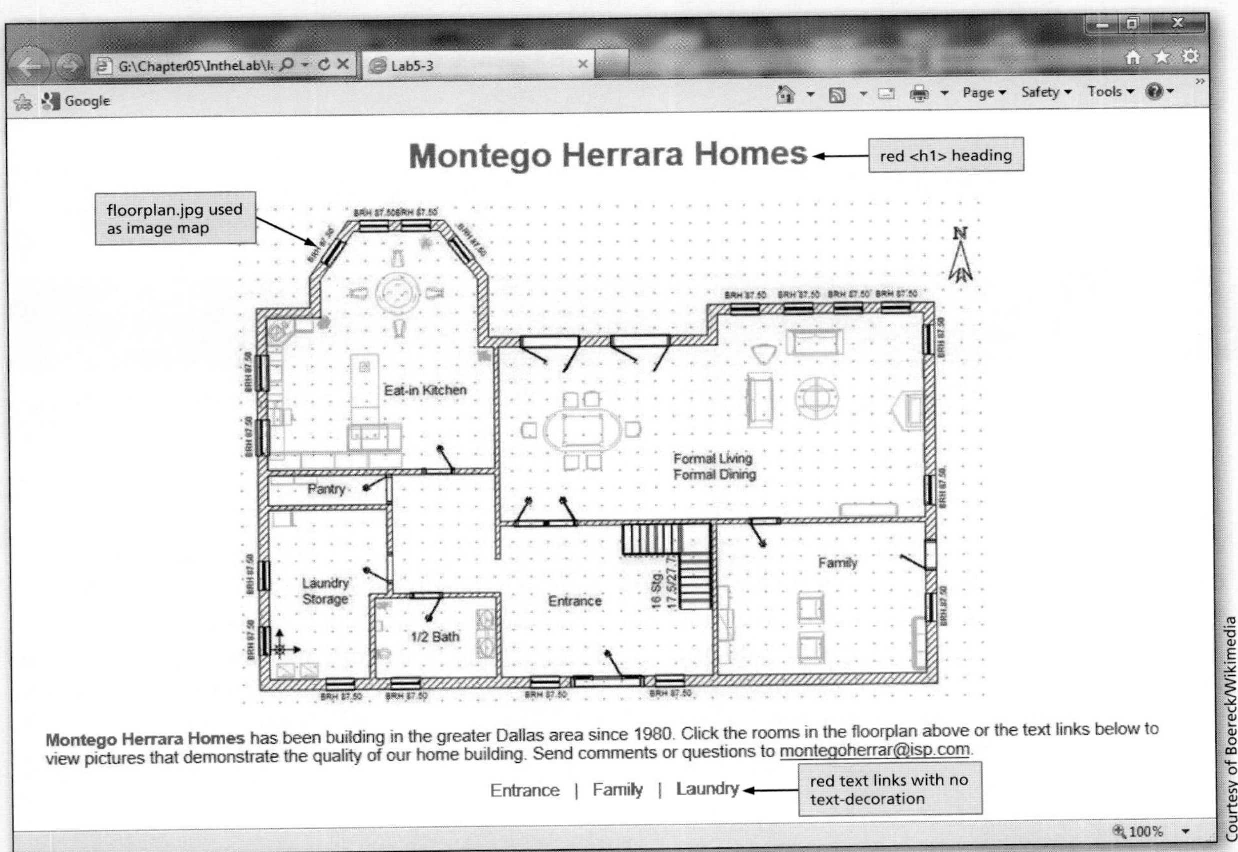

Figure 5–41

Continued >

In the Lab *continued*

Instructions: Perform the following tasks:

1. Using Paint, open the file floorplan.jpg from the Chapter05\IntheLab folder of the Data Files for Students.
2. Using Paint, determine the x- and y-coordinates necessary to create three clickable areas on the map image. Use two rectangular-shaped areas for the Family room and the Entrance. Use a polygonal-shaped area for the Laundry Storage room. Write down these coordinates for later use.
3. Using Notepad++, create a new HTML file with the title Lab 5-3 in the main heading section.
4. Make all headings and links (other than the e-mail link) red. Insert left- and right-margins of 20 pixels. Make the text Arial 11 point font. Links should have no text-decoration. (*Hint:* Use an embedded style sheet for these styles.)
5. Begin the body section by adding the floorplan.jpg image, as shown in Figure 5–41.
6. Use the usemap attribute usemap="#menubar" in the <img> tag.
7. Enter the <map> </map> tags required to create the image map named menubar.
8. Enter the <area> tags required to define three clickable areas on the image floorplan.jpg. Use the x- and y-coordinates determined in Step 2 and set the href attribute to display the images provided in the Data Files (entrance.jpg, family.jpg, and laundry.jpg) when a link is clicked.
9. Save the HTML file in the Chapter05\IntheLab folder using the filename lab5-3solution.html. Validate the Web page. Print the HTML file.
10. Open the file lab5-3solution.html in your browser and test the image map and text links to verify they link to the correct images.
11. Print the main Web page.
12. Submit the completed HTML files and Web pages in the format specified by your instructor.

Cases and Places

Apply your creative thinking and problem-solving skills to design and implement a solution.

1: Analyzing Web Sites for Image Map Use

Academic

Complete an analysis of frequently visited Web sites to discover which sites use image maps for navigation. Some examples of Web sites are: amazon.com, yahoo.com, and many others. Find at least one site that uses image maps and one that does not. Print the home pages of those sites to use as examples. Explain in a paper why you think the use of image maps is appropriate. Also explain why you think the Web site that does not use image maps has other navigation techniques. Submit your paper in the format specified by your instructor.

2: Researching Image Mapping Software

Personal

You are very interested in finding out more information about some of the image mapping software tools listed in Table 5–2 on page HTML 254. Review the information about each tool listed, including any associated costs, free trial version availability, platform(s) supported, and ease of use. If a free trial version is offered at any of the Web sites and you are using your own computer (or your instructor or lab coordinator allows it), download the software and use it to create an image map. Compare the technique of using these tools to the technique used in this chapter using Paint. Write a synopsis of the available products, including any associated costs, free trial version availability, platform(s) supported, and ease of use.

3: Using Image Maps to Link to External Web Sites

Professional

Find images that depict the other rooms in the floor plan used in Lab 3. These images can either be taken during the "building" stage of the house or as the finished product. If you use pictures of the finished product, you may need to change the text in the paragraph on the home page. Create an additional Web page using one of the images (either one of the three provided or a new one). Use that image as an image map and create reasonable hotspots. For instance, you may have a hotspot on the fireplace or a section of the laundry room cabinet that you can zoom in on or use to link to fireplace or cabinet manufacturers.

6 Creating a Form on a Web Page

Objectives

You will have mastered the material in this chapter when you can:

- Define terms related to forms
- Describe the different form controls and their uses
- Use the <form> </form> tags
- Use the <input /> tag
- Create a text box
- Create check boxes
- Create a selection menu with multiple options
- Use the <select> tag
- Use the <option> tag
- Create radio buttons
- Create a textarea box
- Create a Submit button
- Create a Reset button
- Use the <fieldset> and <legend> tags to group form information

6 Creating a Form on a Web Page

Introduction

The goal of the projects completed thus far has been to present information *to* Web site visitors. In this chapter, you will learn how to get information *from* Web site visitors by adding a form for user input.

Using a Web page form for user input reduces the potential for errors because customers enter data or select options from a form included directly on the Web page. A form has input fields to remind users to enter information and limits choices to valid options to avoid incorrect data entry. Forms provide an easy way to collect needed information from Web page visitors.

In this chapter, you will learn how to use HTML to create a form on a Web page. The form will include several controls, including check boxes, a drop-down menu, radio buttons, and text boxes. You will also learn to add Submit and Reset buttons that customers can use to submit the completed form or clear the information previously entered into the form. Finally, you will learn to use the <fieldset> tag to group information on a form in a user-friendly way with the <legend> tag, which is used to add labels to the groups within the form.

Project — Creating Forms on a Web Page

Jin Chen is a music business entrepreneur and lead singer in Blu Wav Music. He and his band play at parties and weddings on the weekends, he has several recordings that music lovers can purchase, and he is a regular guest on a variety of radio shows. Jin wants to get a better idea of what types of music people like to listen to. He also wants to know what radio stations people listen to and where they buy their music. Jin has a Web site that advertises his band and his music. On the Web site, he has a form that visitors can print and fax to him. That effort has not been very successful. He has therefore spoken to you about using a form on the Web to gather information.

The Blu Wav Music Web page form is provided in the Data Files for Students for this chapter. In this project, you will enter HTML tags to modify the static Web page form that the owner of Blu Wav Music, Jin Chen, originally created shown in Figure 6–1a and from it, create a dynamic Web-based form, as shown in Figure 6–1b. This page requests the same information as the static Web page, but is created with a Web-based form that allows users to enter data, select options, and then submit the form to an e-mail address.

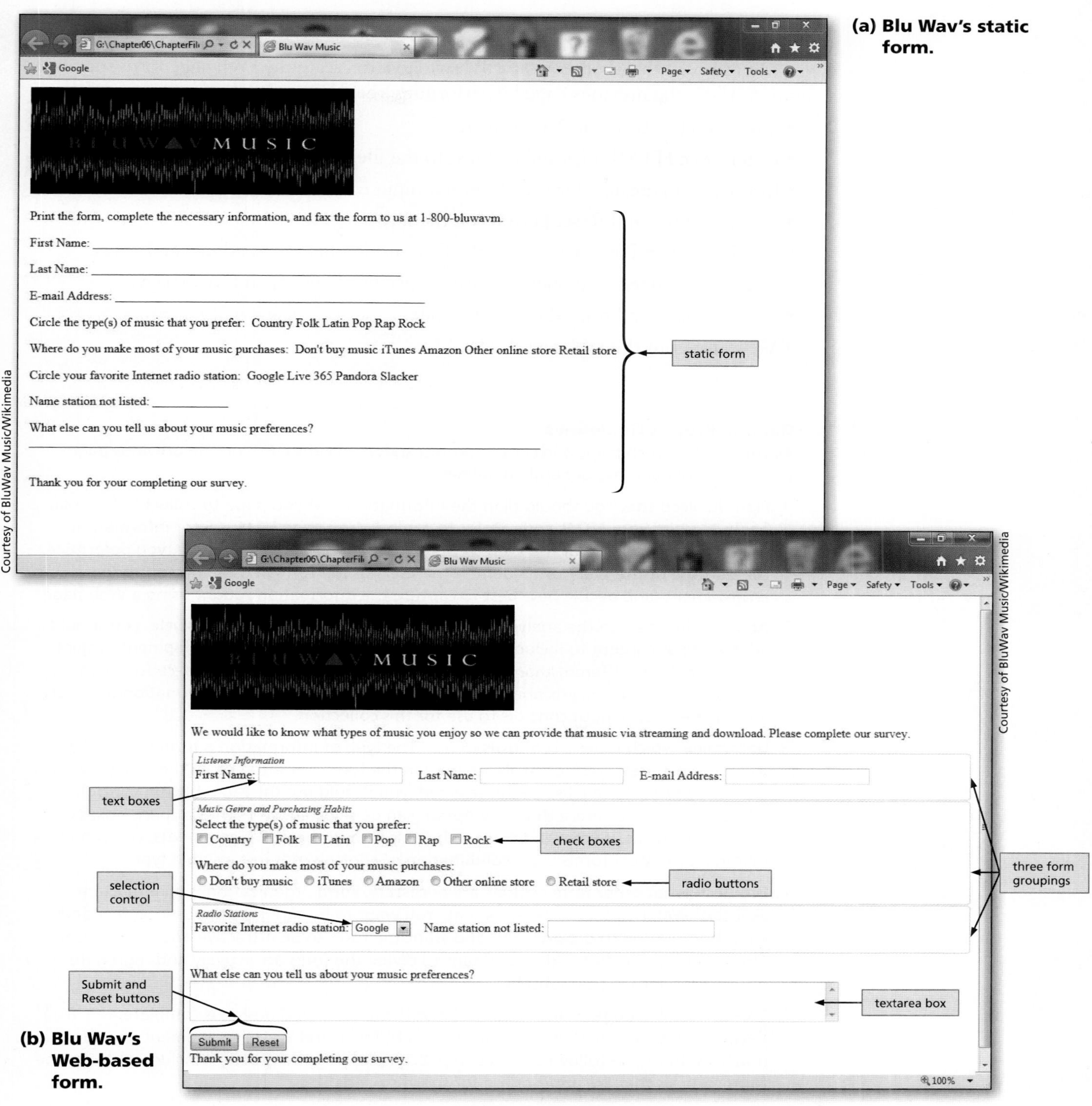
(a) Blu Wav's static form.
Print the form, complete the necessary information, and fax the form to us at 1-800-bluwavm.
First Name:
Last Name:
E-mail Address:
Circle the type(s) of music that you prefer: Country Folk Latin Pop Rap Rock
Where do you make most of your music purchases: Don't buy music iTunes Amazon Other online store Retail store
Circle your favorite Internet radio station: Google Live 365 Pandora Slacker
Name station not listed:
What else can you tell us about your music preferences?
Thank you for your completing our survey.
static form
Courtesy of BluWav Music/Wikimedia
We would like to know what types of music you enjoy so we can provide that music via streaming and download. Please complete our survey.
Listener Information
First Name:
Last Name:
E-mail Address:
Music Genre and Purchasing Habits
Select the type(s) of music that you prefer:
Country Folk Latin Pop Rap Rock
Where do you make most of your music purchases:
Don't buy music iTunes Amazon Other online store Retail store
Radio Stations
Favorite Internet radio station: Google
Name station not listed:
What else can you tell us about your music preferences?
Submit Reset
Thank you for your completing our survey.
text boxes
check boxes
selection control
radio buttons
three form groupings
Submit and Reset buttons
textarea box
(b) Blu Wav's Web-based form.
Courtesy of BluWav Music/Wikimedia

Figure 6–1

Overview

As you read this chapter, you will learn how to create the Web page form shown in Figure 6–1b on the previous page by performing these general tasks:

- Open an HTML file in Notepad++.
- Enter basic HTML tags and add text to the file.
- Insert tags to create a form with several input controls.
- Create Submit and Reset buttons on the form.
- Add interest and organization to the form using <fieldset> and <legend> tags.
- Add an embedded style sheet to format specific elements on a Web page.
- Save, validate, and print the HTML code.
- View and print the Web pages.

Plan Ahead

General Project Guidelines

As you create a Web page, such as the project shown in Figure 6–1 on the previous page, you should follow these general guidelines:

1. **Plan the Web site.** You should plan the information that you hope to collect before you begin to write your HTML code. Refer to Table 1–4 on page HTML 15 for information on the planning phase of the Web Development Life Cycle. In this phase, you determine the purpose of the Web form, identify the users of the form and their computing environment, and decide how best to capture the information sought using a Web page.
2. **Analyze the need.** In the analysis phase of the Web Development Life Cycle, you should analyze what content to include in the Web page form. The Web development project in this chapter is different than the ones completed in other chapters because it contains a form. Part of the analysis phase then includes determining what information to collect and the best form input controls to use for this collection.
3. **Determine which types of controls to use.** The type of information a form is intended to gather dictates which controls are used in the form. For instance, in the case in which only one option from a list can be selected, you should use the radio button control. In the case in which more than one option can be selected, you can use check boxes or selection controls. If you want users to be able to add their own comments, you can use a textarea box. Most forms use a combination of controls, not just a single type.
4. **Establish what other form options are necessary.** Form organization is an important aspect of Web page form development. You want to be sure that the user understands what information to provide. You also want the form to be attractive and easy to use. Consider using fieldset and legend tags to divide the form attractively and segregate information into logical subsets.
5. **Create the Web page form and links.** Once the analysis and design is complete, the Web developer creates the Web page form using HTML. Good Web development standard practices should be followed in this step. Examples of good practices include utilizing the form controls that are appropriate for specific needs.
6. **Test the Web page form.** An important part of Web development is testing to ensure that you are following the standards recommended in the early chapters of this book. In this book, we use the World Wide Web Consortium (W3C) validator that allows you to test your Web page and clearly explains any errors you have. Additionally when testing, you should verify that all controls work as intended. Finally, both the Submit and the Reset buttons should be tested.

When necessary, more specific details concerning the above guidelines are presented at appropriate points in the chapter. The chapter will also identify the actions performed and decisions made regarding these guidelines during the creation of the Web page shown in Figure 6–1.

Web Page Forms

The Blu Wav Music Web page form shown in Figure 6–1b on page HTML 285 shows an example of a dynamic Web page form designed to request specific information from the Web page visitor. A Web page form has three main components:

- Input controls
- A <form> tag, which contains the information necessary to process the form
- A Submit button, which sends the data to be processed

Input Controls

An **input control** is any type of input mechanism on a form. A form may contain several different input controls classified as data or text input controls. Most controls are defined in an HTML form by using the type attribute of the <input /> tag. A **data input control** can be a radio button (radio), a check box (checkbox), a Submit button (submit), a Reset button (reset), or a selection menu (select). A **text input control** allows the user to enter text through the following:

- A **text box** (text), for small amounts of text
- A **textarea box** (textarea), for larger amounts of text
- A **password text box** (password), for entering a password

BTW

Forms

Several HTML guides on the Internet discuss the use of forms on Web pages. Many of these sites are created and maintained at universities. The guides give practical tips on the purpose and use of HTML tags and attributes. To view an HTML guide, use a search engine to search for the phrase "HTML form guide" or a related phrase.

As shown in Figure 6–1b, the form developed in this chapter uses several different data and text input controls.

Of the available input controls, the eight listed in Table 6–1 are used most often in form creation.

Table 6–1 Form Input Controls

Control	Function	Remarks
text	• Creates a single-line field for a relatively small amount of text	• Indicates both the size of the field and the total maximum length
password	• Identical to text boxes used for single-line data entry	• Echoes (or masks) the entered text as bullets
textarea	• Creates a multiple-line field for a relatively large amount of text	• Indicates the number of rows and columns for the area
select	• Creates a drop-down menu of choices from which a visitor can select an option or options	• Indicates the length of the list in number of rows
checkbox	• Creates a single item or a list of items	• Indicates a single item that can be checked • Indicates a list of more than one item that can be chosen
radio	• Creates a list item	• Indicates only one item in a list can be chosen
submit	• Submits a form for processing	• Tells the browser to send the data on the form to the server
reset	• Resets the form	• Returns all input controls to the default status

A **text control** creates a text box that is used for a single line of input (Figure 6–2 on the next page). The text control has two attributes:

- **size**, which determines the number of characters that are displayed on the form
- **maxlength**, which specifies the maximum length of the input field

For example, the first line of the code below creates a text box to input the user's last name and the second line creates a text box to input the user's password:

```
<p>Last Name: <input name="lastname" type="text" size="25" /></p>
<p>Password: <input name="password" type="password" size="12" /></p>
```

A **password control** also creates a text box used for a single line of input (Figure 6–2), except that the characters entered into the field can appear as asterisks or bullets. A password text box holds the password entered by a visitor. The password appears as a series of characters, asterisks, or bullets as determined by the Web developer, one per character for the password entered. This feature is designed to help protect the visitor's password from being observed by others as it is being entered.

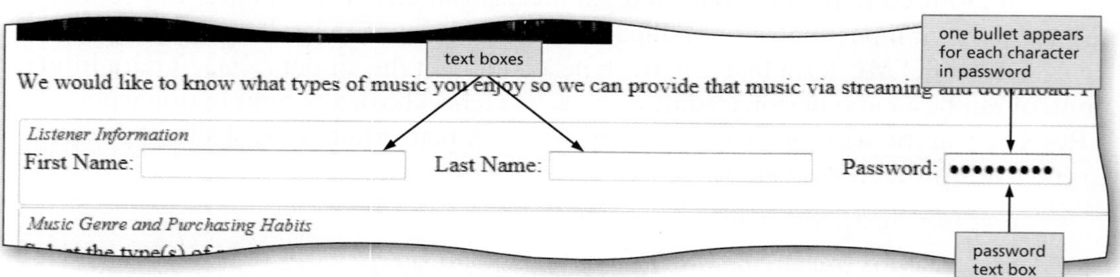

Figure 6–2 Text and password text controls.

The maximum length of the field may exceed the size of the field that appears on the form. For example, consider a field size of three characters and a maximum length of nine characters. If a Web page visitor types in more characters than the size of the text box (three characters), the characters scroll to the left, to a maximum of nine characters entered.

A **checkbox control** allows a Web page visitor to (a) select one item from a single-item list or (b) select more than one choice from a list of choices (Figure 6–3). Each choice in a check box list can be either on or off. By default, all check boxes are deselected. The default can be changed so a particular check box is preselected as the default, by using the checked attribute and value (checked="checked") within the <input /> tag. Here is sample code for a checkbox control. The first sample shows how to create a check box for the type choice Country music. The second sample code shows that the Folk music type is selected (or checked) when the Web page is loaded.

```
<input name="musictype" type="checkbox" value="country"
/>Country

<input name="musictype" type="checkbox" checked="checked"
value="folk" />Folk
```

> **BTW**
> **Radio Buttons**
> Old-time car radios were operated by a row of large black plastic buttons. Push one button, and you would get one preset radio station. You could push only one button at a time. Radio buttons on forms work the same way as the old-time radio buttons—one button at a time. With check boxes, more than one option can be selected at a time.

A **radio control** limits the Web page visitor to only one choice from a list of choices (Figure 6–3). Each choice is preceded by a **radio button**, or option button, which typically appears as an open circle. When the visitor selects one of the radio buttons, all other radio buttons in the list are automatically deselected. By default, all radio buttons are deselected. To set a particular button as the default, you use the checked value within the <input /> tag. Here is the sample code to create two radio controls:

```
<input name="purchases" type="radio" value="none" />Don't buy music
<input name="purchases" type="radio" value="itunes" />iTunes
```

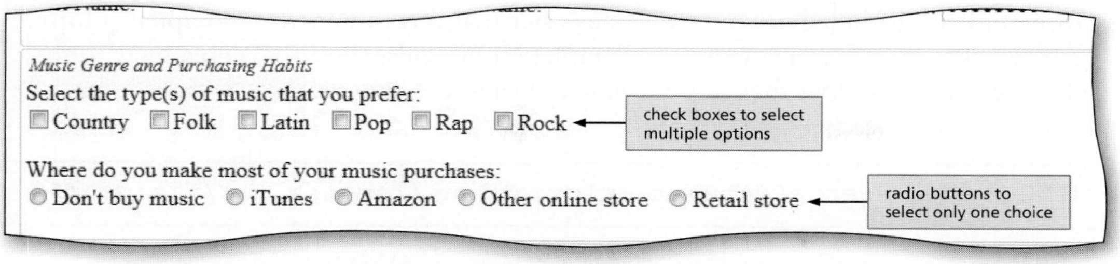

Figure 6–3 Checkbox and radio button controls.

A **select control** creates a selection menu from which the visitor selects one or more choices (Figure 6–4). This prevents the visitor from having to type information into a text or textarea field. A select control is suitable when a limited number of choices are available. The user clicks the list arrow to view all the choices in the menu. When clicked, the default appears first and is highlighted to indicate that it is selected. The select control does not use the <input /> tag, but rather the <select> and <option> tags. Here is sample code for a select control:

```
<select name="station">
     <option>Google</option>
     <option>Live 365</option>
     <option>Pandora</option>
     <option>Slacker</option>
</select>
```

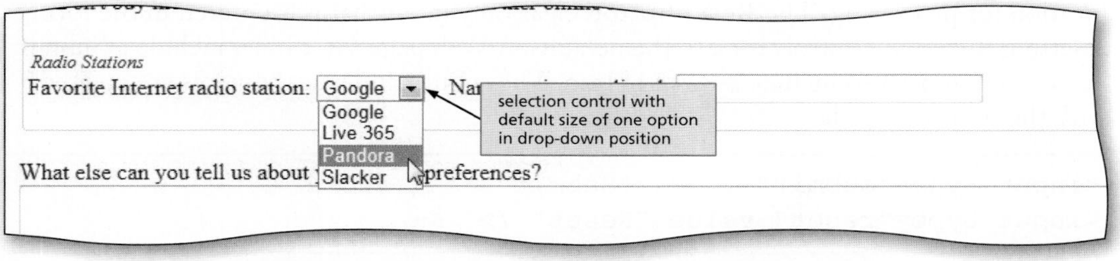

Figure 6–4 Different options for selection controls.

A **textarea control** creates a field that allows multiple lines of input (Figure 6–5). Textarea fields are useful when an extensive amount of input is required from, or desired of, a Web page visitor. Note that the textarea control uses the <textarea> tag instead of the <input /> tag. There are six new textarea attributes with HTML5. These are all listed in Appendix A. In addition to these, the textarea control has two primary attributes:

- **rows**, which specifies the number of rows in the textarea field
- **cols**, which specifies the number of columns in the textarea field

A textarea control is created with the following code:

```
What else can you tell us about your music preferences?
<textarea name="other" rows="3" cols="100"></textarea>
```

The **fieldset control** (Figure 6–5 on the next page) is not an input control but helps to group related form elements together. This makes the form easier to read and complete. The form segment in Figure 6–5 shows three groupings: two with left-aligned legends and one with a right-aligned legend. Using fieldset tags to segregate information immediately allows the Web page visitor to see that two (or more) categories of

> **BTW**
> **Textareas**
> To create a textarea, the Web developer specifies the number of rows and columns in which the Web page visitor can enter information. You can specify the dimensions using the rows and cols attributes within the textarea tag. You can also use CSS height and width properties to set the dimensions. The maximum number of characters for a textarea is 32,700. It is a good rule to keep the number of columns in a textarea to 50 or fewer. Using that as a limit, the textarea will fit on most screens.

information are included in the form. The easier that it is for a user to complete a form, the more likely it is that he or she will complete it. A fieldset control is created with the following code; note that the ... in the code indicates the area in which various input controls would be coded:

```
<fieldset><legend>Listener Information</legend>...</fieldset>
```

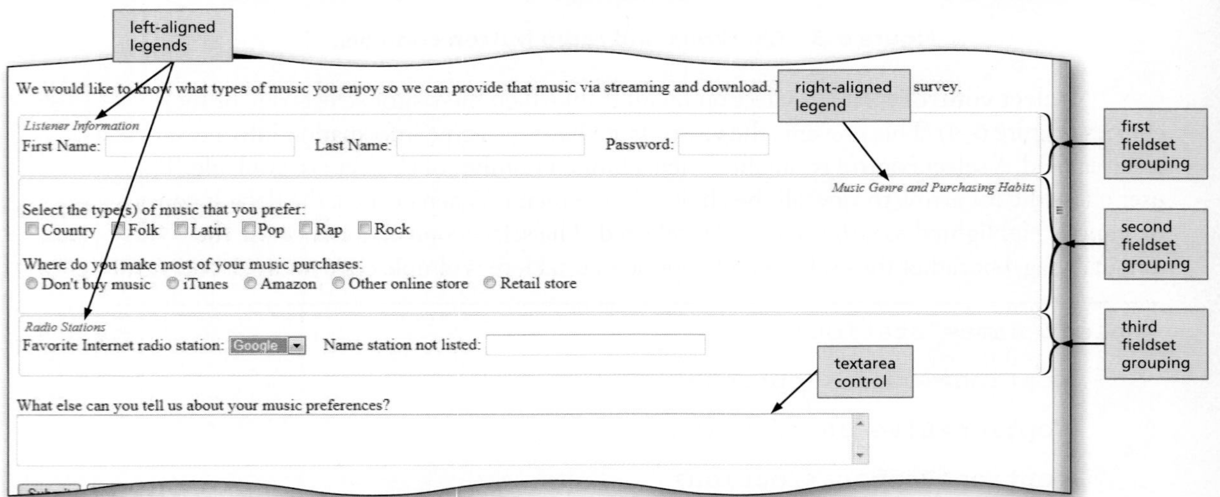

Figure 6–5 Fieldset and textarea controls.

The **submit control** and the **reset control** create the Submit and Reset buttons, respectively (Figure 6–6). The **Submit button** sends the information to the appropriate location for processing. The **Reset button** clears any input that was entered in the form, resetting the input controls back to the defaults. A Web page form must include a Submit button, and most also include a Reset button. The submit and reset controls are created with the following code:

```
<input type="submit" value="Submit" />
<input type="reset" value="Reset" />
```

Submit and Reset buttons

Submit Reset

Thank you for your completing our survey.

Figure 6–6 Submit and Reset button controls.

Regardless of the specific type, each input control has one or two attributes that are used more frequently than the others:

- **name**, which identifies the specific information that is being sent when the form is submitted for processing. All controls have a name.
- **value**, which is the type of data that is contained in the named input control (that is, the data that the Web page visitor enters). All controls except textarea also have a value attribute. For a textarea field, no value attribute is possible because of the variability of the input.

When a Web page visitor clicks the Submit button on the form, both the control name and the value of the data contained within that control are sent to the server to be processed.

HTML Tags Used to Create Forms

Form statements start with the <form> tag and end with the </form> tag. The input controls in a form are created using either HTML tags or attributes of HTML tags. For example, the select and textarea controls are created using the HTML tags <select> and <textarea>, respectively. Other input controls are created using attributes of HTML tags. For example, the text boxes, check boxes, radio buttons, and Submit and Reset buttons all are created using the type attribute of the <input /> tag. Table 6–2 lists the HTML tags used to create the form in this chapter. Any combination of these elements can be used in a Web page form.

Table 6–2 HTML Tags Used to Create Forms

Tag	Function	Remarks
<fieldset> </fieldset>	Groups related controls on a form	Optionally used for readability
<form> </form>	Creates a form that allows user input	Required when creating forms
<input />	Defines the controls used in the form, using a variety of type attribute values	Required for input controls
<legend> </legend>	Defines the caption that is displayed in the grouping borders	Optionally used when using <fieldset> tags
<option> </option>	Specifies a choice in a <select> tag	Required, one per choice
<select> </select>	Creates a menu of choices from which a visitor selects	Required for selection choices
<textarea> </textarea>	Creates a multiple-line text input area	Required for longer text inputs that appear on several lines

Attributes of HTML Tags Used to Create Forms

Many of the HTML tags used to create forms have several attributes. Table 6–3 lists some of the HTML tags used to create forms, along with their main attributes and functions. All tags and attributes are listed in Appendix A. HTML5 includes new attributes for the <input /> tag. Many of these are not yet supported by browsers, however.

Table 6–3 Attributes and Functions of HTML Tags Used to Create Forms

Tag	Attribute	Function
<form> </form>	action	• URL for action completed by the server
	method	• HTTP method (post)
	target	• Location at which the resource will be displayed
<input />	alt	• Alternative text for an image control
	checked	• Sets a radio button or check box to a checked state (only one can be checked)
	disabled	• Disables a control
	maxlength	• Maximum number of characters that can be entered
	name	• Name of the control
	readonly	• Specifies that an element should be read-only; meaning not editable; can be used with value attribute so text box or other input control has content
	size	• Number of characters of an <input /> element that appear on the form
	src	• Specifies the URL of an image to use as a submit button
	type	• Type of input control (text, password, checkbox, radio, submit, reset, file, hidden, image, button, among others)
	value	• Value submitted if a control is selected (required for radio and checkbox controls)

Table 6–3 Attributes and Functions of HTML Tags Used to Create Forms (continued)

Tag	Attribute	Function
<option> </option>	selected disabled value	• Specifies whether an option is selected • Disables a control • Value submitted if a control is selected
<select> </select>	name size multiple disabled	• Name of the element • Number of visible options in the select list • Allows for multiple selections in select list • Disables a control
<textarea> </textarea>	name rows cols disabled readonly	• Name of the control • Height in number of rows • Width in number of columns • Disables a control • Specifies that a text area should be read-only; meaning not editable; can be used with value attribute so text box or other input control has content

Creating a Form on a Web Page

In this chapter, you will modify the static Web page form used in the Blu Wav Music Web site. The file, bluwavform.html, currently contains only text and does not utilize a form or form controls (Figure 6–1a on page HTML 285). Using this static form is inconvenient for the user, who must print the form, complete the required information, and then fax that information to the phone number listed in the opening paragraph of text.

The file, bluwavform.html, is stored in the Data Files for Students for this chapter. See the inside back cover of this book for instructions on downloading the Data Files for Students, or contact your instructor for information about accessing the required file. After opening this file in Notepad++, you will enter HTML code to convert this static Web page into the dynamic Web page form shown in Figure 6–1b on page HTML 285.

Plan Ahead

Processing form information.
One of the most important issues to determine when creating a Web page form is what to do with the information once it is entered. One way to process the information is to use a CGI script, which is code that has been previously written in a language other than HTML. The information collected from forms is often used to feed databases. A CGI script provides a much better way to process that information. For the scope of this book, we use the second method to process information, the post. The post can be used to send the information to an e-mail address.

- **Using a CGI script.** This action is beyond the scope of this book, but it is the more efficient way to handle the information input into the Web page form. A Web developer would have to find out what script capabilities reside on the server in order to utilize it.
- **Posting to an e-mail address.** Because we do not know what CGI scripts are available on the Web servers at your location, we will utilize the e-mail posting technique in this chapter. The information posted to an e-mail address is not readily usable, so other steps will have to be taken to utilize the data coming in via an e-mail message.

To Start Notepad++ and Open an HTML File

The following steps start Notepad++ and open the HTML file, bluwavform.html.

1. Start Notepad++ and, if necessary, maximize the window.
2. With a USB drive plugged into your computer, click File on the menu bar and then click Open.
3. If necessary, navigate to the Chapter06\ChapterFiles folder on the USB drive.
4. Click bluwavform.html in the list of files.
5. Click the Open button to open the bluwavform.html file in Notepad++ (Figure 6–7).

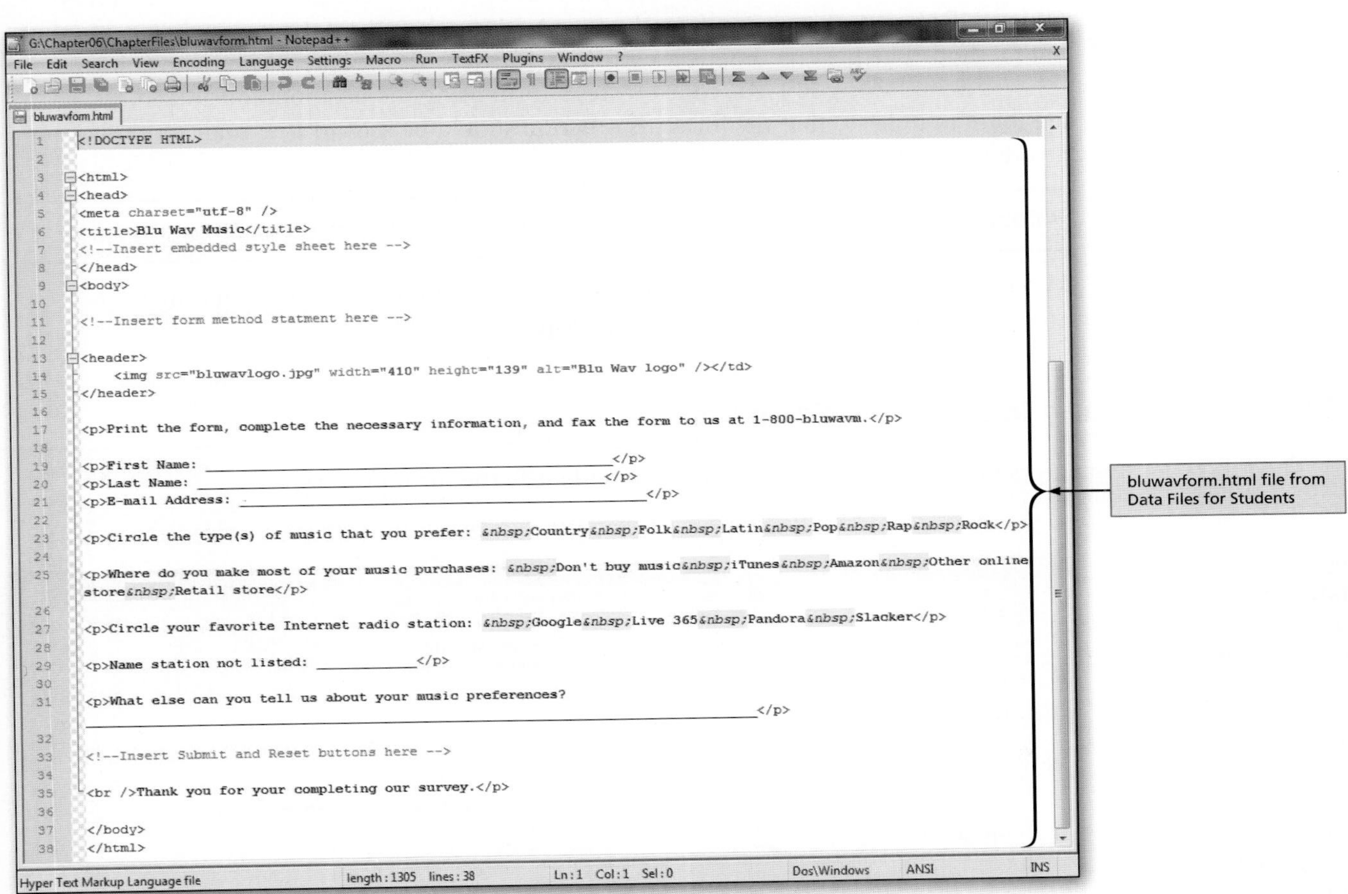

```
<!DOCTYPE HTML>

<html>
<head>
<meta charset="utf-8" />
<title>Blu Wav Music</title>
<!--Insert embedded style sheet here -->
</head>
<body>

<!--Insert form method statment here -->

<header>
    <img src="bluwavlogo.jpg" width="410" height="139" alt="Blu Wav logo" /></td>
</header>

<p>Print the form, complete the necessary information, and fax the form to us at 1-800-bluwavm.</p>

<p>First Name: ________________________________________________</p>
<p>Last Name: ________________________________________________</p>
<p>E-mail Address: _____________________________________________</p>

<p>Circle the type(s) of music that you prefer:  Country Folk Latin Pop Rap Rock</p>

<p>Where do you make most of your music purchases:  Don't buy music iTunes Amazon Other online store Retail store</p>

<p>Circle your favorite Internet radio station:  Google Live 365 Pandora Slacker</p>

<p>Name station not listed: ____________</p>

<p>What else can you tell us about your music preferences?
________________________________________________________________________________</p>

<!--Insert Submit and Reset buttons here -->

<br />Thank you for your completing our survey.</p>

</body>
</html>
```


Figure 6–7

Creating a Form and Identifying the Form Process

When adding a form to a Web page, the first steps are creating the form and identifying how the form is processed when it is submitted. The start <form> and end </form> tags designate an area of a Web page as a form. Between the <form> and </form> tags, form controls can be added to request different types of information and allow the appropriate input responses. A form can include any number of controls.

The **action attribute** of the <form> tag specifies the action that is taken when the form is submitted. Information entered in forms can be sent by e-mail to an e-mail address or can be used to update a database. Although the e-mail option is functional, many Web sites process information from forms using Common Gateway Interface (CGI) scripting.

BTW

CGI Scripts
Using CGI scripts to process forms is a much more efficient way to handle the data that is sent from a form. Many Web sites have free sample CGI scripts for Web developers to use. Search the Web for relevant CGI information and free samples.

A **CGI script** is a program written in a programming language (such as PHP or Perl) that communicates with the Web server. The CGI script sends the information input on the Web page form to the server for processing. Because this type of processing involves programming tasks that are beyond the scope of this book, the information entered in the form created in this chapter will be submitted in a file to an e-mail address. The e-mail address will be specified as the action attribute value in the <form> tag.

> **BTW** **Mailto Restrictions**
> Some schools and organizations restrict the use of the mailto action. This is something that you need to test in order to determine whether it will work in your situation.

The **method attribute** of the <form> tag specifies the manner in which the data entered in the form is sent to the server to be processed. Two primary ways are used in HTML: the get method and the post method. The **get method** sends the name-value pairs to the end of the URL indicated in the action attribute. The **post method** sends a separate data file with the name-value pairs to the URL (or e-mail address) indicated in the action attribute. Most Web developers prefer the post method because it is much more flexible. You need to be cautious when using the get method. Some Web servers limit a URL's size, so you run the risk of truncating relevant information when using the get method. The post method is used for the forms in this chapter.

The following HTML code creates a form using the post method and an action attribute to indicate that the form information should be sent to an e-mail address in an attached data file:

```
<form method="post" action="mailto:bluwav@isp.com">
```

When the form is submitted, a file containing the input data is sent as an e-mail attachment to the e-mail address bluwav@isp.com.

To Create a Form and Identify the Form Process

The following step enters HTML code to create a form and identify the form process.

1

- Highlight the statement <!--Insert form method statement here --> on line 11.
- Type `<form method="post" action="mailto:bluwav@isp.com">` to replace the highlighted statement with the new tag.
- Click the blank line 36 and press the ENTER key.
- Type `</form>` but do not press the ENTER key (Figure 6–8).

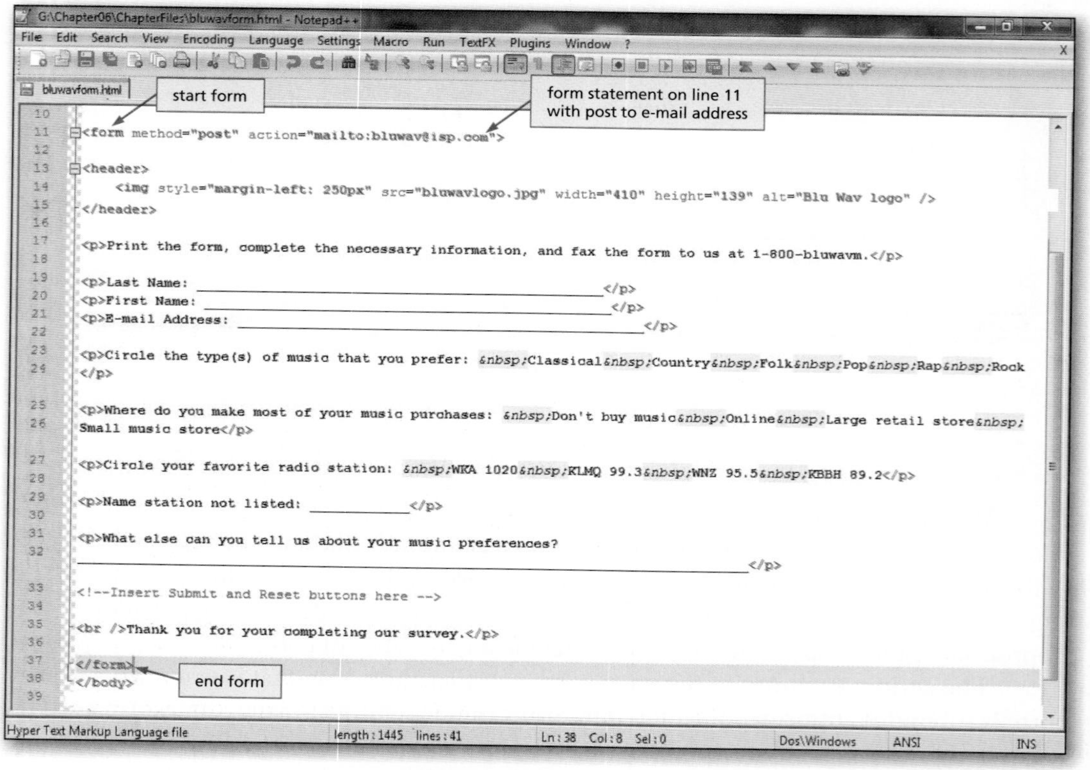

start form

form statement on line 11 with post to e-mail address

end form

Figure 6–8

To Change the Text Message

The next step in updating the static Web page form is to modify the text that tells the user to submit the questionnaire by fax. Notice that Blu Wav logo is already in the file on line 14. Table 6–4 shows the new HTML code used to provide information to users on the purpose of the form.

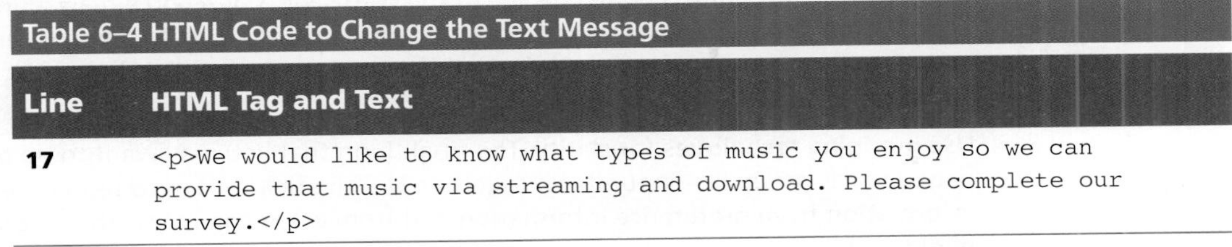

Table 6–4 HTML Code to Change the Text Message

Line	HTML Tag and Text
17	`<p>We would like to know what types of music you enjoy so we can provide that music via streaming and download. Please complete our survey.</p>`

The following step changes the text message to provide instructions on how to use the form.

1

- Highlight line 17.
- Enter the HTML code shown in Table 6–4, but do not press the ENTER key (Figure 6–9).
- Highlight lines 19 through 32 and then press the DELETE key; the cursor should then be positioned on line 19 (Figure 6–9).

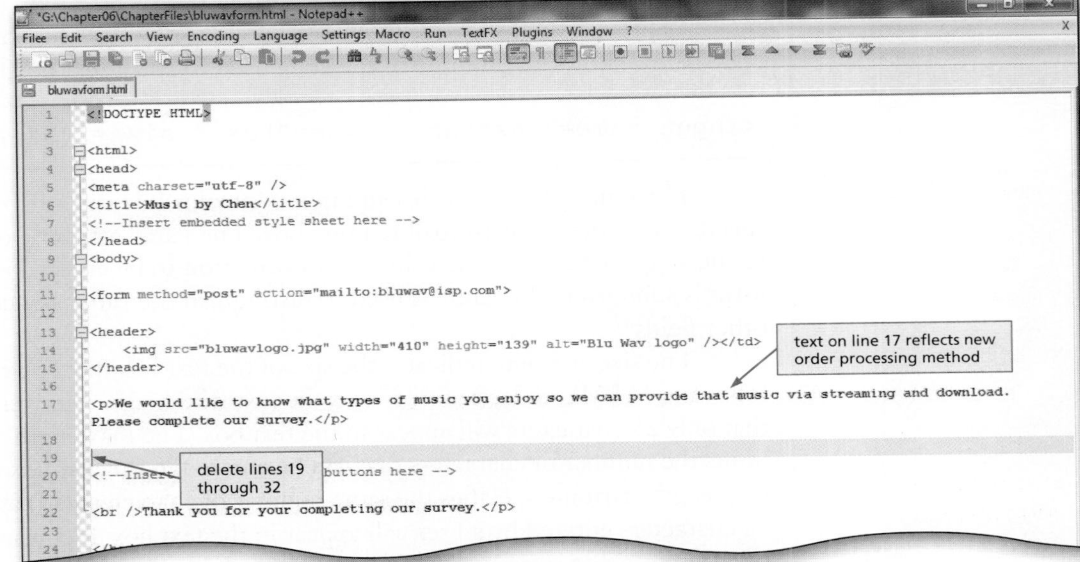

Figure 6–9

Plan Ahead

Form controls.

Before creating a Web page form, you should plan how you want to format it. By effectively utilizing input controls, you can call attention to important data-collection areas on the Web page without overpowering it. Creating an effective form includes:

1. **Determine what data to collect.** In the case of a form designed to collect information, you need the visitor's name and e-mail address. Make sure to provide enough space for each field so that you do not cut out important information. For instance, a last name field only 5 characters long may cut out much of a person's last name.
2. **Determine what types of control to use.** For data such as name and e-mail address, you need text input areas. For data such as favorite Internet radio station, there is generally a limited subset (e.g., Google, Live 365, Pandora, and Slacker), so a selection control is appropriate. When you ask what kind of music the visitor is interested in listening to or buying, you can use check boxes, which allow multiple selection. In the case of a question with only one appropriate answer (e.g., select your favorite), a radio button is more appropriate.

(continued)

(continued)

3. **Lay out the input areas effectively.** One of the first input items you may want is the visitor's name and e-mail address information. That should go to the top of the page. Also, you can group information together on the same line if it makes sense to make the Web page form short enough that visitors do not have to scroll much. Notice in our form that the last name/first name/e-mail address are on one line of the Web page. Collecting e-mail addresses is a great way to continue communication with visitors or customers. A company can e-mail newsletters, coupons, and general information to customers once they have their e-mail addresses.
4. **Use grouping techniques for clarity.** The final thing that you may want to do on a Web page form is group like input items together. Use the fieldset tag to segregate personal information from preference information and from other comments that the visitor might make.

Adding Text Boxes

As previously discussed, a text box allows for a single line of input. The HTML code below shows an example of the code used to add a text box to a form:

```
<input name="lastname" type="text" size="25" />
```

The <input /> tag creates an input control, while the attribute and value type="text" specifies that the input control is a text box. The name attribute of the input control is set to the value lastname, to describe the information to be entered in this text box. When the form is submitted, the name is used to distinguish the value associated with that field from other fields.

The size attribute indicates the size of the text box that appears on the form. In the following HTML code, size="25" sets the text field to 25 characters in length, which means that only 25 characters will appear in the text box. The maxlength attribute maxlength="25" limits the number of characters that can be entered in the text box to 25 characters. The maxlength attribute specifies the same number of characters (25) as the size attribute (25), so all characters entered by a user will appear in the text box. If you specify a maximum number of characters that is greater than the number of characters specified in the size attribute, the additional characters scroll to the right in the text box as the user enters them.

To Add Text Boxes

The next step in creating the form is to add three text boxes to the form for users to enter last name, first name, and e-mail address. Table 6–5 shows the HTML code to add three text boxes to the form. Each text box has a size of 25 characters so that you provide enough room for your visitor to add the information. No maxlength attribute is specified, which means users can enter text items longer than 25 characters, but only 25 characters will display in the text box. As you learned in the last chapter, the special character   (nonbreaking space) is used to provide space between the text boxes and the labels.

Table 6–5 HTML Code to Add Text Boxes

Line	HTML Tag and Text
19	`<p>First Name: <input name="firstname" type="text" size="25" />    `
20	`Last Name: <input name="lastname" type="text" size="25" />    `
21	`E-mail Address: <input name="email" type="text" size="25" /></p>`

The following step adds text boxes to the form.

1

- If necessary, click line 19 and indent one TAB stop.
- Enter the HTML code shown in Table 6–5 and then press the ENTER key twice (Figure 6–10).

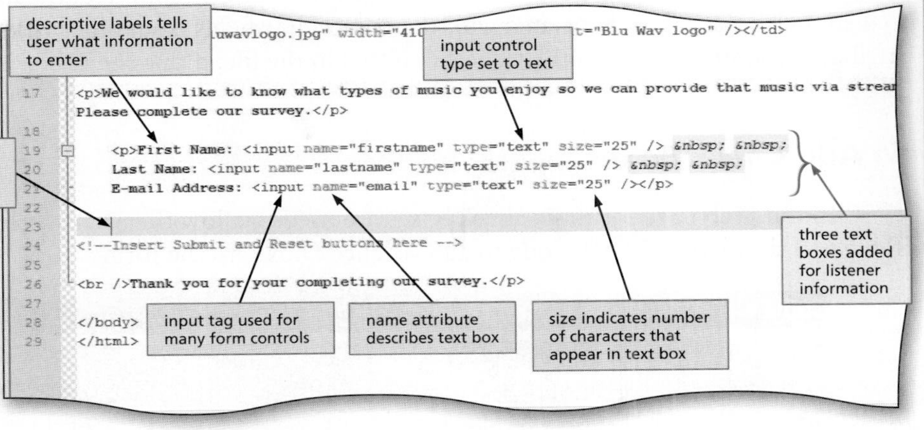

Q&A How do I know what size to make each field?

Determine a reasonable field size for the various input areas. For instance, it would not be wise to allow only 10 characters for the last name, because last names can be more than 10 characters. To improve your judgment for field sizes, observe online and paper forms that you complete. Also, think of long street or city names and try those in the forms that you create.

Q&A What is the default value if I do not specify the type in my <input /> tag?

The default type for the <input /> tag is a text box. Therefore, if the type attribute is not used in the <input /> tag, it creates a text box.

Figure 6–10

To Save an HTML File

Because you opened a file that was already created, you can press the CTRL+S keys to save what you have done so far. Do this frequently throughout your projects.

1 With the USB flash drive connected to one of the computer's USB ports, hold down the CTRL key and then press the S key.

Other Ways

1. Click File, then Save
2. Click Save icon on Notepad++ toolbar

Adding Check Boxes

The next step is to add six check boxes to the form. Check boxes are similar to radio buttons, except they allow multiple options to be selected. Radio buttons should be used when only one option can be selected, while check boxes should be used when the user can select more than one option.

The HTML code below shows an example of the code used to add a check box to a form:

```
<input name="musictype" type="checkbox" value="country"
/>Country
```

The <input /> tag creates an input control, while the attribute and value type="checkbox" specifies that the input control is a check box. The name attribute of the input control is set to the value musictype. When the form is submitted, the name is used to distinguish the values associated with these checkbox fields from other fields. The value attribute "country" indicates the value submitted in the file, if this check box is selected.

To Add Check Boxes

In the Web page form, six check boxes are used to allow the user to select one or more types of music to add. Table 6–6 shows the HTML code to add six check boxes to the form.

Table 6–6 HTML Code to Add Check Boxes

Line	HTML Tag and Text
23	` Select the type(s) of music that you prefer:`
24	` <input name="musictype" type="checkbox" value="country" />Country  `
25	`<input name="musictype" type="checkbox" value="folk" />Folk  `
26	`<input name="musictype" type="checkbox" value="latin" />Latin  `
27	`<input name="musictype" type="checkbox" value="pop" />Pop  `
28	`<input name="musictype" type="checkbox" value="rap" />Rap  `
29	`<input name="musictype" type="checkbox" value="rock" />Rock`

The following step enters HTML code to add check boxes to the form.

1

- Check that the insertion point is on Line 23 and indented one Tab stop.
- Enter the HTML code shown in Table 6–6 and then press the ENTER key twice (Figure 6–11).

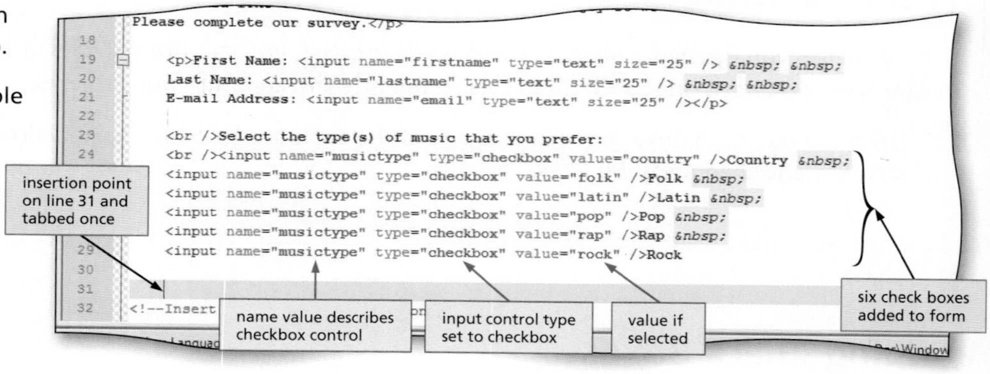

Figure 6–11

Q&A How do I determine whether to list fields on the same line or use a line break or paragraph break between fields?

Consider the "real estate" (the amount of space available) of the Web page itself. If you have an especially long form that the visitor has to scroll down, consider positioning the fields across, rather than down the form. You do not want to crowd the information, but you also do not want to force the visitor to scroll excessively.

Adding Radio Buttons

The next step is to add radio buttons to the form. Remember that radio buttons are appropriate to use when a user can select only one choice from a set of two or more choices. Although questions with a Yes or No answer are perfect for the use of radio buttons, other types of questions are appropriate as well. In the case of selecting where they make most of their music purchases, users are asked to select one choice from five options. On the Web page form radio buttons allow users to select a one-choice answer to a question.

To Add Radio Buttons

Table 6–7 contains the HTML code to add a set of radio buttons to the Web page form.

Table 6–7 HTML Code to Add Radio Buttons

Line	HTML Tag and Text
31	<p>Where do you make most of your music purchases:
32	 <input name="purchases" type="radio" value="none" />Don't buy music
33	<input name="purchases" type="radio" value="itunes" />iTunes
34	<input name="purchases" type="radio" value="amazon" />Amazon
35	<input name="purchases" type="radio" value="online" />Other online store
36	<input name="purchases" type="radio" value="retail" />Retail store
37	</p>

The following step adds three sets of radio buttons to the form.

1

- Check that the insertion point is on Line 31, and indented one Tab stop.
- Enter the HTML code shown in Table 6–7 and then press the ENTER key twice (Figure 6–12).

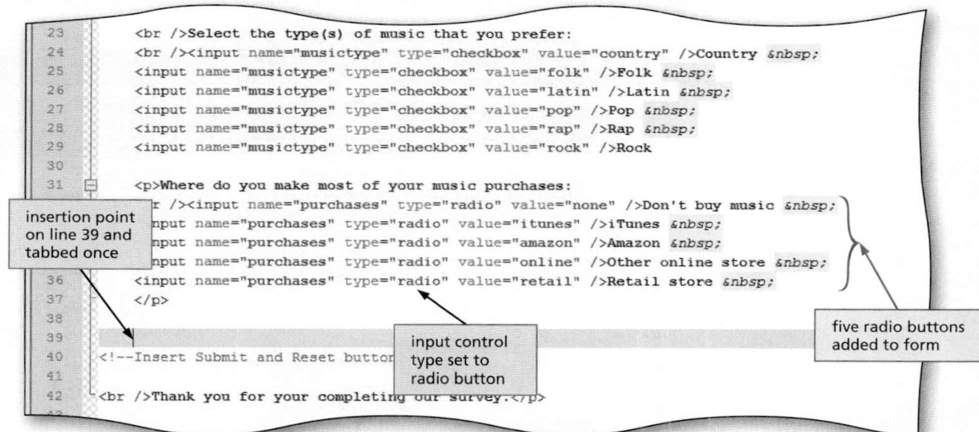

Figure 6–12

Q&A Could I have used check boxes for this control, rather than radio buttons?

You could have used check boxes, but it would not make sense for this information. In this case, a single option is appropriate, one choice as the user's favorite. When you use check boxes in a form, users will assume that they can make multiple selections. Make a point of becoming familiar with the user interface standards used in most Web development.

Adding a Selection Menu

A select control is used to create a selection menu from which the visitor selects one or more choices. A select control is suitable when a limited number of choices are available. Figure 6–13 on the next page shows the basic selection menu used in the form, with four Internet radio stations (Google, Live 365, Pandora, and Slacker) as the choices in the list. Because this is a short list (four items), you could have used radio buttons for the same purpose. Selection menus are often used in lieu of check boxes because of limited "real estate" (or space) on the Web page. Selection boxes are often used for credit card information because there is a limited number of credit card networks. The topic of accepting credit cards via online forms is a serious one. See BTW on this page for more information.

BTW **Security**
Security is an important issue to understand, especially when you are collecting credit card information. Search the Web for specific information concerning the usage of the SSL-encrypted HTTPS protocol versus the unencrypted HTTP protocol.

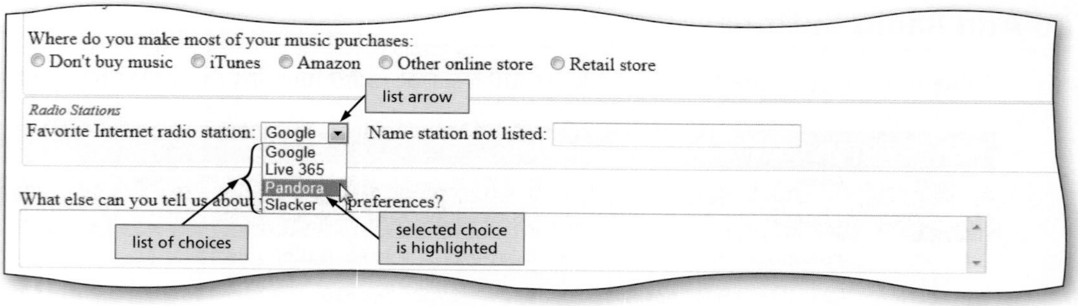

Figure 6–13 Select control.

If you do not specify a size attribute in the <select> tag, only one option is displayed, along with a list arrow, as shown in Figure 6–13. When the list arrow is clicked, the selection menu displays all the selection options. When the user selects an option, such as Pandora, in the list, it appears as highlighted.

To Add a Selection Menu

Table 6–8 shows the HTML code used to create the selection menu shown in Figure 6–13.

Table 6–8 HTML Code to Add a Selection Menu

Line	HTML Tag and Text
39	<p>Favorite Internet radio station:
40	<select name="station">
41	<option>Google</option>
42	<option>Live 365</option>
43	<option>Pandora</option>
44	<option>Slacker</option>
45	</select>

The following step adds a selection menu to the Web page form.

1

- Check that the insertion point is on Line 39, indented one Tab stop.
- Enter the HTML code shown in Table 6–8 and then press the ENTER key twice (Figure 6–14).

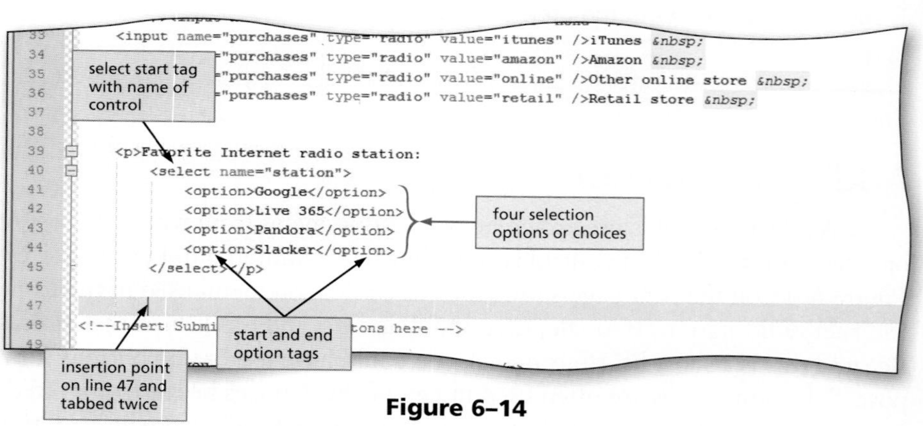

Q&A How do I know what control type to use?

Consider the Web page "real estate," together with usability. If you have 20 options, it may not make sense to use a select control. With the four radio station options it makes sense to use a select control, as users are familiar with this model. You can also look at the types of controls other Web developers use, and apply those that make sense for your situation.

Figure 6–14

Understanding Advanced Selection Menus Selection menus have many variations beyond the simple selection menu used in the Web page form. Table 6–3 on page HTML 292 lists several attributes for the <select> tag. Using these attributes, a selection menu can be set to display multiple choices or only one, with a drop-down list to allow a user to select another choice. A selection menu can also be defined to have one choice preselected as the default.

Figure 6–15 shows samples of selection menus. The HTML code used to create each selection menu is shown in Figure 6–16 on the next page.

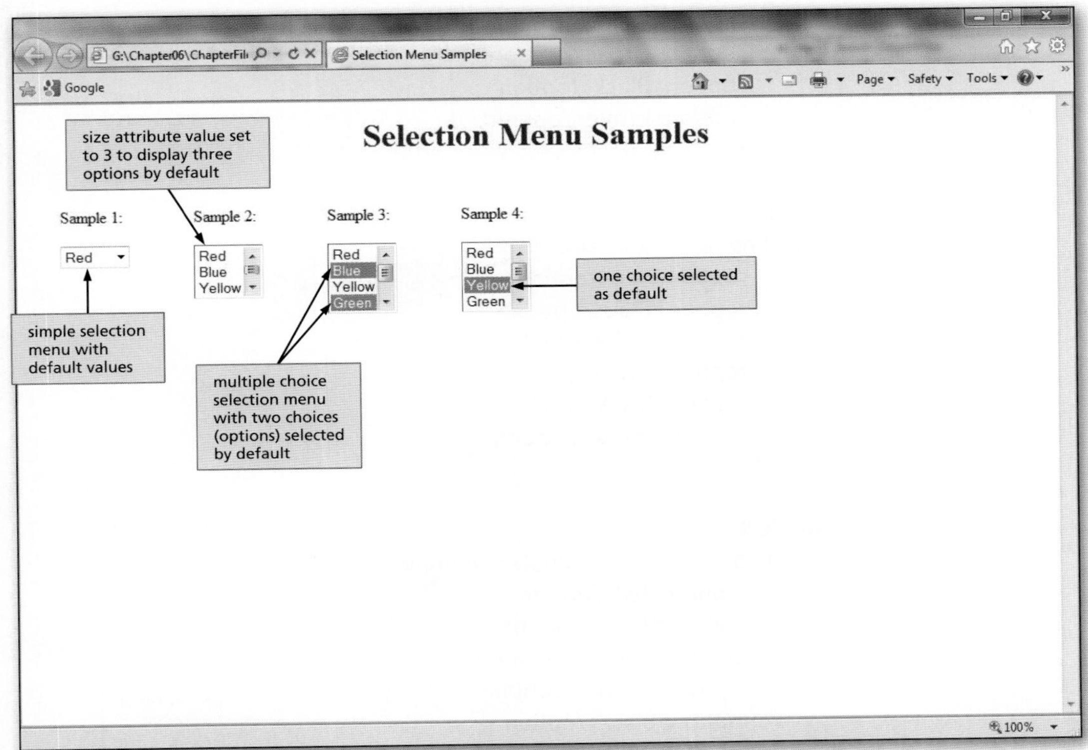

Figure 6–15 Sample selection controls with variations.

The selection menu in Sample 1 is a basic selection menu, with no attributes specified other than the name and the list options. This resulting selection menu uses a list menu that allows users to select one choice from the list. No choice is selected by default. The selection menu in Sample 2 uses a size attribute value of 3 to indicate that three choices should appear in the menu at startup. A user can use the up and down scroll arrows to view other choices in the list. The selection menu in Sample 3 uses the multiple attribute to allow a user to select more than one choice in the list. To select multiple choices, a user must first select one choice and then press and hold the CTRL key while clicking other choices in the list. If a user wants to select several consecutive choices, he or she can select the first choice and then press and hold the SHIFT key while selecting the last choice. All choices between the first choice and last choice automatically will be selected. The selection menu in Sample 4 also contains the multiple attribute, so one or more choices can be selected. In addition, Sample 4 provides an example of one choice (in this case, Yellow) being selected at startup. As shown in the HTML code in Figure 6–16 on the next page, the selected attribute is included in the <option> tag for Yellow, to indicate that Yellow should be selected at startup.

BTW

Options
The <select> and <option> tags are useful when you have a limited number of choices from which a Web page visitor can select. If the number of options becomes too large, however, the list is difficult to read. A better idea might be to group together like options into submenus. You can use the <optgroup> tag before the first <option> tag in the first group that you want to use in a submenu. After the last option in that group, use the </optgroup> tag.

The purpose of the selection menu dictates which type of selection menu should be used and the HTML code required to create that select control. Using the basic tags and attributes shown in Figure 6–16, you can create a wide variety of selection menus to suit almost any purpose.

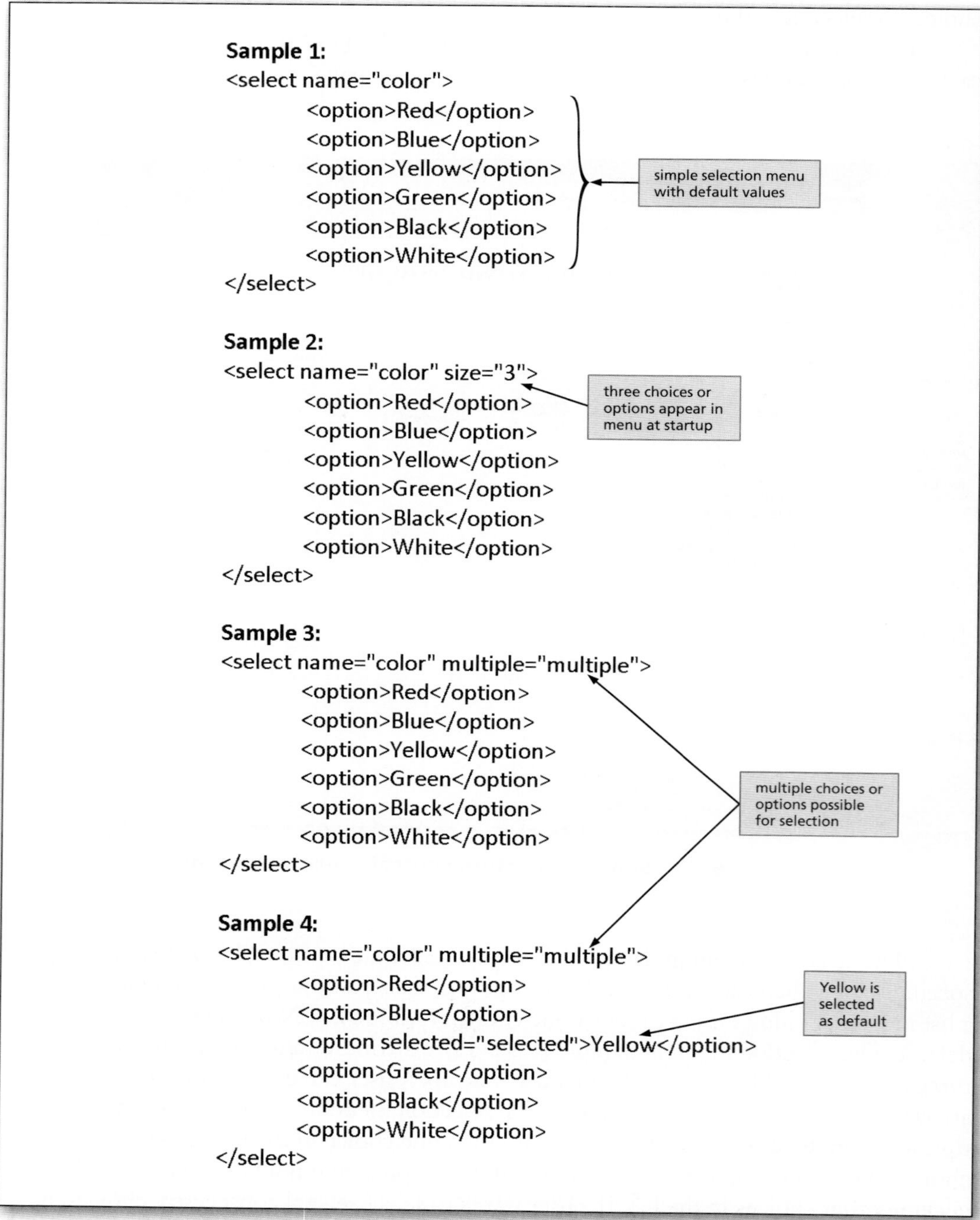

Figure 6–16 HTML code to create selection menus.

To Add an Additional Text Box

The next step in creating the Web page form is to add one more text box for an Internet radio station not listed in the selection menu. You again use the nonbreaking space ( ) special character to move the text box over more than one space from the selection menu. Table 6–9 shows the HTML code used to add the additional text box. A text field is used rather than a textarea field because the user needs to enter only one row of characters.

Table 6–9 HTML Code to Add Additional Text Boxes

Line	HTML Tag and Text
47	Name station not listed:
48	<input name="additstation" type="text" size="30" maxlength="30" />

The following steps add an additional text box to the Web page form.

1. Check that the insertion point is on Line 47, indented one Tab stop.
2. Enter the HTML code shown in Table 6–9 and then press the ENTER key twice (Figure 6–17). Align the insertion point at the beginning of Line 50.

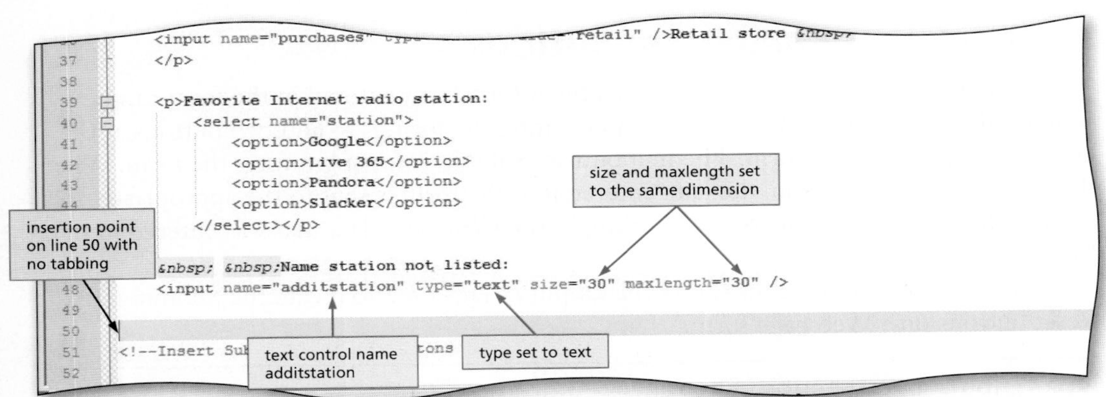

Figure 6–17

> **BTW**
> **Feedback**
> One good use of forms is to get feedback from your visitors. Suggestions from visitors not only can help improve the Web site, but can give your visitors the sense that you care about their opinions. Taking visitor feedback into account leads to better customer satisfaction.

Adding a Textarea Box

A textarea box is added next. Remember that a textarea is used when you want a multiple-row input area. The text control only allows a user to input one row of information. For multiple rows, use the textarea control.

The form includes a textarea that allows the user to add additional comments about their music preferences. Because the response can be longer than just one line, a textarea control is used.

To Add a Textarea Box

The next step is to add a textarea to the form. You use a textarea because you want the user to be able to input more than one line. Table 6–10 contains the tags and text to specify a textarea for multiple-line input.

Table 6–10 HTML Code to Add a Textarea

Line	HTML Tag and Text
50	 What else can you tell us about your music preferences?
51	 <textarea name="other" rows="3" cols="100"></textarea>

The following step adds a textarea to the form.

1

- If necessary, click line 50.
- Enter the HTML code shown in Table 6–10 and then press the ENTER key (Figure 6–18).

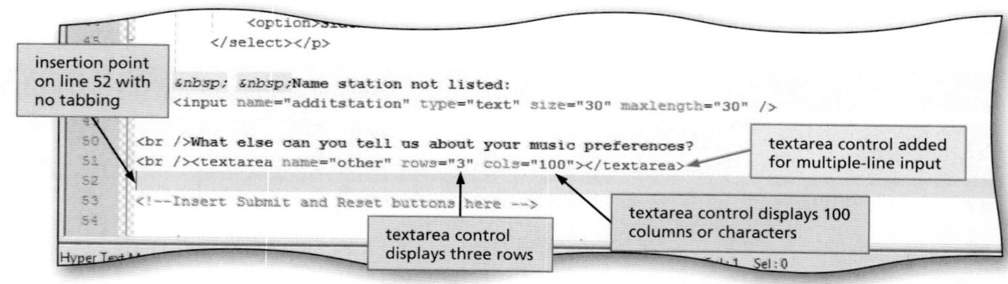

Figure 6–18

Q&A How do I know how big to make the textarea box?

Again, you need to look at the standards used in most Web development. You also have to view the textarea box in the browser to see how the size affects the Web page form. For instance, if we had made the number of rows 4, rather than 3, the Web page visitor would not have seen the "Thank you for completing our survey." message on the bottom of the page. That is something that you want the visitor to see without scrolling. Of course, like other tags, you can use CSS styles to size the textarea box.

BTW **Submit and Reset Buttons**

A simplistic, default button is created when you use the type="submit" attribute and value or the type="reset" attribute and value within the <input /> tag. The <button> tag can also be used to create a submit button. The <button> tag gives you the option of using an image for the button, rather than using the default button style. The appearance of the button text can be changed with the <style> tag. These tags give you more flexibility when creating submit or reset buttons.

Adding Submit and Reset Buttons

The form controls are useless unless the information entered in the form can be submitted for processing. The next step in creating the form is to add two buttons at the bottom of the Web page form. The first button, Submit, is for submitting the form. When the visitor clicks this button, the data entered into the form is sent to the appropriate location for processing. The second button, Reset, clears any data that was entered in the form.

The HTML code below shows the <input /> tags used to create the Submit and Reset buttons on a Web page form:

```
<p><input type="submit" value="Submit" />
<input type="reset" value="Reset" /></p>
```

The first line of HTML code creates a Submit button on the Web page form. A Submit button is created by using the attribute type="submit" in an <input /> tag. The value attribute is used to indicate the text that should appear on the button face — in this case, Submit.

When a user clicks the Submit button, all data currently entered in the form is sent to the appropriate location for processing. The action taken when a form is submitted is based on the method and action attributes specified in the <form> tag. In the <form> tag at the start of this form, the HTML code set the form attributes to method="post" and action="mailto:bluwav@isp.com". Thus, when a user clicks the Submit button, a data file that contains all the input data automatically is sent as an e-mail attachment to the e-mail address bluwav@isp.com. By default, the data file is named Postdata.att.

The code below shows a sample of the data file that is sent to the e-mail address, when using the post method. In this sample, the user checked the radio button for Folk music as a type that they like, iTunes as the place where they purchase most of their music, and Pandora as their favorite Internet radio station:

```
musictype=Folk&purchases=iTunes&station=Pandora
```

The data entered in the form appears in the data file as name-value pairs — the name of the control as specified in the name attribute, followed by the value entered or selected in the control. In the above example, the user selected the Folk music option in the check box selection, which is controlled by the field named musictype. The user then clicked the radio button option for the iTunes option, which is controlled by the field named purchases. The user also selected the radio station Pandora in the selection menu. An ampersand (&) strings together all of the name-value pairs to make them easier to read. The receiver of this e-mail could take the information in this format and decipher what is being requested. A simple program, written in a different programming language such as C++ or Java, could be developed that reads the information in the e-mail and transforms it into a more usable format. As mentioned earlier in the chapter, a CGI script is a better way to collect large amounts of information from forms, but that is beyond the scope of this book.

The Reset button is also an important part of any form. Resetting the form clears any information previously typed into a text box or textarea and resets radio buttons, check boxes, selection menus, and other controls to their initial values. As shown in the second line of the HTML code above, a Reset button is created by using the attribute type="reset" in an <input /> tag. The value attribute is used to indicate the text that should appear on the button face — in this case, Reset.

To Add Submit and Reset Buttons

The following step adds a Submit button and a Reset button to the form.

1

- Highlight the statement <!--Insert Submit and Reset buttons here --> on line 53.
- Type `<p><input type="submit" value="Submit" />` to create the Submit button and then press the ENTER key.
- Type `<input type="reset" value="Reset" />` to create the Reset button. Do not press the ENTER key (Figure 6–19). Save your code.

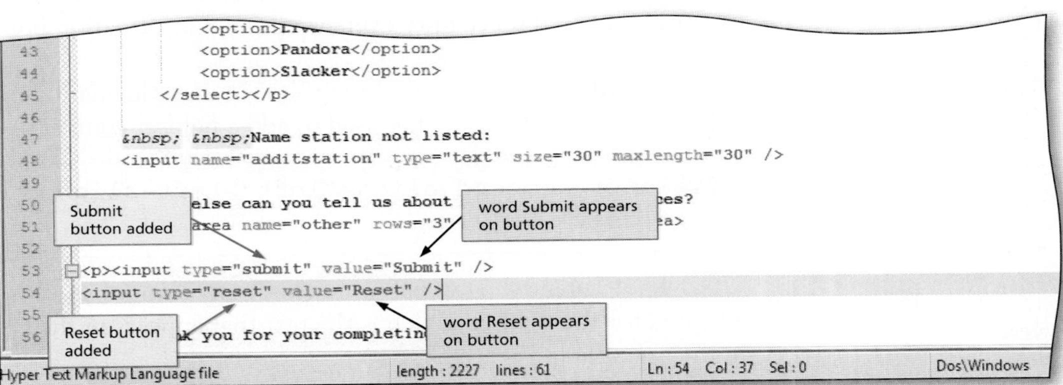

Figure 6–19

Q&A That submit option seems very easy to use. Do I need to do anything else in order to process the data?

No, the Submit button works in conjunction with the statements that you provided in your form tag in order to process the data entered.

Q&A Why do I need the Reset button?

It is always best to provide a Reset button next to the Submit button. This is useful to clear all of the data entered in case your visitors want to start over or if they change their minds or make mistakes.

Q&A If a visitor uses the Reset button, what does that do to default values that I have included in the tags?

Reset will set those default values back to the original values included in the tags. In other words, if you use a default value, Reset does not clear that value.

Plan Ahead

Organizing a form.
When using fieldset tags to separate and organize information on a form, consider the following:

- **Required versus optional information.** You can group all required information into one section of the form and place all optional information into another grouping. By doing this, you immediately call attention to the required information on the form.
- **General organization.** It can be helpful to enhance the look and feel of the form with groupings. Especially in the case of a long form, using separators helps direct the visitors' attention.

BTW

Groupings
An important part of good Web design is to make a form easy to use. Your Web site visitors are more likely to complete a form if they readily understand the information that is being requested. You can use the <fieldset> tag to group like information together.

Organizing a Form Using Form Groupings

An important aspect of creating a Web page form is making the form easy for Web site visitors to understand. Grouping similar information on a form, for example, makes the information easier to read and understand — and, as a result, easier to complete. Grouping is especially helpful in cases where some information is required and some is optional. In online order forms, for example, all the personal information is required (for example, name, address, and credit card number). On the other hand, an online order form may include an item (such as age or gender) that a visitor does not want to list. Therefore, that is optional information.

In the form developed in this chapter, there really is no required information. A visitor is not placing an order, but just identifying preferences. The groupings in this case are not based on required versus optional information but instead organizes like items together.

A **fieldset** control is used to group similar information on a form. The HTML code below shows the <fieldset> tag used to add a fieldset control to a Web page form:

```
<fieldset><legend align="left">Left-aligned legend</legend>
</fieldset>
```

The <legend> tag within the fieldset tag is optional. Using the <legend> tag creates a legend for the fieldset, which is the text that appears in the grouping borders, as shown in the example in Figure 6–20.

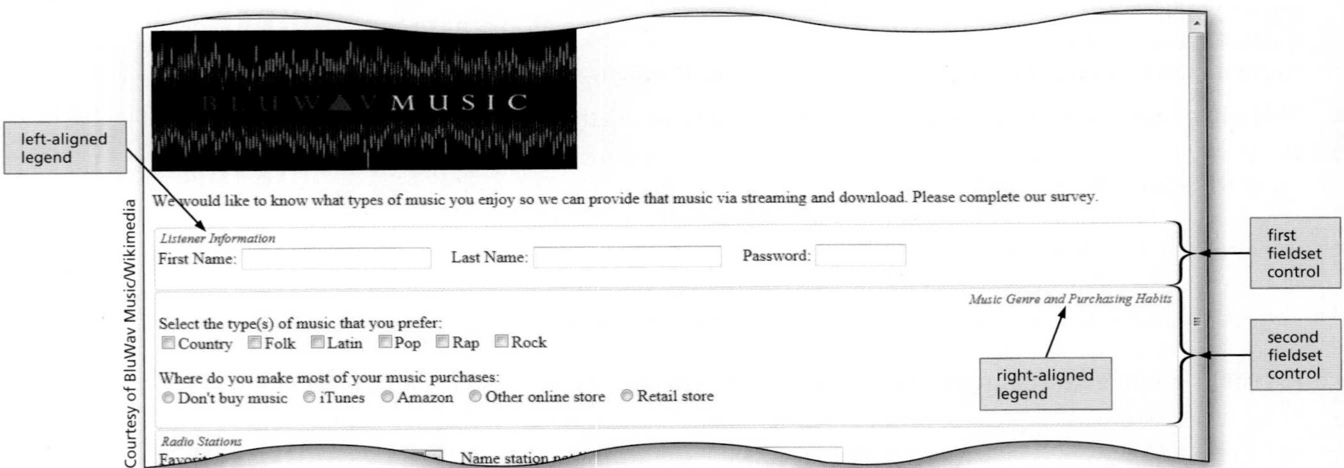

Figure 6–20 Fieldset controls on a form.

In the Web page form you will add three fieldset controls to group similar information on the form. The first fieldset control is used to group listener information, as shown in Figure 6–21. The first fieldset control has the legend, Listener Information, aligned to the left. The second fieldset control is used to group music genre and purchasing habits information. The second fieldset control has the legend, Music Genre and Purchasing Habits, aligned to the left. The third fieldset control, used to group the radio station information, has the legend, Radio Station, aligned to the left. These groupings divide the form so it is more readable and clearly separates like information.

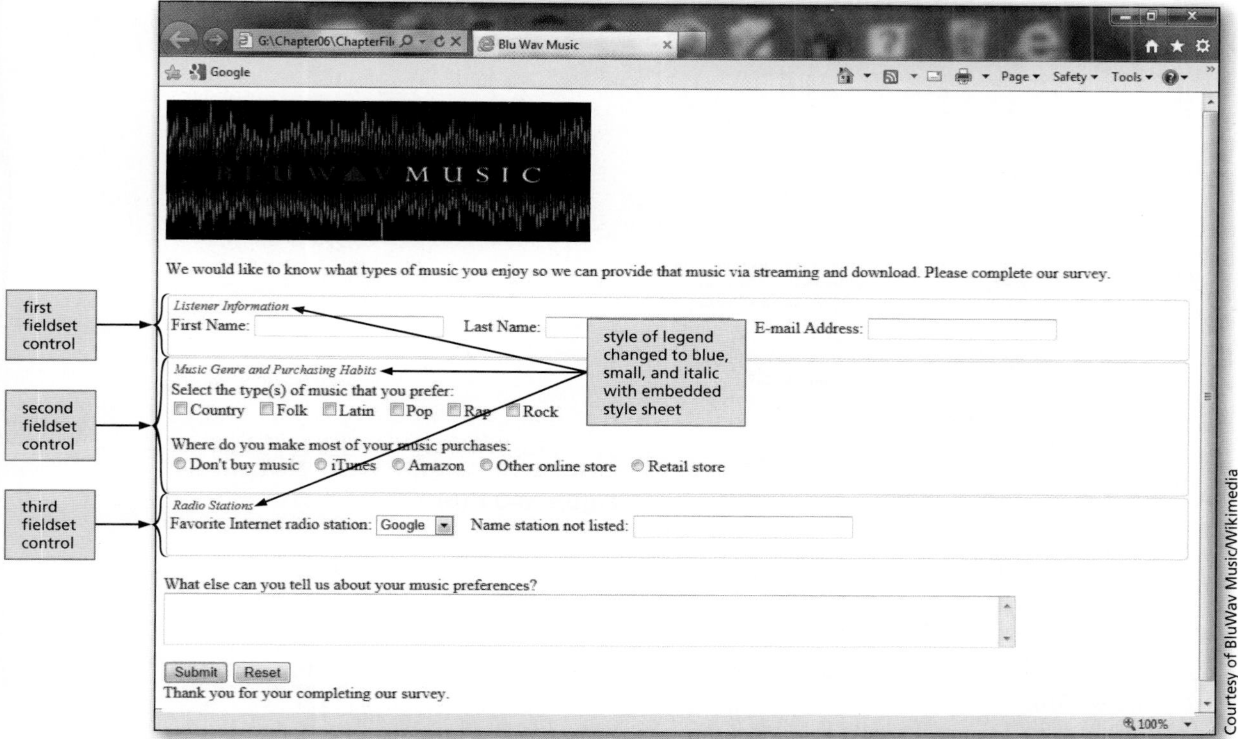

Figure 6–21 Blu Wav Music completed Web page.

To Add Fieldset Controls to Create Form Groupings

The following steps add three sets of fieldset tags to create information groupings on the Web page form.

1

- Click just before <p>First Name at the beginning of line 19, and then press the ENTER key.
- Move the insertion point back up to line 19. If necessary, use the BACKSPACE key to move back to the left margin. Type `<fieldset><legend>Listener Information</legend>` as the tag to begin the first fieldset.
- Click just after the </p> on line 22, and then press the ENTER key.
- If necessary, use the BACKSPACE key to move back to the left margin, type `</fieldset>` on line 23 to end the first fieldset, and then press the ENTER key (Figure 6–22a).

```
   ...complete our survey.</p>
18
19 <fieldset><legend>Listener Information</legend>
20     <p>First Name: <input name="firstname" type="text" size="25" />    
21     Last Name: <input name="lastname" type="text" size="25" />    
22     E-mail Address: <input name="email" type="text" size="25" /></p>
23 </fieldset>
24 |
25
26     <br />Select the type(s) of music that you prefer:
27     <br /><input name="musictype" type="checkbox" value="country" />Country  
28     <input name="musictype" type="checkbox" value="folk" />Folk  
29     <input name="musictype" type="checkbox" value="latin" />Latin  
       <input name="musictype" type="checkbox" value="pop" />Pop  
       <input name="musictype" type="checkbox" val...
```


Figure 6–22 (a)

2

- With the insertion point on line 25 (leave a blank line on 24), type `<fieldset><legend>Music Genre and Purchasing Habits</legend>` to start the second fieldset.
- Click to the right of the </p> on line 40 and then press the ENTER key.
- If necessary, use the BACKSPACE key to move back to the left margin, type `</fieldset>`, and then press the ENTER key.
- On line 43 (leave a blank on line 42), type `<fieldset><legend>Radio Stations</legend>` to start the third fieldset.
- Click to the right of the /> on line 53 and then press the ENTER key.
- If necessary, use the BACKSPACE key to move back to the left margin, and type `</fieldset>` to end the third fieldset (Figure 6–22b).

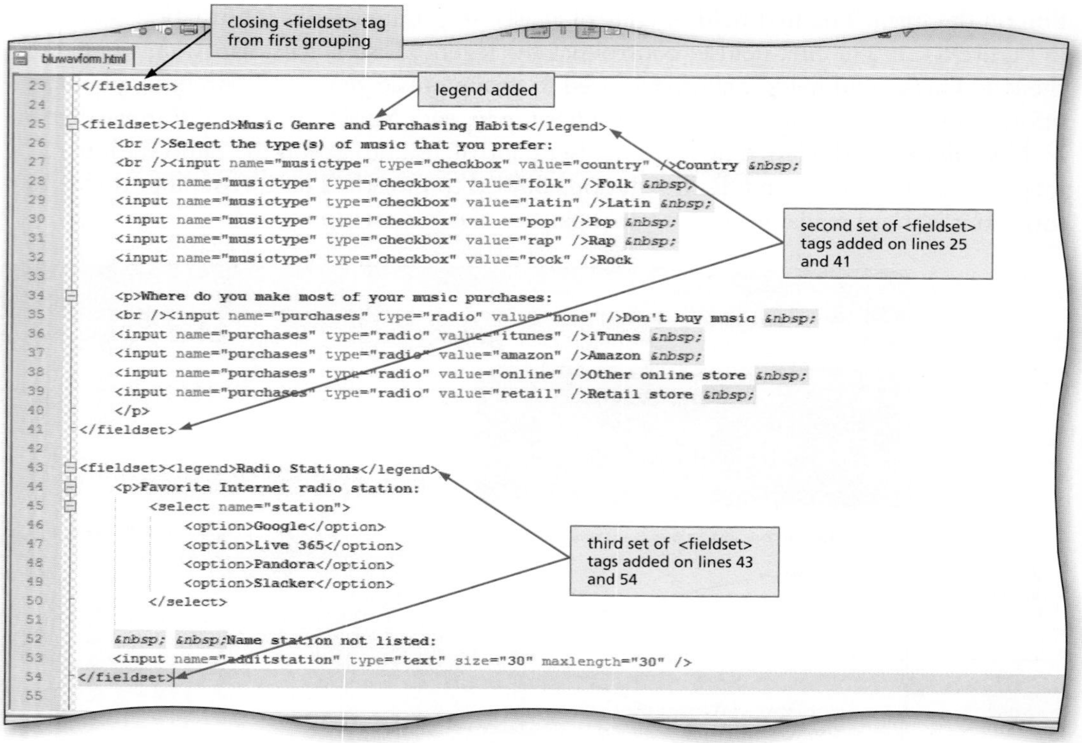

```
23 </fieldset>
24
25 <fieldset><legend>Music Genre and Purchasing Habits</legend>
26     <br />Select the type(s) of music that you prefer:
27     <br /><input name="musictype" type="checkbox" value="country" />Country  
28     <input name="musictype" type="checkbox" value="folk" />Folk  
29     <input name="musictype" type="checkbox" value="latin" />Latin  
30     <input name="musictype" type="checkbox" value="pop" />Pop  
31     <input name="musictype" type="checkbox" value="rap" />Rap  
32     <input name="musictype" type="checkbox" value="rock" />Rock
33
34     <p>Where do you make most of your music purchases:
35     <br /><input name="purchases" type="radio" value="none" />Don't buy music  
36     <input name="purchases" type="radio" value="itunes" />iTunes  
37     <input name="purchases" type="radio" value="amazon" />Amazon  
38     <input name="purchases" type="radio" value="online" />Other online store  
39     <input name="purchases" type="radio" value="retail" />Retail store  
40     </p>
41 </fieldset>
42
43 <fieldset><legend>Radio Stations</legend>
44     <p>Favorite Internet radio station:
45         <select name="station">
46             <option>Google</option>
47             <option>Live 365</option>
48             <option>Pandora</option>
49             <option>Slacker</option>
50         </select>
51
52        Name station not listed:
53     <input name="additstation" type="text" size="30" maxlength="30" />
54 </fieldset>
55
```

Figure 6–22 (b)

Q&A

Are there other options such as colored borders that I can use with the <fieldset> tag?

Yes, you can set the margins, font, colors, etc. for the <fieldset> tag. You can use an inline, embedded, or external Cascading Style Sheet (CSS) for those options.

Adding an Embedded Style Sheet

The next step in creating the Web page form is to add an embedded style sheet to improve the look of the legends in all three field groupings. Figure 6–23a shows the Web page as it displays currently without the change in legend style. Note that the default position for the legend is on the left, and the legend is the default color, black. Figure 6–23b shows the Web page with the new style for the legends as inserted in the embedded style sheet. Remember that an embedded style sheet changes the style for a single Web page. The embedded style sheet is inserted within the <style></style> container in the <head> section of the Web page.

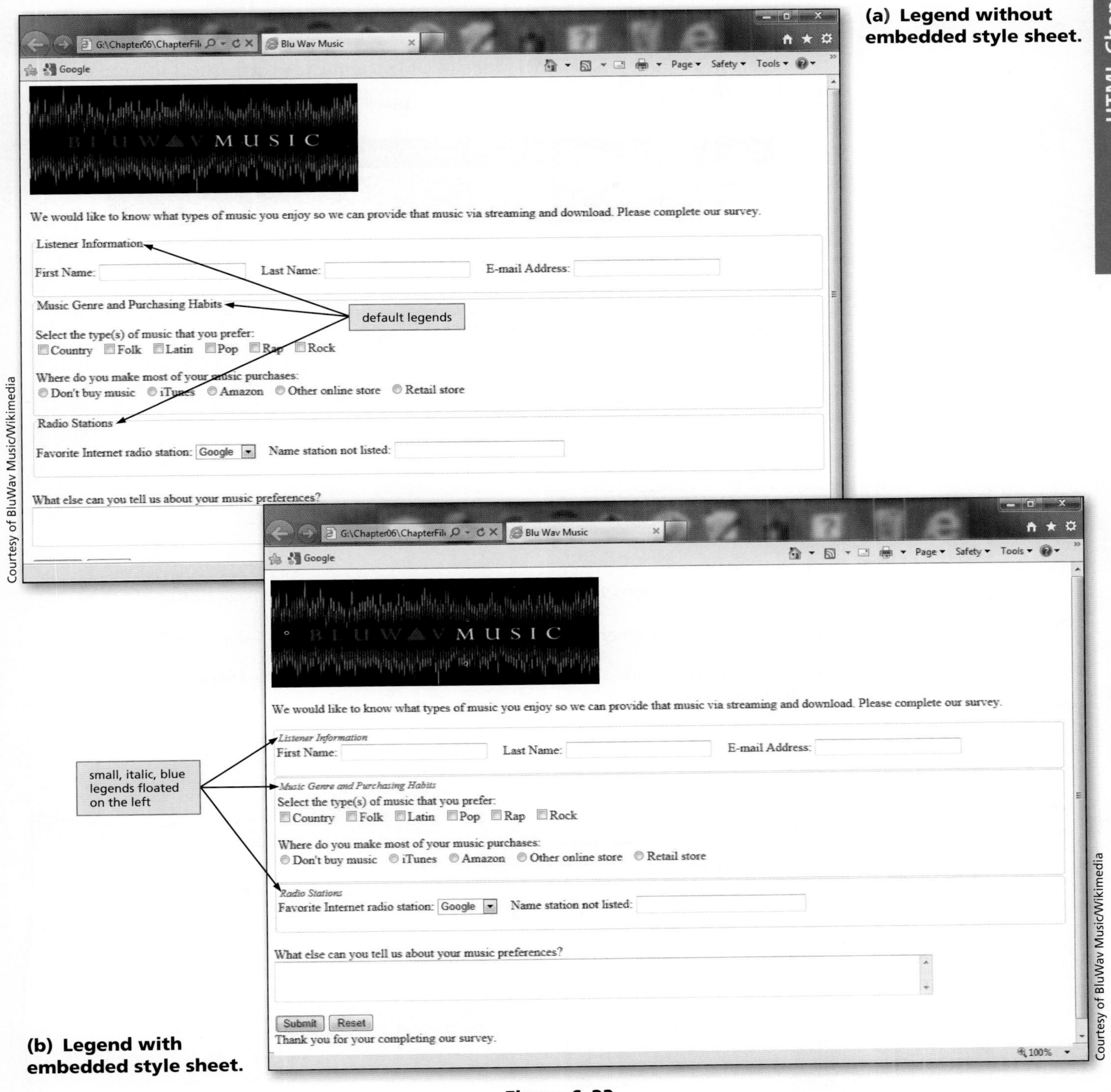

Figure 6–23

In this style sheet, you will change the color, font-style, and font-size of the legend (lines 10 through 13), making it blue and smaller than the surrounding text. You will also use the float property (line 10) to align the legend on the left. In Chapter 3, you used the float property to align images relative to the Web page text. The float property indicates in which direction (in this case left or right) to display (or float) an element (the legend) being inserted on a Web page. It can be an effective Web development practice to use an alignment element such as float so that you can easily change the alignment if you choose.

To Add an Embedded Style Sheet

Table 6–11 shows the HTML code to add an embedded style sheet to format the legends for the form fields.

Table 6–11 HTML Code to Add an External Style Sheet	
Line	**HTML Tag and Text**
7	`<style type="text/css">`
8	`<!--`
9	
10	`legend {float: left;`
11	`color: #0000fe;`
12	`font-style: italic;`
13	`font-size: small;}`
14	
15	`-->`
16	`</style>`

The following steps add an embedded style sheet to the Web page form.

1. Highlight the statement <!--Insert embedded style sheet here --> on line 7.
2. Enter the HTML code shown in Table 6–11, but do not press the ENTER key on line 16 (Figure 6–24).

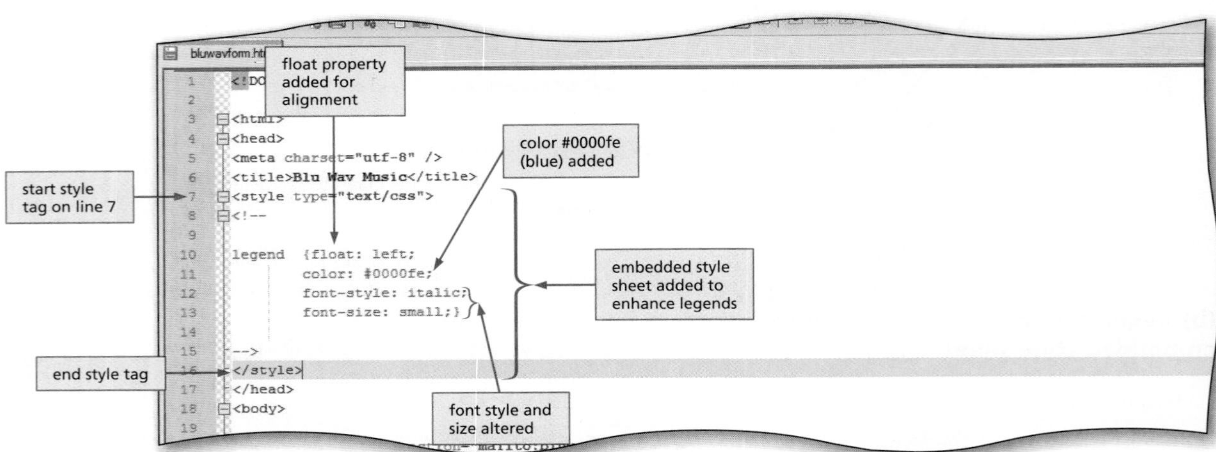

Figure 6–24

To Save the HTML File

With the Web page form complete, the HTML file should be saved. The following step saves the bluwav.html file on the USB drive.

1. With a USB drive plugged into your computer, click File on the menu bar and then click the Save button to save the bluwav.html file.

To Validate, View, and Test a Web Page

After completing the Blu Wav Music Web page form, you should validate the code, and view and test it in a browser to confirm that the Web page appears as desired and that the controls function as expected. Note that you cannot test the Submit button because it automatically generates an e-mail message to bluwav@isp.com, which is a nonexistent e-mail address. When you are collecting information from an online form, it is very important to test that the information is accurate. It is beyond the scope of this book to address validation issues related to server-side processing. After testing the controls, the Web page and the HTML code should be printed for future reference. The following steps validate, view, and test a Web page.

1. Validate the bluwav.html file by file upload at validator.w3.org.
2. In Internet Explorer, click the Address bar, type `G:\Chapter06\ChapterFiles\bluwav.html` or the location of your file, and then press the ENTER key to display the completed form for Blu Wav Music (Figure 6–25 on the next page).
3. Review the form to make sure all spelling is correct and the controls are positioned appropriately.
4. Test all of the text boxes on the form. Try to type more than the maximum number of allowable characters in the additional radio station text box.
5. Click the check boxes to test them. You should be able to choose one, two, or any number of the boxes at the same time because check boxes are designed to select more than one option.
6. Test the selection control by clicking the list arrow and selecting one of the options.
7. Click the radio buttons to test them. You should be able to make only one choice (Don't buy music, iTunes, Amazon, Other online store, or Retail store).
8. Test the textarea by entering a paragraph of text. Verify that it allows more characters to be entered than are shown in the textarea.
9. Click the Reset button. It should clear the form and reset all controls to their original (default) state.

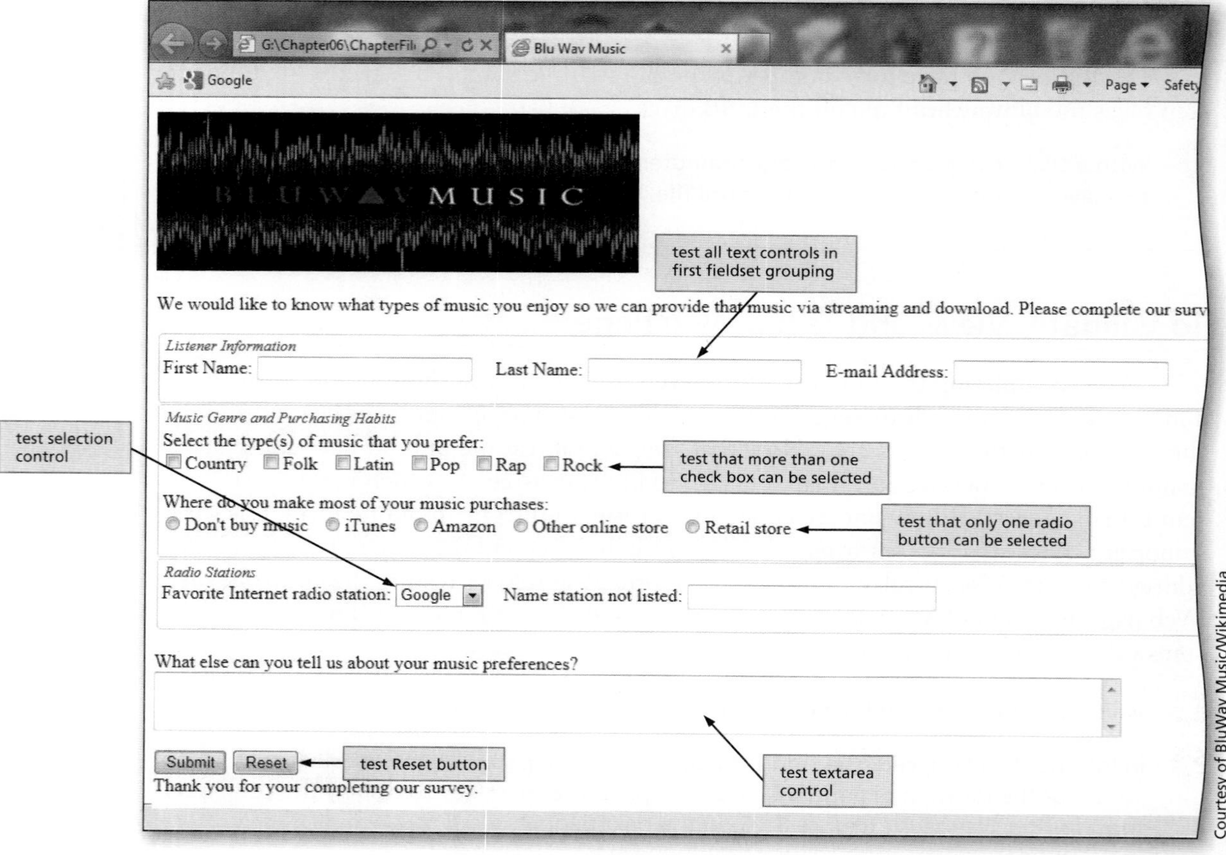

Figure 6–25

To Print a Web Page and HTML

1. Print the Web page.
2. Activate Notepad++ and print the HTML file (Figure 6–26).

```
<!DOCTYPE HTML>

<html>
<head>
<meta charset="utf-8" />
<title>Blu Wav Music</title>
<style type="text/css">
<!--

legend {float: left;
        color: #0000fe;
        font-style: italic;
        font-size: small;}

-->
</style>
</head>
<body>

<form method="post" action="mailto:bluwav@isp.com">

<header>
    <img src="bluwavlogo.jpg" width="410" height="139" alt="Blu Wav logo" />
</header>

<p>We would like to know what types of music you enjoy so we can provide that music via
streaming and download. Please complete our survey.</p>

<fieldset><legend>Listener Information</legend>
    <p>First Name: <input name="firstname" type="text" />    
    Last Name: <input name="lastname" type="text" size="25" />    
    E-mail Address: <input name="email" type="text" size="25" /></p>
</fieldset>

<fieldset><legend>Music Genre and Purchasing Habits</legend>
    <br />Select the type(s) of music that you prefer:
    <br /><input name="musictype" type="checkbox" value="country" />Country  
    <input name="musictype" type="checkbox" value="folk" />Folk  
    <input name="musictype" type="checkbox" value="latin" />Latin  
    <input name="musictype" type="checkbox" value="pop" />Pop  
    <input name="musictype" type="checkbox" value="rap" />Rap  
    <input name="musictype" type="checkbox" value="rock" />Rock

    <p>Where do you make most of your music purchases:
    <br /><input name="purchases" type="radio" value="none" />Don't buy music  
    <input name="purchases" type="radio" value="itunes" />iTunes  
    <input name="purchases" type="radio" value="amazon" />Amazon  
    <input name="purchases" type="radio" value="online" />Other online store  
    <input name="purchases" type="radio" value="retail" />Retail store  
    </p>
</fieldset>

<fieldset><legend>Radio Stations</legend>

    <p>Favorite Internet radio station:
        <select name="station">
            <option>Google</option>
            <option>Live 365</option>
            <option>Pandora</option>
            <option>Slacker</option>
        </select>

       Name station not listed:
        <input name="additstation" type="text" size="30" maxlength="30" /></p>

</fieldset>

<br />What else can you tell us about your music preferences?
<br /><textarea name="other" rows="3" cols="100"></textarea>

<p><input type="submit" value="Submit" />
<input type="reset" value="Reset" />

<br />Thank you for your completing our survey.</p>

</form>
</body>
</html>
```

Figure 6–26

BTW

Quick Reference
For a list of HTML tags and their associated attributes, see Appendix A at the back of this book, or visit the HTML Quick Reference on the Book Companion Site Web page for this book at www.cengagebrain.com. For a list of CSS properties and values, see Appendix D at the back of this book or visit the Book Companion Site Web page.

To Quit Notepad++ and a Browser

1. In Notepad++, click the File menu, then Close All.
2. Click the Close button on the Notepad++ title bar.
3. Click the Close button on the browser title bar. If necessary, click the Close all tabs button.

Chapter Summary

In this chapter, you have learned how to convert a static Web page to a dynamic Web page form with various controls for user input. The items listed below include all the new HTML skills you have learned in this chapter.

1. Create a Form and Identify the Form Process (HTML 294)
2. Add an Image and Change the Text Message (HTML 295)
3. Add Text Boxes (HTML 296)
4. Add Check Boxes (HTML 298)
5. Add Radio Buttons (HTML 299)
6. Add a Selection Menu (HTML 300)
7. Add a Textarea Box (HTML 303)
8. Add Submit and Reset Buttons (HTML 305)
9. Add Fieldset Controls to Create Form Groupings (HTML 307)

Learn It Online

Test your knowledge of chapter content and key terms.

Instructions: To complete the following exercises, please visit `www.cengagebrain.com`. At the `CengageBrain.com` home page, search for *HTML5 and CSS 7th Edition* using the search box at the top of the page. This will take you to the product page for this book. On the product page, click the Access Now button below the Study Tools heading. On the Book Companion Site Web page, select Chapter 6, and then click the link for the desired exercise.

Chapter Reinforcement TF, MC, and SA
A series of true/false, multiple choice, and short answer questions that test your knowledge of the chapter content.

Flash Cards
An interactive learning environment where you identify chapter key terms associated with displayed definitions.

Practice Test
A series of multiple choice questions that test your knowledge of chapter content and key terms.

Who Wants To Be a Computer Genius?
An interactive game that challenges your knowledge of chapter content in the style of a television quiz show.

Wheel of Terms
An interactive game that challenges your knowledge of chapter key terms in the style of the television show, *Wheel of Fortune*.

Crossword Puzzle Challenge
A crossword puzzle that challenges your knowledge of key terms presented in the chapter.

Apply Your Knowledge

Reinforce the skills and apply the concepts you learned in this chapter.

Creating a Course Evaluation Web Page Form

Instructions: Start Notepad++. Open the file apply6-1.html from the Chapter06\Apply folder of the Data Files for Students. See the inside back cover of this book for instructions on downloading the Data Files for Students, or contact your instructor for information about accessing the required files. This sample HTML file contains all of the text for the Course Evaluation Survey Web page shown in Figure 6–27. You will add the necessary tags to make the Web page form.

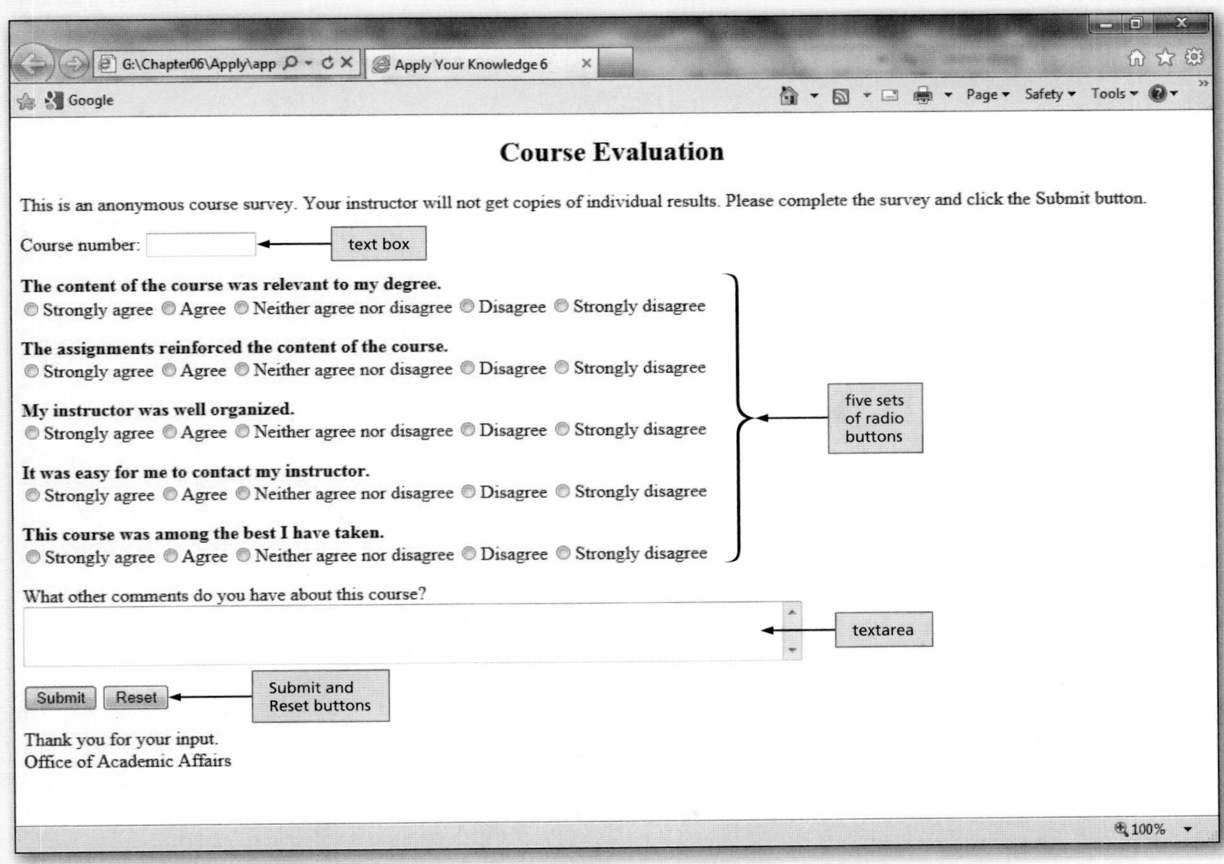

Figure 6–27

Perform the following tasks:

1. Using Notepad++, add the HTML code necessary to make the Web page look similar to the one shown in Figure 6–27. Controls used in the form include:
   a. One text box for Course number
   b. Five sets of five radio buttons for course evaluation options
   c. A textarea box with 3 rows and 80 columns
2. Include the HTML code to add Submit and Reset buttons.
3. Use the post method to send an e-mail to email@isp.com.
4. Save the revised document as apply6-1solution.html.
5. Validate your HTML code and test all controls.
6. Print the Web page and HTML.
7. Submit the solution in the format specified by your instructor.

STUDENT ASSIGNMENTS

Extend Your Knowledge

Extend the skills you learned in this chapter and experiment with new skills.

Creating a Web Page Restaurant Questionnaire

Instructions: Start Notepad++. Create the Web page questionnaire for Sahani's Blue Crab Diner by adding the heading, text, form controls, and groupings, as shown in Figure 6–28.

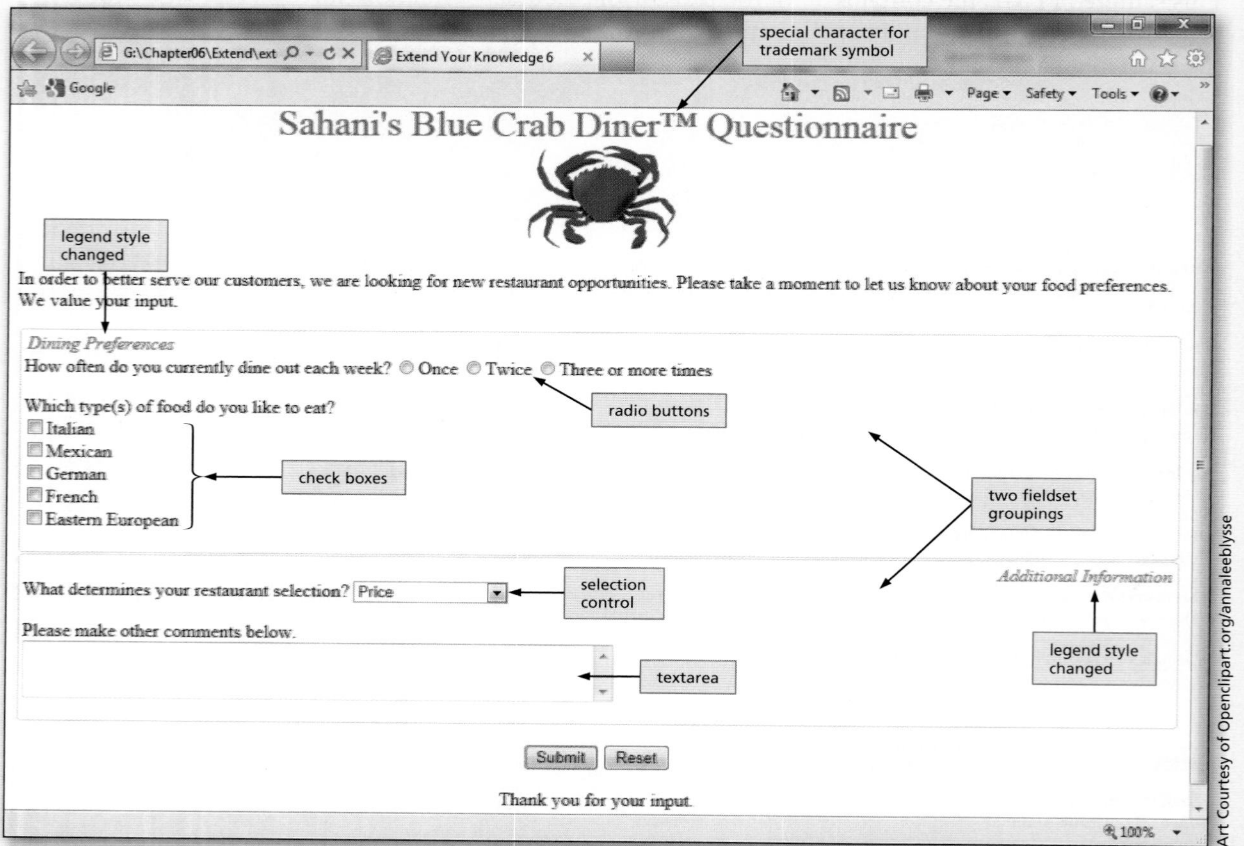

Figure 6–28

Perform the following tasks:

1. Using Notepad++, create the Web page, adding any HTML code necessary to make the Web page look similar to the one shown in Figure 6–28. The code should include:
   a. A heading that includes an xx-large font-size and color #137b95. Also add a special character. (*Hint:* See Appendix F.) Include the blue_crab.png image beneath the heading.
   b. Three radio buttons for the number of times the visitor eats out.
   c. Five check boxes for the types of food the visitor eats.
   d. A selection box with three options for factors that determine where they eat: Price, Proximity to home, Quality of food.
   e. A textarea box with three rows and 60 columns.
2. Add the HTML code necessary to add two groupings with the legends as shown. Use an embedded style sheet with classes or inline styles to change the legends to #137b95 and italics. Align the first legend to the left and the second to the right.

3. Include the HTML code necessary to add Submit and Reset buttons.
4. Save the revised file using the filename extend6-1solution.html.
5. Validate your HTML code.
6. Print the revised HTML file.
7. View the Web page in your browser and test all controls.
8. Print the Web page.
9. Submit the files in the format specified by your instructor.

Make It Right

Analyze a document and correct all errors and/or improve the design.

Correcting the Annual Customer Survey Web Page

Instructions: Start Notepad++. Open the file makeitright6-1.html from the Chapter06\MakeItRight folder of the Data Files for Students. See the inside back cover of this book for instructions on downloading the Data Files for Students, or contact your instructor for information about accessing the required files. The Web page is a modified version of what you see in Figure 6–29. Make the necessary corrections to the Web page to make it look like the figure. Use the image oceansidelogosm.jpg at the top of the Web page to the left of the xx-large heading. Apply the following styles to the <h2> tag: "margin-left: 5px" "vertical-align: 50px". (*Hint:* Use the <span> tag for that.) Also apply the following style to the <img /> tag: margin-left: 250px. The textarea shown displays three rows and 60 columns. Save the file as makeitright6-1solution.html.

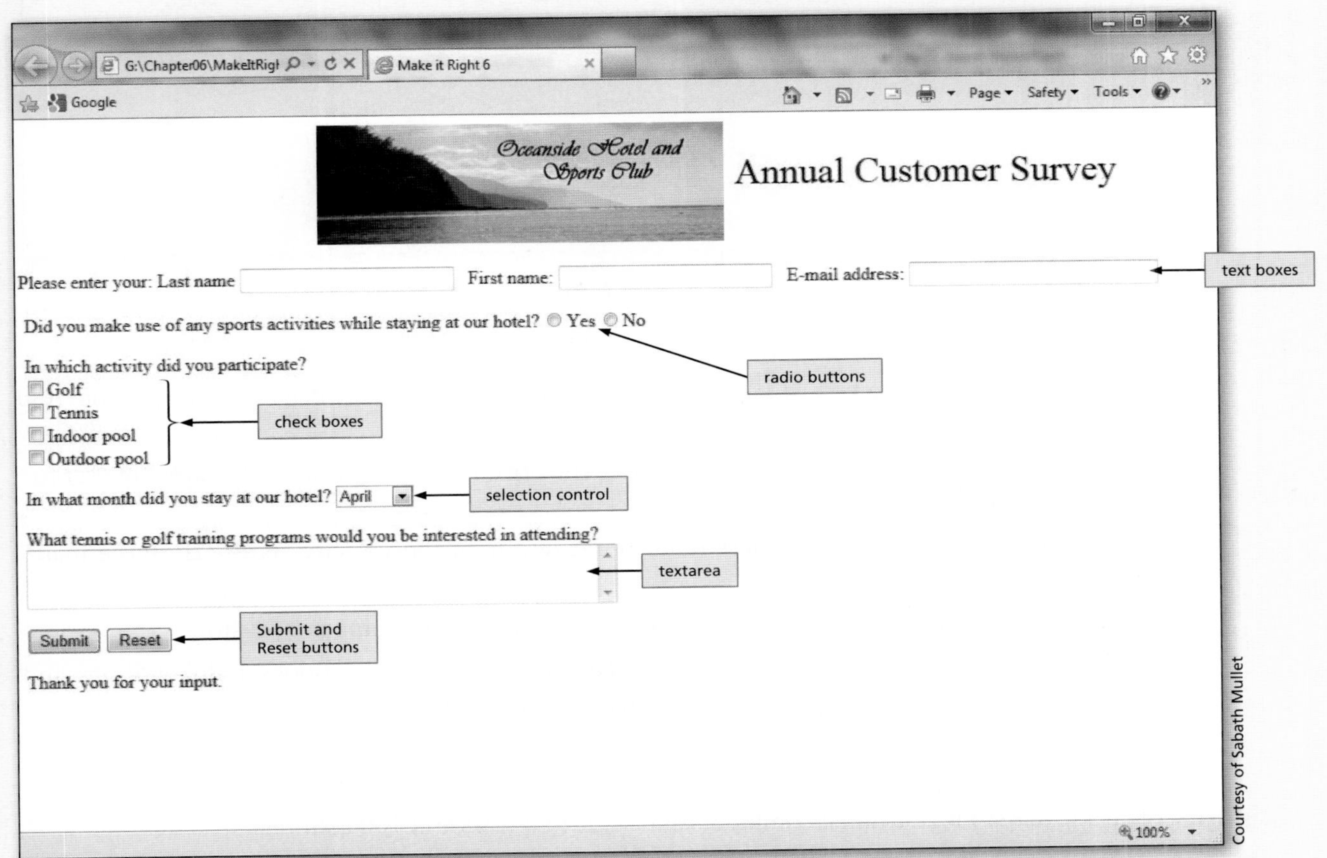

Figure 6–29

STUDENT ASSIGNMENTS

In the Lab

Lab 1: Creating a School Bookstore Survey

Instructions: The staff of the school bookstore wants to survey students about their book-buying habits to determine where they purchase their books. The staff has asked you to create a Web page form that contains the questions shown in Figure 6–30.

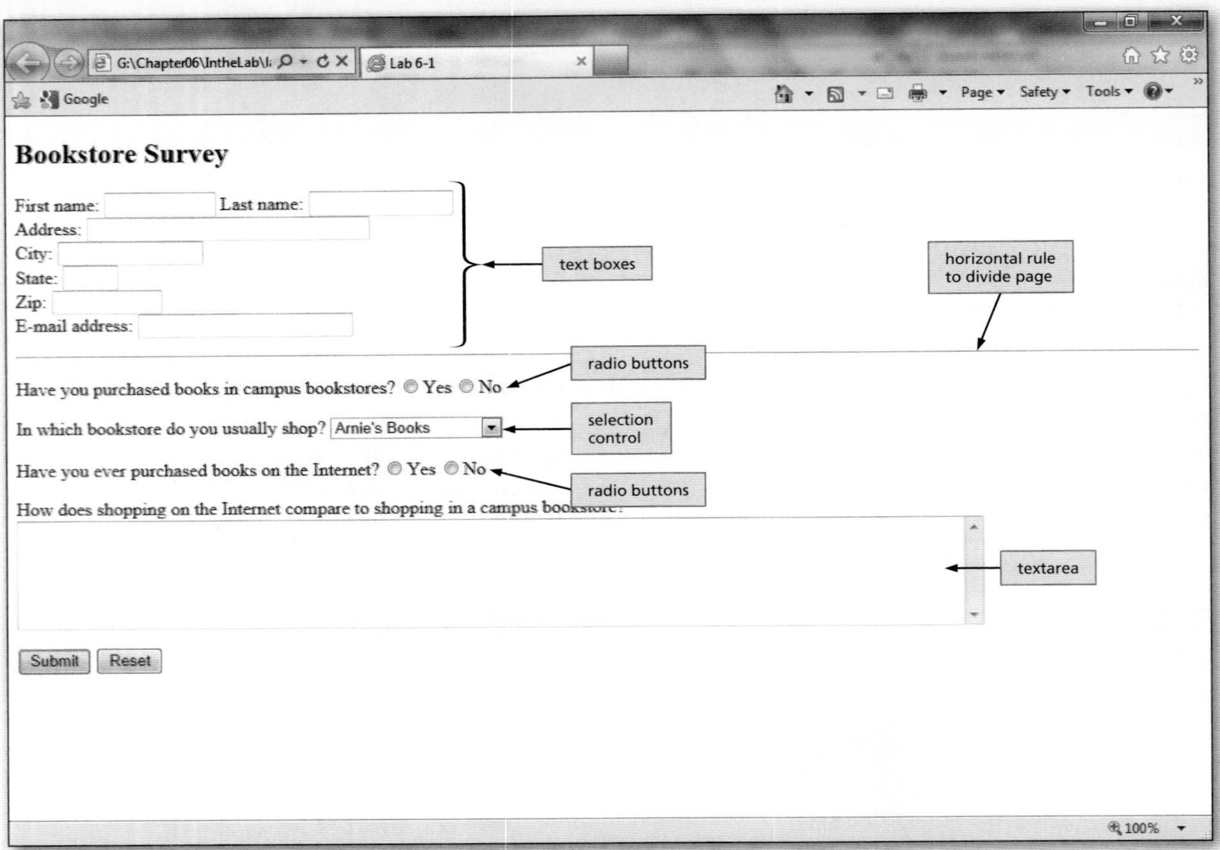

Figure 6–30

Perform the following tasks:

1. Using Notepad++, create a new HTML file with the title Lab 6-1 in the main heading section. Add the Web page h2 heading Bookstore Survey at the top of the page.
2. Create a form and identify the form process using the post method with the action attribute set to mailto:email@isp.com.
3. Add seven text boxes for first name, last name, home or school address, city, state, ZIP, plus e-mail address.
4. Add two radio buttons for users to say whether or not they use the campus bookstore.
5. Add a selection menu with three options of your choosing (or use Arnie's Books, Lafollet Shops, and University Bookstore) for users to select the bookstore in which they shop.
6. Create a second set of radio buttons for users to say whether they have purchased books on the Internet.
7. Create a textarea for additional comments and set it to 6 rows and 100 columns.
8. Add Submit and Reset buttons at the bottom of the Web page form.

9. Save the HTML file in the Chapter06\IntheLab folder using the filename lab6-1solution.html. Validate the Web page. Print the HTML file.
10. Open the lab6-1solution.html file in your browser and test all controls except the Submit button.
11. Print the Web page.
12. Submit the files in the format specified by your instructor.

In the Lab

Lab 2: Penelope's Music House Survey

Instructions: Penelope's Music House is looking for information on their customers' lesson needs. They want to know what type of music lessons customers take now, how much they practice each week, and what other music lessons they would like to have. The company has asked you to create the survey as a Web page form, as shown in Figure 6–31.

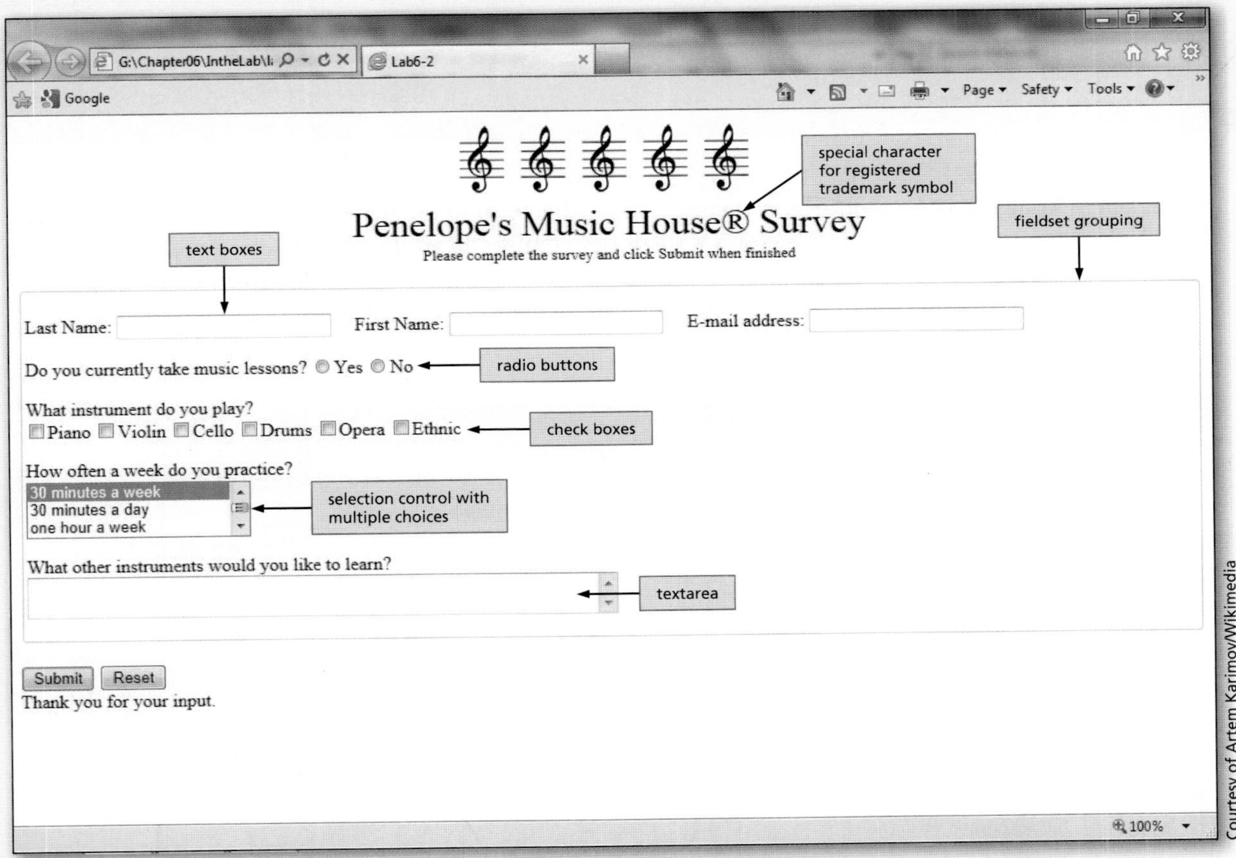

Figure 6–31

Perform the following tasks:

1. Using Notepad++, create a new HTML file with the title Lab 6-2 in the main heading section.
2. Create a form and identify the form process using the post method with the action attribute set to mailto your e-mail address (if you do not have an e-mail address, use email@isp.com).
3. Create a heading for the Web page. First, insert the image music_clef_sm.png five times across the top of the Web page. Then add a heading with an xx-large font size followed by instructions in a small font size. Include the special character shown in Figure 6–31. Center the heading.
4. Add three text boxes for last name, first name, and e-mail address.

Continued >

STUDENT ASSIGNMENTS

In the Lab *continued*

5. Add a set of radio buttons to ask if customers take lessons, and six check boxes for users to select their instrument(s).
6. Add a selection menu that initially displays three rows. One of the menu options should be selected at startup.
7. Insert a 2-row, 60-column textarea for users to provide additional suggestions.
8. Add a Submit button and a Reset button at the bottom of the Web page form.
9. Add fieldset as shown in Figure 6–31. Note that there is no legend on the fieldset for this Web page.
10. Save the HTML file in the Chapter06\IntheLab folder using the filename lab6-2solution.html. Validate the Web page. Print the HTML file.
11. Open the lab6-2solution.html file in your browser and test all controls except the Submit button.
12. Print the Web page.
13. Submit the files in the format specified by your instructor.

In the Lab

Lab 3: Using Fieldset Controls to Organize a Form

Instructions: Your manager at Horizon Learning has asked you to create a Web page form that novice HTML developers can use as a model for a well-designed, user-friendly form. Having created forms for several different Web sites, you have learned that using fieldset controls to group form controls results in a well-organized, easily readable form. Create a Web page form that utilizes three fieldset controls, like the one shown in Figure 6–32.

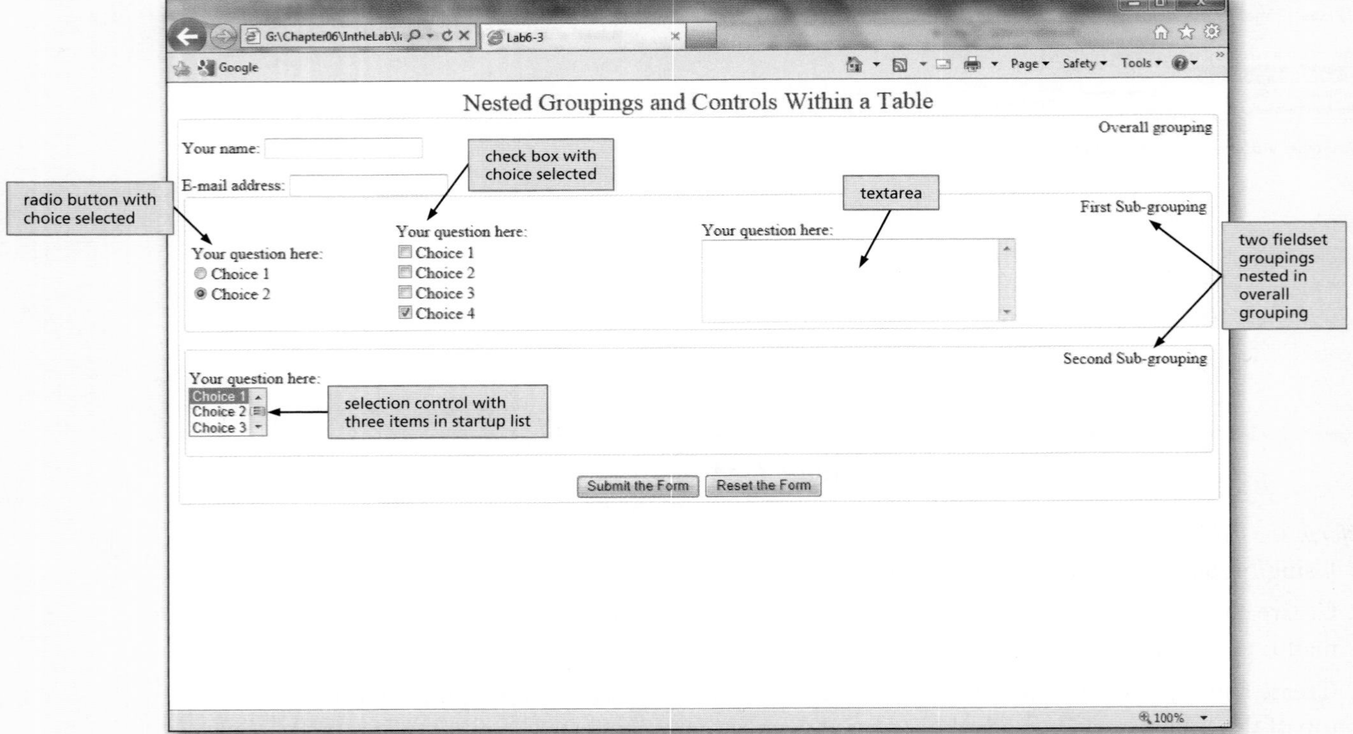

Figure 6–32

Perform the following tasks:

1. Using Notepad++, create a new HTML file with the title Lab 6-3 in the main heading section.
2. Add the Web page heading Nested Groupings and Controls Within a Table.
3. Create a form and identify the form process using the post method with the action attribute set to mailto your e-mail address (if you do not have an e-mail address, use email@isp.com).
4. Add two text boxes for name and e-mail address.
5. Add two radio buttons, with Choice 2 preselected, as shown in Figure 6–32, together with four check boxes with Choice 4 selected.
6. Add a 5-row, 35-column textarea, as shown in Figure 6–32.
7. Insert a selection menu with options of Choice 1 through Choice 4. Set the selection menu to display three rows and have Choice 1 preselected as the default option. Allow the user to select multiple options.
8. Add a Submit button that says Submit the Form and a Reset button that says Reset the Form at the bottom of the Web page form.
9. Add three fieldset controls to group the form controls, as shown in Figure 6–32. Nest the two subgroupings within the main grouping.
10. Save the HTML file in the Chapter06\IntheLab folder using the filename lab6-3solution.html. Validate the Web page. Print the HTML file.
11. Open the lab6-3solution.html file in your browser and test all controls except the Submit button.
12. Print the Web page.
13. Submit the files in the format specified by your instructor.

Cases and Places

Apply your creative thinking and problem-solving skills to design and implement a solution.

1: Changing a Paper Form to an Online Form

Academic

As part of your Web development project, your instructor has asked you to find a static form that is currently in use by your school administration, a school club, or another organization. Any printed form that you complete as a student is a good option for this exercise. Convert this static form to a dynamic Web page form. Start by designing the form on paper, taking into consideration the fields that are the most appropriate to use for each input area. Once your design is complete, use HTML to develop the Web page form. Test the form, and once testing is done, show the form to several people from the organization that controls the form. Explain to them why it is better to collect information using a dynamic Web page form, rather than a printed, static form. Discuss the possible negatives about using an online (vs. a paper) form as well. As one example, what happens with forms that require a student's signature if the forms are online?

2: Making a Form Easier to Use

Personal

Your uncle's car club wants to collect information from club members. Search the Internet for two or three examples of Web page forms used to collect information from club members. Print the forms as examples. If you were the Web developer for these Web sites, how would you update the forms to gather more information or make the forms easier to use? Using the example Web pages that you have found, draw a sketch of a Web page form design for a car club. Develop the Web page form as an example to share with your uncle.

Continued >

Cases and Places *continued*

3: Learning About Advanced Form Processing

Professional

You work in the Web development department for a small company in your community. You are interested in learning the latest programming techniques so you can stay current with the technology. In this chapter, data from a form was sent in a file to an e-mail address. The chapter mentioned CGI scripts and the PHP and Perl programming languages as better, more secure methods to use for processing the information submitted in a form. While CGI scripts and Perl programming are beyond the scope of this book, they are important topics to study. Search the Web to find additional information about CGI scripts, PHP, and Perl used in conjunction with forms. Try to find online tutorials that explain how to use these techniques. What other options are available for collecting information online? Develop a Web page that lists links to various Web sites that discuss these topics. Under each link, write a brief paragraph explaining the purpose of each Web site and why it is important to review.

7 Using Advanced Cascading Style Sheets

Objectives

You will have mastered the material in this chapter when you can:

- Add an embedded style sheet to a Web page
- Change the body and link styles using an embedded style sheet
- Create a drop-down menu using an embedded style sheet
- Change the color and font styles of the drop-down menus
- Create an external style sheet
- Change the paragraph margins and font styles using an external style sheet
- Create a pop-up effect using an external style sheet
- Use classes, pseudoclasses, and divisions for the pop-up effect
- Use the <link> tag to insert a link to an external style sheet
- Add an external style sheet for printing Web pages

7 Using Advanced Cascading Style Sheets

Introduction

In previous chapters, you used HTML tags and Cascading Style Sheets (CSS) to change the way a Web page appears in a Web browser, such as adding italic, bold, colors, headings, and tables. This is also known as the style of the Web page. In this chapter, you will expand your knowledge of CSS to give added functionality to your Web pages. You will insert drop-down menus for your Web site visitors to use for navigation. This advanced technique is done with more complex CSS code. You will also add pop-up image effects using an advanced CSS technique. Using CSS is a better way to format your Web pages as opposed to using tables. You have more flexibility using CSS versus tables for Web page structure.

Project — Using Advanced Cascading Style Sheets

Jared Adam's Adventure Travel had a Web site created several years ago. Although the Web site is well-designed and effective, they now want to improve their Web site with drop-down menus and image effects. They hire you to enhance their Web site using advanced Cascading Style Sheets (CSS).

At Mr. Adam's request, you use advanced Cascading Style Sheets to add a drop-down menu, as shown in Figure 7–1b. Recognizing that the Jared Adam's Adventure Travel Web site will continue to grow, you suggest that you modify the Web site to use embedded and external Cascading Style Sheets (CSS). You explain to him that Cascading Style Sheets maintain a consistent look across a Web site — especially Web sites that contain many pages, and can give the pages a more polished look. You suggest that you create an external style sheet that is linked to the other Web pages. This style sheet, which can be easily linked into all pages in the Web site, is used to give the images on the Web page a pop-up effect (Figure 7–1b). Additionally, you would like to create a second external style sheet that can be used when printing, to print only the content of a Web page and not the navigation bar. Mr. Adam is supportive of the plan and encourages you to start as soon as possible.

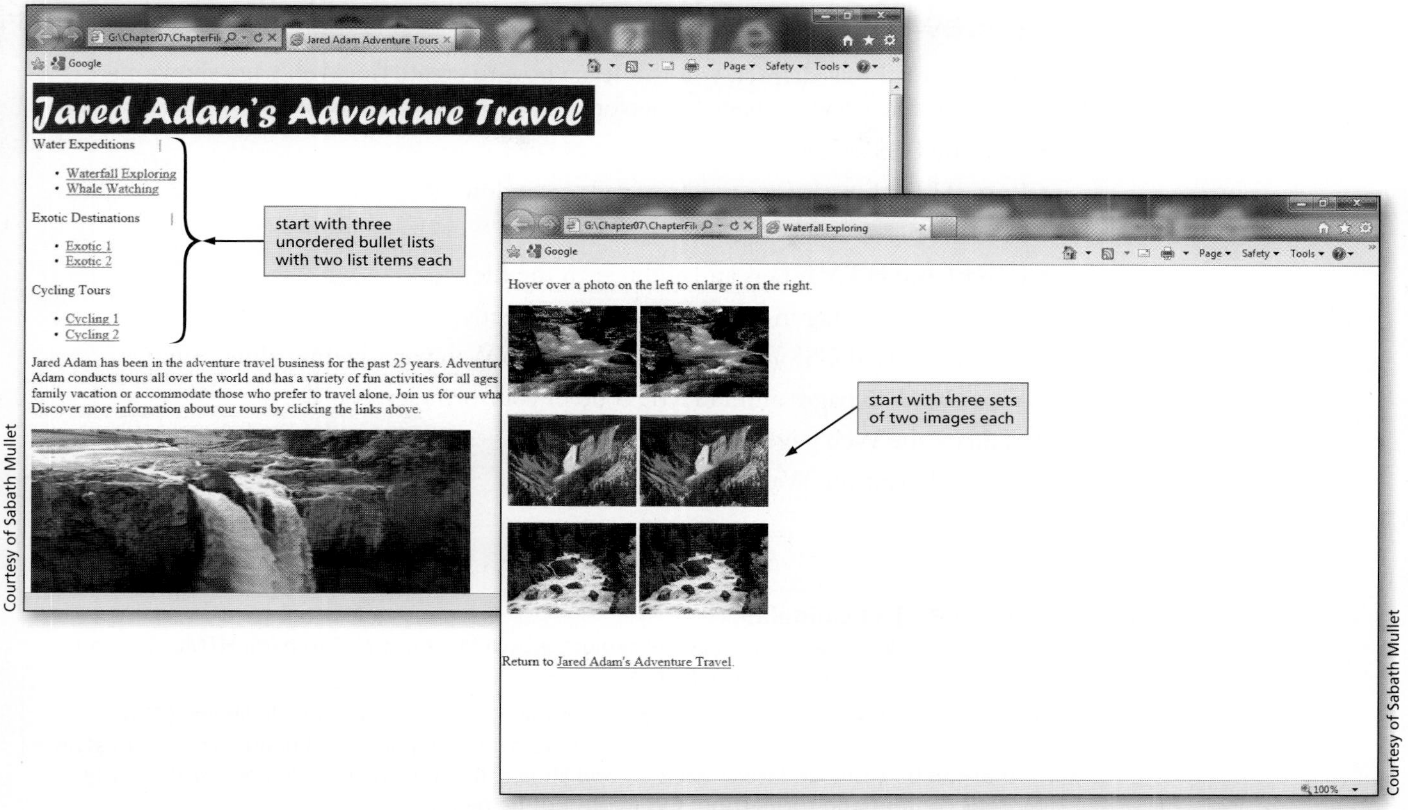
Jared Adam's Adventure Travel
Water Expeditions
Waterfall Exploring
Whale Watching
Exotic Destinations
Exotic 1
Exotic 2
Cycling Tours
Cycling 1
Cycling 2
start with three unordered bullet lists with two list items each
Hover over a photo on the left to enlarge it on the right.
start with three sets of two images each
Return to Jared Adam's Adventure Travel.
Courtesy of Sabath Mullet
Courtesy of Sabath Mullet

(a) Web pages without style sheets.

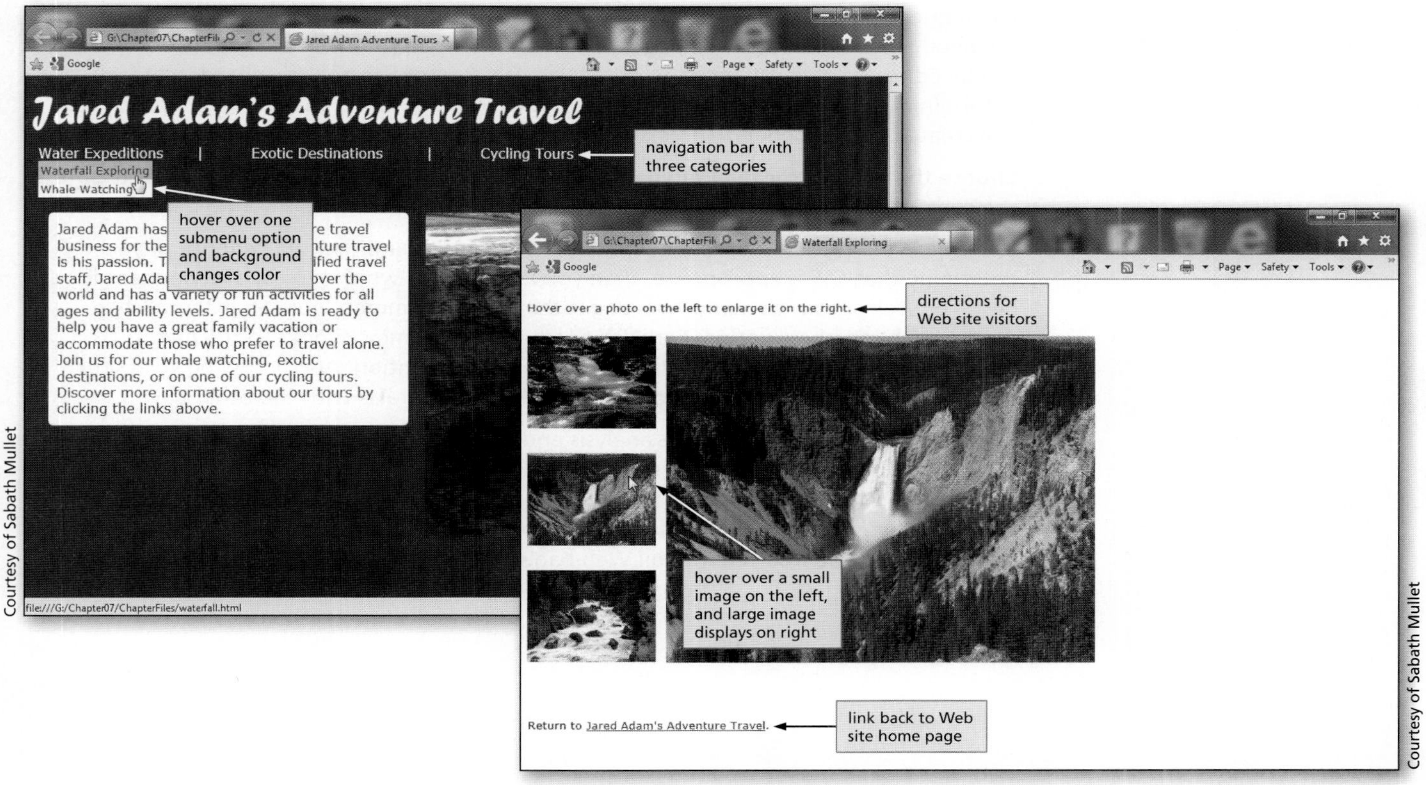
Jared Adam's Adventure Travel
Water Expeditions | Exotic Destinations | Cycling Tours
navigation bar with three categories
Waterfall Exploring
Whale Watching
hover over one submenu option and background changes color
Hover over a photo on the left to enlarge it on the right.
directions for Web site visitors
hover over a small image on the left, and large image displays on right
Return to Jared Adam's Adventure Travel.
link back to Web site home page
Courtesy of Sabath Mullet
Courtesy of Sabath Mullet

(b) Web pages with style sheets.

Figure 7–1

Overview

As you read this chapter, you will learn how to create the Web page shown in Figure 7–1 on the previous page by performing these general tasks:

- Plan the CSS structure.
- Enter HTML code into the Notepad++ window.
- Save the file as an HTML file.
- Enter basic HTML tags and add text to the file.
- Use the <style> tag in an embedded style sheet.
- Create external CSS files that are linked into Web pages with a <link /> tag.
- View the Web pages and HTML code in your browser.
- Validate the Web pages.
- Test and print the Web pages.

Plan Ahead

General Project Guidelines

As you create Web pages, such as the project shown in Figure 7–1 on page HTML 325, you should follow these general guidelines:

1. **Plan the Web site**. First, you should determine if using Cascading Style Sheets (CSS) is appropriate for your Web site. If you have several Web pages and need a consistent style that can be easily updated, CSS is a good choice. If you have a single page with mostly static content and formatting, CSS might not be needed.
2. **Analyze the need.** In the analysis phase of the Web Development Life Cycle, you should analyze what content to include in the Web page. Chapter 7 introduces advanced CSS techniques that can be used for Web development. Using style sheets can eliminate the need to edit multiple Web pages for simple changes. An external style sheet can be edited to make changes across a Web site. Part of the analysis phase includes determining how the multiple Web pages work together using CSS. In this chapter, you will create both embedded and external style sheets.
3. **Choose the content for the Web page.** With a multiple-page Web site, you can distribute the content as needed throughout the Web site.
4. **Determine the type of style sheets to use for the pages and their precedence.** If you determine that CSS is appropriate, then you must decide which type(s) of style sheet is best. For Web sites with many Web pages that have a common look, an external style sheet may be the best option. For Web sites with few common looks to the pages, using embedded or inline style sheets may be a better option. Also, knowing style sheet precedence helps you to understand how each style interacts with the others.
5. **Create the style sheets**. Once the analysis and design is complete, the Web developer creates the Web page using CSS. Good Web development standard practices should be followed in this step. Embedded and inline style sheets are used within particular Web pages. An external style sheet must first be created and saved as a .css file. Then a link statement must be inserted into all Web pages that will use the external style sheet.

(continued)

6. **Test all Web pages within the Web site.** An important part of Web development is testing to assure that you are following the coding standards discussed earlier in the book. In this book, you use the World Wide Web Consortium (W3C) validator that allows you to test your Web page and clearly explains any errors you have. As defined earlier in the book, one validator is used for all .html files, and another is used for all .css files. In addition to the validation process, you should test the Web pages themselves in the browser. When testing, you should also check all content for accuracy and ensure that all links work as intended.

When necessary, more specific details concerning the above guidelines are presented at appropriate points in the chapter. The chapter also will identify the actions performed and decisions made regarding these guidelines during the creation of the Web page shown in Figure 7–1 on page HTML 325.

Plan Ahead

Using Style Sheets

As you learned in earlier chapters, although HTML allows Web developers to make changes to the structure, design, and content of a Web page, HTML is limited in its ability to define the appearance, or style, across one or more Web pages. As a result, Cascading Style Sheets (CSS) were created. With CSS, you can establish a standard look for all Web pages in a Web site. Using CSS, you avoid the tedious steps of adding repetitive codes to format the same types of information. For example, instead of making all paragraphs of text 10pt Verdana in individual <p> tags, you can define that style in an external style sheet (.css file) and link that external file to all Web pages. CSS is also perfect for formatting Web pages, but without using HTML table tags. As mentioned earlier in the book, tables should not be used to format Web pages; CSS should be used instead.

A style is a rule that defines the appearance of an element on a Web page, and a style sheet is a series of rules that defines the style for a Web page or an entire Web site. There are three types of CSS: inline, embedded (or internal), and external (or linked). In previous chapter projects, you have used all three types to alter the appearance of a Web page or pages by changing characteristics such as font-family, font-size, margins, and link specifications. In this chapter, you will learn to use more advanced CSS features to add functionality to Web pages.

First, an embedded style sheet is used to add a drop-down menu to the home page of the Web site (Figure 7–2a on the next page). You use an embedded style sheet in this case because the menu appears only on the home page. An external style sheet (Figure 7–2b) is created for printing and is linked into the home page, jaredadam.html. With these style sheets added, the Jared Adam's Adventure Travel home page is attractive, polished, and professional looking (Figure 7–2c). An external style sheet is then created to add a pop-up effect in the other Web pages in the Web site (Figure 7–2d). You use an external style sheet because the style will be the same across several Web pages. That external style sheet is linked into the waterfall exploring and whale watching pages to give the pop-up effect shown in Figure 7–2e.

BTW

CSS
The World Wide Web Consortium (W3C) has a wealth of information about Cascading Style Sheets (CSS). You can find out what is new with CSS, access CSS testing suites, and find links to CSS authoring tools from this Web site. For more information, visit the W3C Web site and search for CSS.

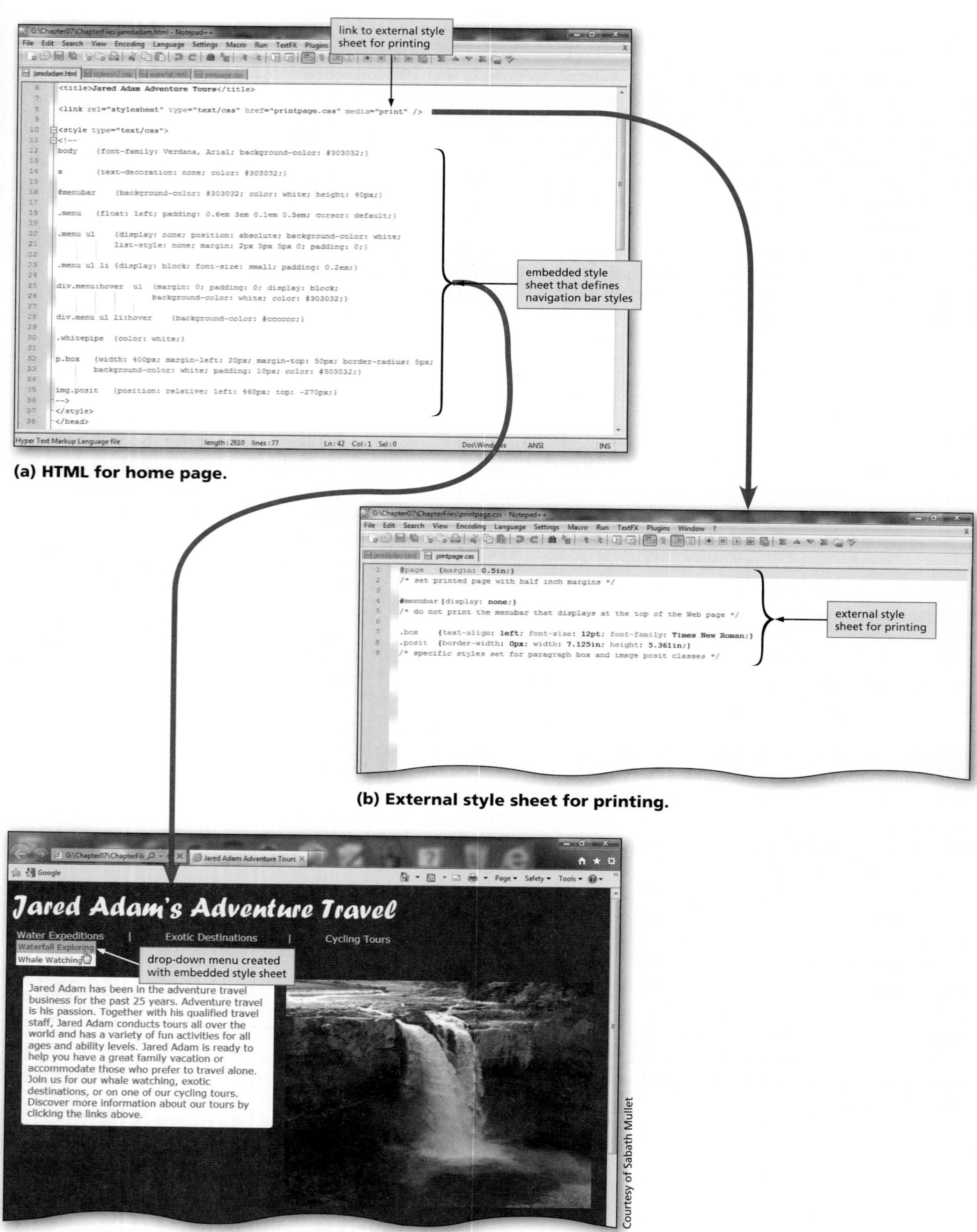

(a) HTML for home page.

(b) External style sheet for printing.

(c) Home page with embedded and external style sheets.

Figure 7–2

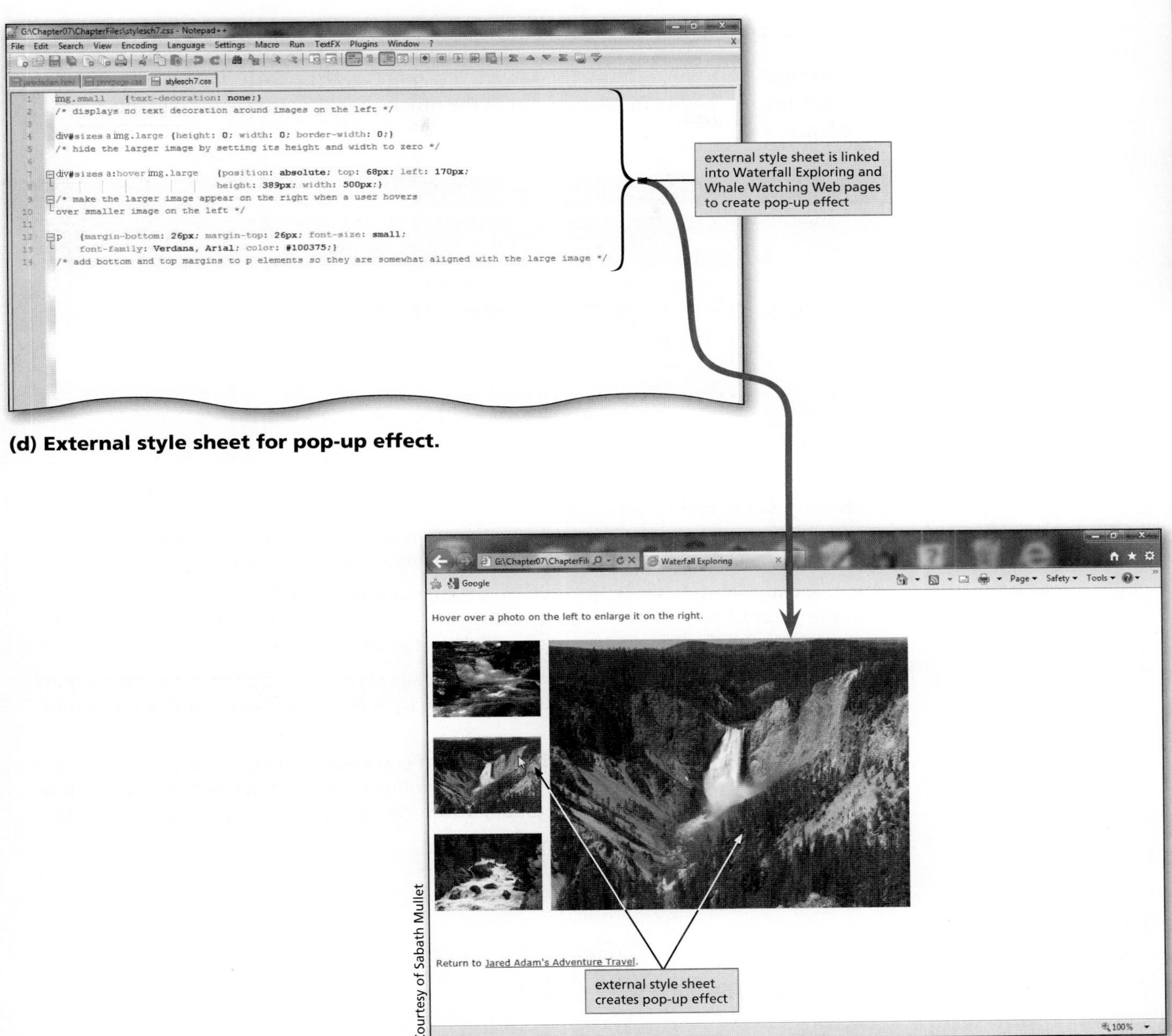

(d) External style sheet for pop-up effect.

(e) Secondary Web page with link to external style sheet.

Figure 7–2 (continued)

Style Sheet Precedence Review

As discussed in previous chapters, each style sheet type has a different level of precedence or priority in relationship to the others. Table 7–1 reviews style sheet precedence.

Table 7–1 Style Sheet Precedence

Type	Level and Precedence
Inline	• Changes the style within an individual HTML tag • Overrides embedded and external style sheets
Embedded	• Changes the style of one Web page • Overrides external style sheets
External	• Changes the style of multiple pages in a Web site

Plan Ahead

Identify what style sheets to use.

The first step to consider when using style sheets is to lay out a plan that takes style sheet precedence into account. This project uses only embedded and external style sheets.

- **Use external style sheets for styles that you want across the Web site.** As mentioned, the greatest benefit of CSS is the ability to identify a style across a Web site. For Web pages in which you want a common look, use external style sheets.
- **Use embedded style sheets for single Web page styles.** This type of style sheet is good to use if you want the style to just affect one (or a few) Web pages, and not all pages across the Web site.
- **Use inline style sheets for individual styles.** If you want to change the style of one or a few sections of one Web page, then using inline style sheets is the most appropriate. If the style is intended for most (or all) of the Web pages, you may want to switch to embedded or external style sheets.

Adding Style Sheets to the Jared Adam's Adventure Travel Site

The Jared Adam's Adventure Travel Web site for this chapter consists of six files (excluding image files), as shown in Table 7–2. The first Web page, jaredadam.html, is the home page of the Web site. The jaredadam.html file contains the navigation bar at the top of the Web page. It also contains the company logo and the home page content.

Table 7–2 Files Used for the Chapter 7 Project

File Name	Purpose and Display Specifics at Startup	Changes Made in Chapter 7
jaredadam.html	• Home page of the Web site • Contains an unordered list of navigation options, an image logo, and a paragraph of text	• Add an embedded style sheet that creates a drop-down menu • Position paragraph of text and image by defining styles for margins, background color, and padding
waterfall.html	• Contains the HTML tags, content, and images that are needed for the pop-up effect	• Add a link to an external style sheet that displays a large image when a user hovers the mouse over a smaller version of the image

Table 7–2 Files Used for the Chapter 7 Project (continued)

File Name	Purpose and Display Specifics at Startup	Changes Made in Chapter 7
whale.html	• Contains the HTML tags, content, and images that are needed for the pop-up effect	• Add a link to an external style sheet that displays a large image when a user hovers over the smaller image
stylesch7.css	• Nothing at startup; created from scratch	• Create an external style sheet • Save as a .css file
printpage.css	• Nothing at startup; created from scratch	• Create an external style sheet • Save as a .css file
ch7sample.html	• Dummy Web page that contains initial HTML code and link statement to external style sheet	• Nothing is done to this Web page in the chapter; you can use it as a starting point for additional Web pages

In this project, you will add different types of style sheets to the Web pages in the Jared Adam's Adventure Travel Web site. To add the style sheets, you will make changes to three of the Web pages stored in the Chapter07/ChapterFiles folder of the Data Files for Students: jaredadam.html, waterfall.html, and whale.html. You will also create two external style sheet files, stylesch7.css and printpage.css. In addition to the files listed in Table 7–2, all image files needed for the chapter project are stored in the Data Files for Students. See the inside back cover of this book for instructions on downloading the Data Files for Students, or contact your instructor for information about accessing the required files.

Plan Ahead

Creating an Embedded Style Sheet.

You use an embedded style sheet if you want to set the styles within a Web page. In the case of this Web site, you want to create a navigation bar with a drop-down menu on the home page only. You design that menu on the home page by creating an embedded style sheet.

- **Determine which Web pages vary enough that an embedded style sheet makes sense.** You may have only one or even just a few Web pages in a Web site that will vary slightly from all other pages. In this case, an embedded style sheet makes sense. If there are styles that are to be repeated in that one Web page (or in a few pages), you would be better off using an embedded style sheet rather than a series of inline styles. For instance, if you want all paragraphs of text to have the same style within one Web page, then it makes more sense to embed that style rather than add the style to each paragraph tag within the Web page.
- **Copy an embedded style sheet into other Web pages.** If you have a few Web pages that should have the same style, insert the embedded sheet in one Web page, save, validate, and test it. Once you have verified that it works as you intend, then you can copy/paste the embedded style sheet into the other Web pages.
- **Change to an external style sheet when necessary.** If you find that the style from the embedded style sheet is used on more Web pages as time goes on, you should create an external style sheet and link it into all Web pages in which you had previously inserted an embedded style sheet. For instance, if you decide that you want to have the drop-down menu on all Web pages in the Web site, you should move the code in the embedded style sheet to an external style sheet and link that external style sheet into all Web pages in the Web site.

Adding a Navigation Bar with an Embedded Style Sheet

The first step in adding style sheets to the Jared Adam's Adventure Travel Web site is to add an embedded style sheet to the home page of the Web site, jaredadam.html. First, the HTML file jaredadam.html must be opened in Notepad++. Then you enter the code for the embedded style sheet. Figure 7–3a shows the home page in the default style (without a style sheet) as provided in the Data Files for Students, and Figure 7–3b shows the same Web page after the embedded style sheet has been added.

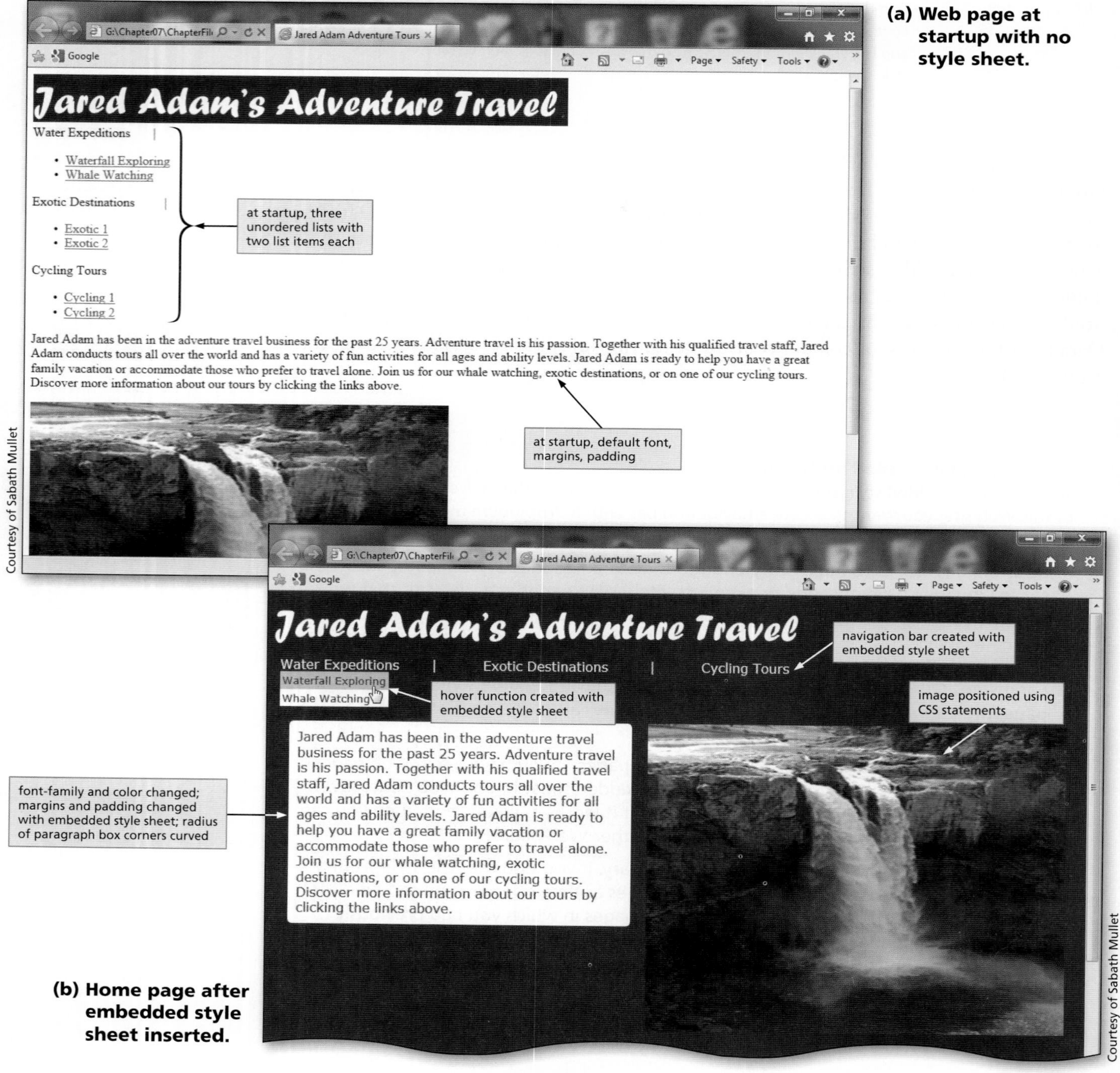

(a) Web page at startup with no style sheet.

(b) Home page after embedded style sheet inserted.

Figure 7–3

To Start Notepad++ and Open an HTML File

1. Start Notepad++ and, if necessary, maximize the window.
2. With the USB drive plugged into your computer, click File on the menu bar and then click Open.
3. If necessary, navigate to the Chapter07\ChapterFiles folder on the USB drive.
4. Double-click jaredadam.html in the list of files to open the file shown in Figure 7–4.

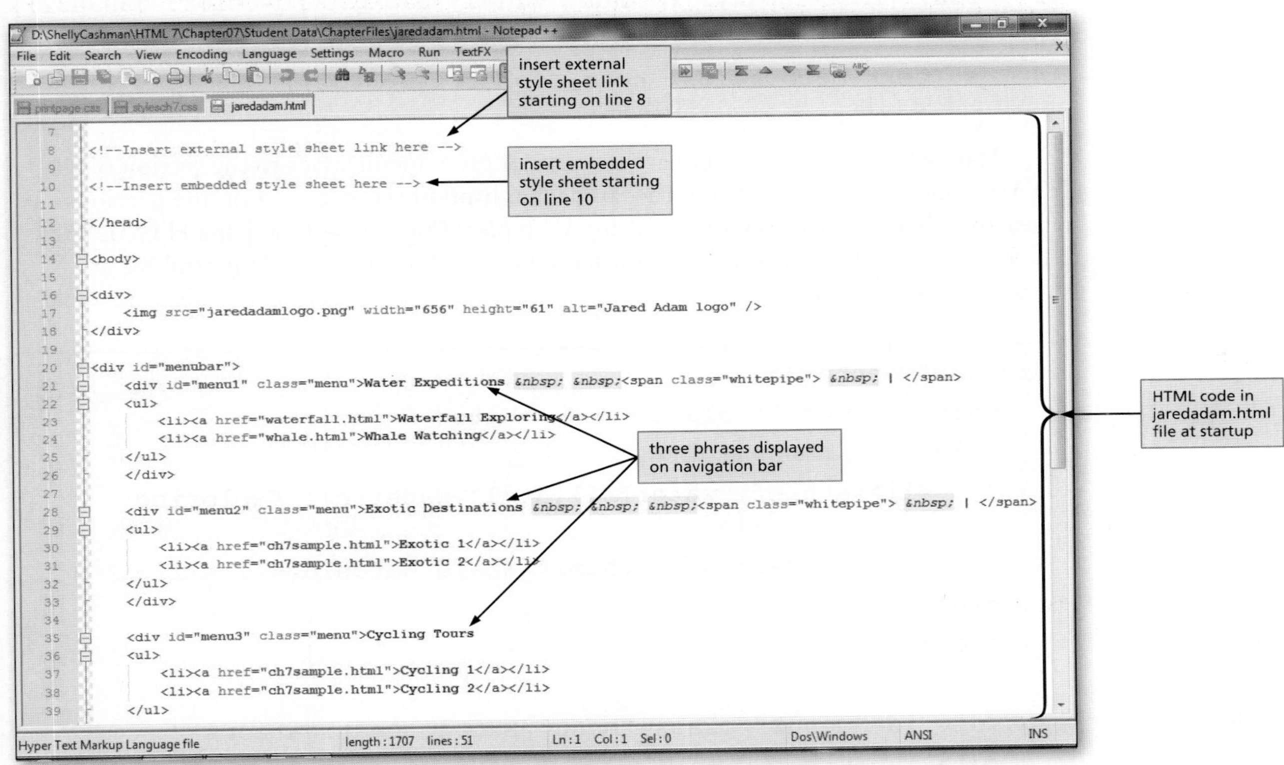

Figure 7–4

Setting the Body Style and Link Style, and Adding a Drop-down Menu

Before you enter the code for the embedded style sheet, you should understand a little more about the styles you are setting.

The code for an embedded style sheet must be inserted between a start <style> tag and an end </style> tag, which are positioned within the head element. Within the style tag container, Web developers generally follow the coding practice to add an HTML start comment code <!-- and end comment code -->. The beginning and ending HTML comment lines hide any script language that an older browser cannot interpret.

First we will review sections of the embedded CSS code that you will add and review how each section helps to create the home page of Jared Adam's Adventure Travel. This code will enhance the three unordered lists displayed at the top of the Web page by creating a navigation bar (see Figure 7–3b on the previous page) with the words Water Expeditions, Exotic Destinations, and Cycling Tours. It will also improve the appearance of the two list items within each unordered list that are used as submenus.

> **BTW**
> **Word Spacing**
> The CSS word-spacing property is a good way to add additional space between words. You can use any of the length units including: inches, centimeters, millimeters, points, picas, ems, x-height, and pixels.

Figure 7–3b on page HTML 332 shows the two list items: Waterfall Exploring and Whale Watching. Notice the white background color on the submenu, which differs from the dark background color used on the navigation bar. Using CSS to apply the background colors gives the appearance of a menu and submenu system. You could use graphical images here as well. For instance, you could create a navigation bar using button images to give this same menu and submenu effect.

The embedded style sheet code below sets the font-family throughout the Web page by use of the body element (Line 12). Line 14 sets the link color and turns text-decoration (i.e., underline) off. (Line 13 is intentionally left blank.)

```
12   body {font-family: Verdana, Arial; background-color: #303032;}
13
14   a {text-decoration: none; color: #303032;}
```

It may help for you to compare the uses of these menu styles to the section of HTML code (below) provided in the jaredadam.html file (Figure 7–4 on the previous page), together with viewing the resulting Web page (Figure 7–3b on page HTML 332). The structure of the divisions and unordered lists used in the jaredadam.html file at start-up are as follows:

```
<div id="menubar">
    <div id="menu1" class="menu">Water Expeditions
    <ul>
        <li><a href="waterfall.html">Waterfall Exploring
            </a></li>
        <li><a href="whale.html">Whale Watching</a></li>
    </ul>
    </div>

    <div id="menu2" class="menu">Exotic Destinations
    <ul>
        <li><a href="ch7sample.html">Exotic 1</a></li>
        <li><a href="ch7sample.html">Exotic 2</a></li>
    </ul>
    </div>

    <div id="menu3" class="menu">Cycling Tours
    <ul>
        <li><a href="ch7sample.html">Cycling 1</a></li>
        <li><a href="ch7sample.html">Cycling 2</a></li>
    </ul>
    </div>
</div>
```

Notice that all three navigation bar options (Water Expeditions, Exotic Destinations, Cycling Tours) are placed within a division (section) of the Web page, as shown by the <div> and </div> tags. This division is given the id name menubar. You will insert the embedded CSS code shown below within the <style> </style> container to define the menubar id and menu class.

```
16    #menubar {background-color: #303032; color: white; height:
      40px;}
17
18    .menu {float: left; padding: 0.6em 3em 0.1em 0.5em;
      cursor: default;}
```

Note that lines 16 and 18 define the styles that are to be used for id="menubar" and class="menu" in the CSS code. There are also three unordered lists within this same division (for Water Expeditions, Exotic Destinations, and Cycling Tours), each containing two list items. Those unordered lists each use the class="menu" (see lines 21, 28, and 35). Therefore, the styles defined in the CSS code lines 16 and 18 are reflected in the submenu list items from the three unordered lists.

Lines 16 through 18 set the styles for the drop-down menu that will display at the top of the Web page, as shown in Figure 7–6a on page HTML 337. In line 16, you set the background color, text color, and height, of an element named menubar that will be used in a <div> tag. The background color is set to #303032, while the text color is set to white. Line 16 also sets the height of the area to 40 pixels. The height is something that you can adjust as you develop the Web page. You need to determine how much space you want relative to the default font size.

Line 18 sets the styles for a class named menu. The first style statement floats the text to the left. The padding property uses the "shorthand property" code. The **shorthand property** allows a Web developer to shorten the code. Instead of using padding-top, padding-bottom, padding-right, and padding-left, you can specify all the padding values in one property. The padding property can have from one to four values. Table 7–3 shows the shorthand statement together with the resulting values.

BTW

Line Height
The CSS line-height property gives you the ability to control line height. With this property, you can control the vertical spacing between lines of text. There are three different ways to add the line-height value: by number, by length, and by percentage. If you specify by number, the browser uses the font-size property to determine the space. You can use em and pt with the length value to set a fixed line height. Finally, you can determine the line spacing using a percentage.

BTW

Shorthand Properties
Shorthand properties are great to use and make your CSS code very efficient. You can use shorthand properties with many different elements, including padding, borders, margins, and fonts. See the w3.org Web site for helpful information about shorthand properties.

Table 7–3 Shorthand Properties

Padding Property Statement	Resulting Values
padding: 25px 50px 75px 100px;	top padding is 25px right padding is 50px bottom padding is 75px left padding is 100px
padding: 25px 50px 75px;	top padding is 25px right and left paddings are 50px bottom padding is 75px
padding: 25px 50px;	top and bottom paddings are 25px right and left paddings are 50px
padding: 25px;	all four paddings are 25px

BTW

Em Units
The em is a very useful unit in CSS, because it adapts automatically to the font size that the Web page visitor uses.

BTW

Measurement Values
When is it best to use the "em" measurement versus using the "pt" measurement? There are many advanced Web page design resources available that discuss this topic. The main goal with any measurement value is to design a Web page so that it is legible.

Notice also that you are setting the padding in the statement to an "em" measurement value. Table 7–4 describes the units that can be used by Web developers.

Table 7–4 Measurement Values

Unit	Description
%	percentage
in	inch
cm	centimeter
mm	millimeter
em	1em is equal to the current font size; 2em means 2 times the size of the current font. For example, if an element is displayed with a font of 12 pt, then 2em is 24 pt
ex	one ex is the x-height of a font (x-height is usually about half the font size)
pt	point (1 pt = 1/72 inch)
pc	pica (1 pc = 12 points)
px	pixels (a dot on the computer screen)

Line 18 also sets the cursor to the default value using cursor: default as the statement. If you do not have this statement, then you would not see a cursor as shown in Figure 7–5a. With this cursor code statement inserted, you see the cursor as shown in Figure 7–5b.

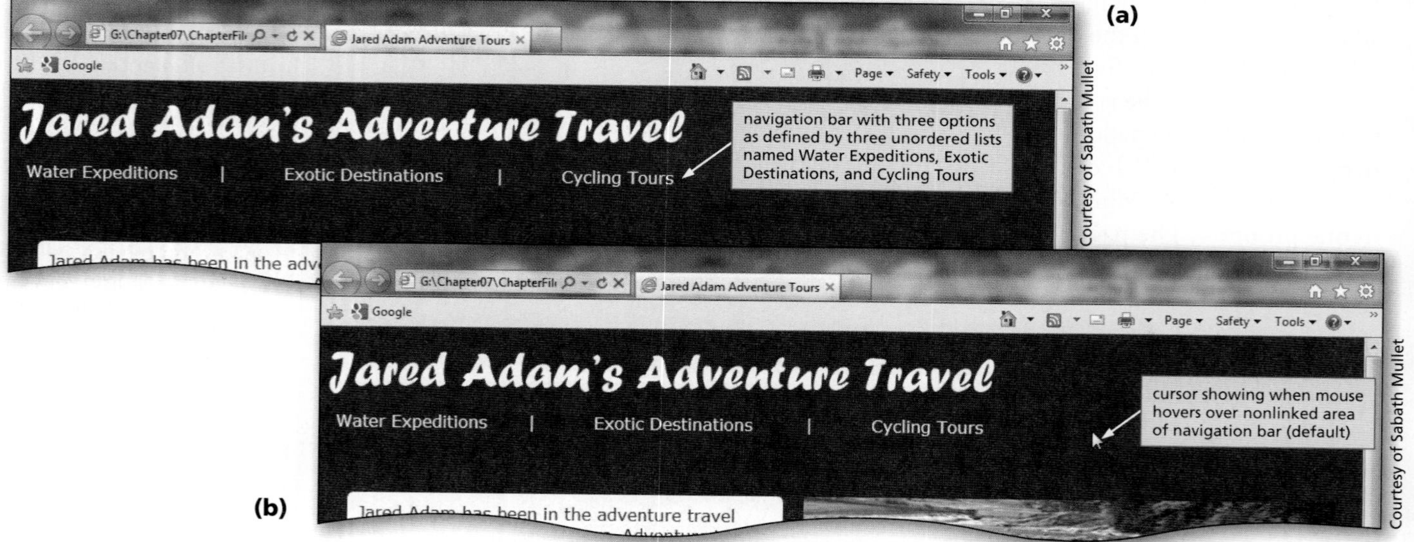

Figure 7–5

The next section of code that you will add to the jaredadam.html embedded style sheet (lines 20 through 28 shown below) specifies additional styles for the navigation bar and submenus.

```
20   .menu ul   {display: none; position: absolute;
                background-color: white;
21              list-style: none; margin: 2px 5px 5px 0;
                padding: 0;}
22
```

```
23    .menu ul li        {display: block; font-size: small;
                          padding: 0.2em;}
24
25    div.menu:hover ul{margin: 0; padding: 0; display: block;
26                      background-color: white; color: #303032;}
27
28    div.menu ul li:hover    {background-color: #cccccc;}
```

Figure 7–5b shows the navigation bar with the inserted code above. Figure 7–6a shows the navigation bar when the pointer is on the Water Expeditions option. This is defined with the style statements on lines 20 and 21 in the CSS code. Figure 7–6b shows the navigation bar when a Web site visitor hovers over the Whale Watching list item in the Water Expeditions list. This style is defined on lines 25 through 28 where the hover pseudoclass is used.

> **BTW**
> **CSS Pseudoclasses**
> To expand the possibilities of CSS, you can use pseudoclasses (e.g., the link hover). When used effectively, CSS pseudoclasses are used to add special effects to some selectors.

Figure 7–6

The CSS code in the embedded style sheet contains some properties you are familiar with from previous chapters and some that are new. Line 20 in the CSS code sets a style for the unordered lists (ul) in the menu class. It starts by setting display to none. When the Web page loads (i.e., before the user hovers over the menu), the unordered lists will not display (Figure 7–5b on the previous page). The position property is used to position an element on the Web page. If you do not use the position property, the elements display on the Web page in the order in which they appear. For example, if you have a line of text entered in your HTML code, and then you insert an image in the code, the text appears on the Web page before the image. The position: absolute property in line 20 sets the style so that the menu text remains constant and does not move. Table 7–5 on the next page lists the available property values for position.

Table 7–5 Position Property Values

Property Values	Value Description
absolute	Generates an absolutely positioned element, positioned relative to the first parent element that has a position other than static
fixed	Generates an absolutely positioned element, positioned relative to the browser window
relative	Generates a relatively positioned element, positioned relative to its normal position, so "left: 10" adds 10 pixels to the element's left position
static	Default; no position; the element occurs in the normal flow
inherit	Specifies that the value of the position property should be inherited from the parent element

When you add the list-style: none property in line 21, you turn off the display of the disc that is the default bullet for an unordered list. The margin: 2px 5px 5px 0 code is a shorthand property statement for margins. When you set the display: block style on lines 23 and 25, the ul element will generate a block box (line break) before and after the element. On line 30 (shown below) you will create a class named "whitepipe":

```
30    .whitepipe {color: white;}
```

The whitepipe class sets the color of the pipe symbol used in between the menu options to white. We set that pipe symbol to white so that it will display against the dark background.

In the final section of the embedded style sheet (lines 32 through 35) you will set the styles for the content (text and image) that displays beneath the navigation bar.

```
32    p.box {width: 400px; margin-left: 20px; margin-top: 50px;
             border-radius: 5px;
33           background-color: white; padding: 10px; color:
             #303032;}
34
35    img.posit {position: relative; left: 460px; top: -270px;}
```

Lines 32 and 33 create a paragraph class named "box" that describes the style of the box surrounding the paragraph of text. The width of the box is 400 pixels with a left margin of 20 pixels and a top margin of 50 pixels as shown in Figure 7–7a. The border-radius is set to 5 pixels which gives the box rounded corners. The background color is white with gray (#303032) text. Line 35 creates a class named "posit" that positions the image in a relative position from the left by 460 pixels and from the top at –270 pixels. Figure 7–7b shows the same image positioned from the bottom of the paragraph box by 50 pixels.

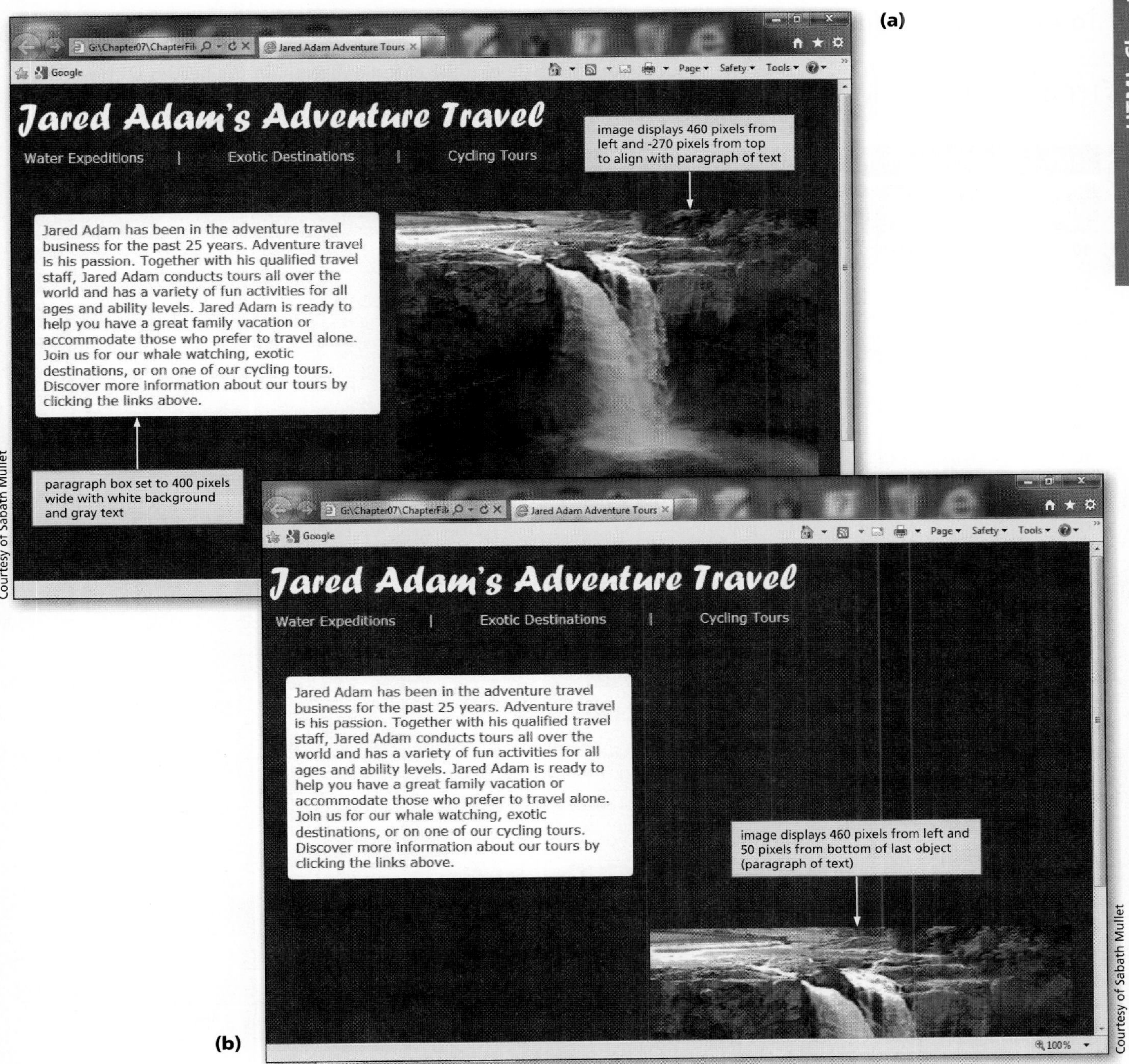

(a)
G:\Chapter07\ChapterFil
Jared Adam Adventure Tours
Google
Page
Safety
Tools
Jared Adam's Adventure Travel
Water Expeditions | Exotic Destinations | Cycling Tours
image displays 460 pixels from left and -270 pixels from top to align with paragraph of text
Jared Adam has been in the adventure travel business for the past 25 years. Adventure travel is his passion. Together with his qualified travel staff, Jared Adam conducts tours all over the world and has a variety of fun activities for all ages and ability levels. Jared Adam is ready to help you have a great family vacation or accommodate those who prefer to travel alone. Join us for our whale watching, exotic destinations, or on one of our cycling tours. Discover more information about our tours by clicking the links above.
paragraph box set to 400 pixels wide with white background and gray text
Courtesy of Sabath Mullet
(b)
G:\Chapter07\ChapterFil
Jared Adam Adventure Tours
Google
Page
Safety
Tools
Jared Adam's Adventure Travel
Water Expeditions | Exotic Destinations | Cycling Tours
Jared Adam has been in the adventure travel business for the past 25 years. Adventure travel is his passion. Together with his qualified travel staff, Jared Adam conducts tours all over the world and has a variety of fun activities for all ages and ability levels. Jared Adam is ready to help you have a great family vacation or accommodate those who prefer to travel alone. Join us for our whale watching, exotic destinations, or on one of our cycling tours. Discover more information about our tours by clicking the links above.
image displays 460 pixels from left and 50 pixels from bottom of last object (paragraph of text)
100%
Courtesy of Sabath Mullet

Figure 7–7

To Add an Embedded Style Sheet

Table 7–6 shows the CSS code for the embedded style sheet to be entered directly in the header section of the HTML code for the home page, jaredadam.html.

Table 7–6 Code for an Embedded Style Sheet

Line	CSS Code
10	<style type="text/css">
11	<!--
12	body {font-family: Verdana, Arial; background-color: #303032;}
13	
14	a {text-decoration: none; color: #303032;}
15	
16	#menubar {background-color: #303032; color: white; height: 40px;}
17	
18	.menu {float: left; padding: 0.6em 3em 0.1em 0.5em; cursor: default;}
19	
20	.menu ul {display: none; position: absolute; background-color: white;
21	list-style: none; margin: 2px 5px 5px 0; padding: 0;}
22	
23	.menu ul li {display: block; font-size: small; padding: 0.2em;}
24	
25	div.menu:hover ul {margin: 0; padding: 0; display: block;
26	background-color: white; color: #303032;}
27	
28	div.menu ul li:hover {background-color: #cccccc;}
29	
30	.whitepipe {color: white;}
31	
32	p.box {width: 400px; margin-left: 20px; margin-top: 50px; border-radius: 5px;
33	background-color: white; padding: 10px; color: #303032;}
34	
35	img.posit {position: relative; left: 460px; top: -270px;}
36	-->
37	</style>

The following step adds the embedded style sheet to the Web page jaredadam.html.

1

- Highlight the comment <!--Insert embedded style sheet here -->, on line 10.
- Enter the CSS code shown in Table 7–6 (Figure 7–8).

```
10 <style type="text/css">
11 <!--
12 body     {font-family: Verdana, Arial; background-color: #303032;}
13
14 a        {text-decoration: none; color: #303032;}
15
16 #menubar     {background-color: #303032; color: white; height: 40px;}
17
18 .menu    {float: left; padding: 0.6em 3em 0.1em 0.5em; cursor: default;}
19
20 .menu ul     {display: none; position: absolute; background-color: white;
21              list-style: none; margin: 2px 5px 5px 0; padding: 0;}
22
23 .menu ul li {display: block; font-size: small; padding: 0.2em;}
24
25 div.menu:hover  ul  {margin: 0; padding: 0; display: block;
26                     background-color: white; color: #303032;}
27
28 div.menu ul li:hover    {background-color: #cccccc;}
29
30 .whitepipe  {color: white;}
31
32 p.box   {width: 400px; margin-left: 20px; margin-top: 50px; border-radius: 5px;
33         background-color: white; padding: 10px; color: #303032;}
34
35 img.posit   {position: relative; left: 460px; top: -270px;}
36 -->
37 </style>
38 </head>
39
```

sets styles for Web page body and all links
sets styles for id named menubar
sets styles for unordered lists
sets styles for hover function
sets styles for class named whitepipe
sets styles for class named box to position the image
sets styles for class named posit to position the image

Figure 7–8

Q&A What is an easy way to find out what fonts are supported on your computer system?

One way is to review the font names and examples as they appear in an application such as in the Font group in Microsoft Word. You may want to try different fonts and sizes in an application such as Word to see what they look like. You can save a document as a Web page in Word and view it in the browser as well.

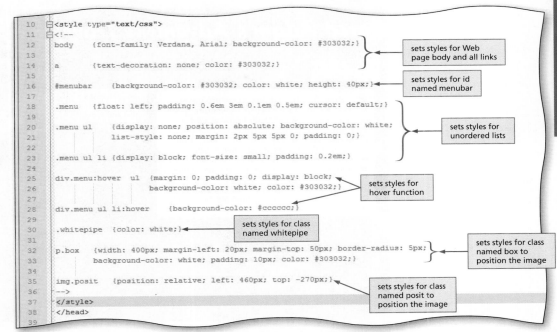

Q&A Why would I want to use the "hover" technique for links?

Using hover adds interactivity and in this case helps to highlight the menu and submenu structure for the user.

Experiment

- Remove the position: absolute property and value in line 20, save the file, and then open it in your browser. Notice how this change affects the phrases, Exotic Destinations and Cycling Tours, when you hover over the phrase, Water Expeditions. Put the statement back in.

To Save, Validate, and View an HTML File

After you have added the embedded style sheet to the jaredadam.html Web page, you should save the HTML file and view the Web page to review the style changes.

1. With the USB drive plugged into your computer, click File on the menu bar and then click Save.
2. Validate the Web page using the W3C validation service.
3. Open the jaredadam.html file in the Web browser to show the completed navigation bar, as shown at the top of the jaredadam.html Web page (Figure 7–9 on the next page).

BTW **Font Families**
You also can specify font-weight using numerical values from 100 to 900. Normal text that is not bold has a value of 400. Each larger number is at least as bold as the one above it, and 900 is the boldest option of the font. The browser interprets each value as it displays the Web page.

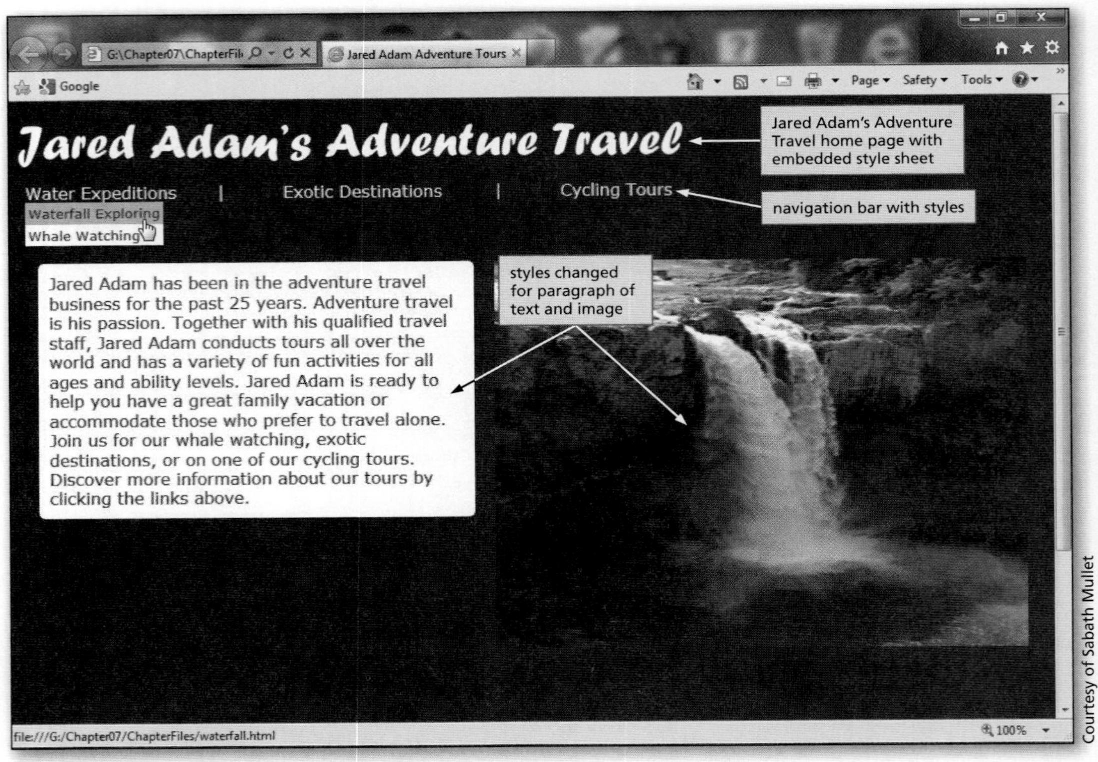

Figure 7–9

Plan Ahead

Creating an External Style Sheet

The external style sheet is the most powerful and the lowest precedence style sheet. With this style sheet, you can easily create a common look across a Web site by creating the external (.css) style sheet and linking it into all other Web pages. In this project, you have multiple pages where you want images to display a larger version when you hover over them.

- **Create the external style sheet.** The first step is to create the file itself. This file, which contains all of the style statements that you want, has to be saved with a filename extension of .css. Make sure to store this file in the same folder as the other Web pages.
- **Link the external style sheet into the Web pages.** The second step is to link the external style sheet (.css file) into the Web pages where you want it. The link statement is placed between the <head> and </head> tags.
- **Add comments to your code as needed.** The CSS code added to this external style sheet is complex. Comments help you remember and explain what you have done. The comments will not display on the Web page, but they will stay in the file with the CSS code.

Adding Pop-up Images with an External Style Sheet

As you learned in previous chapters, an external style sheet is a separate text file that contains the style statements that define how the Web page elements will appear across multiple pages. After you create the text file with all of the desired style statements and comments, you save the file with the file extension .css to identify it as a CSS file. You then use a <link> tag to link the external style sheet to the Web pages to which you want to apply the style.

Structuring the Web Page

It is useful to understand how you can structure your Web page by dividing it into logical sections. In previous chapters, you used <div> </div> tags for structure. Specifically, you aligned images by placing the image element within the tag. You also set specific styles using the <div> </div> tags. When you use the <div> </div> tags, you are able to design a layout that uses CSS, including inserting images.

When structuring your Web pages, it is also useful to understand the concept of the CSS box model. The **box model** describes the structure of the elements that are displayed on the Web page. Once you have positioned the box on the Web page, you can control its appearance by manipulating its padding, borders, and margins, as shown in Figure 7–10. The **margin** specifies the space between the element and other content on the Web page. The **border** is what surrounds the element content. The **padding** is the space between the content of the element and the box border. These four elements (content, padding, border, and margin) determine how the element content is displayed in the browser.

BTW

The Box Model
The CSS box model is an important concept to understand. Determining an effective structure of your Web pages involves correctly determining the box model controls. Search the Web for the term "box model" to find numerous resources that discuss box model control principles.

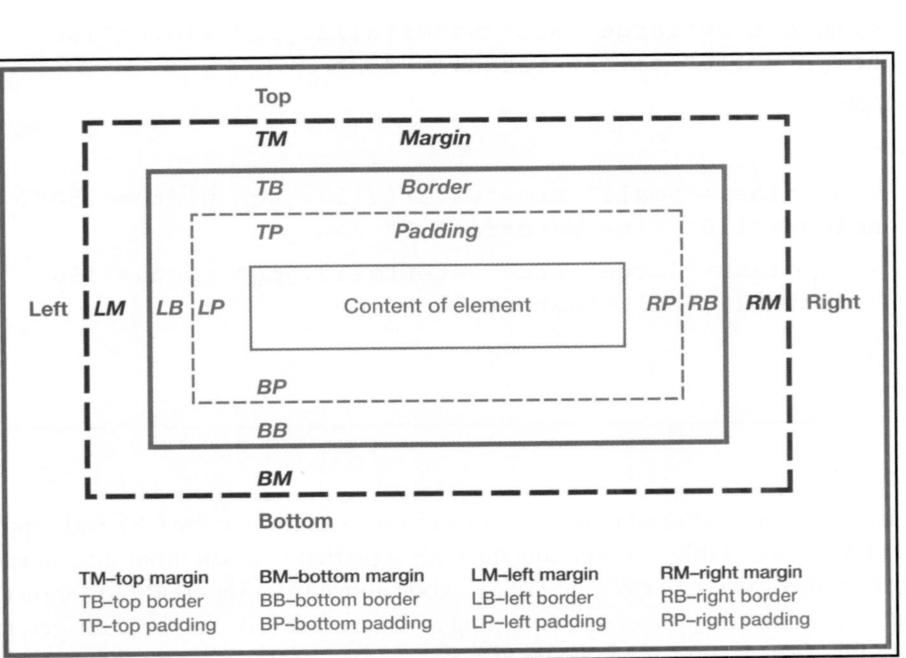

Figure 7–10

You will manipulate some of these characteristics (border, margin-bottom, margin-top) in the external style sheet completed in this section of the chapter. You will also use the <div> </div> tags to divide the Web page to allow the pop-up effect.

BTW

Box Model Troubleshooting
You can also find an abundance of information on the box model troubleshooting tools like those in Firebug or Google Chrome Developer Tools.

Creating a Pop-up Image Using Cascading Style Sheets

The CSS code for the external style sheet defines a new style that provides a pop-up image effect on a Web page. In this case, you will add link and hover functionality that allows a Web site visitor to hover (i.e., move the mouse pointer) over an image and display a larger version of the image.

The two files used for the pop-up effect, waterfall.html and whale.html, are stored in the Data Files for Students. These files are all ready to use for the pop-up effect but need to have the link statements inserted after the external style sheet is created and saved. It helps to look at the code in one of those files (waterfall.html) to see how the CSS code you will enter is used in the HTML file. The HTML code from waterfall.html follows:

```
<div id="sizes">
<p><a>
      <img class="small" src="waterfall1.jpg" width="150"
      height="110" alt="Waterfall 1" />
      <img class="large" src="waterfall1.jpg" width="150"
      height="110" alt="Waterfall 1" />
</a></p>
<p><a>
      <img class="small" src="waterfall2.jpg" width="150"
      height="110" alt="Waterfall 2" />
      <img class="large" src="waterfall2.jpg" width="150"
      height="110" alt="Waterfall 2" />
</a></p>
<p><a>
      <img class="small" src="waterfall3.jpg" width="150"
      height="110" alt="Waterfall 3" />
      <img class="large" src="waterfall3.jpg" width="150"
      height="110" alt="Waterfall 3" />
</a></p>
</div>
```

BTW

External Style Sheet Validator
For the external style sheet, be sure to use the CSS validator found at the w3.org validation service at jigsaw.w3.org/css-validator/#validate_by_upload.

There are two areas that need to be discussed to understand how the CSS code applies to the HTML code. Table 7–7 contains the CSS code that you will input into an external style sheet named stylesch7.css. The HTML code above from waterfall.html shows a division with an id named sizes and two <img /> tags for each of the three images, as shown in Figure 7–1b on page HTML 325.

Table 7–7 defines the styles for the id named "sizes" as used in the waterfall.html code. Line 1 in Table 7–7 creates a class named "small" that is used with the image element. Lines 4 and 7 identify a class named "large" that also will be used with the image element as shown in the waterfall.html code above. Note that line 4 identifies the styles for a link of an image for a class named large (an img.large), as used in the division with id sizes. Line 4 also tells the browser to set the large image size to height of zero and width of zero. The net effect of this is that the large image does not display at startup.

Line 7 targets the same elements (a and img) and the same class (large), but this time it sets styles for the hover pseudoclass (a:hover). This style statement tells the browser to enlarge the image with class name large when a user hovers over the small image. The "large" version of the image is set to an absolute position 68 pixels from the top of the browser window and 170 pixels from the left of the window. The height of the image when enlarged is 389 pixels, while the width is 500 pixels. This CSS code enlarges an image, but you can also display text or other elements using this same basic code structure.

To Create an External Style Sheet

To create an external style sheet, you will open a new text file and enter CSS code shown in Table 7-7. After coding the style statements, you will save the file with the file extension .css to identify it as a CSS file.

Table 7–7 Code for an External Style Sheet

```
img.small            {text-decoration: none;}
/* displays text decoration around images on the left */

div#sizes a img.large       {height: 0; width: 0; border-width: 0;}
/* hide the larger image by setting its height and width to zero */

div#sizes a:hover img.large       {position: absolute; top: 68px; left: 170px;
                                   height: 389px; width: 500px;}
/* make the larger image appear on the right when a user hovers
over smaller image on the left */

p        {margin-bottom: 26px; margin-top: 26px; font-size: small;
         font-family: Verdana, Arial; color: #100375;}
/* add bottom and top margins to p elements so they are aligned with the large image */
```

The following step creates an external style sheet to define Web page style.

1

- If necessary, click the Notepad++ button on the taskbar. Click File on the menu bar and then click New.
- Enter the CSS code as shown in Table 7–7.
- Save the file as stylesch7.css (Figure 7–11).
- Validate the CSS file (at jigsaw.w3.org/css-validator/#validate_by_upload) and then print it.

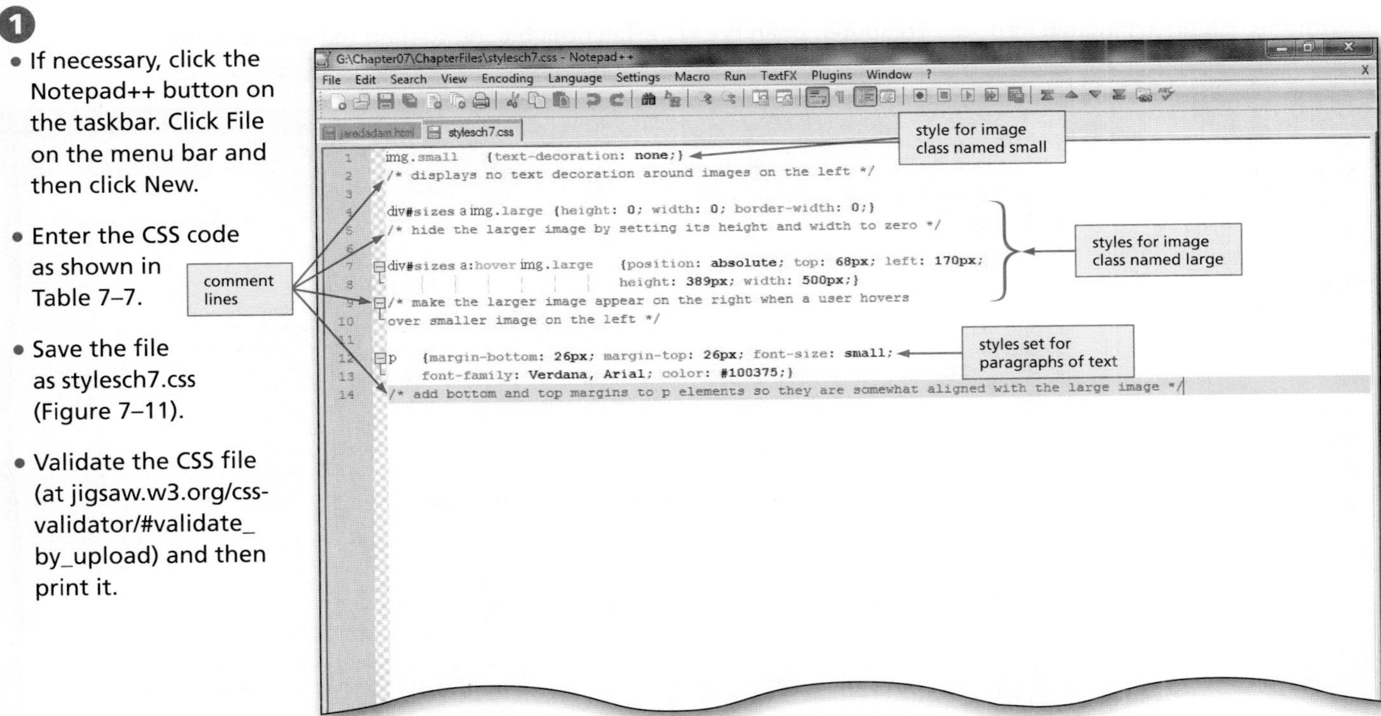

Figure 7–11

Linking to an External Style Sheet

You now want to add this pop-up image effect to two Web pages in the Jared Adam's Adventure Travel Web site: waterfall.html and whale.html. Linking the external style sheet to each of these Web pages gives you the capability to enlarge images in a pop-up format.

To link to the external style sheet, a <link> tag must be inserted into each of these two Web pages. The <link> tag used to link an external style sheet is added within the <head> tag of the Web page HTML. The general format of the <link> tag is:

```
<link rel="stylesheet" type="text/css" href="stylesch7.css" />
```

where rel="stylesheet" establishes that the linked document is a style sheet, type="text/css" indicates that the CSS language is used in the text file containing the style sheet, and href="stylesch7.css" provides the name and location (URL) of the linked style sheet. To link a style sheet to a Web page, the <link> tag must use "stylesheet" as the value for the rel property and text/css as the value for the type property. The URL used as the value for the href property varies, based on the name and location of the file used as the external style sheet. The URL used here indicates that the external style sheet, stylesch7.css, is located in the main or root directory of the Web site.

To Link to an External Style Sheet

The following steps add a link to an external style sheet using a <link> tag and then saves, validates, and tests the HTML file.

- If necessary, click the Notepad++ button on the taskbar.
- With the USB drive plugged into your computer, open the waterfall.html file, navigating to the G:\Chapter07\ChapterFiles folder if necessary.
- Highlight the text, <!--Insert external style sheet link statement here --> on line 8.
- Type `<link rel="stylesheet" type="text/css" href="stylesch7.css" />` to enter the link to the external style sheet (Figure 7–12).

G:\Chapter07\ChapterFiles\waterfall.html - Notepad++

File Edit Search View Encoding Language Settings Macro Run TextFX Plugins Window ?

jaredadam.html | stylesch7.css | waterfall.html

```
1  <!DOCTYPE HTML>
2
3  <html>
4  <head>
5  <meta charset="utf-8" />
6  <title>Waterfall Exploring</title>
7
8  <link rel="stylesheet" type="text/css" href="stylesch7.css" />
9
10 </head>
11
12 <body>
13
14 <p>Hover over a photo on the left to enlarge it on the right.</p>
15
16 <div id="sizes">
17 <p><a>
18     <img class="small" src="waterfall1.jpg" width="150" height="110" alt="Waterfall 1" />
19     <img class="large" src="waterfall1.jpg" width="150" height="110" alt="Waterfall 1" />
20 </a></p>
21 <p><a>
22         <img class="small" src="waterfall2.jpg" width="150" height="110" alt="Waterfall 2" />
23         <img class="large" src="waterfall2.jpg" width="150" height="110" alt="Waterfall 2" />
24 </a></p>
25 <p><a>
26     <img class="small" src="waterfall3.jpg" width="150" height="110" alt="Waterfall 3" />
```

link statement to external style sheet stylesch7.css

Figure 7–12

2

- Save the file.
- Validate the Web page using the W3C service.
- Return to the browser window and use the Water Expeditions menu on the navigation bar to select Waterfall Exploring. Hover over each image shown on the Web page (Figure 7–13) to see the changes in the Web page.

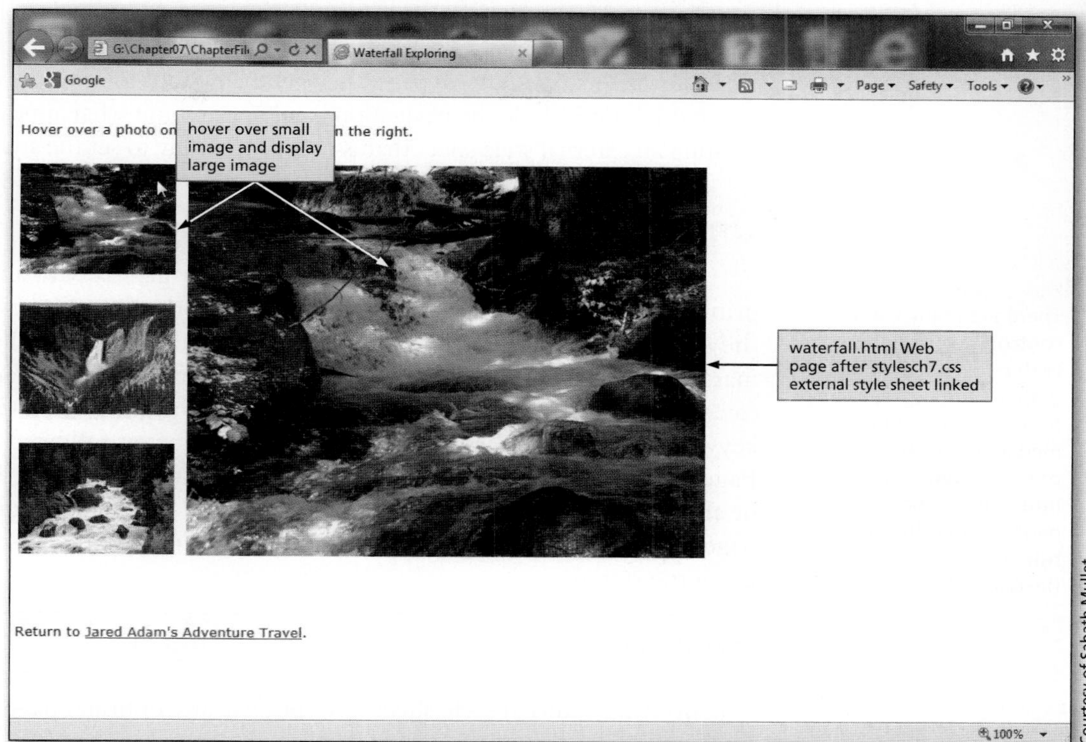

Figure 7–13

To Link the Remaining HTML File to an External Style Sheet

You have linked the waterfall.html page to the external style sheet stylesch7.css. Now you need to link the whale.html Web page to the same style sheet. The following steps add a <link> tag to the Whale Watching Web page and then save and test the file.

1. If necessary, click the Notepad++ button on the taskbar.
2. With the USB drive plugged into your computer, open the whale.html file, navigating to the G:\Chapter07\ChapterFiles folder if necessary.
3. Highlight the text, <!--Insert external style sheet link statement here --> on line 8.
4. Type `<link rel="stylesheet" type="text/css" href="stylesch7.css" />` to enter the link to the external style sheet.
5. Save the file.
6. Open whale.html in a Web browser and test to see that the pop-up image effects are implemented.

Creating an External Style Sheet for Printing

You will next create an external style sheet that will be used for printing a Web page. When Web site visitors print a Web page, they generally want to print the content of the Web page, which does not include the navigation bar. You can limit what appears on the printed page by creating an external style sheet that is used specifically to set the styles for a printed Web page.

Understanding the Page Box Model

BTW

@page Rule
There are many ways to control the printing of a Web page. Paged media (paper or transparencies) differ from continuous media in that the content of the document is split into one or more discrete pages. Using the @page rule gives you the flexibility that you need.

In this external style sheet, you will add a page box with an @page rule to format the printed page. A **page box** is a rectangular region that contains two areas: the page area and the margin area. The page area includes the elements (or boxes) laid out on the page. The margin area surrounds the page area; the page margin area is transparent. Web developers can specify the margins of a page box inside an @page rule. An **@page rule** contains the keyword @page, followed by an optional page selector, followed by a block of declarations. Page selectors give a Web developer the flexibility to designate the first page, all left pages, or all right pages. For instance, you could specify different margins for the first printed page of a Web site. You could therefore use the first pseudoclass in your @page rule by using the statement:

```
@page :first { }
```

The printing external style sheet does not use any optional page selectors. It does include a declaration in the @page rule with the statement:

```
@page {margin: 0.5in;}
```

As with other external style sheets, you must first create the external style sheet, and then you must link that style sheet into the Web page(s) for which you want to use it using the <link /> statement.

To Create an External Style Sheet for Printing

Table 7–8 shows the code for the external style sheet for printing.

Table 7–8 Code for a Print Style Sheet

Line	CSS Code
1	`@page {margin: 0.5in;}`
2	`/* set printed page with half inch margins */`
3	
4	`#menubar {display: none;}`
5	`/* do not print the menubar that displays at the top of the Web page */`
6	
7	`box {text-align: left; font-size: 12pt; font-family: Times New Roman;}`
8	`posit {border-width: 0px; width: 7.125in; height: 5.361in;}`
9	`/* specific styles set for paragraph box and image posit classes */`

Lines 2, 5, and 9 are all comment lines. They are important because they explain the code above them. Line 4 indicates that the id named menubar should not display (or print). Lines 7 and 8 define the parameters for printing of the box and posit classes.

The following step creates an external style sheet to define how a Web page will print.

1

- If necessary, click the Notepad++ button on the taskbar. Click File on the menu bar and then click New.
- Enter the CSS code as shown in Table 7–8.
- With the USB drive plugged into your computer, save the file as `printpage.css`. If necessary, navigate to the Chapter07\ChapterFiles folder on your USB drive (Figure 7–14).
- Print the CSS code.

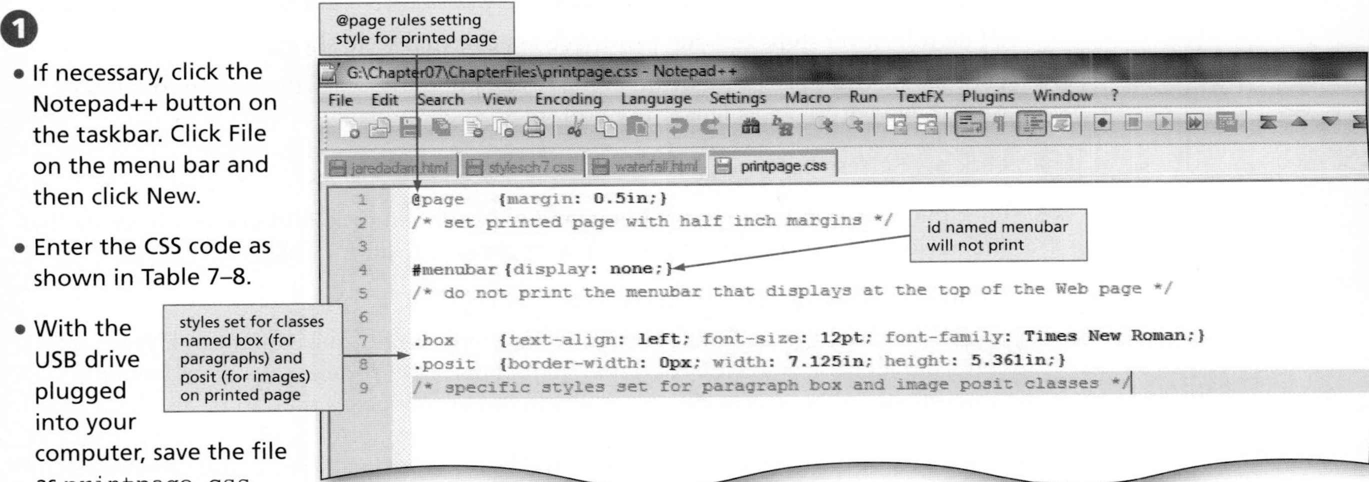

Figure 7–14

To Link to an External Style Sheet

The following steps add a link to an external style sheet using a <link> tag and then save the HTML file.

1. Click the jaredadam.html tab in Notepad++.
2. Highlight the comment <!--Insert external style sheet link here --> on line 8.
3. Type `<link rel="stylesheet" type="text/css" href="printpage.css" media="print" />` to enter the link to the external style sheet (Figure 7–15).
4. Save and print the file.

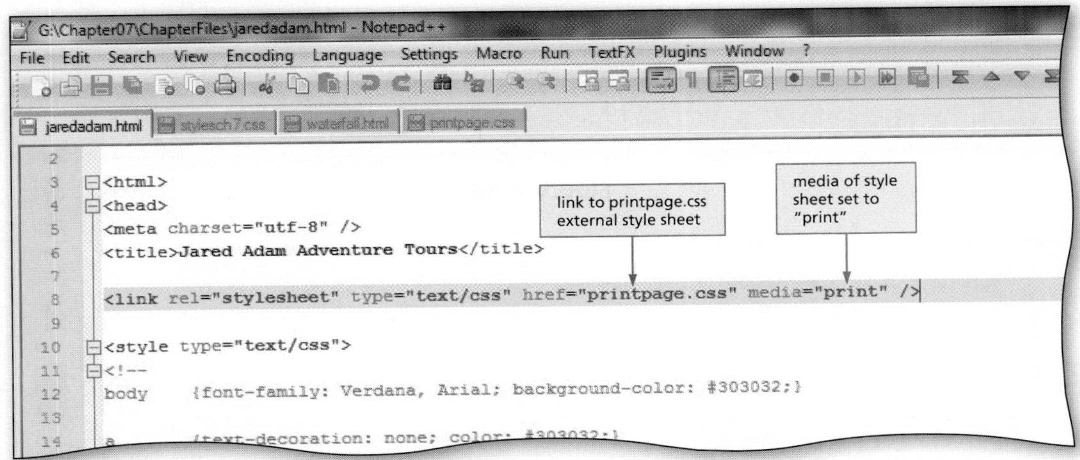

Figure 7–15

To Test the External Style Sheet

The following steps test the printpage.css external style sheet.

1. Click the Internet Explorer button in the taskbar and then click the Return to Jared Adam's Adventure Tours link at the bottom of the Web page.
2. Click the Refresh button.
3. Click the Print icon arrow in the Command bar and then click Print preview to verify that the navigation bar does not appear in print preview (Figure 7-16).

Q&A

What other styles might be appropriate for printing?

As mentioned above, Web site visitors generally want to print the content of a Web page, not necessarily the format. You therefore might want to change the way that headings (h1 through h6) print. You could add a style to the printpage.css that prints all headings in one particular size (perhaps slightly larger than the general content of the Web page). You also might want to vary the margins from the Web page as displayed in the browser versus the margins on a printed page.

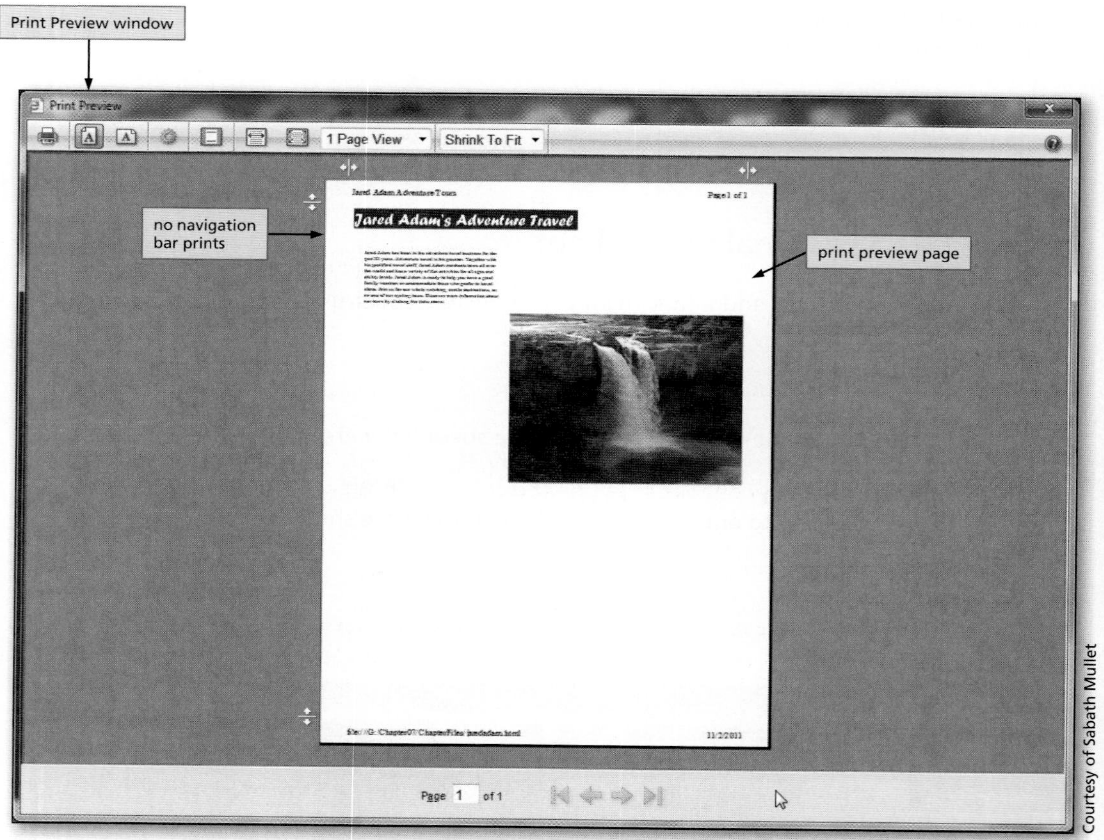

Figure 7–16

To Quit Notepad++ and a Browser

After you have viewed and printed the HTML and CSS files, the project is complete.

1. Close all open browser windows.
2. Click File on the Notepad++ menu bar and then click Close All.
3. Click the Close button on the Notepad++ window title bar.

BTW

Quick Reference
For a list of CSS properties and values, see the CSS Quick Reference (Appendix D) at the back of this book, or visit the Book Companion Site Web page for this book at www.cengagebrain.com.

Chapter Summary

In this chapter, you have learned how to add advanced CSS features in embedded and external style sheets to add functionality and give your Web pages a consistent and polished look. The items listed below include all the new HTML and CSS skills you have learned in this chapter.

1. Add an Embedded Style Sheet (HTML 340)
2. Create an External Style Sheet (HTML 345)
3. Link to an External Style Sheet (HTML 346)
4. Create an External Style Sheet for Printing (HTML 348)

Learn It Online

Test your knowledge of chapter content and key terms.

Instructions: To complete the following exercises, please visit `www.cengagebrain.com`. At the CengageBrain.com home page, search for *HTML5 and CSS 7th Edition* using the search box at the top of the page. This will take you to the product page for this book. On the product page, click the Access Now button below the Study Tools heading. On the Book Companion Site Web page, select Chapter 7, and then click the link for the desired exercise.

Chapter Reinforcement TF, MC, and SA

A series of true/false, multiple choice, and short answer questions that test your knowledge of the chapter content.

Flash Cards

An interactive learning environment where you identify chapter key terms associated with displayed definitions.

Practice Test

A series of multiple choice questions that test your knowledge of chapter content and key terms.

Who Wants To Be a Computer Genius?

An interactive game that challenges your knowledge of chapter content in the style of a television quiz show.

Wheel of Terms

An interactive game that challenges your knowledge of chapter key terms in the style of the television show, *Wheel of Fortune*.

Crossword Puzzle Challenge

A crossword puzzle that challenges your knowledge of key terms presented in the chapter.

STUDENT ASSIGNMENTS

Apply Your Knowledge

Reinforce the skills and apply the concepts you learned in this chapter.

Adding Menus to an Egyptian Web Site

Instructions: Start Notepad++ and a browser. Using your browser, open the apply7-1.html file from the Chapter07\Apply folder of the Data Files for Students. See the inside back cover of this book for instructions on downloading the Data Files for Students, or contact your instructor for information about accessing the required files. The apply7-1.html file is the partially completed HTML file needed for this exercise. Figure 7–17 shows the Apply Your Knowledge Web page as it should appear in the browser after the necessary code is added.

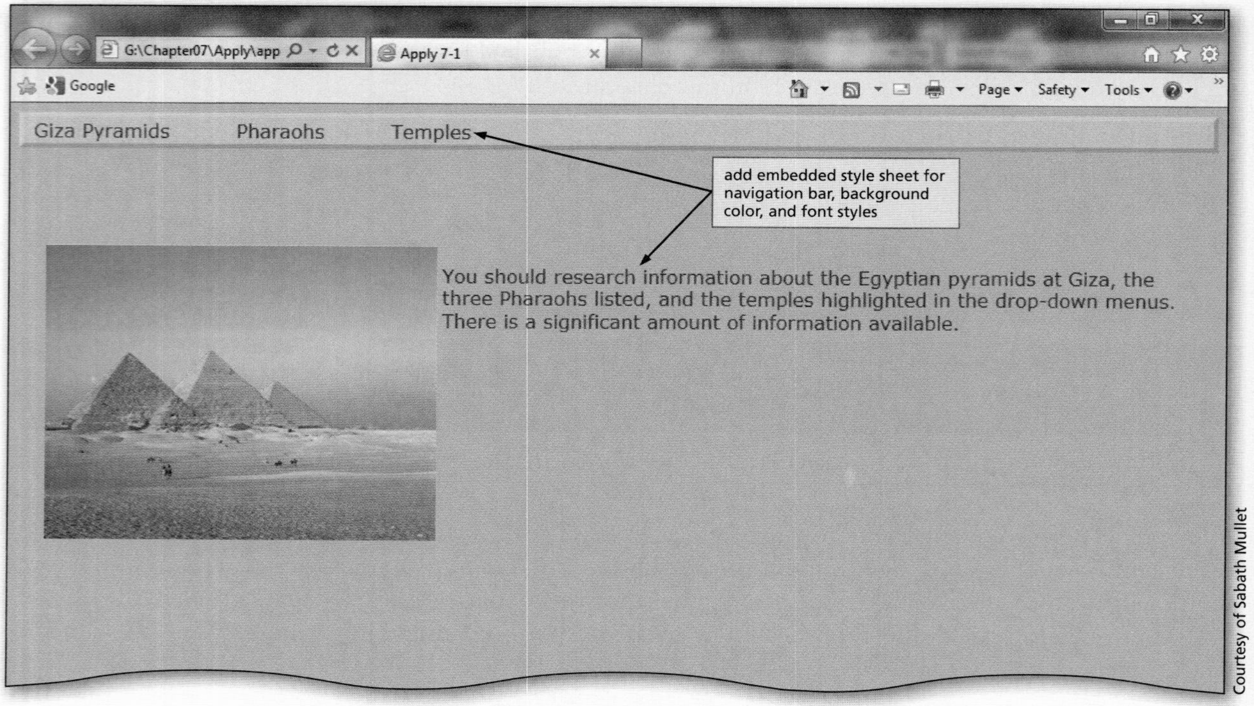

Figure 7–17

Perform the following tasks:

1. Examine the HTML file and its appearance in the browser.
2. Embed the following style sheet into the apply7-1.html file:

```
body       {font-family: Verdana, Arial, sans-serif;
           background: #edbf79;}
a          {text-decoration: none; color: #5a3702;}
#menubar   {border-top: 4px solid #f4dab2; border-right: 4px
           solid #e0a140; border-bottom: 4px solid #e0a140;
           border-left: 4px solid #f4dab2; background-color:
           #f5cb8a; color: #5a3702; height: 23px;}
.menu      {float: left; padding: 0.1em 3em 0.1em 0.5em;
           cursor: default;}
```

```
.menu ul               {display: none; position: absolute;
                       background-color: #f4dab2; color: #5a3702;
                       list-style: none; margin: 0.1em 0 0 0; padding: 0;}
.menu ul li            {display: block; font-size: small; padding: 0.2em;}
div.menu:hover ul      {margin: 0; padding: 0; display: block;
                       border-bottom: .15em solid #e0a140; border-left:
                       .15em solid #e0a140;}
div.menu ul li:hover   {background-color: #e0a140;}
div.content            {margin-left: 20px; margin-right: 20px;
                       padding-top: 8%; color: #5a3702;}
```

3. Insert the necessary HTML in the body of the Web page to utilize the classes within the embedded style sheet. (*Hint:* Refer to the chapter project to help you determine where these classes should be inserted.)
4. Save the file as apply7-1solution.html, validate the code, and print the file.
5. View and print the Web page in your browser.
6. Submit the solution in the format specified by your instructor.

Extend Your Knowledge

Extend the skills you learned in this chapter and experiment with new skills.

Creating an External Style Sheet

Instructions: You will create and save an external style sheet, and then link it to the file extend7-1.html from the Chapter07\Extend folder of the Data Files for Students. See the inside back cover of this book for instructions on downloading the Data Files for Students, or contact your instructor for information about accessing the required files. This HTML file contains all of the text for the Web page shown in Figure 7–18.

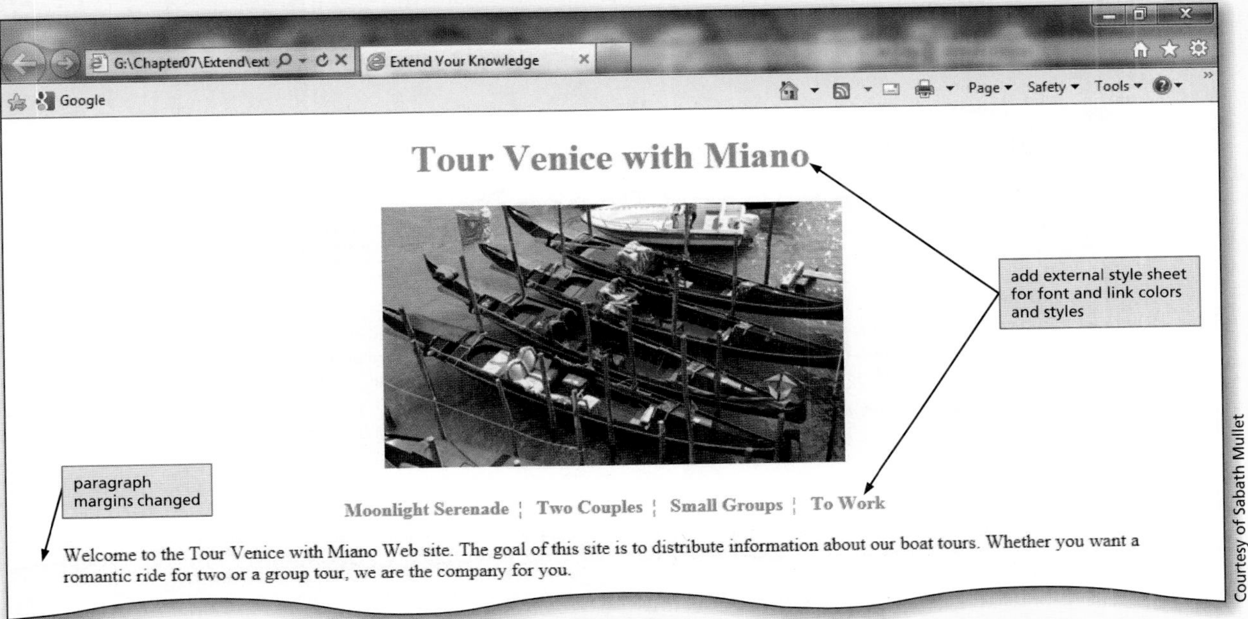

Figure 7–18

Continued >

Extend Your Knowledge *continued*

Perform the following tasks:

1. Start a new file in Notepad++, and add the following CSS code to create a new external style sheet that specifies the following:
   a. all links red in color, bolder weight, and no text-decoration
   b. h1 headings in red, paragraph left and right margins 40 pixels
   c. hover color blue with a red background
2. Save the file as extend7-1styles.css and print the file.
3. Open the extend7-1.html file from the Data Files for Students and add a link statement to the external style sheet extend7-1styles.css.
4. Save the file as extend7-1solution.html, validate the code, and then print the file.
5. Open the extend7-1solution.html file in the browser and print the Web page.
6. Submit the solution in the format specified by your instructor.

Make It Right

Analyze a document and correct all errors and/or improve the design.

Correcting the Halloween Night Dinner and Dance Web Page

Instructions: Start Notepad++. Open the file makeitright7-1.html from the Chapter07\MakeItRight folder of the Data Files for Students. See the inside back cover of this book for instructions on downloading the Data Files for Students, or contact your instructor for information about accessing the required files. The Web page is a modified version of what you see in Figure 7–19, but it contains errors, including in the CSS code. The heading should be in italics, and the last paragraph should be italic and size small. Make the necessary corrections to the Web page to make it look like the figure.

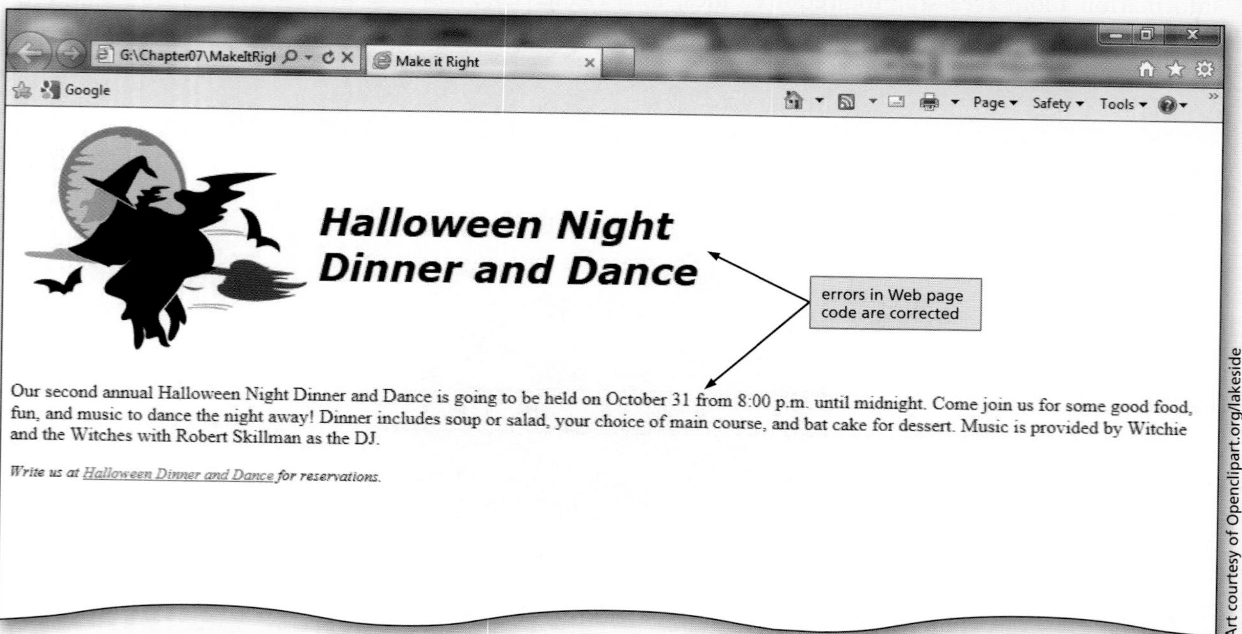

Figure 7–19

In the Lab

Lab 1: Creating an External Style Sheet for Printing

Instructions: You have been asked to create a style sheet that can be used for printing across a number of people's personal Web pages. You decide to set the printing styles in an external style sheet so that it can easily be linked to any number of Web page files. You use the lab7-1.html file for this exercise. The HTML code is completed for the Web page, as shown in Figure 7–20a. You should create the external style sheet that results in Figure 7–20b.

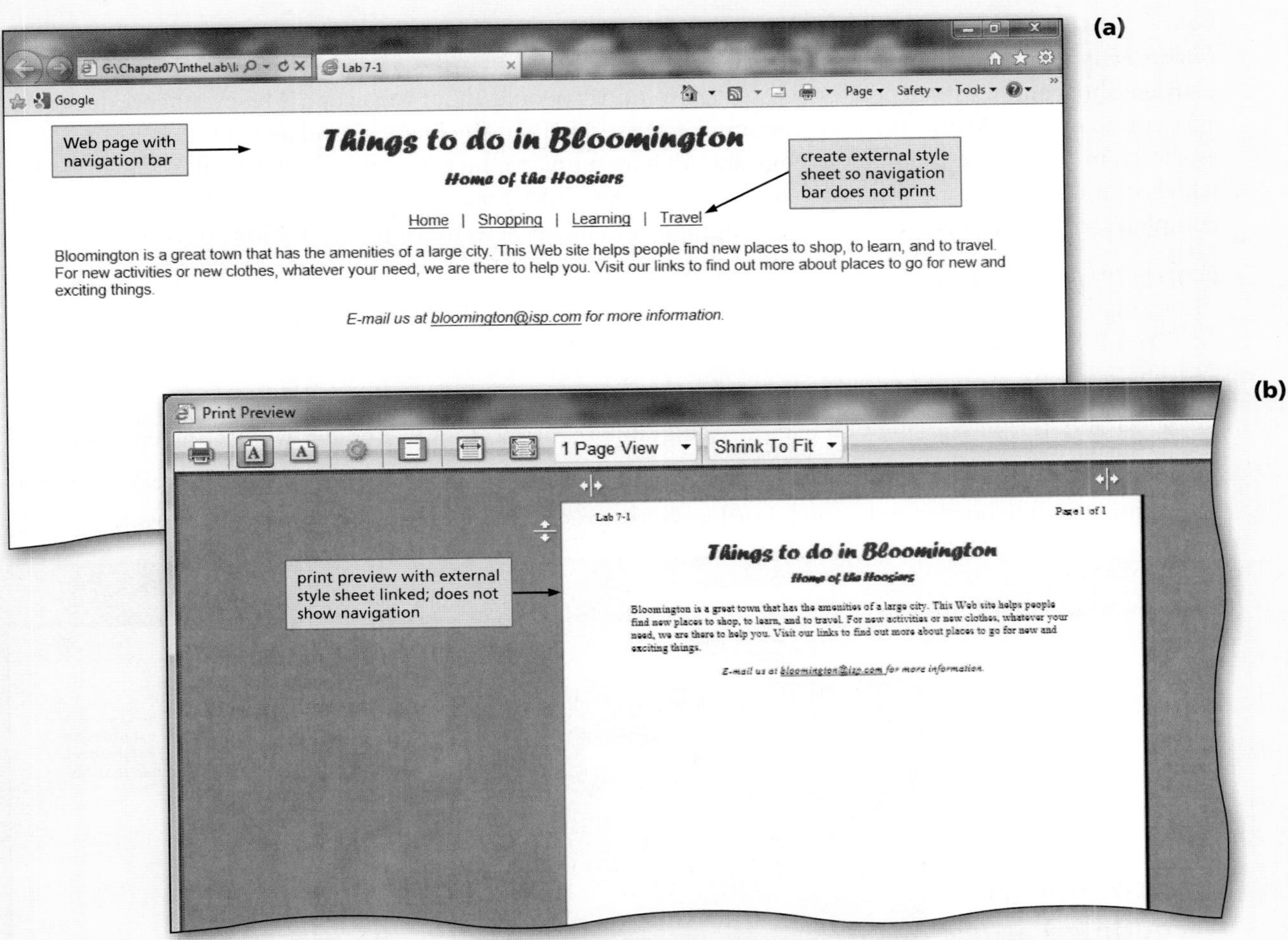

Figure 7–20

Perform the following tasks:

1. Using Notepad++, create a new file for an external style sheet that is used for printing.
2. Using CSS, create the style structure so that the navigation bar on the Web page is not printed. (*Hint:* Use the menubar id.) Also, align the content of the Web page on the left with a font size of 12 points in Times New Roman font for the printed page. (*Hint:* Use the content class.)
3. Save the file as lab7-1print.css.
4. Open the HTML file lab7-1.html and add a link to the external style sheet, lab7-1print.css.
5. Save the HTML file as lab7-1solution.html. Validate the file and then print it.

Continued >

In the Lab *continued*

6. Open the file, lab7-1solution.html in the browser. Use Print Preview to test if printing your external style sheet works correctly.
7. Print the Print Preview view of the Web page.
8. Submit the solution in the format specified by your instructor.

In the Lab

Lab 2: Adding External and Inline Style Sheets

Instructions: Your family business, Marsh Vineyards Wedding Parties, is participating in the Home and Garden Show and wants to create a Web page to notify people about the event. The event coordinator asks you to create a Web page that contains information about the business and an e-mail address link, as shown in Figure 7–21. The Web page should have a link to the external style sheet, lab7-2styles.css, which is in the Chapter07\IntheLab folder of the Data Files for Students. The external style sheet is not complete, so you must add the h1, h2, paragraph, and image selectors and declarations to complete it.

Perform the following tasks:

1. Using Notepad++, open the HTML file lab7-2styles.css in the Chapter07\IntheLab folder of the Data Files for Students.
2. Add the following styles to the external style sheet:
   a. h1 and h2: "Baskerville Old Face", "Calligrapher", "Arial" font in a bolder weight and color green
   b. paragraphs: "Baskerville Old Face", "Calligrapher" font, color of black, with a 10 pixel left margin
   c. img: double border style, thick border width, green border color, with a 10 pixel margin

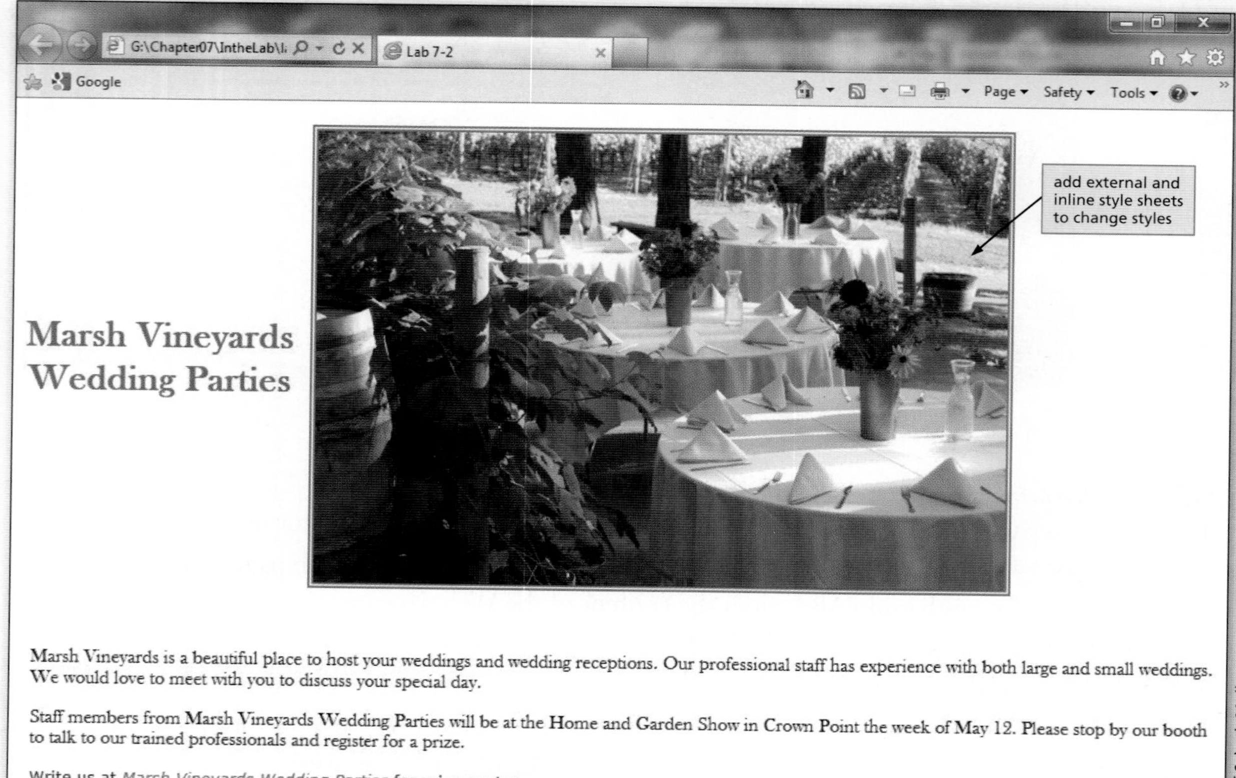

Courtesy of Sabath Mullet

Figure 7–21

3. Save the file using the same filename.
4. Using Notepad++, open the HTML file lab7-2.html.
5. Add the link necessary to apply the styles from the lab7-2styles.css external style sheet.
6. Add an inline style sheet to the last paragraph of text that sets the font to Verdana and size 10pt.
7. Within the table provided, insert an <h1> heading tag, center-aligned with an inline style, that contains the words Marsh Vineyards Wedding Parties with a line break as indicated. Add the image centertables.jpg in a data cell to the right of the heading. Be sure to include the alt, height, and width attributes for the image.
8. Save the file as lab7-2solution.html, validate the file, and print it.
9. Open the lab7-2solution.html file in your browser and print the Web page.
10. Submit the solution in the format specified by your instructor.

In the Lab

Lab 3: Developing an External Style Sheet for Pop-up Text

Instructions: You just climbed Mount Rainier and are excited to share your pictures online. You decide to display three pictures that help tell your climbing story using pop-up text that displays beneath the picture, as shown in Figure 7–22. The file lab7-3.html is an HTML file that contains some of the structure of the Web page and is included in the Chapter07\IntheLab folder of the Data Files for Students. In this exercise, you will create an embedded style sheet that displays text under each mountain image when a user hovers over the image. Research a Mount Rainier climb to get an idea of what information to use in your pop-up text.

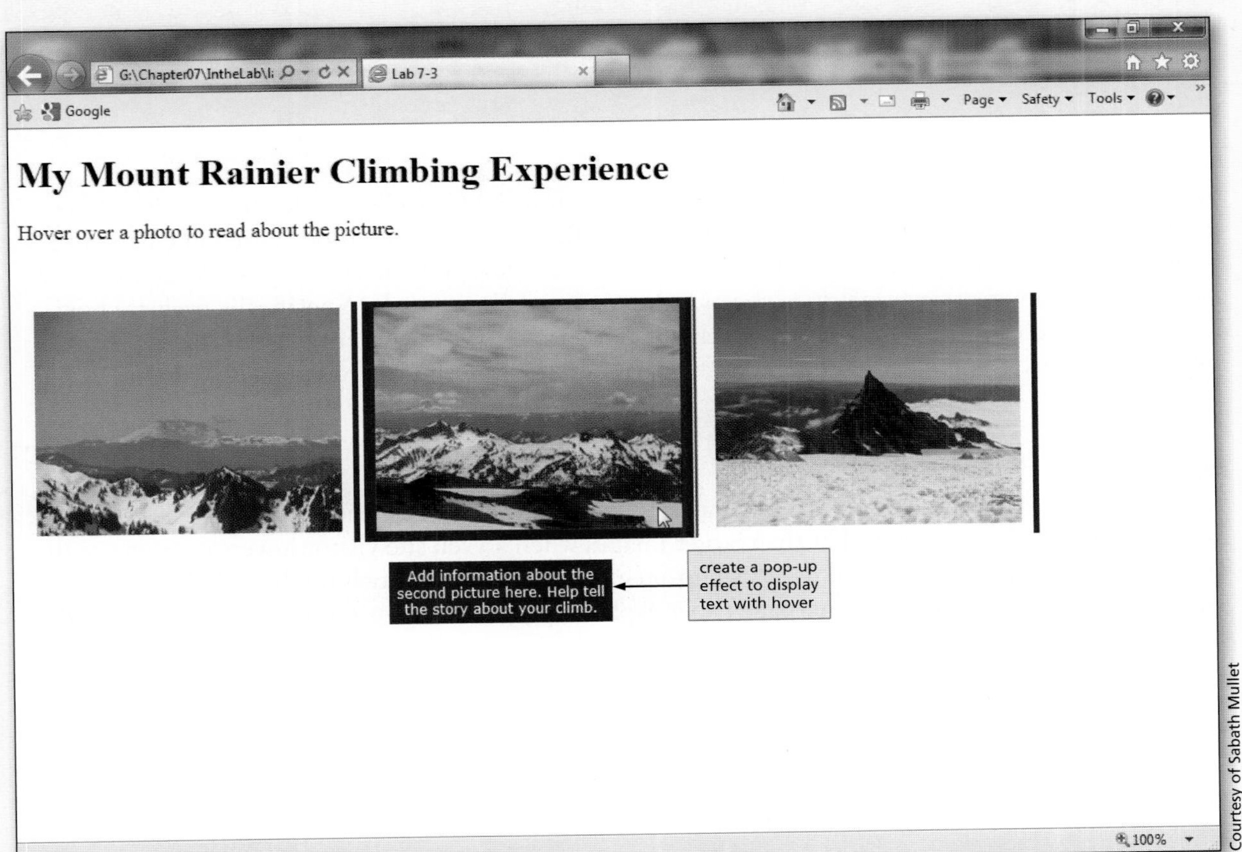

Figure 7–22

Continued >

In the Lab *continued*

Perform the following tasks:

1. Open the lab7-3.html file in Notepad++.
2. Add an embedded style sheet to set the following:
   a. links class (no pseudoclasses): position of the text should be absolute and 150 pixels from the top; the text should display in a block, center-aligned in bold with 1em sans-serif; padding of text should be 5 and 10 pixels with margins of 0, 0, and 1 pixel; border-width should be 0 with text-decoration of none; right border should be 5 pixels in solid navy
   b. links class hovered: background is navy with a 5 pixels double border in white
   c. span tag (no pseudoclasses): there should be no display
   d. span tag hovered: text should display in a block with an absolute poition from the top of 220 pixels, left of 550 and width of 180 pixels; the padding should be 5 pixels with a margin of 10 pixels; text color white and background navy; the font should be 12 pixels in Verdana sans-serif and aligned in the center of the block
3. Add the Mount Rainier climb information to your HTML file.
4. Save the file as lab7-3solution.html, validate it, and then print the HTML code.
5. Open the Web page in your browser to test that the pop-up text displays when you hover over each mountain image, as shown in Figure 7–22 on the previous page. Print the Web page.
6. Submit the solution in the format specified by your instructor.

Cases and Places

Apply your creative thinking and problem-solving skills to design and implement a solution.

1: Finding CSS Information Online

Academic

Browse the Internet to find two Web sites that discuss advanced Cascading Style Sheets (CSS). How else can CSS be used in your Web development that differs from how it has been used in Chapters 2 through 7? What other properties and values can you use to format your Web pages? What are other ways that you can create external style sheets to be used for printing only? Specifically evaluate how CSS3 can be used with the browsers to which you have access. Write a brief report on each Web site, including the URL, and be prepared to discuss what other advanced CSS you would like to utilize.

2: Applying Pop-up Text

Personal

Create a Web site that utilizes several of your own pictures. Use the basic pop-up techniques covered in this chapter to display text rather than larger images when a Web site visitor hovers over one of the images. Determine how you could use this pop-up effect for text and why it might be helpful in your own Web development. Write a one-page paper explaining your thoughts on pop-up effects created using CSS.

3: Completing the Jared Adam's Adventure Travel Web Site

Professional

In this exercise, you will complete the Jared Adam's Adventure Travel Web site. There are four links to the dummy Web page, chapter7sample.html, provided in the Data Files for Students in the Chapter7\ChapterFiles folder. The sample Web page is accessed via two links that drop down from the Exotic Destinations menu selection and two links that drop down from the Cycling Tours menu selection. As a first step, determine if the Exotic Destinations and Cycling Tours menu items are of interest. If not, determine other categories to replace Exotic Destinations and Cycling Tours (remember, this is an "Adventure Travel" Web site) and identify drop-down submenu categories to replace Exotic 1 and Exotic 2 and Cycling 1 and Cycling 2. Once you determine which categories to include, search through your travel photos or take pictures of appropriate "adventure" activities to complete the Web site.

8 Adding Multimedia Content to Web Pages

Objectives

You will have mastered the material in this chapter when you can:

- Describe the benefits and limitations of multimedia in Web sites
- Identify audio and video formats
- Describe parameters for embedded multimedia
- Add an audio clip to a Web page using the HTML5 audio element
- Add a video clip to a Web page using the HTML5 video element

8 Adding Multimedia Content to Web Pages

Introduction

In previous chapters, you used HTML tags and CSS code to change the way a Web page is displayed in a Web browser. You learned how to collect data from Web site visitors using Web page forms. You also learned advanced CSS techniques to create drop-down menus and pop-up effects. In this chapter, you will learn how to insert multimedia content in the form of audio and video clips.

Project — Adding Multimedia to an English Literature Class Web Site

In your English literature class, you are studying the poems of Henry Wadsworth Longfellow. To make the 19th century poet seem more real, your class created a Web site that shows the home where Longfellow lived for almost 50 years. Your instructor, Mr. Angelo Garcia, would like you to enhance that Web site by including audio and video clips.

The English literature class Web site consists of a home page (Figure 8–1a) and two linked Web pages (Figures 8–1b and 8–1c). The home page contains a picture of the Longfellow home together with a horizontal navigation bar. The navigation bar links to two additional pages. One Web page that you will create has a short video clip of the historical Longfellow home in Cambridge, Massachusetts. The other Web page contains an audio of a Longfellow poem that describes changes when revisiting a place after a long absence. You feel that the addition of multimedia files (one audio and one video) might help make Mr. Garcia's English literature class Web site more engaging for the students. It is one thing for a student to see a picture or read a poem, but it may have greater impact to see a video of the actual home and hear a poem written by Longfellow read aloud. Multimedia content can provide this type of valuable experience. Because the use of multimedia content is complex, you must first research how to add multimedia to Web pages. Mr. Garcia is supportive of the plan and encourages you to start as soon as possible.

Overview

As you read this chapter, you will learn how to add the multimedia content to the two Web pages shown in Figures 8–1b and 8–1c by performing these general tasks:

- Plan the use of multimedia in the Web site
- Enter the HTML code to insert an audio clip
- Enter the HTML code to insert a video clip
- Save the files as HTML files
- View the Web pages and HTML code in your browser
- Validate the Web pages
- Test and print the Web pages

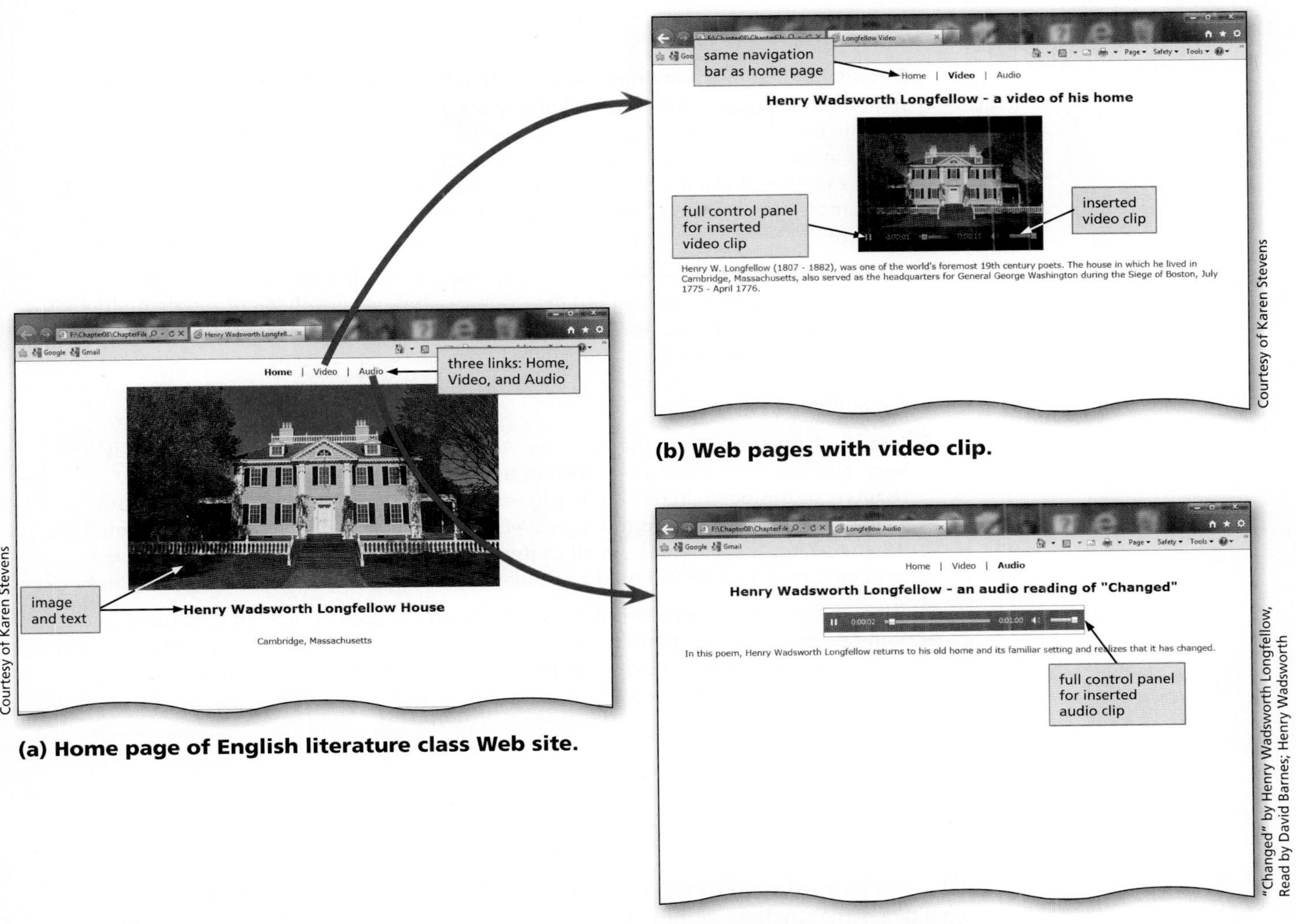

(a) Home page of English literature class Web site.

(b) Web pages with video clip.

(c) Web page with audio clip.

Figure 8–1

Plan Ahead

General Project Guidelines

As you create Web pages, such as the chapter project shown in Figure 8–1, you should follow these general guidelines:

1. **Plan the Web site**. First, you should determine if using multimedia content is appropriate for your Web site. If your subject matter is such that audio or video would enhance the visitors' experience, multimedia is a good choice.
2. **Analyze the need**. In the analysis phase of the Web Development Life Cycle, you should analyze what content to include on the Web page. Chapter 8 introduces a new Web development technique, adding multimedia content to your Web page; this technique can enhance the text and graphics content that you have developed in other chapters.
3. **Choose the content for the Web page**. You always want your content to add positively to your Web site visitors' experience. You therefore have to assess multimedia content just as you would text or graphics content. Many sources of content are available for Web sites. You can create your own video and audio clips easily and insert those into the appropriate Web pages. You can also take advantage of audio and video clips available online, after reviewing any copyright restrictions.

Plan Ahead

(continued)

4. **Determine the type of multimedia to incorporate into your Web pages**. The type of multimedia that you select is based on the purpose of the content. If you want to provide background music, an audio clip is fine; there would be no need for a video clip in this instance. For more complex topics though, a video clip might be more effective. As an example, if you are explaining to someone where middle C is on the piano, a video clip is more appropriate. If you want to give someone the experience of hearing a speech that does not explain things in a "how to" approach, then an audio clip is acceptable.
5. **Create or find the multimedia content and insert it into the Web site**. Once the analysis and design are complete, the Web developer creates or finds the appropriate multimedia content for the Web site. Again, consider public domain content sources. Otherwise, developing multimedia content on your own might be a fun experience. Good Web development standard practices should be followed in the steps that you take to insert the multimedia.
6. **Test all Web pages within the Web site**. An important part of Web development is testing to assure that you are following the standards recommended in the early chapters of this book. In this book, you use the World Wide Web Consortium (W3C) validator that allows you to test your Web page and clearly explains any errors you have. When testing, you should check all content for accuracy. Finally, all of the Web pages with multimedia content should be validated per the standards set throughout this book.

When necessary, more specific details concerning the above guidelines are presented at appropriate points in the chapter. The chapter will also identify the actions performed and decisions made regarding these guidelines during the creation of the Web page shown in Figure 8–1 on the previous page.

Using Multimedia

The popularity of the World Wide Web (the Web) is due in part to the ability to view Web pages that include graphic images, audio, and video. These additions can be wonderful for a Web site and give the users more enhanced and enjoyable browsing experiences. Sometimes, however, the addition of multimedia can distract from the Web site message. Always remember the purpose of the Web site. If the multimedia content enhances that purpose, it should be included. If the multimedia content distracts from the purpose of the Web site, then you should reconsider using it.

Multimedia is defined as the combination of text, sound, and video to express an idea or convey a message. In the early days of the Internet, it was somewhat prohibitive to use multimedia on the Web. Most people connected to the Internet using a modem and a standard telephone line, so the bandwidth (i.e., the capacity for data transfer) was not there to accommodate the large files required for audio, video, and even some graphic images. The Web of yesterday was mostly text-based with a few background colors and small graphic images. Today, most people have broadband Internet connections with a much greater capacity for data transfer. Multimedia Web pages that include large graphics, audio, and video are common.

Multimedia is used widely on Web pages. Many companies utilize videos to show potential customers new products or how to use their existing products. You may be able to review a medical procedure online before having the procedure done yourself. You can view clips of movies or hear segments of audio recordings from Web pages that provide content in those formats. **Podcasts**, a series of audio or video clips that are released in a sequence, are becoming more prevalent in both academic and corporate settings. Additionally, some instructors rely on multimedia content to stress important aspects of a class. It is important to determine where multimedia content may enhance the learning or viewing experience. You do not want to divert your Web site visitors with distracting multimedia. The Web site enhanced in this chapter highlights an important 19th century American poet. To improve the user experience, you will insert an audio clip and a video clip on two different Web pages. These clips enhance the content of each Web page nicely; they do not distract from the message.

This chapter provides an introduction to the use of multimedia in Web development. The chapter focuses on two different forms of multimedia: audio and video. Other multimedia formats exist, but are not covered in this chapter, including Java applets, Flash, and automated slideshows. The finished Web pages (Figure 8–2a and 8–2b) contain relevant audio and video clips that provide valuable multimedia content.

BTW

Slideshows, Java, and Flash

You can easily create a slideshow from your pictures using most movie editing software. A Java applet is a program written in the Java programming language that can be included in a Web page. Adobe Flash is a popular multimedia platform not discussed in this chapter. Search the Web for more information on these formats.

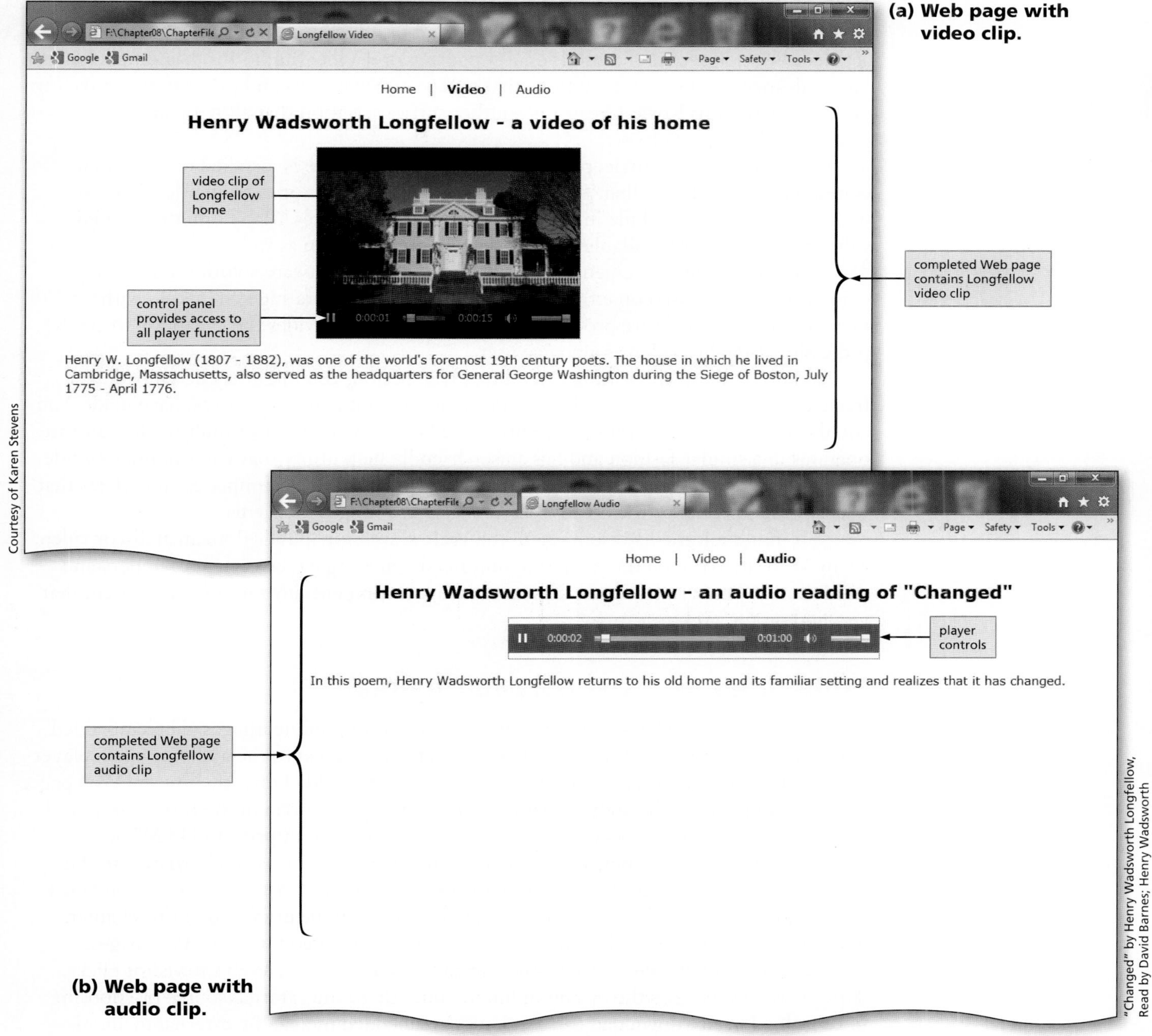

(a) Web page with video clip.

(b) Web page with audio clip.

Figure 8–2

BTW

Multimedia Sources
Search the Web for public domain sources of audio and video clips that you can use in your projects. Determine a way to keep track of the site, the specific copyright and licensing language, and the clips that you download. This is a great way to make sure that you follow the guidelines required by creators of the audio and video clips.

Creating or Finding Multimedia Files

You can obtain multimedia files by creating them yourself or finding files that are already available. The good thing about creating your own multimedia files is that you do not have to be concerned with copyright or licensing agreements. The bad thing about creating your own multimedia files is that they may not be the same quality as those that are created professionally. You can create your own audio files using a microphone and software designed to edit digital files. Many software options are available today for audio and video creation and editing. If you do use any portion of files that have been professionally developed, be certain that you understand and follow the copyright and licensing requirements.

For video files, a digital camcorder, a digital camera, or even a smartphone, allow you to create clips that can be used on a Web page. This is what has made video Web sites such as YouTube so popular. For the Windows environment, Windows Live Movie Maker is available for download from the Microsoft Web site as part of Windows Live Essentials. MAGIX Movie Edit Pro software and training is available for a fee, with an active online community for additional support. Corel VideoStudio Pro has simple and more advanced menu system options that novice movie editors and professionals alike can utilize comfortably. Roxio Creator is another software option that allows you to create professional-quality videos.

For Mac users, iMovie, part of the iLife software suite, is installed on most new computers and is an excellent option. Final Cut Pro X offers professional-level editing with a new interface and file import and organization features. Many other multimedia software products are available for the Mac operating system as well.

Adobe Premiere Elements is another highly rated software solution for movie editing that can be used on either the Mac or Windows operating systems. As with many multimedia software products, Premier Elements provides the capability to create professional-quality video as a novice user.

Many of these application offer a free trial period. You might try downloading a free trial of the software, if available, and using it to edit a movie that you have made. You could even try a few different programs to see how they work. Most multimedia software operates in a similar fashion and has a user-friendly help utility that you can use to guide you through the process of editing. Most products also provide templates and effects that you can use to enhance the creative aspects of presenting multimedia.

To find multimedia resources on the Web, search for "public domain audio or video." Many Web sites contain these types of multimedia files. Again, be certain to understand and follow the copyright license agreements that accompany any multimedia content that you find on the Web.

Embedded vs. External Multimedia

Embedding media is similar in concept to inserting inline images. The embedded media files appear within the Web page and users have access to the audio or video player controls right on the page. Because the media file is embedded directly into the Web page, you can complement the audio or video clip resource with surrounding text or graphical images. The <object> tag was used to insert embedded content prior to HTML5. HTML5 introduces two new tags, <audio> and <video>, to use as an alternative to the <object> tag. However, as of the writing of this book, not all browsers support the new tags. All three tags—<object>, <audio>, and <video>—will be discussed in this chapter. This gives you more flexibility to incorporate audio and video into your Web pages.

External media files are accessed through a link that your Web site visitor clicks. This gives your visitors the option of linking directly to the external source or choosing to download or not download the file. Unlike embedded media, the external media is displayed out of context with the Web page that calls it. The <embed> tag is used to place external interactive content or a plug-in on the Web page. Using external links is a Web development practice that is used often, such as the many video resources in Web sites such as YouTube. External media files are frequently used, and the embed element defines a container for an external application or interactive content (a plug-in). This element is new to HTML5 and is supported by all browsers. Figure 8–3 shows how the the new <video> tag is used to embed a video clip of Longfellow's house. The video is supplemented with a heading, text, and navigation bar.

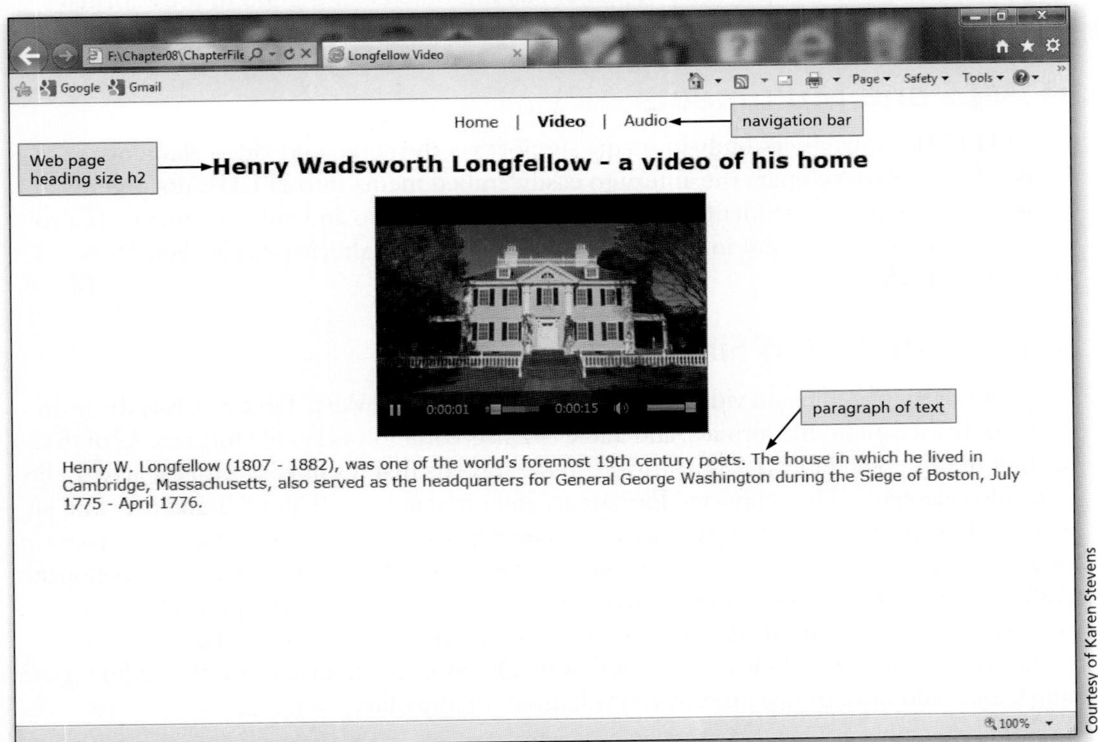

Figure 8–3 Completed Web page at launch with video clip.

Media Players and Plug-Ins

The functionality of a browser includes the ability to display text and the graphics formats discussed in earlier chapters. In order to play an audio or video file, some browsers need the help of an application called a media player or a plug-in. A **media player** is computer software that is used to play multimedia files. Most software media players support an array of media formats, including both audio and video files. This chapter uses an .mp3 audio file and an .mp4 video file. Both can be played by the Internet Explorer browser. The Windows Media Player, also discussed in this chapter, plays both audio and video. Windows Media Player is included with Microsoft Windows. The Mac operating system comes with QuickTime Player for playing movies, while iTunes can be downloaded for Windows or Mac OS to play a variety of media formats.

A **plug-in** (also called an add-in or add-on) is extra software that is added to the browser (or other program) to provide a capability that is not inherent to the program (the browser in this case). In other words, for an embedded media file to work in a browser, the Web site visitor needs to have the correct plug-in. Most browsers have a variety of plug-ins installed, but the Web site visitor can also download and install necessary plug-ins from the browsers' manufacturers. Common plug-ins are Windows Media Player, Apple QuickTime Player, Adobe Flash, Microsoft Silverlight, and Adobe Acrobat.

Internet Explorer (IE; used in this book) utilizes proprietary ActiveX controls. When IE encounters a multimedia file, it searches for the appropriate ActiveX control. If it cannot find it, users are most often asked if they want to install that control. Some

BTW

Plug-ins and Add-Ons
Investigate what plug-ins are available for the version of browser that you use. (In Internet Explorer, display the Command bar, click on the Tools menu, then select Manage add-ons.) Search the Web for information about the listed add-ons and determine if there are other add-ons that would be helpful that you can download.

BTW

Updating or Installing Plug-ins
Your Web site visitors might not have the plug-ins that are required to play the multimedia content on your Web site. Many Web sites discuss how to best provide users with access to such software.

browsers direct users to the Web site from which they can download the required plug-in. A suggestion to Web developers is to utilize common formats, such as .wmv, .mp4, .flv, and .mp3. It is also a good idea to let your users know what format is being used. If the plug-in is not installed, IE generally provides the capability to install it. Many Web sites today also provide a link to the appropriate manufacturer for an ActiveX control needed to play the file.

As you will see in the following section, the various audio and video formats can be played on a variety of players. For embedded multimedia, it is good to use a format supported by multiple players.

HTML5 and Multimedia

HTML5 introduces built-in media support via the audio and video elements. This offers Web developers the ability to easily embed media into HTML documents. This chapter will teach students how to utilize the new audio and video elements. It also discusses the object element in-depth so that students have alternatives in their Web development efforts.

Audio and Video File Formats

A variety of audio and video formats can be used on the Web. Table 8–1 lists the most commonly used audio file formats, and Table 8–2 lists common video file formats. As of the writing of this book, HTML5 is restrictive in the formats that it supports with the new audio and video elements. The supported formats are indicated in both Tables 8–1 and 8–2 with an asterisk. Understand that there are many software applications available that convert from one audio (or video) format to another though which is another option for a Web developer. Audio files that are used on the Web often utilize file compression techniques. This reduces the size of the file, but it can also diminish the sound quality. Uncompressed audio formats included in Table 8–1 include .aiff, .au, and .wav. The three main formats for the audio tag are: .mp3, .ogg, and .wav. In this project, you will insert an .mp3 file.

Table 8–1 Common Audio File Formats

Format	File Extension	Description
AIFF	.aiff	• The standard audio file format developed by Apple • As a noncompressed and lossless format, it uses more disk space than the MP3 format
AU	.au	• The standard audio file format used by Sun, UNIX, and Java • Can be compressed
MIDI	.mid .rmi	• Musical Instrument Digital Interface (MIDI) • Limited to electronic musical instruments (such as synthesizers) and other electronic equipment • Can be much smaller in size than other formats
MP3*	.mp3	• One of the most popular formats for music storage • Compresses files to approximately 1/10 the size of uncompressed files
MP4*	.mp4	• Created on basis of the QuickTime format; used for audio and video • Is a quicker, faster, high-quality media • Not supported by Windows Media Player
Ogg*	.ogg	• Maintained by Xiph.Org Foundation • Designed to provide for efficient streaming and high-quality digital multimedia • Can be used with <audio> tag
RealAudio	.ra .ram	• Designed for streaming audio over the Internet; declining use • Sound quality not as good as other formats
WAV*	.wav	• Standard audio format for Windows • Commonly used for storing uncompressed CD-quality sound files • Compression is available to reduce file size

*Supported by HTML5 <audio> tag

The video format that you choose depends on the visitors you expect to visit your Web site. Are most of your Web site visitors users of Macs or PCs? What is the level of computer (e.g., amount of RAM or cache) and connection speed (e.g., broadband) for your average user? In this project, you will insert an .mp4 file on a Web page.

Table 8–2 Common Video File Formats

Format	File Extension	Description
AVI	.avi	• Audio / Video Interleaved • Developed by Microsoft to use with Windows • Can contain both audio and video data
Flash	.swf	• Small Web Format • Can contain audio, video, or animations • Requires Adobe Flash Player
Flash Video	.flv .f4v	• Developed by Adobe • Format of choice for embedded video on the Web • Used by YouTube and Hulu
MPEG	.mpg .mpeg .mp3	• Moving Picture Experts Group • Can be highly compressed resulting in small file size • Supported by most major browsers
MP4*	.mp4	• Created on basis of QuickTime format; used for audio and video • Is a quicker, faster, high-quality media • Not supported by Windows Media Player
Ogg*	.Ogg	• Maintained by Xiph.org Foundation • Designed to provide for efficient streaming and high-quality digital multimedia • Can be used with HTML5 <video> tag
QuickTime	.mov	• Developed by Apple for both Windows and Mac operating systems • File compression can result in smaller file size • Requires QuickTime Player or Adobe Flash Player, which are easily downloaded
RealVideo	.rm .rv	• Proprietary video format developed by RealNetworks • Requires RealPlayer
WebM*	.webm	• Developed by Google • Royalty free, open format • Can be used with HTML5 <video> tag
Windows Media	.wmv	• Developed by Microsoft • Originally designed for Internet streaming applications • Requires Windows Media Player or RealPlayer

*Supported by HTML5 <video> tag

Adding an Audio File to a Web Page

Mr. Garcia's English literature class Web site consists of three files. The first Web page, longfellow.html, is the home page, which contains an image of the Longfellow home and a horizontal navigation bar. This Web page will not change. The next Web page, longfellow-audio.html, is the Web page file into which you will insert an audio file, longfellow-audio.mp3. The third page, longfellow-video.html, will contain the video clip, longfellow-video.mp4. All Web pages in this Web site are linked to the external style sheet, stylesch8.css. The external style sheet file is also not changed. Please review the file, however, so that you are familiar with the styles used in the Web site. Pay special attention to the classes that are named in the external style sheet and review how those classes are used in the longfellow-audio.html and longfellow-video.html files.

BTW

Audio Clips
Many good Web design sites discuss the use of audio clips in Web development. Search for ideas of how you can most effectively utilize an audio clip.

New HTML5 Multimedia Tags

As mentioned earlier, HTML5 has two new tags for multimedia: the <audio> and <video> tags. These tags take the place of the <object> tag discussed in the next sections. We keep the <object> tag information in the book because of the limitations of the new HTML5 tags. With this knowledge, you can fall back on the <object> tag to embed audio and video clips. You will use both the <audio> and <video> tags to insert the clips for this project, so both of these tags are discussed later in the chapter.

The Object Tag

The object element supports many different media types, including: pictures, sounds, videos, as well as other objects. The term **object** is used to describe the things that people want to place in HTML documents. Appendix A lists the attributes that can be used with the <object> tag. The purpose of the <object> tag is to support plug-ins. The plug-ins launched by the <object> tag can be used to play audio and video. The object element references a plug-in for playing audio, and that the features of the plug-in can be defined by the <param> tag. Tables 8–1 and 8–2 detailed some of the media players that are used to playback specific audio and video file formats.

The code for inserting an audio file using the <object> tag is as follows:

```
<object data="longfellow-audio.mp3" height="45" width="250">
        <param name="URL" value="longfellow-audio.mp3" />
</object>
```

The object statement includes the **height** and **width** attributes—that is, the height and width of the object in pixels. You will include the height and width when specifying the audio file to identify the view of the player control panel that you want to display. Table 8–3 shows how the control panel will appear at different widths. In all cases in Table 8–3, the height of the object is 45 pixels, which provides enough height to display the player control vertically. (Note that these are not exact numbers, but suggestions for a width that displays the image in the right column.) You can experiment with the width and height to see what might best fit your application. As with most Web development decisions, your purpose would dictate why you would select a specific width. For instance, if you wanted to allow Web site visitors to only play and pause the audio clip, without being able to vary the volume, you would set the width to 42 pixels.

Table 8–3 Control Panel Views for Windows Media Player

Width Setting	Resulting Control Display	Image
42 pixels	Displays the fast forward and play/pause buttons	
66 pixels	Displays the rewind, fast forward, play/pause, and stop buttons	
118 pixels	Adds the previous and next buttons	
250 pixels	Adds a volume control (full control panel)	

Figure 8–4 shows how the various width dimensions display the player control relative to the Web page.

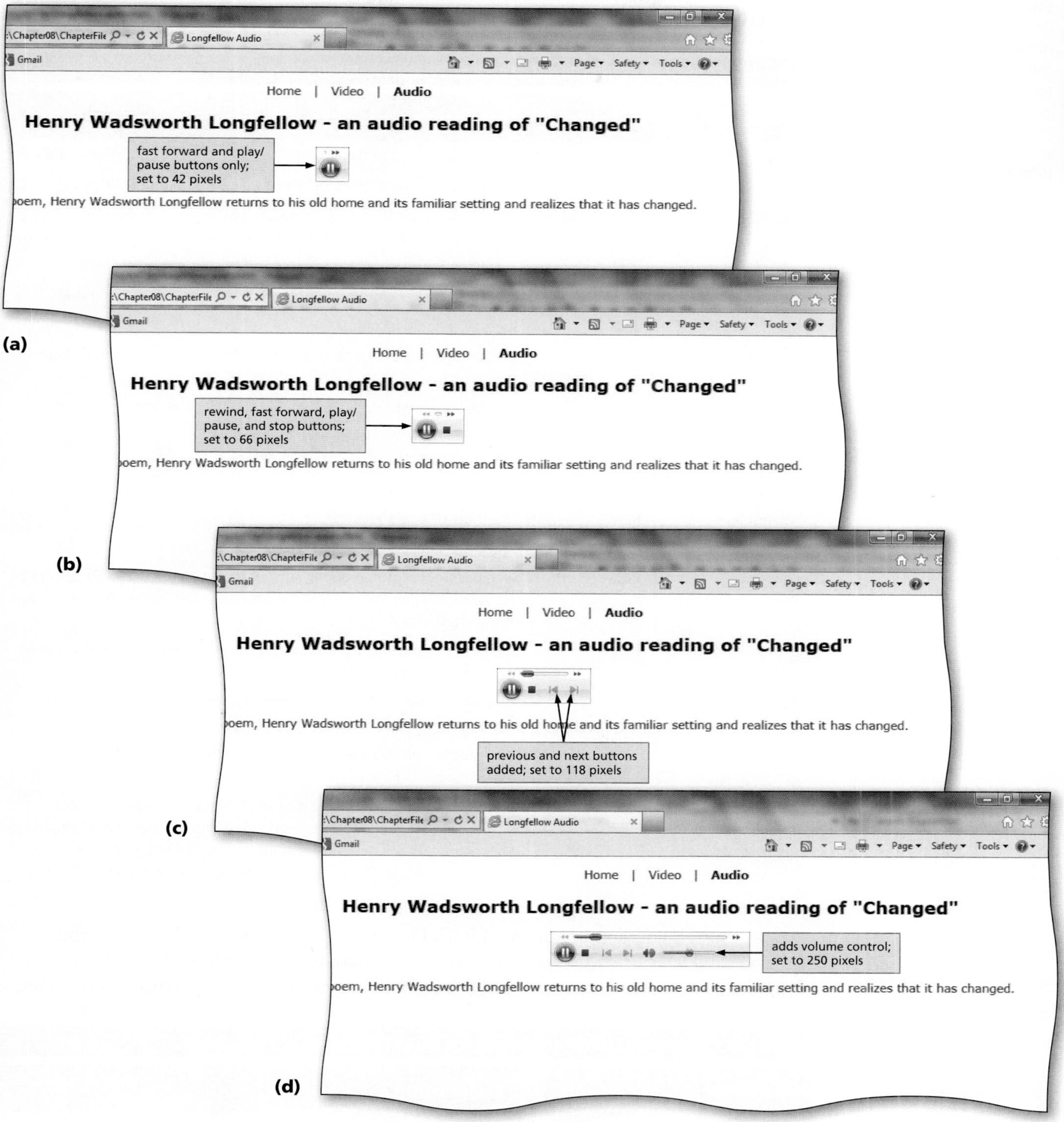

Figure 8–4

BTW

Parameters
Many other object parameters are available that are not discussed in this chapter. The various ActiveX controls have different parameters that can be used with that control. Review online what other parameters might be effective for you to use in your Web development.

Object Tag Parameters

Each type of media player has various <object> tag parameters that can be used. A **parameter** identifies the behavior and appearance of the object to which you assign the parameters. Table 8–4 lists the most commonly used parameters for Windows Media Player.

Table 8–4 Commonly Used Parameters for Windows Media Player

Parameter	Default	Description
autostart	true	Specifies whether the current media item begins playing automatically
balance	0	Specifies the current stereo balance; values range from –100 to 100
baseURL	[no default]	Specifies the base URL used for relative path resolution with URL script commands that are embedded in media items
enabled	false	Specifies whether the Windows Media Player control is enabled
fullscreen	false	Specifies whether video content is played back in full-screen mode
mute	false	Specifies if audio is muted
playcount	1	Specifies the number of times a media item will play; minimum value of one
rate	1.0	Specifies the playback rate; 0.5 equates to half the normal playback speed, 2 equates to twice
showaudiocontrols	true	Sets if the audio controls should show
showcontrols	true	Sets if the player controls should show
showdisplay	false	Sets if the display should show
showstatusbar	false	Sets if the status bar should show
stretchtofit	false	Specifies whether video displayed by the control automatically sizes to fit the video window, when the video window is larger than the dimensions of the video image
uimode	full	Specifies which controls are shown in the user interface; possible values: invisible, none, mini, full
URL		Specifies the name of the media item to play; you can specify a local filename or a URL
volume	[last setting; 0–100]	Zero specifies no volume and 100 specifies full volume
windowlessvideo	false	Specifies or retrieves a value indicating whether the Windows Media Player control renders video in windowless mode; when windowlessvideo is set to true, the player control renders video directly in the client area, so you can apply special effects or layer the video with text

Although you do not add any QuickTime video clips to any Web pages in this chapter, Table 8–5 lists the most commonly used parameters for QuickTime. To see complete parameters for any player, review them online at the manufacturers' Web sites.

Table 8–5 Commonly Used Parameters for QuickTime

Parameter	Default	Description
autoplay	true	Specifies whether the current media item begins playing automatically
bgcolor	[no default]	Sets the background color for the object
controller	true	Specifies if the player controls should show
endtime	[no default]	Specifies the time in the clip at which the video ends

Table 8–5 Commonly Used Parameters for QuickTime (continued)		
Parameter	**Default**	**Description**
loop	false	Plays the clip in a continuous loop
starttime	[no default]	Specifies the time in the clip at which the video begins
volume	[last setting]	Sets the initial audio volume

In the sample code (repeated below), one parameter is added in the <object> </object> container for the audio clip.

```
<object data="longfellow-audio.mp3" height="45" width="250">
        <param name="URL" value="longfellow-audio.mp3" />
</object>
```

The URL parameter, as shown in Table 8–4, identifies what audio clip is to be played. In this case, you are inserting an MPEG (.mp3) file. This is a recording in which Longfellow's poem "Changed" is read. As soon as you open the Web page with this <object> statement, the longfellow-audio.mp3 audio clip starts immediately (note the autostart default in Table 8–4). As stated before, the purpose of the Web site dictates what parameters you use. Think about yourself as a Web site visitor. How do you feel when a loud audio clip plays as soon as you enter a Web site? What do you think if you have no option to pause or stop the clip? Always consider your own browsing habits, likes, and dislikes when you design Web sites. If you did not want to start the .mp3 file automatically, you would add a <param name="autostart" value="false" /> statement within the <object> </object> container. With this audio clip insertion, you do provide the player control panel that gives the user the opportunity to pause or stop the audio clip.

The HMTL5 <audio> Tag

One of the most long-awaited features in HTML5 is the audio element. The <audio> tag is used to define sound, such as music or other audio streams. At the writing of this book, the <audio> tag is supported in all major browsers. If you use an older browser that doesn't support the <audio> tag, you can fall back to using the <object> tag. The negative about this new tag is that it does not currently support all audio formats. However, you can use a variety of software applications to convert from one audio form to another. Table 8–6 shows the attributes and values that can be used with the <audio> tag.

Table 8–6 Attributes for <audio> Tag		
Attribute	**Value**	**Description**
autoplay	autoplay	Specifies that the audio will start playing as soon as it is ready
controls	controls	Specifies that audio controls should be displayed (such as a play/pause button, etc.)
loop	loop	Specifies that the audio will start over again, every time it is finished
preload	auto metadata none	Specifies if and how the author thinks the audio should be loaded when the page loads
src	*URL*	Specifies the URL of the audio file

The sample code below shows how to use the <audio> tag to insert an audio file named longfellow-audio.mp3.

```
<audio controls="controls" autoplay="autoplay">
   <source src="longfellow-audio.mp3" type="audio/mp3" />
   If you are reading this, your browser does not support the
   HTML5 audio element.
</audio>
```

The controls attribute adds audio controls, like play, pause, and volume. It can be set up in any of the three following ways:

- <audio controls="controls">
- <audio controls>
- <audio controls=" ">

Similarly, the autoplay attribute can be set up in any of these ways:

- <audio autoplay>
- <audio autoplay="autoplay">
- <audio autoplay=" ">

You can use the src attribute in the <audio> tag itself as shown in the sample below:

```
<audio controls autoplay src="longfellow-audio.mp3">
   If you are reading this, your browser does not support
   the HTML5 audio element.
</audio>
```

However, in order to make the <audio> tag work in all browsers, you should use the source elements inside the audio element. The source elements can link to different audio files. The browser will use the first recognized format. An example of an <audio> tag with multiple <source> tags is shown below:

```
<audio controls="controls" autoplay="autoplay">
   <source src="longfellow-audio.mp3" type="audio/mp3" />
   <source src="longfellow-audio.ogg" type="audio/ogg" />
</audio>
```

Browsers that do not support the audio element will ignore the <audio> tag. You should always insert text content between the <audio> and </audio> tags, which will display if the browser does not support the tag.

Regarding the other attributes that you do not see in these examples, the preload attribute tells the browser to begin downloading the audio immediately when the element is encountered. The loop attribute restarts the audio immediately once it has finished playing. These can both be useful attributes depending on the audio clip and the purpose of the Web site.

Because this book is designed to highlight HTML5, you will use the new audio element to insert the Longfellow audio clip. (Note that you could have used the object element as shown in the examples above to insert the same audio clip.) As mentioned, most browsers today support the audio element, and the audio clip is in a format supported by the new tag (.mp3). You could use either element to accomplish the same task.

Plan Ahead

Inserting an audio file.

You would insert an audio file into a Web page if you want your Web site visitors to be able to hear content or background music. In the case of this Web site, you will insert an audio clip of a reading of the Longfellow poem "Changed."

- **Determine the area on the Web page into which you want to insert the audio clip**. This was a simple task for the Web site under development. There is a longfellow-audio.html Web page that discusses the poem. You center the controls of the audio clip by using the class "audio" that is defined in the stylesch8.css external style sheet.
- **Decide which attributes (if any) that you should use**. For this audio clip, you want the audio clip to start automatically when the Web page is opened. The Web site visitors will have the ability to pause, stop, or replay the audio clip using the default player control panel provided.

To Start Notepad++ and Open an HTML File

1. Start Notepad++ and, if necessary, maximize the window.
2. With the USB drive plugged into your computer, navigate to the Chapter08\ChapterFiles folder.
3. Double-click longfellow-audio.html in the list of files to open the file shown in Figure 8–5.

Q&A What is the purpose for the "audio" class on line 23?

This is a class identified in the external style sheet, stylesch8.css, to which you link on line 8. If you have not already done so, you should review that external style sheet. All classes (on lines 15–17, 23, and 27) are created in that external style sheet.

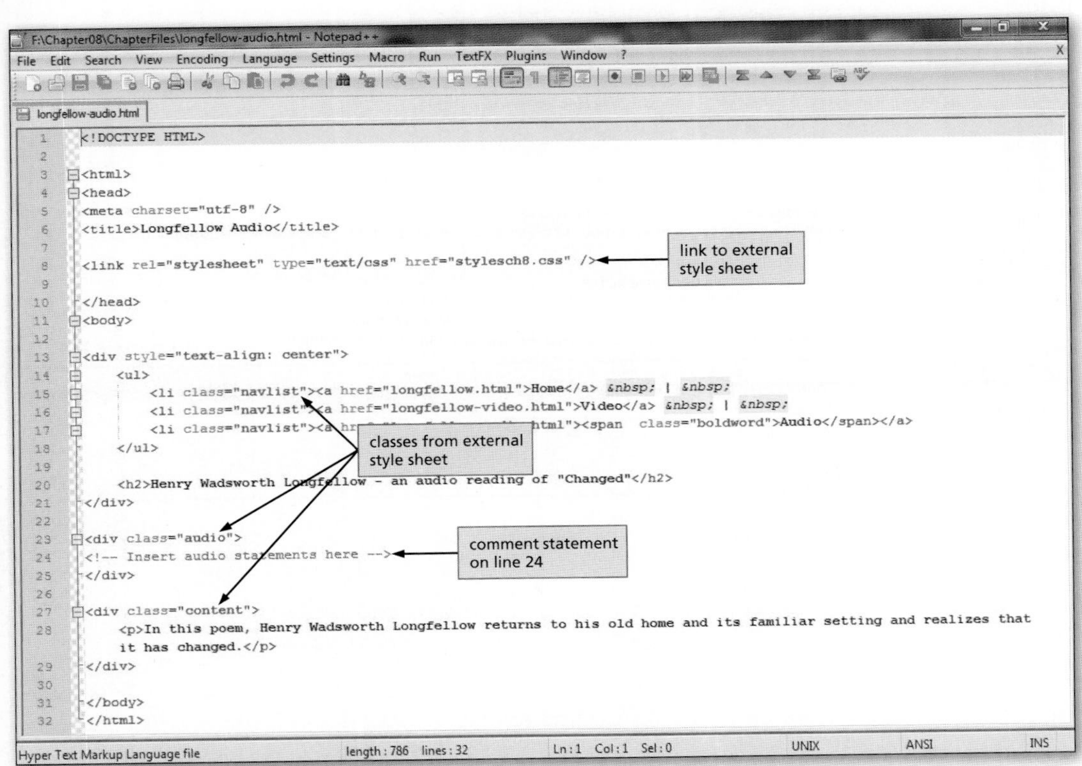

Figure 8–5

To Add an Audio Clip to a Web Page

The longfellow-audio.html Web page file is complete except for the <audio> and <source> statements, which will be added next. Table 8–7 shows the HTML code for this statement.

Table 8–7 HTML Code to Add Audio Clip Statements

Line	HTML Code
24	`<audio controls="controls" autoplay="autoplay">`
25	
26	`    <source src="longfellow-audio.mp3" type="audio/mp3" />`
27	`    If you are reading this, it is because your browser does not support the HTML5 audio element.`
28	
29	`</audio>`

The following step adds an audio clip to the Longfellow audio Web page.

1

- Highlight the words <!-- Insert audio statements here --> on line 24.
- Enter the HTML code in Table 8–7, indenting as shown.
- Save the file (Figure 8–6).

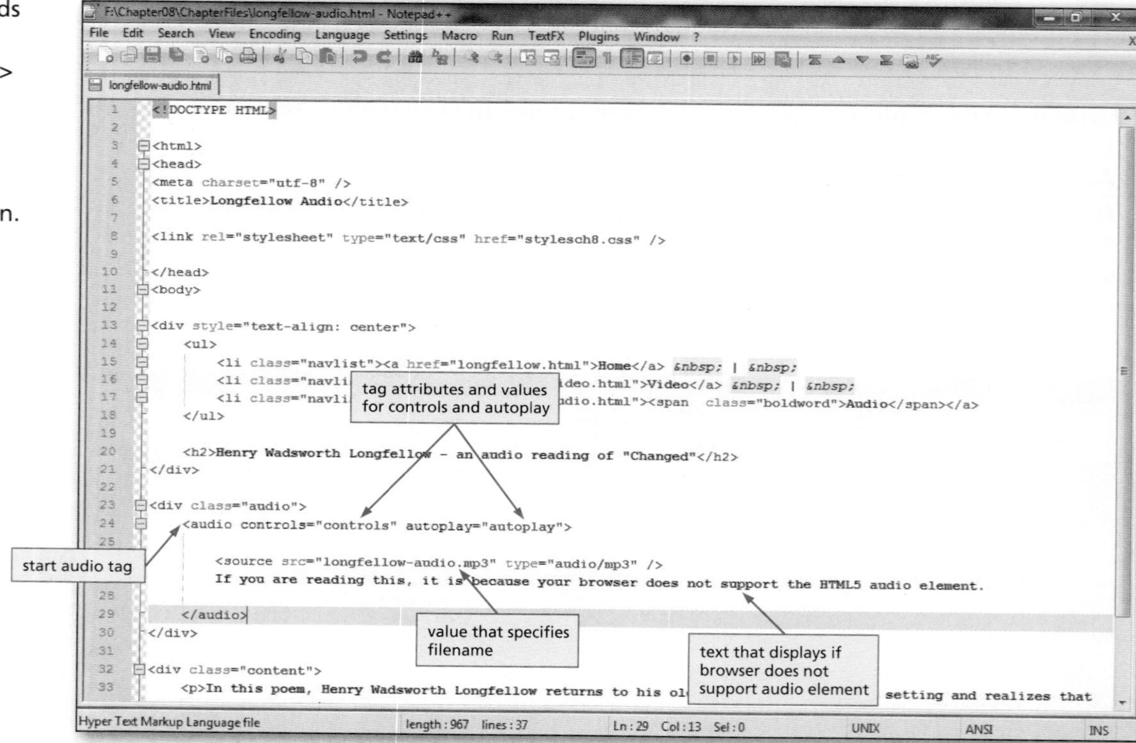

Figure 8–6

To Validate and View a Web Page Using ActiveX Controls

As always, you should validate and then view your pages. When you try to link to the Longfellow Audio Web page, it is likely that your browser will block the page's ActiveX content and display a security notification. **ActiveX controls** are small programs that are used extensively on the Internet. They can make browsing more enjoyable by providing toolbars, audio, video, animated content, and more. These programs can malfunction, however, or give you content you don't want. In some cases, these programs can be used to collect information from your computer in ways you might not approve of: possibly damage information on your computer, install software on your computer without your consent, or allow someone else to control your computer remotely. Given these risks, you should only install an ActiveX control or add-on if you completely trust the publisher and the Web site offering it. Internet Explorer sets security to high by default. This prohibits ActiveX controls from running without your intervention. The following steps validate the Web page, and then respond to the security notification in Internet Explorer to view the Web page.

1

- Validate the longfellow-audio.html Web page using the W3C validation service.
- With the USB drive plugged in to your computer, navigate to the Chapter08\ChapterFiles folder and open the longfellow.html file in the Web browser to display the home page of this Web site. Click the Audio link to navigate to the newly saved file.
- Because of Internet Explorer's high level of security, you get a notification in the gold bar at the bottom of the browser (Figure 8–7).

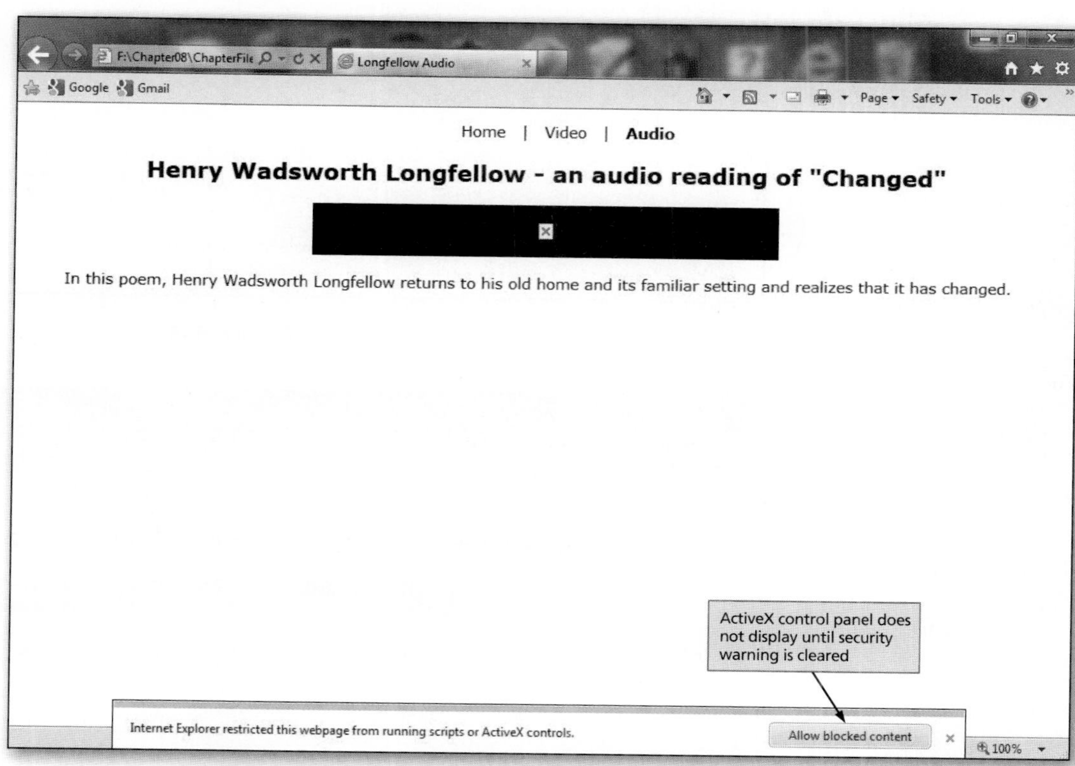

Figure 8–7

Q&A

Will the ActiveX controls and security notification appear if I use a browser other than Internet Explorer?

No. ActiveX controls only display in the Internet Explorer Web browser.

• Click the 'Allow blocked content' button in the gold bar at the bottom of the browser window (Figure 8–8).

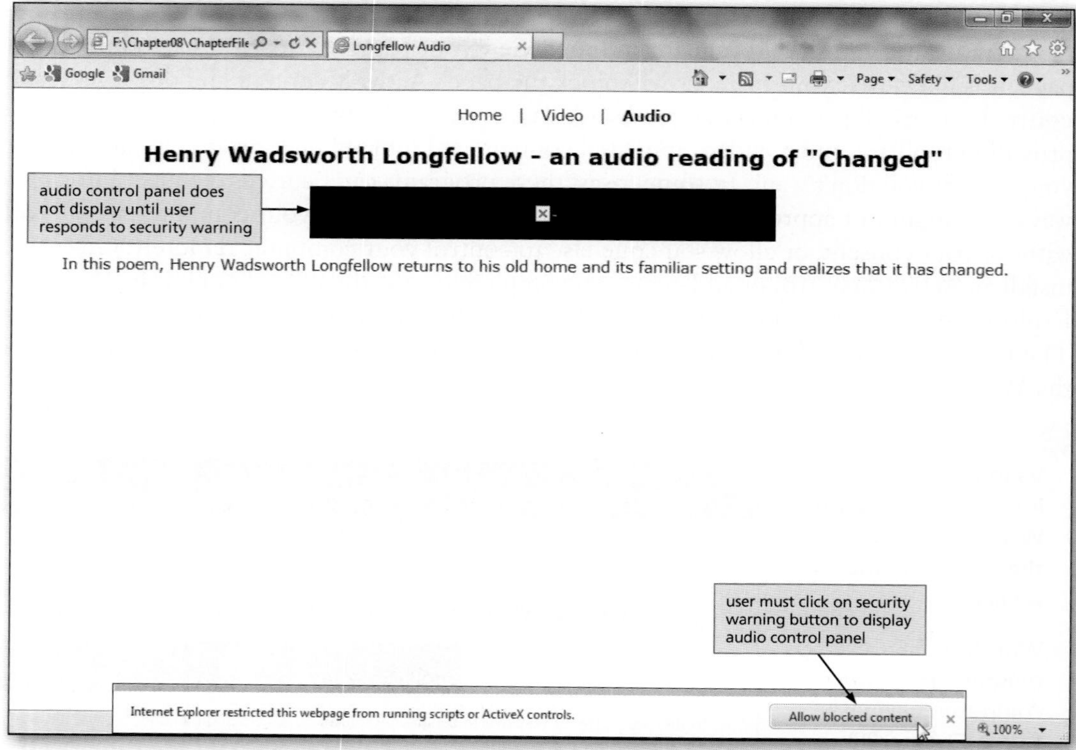

Figure 8–8

3

• The completed Web page displays with audio controls (Figure 8–9).

Q&A Do I have to respond to the security questions for each page in a Web site?

No, you are asked to respond just once within a given Web site. For example, if you were to open the longfellow-video.html Web page next (once the video clip is inserted), you would not be asked those security questions.

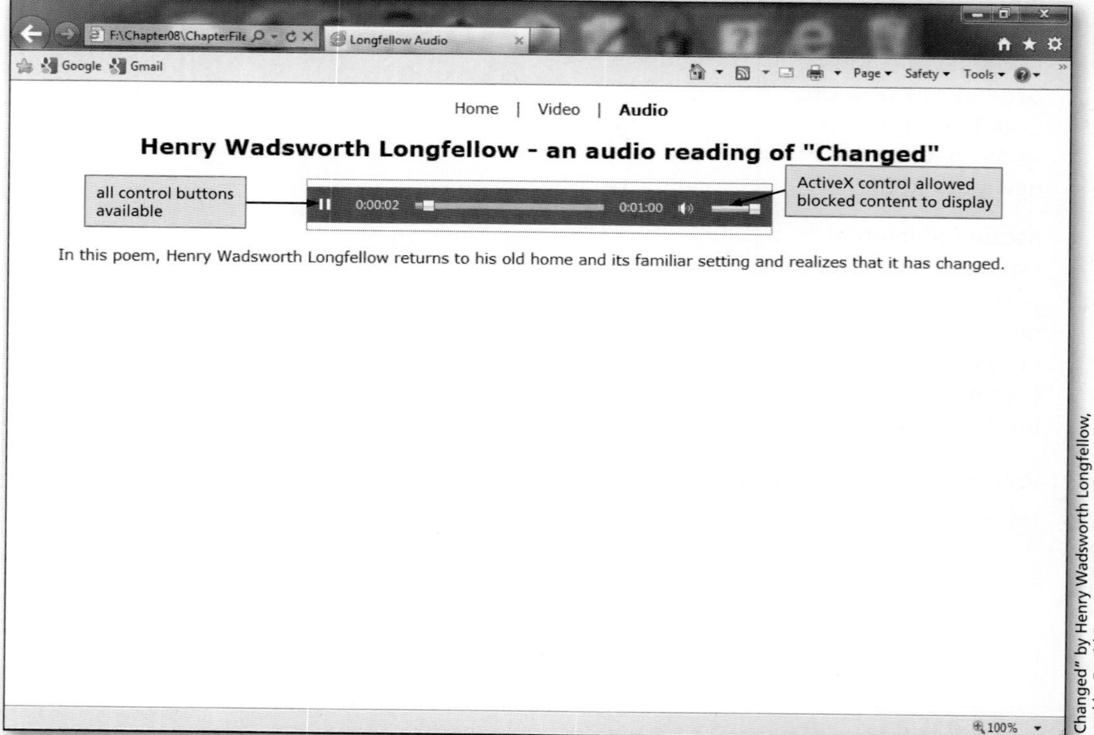

Figure 8–9

"Changed" by Henry Wadsworth Longfellow, Read by David Barnes; Henry Wadsworth

To Print a Web Page and an HTML File

1. Print the Longfellow Audio Web page from the browser (Figure 8–10).
2. Click the Notepad++ button on the taskbar.
3. Print the longfellow-audio.html file from Notepad++.

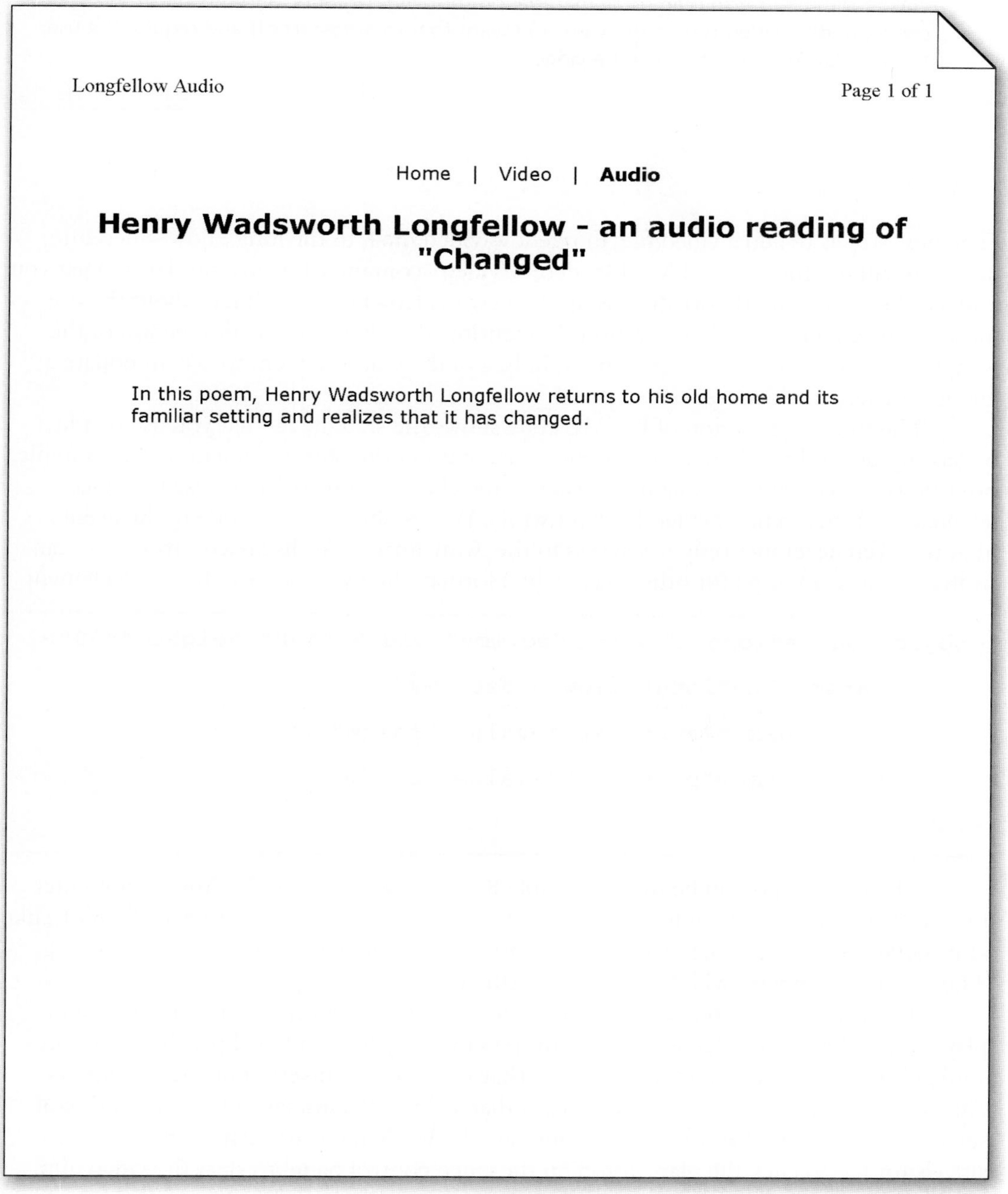

Longfellow Audio

Page 1 of 1

Home | Video | **Audio**

Henry Wadsworth Longfellow - an audio reading of "Changed"

In this poem, Henry Wadsworth Longfellow returns to his old home and its familiar setting and realizes that it has changed.

Figure 8–10

Plan Ahead

Inserting a video clip.
Video clips can add valuable content to a Web page. There are many uses for video clips. Companies use clips for training or to convey messages from the CEO. Instructors use videos to help students better understand complex topics in online classes. Many people use video clips just for fun on their personal Web sites or on YouTube.

- **Utilize video clips that enhance the content of the Web page.** In the chapter project, a video clip of a historical home adds value to the Web page.
- **Determine whether to utilize the autostart parameter.** Sometimes you want to encourage the user to read some material on the Web page first and then view the corresponding video clip. In this case, you want to turn autostart off and require the user to click play in order to watch the video.

BTW

Video Clips
Video clips can have a large file size depending on the length and the quality of the clip. Search for information about rules-of-thumb for file sizes when video clips are incorporated into a Web site.

Adding a Video Clip to a Web Page

The next step is to add a video file, longfellow-video.mp4, to the longfellow-video.html file. You will use the new HTML5 <video></video> container for this, similar to what you did for the audio clip. Before discussing the new <video> tag, we will talk about the use of the <object> tag for video insertion. As mentioned earlier in the audio section of the chapter, you may use the object element in lieu of the video element to accommodate a greater variety of video formats.

The following section of HTML code shows the statements that you use to add a video clip using the <object> tag. Because we are using the object element in this example, we can use a .wmv file as explained earlier in the chapter. You could not use the video element with that type of video format (.wmv). We are showing this code in the event that the Web developer only has access to the .wmv format. As discussed earlier, you can convert that to an .mp4 (or other acceptable) format, then you can use the video element.

```
<object data="longfellow-video.wmv" width="400" height="400">
      <param URL="longfellow-video.wmv" />
      <param name="autostart" value="false" />
      <param name="playcount" value="3" />
</object>
```

The parameters can be found in Table 8–4 on page HTML 372. You do not enter the width and height attributes this time so that you can see what this movie clip looks like at its default size. You can, however, add width and height attributes in the <object> tag. This is something with which you can experiment.

The three parameters used for the video clip insertion are: URL, autostart, and playcount. The source element is used in the same way for a video clip as it was for an audio clip. It tells the name of the object that you want to insert. The default for the autostart parameter is "true," which means that a clip will automatically start unless you set autostart to "false" as seen in the code sample. With autostart turned off, your Web site visitor has to click the play button on the video control panel to start the video clip. The playcount is the number of times that the video will play. The default is 1 time. Just as with other decisions that are made during the analysis phase of the Web development life cycle, you have to decide what is best for your application. Do you want the video clip to start as soon as the Web page is opened, or is it best to require your user to start it?

The HTML5 <video> Tag

Until now, there has not been a standard for showing a video on a Web page — most videos are shown through a plug-in (like Adobe Flash). The problem is that different browsers may have different plug-ins or only recognize specific video formats. There are three different tags that you can use to incorporate video: <embed>, <object>, and <video>. You would have to add all three elements and utilize different video formats to make sure your video will play in all browsers (Internet Explorer, Chrome, Firefox, Safari, Opera) and on all hardware (PC, Mac, iPad, iPhone). In this project, we will discuss the embed and object elements and we will utilize the video element to add a video clip.

The purpose of the <embed> tag is to embed multimedia elements in HTML pages. The problems with the <embed> tag are: it is unknown to HTML 4 and will not validate correctly; if the browser does not support Flash, your video will not play; iOS devices such as the iPad and iPhone cannot display Flash videos; and, if you convert the video to another format, it will still not play in all browsers.

The purpose of the <object> tag is to embed multimedia elements in HTML pages. The chapter contains a significant amount of information about the object element. Although the code with an <object> tag will validate correctly, there are also problems associated with this option: if the browser does not support Flash, your video will not play; iOS devices such as the iPad and iPhone cannot display Flash videos; and if you convert the video to another format, it will still not play in all browsers.

Using the <video> Tag

HTML5 defines a new element that specifies a standard way to embed a video or movie on a Web page: the video element. The tag is used to specify a video, such as a movie clip or other video streams. It is supported by most browsers, but review Table 8–2 on page HTML 369 to see what formats the video element supports. Just as with audio clips, there are numerous software applications that allow you to convert video from one format to another. There are, however, problems with using the video element: you must convert your videos to one of the supported formats; the video element does not work in older browsers; and the video element does not validate in HTML 4 and XHTML. Table 8–8 lists the attributes and values that can be used with the <video> tag.

Table 8–8 Attributes for <video> Tag

Attribute	Value	Description
autoplay	autoplay	Specifies that the video will start playing as soon as it is ready
controls	controls	Specifies that video controls should be displayed (such as a play/pause button, etc.)
height	*pixels*	Sets the height of the video player
loop	loop	Specifies that the video will start over again, every time it is finished
muted	muted	Specifies that the audio output of the video should be muted
poster	*URL*	Specifies an image to be shown while the video is downloading, or until the user hits the play button
preload	auto metadata none	Specifies if and how the author thinks the video should be loaded when the page loads
src	*URL*	Specifies the URL of the video file
width	*pixels*	Sets the width of the video player

The following sample code shows how to use the <video> tag to insert a video file named longfellow-video.mp4 in a Web page.

```
<video width="320" height="240" controls="controls">
   <source src="longfellow-video.mp4" type="video/mp4" />
   If you are reading this, your browser does not support the
   HTML5 video element.
</video>
```

It is a good idea to always include width and height attributes. If height and width are set, the space required for the video is reserved when the page is loaded. However, without these attributes, the browser does not know the size of the video and cannot reserve the appropriate space for it. The effect will be that the page layout will change during loading, when the video loads.

As with the audio element, the controls attribute adds video controls, like play, pause, and volume. It can be set up in any of the three following ways:

- <video controls="controls">
- <video controls>
- <video controls=" ">

You can use the src attribute in the video element itself as shown in the sample below:

```
<video controls autoplay src="longfellow-video.mp4">
   If you are reading this, your browser does not support the
   HTML5 video element.
</video>
```

Also, as you did with the audio element, you should use the source elements inside the video element. The video element allows multiple source elements. The source elements can link to different video files. The browser will use the first recognized format. An example of a <video> tag with multiple <source> tags is shown below:

```
<video controls="controls" autoplay="autoplay">
   <source src="longfellow-video.mp4" type="video/mp4" />
   <source src="longfellow-video.ogg" type="video/ogg" />
</video>
```

Browsers that do not support the video element will ignore the <video> tag. You should always insert text content between the <video> and </video> tags, which will display if the browser does not support the <video> tag.

Because this book is designed to highlight HTML5, you will use the new video element to insert the Longfellow video clip. (Note that you could have used the object element as shown in the examples above to insert the same video clip.) As mentioned, most browsers today support the video element, and the video clip is in a format supported by the new tag (.mp4). However, that clip was converted from a .wmv (Windows Media format) to a format supported by the video element (.mp4) using a software application that converted the formats. When creating a Web page, you can choose to use the object element together with a .wmv file or the video element (as is done in this project) together with an .mp4 file to accomplish the same task.

To Add a Video Clip to a Web Page

To add the video file, longfellow-video.mp4, to the longfellow-video.html file, you will use the <video></video> container, just as you did for the audio clip, but with different attributes. Table 8–9 shows the code to add the video clip.

Table 8–9 HTML Code to Add Video Clip

Line	HTML Code
24	`<video width="320" height="240" controls="controls">`
25	
26	`<source src="longfellow-video.mp4" type="video/mp4" />`
27	`If you are reading this, it is because your browser does not support the HTML5 video element.`
28	
29	`</video>`

1

- If necessary, click the Notepad++ button on the taskbar.
- Open the longfellow-video.html file from the Chapter08\ChapterFiles folder (Figure 8–11).

```
1  <!DOCTYPE HTML>
2
3  <html>
4  <head>
5  <meta charset="utf-8" />
6  <title>Longfellow Video</title>
7
8  <link rel="stylesheet" type="text/css" href="stylesch8.css" />
9
10 </head>
11 <body>
12
13 <div style="text-align: center">
14     <ul>
15         <li class="navlist"><a href="longfellow.html">Home</a>   |  
16         <li class="navlist"><a href="longfellow-video.html"><span  class="boldword">Video</span></a>   |
            
17         <li class="navlist"><a href="longfellow-audio.html">Audio</a>
18     </ul>
19
20     <h2>Henry Wadsworth Longfellow - a video of his home</h2>
21 </div>
22
23 <div class="movie">
24 <!-- Insert video statements here -->
25 </div>
26
27 <div class="content">
28     <p>Henry W. Longfellow (1807 - 1882), was one of the world's foremost 19th century poets. The house in which
       he lived in Cambridge, Massachusetts, also served as the headquarters for General George Washington during the
       Siege of Boston, July 1775 - April 1776.</p>
29 </div>
30
```

Hyper Text Markup Language file | length : 910 lines : 32 | Ln : 1 Col : 1 Sel : 0 | UNIX | ANSI | INS

HTML code in longfellow-video.html file

comment on line 24 where object tag is inserted

Figure 8–11

2

- Highlight the words <!—Insert the video statements here --> on line 24.
- Enter the HTML code shown in Table 8–9 (Figure 8–12).
- Save the file.

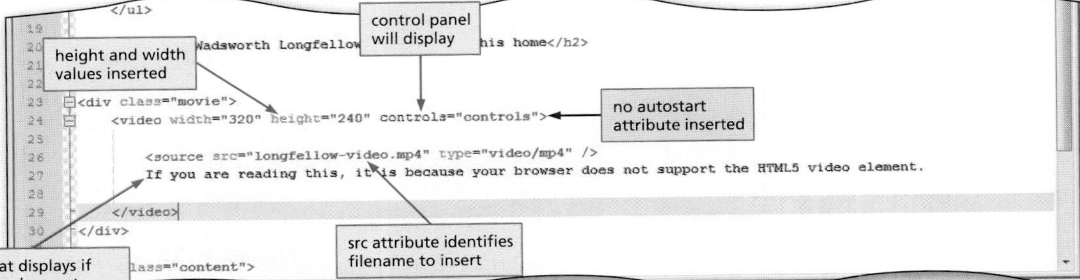

Figure 8–12

To Validate and View a Web Page

After you have added the video clip to the longfellow-video.html Web page file, you need to validate the file and view the Web page to review the style changes.

1. Validate the Web page using the W3C validation service.
2. Return to the Web site home page and click the navigation link for the longfellow-video.html file in the browser to view the changes. Figure 8–13a shows how the video displays at start-up with no controls. When the pointer hovers over the video, the controls display as shown in Figure 8–13b.

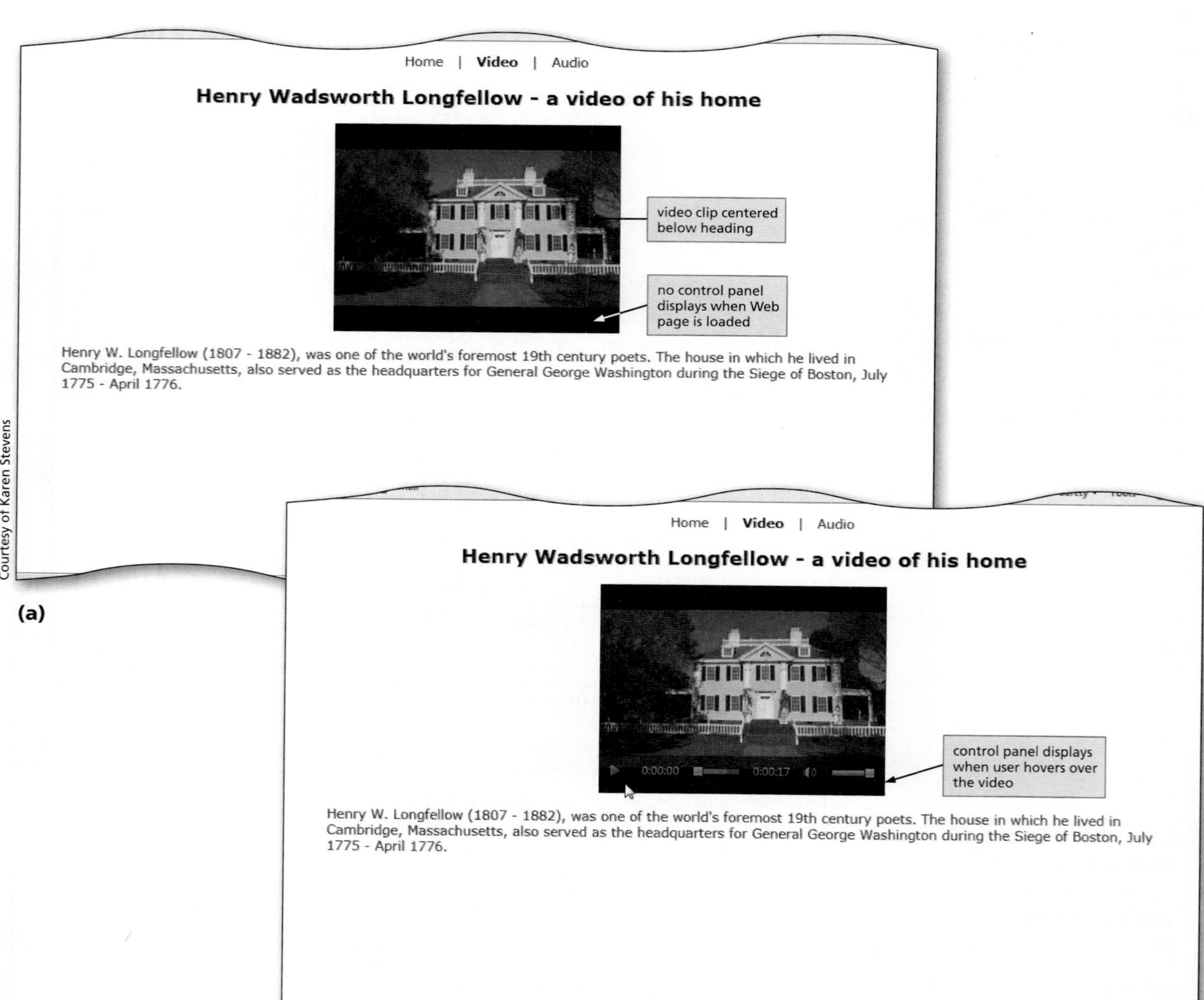

Figure 8–13

To Print a Web Page and HTML File

1. Print the Longfellow Video Web page from the browser.
2. Print the Notepad++ longfellow-video.html file (Figure 8–14).

BTW

Quick Reference
For a list of HTML tags and their associated attributes, see Appendix A at the back of this book, or visit the HTML Quick Reference on the Book Companion Site Web page for this book at www.cengagebrain.com.

```
<html>
<head>
<meta charset="utf-8" />
<title>Longfellow Video</title>

<link rel="stylesheet" type="text/css" href="stylesch8.css" />

</head>
<body>

<div style="text-align: center">
    <ul>
        <li class="navlist"><a href="longfellow.html">Home</a>   |  
        <li class="navlist"><a href="longfellow-video.html"><span  class="boldword">
        Video</span></a>   |  
        <li class="navlist"><a href="longfellow-audio.html">Audio</a>
    </ul>

    <h2>Henry Wadsworth Longfellow - a video of his home</h2>
</div>

<div class="movie">
    <video width="320" height="240" controls="controls">

        <source src="longfellow-video.mp4" type="video/mp4" />
        If you are reading this, it is because your browser does not support the HTML5
        video element.

    </video>
</div>

<div class="content">
    <p>Henry W. Longfellow (1807 - 1882), was one of the world's foremost 19th century
    poets. The house in which he lived in Cambridge, Massachusetts, also served as the
    headquarters for General George Washington during the Siege of Boston, July 1775 -
    April 1776.</p>
</div>

</body>
</html>
```

Figure 8–14

Chapter Summary

In this chapter, you have learned how to embed audio and video files in your Web pages. The items listed below include all the new HTML skills you have learned in this chapter.

1. Add an Audio Clip to a Web Page (HTML 376)
2. Validate and View a Web Page Using ActiveX Controls (HTML 377)
3. Add a Video Clip to a Web Page (HTML 383)

STUDENT ASSIGNMENTS

Learn It Online

Test your knowledge of chapter content and key terms.

Instructions: To complete the following exercises, please visit www.cengagebrain.com. At the CengageBrain.com home page, search for *HTML5 and CSS 7th Edition* using the search box at the top of the page. This will take you to the product page for this book. On the product page, click the Access Now button below the Study Tools heading. On the Book Companion Site Web page, select Chapter 8, and then click the link for the desired exercise.

Chapter Reinforcement TF, MC, and SA

A series of true/false, multiple choice, and short answer questions that test your knowledge of the chapter content.

Flash Cards

An interactive learning environment where you identify chapter key terms associated with displayed definitions.

Practice Test

A series of multiple choice questions that test your knowledge of chapter content and key terms.

Who Wants To Be a Computer Genius?

An interactive game that challenges your knowledge of chapter content in the style of a television quiz show.

Wheel of Terms

An interactive game that challenges your knowledge of chapter key terms in the style of the television show *Wheel of Fortune*.

Crossword Puzzle Challenge

A crossword puzzle that challenges your knowledge of key terms presented in the chapter.

Apply Your Knowledge

Reinforce the skills and apply the concepts you learned in this chapter.

Adding a Background Sound

Instructions: Start Notepad++ and a browser. Using your browser, open the apply8-1.html file from the Chapter08\Apply folder of the Data Files for Students. See the inside back cover of this book for instructions on downloading the Data Files for Students, or contact your instructor for information about accessing the required files. Figure 8–15 shows the Apply Your Knowledge Web page as it should appear in the browser after the necessary code is added.

Courtesy of LadyofHats, Wikimedia

Figure 8–15

Perform the following tasks:

1. With the apply8-1.html file open in Notepad++, add the 04geeseflyhonk.mp3 audio clip with the following options:
   a. Use the new audio element to insert the audio clip in such a way that no control panel displays.
   b. Set the audio clip to continuously repeat.
2. Save the file as apply8-1solution.html. Validate the code and print the file.
3. Submit the solution in the format specified by your instructor.

Extend Your Knowledge

Extend the skills you learned in this chapter and experiment with new skills.

Inserting Multiple Audio Files on a Single Web Page

Instructions: Start Notepad++. Open the file extend8-1.html from the Chapter08\Extend folder of the Data Files for Students. See the inside back cover of this book for instructions on downloading the Data Files for Students, or contact your instructor for information about accessing the required files. Save the file as extend8-1solution.html. This file contains the Web page shown in Figure 8–16.

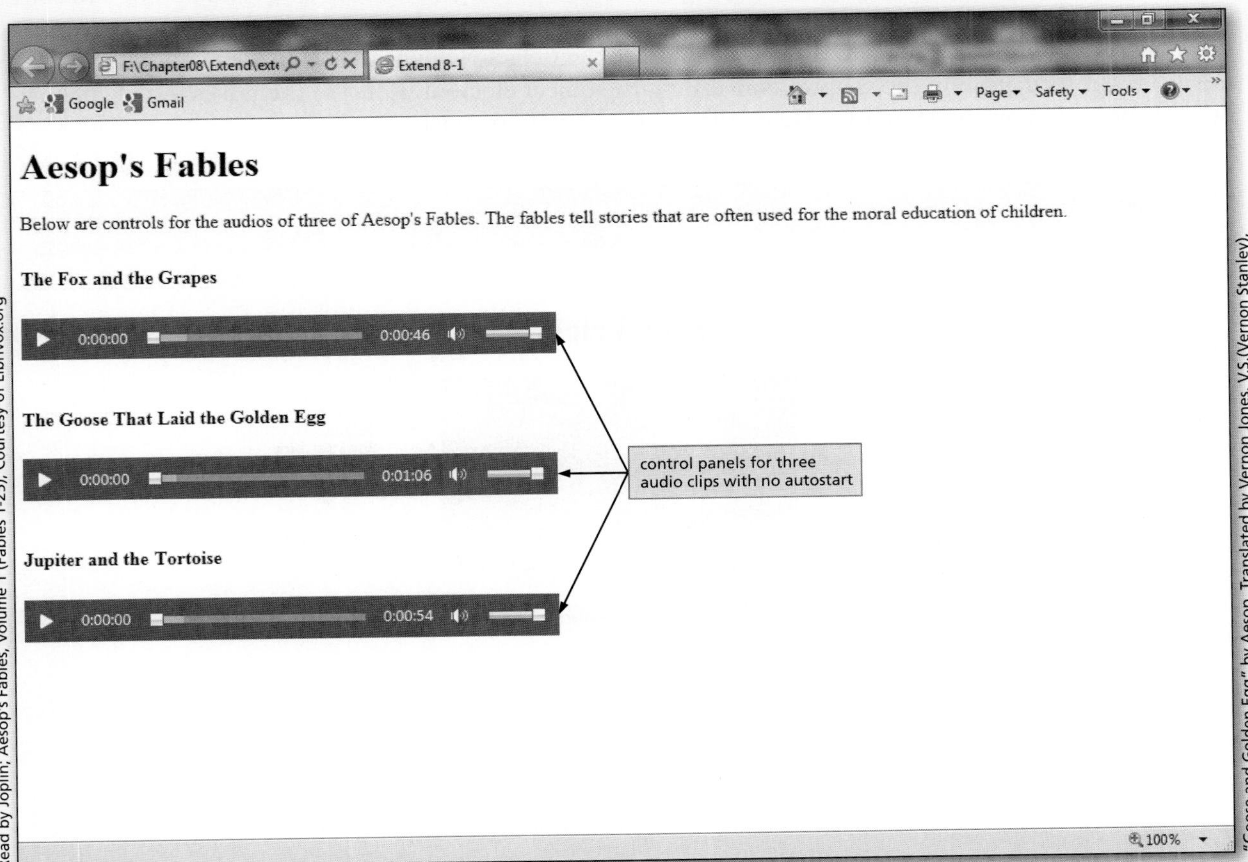

Figure 8–16

Continued >

Extend Your Knowledge *continued*

Perform the following tasks:

1. There are three paragraphs of text in the extend8-1.html file that list the titles of the fables. With the file open in Notepad++, use the HTML5 audio element to add the three audio clips (foxfable.mp3, goosefable.mp3, and jupiterfable.mp3) below the relevant headings.
2. Insert the audio clip in such a way that the control panel for each audio clip displays.
3. Save the file as extend 8-1solution.html; validate the code; print the file.
4. Submit the solution in the format specified by your instructor.

Make It Right

Analyze a document, and correct all errors and/or improve the design.

Correcting the Dog Tricks Web Page

Instructions: Start Notepad++. Open the file makeitright8-1.html from the Chapter08\MakeItRight folder of the Data Files for Students and save it as makeitright8-1solution.html. See the inside back cover of this book for instructions on downloading the Data Files for Students, or contact your instructor for information about accessing the required files. The Web page is a modified version of what you see in Figure 8–17, but it contains some errors. The dogtricks.wmv video should not autostart and should display with the control panel. Make the necessary corrections to the Web page to make it look like the figure. For this exercise, you should use the object element to add a video clip. If necessary, review the information in the chapter concerning the object element. Refer to the tables in the chapter with information on the Windows Media Player to complete the task.

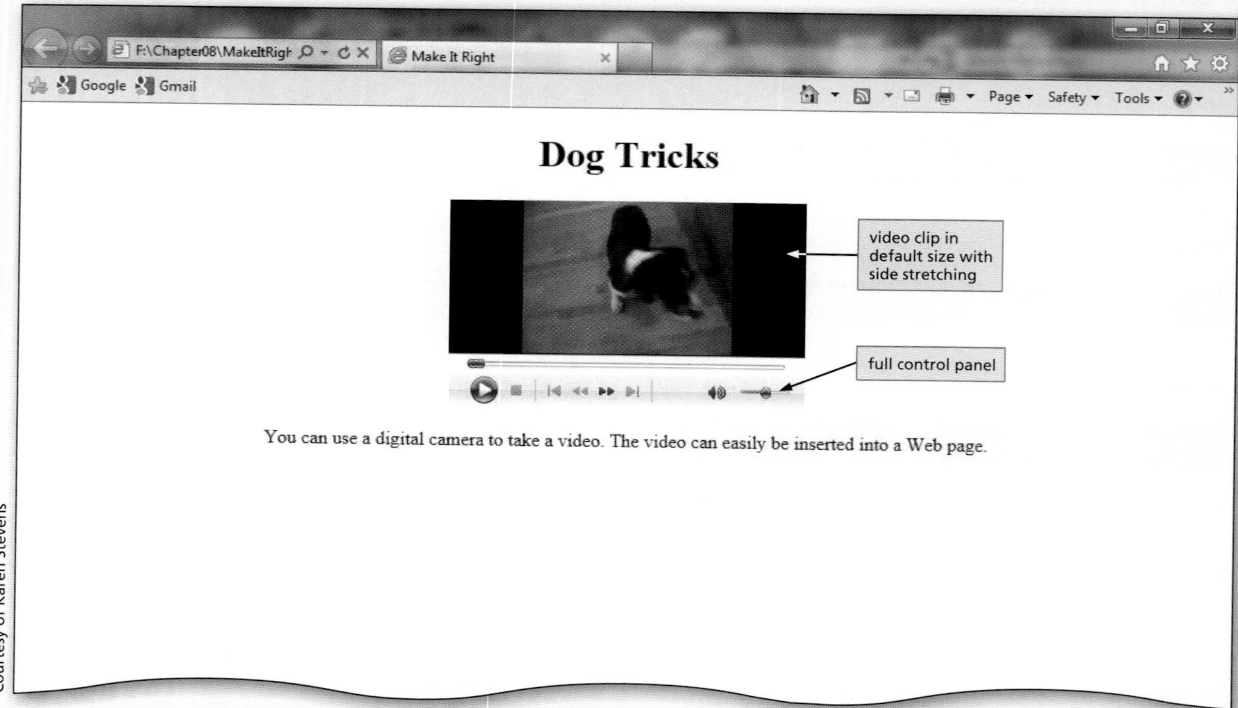

Courtesy of Karen Stevens

Figure 8–17

In the Lab

Lab 1: A Spooky Poem

Instructions: Your English literature teacher would like to see an example of how an audio clip of a poem would sound on a Web page. She wants to be able to pause, stop, and replay the audio clip, as shown in Figure 8–18.

Figure 8–18

Perform the following tasks:

1. Using Notepad++, open the HTML file lab8-1.html in the Chapter08\IntheLab folder of the Data Files for Students.
2. Add the audio clip, ghostshighnoon.mp3, to the Web page.
3. Add the <audio> attribute to start this audio clip automatically.
4. Add the attribute needed to display controls for the audio clip.
5. Save the HTML file in the Chapter08\IntheLab folder as lab8-1solution.html. Validate the file and then print it.
6. Test the Web page in Internet Explorer.
7. Submit the solution in the format specified by your instructor.

In the Lab

Lab 2: Whooping Crane Video

Instructions: Your biology class is learning about bird migration. You have read about how some researchers are attempting to reintroduce Whooping Cranes in the U.S. and help Whooping Cranes raised in captivity participate in migration. You have found a video clip that shows these efforts in progress. You decide to create a Web page that will show this video, as shown in Figure 8–19.

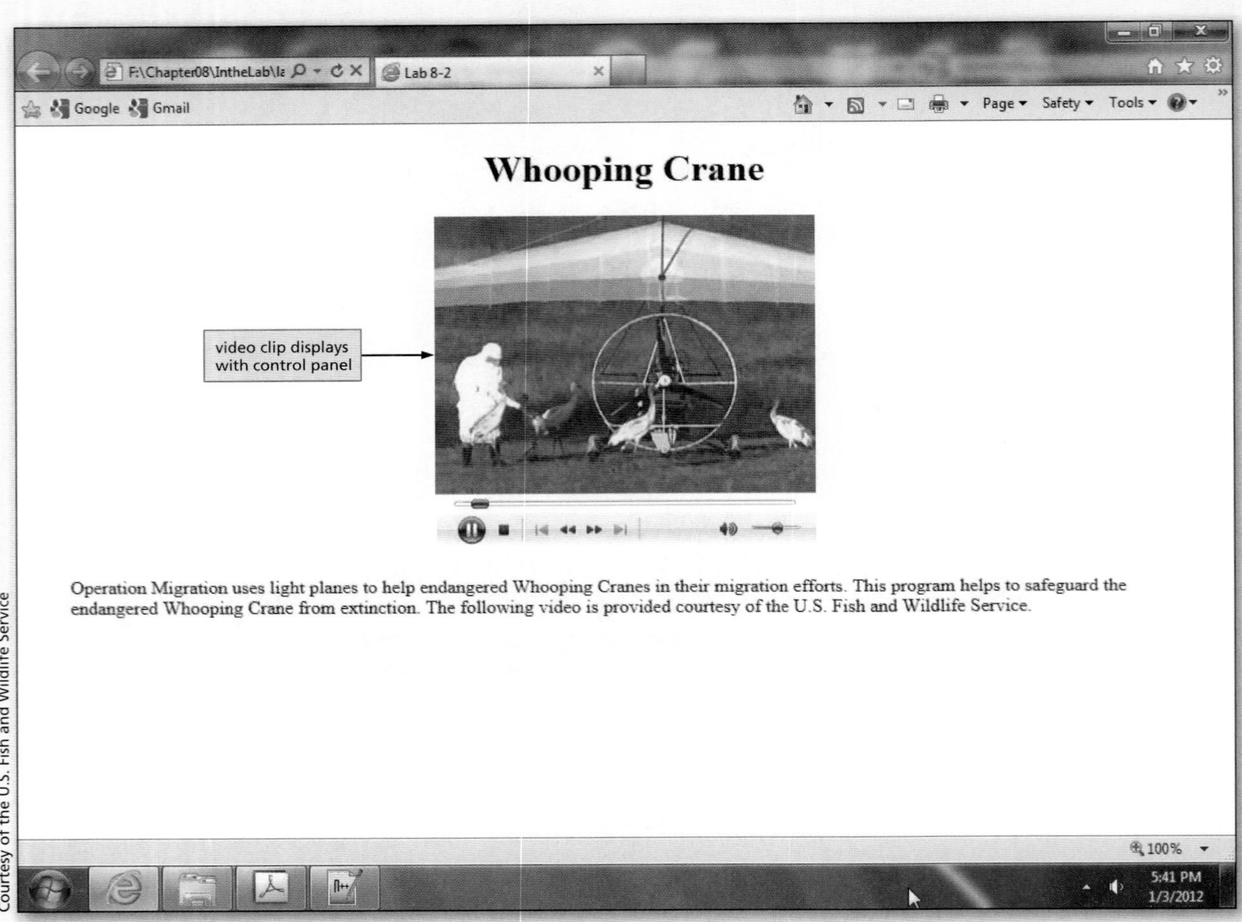

Figure 8–19

Perform the following tasks:

1. Using Notepad++, open the HTML file lab8-2.html in the Chapter08\IntheLab folder of the Data Files for Students.
2. Add the video clip whooper.wmv to the Web page using the object element.
3. Do not allow this video to start automatically and display the player controls.
4. Save the HTML file in the Chapter08\IntheLab folder as lab8-2solution.html. Validate the file and then print it.
5. Test the Web page in Internet Explorer.
6. Submit the solution in the format specified by your instructor.

In the Lab

Lab 3: Adding a Video Clip

Instructions: Your history teacher has asked everyone in class to find one interesting fact from a government Web site. You find a video clip that discusses beekeeping at the White House, and you think a Web page showing that clip would be interesting to the other students. The file lab8-3.html is included in the Chapter08\IntheLab folder of the Data Files for Students.

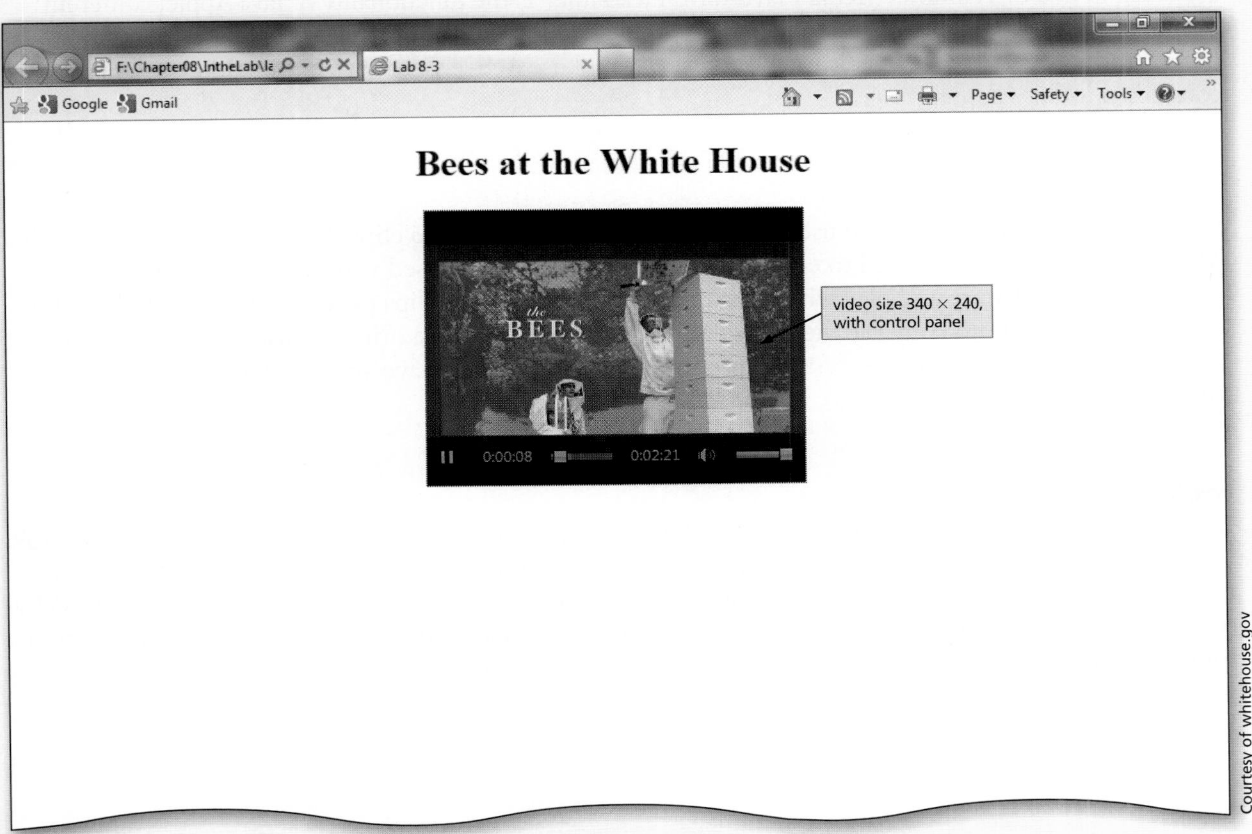

Figure 8–20

Perform the following tasks:

1. Open the file lab8-3.html in Notepad++. Save the file as lab8-3solution.html.
2. Insert the WH_bees.mp4 file as the video. Set the width to 320 and height to 240 and display the player controls. The video should not start automatically. There should be a control panel on the Web page, as shown in Figure 8–20.
3. Include a line of text that is displayed in the event that the user's browser does not support the video element.
4. Save the file, validate it, and then print it.
5. Test the Web page in Internet Explorer.
6. Submit the solution in the format specified by your instructor.

Cases and Places

Apply your creative thinking and problem-solving skills to design and implement a solution.

1: Finding Multimedia Information Online

Academic

Search on the Internet for an ActiveX control other than those discussed in this chapter. Why would you use Flash in lieu of Windows Media Player or QuickTime? Is the functionality of Java Applets different from or similar to the functionality of Windows Media Player or QuickTime? How does RealAudio differ from its competition? Determine when you would use ActiveX controls in the exercises you have completed in this chapter.

2: Movie-Making Software

Personal

Search for software that you can use to make or edit movie and audio clips that offers free trial periods. Most software that can be used to edit or make movies can also be used with audio files. If possible, download that software and play with it, using the video and audio clips provided in the Data Files for Students. Make sure to copy the file that you plan to use and save the original, just in case something happens. As you work with the software, use the Help utility if you have any problems. Demonstrate the software to the class.

3: Multimedia Formats

Professional

Review the audio and video formats listed in Tables 8–1 and 8–2 on pages HTML 368 and HTML 369. In this chapter, you used the following types of files: .mp3, .mp4, and .wmv. What are the benefits of these other formats? How are these formats better or worse than the formats used in the chapter? Why would you use one format over the other? How prevalent is one media format over the others? Search online for audio or video clips in at least three of the other formats.

Special Feature 2
Converting Frames on Your Web Site

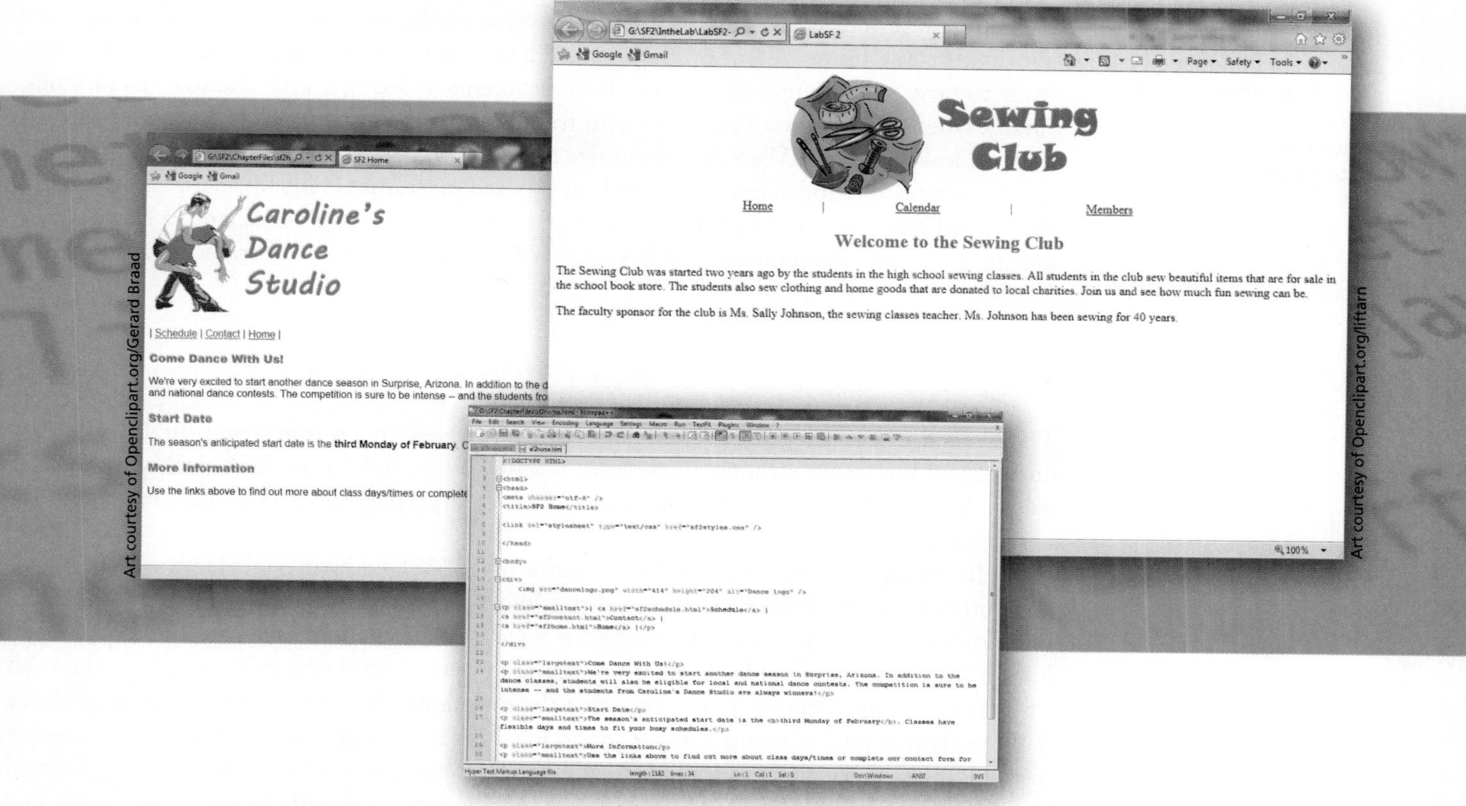

Art courtesy of Openclipart.org/Gerard Braad

Art courtesy of Openclipart.org/liftarn

Objectives

You will have mastered the material in this special feature when you can:

- Define terms related to frames
- Identify all parts of a framed Web site structure
- Discuss the purpose and design of a frame definition file
- Determine a structure to replace frames on a Web site
- Develop a Web site to replace frames

Introduction

A **frame** is a rectangular area of a Web page — essentially, a window — in which a separate Web page can be displayed. Frames allow a user to display several Web pages at one time in a single browser window. Each frame displays a different, individual Web page, each of which is capable of interacting with other Web pages. Web pages that include frames look and act differently from Web pages created in previous projects. Frames are not used in the projects in this book because HTML5 does not support the frame tags. Web pages with frames will therefore not validate with an HTML5 doctype. Additionally, and just as importantly, many screen readers, such as those used by visually impaired people, have difficulty displaying a Web site that uses frames. The Americans with Disabilities Act (ADA) standards recommend that frames not be used for Web sites. In addition to problems with devices for the disabled, there are other potential problems with the use of frames for Web development. Frames can cause problems when people bookmark or add the Web page as a favorite. It is the frame definition that is stored, and that may not be the page that the user wants to save. Search engines may also have problems indexing a Web site that uses frames. Finally, when users print a Web page with frames, they may not get what they see on the screen. However, many Web sites do utilize a frame structure, and as a Web developer, you may be responsible for maintaining Web sites based on frames. This Special Feature explains frames and how they are used, and shows you how to convert Web sites from a frame structure to better accommodate ADA standards and to address other frame-related issues.

BTW

Americans with Disabilities Act
Review the Web site dedicated to this act, ada.gov. It contains a wealth of information on the standards related to this act, including information about Web site functionality.

Project — Converting Frames

The Web site presented in this Special Feature is based on a frame structure. In order to understand the frame structure, you have to know what the frame definition is and how it works. You also have to understand how the other Web pages in a Web site are related to the frame definition file.

In this Special Feature, you review frame-based Web pages provided in the Data Files for Students. See the inside back cover of this book for instructions on downloading the Data Files for Students, or contact your instructor for information about accessing the required files. Figure 1a shows the initial Web site using frames. A blue dashed line indicates where the Web page is divided into frames. You can see that the top frame (the section of the Web page above the blue dashed line) contains a dance studio logo and a navigation bar. The bottom frame (the section of the Web page beneath the blue dashed line) contains the Web page content. You will look at the frame definition file (Figure 1b) and see how it works with the other files in the Web site. You are then introduced to options that can take the place of a frame structure. Finally, you will redesign the Web site to look similar but remove the frames (Figures 1c and 1d).

Overview

As you read through this feature, you will learn how to assess the frame definition file that creates the Web site shown in Figure 1a. You will then convert the Web site structured with frames (Figure 1b) to a Web site structured without frames, using techniques that you have previously studied (Figures 1c and 1d). You will complete this by performing these general tasks:

- Determine the use of a frame definition file to structure a Web site.
- Identify what Web design methods could be used to restructure the Web site.
- Make the changes necessary to the Web pages provided to restructure the Web site.
- Validate and test the Web pages.

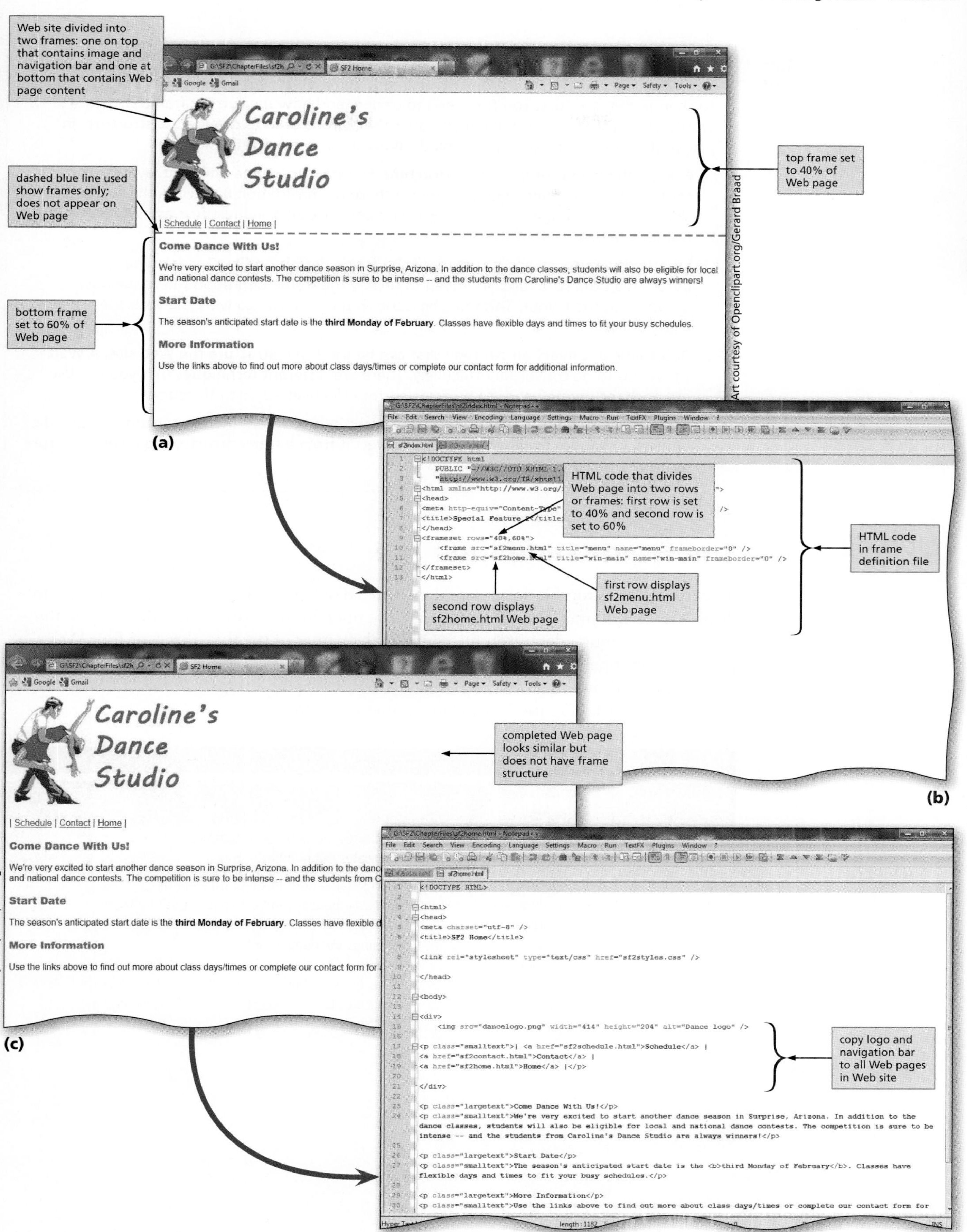

Web site divided into two frames: one on top that contains image and navigation bar and one at bottom that contains Web page content
Caroline's Dance Studio
| Schedule | Contact | Home |
dashed blue line used show frames only; does not appear on Web page
top frame set to 40% of Web page
Come Dance With Us!
We're very excited to start another dance season in Surprise, Arizona. In addition to the dance classes, students will also be eligible for local and national dance contests. The competition is sure to be intense -- and the students from Caroline's Dance Studio are always winners!
Start Date
The season's anticipated start date is the third Monday of February. Classes have flexible days and times to fit your busy schedules.
More Information
Use the links above to find out more about class days/times or complete our contact form for additional information.
bottom frame set to 60% of Web page
(a)
HTML code that divides Web page into two rows or frames: first row is set to 40% and second row is set to 60%
HTML code in frame definition file
first row displays sf2menu.html Web page
second row displays sf2home.html Web page
(b)
completed Web page looks similar but does not have frame structure
(c)
copy logo and navigation bar to all Web pages in Web site
(d)
Art courtesy of Openclipart.org/Gerard Braad

Figure 1

Plan Ahead

General Project Guidelines

The Web pages used in this project are already completed with a frame structure. In order to change the structure, you first need to understand how the current frame structure works. Then you can determine techniques that can be used to change the structure. In preparation for this project, you should follow these general guidelines:

1. **Review the layout of the frame structure.** Frames can assume different layouts. You could have a two-frame layout in which there is a navigation bar across the top or left side of the Web page or a three- or four-frame layout. You must first assess the existing frame structure.
2. **Identify the purpose and structure of the frame definition file.** Once you have determined the structure, you need to review the frame definition file to see how it applies to the layout. This must be done so that you can convert the Web site appropriately.
3. **Determine a conversion strategy that can be used to restructure the Web site.** A Web site needs to be converted effectively. There are different techniques that you can use, but each technique needs to be assessed for effectiveness and efficiency.
4. **Make the necessary changes.** Once your technique is determined, you need to make the necessary changes to the Web site to convert it from a frame structure to a new structure (as developed in all chapters of this book).

The Frame Definition File

The frame definition file structures the frame layout and tells the browser which file to display in each frame. This is the file that you open in the browser in order to view the Web site. The frame definition file contains the names of the two, three, or four Web pages that are opened in frames when the page is loaded.

Table 1 shows the frame tags and attributes, which were part of the HTML 4 specification, that were used to create a frame structure.

Table 1 Frame Tag Attributes

Tag	Attribute	Function
`<frameset>`	cols rows	• Indicates the number of columns • Indicates the number of rows
`<frame>`	frameborder marginheight marginwidth name noresize scrolling src	• Turns frame borders on or off (1 or 0) • Adjusts the top and bottom margins of a frame • Adjusts the left and right margins of a frame • Defines the name of a frame • Locks the borders of a frame to prohibit resizing • Specfies whether or not scroll bars will be displayed • Indicates the Web page or other file to be displayed in the frame

The HTML code that creates this frame structure for the Web page shown in Figure 1a on page HTML 395 is contained in the sf2index.html frame definition file, and is as follows (line numbers have been added):

```
1    <!DOCTYPE html
2       PUBLIC "-//W3C//DTD XHTML 1.0 Frameset//EN"
3       "http://www.w3.org/TR/xhtml1/DTD/xhtml1-frameset.dtd">
4    <html xmlns="http://www.w3.org/1999/xhtml" xml:lang="en"
     lang="en">
5    <head>
6    <meta http-equiv="Content-Type" content="text/html;
     charset=utf-8" />
7    <title>Special Feature 2</title>
8    </head>
9    <frameset rows="40%,60%">
10   <frame src="sf2menu.html" title="menu" name="menu"
     frameborder="0" />
11   <frame src="sf2home.html" title="win-main" name="win-main"
     frameborder="0" />
12   </frameset>
13   </html>
```

Note that there are several differences between the initial HTML statements in this file as compared to what you have created throughout the book. Lines 2 and 3 are eliminated in the HTML5 doctype statement; line 4 is changed in HTML5. In this frame sample code, it is necessary to declare a doctype of Frameset, as shown in line 2. The <meta> statement on line 6 is also different in this code sample from what you have created in all other HTML files. All of the other files provided for this project already contain the expected HTML5 doctype and meta tags.

In the code above, also notice that one frameset (line 9) is inserted that contains two rows (top and bottom) that create two sections (or frames) of 40% and 60% of the Web page, respectively. (If you wanted to structure the frames with the navigation frame on the left and the content frame on the right, you would change the attribute "rows" in the frameset line of code to "cols" instead and adjust the percentages as needed.) There will always be one frame for each <frame /> tag that is used. That is, the <frame /> tag defines one particular window (or frame) within a frameset. Each frame in a frameset can have different attributes, such as border, scrolling, the ability to resize, etc., but each frame contains only one Web page at a time as described below.

When the Web page loads (on lines 10 and 11 of the code), you see that the sf2menu.html file opens in the first (top) frame, and the sf2home.html file opens in the second (bottom) frame (or row). In other words, the top frame (sf2menu.html, which contains the logo and navigation bar) displays in the top 40% of the Web page, while the content frame (or section) named sf2home.html displays in the bottom 60% of the Web page. Also note that line 11 gives that frame the target name "win-main" as an identifier. The name "win-main" is used by the sf2menu.html file (shown later) as the target frame in which all content is displayed.

BTW

Framesets
A frameset can be thought of as a window with various windowpanes. Within each pane is a separate Web page. The frame definition file is the HTML file that defines the Web pages that are displayed in the individual panes. Every Web page used in a frameset can be viewed independently in the browser as well as within the frameset.

To View a Web Site with Frames

To view the Web site with frames used in this project, you will open the sf2index.html frame definition file in the browser. Then you will open the HTML file and compare this Web site to the code shown in the frame definition file.

- With a USB drive plugged into your computer, start your browser.
- Open the sf2index.html file in the SF2\ChapterFiles folder of the Data Files for Students (Figure 2).
- Click the navigation links (Schedule, Contact, and Home) to view the entire Web site.

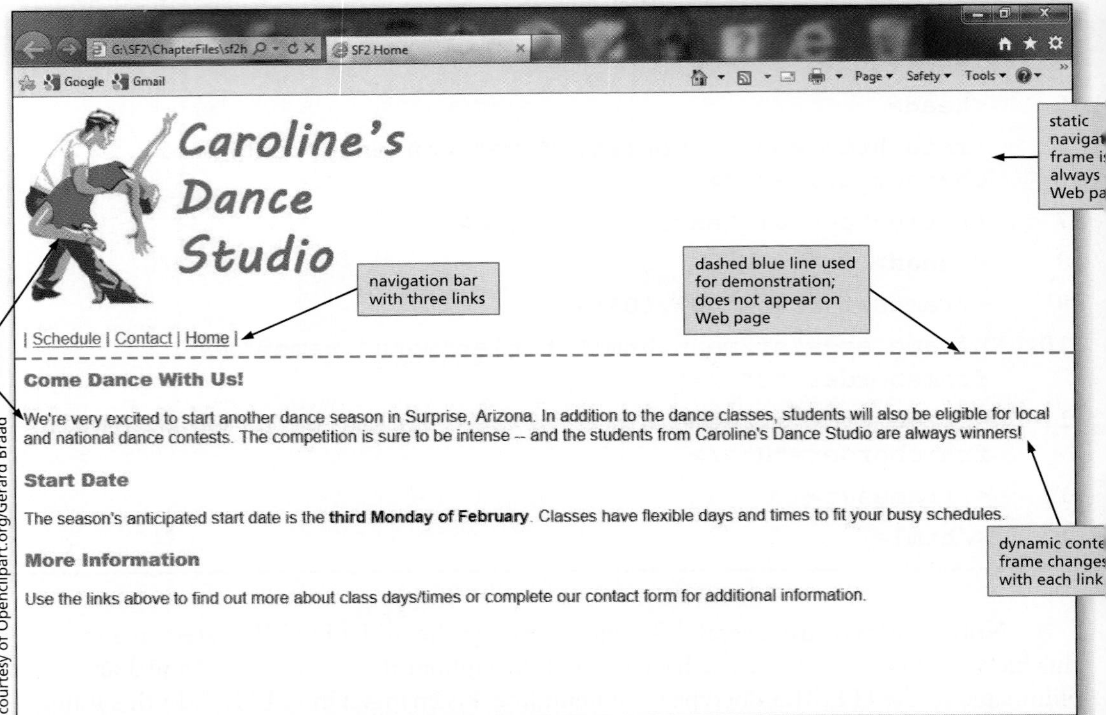

Figure 2

2

- Start Notepad++ and open the sf2index .html frame definition file in the SF2\ ChapterFiles folder of the Data Files for Students (Figure 3).

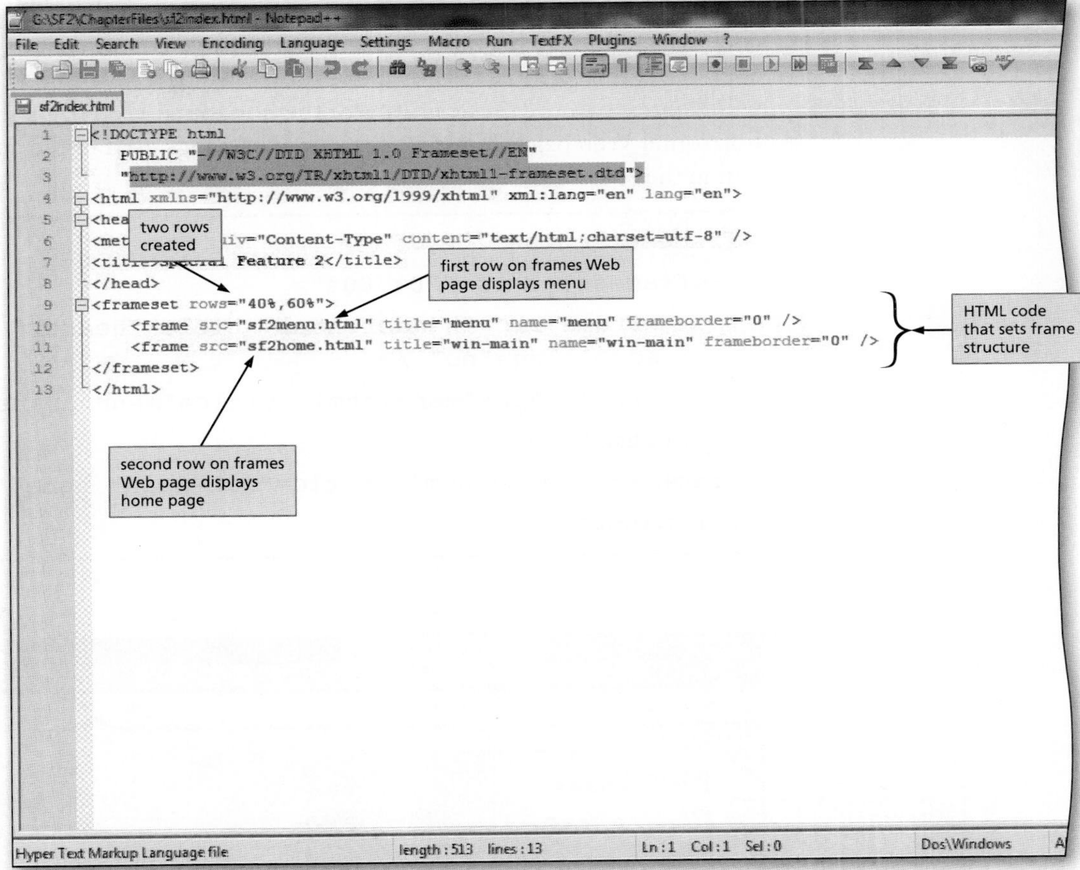

Figure 3

Q&A

How can you tell that this Web site uses frames?

The only way to be completely sure that the structure uses frames is to open the Web page source code. You immediately see that the structure of the Web page (shown in Figure 3) is developed in frames. In this Web site, the dance studio logo and the navigation bar are always present on the top section (or frame) of the Web page, and this section is static (i.e., it always remains the same). The content from the sf2home.html file displays in the bottom frame (the target named "win-main"). A Web site visitor can click any of the three menu items (Schedule, Contact, Home), and the content from those Web pages displays in the dynamic (i.e., changing) target "win-main" (the bottom frame) of the Web page.

Frame Layouts

Frame layouts can be designed in a variety of ways. The goal and purpose of the Web site determine which layout is appropriate. For example, the Caroline's Dance Studio Web site uses a basic two-frame structure, as shown in Figures 2 and 3. The navigation on the top remains constant, and the content frame on the bottom changes.

Figure 4 shows a three-frame structure, often used to display a company logo (top) in the third frame. To create a three-frame structure as shown in Figure 4, the HTML code is as follows. This time, you will identify two columns first (one is 25% of the vertical Web page; the other is 75% of the vertical Web page). Within the first column, you will identify two rows (one is 20% of the horizontal Web page; the other is 80% of the horizontal Web page). There are two frameset tags used in the code because these tags define the structure of the frames within a window.

```
<frameset cols="25%,75%">
   <frameset rows="20%,80%">
      <frame src="header.html" title="header" name="header"
      scrolling="no" />
      <frame src="menu.html" title="menu" name="menu" />
   </frameset>
<frame src="home.html" title="win-main" name="win-main" />
</frameset>
```

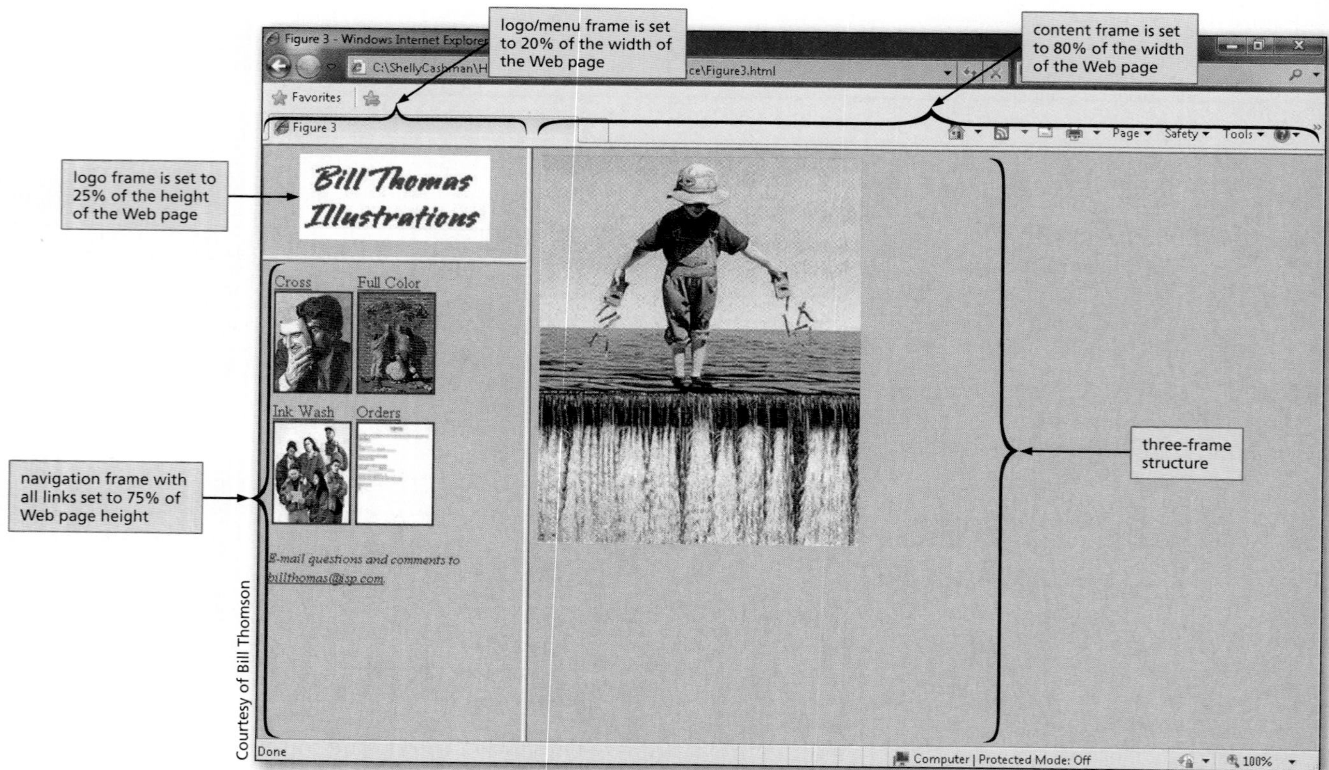

logo/menu frame is set to 20% of the width of the Web page
content frame is set to 80% of the width of the Web page
logo frame is set to 25% of the height of the Web page
navigation frame with all links set to 75% of Web page height
three-frame structure
Bill Thomas Illustrations
Cross
Full Color
Ink Wash
Orders
E-mail questions and comments to billthomas@isp.com
Courtesy of Bill Thomson

Figure 4

A four-frame structure, as shown in Figure 5, can be used to split a header image from the header text. The HTML code needed to create the four-frame structure shown in Figure 5 is as follows. This time, you will identify two rows first with two columns in each row.

```
<frameset rows="30%,70%">
   <frameset cols="25%,75%">
      <frame src="logo.html" title="logo" name="logo" />
      <frame src="header.html" title="header" name="header" />
   </frameset>
   <frameset cols="25%,75%">
      <frame src="menu.html" title="menu" name="menu" />
      <frame src="home.html" title="win-main" name="win-main"/>
   </frameset>
</frameset>
```

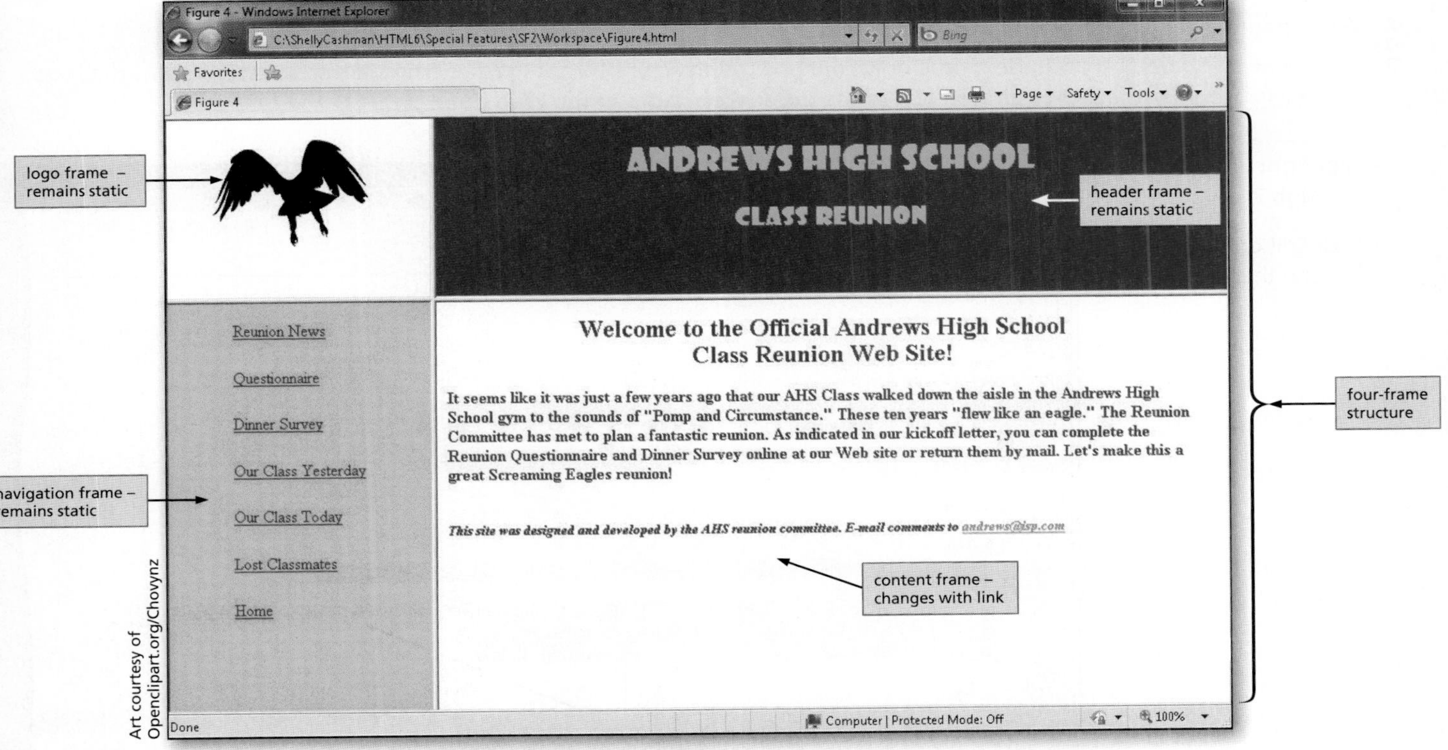

Figure 5

Determining a Conversion Strategy

Now that you understand the purpose and organization of the frame definition file, you must decide how to convert the Web site from a frame structure to an ADA-compliant structure. You have several methods to choose from to accomplish this conversion. One way is similar to what you did in the Chapter 7 project, using the <div> </div> tags to provide a pop-up window when a user hovers over an image. Here, however, you want the content of a second Web page to remain visible all the time, not just when a user hovers over it. Using the <div> tag, you can lay out a Web page so that a menu remains constant in one division (or section), and the content displays in a second division (or section) of the Web page. That is fine, but it means that you must have all content in one Web page. That is not an efficient way to convert from frames for this project.

A second way to convert from a frame structure is to copy the static portion of the Web page (the image and the navigation bar) to all pages in the Web site. The sf2menu.html file contains the logo and the navigation bar for this Web site. You will open this file and copy the logo and navigation bar code and paste it into the sf2home.html, sf2schedule.html, and sf2contact.html Web pages.

To Copy HTML Code for a Navigation Bar

The following step copies the necessary navigation bar code from the sf2menu.html file.

1

- If necessary, start Notepad++.
- With a USB drive plugged into your computer, open the sf2menu.html file in the SF2\ChapterFiles folder.

Q&A Why open this file and not edit the frame definition file, sf2index.html?

The frame definition file, sf2index.html, only contains the structure for the frames. The sf2menu.html contains the logo and navigation bar that you want to copy to the other Web pages in the Web site.

- Highlight lines 14 through 21 (Figure 6).
- Click Edit on the menu bar and then click Copy.

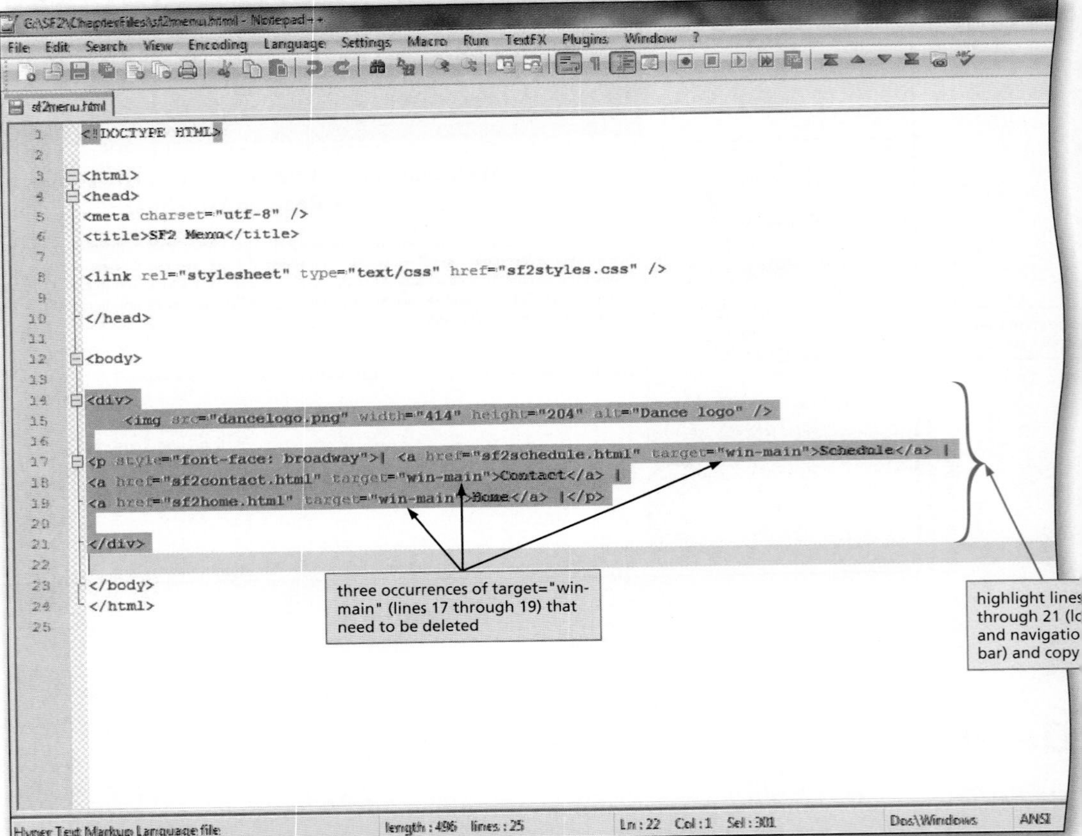

Figure 6

To Paste Code into the Home Page and Edit the Code

The following step pastes the code copied above into the home page and edits the code to remove the target property.

- In Notepad++, open the sf2home.html file in the SF2\ChapterFiles folder on the USB drive.
- Click after the > in the <body> tag on line 12 and press the ENTER key twice.
- Click Edit on the menu bar and then click Paste.
- Delete the code target="win-main" on lines 17, 18, and 19 (Figure 7).
- Click the Save button on the toolbar to save the sf2home.html file with the new code.

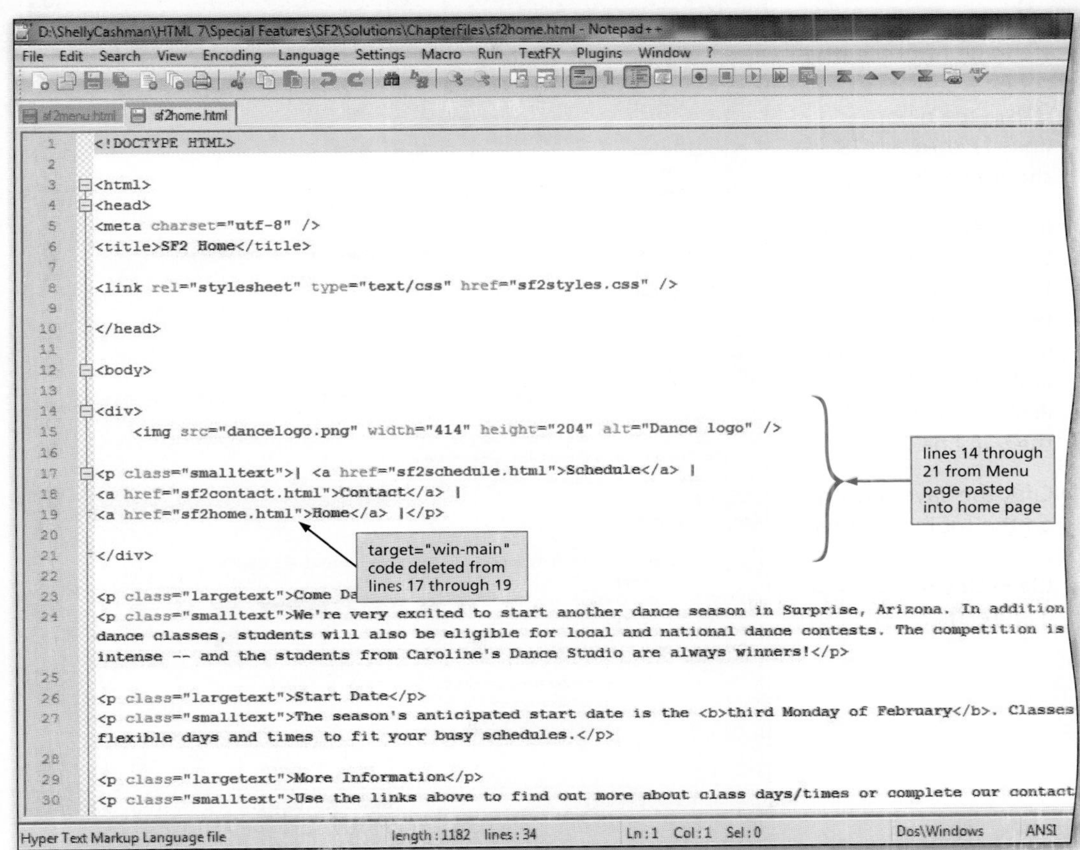

Figure 7

Q&A By copying and pasting this code, I can provide the same look to my Web site visitors as a frame structure, right?

Yes, your Web site will operate in the same manner without the frame structure, with the image and the navigation bar across the top of the Web page and the content changing on the bottom part.

Q&A Why do I have to remove the target="win-main" code?

The target is named to support the dynamic (i.e., changing) frame within the frame structure. Because there is now only one Web page representing the home page and no frame structure, you do not need to identify the target frame.

To Copy and Paste Code into the Schedule and Contact Web Pages

The following steps copy and paste the navigation bar code into the Schedule and Contact Web pages.

1

- Copy lines 14 through 21 in the newly saved sf2home.html file (the code target ="win-main" on lines 17 through 19 should be deleted).
- In Notepad ++, open the sf2schedule.html file. Click line 13 and press the ENTER key once. Paste the copied eight lines of code. Press ENTER once after the > in line 21.
- Click the Save button on the toolbar to save the sf2schedule.html file with the new code (Figure 8).

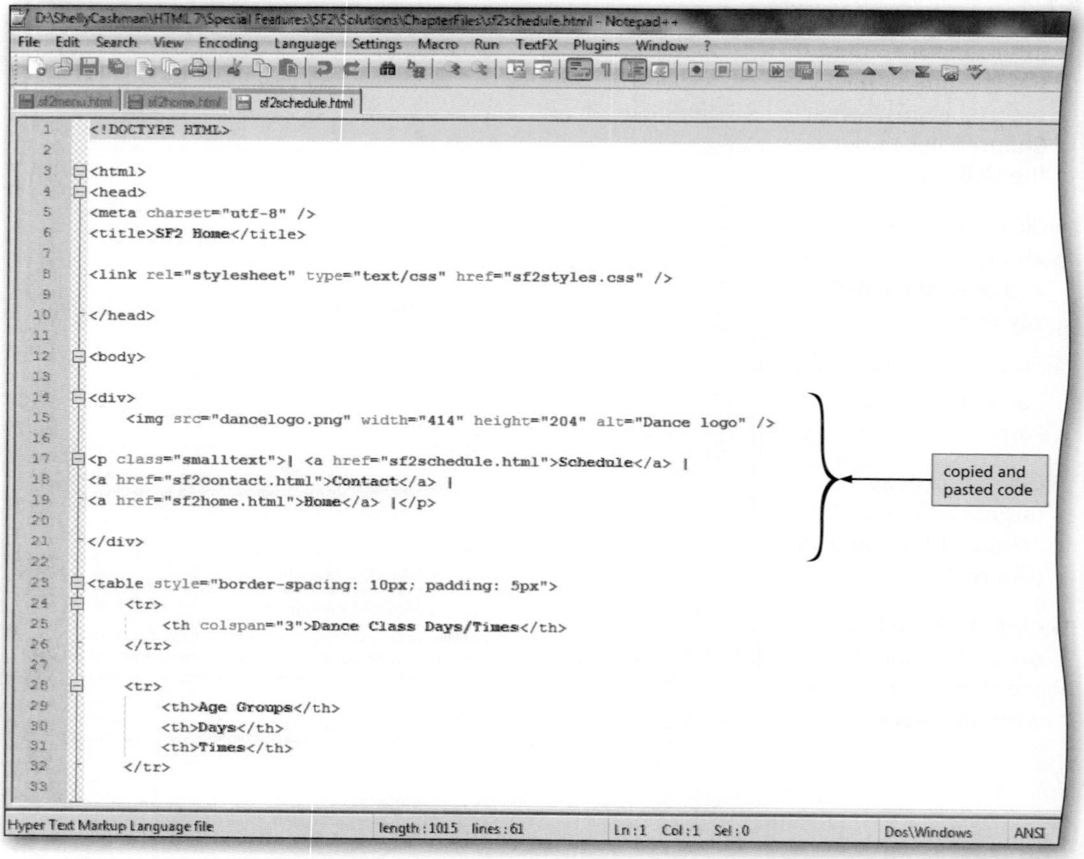

```
1  <!DOCTYPE HTML>
2
3  <html>
4  <head>
5  <meta charset="utf-8" />
6  <title>SF2 Home</title>
7
8  <link rel="stylesheet" type="text/css" href="sf2styles.css" />
9
10 </head>
11
12 <body>
13
14 <div>
15     <img src="dancelogo.png" width="414" height="204" alt="Dance logo" />
16
17 <p class="smalltext">| <a href="sf2schedule.html">Schedule</a> |
18 <a href="sf2contact.html">Contact</a> |
19 <a href="sf2home.html">Home</a> |</p>
20
21 </div>
22
23 <table style="border-spacing: 10px; padding: 5px">
24     <tr>
25         <th colspan="3">Dance Class Days/Times</th>
26     </tr>
27
28     <tr>
29         <th>Age Groups</th>
30         <th>Days</th>
31         <th>Times</th>
32     </tr>
33
```

copied and pasted code

Figure 8

2

- Open the sf2contact.html file. Click line 13 and press the ENTER key twice. Move the insertion point back to line 14 and paste the same eight lines of code.
- Click the Save button on the toolbar to save the sf2contact.html file with the new code.

To Validate and Print a Document

You are finished entering the lines of code needed for the logo and navigation bar. You now need to validate and print the files.

1. Validate sf2home.html, sf2schedule.html, and sf2contact.html using the w3.org validation service.
2. Once the files are all successfully validated, print the files.

To View the Web Site in the Browser

As with all other projects, it is important to view the Web pages in the browser and test all links. After converting the Web site structure, you will open the sf2home.html file as your starting point rather than the frame definition file sf2index.html. With the change from the frame structure to the new Web site structure, you will eliminate the sf2index.html file from the Web site.

1. If necessary, start your browser. Open the file sf2home.html in the browser (Figure 9).
2. Test all links by clicking the Schedule, Contact, and Home links.

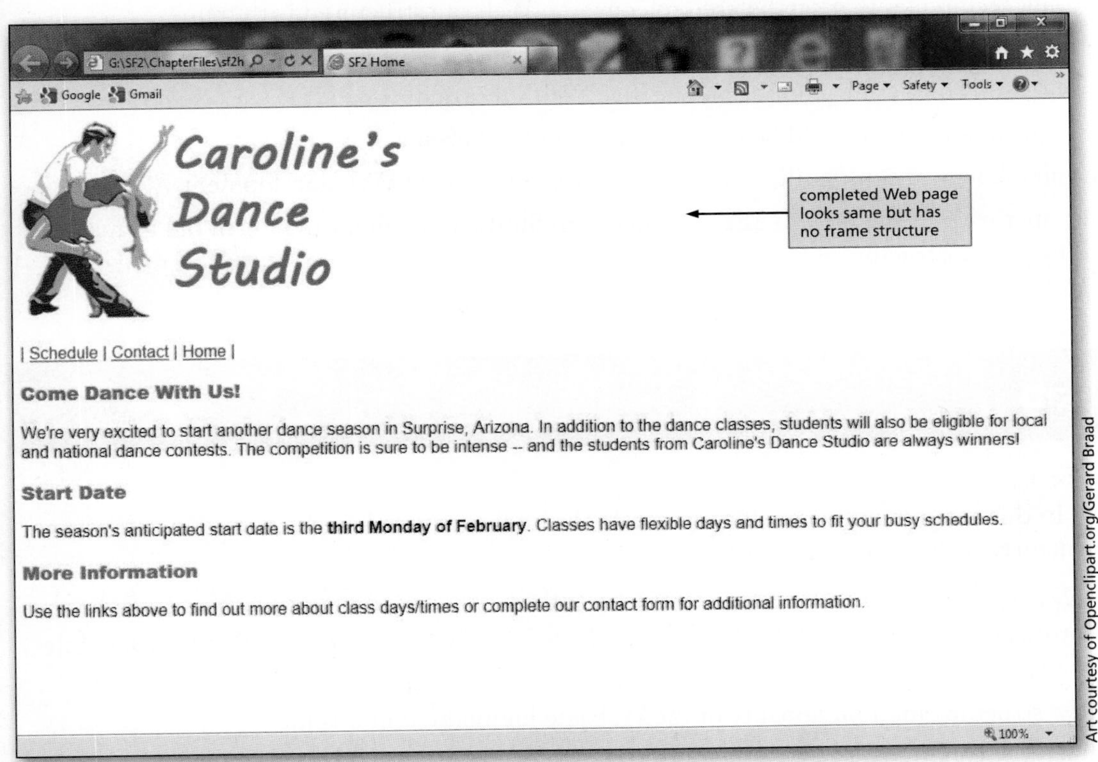

Figure 9

Feature Summary

In this feature, you have learned how to convert a frame-structured Web site to one in which frames are not used. This is an important aspect of Web development because of the ADA compliance standards that do not fully support frames. The items listed below include all the new Web development skills you have learned in this feature.

1. View a Web Site with Frames (HTML 398)
2. Copy HTML Code for a Navigation Bar (HTML 402)
3. Paste Code into the Home Page and Edit the Code (HTML 403)
4. Copy and Paste Code into the Schedule and Contact Web Pages (HTML 404)

In the Lab

Design and/or create a document using the guidelines, concepts, and skills presented in this chapter. Labs are listed in order of increasing difficulty.

Lab 1: Determining Another Way to Convert from Frames

Instructions: Your assignment is to research frame conversion strategies and determine another way to convert a Web site from a frame structure to a nonframe structure.

Perform the following tasks:

1. Search online for information about ADA compliance issues related to frames.
2. Review other techniques that can be used to convert a Web site structured with frames.
3. Write a paper that addresses the topics discussed in this Special Feature. Your paper should:
   a. Specify reasons frames may not be an effective Web site structure
   b. Identify techniques that could be used to restructure a Web site
   c. Determine how you could utilize these techniques in your own Web development
4. Save the paper with the name Lab SF2-1 Conversion Strategies. Submit the file in the format specified by your instructor.

In the Lab

Lab 2: Convert a Second Web Site

Instructions: In this assignment, you will convert a Web site that is based on the frame structure to a nonframe structure, as shown in Figure 10.

Perform the following tasks:

1. In your browser, open the LabSF2-2.html file in the SF2\IntheLab folder found in the Data Files for Students.
2. Review the structure and functionality of the Web site highlighted in this file.
3. Determine how you can restructure the Web site by converting from its current frame structure. Your conversion strategy can be that which is used in this Special Feature or another strategy that you found in your research in Lab 1.
4. Make the changes to the Web pages in the Web site. Save the new file as LabSF2-2solution.html, validate all files, test the site, and print the pages of the modified site.
5. Submit the files in the format specified by your instructor.

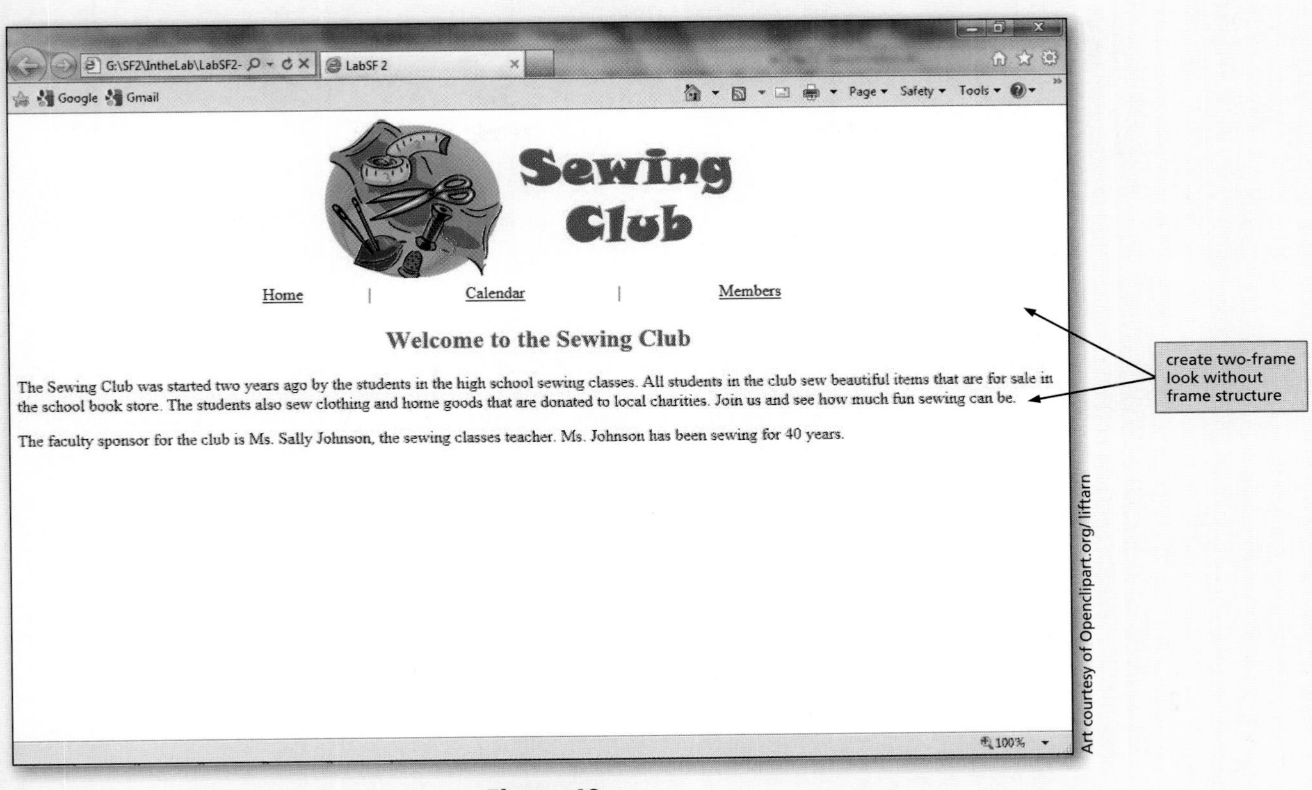
G:\SF2\IntheLab\LabSF2-
LabSF 2
Google
Gmail
Page
Safety
Tools
Sewing
Club
Home
Calendar
Members
Welcome to the Sewing Club
The Sewing Club was started two years ago by the students in the high school sewing classes. All students in the club sew beautiful items that are for sale in the school book store. The students also sew clothing and home goods that are donated to local charities. Join us and see how much fun sewing can be.
The faculty sponsor for the club is Ms. Sally Johnson, the sewing classes teacher. Ms. Johnson has been sewing for 40 years.
100%
create two-frame look without frame structure
Art courtesy of Openclipart.org/ liftarn

Figure 10

9 Integrating JavaScript and HTML5

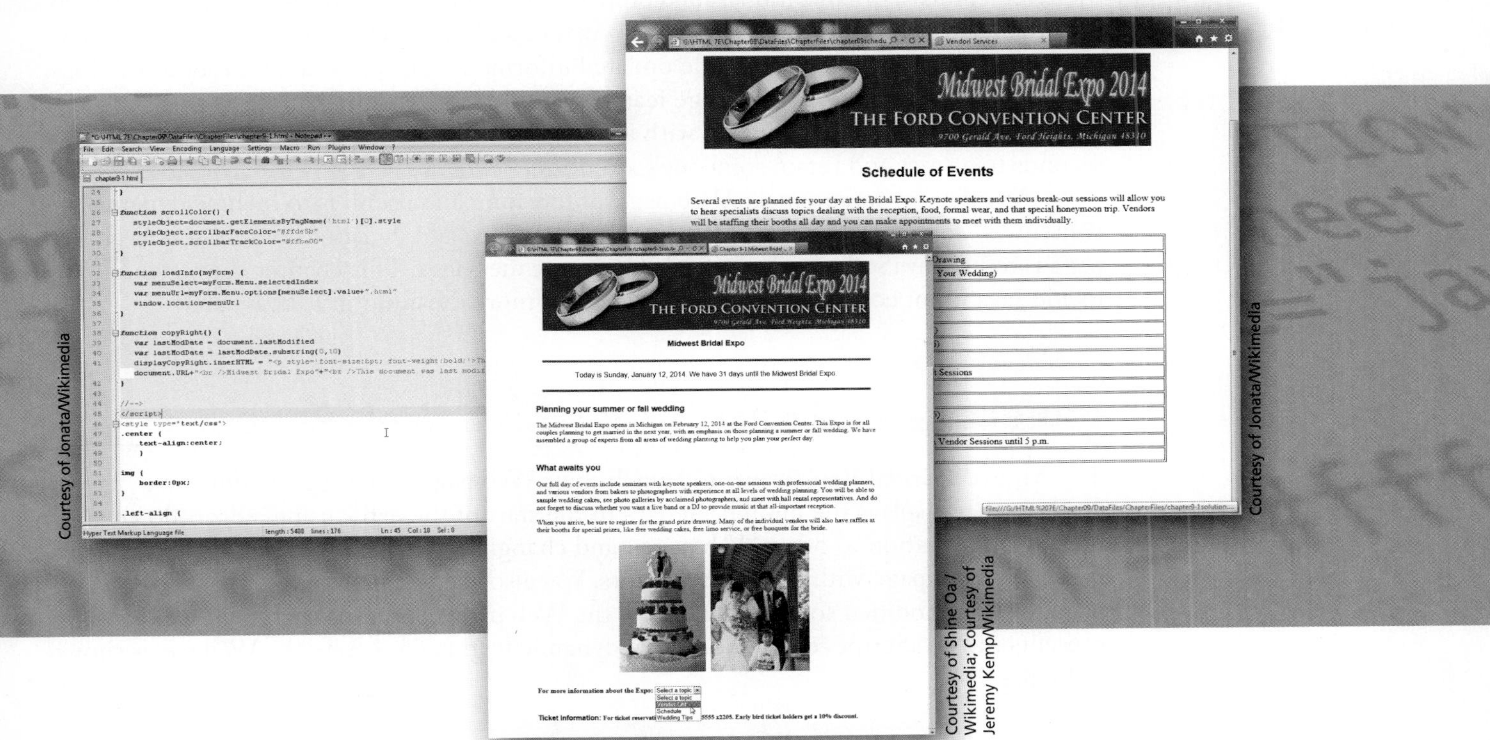

Courtesy of Jonata/Wikimedia

Courtesy of Jonata/Wikimedia

Courtesy of Shine Oa / Wikimedia; Courtesy of Jeremy Kemp/Wikimedia

Objectives

You will have mastered the material in this chapter when you can:

- Describe JavaScript and how it can be integrated with HTML5
- Describe how the <div> tag container is used to display text
- Describe a valid JavaScript user-defined function
- Write the code to create a <script> section on a Web page
- Define and describe JavaScript variables
- Extract the current system date
- Calculate the number of days from the current date to a future date
- Use the innerHTML property to display a dynamic message to a Web page
- Write a user-defined JavaScript function that changes the color of the browser's scroll bar
- Write a user-defined JavaScript function to open a Web page from a <select> tag <option> value
- Use the lastModified property to display the date the document was last modified
- Use an event handler to invoke a JavaScript user-defined function when a Web page is loaded

9 Integrating JavaScript and HTML5

Introduction

Many individuals, organizations, and companies rely on their Web sites as a key vehicle to communicate with friends, members, and current and future customers. Web pages often announce upcoming events, provide updated information, or act as a sales tool or catalogs. Regardless of the content, Web page features should spark visitors' interests and entice them to return to the Web site. As with an advertisement, a Web page has six to seven seconds to attract and retain someone's attention.

An effective way to make Web pages interesting and useful is to include dynamic content to make the Web page interactive. One way to add dynamic content to a Web page is to use JavaScript code to display dynamic messages. This chapter shows you how to add JavaScript code to a Web page to make it more dynamic and attractive.

Project — Midwest Bridal Expo Web Page

The Midwest Bridal Expo wants to launch their Web page. You suggest adding a dynamic message that displays the number of days to the start of the expo, using a drop-down menu for navigation to other Web pages, and changing the scroll bar color to help balance the look of the page with the banner colors. You also suggest including the date the Web page was last modified so that users know the Web page content is current. Chapter 9 presents the JavaScript code to add these dynamic features to create the Web pages shown in Figure 9–1.

Overview

As you read through this chapter, you will learn how to integrate JavaScript onto a Web page, as shown in Figure 9–1, by performing these general tasks:

- Write a JavaScript function to display a dynamic message in a <div> container
- Write a JavaScript function to change the color of the scroll bar
- Write a JavaScript function to use a drop-down menu to link to new Web pages
- Write a JavaScript function to display the date the Web page was last modified and a copyright message in a <div> container

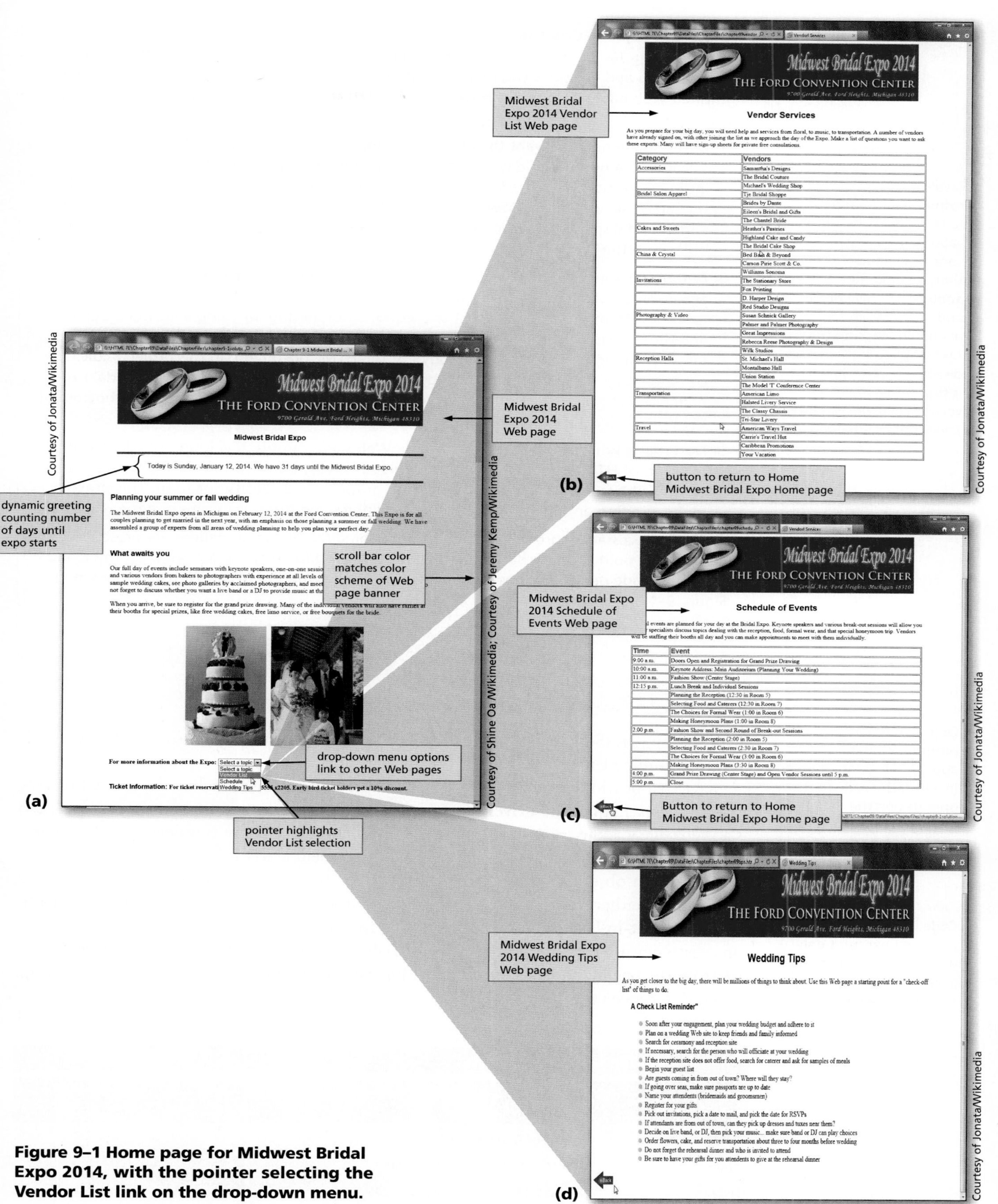

Figure 9–1 Home page for Midwest Bridal Expo 2014, with the pointer selecting the Vendor List link on the drop-down menu.

Plan Ahead

General Project Guidelines

When adding JavaScript or any scripting language to a Web page document, the actions you perform and decisions you make will affect the appearance and characteristics of the finished Web page. Before you write the JavaScript code, you should follow these general guidelines:

1. **Determine what you want the code to accomplish.** The JavaScript tasks in this chapter calculate the number of days to a future date and display a dynamic message that includes the current date and number of days until another date, change the color of the scroll bar, use a drop-down menu (HTML tag <select/options>) to link to other Web pages, and display a copyright notice and date the Web page was last modified at the bottom of the Web page.
2. **Determine where on the Web page you want the code to appear.** JavaScript code should always be placed in the <head> section of the HTML code. To display messages at specific locations, JavaScript can send text to a <div> container tag. By using a <div> container and the innerHTML property, a JavaScript user-defined function can display dynamic messages at any location in the <body> of the HTML document. In this project, <div> container tags are used to display a dynamic message beneath the Midwest Bridal Expo banner and to display the date last modified and copyright information at the bottom of the Web page.
3. **Determine where you want to store the Web page during development**. The storage location of HTML code and associated images is very important. A best practice is to create folders to organize HTML files and graphics in a specific location. This practice makes finding and maintaining links to graphics and other Web site pages easy.

When necessary, more specific details concerning the above guidelines are presented at appropriate points in the chapter. The chapter will also identify the actions performed and decisions made regarding these guidelines during the creation of the Web page shown in Figure 9–1 on the previous page.

BTW **JavaScript Advantages and Disadvantages**
JavaScript allows for faster response in client pages to requests such as form validation. JavaScript code downloads faster than other kinds of applets, like Java or Flash, and no extra plug-in is needed to execute the JavaScript code. The main disadvantage to JavaScript is that some browser versions may not execute JavaScript as intended.

JavaScript

Before adding JavaScript code to your Web page, you should understand some basics about the programming language. **JavaScript** is an event-driven, object-based programming language that provides various types of functionality to Web pages, such as the ability to interact with the user. An **event-driven** programming language is one that responds to events, such as a Web page loading or a user clicking a Submit button. JavaScript is **object-based** because it is a scripting language that uses built-in objects that belong to the browser.

Built-in objects are values that are common to a browser (arrays, dates, strings, etc.), which neither depend on nor belong to another object. Table 9–1 contains a general list of the built-in JavaScript objects common to many browsers. JavaScript developers can create new objects based on the built-in objects, and the new objects inherit properties from the original objects. For more information about these objects, see the JavaScript Quick Reference in Appendix G.

BTW **Object-Oriented Programming (OOP)**
Object-oriented programming is an approach to programming in which the code that operates on the data is packaged into a single unit called an object.

BTW **Event-Driven Programming**
Code in event-driven programs executes only when a certain event, such as clicking a button, triggers the code to execute.

Table 9–1 Built-In JavaScript Objects

Object	Description
Array	Returns an ordered set of values
Boolean	Converts objects to Boolean values
Date	Accesses the system time and date
Document	Represents the content of a browser's window

Table 9–1 Built-In JavaScript Objects (continued)

Object	Description
DOM	All elements related to the Document Object Model
Function	Accesses information about specific functions
History	Keeps track of Web pages visited
Location	Switches to a new Web page
Math	Performs calculations
Navigator	Obtains information about the current Web browser
Number	Supports special constants
Object	Creates an Object wrapper
RegExp	Describes patterns of characters
Screen	Gives platform-specific information about the user's screen
String	Represents a set of characters
Window	Represents a browser window

JavaScript objects have properties and methods. **Properties** are attributes that describe an object's characteristics. As shown in Table 9–2, an object and its property are written by separating the object from its property with a period. A specific value can be assigned to a property, as shown in the following example:

```
truck.style="pickup"
```

where the truck is the object, style is the property, and pickup is the value assigned to the property.

BTW **Other Scripting Languages**
Although JavaScript and VBScript are the two main client-side script languages used today, there are over a dozen other scripting languages that work on specific platforms or operating systems. For example, PHP and Perl. Perl stands for Practical Extraction and Report Language, and was developed by Larry Wall in 1987 while at Unisys.

Table 9–2 Object and Property

General form:	object.property
Comment:	where the *object* is stated first, then a period, then the descriptive *property*. A value can be assigned to the property, or the property can return a value, as shown in the examples below. In some cases, an object can be a property of a superior object, such as a text field that belongs to a form.
Examples:	myForm.fname.style.backgroundColor="#ff0000" browser=navigator.appName

Methods are actions that an object can perform. For example, methods associated with the truck object might be style, color, and model. An object and one of its methods would be written as:

```
truck.load()
```

where truck is the object and load is a method of the truck object. Methods are followed by parentheses, which may be empty, or may contain an argument.

An **argument** is a value given to a method. Some methods require arguments, and others do not. For example, given a truck object and the load() method, the argument "firewood" describes the material with which the truck may be loaded and would be written as:

```
truck.load("firewood")
```

where the argument "firewood" describes the material loaded into the truck.

BTW **Object Inheritance**
Once a built-in object has been converted to a new object, the new object inherits all the properties and methods available to the original object.

As shown in Table 9–3, the general form of writing an object with its method is similar to writing objects and properties.

BTW

JavaScript Methods and Arguments
Not all JavaScript methods require an argument. In fact, with some methods, if an argument is used, it generates an error.

Table 9–3 Object and Method

General form:	objectname.method(argument values)
Comment:	where *objectname* is the object, *method* is the action, and *argument values* are optional items or instructions the method should use. A period separates the object name from the method.
Examples:	window.open(Url, "", "toolbar=no,width=500,height=400,status=no,resize=yes") window.alert("This is a message") var ToDayDate=Date.toString( )

BTW

JavaScript Help
Many Web sites provide help for JavaScript developers. To find such Web sites, search for keywords such as "JavaScript Tutorials" or "JavaScript Help" in any good search engine.

User-Defined Functions

A **function** is JavaScript code that is written to perform certain tasks repeatedly. A **user-defined function** is JavaScript code written by a Web developer to perform a particular task. The function can be used whenever that task is needed, eliminating the need to repeat the code several times throughout an application. Functions replace large sets of JavaScript code that are too large to fit within an HTML attribute. Functions are placed in a JavaScript section within the <head> section of the HTML code.

JavaScript objects exist in a hierarchy starting with the window object. Other objects, such as document, navigator, and history belong to the window object. These objects are built-in and the methods that are associated with them are often referred to as built-in functions. These include alert(), close(), open(), and print(). These functions actually belong to the Window object. Because the Window object is assumed, developers often call them built-in functions. For a complete list of built-in functions, see the JavaScript Quick Reference in Appendix G.

In this project, user-defined functions use generic container tags to display dynamic information. A **container** is an HTML tag that identifies a section of HTML code using the id attribute so content of the tag can be set or defined by the use of the innerHTML property. The <div> tag container defines a division or section of code that groups similar elements together. To uniquely identify this <div> container, use an id attribute, with a unique id value not used by any other tag. In this project, the id value will be used by JavaScript to assign text to that container. Because an empty division contains no other tags or text, it can be used to dynamically display text at a particular location within a Web page.

Most JavaScript user-defined functions are called or invoked using event handlers. An event is the result of an action, such as a mouse click or a Web page loading into the browser. An **event handler** is JavaScript's way to associate an action with a function. In this project, you first write the functions, and then the event handlers that will associate the functions with specific events, such as loading the Web page.

Plan Ahead

Create a <div> tag container to display a dynamic message.
To display a dynamic message on a Web page, you must:

- **Identify the location within the Web page where you want a dynamic message to display.** In this Web page, you determine to place the dynamic message between the two horizontal lines beneath the banner.
- **Create a <div> tag container for your message.** You need to create a <div> tag container with an id attribute, which will identify that division as separate from any other <div> tag and act as a holding location for the message. This container, working in conjunction with the innerHTML property, will display the dynamic message.

To Open an Existing HTML File

The following steps open the chapter9-1.html file included in the Data Files for Students, in which you will place the <div> tag container.

1. Start Notepad++, and, if necessary, maximize the window.
2. Click View on the menu bar. If the word wrap command does not have a check mark next to it, click word wrap.
3. With a USB flash drive plugged into your computer, click File on the menu bar and then click Open on the File menu.
4. Navigate to the Chapter09\ChapterFiles folder on the USB drive.
5. Double-click chapter9-1.html in the list of files to display the HTML code for the chapter9-1.html Web page, as shown in Figure 9–2.

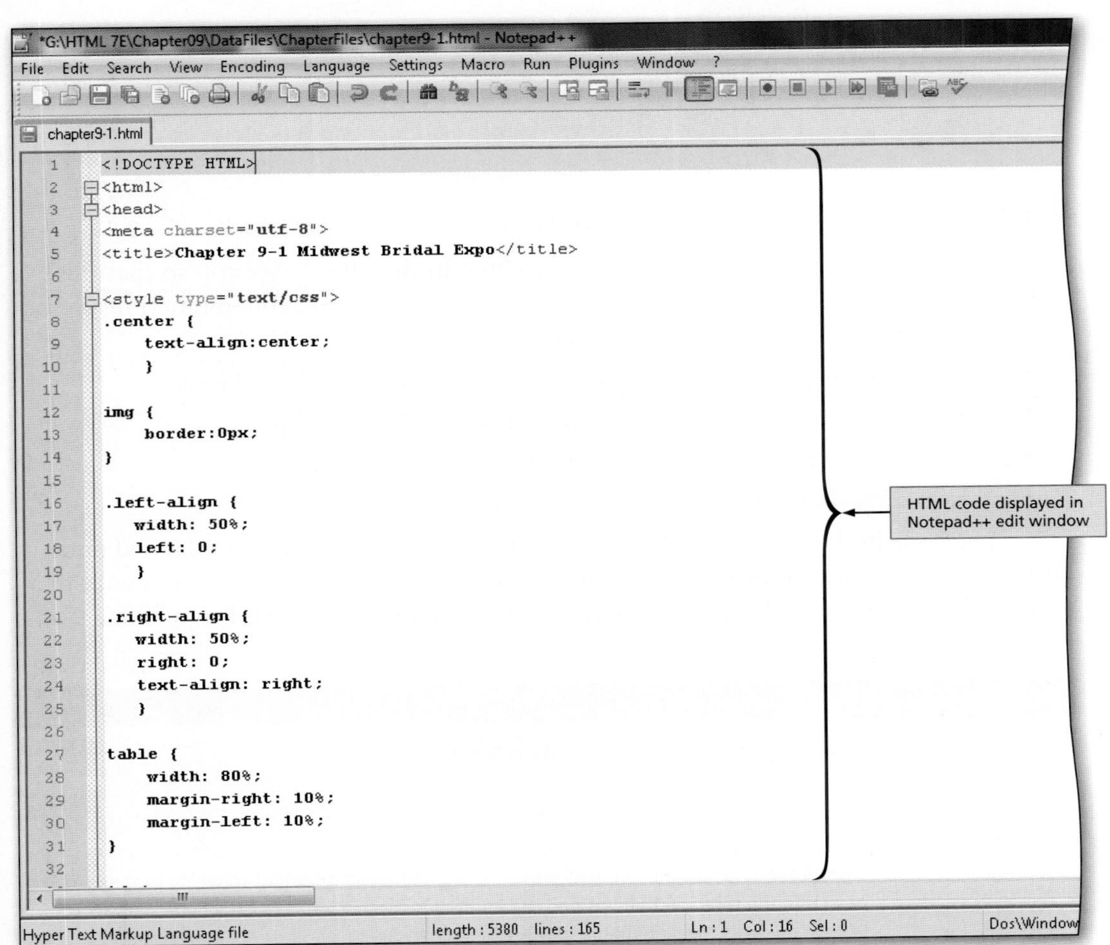

Figure 9–2

To Enter a <div> Tag Container

The following step enters the <div> tag with the id attribute. No other tags or text are needed between the beginning <div> and the closing </div> tag.

- Click the blank line at line 44 and type `<div id= "displayCountDown">` and press ENTER.
- Type `</div>` and do not press ENTER (Figure 9–3).

```
34        padding: 5px;
35    }
36
37    </style>
38    </head>
39    <body>
40    <div class="center">
41    <p><img src="chapter9-1banner.jpg"          160" alt="Bridal Expo Banner"></p>
42    <p style="font-family:Arial, Helvet         t-size:18px; font-weight:bold;">Midwest Bridal Expo</p>
43    <img src="hrimg-wedding-burgundy.jp         t="5" alt="hr">
44    <div id="displayCountDown">
45    </div>
46    <img src="hrimg-wedding-burgundy.jpg" width="750" height="5" alt="horizonal rule">
47    </div>
48    <table c          ">
49      <tr>
50        <td colspan="2">
51        <p style="font-weight:bold; font-family:Arial, sans-serif; font-size:14pt">Planning your summer or fall wedding<,
52        <p style="font-family: 'Times New Roman', Times, serif; font-size:12pt">The Midwest Bridal Expo opens in Michigai
53
```

press ENTER key at end of line 44, not line 45
insertion point

Figure 9–3

> **BTW**
> **Placing JavaScript Functions in the <head> Section**
> Always place your JavaScript functions in the <head> section to ensure they are loaded completely before they are called.

Writing User-Defined Functions

User-defined functions are normally written in the <head> section so that this code is loaded before the remainder of the Web page. The user-defined functions in the Midwest Bridal Expo Web page do the following:

- Calculate and display the number of days until the Midwest Bridal Expo.
- Change the color of the scroll bar to match the Web page colors.
- Display the date the Web page was last modified.
- Create a drop-down menu linking to other Web pages.

The code in the user-defined function in the <head> section is not executed until a JavaScript statement calls or invokes the function. To call a function means to invoke or execute the function. The general form of a user-defined function is shown in Table 9–4.

Table 9–4 User-Defined Functions

General form:	function functionName(optional parameters) {
	    JavaScript Code
	}

Comment:	where **function** is the keyword that designates the function, the *functionName* is the name of the user-defined function, and the *optional parameters* represent values or properties passed to the function that will be used by the function in the JavaScript code. *JavaScript Code* represents the statements that execute when the function runs.

Examples:	function showBrowserName() {
	    alert("You are using" +navigator.appname)
	}
	function getSum(myform) {
	    var sum= document.Calculator.Amount1.value+document.Calculator.Amount2.value
	}

Table 9–5 shows the naming conventions for a function name with valid and invalid examples. A function name must begin with a letter or an underscore; it may contain numerals, but may not contain any spaces, punctuation (such as periods or commas), or reserved words. Data, as variables, are passed to a function in order for the function to process data and return a result.

Table 9–5 Valid Function Names

Rule	Valid Function Names	Invalid Function Names
Must start with a letter or underscore	verifyForm() _3Ddisplay()	3Ddisplay()
No periods allowed or other punctuation allowed	get_Cookie()	make.cookie() valid,form()
No spaces allowed	calcPayment()	calc payment()
No hyphens allowed	popWind() pop_Wind()	pop-upWindow()

Plan Ahead

To display a message with the current date and the number of days until a specific future date, you must:

- **Create the <script> section in the <head> section.** In this project, the <script> sections will be placed in the <head> section.
- **Define variables.** Using variables allows you to work with the system date, which changes daily, to calculate the number of days from today to the Midwest Bridal Expo.
- **Calculate the number of days until the Midwest Bridal Expo.** To calculate the number of days to the Wedding Expo, you write code to subtract the current date from the future date.
- **Display a message string.** Use the innerHTML property to place the message on the Web page. The innerHTML property allows you to change the contents of the text that appears between an opening and closing of an HTML tag.
- **Close the <script> section.** All HTML tags must have a closing tag. If you fail to close the <script> section, you will have undesired results.
- **Add the event handlers.** The event handlers call the function to display a dynamic message when the Web page loads.

Inserting <script> Tags in the <head> Section

Although JavaScript code can be placed anywhere in the HTML code in a <script> section, developers follow the coding practice and place user-defined functions and variables in the <head> section. Placing the JavaScript code in the <head> section ensures that all the JavaScript is loaded and interpreted before the user can begin using the Web page.

In this chapter, you will only use JavaScript features that work in the latest version of Microsoft Internet Explorer. JavaScript sections always start with a <script> tag, which indicates the language being used. Similar to other HTML tags, the JavaScript <script> tag has a start <script> tag and an end </script> tag.

The general form of the script tag is shown in Table 9–6 on the next page. The <script> tag supports several attributes, including src, type, and defer. In the past, the start <script> tag was written as <script language="JavaScript">, but, as noted in the Table 9–6 example, the preferred style is to use the type attribute. If the type or language attribute is omitted, most browsers default to JavaScript.

The <!-- HTML comment line after the <script> tag is used to hide the JavaScript code in the event a browser does not recognize the JavaScript code. Like all other HTML tags, it must be closed (using the format -->).

BTW

Script Sections
Many Web developers recommend inserting the start <script> tag and the end </script> tag immediately as the Web page is modified or constructed. The important rule to remember is that a complete set of <script> tags must be included, both <script> and </script>.

BTW

HTML Comments within JavaScript
Within a <script> section, an HTML comment is often added to hide the JavaScript from old browsers. The HTML comment is a tag that begins with <!-- and ends with -->. If the HTML comment is not closed properly in the <script> section, then that could cause the remainder of the Web page to not display in the browser.

Table 9–6 JavaScript Section

General form:	<script src="url" type="valid MIME type" async="async" defer charset="character set" >
Comments:	where **script** is the script tag, *src* specifies the location of an external script URL, *type* indicates the valid MIME type or specific scripting language, language is a deprecated attribute in HTML5, and *defer* is a Boolean attribute that indicates whether the script is going to generate any document content. The type attribute is supported by HTML5 and the XHTML and XML standards. The src, async, charset, and defer attributes are optional.
Example:	<script type="text/javascript"> <!- -Hide from old browsers miscellaneous JavaScript code //--> </script>

To Enter the Start <script> and Comment Tags

The following step enters the <script> and HTML comment tags.

1

- In the Notepad++ file chapter9-1.html, click line 6 (a blank line).
- Type `<script type="text/javascript">` as the beginning of the script and then press the ENTER key.
- Type `<!--Hide from old browsers` and then press the ENTER key to put the insertion point on line 8 (Figure 9–4).

Figure 9–4

Q&A

Is it really necessary to add the comment, <!--Hide from old browsers?

Although JavaScript has been added to browsers since the second and third releases of Internet Explorer and Netscape, conventional wisdom suggests that programmers take into consideration all possibilities, which means, there may be someone still not using a JavaScript-capable browser. This may be especially true in mobile devices.

BTW

JavaScript Comments
Comments can be added to JavaScript in two ways. The double slash [//] is used to indicate a comment for a single line. The double slash [//] is also used to close and hide the end HTML comment in the <script> section. To comment multiple lines with a script, begin the comment with a slash and asterisk [/*] and place an asterisk and slash [*/] to end the comment lines.

Using JavaScript Variables

As in other programming languages, JavaScript uses variables to store values temporarily in internal memory. A variable's value can change, depending on the results of an expression or data entered by a user from a form. Variables must have a unique name, and must follow the same naming conventions as user-defined functions. JavaScript variable names are case sensitive, which means the variable name months is different from the variable name Months. Table 9–7 shows the rules with valid and invalid variable name examples.

Table 9–7 Naming Conventions for JavaScript Variables

Rule	Valid Name Examples	Invalid Name Examples
Name must begin with a letter or underscore	menu	$menu
Rest of name must be letters, numerals, or underscores	Last_Name	Last-name
Name may not use spaces, hyphens, or punctuation	ZipCode	zip.code or zip code
Name may not contain JavaScript objects, properties, and reserved words	xNow	Date

JavaScript variables are considered global, unless the variable is defined within a user-defined function, in which case it is considered a local variable. **Global** means that the variable value is available for use anywhere inside the HTML file Web page. To define a variable as global, it must be declared in the <script> section before any of the user-defined functions. **Local** means that the variable's value is available only in the function in which it is defined.

A variable's **data type**, the type of data it stores, such as text or numbers, must be known so the computer knows how to store and manipulate the data. JavaScript has four data types: numeric, string, date, or Boolean. **Numeric data types** hold numbers. **String data types** are variables that hold characters or a combination of letters, numbers, or symbols. **Date data types** contain a date and time. **Boolean data types** contain logical data that can be one of two values, such as True/False or Yes/No.

JavaScript variables are **loosely typed**, which means they do not have to be assigned an initial specific data type as in other programming languages. Instead, JavaScript defines the data type by declaring the variable with an initial value. This feature allows variables to be flexible and store any data type. Web developers, however, do not recommend changing a variable's data type in the middle of JavaScript code. This action may create an error, which can be very difficult to find. Table 9–8 shows the general form of declaring a variable and assigning a value to it.

BTW

Undefined Variables
If a variable's value, which has not been defined or declared previously, is used or displayed on the Web page, JavaScript assigns the value "undefined" to that variable. An undefined variable can cause errors in mathematical calculations.

Table 9–8 Assigning Values to Variables

General form:	var variableName=value
Comment:	where **var** is an optional keyword to designate a variable; *variableName* is a valid variable name; and *value* is the string, numeric, date, or Boolean value being assigned to the variable
Examples:	var FilmStyle="Drama" // This variable is a string data type var length=6.5 // This variable is a numeric data type var finished=true // This variable is a Boolean data type

In the examples in Table 9–8, the keyword var, meaning variable, appears before the variable name. A **keyword**, or **reserved word**, is a word with special meaning in a programming language. The JavaScript var keyword is optional for global variables; however, it is good programming practice to precede the variable name with the var keyword the first time it is defined. In addition, the var keyword is required for local variables defined within a function.

Plan Ahead

For the dynamic greeting on the home page, you need to calculate the number of days between two dates. A computer's system date is not stored in a string format that can be easily used by displaying the contents of the Date() object, so it must be broken apart to extract the day of the week, date, year, and time. First, you must extract information about the current date using the following steps:

- Obtain the current system date with the Date() object and create a new object instance by assigning the current date to a variable.
- Use the toLocaleString() method to convert the date to a string to be manipulated.
- Use the indexOf() method to find the space between the month and the day of the week to extract the month.
- Use the substring() method to extract the day of the week from the string.
- Use the substring() method to extract the remainder of the date from the string.
- Use the indexOf() method to locate the position of the year in the string.
- Use the substring() method to extract the day of the week.
- Use the substring() method to extract the current year.
- Use the substr() method to extract the year from the string.

Extracting the Current System Date

The built-in Date() object accesses the current system date and time. On the Midwest Bridal Expo Web page, the Date() object and several of its methods are used to extract the current system date and then display it on the Web page as part of the greeting.

To manipulate the Date() object, a new object instance must be created. Table 9–9 shows the general form of the JavaScript statement to create a new object instance, which uses the new keyword and assigns the built-in object to a variable. This variable is referred to as an **object instance variable**.

BTW — Date() Object
The Date() object can use three other methods to build a string for a current date: getDate(), getMonth(), or getFullYear(). The getDate() method returns the date in the month; getMonth() returns the value of the month as a number from 0 to 11 with 0 representing January; and the getFullYear() method returns the four digit year. Because the getMonth() method returns an integer that represents the month, the developer must add 1 to the result to get the current month.

Table 9–9 Creating a New Object Instance

General form:	var variableName=new Builtin_Object
Comments:	where *variableName* is the name of the new object instance, **new** is the required keyword, and *Builtin_Object* is the name of the object from which the new object instance is to be created
Examples:	var sysDate=new Date() var sysDate=new Date("February 12, 2014")

The Date() object also allows developers to enter a specific date and time other than the current system date and time. The first example shown in Table 9–9 has no specific date value provided, thus the Date() object accesses the current system date and time from the computer and stores it in the object instance variable sysDate. In the second example in Table 9–9, the Date() object has a specific date value enclosed within quotation marks inside the parentheses and that value (February 12, 2014) is assigned to the object instance variable sysDate.

BTW — Extracting the System Date
The results in extracting the date are based upon the how the system date is stored. Individual users and other countries may use different computer settings. The default display is: Day Month Date Year HH:MM:SS AM/PM.

Converting the System Date to a String To use the date and time value stored in the variable sysDate, the variable must first be converted to a string, or a series of characters. To convert the date to a string, you use the toLocaleString() method. Table 9–10 shows the general form of the toLocaleString() method.

Table 9–10 toLocaleString() Method

General form:	var variable=dateString.toLocaleString()
Comment:	where *dateString* is an object instance and the **toLocaleString()** method converts an object instance of the Date() to a string using the default display format used on the client computer. The default display format for the Date() object is Day of the Week Month Date Year HH:MM:SS.
Example:	var curDate=sysDate.toLocaleString()
Result:	curDate contains the date and time stored as: Day of the Week Month Date Year HH:MM:SS

Once the current system date has been converted to a string, the JavaScript indexOf(), substring(), and substr() methods can be used to extract the day of the week, the month, date, the year, and the hours (HH), minutes (MM), and seconds (SS) to be displayed on the Web page.

Using the indexOf() Method The indexOf() method returns the position of the first occurrence of a specified value in a string. Table 9–11 explains how the indexOf() method searches a string for a particular value, which is enclosed within the quotation marks, and then returns the relative location of the value within the string. If the search finds the value in the search string object, the indexOf() method returns the relative position of the value within the string object, typically an integer. If the search value is not found, the indexOf() method returns a negative one (–1). It is important to note that the first item in a string will be given the value of zero, not one.

Table 9–11 indexOf() Method

General form:	var position=stringValue.indexOf("x")
Comment:	where *stringValue* is a string in which a search is conducted, *x* is the value to be searched for within the stringValue, and *position* is the variable that is assigned the location of x in the string. The value x must be a literal value.
Examples:	curDate="February 12, 2014" dateLocate=curDate.indexOf(",")
Result:	returns the relative position of the comma found in the string value of curDate: 11

BTW

Using the Current Year in indexOf()
When extracting the system date and comparing it to another day, the date you search for in the system Date in the indexOf() method must match the current year, or you will received incorrect results.

Using the substring() Method to Extract the Month from a String The substring() method uses two parameters (x,y), where x is the starting point of the string and y is the location of the last character needed. If only an x parameter is given, the substring() method returns all the characters starting at that position through the end of the string. Table 9–12 describes the general form of the substring() method. To extract the year 2014 from the string using the substring() method, the JavaScript code would be written as:

```
birthDay.substring(17,20)
```

Table 9–12 substring() Method

General form:	var variable=string.substring(x,y)
Comment:	where *string* is any string object. The **substring** method extracts a portion of a string, starting at location *x* and ending at location *y*. x and y may be constants or variables.
Example:	weekDay=dayofweek.substring(0, dateLocate)
Result:	the variable weekDay contains the substring result giving the current day of the week

Using the substr() Method The substr() method is similar to the substring() method, in that it extracts part of a string. Although the methods perform similar functions in JavaScript, they differ in how they use parameter values. The substring() method uses the exact byte locations in a string to extract part of the string between the x and y locations, whereas the substr() method uses a length value to extract y number of characters starting at x location. Table 9-13 describes the substr() method. To extract the year 2014 from the string using the substr() method, the JavaScript code would be written as:

```
birthDay.substr(yearLocate, 4)
```

Table 9–13 substr() Method

General form:	var variable=string.substr(x,y)
Comment:	where *string* is any string object instance. This method extracts a portion of a string, starting at location *x* for a length of *y*. x and y may be constants or variables.

Example:	var dayofweek = today.toLocaleString() //Converts date into string as: Day, Month Date, Year HH:MM:SS AM/PM
	yearLocate=dayofweek.indexOf("2014")
	year=dayofweek.substr(yearLocate, 4)

Result:	the variable year contains the four-digit year

Both the substring() and substr() methods use relative addressing as a means of locating characters in a string. A **relative address** is the location of a byte in a string of bytes, as defined by its position relative to the first byte in that string. As an example, assume the data in Table 9–14 is a string value stored in the variable birthDay. The address of the first byte in a string of characters is zero (0).

Table 9–14 Relative Addressing

S	u	n	d	a	y	,		M	a	r	c	h		9	,		2	0	1	4
0	1	2	3	4	5	6	7	8	9	10	11	12	13	14	15	16	17	18	19	20

Table 9–15 shows the JavaScript code used to extract the system date for the Midwest Bridal Expo Web page. The JavaScript code uses the toLocaleString(), substr(), substring(), and indexOf() methods of the Date() object to obtain the current system date and then extract the weekday, the date, the month, and the year. Once these values have been extracted and assigned to variables, they can be displayed on the Web page.

Table 9–15 Code to Extract the System Date

Line	Code
8	`function countDown() {`
9	`    var today = new Date()`
10	`    var dayofweek = today.toLocaleString()`
11	`    dayLocate = dayofweek.indexOf(" ")`
12	`    weekDay = dayofweek.substring(0, dayLocate)`
13	`    newDay = dayofweek.substring(dayLocate)`
14	`    dateLocate = newDay.indexOf(",")`
15	`    monthDate = newDay.substring(0, dateLocate+1)`
17	`    yearLocate = dayofweek.indexOf("2014")`
18	`    year = dayofweek.substr(yearLocate, 4)`

Line 8 starts the JavaScript user-defined function, countDown(). The function must include the open brace. Line 9 creates the new date object instance variable, today, and assigns the current system date and time to the variable. Line 10 converts the date and time value stored in the today variable to a string, using the toLocaleString() method and assigns it to the dayofweek variable. To find the day of the week in the string, the indexOf() method in line 11 looks for the first blank space in the string. Line 12 uses the substring() method to extract the day of the week, while line 13 extracts the remainder of the string, which includes the month, day, year, and time. (Remember that when the substring() method is used with one variable, the data extraction starts at the position of the given variable and goes all the way through the end of the string.) Line 14 looks for the comma that separates the date from the year using the indexOf() method. Using the address of the comma, the substring() method in line 15 extracts the date. To find the year, line 16 uses the indexOf() method and the current year to determine the starting address of the year. When inserting the date at line 16, you must use the current year. Line 17 uses the substr() method, using the starting address from the indexOf() method and length of the year, which is four characters long.

To Extract the Current System Date Using the Date() Object

This step writes JavaScript code that uses the Date() object and its methods to extract the current system date.

1

- If necessary, activate the Notepad++ window.
- If necessary, click line 8 below the <!--Hide from old browsers statement.
- Enter the JavaScript code shown in Table 9–15, indenting as shown. Press ENTER at the end of each complete line of code. If the current year is different from 2014, replace 2014 with the current year in the indexOf() method on line 16.
- After typing the last line in Table 9–15, press the ENTER key twice to leave space for additional JavaScript code.
- Compare what you typed to Figure 9–5. Correct any errors before proceeding.

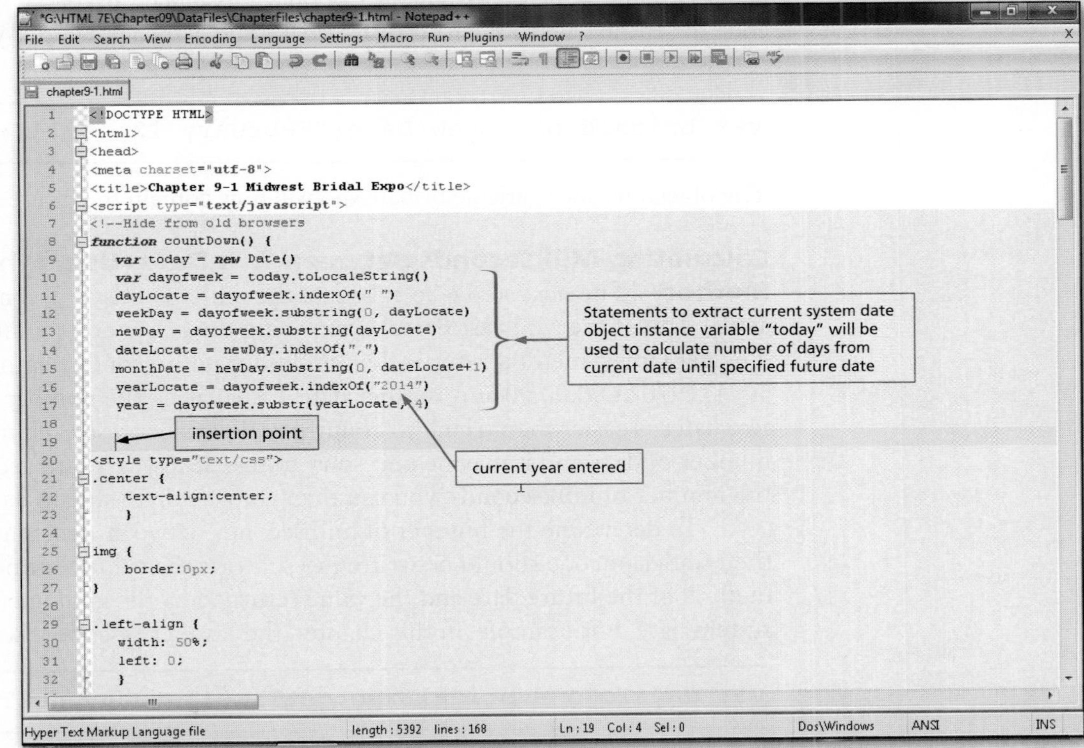

Figure 9–5

Q&A Why is some of the code in Figure 9–5 indented?

The code is indented with the SPACEBAR for ease of reading. It does not affect the execution of the code. You may want to indent sections of code to make it easier to identify.

Q&A What happens if a different year is entered in the indexOf() method than what is in the system?

The year will never match and JavaScript returns unusual looking results, but not as an error message.

Plan Ahead

The steps required to calculate a future date for a dynamic greeting include:

- Create a Date() object instance with the future date and the current date.
- Use the getTime() method on the current and future date, calculate the milliseconds between the current date and the future date by subtracting the current getTime() date from the future getTime() date.
- Convert the number of milliseconds to days using the Math.ceil() method to round up to the next integer.

Calculating the Number of Days Until a Future Event

Calculating the number of days until a future date can be useful for a dynamic greeting. With the Midwest Bridal Expo Web page, each time users view the Web page in a browser, the Web page displays a greeting that notifies them of the number of days until the Midwest Bridal Expo.

Creating a Date() Object Instance to Store a Future Date To calculate the number of days until a future date, an object instance of the Date() object must be created using the future date. As previously discussed, the Date() object can have a specific literal date as a value, which is assigned to an object instance variable. For example, the JavaScript code to set the date to the Midwest Bridal Expo, which is February 12, 2014, is written as follows:

```
var bridalExpo = new Date("February 12, 2014")
```

The object instance variable bridalExpo will now contain the future date of February 12, 2014.

Calculating Milliseconds Between Two Dates Using the getTime() Method The next step is to calculate the milliseconds between the current date and the actual date of the Midwest Bridal Expo using the getTime() method of the Date() object. The getTime() method returns the number of milliseconds that have elapsed since January 1, 1970 at 00:00:00 and another date. Calculating the number of milliseconds between two dates is easier than trying to count actual days because each month has a different number of days and it may be necessary to take leap years into account. After determining the number of milliseconds, you can then convert that value to days.

To determine the number of milliseconds between a current date and another date, the JavaScript code should be written to subtract the value returned by the getTime() method of the future date and the value returned by the getTime() method of the current system date. For example, in this chapter, the JavaScript code is written as follows:

```
var daysToGo = bridalExpo.getTime()-today.getTime()
```

where the variable daysToGo will contain the number of milliseconds between the future date and the current system date.

Converting Milliseconds to Days and Rounding Up Using the ceil() Method After calculating the number of milliseconds between the current date and the Midwest Bridal Expo, the next step is to convert the milliseconds to days. To convert milliseconds to days, the JavaScript code is written to divide the number of milliseconds stored in the daysToGo variable by the product of 1000*60*60*24. This expression represents the 1,000 milliseconds in a second, the 60 seconds in a minute, the 60 minutes in an hour, and the 24 hours in a day.

The value returned from the calculation daysToGo/(1000*60*60*24) will probably contain a decimal value. The Midwest Bridal Expo Web page, however, should display the number of days to the Midwest Bridal Expo as an integer value. The ceil() method of the Math object is used to round up to the nearest integer (for example, if the result is 12.843 days, 13 will display because of the ceil() method). The general form of the ceil() method is shown in Table 9–16.

Table 9–16 Math ceil() Method	
General form:	var variable=ceil(value)
Comment:	where *value* may be the result of any calculation. The **ceil()** method returns a value that rounds the value up to the next highest integer.
Examples:	var myResult=ceil(−3.8) var myNumber=ceil(4.179)
Result:	myResult is −3 myNumber is 5

The JavaScript code for the Midwest Bridal Expo Web page is written as follows:

```
var daysToBridalExpo = Math.ceil(daysToGo/(1000*60*60*24))
```

which first finds the product of 1000*60*60*24, then divides the value stored in the daysToGo variable by this product, and then raises the result (rounds up) to the next highest integer.

To Calculate the Number of Days to a Future Date

The code to calculate the number of days to a future date is shown in Table 9–17. Line 19 creates the bridalExpo object from the future date of the Midwest Bridal Expo in 2014. Line 20 subtracts the number of milliseconds of the current date (today.getTime()) from the future date (bridalExpo.getTime()). Line 21 converts the number of milliseconds to days.

Table 9–17 Code to Calculate the Number of Days to the Midwest Bridal Expo

Line	Code
19	`var bridalExpo = new Date("February 12, 2014")`
20	`var daysToGo = bridalExpo.getTime()-today.getTime()`
21	`var daysToBridalExpo = Math.ceil(daysToGo/(1000*60*60*24))`

The step on the next page enters the code to calculate the number of days to the Midwest Bridal Expo.

1

- If necessary, click line 19.
- Enter the JavaScript code shown in Table 9–17 on the previous page. Enter the current year's Midwest Bridal Expo date in line 19, if necessary. Press ENTER at the end of each complete line of code.

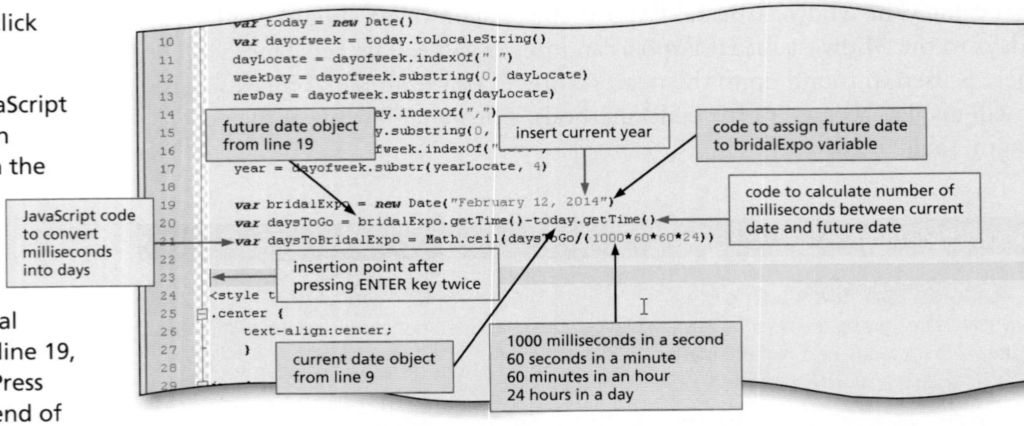

```
   var today = new Date()
10 var dayofweek = today.toLocaleString()
11 dayLocate = dayofweek.indexOf(" ")
12 weekDay = dayofweek.substring(0, dayLocate)
13 newDay = dayofweek.substring(dayLocate)
14              ay.indexOf(",")
15              y.substring(0,
16              fweek.indexOf("
17 year = dayofweek.substr(yearLocate, 4)
18
19 var bridalExpo = new Date("February 12, 2014")
20 var daysToGo = bridalExpo.getTime()-today.getTime()
21 var daysToBridalExpo = Math.ceil(daysToGo/(1000*60*60*24))
22
23
24 <style t
25 .center {
26    text-align:center;
27    }
28
```

future date object from line 19

insert current year

code to assign future date to bridalExpo variable

code to calculate number of milliseconds between current date and future date

JavaScript code to convert milliseconds into days

insertion point after pressing ENTER key twice

current date object from line 9

1000 milliseconds in a second
60 seconds in a minute
60 minutes in an hour
24 hours in a day

Figure 9–6

- After typing the last line in Table 9–17, press the ENTER key twice (Figure 9–6).
- Compare what you typed to Figure 9–6. Correct any errors before proceeding.

Q&A Can a date only be entered as "February 12, 2014" in the Date() object?

The date can also be entered as 2014, 1, 12 in the Date() object. Because the Date() object starts numbering the months with 0, that means February is 1.

Q&A What happens if I enter a date for the Midwest Bridal Expo that is in the past?

Entering a date that is in the past, prior to today's date, will result in a negative number in the countdown display.

Plan Ahead

Using JavaScript to write dynamic text to a Web page.
Before writing dynamic text to a Web page, you need to determine what your message will say and how you will format it for display. Most messages will be a combination of text strings and variables. Text can be formatted using standard HTML tags or using inline styles. Inline styles can be placed in <p> or <span> tags to format text.

BTW **JavaScript Strings**
The recommended maximum length of a string is 256 characters or bytes. This limit is based on a limit of older browsers.

Displaying Text and Variable Values to a Web Page with innerHTML

After the number of days until the Midwest Bridal Expo has been calculated, this data can be written on the Web page using JavaScript. To write data directly to the Web page, JavaScript can use the write() or writeln() methods of the document object. These methods, however, are not useful in user-defined functions located in the <head> section. For this reason, most developers do not use the write() or writeln() methods and they should be avoided if possible. Instead, to display text at a specific location, developers use the innerHTML property in association with the id value of a <div> tag container. The innerHTML property allows dynamic content to be placed in the container associated with the unique tag id. (Note that the Firefox browser does not recognize the innerHTML property.) Table 9–18 shows the general form of the innerHTML property.

BTW **JavaScript writeln() Method**
The writeln() method works only in HTML tags that either are sensitive to the new line character ("/n") or the carriage return, line feed, such as the <textarea> tag.

Table 9–18 innerHTML Property	
General form:	tag_id.innerHTML="text string"
Comment:	where *tag_id* is the id attribute assigned to the designated container tag, and *text string* is any combination of HTML tags, text, and variables
Examples:	displayCountDown.innerHTML = "Today is "+weekDay+" "+monthDate+" "+year+". We have "+daysToBridalExpo+" days until the Midwest Bridal Expo."

To display the contents of a variable as part of a text string, JavaScript can concatenate text and variables to create a seamless string of characters. **Concatenate** means to join or link together. The symbol for concatenation is the plus sign (+).

To Display Text and Variable Values to a Web Page Using innerHTML

Table 9–19 shows the code to write a simple welcome message that concatenates text with the values stored in several variables. In line 23, the innerHTML property is used to place data directly into a Web page in the <p> tag container. The text message string encloses the HTML tag in quotation marks within the text message string. The plus sign (+) concatenates the three variables weekDay, monthDate, and year together, along with the text message and variable daysToBridalExpo. Placement of quotation marks is important and you must include closing HTML tags. Line 24 is the closing brace for the countDown() user-defined function.

Table 9–19 Code to Write a Message to the Web Page

Line	Code
23	`displayCountDown.innerHTML = "<p style='font-size:12pt; font-family:helvetica;'>Today is "+weekDay+" "+monthDate+" "+year+". We have "+daysToBridalExpo+" days until the Midwest Bridal Expo.</p>"`
24	`}`

The following step displays text and variables using the innerHTML property.

1

- Click line 23, if necessary.
- Enter the JavaScript code shown in Table 9–19 to create the message text with the stored values. Press the ENTER key only at the end of each complete line of code.
- Press the ENTER key once more after the last } on line 24 to leave a blank line between user-defined functions (Figure 9–7).

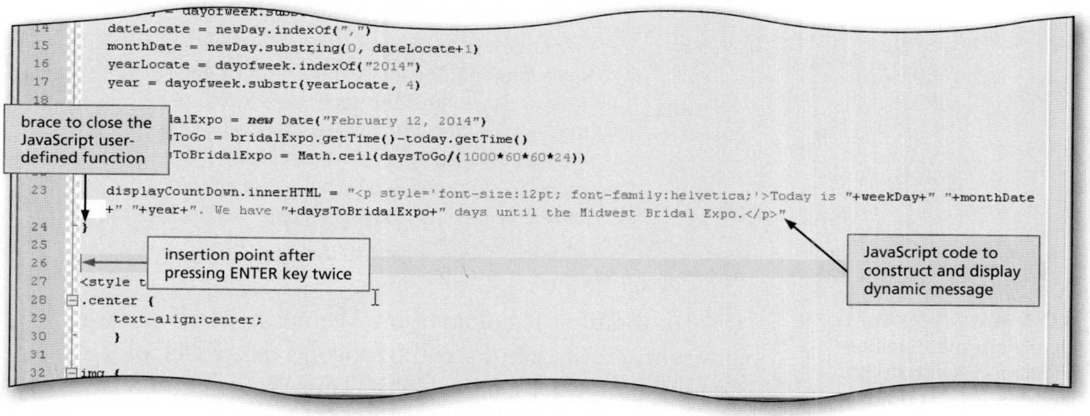

Figure 9–7

Q&A Can the innerHTML property be used for anything else?

The innerHTML property can retrieve the contents of any tag that has an id attribute. The id attribute values must be unique for each tag.

Q&A How does JavaScript know to concatenate instead of add when it sees the plus sign (+)?

When the JavaScript interpreter identifies the values surrounding a plus sign (+) and they are not numeric values, it will attempt to join them together.

Plan Ahead

Changing the color of the browser scroll bar.
The scroll bar color can be changed with a JavaScript user-defined function. To change the scroll bar color, follow these guidelines:

- JavaScript must have access to the object (the scroll bar). Use the getElementsByTagName() method of the document object to assign the "HTML" object to a variable. The getElementsByTagName() method returns an array of elements belonging to the identified object and all associated properties to that object.
- Using the variable as an object, JavaScript can set values to the various scroll bar properties: FaceColor, ArrowColor, HighlightColor, 3DlightColor, DarkshadowColor, TrackColor, and ShadowColor.
- Assign a color that matches or complements the colors on the Web page to at least the FaceColor and TrackColor.

Changing the Color of the Browser Scroll Bar

Currently, Cascading Style Sheets (CSS) do not have an official standard style for changing colors of the browser scroll bar that is recognized by all browsers. To modify the scroll bar, JavaScript needs to know the object so it can assign new style values. You use the getElementsByTagName() method to obtain a list of any type of HTML element. In this instance, the getElementsByTagName() method will identify the scroll bar object and assign it to a variable, which can then be modified by JavaScript. Table 9–20 shows the general form of the getElementsByTagName() method.

BTW
Color Values
For the most flexibility in using colors, Web developers suggest using either the hexadecimal version or the rgb() method version to assign a color. Be careful in using a standard color name. Color names like "lightblueaqua" may not be recognized by the style property.

Table 9–20 getElementsByTagName() Method

General form:	document.getElementsByTagName('html')
Comments:	where **getElementsByTagName()** is a method of the document object and 'html' is the object to be returned. The tag element must be entered as a string in single quotation marks and is case sensitive. The 'html' tag is used to access the entire Web page document, which allows modification through the styleObject variable using CSS selectors. The returning values are returned in an array format, so that each element can be referenced individually by an array value. The returned value can also use any properties associated with that value. The example shows the method to create an object of the html tag styles named styleObject.
Example:	styleObject=document.getElementsByTagName('html')[0].style

To modify the colors of the Web page scroll bar, use the styleObject object name with the standard scroll bar properties: FaceColor, ArrowColor, HighlightColor, 3DlightColor, DarkshadowColor, TrackColor, and ShadowColor. For example, to change the FaceColor of the scroll bar write

```
styleObject.scrollbarFaceColor="#ffde5b"
```

where the color must be written as a standard color name, a hexadecimal value, or defined by using the rgb() values method.

On the Midwest Bridal Expo Web page, the scroll bar colors are changed so the scroll bar is orange and the scroll bar track is yellow.

BTW
CSS and Scroll Bars
Only Internet Explorer will modify the scroll bar properties using JavaScript and the getElementsByTag() method associated with the <html> tag. All other browsers will ignore this set of code and not modify the scroll bar.

To Enter the User-Defined Function to Change the Browser Scroll Bar Color

Table 9–21 shows the code to change the scroll bar colors. Line 26 defines the function as scrollColor(). Line 27 defines the style property of the <html> tag and assigns it to an object, so face color and track color can be changed in lines 28 and 29. Line 28 changes the color of the scroll bar face to orange using a hexadecimal value. Line 29 changes the scroll bar track color to yellow using a hexadecimal value. Line 30 closes the scrollColor() function.

Table 9–21 Code to Change the Browser Scroll Bar Color

Line	Code
26	`function scrollColor() {`
27	`styleObject=document.getElementsByTagName('html')[0].style`
28	`styleObject.scrollbarFaceColor="#ffde5b"`
29	`styleObject.scrollbarTrackColor="#ffba00"`
30	`}`

The following step enters the user-defined function to change the browser scroll bar color in the <head> section.

1

- If necessary, click blank line 26.
- Enter the JavaScript code shown in Table 9–21.
- Press the ENTER key twice after the last } to leave a blank line between user-defined functions (Figure 9–8).

scrollColor() function changes color of browser scroll bar and scroll bar track to yellow and gold, respectively

insertion point after pressing ENTER key twice

Figure 9–8

Plan Ahead

Using the select list as a drop-down menu.
To use a <select> list as a drop-down menu, a user-defined function must make use of the following:

- The window's location property (window.location), to which a URL can be assigned, and which changes the location of the Web page in the browser.
- The selectedIndex property to identify which item was selected from the drop-down menu.

Using the selectedIndex Property and the Location Object to Link to a New URL

As shown in Figure 9–1 on page HTML 411, the Midwest Bridal Expo Web page also includes a <select> list that allows users to select items from a drop-down menu. Depending on the item chosen in the select list, the code will link users to one of three Web pages containing a vendor list, the schedule, or wedding tips.

When a user selects an item in the select list, the selectedIndex property of the select list returns the value of the selected item, which in this case is a URL of another Web page. The selectedIndex values of the items in a select list are considered to be numbered, starting with zero for the first item. The second item is number one, and so on. Table 9–22 shows the general form of the selectedIndex property.

BTW

The selectedIndex Property
The selectedIndex property cannot be used alone; it must be used in full reference to the particular select list, the form it belongs to, and its options.

Table 9–22 selectedIndex Property

General form:	var varname=formName.SelectListName.selectedIndex
Comments:	where *varname* is a variable, *formName* is the identifier of the form that holds the select list, *SelectListName* is the name of the select list, and **selectedIndex** is a property that returns an integer corresponding to the position of the item in the list
Example:	var menuSelect=myForm.Menu.selectedIndex

As you learned in earlier chapters, the text that appears for each item in a select list is enclosed in <option> tags. The option tag also supports a value attribute, as shown in the code in Figure 9–9. The value in the value attribute describes the item and can be assigned to a variable.

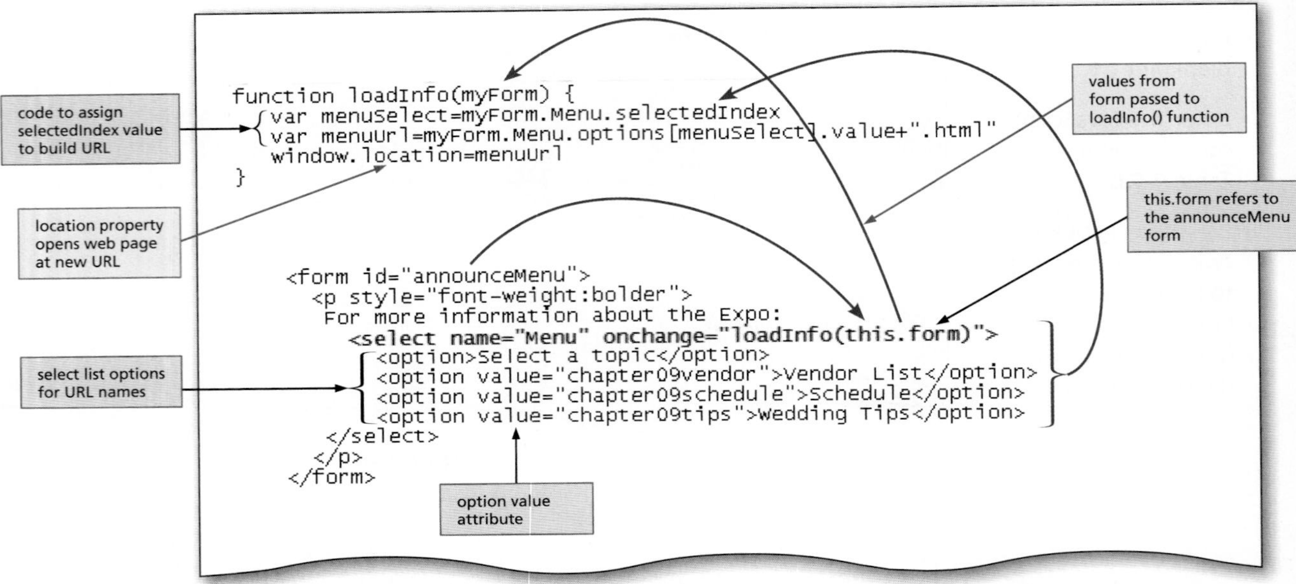

Figure 9–9 Relationship between HTML form object and JavaScript function.

This variable can then be used to assign the new Web page location to the window's location property. This statement will load a new URL into the browser. Table 9–23 shows the general form of the location property.

Table 9–23 Location Property

General form:	object=window.location or window.location=URL
Comments:	where *object* is a variable or some other object that can display the URL of the current window, and *URL* is the address of the Web page to display. The use of the window object is optional.
Examples:	myform.textbox.value=window.location location=http://www.cengagebrain.com

In order to use a select list as navigation, you need to create a function that will determine which option the user selects and results in the chosen page being loaded in the browser. Table 9–24 shows the JavaScript code for a loadInfo() function that uses the selected value to determine which item in a list was selected, assigns the value attribute for that item, and then uses that variable to create a URL.

Table 9–24 Code to Change Location

Line	Code
32	`function loadInfo(myForm) {`
33	`    var menuSelect=myForm.Menu.selectedIndex`
34	`    var menuUrl=myForm.Menu.options[menuSelect].value+".html"`
35	`    window.location=menuUrl`
36	`}`

The selectedIndex property is then used on the object name of the select list and the form provided in the data file. Line 32 defines the function name. The form object, myForm, is passed to the function from the select list name attribute. In line 33, the selectedIndex statement assigns the numerical value of the item selected from the list to the variable menuSelect. In this line, menuSelect is a variable name, myForm is the identifier of the form that holds the select list, and Menu is the name of the select list. The options property of Menu refers to the <option> tag in the select list, while selectedIndex indicates the integer value of the item selected in the select list. Line 34 concatenates the value attribute of the selected item (menuSelect) with the file extension .html to create a URL. The URL name is concatenated to the .html filename extension using the plus sign (+). Line 35 uses that URL to load that Web page into the browser window. Line 36 closes the function.

To Enter the User-Defined Function to Link to a New URL Using the Drop-Down Menu

The following step enters the user-defined function to link to a new URL using the drop-down menu. (Note that the <option> tags are included in the Data File.)

1

- Click line 32 if necessary.
- Enter the JavaScript code shown in Table 9–24 to enter the options and links for the drop-down menu.
- Press the ENTER key twice after line 36 (Figure 9–10).

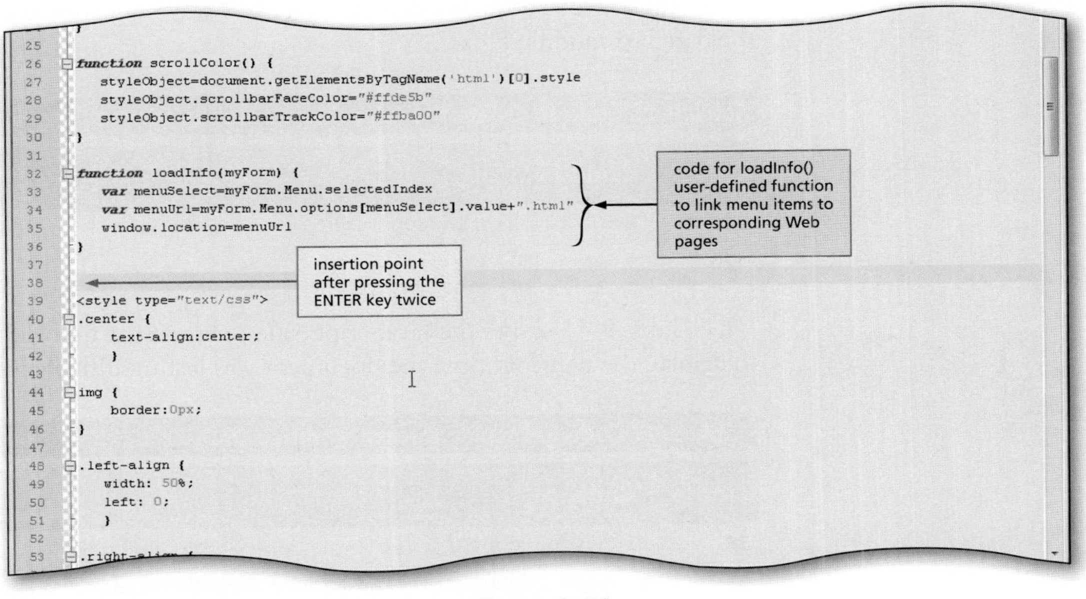

code for loadInfo() user-defined function to link menu items to corresponding Web pages

insertion point after pressing the ENTER key twice

Figure 9–10

Plan Ahead

Writing the date last modified on the Web page.

The date the Web page was last modified indicates how current the information is. When writing this content, you should follow these guidelines:

- Determine what your message will be. Many Web pages display a copyright notice with the date last modified.
- Create a <div> tag container with the id displayCopyRight.
- Create a text message string enclosed in quotation marks and include the document.lastModified property with the text string.
- Use the innerHTML property to assign the message to the <div> tag container.

BTW

The lastModified Property

The lastModified property may return different values than expected with older browsers and unknown Web servers.

Displaying the Date the Document Was Last Modified

Most Web developers agree that a Web page should display the date the Web page was last modified, so visitors are aware of how current the Web page content is. For the Midwest Bridal Expo Web page, the date last modified should appear at the bottom of the page in a smaller font to keep the message from distracting the user (see Figure 9–1 on page HTML 411).

JavaScript provides an easy way to display the date by using the lastModified property of the document object. The lastModified property displays the date in the form of mm/dd/yyyy followed by the time in the form of hh:mm:ss. Table 9–25 shows the general form of the lastModified property of the document.

Table 9–25 lastModified Property

General form:	document.lastModified
Comment:	where **lastModified** is a property of the document object that returns the date the document was last saved
Example:	var lastDateModified= document.lastModified

Table 9–26 shows the code to place the <div> tag container for the copyright and the date last modified text.

Table 9–26 Code to Create the <div> Tag Container for the Copyright and Date Last Modified

```
<div id="displayCopyRight">
</div>
```

Table 9–27 shows the JavaScript code to create the user-defined function, copyRight(), to display the date and time the document was last modified and a copyright message.

Table 9–27 Code to Display the lastModified Date

```
function copyRight() {
   var lastModDate = document.lastModified
   var lastModDate = lastModDate.substring(0,10)
   displayCopyRight.innerHTML = "<p style='font-size:8pt; font-weight:
   bold;'>The URL of this document is "+document.URL+"<br />Midwest Bridal
   Expo"+"<br />This document was last modified "+lastModDate+".</p>"
}
```

Line 38 defines the copyRight() function. Line 39 assigns the date the Web page was last modified and assigns it to a temporary variable, lastModDate. Line 40 uses the substring() method to extract the date portion only. Line 41 uses the innerHTML property to assign the message string to the <div> tag container. The document.URL displays the Web address of this document. Line 42 closes the function.

To Include the Date Last Modified and a Copyright Message in a Text String

The following steps enter JavaScript code to include the date last modified and a copyright message in a text string.

1

- Scroll down and click line 119.
- Enter the JavaScript code In Table 9–26. Do not press the ENTER key after the last line.

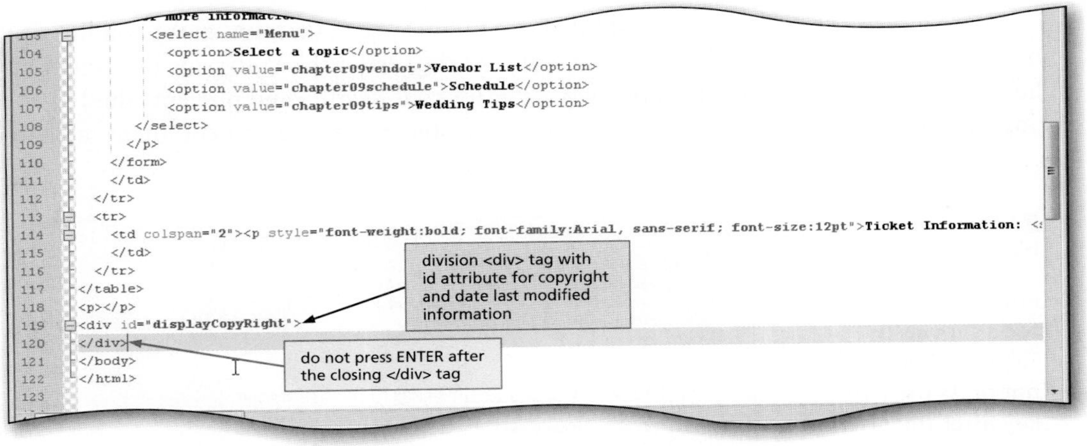

division <div> tag with id attribute for copyright and date last modified information

do not press ENTER after the closing </div> tag

Figure 9–11

2

- Scroll up and click line 38.
- Enter the JavaScript code shown in Table 9–27.
- Press the ENTER key after each line, and press the ENTER key twice after the } in line 42 (Figure 9–12).

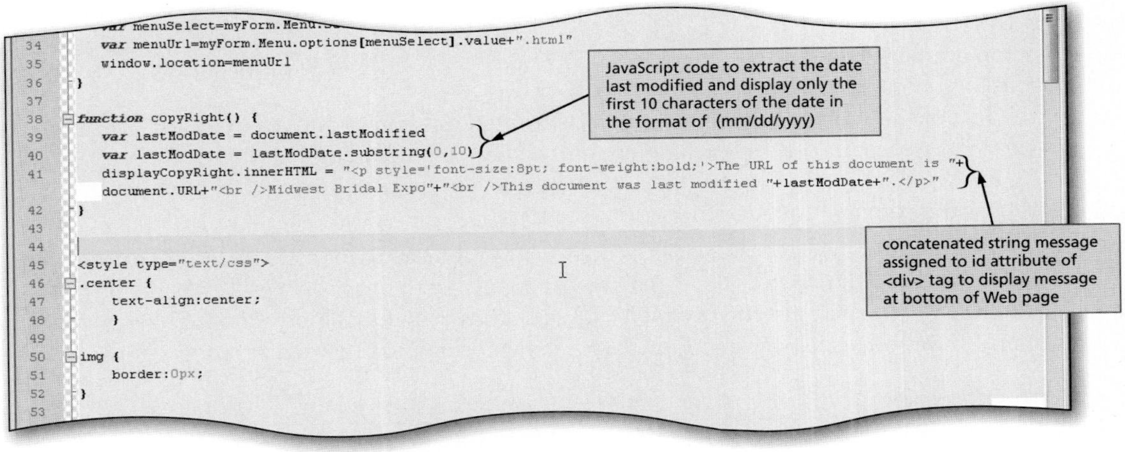

JavaScript code to extract the date last modified and display only the first 10 characters of the date in the format of (mm/dd/yyyy)

concatenated string message assigned to id attribute of <div> tag to display message at bottom of Web page

Figure 9–12

Completing the JavaScript Section

As you know, all HTML tags must have start and end tags to separate them from other page elements. To complete this section of JavaScript code, it is necessary to add the end comment tag and the end </script> tag.

To Enter the End Comment and End </script> Tags

Table 9–28 shows the code used to close the start <script> tag on line 6 and the start comment tag on line 7, as entered in Figure 9–4 on page HTML 418.

Table 9–28 Closing the Script Section

Line	Code
44	`//-->`
45	`</script>`

Line 44 ends the comment, <!--Hide from old browsers, that was started on line 7. If the HTML comment line is used and it is not closed properly, it will read the rest of the Web page document as part of the comment. The end </script> tag on line 45 ends the JavaScript code section and prevents the HTML code that follows from being interpreted as JavaScript code. The following step enters the end comment tag and the end </script> tag.

- If necessary, click blank line 44.
- Enter the JavaScript code shown in Table 9–28 and do not press the ENTER key after the last line (Figure 9–13).

```
37
38  function copyRight() {
39      var lastModDate = document.lastModified
40      var lastModDate = lastModDate.substring(0,10)
41      displayCopyRight.innerHTML = "<p style='font-size:8pt; font-weight:bold;'>The URL of this document is "+
        document.URL+"<br />Midwest Bridal Expo"+"<br />This document was last modified "+lastModDate+".</p>"
42  }
43
44  //-->
45  </script>
46  <style type="text/css">
47  .center {
48      text-align:center;
49      }
50
51  img {
52      border:0px;
53  }
54
```


Figure 9–13

Q&A What happens if a <script> section is not closed properly?

If the HTML comment line is used and it is not closed properly, the rest of the Web page document will be treated as a comment. When the user attempts to view the Web page, nothing will appear after that comment line.

Q&A Why is the comment needed in <script> sections?

Some browsers or mobile Web devices do not interpret JavaScript code correctly, so the comment hides the JavaScript code. If the comment line is not closed properly, the Web page may not display from the point of the comment forward, thus giving the impression the Web page is blank. If this occurs, always check to ensure the end comment tag was included.

Plan Ahead

Using event handlers to call user-defined functions.

Event handlers must be placed with the object (such as a button, drop-down menu, or HTML tag) that controls the event. In this chapter, the events are load and change, so you use the event handlers onLoad and onChange to call the user-defined functions. In this chapter, you will:

- Place the onLoad event handler in the <body> tag.
- Place the onChange event handler in the <select> tag that starts the drop-down menu.

Calling JavaScript Functions Using Event Handlers

Now that you have added user-defined functions to count down to a certain date, changed the scroll bar color, used a drop-down menu, and added the date last modified at the bottom of the page, you need to add code that calls these functions when the Web page is loaded. JavaScript has two basic methods to call functions. One method to call a function is to use event handlers and object methods. The other method is to code the function name in a JavaScript section at the logical point of execution. The user-defined functions written in this chapter execute using event handlers.

As you have learned, an event is the result of an action, such as a mouse click or a window loading. An event handler is a way to associate that action with a function. For example, when a user clicks a button or a check box, a JavaScript user-defined function may be associated with that event. The associated function will execute if the event is captured and then triggers, or calls, the JavaScript user-defined function. The general form of an event handler is shown in Table 9–29.

Table 9–29 Event Handlers

General form:	<tag attribute eventhandler="JavaScript code">
Comment:	where *tag* is the HTML tag; *attribute* is a property of the tag that can have a value assigned to it, *eventhandler* is the name of the JavaScript event handler, and *JavaScript code* is the instruction to execute, usually in the form of a function name
Example:	<body onLoad="scrollColor()">

JavaScript event handlers make Web pages more dynamic and interactive by allowing JavaScript code to execute only in response to a user action, such as a mouse click or selection of an item in a list. For a complete list of event handlers, see the JavaScript Quick Reference in Appendix G. You use the onLoad and onChange event handlers in the Midwest Bridal Expo Web page.

To have a JavaScript user-defined function execute automatically when a page loads, use the onLoad event. The onLoad event handler triggers the associated function when the Web page has completed loading into the browser. The onChange event handler triggers when the value of an object changes. For example, when the user selects a list item in the select list, the value of the select list is changed.

To Associate User-Defined Functions with the OnLoad Event

The following steps enter JavaScript code to associate the countDown(), scrollColor(), and copyRight() user-defined functions with the onLoad event.

- Click to the right of the y in the <body> tag in line 78, as shown in Figure 9–14.

```
73     padding: 5px;
74   }
75
76 </style>
77 </head>
78 <body>
79 <div class="center">
80 <p><img src="chapter9-1banner.jpg" width="747" height="160" alt="Bridal Expo Banner"></p>
81 <p style="font-family:Arial, Helvetica, sans-serif; font-size:18px; font-weight:bold;">Midwest Bridal Expo</p>
82 <img src="hrimg-wedding-burgundy.jpg" width="750" height="5" alt="hr">
83 <div id="displayCountDown">
84 </div>
85 <img src="hrimg-wedding-burgundy.jpg" width="750" height="5" alt="horizonal rule">
86 </div>
```

insertion point in <body> tag; press SPACEBAR once to begin adding onLoad event handler

Figure 9–14

- Press the SPACEBAR once and then type `onLoad="scrollColor(); countDown(); copyRight()"` within the <body> tag. Do not press the ENTER key (Figure 9–15).

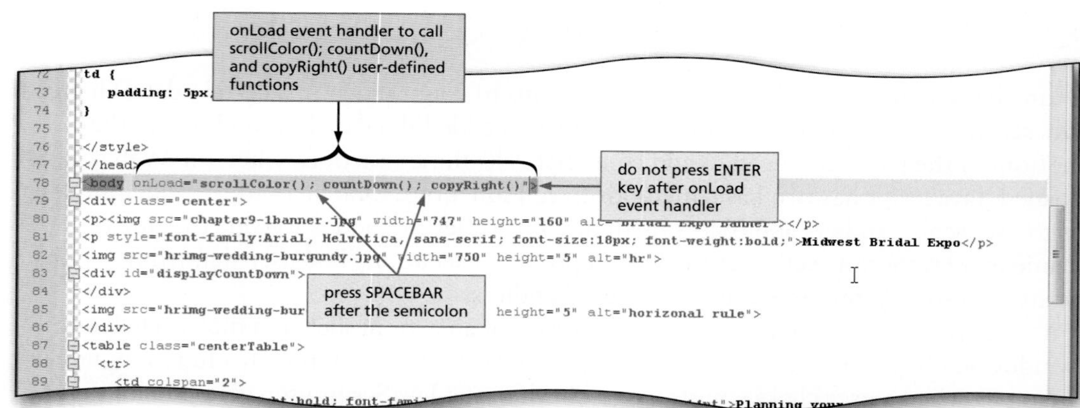

Figure 9–15

To Associate a User-Defined Function with the OnChange Event

When the user selects an item in the select list (changes the value of the select list), this change triggers the associated user-defined function loadInfo(). The this.form parameter in the function call sends the values of the <option> tags to the function. The following step associates the user-defined function loadInfo() with the onChange event.

- Scroll to line 110 and click to the right of "Menu".
- Press the SPACEBAR once and then type `onChange="loadInfo(this.form)"` within the <select> tag. Do not press the ENTER key (Figure 9–16).

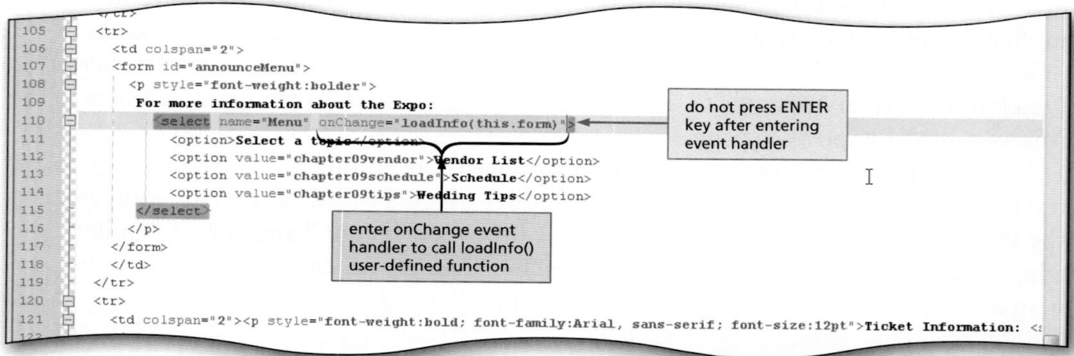

Figure 9–16

To Save an HTML File

With the first section of JavaScript code for the Midwest Bridal Expo Web page complete, you should save the file.

1. Click File on the menu bar, click Save, and then type `chapter9-1solution.html` in the File name text box (do not press ENTER).
2. Navigate to the storage device and folder (Chapter09\ChapterFiles) where you save your Data Files and then click the Save button in the Save As dialog box to save the file.

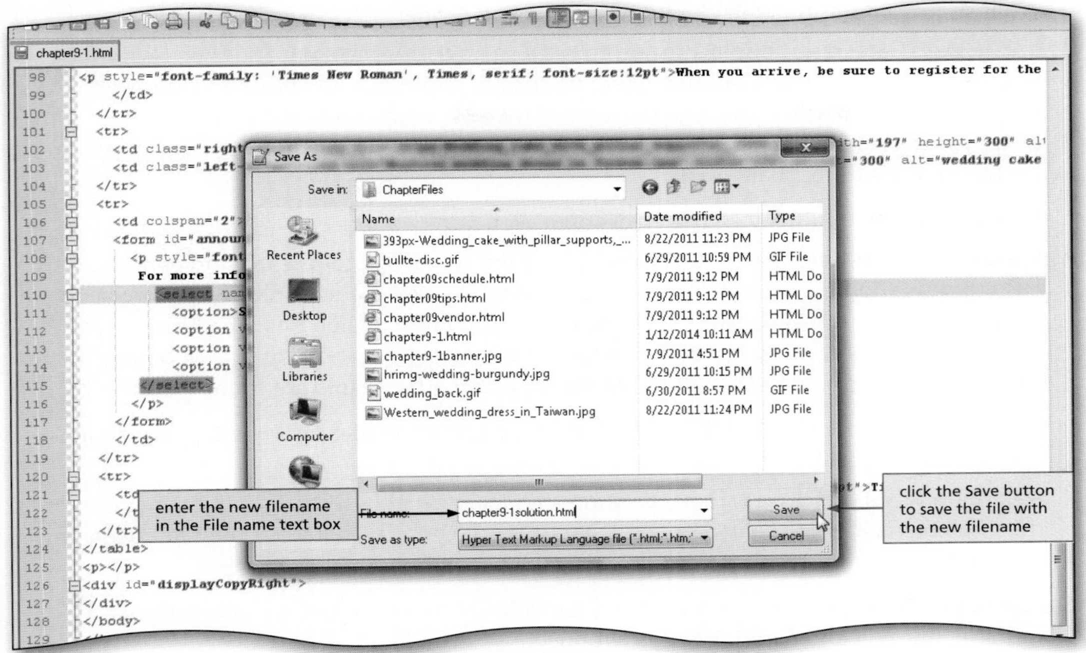

Figure 9–17

To Test the Completed Web Page

Once you complete your JavaScript code, you should test the code in a browser. The following steps open a browser, such as Internet Explorer, and load the chapter9-1solution.html Web page to test if the JavaScript works correctly.

1. Open Internet Explorer and type `G:\Chapter09\ChapterFiles\chapter9-1solution.html` in the Address box.
2. Press ENTER to display the Web page (Figure 9–18a). If a security message appears, click the 'Allow blocked content' button. (If you are running IE 8 or lower, your security message may be different.)
3. Select Vendor List in the drop-down menu to display the Vendor List Web page.
4. Click the Back button on the lower-left corner of the Web page or the Back button on the Standard toolbar to return to the Midwest Bridal Expo home page.
5. Select Wedding Tips in the drop-down menu (Figure 9–18b) to display the Wedding Tips Web page.
6. Click the Back button on the lower-left corner of the Web page or the Back button on the Standard toolbar to return to the Midwest Bridal Expo home page.
7. Select Schedule from the drop-down menu to display the Bridal Expo Schedule of Events Web page.
8. Click the Back button on the lower-left corner of the Web page or the Back button on the Standard toolbar to return to the Midwest Bridal Expo home page.

Q&A

Should I always allow a Web page running an ActiveX control to load?

For the Web page you just created, or one you are familiar with, you can let the ActiveX control execute. If you are not familiar with a Web site, however, it is not advisable to let them run.

Q&A What should I do if the Web page is not displaying properly?

If your Web page is not displaying correctly, close any error message and then click the Notepad++ button on the taskbar. Check your JavaScript code according to Figures 9–3 through 9–17 on pages HTML 416 through HTML 437. Correct any errors, save the file, click the Internet Explorer taskbar button to activate the browser, and then click the Refresh button on the Address bar.

Q&A Is there any way to display all the errors on a Web page at once?

Internet Explorer does not offer this feature. If the JavaScript code is missing periods, is missing quotation marks, or has misspelled words, the Web page displays with errors. To continue loading the Web page, click the OK button in the dialog box. The browser will cease to process any more JavaScript code, but will load what it can of the Web page. After you fix the errors, refresh the Web page to see if any other errors are found.

Q&A How come no other browser (Firefox, Chrome, or Safari) besides Internet Explorer changes the scroll bar colors?

According to various Web forums, only Internet Explorer allows changes to be made to the scroll bar colors. In reality, the scroll bars are not considered part of the Web page only the browser, and only IE contains the ability to change browser color.

Q&A I cannot get the dynamic message to display in Mozilla Firefox, but it will in Internet Explorer, Chrome and Safari. What is wrong?

The innerHTML property was not recognized by early versions of Firefox; however, at the time of this writing, there is no indication in various Web forums that the current versions do either.

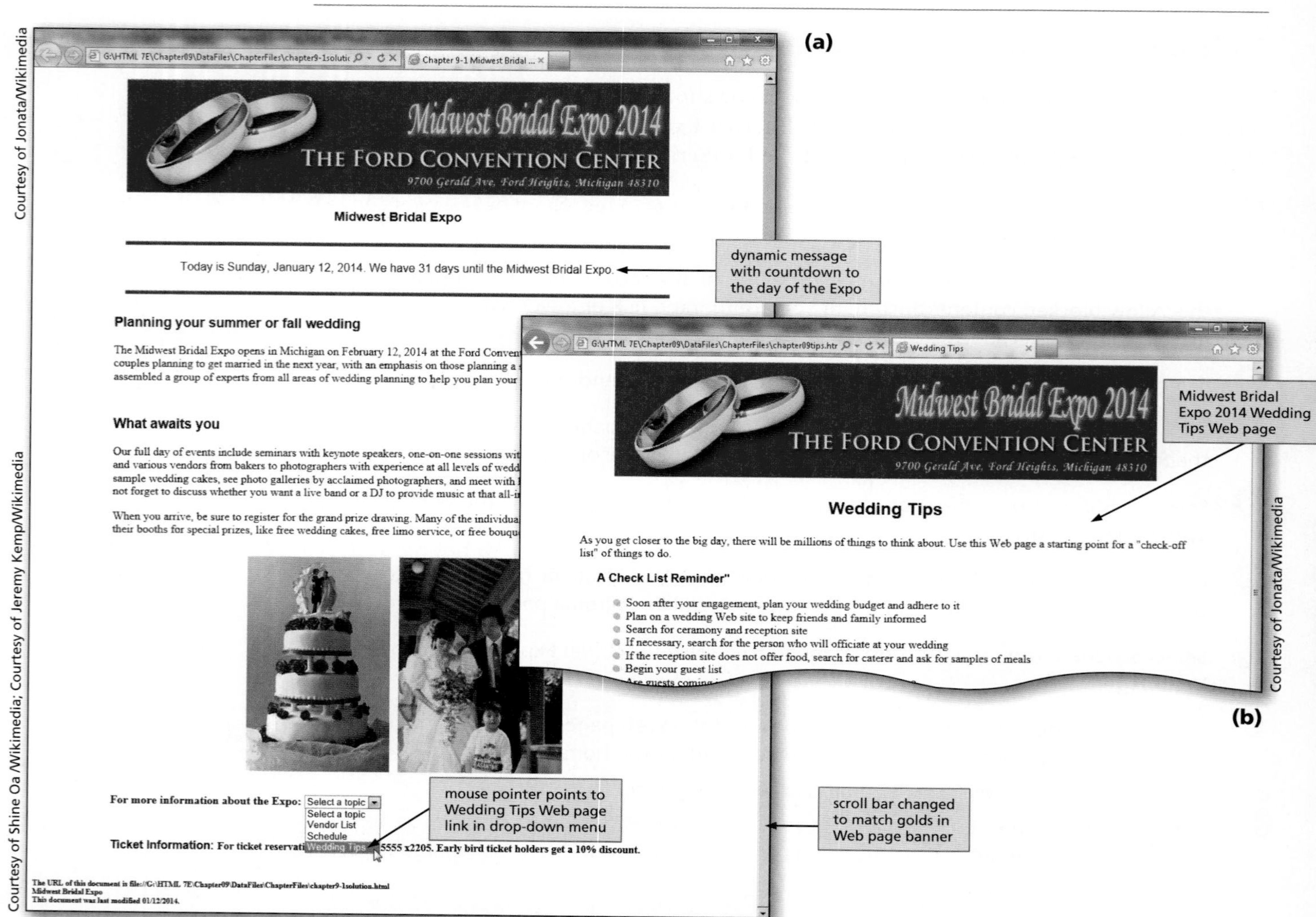

Figure 9–18

To Validate a Web Page

Now that you have tested the Web page and made sure the JavaScript works as desired, you should validate the page at the w3.org Web site.

1. Open Internet Explorer, navigate to the Web site `validator.w3.org`, and then click the Validate by Upload tab.
2. Click the Browse button.
3. Locate the chapter9-1solution.html file on your storage device, click the filename, and then click the Open button on the Choose File to Upload dialog box.
4. Click the Check button to validate the file.

Q&A When I validated, it said it passed as HTML5, but it had a warning?

Because HTML5 has not been finalized and adapted by all browsers, the warning just lets you know that your markup is valid for HTML5, but it may encounter problems with any browser that does not adhere to HTML5 specifications.

To Print an HTML File

After completing and testing the Web page, you should print the HTML file using Notepad++ for future reference.

1. Click the Notepad++ icon on the taskbar and click the chapter9-1solution.html tab to activate the file.
2. Click File on the menu bar and then click Print. Click the Print button in the Print dialog box.

To Quit Notepad++ and the Browser

1. In Notepad++, click the File menu, then Close All.
2. Click the Close button on the Notepad++ window title bar.
3. Click the Close button on all open browser windows.

BTW **Quick Reference**
For a list of JavaScript statements and their associated attributes, see the JavaScript Quick Reference (Appendix G) at the back of this book, or visit the JavaScript Quick Reference Web page at www.cengagebrain.com.

Chapter Summary

In this chapter, you learned basic JavaScript concepts and how to write and insert JavaScript code to make your Web page more dynamic and interactive. The items listed below include all the new HTML and JavaScript skills you have learned in this chapter.

1. Enter a <div> Tag Container (HTML 416)
2. Enter the Start <script> and Comment Tags (HTML 418)
3. Extract the Current System Date Using the Date() Object (HTML 423)
4. Calculate the Number of Days to a Future Date (HTML 425)
5. Display Text and Variable Values to a Web Page Using innerHTML (HTML 427)
6. Enter the User-Defined Function to Change the Browser Scroll Bar Color (HTML 428)
7. Enter the User-Defined Function to Link to a New URL Using the Drop-Down Menu (HTML 431)
8. Include the Date Last Modified and a Copyright Message in a Text String (HTML 433)
9. Enter the End Comment and End </script> Tags (HTML 434)
10. Associate User-Defined Functions with the onLoad Event (HTML 435)
11. Associate a User-Defined Function with the onChange Event (HTML 436)

Learn It Online

Test your knowledge of chapter content and key terms.

Instructions: To complete the following exercises, please visit www.cengagebrain.com. At the CengageBrain.com home page, search for *HTML5 and CSS, 7th Edition* using the search box at the top of the page. This will take you to the product page for this book. On the product page, click the Access Now button below the Study Tools heading. On the Book Companion Site Web page, select Chapter 9, and then click the link for the desired exercise.

Chapter Reinforcement TF, MC, and SA

A series of true/false, multiple choice, and short answer questions that test your knowledge of the chapter content.

Flash Cards

An interactive learning environment where you identify chapter key terms associated with displayed definitions.

Practice Test

A series of multiple choice questions that test your knowledge of chapter content and key terms.

Who Wants To Be a Computer Genius?

An interactive game that challenges your knowledge of chapter content in the style of a television quiz show.

Wheel of Terms

An interactive game that challenges your knowledge of chapter key terms in the style of the television show, *Wheel of Fortune*.

Crossword Puzzle Challenge

A crossword puzzle that challenges your knowledge of key terms presented in the chapter.

Apply Your Knowledge

Reinforce the skills and apply the concepts you learned in this chapter.

Adding User-Defined Functions

Instructions: Start Notepad++. Open the file apply9-1.html from the Chapter09\Apply folder of the Data Files for Students. See the inside back cover of this book for instructions on downloading the Data Files for Students, or contact your instructor for information about accessing the required files.

The apply9-1.html file is a partially completed HTML file that you will use for this exercise. Figure 9–19 shows the Apply Your Knowledge Web page as it should be displayed in a browser after the JavaScript has been added. This problem requires using JavaScript to change the scroll bar color, to display a dynamic message, and display copyright information and the date the Web page was last modified. The problem also requires adding event handlers in the <body> tag to invoke the JavaScript user-defined functions.

Perform the following tasks:

1. Using Figure 9–3 on page HTML 416 as a guide, enter a <div> tag with an id name of countDown between the two orange divider images (hrimg-summercamp.jpg) at line 50.
2. Enter the beginning of a JavaScript code section for a user-defined function in the <head> section of the Web page before the <style> tag. Be sure to include a comment line to hide the JavaScript from old browsers.
3. Using the code in Tables 9–15, 9–17, and 9–19 on pages HTML 422, 425, and 427 as a guide, write a JavaScript user-defined function to display the countdown message shown in Figure 9–19. Use your own current and future dates for this Web page.

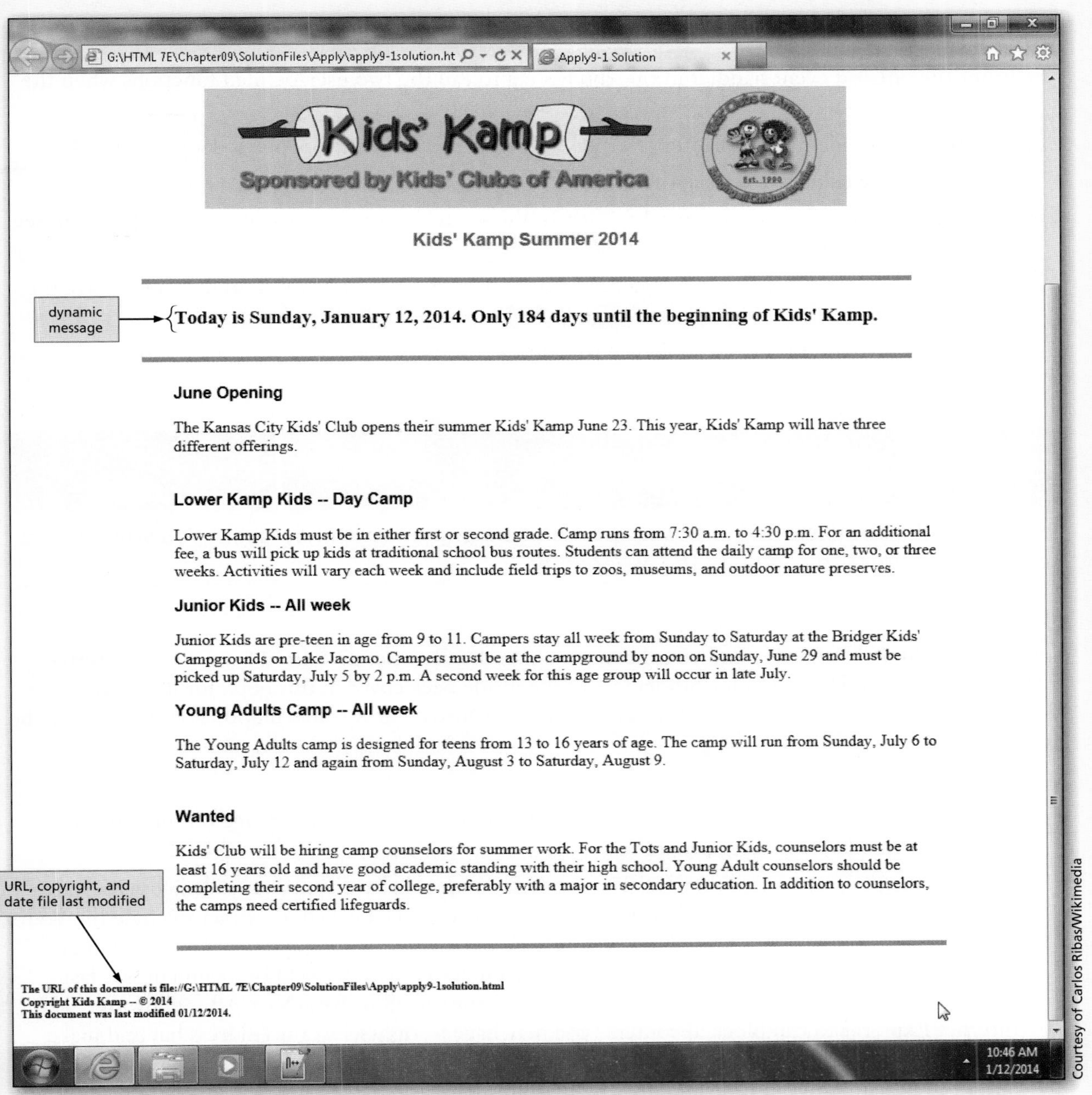

Figure 9–19

4. Make sure to enter the closing brace for the function, followed by the closing HTML tags to close the <script> section.
5. Using the code in Table 9–26 on page HTML 432 as a guide, enter the code to create a <div> tag container with an id attribute of copyrightdate after the end </table> tag and before the end </body> tag.
6. Using the code in Table 9–27 on page HTML 432 as a guide, write a user-defined function using the <div> tag container, using the id attribute copyrightdate, and the innerHTML property to display the document URL, a copyright message, and the date the document was last modified at the bottom of the Web page, as shown in Figure 9–19. (*Hint:* To add a copyright symbol enter © in your text.)

Continued >

Apply Your Knowledge *continued*

7. Enter the onLoad event handler in the <body> tag to call the two user-defined functions when the Web page loads.
8. Save the revised file in the Chapter09\Apply folder using the filename apply9-1solution.html.
9. Validate the file using the w3.org validator.
10. View and test the Web page in your browser. In this exercise, you must use Internet Explorer to see the countdown message.
11. If any errors occur, check the code against Steps 1 through 7, make any required changes, save the file using the same filename, and then refresh the Web page in the browser.
12. Submit the revised HTML file and Web page in the format specified by your instructor.

Extend Your Knowledge

Extend the skills you learned in this chapter and experiment with new skills. You will need to search the Internet to complete the assignment.

Learning More about Displaying Messages

Instructions: Start Notepad++ and your browser. Open the file extend9-1.html from the Chapter09\Extend folder of the Data Files for Students. See the inside back cover of this book for instructions on downloading the Data Files for Students, or contact your instructor for information about accessing the required files.

Perform the following tasks:

1. Search the Internet for the JavaScript instructions on how to display a message on the status bar of your browser. (*Hint:* Look for properties of the Windows object.)
2. Add the <script> section and then write the code for a user-defined function, called copyRight(), which would use the lastModified property and the substring() method to extract the date the Web page was last modified and saved. However, instead of placing the message in a <div> container, create a copyright message: "© Copyright Denver Opera House 2014. This document was last modified" followed by the date, and assign it to the browser status bar. (*Note:* After allowing Internet Explorer to run blocked content, you may have to right-click the Address bar and make sure the status bar is checked. If the status bar still does not display, you may have click the Refresh button to reload the Web page and display the status bar.)
3. Search the Internet for the proper scroll bar names for the arrow and shadow color. Using the code in Table 9–21 on page HTML 429 as a guide, enter the code for a user-defined function called newScroll() to change the scroll bar colors to the hexadecimal values shown in Table 9–30.

Table 9–30 Scroll Bar Colors
scroll bar face color: #603520
scroll bar arrow color: #bf853f
scroll bar track color: #ffffff
scroll bar shadow color: #a66030

4. Locate the blank line between the divider line images and enter the <div> tag container for the dynamic message. Use an id attribute "displayDate" and include a class attribute, center, which is defined in the CSS code.

5. Using the code from Tables 9–15, 9–17, and 9–19, write the user-defined function to display the dynamic message shown in Figure 9–20. Pick a date about 30 days from the current date to use in the calculation.
6. The <div> tag is not the only container tag. What other tag can be used to contain items? After the last row of the table and before the end </body> tag, enter a container tag with an id attribute of footer_Msg. Include a class attribute called "footertext," which already exists in the CSS code.
7. Write the JavaScript user-defined function, footerMsg(), to display the opera house address as follows in the footer container:

   The Denver Opera House

   900 Market Street

   Denver, CO 80205
8. Add the onLoad event handler to the <body> tag to call all the user-defined functions when the Web page loads.
9. Save the revised file in the Chapter09\Extend folder using the filename extend9-1solution.html.
10. Validate the file using the w3.org validation Web page.
11. View and test the Web page in Internet Explorer.
12. If any errors occur, check the code against Steps 1 through 8, make any required changes, save the file using the same filename, and then refresh the Web page in the browser.
13. Submit the revised HTML file and Web page in the format specified by your instructor.

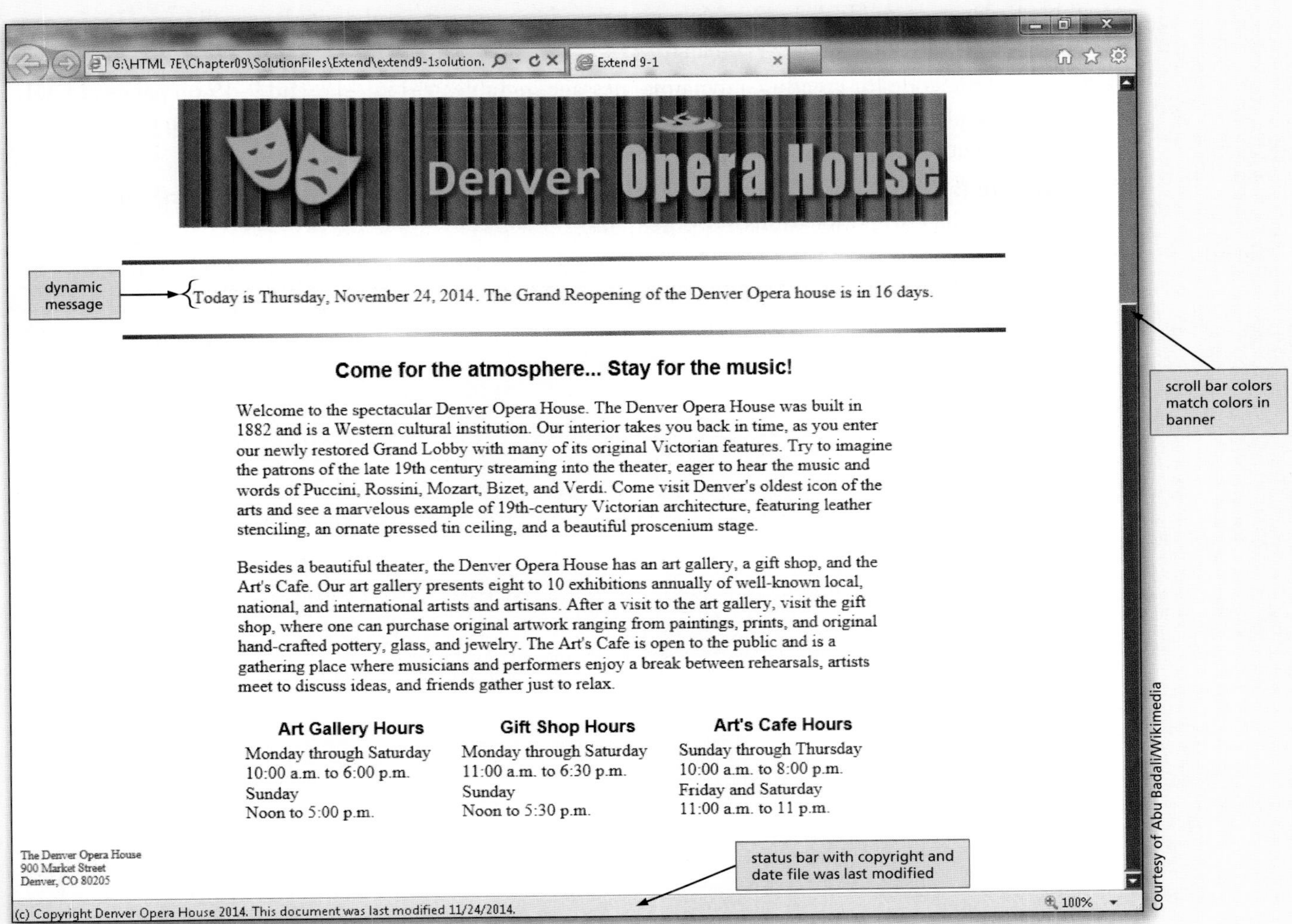

Figure 9–20

Make It Right

Analyze the JavaScript code on a Web page and correct all errors.

Correcting Syntax Errors and Inserting Missing Code

Instructions: Start your browser. Open the file makeitright9-1.html from the Chapter09\MakeItRight folder of the Data Files for Students. See the inside back cover of this book for instructions for downloading the Data Files for Students, or see your instructor for information on accessing the files required in this book.

The Web page shown in Figure 9–21 is an announcement for a Memorial Day sale at Frank's Fix-it Hardware. This Web page has four errors that you are to find and correct.

Perform the following tasks:

1. When you open the make9-1.html file in the browser, you will notice that the scroll bar did not change color, the dynamic message did not display between the horizontal lines, and the copyright and date last modified did not display. After you find and fix the error that will display the dynamic message, the date will include the time. You must remove the time from the message and only display the date.
2. Start Notepad++. Open the make9-1.html file. Save the HTML file in the Chapter09\MakeItRight folder using the filename make9-1solution.html.
3. Compare the code in the user-defined function to the code to change the scroll bar color in Table 9–21 on page HTML 429. Make the changes necessary to change the scroll bar color in the Frank's Fix-it Hardware Web page.
4. Compare the code for creating a dynamic message in Tables 9–15, 9–17, and 9–19 on pages HTML 422, 425, and 427, to the code in the HTML file for the Frank's Fix-it Hardware Web page, and make corrections as necessary.
5. Make sure the user-defined functions are called properly by the correct event handlers and that they are in the correct locations.
6. Save the corrected HTML file and test it using your browser. If errors occur, check your code and save again. Your Web page should look similar to Figure 9–21.
7. Submit the revised HTML file and Web page in the format specified by your instructor.

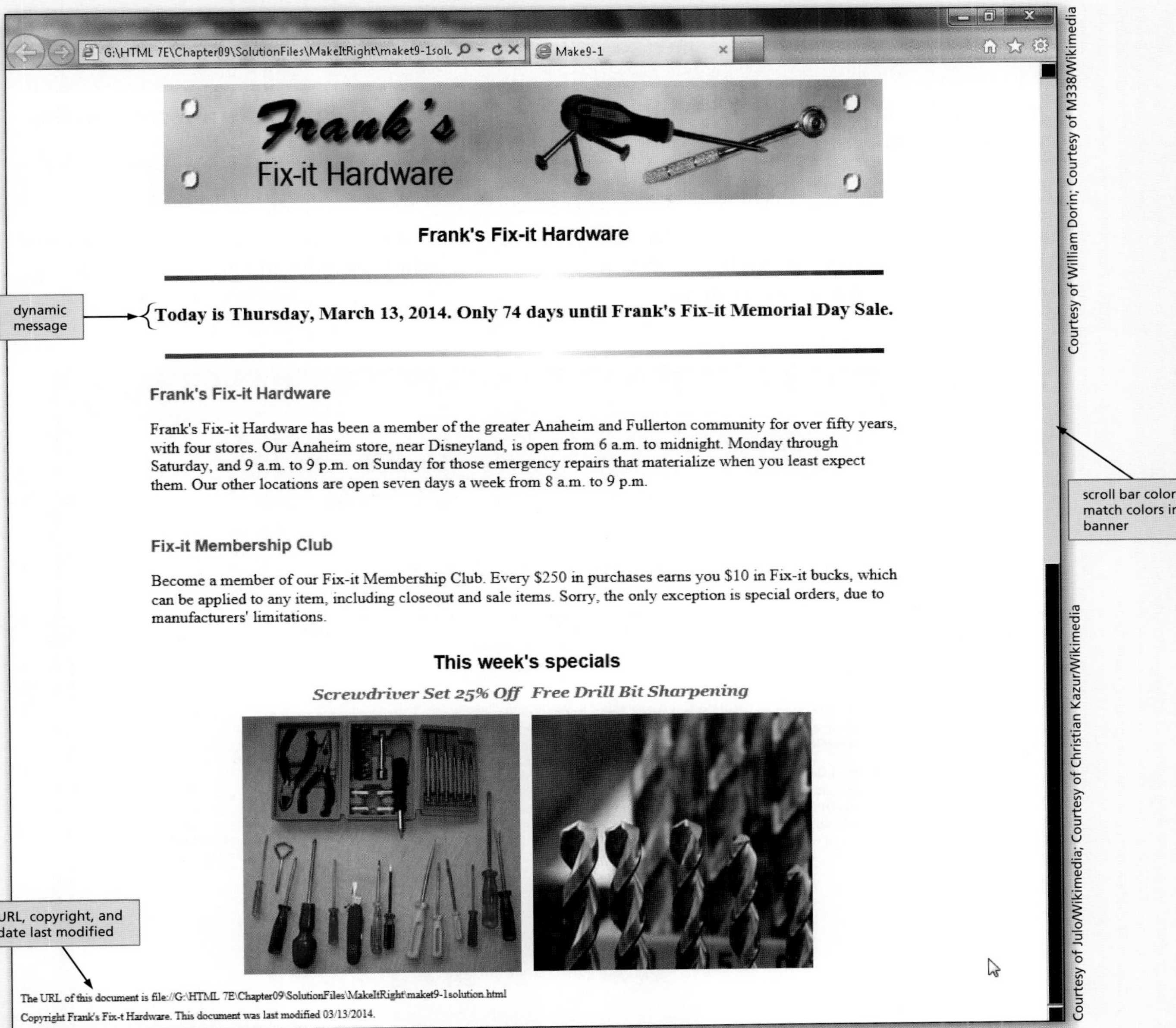

Courtesy of William Dorin; Courtesy of M338/Wikimedia

Courtesy of Julo/Wikimedia; Courtesy of Christian Kazur/Wikimedia

Figure 9–21

In the Lab

Design and/or create a Web page using the guidelines, concepts, and skills presented in this chapter. Labs are listed in order of increasing difficulty.

Lab 1: Creating a Web Page for Dorin and Dodaro Accounting Firm

Instructions: You work for Dorin and Dodaro Accounting Firm and have been asked to create their new Web site. You will create the Web page shown in Figure 9–22, which includes adding a dynamic message and changing the color of the scroll bar.

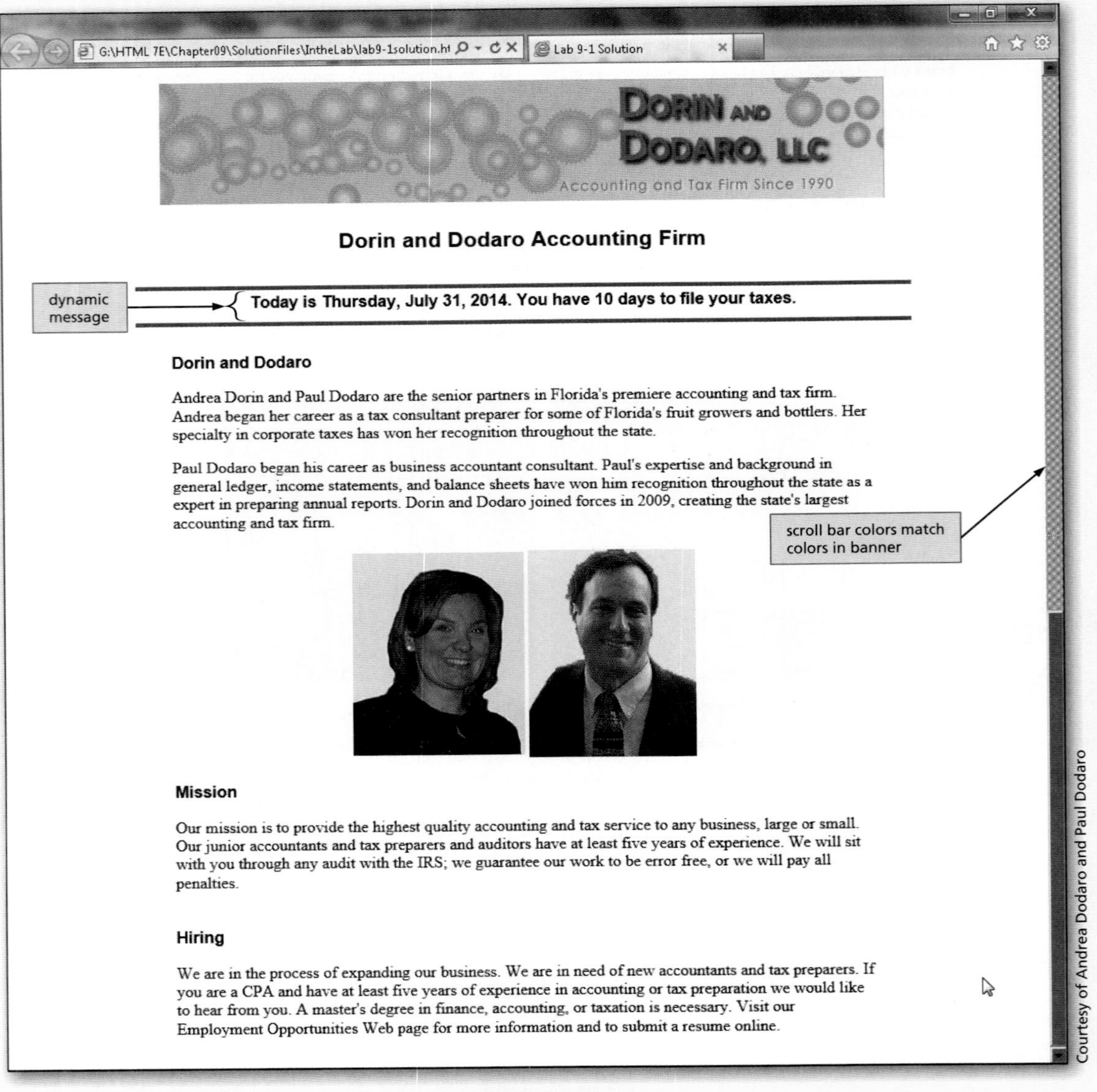

Figure 9–22

Perform the following tasks:

1. Start Notepad++ and open the lab9-1.html file from the Chapter09\IntheLab folder of the Data Files for Students. Save the file as lab9-1solution.html.
2. Start a new <script> section in the <head> section under the <title> tag. Write a JavaScript user-defined function to change the scroll bar colors called scrollColor(). Use the code in Table 9–21 on page HTML 429 as a guide, and use the following color values for the scroll bar face and track colors:

   face color: #857040

   track color: #f4efe9
3. Insert a <div> container using the id taxDay, and the CSS class, taxmessage. Insert this <div> between the hrimg-red.gif <img> dividers.
4. Write a JavaScript user-defined function called taxMsg() to calculate the date until taxes are due. Use the code in Tables 9–15, 9–17, and 9–19 on pages HTML 422, 425, and 427 as a guide. Ask your instructor for which date to use, April 15th or the end of a quarter. Have the message display as follows: Today is Day, Month, Year. You have N days to file your taxes. Replace Day, Month, and Year with the current date information, and N should be the number of days until the date taxes are due.
5. Add the proper event handlers to the <body> tag to call the scrollColor() and taxMsg() user-defined functions when the Web page loads.
6. Save the completed HTML file, validate it, and test it using your browser. If an error occurs, check your code and save and test again.
7. Submit the completed HTML file and Web page in the format specified by your instructor.

In the Lab

Lab 2: Tao Health Foods

Instructions: You are the Web developer at Tao Health Foods. The company is opening a new store and wants to announce the grand opening on their Web site. You decide to add a dynamic announcement to count down to the grand opening. You decide to use a drop-down menu to link to other pages of information. To make the Web page more colorful you change the color of the scroll bar. At the bottom of the Web page you want to add URL information with the date last modified. The Web page should appear as in Figure 9–23 on the next page.

Continued >

In the Lab *continued*

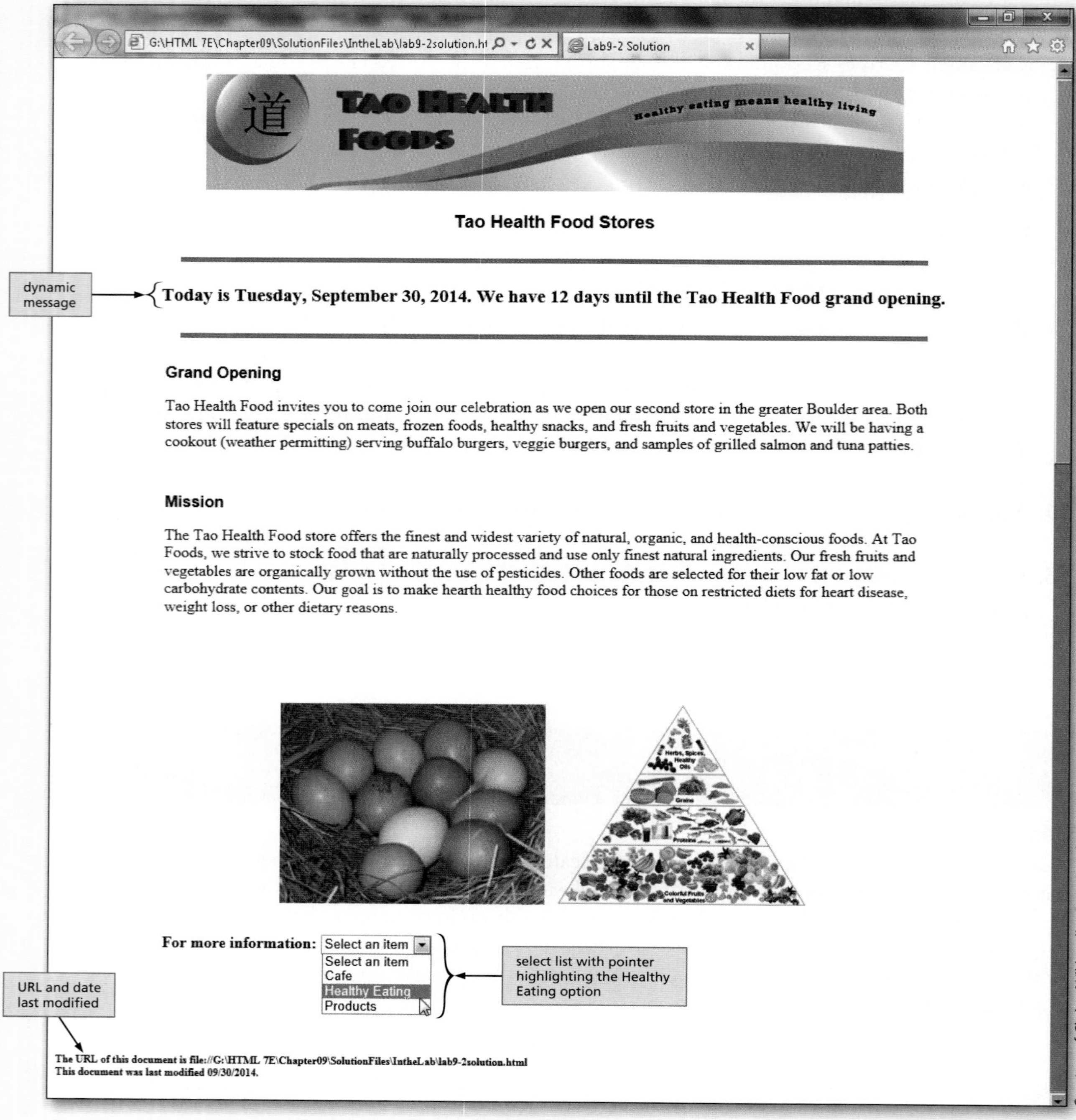

G:\HTML 7E\Chapter09\SolutionFiles\IntheLab\lab9-2solution.ht
Lab9-2 Solution

TAO HEALTH FOODS
Healthy eating means healthy living

Tao Health Food Stores

dynamic message

Today is Tuesday, September 30, 2014. We have 12 days until the Tao Health Food grand opening.

Grand Opening

Tao Health Food invites you to come join our celebration as we open our second store in the greater Boulder area. Both stores will feature specials on meats, frozen foods, healthy snacks, and fresh fruits and vegetables. We will be having a cookout (weather permitting) serving buffalo burgers, veggie burgers, and samples of grilled salmon and tuna patties.

Mission

The Tao Health Food store offers the finest and widest variety of natural, organic, and health-conscious foods. At Tao Foods, we strive to stock food that are naturally processed and use only finest natural ingredients. Our fresh fruits and vegetables are organically grown without the use of pesticides. Other foods are selected for their low fat or low carbohydrate contents. Our goal is to make hearth healthy food choices for those on restricted diets for heart disease, weight loss, or other dietary reasons.

For more information: Select an item
Select an item
Cafe
Healthy Eating
Products

select list with pointer highlighting the Healthy Eating option

URL and date last modified

The URL of this document is file://G:\HTML 7E\Chapter09\SolutionFiles\IntheLab\lab9-2solution.html
This document was last modified 09/30/2014.

Figure 9–23

Courtesy of Nyo/Wikimedia

Courtesy of Christa/Wikimedia; Courtesy of Spmallare/Wikimedia

Perform the following tasks:

1. Start Notepad++ and open the lab9-2.html file from the Chapter09\IntheLab folder of the Data Files for Students, and save the file as lab2-1solution.html.
2. Start a new <script> section in the <head> section, on the line following the <title> tag, for four user-defined functions. Write a JavaScript function to change the scroll bar colors called healthFoodScroll(). Use the code in Table 9–21 as a guide, and use the following color values for the scroll bar face and track colors:

   face color: #e88028

   track color: #d15900
3. Using the code in Table 9–24 on page HTML 431 as a guide, write a JavaScript function called menuLinks() that uses the <select> list infoMenu to go to a different Web page.
4. Enter the HTML code to create a <div> tag with an id attribute of displayCountDown between the two orange divider line images, hrimg-healthy.gif.
5. Write a JavaScript user-defined function called grandOpening() to take the current date and calculate the number of days until the grand opening. Use a future date associated with the current date in your code. The script code should display a dynamic message, as shown in Figure 9–23.
6. Before the closing </body> tag, enter the HTML code to create a container tag of your choice with an id attribute of displayCopyRight.
7. Using the code in Table 9–27 on page HTML 432, write the JavaScript user-defined function to display a copyright message and the date the Web page was last modified.
8. Add the event handler in the appropriate HTML tag to call the healthFoodScroll(), grandOpening(), and copyRight() functions when the Web page loads. Add the onChange() event handler to call the menuLinks() function in the <select> tag when the user selects an item from the drop-down menu.
9. Save the completed HTML file, validate it, and test it using your browser. If an error occurs, check your code and save and test again.
10. Submit the completed HTML file and Web page in the format specified by your instructor.

In the Lab

Lab 3: World Travel Expo Web Page

Instructions: You are the Web developer for World Travel and have been asked to update their Web page for their annual World Travel Expo. You will create a Web page, shown in Figure 9–24, that announces the upcoming World Travel exposition.

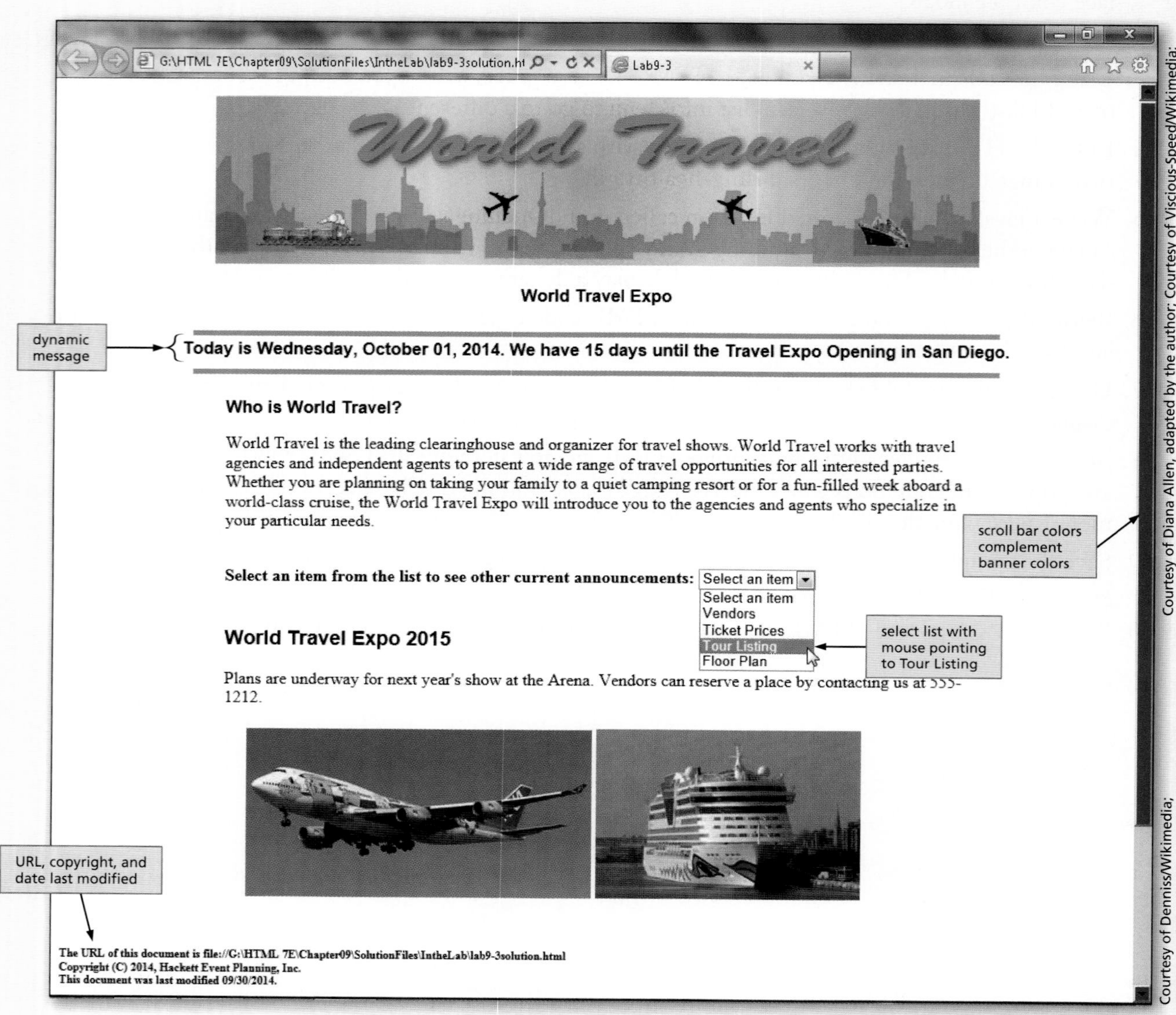

Figure 9–24

Perform the following tasks:

1. Start Notepad++ and open the lab9-3.html file from the Chapter09\IntheLab folder. Save the file as lab9-3solution.html.
2. Using the techniques learned in this chapter, write the JavaScript code to create a dynamic message with a countdown, change the scroll bar color, and use the selectedIndex in the <select> tag to link to new Web pages. The menu links are Vendors, Ticket Prices, Tour Listing, and Floor Plan. In addition, add the URL, a copyright notice, and the date the Web page was last modified. Use a future date near the current date for this lab. Use #20409a for the scroll bar face color and #ffde20 for the scroll bar track color.
3. Save the completed HTML file, validate it, and test it using your browser. If an error occurs, check your code and save and test again.
4. Submit the completed HTML file and Web page in the format specified by your instructor.

Cases and Places

Apply your creative thinking and problem-solving skills to design and implement a solution.

Note: To complete these assignments, you may be required to use the Data Files for Students. See the inside back cover of this book for instructions on downloading the Data Files for Students, or contact your instructor for information about accessing the required files.

1: Learning about Browsers

Academic

Pick one of the following browsers: Internet Explorer, Netscape, Firefox, Chrome, Safari, Opera, or the Mozilla project. Research and develop a brief history (include a time line of versions) of your chosen browser. Create a PowerPoint presentation lasting around five minutes detailing what you found. Start with a time line with the name of the original browser and include the various versions over the years along with when they were released (include versions for the Mac OS, if they exist). Describe the improvements provided with each upgrade for each browser. In your research, include which of the various W3C specifications are supported by that browser (XHTML, HTML5, XML, etc). As noted in this chapter, only Internet Explorer allows a programmer to dynamically modify the scroll bar. Search forums or Web sites to find discussions on why the browser you chose will or will not allow access to the scroll bar. Did your research reveal any other parts of the browser that can or cannot be modified?

2: Creating a Personal Web Page

Personal

Many families have begun sharing information via the Internet. Consider your own family and friends, and then use the concepts and techniques presented in this chapter to create a Web page that announces a birthday, wedding, anniversary, family reunion, or other special family event. Use a dynamic message to display the current date and the number of days to the event. Make your page long enough (perhaps add several photos) so that the scroll bar is active and write the JavaScript user-defined function to change the scroll bar color. Create a drop-down menu to link to other Web pages that you have created or that already exist, such as links to family or friends who have Web pages. Add a copyright notice and add the date the page was last modified at the bottom in small print. Be sure to check the spelling and grammar on the Web pages that you create.

Continued >

Cases and Places *continued*

3: Creating a Web Page for the Green Bay Shopper

Professional

As a summer intern for the Green Bay Shopper (a local weekly ad paper), you have been asked to create the home page for the shopper. You can use the case9-3banner.jpg as the page banner. You can use the four ad images on the home page to give the page enough length so that the scroll bar displays. Use paragraphs and lists provided in the case9-3lorem_ipsum text file for text copy in the pages.

The home page should have a drop-down menu with links to real estate, coupons, and personal ad Web pages. The home page should change the scroll bar face color to #999999 and the track color to #cccccc. Create a dynamic message indicating the number of days to either a fall event (Halloween, Thanksgiving, or Christmas) or a spring event (Valentine's Day, St. Patrick's Day, or Memorial Day), placed between two divider lines (case9-3divider.jpg). Add a copyright message with the date the Web page was last modified that displays in the status bar of Internet Explorer.

For the real estate Web page, use the three house photos and a paragraph of the lorem ipsum text as the description of each house. For the coupons page, create a 2×2 table that displays goods in one column and a percent discount in the other column. For the personal ads, just create a single column table with four rows and place a paragraph of the lorem ipsum text in each row.

10 Creating Pop-Up Windows, Adding Scrolling Messages, and Validating Forms

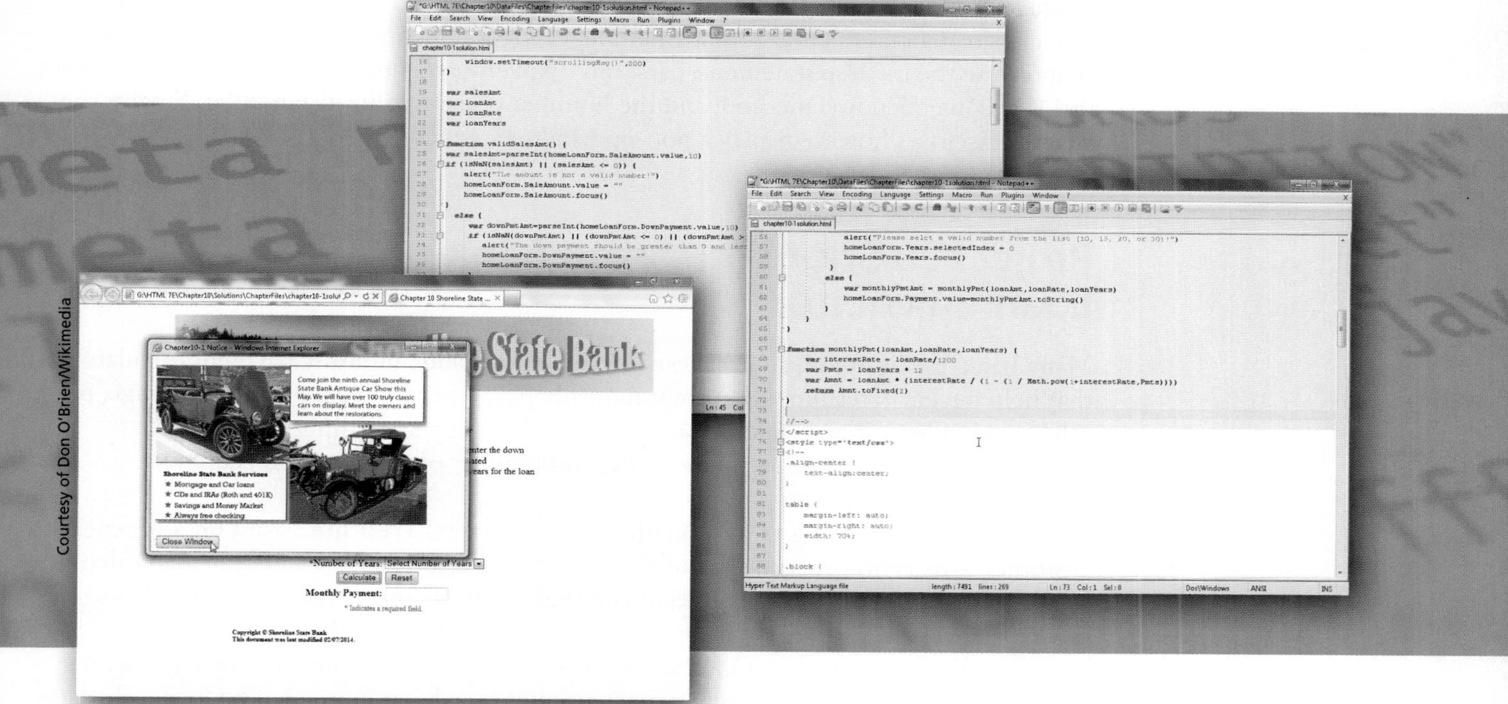
Courtesy of Don O'Brien/Wikimedia

Objectives

You will have mastered the material in this chapter when you can:

- Write a JavaScript user-defined function to display a scrolling message
- Write a JavaScript user-defined function to validate form data
- Write a JavaScript user-defined function to calculate a total loan amount based on a sales amount and down payment
- Write a JavaScript user-defined function to calculate monthly loan payments
- Define if and if...else statements, conditionals, and operands
- Write a JavaScript user-defined function to format output in a text field
- Describe how to open a pop-up window

10 Creating Pop-Up Windows, Adding Scrolling Messages, and Validating Forms

Introduction

In Chapter 9, you learned how to integrate JavaScript into an HTML5 document using variables and objects, and how to write JavaScript user-defined functions called by event handlers. This chapter reinforces these skills and shows you how to create a scrolling message that displays a text message in a form text field, and how to use JavaScript to validate the data users enter into forms. The validation techniques discussed in this chapter use the if…else statement; parseInt(), parseFloat(), and isNaN() built-in functions; the Math object's pow() method; and the Number object's toFixed() method. Finally, the chapter discusses how to display a pop-up window.

Project — Shoreline State Bank Loan Calculator

Many bank, credit union, and real estate Web sites include monthly payment calculators that help buyers determine what their monthly payments will be for a car, mortgage, or other type of loan. These calculators generally allow buyers to input basic loan information — loan amount, interest rate, and number of years — that is used to estimate the monthly payment.

Shoreline State Bank has decided to improve its Web site based on a recent customer-satisfaction survey. One of the most-requested items was a simple loan calculator that would allow customers to estimate their monthly mortgage payments. As one of the Web developers, you have been assigned to create this new Web page.

You decide to create an interactive form that allows customers to enter the selling price of the house and the down payment amount in a dollar amount. The form calculates the mortgage loan amount and then allows the user to enter the loan interest rate and select the number of years for the loan from a drop-down menu. When the user clicks the Calculate button, the monthly mortgage payment displays. A Reset button allows the user to restart and try different values. You also decide to add a simple scrolling message, in which the bank says that some used car loans can be made for 100% of the purchase price. In addition, the bank wants a pop-up window to promote the upcoming antique auto show and to list some of their popular bank services. Figure 10–1 shows the pop-up window, the scrolling message, and the user input form for the loan calculator.

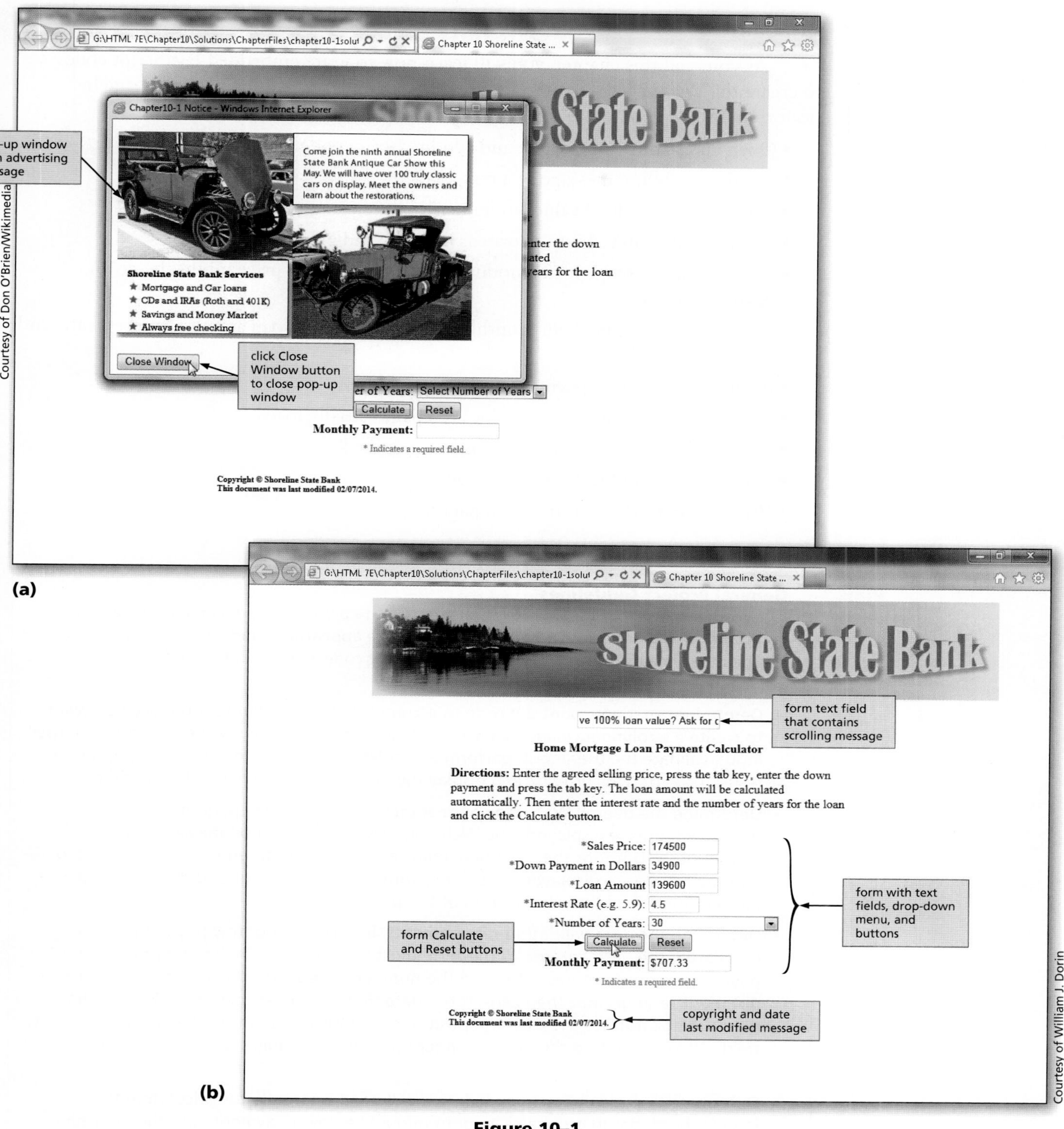

G:\HTML 7E\Chapter10\Solutions\ChapterFiles\chapter10-1solut
Chapter 10 Shoreline State ...
Chapter10-1 Notice - Windows Internet Explorer
pop-up window with advertising message
Come join the ninth annual Shoreline State Bank Antique Car Show this May. We will have over 100 truly classic cars on display. Meet the owners and learn about the restorations.
Shoreline State Bank Services
Mortgage and Car loans
CDs and IRAs (Roth and 401K)
Savings and Money Market
Always free checking
Close Window
click Close Window button to close pop-up window
Select Number of Years
Calculate
Reset
Monthly Payment:
* Indicates a required field.
Copyright © Shoreline State Bank
This document was last modified 02/07/2014.
Courtesy of Don O'Brien/Wikimedia
(a)
Shoreline State Bank
ve 100% loan value? Ask for c
form text field that contains scrolling message
Home Mortgage Loan Payment Calculator
Directions: Enter the agreed selling price, press the tab key, enter the down payment and press the tab key. The loan amount will be calculated automatically. Then enter the interest rate and the number of years for the loan and click the Calculate button.
*Sales Price: 174500
*Down Payment in Dollars 34900
*Loan Amount 139600
*Interest Rate (e.g. 5.9): 4.5
*Number of Years: 30
form Calculate and Reset buttons
Calculate
Reset
Monthly Payment: $707.33
form with text fields, drop-down menu, and buttons
* Indicates a required field.
Copyright © Shoreline State Bank
This document was last modified 02/07/2014.
copyright and date last modified message
(b)
Courtesy of William J. Dorin

Figure 10–1

Overview

As you read this chapter, you will learn how to write embedded JavaScript code to create the Web pages shown in Figures 10–1a and 10–1b on the previous page by performing these general tasks:

- Open an existing HTML file and add JavaScript code.
- Create a scrolling message in a text field.
- Convert the text field values to numeric values using built-in functions.
- Validate data entered into a form as numeric and greater than zero.
- Calculate a mortgage loan amount based on the selling price minus the down payment amount.
- Calculate a mortgage loan monthly payment based on loan amount, interest rate, and number of years.
- Format the monthly payment to display as currency.
- Open a pop-up window when the Web page initially loads.
- Display the date the Web page was last modified.
- Save, validate, and test the Web pages.
- Print the HTML code and Web pages.

Plan Ahead

General Project Guidelines

When adding JavaScript or any scripting language to a Web page document, the actions you perform and decisions you make will affect the appearance and characteristics of the finished Web page. Before you write the JavaScript code, you should follow these general guidelines:

- **Determine what you want the code to accomplish.** For this chapter's project, you want to create a scrolling message in a text field, add a pop-up window, create a form for user input, validate the user input, perform a calculation based on the user input, output a result formatted as currency, and display the date the Web page was last modified.
- **Determine the overall Web page appearance.** When the Web page first loads, a pop-up window is displayed. The Web page also includes a text message that scrolls continuously. Data for the mortgage loan calculation is entered in a form, validated, and the results are displayed in currency format. The copyright and date the page was last modified display at the bottom of the page.
- **Determine the data validation requirements.** Before the monthly payment can be calculated, the data entered in the form must be validated. The selling price, down payment amount, interest rate, and the number of years for the loan must be numeric, not blank, and greater than zero. If the data does not meet these criteria, an alert message box notifies the user and positions the insertion point in the appropriate text field. When validating the down payment amount, it should not be greater than the selling price.
- **Determine the calculations needed.** You will need a formula for calculating the loan amount, based on a sales amount minus the down payment, and the monthly payment. The formulas are given later in the chapter.

When necessary, more specific details concerning the above guidelines are presented at appropriate points in the chapter. The chapter will also identify the actions performed and decisions made regarding these guidelines during the creation of the Web page shown in Figure 10–1.

Inserting a Scrolling Message on a Web Page

A simple way to provide a Web site visitor with information is to add a scrolling text message to a Web page. Companies often use scrolling messages on their Web sites to highlight breaking news, key products, or special promotions. A scrolling text message can appear either in a text field within the Web page or on the status bar in the browser window. Because visitors to a Web page often do not look at the status bar, placing the scrolling message in a prominent place on the Web page is a better location.

A scrolling message has four basic components:

- The display object (a form text field)
- The text message to scroll in the text field
- The position of the next character in the text message
- A time delay

The **display object** identifies where the scrolling message is displayed, which, in this project, is in a form text field. The scrolling **message** is a text string assigned to a variable. The text string is what the user sees when the message is displayed. The **position** is the location of the next character in the text string. The **delay** regulates the speed in which the characters display in the text field.

The first step in creating the scrolling message for the Shoreline State Bank Web page is to create the object that will display the scrolling message. The most common object to display a scrolling message is a text field. The text field must be part of a form object. In the Shoreline State Bank Web page, you will place the form and text field below the banner.

You must name the form using the id attribute and the text field using the name attribute. The <form> id serves as the object and the <input> name serves as a property to be used in the JavaScript code to assign the message string to the text field. The size attribute of the text field indicates the display width of the text field.

BTW
Accessibility Issue
The Web Content Accessibility Guidelines (WCAG) 2.0 of W3.org recommends that scrolling messages have a mechanism to allow the user to stop and start the scrolling. See Appendix C for more information. Stopping text in an <input> text field has unpredictable results. Chapter 11, however, shows how to stop an image scrolling across a page.

To Open an Existing HTML File

As in Chapter 9, you will integrate JavaScript into an existing HTML document. The chapter10-1.html file has an embedded CSS <style> section. The following steps open the chapter10-1.html file included in the Data Files for Students.

1. Start Notepad++, and, if necessary, maximize the window.
2. Click View on the menu bar. If the word wrap command does not have a check mark next to it, click word wrap.
3. With a USB flash drive plugged in to your computer, click File on the menu bar and then click Open on the File menu.
4. Navigate to the Chapter10\ChapterFiles folder on the USB drive.
5. Double-click chapter10-1.html in the list of files to display the HTML code for the chapter10-1.html Web page (Figure 10–2 on the next page).

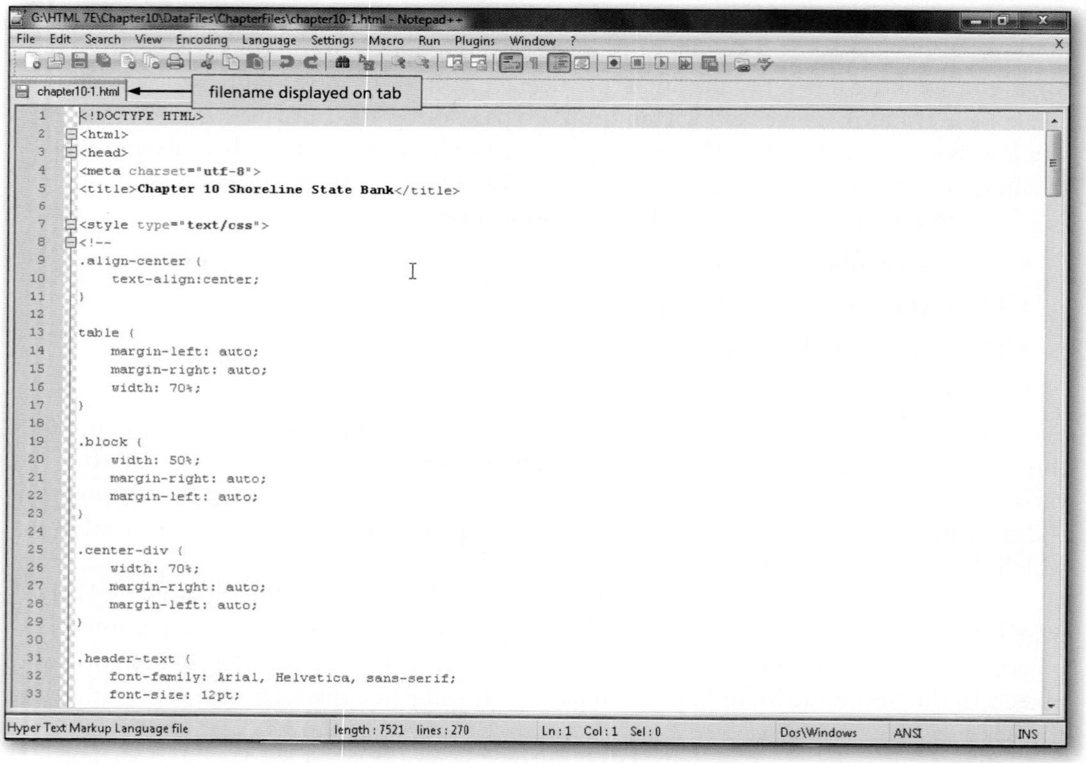

Figure 10–2

To Create a Form Text Field to Display a Scrolling Message

The following step creates a form and a form text field to display a scrolling message. Table 10–1 shows the HTML code to create the form and a text field for the scrolling message.

Table 10–1 Code to Create a Form and a Text Field

Line	Code
67	`<form id="msgForm">`
68	`<p style="text-align:center"><input type="text" name="scrollingMsg" size="25" /></p>`
69	`</form>`

Line 67 starts the form and uses the id attribute to give the form the unique name, msgForm. Line 68 starts with a <p> tag and an inline style that centers the text field. The form input tag is a text type, which creates a text field that can receive data. The text field is named scrollingMsg and is set to a size of 25. Line 69 is the closing </form> tag.

1

- Click the blank line 67 below the <div class="center-div"> tag.
- Enter the HTML code shown in Table 10–1 on the previous page to create the form and text field (Figure 10–3).

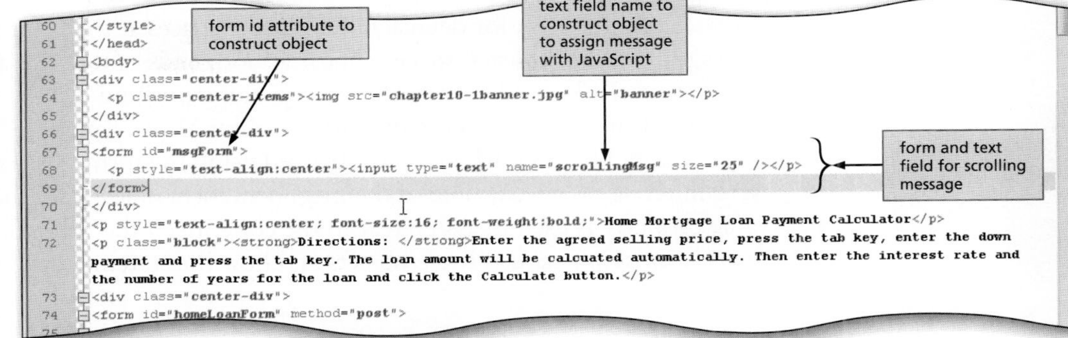

Figure 10–3

Q&A

Can a scrolling message be placed in other Web elements in addition to text fields?

Besides a text field, any object that can have values assigned to it, such as a button, the status bar, or a title bar can be used to display a scrolling text message.

Creating the scrollingMsg() User-Defined Function

The scrollingMsg() function requires two variables and performs five tasks. The two variables are:

- The adMsg variable represents the message.
- The beginPos variable represents the current character in the text message.

The five tasks the scrollingMsg() function performs are:

- Assigns the string message to the display object (which, in this project, is the text field)
- Increments the beginPos variable by 1 to place the next character in the text message in the display object
- Uses an if statement to test for the end of the message
- If the text has scrolled to the end of the message, starts over with the first character
- Makes the display continuous and regulates the speed of the display using the setTimeout() method set to 200 milliseconds

Table 10–2 shows the code to begin the JavaScript section, declare and initialize the adMsg and beginPos variables, declare the scrollingMsg() function, and assign the first characters of the message to the text field.

BTW

Placement of Scrolling Text

Although scrolling text can be assigned to a <div> tag container using the innerHTML property, the <div> tag container does not allow for as much control as a form object like a text field or button.

Table 10–2 Code to Begin the scrollingMsg() Function

Line	Code
6	<script type="text/javascript">
7	<!--Hide from old browsers
8	var adMsg=" ** Did you know some used cars can have 100% loan value? Ask for details! ** "
9	var beginPos=0
10	function scrollingMsg() {
11	msgForm.scrollingMsg.value=adMsg.substring(beginPos, adMsg.length)+adMsg.substring(0,beginPos)

Lines 6 and 7 start the <script> section of the Web page file. Line 8 declares the adMsg variable and assigns the message string, "** Did you know some used cars can have 100% loan value? Ask for details! **" to it. The spaces at the beginning and end of the message string ensure that spaces appear at both ends of the message. Line 9 declares the beginPos variable, used to indicate the beginning position of the text string, and initializes it to zero. Line 10 declares the function scrollingMsg(). Line 11 assigns the message string to the text field object, which is constructed using the form (msgForm), the text field object (scrollingMsg) as an attribute of the msgForm form object, and the value property. The value property is used to assign text to the contents of the text field. Figure 10–4 illustrates the relationship between these objects and how the statement is derived.

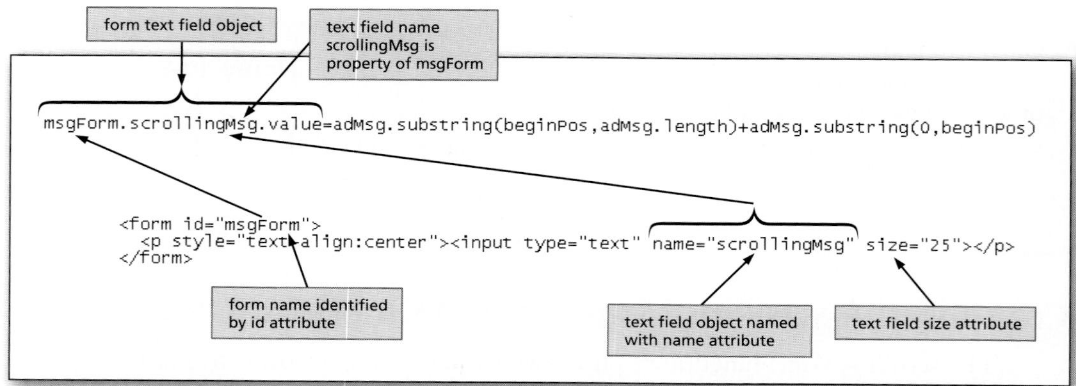

Figure 10–4

The rest of the assignment statement in line 11 uses the substring() method and concatenates the remainder of the adMsg variable to the beginning of the adMsg variable. As you learned in Chapter 9, the substring() method needs two parameters (x,y), where x is the starting point of the string and y is the location of the last character needed. This statement tells the scrollingMsg() function to assign the next character in the string message to the text field, to make the message appear as if it is scrolling.

To Create the scrollingMsg() User-Defined Function

The following step creates the scrollingMsg() user-defined function and defines its variables.

1

- Click line 6, the blank line below the <title> tag.
- Enter the JavaScript code shown in Table 10–2 on the previous page to enter the beginning script tags and define the variables used in the scrolling message, indenting as shown. Press the ENTER key to position the insertion point on line 12 (Figure 10–5).

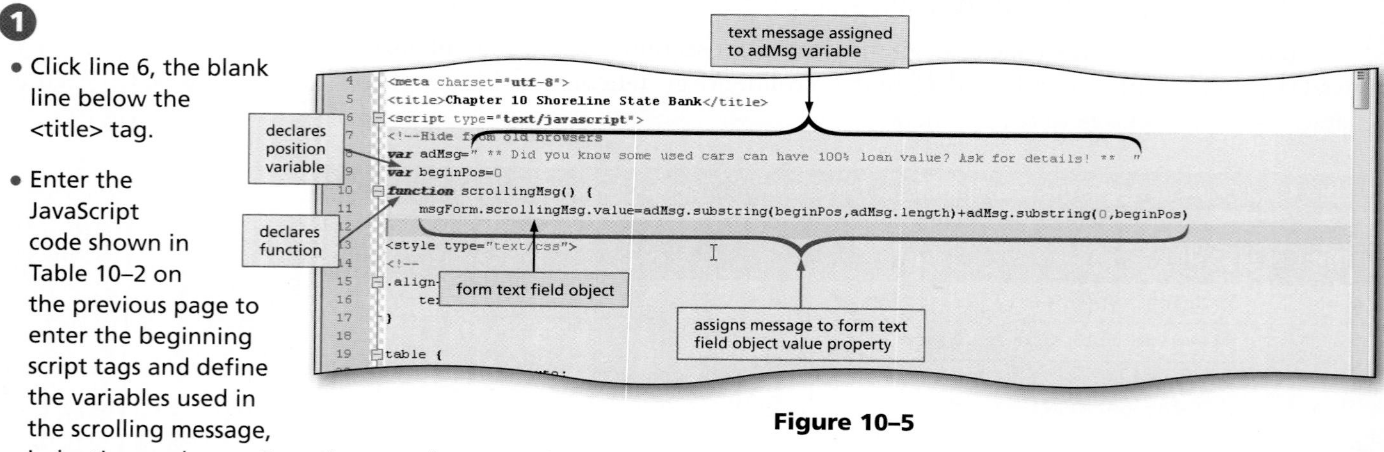

Figure 10–5

Q&A

How can the scrolling message be formatted?

When using an <input> text field, you can format the text using an inline style.

Incrementing the Position Locator Variable After declaring the scrollingMsg() function, the next step is to increment the beginPos variable and append the next character from the message string to the text field. To cause the message to scroll in the text field, the position locator variable (beginPos) must be incremented by one. Table 10–3 describes the various ways JavaScript statements can be used to increment variables.

Table 10–3 Incrementing a Variable

Statement	Explanation
`variable=variable+1`	Executes the expression on the right side of the equal sign and assigns the result to a variable on the left side
`variable+=1`	Adds the number after the equal sign to a variable
`variable++`	Adds 1 to a variable; increments after the assignment
`++variable`	Adds 1 to a variable before the assignment

Once incremented, the new value of the position locator variable, beginPos, allows the substring() method in line 11 to extract the next character in the message string and append it to the end of the message in the text field.

To Enter the Code to Increment the Position Locator Variable

The following step enters the code to increment the position counter.

1

- If necessary, click line 12 and indent under the previous line.
- Type `beginPos= beginPos+1` to increment the position locator by one and then press the ENTER key (Figure 10–6).

```
   <!DOCTYPE HTML>
2  <html>
3  <head>
4  <meta charset="utf-8">
5  <title>Chapter 10 Shoreline State Bank</title>
6  <script type="text/javascript">
7  <!--Hide from old browsers
8  var adMsg=" ** Did you know some used cars can have 100% loan value? Ask for details! **  "
9  var beginPos=0
10 function scrollingMsg() {
11     msgForm.scrollingMsg.value=adMsg.substring(beginPos,adMsg.length)+adMsg.substring(0,beginPos)
12     beginPos=beginPos+1
13     
14 <style type="text/css">
15 <!--
16 .align-center {
17     text-align:center;
18 }
19 
20 table {
```


Figure 10–6

Q&A Why did we write the increment statement this way instead of using one of the other methods?

This method is the most common and easiest for beginners to understand. In addition, developers should use a format that can be recognized by anyone who might have to modify their code after the initial implementation.

Entering an if Statement After incrementing the position location variable (beginPos) by one, the JavaScript code must determine if the current value of beginPos exceeds the length of the message string. An **if statement** is used to test a condition and then take one or more actions, based on the results of the test. The general form of the if statement is shown in Table 10–4 on the next page. The if statement tests a **condition**, which is any comparison of values that evaluates to true or false. If the result of the comparison is true, the JavaScript code within the braces is executed. If the result of the comparison is false, the code after the closing brace is executed.

BTW

Operands in a Conditional Evaluation
An **operand** is a numerical, string, logical, or object data type or value. Operands must be of the same data type, or you will not get a true comparison result.

Figure 10–7 shows the flowchart that corresponds to an if statement. The if statement determines if the current value of the beginPos variable is greater than the length of the message.

BTW

Spaces Between Operators and Operands
Spaces between an operand and operator are optional. It may be easier to read an expression if spaces are used, but they are not necessary.

Table 10–4 if Statement

General form:	`if (condition) {`
	`    JavaScript statements if condition true`
	`}`

Comment:	where *condition* is the comparison of values. All conditions must be placed in parentheses. If the result of the comparison is true, JavaScript executes the statements between the curly braces. If the result of the comparison is false, the JavaScript statements after the closing brace are executed.

Example:	`if (beginPos>adMsg.length) {`
	`        beginPos=0`
	`}`

As shown in the example in Table 10–4, the conditions use symbols called operators to indicate what type of comparisons should be made between the values. Table 10–5 shows the conditional operators used for comparisons. For more information about conditional operators, see the JavaScript Quick Reference in Appendix G.

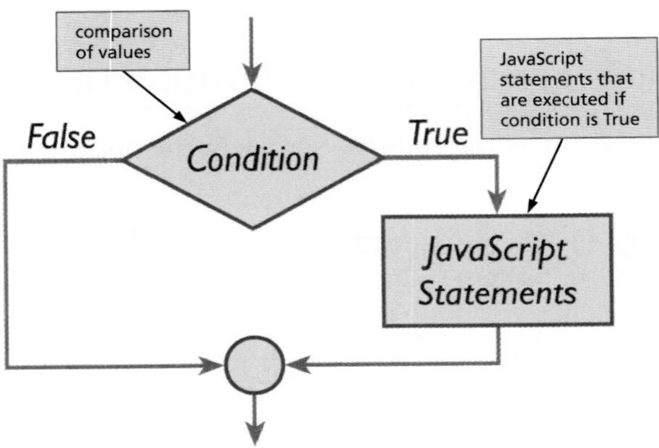

Figure 10–7

BTW

Conditional Operators
Conditional operators are symbols used to compare two values, called operands. The operator compares the two operands and returns a logical value based on whether the comparison is true.

Table 10–5 Conditional Operators

Operators	Example	Results
==	(a==b)	True if a equals b
===	(a=== b)	True if a equals b and the data are of the same type
!=	(a!=b)	True if a does not equal b
!==	(a!==b)	True if a does not equal b and/or the data are not of the same type
>	(a>b)	True if a is greater than b
<	(a<b)	True if a is less than b
>=	(a>=b)	True if a is greater than or equal to b
<=	(a<=b)	True if a is less than or equal to b
&&	(a==b) && (x<y)	True if both conditions are true (a equals b and x is less than y)
||	(a!=b) || (x>=a)	True if either condition is true (a does not equal b or x is greater than or equal to a)
!	!(a<b)	True if a is greater than b; False if a is less than b

The flowchart and sample code shown in Figure 10–8 illustrate how the if statement compares the beginning position variable (beginPos) with the overall length of the message (adMsg.length).

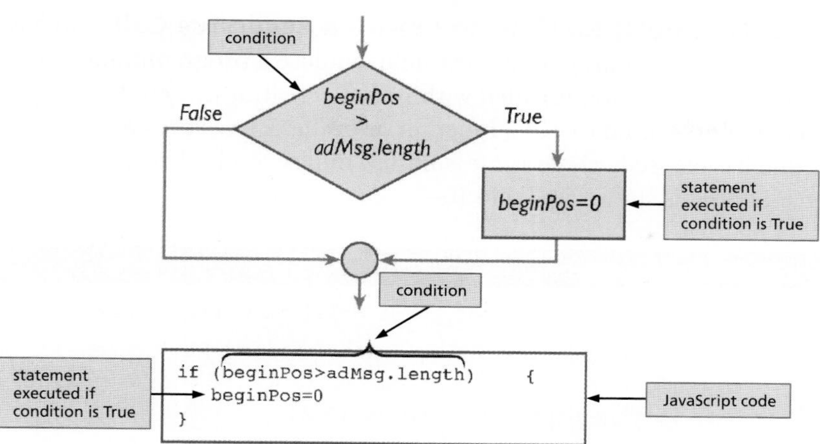

Figure 10–8

If the current value of the beginPos variable exceeds the length of the adMsg variable, the statement assigns the value zero to the beginPos variable. By setting beginPos to zero, the JavaScript code starts over assigning the first character of the string message to the text field, which gives the illusion the text is scrolling in the text field.

To Enter an if Statement

Table 10–6 shows the code to enter an if statement.

Table 10–6 Code to Enter an if Statement

Line	Code
13	`if (beginPos>adMsg.length) {`
14	`   beginPos=0`
15	`}`

The following step enters an if statement.

1

- If necessary, click line 13 and indent under the previous line.
- Enter the code in Table 10–6, indenting as shown, to add the if statement to test the beginPos value, and press the ENTER key (Figure 10–9).

```
   <title>Chapter 10 Shoreline State
6  <script type="text/javascript">
7  <!--Hide from old browsers
8  var adMsg=" ** Did you know some used cars can have 100% loan value? Ask for details! **  "
9  var beginPos=0
10 function scrollingMsg() {
11     msgForm.scrollingMsg.value=adMsg.substring(begi                        ring(0,beginPos)
12     beginPos=beginPos+1
13     if (beginPos>adMsg.length) {
14        beginPos=0
       }

   <style type="text/css">
18 <!--
19 .align-center {
20     text-align:center;
21 }
22
```

insertion point

if statement tests if character position has exceeded length of message

if all characters in message have been used, then start over from beginning character

Figure 10–9

Q&A Do all JavaScript if statements have to be written in this format?

When only one statement follows the condition, like in this example, the statement could have been written as follows: `if (beginPos>adMsg.length) beginPos=0`. Note that the braces have been dropped for just one statement to be executed if the condition is true. If more than one statement needs to be executed, then the braces must be used to create the block of statements.

> **BTW**
> **Recursion**
> In this chapter's project, recursion is used to keep a routine going indefinitely or until some other function is called to stop it. Normally, a recursive function should have a mechanism that terminates the function when it completes its task.

Using the setTimeout() Method to Create a Recursive Call To have the message text scroll continuously in the text field, you use a programming technique called **recursion**, in which a function is called within itself, creating an "endless loop." The setTimeout() method is used to call a function or evaluate an expression after a specified amount of time has elapsed, which is measured in milliseconds. The general form of the setTimeout() method is shown in Table 10–7.

Table 10–7 setTimeout() Method	
General form:	`setTimeout("instruction", time delay in milliseconds)`
Comment:	where *instruction* is any valid JavaScript statement and time delay is expressed in number of milliseconds
Example:	`window.setTimeout("scrollingMsg()",200)`

The recursive call of the scrollingMsg() user-defined function by the setTimeout() method continuously displays characters and regulates the speed of the characters displaying in the text field.

To Add the setTimeout() Method to Create a Recursive Call

The following step adds the setTimeout() method to create a recursive call to the scrollingMsg() function, which will control how fast the characters in the scrolling message are displayed.

1

- If necessary, click line 16 and indent under the previous line of code, type `window.setTimeout ("scrollingMsg()", 200)` to call scrollingMsg() from within itself, and then press the ENTER key.
- Align the insertion point under the function statement, type } on line 17 to close the function, and then press the ENTER key two times (Figure 10–10).

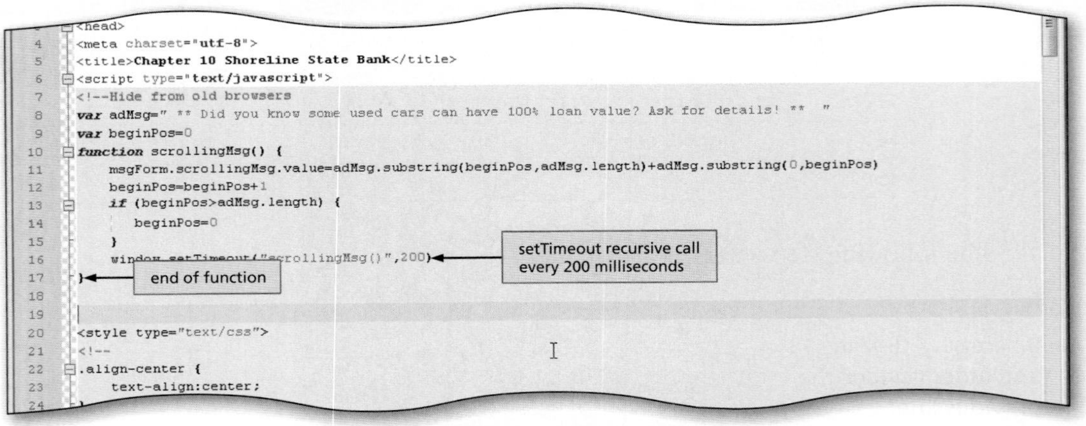

```
   <head>
4  <meta charset="utf-8">
5  <title>Chapter 10 Shoreline State Bank</title>
6  <script type="text/javascript">
7  <!--Hide from old browsers
8  var adMsg=" ** Did you know some used cars can have 100% loan value? Ask for details! **  "
9  var beginPos=0
10 function scrollingMsg() {
11     msgForm.scrollingMsg.value=adMsg.substring(beginPos,adMsg.length)+adMsg.substring(0,beginPos)
12     beginPos=beginPos+1
13     if (beginPos>adMsg.length) {
14        beginPos=0
15     }
16     window.setTimeout("scrollingMsg()",200)
17 }
18
19
20 <style type="text/css">
21 <!--
22 .align-center {
23     text-align:center;
24
```

setTimeout recursive call every 200 milliseconds

end of function

Figure 10–10

> **Q&A**
> How do you know how fast to make the scrolling?
> The best way is to try several different speeds and ask potential users to look at it and indicate their preference.

> **Q&A**
> What if you changed the number from 200 to 2000?
> The text would display one character every two seconds and would be too boring to watch, you would lose the interest of your user.

To Complete a JavaScript Section

The following steps enter the JavaScript code to complete the <script> section.

1. If necessary, click line 19, and position the insertion point to line up under the <script> tag on line 6.
2. Type `//-->` to close the comment to hide the JavaScript and then press the ENTER key.
3. Type `</script>` to close the <script> section, but do not press the ENTER key (Figure 10–11).

Q&A

Can I use one hyphen and the greater than sign to end the comment?

No, it must be two hyphens and the greater than sign to close the comment.

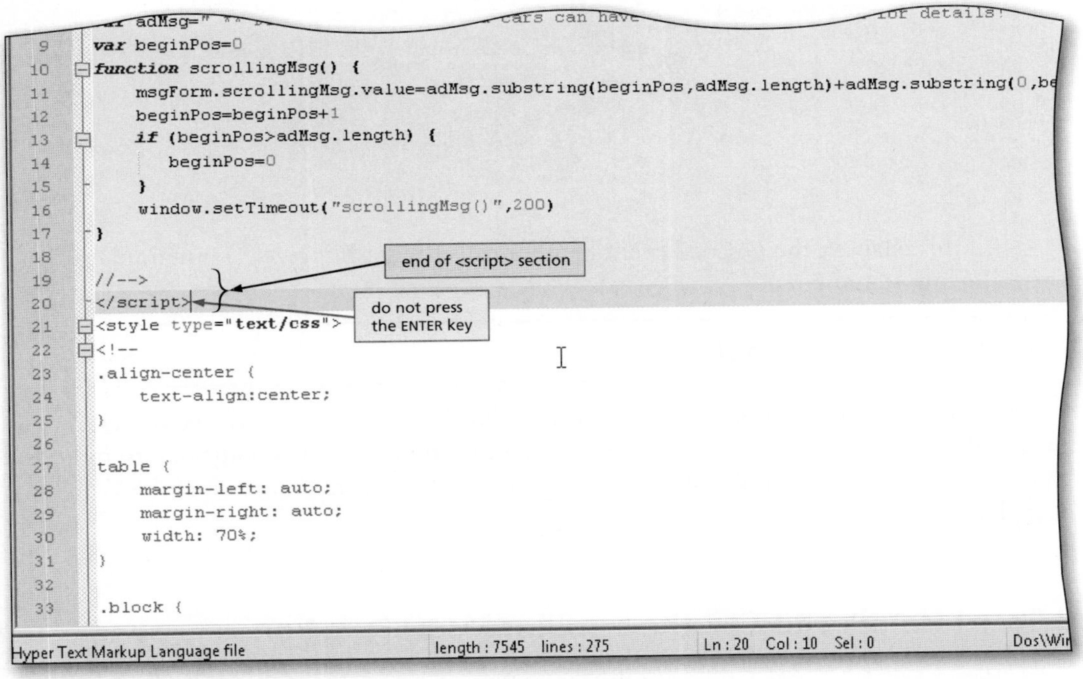

```
9   var beginPos=0
10  function scrollingMsg() {
11      msgForm.scrollingMsg.value=adMsg.substring(beginPos,adMsg.length)+adMsg.substring(0,be
12      beginPos=beginPos+1
13      if (beginPos>adMsg.length) {
14          beginPos=0
15      }
16      window.setTimeout("scrollingMsg()",200)
17  }
18
19  //-->
20  </script>
21  <style type="text/css">
22  <!--
23  .align-center {
24      text-align:center;
25  }
26
27  table {
28      margin-left: auto;
29      margin-right: auto;
30      width: 70%;
31  }
32
33  .block {
```

end of <script> section

do not press the ENTER key

Hyper Text Markup Language file | length : 7545 lines : 275 | Ln : 20 Col : 10 Sel : 0 | Dos\Wi

Figure 10–11

Adding an Onload Event Handler

The last step in adding a scrolling message to a Web page is to add an event handler to start the scrolling message when the Web page loads. As discussed in Chapter 9, an **event** is an action, such as a mouse click or a window loading. An **event handler** is a way to associate that action with a function. The event handler that starts the scrolling message is the onLoad event handler and is placed in the <body> tag.

The JavaScript standard uses both uppercase and lowercase in spelling event handlers, as shown in Table 10–8 on the next page. To be HTML5 compliant and to pass HTML5 validation, this text follows the HTML5 standards. Because HTML5 allows for mixed-case attributes, and the JavaScript standard for event handlers is mixed case, this text will use the mixed-case event handlers.

Table 10–8 shows some of the event handlers and the associated objects. As the table indicates, event handlers can be used only with certain objects. For example, the onClick event handler is used to trigger JavaScript code when a user clicks a button or link, while the onLoad event handler is used to trigger JavaScript code when a document is loaded into the browser window. For more information about event handlers, see the JavaScript Quick Reference in Appendix G.

Table 10–8 Objects and Associated Event Handlers

Object	Event Handler
button	`onClick, onDblClick`
document	`onLoad, onUnload`
form	`onSubmit, onReset, onBlur, onKeydown, onKeypress, onKeyup`
hyperlink	`onClick, onMouseover, onMouseout, onDblClick, onMousemove, onMousedown`
image	`onLoad, onAbort, onError, onMousemove, onMousedown`
input box	`onBlur, onChange, onFocus, onKeypress, onKeyup, onKeydown`
Submit button	`onClick`
window	`onLoad, onUnload, onBlur, onFocus`

In this chapter, the onLoad event handler calls the scrollingMsg() function, using the following statement:

```
onLoad="scrollingMsg()"
```

where onLoad is the event handler and the scrollingMsg() function is the code that is executed as the result of the event. The statement is entered in the <body> tag to indicate that the onLoad event handler should call the scrollingMsg() function when the Web page loads.

To Enter the onLoad Event Handler to Call the scrollingMsg() Function

The following step enters the onLoad event handler to call the scrollingMsg() function.

- Click to the right of the y in body in line 76.
- Press the SPACEBAR once.
- Type `onLoad="scrollingMsg();"` to add the event handler and do not press the ENTER key (Figure 10–12).

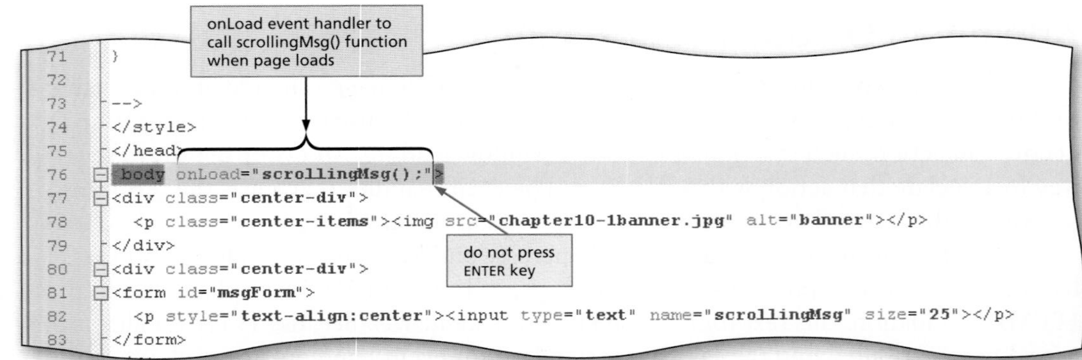

Figure 10–12

To Save an HTML File and Test a Web Page

After completing a section of JavaScript code, you should test your Web page to ensure the code works. You should not continue with the next section until you are sure the scrolling message works correctly. With the code for the scrollingMsg() function complete and the onLoad event handler added to call the function when the Web page loads, you should save the HTML file and test the Web page. The following steps save the HTML file and then test the Web page.

1. Click File on the menu bar, click Save As, and then type `chapter9-10solution.html` in the File name text box (do not press the ENTER key).

2. Navigate to the storage device and folder (Chapter10\ChapterFiles) where you save your Data Files and then click the Save button in the Save As dialog box to save the file.

3. Open Internet Explorer and type `G:\Chapter10\ChapterFiles\chapter10-1solution.html` in the Address box.

4. Press ENTER to display the Web page. If a security message appears at the bottom of the browser window, click the Allow blocked content button. (If you are running Internet Explorer 8 or lower, your security message may be different.) The message should start scrolling in the form text field (Figure 10–13).

5. Before proceeding to the next section, verify that this code works. If you have errors, check your code against Figures 10–3, 10–10, 10–11, and 10–12. Correct any mistakes, save your Web page file, and refresh the browser.

Q&A

What if I do not see a security message?

It may mean that tight restrictions and security are not set on your browser. You may have to refresh your browser or close it and restart the browser.

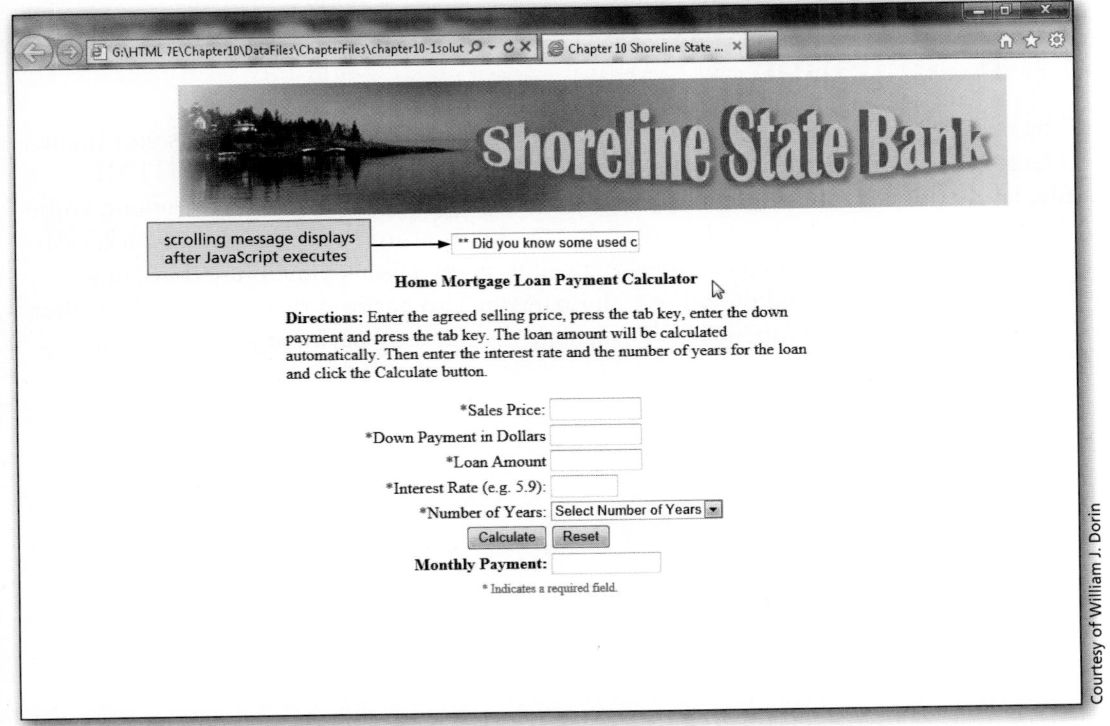

Figure 10–13

Plan Ahead

Validating form input.

The validations and calculations in this project require two separate user-defined functions. In order to calculate the monthly payment, the values entered into the text fields must be valid numbers. A user-defined function called validSalesAmt() performs the following steps to validate the text field entries and calculate the loanAmt:

- Convert the text field value to a numeric value using the parseInt() or parseFloat() function
- Use the isNaN (is Not a Number) function to verify the value is numeric and then verify the value is greater than zero
- Use an if statement to test if the value is not a number or is zero or less, display an error message, clear the text field, and position the insertion point in that text field
- Subtract the down payment amount from the sales amount to calculate the loan amount

To call the validSalesAmt() validation function, an onBlur event handler is added to the form. Once the loan amount is calculated, the user must enter the loan interest rate and the number of years to pay the loan off. The valid number of years are displayed on the form in a <select> list, but the validation must still verify a number was selected. A user-defined function called CalcLoanAmt() follows these steps to validate the text field and <select> list entries and calculate the monthly payment:

- For the loan rate, convert the loan rate text field value to a numeric value using the parseInt() or parseFloat() function
- If the value is not a number or is zero or less, display an error message, clear the text field, and position the insertion point in that text field
- For the loan years, convert the years text field value to a numeric value using the parseInt() function
- Use the isNaN (is Not a Number) function to verify a valid value was selected from the drop-down menu

BTW

Validating Web Form Data

Web developers use multiple techniques to validate Web forms using JavaScript. Some developers choose to validate each item as it is entered by using a combination of onchange event handlers and user-defined functions. It is important to validate Web forms because some Web databases are sensitive to invalid data and may crash, or mathematical formulas may cease to function when using invalid data.

Adding a Loan Calculator with Validation

The mortgage loan payment calculator form shown in Figure 10–14 requests user input. The form, which is named homeLoanForm, has already been created in the HTML file. JavaScript code must be added to validate the input, calculate the loan amount, and display the results in the homeLoanForm form. In order for the calculator to work, each text field must have a valid data entry. You will write two user-defined functions, one called validSalesAmt() and the other CalcLoanAmt(), to perform these three tasks. Other JavaScript user-defined functions will calculate the monthly payment and display the formatted results.

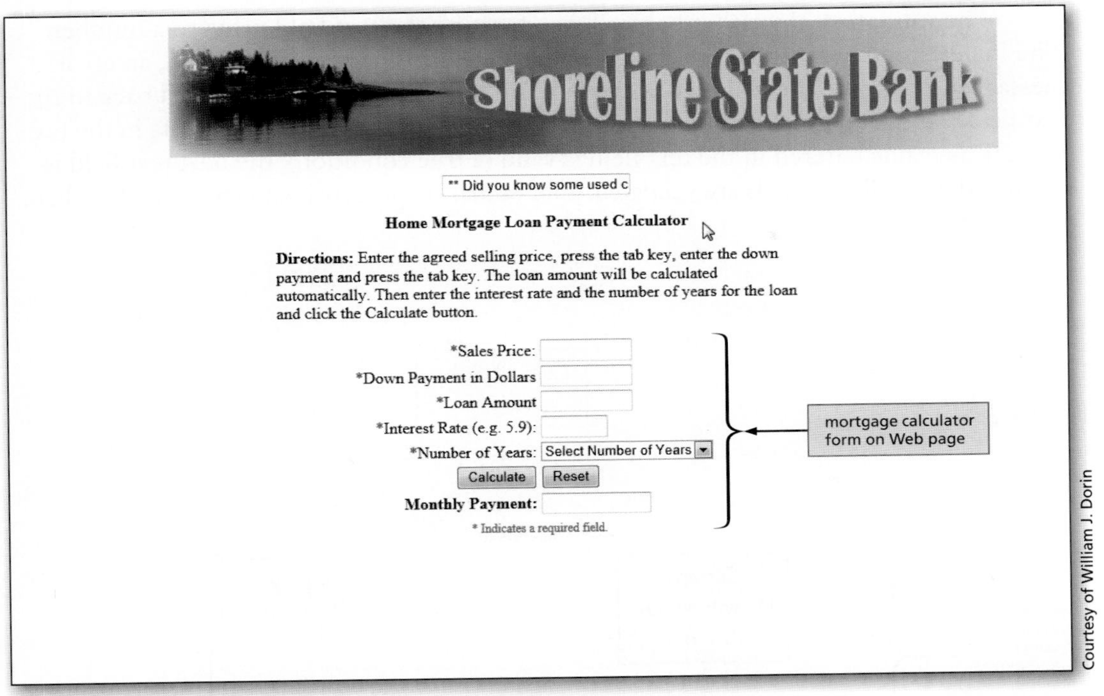

Courtesy of William J. Dorin

Figure 10–14

Validating Forms Using Nested if...else Statements

You can use different techniques to validate forms. This chapter uses a series of nested if…else statements. The if…else statement is like the if statement except that it specifies statements to execute if the condition is false, as shown in the flowchart in Figure 10–15. Much like the if statement, an if…else statement tests a condition. If the condition is true, the statements between the curly braces after the if statement execute. If the condition is false, the statements between the braces after the else statement execute.

BTW

if and if…else Statements
JavaScript if and if…else statements are an integral part of the programming language. These statements control the flow of logic or execution of expressions based on the result of a conditional test.

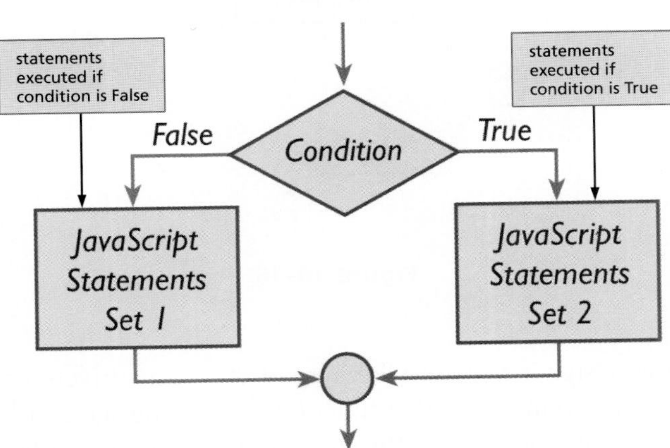

Figure 10–15

The validation algorithm begins by converting the text field value to a number. The if…else statement tests if the value entered in a text field is valid. If false, an error message is displayed, the text field is cleared, and the insertion point is placed back in the text field. This prevents the user from continuing until the user enters valid data in the text field. If the value entered in the text field is valid (a true condition), the next text field is examined until all text fields are validated. The validation process is shown in the flowchart in Figure 10–16.

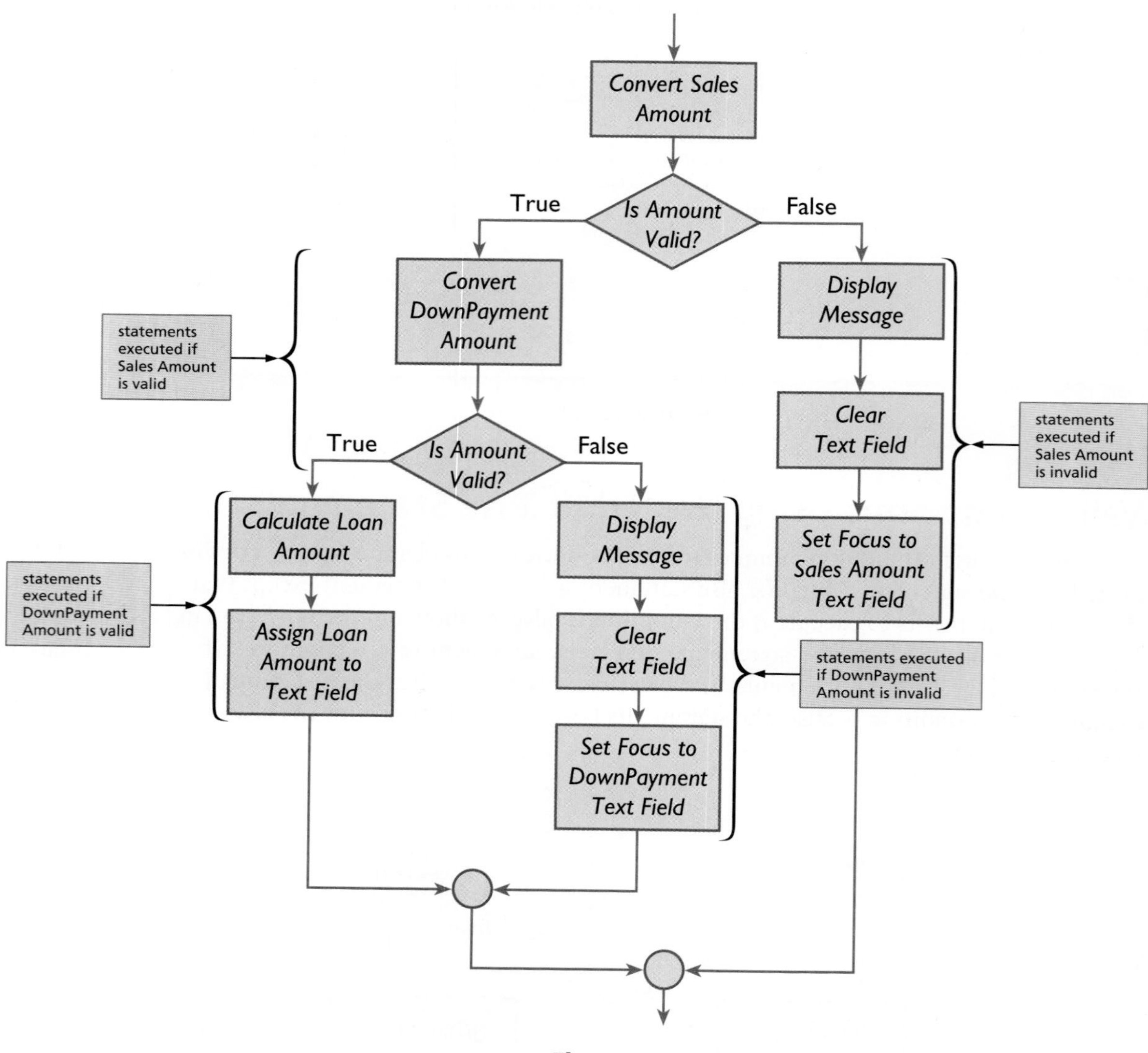

Figure 10–16

This validation design is necessary because of the event-driven nature of JavaScript. When a user triggers an event that calls a function, processing stays within that function until all statements execute. Because all the statements execute in a function, the form validation routine uses nested if…else statements to ensure each text field is validated correctly. By nesting if…else statements, you can place an if…else statement inside another, as shown in Figure 10–17.

```
if (dollarLen > 3) {
  while (dollarLen > 0) {
        tempDollars = dollars.substring(dollarLen - 3,dollarLen)
        if (tempDollars.length == 3) {
           formatDollars = ","+tempDollars+formatDollars
           dollarLen = dollarLen - 3
        } else {
             formatDollars=tempDollars+formatDollars
             dollarLen = 0
        }
  }
     if (formatDollars.substring(0,1) == ",")
        dollars = formatDollars.substring(1,formatDollars.length)
     else
        dollars = formatDollars
}
```

statements executed if first if statement is True

statements executed if the if statement is True

statements executed if the if statement is False

Figure 10–17

Using Built-In Functions to Validate Data

When validating data, the JavaScript code may have to evaluate several criteria — for example, to ensure that a text field is not blank or that it contains numeric data (not text or characters). HTML forms accept data entered into a text field as text character data, which means that the values must be converted to a number before they can be tested or validated. Table 10–9 describes the two built-in functions, parseInt() and parseFloat(), used to convert values and one function, isNaN(), used to test if the converted value is a number.

BTW — Number Base
Radix is the number base to which the integer value should be converted. A number base represents the number of digits and the placement of digits. We use base 10 for our decimal system. Base 2 is binary, base 8 is octal, and base 16 is hexadecimal.

BTW — parseFloat() and parseInt() Built-in Functions
The parseFloat() function is a built-in function that parses a string argument and converts the value into a decimal floating-point number. If the first character cannot be converted to a number, the result is NaN, which means "not a number." The parseInt() built-in function converts a value to an integer. If a value of 12Wre is entered, parseInt() will convert to 12.

Table 10–9 Built-In Functions: parseInt(), parseFloat(), isNaN()

General form:	`variable = parseInt(value, base)`
Comment:	converts to an integer. *Value* is any string, which can be a variable or literal; *base* is the number base to which you want the string converted. A base of 2 means binary base number, an 8 means octal, and a 10 means decimal. The function returns an integer value, stripping the value after the decimal point.
Example:	`parseInt(loanAmount,10)`
General form:	`variable = parseFloat(value)`
Comment:	converts to a floating point number. *Value* is any string, which can be a variable or literal, representing a floating-point number. A floating-point number is one with a fractional or decimal value (including percentages). The function returns the value as a floating-point number.
Example:	`parseFloat(loanAmount)`
General form:	`isNaN(value)`
Comment:	isNaN means is Not a Number. *Value* is any value, which can be a variable or literal. The function returns a Boolean condition of true or false.
Example:	`isNaN(loanAmount)`

Figure 10–18 on the next page shows how the values of the form are passed to the validSalesAmt() user-defined function.

BTW

isNaN() Built-in Function
The isNaN() built-in function, which tests whether a value is not a number, is the only function that tests a numeric value as the argument. The test uses the NOT operator and returns a Boolean value of true or false.

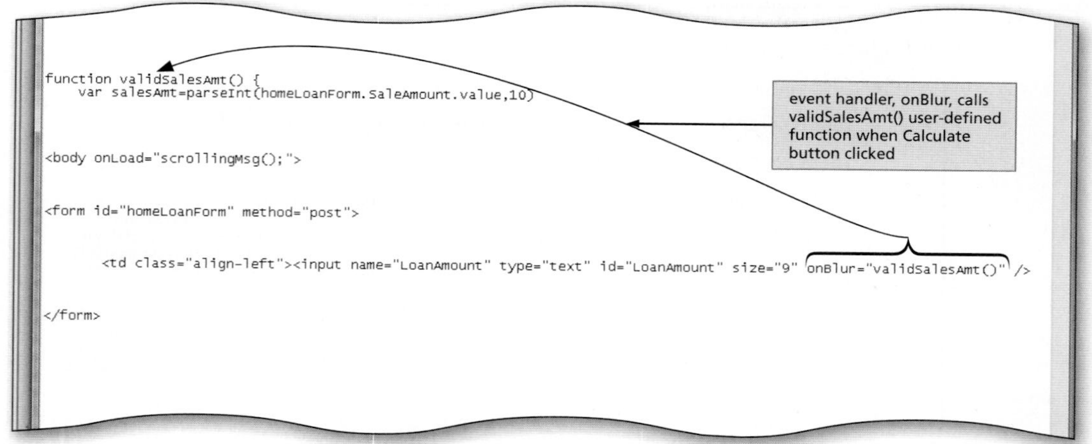

Figure 10–18

Table 10–10 shows the general form of the JavaScript statement used to assign a null, or other, value to a text field object within a form.

Table 10–10 Assignment Statement	
General form:	`document.formname.textfieldname.value=variable_or_literal`
Comment:	where *formname* is the name of the form; *textfieldname* is the name of a text field in the form; value is the attribute; and *variable_or_literal* is the value assigned to the text field.

Examples:	`document.LoanForm.Amount.value=LoanAmt`
	`document.LoanForm.Amount.value="12500"`
	`document.LoanForm.Amount.value=""`

To place the insertion point back in a specific text field in the form, the focus must be set for that text field. Setting the focus means giving attention to an object. JavaScript uses the **focus() method** to give attention to an object. When the focus is set to an object, such as the Amount text field, the JavaScript statement automatically positions the insertion point in the text field. Table 10–11 shows the general form of the focus() method.

Table 10–11 focus() Method	
General form:	`document.formname.objectname.focus()`
Comment:	where *formname* is the name of the form that contains the object; and *objectname* identifies the object to which focus should be set.
Examples:	`document.LoanForm.Amount.focus()`

The first step in creating this validation function is to define the variables that will be needed. Table 10–12 shows the code to define the variables for the validSalesAmt() and CalcLoanAmt() user-defined functions.

Table 10–12 Code for validSalesAmt() Function to Validate the Loan Amount

Line	Code
19	`var salesAmt`
20	`var loanAmt`
21	`var loanRate`
22	`var loanYears`

Lines 19 through 22 declare the variables that will be used in the two user-defined functions. Table 10–13 shows the code to enter the validSalesAmt() user-defined function and the statements necessary to validate and calculate the mortgage loan amount based on the sales amount minus the down payment amount using the parseInt() and isNaN() functions.

Table 10–13 Code for validSalesAmt() Function to Validate and Calculate the Loan Amount

```
Line  Code
24    function validSalesAmt() {
25        var salesAmt=parseInt(homeLoanForm.SaleAmount.value,10)
26        if (isNaN(salesAmt) || (salesAmt <= 0)) {
27            alert("The sales price is not a valid number!")
28            homeLoanForm.SaleAmount.value = " "
29            homeLoanForm.SaleAmount.focus()
30        }
31        else {
32            var downPmtAmt=parseInt(homeLoanForm.DownPayment.value,10)
33            if (isNaN(downPmtAmt) || (downPmtAmt <= 0) || (downPmtAmt > salesAmt)) {
34                alert("The down payment should be greater than 0 and less than the sales amount!")
35                homeLoanForm.DownPayment.value = " "
36                homeLoanForm.DownPayment.focus()
37            }
38            else {
39                loanAmt = salesAmt-downPmtAmt
40                homeLoanForm.LoanAmount.value = loanAmt
41                homeLoanForm.Rate.focus()
42            }
43        }
44    }
```

Line 24 declares the validSalesAmt() function and uses the values entered or selected in the LoanForm. Line 25 assigns the data entered in the SaleAmount text field to the salesAmt variable and the parseInt() function converts that value to an integer. The if statement beginning on line 26 tests if the value for the salesAmt variable is not a number or if the value entered is less than or equal to zero. If the result of the condition is true (that is, the value entered is not a number or it is a negative number), the function notifies the user with an alert message (line 27) that the sales amount is not valid, clears the data entered in the SaleAmount text field (line 28), and then sets the focus back to the SaleAmount text field (line 29). The brace in line 30 closes the if statement.

Because an event must be executed until completion, the validSalesAmt() function validates all the entered values. Line 31 continues with the else statement to validate the down payment amount. Line 32 converts the DownPayment value to an integer assigned the downPmtAmt variable. The if statement at line 33 tests if the downPmtAmt is a number and greater than zero but less than or equal to the salesAmt. If any of the compound conditions is false, line 34 displays the alert error message. Line 35 clears the input text field, and line 36 sets the focus back to the DownPayment input text field.

Line 37 closes the if statement. Line 38 starts the else statement block, which processes the valid data. Line 39 calculates the loan amount by subtracting the down payment value from the sales amount. Line 40 assigns the loan amount to the LoanAmount input text field to display on the form. Line 41 sets the focus to the interest rate input text field to continue processing the form.

To Add the validSalesAmt() Function with Nested if...else Statements to Validate Form Data

The following step enters the validSalesAmt() user-defined function and the if...else statements that validate the amounts entered in the SaleAmount and DownPayment text fields and calculates the loan amount.

- If necessary, click the Notepad++ button on the taskbar to display chapter10-1solution .html in the Notepad++ window.
- Click line 18.
- Press the ENTER key once to create a blank line, and position the insertion point on line 19.
- Enter the JavaScript code shown in Table 10–12 on page HTML 472, indenting as shown to enter the code to define the variables for the user-defined functions.

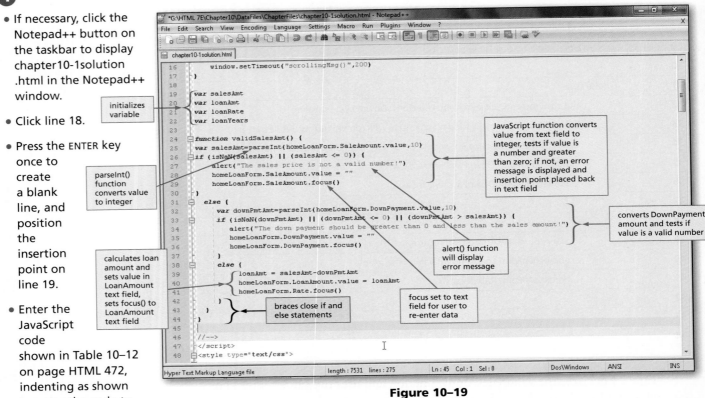

*G:\HTML 7E\Chapter10\DataFiles\ChapterFiles\chapter10-1solution.html - Notepad++

File Edit Search View Encoding Language Settings Macro Run Plugins Window ?

chapter10-1solution.html

```
16        window.setTimeout("scrollingMsg()",200)
17    }
18
19    var salesAmt
20    var loanAmt
21    var loanRate
22    var loanYears
23
24    function validSalesAmt() {
25    var salesAmt=parseInt(homeLoanForm.SaleAmount.value,10)
26    if (isNaN(salesAmt) || (salesAmt <= 0)) {
27        alert("The sales price is not a valid number!")
28        homeLoanForm.SaleAmount.value = ""
29        homeLoanForm.SaleAmount.focus()
30    }
31      else {
32        var downPmtAmt=parseInt(homeLoanForm.DownPayment.value,10)
33        if (isNaN(downPmtAmt) || (downPmtAmt <= 0) || (downPmtAmt > salesAmt)) {
34            alert("The down payment should be greater than 0 and less than the sales amount!")
35            homeLoanForm.DownPayment.value = ""
36            homeLoanForm.DownPayment.focus()
37        }
38        else {
39            loanAmt = salesAmt-downPmtAmt
40            homeLoanForm.LoanAmount.value = loanAmt
41            homeLoanForm.Rate.focus()
42        }
43      }
44    }
45
46    //-->
47    </script>
48    <style type="text/css">
```

Hyper Text Markup Language file | length : 7531 lines : 275 | Ln : 45 Col : 1 Sel : 0 | Dos\Windows | ANSI | INS

initializes variable

parseInt() function converts value to integer

calculates loan amount and sets value in LoanAmount text field, sets focus() to LoanAmount text field

JavaScript function converts value from text field to integer, tests if value is a number and greater than zero; if not, an error message is displayed and insertion point placed back in text field

converts DownPayment amount and tests if value is a valid number

alert() function will display error message

focus set to text field for user to re-enter data

braces close if and else statements

Figure 10–19

- Press the ENTER key twice after line 22.
- Enter the JavaScript code shown in Table 10–13 on the previous page, indenting as shown to enter the code for the user-defined function validSalesAmt(), which validates the data entered and calculates the loan amount based on the sales amount minus the down payment value.
- Press the ENTER key once after line 44 (Figure 10–19).

Q&A

Are spaces necessary around equal signs in JavaScript statements?

No, spaces are not required. You can write one line of code with spaces around the equal signs and another without spaces and it will not make any difference.

To Enter the onBlur Event Handler to Call the validSalesAmt() Function

After adding the user-defined function to validate the sales price and the down payment values and calculate the loan amount, you need to add an onBlur event handler to invoke the validSalesAmt() function when the user presses the Tab key or clicks the Interest Rate text field. Moving the insertion point to another form field or object after the down payment value is entered means the text field no longer has the focus, which is called blur. The following step enters the onBlur event handler to call the validSalesAmt() function.

- Scroll down to the HTML code for the form and then click line 127 right after the closing quote in the size="9" attribute and before the rightmost /> bracket.
- Press the SPACEBAR once.
- Type `onBlur="validSalesAmt()"` to add the event handler to the DownPayment text field, but do not press the ENTER key (Figure 10–20).

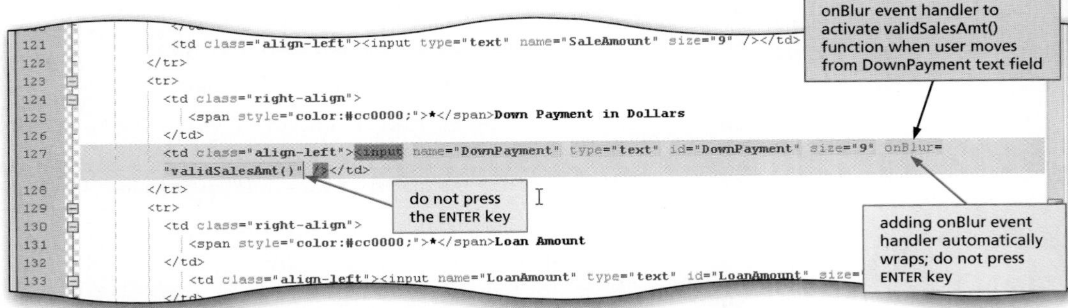

Figure 10–20

Validating the Interest Rate and the Number of Years for the Loan

The CalcLoanAmt() user-defined function is used to validate the interest rate and number of years of the loan. The code for CalcLoanAmt() is shown in Table 10–14. This function is called after the user enters the interest rate value, selects the number of years from the drop-down menu, and then clicks the Calculate button.

Table 10–14 Code to Validate the Interest Rate

Line	Code
46	`function CalcLoanAmt() {`
47	`    loanRate=parseFloat(homeLoanForm.Rate.value)`
48	`    if (isNaN(loanRate) || (loanRate <= 0)) {`
49	`        alert("The interest rate is not a valid number!")`
50	`        homeLoanForm.Rate.value = ""`
51	`        homeLoanForm.Rate.focus()`
52	`    }`

Line 46 declares the user-defined function CalcLoanAmt. This function is called when the user clicks the Calculate button. Line 47 passes the value in the Interest Rate text field to the loanRate variable, and converts it to a floating-point number using the parseFloat() function. Because the interest rate is a floating-point number, you must use the parseFloat() function to keep the interest rate a floating-point number.

The if statement in line 48 tests the loanRate variable to determine if it is a number or if the value is less than or equal to zero. If the result of the condition is true, an alert message (line 49) notifies the user that the interest rate is not valid. Line 50 clears the data entered in the Interest Rate text field, and then line 51 sets the focus back to the Interest

> **BTW**
> **Domain**
> A domain is a range of acceptable values for a field or column in a database. Using an HTML select list can ensure that accurate values are entered.

Rate text field. The brace in line 52 closes the if statement. If the loanRate data is valid, the function then proceeds to validate the number of years.

Table 10–15 shows the code used to validate the value selected in the Years drop-down list.

Table 10–15 Code to Convert and Validate the Years Entered Value

<table>
<tr><th>Line</th><th>Code</th></tr>
<tr><td>53</td><td><code>else {</code></td></tr>
<tr><td>54</td><td><code>loanYears=homeLoanForm.Years.value</code></td></tr>
<tr><td>55</td><td><code>if (isNaN(loanYears) || (loanYears < 1 || loanYears > 30)) {</code></td></tr>
<tr><td>56</td><td><code>alert("Please select a valid number from the list (10, 15, 20, or 30)!")</code></td></tr>
<tr><td>57</td><td><code>homeLoanForm.Years.selectedIndex = 0</code></td></tr>
<tr><td>58</td><td><code>homeLoanForm.Years.focus()</code></td></tr>
<tr><td>59</td><td><code>}</code></td></tr>
<tr><td>60</td><td><code>}</code></td></tr>
<tr><td>61</td><td><code>}</code></td></tr>
</table>

Line 53 is an else statement that executes the statements if the if condition on line 48 is false. Line 54 receives the selected value from the drop-down menu. The if statement beginning in line 55 checks the condition to determine if the loanYears value entered is a number, or is less than one, or is greater than 30. If the number of years is not valid, line 56 displays a message and line 57 sets the selectedIndex to 0. Line 58 places the focus back in the Years drop-down menu. The braces in lines 59 through 61 close the nested if...else statements and the function.

To Enter the CalcLoanAmt() User-Defined Function

The following step enters the CalcLoanAmt() function to validate the Interest Rate (e.g. 4.75) text field and the Number of Years from the drop-down menu.

- If necessary, click line 45 and then press the ENTER key once.
- Enter the JavaScript code shown in Table 10–14 on the previous page starting on line 46 to validate the interest rate, indenting the code as shown in Figure 10–21.
- Continue on line 53 and enter the JavaScript code shown in Table 10–15 to validate the number of years for the loan, indenting to align the code as shown in Figure 10–21.
- Press the ENTER key to finish the else portions of the nested if...else statements (Figure 10–21).

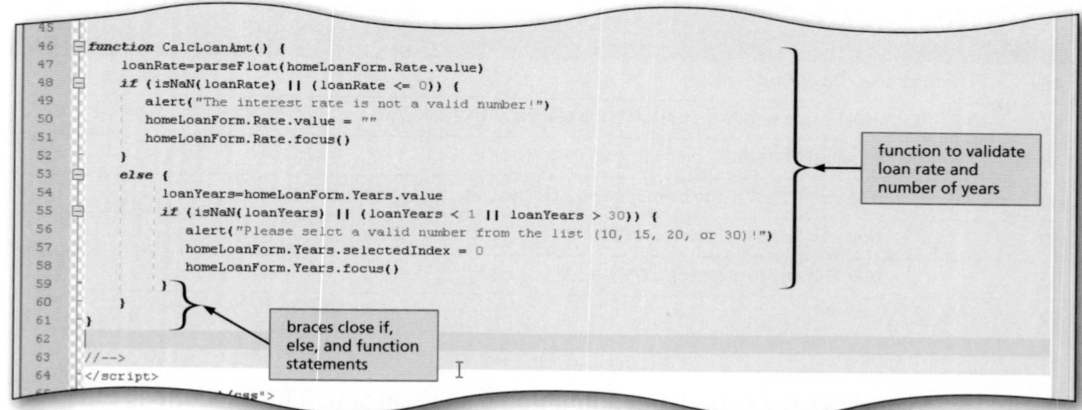

Figure 10–21

> **Q&A**
> Why is the year not converted to a floating point number?
> Most loans, especially mortgage loans, are NOT made on part of a year, so the number of years should be an integer.

To Enter an onClick Event Handler to Call the CalcLoanAmt() Function

The last step in validating the mortgage loan payment calculator is to add an event handler to invoke the CalcLoanAmt() function when the user clicks the Calculate button. After entering all the data in the form, a user clicks the Calculate button, which triggers the CalcLoanAmt() function to validate the interest rate and number of years data entered in the form. The following step enters the onClick event handler to call the CalcLoanAmt() function.

- Scroll down to the HTML code for the form and then click line 174 right after the closing quote in “Calculate” and before the right-most /> bracket.
- Press the SPACEBAR once.
- Type `onClick="CalcLoanAmt()"` to add the event handler to the Calculate button, but do not press the ENTER key (Figure 10–22).

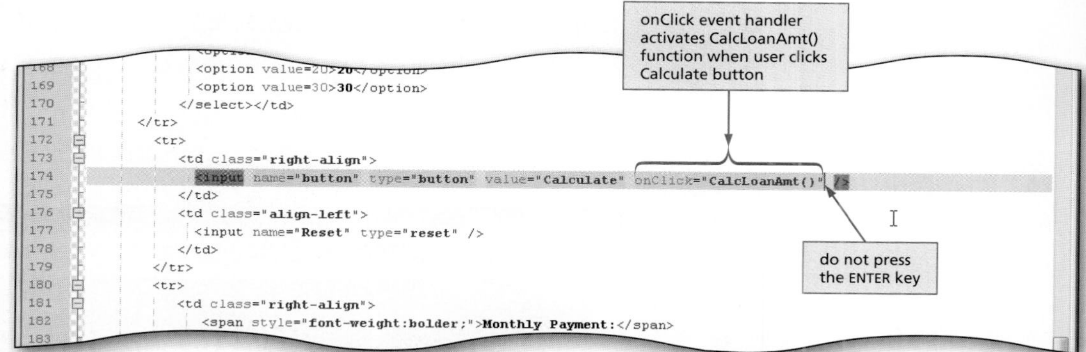
onClick event handler activates CalcLoanAmt() function when user clicks Calculate button
169 <option value=30>30</option>
170 </select></td>
171 </tr>
172 <tr>
173 <td class="right-align">
174 <input name="button" type="button" value="Calculate" onClick="CalcLoanAmt()" />
175 </td>
176 <td class="align-left">
177 <input name="Reset" type="reset" />
178 </td>
179 </tr>
180 <tr>
181 <td class="right-align">
182 <span style="font-weight:bolder;">Monthly Payment:</span>
do not press the ENTER key

Figure 10–22

To Save an HTML File and Test a Web Page

With the JavaScript code for the form validation entered, the Web page can be saved and tested in a browser. The CalcLoanAmt() function will validate the text field entries, but will not yet calculate the monthly payment. The following steps save the HTML file and test the Web page. Do not continue until this code is working properly.

1. With the USB drive plugged into your computer, click File on the menu bar, and then click Save.
2. Click the browser button on the taskbar.
3. Click the Refresh button on the Address bar.
4. When the Web page is displayed, click the Sales Price text field.
5. Enter the test data set 1, as shown in Table 10–16 on the next page, pressing the TAB key to move to the next text field.
6. When an error message appears, click the OK button, and enter a valid number for the missing data.
7. When you have entered the test data set 1, click the Calculate button at the bottom of the form.
8. After completing a set of data, click the Reset button at the bottom of the form.
9. Repeat Steps 5 through 8, using test data sets 2, 3, and 4, as shown in Table 10–16, and respond to any error messages. Figure 10–23 on the next page shows the fourth data set with the error message.

Table 10–16 Mortgage Loan Test Data Set

Data Set	Sales Price	Down Payment	Interest Rate %	Years	Comment
1		23000	4.75	20	The sales price is not a valid number!
2	123900	24800	A	15	The interest rate is not a valid number!
3	190000	19000	3.75	30	No error messages
4	231000	45000	5.375		Please select a valid number from the list (10, 15, 20, or 30)!

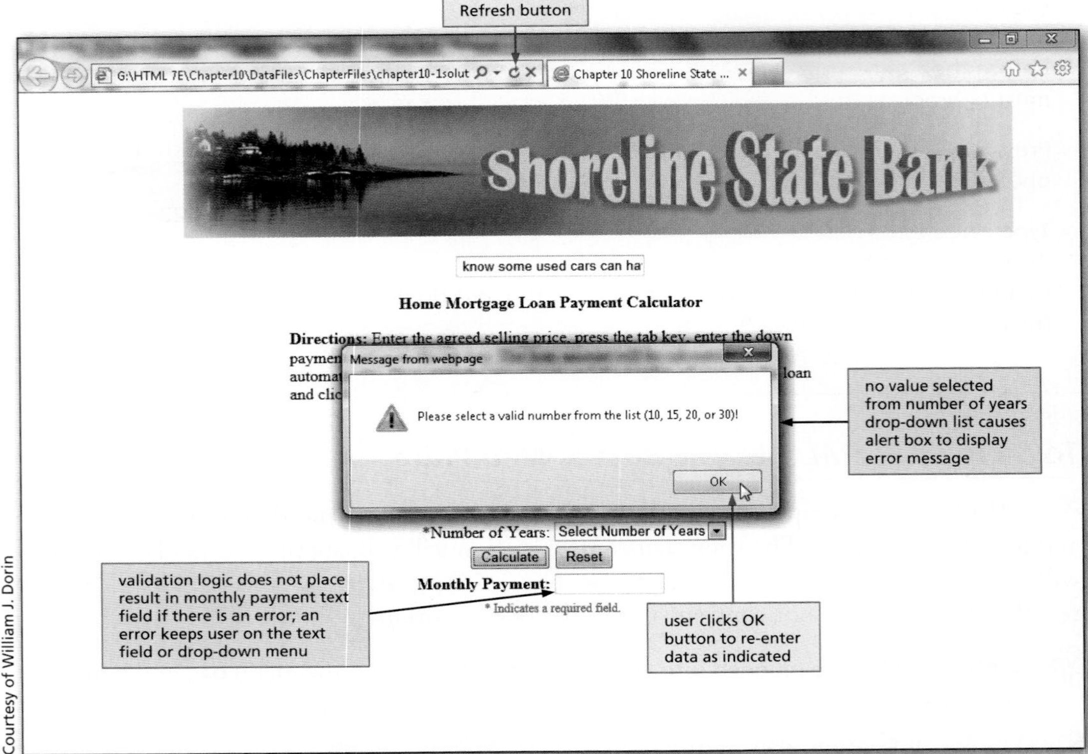

Figure 10–23

Plan Ahead

Calculating the monthly payment.

The monthlyPmt() function requires three parameters: the loan amount (loanAmt), the interest rate (loanRate), and the number of years that the payments will be made (loanYears). These values are passed from the CalcLoanAmt() user-defined function to the monthlyPmt() function. The steps to calculate the monthly payment are as follows:

1. Pass the three variables — loanAmt, loanRate, and loanYears — to the monthlyPmt() function.
2. Convert the annual interest rate to a monthly interest rate (interestRate) by dividing loanRate by 1200
3. Convert the number of years to the number of months of payments (Pmts) by multiplying loanYears by 12
4. Calculate the monthly payment with the following formula:

   loanAmt * (interestRate / (1 - (1 / Math.pow(1+interestRate,Pmts))))
5. Return the monthly payment as a fixed decimal value to two decimal places using the toFixed(2) method.

Adding the Monthly Payment Calculation

With the JavaScript code for the form validation complete, the next step is to add code to the CalcLoanAmt() function to calculate the monthly payment. First, a statement must be added to the CalcLoanAmt() function to call a user-defined function named monthlyPmt(), which calculates the monthly payment. The monthlyPmt() function uses the valid data in the form and calculates the monthly payment. The result is the monthly payment, which is returned as a floating-point value.

The placement of the monthlyPmt() function within the CalcLoanAmt() function is important so that, if a value in a text field is invalid, the function does not attempt to process invalid data and return an undefined result. To place this function properly, one more else statement must be added to the CalcLoanAmt() function, as shown in Table 10–17.

Table 10–17 Code to Call the monthlyPmt() Function

Line	Code
60	`else {`
61	`    var monthlyPmtAmt = monthlyPmt(loanAmt,loanRate,loanYears)`
62	`    homeLoanForm.Payment.value=monthlyPmtAmt.toString()`
63	`}`

Line 60 adds an additional else statement to the nested if...else statements. Line 61 calls the monthlyPmt() function and passes the loan amount, interest rate, and number of years for the loan as variables: loanAmt, loanRate, and loanYears. The result is stored in a temporary variable named monthlyPmtAmt. Line 62 assigns the monthly payment result to the Payment text field on the form using the toString() method to convert the value to a string for display in the text field and for use in the formatting user-defined function, which will be written later. Line 63 is the closing brace for the additional else statement.

To Enter Code to Call the monthlyPmt() Function

The following step enters the final else statement and the function call that passes the required values to the monthlyPmt() function.

- Click the beginning of line 60 and then press the ENTER key to insert a blank line.
- Click the blank line just inserted (line 60).
- Press the SPACEBAR to indent under the closing brace in line 59, then enter the JavaScript code shown in Table 10–17 to call the monthlyPmt() user-defined function and assign the result to the payment text field, but do not press the ENTER key (Figure 10–24).

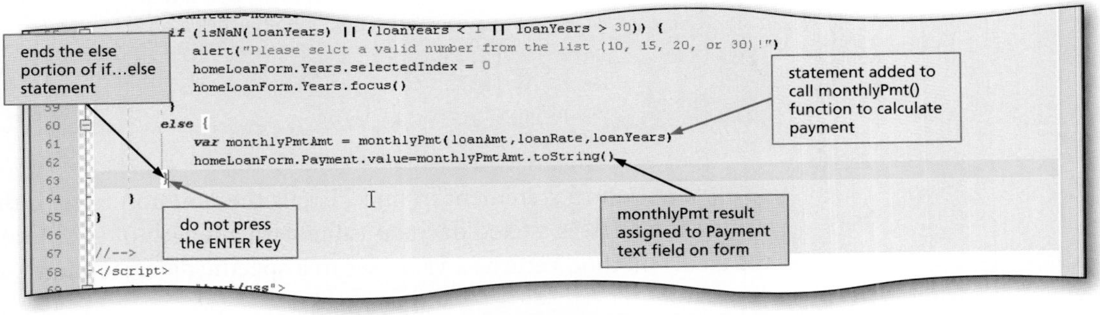

Figure 10–24

Q&A If I try to execute this Web page now, will an error occur?

Yes, because the monthlyPmt() user-defined function has not been written and entered.

Creating the monthlyPmt() User-Defined Function The monthlyPmt() function is a user-defined function that calculates the monthly payment amount. The JavaScript code for the monthlyPmt() function is shown in Table 10–18.

Table 10–18 Code for monthlyPmt() User-Defined Function

Line	Code
67	`function monthlyPmt(loanAmt,loanRate,loanYears) {`
68	`var interestRate = loanRate/1200`
69	`var Pmts = loanYears * 12`
70	`var Amnt = loanAmt * (interestRate / (1 - (1 / Math.pow(1+interestRate,Pmts))))`
71	`return Amnt.toFixed(2)`
72	`}`

BTW

Math Object
The Math object cannot be used to create other objects. Most of the properties of the Math object return preset values. Other properties of the Math object really are methods and act as functions.

Line 67 declares the monthlyPmt() function. Line 68 determines the monthly interest rate percentage by dividing the annual rate by 1200. The result is assigned to the interestRate (interest rate) variable. Line 69 determines the number of monthly payments on the loan, by multiplying the number of years in the loan by 12. The resulting value is assigned to the Pmts variable.

Line 70 is the formula for calculating a monthly payment based on the amount of the loan, the monthly interest percentage, and the number of monthly payments. The mathematical representation of the formula is:

$$\text{loan amount} * (\text{monthly interest rate} / (1 - (1 /(1 + \text{monthly interest rate})^{\text{number of payments}})))$$

JavaScript, however, does not use typical programming language symbols to represent exponentiation in code. Instead, to calculate the expression $(1 + \text{monthly interest rate})^{\text{number of payments}}$, JavaScript uses the pow() method associated with the Math object. Table 10–19 shows the general form of the pow() method.

Table 10–19 Math.pow() Method

General form:	`Math.pow(number, exponent)`
Comment:	where *number* is the value raised to the power of the *exponent* value. The pow() method accepts variables (X,n), constants (2,3), or both (Sidelength,2).

Examples:	`Math.pow(2,3)`
	`Math.pow(X,n)`
	`Math.pow(Sidelength,2)`

The return statement in line 71 tells the function to send the results of the expression back as a fixed decimal value with a length of two. The Number object's toFixed() method returns a value set to a specific decimal length, as shown in Table 10–20.

Table 10–20 Number.toFixed() Method

General form:	`Number.toFixed(digits)`		
Comment:	where *digits* is the exact number of digits after the decimal point. The number is rounded or padded with zeros if necessary.		
Examples:	Pmt = 234.8932	`Pmt.toFixed(3)`	Result: 234.893
	Amt = 843.6778	`Amt.toFixed(2)`	Result: 843.68

To Create the monthlyPmt() Function

The following step enters the monthlyPmt() user-defined function to calculate the monthly payment on a auto loan.

- Click the beginning of line 67 and press the ENTER key once.
- Position the insertion point on the blank line 67 just created.
- Enter the JavaScript code shown in Table 10–18 to write the code to calculate the monthly payment and then press the ENTER key once (Figure 10–25).

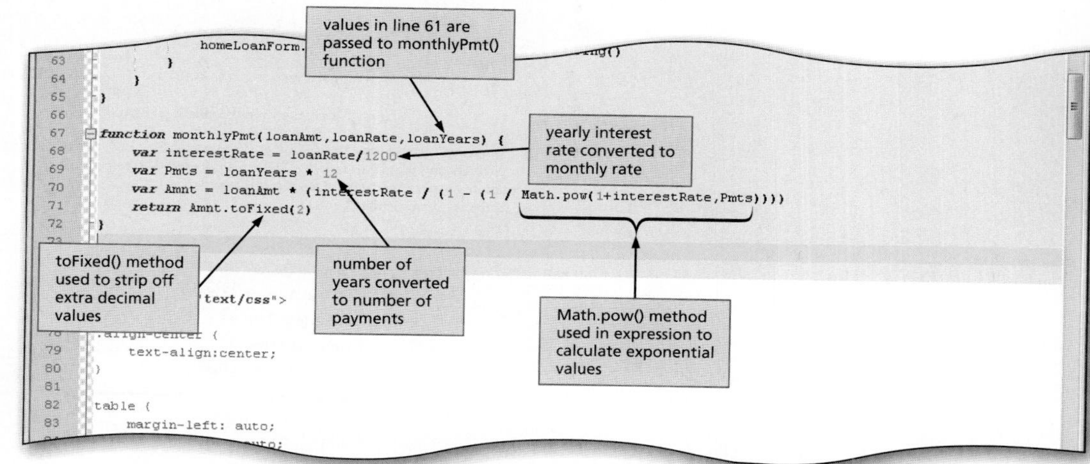

Figure 10–25

To Save an HTML File and Test a Web Page

Now that the monthly payment can be calculated, this is a good place to test the Web page. You should not continue to the next section until this code is working properly. The following steps save the HTML file and test the Web page.

1. With the USB drive plugged into the computer, click File on the menu bar, and then click Save.
2. Click the browser button on the taskbar.
3. Click the Refresh button next to the Address box.
4. Click the Reset button on the form.
5. If necessary, click the Sales Price text field to place the insertion point in the text field.
6. Type 174500 in the Sales Price text field and then press the TAB key.
7. Type 51000 in the Down Payment text field and then press the TAB key. If there are no errors, the Loan Amount of 123500 is calculated and displays in the Loan Amount text field.
8. Type 4.5 in the Interest Rate (e.g. 5.9) text field and then press the TAB key.
9. Select 30 in the Number of Years drop-down menu field and then click the Calculate button (Figure 10–26 on the next page).

Q&A

What if my result was slightly different? Did I do something wrong?

If your result is only a few cents different, it is probably just a difference in the math processor on your computer. If the value is hundreds or even thousands of dollars off, check your formula code on lines 68 through 70.

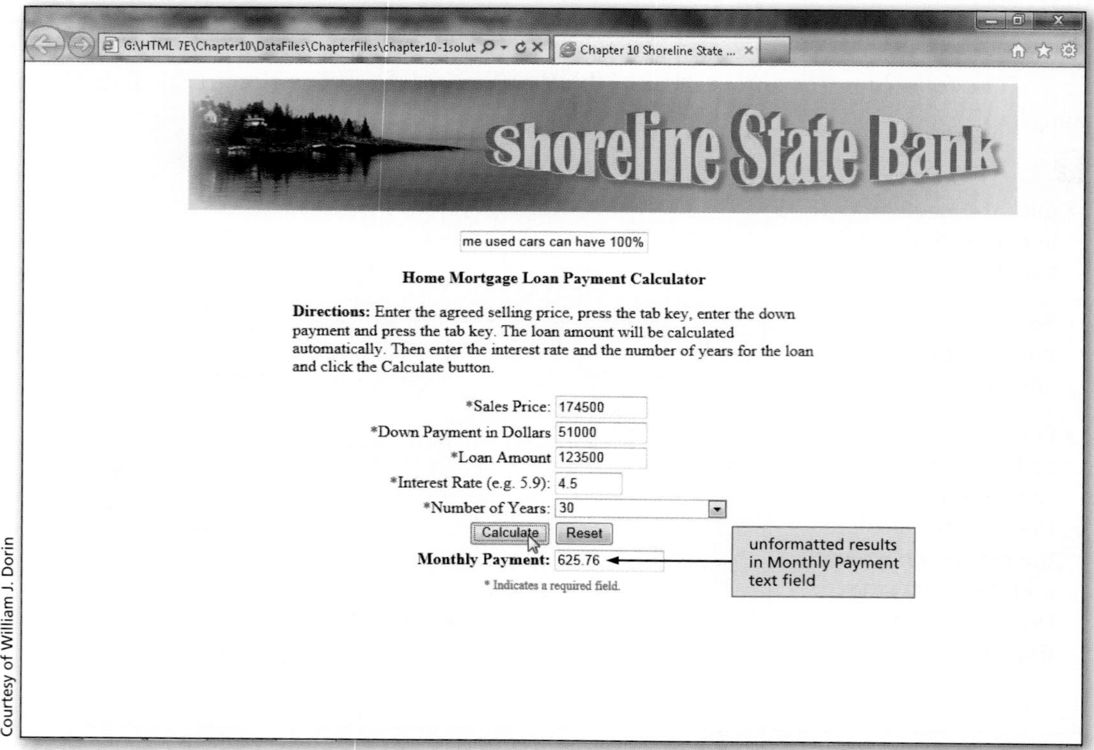

Courtesy of William J. Dorin

Figure 10–26

Plan Ahead

Formatting output results.

To format the result, the dollarFormat() function performs these seven basic steps:

1. Initialize two variables: one to hold the dollars portion of the value and the other to hold the formatted amount
2. Separate the dollars portion from the cents portion by using the split() method
3. The split() method creates an array; the zero element contains the dollar amount
4. Insert commas every three positions in dollar amounts exceeding 999
5. Reconstruct the result string value with two decimal places
6. Insert a dollar sign immediately to the left of the first digit without spaces
7. Return the completed formatted value

The value is assigned to the Monthly Payment text field in the form.

Formatting the Monthly Payment Output as Currency

As shown in Figure 10–26, the loan payment calculator currently displays the monthly payment amount as a value with two decimal places. To set the form to display the monthly payment amount in a currency format with a dollar sign, the dollarFormat() function is used. First, you must enter a statement that passes the resulting string object of the monthly payment CalcLoanAmt() function to the dollarFormat() function. The dollarFormat() function then analyzes the string, adds commas, and returns the number with a dollar sign and two decimal places.

Using the split() Method of the String Object The split() method is used to split a string based on an identified separator and a desired number of "sub" strings. The split() method searches the string object for the separator, which is enclosed within the quotation marks, and for every separator creates a separate sub string. These values are stored in an array. An **array** is a JavaScript object that stores multiple values in one variable name. Arrays are discussed in detail in Chapter 11. Table 10–21 shows the general form of the split() method.

Table 10–21 split() Method

General form:	`var newValue = stringname.split (separator, how many)`
Comment:	where *newValue* Is a variable holding the results of the split; *stringname* is any string object; *separator* is a string value such as a space, comma, or period that can separate a string; and *how many* is the value that indicates how many items will result from the split.

Example:	`phone="555.543.4321"`
	`numbparts=phone.split(".",3)`
	`areacode=numbparts[0]`
	`numbparts[0] contains 555`
	`numbparts[1] contains 543`
	`numbparts[2] contains 4321`

In this chapter, the split() method is used to separate the dollars from the cents at the decimal point in the monthly payment amount. Figure 10–27 provides an example of how the split() method works.

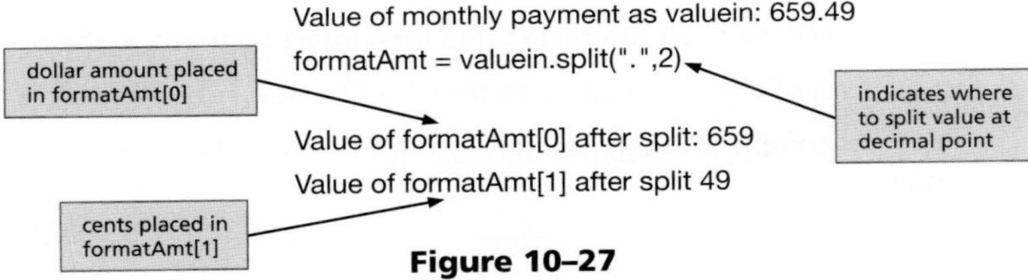

Figure 10–27

Beginning the dollarFormat() Function and Formatting the Dollars Portion The dollarFormat() function initializes the variables that will be used to format value as currency. Most programmers agree it is a good programming practice to clear and initialize variables to ensure the data is valid. Table 10–22 shows the JavaScript code used to add the dollarFormat() function.

Table 10–22 Code for the dollarFormat() Function

Line	Code
74	`function dollarFormat(valuein) {`
75	`var formatValue = ""`
76	`var formatDollars = ""`
77	`formatAmt = valuein.split(".",2)`
78	`var dollars = formatAmt[0]`

Line 74 declares the dollarFormat() function and the valuein variable. Lines 75 and 76 clear the variables used to assemble the formatted output by assigning null (or empty) values. The split() method in line 77 returns the dollar portion of the value and the cents portion into an array called formatAmt. As an array, formatAmt[0] contains the dollar amount, and formatAmt[1] contains the cents. Line 78 assigns the dollar amount to the dollars variable.

To Enter the dollarFormat() Function

The following step enters the dollarFormat() function and initialize the variables.

- Click line 73 and press the ENTER key once.
- On line 74, enter the JavaScript code from Table 10–22 on the previous page to begin the dollarFormat() function and then press the ENTER key (Figure 10–28).

```
72 }
73
74 function dollarFormat(valuein) {
75     var formatValue = ""
76     var formatDollars = ""
77     formatAmt = valuein.split(".",2)
78     var dollars = formatAmt[0]
79
80 //-->
81 </script>
82 <style type="text/css">
83 <!--
84 .align-center {
85     text-align:center;
```

split() used to find decimal point in value by searching for period. 2 indicates into how many items string should be split. Items stored in an array.

dollar amount is stored in element zero [0]

Figure 10–28

Plan Ahead

Using a while loop to insert commas every three digits in a number.
To place a comma every three digits, use a while loop. The following steps describe the logic of the while loop:

1. Extract three digits from the dollar value, starting from the right by subtracting 3 from the length of the dollar value (dollarLen)
2. Verify that three digits have been subtracted and then insert a comma in the output string
3. Decrement the length of the dollar value to look for the next group of three digits
4. The process (loop) is complete when no more groups of three digits exist and the length of dollarLen is zero

Using a while Loop and if...else Statement to Extract the Dollars Portion and Insert Commas A **loop** is a series of statements that executes repeatedly until it satisfies a condition. JavaScript has two types of loops: for loops and while loops. Both types of loops use the logic illustrated by the flowchart in Figure 10–29. Both loops first test a condition to determine if the instructions in the loop are to be executed.

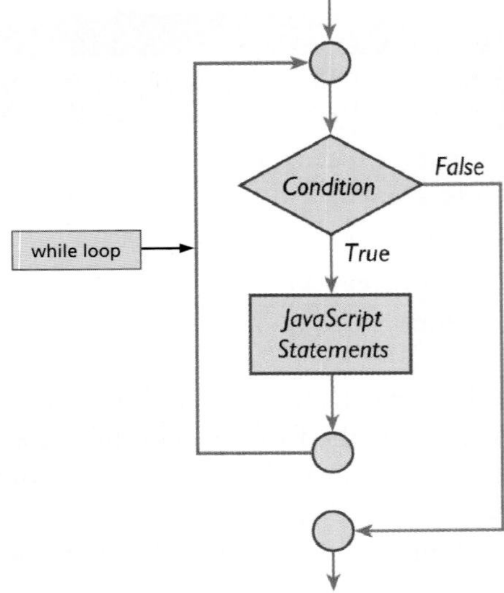

Figure 10–29

The **for loop** relies on a conditional statement using numeric values and thus is often referred to as a counter-controlled loop. Table 10–23 shows the general form of the for loop.

Table 10–23 for Loop

General form:	`for (start; stop; counter-control) {`
	`        JavaScript statements`
	`}`

Comment:	where *start* is a variable initialized to a beginning value; *stop* is an expression indicating the condition at which the loop should terminate; and the *counter-control* is an expression indicating how to increment or decrement the counter. Semicolons separate the three variables.

Examples:	`for (j=1; j<5; j++) {`
	`for (ctr=6; ctr>0; ctr--) {`
	`for (itemx=1; itemx<10; itemx=itemx+2) {`

The **while loop** relies on a conditional statement that either can use a numeric value or a string. Unlike the for loop, which will execute for a specified number of times, the while loop will execute until the specified condition is no longer true. Table 10–24 shows the general form of the while loop.

Table 10–24 while Loop

General form:	`while (condition) {`
	`        JavaScript statements`
	`}`

Comment:	where *condition* is either a numeric value or a string; and the JavaScript statements execute while the result of the condition is true.

Examples:	`while (ctr < 6) {`
	`while (isNaN(temp)) {`
	`while (Response != "Done") {`

In this chapter, the while loop is used in formatting the dollar value of the Monthly Payment value. The dollars portion is represented by the digits to the left of the decimal point. If the dollars portion of the mortgage payment contains more than three digits, commas need to be inserted. Table 10–25 shows the JavaScript statements used to determine the length of the dollar value and placement of the commas.

Table 10–25 Code for Determining the Length of the Dollar Value and Comma Placement

```
var dollarLen = dollars.length
if (dollarLen > 3) {
   while (dollarLen > 0) {
      tempDollars = dollars.substring(dollarLen - 3,dollarLen)
         if (tempDollars.length == 3) {
            formatDollars = ","+tempDollars+formatDollars
            dollarLen = dollarLen - 3
         } else {
               formatDollars = tempDollars+formatDollars
               dollarLen = 0
         }
   }
```

Table 10–25 (continued)

Line	Code
91	`if (formatDollars.substring(0,1) == ",")`
92	`    dollars = formatDollars.substring(1,formatDollars.length)`
93	`else`
94	`    dollars = formatDollars`
95	`}`

Because the dollar portion of the value is still a string, line 79 uses the length property to determine how many digits are in the dollar portion. The if statement at line 80 determines if the dollar portion of the value is longer than three digits. If that is true, then a while loop routine (lines 81 through 90) places a comma every three digits. Line 82 extracts three digits starting from the right by subtracting 3 from the length of the dollar value (dollarLen). The if statement at Line 83 verifies three digits and line 84 inserts a comma in the output string. Line 85 decrements the length of the dollar value to look for the next group of three digits. When no more groups of three digits exist, the length of dollarLen is set to zero (line 88) and the loop terminates at line 90. The statements in lines 91 through 95 prevent the code from inserting a comma if only three digits are to the left of the decimal point.

To Enter an if...else Statement and while Loop to Extract the Dollar Portion of the Output and Insert Commas

The following step enters the if…else statement and while loop to extract the dollar portion of the output and insert commas into the output if needed.

- If necessary, click line 79.
- Enter the JavaScript code as shown in Table 10–25 starting on the previous page, indenting as shown to extract the dollar portion of the output, insert the appropriate commas, and then press the ENTER key (Figure 10–30).

```
77   formatAmt = valuein.split(".",2)
78   var dollars = formatAmt[0]
79   var dollarLen = dollars.length
80   if (dollarLen > 3) {
81       while (dollarLen > 0) {
82           tempDollars = dollars.substring(dollarLen - 3,dollarLen)
83           if (tempDollars.length == 3) {
84               formatDollars = ","+tempDollars+formatDollars
85               dollarLen = dollarLen - 3
86           } else {
87               formatDollars=tempDollars+formatDollars
88               dollarLen = 0
89           }
90       }
91       if (formatDollars.substring(0,1) == ",")
92           dollars = formatDollars.substring(1,formatDollars.length)
93       else
94           dollars = formatDollars
95   }
96
97   //-->
98   </script>
99   <style type="text/css">
100  <!--
```

determines number of digits in dollar amount for placement of commas every 3 digits

determines if commas should be placed every three digits, and places them

strips off any extra commas not needed

Figure 10–30

Reconstructing the Formatted Output and Returning the Formatted Value Next, the JavaScript statements must be written to reconstruct (concatenate) the formatted dollars and cents output into a formatted payment amount value, store the payment amount value in the formatValue variable, and return the formatValue variable. Table 10–26 shows the statements needed to complete this task.

Table 10–26 Code for Reconstructing the Formatted Output and Returning the Formatted Value

Line	Code
96	var cents = formatAmt[1]
97	var formatValue="$"+dollars+"."+cents
98	return formatValue
99	}

Line 96 assigns two decimal values to the cents variable from the formatAmt[1] array. Line 97 reconstructs the values, concatenating a dollar sign ($), the dollars, a decimal point, and the cents. Line 98 returns the formatted value to the CalcLoanAmt() function. Line 99 closes the function.

To Reconstruct the Formatted Output and Return the Formatted Value

The following step reconstructs the formatted output and returns the formatted value to the calling function.

1

- If necessary, click line 96.
- Enter the JavaScript code from Table 10–26, indenting as shown to reconstruct the formatted output and return the formatted value, and then press the ENTER key (Figure 10–31).

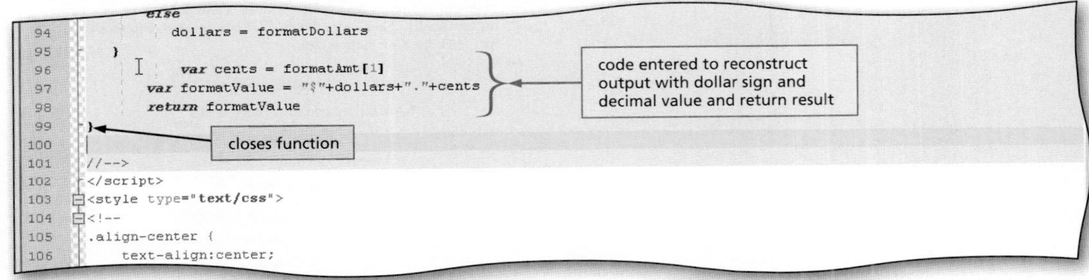

Figure 10–31

To Pass the Monthly Payment Value to the dollarFormat() Function

To have the monthly payment value appear in the Monthly Payment text field formatted as currency, it must be passed to the dollarFormat() function. Because the dollarFormat() function manipulates a string value, the monthly payment result must first be converted to a string using the toString() method. In Chapter 9, the toString() method was used to convert a date value to a string. In this chapter, the toString() method is used to convert the monthly payment to a string that the dollarFormat() function can manipulate.

The following step enters the JavaScript statements needed to pass the monthly payment as a string object to the dollarFormat() function.

- Scroll up to and click line 62 (the line that starts with home LoanForm.Payment.value).
- Position the insertion point before monthlyPmtAmt.toString(), then type `dollarFormat(` without a space.
- Position the insertion point after dollarFormat (monthlyPmtAmt. toString() and type `)` but do not press the ENTER key (Figure 10–32).

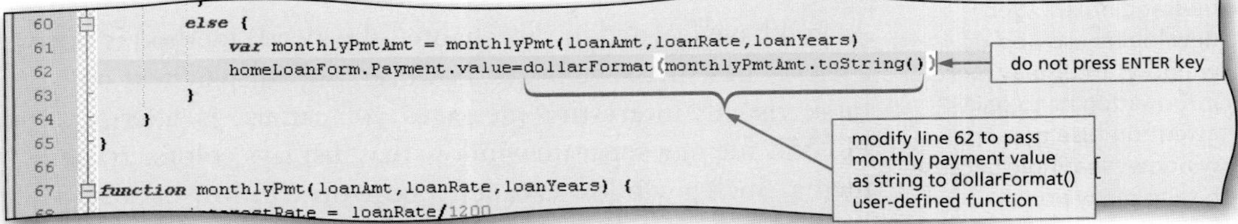

Figure 10–32

To Save an HTML File and Test a Web Page

The following steps save the HTML file and test the Web page.

1. With the USB drive plugged into your computer, click File on the menu bar, and then click Save.
2. Click the browser button on the taskbar.
3. Click the Refresh button.
4. Enter the test data as follows: Sales Price: 174500, Down Payment: 51000, Interest Rate: 5.375, and Number of Years: 30.
5. Click the Calculate button. The result should be formatted as shown in Figure 10–33.

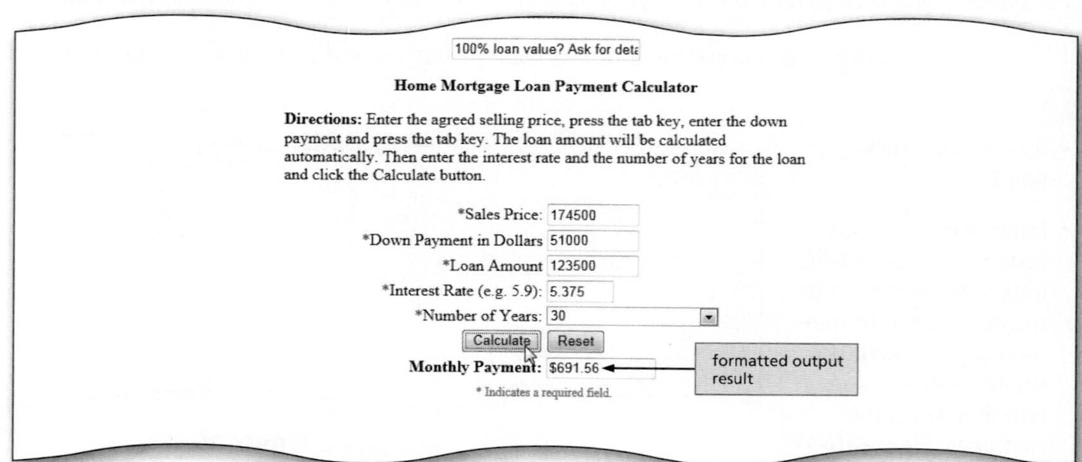

Figure 10–33

Plan Ahead

Planning pop-up windows.
A pop-up window is used to add additional information to a Web page. You must decide what features you want the pop-up window to utilize. Ask yourself these questions:

- Do you want to include the status bar, title bar, address bar, scroll bars, toolbars, and menu bar?
- Do you want the user to be able to resize the window?
- What width and height should the window be?

Each of these properties can be set as properties in the open() method, creating a customized look for that particular pop-up window.

BTW

Pop-up Windows
In addition to alert() message boxes, Web developers use pop-up windows to display more information or to gain attention. Use pop-up windows sparingly because having many pop-up windows can annoy visitors.

Adding a Pop-Up Window

As you have learned in this chapter, the alert() method is one way to display messages to a user. These message boxes, however, only display text on a gray background. To create more visually interesting messages, you can use JavaScript to open and display another HTML file in a separate window that displays colors, graphics, animations, and other media. Such a window is called a **pop-up window** because it appears over the previously opened browser window.

The **open() method** is used to create a pop-up window. Table 10–27 shows the general form of the open() method.

Table 10–27 open() Method

General form:	`var windowname=open("window file name(URL)", "object name", "features")`
Comment:	where *windowname* is an optional name of a window object (required only if you need to refer to the pop-up window in any other Web page); *window file name* is the name of the HTML file; and features describe how the window should appear.
Examples:	`open("chapter10-1notice.html","noticeWin","width=520,height=330")`

As shown in Table 10–27, when adding the open() method to create a pop-up window, all of the pop-up window features must be enclosed within one set of quotation marks. Table 10–28 describes the more commonly used attributes of the open() method, which are used to define pop-up window features. For more information about the open() method, see the JavaScript Quick Reference in Appendix G.

Table 10–28 open() Method Attributes

Feature	Description	Written As
height	States height in pixels	"height=450"
location	Includes address bar	"location=yes"
menubar	Includes menu bar	"menubar=yes"
resize	Allows user to resize	"resizeable=yes"
scrollbars	Includes scroll bars	"scrollbars=yes"
status	Includes status bar	"status=yes"
titlebar	Removes title bar	"titlebar=yes"
toolbar	Includes toolbar	"toolbar=yes"
width	States width in pixels	"width=220"

In this chapter, the open() method is used to open a pop-up window that will display information about Shoreline State Bank services. You will insert code for the popUpNotice function and open() method, and then add an event handler to call the popUpNotice() function when the page is loaded. Earlier in the chapter, the onLoad event handler was associated with the scrollingMsg() function. You will also use the onLoad event handler for the popUpNotice() function. Multiple functions can be associated with the same event handler.

Table 10–29 shows the code to create the user-defined function popUpNotice(). The chapter10-1notice.html file has already been created and is stored in the Chapter10\ChapterFiles folder of the Data Files for Students.

Table 10–29 Code to Open chapter10-1notice.html Pop-Up Window

```
function popUpNotice() {
     open("chapter10-1notice.html","noticeWin","width=520,height=330")
}
```

Line 101 declares the popUpNotice() function. The statement in line 102 opens the chapter10-1notice.html Web page as a pop-up window that is 520 pixels wide and 330 pixels high. Line 103 closes the function.

To Enter the popUpNotice() Function to Open a Pop-Up Window

The following step enters the popUpNotice() user-defined function that contains the open() method to open the chapter10-1notice.html file in a pop-up window.

- Activate the Notepad++ chapter10-1solution .html window.
- Click line 100, the line directly above the //--> tag, and press the ENTER key once.
- On line 101, enter the JavaScript code from Table 10–29 on the previous page, indenting as shown, and press the ENTER key after line 103 (Figure 10–34).

```
        else
94          dollars = formatDollars
95      }
96          var cents = formatAmt[1]
97      var formatValue = "$"+dollars+"."+cents
98      return formatValue
99  }
100
101 function popUpNotice() {
102     open("chapter10-1notice.html","noticeWin","width=520,height=330")
103 }
104
105 //-->
106 </script>
107 <style type="text/css">
108 <!--
109 .align-center {
110     text-align:center;
111 }
112
113 table {
114     margin-left: auto;
115     margin-right: auto;
```

JavaScript statement to open pop-up window

no spaces in Window dimension attributes

Figure 10–34

To Add the Event Handler to Call the popUpNotice() Function

Now you need to add the onLoad event handler to open the pop-up window when the Web page loads. Each function name is enclosed in one set of quotation marks and separated by a semicolon. The following steps add the second function call to the onLoad() event handler.

- Position the insertion point in front of the "> at the end of line 162 (the line that begins <body onLoad=) (Figure 10–35).

```
154     width: 50%;
155     margin-right: auto;
156     margin-left: auto;
157 }
158
159 -->
160 </style>
161 </head>
162 <body onLoad="scrollingMsg();">
163 <div class="center-div">
164   <p class="center-items"><img src="chapter10-1banner.jpg" alt="banner"></p>
165 </div>
166 <div class="center-di
167 <form id="msgForm">
168   <p style="text-alig                    "text" name="scrollingMsg" size="25"></p>
169 </form>
170 </div>
171 <p style="text-align:center; font-size:16; font-weight:bold;">Home Mortgage Loan Payment Calculator</p>
172 <p class="block"><strong>Directions: </strong>Enter the agreed selling price, press the tab key, enter
    payment and press the tab key. The loan amount will be calcuated automatically. Then enter the interest
```

do not press ENTER after typing

click before quotation marks and do not press SPACEBAR before typing

Figure 10–35

2

- Press the SPACEBAR, type `popUpNotice();` to add the call to the popUpNotice() user-defined function to the left of the second quotation mark, but do not press the ENTER key (Figure 10–36).

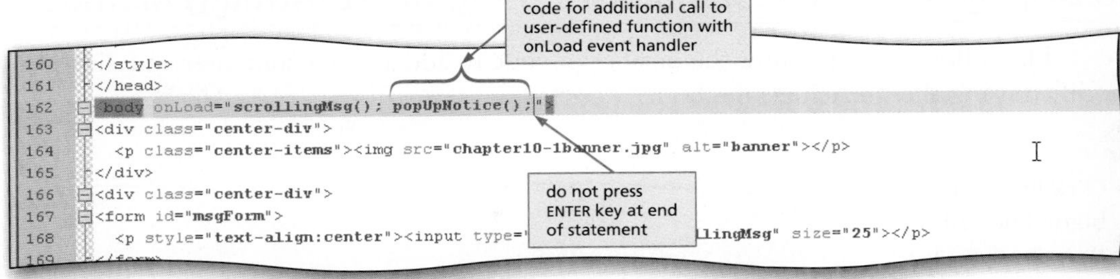
code for additional call to user-defined function with onLoad event handler
</style>
</head>
<body onLoad="scrollingMsg(); popUpNotice();">
<div class="center-div">
<p class="center-items"><img src="chapter10-1banner.jpg" alt="banner"></p>
</div>
<div class="center-div">
<form id="msgForm">
<p style="text-align:center"><input type=
llingMsg" size="25"></p>
do not press ENTER key at end of statement

Figure 10–36

Q&A Is this the only way to open a pop-up window?

An open() method can be placed anywhere in the <script> section in the <head> section. Once the <head> section loads in the browser, it will execute the "stand-alone" open() method, opening a pop-up window. The code must be in the <head> section, however, for this to work properly.

Adding Copyright and the Date Last Modified

As you learned in Chapter 9, the purpose of displaying the date a Web page was last modified is to make sure the user knows how current the information is contained on the Web page. You added JavaScript code to the Midwest Bridal Expo Web page to display the URL, a copyright notice, and the date the file was last modified. The Shoreline State Bank Web page should include similar JavaScript code to display just the date the Web page was modified, not the time.

To display the footer message of the copyright and date the Web page was last modified, you need to insert a <div> tag at the bottom of the Web page. Table 10–30 shows the code for creating the <div> tag container. The embedded style for the displayDateLast id attribute will size the division to 50% of the screen width and place the division in the center of the screen.

Table 10–30 Code to Create a <div> Tag Container

Line	Code
236	<div id="displayDateLast">
237	</div>

To display just the date, the code in Table 10–31 uses the substring() method to grab just the date and display copyright information.

Table 10–31 Code to Display the Date Last Modified Using the substring() Method

Line	Code
105	function copyRight() {
106	var lastModDate = document.lastModified
107	var lastModDate = lastModDate.substring(0,10)
108	displayDateLast.innerHTML = "<h6>Copyright © Shoreline State Bank"+" This document was last modified "+lastModDate+".</h6>"
109	}

Line 105 declares the copyRight() user-defined function. Line 106 assigns the date last modified from the document lastModified property. The substring(0,10) method in line 107 extracts the first 10 characters of the date and time — mm/dd/yyyy — so only the date is displayed, not the time. Line 108 assigns the message string to the <div> tag container using the id attribute, displayDateLast, and the innerHTML property. The text is formatted with the <h6> tag and the <br /> tag places the information on two separate lines.

To Display the Date Last Modified Using the substring() Method

The following steps enter the JavaScript code to add a <div> container and display the date the file was last modified using the substring() method.

1

- Click line 236 (the blank line just above the </body> tag).
- Enter the HTML <div> tag code from Table 10–30, but do not press the ENTER key after line 237 (Figure 10–37).

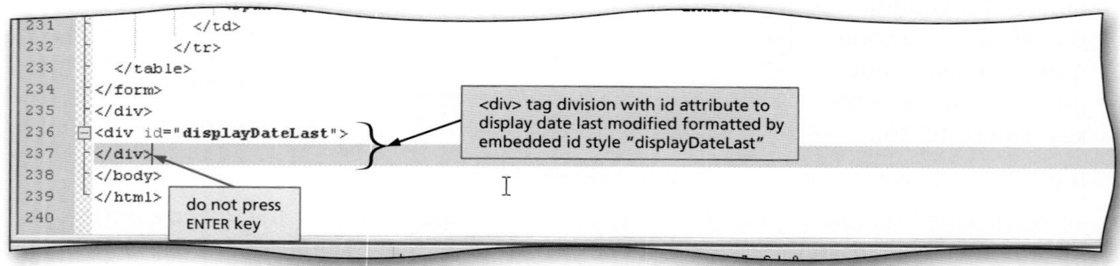

Figure 10–37

2

- Click line 104 and press the ENTER key.
- Enter the JavaScript code from Table 10–31 on the previous page to enter copyright and date-last-modified code, pressing the ENTER key only at the end of each complete line (Figure 10–38).

```
103 }
104
105 function copyRight() {
106     var lastModDate = document.lastModified
107     var lastModDate = lastModDate.substring(0,10)
108     displayDateLast.innerHTML = "<h6>Copyright &copy; Shoreline State Bank"+"<br />This document was last modified "+lastModDate+".</h6>"
109 }
110
111 //-->
112 </script>
113 <style type="text/css">
114 <!--
115 .align-center {
```

code to insert copyright and date last modified on Web page

Figure 10–38

3

- Position the insertion point in front of the "> at the end of line 168 (the line that contains the <body> tag).
- Press the SPACEBAR, type `copyRight()` after popUpNotice() to add the call to the copyRight() user-defined function to the <body> tag, and do not press the ENTER key (Figure 10–39).

code for additional call to user-defined function with onLoad event handler

```
165 -->
166 </style>
167 </head>
168 <body onLoad="scrollingMsg(); popUpNotice(); copyRight()">
169 <div class="center-div">
170   <p class="center-items"><img src="chapter10-banner.jpg" alt="
171 </div>
172 <div class="center-div">
173 <form id="msgForm">
174   <p style="text-align:center"><input type="text" name="scrollingMsg" size="25"></p>
```

do not press ENTER key at end of statement

Figure 10–39

To Save an HTML File, Test a Web Page, and Print the HTML File

The code for the Shoreline State Bank Web page with a loan payment calculator and pop-up window is complete. Now you should save the HTML file, test the JavaScript code using a Web browser, and then print the HTML file.

1. With the USB drive plugged into your computer, click File on the menu bar, and then click Save.
2. Click the browser button on the taskbar.
3. Click the Refresh button on the browser toolbar.
4. If necessary, click the Allow blocked content button. (If you are running Internet Explorer 8 or lower, your security message may be different.)

5. If the same security message displays on the pop-up window, click the Allow blocked content button, then click the Close Window button to close the pop-up window.

6. If necessary, scroll down to verify that the bottom of the Web page displays the date the page was last modified (the date the file was saved), as shown in Figure 10–40.

7. Return to Notepad++ and print the HTML file.

Q&A My Security message disappeared before I could click the button, what happened?

If the security message disappeared before you could click the 'Allow blocked content' button, refresh the Web page and the security message should display.

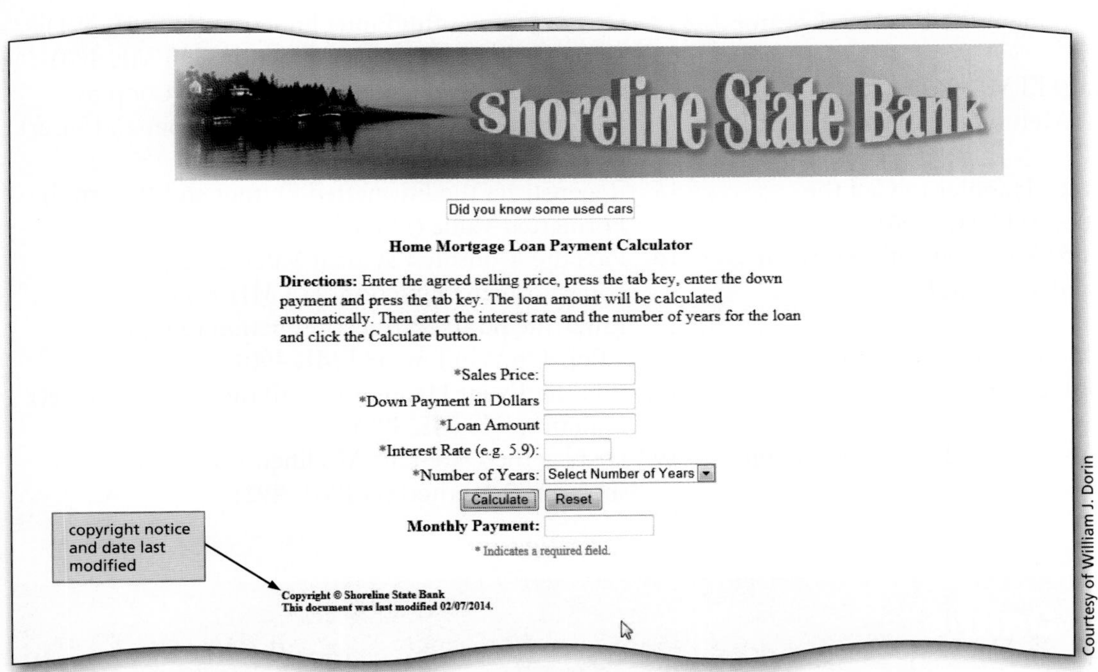

Figure 10–40

To Validate a Web Page

1. Open Internet Explorer, navigate to the Web site validator.w3.org, and then click the Validate by File Upload tab.

2. Click the Browse button.

3. Locate the chapter10-1solution.html file on your storage device, click the filename, and then click the Open button in the Choose File to Upload dialog box.

4. Click the Check button.

To Quit Notepad++ and a Browser

1. In Notepad++, click the File menu, then Close All.

2. Click the Close button on the Notepad++ title bar.

3. Click the Close button on the browser title bar. If necessary, click the Close all tabs button.

BTW

Quick Reference

For a list of JavaScript statements and their associated attributes, see the JavaScript Quick Reference (Appendix G) at the back of this book, or visit the JavaScript Quick Reference on the Book Companion Site Web page for this book at www.cengagebrain.com.

Chapter Summary

This chapter described how to write JavaScript to create a scrolling message, a pop-up window, and if and if...else statements; how to pass values to a user-defined function; how to validate the data entered into a form and convert text to numeric values using the parseInt(), parseFloat(), and isNaN() built-in functions; and how to format string output results to display as currency. The items listed below include all the new JavaScript skills you have learned in this chapter.

1. Create a Form Text Field to Display a Scrolling Message (HTML 458)
2. Create the scrollingMsg() User-Defined Function (HTML 460)
3. Enter the Code to Increment the Position Locator Variable (HTML 461)
4. Enter an if Statement (HTML 463)
5. Add the setTimeout() Method to Create a Recursive Call (HTML 464)
6. Enter the onLoad Event Handler to Call the scrollingMsg() Function (HTML 466)
7. Add the validSalesAmt() Function with Nested if... else Statements to Validate Form Data (HTML 474)
8. Enter the onBlur() Event Handler to Call the validSalesAmt() Function (HTML 475)
9. Enter the CalcLoanAmt() User-Defined Function (HTML 476)
10. Enter an onClick() Event Handler to Call the CalcLoanAmt() Function (HTML 477)
11. Enter Code to Call the monthlyPmt() Function (HTML 479)
12. Create the monthlyPmt() Function (HTML 481)
13. Enter the dollarFormat() Function (HTML 484)
14. Enter an if...else Statement and while Loop to Extract the Dollar Portion of the Output and Insert Commas (HTML 486)
15. Reconstruct the Formatted Output and Return the Formatted Value (HTML 487)
16. Pass the Monthly Payment Value to the dollarFormat() Function (HTML 487)
17. Enter the popUpNotice() Function to Open a Pop-Up Window (HTML 490)
18. Add the Event Handler to Call the popUpNotice() Function (HTML 490)
19. Display the Date Last Modified Using the substring() Method (HTML 492)

Learn It Online

Test your knowledge of chapter content and key terms.

Instructions: To complete the following exercises, please visit www.cengagebrain.com. At the CengageBrain.com home page, search for *HTML5 and CSS 7th Edition* using the search box at the top of the page. This will take you to the product page for this book. On the product page, click the Access Now button below the Study Tools heading. On the Book Companion Site Web page, select Chapter 10, and then click the link for the desired exercise.

Chapter Reinforcement TF, MC, and SA

A series of true/false, multiple choice, and short answer questions that test your knowledge of the chapter content.

Flash Cards

An interactive learning environment where you identify chapter key terms associated with displayed definitions.

Practice Test

A series of multiple choice questions that test your knowledge of chapter content and key terms.

Who Wants To Be a Computer Genius?

An interactive game that challenges your knowledge of chapter content in the style of a television quiz show.

Wheel of Terms

An interactive game that challenges your knowledge of chapter key terms in the style of the television show, *Wheel of Fortune*.

Crossword Puzzle Challenge

A crossword puzzle that challenges your knowledge of key terms presented in the chapter.

Apply Your Knowledge

Reinforce the skills and apply the concepts you learned in this chapter.

Instructions: Start Notepad++. Open the file apply10-1.html from the Chapter10\Apply folder of the Data Files for Students. See the inside back cover of this book for instructions on downloading the Data Files for Students, or contact your instructor for information about accessing the required files.

The apply10-1.html file is a partially completed HTML file for the Crab Apple Heights Elementary School that you will use for this exercise. You will use JavaScript to create a scrolling message and validate three text fields: parent or guardian name, cell phone, and e-mail address. The parent name and cell phone fields must not be blank. The e-mail address must include an @ sign for a valid e-mail address. You must add the event handler in the <body> tag to call the scrolling message function and the event handler in the Submit button to call the validate function. Figure 10–41 shows the Apply Your Knowledge Web page as it should be displayed in a browser after the JavaScript has been added.

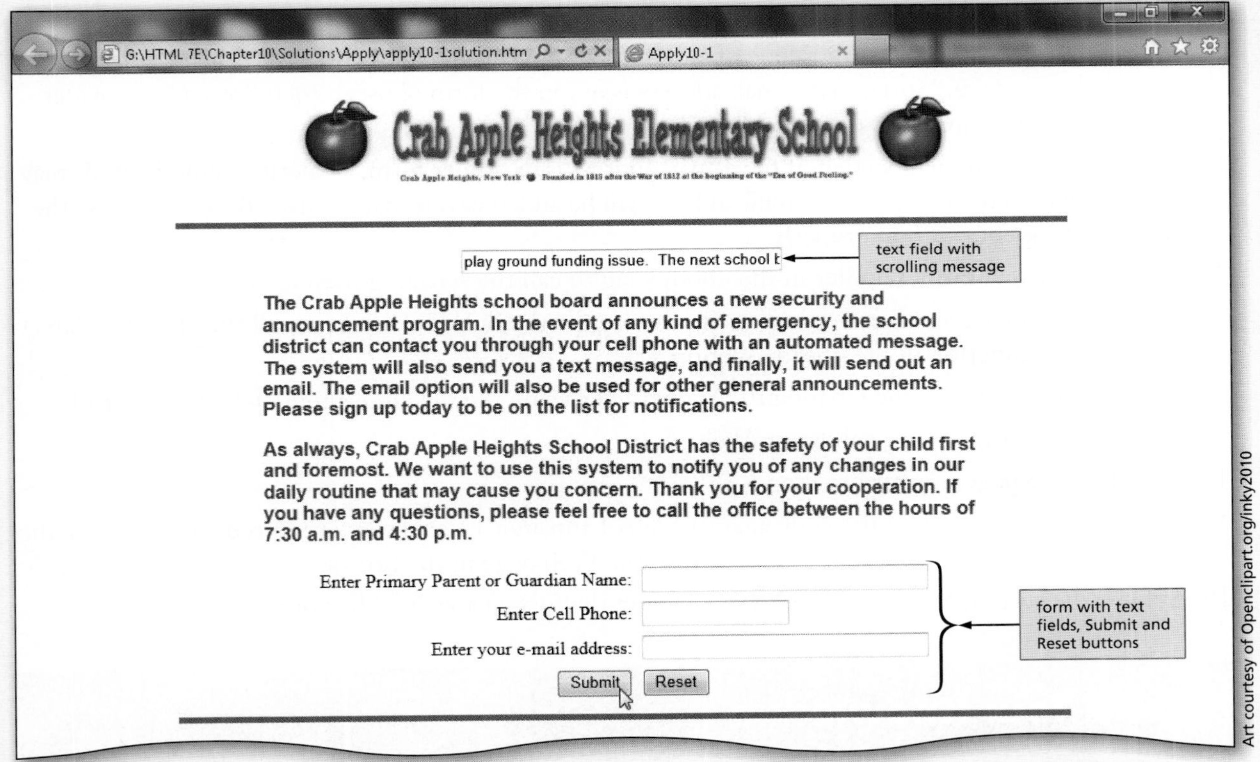

Figure 10–41

Perform the following tasks:

1. Enter the beginning of a JavaScript code section for a user-defined function in the <head> section of the Web page.
2. Using the code presented in Table 10–1 on page HTML 458 as a guide, enter a form for the scrolling message after the <div> tag following the brown divider line. Use Message as the name of the form and msgBox as the name of the text field.
3. Using the code in Tables 10–2, 10–6, and Figure 10–10 on pages HTML 459, 463, and 464, respectively, as a guide, write a JavaScript user defined function called scrollingMsg() to display the following text string, "The next school board meeting will discuss the playground funding issue." Be sure to leave a space before and after the text string message.

Continued >

Apply Your Knowledge *continued*

4. Assign this text string to a variable named Msg.
5. Use the variable name startAt as the position locator for the message.
6. In the setTimeout() method used to call the scrollingMsg() function, use 300 milliseconds as the time delay.
7. Declare a new user-defined function named emailValidate(emailForm).
8. Use an if statement to verify that the parent or guardian name text field (parent) is not blank by testing if the length of the text field is less than 1. If the field is blank, use an alert to notify the user with the message, "Please enter a parent or family name."
9. Use an if statement to verify that cell phone text field is not blank by testing if the length of the text field is less than 1. If the field is blank, use an alert to notify the user with the message, "Please enter a cell phone number in the format of xxx-xxx-xxxx to receive text messages."
10. Use the indexOf() method to determine if an @ sign is in the e-mail text field. Assign the result of the indexOf() method to a variable named atSign.
11. Enter an if statement to test the value of atSign. If atSign is less than 0, then use an alert() method to display the message, "Sorry, that e-mail address is not in the form of userID@ followed by provider name. Please re-enter your e-mail address."
12. Enter the else statement so that, if the e-mail address is in proper form, an alert() method will display the message, "Thank you. Your e-mail address will be added to our mailing list." Be sure to close the JavaScript <script> section properly.
13. Enter the proper event handler in the <body> tag to call the scrolling message function.
14. Enter the proper event handler in the <input> tag for the Submit button to call the emailValidate() user-defined function in the <head> section.
15. Save the revised file in the Chapter10\Apply folder using the filename apply10-1solution.html.
16. Validate using the w3.org validation Web page.
17. Test the Web page in your browser.
18. If any errors occur, check the code against Steps 1 through 14, make any required changes, save the file using the same filename, and then refresh the Web page in the browser.
19. Submit the revised HTML file and Web page in the format specified by your instructor.

Extend Your Knowledge

Extend the skills you learned in this chapter and experiment with new skills. You will need to search the Internet to complete the assignment.

Learning More About Displaying Messages

Instructions: Start Notepad++ and your browser. Open the file extend10-1.html from the Chapter10\Extend folder of the Data Files for Students. See the inside back cover of this book for instructions on downloading the Data Files for Students, or contact your instructor for information about accessing the required files.

The extend10-1.html file is a partially completed HTML file that you will use for this exercise. Figure 10–42 shows the Extend Your Knowledge Web page as it should be displayed in a browser after the JavaScript has been added.

A number of Web sites use forms where part of the form or a button is "disabled" by being grayed out or not visible until a response to a question or an option button or check box item has been selected. Once the question, option button, or check box has been filled or selected a button, text field, or image may become visible or usable.

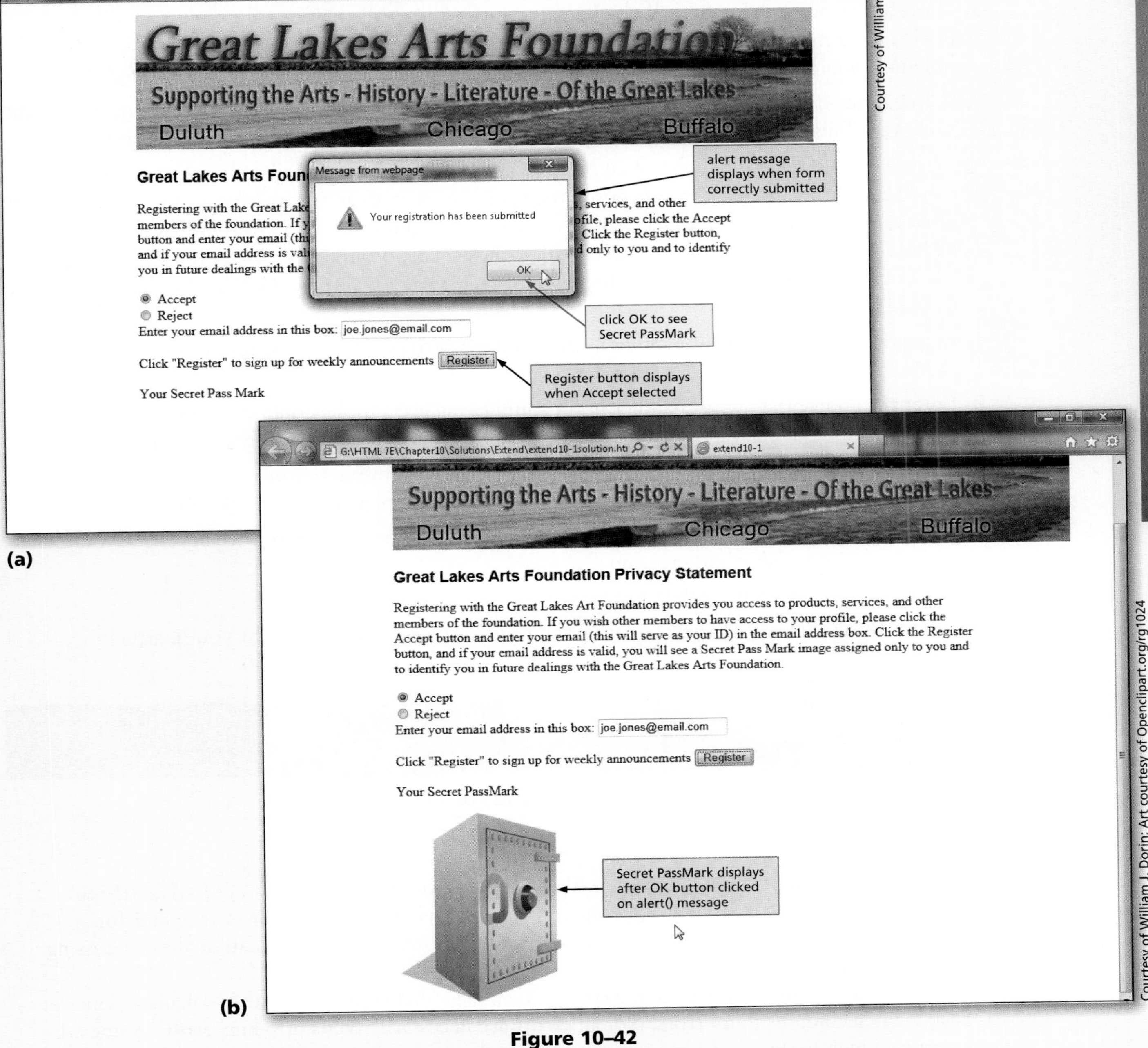

Figure 10–42

Search the Internet to find out how to disable and enable a text field and a button and how to hide an image with an HTML attribute and style. Then, search for the JavaScript code to disable and activate the text field and button when an option button has been selected. (You will need to disable fields and buttons and hide the image when you reload the Web page.) When the text field and button display, the user will enter an e-mail address, which must be valid, then a PassMark image will be displayed. (*Hint:* Look for the style.display with the getElementById() method.)

Perform the following tasks:

1. Save the file extend10-1.html as extend10-1solution.html.
2. Create a <script> section in the <head> section for three user-defined functions: disableItems(), accept_it(), and register().

Continued >

Extend Your Knowledge *continued*

3. Write a user-defined function, disableItems(), which will be called by an onload event handler, to disable the e-mail text box, the submitreg button, the emailfield, and the PassMark image. This function should also make sure the acceptpolicy and rejectpolicy radio buttons are enabled.
4. Write a user-defined function, named accept_it(), that is called when the acceptpolicy option button is clicked. This function should enable the emailfield and the register (submitreg) button.
5. Write a user-defined function, called register(), that validates the e-mail address entered into the emailfield. If the e-mail address is not in the proper form with an @ sign, display the following error message: "Sorry, that e-mail address is not in a valid format. Please re-enter your e-mail address." Place focus back on the emailfield. If the e-mail address is in the correct format, display the message:" Your registration has been submitted," and then display the PassMark image (extend10-1safe.jpg).
6. Enter the appropriate event handler in the <body> tag to call the disableItems() function when the Web page is loaded.
7. Enter the appropriate event handler in the <input> tag acceptpolicy option button to call the accept_it() user-defined function when the user clicks the acceptpolicy option button.
8. Enter the appropriate event handler in the <input> tag submitreg button to call the register() user-defined function to validate the e-mail address and display the PassMark image.
9. Save the completed HTML file and test it using your browser. If an error occurs, check your code from Steps 2 through 8 and save and test again.
10. Validate using the w3.org validation Web page.
11. Submit the completed HTML file and Web page in the format specified by your instructor.

Make It Right

Analyze the JavaScript code on a Web page and correct all errors.

Correcting Syntax Errors and Inserting Missing Code

Instructions: Start your browser. Open the file make10-1.html from the Chapter10\MakeItRight folder of the Data Files for Students. See the inside back cover of this book for instructions for downloading the Data Files for Students, or contact your instructor for information about accessing the required files.

The make10-1.html Web page is a college Web page that allows students to calculate semester expenses, which contains four errors. Not all errors are necessarily typos or syntax errors. Some are logic errors, which means a statement may be executed out of order, is missing, or, in the case of JavaScript, is using an incorrect property or method.

Use the following information as background for your corrections. The number of credit hours to select from the drop-down menu is 14, and enter 1800 for the total expenses. The corrected Web page is shown in Figure 10–43.

Perform the following tasks:

1. Refresh the Web page in the browser and look at the error messages. (*Hint:* You may have to enable Internet Explorer script debugging to see the errors. Use the Internet options command on the Tools menu, click the Advanced tab, and then in the Settings box, Browsing category, deselect the 'Disable script debugging (Internet Explorer)' check box.)

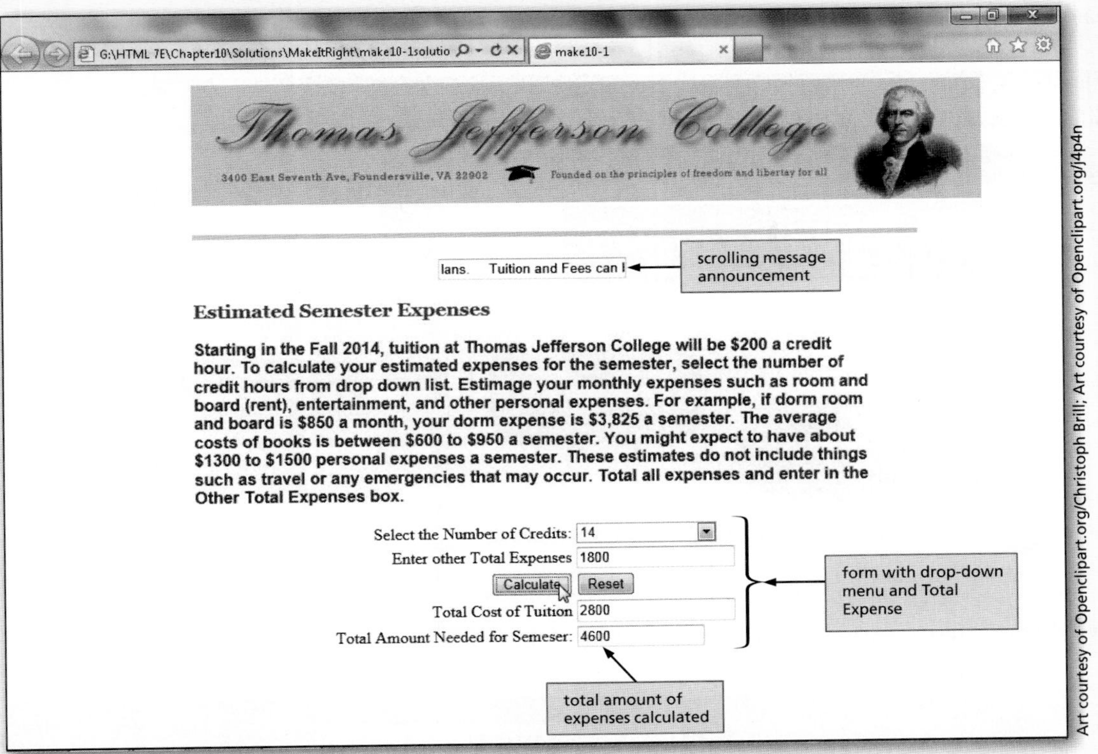

Figure 10–43

2. Correct any misspelled variable names, function, and object names. Search for any logic errors that may be in the JavaScript code that produce incorrect results.
3. Make sure validation of the form input is correct.
4. Make sure all user-defined functions are being called properly.
5. Save the corrected HTML file as make10-1solution.html, test using your browser, and then validate the Web page. If an error still occurs, check your code from Steps 1 through 4 and save again.
6. Submit the revised HTML file and Web page in the format specified by your instructor.

In the Lab

Design and/or create a Web page using the guidelines, concepts, and skills presented in this chapter. Labs are listed in order of increasing difficulty.

Lab 1: Danyi's Donuts

Instructions: Your sister, Danyi, has opened a donut shop. She asks if you can create a Web page that will calculate the cost of a donut order. The user will select the type of donut from a drop-down menu and enter the number of donuts they want. When the user clicks the calculate button, it will validate the data entered and calculate the cost of the donuts. A sample solution is shown in Figure 10–44 on the next page.

Continued >

In the Lab *continued*

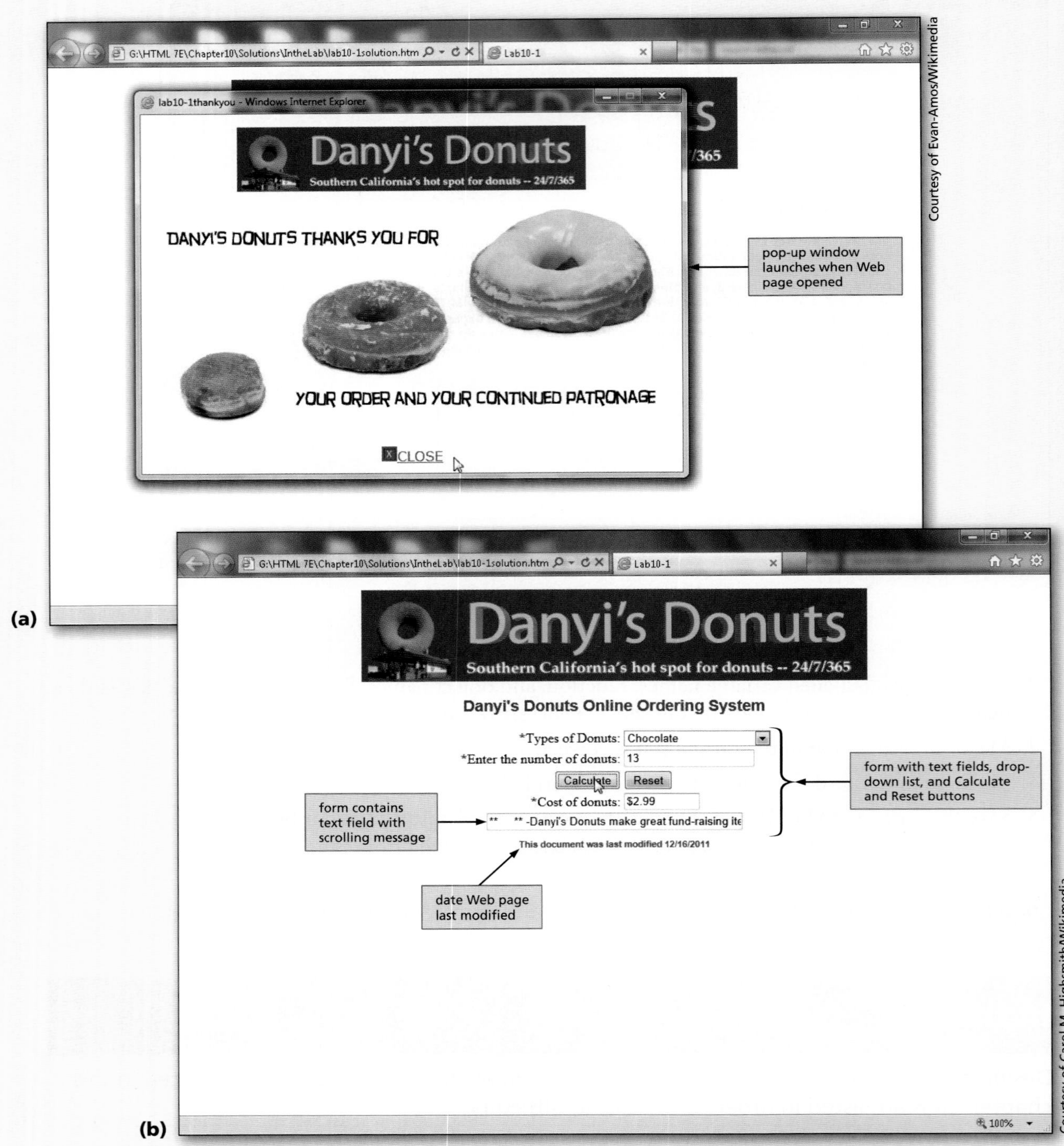

Figure 10–44

Instructions: Perform the following tasks:

1. Start Notepad++ and open the lab10-1.html file from the Chapter10\IntheLab folder of the Data Files for Students.
2. Save the file as lab10-1solution.html.
3. Create a <script> section in the <head> section for user-defined functions.
4. Create a form for a scrolling message. Use the text ** -Danyi's Donuts make great fund-raising items.- ** as the message.
5. Place the form for the message box text field beneath the donutOrder form table at line 100. Use "msgBox" for the form name and use the embedded style sheet, center-items, to center the form on the page. Name the input text field "Message" and make the width 45.
6. Using the form named donutOrder, write the JavaScript code to validate the drop-down menu and the text field values in the form. Use nested if statements to validate that the donutType was selected and that the count is a valid numeric value.
7. Display a message if the donut type is not selected and the number of donuts is not numeric, clear the text field, and use the focus() method to position the insertion point back in that text field.
8. If the values are valid, compute the cost of the donuts by multiplying the selected type of donuts times the number ordered. Assign the value to a variable totalCost.
9. Assign the totalCost to itself using the toFixed() method to set two decimal places.
10. Use the code in Tables 10–22, 10–25, and 10–26 on pages HTML 483 through HTML 487 as a guide to display the result in currency format in the donutCost text field.
11. Add a function called thankyouWindow to display the pop-up window, lab10-1thankyou.html.
12. Add a function called lastModifiedMsg to display the date the document was last modified in the <div id="footer"> tag.
13. Be sure to add the appropriate event handlers where required.
14. Save the revised lab10-1solution.html file.
15. Test the Web page in your browser.
16. Validate the Web page using the w3.org validation Web page.
17. If any errors occur, check the code against Steps 3 through 14, make any required changes, save the file using the same filename, and then refresh the Web page in the browser.
18. Submit the revised HTML file and Web page in the format specified by your instructor.

STUDENT ASSIGNMENTS

In the Lab

Lab 2: Circle Cement

Instructions: You are the Webmaster for Circle Cement. A number of customers have been asking for a way to calculate how much cement they need to order for a job. Management has asked you to create an interactive Web page that will allow customers to input the length, width, and depth of concrete needed and calculate the number of yards. The Web page has a scrolling message and validates the data entered into the form as numeric. The calculated number of yards needed is truncated to two decimal places and displayed in the text field yards. Add the JavaScript to make the Web page appear as in Figure 10–45.

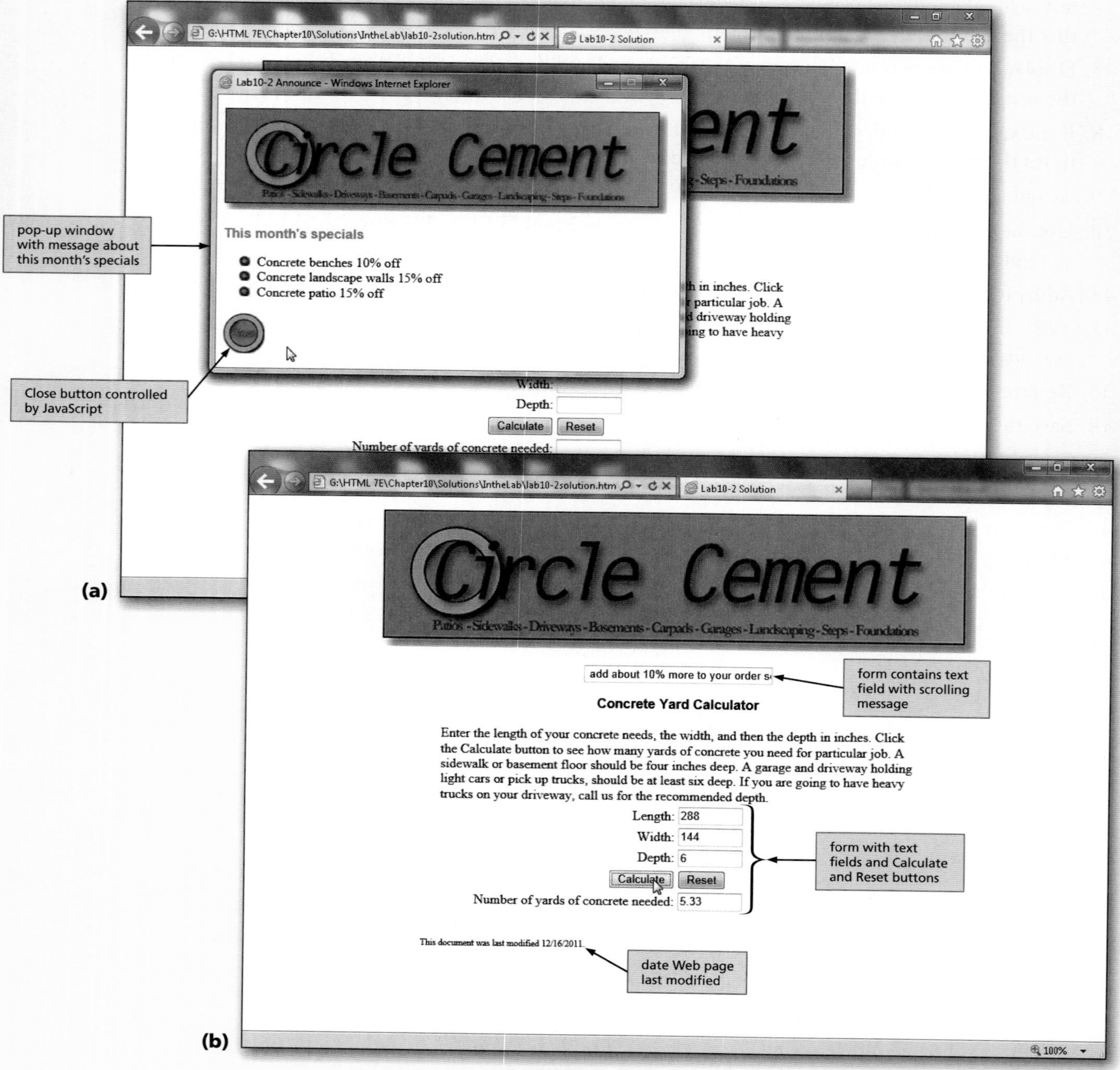

Figure 10–45

Perform the following tasks:

1. Start Notepad++ and open the file lab10-2.html from the Chapter10\IntheLab folder of the Data Files for Students.
2. Save the file as lab10-2solution.html.
3. Using the code from Table 10–1 on page HTML 458 as a guide, create a form with one text field for a scrolling message between the <div> tags at line 55. Name the form msgForm, the input text field messageBox, and make the text field size 32.
4. Create a <script> section in the <head> section for the user-defined functions.
5. Using the code presented in Figures 10–4 through 10–10 on pages HTML 460 through HTML 464 as a guide, write the user-defined function called textMsg(). Assign the message string "*** Remember, you should add about 10% more to your order so you do not run short. ***" to a variable named concreteMsg.
6. Use 200 for the setTimeout() method to recursively call the textMsg() function.
7. Using the code in Tables 10–14 and 10–15 on pages HTML 475 and HTML 476 as a guide, write the JavaScript user-defined function concreteCalc() to validate the data entered into the form as numeric and not less than 0.
8. Assign the length value to iLength, the width value to iWidth, and the depth value to iDepth.
9. Once the data is validated as numeric, calculate the cubicInches by multiplying iLength times iWidth times iDepth. Calculate the cubicFeet by dividing the cubicInches by 1728. Calculate the cubicYards by dividing the cubicFeet by 27.
10. Assign the cubicYards to the yards text field using the toFixed() method with 2 decimal places.
11. If an error occurs, check your code from Steps 3 through 10 and save and test again. Do not continue unless there are no errors.
12. Using the code in Table 10–29 on page HTML 489, write a user-defined function that opens a pop-up window using the file lab10-2announce.html. Set the window size to 545 pixels wide by 330 pixels high.
13. Use the code in Table 10–30 on page HTML 491 as a guide to enter a <div> tag with an id concreteLastDate, and an inline style of margin-left 20% before the closing </body> tag.
14. Use the code in Table 10–31 on page HTML 491 as a guide to enter the user-defined function to display the date the Web page was last modified, as shown in Figure 10–45.
15. Be sure to enter the event handlers as needed in the form and the <body> tag.
16. Save the completed HTML file, validate, and test the Web page using your browser using the values shown in Figure 10–45.
17. If an error occurs, check your code from Steps 12 through 16, save, and test again.
18. Submit the completed HTML file and Web page in the format specified by your instructor.

In the Lab

Lab 3: Consumer Credit Counselors

Instructions: You are the Webmaster for Consumer Credit Counselors, a not-for-profit organization. As a benefit for credit-conscious individuals, a Web page will allow users to enter the amount of their credit card debt, their interest rate, and their minimum monthly payment to calculate the number of months needed to pay off their credit cards. This Web page will have a scrolling message, "** The higher your monthly payments, the quicker you can pay off your debt.**" When the Web page loads, a pop-up window will display some basic information about Consumer Credit Counselors. The Web page will validate the data entered into the form as numeric and greater than zero and display the number of months needed to pay off the credit card debt.

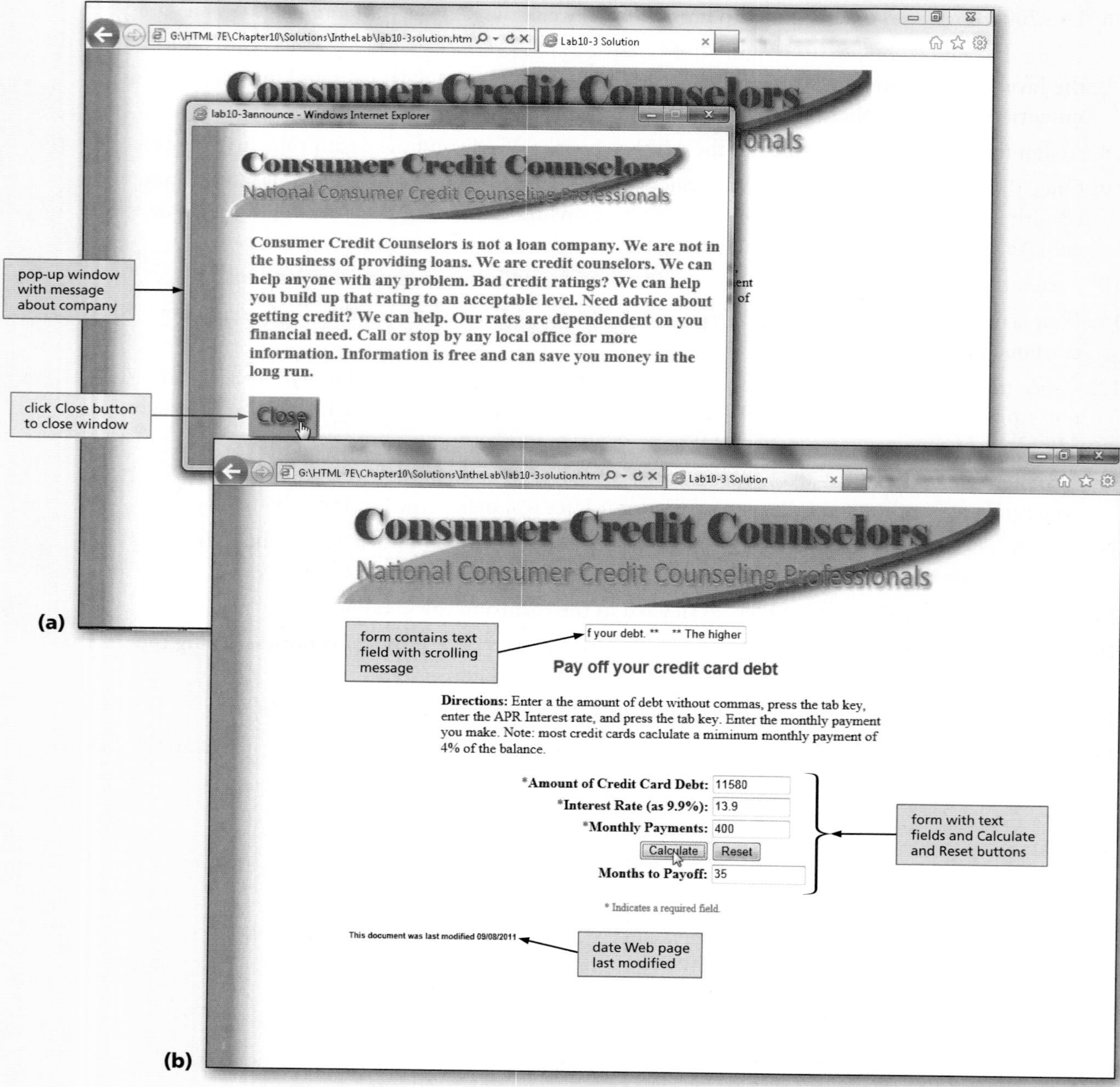

Figure 10–46

Perform the following tasks:

1. Start Notepad++ and open the lab10-3.html file from the Chapter10\IntheLab folder of the Data Files for Students. Save immediately as lab10-3solution.html.
2. Using the techniques learned in this chapter, write the JavaScript code to create a scrolling message, validate the data entered into the form, and calculate the number of months to pay off a debt making a specific monthly payment. Place the scrolling message form text field in the blank line after the banner image, and use the embedded style sheet class, align-center, to center the form. Add the date the Web page was last modified in the blank line before the </body> tag at the bottom of the Web page. Use either a <div> or <footer> tag with an inline style with a left margin of 25% and the id attribute, lastDate. A pop-up window should display with a message as indicated in Figure 10–46a. The pop-up window size is 600 pixels wide by 390 pixels high. The pop-up filename is lab10-3announce.html.
3. Save the completed HTML file, validate, and test it using your browser. If an error occurs, check your code, save, and test again.
4. Submit the completed HTML file and Web page in the format specified by your instructor.

Cases and Places

Apply your creative thinking and problem-solving skills to design and implement a solution.

Note: To complete these assignments, you may be required to use the Data Files for Students. See the inside back cover of this book for instructions on downloading the Data Files for Students, or contact your instructor for information about accessing the required files.

1: Creating a Stock Market Club Web Page

Academic

You are a member of your campus Stock Market Club. Because you have had a course in Web design and Web programming, they have asked you to create a Web page that allows a user to enter a current stock quote price and the number of shares of the five stocks your club has chosen to track. Your Web page form should validate that the data entered is numeric and should display a total cost of shares purchased, formatted with commas and dollar signs.

You should search the Internet for a widget or badge (such as Yahoo! Finance at finance.yahoo.com/badges). Follow the steps for creating the HTML code to embed the stock quotes on your page. Use your five stocks as the stock symbols. (Search the Internet to find the stock symbols you want to use.) Use this page as a pop-up window that launches when the Web page is loaded.

2: Calculating Your GPA

Personal

Quite often, students like to track their own semester GPA. Check with your school, but most schools that use a plus/minus grade system assign the following values to letter grades: A+ = 4, A = 4, A- = 3.7, B+ = 3.3, B = 3, B- = 2.7, C+ = 2, C- = 1.7, D+ = 1.3, D = 1, D- = .7, F = 0. Grades of W, I, P are not calculated in a GPA.

Create a form that allows you to enter from four to six courses. For each course have a text box to accept the letter grade. Next to the letter grade, have a text field that accepts the credit hours for the course. Include Calculate GPA and Reset buttons. When you click the Calculate GPA button, the JavaScript function needs to verify that a valid grade letter has been entered and then accumulate the number of grade points. At the same time, you need to accumulate the credit hours.

Continued >

STUDENT ASSIGNMENTS

Cases and Places *continued*

To calculate the GPA, divide the number of grade points by the total number of credit hours. Display your GPA using an alert() function. As you verify the grades, you should convert the letter in the text field to upper case to be consistent. In addition, you are only looking for letter grades of A+, A, A-, and so on. Not every course needs a grade so you should not enter W, I, or P grades.

3: Creating a Web page for a Real Estate Web site

Professional

You are an intern at the Shoreline State Bank. The bank has received numerous questions about the loan calculator Web page. Customers want to be able to enter the sale price, a down payment percentage (not a dollar value), and calculate the mortgage amount based on the down payment. In addition, they wish to have the amount of Personal Mortgage Insurance (PMI) calculated and added to the form.

Create a separate function that validates Selling Price and Percent Down (for Down Payment) text fields as valid numbers. Calculate the down payment by multiplying the down payment percentage times the selling price and subtracting that value from the selling price. Use an onBlur event handler to call this function after the percent down value is entered. *Hint:* Selling Price - (Selling Price * (Percent Down/100)).

Use the original form from the chapter project, add the text field, and use the original event handler to call the Calc() user-defined function. Add the calculation to test if the percent down is less than 20% to calculate the PMI. The monthly PMI is calculated by taking the mortgage amount * .005 and dividing the product by 12 to get the monthly amount.

1 Using DOM to Enhance Web Pages

Courtesy of William J. Dorin; Art courtesy of Openclipart.org/John Olsen; Courtesy of the Bernice P. Bishop Museum, Wikimedia; Courtesy of Will Murray, Wikimedia; Courtesy of Will Murray, Wikimedia; Courtesy of the Bernice P. Bishop Museum, Wikimedia; Courtesy of Kriplozoik, Wikimedia

Objectives

You will have mastered the material in this chapter when you can:

- Define the Document Object Model (DOM)
- Use the Math.random() method to display a different image on a Web page every time the Web page is loaded
- Describe how mouse event handlers control image rollovers
- Integrate Cascading Style Sheets (CSS) with JavaScript statements to position elements on a Web page
- Use the JavaScript setTimeout() and clearTimeout() methods to control a floating image on a page
- Call JavaScript functions directly using the JavaScript command
- Use onMouseOver and onMouseOut event handlers to control pop-up captions
- Integrate the <div> tag in JavaScript statements for pop-up captions
- Define an array and describe how to create an array instance
- Create a slide show using image objects

11 Using DOM to Enhance Web Pages

Introduction

BTW

The Document Object Model (DOM)
The Document Object Model (DOM) is an application programming interface (API) that identifies interfaces, semantics, and relationships, and allows JavaScript and other languages to dynamically manipulate and update the structure of the underlying document. The core parts of the DOM are the scripting language, the markup language, and style sheets. The DOM's simple and hierarchical naming system makes certain objects on a Web page, such as images, forms, and layers, accessible to scripting languages, which allow the appearance of the Web page to fit a specified circumstance.

In Chapter 10, you learned to write JavaScript user-defined functions to add scrolling messages and pop-up windows to your Web site, to validate user entries on Web forms, to make calculations from user input, and to format output to a text field. This chapter builds on those skills and others you have learned so far by introducing the **Document Object Model (DOM)**, a combination of technologies that includes HTML, Cascading Style Sheets (CSS), and a scripting language, such as JavaScript, which used to be referred to as DHTML. The DOM will make your Web pages more dynamic. In this chapter, you will use DOM to manipulate image objects. You will create four Web pages that incorporate a navigation bar using image rollovers, display a random image when a Web page loads, showcase a slide show, use a floating image as a link to a pop-up window, and use pop-up captions to display additional information.

Project — The Hickory Oaks Forest Preserve Web Site

You are on the Web development team for Hickory Oaks Forest Preserve, which is redesigning its Web site to incorporate DOM technology. The new design includes a navigation bar that uses image rollovers as links to three different Web pages about the nature center, the gift shop, and the trails. For consistency, every Web page uses the same navigation bar. The home page uses a random number generator to display a different image every time the user reloads the page.

To make the Hickory Oaks Forest Preserve Web site more interesting, you will have the Nature Center Web page automatically start a slide show displaying different images of trees. You will have the Gift Shop Web page use a floating image to add animation to the page, which stops when the user places the mouse over the image and starts up again when the user moves the mouse off the image. If the user clicks the floating image, a pop-up window displays with a coupon. For the Trails Web page, you will add pop-up captions providing more information about certain aspects of the trails. A **pop-up caption** is text that appears when you hover the mouse pointer over an item on the screen; the text provides additional information about the item. The Web pages provided in the Data Files for Students contain embedded CSS to format and place text and images. Later in the chapter, you will enter additional CSS selectors and properties related to the pop-up captions and images.

Figure 11–1 shows the completed Hickory Oaks Forest Preserve Home page and the three supporting Web pages with dynamic elements.

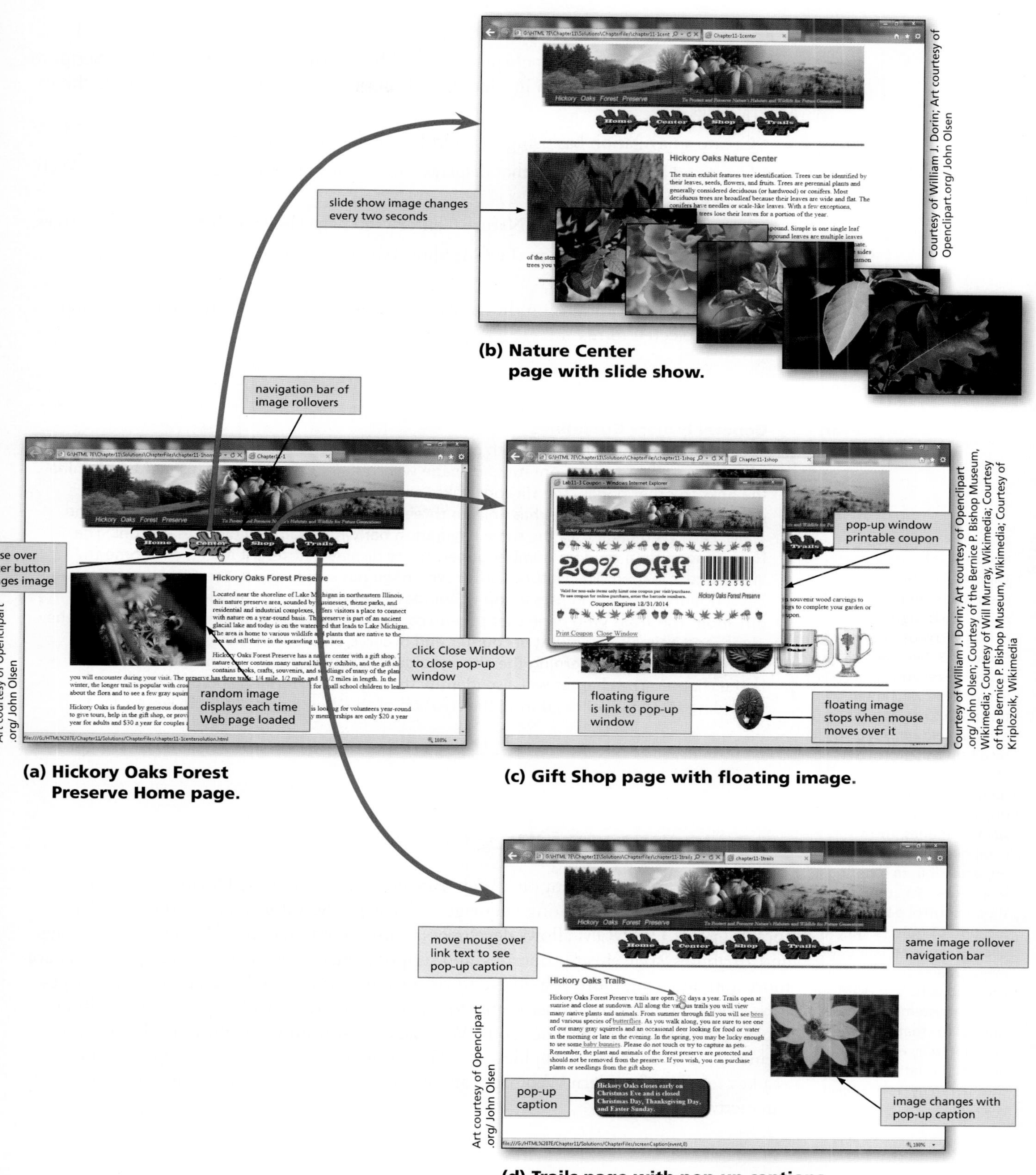
slide show image changes every two seconds
navigation bar of image rollovers
mouse over Center button changes image
random image displays each time Web page loaded
click Close Window to close pop-up window
pop-up window printable coupon
floating figure is link to pop-up window
floating image stops when mouse moves over it
move mouse over link text to see pop-up caption
same image rollover navigation bar
pop-up caption
image changes with pop-up caption
Hickory Oaks Nature Center
Hickory Oaks Forest Preserve
Hickory Oaks Trails
20% Off
Coupon Expires 12/31/2014
Print Coupon Close Window
Hickory Oaks closes early on Christmas Eve and is closed Christmas Day, Thanksgiving Day, and Easter Sunday.
Courtesy of William J. Dorin; Art courtesy of Openclipart.org/ John Olsen
Courtesy of William J. Dorin; Art courtesy of Openclipart.org/ John Olsen; Courtesy of the Bernice P. Bishop Museum, Wikimedia; Courtesy of Will Murray, Wikimedia; Courtesy of the Bernice P. Bishop Museum, Wikimedia; Courtesy of Kriplozoik, Wikimedia
Art courtesy of Openclipart.org/ John Olsen

(a) Hickory Oaks Forest Preserve Home page.

(b) Nature Center page with slide show.

(c) Gift Shop page with floating image.

(d) Trails page with pop-up captions.

Figure 11–1

Overview

As you read through this chapter, you will learn how to use DOM with JavaScript to create dynamic pages as shown in Figure 11–1 on the previous page by performing these general tasks:

- Create a navigation bar using image rollovers for all Web pages.
- Create a Home Web page that displays a different random image each time the Web page is loaded.
- Create a slide show on the Nature Center Web page showing different types of trees.
- Create a floating image on the Gift Shop Web page that also serves as a link to launch a pop-up window.
- Create pop-up captions on the Trails Web page to provide additional information about selected terms.

Plan Ahead

General Project Guidelines
In creating a complex Web site with multiple Web pages, you should determine what pages will be created and what content each page will contain. In addition, you should determine the links to other pages. The Hickory Oaks Forest Preserve Web site contains four Web pages. The main Home page has links to three other pages: Nature Center, Gift Shop, and Trails. Each Web page uses the same navigation bar with image rollovers as buttons. The Home page uses a random number generator to display a different image each time the Web page is loaded. The Nature Center Web page has a slide show. The Gift Shop Web page has a floating image and uses a pop-up window that displays a coupon for the preserve's gift shop. The Trails Web page uses pop-up captions to provide more information about the plants and animals you might encounter and observe on the trail. When necessary, more specific instruction concerning the above guidelines is presented at appropriate points in the chapter. The chapter will also identify the actions performed and decisions made regarding these guidelines during the creation of the Web pages shown in Figure 11–1.

BTW

Document Object Model Techniques
The DOM techniques used to create these Web pages are designed for use in Microsoft Internet Explorer 9. Because not all browsers recognize objects in the same way, these techniques may not work or may yield unexpected results in other browsers. The DOM hierarchical naming system makes objects on a Web page, such as images, form components, layers, and so on, accessible to scripting languages. Because style sheets control position or location of objects, they allow a scripting language even greater control over these objects. The DOM naming system uses these objects to create a tree-like hierarchy of parent and child relationships. In this hierarchy, each object is a node.

The Document Object Model (DOM)

Each section and component on a Web page is an object, and the Document Object Model (DOM) allows scripting languages such as JavaScript to access and manipulate those objects. The DOM allows developers to use a combination of HTML objects, tags and attributes, style sheet properties, and scripting languages to create Web pages that are more animated and more responsive to visitor interaction than basic HTML Web pages.

With DOM, a developer is able to identify objects, such as graphics, and position, replace, or move them anywhere on a Web page. **Positioning** specifies the placement of elements, such as text and graphics, on a Web page. Dynamic positioning of elements is a key feature of modern Web pages and makes the Web pages more appealing and interactive.

To Open an Existing HTML File in Notepad++

In this chapter, the partially completed HTML code for the Home Web page is provided in the Data Files for Students in the file chapter11-1home.html, which includes an embedded CSS <style> section. You will begin by opening this file in a new Notepad++ window.

1. Start Notepad++, and, if necessary, maximize the window. Verify that word wrap is on.
2. With a USB flash drive plugged in to your computer, click File on the menu bar and then click Open.
3. Navigate to the Chapter11\ChapterFiles folder on the USB drive.
4. Double-click chapter11-1home.html in the list of files to display the HTML code for the chapter11-1home.html Web page, as shown in Figure 11–2.

BTW

Document Object Model Hierarchy Nodes

The DOM naming system uses a treelike hierarchy of parent and child relationships where each object is a node. A **node** is a point in a treelike structure that indicates the relationship between objects. The <html> tag is the root node, and the <body> tag is a child to the <html> tag node. These relationships allow an object to become a child of another object, and the relationship between the document object and the objects within a Web page is what gives Web developers access to every aspect of the Web page.

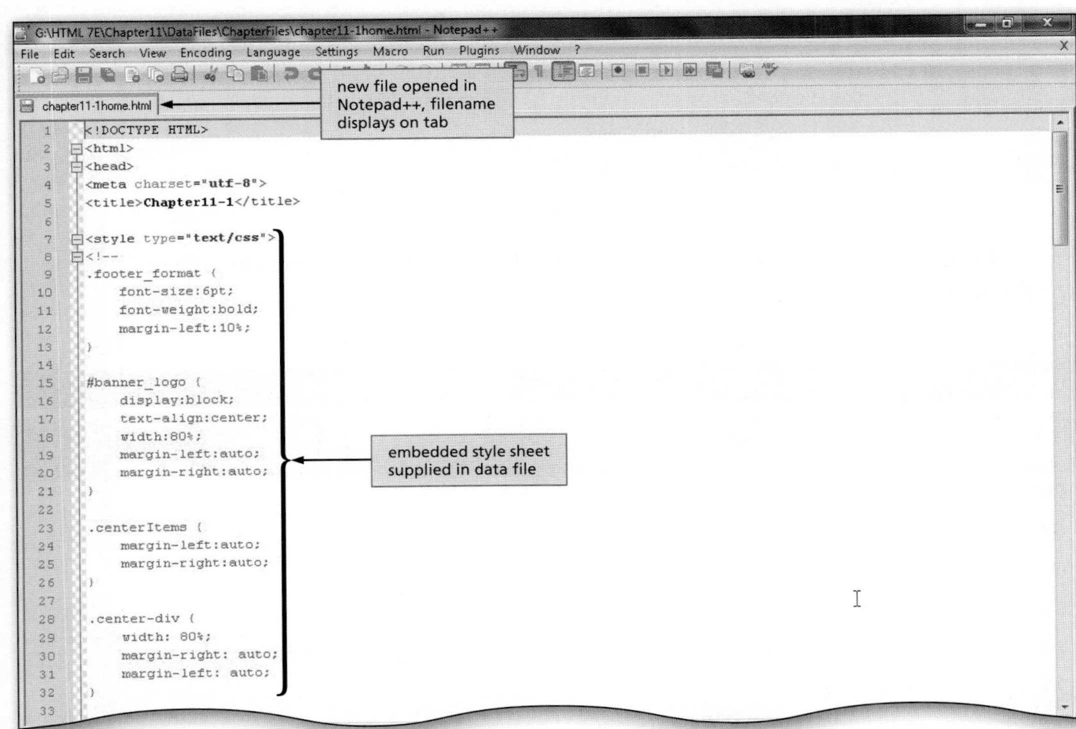

Figure 11–2

Plan Ahead

Creating the navigation bar with image rollovers.

To create and utilize the navigation bar on the Hickory Oaks Forest Preserve Web site, create the following items:

- A set of images used as buttons, to represent the mouse state: up-state, over-state, and down-state
- A table with one row and as many data table cells as needed for each button
- JavaScript user-defined functions associated with each mouse event handler

The buttons should be named the same way including its state (up, over, down) as part of the name. For example, chapter11-1home_down.jpg includes the button text (home) and its state (down) when clicked. The name will be used to select the correct button to match the event handler calling the image rollover user-defined function.

Creating the Navigation Bar

The first step in updating the Hickory Oaks Forest Preserve Web site is to create the graphics needed for the buttons. In this case, a graphic designer has created and supplied the images. The button image names should relate to the mouse state: up, down, or over. The navigation bar is an HTML table with one table row (<tr>), and four table data cells (<td>) that will contain the images (<img>) and event handlers to call a user-defined function to change the button depending on the action of the mouse. In addition, in each table data cell, an anchor tag (<a href>) makes the image a link to another Web page.

Within each table data cell the <img> tag contains an id attribute to identify that image as an object. Table 11–1 reviews the general form of the <img> tag.

BTW

Making Web Pages Dynamic with DOM
Using JavaScript takes away the dependence on the server to produce interesting effects and animation on a Web page. As the content of the Web page grows or changes, so does the appearance and presentation of the Web page.

BTW

Tag Name Attribute
Because the name attribute is deprecated in HTML5 for the <img> tag, JavaScript must use the getElementByID method to access the image object.

Table 11–1 General Form of <img> Tag to Create Image Object

General form:	<img src="img_Filename" id="Object_name" alt="alternative text" />
Comment:	where the *source* (img_Filename) represents the filename of the image that initially is displayed at the location where the tag appears. The **id** attribute identifies the object for JavaScript. To be HTML5 compliant, <img> tags need an **alt** attribute, which is alternative text that appears if the graphic does not load. In addition, HTML5 requires that empty tags like <img> must include the closing / symbol within the tag.
Example:	<img src="chapter11-1home_up.gif" id="home" alt="home" />

Table 11–2 shows the code to enter the HTML table to create the image objects for the image rollover navigation bar.

Table 11–2 HTML Code to Create the Table to Contain a Navigation Bar

```
<table class="centerItems">
  <tr>
  <td>
  <a href="#">
  <img src="chapter11-1home_up.gif" id="home" alt="home"/></a>
  </td>
  <td>
  <a href="chapter11-1centersolution.html">
  <img src="chapter11-1center_up.jpg" id="center"
  alt="nature center"/></a>
  </td>
  <td>
  <a href="chapter11-1shopsolution.html">
  <img src="chapter11-1shop_up.gif" id="shop" alt="gift shop"/></a>
  </td>
  <td>
```

Table 11–2 HTML Code to Create the Table to Contain a Navigation Bar (continued)

Line	Code
81	<a href="chapter11-1trailssolution.html">
82	<img src="chapter11-1trails_up.gif" id="trails" alt="trails" /></a>
83	</td>
84	</tr>
85	</table>

Line 66 starts the table that holds the navigation bar. The class attribute centerItems will center the table on the page based on a style sheet selector and rule. Line 67 starts the only table row. Lines 68, 72, 76, and 80 start a new column or data cell tag (<td>) to hold each image. Lines 71, 75, 79, and 83 close the data cell </td> tag. Lines 69, 73, 77, and 81 include an <a href> tag to link to each of the four Web pages. Lines 70, 74, 78, and 82 contain the <img> tag with the image of the button in its "up state." Line 84 closes the row </tr> tag and line 85 closes the </table>.

To Create an HTML Table to Contain the Navigation Bar

The following step enters the HTML code to create the navigation bar.

1

- Click line 66 (the blank line after the </div> tag).
- Enter the HTML code shown in Table 11–2 to create the HTML table for the navigation bar, indenting as shown. Do not press the ENTER key after the </table> tag on line 85 (Figure 11–3).

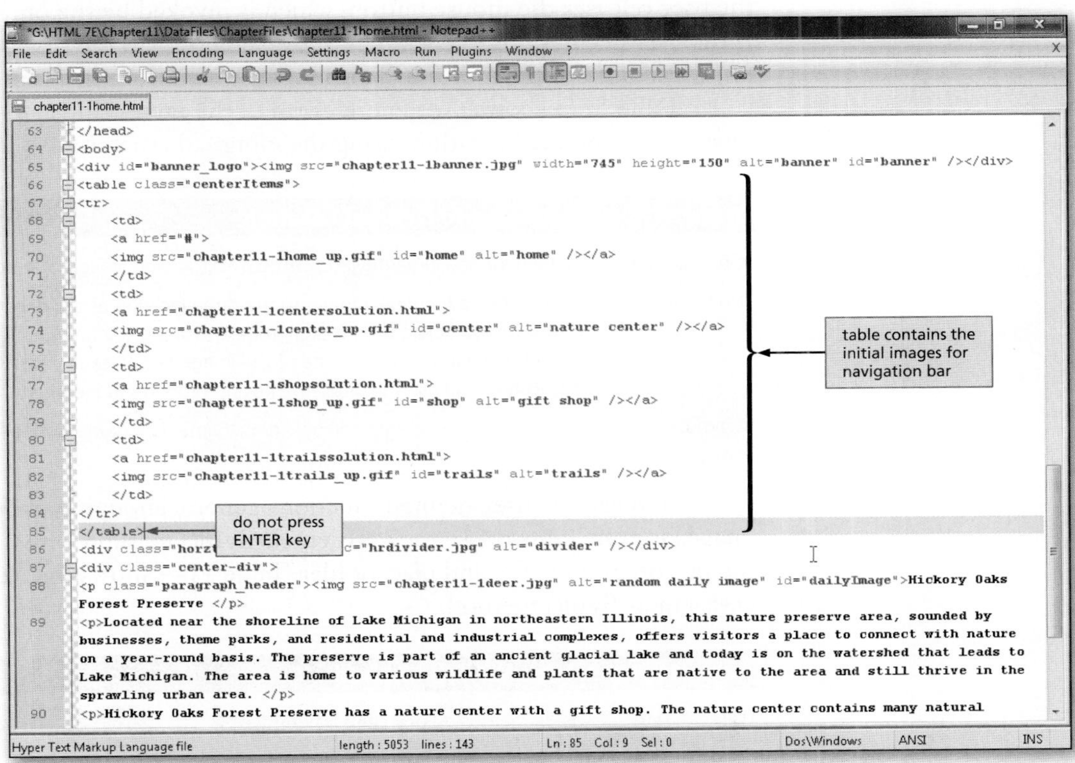

Figure 11–3

Plan Ahead

Creating the user-defined functions for the image rollovers.
To make the navigation bar on the Hickory Oaks Forest Preserve Web site work, three user-defined functions must be written for the mouse events, one for each state of the navigation button. The mouse event handlers you will use are onMouseOver, onMouseDown, onMouseUp, and onMouseOut. The same function will be used for onMouseUp and onMouseOut. Each function will do the following:

- Use the button name, the state of the mouse (over, down, up, and out) associated with the event handler, and the filename extension to construct the associated graphic filename for that state
- Use the getElementById() method to assign the filename to the correct image location

The id attribute with the <img> tag is used by the getElementById() method to identify the correct button. When the function code is complete, the mouse event handlers are added to the <img> tags to invoke the appropriate image rollover function.

Creating the JavaScript User-Defined Functions for the Image Rollovers

You will write a user-defined function for each of the three states (up, over, and down) of the button associated with a particular mouse event: a function named overButton() for when the mouse is hovering over the button, which is invoked by the onMouseOver event handler; a function named downButton() for when the user clicks the button, which is invoked by the onMouseDown event handler; and a function named upButton() for when the user releases the mouse button, which is invoked by the onMouseUp event handler. If the user decides not to click that button, and moves the mouse off the button, the onMouseOut event handler will also invoke the upButton() user-defined function.

Table 11–3 shows the general form of the JavaScript statement to assign a new image to the defined location, using the <img> id attribute as part of the object.

Table 11–3 Assign Image to Defined Location

General form:	document.getElementById(id_attribute).src="new image filename"
Comment:	where the new image appears in the same location as the original by assigning a new filename to the image object source (src) property. The objectname in the JavaScript code must match the object name in the id attribute of the image tag. Because the name attribute is depreciated in the <img> you use the getElementbyId() property to identify the objectname.
Example:	document.getElementById(img).src="chapter11-1home_over.gif"

To make the user-defined functions generic enough to work with all the possible images for one button, use the getElementById() method with a variable to identify the button graphic file and placeholder. Table 11–4 shows the general form of the getElementById() method.

Table 11–4 getElementById() Method

General form:	getElementById('id_value') getElementById(variable)
Comments:	where **getElementById()** is a method that returns the object with that specific id. The *id value* must be entered in quotation marks or as a valid variable name. As a string in quotation marks, it is case-sensitive and must match exactly the tag id attribute. The returned value also can use any properties associated with that value. The example below shows the method to assign a new graphic file to an image placeholder, using a variable name (img) in the method.
Example:	buttonImg="chapter11-1"+img+"_over.jpg" document.getElementById(img).src=buttonImg

The code for each of the functions is shown in Table 11–5. The functions will be associated with mouse event handlers, so when the user places the mouse over a button, clicks a button, releases a button, or moves the mouse off a button, the button changes to the appropriate image.

Table 11–5 JavaScript Code for User-Defined Functions

Line	Code
6	`<script type="text/javascript">`
7	`<!-- Hide from old browsers`
8	`function overButton(img) {`
9	`buttonImg="chapter11-1"+img+"_over.gif"`
10	`document.getElementById(img).src=buttonImg`
11	`}`
12	
13	`function downButton(img) {`
14	`buttonImg="chapter11-1"+img+"_down.gif"`
15	`document.getElementById(img).src=buttonImg`
16	`}`
17	
18	`function upButton(img) {`
19	`buttonImg="chapter11-1"+img+"_up.gif"`
20	`document.getElementById(img).src=buttonImg`
21	`}`
22	
23	`//-->`
24	`</script>`

Line 6 starts a JavaScript section. Line 7 is a standard HTML comment to hide the JavaScript code from older browsers. Line 8 defines the user-defined function, overButton() with the parameter img. Img is passed to the function to create the name of the image file needed for that event. Line 9 constructs the image filename using the parameter, and line 10 uses the getElementById to assign the new file image to the <img> tag using the src property. Lines 13 and 18 define the downButton() and upButton() functions. Lines 14 and 19 construct the appropriate image filename, and lines 15 and 20 assign the new image to the <img> tag. Lines 11, 16, and 21 close the functions, and lines 23 and 24 close the comment and the JavaScript section.

To Create User-Defined Functions for Image Rollovers

The following step enters the code to create the user-defined functions for the image rollovers.

1

- Click line 6 (the blank line after the title code).
- Enter the code from Table 11–5 on the previous page to create the JavaScript user-defined functions for each button, indenting as shown. Do not press the ENTER key after the closing </script> tag (Figure 11–4).

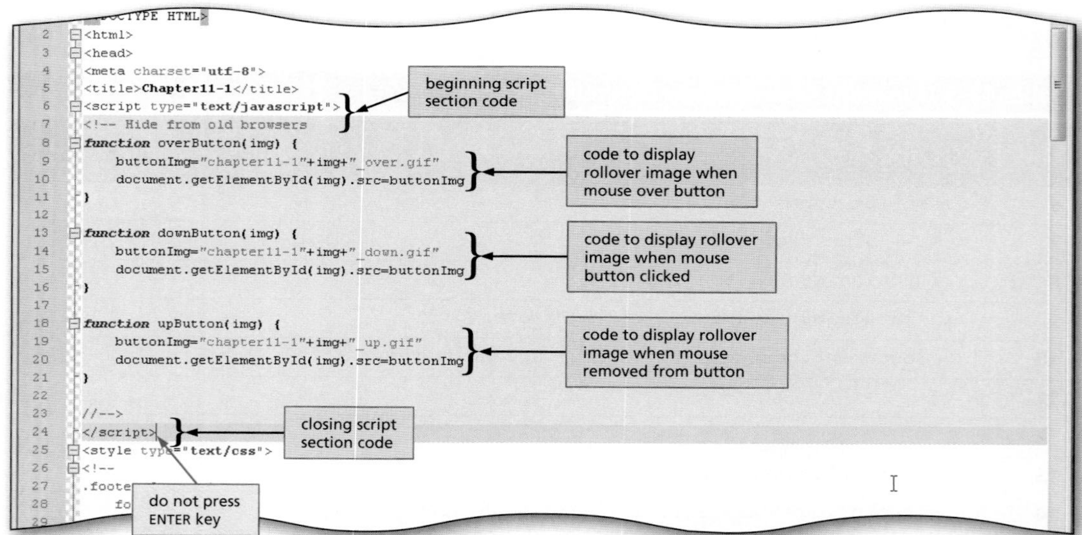

Figure 11–4

To Enter Mouse Event Handlers to Invoke User-Defined Functions

The next step is to enter the mouse event handlers in the <img> tags. Table 11–6 shows the code to add the mouse event handlers to the <img> tags.

Table 11–6 Code to Enter the Mouse Event Handlers in the <img> Tags

Line	Code
88	`onMouseOver="overButton('home')" onMouseDown="downButton('home')" onMouseOut="upButton('home')" onMouseUp="upButton('home')"`
...	
92	`onMouseOver="overButton('center')" onMouseDown="downButton('center')" onMouseOut="upButton('center')" onMouseUp="upButton('center')"`
...	
96	`onMouseOver="overButton('shop')" onMouseDown="downButton('shop')" onMouseOut="upButton('shop')" onMouseUp="upButton('shop')"`
...	
100	`onMouseOver="overButton('trails')" onMouseDown="downButton('trails')" onMouseOut="upButton('trails')" onMouseUp="upButton('trails')"`

Line 88 adds the mouse event handler for the Home button. Line 92 adds the mouse event handler for the Center button. Line 96 adds the mouse event handler for the Shop button. Line 100 adds the mouse event handler for the Trails button.

The following steps enter the code for the mouse event handlers to invoke the associated user-defined functions for the image rollovers. Note that each line of code may wrap to a second line in Notepad++.

1

- Click line 88 and position the insertion point after the alt="home" attribute.
- Press the SPACEBAR and enter the code shown in Table 11–6 for line 88 to enter all the mouse event handlers associated with image rollovers for the Home button. Do not press the ENTER key when finished.

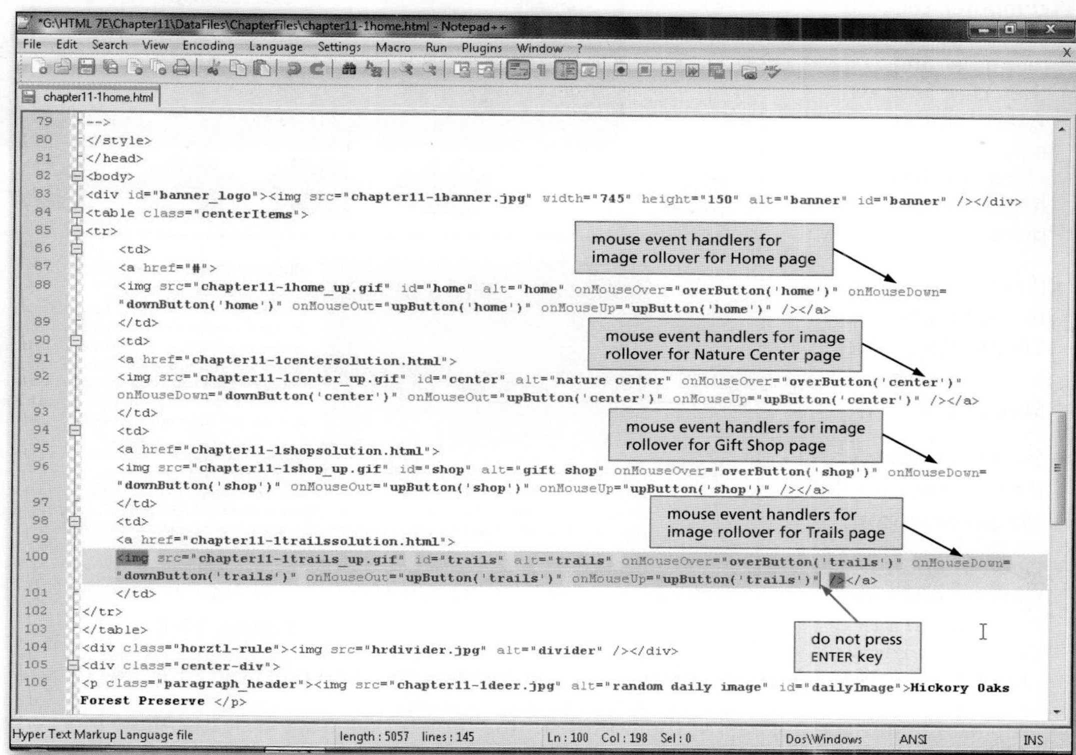

Figure 11–5

- Click line 92 and position the insertion point after the alt="nature center" attribute.
- Press the SPACEBAR and enter the code shown in Table 11–6 for line 92 to enter all the mouse event handlers associated with image rollovers for the Center button. Do not press the ENTER key when finished.

- Click line 96 and position the insertion point after the alt="gift shop" attribute.
- Press the SPACEBAR and enter the code shown in Table 11–6 for line 96 to enter all the mouse event handlers associated with image rollovers for the Shop button. Do not press the ENTER key when finished.

- Click line 100 and position the insertion point after the alt="trails" attribute.
- Press the SPACEBAR and enter the code shown in Table 11–6 for line 100 to enter all the mouse event handlers associated with image rollovers for the Trails button. Do not press the ENTER key when finished (Figure 11–5).

To Save and Test the Hickory Oaks Forest Preserve Web Page Navigation Bar

The code for the Hickory Oaks Forest Preserve Web page navigation bar is complete. Now you should save the HTML file and then test the JavaScript code using a Web browser. The following steps save and test the Hickory Oaks Forest Preserve Web page.

1

- With a USB drive plugged into your computer, click File on the Notepad++ menu bar and then click Save As. Type `chapter11-1homesolution.html` in the File name text box (do not press the ENTER key).
- If necessary, navigate to the Chapter11\ChapterFiles folder, and then click the Save button.
- Start your browser. If necessary, click the Maximize button.
- Open Internet Explorer and type `G:\chapter11\ChapterFiles\chapter11-1homesolution.html` in the Address box and then press the ENTER key (Figure 11–6).
- If a security message appears at the bottom of the browser window, click the Allow blocked content button. (If you are running Internet Explorer 8 or lower, your security message may be different.)

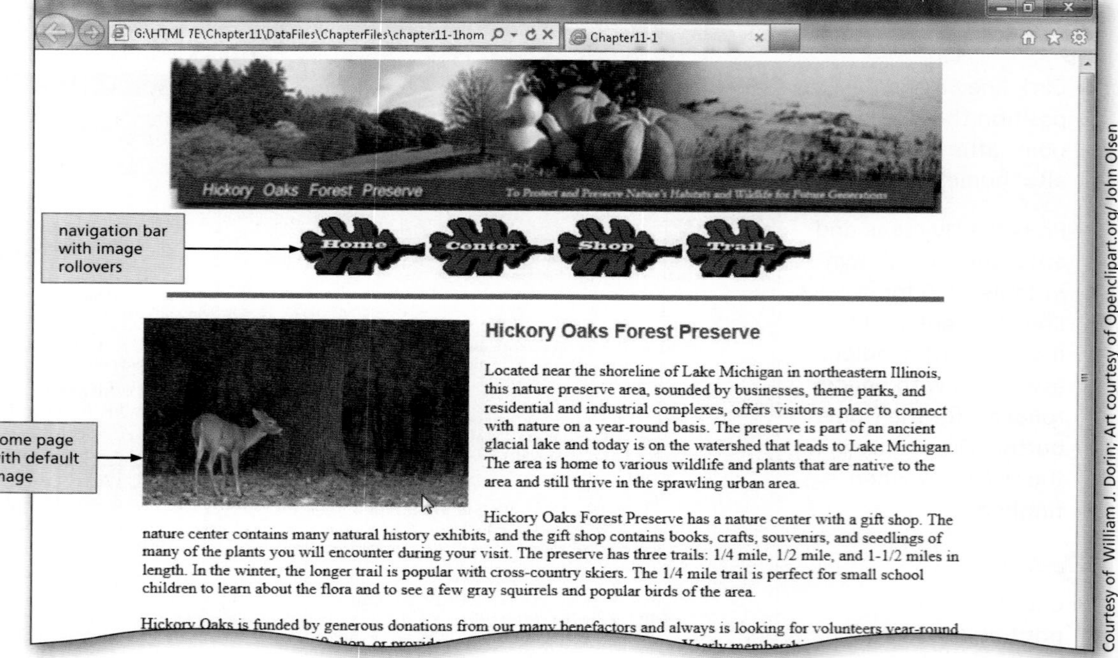

Figure 11–6

2

- Position the mouse pointer over the Home button. The button image should change color, as in Figure 11–7.

Figure 11–7

3

- Click the Home button. The button image should change color (Figure 11–8).

Figure 11–8

Plan Ahead

Creating a random image generator with a user-defined function.
A random image generator will display a new image in the image placeholder every time the Web page is loaded. To create a user-defined function to display random images, the following steps and programming logic must be followed.

- Determine the location for an image object
- Determine the image to be used as the default image
- Make sure each image is as close to the same size as possible
- Write the user-defined JavaScript function using the following logic:
  1. Define a list of images in an array object making the first element blank or null
  2. Determine the maximum random number size by subtracting 1 from the array length
  3. Use the Math.ceil() and Math.random() methods to create the random number
  4. Assign the array value using the random number as a subscript to the image placeholder
  5. Add the onLoad event handler to the <body> tag to invoke the user-defined function when the Web page is loaded

In the Home Web page, the first element in the array is blank or null because it is element zero, and the Math.ceil() method will never return a zero with the Math.random() method. Thus, that image would never be used or displayed.

Creating the User-Defined Function Random Number Generator

The first step in creating the random image on the Home Web page is to create a list in which to store the filenames of the images that will be selected by the random number generator: chapter11-1b_bee3.jpg, chapter11-1blackant.jpg, chapter11-1deer.jpg, chapter11-1dragonfly1.jpg, chapter11-1gray_squirrel.jpg, and chapter11-1monarch.jpg. (These files can be found in the Data Files for Students.) JavaScript, like other programming languages, uses a data structure called an array to work with lists of data. An **array** is a collection of data items, represented by one variable name. This variable is called the **array name**. Each of the individual data items is called an element, and a subscript references the individual data items in the array. A **subscript** is a number that designates a single occurrence of an array element.

Arrays are built-in objects. To create an array and fill that array with data, create an object instance of the Array object. Recall from Chapter 9 that an **object instance** is a new JavaScript object created from a built-in object. Table 11–7 shows the general form for creating an array object instance from the Array object.

BTW

Arrays
JavaScript arrays are not a fixed length like in other programming languages. New elements can be added to the array without having to redefine the structure. Remember, also, that JavaScript is a loosely typed language and does not require variables to be declared as a data type. Thus, you can store string, numeric, or Boolean values to the same array.

Table 11–7 Create an Array

General form:	var myarrayname=new Array()
Comment:	where **Array** is a built-in object and the **new** command creates a new object instance of the array. Data items may fill an array in one of two ways: (1) by placing the data directly in the array object; or (2) by assigning the items separately.
Examples:	var randomImage = new Array ("", "chapter11-1b_bee3.jpg", "chapter11-1blackant.jpg", "chapter11-1deer.jpg","chapter11-1dragonfly1.jpg") or var randomImage=new Array() randomImage[0]="" randomImage[1]="chapter11-1b_bee3.jpg" randomImage[2]="chapter11-1blackant.jpg" randomImage[3]="chapter11-1deer.jpg" randomImage[4]="chapter11-1dragonfly1.jpg"

Subscripts are placed after the array name in square [ ] brackets, as shown in the example in Table 11–7. A subscript must be any valid JavaScript variable or numeric literal value. The first element in a JavaScript array always is element zero [0].

After the data elements are assigned to the array, the JavaScript code can retrieve or use the data by referencing the array name with the subscript. As shown in Figure 11–9, the data in an array is stored sequentially. For example, to reference the second element (chapter11_1blackant.jpg), the JavaScript code uses the contents of randomImage[1]. To reference the third element in the array, the JavaScript code uses the contents of randomImage[2].

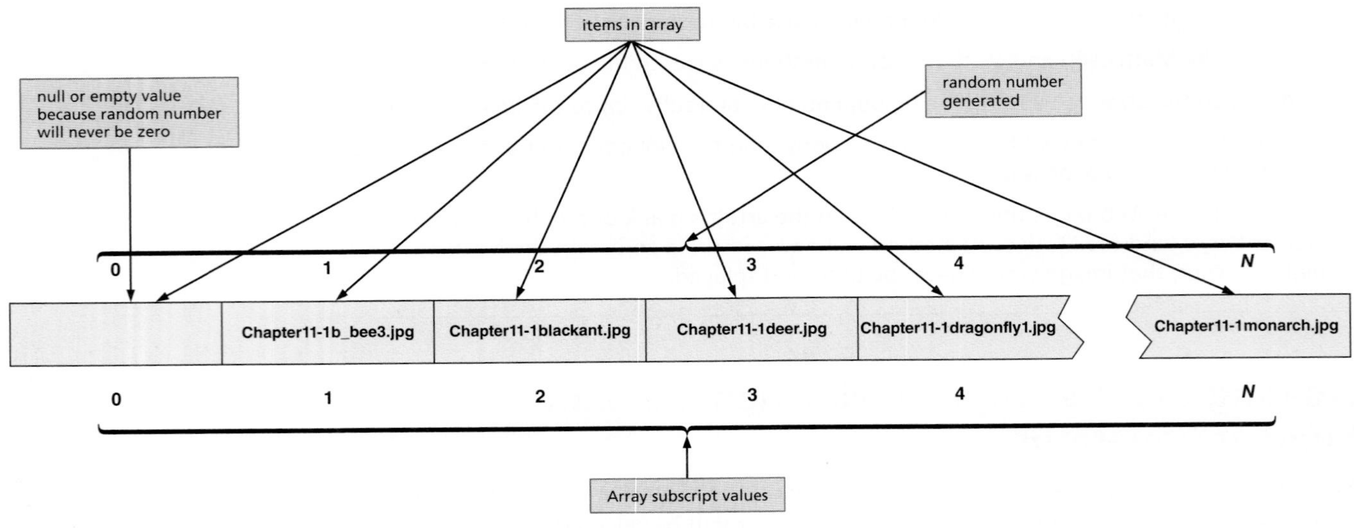

Figure 11–9

The next step in updating the Hickory Oaks Forest Preserve Home page is to create the user-defined function to display an image from an array using a random number generator. With this function, the Web page will show a different image every time the page is loaded. Table 11–8 shows the code for the creating the array object, generating the random number, and assigning the new image to the image placeholder.

Table 11–8 Code for User-Defined Functions to Create a Randomly Displayed Image

Line	Code
23	`var randomImage = new Array ("", "chapter11-1b_bee3.jpg", "chapter11-1blackant.jpg", "chapter11-1deer.jpg", "chapter11-1dragonfly1.jpg", "chapter11-1gray_squirrel.jpg", "chapter11-1monarch.jpg")`
24	`function rndimage() {`
25	`rndnumsize=randomImage.length-1`
26	`var randomnumber=Math.ceil(Math.random()*rndnumsize)`
27	`document.getElementById("dailyImage").src=randomImage[randomnumber]`
28	`}`

Line 23 creates the array object, randomImage, with one null element and six image filenames. The null element is created by an empty set of quotation marks (""). Line 24 declares the user-defined function, rndimage(). Line 25 determines the maximum value of the random number by taking the size of the array (randomImage.length) and subtracting 1 from that size. This subtraction is necessary because an array's first element is identified as element zero. Line 26 generates the random number using the Math.ceil() method and Math.random() methods. The Math.random() method generates a number between 0 and 1. The result is multiplied by the array size, which in this case is seven, minus one to give us six (the rndnumsize).

The multiplication by the array size provides a number between 1 and 7, and the Math.ceil() method will round the value to the next integer, which is assigned to the variable randomnumber. The randomnumber value is used in line 27 to assign an array element to the image placeholder. Line 28 closes the function.

To Enter a Random Number Generator User-Defined Function

The following step enters the user-defined function, rndimage(), to randomly assign an image to the image placeholder.

1

- Click line 22 and press the ENTER key once.
- On line 23, enter the JavaScript code shown in Table 11–8 to create the user-defined function to randomly assign an image to the image placeholder, as shown in Figure 11–10.
- Press the ENTER key once.

```
20      document.getElementById(img).src=buttonImg
21  }
22
23  var randomImage = new Array ("", "chapter11-1b_bee3.jpg", "chapter11-1blackant.jpg", "chapter11-1deer.jpg",
    "chapter11-1dragonfly1.jpg", "chapter11-1gray_squirrel.jpg","chapter11-1monarch.jpg")
24  function rndimage() {
25      rndnumsize=randomImage.length-1
26      var randomnumber=Math.ceil(Math.random()*rndnumsize)
27      document.getElementById("dailyImage").src=randomImage[randomnumber]
28  }
29
30  //-->
31  </script>
32  <style type="text/css">
33  <!--
34  .footer_format {
35      font-size:6pt;
36      font-weight:bold;
```

null entry because zero element is never generated

line 23 fills array of images for random display

Math.random() function generates random number

random number used to pick image from array and display on Web page

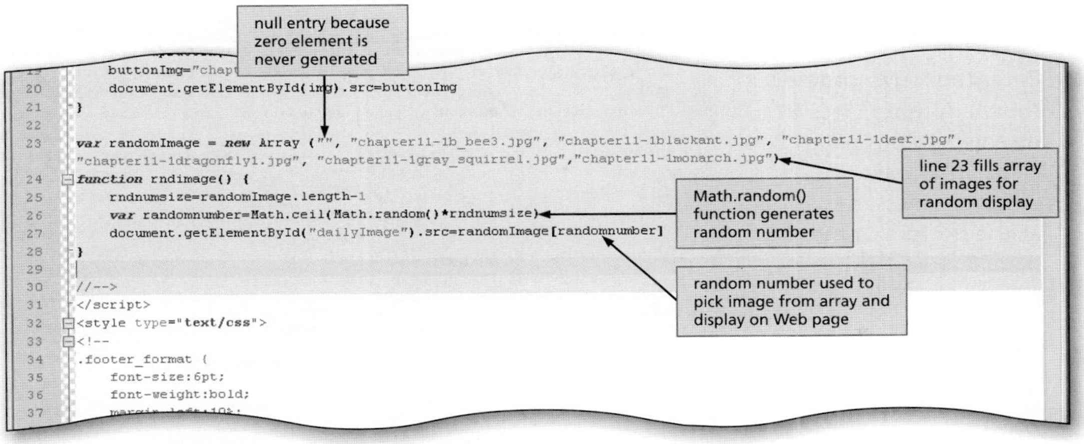

Figure 11–10

To Enter Code to Show Copyright Information and Date Last Modified

As shown in Figure 11–1a on page HTML 509, the Hickory Oaks Forest Preserve Home page displays copyright information, the date the file was last modified, and the URL at the bottom of the Web page. To show just the date, without the time, the JavaScript code uses the substring() method, which was introduced in Chapter 10. First, however, a <div> or <footer> container tag with an id attribute must be inserted in the HTML code where the message is to display. Table 11–9 shows the HTML code for the <footer> tag with the id attribute and class attribute for formatting the copyright display. By adding a class attribute, a style sheet entry can format the text for this container, eliminating the need for an inline style.

Table 11–9 Code for <footer> Tag with the id and class Attributes

Line	Code
119	`<footer id="displayCopyRight" class="footer_format">`
120	`</footer>`

Table 11–10 on the next page shows the JavaScript code for the <script> section to show the copyright information and date the Web page was last modified.

Table 11–10 Code to Show the Date Last Modified

Line	Code
30	`function copyRight() {`
31	`var lastModDate = document.lastModified`
32	`var lastModDate = lastModDate.substring(0,10)`
33	`displayCopyRight.innerHTML = "The URL of this document is "+document.URL+" Hickory Oaks Forest Preserve"+"  This document was last modified "+lastModDate +".</p>"`
34	`}`

The following steps enter the HTML <footer> tag and the JavaScript user-defined function to show copyright information and the date the file was last modified using the substring() method so it is displayed at the bottom of the Web page.

- Click line 119.
- Enter the HTML code shown in Table 11–9 on the previous page to position the copyright message at the bottom of the page (Figure 11–11).

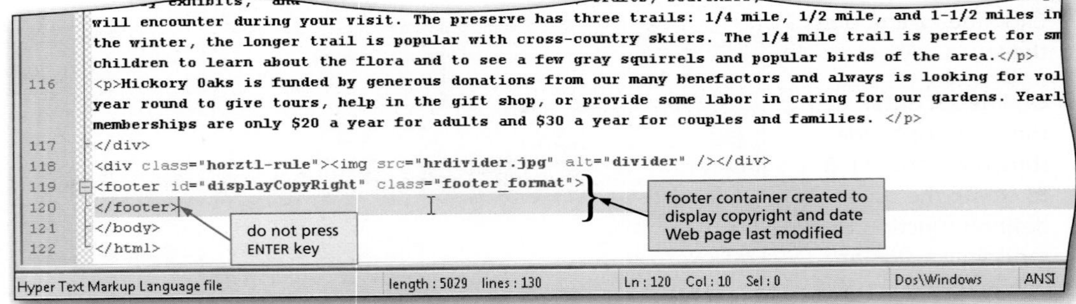

Figure 11–11

- Click line 29 and then press the ENTER key.
- On line 30, enter the JavaScript code shown in Table 11–10 and then press the ENTER key (Figure 11–12).

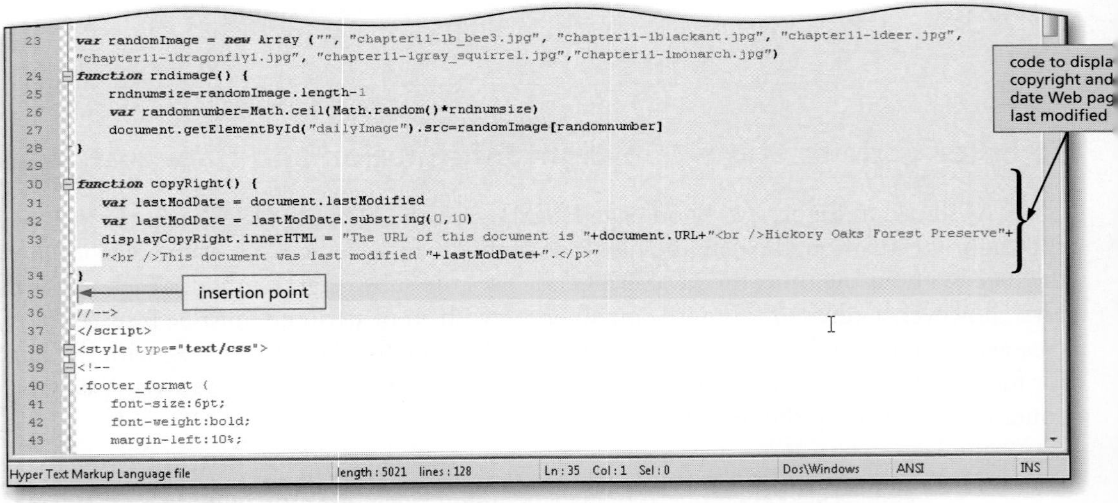

Figure 11–12

To Enter onLoad Event Handlers in the <body> Tag

With the code for the user-defined functions entered to display the random pictures, the copyright information, and the date last modified, the final step is to add the onLoad event handlers in the <body> tag to invoke the rndimage() and copyRight() user-defined functions. The following step enters the event handlers in the <body> tag.

1

- In line 95, click after the y in the word body.
- Press the SPACEBAR once and type `onLoad= "rndimage(); copyRight();"` before the >.
- Do not press the ENTER key at the end (Figure 11–13).

```
90  }
91
92  -->
93  </style>
94  </head>
95  <body onLoad="rndimage(); copyRight();">
96  <div id="banner_logo"><img src="chapter11-1banner.jpg" width="745" height="150" alt="banner" id="banner" /></div>
97  <table class="centerItems">
98  <tr>
99      <td>
100     <a href="#">
101     <img src="chapter11-1home_up.gif" id="home" alt="home" onMouseOver="overButton('home')" onMouseDown=
        "downButton('home')" onMouseOut="upButton('home')" onMouseUp="upButton('home')" /></a>
102     </td>
103     <td>
```


Figure 11–13

To Save an HTML File and Test a Web Page

With the code for the user-defined functions and the JavaScript section for the copyright information and the date last modified complete, you should save the HTML file and test the Web page. The following steps save the HTML file and then test the Hickory Oaks Forest Preserve Home page.

1. With a USB drive plugged into your computer, click File on the menu bar and then click Save to save the Chapter11-1homesolution.html file.
2. Click the Internet Explorer button on the taskbar and click the Refresh button on the browser window.
3. If necessary, scroll down to the see the bottom of the Web page and the copyright information.
4. Move the mouse over the Center button, but do not click the mouse. Note that the image changes.
5. Click the Refresh button to see a different nature image generated by the random number generator user-defined function (Figure 11–14).

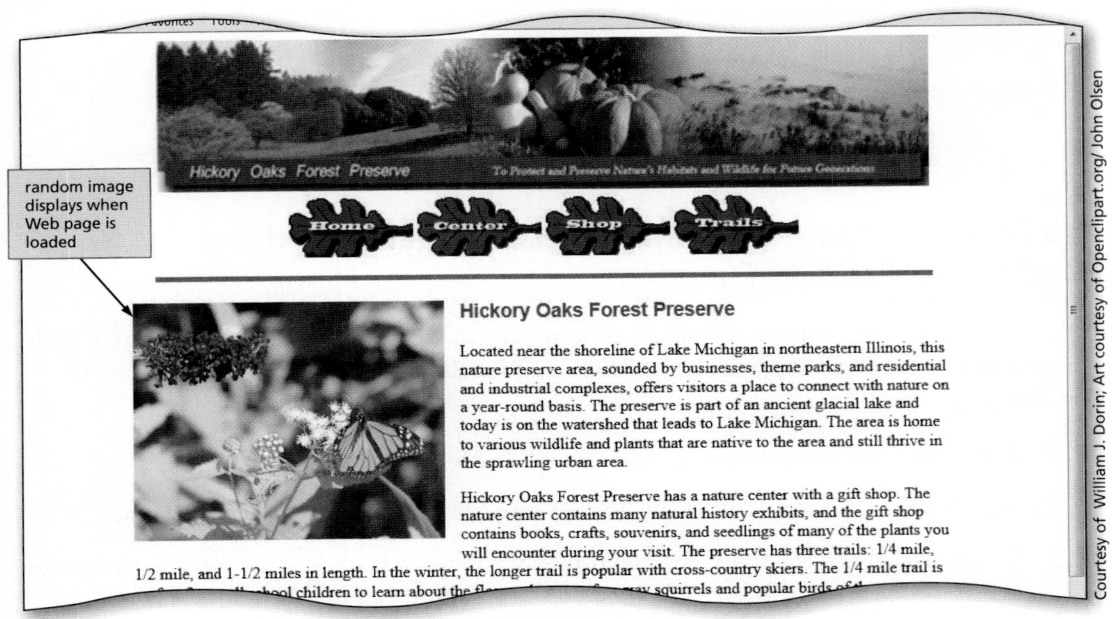

Figure 11–14

Plan Ahead

Creating an automatic slide show.
Instead of having only one image on a page, many Web sites include slide shows to display multiple images. The intent is to grab the visitors' attention and keep them on the page. To include a slide show that will start automatically when the Nature Center page opens, you need to do the following:

- Determine the location for an image object
- Determine the images to be used
- Write the user-defined JavaScript function using the following logic:
  1. Define a list of images in an array object
  2. Establish a counter
  3. Increment the counter by 1
  4. Test the counter against the number of items in the list
  5. Assign the list element, based on the current counter value, to the image object
  6. Call the function again using the setTimeout() method
- Add the event handler to call the function

Creating a Slide Show on the Nature Center Web Page

As shown in Figure 11–1b on page HTML 509, the Nature Center Web page contains a slide show. A **slide show** is a set of images, all the same size, that are displayed in the same location for a few seconds, one after the other, to create the appearance that the images are rotating. The slide show in this chapter continuously runs, with no controls.

To Open an Existing HTML File in Notepad++

In this chapter, the partially completed HTML code for the Nature Center Web page is provided in the Data Files for Students. To modify this Web page, the file chapter11-1center.html must be opened in a new Notepad++ window.

1. If necessary, start Notepad++.
2. Open the chapter11-1center.html file in the Chapter11\ChapterFiles folder.

To Copy and Paste the Navigation Bar, Event Handlers, and Image Rollover Functions

To maintain consistency in looks among all the Web pages, the Nature Center Web page should use the same navigation bar created for the Hickory Oaks Forest Preserve Home page.

1. If necessary, open the chapter11-1homesolution.html file in Notepad++.
2. Copy the HTML <table> code from lines 97 through 116 to copy the navigation bar.
3. Click line 63 in the chapter11-1center.html file and paste the code to insert the navigation bar from Table 11–2 on page HTML 512 into the Nature Center Web page file.

4. Modify line 66 to replace the # symbol with `chapter11-1homesolution.html`.

5. Modify line 70 to replace chapter11-1centersolution.html with the # symbol.

6. In the chapter11-1homesolution.html file, copy the JavaScript code from lines 6 through 22. Return to the chapter11-1center.html file and insert the copied code for the navigation bar image rollovers on line 6 and then press the ENTER key. On line 23 type `//-->`, and press the ENTER key. On line 24 type `</script>` and do not press the ENTER key (Figure 11–15).

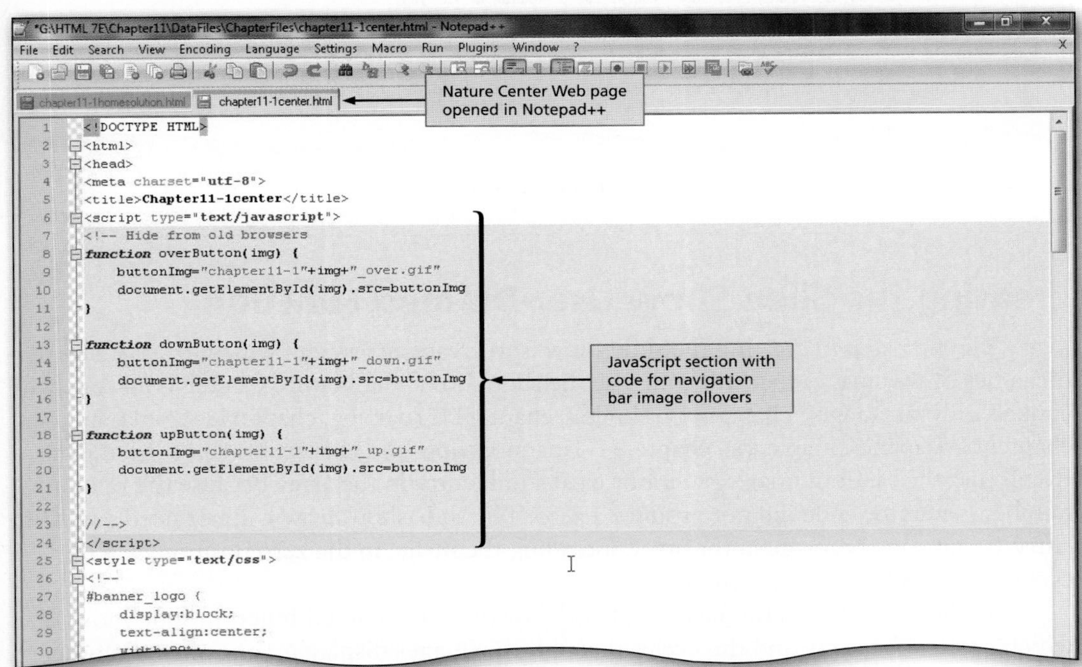

Figure 11–15

Creating and Placing an Image Object

The first step in creating a slide show is to determine the location of the slide show images. To define the image for the user-defined function, you must add the name attribute and value. The name attribute allows JavaScript to assign a new graphic image to the same location as the original image. This technique is the same as in Table 11–1 on page HTML 512. A new graphic file is assigned the image placeholder as described in Table 11–3 on page HTML 514.

To Create an Image Object

The initial image is placed following a <p> tag in the body of the text. The id attribute will be used by the getElementById() method to assign a new image to this location. In addition, an id selector in the embedded style sheet will make the image "float" to the left of the text. Table 11–11 shows the HTML code to place the image object in the data cell in the Web page.

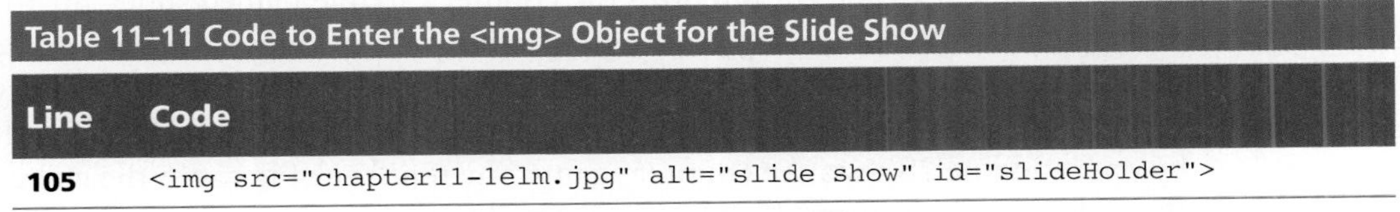

Table 11–11 Code to Enter the <img> Object for the Slide Show

Line	Code
105	`<img src="chapter11-1elm.jpg" alt="slide show" id="slideHolder">`

The following step creates an image object at a specific location on a Web page.

1

- Position the insertion point on line 105 after the <p class= "paragraph_header"> tag.
- Enter the code in Table 11–11 on the previous page to define and place the initial image and do not press the ENTER key at the end of the line (Figure 11–16).

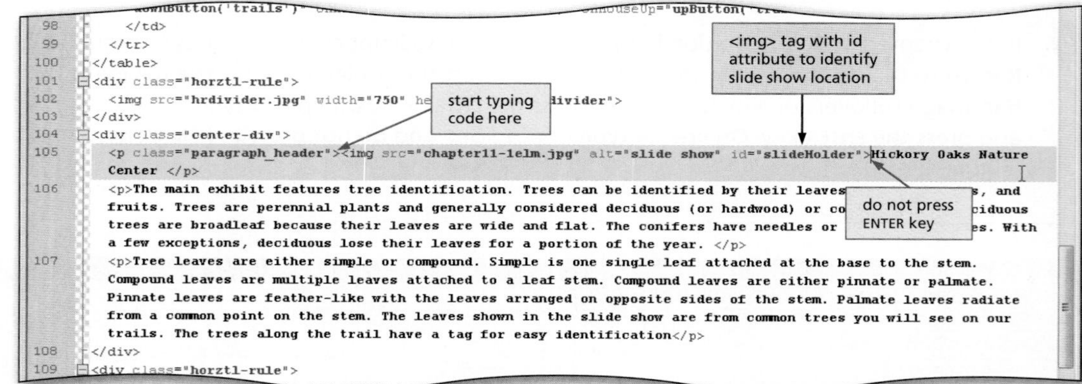

Figure 11–16

Creating the Slide Show User-Defined Function

The first step in creating the slide show is to create an array in which to store the filenames of the images that will compose the slide show. The Nature Center Web page will contain only six images: chapter11-1elm.jpg, chapter11-1oak.jpg, chapter11-1ginko.jpg, chapter11-1japanesemaple.jpg, chapter11-1magnolia.jpg, and chapter11-1blue_bean.jpg. Recall that the random image generator used a null entry in the array because the random number generator code did not produce a zero. The slide show array will not need a null entry, because every image in the array, including the image in the zero position, will be cycled through by the JavaScript code.

Table 11–12 shows the JavaScript code for the user-defined function slideShow(), which creates the array and the cycles through the images displaying one after the other.

Table 11–12 Code to Create the slideShow() Function

Line	Code
23	`var slides=new Array("chapter11-1elm.jpg", "chapter11-1oak.jpg", "chapter11-1ginko.jpg", "chapter11-1japanesemaple.jpg", "chapter11-1magnolia.jpg", "chapter11-1blue_bean.jpg")`
24	
25	`var slideCntr=slides.length-1`
26	`function slideShow() {`
27	`slideCntr+=1`
28	`if (slideCntr==slides.length) slideCntr=0`
29	`document.getElementById("slideHolder").src = slides[slideCntr]`
30	`setTimeout("slideShow()",2000)`
31	`}`

Line 23 begins by creating an array named slides, with six image filenames set as the data elements. Line 25 initializes the counter variable named slideCntr to the number of elements in the table using the length property slides.length. One is subtracted from the length so the counter does not exceed the number of elements in the array on line 27. Line 26 declares the user-defined function slideShow(). Line 27 increments the slideCntr by one, and line 28 tests the counter against the number of items in the array, using the slides.length property. If slideCntr is equal to the number of elements in the array, line 28 assigns a zero (0) to slideCntr, which reinitializes the counter to the first element of the array. Using the length property allows a developer to add or subtract images in the array without having to change other lines of code. Line 29 assigns the contents of slides[slideCntr] to the image object, identified by the getElementById() method, so the new image is displayed. The function then uses the setTimeout() method on line 30 to make a recursive call to itself after a two-second delay. The brace (}) on line 31 completes the slideShow() function.

To Create a User-Defined Function to Add a Slide Show

The following step enters the slideShow() function to create a slide show on the Nature Center page.

- Click blank line 22, press the ENTER key once, and then enter the JavaScript code (on line 23) shown in Table 11–12 to create the slideShow() user-defined function, indenting as shown (Figure 11–17).
- Press the ENTER key once after the closing brace to complete the user-defined function.

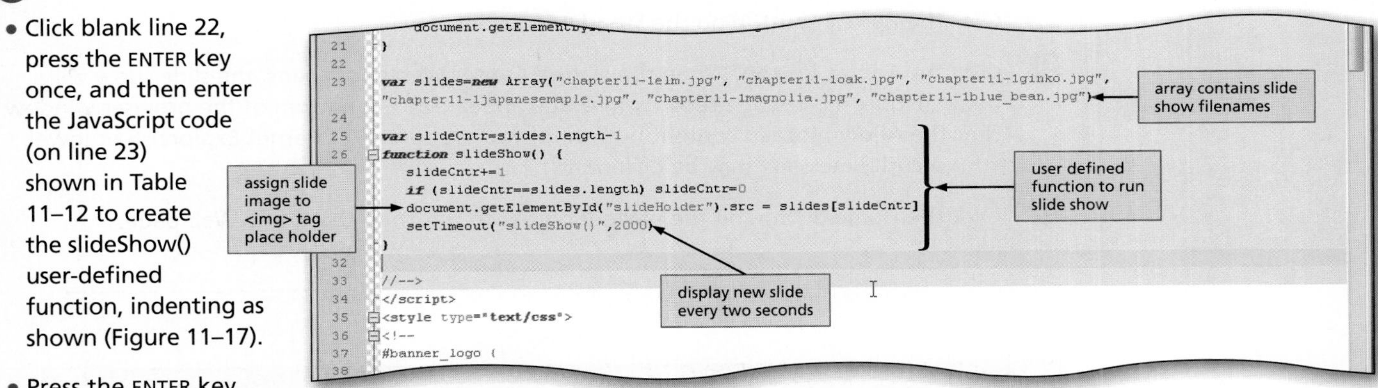

Figure 11–17

To Enter an OnLoad Event Handler to Call a Function

The next step is to enter the onLoad event handler that calls the slideShow() function when the Nature Center Web page loads. To call the slideShow() user-defined function initially, an onLoad event handler is placed in the <body> tag. The following steps enter the onLoad event handler to call the slideShow() function.

1. Position the insertion point between the y and the > symbol in the <body> tag on line 89.
2. Press the SPACEBAR once.
3. Type `onLoad="slideShow();"` to enter the onLoad event handler in the <body> tag, and do not press the ENTER key (Figure 11–18).

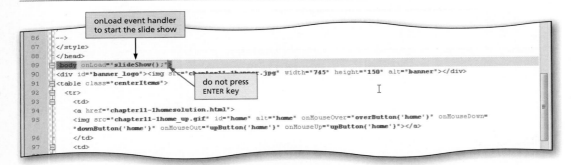

onLoad event handler to start the slide show

```
86 -->
87 </style>
88 </head>
89 <body onLoad="slideShow();">
90 <div id="banner_logo"><img src="chapter11-1banner.jpg" width="745" height="150" alt="banner"></div>
91 <table class="centerItems">
92 <tr>
93 <td>
94 <a href="chapter11-1homesolution.html">
95 <img src="chapter11-1home_up.gif" id="home" alt="home" onMouseOver="overButton('home')" onMouseDown="downButton('home')" onMouseOut="upButton('home')" onMouseUp="upButton('home')"></a>
96 </td>
97 <td>
```

do not press ENTER key

Figure 11–18

To Save an HTML File and Test a Web Page

With the code for the Nature Center Web page complete, the HTML file should be saved and the Web page should be viewed in a browser to confirm the Web page appears and functions as desired.

1. With a USB drive plugged into your computer, click File on the menu bar and then click Save As on the File menu.
2. Type `chapter11-1centersolution.html` in the File name text box to save the file with a new name, and then click the Save button in the Save As dialog box.
3. Click the Internet Explorer button on the taskbar and display the Hickory Oaks Forest Preserve Home page.
4. Click the Refresh button on the Standard toolbar.
5. Click the Center button. When the Nature Center Web page loads, the slide show will begin (Figure 11–19). If a security message appears at the bottom of the browser window, click the Allow blocked content button. (If you are running Internet Explorer 8 or lower, your security message may be different.)
6. Click the Home button on the navigation bar to return to the Home Web page.

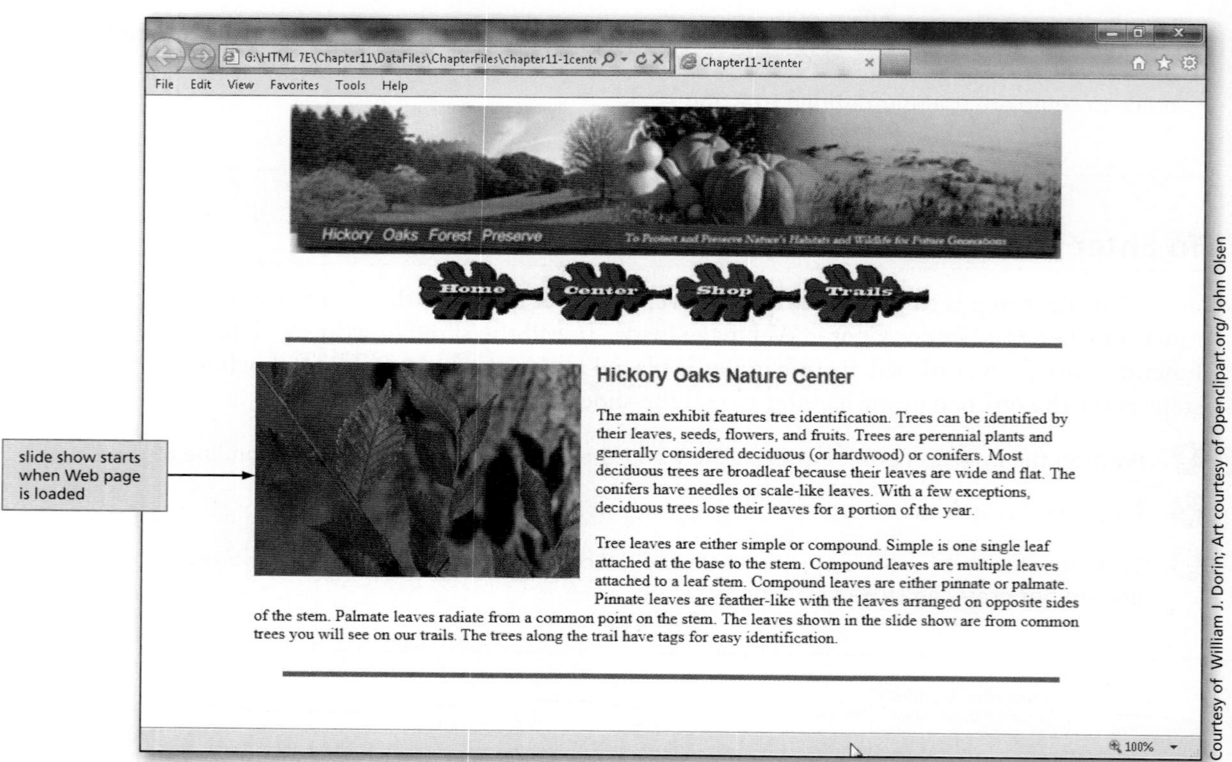

Figure 11–19

Plan Ahead

Creating a floating image.
The position of the floating image on the Web page is based on a screen resolution of 1024 × 768. Different screen resolutions will need to adjust the positioning values. In this chapter, the JavaScript code used to create a floating image includes four user-defined functions that do the following:

- Have an image float from right to left (floatingImage() function)

  The following steps detail the programming logic for the floatingImage() function:

  1. Decrement the left pixel position by 10
  2. Test left pixel position to determine if it is off the screen
  3. If left pixel < 150, reset to the right side of the screen (950) based on the screen resolution of 1024 by 768
  4. Use the <div> tag's id attribute to assign the calculated value of the left pixel to the pixelLeft property of the <div> tag object
  5. Assign the setTimeout() method used to call the floatingImage() function to a variable so the clearTimeout() method can be used to stop the scrolling
- Stop the image from scrolling (stopFloat() function) with the clearTimeout() method
- Restart the image scrolling (restartFloat() function) using the setTimeout() method
- Open a pop-up window for the coupon offer (coupon() function) using the open() method

Adding a Floating Image to the Gift Shop Web Page

The Gift Shop Web page (Figure 11–1c on page HTML 509) highlights the gift shop at the Hickory Oaks Forest Preserve. The Web page has an image that scrolls from right to left, and if the user clicks the image, a pop-up window displays with a coupon. When a visitor places the mouse over the image, it stops scrolling. When the mouse is moved off the floating image, it starts scrolling again. The image stops by using the clearTimeout() method and the mouse pointer becomes a hand by using an embedded style in the <img> tag. The floating image is a link to the Coupon Web page that is displayed as a pop-up window.

To Open an Existing HTML File in Notepad++

To move or float an image, it is placed in a <div> tag layer that is referenced by the user-defined functions. The floating image is positioned after images on the page to fill some of the blank space and to avoid overlaying any other text. To begin, the Gift Shop Web page must be opened.

1. If necessary, start Notepad++.
2. Open the chapter11-1shop.html file in the Chapter11\ChapterFiles folder.

To Copy and Paste the Navigation Bar, Event Handlers, and Image Rollover Functions

To maintain consistency in looks among all the Web pages, the Gift Shop Web page should use the same navigation bar, event handlers, and image rollover functions created for the Hickory Oaks Forest Preserve Home page.

1. Open the chapter11-1homesolution.html file in Notepad++ in the Chapter11\ChapterFiles folder, if necessary.
2. Copy the HTML <table> code from lines 97 through 116 (the HTML code and mouse event handlers for the navigation bar).
3. In the chapter11-1shop.html file, click line 62 and paste the code to create the navigation bar.
4. Modify line 65 to replace the # symbol with `chapter11-1homesolution.html`.
5. Modify line 74 to replace the chapter11-1shopsolution.html with a # symbol.
6. In the chapter11-1homesolution.html file, copy the JavaScript code from lines 6 through 21. Return to the chapter11-1gifts.html file and insert the copied code for the navigation bar image rollovers on line 6. After the } brace, press the ENTER key twice. Add the closing HTML comment (//-->) and the closing `</script>` tags on lines 23 and 24 and do not press the ENTER key (Figure 11–20).

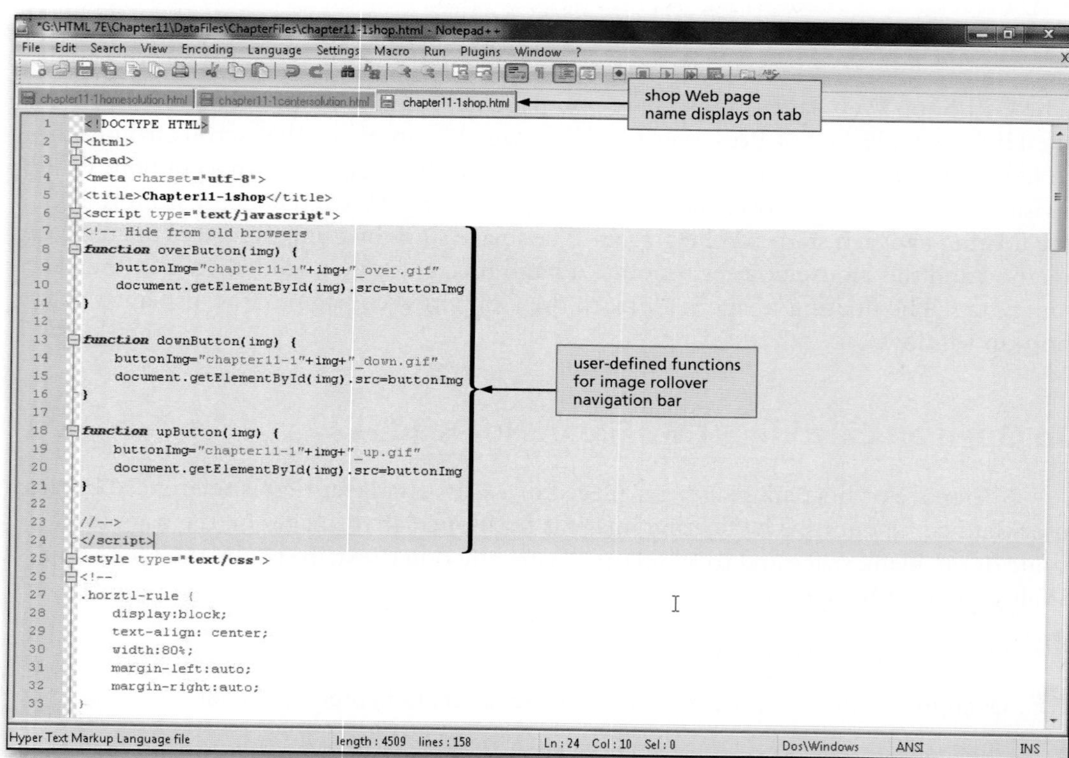

Figure 11–20

Entering the floatingImage(), stopFloat(), and restartFloat()Functions

The next step is to enter the code to have the image float across the screen on the Gift Shop Web page from right to left, to stop floating when the mouse is over the image, and to restart floating when the mouse moves off the image. Table 11–13 shows the code for the floatingImage() function.

Table 11–13 Code for the floatingImage() Function

Line	Code
23	`var leftPX=950`
24	`function floatingImage() {`
25	`leftPX-=10`
26	`if (leftPX<-150) leftPX=950`
27	`document.getElementById('floatImg').style.pixelLeft=leftPX`
28	`imager=setTimeout("floatingImage()",100)`
29	`}`

Line 23 assigns 950 to the variable leftPX to represent the right side of the screen for the screen resolution 1024 by 768. Line 24 declares the function, floatingImage(). Line 25 decrements the leftPX variable by 10 pixels. Line 26 tests the value of leftPX to see if it has extended past the end of the screen. The value −150 was chosen to allow the image to scroll completely off the screen before starting over at the right. If the value is less than −150, leftPX is assigned 950 so the image can start from the right again.

Line 27 assigns the value of leftPX to the pixelLeft property of the image object, identified by the getElementbyId('floatImg') object. Line 28 assigns the recursive call of the setTimeout() method to a variable so the floating image can be stopped with an onMouseOver event handler calling a different function. Line 29 closes the function code.

BTW

Simple Animation on a Web Page with JavaScript
Animation can be created by moving objects associated with a division (layer). By repeatedly changing the position and placement of the division in a recursive user-defined function, the object moves.

To Enter the floatingImage() Function

The following step enters the floatingImage() function.

1

- Click line 22 and press the ENTER key.
- On line 23, enter the JavaScript code as shown in Table 11–13 to enter the floatingImage() user-defined function, indenting as shown.
- Press the ENTER key twice to place the insertion point on line 31 (Figure 11–21).

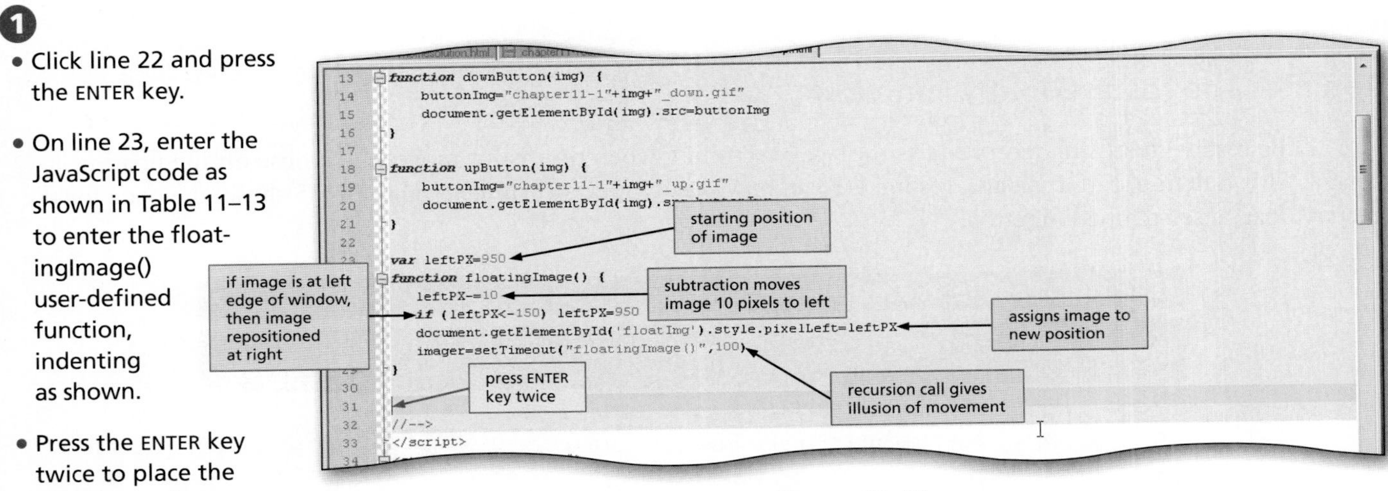

Figure 11–21

To Enter the stopFloat() Function

The stopFloat() function stops the image from floating when the visitor moves the mouse over the image. The function, stopFloat(), responds to an onMouseOver event handler. Table 11–14 shows the JavaScript code for the stopFloat() function.

Table 11–14 Code for the stopFloat() Function

Line	Code
31	`function stopFloat() {`
32	`        clearTimeout(imager)`
33	`}`

Line 31 defines the stopFloat() user-defined function. The clearTimeout() method on line 32 stops the floating image by clearing the imager variable used in the recursive call made by the setTimeout() method on line 28 in Table 11–13. Line 33 closes the stopFloat() function.

The following step enters the stopFloat() user-defined function.

- If necessary, click line 31.
- Enter the code shown in Table 11–14 to create the stopFloat() user-defined function, indenting as shown.
- Press the ENTER key twice to position the insertion point on line 35 (Figure 11–22).

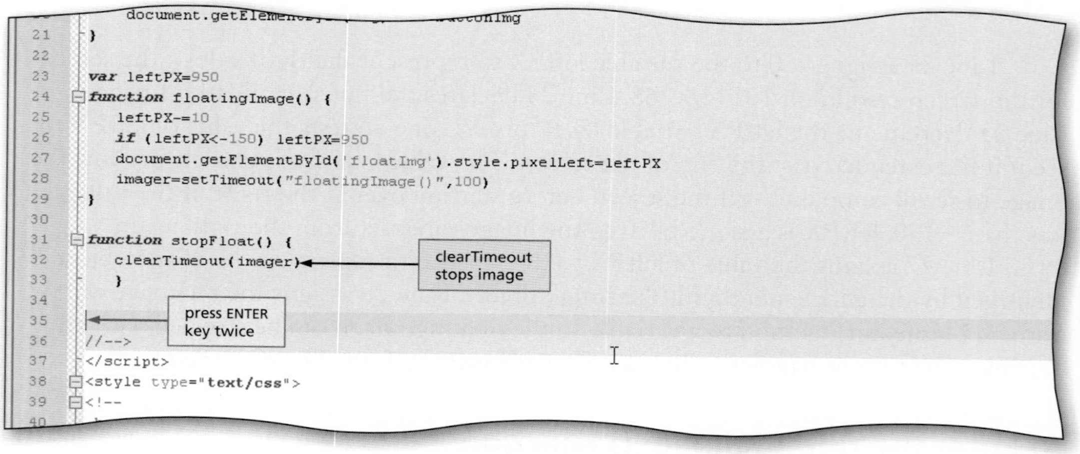

Figure 11–22

To Enter the restartFloat() Function

The restartFloat() function restarts the image scrolling when the visitor moves the mouse off the floating image. This function, restartFloat(), responds to an onMouseOut event handler. Table 11–15 shows the code for the restartFloat() user-defined function.

Table 11–15 Code for the restartFloat() Function

Line	Code
35	`function restartFloat() {`
36	`        setTimeout("floatingImage()",100)`
37	`}`

Line 35 declares the function. Line 36 uses the setTimeout() method to call the floatingImage() user-defined function. Line 37 closes the restartFloat() function code.

The following step enters the user-defined function restartFloat().

1

- If necessary, click line 35.
- Enter the code shown in Table 11–15 to create the restartFloat() user-defined function, indenting as shown.
- Press the ENTER key twice to place the insertion point on line 39 (Figure 11–23).

```
var leftPX=950
function floatingImage() {
    leftPX-=10
    if (leftPX<-150) leftPX=950
    document.getElementById('floatImg').style.pixelLeft=leftPX
    imager=setTimeout("floatingImage()",100)
}

function stopFloat() {
    clearTimeout(imager)
    }

function restartFloat() {
    setTimeout("floatingImage()",100)
}

//-->
```

setTimeout() restarts floating image by calling the original user-defined function

press ENTER key twice

Figure 11–23

To Enter the coupon() Function

The fourth user-defined function added to the Gift Shop Web page is the coupon() function, which opens the coupon pop-up window when the user clicks the floating image. Table 11–16 shows the code for the coupon() function.

Table 11–16 Code for the coupon() Function

Line	Code
39	`function coupon() {`
40	`window.open("chapter11-1coupon.html", "coupon", "width=525,height=360")`
41	`}`

Line 39 declares the function. Line 40 uses the open() method to open the Coupon Web page as a pop-up window. The attributes settings size the window to a width of 525 pixels and a height of 360 pixels. This window does not need any menu or scroll bars. Line 41 closes the function.

The following step enters the coupon() user-defined function.

- If necessary, click line 39 and enter the code shown in Table 11–16 to create the coupon() user-defined function, indenting as shown.
- Press the ENTER key once after line 41 (Figure 11–24).

```
    setTimeout("floatingImage()",100)
}

function coupon() {
  window.open("chapter11-1coupon.html", "coupon", "width=525,height=365")
}

//-->
</script>
<style type="text/css">
<!--
.horztl-rule {
    display:block;
    text-align: center;
```

opens pop-up window with coupon

press the ENTER key once

Figure 11–24

To Enter an Embedded Style Sheet to Format the Floating Image

The next step is to add an id selector to the embedded CSS to place the floating image. The style sheet uses the id selector, floatImg, which later will be associated with the <div> tag container to position the image. The embedded style sheet sets the position to absolute, and 950 pixels from the left side of the screen. The following step enters the id selector in the embedded style sheet used to position the floating image on the Gift Shop Web page.

1

- Click the blank line 91 and then press the ENTER key.
- Type `#floatImg {` to create the id selector and then press the ENTER key.
- Indent as shown in Figure 11–25, then type `position: absolute; left:950 px;` to define the initial position of the image, and then press the ENTER key.
- Move to the left margin and type `}` to close the #floatImg id selector, and then press the ENTER key (Figure 11–25).

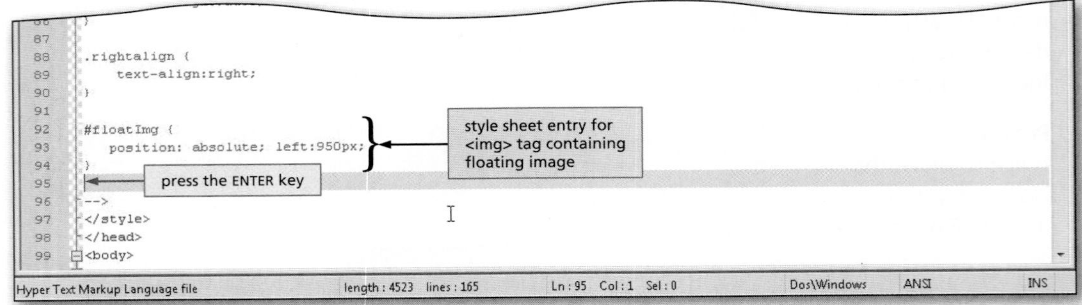

Figure 11–25

> **BTW**
> **The Purpose of the <div> Tag**
> The <div> tag is called a container, and is used to format the layout of sections or divisions of text needing the same style. Web developers often describe divisions as layers because they can be placed on top of each other and revealed dynamically as needed.

> **BTW**
> **Moving Objects**
> Object positions can be dynamically modified within a division (<div>) or a span (<span>) tag using a scripting language. Differences in browsers may cause a division to appear slightly lower or higher than originally intended by the developer.

Entering an Image Object for the Floating Image Using the <div> and <img> Tags

The next step is to add the floating image. First, a <div> tag container must be added on the Web page. The <div> tag uses the id selector, #floatImg, to indicate where the image should be initially positioned. The <div> tag layer becomes the image object whose pixelLeft property is modified to change the position of the image to float across the page. Table 11–17 shows the HTML code for the <div> tag and image tags that must be added to the Web page table.

Table 11–17 Code to Add the Floating Image <div> Tag

Line	Code
137	`<div id="floatImg">`
138	`<img src="chapter11-1floatingplaque.gif" alt="scrolling plaque" style="cursor:pointer;" onMouseOver="stopFloat()" onMouseOut="restartFloat()" onClick="coupon()" />`
139	`</div>`

Line 137 starts the <div> tag with the floatImg id selector attribute (id="floatImg"). Line 138 is the <img> image tag with three event handlers. This line must be typed without any line breaks. The onMouseOver event handler calls the stopFloat() user-defined function to stop the movement. When the visitor moves the mouse off the image, the onMouseOut event handler calls the restartFloat() user-defined function. The onClick event handler calls the coupon() user-defined function, which displays a pop-up window with a coupon. The style attribute will cause the mouse pointer to change to a hand when the mouse is over the image. Line 139 is the closing </div> tag.

To Enter <div> and <img> Tags for the Floating Image

The following step shows how to enter the <div> and <img> tags.

1

- Click line 137 to place the insertion point on the blank line before the </body> tag.
- Enter the HTML code shown in Table 11–17 to create the <div>, <img>, and </div> tags for the floating image at this position on the Web page (Figure 11–26).

```
    and mugs. Pick up a bottle of wine as a gift for your host or hostess when invited to a dinner party. Like to
    picnic? We have a picnic basket with a special insulated pocket for keeping your favorite wine slightly
    chilled. Click the scrolling image of the wooden plaque to display a coupon.</p></td>
127   </tr>
128   <tr>
129     <td><img src="chapter11-1alice_oakleaf-hydrangia.jpg" alt="feature image" /></td>
130     <td><img src="chapter11-1rose.jpg" width="160" height="107" alt="rose" /></td>
131     <td ><img src="chapter11-1plaque2.gif" width="120" height="105" alt="gift 2" /></td>
132     <td ><img src="chapter11-1mug2.gif" width="131" height="107" alt="coffee mug" /></td>
133     <td ><img src="chapter11-1mug1.gif" width="86" height="120" alt="gift 3" /></td>
134   </tr>
135 </table>
136 <div class="horztl-rule"><img src="hrdivider.jpg" width="750" height="5" alt="divider" /></div>
137  <div id="floatImg">
138    <img src="chapter11-1floatingplaque.gif" alt="scrolling plaque" style="cursor:pointer;" onMouseOver=
       "stopFloat()" onMouseOut="restartFloat()" onClick="coupon()" />
139 </div>
140 </body>
141 </html>
```

<div> tag container with <img> tag and mouse event handlers for floating image

do not press the ENTER key

do not press the ENTER key to start a new line

Hyper Text Markup Language file | length : 4523 lines : 165 | Ln : 139 Col : 7 Sel : 0 | Dos\Windows | ANSI | INS

Figure 11–26

To Add an OnLoad Event Handler to Call the floatingImage() Function

The final step in modifying the Gift Shop Web page is to enter the onLoad event handler to call the floatingImage() user-defined function as soon as the Web page is loaded. The following step adds the onLoad event handler to the <body> tag.

- Click line 99.
- Position the insertion point between the y in body and the > symbol and press the SPACEBAR once.
- Type `onLoad="floatingImage();"` and do not press the ENTER key (Figure 11–27).

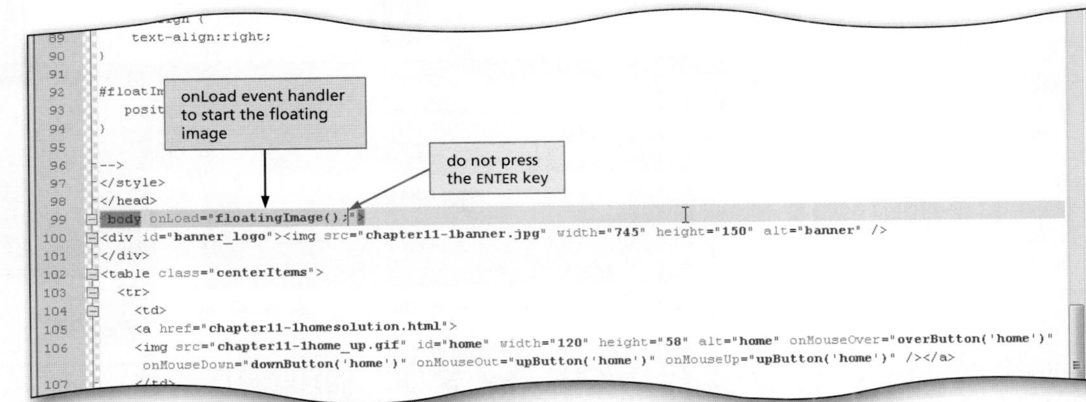

Figure 11–27

To Save an HTML File and Test a Web Page

With the code for the Gift Shop Web page complete, the HTML file should be saved and the Web page should be viewed in a browser to confirm the Web page appears and functions as desired.

1 With a USB drive plugged into your computer, click File on the menu bar, and then click Save As on the File menu.

2 Type `chapter11-1shopsolution.html` in the File name text box to save the file with a new name, and then click the Save button in the Save As dialog box.

3. Click the Internet Explorer button on the taskbar.
4. Type `G:\chapter11\ChapterFiles\chapter11-1shopsolution.html` in the Address box, and then press the ENTER key. If a security message appears at the bottom of the browser window, click the Allow blocked content button. (If you are running Internet Explorer 8 or lower, your security message may be different.)
5. When the Gift Shop Web page loads, an artistic wooden plaque image begins to float across the page from right to left.
6. Place your mouse over the floating image. The image will stop floating (Figure 11–28a).
7. Click the floating image. The coupon pop-up window appears (Figure 11–28b).

(a) Floating image of wooden plaque.

Courtesy of William J. Dorin; Courtesy of the Bernice P. Bishop Museum, Wikimedia; Courtesy of Will Murray, Wikimedia

(b) Pop-up window with coupon.

Courtesy of William J. Dorin; Art courtesy of Openclipart.org/ John Olsen; Courtesy of the Bernice P. Bishop Museum, Wikimedia; Courtesy of Will Murray, Wikimedia; Courtesy of Kriplozoik, Wikimedia

Figure 11–28

Plan Ahead

Creating Pop-up Captions

Creating a pop-up caption requires the following steps:

- Entering the JavaScript code for the user-defined function, popupCaption(), that is associated with a particular image

  The following steps detail the programming logic for the popupCaption() function:

  1. Define the image file using the element id
  2. Construct the pop-up object and determine the state (hidden or visible)
  3. If visible, hide the pop-up captions and restore the original image
  4. If hidden, show the pop-up captions with the new image
- Entering the embedded style sheet
- Entering the <a> tags and event handlers for each of the four terms
- Entering the <div> tags containing the pop-up captions text and style sheet attributes that format the appearance of the pop-up captions text

Creating Pop-up Captions on the Trails Web Page

The Trails Web page includes four elements that appear as hyperlinks on the Web page: 362, bees, butterflies, and baby bunnies. When the user places the mouse over these hyperlinks, a pop-up caption will display as a new image appears. Figure 11–1d on page HTML 509 shows an example of a pop-up caption.

The four words appear as hyperlinks by using the anchor tag <a> embedded with JavaScript statements and event handlers to call the user-defined function popupCaption(). The popupCaption() user-defined function uses a combination of JavaScript objects and properties, in conjunction with associated style sheet definitions, to show the caption text. Each pop-up caption is defined by <div> tags with id and class attributes that work in conjunction with the style sheet.

To Open an Existing HTML File in Notepad++

Now you will open the Trails HTML file in Notepad++ to enter the JavaScript user-defined function, the style sheet information, the <a> tag, the event handlers to call the JavaScript function, and the <div> tags containing the pop-up caption text.

1. If necessary, start Notepad++.
2. Open the chapter11-1trails.html file in the Chapter11\ChapterFiles folder.

To Copy and Paste the Navigation Bar, Event Handlers, and Image Rollover Functions

To maintain consistency in looks among all the Web pages, the Trails Web page should use the same the navigation created for the Hickory Oaks Forest Preserve Home page.

1. If necessary, open the chapter11-1homesolution.html in Notepad++ in the Chapter11\ChapterFiles folder.

2. Copy the HTML <table> code from lines 97 through 116 for the HTML code and mouse event handlers for the navigation bar.

3. In the chapter11-1trails.html file, click line 60 and paste the code to create the navigation bar.

4. Modify line 64 to replace the # symbol with `chapter11-1homesolution.html`.

5. Modify line 76 to replace the chapter11-1trailssolution.html with a # symbol.

6. In the chapter11-1homesolution.html file, copy the JavaScript code from lines 6 through 21. Return to the chapter11-1tours.html file and insert the copied code on line 6, and then press the ENTER key twice. Add the closing HTML comment (//-->) and the closing `</script>` tags on lines 23 and 24 (Figure 11–29).

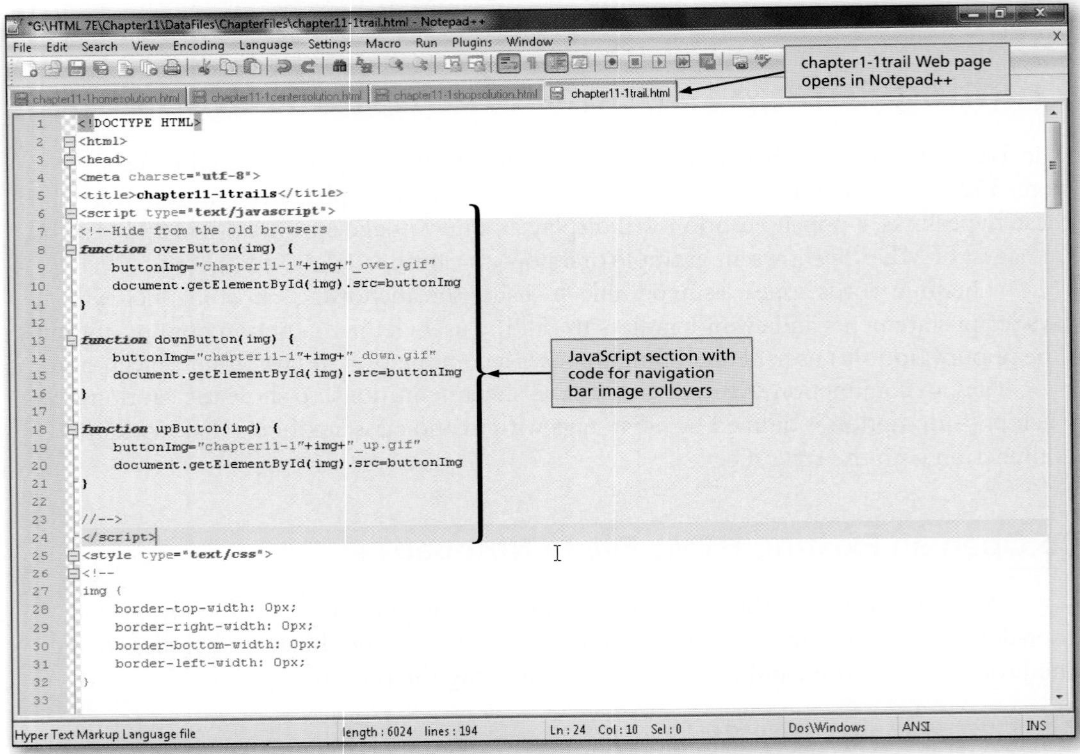

Figure 11–29

Creating the popupCaption() User-Defined Function

The JavaScript code for the popupCaption() user-defined function is written in such a way that it can be used for all pop-up captions. The function will accept two parameters from the event handlers and display the appropriate pop-up caption. Table 11–18 shows the JavaScript code used to create the popupCaption() function.

BTW

The eval() Statement
The eval() statement, short for evaluator, executes an expression as if it were originally written as language code. The eval() statement is useful in executing JavaScript statements using data whose value is not known at the time the Web page loads, such as the size of a window.

Table 11–18 Code to Create popupCaption() Function

<table>
<tr><th>Line</th><th>Code</th></tr>
<tr><td>23</td><td>function popupCaption(evnt,currElement) {</td></tr>
<tr><td>24</td><td>   var imgShow="chapter11-1"+currElement+".jpg"</td></tr>
<tr><td>25</td><td>   var documentObj=document.getElementById(currElement).style</td></tr>
<tr><td>26</td><td>   if (currElement!=0) {</td></tr>
<tr><td>27</td><td>   var state=documentObj.visibility</td></tr>
<tr><td>28</td><td>   if (state=="visible" || state=="show") {</td></tr>
<tr><td>29</td><td>   documentObj.visibility="hidden"</td></tr>
<tr><td>30</td><td>   document.getElementById("trailImage").src="chapter11-1trailImg1.jpg"</td></tr>
<tr><td>31</td><td>   }</td></tr>
<tr><td>32</td><td>   else {</td></tr>
<tr><td>33</td><td>   documentObj.visibility="visible"</td></tr>
<tr><td>34</td><td>   document.getElementById("trailImage").src=imgShow</td></tr>
<tr><td>35</td><td>   }</td></tr>
<tr><td>36</td><td>   }</td></tr>
<tr><td>37</td><td>}</td></tr>
</table>

Line 23 declares the popupCaption() user-defined function and assigns two parameter values: the event value (evnt), and the element name or id (currElement). Later in the chapter, the code for the onMouseOver and onMouseOut event handlers, which pass values to the function for these parameters, will be entered. The event value indicates if the mouse pointer is moved over or off the hyperlink or if the hyperlink is clicked. If the visitor clicks the mouse, the function receives the null parameter as the event value, which does not trigger an event. The name or id parameter passed to the function indicates the style sheet selector to be used with the associated text in the <div> tags.

Line 24 uses currElement and constructs a graphic filename associated with the pop-up caption, and is used to display an image associated with the caption. Line 25 defines one local variable, documentObj, that will be used to show or hide the caption. Line 26 tests the value of currElement to determine which link element the mouse is over. If the value is greater than 0, line 27 defines the current state of the element with style property, visibility.

Line 28 then tests if the state is visible or show. If the caption is already showing, the visibility property of the caption is set to "hidden," (line 29), and the original trail image is shown (line 30); line 29 completes the if statement and the else (line 32) begins the code to display the pop-up caption (line 33) with the associated trail image (line 34). The currElement in mouse event handlers is the name of the trail image and the <div> tag id attribute that contains the pop-up caption text. Line 35 closes the else. Line 36 closes the if at line 26, and line 37 closes the function at line 23. The position of the caption is fixed and set by the CSS id selectors. These captions display below the body text and to the left of the new image that displays on the page.

To Enter the popupCaption() Function

The following step enters the code for the popupCaption() user-defined function.

1

- Click line 22 and press the ENTER key once.
- Enter the code shown in Table 11–18 on the previous page to create the popupCaption() function, indenting as shown, and then press the ENTER key once to place the insertion point on line 38 (Figure 11–30).

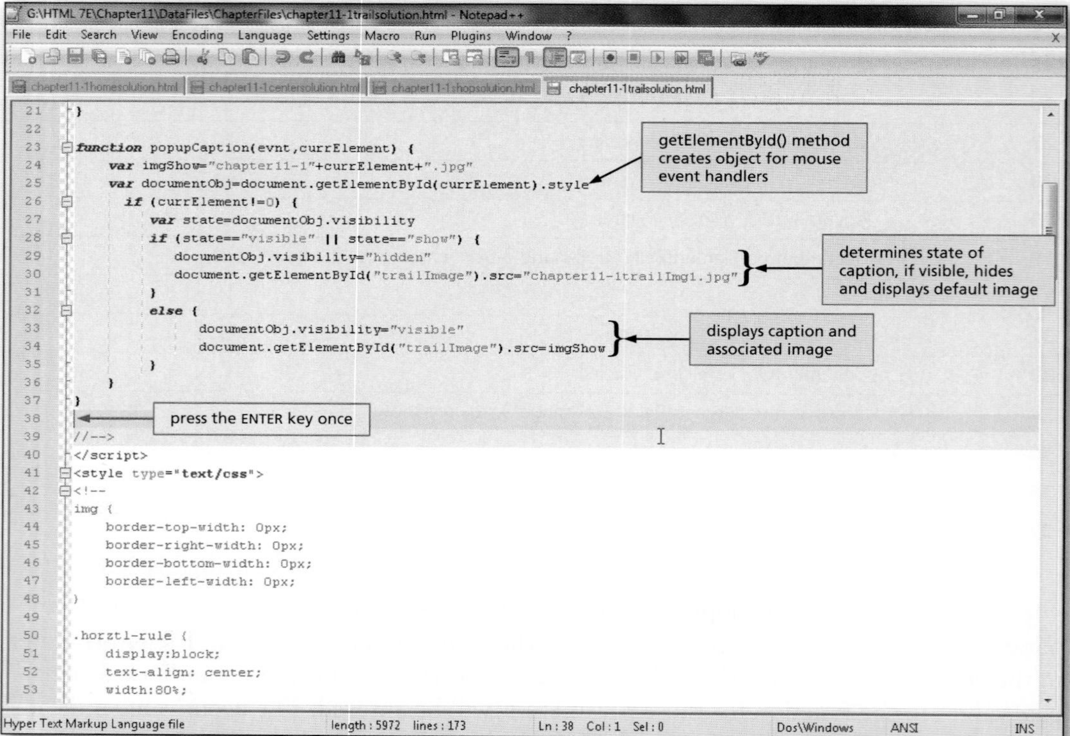

Figure 11–30

Adding an Embedded Style Sheet Using id and Class Properties

> BTW
> **id and class Selectors**
> Recall from earlier chapters that an id selector is used to identify one element, and the class can be used to identify more than one. The class selector must be notated by the class attribute in the HTML tag. In the normal hierarchy of cascading selectors, the id selector has a higher priority than attribute selectors.

The embedded style sheets used on the Trails Web page employ the id and class selectors to define the style for each of the four pop-up captions. Each caption is identified uniquely using an id attribute and value, so the popupCaption() function can ensure that only one caption appears at a time. An id selector is used in a style sheet much like a class selector — except that the id selector is entered with a preceding pound sign (#).

In the Trails Web page, the <div> tag is used to enclose the text that appears in the pop-up captions. In this use, the <div> tag is referred to as a container. A **container** means that the text is grouped together. Text enclosed within the <div> tag is referred to as **inline**. The id and class attributes are used in the <div> tag to associate the selectors in the embedded style sheet with each of the four pop-up captions.

The popupCaption() user-defined function needs two parameters: evnt and currElement. For each pop-up caption, the evnt parameter indicates the type of event, using an onMouseOver or onMouseOut event handler, and the currElement parameter passes the style sheet id selector. Figure 11–31 illustrates the relationship between the event handler function call, the associated selector in the style sheet, and the text in the <div> tag. The <div> tag contains an id attribute, which is the style sheet selector, and the style sheet class, which indicates how to format the displayed pop-up caption text. Thus, to apply a style to the pop-up captions, the embedded style sheet uses the id attribute value as the selector.

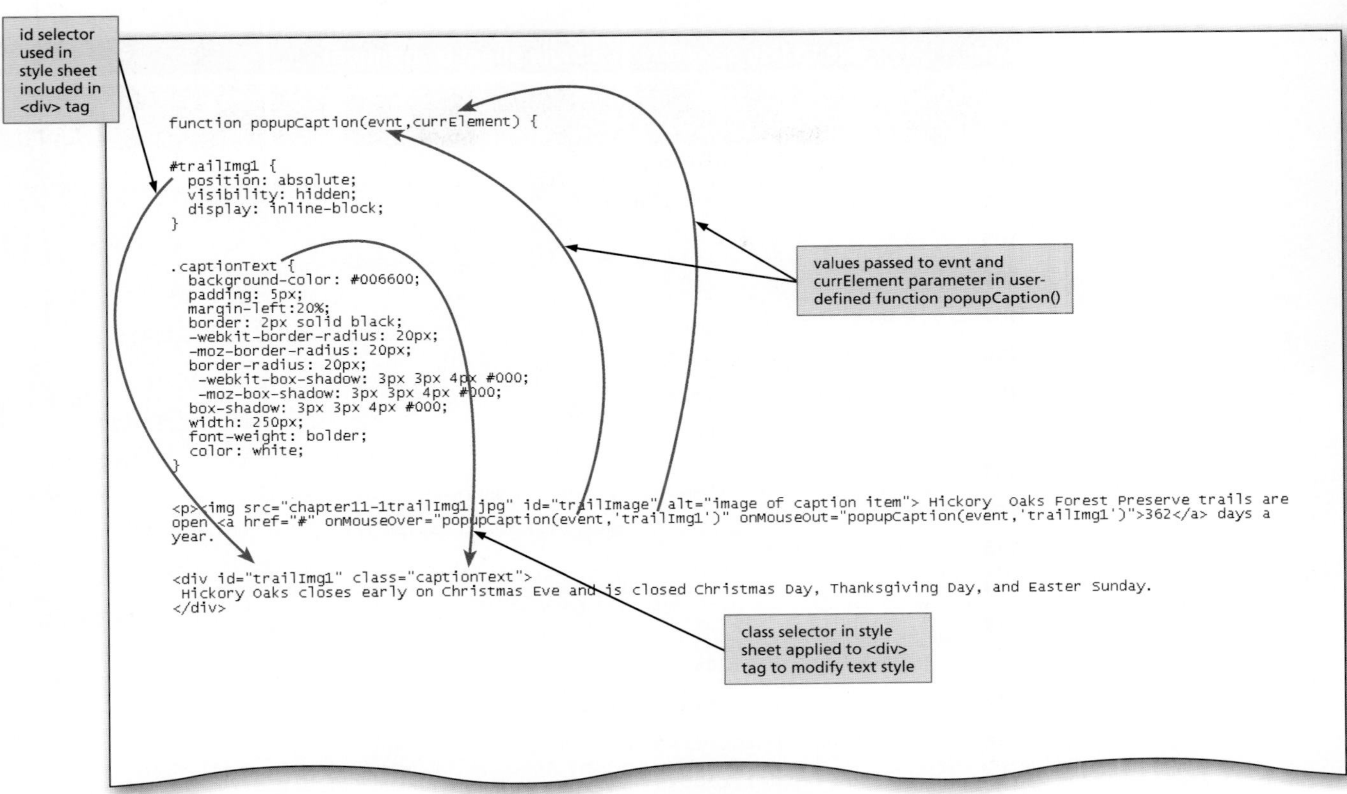

id selector used in style sheet included in <div> tag
function popupCaption(evnt,currElement) {
#trailImg1 {
position: absolute;
visibility: hidden;
display: inline-block;
}
.captionText {
background-color: #006600;
padding: 5px;
margin-left:20%;
border: 2px solid black;
-webkit-border-radius: 20px;
-moz-border-radius: 20px;
border-radius: 20px;
-webkit-box-shadow: 3px 3px 4px #000;
-moz-box-shadow: 3px 3px 4px #000;
box-shadow: 3px 3px 4px #000;
width: 250px;
font-weight: bolder;
color: white;
}
<p><img src="chapter11-1trailImg1.jpg" id="trailImage" alt="image of caption item"> Hickory Oaks Forest Preserve trails are open <a href="#" onMouseOver="popupCaption(event,'trailImg1')" onMouseOut="popupCaption(event,'trailImg1')">362</a> days a year.
<div id="trailImg1" class="captionText">
Hickory Oaks closes early on Christmas Eve and is closed Christmas Day, Thanksgiving Day, and Easter Sunday.
</div>
values passed to evnt and currElement parameter in user-defined function popupCaption()
class selector in style sheet applied to <div> tag to modify text style

Figure 11–31

The popupCaption() function code uses these values to show the pop-up caption at the position defined by the trailImg1 selector in the style sheet. The embedded style sheet on the Trails Web page has four id selectors — trailImg1 through trailImg4 — to set the position at which each pop-up caption appears. It also defines a style for the class captionText, which defines the format of the pop-up caption text. Table 11–19 shows the embedded style sheet code used to set the position of the pop-up caption and format the caption text.

> **BTW**
> **When to use <div> and <span> Container Tags**
> The <div> tag groups items as a block, and the <span> tag groups items inline. Inline refers to the fact that the <span> tag does not do any formatting of its own. For example, the <div> tag will cause a paragraph break, and the <span> tag will not. Using the <span> tag allows changing styles within a division or paragraph.

Table 11–19 Code to Use Selectors in a Style Sheet

Line	Code
89	`#trailImg1 {`
90	`position: absolute;`
91	`visibility: hidden;`
92	`display: inline-block;`
93	`}`
94	
95	`#trailImg2 {`
96	`position: absolute;`
97	`visibility: hidden;`
98	`display: inline-block;`
99	`}`
100	
101	`#trailImg3 {`
102	`position: absolute;`

Table 11–19 Code to Use Selectors in a Style Sheet (continued)

Line	Code
103	visibility: hidden;
104	display: inline-block;
105	}
106	
107	#trailImg4 {
108	position: absolute;
109	visibility: hidden;
110	display: inline-block;
111	}
112	
113	.captionText {
114	background-color: #006600;
115	padding: 5px;
116	margin-left:20%;
117	border: 2px solid black;
118	-webkit-border-radius: 20px;
119	-moz-border-radius: 20px;
120	border-radius: 20px;
121	-webkit-box-shadow: 3px 3px 4px #000;
122	-moz-box-shadow: 3px 3px 4px #000;
123	box-shadow: 3px 3px 4px #000;
124	width: 250px;
125	font-weight: bolder;
126	color: white;
127	}

Lines 89, 95, 101, and 107 declare the id selectors for each of the four trail images (trailImg1 through trailImg4). Lines 90, 96, 102, and 108 set the position attribute to absolute. Lines 91, 97, 103, and 109 use the visibility attribute (hidden) to hide the pop-up caption. Lines 92, 98, 104, and 110 indicate that the display will be an inline-block.

Line 113 starts the class selector, captionText, to define how the pop-up caption text should display. Line 114 sets the background color to a darker shade of green. Line 115 sets padding to five pixels. Line 116 indicates the pop-up caption should display with a left margin 20% of the width of the browser window. Lines 117 through 124 describe the features of the display box. The border is two pixels thick, with a 20 pixel radius for rounded corners. Lines 120 to 122 describe the drop shadow for the display of the pop-up caption. Line 125 indicates the text should be bolder, and line 126 sets the text color to white. Line 127 closes the captionText class selector.

To Enter Cascading Style Sheet id and Class Selectors for the Pop-up Captions

The following steps enter the Cascading Style Sheet id and class selectors for the pop-up captions.

1

- Click line 88 and press the ENTER key.
- Enter the code shown in Table 11–19 starting on the previous page from lines 89 to 111 to enter the id selectors in the embedded style sheet, indenting as shown. Press the ENTER key twice to position the insertion point on line 113 (Figure 11–32).

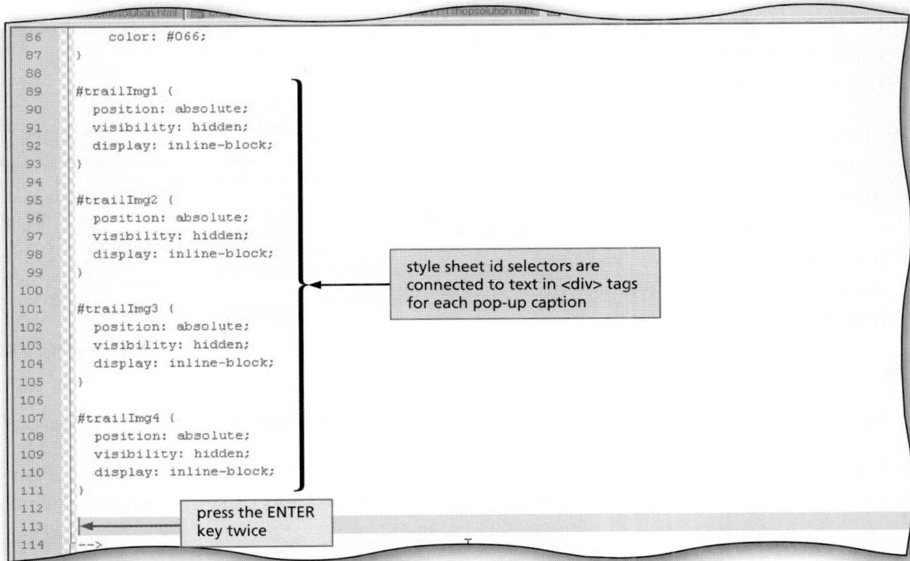
color: #066;
}
#trailImg1 {
position: absolute;
visibility: hidden;
display: inline-block;
}
#trailImg2 {
position: absolute;
visibility: hidden;
display: inline-block;
}
#trailImg3 {
position: absolute;
visibility: hidden;
display: inline-block;
}
#trailImg4 {
position: absolute;
visibility: hidden;
display: inline-block;
}
-->
style sheet id selectors are connected to text in <div> tags for each pop-up caption
press the ENTER key twice

Figure 11–32

2

- Continuing on line 113, enter the code shown in Table 11–19 from lines 113 through 127 to enter the styles for the class captionText, indenting as shown, and then press the ENTER key after line 127. (Figure 11–33).

```
113 .captionText {
114   background-color: #006600;
115   padding: 5px;
116   margin-left:20%;
117   border: 2px solid black;
118   -webkit-border-radius: 20px;
119   -moz-border-radius: 20px;
120   border-radius: 20px;
121     -webkit-box-shadow: 3px 3px 4px #000;
122     -moz-box-shadow: 3px 3px 4px #000;
123   box-shadow: 3px 3px 4px #000;
124   width: 250px;
125   font-weight: bolder;
126   color: white;
127 }
128
```

selector for pop-up caption text so all text is formatted the same

press the ENTER key once

Figure 11–33

Q&A In this code for the style sheet, both color names and hexidecimal codes are used. What is the difference?

No difference exists. Most browsers will recognize the standard colors by name. Other colors must be entered using their hexidecimal values.

To Add Links and Event Handlers to Call the popupCaption() Function

The four terms, highlighted as links in the Trails Web page, must have onMouseOver and onMouseOut event handlers code associated with these <a href> tags to call the popupCaption() user-defined function. The popupCaption() function changes the image on the Web page and displays the pop-up caption when the visitor places the mouse over the hyperlink.

Normally, a link is associated with a URL, so when the visitor clicks the hyperlink, the browser shows a new Web page. This Web page uses links associated with the onMouseOver and onMouseOut event handlers to show the pop-up caption when a user points to the link. The <a href="#"> is used so the browser will not show a new Web page if a user accidentally clicks the link.

The following steps enter the pop-up caption links and the onMouseOver and onMouseOut event handlers to call the popupCaption() function.

1

- In line 157, position the insertion point before the number 362 in the first sentence.
- Type <a href="#" onMouseOver="popupCaption(event,'trailImg1')" onMouseOut="popupCaption(event,'trailImg1')"> to enter the link for the 362 pop-up caption. Do not press the ENTER key.
- Click immediately to the right of the number 362, and type </a> to close the <a> anchor tag. Do not press the ENTER key (Figure 11–34).

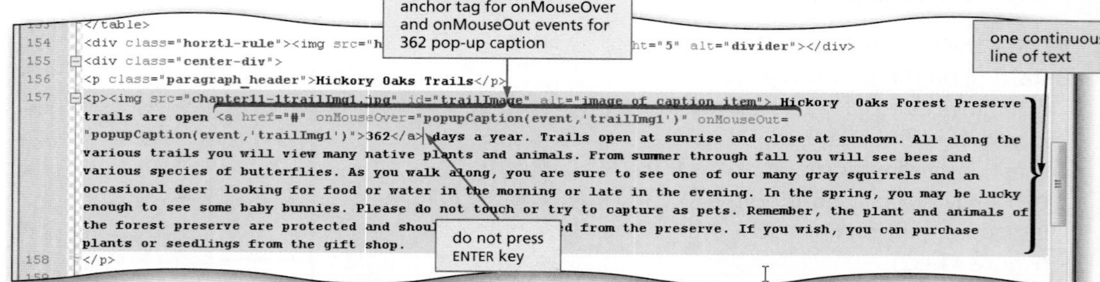

Figure 11–34

- Farther in the same line and paragraph, position the insertion point just before the word bees.
- Type <a href="#" onMouseOver="popupCaption(event,'trailImg2')" onMouseOut="popupCaption(event,'trailImg2')"> to enter the link for the bees pop-up caption. Do not press the ENTER key.
- Click to the right of the word bees and type </a> to close the <a> anchor tag. Do not press the ENTER key (Figure 11–35).

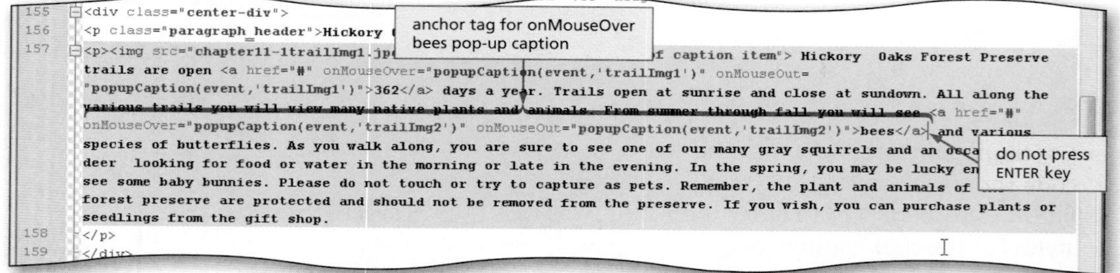

Figure 11–35

3

- Farther in the same paragraph, position the insertion point before the word butterflies.
- Type <a href="#" onMouseOver="popupCaption(event,'trailImg3')" onMouseOut="popupCaption(event,'trailImg3')"> to enter the link for the butterflies pop-up caption. Do not press the ENTER key. Click to the right of the words butterflies and type </a> to the <a> anchor tag. Do not press the ENTER key.
- Farther in the same paragraph, position the insertion point before the words baby bunnies.
- Type <a href="#" onMouseOver="popupCaption(event,'trailImg4')" onMouseOut="popupCaption(event,'trailImg4')"> to enter the link for the baby bunnies pop-up caption. Do not press the ENTER key. Click to the right of the words baby bunnies and type </a> to the <a> anchor tag. Do not press the ENTER key (Figure 11–36).

Q&A The pop-up caption selectors all have the same features. Why must we use so many?

Each pop-up caption must have its own selector to be identified by the pop-up caption code and to match the text in the <div> containers.

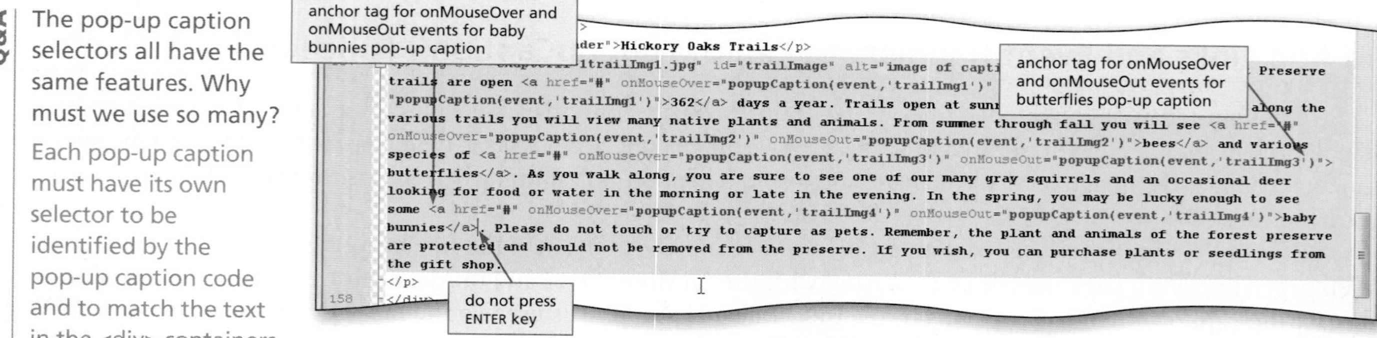

Figure 11–36

Q&A What does the pound sign (#) mean in the <a href> tag?

The # sign means it is a null link, and will not attempt to link to another URL.

Entering the <div> Tags Containing Pop-up Caption Text

The text that appears in each of the four pop-up captions on the Trails Web page is enclosed in <div> tags. The <div> tags use the id and class attributes to associate the pop-up captions with the embedded style sheet declarations that control the appearance of the text in the caption. Table 11–20 shows the HTML code used to enter the <div> tags that define the caption text.

Table 11–20 Code for <div> Tags Containing captionText Text

Line	Code
160	`<div id="trailImg1" class="captionText">`
161	`Hickory Oaks closes early on Christmas Eve and is closed Christmas Day, Thanksgiving Day, and Easter Sunday.`
162	`</div>`
163	`<div id="trailImg2" class="captionText">`
164	`A wide variety of bees and wasps frequent our flower gardens This bumble bee is one example.`
165	`</div>`
166	`<div id="trailImg3" class="captionText">`
167	`Butterflies often visit our gardens, you'll see Monarch, Hoary Edges, and swallowtails of all varieties.`
168	`</div>`
169	`<div id="trailImg4" class="captionText">`
170	`Baby rabbits are called kits. As many as 12 can be in a litter.`
171	`</div>`

Line 160 is the <div> tag with the trailImg1 id selector and captionText class selector. Line 161 contains the text for the pop-up text when the mouse is over the 362 link. Line 163 is the <div> tag for the trailImg2 id selector and captionText class selector. Line 164 is the pop-up text for the bees link. Line 166 is the <div> tag with the trailImg3 id selector and captionText class selector. Line 167 is the text for the butterfly link. Line 169 is the <div> tag with the trailImg4 id selector and captionText class selector. Line 170 is the text for the baby bunnies link. Lines 162, 165, 168, and 171 close the <div> tags.

To Enter <div> Tags Containing Pop-up Caption Text

The following step enters the <div> tags containing the pop-up caption text.

1

- Click line 160, between the closing </div> tag and the closing </body> tag.
- Enter the code shown in Table 11–20 to create <div> containers for the pop-up caption text. Do not press ENTER after the </div> tag on the last line (Figure 11–37).

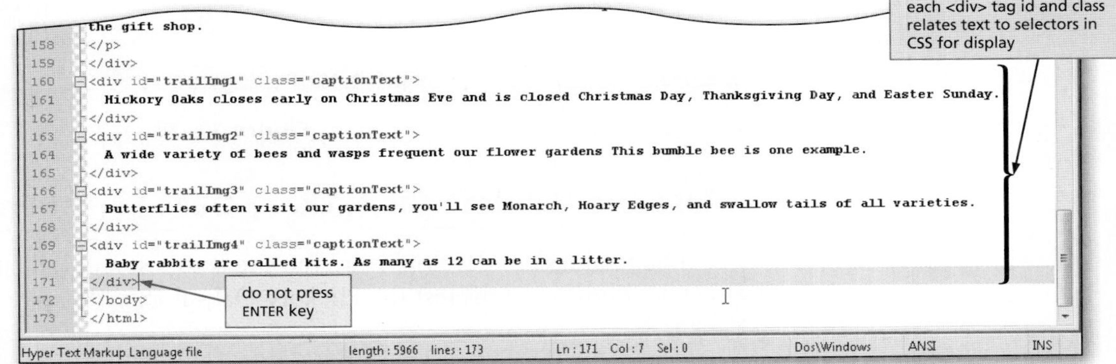

Figure 11–37

To Save an HTML File and Test the Trails Web Page

After the JavaScript code for the Trails Web page is complete, the HTML file should be saved and the Web page should be viewed in a browser to confirm the Web page appears as desired and that pop-up captions and the new images display correctly.

1. With a USB drive plugged into your computer, click File on the menu bar and then click Save As.
2. Type `chapter11-1trailssolution.html` in the File name text box and then click the Save button.
3. Click the Internet Explorer button on the status bar.
4. Type `G:\chapter11\ChapterFiles\chapter11-1trailssolution.html` in the Address box and then press the ENTER key. If a security message appears at the bottom of the browser window, click the Allow blocked content button. (If you are running Internet Explorer 8 or lower, your security message may be different.)
5. When the trails Web page is displayed, move the mouse pointer over the link 362 to view the new image and pop-up caption.
6. Next, position the mouse pointer over the bees link, and then the baby bunnies link to test the pop-up captions and images.
7. Move the mouse pointer over the word butterflies to view the new image and pop-up caption, as shown in Figure 11–38.

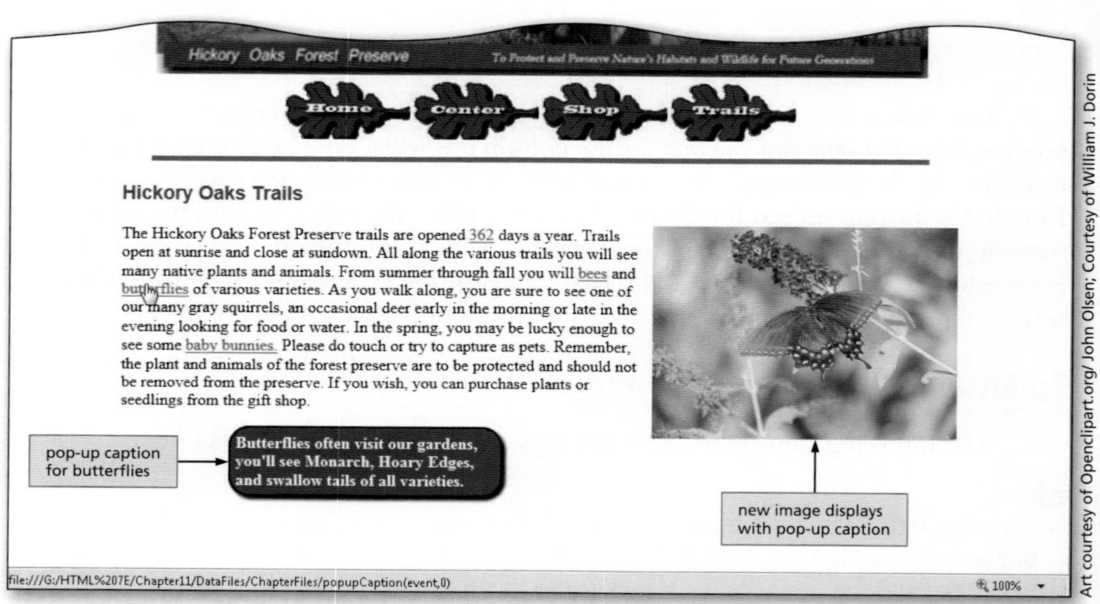

Figure 11–38

To Test and Validate the Hickory Oaks Forest Preserve Web Pages

The final task in developing a Web site is to test and validate all the Web pages and links. The following steps test the Hickory Oaks Forest Preserve Web pages.

1. Click the address box and type `G:\chapter11\chapter11-1homesolution.html` and press the ENTER key. If a security message appears at the bottom of the browser window, click the Allow blocked content button. (If you are running Internet Explorer 8 or lower, your security message may be different.)

2. Position the mouse over the Center, Shop, and Trails buttons to make sure each one functions properly.
3. Click the Shop button. Check to see that the floating image moves across the screen of the Gift Shop page.
4. Move the mouse over the floating image to ensure it stops, and then click the image to display the coupon pop-up window.
5. Click the Print Coupon link in the pop-up coupon window, and then click the Cancel button in the Print dialog box. Click Close to close the pop-up window.
6. Click the Center button. After the slide show plays, click the Trails button.
7. Drag the mouse over the underlined terms to verify the new images and pop-up captions display, and then click the Home button.
8. Validate the Chapter 11 Hickory Oaks Forest Preserve Web pages using validator.w3.org.

BTW

Quick Reference
For a list of JavaScript statements and their associated attributes, see the JavaScript Quick Reference (Appendix G) at the back of this book, or visit the JavaScript Quick Reference on the Book Companion Site Web page for this book at www.cengagebrain.com.

To Quit Notepad++ and a Browser

1. In Notepad++, click the File menu, and then Close All.
2. Click the Close button on the Notepad++ title bar.
3. Click the Close button on the browser title bar. If necessary, click the Close all tabs button.

Chapter Summary

Chapter 11 introduced the concepts of the Document Object Model (DOM), a combination of technologies that include HTML, Cascading Style Sheets (CSS), and a scripting language, such as JavaScript. Using the DOM, you learned how to create a navigation bar with image rollovers, display a random image from an array of images, create and display a slide show that automatically starts when a Web page is loaded, create a floating image that also serves as a link to a pop-up window, and how to use pop-up captions to add more information about terms on a Web page. The items listed below include all the new skills you have learned in this chapter.

1. Create an HTML Table to Contain the Navigation Bar (HTML 513)
2. Create User-Defined Functions for Image Rollovers (HTML 516)
3. Enter Mouse Event Handlers to Invoke User-Defined Functions (HTML 517)
4. Save and Test the Hickory Oaks Forest Preserve Web Page Navigation Bar (HTML 517)
5. Enter a Random Number Generator User-Defined Function (HTML 521)
6. Enter Code to Show Copyright Information and Date Last Modified (HTML 521)
7. Enter OnLoad Event Handlers in the <body> Tag (HTML 522)
8. Create an Image Object (HTML 525)
9. Create a User-Defined Function to Add a Slide Show (HTML 527)
10. Enter an OnLoad Event Handler to Call a Function (HTML 527)
11. Enter the floatingImage() Function (HTML 531)
12. Enter the stopFloat() Function (HTML 532)
13. Enter the restartFloat() Function (HTML 532)
14. Enter the coupon() Function (HTML 533)
15. Enter an Embedded Style Sheet to Format the Floating Image (HTML 534)
16. Enter <div> and <img> Tags for the Floating Image (HTML 535)
17. Add an OnLoad Event Handler to Call the floatingImage() Function (HTML 535)
18. Enter the popupCaption() Function (HTML 540)
19. Enter Cascading Style Sheet id and Class Selectors for the Pop-up Captions (HTML 543)
20. Add Links and Event Handlers to Call the popupCaption() Function (HTML 543)
21. Enter <div> Tags Containing Pop-up Caption Text (HTML 545)

Learn It Online

Test your knowledge of chapter content and key terms.

Instructions: To complete the following exercises, please visit www.cengagebrain.com. At the CengageBrain.com home page, search for *HTML5 and CSS 7th Edition* using the search box at the top of the page. This will take you to the product page for this book. On the product page, click the Access Now button below the Study Tools heading. On the Book Companion Site Web page, select Chapter 11, and then click the link for the desired exercise.

Chapter Reinforcement TF, MC, and SA

A series of true/false, multiple choice, and short answer questions that test your knowledge of the chapter content.

Flash Cards

An interactive learning environment where you identify chapter key terms associated with displayed definitions.

Practice Test

A series of multiple choice questions that tests your knowledge of chapter content and key terms.

Who Wants To Be a Computer Genius?

An interactive game that challenges your knowledge of chapter content in the style of a television quiz show.

Wheel of Terms

An interactive game that challenges your knowledge of chapter key terms in the style of the television show, *Wheel of Fortune*.

Crossword Puzzle Challenge

A crossword puzzle that challenges your knowledge of key terms presented in the chapter.

Apply Your Knowledge

Reinforce the skills and apply the concepts you learned in this chapter.

Instructions: Start Notepad++. Open the file apply11-1.html from the Chapter11\Apply folder of the Data Files for Students. See the inside back cover of this book for instructions on downloading the Data Files for Students, or contact your instructor for information about accessing the required files.

The apply11-1.html file is a partially completed HTML file that you will use for this exercise. Figure 11–39 on page HTML 550 shows the Apply Your Knowledge Web page as it should be displayed in a browser after the JavaScript code has been added.

Perform the following tasks:

1. Using the JavaScript code in Table 11–18 on page HTML 539 as a guide, create a user-defined function to create pop-up captions and to change the image on the left side of the body text. The id attribute for the image provided is making_steel; use this id in the getElementById() method in the user-defined function. Use the original image, apply11-1steelmill.jpg as the image to display when the mouse is off the linked term.
2. Using the CSS code in Table 11–19 on page HTML 541 as a guide, add a CSS selector for each pop-up caption and image. Use #smelting, #H_Bessemer, #taconite, #limestone, #coke_oven, and #rolled_coil to match the images provided.

3. Using the code associated with Figure 11–34 on page HTML 544 enter the <a href> tags for each of the words to be linked as shown in Table 11–21.

Table 11–21

Linked Word	<a href> tag
smelting	<a href="#" onMouseOver="popUp(event,'smelting')" onMouseOut="popUp(event,'smelting')">
Sir Henry Bessemer	<a href="#" onMouseOver="popUp(event,'H_Bessemer')" onMouseOut="popUp(event,'H_Bessemer')">
taconite	<a href="#" onMouseOver="popUp(event,'taconite')" onMouseOut="popUp(event,'taconite')">
limestone	<a href="#" onMouseOver="popUp(event,'limestone')" onMouseOut="popUp(event,'limestone')">
coke	<a href="#" onMouseOver="popUp(event,'coke_oven')" onMouseOut="popUp(event,'coke_oven')">
rolled	<a href="#" onMouseOver="popUp(event,'rolled_coil')" onMouseOut="popUp(event,'rolled_coil')">

Be sure to add the closing </a> after the linked word.

4. Using the code in Table 11–20 on page HTML 545 as a guide, write the <div> tags for each linked word. Table 11–22 contains the tag id, class, and text for the pop-up captions. Place the HTML code in the blank line after the HTML comment <!-- div tags for pop-up captions -->. Be sure to close the <div> tags.

Table 11–22

div tag id	class	Caption
smelting	captionText	Smelting is the process of melting an ore to get the metal out of it.
H_Bessemer	captionText	Henry Bessemer bought the patent from William Kelly, who invented the process in 1851. The Bessemer process blows air through the molten iron ore to remove impurities.
taconite	captionText	Taconite is iron ore ground into a powder and combined with clay and limestone, which is rolled into pellets and submitted to high temperatures to increase durability.
coke_oven	captionText	Coke is coal that has been baked in an oven.
limestone	captionText	Limestone is sedimentary rock, formed primarily of various calcium carbonate crystals of calcite and aragonite.
rolled_coil	captionText	This roll of steel may be headed to an auto manufacturer or used to make refrigerators, washers, and dryers.

5. Save the revised file in the Chapter11\Apply folder using the filename apply11-1solution.html.
6. Start your browser. Enter the URL G:\Chapter11\Apply\apply11-1solution.html to view and test the Web page in your browser. Validate the Web page.
7. If any errors occur, check the code against Steps 1 through 4, make any required changes, save the file using the same filename, and then refresh the Web page in the browser.
8. Submit the revised HTML file and Web page in the format specified by your instructor.

Continued >

Apply Your Knowledge *continued*

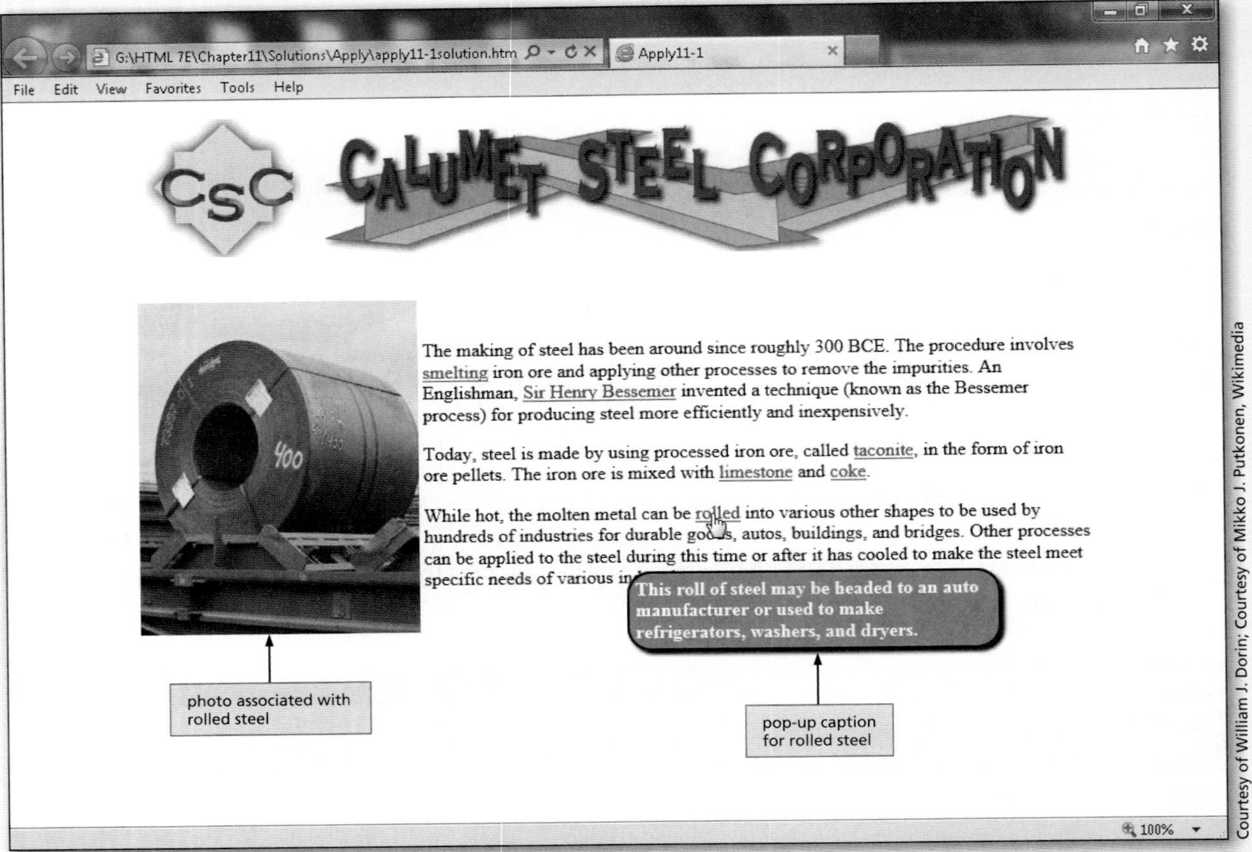

Courtesy of William J. Dorin; Courtesy of Mikko J. Putkonen, Wikimedia

Figure 11–39

Extend Your Knowledge

Extend the skills you learned in this chapter and experiment with new skills. You will need to search the Internet to complete the assignment.

Learning More About Moving or Floating Objects

Instructions: Start Notepad++ and your browser. Open the file extend11-1.html from the Chapter11\Extend folder of the Data Files for Students. See the inside back cover of this book for instructions on downloading the Data Files for Students, or contact your instructor for information about accessing the required files.

The code in Table 11–13 moves an object across the Web page 10 pixels at a time by modifying the pixelLeft style of the getElementById() object. An object can be moved from one location on the screen to another by simply setting the pixelLeft to a specific location, using mouse events to call appropriate user-defined functions. This Web page also takes the floating object used in the chapter and instead of having the object float from left to right or right to left, the user-defined function is modified to make the object float from top to bottom. To make the Web page more interesting, the floating object is randomly picked each time the Web page is loaded. The initial images (bowling ball, pins, and random bowling pin placement images) are placed in the correct locations in the data file. In addition, the CSS selectors and values are provided for these images.

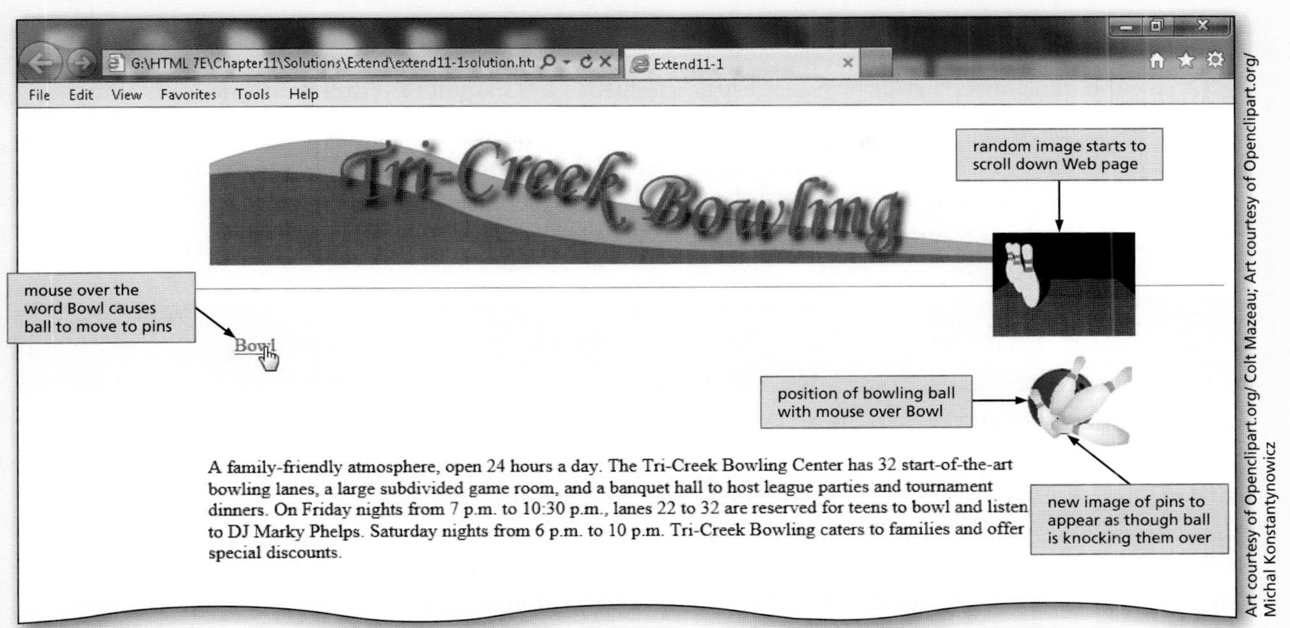

Art courtesy of Openclipart.org/ Colt Mazeau; Art courtesy of Openclipart.org/ Michal Konstantynowicz

Figure 11–40

Perform the following tasks:

1. Open the extend11-1.html data file and save it immediately as extend11-1solution.html.
2. Using line 27 from Table 11–13, which sets the position of the image, as a guide, write a user-defined function called moveRight() to move the bowling ball object to the right at the position of the bowling pins. Assign the image file extend11-1pinsdown.gif to the pins object.
3. Write a user-defined function called moveBack() to move the bowling ball object back to its original position on the left side of the Web page. Assign the image file extend11-1pinsup.gif to the pins object.
4. Add the following id selectors in the embedded CSS called pins and bowling_ball. Set the pins properties as follows: position: absolute; left: 900px; top: 217px. Set the bowling_ball properties as follows: position: absolute; left: 200px; top: 225px.
5. A <span> tag with the id ImgText preceeds the word Bowl. Add another CSS id selector (ImgText) to the embedded style sheet for this id. Set the properties as follows: position: absolute; left: 10; top: 196px.
6. After the <span> tag, insert in the <a href="#"> tag the mouse events to call the moveRight() and moveBack() user-defined functions.
7. The apDiv1 selector places an image to the right of the banner using an id of splits. Write the user-defined function called selectImg() to assign a random image to the splits image. These images are of various types of splits that can be left in bowling. The filenames are as follows: extend11-1_2-4-7.gif, extend11-1_4-7-8.gif, extend11-1_4-10.gif, extend11-1_5.gif, extend11-1_6-10.gif, and extend11-1_7-10.gif. After assigning the random image, call a user-defined function called dropImage().
8. Write the user-defined function, dropImage() to make the randomly selected split image drop from the top to the bottom of the screen. Modify the code in Table 11-13 by changing the leftPX to topPX, test if the topPX > 600. If the image is at the bottom of the Web page, reset topPX to 10 and stop the scroll with the clearTimeout() method. To move the image from top down, use the getElementById() on the apDiv1, setting the style.pixelTop to the topPX value. Do not forget to use recursion to call the dropImage() function from within itself.

Continued >

Extend Your Knowledge *continued*

9. Save the file and start your browser. Enter the URL G:\Chapter11\Extend\extend11-1solution.html to view and test the Web page in your browser.
10. If any errors occur, check the code against Steps 1 through 8, make any required changes, save the file using the same filename, and then refresh the Web page in the browser.
11. Submit the revised HTML file and Web page in the format specified by your instructor.

Make It Right

Analyze the JavaScript code on a Web page and correct all errors.

Correcting Syntax Errors and Inserting Missing Code

Instructions: Start your browser, and open the file make11-1.html from the Chapter11\MakeItRight folder of the Data Files for Students in the browser. See the inside back cover of this book for instructions on downloading the Data Files for Students, or contact your instructor for information about accessing the required files. The file is a Web page for the Amateur Meteorological Society that contains five errors. The errors can be in the form of syntax, logic, or missing code. The corrected page appears as shown in Figure 11–41.

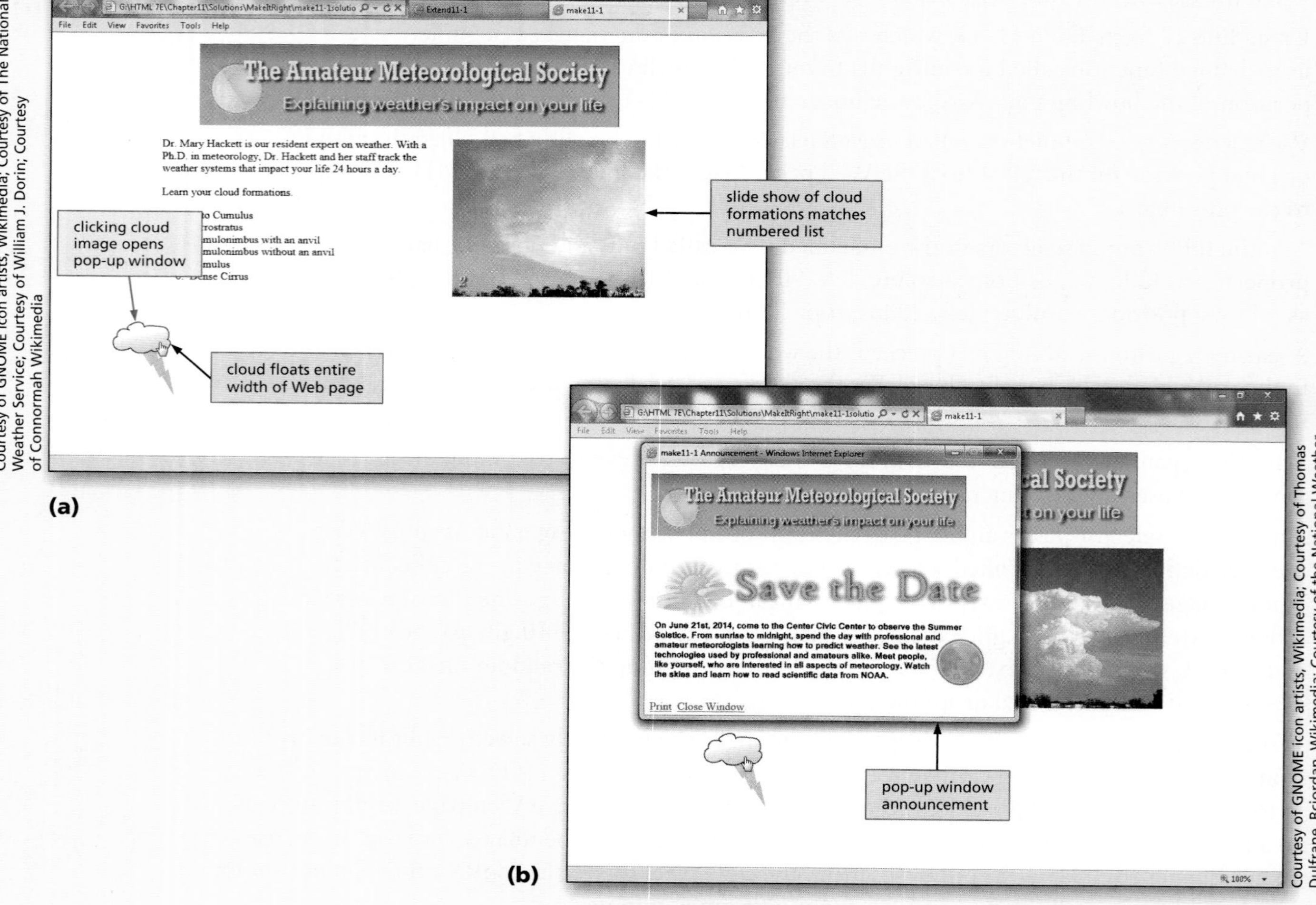

Figure 11–41

Perform the following tasks:

1. Start Notepad++. Open the make11-1.html file and save the file as make11-1solution.html.
2. The floatImage() user-defined function has one error. The lightning cloud on the left should scroll the entire width of the Web page. Find the error in the floatImage() function so that the lightning cloud scrolls the entire width of the Web page.
3. When the mouse is placed over the floating lightning cloud, it does not stop. Compare code in Tables 11–13 and 11–14 and find the error.
4. When the slide show tries to find an image, there is an error. All the images are supplied, so it is not a missing image. Find the error related to the cloudSlideShow() user-defined function.
5. When the lightning cloud image is clicked, it should open a pop-up window announcement by calling the user-defined function conference().
6. Correct these errors, and then save the corrected HTML file. Test the corrected Web page using your browser. If you still have an error, check your code, save, and test again (*Hint:* check the onLoad event handler in the <body> tag).
7. Submit the revised HTML file and Web page in the format specified by your instructor.

In the Lab

Design and/or create a Web page using the guidelines, concepts, and skills presented in this chapter. Labs are listed in order of increasing difficulty.

Lab 1: Town of Madison Parks and Recreation

Instructions: You are a summer intern for the Town of Madison's Parks and Recreation Department. Your supervisor wants to create a Web page to announce some free classes for DIY home owners sponsored by Schillingburg Lumber and Hardware. The Web page needs an image rollover with a light switch that is on or off, and when the image is clicked, a pop-up window displays with an announcement about a weekly raffle being held at the store. The Web page has an unordered list of the classes: installing ceramic tile, repairing broken light switches, replacing torn screens, and fixing leaky faucets. When the user moves the mouse over the selected word, a new image replaces the wrench and hammer illustration and a pop-up caption displays (Figure 11–42).

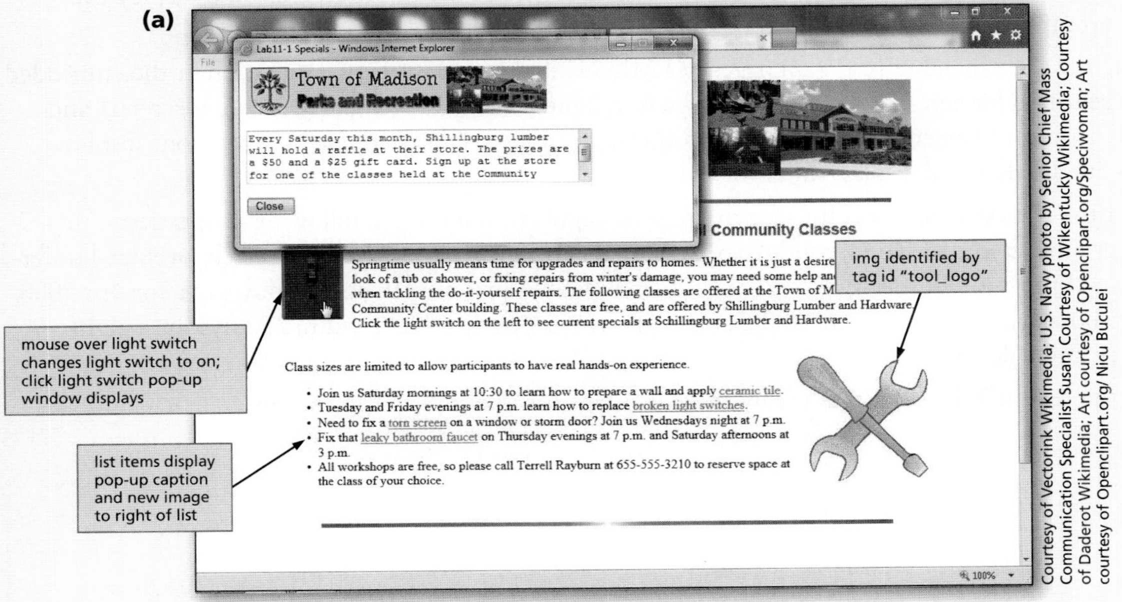

Courtesy of Vectorink Wikimedia; U.S. Navy photo by Senior Chief Mass Communication Specialist Susan; Courtesy of Wikentucky Wikimedia; Courtesy of Daderot Wikimedia; Art courtesy of Openclipart.org/Speciwoman; Art courtesy of Openclipart.org/ Nicu Buculei

Figure 11–42

Continued >

STUDENT ASSIGNMENTS

In the Lab *continued*

(b)

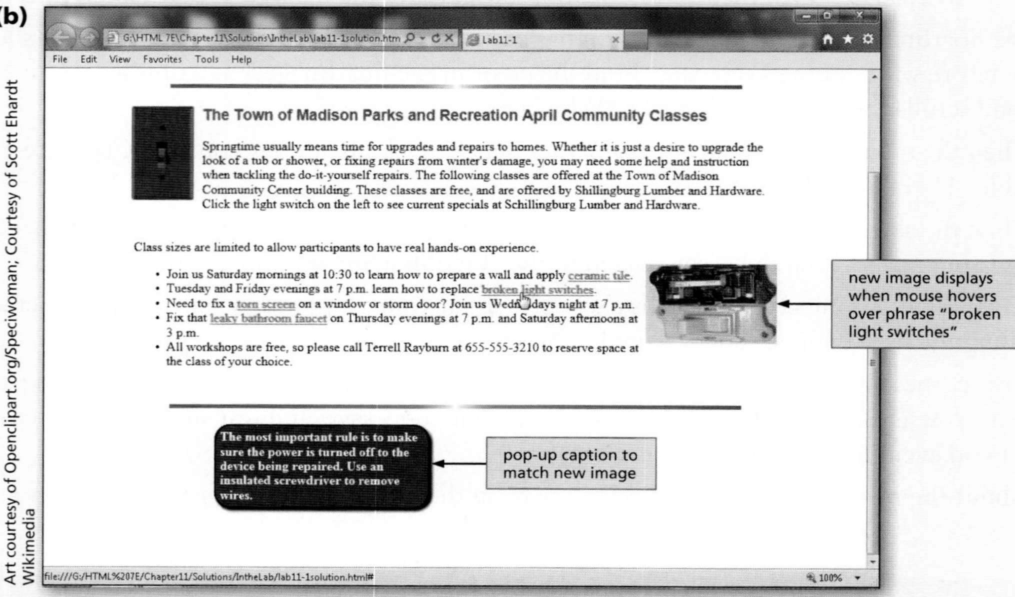

Art courtesy of Openclipart.org/Speciwoman; Courtesy of Scott Ehardt Wikimedia

Figure 11–42 *(continued)*

Perform the following tasks:

1. Start Notepad++ and open the file lab11-1.html from the Chapter11\IntheLab folder of the Data Files for Students.
2. Save the file as lab11-1solution.html.
3. Start a <script> section in the <head> section below the <title> tag on line 6.
4. Using a modified version of the code presented in Table 11–5, write two JavaScript functions called turnSwitchOn() and turnSwitchOff() to change the switch image when the mouse is over or off the image. Pass the id lightswitch to the function for use in the getElementById() method using the parameter img.
5. Using the code in Table 11–18 on page HTML 539 as a guide, write a JavaScript function called caption() to replace the tool logo image on the right side of the unordered list and display the pop-up caption.
6. Using the code in Table 11–19 on pages HTML 541 and HTML 542 as a guide, enter the embedded CSS selectors for ceramic tile (#ceramic), broken light switch (#switch), torn screen (#screen), and leaky bathroom faucet (#faucet). Use the following properties for each selector: position: absolute, visibility: hidden, and display: inline-block.
7. Enter the class selector moreInfo for the pop-up captions, and use the following properties: background-color: #3d3d3d, padding: 5px, margin-left:20%, border: 2px solid black, -webkit-border-radius: 20px, -moz-border-radius: 20px, border-radius: 20px, -webkit-box-shadow: 3px 3px 4px #000, -moz-box-shadow: 3px 3px 4px #000, box-shadow: 3px 3px 4px #000, width: 250px, font-weight: bolder, and color: white.
8. Use the text in Table 11–23 to create the <div> tags for the pop-up caption text.

Table 11–23

```
<div id="ceramic" class="moreInfo">
Ceramic tile in a bath or kitchen is easy to install and easy to keep clean. Decorative tile
adds a nice touch to any decor.
</div>
<div id="switch" class="moreInfo">
The most important rule is to make sure the power is turned off to the device being repaired.
Use an insulated screwdriver to remove wires.
</div>
<div id="screen" class="moreInfo">
You can make emergency repairs with waterproof glue and small pieces of screening for
patches.
</div>
<div id="faucet" class="moreInfo">
Turn off the water and open the faucet to allow any excess water to drain into the sink.
Cover the sink with a towel or cloth to protect it from tools that may be dropped and to
prevent the small parts from going into the drain. Wrap the jaws of wrenches with tape to
protect the faucet's finish.
</div>
```

9. Add the <a href> anchor tags to the unordered list of the classes offered: ceramic tile, broken light switches, torn screen, and leaky bathroom faucet for the mouse over and mouse out event handlers to call the caption() function written in step 5.
10. Use the code in Table 11-16 on page HTML 533 as a guide to write a user-defined function called specialsPage() to open a pop-up window to display lab11-1specials.html. To call the pop-up window specials, add the code JavaScript:specialsPage() in the <a href> tag associated with the light switch rollover image.
11. Save the completed HTML file and test it using your browser. If an error occurs, check your code from Steps 3 through 10, save, and test again.
12. Validate your Web page, and submit the completed HTML file and Web page in the format specified by your instructor.

In the Lab

Lab 2: Sierra Gem and Stone Society

Instructions: You are a member of the Sierra Gem and Stone Society. The organization would like to have a Web presence, so they have asked you to create a Web page. You decide to create a page that displays a random image on the left of the body text, and runs a slide show of various crystal and geodes formations on the right. In the body of the text is a reference to Pangea. When the user places the mouse over the word, a small image of Pangea displays with a pop-up caption. You are to add the JavaScript code to make these Web pages appear as shown in Figure 11–43 on the next page.

Continued >

In the Lab *continued*

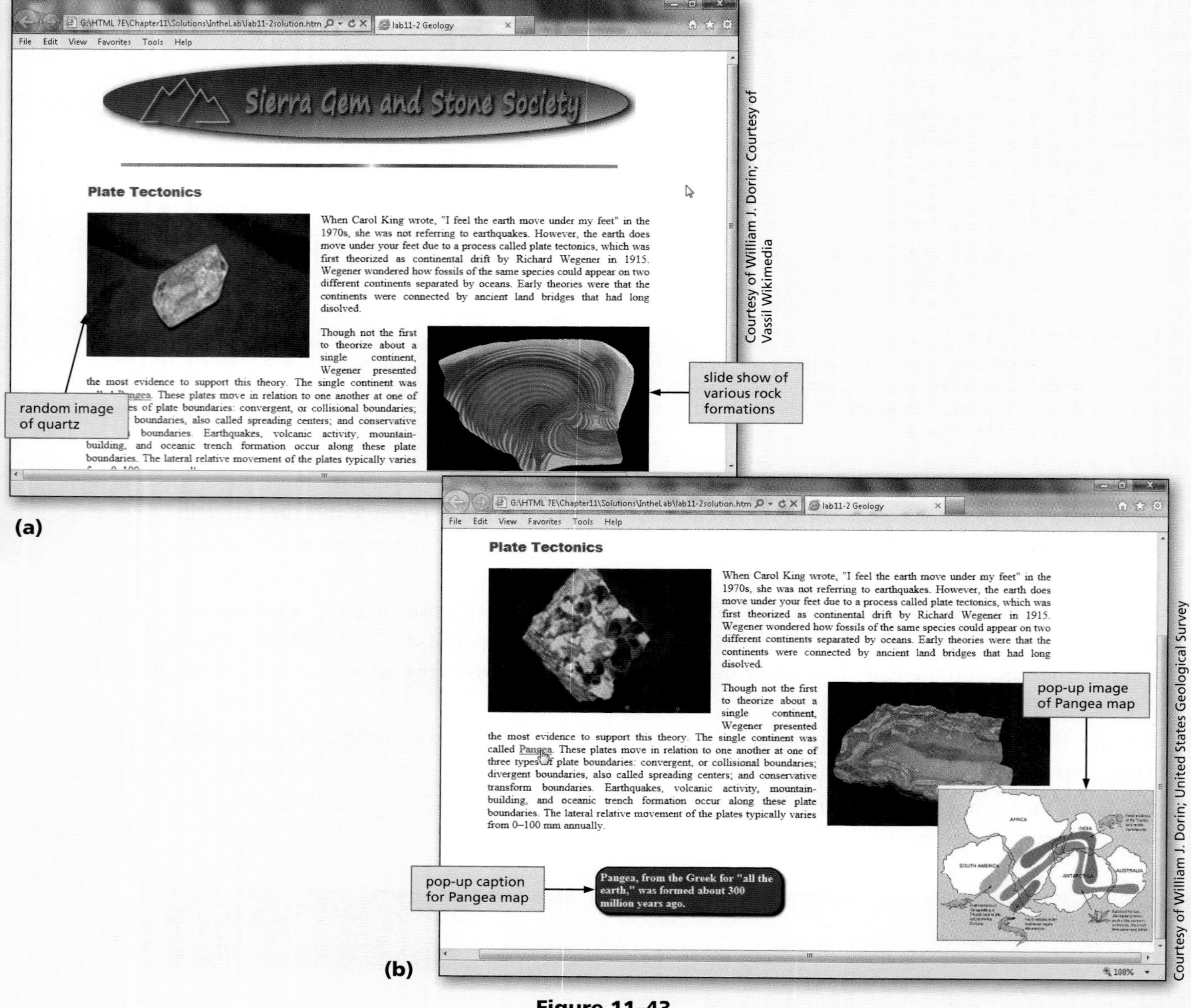

Figure 11–43

Perform the following tasks:

1. Start Notepad++ and open the file lab11-2.html from the Chapter11\IntheLab folder of the Data Files for Students.
2. Save the file as lab11-2solution.html.
3. Use the code in Table 11–8 on page HTML 520 as a guide to display a random image to the left of the body text. The <img> tag id attribute is randomImg for assigning a new random image each time the Web page loads.
4. Use the following files for the random image array (randomImage): lab11-2quartz1.jpg, lab11-2quartz2.jpg, lab11-2quartz3.jpg, lab11-2quartz4.jpg, lab11-2quartz5.jpg, lab11-2quartz6.jpg, and lab11-2quartz7.jpg.

5. Use the code in Table 11–12 on page HTML 526 to create the slide show to the right of the body text. The <img> tag id attribute is slideHolder for assigning the next image in the slide array.
6. The filenames for the slide show array (slides) are lab11-2agate1.jpg, lab11-2agate2.jpg, lab11-2amethyst-geode.jpg, lab11-2carmel-ooids.jpg, lab11-2flint.jpg, and lab11-2petrified_wood.jpg.
7. Use the code in Table 11–18 to create a pop-up caption that also displays the hidden image, which is the map of Pangea, along with the caption text. To display the map, use the getElementById() with <img> tag id attribute pangea_map, to set the properties of style.visibility to hidden or visible, depending on the state.
8. Enter the embedded style sheet selector, #pangea for the pop-up caption. Use the following attributes and properties: position: absolute; visibility: hidden; display: inline-block.
9. Enter the embedded style sheet class selector, .pangeaText for the pop-up caption. Use the following attributes and properties: background-color: #006600; padding: 5px; margin-left: 25%; border: 2px solid black; -webkit-border-radius: 20px; -moz-border-radius: 20px; border-radius: 20px; -webkit-box-shadow: 3px 3px 4px #000; -moz-box-shadow: 3px 3px 4px #000; box-shadow: 3px 3px 4px #000; width: 250px; font-weight: bolder; color: white.
10. Before the closing </body> tag, enter the following <div> tag for the pop-up caption text: <div id="pangea" class="pangeaText"> Pangea, from the Greek for "all the earth," was formed about 300 million years ago. </div>.
11. Save the completed HTML file as lab11-2solution.html.
12. Test the completed Web page by loading the lab11-2solution.html in your browser. Click the Pangea link to see the pop-up caption and image. Make sure the slide show is not missing any images. Reload the page and make sure a new random image displays. If an error occurs, check your code from Steps 3 through 10, save, and test again.
13. Validate your Web pages, and submit the completed HTML files and Web pages in the format specified by your instructor.

In the Lab

Lab 3: Hickory Oaks Bird Sanctuary

Instructions: You are a volunteer at the Hickory Oaks Bird Sanctuary. The director knows of your classes in Web page development and asks you build a Web site that showcases the bird sanctuary. He wants a total of four Web pages, including a Home page, Birds, Bird Count, and Supplies shop page. He wants to use image rollovers for a navigation bar. The Home page is an overall description of the Hickory Oaks Bird Sanctuary and displays a random image every time the page is loaded. The Birds page describes the mission of the sanctuary and contains a slide show of various species of birds that may be seen at different times of the year. The Bird Count page seeks volunteers to count birds. The body of the page has four terms marked as links, so that when a user moves a mouse over the term, a pop-up caption displays and new image displays to the right of the body text. The Supplies page has a floating image, an eagle, that moves left to right beneath a set of images. When the user moves the mouse over the eagle, it stops. When the mouse is moved off, it continues to move across the Web page. If the user clicks the eagle, a pop-up window displays a coupon (Figure 11–44 on the next page).

Continued >

STUDENT ASSIGNMENTS

In the Lab *continued*

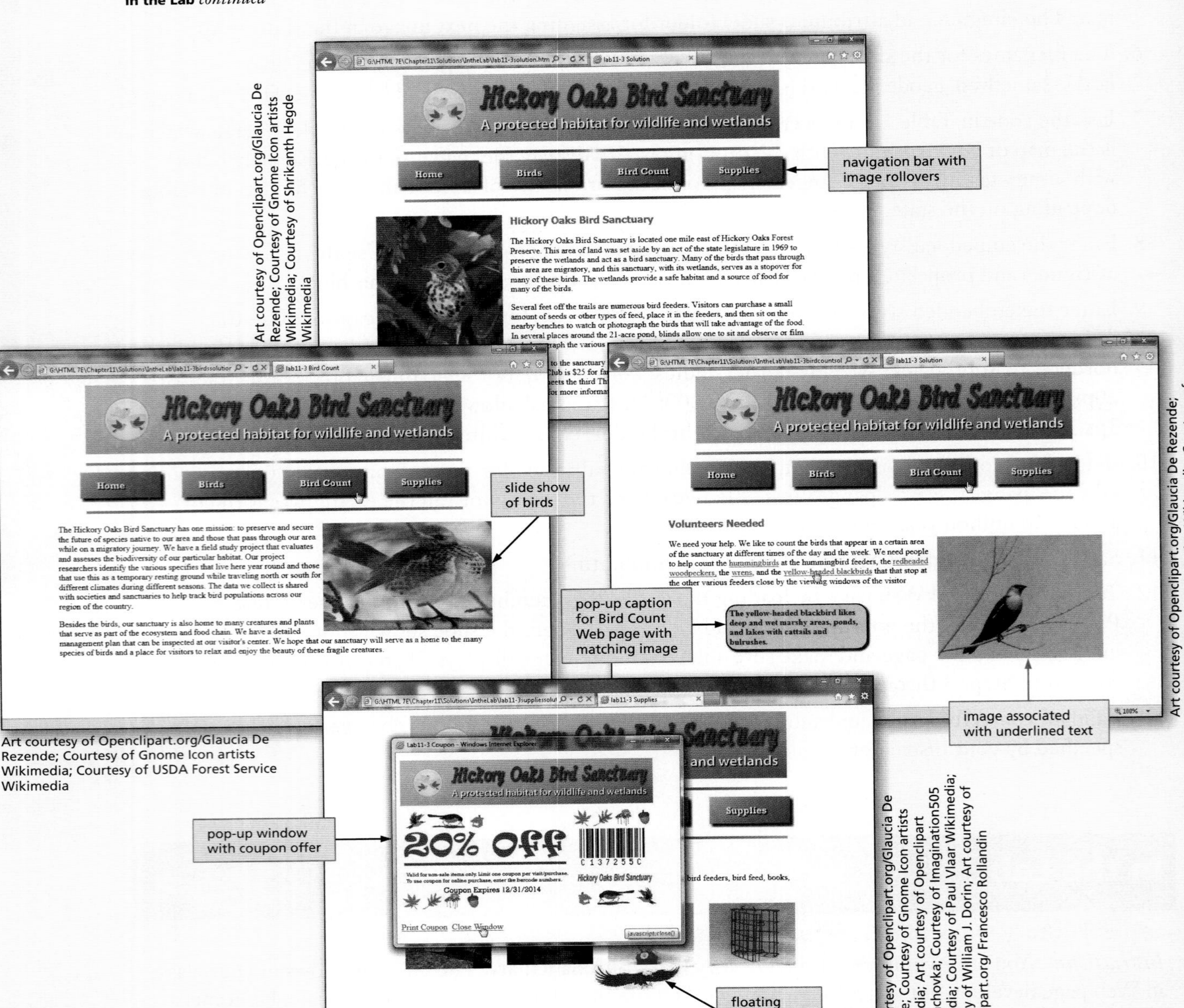

Figure 11–44

Perform the following tasks:

1. Start Notepad++ and open the lab11-3.html file. Save it immediately as lab11-3solution.html.
2. Using the techniques learned in this chapter, create the table to create a navigation bar using the images provided to create the navigation bar for the home page (lab11-3solution.html). The images are for the Home, Birds, Bird Count, and Supplies Web pages. You will find an embedded CSS style sheet with tag, class, and id selectors for the images, table, divisions, and text.
3. Using the techniques learned in this chapter, write the JavaScript code to change the image for a mouse down event handler and for the mouse up and out event handlers for the navigation bar. For the onMouseDown event handler, link to the appropriate Home, Birds, Bird Count, and Supplies Web pages.

4. Save the file as lab11-3solution.html to be used as the Home Web page.
5. Open the lab11-3birds.html and add the table, the JavaScript code, and mouse event handlers to create a navigation bar.
6. Write the JavaScript code to create the slide show. The <img> id is slideshow for assigning the next image in the slide show. The images are lab11-3cedarwaxwing.jpg, lab11-3easternkingbird.jpg, lab11-3fieldfarethrush.jpg, lab11-3flycatcher.jpg, lab11-3kingfisher.jpg, and lab11-3mallard.jpg.
7. Save the Web page as lab11-3birds_solution.html.
8. Open the lab11-3birdcount.html file and add the table, the JavaScript code, and mouse event handlers to create the image rollover navigation bar.
9. Write the JavaScript code to display pop-up captions for each of the bird types. Use the image file lab11-3osprey.jpg as the default image. Use lab11-3hummingbird.jpg for the humming bird link, use lab11-3red-headed_woodpecker for the redheaded woodpecker, use lab11-3wren.jpg for the wrens link, and use lab11-3yellow-headedblackbird.jpg for the yellow-headed black birds link. Use the text in Table 11–24 for the pop-up captions and the embedded CSS id and class selectors.

Table 11–24 Pop-up Caption Text
id: hummingbird class: birdText Text: Did you know there are 343 species of hummingbirds in the western hemisphere?
id: red-headed_woodpecker class: birdText Text: This is the only woodpecker with an entirely red head and neck in North America.
id: wren class: birdText Text: The loss of wetlands is the primary reason for the decline in wren populations.
id: yellow-headblackbird class: birdText Text: The yellow-headed blackbird likes deep and wet marshy areas, ponds, and lakes with cattails and bulrushes.

10. Save the HTML file as lab11-3birdcount_solution.html.
11. Open the lab11-3supplies.html file and add the table, the JavaScript code, and mouse event handlers to create the navigation bar.
12. Write the JavaScript code to make an image (lab11-3_eagle.jpg) float across the page from left to right. The image is in a <div> tag container with an id of flyingEagle.
13. Add the JavaScript user-defined functions to stop the image when the mouse is over the flying eagle image and to continue moving the image when the mouse is off of the flying eagle. Write the user-defined function to open the lab11-3coupon.html in a new window setting the width to 525 and the height to 365.
14. Be sure to add the appropriate event handlers to invoke the user-defined functions to all the Web pages.
15. Save the completed HTML file as lab11-3supplies_solution.html.
16. With all the Web pages saved, test them using your browser. If an error occurs, check your code, save, and test again.
17. Validate your Web pages and submit the completed HTML files and Web pages in the format specified by your instructor.

Cases and Places

Apply your creative thinking and problem solving skills to design and implement a solution.

Note: To complete these assignments, you may be required to use the Data Files for Students. See the inside back cover of this book for instructions on downloading the Data Files for Students, or contact your instructor for information about accessing the required files.

1: Hurricane Slide Show

Academic

Starting with www.nhc.noaa.gov/aboutnames.shtml, create a Web page slide show covering the following topics. List the topics or questions as an unordered list. Select a word or phrase in the list to act as a pop-up tip.

The list:

- Who creates the Atlantic basin hurricane name list and when did they start naming hurricanes?
- What is the Saffir-Simpson scale and what are the sustained winds for each level?
- Who or what are the "hurricane hunters?"
- What year had the most named storms?
- How many category-5 hurricanes made landfall in the U.S. and what were their names?

Use images you find on Wikimedia (commons.wikimedia.org/wiki/Main_Page) or the nhc.noaa.gov Web pages to create the images for the slide show. Change the image when the user places the mouse over the selected word or words in the unordered list.

2: Creating a Personal Web Page

Personal

Use a personal or family event such as a graduation, birthday, anniversary, wedding, or other family event to create a personal Web page with a slide show of at least six images. Use pop-up captions to emphasize some aspect of the images.

3: Using JavaScript to Drag and Drop an Image on a Web Page

Professional

You are a newly hired intern at Secure Micro. They are looking to launch their Web site and you have been asked to come up with a unique introduction to the home page. You have learned how to create Web pages that randomly display an image at a set location, changed an image every few seconds (a slide show) in a set location, used a hyperlink to display a new image with a pop-up caption, and if you did the Extend Your Knowledge exercise, you learned how to change the position of an image. This chapter did not show you how to use drag and drop to move an image around the screen.

Case11-3drag-n-drop.html contains three images: case11-3_computer_worm, case11-3_monitor, and case11-3_hypodermic. The images are placed on the Web page and any relevant style sheet values have been set to properly identify the image objects.

The JavaScript Kit Web site (javascriptkit.com/howto/drag.shtml) contains a simple set of JavaScript code that will allow you to drag the hypodermic needle over the virus-infected computer monitor. You only need to copy and paste the code to drag-n-drop html file, and modify the code to use the case11-3_hypodermic and case11-3_monitor images. You will need to change the .drag style to inoculate, and change classname in the drags() user-defined function to inoculate. Be sure to leave credit for the code to the JavaScript Kit Web site, as listed in the code. You should change the <script> tag to be HTML5 compliant. In addition, use the code in the chapter that "floats" an image across the screen to float the chapter11-3_computer_worm image across the page from right to left. Save this page as case11-3drag-n-drop_solution.html.

12 Creating and Using XML Documents

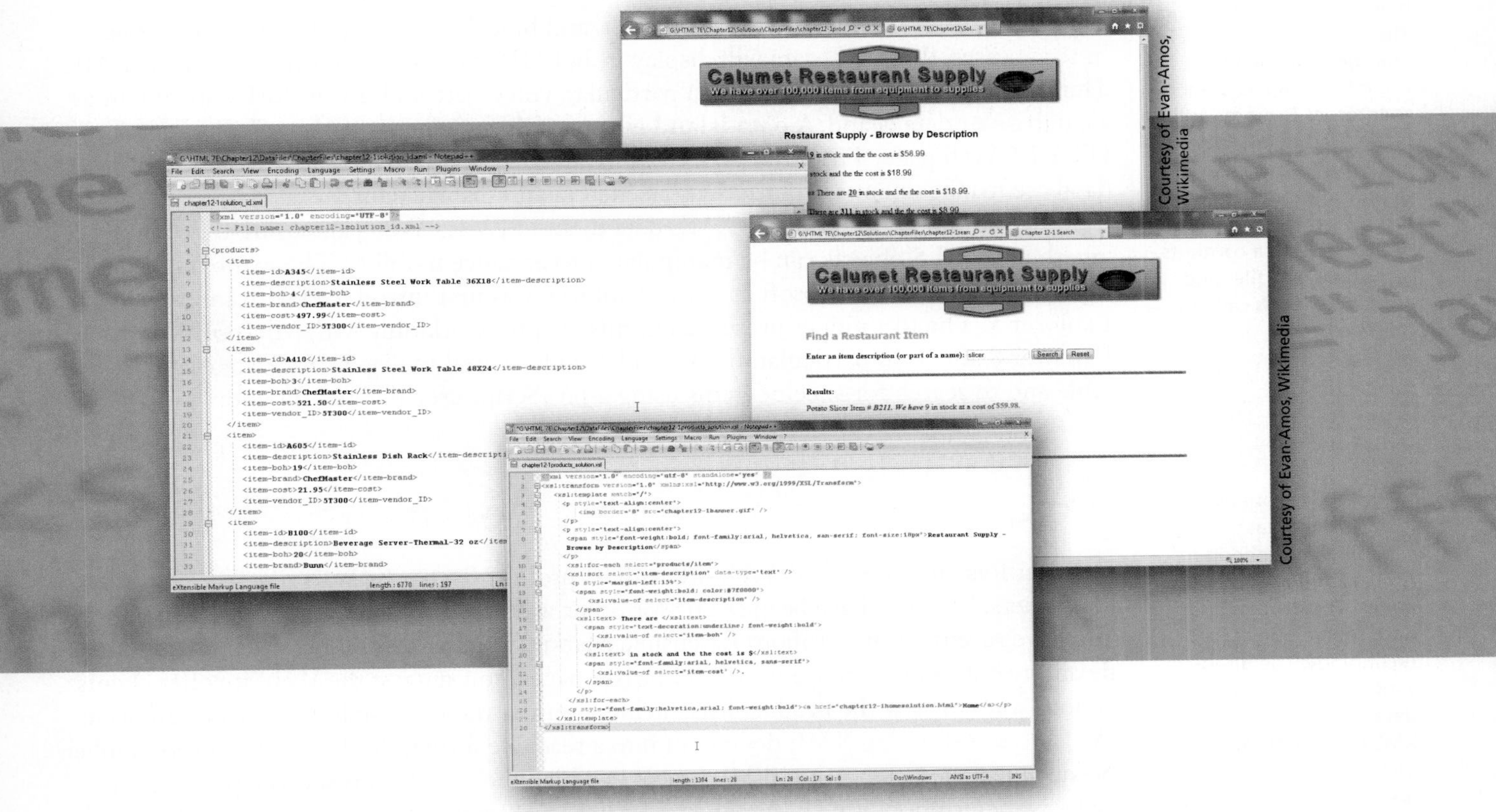

Objectives

You will have mastered the material in this chapter when you can:

- Describe how XML differs from HTML
- Describe an XML document instance and the rules for creating a well-formed and valid XML document
- Define the purpose of the processing instruction, the document prolog, and the document instance
- Describe and create an XML Schema Definition (XSD) language file
- Create and bind an XSL style sheet file to an XML document
- Discuss the uses of an XML data island in Internet Explorer
- Discuss the built-in table element methods for displaying an XML document in a table
- Create a JavaScript user-defined function to search an XML document

12 Creating and Using XML Documents

BTW **Internet Explorer and Data Islands**
Data Island were first used in Internet Explorer 5. The <xml> tag, used to link the XML file with the HTML page is unique to Internet Explorer and is still used in Internet Explorer 9. To use data islands in other browsers requires embedding the entire XML data contents into the HTML file, and creating what is called a "data block."

Introduction

In this chapter, you will learn how to create XML data files for use as stand-alone Web pages, format files using an XSL style sheet, and bind XML files to HTML5 Web pages. In some cases, the XML data will display in HTML5 tables, and in other cases, the XML data will display in other formats. In particular, you create and use an XML document as a database or data island. A **data island** is a set of data elements separate from the main HTML5 Web page. The advantage to using an XML data island is the reduction of database management system activity needed just to display data.

By binding or linking the XML data to an HTML5 Web page using the <xml> tag, the HTML5 objects can be manipulated to enhance usability. The <xml> tag, which is particular only to Microsoft Internet Explorer, was first introduced with Internet Explorer 5. The techniques presented in this chapter work only with Microsoft Internet Explorer 8 and 9. In particular, the HMTL5 code is used to display the data island in a table and to search for specific items using a JavaScript user-defined function.

BTW **XML as a Data Island**
A data island has the capability of embedding XML documents in HTML pages. The process uses data source object (dso) technology. The disadvantage to using an XML data island is that the XML documents are static. Client-side processing does not allow real-time updates to the XML document on the server.

Project — Creating an XML Document

Calumet Restaurant Supply's Web site with its product list has been a great success. Customers, however, have been asking for other ways to browse or search the product list. You have recently learned about Extensible Markup Language (XML), which offers some flexibility not found with traditional HTML5 pages. You suggest the Web site offer clients various ways to view the product lists, including using the Extensible Stylesheet Language (XSL) to transform an XML document into a readable format displayed by item-id number. Next, you suggest using an HTML5 table in which the user can browse the products in order by description. Finally, you suggest using JavaScript to allow a user to search for products by an item description.

The Web pages shown in Figure 12–1 demonstrate three different applications of the same XML document. Figure 12–1a shows Calumet Restaurant Supply's home page containing three links: one link opens an XML page in a browser displaying a list of all the available products formatted by an XSL style sheet in item-description order (Figure 12–1b). The next link displays the XML data in a table in item-id order (Figure 12–1c). The last link displays a Web page to search for products by any part of the item description (Figure 12–1d).

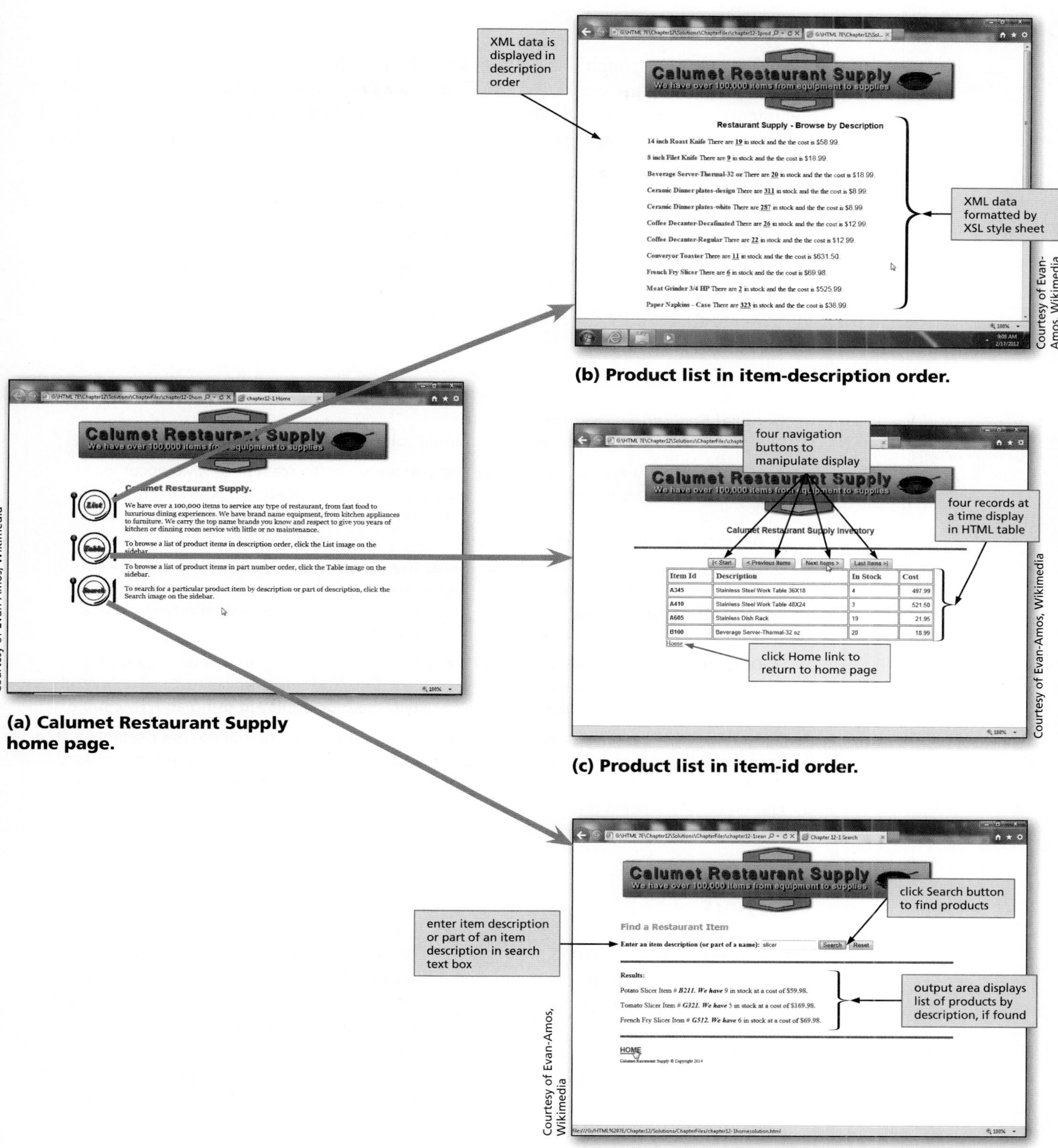

XML data is displayed in description order
Calumet Restaurant Supply
We have over 100,000 items from equipment to supplies
Restaurant Supply - Browse by Description
XML data formatted by XSL style sheet
Courtesy of Evan-Amos, Wikimedia
four navigation buttons to manipulate display
four records at a time display in HTML table
Calumet Restaurant Supply Inventory
click Home link to return to home page
click Search button to find products
Find a Restaurant Item
enter item description or part of an item description in search text box
output area displays list of products by description, if found

(b) Product list in item-description order.

(c) Product list in item-id order.

(a) Calumet Restaurant Supply home page.

(d) Search by description or part of description.

Figure 12–1

Overview

As you read through this chapter, you will learn how to create well-formed and valid XML documents (creating an XML Schema Definition), format and display XML documents using an XSL style sheet, display an XML document in a Web page table, and search for restaurant supply products using JavaScript by performing these general tasks:

- Create an XML Schema Definition (XSD) file.
- Create an XSL style sheet to format the output of an XML document.
- Bind an XSL style sheet to an XML document.
- Bind an XML document to an HTML document as a data island, and display XML data in an HTML table.
- Create a JavaScript function to search for items in an XML document data island.

Plan Ahead

General Project Guidelines
When creating an XML document, you should follow these general guidelines:

1. **Determine what type of XML document you are going to create.** An XML document should follow the form of the desired output. If you are creating a text document, like a memo or a database of inventory items, the XML document should conform to the general form of that type of document.
2. **Determine the contents of the document.** The contents may be created from an existing document or database. Many applications can create XML documents automatically, or the XML document may have to be created manually. In either case, the type of data must be defined with an XML Schema Definition file.
3. **Determine how the document will be displayed.** If the document will be displayed on a Web page, you must think about how to format its contents for display. For example, the document may be formatted with an XSL style sheet or displayed using an HTML table.

When necessary, more specific details concerning the above guidelines are presented at appropriate points in the chapter. The chapter will also identify the actions performed and decisions made regarding these guidelines during the creation of the Web pages shown in Figure 12–1 on the previous page.

XML vs. HTML5

The first Web pages developed with HTML presented static information and allowed linking to other Web pages with additional information. In early Web development, data was converted into forms used in HTML documents. If the data changed, the Web documents had to be changed. As the need arose for more dynamic Web pages that would present current data and allow users to interact with that data, Web developers began relying on various database management systems (DBMSs) to store and retrieve data. Some popular DBMS systems include Oracle, Microsoft SQL Server, MySQL, ObjectStore, and PostgreSQL. Each DBMS uses various programming language interfaces within HTML documents to access data.

Formatting that data in an HTML document, however, could be problematic. Data could be in the format of simple text, a table of rows and columns, or a hierarchical structure with complex relationships. It could be in the form of tables, e-mails, and reports. The **Extensible Markup Language (XML)** was developed to provide a way to share all various types of data in one clear and efficient method. XML provides a common format for all types of data that can be used by anyone using software that can read XML, such as a Web browser. XML also provides a way to separate the data from the HTML document, so that when the data is updated, the HTML document simply displays the new data, allowing for dynamic Web pages that change as the data changes.

Designing XML Documents

XML uses tags to describe the structure of a document and its contents. XML tags do not format the display of text as with an HTML document. XML provides a flexible way for organizations to share common data and to integrate data with Web pages. The main XML document created in this chapter is a list of products available at Calumet Restaurant Supply, which will serve as a database (or data island). The XML data will be formatted by XSL or bound to an HTML Web page for display in a table and searched using JavaScript.

Formatting XML documents for display on a Web page requires binding or linking a style sheet to the XML document, which formats the elements of the XML document as they appear in a browser. An XML document can be formatted with Cascading Style Sheets (CSS) or an Extensible Stylesheet Language (XSL) style sheet. **Extensible Stylesheet Language (XSL)** is used to create style sheets for formatting structured XML data. XSL style sheets provide more flexibility and control over XML documents than CSS. While CSS can format individual XML elements, XSL can control the order of elements or add other information. Most developers prefer XSL style sheets over CSS for formatting XML documents.

BTW

XML

Like HTML, XML is a subset of Standard Generalized Markup Language (SGML). SGML gives developers the ability to create their own elements. XML inherits this ability from SGML. XML does not replace HTML, but it provides a means to extend and enhance the use and appearance of a document. Developers can create XML documents manually using any editor, or generate an XML document using existing tables in a Microsoft SQL Server or Microsoft Access database, and then bind them to their Web pages.

XML Standards

As you learned in Chapter 1, the World Wide Web Consortium (W3C) oversees and develops standards for Web development. To help ensure consistency among the discipline-specific tags created in XML, the W3C has defined a set of standards, or goals, for XML, shown in Table 12–1. The goals provide a framework for all future XML development and XML-related, discipline-specific markup languages.

BTW

Benefits of XML to HTML5

XML development standards have influenced HTML standards. One version of HTML, XHTML (now in version 2.0) was created to provide a seamless relationship between XML and its presentation on the World Wide Web. One aspect of this development is the required reliance on style sheets for formatting the display of Web pages. The development of HTML5 and CSS3 brings the HTML language more in line with XML standards.

Table 12–1 Design Goals for XML

1.	XML shall be straightforwardly usable over the Internet.
2.	XML shall support a wide variety of applications.
3.	XML shall be compatible with SGML.
4.	It shall be easy to write programs that process XML documents.
5.	The number of optional features in XML is to be kept to the absolute minimum, ideally zero.
6.	XML documents should be human-legible and reasonably clear.
7.	The XML design should be prepared quickly.
8.	The design of XML shall be formal and concise.
9.	XML documents shall be easy to create.
10.	Terseness in XML markup is of minimal importance.

Using XML documents as databases is just one of the many ways Web developers use XML. The creation and use of these databases is the central focus of this chapter. As the W3C group continues to develop XML standards, businesses and organizations will find numerous new uses for XML. An important goal of XML is to allow the creation of discipline-specific markup language tags. Table 12–2 on the next page is a partial list of uses and extended markup languages created using XML.

BTW **Uses of XML**
XML is not limited to use in Web databases. There are over a hundred industries using some form of XML, ranging from accounting and finance to weather.

Table 12–2 Real-World Uses of XML

Use	Description of Extended Markup Languages
Define databases	Use labels and fields to store and display data in a variety of ways
Give structure to documents	Provide structure to elements in books and plays, such as indexes or scene directions
Provide Web services	Execute Web services (functions) over a network with the Simple Object Access Protocol (SOAP) and Web Services Description Language (WSDL)
Exchange financial information	Exchange information among various applications using Open Financial Exchange (OFX)
Store voice scripts	Store voice mail messages or regular daily messages
Annotate maps	Add place marks, shapes, and paths to a map using Keyhole Markup Language (KML), an XML markup language
Format mathematical formulas	Format math and science content markup with MathML
Define standard document format for businesses	Allow business partners to share a standard library of XML business documents, such as purchase orders and invoices; identify the documents exchanged in a particular context using Universal Business Language (UBL)
Create Web pages that are valid XML	Transition to XHTML following XML standards and tools
Edit open source documents	Open Document Format (ODF) is a file format for word processing, spreadsheets, and presentation software
Display electronic texts	Use XHTML and XML to display contents of eBooks and ePub devices

BTW **Purpose of the XML Parser**
The XML parser is necessary to create, read, update, or manipulate an XML document. Most modern Web browsers contain various parsers for scripting languages and XML.

Syntax Rules

XML documents must be well-formed to be processed by an application. For an XML document to be **well-formed**, it must adhere to the basic syntax rules for XML, as listed in Table 12–3. Before an XML document is displayed in an application, the document must be parsed. A **parser** is an XML processor that verifies the document follows the syntax rules for a well-formed document and converts the document into a tree of elements. Most modern Web browsers contain XML parsers. For more information on XML syntax, see the XML Quick Reference in Appendix H.

BTW **Generic Identifier**
An element consists of tags based on names that a developer provides or defines. The name that a developer provides for the tags is called the **generic identifier (GI)**. When choosing generic identifiers to name document elements, a developer must follow two simple rules: (1) The name must begin with a letter or underscore (_) and may contain letters, numbers, periods, hyphens, or underscores; and (2) a prefix of XML or the use of colons is reserved for future, anticipated standardization.

Table 12–3 XML Syntax Rules

Rule	Comment	Example
XML is case sensitive.	Use any case — uppercase, lowercase, or mixed — but be consistent.	Correct: <Root></Root> or <root></root> or <ROOT></ROOT> Incorrect: <Root></ROOT>
All tags must have a closing tag.	All tags, including empty tags, must have a closing tag. Empty tags are allowed a special form. Empty tags have no content, such as and <img> tags.	<p>This is a paragraph</p> <name>Susan</name>
All documents must have a root element.	Include the root or start tag that begins a document.	<root> <child></child> </root>
Elements must be nested.	Elements cannot stand alone unless they are the only root element.	<club> <name>Spanish</name> </club>
Attribute values must be enclosed in quotation marks.	Use single or double quotation marks, but be consistent.	<Image picture="icon.jpg" />
With XML, white space is preserved.	Spaces between words within tags are preserved.	No need for ASCII characters ( ) to add spaces

This chapter shows how to create well-formed documents manually. Figure 12–2a shows a simple XML document created in Notepad ++. When displayed in or parsed by a browser or application (Figure 12–2b), this XML document may have little meaning to a user. Linking the XML document to an XSL style sheet (Figure 12–2c) enables the browser to display the document in a more readable format (Figure 12–2d).

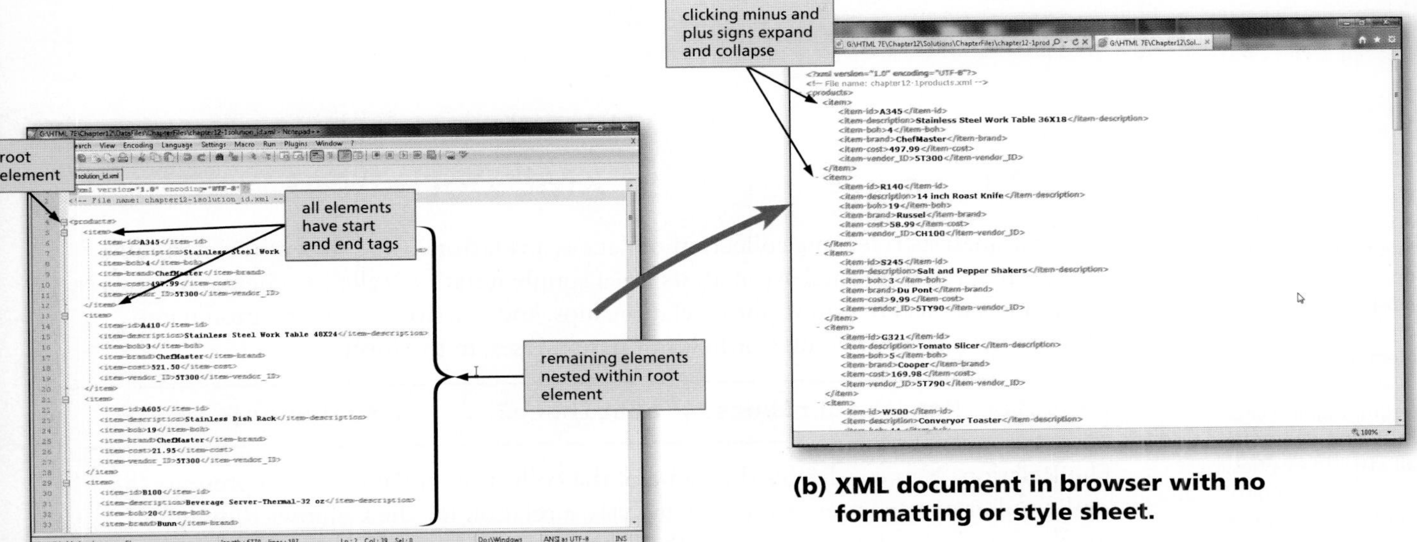

(a) XML document text in Notepad++.

(b) XML document in browser with no formatting or style sheet.

code for XSL style sheet

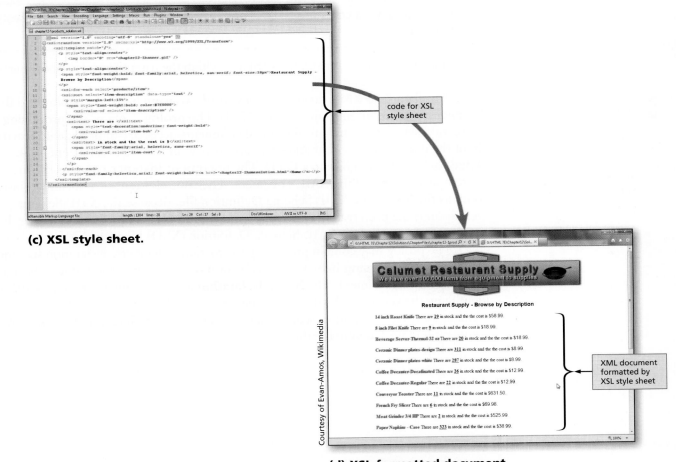

(c) XSL style sheet.

XML document formatted by XSL style sheet

Courtesy of Evan-Amos, Wikimedia

(d) XSL formatted document.

Figure 12–2

Plan Ahead

Creating a well-formed XML document.

The following tasks are necessary to create a well-formed XML document, as described in the next section:

1. Identify the tags to describe the document content and create the XML Schema Definition (XSD).
2. Create the prolog.
3. Create the document instances.

BTW

Well-Formed Documents

A well-formed document meets certain criteria: the document must have at least one root element, and it must nest child elements in the root; every tag must have a beginning and closing tag, including empty tags; and all attribute values must be enclosed in quotation marks, either single or double, but they must be consistent.

Creating a Well-Formed XML Document

Database analysts refer to a collection of data as a **relation**. To represent the attributes or fields in a relation, database analysts use a simple notation, called a schema. A database **schema** is a logical design to show relationships, and is written as the relation name followed by a list of attributes or fields in parentheses, in the form:

```
Relation_Name (attribute1, attribute2..., attributen)
```

The Relation_Name indicates the name of the collection of data, and *n* represents the total number of attributes. After data analysis, a relation for the Calumet Restaurant Supply store is developed, and using the notation style above, the logical schema design for the XML document is written as

```
item (item-id, item-description, item-boh, item-brand, item-cost,
item-vendor_ID)
```

The name of the relation is item; the attributes within the parentheses describe things about the each item.

BTW

The XML Prolog

Every XML document must have a prolog. The prolog must contain at least one line — a declaration statement — identifying the document as an XML document: <?xml version="1.0"?>.

A well-formed XML document consists of two main parts: the prolog and the document instance or elements (Figure 12–3). The **prolog** contains the processing instruction statements and any additional comments necessary to provide information about the document's content and structure such as an optional Document Type Definition (DTD) or a link to a DTD. The **document instance** contains the main content or elements of the XML document. The **root element** of a document instance contains the link to the XML Schema Definition file. Because the XML Schema Definition is the preferred method for forming an XML document, this chapter discusses how to create and link an XML Schema Definition (XSD) file to an XML file.

The prolog may contain processing instruction statements, declaration statements, or comments. A **processing instruction** is one or more instructions passed to the application using the XML document. The **XML declaration** is a processing instruction statement identifying the version of XML used in the document. The prolog shown in Figure 12–3 contains an XML declaration, which is a processing instruction on line 1 followed by a comment on line 2 identifying the file.

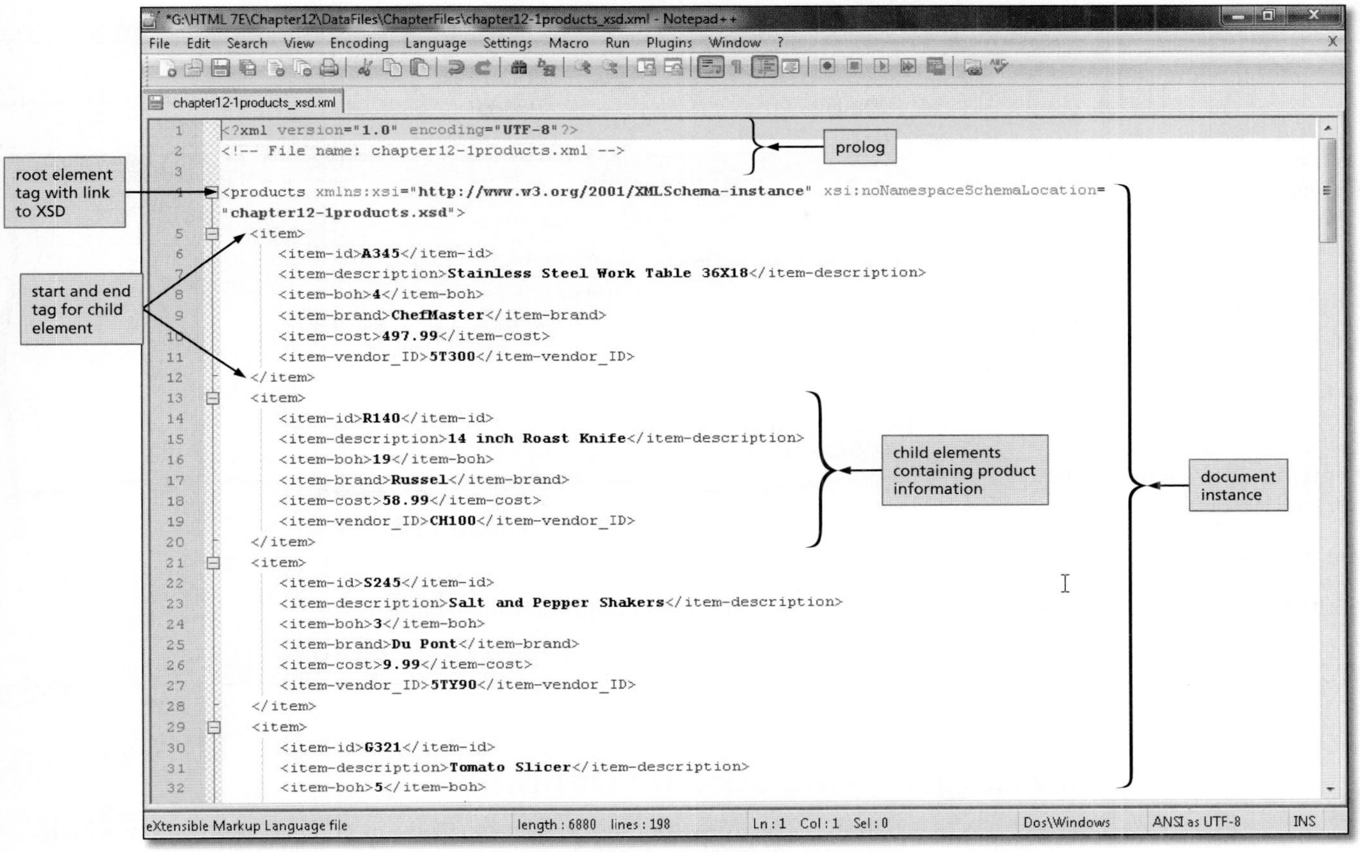

*G:\HTML 7E\Chapter12\DataFiles\ChapterFiles\chapter12-1products_xsd.xml - Notepad++

```
<?xml version="1.0" encoding="UTF-8"?>
<!-- File name: chapter12-1products.xml -->

<products xmlns:xsi="http://www.w3.org/2001/XMLSchema-instance" xsi:noNamespaceSchemaLocation=
"chapter12-1products.xsd">
    <item>
        <item-id>A345</item-id>
        <item-description>Stainless Steel Work Table 36X18</item-description>
        <item-boh>4</item-boh>
        <item-brand>ChefMaster</item-brand>
        <item-cost>497.99</item-cost>
        <item-vendor_ID>5T300</item-vendor_ID>
    </item>
    <item>
        <item-id>R140</item-id>
        <item-description>14 inch Roast Knife</item-description>
        <item-boh>19</item-boh>
        <item-brand>Russel</item-brand>
        <item-cost>58.99</item-cost>
        <item-vendor_ID>CH100</item-vendor_ID>
    </item>
    <item>
        <item-id>S245</item-id>
        <item-description>Salt and Pepper Shakers</item-description>
        <item-boh>3</item-boh>
        <item-brand>Du Pont</item-brand>
        <item-cost>9.99</item-cost>
        <item-vendor_ID>5TY90</item-vendor_ID>
    </item>
    <item>
        <item-id>G321</item-id>
        <item-description>Tomato Slicer</item-description>
        <item-boh>5</item-boh>
```

eXtensible Markup Language file | length : 6880 lines : 198 | Ln : 1 Col : 1 Sel : 0 | Dos\Windows | ANSI as UTF-8 | INS

Figure 12–3

The document instance contains the main content or elements of the XML document and provides a logical structure for the document. An **instance** is an occurrence of XML elements. The XML document must include at least one instance, or occurrence, of an element. The main element is the root element and may contain one or more subelements or **child elements**. This parent-child relationship between elements gives XML its hierarchical, treelike structure, as shown in Figure 12–4.

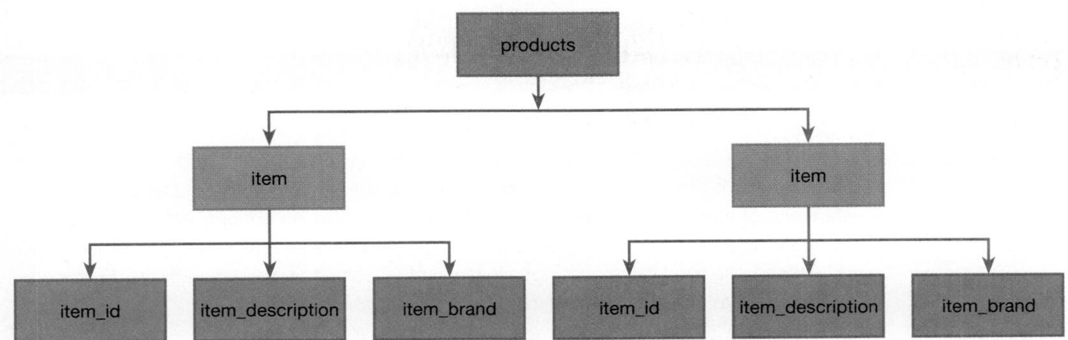

Figure 12–4

To Start Notepad++ and Create a New XML Schema Document

The following step uses Notepad++ to create a new XML Schema document.

- Start Notepad++, and, if necessary, maximize the Notepad++ window. If the word wrap feature is not enabled, enable it.
- With the USB drive plugged into your computer, click File on the menu bar, and then click Save As on the File menu.
- If necessary, navigate to the Chapter12\ChapterFiles folder on your storage device.

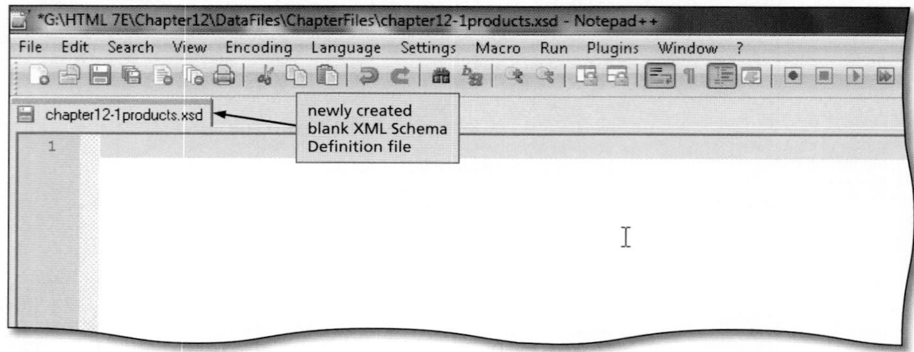

Figure 12–5

- Type `chapter12-1products.xsd` in the File name text box.
- Click the Save button in the Save As dialog box to save the Schema Definition file (Figure 12–5).

Creating an XML Schema Definition

An **XML Schema Definition** describes the structure of an XML document, which includes the data types. An XML Schema Definition is more useful than a Document Type Definition (DTD), because DTDs do not describe the data types. In addition, the DTD is not able to enforce that a specific data type, such as a date, is being implemented. Because of these limitations, XML standards prefer the use of an XML Schema Definition to describe an XML file.

XML Schema Definitions are XML files, and as such, they must conform to the same rules that any XML document must follow. Tags must have a beginning and end tag, though many XML Schema Definitions will use an empty tag with attributes. The rules for attributes must be followed: they must be lowercase and values must be enclosed in quotation marks. The basic component of an XML Schema Definition is the element. Table 12–4 shows the basic format of an XML Schema Definition <element> tag.

Table 12–4 General Form of an XML Schema Definition Element	
General form:	<xs:element name="field name" type="data type" />
Comment:	**xs:** is a namespace, to differentiate this element from any other element that may have the same name. The **name** is an attribute to define the field name; **type** is an attribute to state one of the valid data types. Simple elements may have an optional default or fixed attributes to assign a default value to a field. The default value is assigned if no other value is assigned; the fixed value does not allow any other value to be assigned. Most developers use xs or xsd as a default namespace. This text uses xs.
Examples:	<xs:element name="item-brand" type="xs:string" />

Elements in an XML Schema Definition can be either simple type or complex type. A **simple type** element is one that contains only text. A **complex type** element is one that contains sub or child elements and/or attributes, which themselves contain data. Table 12–5 compares simple type and complex type elements.

Table 12–5 XML Simple Type and Complex Type Elements

Type	Description and XML Element	XML Schema
Simple	an XML element that contains only text <first_name>Bill</first_name>	<xs:element name="first_name" type="string" />
Complex	an XML element that contains child elements or attributes <products> <item> <item-id>A345</item-id> </item> </products>	<xs:element name="products"> <xs:complexType> <xs:sequence> <xs:element name="item" type="childType" minOccurs="1" maxOccurs="unbounded" /> </xs:sequence> </xs:complexType> </xs:element>

The definition of elements in the schema must include the data type. XML Schema Definition has several built-in data types shown in Table 12–6. From this list of simple data types, a developer can build custom data types. Custom data types begin with a base data type and include restrictions in the form of domain (range of valid values), length, or number of characters or digits (patterns).

Table 12–6 XML Schema Definition Data Types

Data Types	Description
String	data is any set of characters
Integer	data is any whole number not a fraction
Decimal	data is any number that contains a decimal fraction
Date	represent the date as YYYY-MM-DD
Boolean	binary logic of true or false, yes or no, on or off
Binary	a set of binary codes in groups of eight
AnyURI	a valid URI Internet address

Custom data types are quite common in database systems. These data types help in validating data fields, to reduce erroneous data entry. Table 12–7 shows an example custom data type. The example shows a custom data type field called age_range, which has a domain between 18 and 70. A **domain** is a set of valid values for a database field.

Table 12–7 XML Custom Data Types

Custom Data Type Example

```
<xs:simpleType name="age_range">
   <xs:restriction base=xs:integer">
      <xs:minInclusive value="18" />
      <xs:maxInclusive value="70" />
   </xs:restriction>
</xs:simpleType>
<xs:element name="employee">
   <xs:complexType>
      <xs:sequence>
         <xs:element name="employment_age" type="age_range" />
      </xs:sequence>
   </xs:complexType>
</xs:element name="employee">
```

An XML Schema Definition is an XML file and starts with an XML processing statement. The general form of the XML processing instruction is shown in Table 12–8.

Table 12–8 General Form of a Processing Instruction

General form:	<?target attribute1="value" attribute2="value"?>
Comment:	The **?** identifies this as a processing instruction. The *target* is the name of the application. The *attributes* and *values* tell the processor how to handle the statement. The values assigned to the attributes can be enclosed in single or double quotation marks, as long as they are consistent.
Examples:	<?xml?> <?xml version="1.0"?> <?xml version="1.0" encoding="UTF-8" standalone="yes"?>

The next statement in the XML Schema Definition is the <xs:schema> root element. This statement contains a namespace declaration. Table 12–9 shows a simple root element with namespace declaration for a single XML file.

Table 12–9 General Form of a Root Element

Root element:	<xs:schema xmlns:xs="http://www.w3.org/2001/XMLSchema" [targetNamespace="URI" xmlns="URI" elementFormDefault="qualified"] >
Comment:	The **xs** is the namespace. The **xmlns** is XML namespace location and associates the xs to the schema of all schemas at the w3.org Web site. The most commonly used namespaces are xs or xsd. The optional elements within the brackets include *targetNamespace* that associates other namespace items with the designated URI. The **xmlns** defines the default namespace location and the *elementFormDefault* indicates the definition must be a qualified namespace.
Example	<xs:schema xmlns:xs="http://www.w3.org/2001/XMLSchema">

Developers add documentation to their XML Schema Definition files using the <annotation> and <documentation> tags. Documentation should include descriptions of all changes made to files by whom and when. In the XML Schema Definition, <annotation> and <documentation> tags are used. Table 12–10 describes the general format of the <annotation> and <documentation> tags in an XML Schema Definition file.

Table 12–10 General Form of Annotation and Documentation Elements

General form:	<namespace:annotation [id="value" | other attributes]> <namespace:documentation [source=URI | xml:lang="language"> Descriptive text </namespace:documentation> </namespace:annotation>
Comment:	The **<annotation>** element is the top-level tag for descriptive documentation. The <annotation> tag may have an optional id or other nonschema attributes. The **<documentation>** element denotes that the text within the opening and closing tags is nonschema data. The <documentation> tag may have an optional Web source of information. The xml:lang attribute identifies the language of the documentation content.
Examples:	<xs:annotation> <xs:documentation> This XSD describes the data structure of Calumet Restaurant Supply products created July 13, 2014 by S.Sims. </xs:documentation> </xs:annotation>

To Enter the Code for the Prolog, Root, Annotation, and Documentation Elements

Table 12–11 shows the code to begin a new XML Schema Definition with a prolog, root, annotation, and documentation elements.

Table 12–11 Code for the Prolog, Root, Annotation, and Documentation Elements

Line	Code
1	<?xml version="1.0" encoding="utf-8" standalone="yes" ?>
2	
3	<xs:schema xmlns:xs="http://www.w3.org/2001/XMLSchema">
4	
5	<xs:annotation>
6	<xs:documentation>
7	This XSD describes the data structure of Calumet Restaurant Supply product listing created July 13, 2014 by S.Sims.
8	</xs:documentation>
9	</xs:annotation>
10	
11	</xs:schema>

Line 1 is a standard XML processing statement. Line 3 is the <schema> root tag and assigns namespace declaration from the w3.org Web site. Line 5 is the beginning <annotation> tag for documentation. Line 6 is the <documentation> tag. Line 7 is the description of this file. Lines 8 and 9 close the tags started on lines 5 and 6. Line 11 is the closing <schema> tag.

The following step enters the code for the prolog, root, annotation, and documentation elements.

1

- If necessary, click line 1.
- Enter the XML code shown in Table 12–11 to create the beginning of the XML Schema Definition with the prolog, root, annotation, and documentation elements, as shown in Figure 12–6.

Q&A Why is the closing root tag included?

It is included so you do not forget to add it at the end of the schema, thus causing an error when the schema is validated.

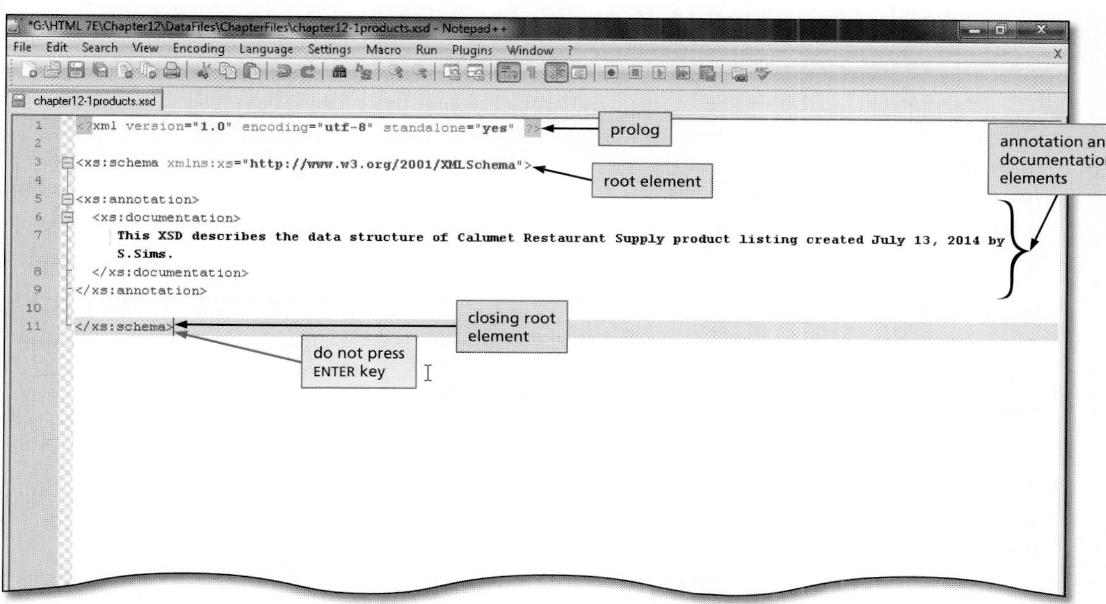

Figure 12–6

Defining the Parent Element

The next part of the schema defines the parent element, <products>. This element is a complex type because it contains a child element, <item>. The attributes of minOccurs and maxOccurs indicate the cardinality. **Cardinality** is the number of relationships between a parent and child element. The minOccurs attribute indicates that at least one item must exist, and the maxOccurs attribute of unbounded indicates there can be an infinite number of items.

To Enter Code for the <products> Element

Table 12–12 shows the code for inserting the parent element.

Table 12–12 Code for Inserting the <products> Element

Line	Code
11	<xs:element name="products">
12	<xs:complexType>
13	<xs:sequence>
14	<xs:element name="item" type="childType" minOccurs="1" maxOccurs="unbounded" />
15	</xs:sequence>
16	</xs:complexType>
17	</xs:element>

Line 11 is an <element> tag that defines the products element in the XML document. Line 12 indicates this is a complex data type element with children. The <sequence> tag at line 13 indicates the following elements must appear in sequence. Only one element is identified in line 14, and that is item with the minOccurs and maxOccurs attributes, used to define cardinality. Lines 15, 16, and 17 close the element tags in 13, 12, and 11, in order.

The following step enters the code for the parent element.

- Click line 10 and press the ENTER key once to place the insertion point on a blank line 11.
- Enter the XML code shown in Table 12–12 to add the <products> element tags.
- Press the ENTER key twice after line 17 (Figure 12–7).

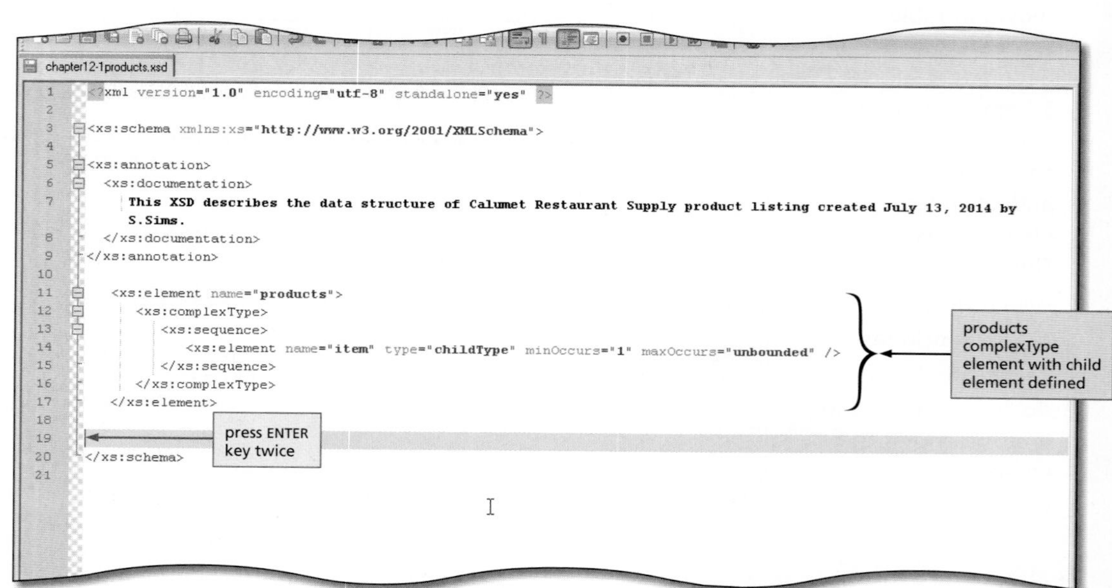

Figure 12–7

Defining and Inserting the Child Elements

The next part of the schema defines the child elements, which are defined as <complexType> elements using a group element. Table 12–13 describes the basic form of a <group> element.

Table 12–13 General Form of a Group Element

Group element:	<namespace:group [id=ID name=Name ref=referencedName maxOccurs=positive Integer minOccurs=zero or any positive Integer any attributes] >
Comment:	The **group** element indicates a series of elements are part of a larger group element. The **id** is a unique name. The **name** specifies the name for the group and is used only when the element is the parent of the group. **Ref** relates this group to another group element. The name and ref attributes cannot be used together. The **minOccurs** and **maxOccurs** indicate a valid range of values that can occur with a minimum of zero (minOccurs) to infinity as defined by unbounded in maxOccurs. The *any* attributes are any non-XML attributes.
Example	<xs:group ref="childElements" />

To Enter Code for the <complexType> Element

The code in Table 12–14 shows the XML Schema Definition element tags to define the group elements.

Table 12–14 Code for Inserting the <complexType> Elements

Line	Code
19	`<xs:complexType name="childType">`
20	`   <xs:group ref="childElements" />`
21	`</xs:complexType>`

Line 19 is a <complexType> element that indicates the following element is a child element. Line 20 expands this definition by indicating with a <group> tag that the group elements belong to a child element, which is <item>. Line 21 closes the <complexType> element. The following step enters the code for the <complexType> element.

1

- If necessary, click line 19.
- Enter the XML code shown in Table 12–14 to enter the <complexType> element to define the group elements.
- Press the ENTER key twice after line 21 and position the insertion point at the beginning of line 23 (Figure 12–8).

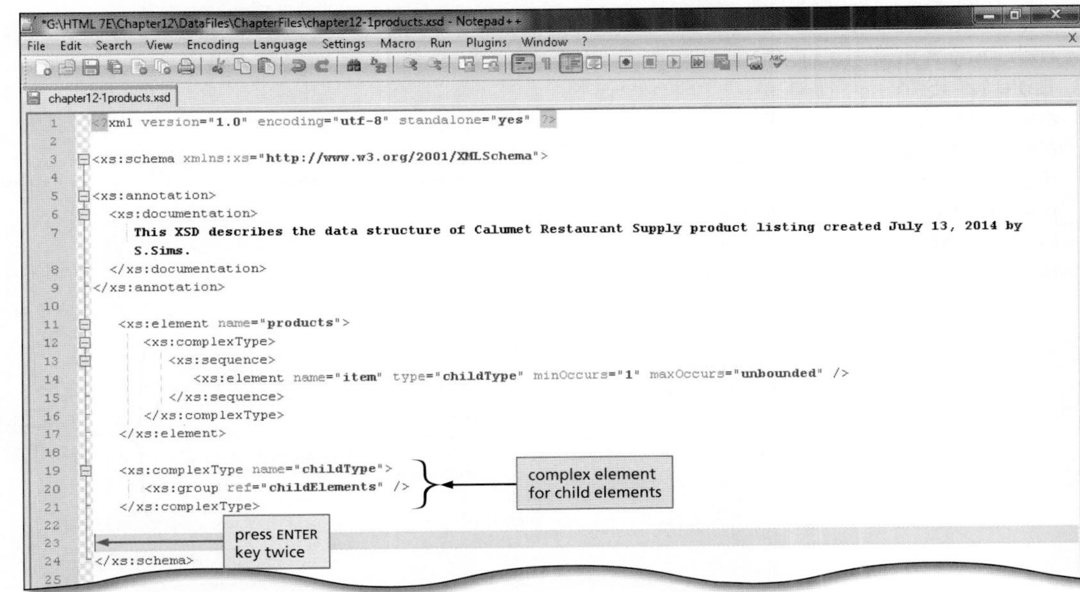

Figure 12–8

To Enter Code for the Child Group Elements

The last <group> element lists the individual elements that belong to the <item> element. The <item> element is a child of the <products> element, and each item instance has elements that describe the item. These descriptive (or <sequence>) elements are child elements of the <item> element. The code in Table 12–15 contains the group element and the <sequence> elements for each individual item and that item's data type.

Table 12–15 Code for Inserting the <group> Element

Line	Code
23	`<xs:group name="childElements">`
24	`   <xs:sequence>`
25	`      <xs:element name="item-id" type="xs:string" />`
26	`      <xs:element name="item-description" type="xs:string" />`
27	`      <xs:element name="item-boh" type="xs:integer" />`
28	`      <xs:element name="item-brand" type="xs:string" />`
29	`      <xs:element name="item-cost" type="xs:decimal" />`
30	`      <xs:element name="item-vendor_ID" type="xs:string" />`
31	`   </xs:sequence>`
32	`</xs:group>`

Line 23 is the <group> element that relates the <sequence> items to the child element (item), which is referenced by the name childElements on line 20. Line 24 starts the <sequence> elements. Recall that elements after a <sequence> element must be in order as they exist in the XML file. Lines 25 through 30 are element tags that name the individual fields and define their data type. Line 31 closes the <sequence> tag and line 32 closes the <group> tag. The closing </xs:schema> element (line 34 in Figure 12–9) was entered with the prolog in Table 12–11 so it would not be forgotten.

The following step enters the code for the <group> element to define the childElements that belong to the <item> element.

- If necessary, click line 23.
- Enter the XML code shown in Table 12–15 to enter the <group> element to define the childElements, pressing the ENTER key once after line 32 (Figure 12–9).

```
chapter12-1products.xsd
4
5  <xs:annotation>
6    <xs:documentation>
7      This XSD describes the data structure of Calumet Restaurant Supply product listing created July 13, 2014 by
       S.Sims.
8    </xs:documentation>
9  </xs:annotation>
10
11   <xs:element name="products">
12     <xs:complexType>
13       <xs:sequence>
14         <xs:element name="item" type="childType" minOccurs="1" maxOccurs="unbounded" />
15       </xs:sequence>
16     </xs:complexType>
17   </xs:element>
18
19   <xs:complexType name="childType">
20     <xs:group ref="childElements" />
21   </xs:complexType>
22
23   <xs:group name="childElements">
24     <xs:sequence>
25       <xs:element name="item-id" type="xs:string" />
26       <xs:element name="item-description" type="xs:string" />
27       <xs:element name="item-boh" type="xs:integer" />
28       <xs:element name="item-brand" type="xs:string" />
29       <xs:element name="item-cost" type="xs:decimal" />
30       <xs:element name="item-vendor_ID" type="xs:string" />
31     </xs:sequence>
32   </xs:group>
33
34 </xs:schema>
35
length : 1153
```


Figure 12–9

To Save and Validate an XML Schema Definition File

The following steps resave the XML Schema Definition file and check that it is a valid XML document.

- With the USB drive plugged into your computer, save the XSD Schema Definition file.
- Close the chapter12-1products.xsd file, but don't close Notepad++.
- Start your browser, type `www.w3.org/2001/03/webdata/xsv` in the Address box and then press the ENTER key.
- Scroll down to find the section that begins with "Use this form only if you are behind a firewall or have a schema to check which is not accessible via the Web" as shown in Figure 12–10.

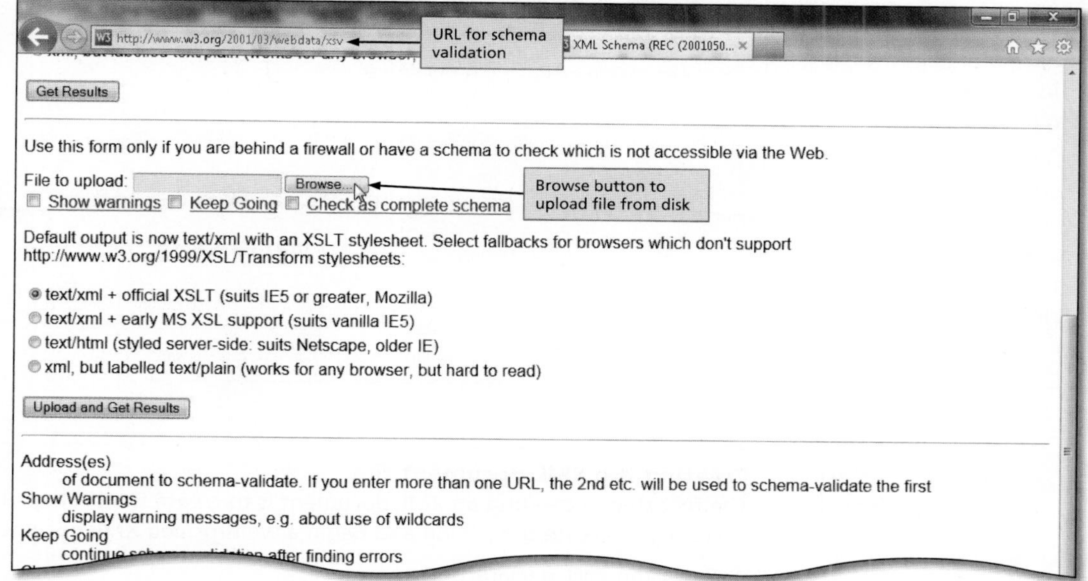

Figure 12–10

- Click the Browse button and navigate to your USB drive.
- Double-click the chapter12-1 products.xsd file to select the XML Schema Definition file for the validation Web page.
- Click the Show warnings and Keep Going check boxes, but not the Check as complete schema check box (Figure 12–11).

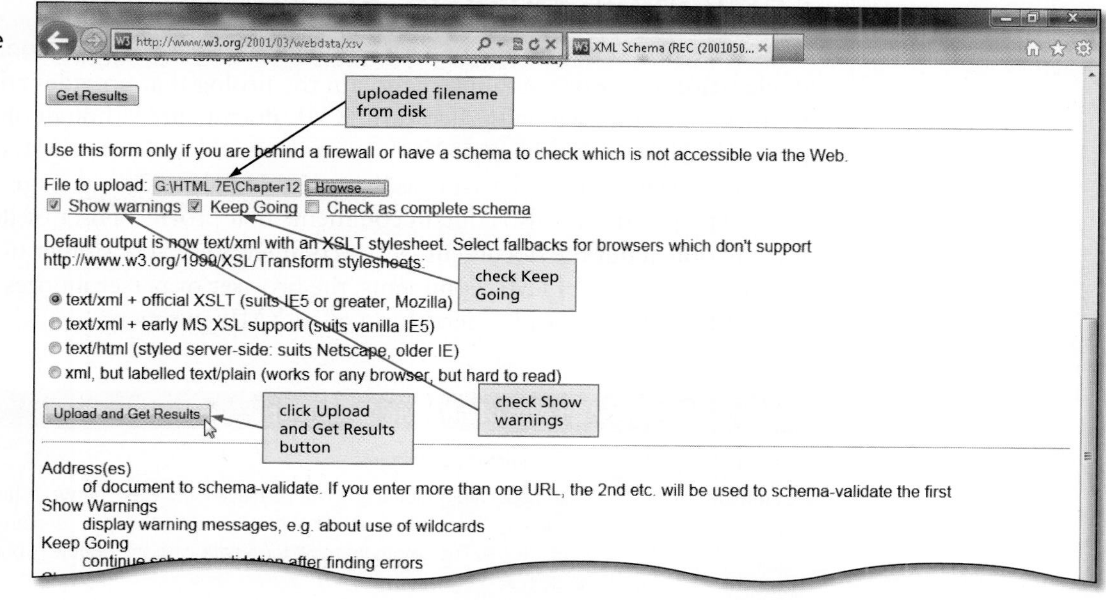

Figure 12–11

Q&A Why didn't we click the Check as complete schema check box?

This should be checked if the schema and the XML file are going to be validated together. We have not yet completed the XML file.

- Click the Upload and Get Results button. A valid XML Schema Definition will have no error messages (Figure 12–12).

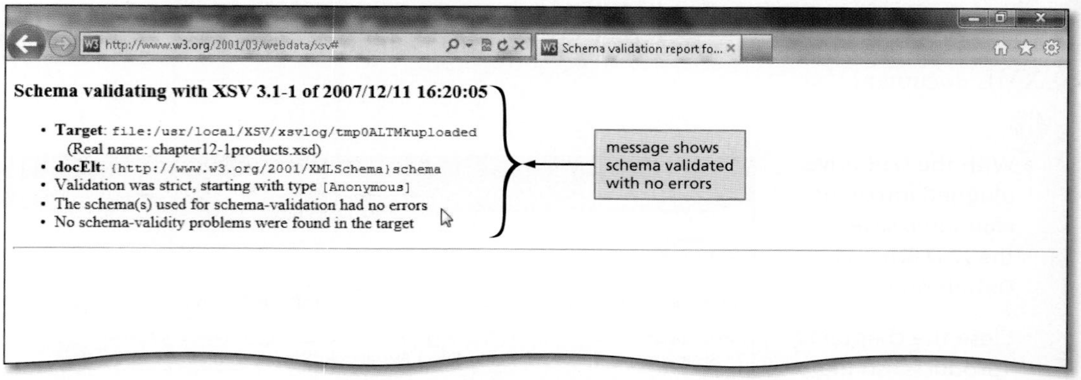

Figure 12–12

Q&A

I have an error; the file did not validate. What do I do?

You need to check your code and make sure everything is spelled and formatted as indicated in the tables. Check for missing tags or tags not closed properly.

Plan Ahead

Creating the XML document file.
The first step in creating an XML document is to create the prolog. The following tasks are necessary to create the prolog and begin a well-formed XML document:

1. Enter the XML declaration.
2. Enter an XML comment (HTML comment tag) to identify the name of the XML file as documentation.

Creating the Prolog in an XML Document

The first statement in an XML prolog is the XML declaration. The **XML declaration** is a processing instruction in the prolog that provides additional information to the application that will process the XML document. Although optional, the first processing instruction in most XML document prologs is the XML declaration. This processing statement is the same as described in Table 12–8 on page HTML 572.

The prolog can also contain comments that provide a user or developer with information about the document. XML comments are very similar in form to HTML comments. As with HTML comments, the browser or parser ignores the XML comments. Table 12–16 presents the general form of an XML comment.

Table 12–16 General Form of an XML Comment

General form:	<!- - comment statements -->
Comment:	Comments are optional and can be placed anywhere between tags, but not within a tag. Comments must begin with the left angle bracket (<), an exclamation point (!), and double hyphens (--). The comment must terminate with the double hyphens (--) and the right angle bracket (>).
Valid example:	<!- - File Name: chapter12-1products.xml - -> <Tag><!- - Comment about tag --></Tag>
Invalid example:	<Tag <!- - This tag is new -->>Data</Tag>

To Create a New XML Document and Enter the Prolog Code

The code in Table 12–17 contains the code for the prolog in the XML file.

Table 12–17 Code for the Prolog

Line	Code
1	<?xml version="1.0" encoding="utf-8" standalone="yes" ?>
2	<!-- File Name: chapter12-1products.xml -->

Line 1 is the XML declaration that identifies this as an XML document using XML version 1.0, uses the utf-8 coding standard, and identifies that this is a stand-alone file. Line 2 is a comment stating the name of the XML file. Prior to the recommendation by W3C, a Document Type Definition (DTD) would follow. Because this text follows the current recommendation to use the XML Schema Definition, the XSD file created previously will be attached in the document instance code. The following steps create a new XML document using Notepad++ and enters the prolog code.

- If necessary, activate the Notepad++ window.
- If necessary, click File on the menu bar, then click New to create a new Notepad++ document.
- With the USB drive plugged into your computer, click File on the menu bar, and then click Save As.
- If necessary, navigate to the Chapter12\ChapterFiles folder on UDISK (G:).
- Type `chapter12-1products.xml` in the File name text box.
- Click the Save button in the Save As dialog box (Figure 12–13).

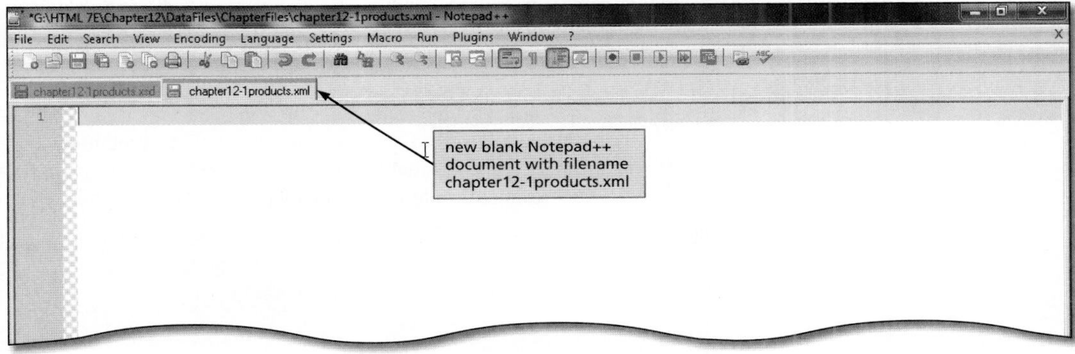

Figure 12–13

2

- If necessary, click line 1.
- Enter the XML code shown in Table 12–17 to create the prolog and press the ENTER key twice (Figure 12–14).

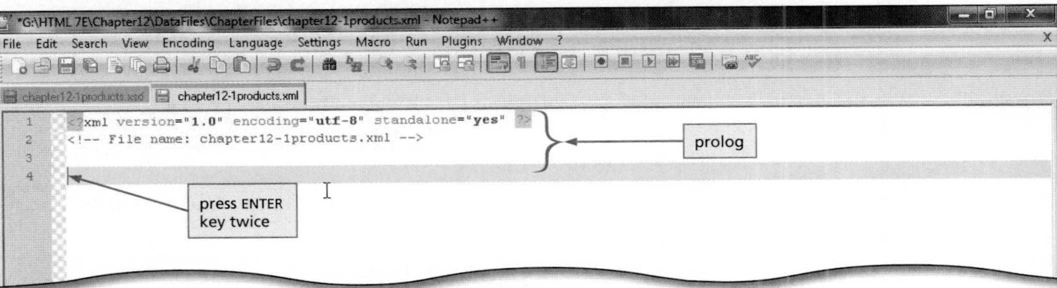

Figure 12–14

Q&A Why isn't the link to the XSD file in the prolog?

It will be entered as part of the root element of the document instance.

Plan Ahead

Creating a document instance.

The main data of an XML document is the document instance. The document instance is all the components of the document, whether the document is free-form text or a database. When creating the document instance, a designer should complete the following tasks:

- Use the relation or logical schema with attributes created in the XML Schema Definition.
- Determine if namespaces are necessary if duplicate identifier names are used.
- Identify the data values for the various XML elements.

Creating the Document Instance in an XML Document

The second part of an XML document is the document instance, or elements. The document instance section contains the document elements and actual content or data. There must be one root element with all other elements nested inside the root. This format creates a hierarchical, treelike structure. This structure defines the XML document as a well-formed document. Table 12–18 shows the general form of an element tag.

Table 12–18 General Form of an Element Tag

General form:	<element start tag>element contents</element end tag>
Comment:	XML documents require start and end element tags. The element tag name must be a valid name. The tag describes the type of content represented by the element (for example, item-description, item-brand). Start and end tags must match exactly in spelling and case. The element contents or data are the text entered between the tags.
Examples:	<item-description>Stainless Steel Work Table 36X18</item-description> <item-brand>ChefMaster</item-brand> <item-cost>497.99</item-cost>

To Start Entering a Document Instance in an XML Document

As shown in Table 12–19, item-id, item-description, item-boh, item-brand, item-cost, and item-vendor_ID are all child elements within the <item> element. The item element is a child element nested within the <products> root element.

Table 12–19 Code for Inserting the Document Instance

```
<products xmlns:xsi="http://www.w3.org/2001/XMLSchema-instance"
xsi:noNamespaceSchemaLocation="chapter12-1products.xsd">
  <item>
    <item-id>A345</item-id>
     <item-description>Stainless Steel Work Table 36X18</item-description>
     <item-boh>4</item-boh>
     <item-brand>ChefMaster</item-brand>
     <item-cost>497.99</item-cost>
     <item-vendor_ID>5T300</item-vendor_ID>
  </item>
```

Line 4 represents the root element of the XML document, with the start <products> tag and the code that identifies and binds the XML Schema Definition file to this XML document. Line 5 defines the <item> element. Lines 6 through 11 are the child elements of the <item> element, with one instance for each occurrence of a data item. Line 12 is the </item> element end tag. The following step enters the document instance in the XML document, chapter12-1products.xml.

1

- If necessary, click line 4.
- Enter the XML code shown in Table 12–19 to create the root and first document instance. Press the ENTER key after line 12 (Figure 12–15).

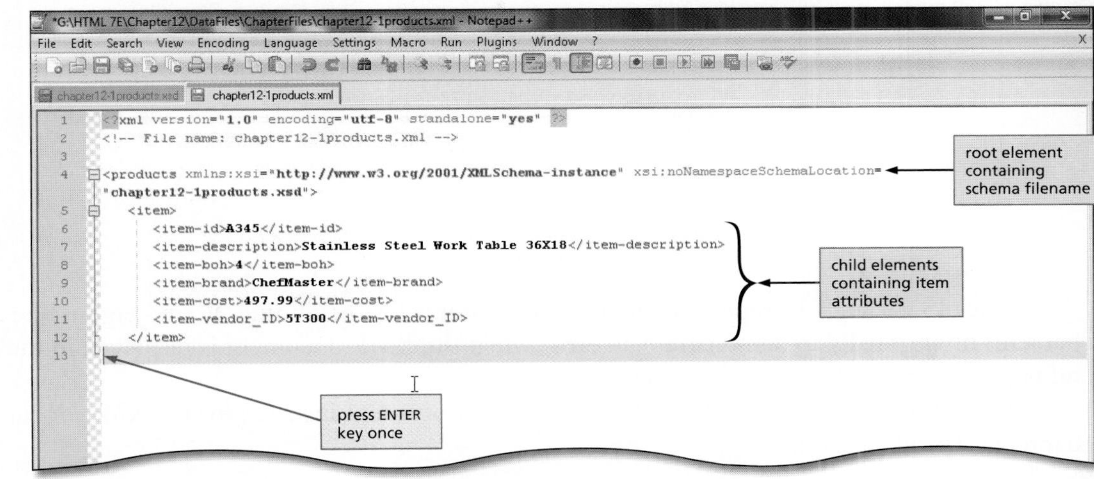

Figure 12–15

Q&A When I enter line 4, when should I press ENTER?

Type line 4 as one continuous line, and do not press the ENTER key until the end of the line. Where line 4 wraps to the next line on your screen may differ from Table 12–19 or Figure 12–15.

To Finish Entering a Document Instance in an XML Document

To complete the document instance, the remaining elements for each item record in the list are entered using the same format, as shown in Table 12–20.

Table 12–20 Code for Completing the Document Instance

Line	Code
13	`<item>`
14	`    <item-id>R140</item-id>`
15	`    <item-description>14-inch Roast Knife</item-description>`
16	`    <item-boh>19</item-boh>`
17	`    <item-brand>Russel</item-brand>`
18	`    <item-cost>58.99</item-cost>`
19	`    <item-vendor_ID>CH100</item-vendor_ID>`
20	`</item>`
21	`<Item>`
22	`    <item-id>S245</item-id>`
23	`    <item-description>Salt and Pepper Shakers</item-description>`
24	`    <item-boh>3</item-boh>`
25	`    <item-brand>Du Pont</item-brand>`
26	`    <item-cost>9.99</item-cost>`
27	`    <item-vendor_ID>5TY90</item-vendor_ID>`
28	`</item>`
29	`<item>`

Table 12–20 Code for Completing the Document Instance (continued)

Line	Code
30	`<item-id>G321</item-id>`
31	`<item-description>Tomato Slicer</item-description>`
32	`<item-boh>5</item-boh>`
33	`<item-brand>Cooper</item-brand>`
34	`<item-cost>169.98</item-cost>`
35	`<item-vendor_ID>5T790</item-vendor_ID>`
36	`</item>`
37	`</products>`

Lines 13 through 36 repeat elements for each item. The beginning <Item> tag on line 21 has an uppercase I character intentionally to demonstrate an error when the XML document is displayed in the browser. Line 37 is the end tag for the root element, </products>.

The following step enters the remainder of the document instance for the XML document, chapter12-1products.xml.

- If necessary, click line 13 and indent as shown in Figure 12–16.
- Enter the XML code shown in Table 12–20 with the error on line 21 to finish creating the document instance and do not press the ENTER key (Figure 12–16).

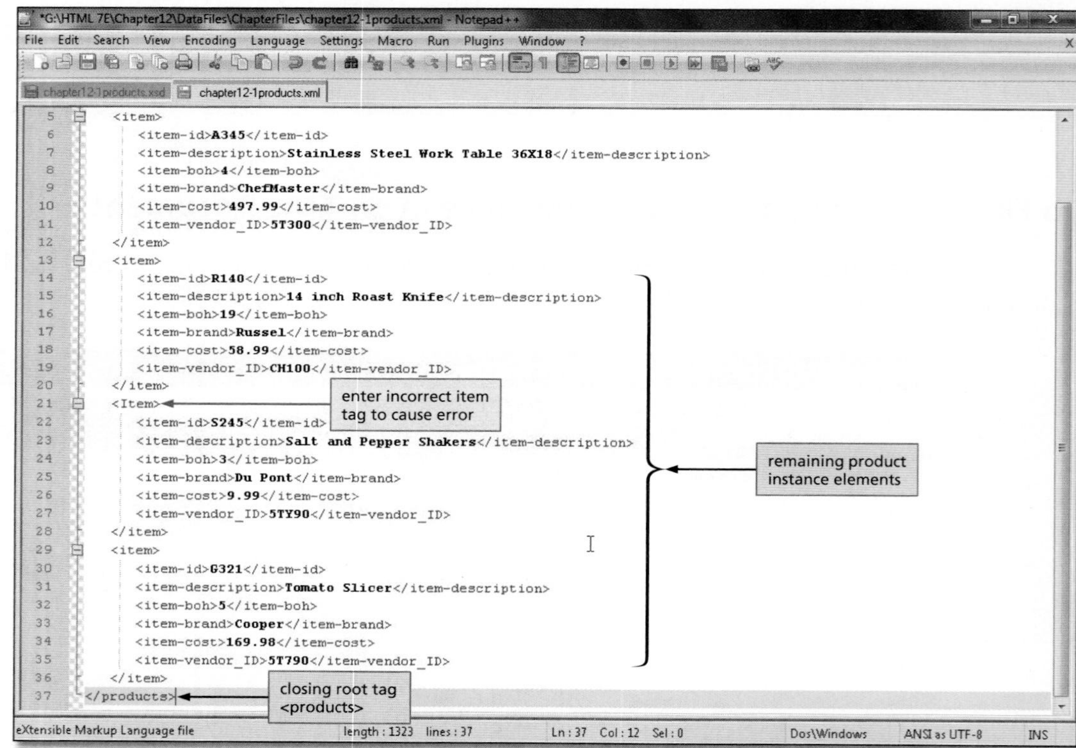

Figure 12–16

To Save and Test an XML Document in a Browser

The following steps save and test the XML document.

1. Save the completed chapter12-1products.xml document.
2. Start your browser. If necessary, click the Maximize button.
3. Type `G:\Chapter12\ChapterFiles\chapter12-1products.xml` in the Address bar and then press the ENTER key to display the completed document (Figure 12–17).

Q&A The document did not display as expected. What happened?

The tag on line 21 is not correct and prevents the XML data from displaying properly.

Q&A This error was made on purpose, so we know the line number. How do I find the line number of an accidental error?

In Internet Explorer 9, press the F12 key. At the bottom of the browser a new window displays. Click the Browser Mode: IE9 button on the toolbar and then click Internet Explorer 9: Compatibility View. This will not display the line number of the error, but will give you a hint at what element may be wrong. The Firefox, Chrome, and Safari browsers will display the error with a line number.

Q&A Will the browser show all the errors at one time?

Unfortunately, you will have to correct each error as it is found by the browser; the browser parser stops processing when it encounters the first error.

BTW

How Internet Explorer Displays Prolog

In Internet Explorer 9, the prolog statement <?xml version="1.0" encoding="utf-8" standalone="yes" ?> will display as <?xml version="1.0" encoding="utf-8" standalone="true" ?>. The root element <products xmlns:xsi="http://www.w3.org/2001/XMLSchema-instance" xsi:noNamespaceSchemaLocation="chapter12-1products.xsd"> will display as <products xsi:noNamespaceSchemaLocation="chapter12-1products.xsd" xmlns:xsi="http://www.w3.org/2001/XMLSchema-instance"> and not as typed.

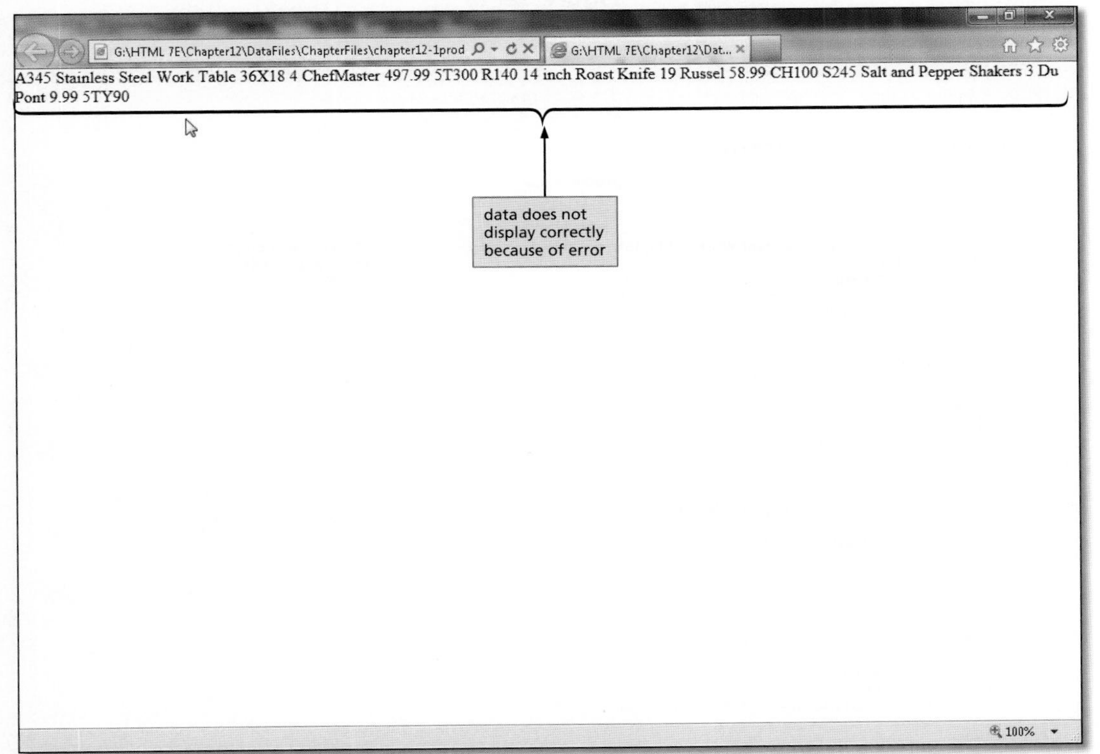

Figure 12–17

To Correct a Tag Error and Retest an XML Document

The following steps correct the tag error and retest the XML document.

- Click the Notepad++ button on the taskbar.
- Click line 21.
- Replace the uppercase I with a lowercase i (Figure 12–18).

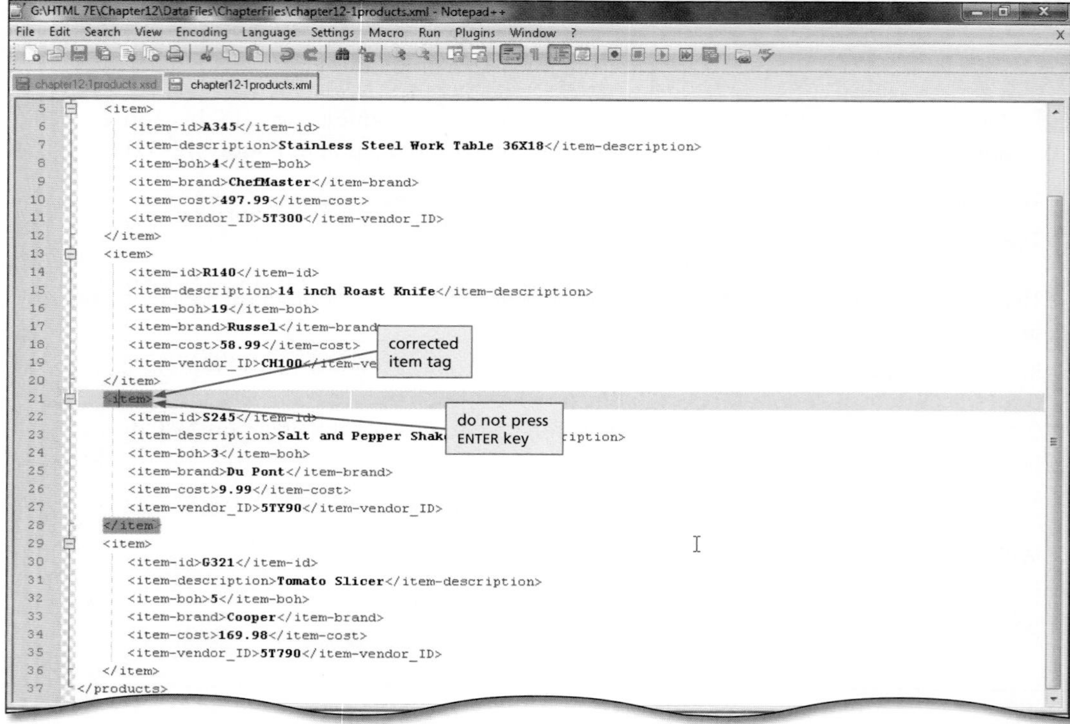

Figure 12–18

- Save the corrected file.
- Activate the browser.
- Click the Refresh button on the Address bar to display the corrected page (Figure 12–19).
- If a security message appears, click the 'Allow blocked content' button. (If you are running Internet Explorer 8 or lower, your security message may be different.)

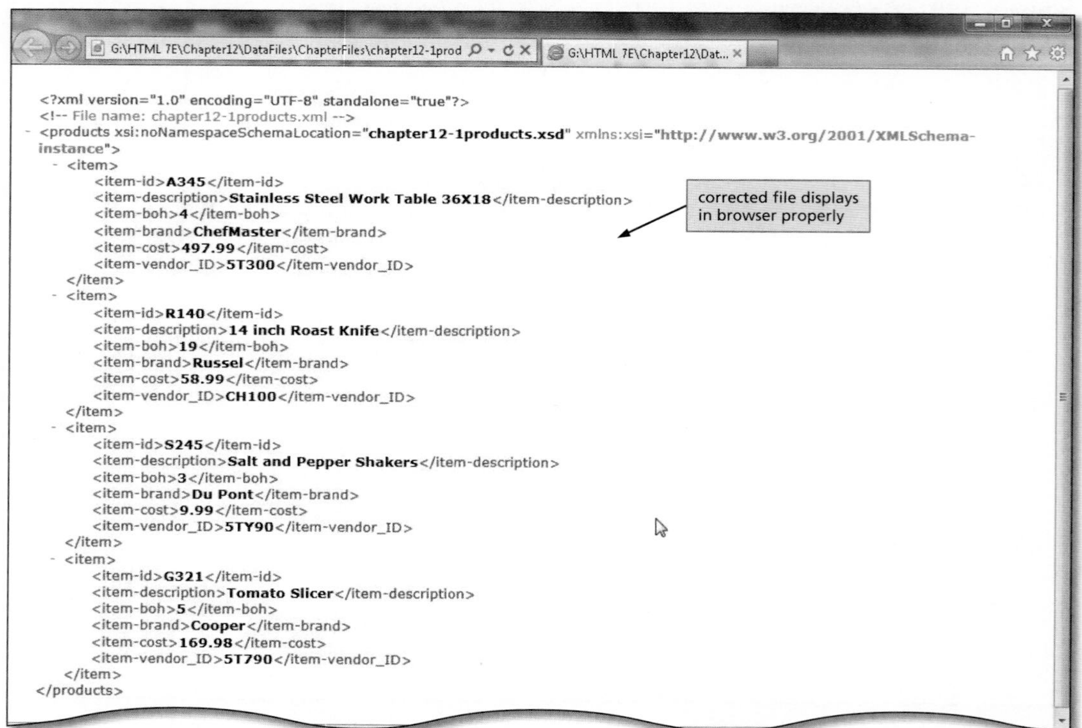

Figure 12–19

What are the minus signs by the <products> and <item> tags?

The minus signs preceding the tags <products> and <item> indicate the level or node (root or child) of the data. A user can collapse or expand the levels of the document by clicking a plus sign to expand or a minus sign to collapse. An unformatted XML document is difficult to read.

3

- Click the minus sign in front of the second and fourth <item> tags to collapse both instances in the list (Figure 12–20).
- Click the plus sign in front of the second <item> tag to expand that instance.

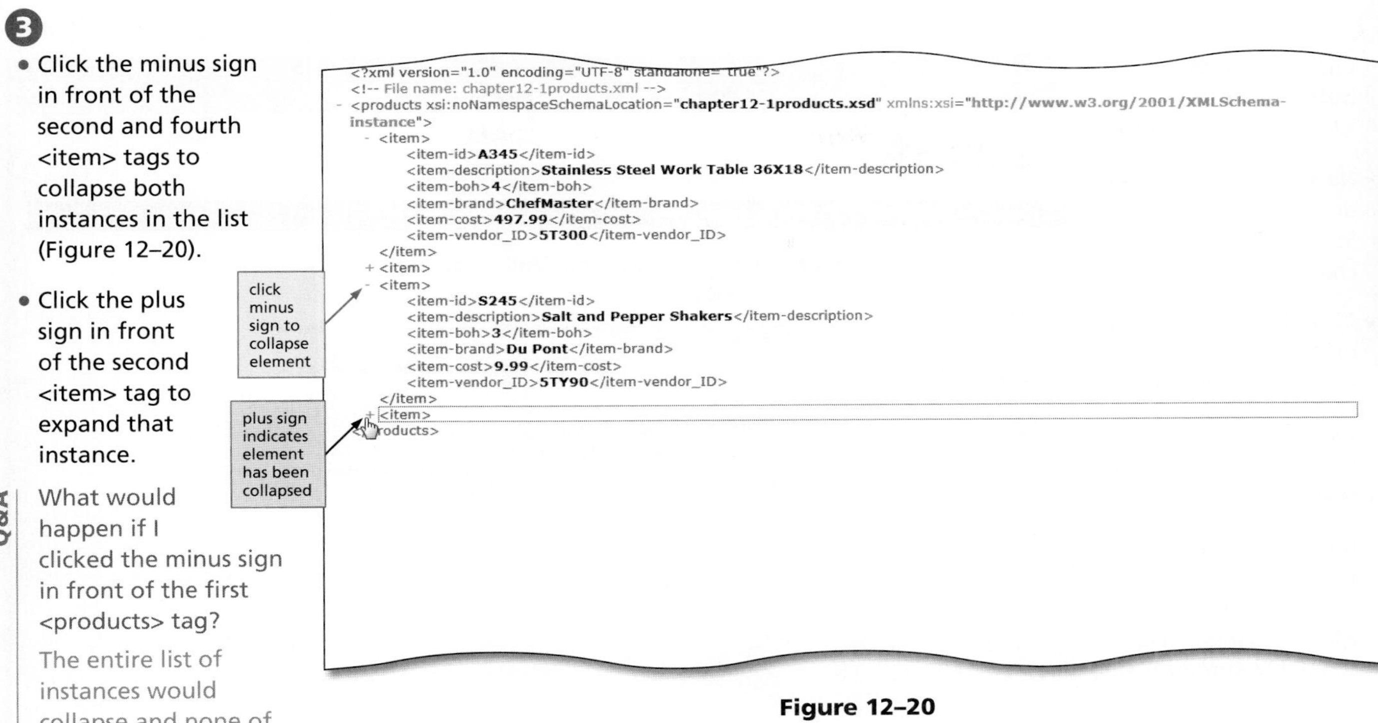

click minus sign to collapse element
plus sign indicates element has been collapsed

Q&A What would happen if I clicked the minus sign in front of the first <products> tag?

The entire list of instances would collapse and none of the child <item> tags would be visible.

Figure 12–20

To Validate XML and XSD Files

Once the XSD and XML files are created and bound together with the <xml> tag you should validate that the XSD does define the XML instance. The following steps validate the XSD and XML files using a Web site that offers this service.

1

- If necessary, activate your browser.
- Click the Address bar.
- Type `www.corefiling.com/opensource/schemaValidate.html` and then press the ENTER key to load the Web page (Figure 12–21).

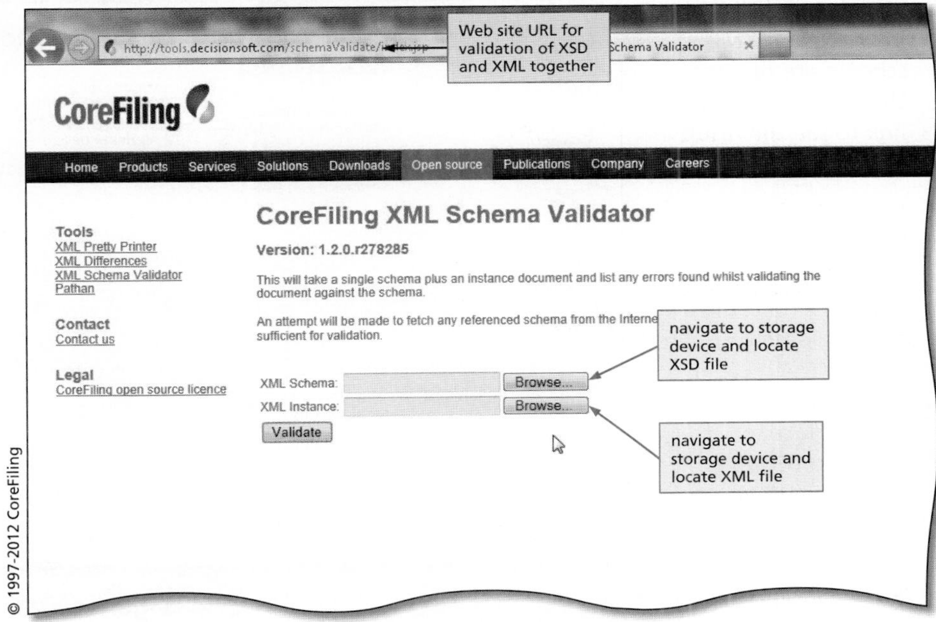

Web site URL for validation of XSD and XML together
navigate to storage device and locate XSD file
navigate to storage device and locate XML file
CoreFiling XML Schema Validator

Figure 12–21

- Click the Browse button next to the XML Schema text box.
- Navigate to your storage device and locate the XML Schema Definition file, chapter12-1products.xsd.
- Click the Open button on the Choose File to Upload dialog box.
- Click the Browse button next to the XML Instance text box.
- If necessary, navigate to your storage device and locate the XML document file, chapter12-1products.xml.
- Click the Open button.

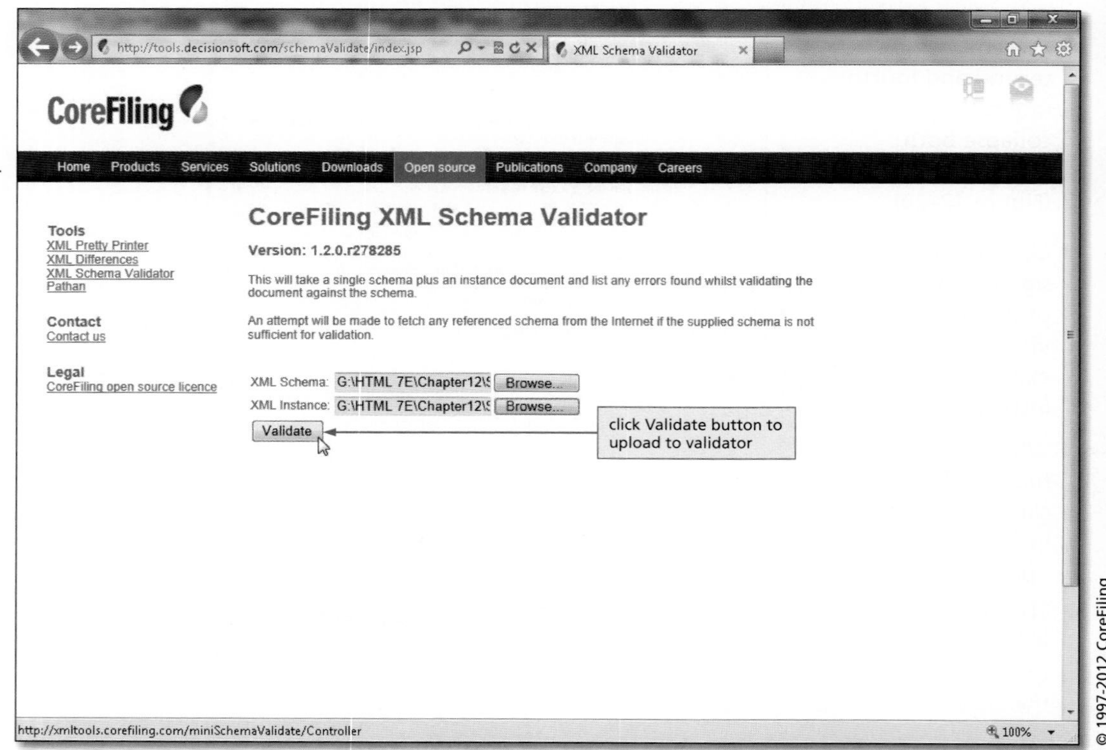

Figure 12–22

- Click the Validate button on the XML Schema Validator to upload the files.
- When the Web page indicates the XML instance and XML schema are present, click the Click here link to see the results (Figure 12–23).

Q&A What do I do if it returns errors?

Look at the line numbers indicated, and compare your code to the code in Figures 12–9 and 12–18, make any corrections, and then repeat Steps 1 through 3.

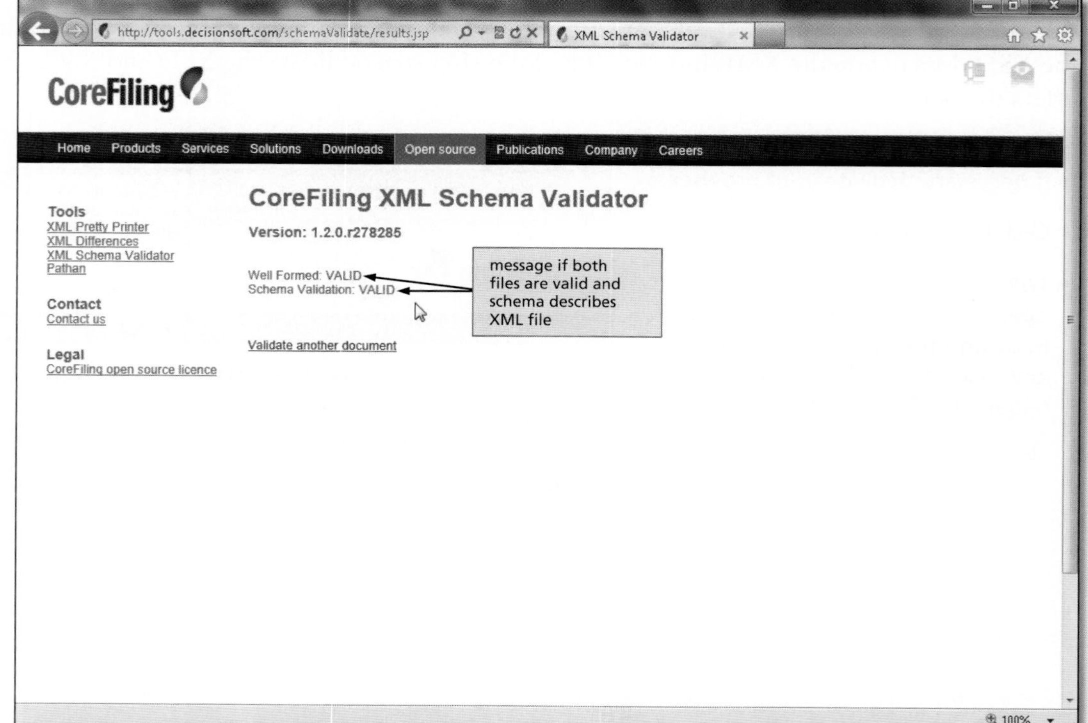

Figure 12–23

Formatting and linking an XSL style sheet to an XML document.
XSL style sheets are used to transform an XML document into a more stylized document. To create an XSL document, perform these tasks:

1. Determine the XML document elements that will be displayed and how you want them to appear.
2. Determine the XSL elements:
   a. Determine if the <template> element will use all or only some elements.
   b. Determine the for-each elements.
   c. Determine the style for each XSL value-of element and format with <span> tags and inline styles.
   d. Determine if sorting is required and which XML element to use as a sort key.
   e. Determine any descriptive text that is needed.
3. Link the XSL style sheet to the XML document.

Plan Ahead

Formatting an XML Document Using an XSL Style Sheet

This section outlines the techniques needed to format the display of an XML document using the Extensible Stylesheet Language (XSL) and to bind the XML document to the XSL style sheet. Recall that the List link on the home page is an image that links to an XML document that will display the products in description order. (Figure 12–1b on page HTML 563). The output and display of this XML document are defined using an XSL style sheet that sets each record to be displayed in a list, sorted in ascending order by the <item-description> element.

BTW

XSL
XSL is three languages: one to transform XML (XSLT), one to define XML parts or patterns (XPath), and one to format objects and define the XML display (XSL). An XSL style sheet assumes that the associated XML document uses a hierarchical structure, which contains a root element, child elements, and any optional attributes, namespaces, processing statements, or comments. An XSL style sheet cannot transform any other type of document, such as Word, PDF, or PostScript files, into HTML documents.

To Open an XML Document and Save It with a New Name

Instead of the .xml file you started, you will continue with a file supplied in the Data Files for Students that is similar but contains additional product items. The next steps are to open that document, save it with a new name, and then create the XSL style sheet to format and place the item listing in the desired order. See the inside back cover of this book for instructions on downloading the Data Files for Students, or contact your instructor for information about accessing the required files.

The following steps open a text document, chapter12-1data.txt, and save it as chapter12-1products_solution.xml.

1. Activate the Notepad++ window. Right-click the chapter12-1products.xml file tab, and click Close on the shortcut menu.
2. With the USB drive plugged into your computer, click File on the menu bar, and then click Open on the File menu.
3. If necessary, navigate to the Chapter12\ChapterFiles folder on the USB drive. Click All types (*,*) in the Save as type drop-down list.
4. Double-click chapter12-1data.txt in the list of files.
5. Click File on the menu bar, and then click Save As on the File menu.

6 If necessary, navigate to the Chapter12\ChapterFiles folder on UDISK (G:).

7 Type `chapter12-1products_solution.xml` in the File name text box and then click the Save button.

BTW

The XSL stylesheet Element

The xsl:stylesheet or xsl:transform element must have a version number and should be written as follows: <xsl:stylesheet version="1.0" xmlns:xsl="http://www.w3.org/1999/XSL/Transform"> or <xsl:transform version="1.0" xmlns:xsl="http://www.w3.org/1999/XSL/Transform">. The version number is required because the namespace code, xmlns:xsl="http://www.w3.org/1999/XSL/Transform", indicates the use of the official W3C specification.

Creating an XSL Style Sheet

As previously stated, an XML document can be formatted with CSS or XSL style sheets. Most Web developers agree that formatting with CSS is impractical and prefer to use XSL style sheets. An XSL style sheet performs two actions: it formats and transforms XML documents. An XSL style sheet can **transform** an XML document by instructing the browser or parser to output the XML document in a completely different form. XSL takes the XML document, called a **source**, and produces completely different output, called a **result tree**.

An XSL style sheet uses syntax similar to the syntax used for XML documents and has the same hierarchical, treelike structure as other XML documents. Each of the style sheet elements in an XSL style sheet must use the namespace prefix, **xsl**, to distinguish the XSL elements from XML elements. To define the namespace, after the prolog statement, the first element is the root element. The root element in an XSL style sheet is the <xsl:stylesheet> or the <xsl:transform> tag, and must include a version. The general format of these root elements is shown in Table 12–21. For a complete list of XSL style sheet elements, see the XML Quick Reference in Appendix H.

Table 12–21 General Form of the stylesheet Element in an XSL Style Sheet	
General form:	<xsl:stylesheet xmlns:prefix="URL" language="language"> ... *(other stylesheet code)* </xsl:stylesheet> or <xsl:transform version="v.x" xmlns:prefix="URL" language="language"> ... *(other stylesheet code)* </xsl:transform>
Comment:	The **stylesheet** (or **transform**) element is the root element of an XSL style sheet. The *prefix* defines the xml namespace (xmlns). The namespace allows duplicate names to be used in a document. The *URL* indicates the official XSL specification as recommended by the W3C. The language attribute is optional. The stylesheet or transform element must be closed at the end of the document by the end tag, </xsl:stylesheet> or </xsl:transform>.
Examples:	(1) <xsl:stylesheet xmlns:xsl="http://www.w3.org/TR/WD-xsl"> (2) <xsl:transform version="1.0" xmlns:xsl="http://www.w3.org/1999/XSL/Transform">

The **stylesheet** or **transform element** establishes a namespace, so the remaining elements, such as the template, can use names that will not be confused with other elements. A **template** is an instruction that identifies the elements in a document that should be transformed or converted and then specifies how the element should be transformed. The browser refers to the template when displaying a particular element in the XML document. The template is the most important part of the XSL style sheet, and the XSL style sheet must include at least one template element. Table 12–22 shows the general form of the template element.

Table 12–22 General Form of the template Element

General form:	<xsl:template match="pattern" language="language"> ... *(other stylesheet code)* </xsl:template>
Comment:	The *pattern* indicates the XML element or node. A pattern of "/" indicates that the entire document will be displayed. The template element needs an end element.
Example:	<xsl:template match="/"> ... *(other stylesheet code)* </xsl:template>

BTW

The XSL template Element
The XSL template element associates each output with an input. The match="/" attribute defines the entire document.

To Start Creating an XSL Style Sheet

This XSL style sheet will display the items in order by item description, using the <item-description> tag element in the XML file. Table 12–23 shows the code for the processing instruction, an XML declaration, a stylesheet element, and a template element in an XSL style sheet.

Table 12–23 Code for Creating an XSL Style Sheet

Line	Code
1	`<?xml version="1.0" encoding="utf-8" standalone="yes" ?>`
2	`<xsl:transform version="1.0" xmlns:xsl="http://www.w3.org/1999/XSL/Transform">`
3	`    <xsl:template match="/">`

Line 1 is the XML declaration that identifies this as an XML document using XML version 1.0. Line 2 is the XSL stylesheet element used to define the namespace, xsl, for the remaining elements. Line 3 defines the template pattern, using a "/" to indicate that the template applies to the entire XML document. The following step begins creating an XSL style sheet.

- If necessary, activate the Notepad++ window.
- Click File on the menu bar, and then New to start a new Notepad++ document.
- With your USB drive plugged into your computer, click File on the menu bar, and then click Save As. If necessary, navigate to the Chapter12\ChapterFiles folder.

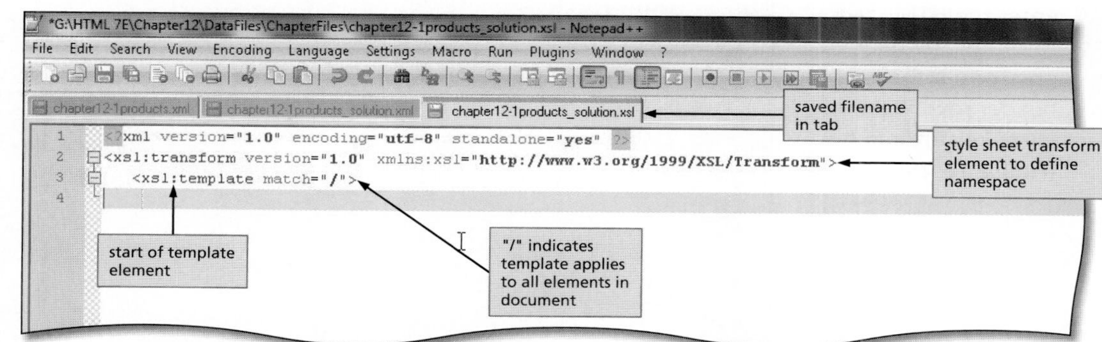

Figure 12–24

- Type `chapter12-1products_solution.xsl` in the File name text box and then click the Save button.
- Enter the code shown in Table 12–23 to start the XSL style sheet, and then press the ENTER key once after line 3 (Figure 12–24).

Q&A What happens if more than one XSL style sheet is linked to an XML document?

If more than one XSL style sheet is linked to an XML document, the first XSL style sheet the browser reads is used and the others are ignored.

Q&A Can an XSL style sheet and Cascading Style Sheet both be linked to an XML document?

If an XSL style sheet and a Cascading Style Sheet are both linked to an XML document, the XSL style sheet is used and the Cascading Style Sheet is ignored.

To Enter HTML Code to Display the Banner and Header Text in a Web Page

The next step is to enter the HTML tags that will display the banner and header text in the browser. The <p> and <span> tags will use inline CSS styles to format and center the banner and text on the Web page. This code must be placed after the <template> tag and is shown in Table 12–24.

Table 12–24 Code for the HTML Tags to Center the Banner and Header Text

Line	Code
4	`<p style="text-align:center">`
5	`  <img border="0" src="chapter12-1banner.gif" />`
6	`</p>`
7	`<p style="text-align:center">`
8	`  <span style="font-weight:bold; font-family:arial, helvetica, san-serif; font-size:18px">` `  Restaurant Supply - Browse by Description</span>`
9	`</p>`

Line 4 is a paragraph tag with a style attribute to center the banner <img> in line 5. The closing </p> tag is after the <img> tag. Line 7 is a new <p> tag with a style attribute to center the Web page header text. The <span> tag in line 8 contains the inline style to format the header text as bold, Arial font, and size 18. Line 8 also contains the header text and the closing </span> tag. Line 9 is the closing </p> tag. The following step enters the HTML tags to center the banner and center and format the header text.

- If necessary, click line 4.
- Enter the code shown in Table 12–24 to enter the HTML tags to center the banner and format the header text. Press the ENTER key after line 9 (Figure 12–25).

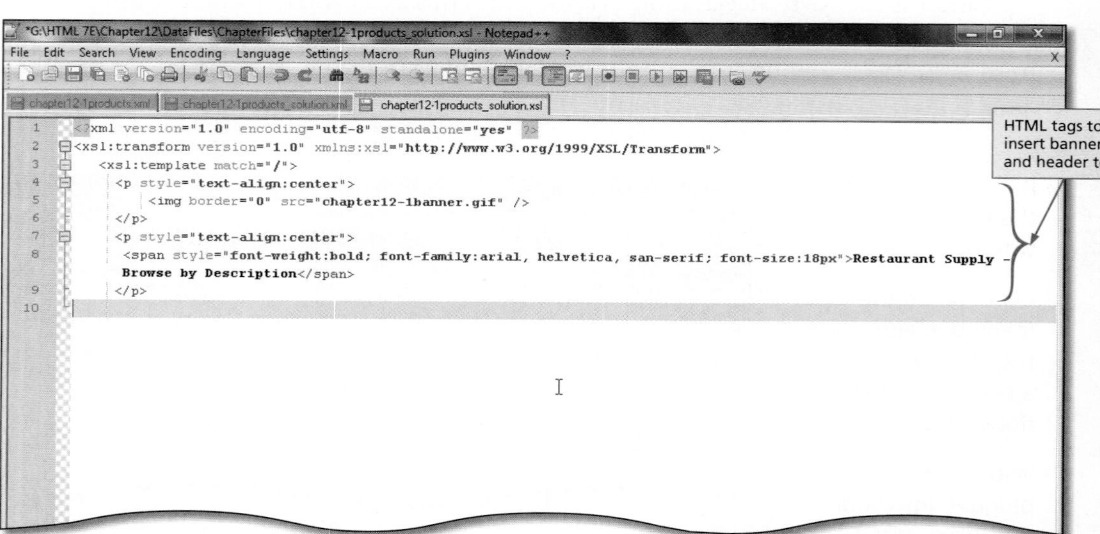

Figure 12–25

Using XSL Style Sheet Tags

By combining the XSL elements and XML markup tags, an XSL style sheet tells the browser how to transform and format the XML document to display records in paragraph format on the Web page. In this project, you will use the for-each, sort, text, and value-of XSL style sheet tags. The **for-each** element makes each element appear in the list, and associates each child element <item> related with the <products>. This association identifies the XML elements that should appear in the items list on the Web page. Table 12–25 shows the general form of the for-each element.

Table 12–25 General Form of the for-each Element

General form:	<xsl:for-each select="pattern">
Comment:	The **for-each** element returns the associated child element's data identified by the **select** attribute pattern. As the for-each cycles through the data, each of the child nodes contained in the pattern name becomes the current node element or record.
Example:	<xsl:for-each select="products/item">

BTW

The XSL for-each Element
The for-each element allows a developer to "loop" through a set of XML data. The use of the for-each selects every item in a set of nodes. In the event of multiple items, the first value is used.

XSL style sheets allow for a more free-form, yet organized, display of data. To display the items in order by item description, use the sort element as shown in Table 12–26.

Table 12–26 General Form of the sort Element

General form:	<xsl:sort [select="value" lang="token" data-type="value" order="ascending|descending" case-order="upper-first|lower-first"] />
Comment:	The **sort** element has five optional attributes: select, lang, data-type, order, and case-order. The **select** attribute value indicates on which element to sort; **lang** indicates the language of the sort keys. The system default language is assumed. **Data-type** is used to indicate the data type of the select value (alphabetic or numeric). In an alphabetic sort, numbers are sorted alphabetically, meaning 100 comes before 99. Numeric data types sort numbers in their correct numeric order. **Order** indicates ascending (default) or descending. **Case-order** indicates if uppercase or lowercase order should be first.
Example:	<xsl:sort select="item-description" data-type="text" />

BTW

The XSL sort Element
If the select attribute is omitted, the XSLT processor sorts on all the elements as a string as the sort key.

In conjunction with the for-each element, XSL uses the <xsl:text> tag to display text on a page. Any text placed between the <xsl:text> and closing </xsl:text> tags will display based on the formatting of any HTML tags. Recall that spaces in XML documents are kept, unlike in HTML documents where special codes must be used to insert a space.

To display any element values from the XML document, the XSL style sheet uses the XSL value-of element to display each instance within the item list. Table 12–27 shows the general form of the XSL value-of element.

Table 12–27 General Form of the value-of Element

General form:	<xsl:value-of select="pattern" />
Comment:	The **value-of** element indicates that the page should display the value for the specified element. The *pattern* value of the select attribute identifies the name of the specific element used in the output.
Example:	<xsl:value-of select="item-description" />

BTW

The XSL value-of Element
The value-of element transfers the value of the designated XML tag (field) to the output document.

To Add XSL Style Sheet Tags

Table 12–28 on the next page shows the code for the remainder of the XSL to sort the data by item-description in ascending order and display the item-description, item-boh, and item-cost in a sentence format on the Web page.

Table 12–28 Code for Adding the for-each, sort, text, and value-of XSL Style Sheet Tags

Line	Code
10	<xsl:for-each select="products/item">
11	<xsl:sort select="item-description" data-type="text" />
12	<p style="margin-left:15%">
13	<span style="font-weight:bold; color:#7f0000">
14	<xsl:value-of select="item-description" />
15	</span>
16	<xsl:text> There are </xsl:text>
17	<span style="text-decoration:underline; font-weight:bold">
18	<xsl:value-of select="item-boh" />
19	</span>
20	<xsl:text> in stock and the cost is $</xsl:text>
21	<span style="font-family:arial, helvetica, sans-serif">
22	<xsl:value-of select="item-cost" />.
23	</span>
24	</p>
25	</xsl:for-each>
26	<p style="font-family:helvetica,arial; font-weight:bold"> <a href="chapter12-1home_solution.html">Home</a></p>
27	</xsl:template>
28	</xsl:transform>

Line 10 is the <for-each> tag that cycles through the XML file displaying each individual instance. Line 11 is the <sort> tag that directs the elements to be displayed in sorted order on the description using the <item-description> element. The paragraph <p> tag on line 12 displays each record on a separate line, indented by 15 percent of window width from the left margin. Line 13 is a <span> tag with an embedded style sheet used to set the font-weight to bold and the color to #7f0000. Line 14 uses the value-of select attribute to display the value for the item-description element. Line 15 closes the <span> tag started on line 13, so the next text displayed does not use the same style.

Line 16 uses the text attribute to insert the text "There are" between the item-desciption and the item-boh value displayed by line 18. The inline style in line 17 displays the item-boh (number in stock) bold and underlined. Line 20 inserts the text "in stock and the cost is $" and the <span> tag on line 21 uses an embedded style sheet to set the font of the item-cost, which is displayed with the <value-of> tag in line 22. Line 23 closes the <span>.

Line 24 closes the <p> tag on line 12. Line 25 closes the for-each element. Line 26 is a <p> tag with an embedded style followed by an <a href> tag to create a link back to the home page. Line 27 closes the <xsl:template> tag on line 3. Line 28 closes the <xsl:transform> tag on line 2, which began the XSL markup tag elements.

The following step enters the remaining code to complete the XSL style sheet.

1

- If necessary, click line 10.
- Enter the code shown in Table 12–28, indenting as shown, to complete the XSL style sheet (Figure 12–26).
- Save the XSL style sheet file.

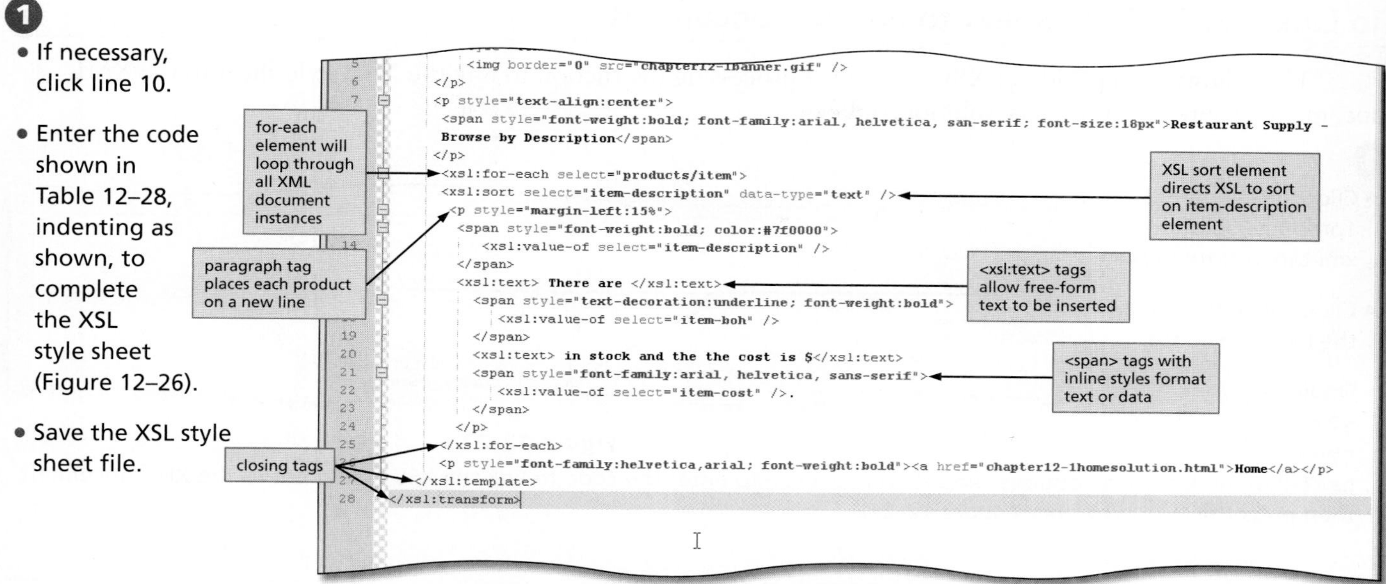

Figure 12–26

Linking an XSL Style Sheet to an XML Document

With the XSL file saved, the next step is to link the XSL style sheet to the XML document. For this part of the project, you will link the chapter12-1products_solution.xsl style sheet to the chapter12-1products_solution.xml file that you previously saved from the Data Files for Students. Linking an XSL style sheet to an XML document requires an xml-stylesheet processing instruction. Table 12–29 shows the general form of this xml-stylesheet processing instruction.

Table 12–29 General Form of the xml-stylesheet Processing Instruction

General form:	<?xml-stylesheet type="text/xsl" href="file path"?>
Comment:	The processing instruction used to link an XSL style sheet contains the **xml-stylesheet type** attribute. The value, text/xsl, indicates that this is an XSL file. The **href** attribute indicates the external path or URI of the XSL file.
Example:	<?xml-stylesheet type="text/xsl" href="chapter12-1products_solution.xsl"?>

XSL style sheet processing instructions are usually entered in the prolog of the XML document.

To Link an XSL Style Sheet to an XML Document

The following step adds an XSL style sheet processing instruction to link the XSL style sheet to the XML document, chapter12-1products_solution.xml.

- Click the chapter12-1products_solution.xml tab in Notepad++.
- Click line 3, then press the ENTER key once.
- On line 4, type `<?xml-stylesheet type="text/xsl" href="chapter12-1products_solution.xsl"?>` to enter the code to link the XSL style sheet to the XML document, then press the ENTER key once (Figure 12–27).

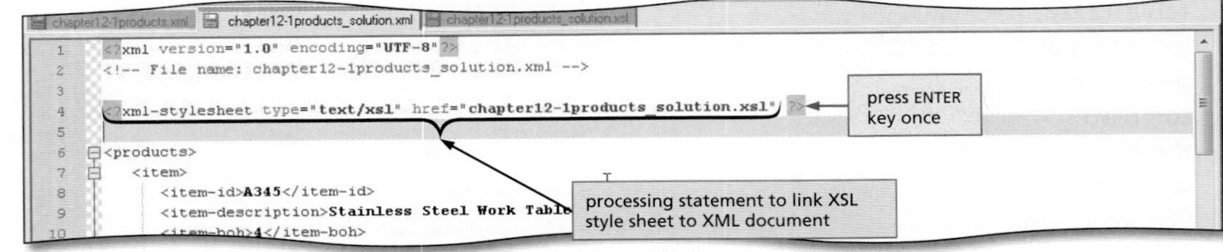

Figure 12–27

To Save and Test an XML Document Formatted Using an XSL Style Sheet

Once the XSL style sheet is complete and the processing instruction is added to the XML document, you should save and test the XML document in a browser. The following step saves and tests the XML document formatted using an XSL style sheet.

- Save the chapter12-1products_solution.xml file.
- Activate the browser.
- Click the Address bar.
- Type `G:\Chapter12\ChapterFiles\chapter12-1products_solution.xml`, and then press the ENTER key to display the XML document formatted by the XSL style sheet in item-description order (Figure 12–28).

Q&A What should I do if there is an error?

Check your code against Figures 12–25 and 12–26, save the XSL file, and then refresh the browser display.

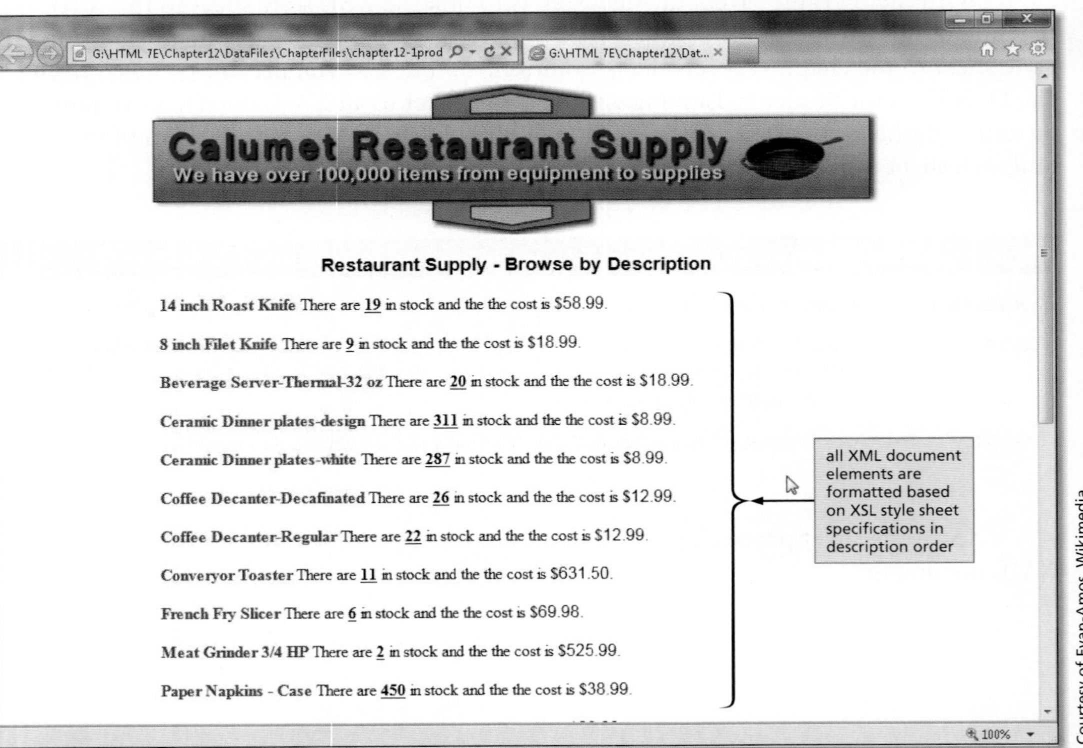

Courtesy of Evan-Amos, Wikimedia

Figure 12–28

To Close the XML and XSL Files in Notepad++

Once the XSL style sheet is complete and the XML file displays properly, you should close the XSL and the XML files in Notepad++. The following steps close the open files in Notepad++.

1. With the Notepad++ window active, right-click the chapter12-1products_solution.xml file tab, and click Close on the shortcut menu.
2. Right-click the chapter12-1products.xml file tab and click Close on the shortcut menu.
3. Close the chapter12-1products_solution.xsl file.

Plan Ahead

Displaying XML data in an HTML table.
Long lists of data can be tedious to look at. Dividing a list into manageable pages using a table can make the data easier to read. To plan a table:

- Determine the number of rows to display on each Web page.
- Determine the ID names to associate the objects properly with the table.
- Create the navigation control buttons for the table.
- Determine any style formatting for the data in the table.

Using an HTML Table with Paging to Display XML Data

The second hyperlink on the Calumet Restaurant Supply home page (Figure 12–1c on page HTML 563) is Table. This Web page displays a list of available product items in a table in item-id order (Figure 12–29) using the XML file as a data island. Recall that a data island is a set of data elements separate from the HTML Web page. The HTML Web page binds with the XML document and displays each record element in an HTML table. In Internet Explorer, the <table> tag has a nonstandard attribute, datapagesize, which dictates the number of rows that can be displayed. This attribute works only in Internet Explorer. The Web page has four buttons that use built-in browser functions, allowing users to navigate forward and backward through the table rows or to move to the first or last page.

BTW

Linking XML Data Island File
When using this method to create an XML data island, the XML file should not have any links to XSL style sheets nor should the root element have a link to any XSD schema file.

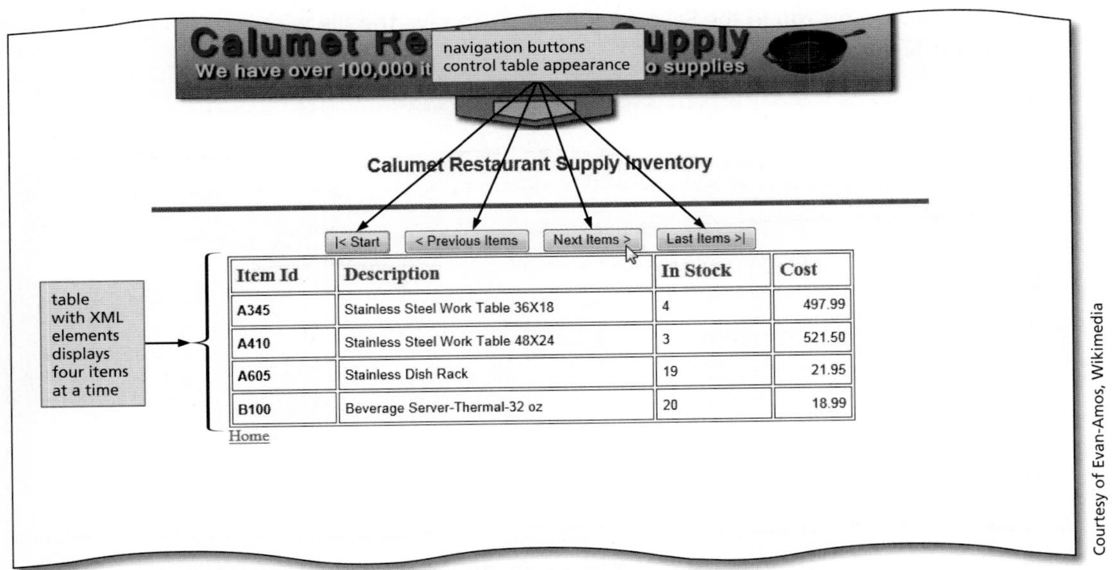

Courtesy of Evan-Amos, Wikimedia

Figure 12–29

BTW
Data Binding
Data binding consists of four major pieces: the data source object (DSO), data consumers, the binding agent, and the table repetition agent.

Linking an XML document to an HTML Web page requires the use of the HTML element <xml> to create a data island. The <xml> tag also works only in Internet Explorer. A unique name represents the data island in the XML element, called a **data source object (dso)**. Table 12–30 shows the general form of the <xml> element. Because the <xml> tag is unique to Internet Explorer, this HTML Web page will not validate properly from the w3.org validation page.

Table 12–30 General Form of the HTML <xml> Element

General form:	<xml id="name" src="URL"></xml>
Comment:	The <xml> element is a Microsoft extension and may not be recognized by browsers other than Internet Explorer. The id attribute value, *name*, must be a unique name, and it must represent the data source. Web developers use the prefix **dso** before any name value to indicate that it is the data source object. The *URL* is the location and name of the XML data file. The <xml> element must have an end element.
Example:	<xml id="dsoTableList" src="chapter12-1product_id.xml"></xml>

BTW
The <xml> Tag and Validation
The <xml> tag is unique to Internet Explorer. This tag is what links or binds an XML document to the Web page. This tag is not recognized by other browsers, so when validating the HTML pages, this tag will be identified as invalid.

When the browser opens the HTML Web page, the XML parser reads and parses the XML data. The browser then creates a data island or data source object (dso), which handles and manipulates the XML data as a recordset. A **recordset** is a collection of data records and their fields. The Internet Explorer browser also contains several built-in methods, properties, and events that are automatically associated with the recordset.

To Create an HTML Document to Display XML Data in a Table

The following steps create the HTML document to display the XML data in a table.

1. Activate the open Notepad++ window.
2. With a USB drive plugged into your computer, open the file chapter12-1table.html from the Chapter12\ChapterFiles folder.
3. Click File on the menu bar, and then click Save As.
4. Type `chapter12-1table_solution.html` in the File name text box.
5. Click the Save button in the Save As dialog box to save the file with a new name (Figure 12–30).

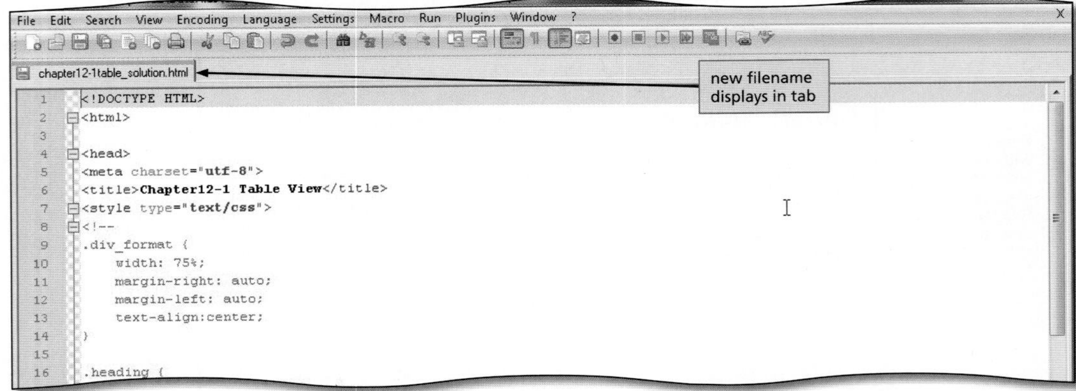

Figure 12–30

To Enter Code to Link an XML Document with an HTML Web Page

Because embedding the binding tags for an XSD or XSL file prevents the HTML table from reading the XML file, this section will use a different XML file provided in the Data Files for Students, chapter12-1product_id.xml. This file is in item-id order. The following step binds this XML file with an HTML Web page.

1

- With the chapter12-1table_solution.html Notepad++ window active, click line 3.
- Type `<xml id="dsoTableList" src="chapter12-1product_id.xml"></xml>` to link the XML document to the HTML Web page. Do not press the ENTER key (Figure 12–31).

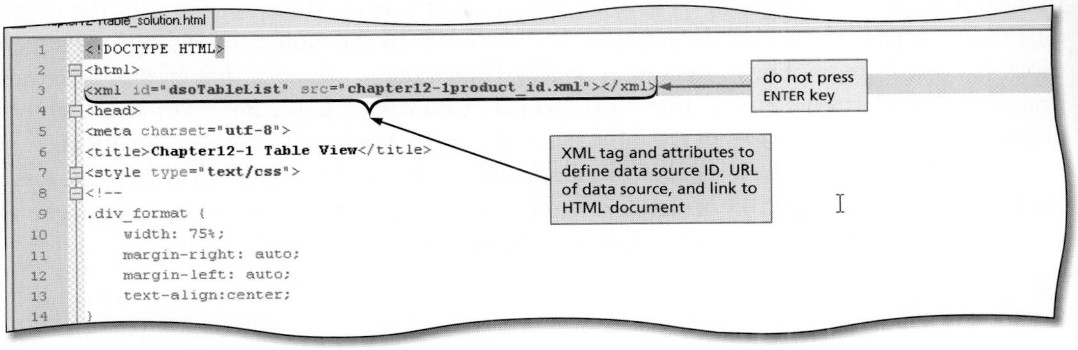

do not press ENTER key

XML tag and attributes to define data source ID, URL of data source, and link to HTML document

Figure 12–31

Adding Navigation Controls

The next step is to enter code to add the four navigation buttons that allow a user to manipulate the number of records that display on the HTML Web page. Each of the four buttons calls an element method that will display the records in the table. Table 12–31 lists four table element methods.

Table 12–31 Table Element Methods

Method	Action	Example Code
firstPage	Displays the first page of records	TableName.firstPage()
previousPage	Displays the previous page of records	TableName.previousPage()
nextPage	Displays the next page of records	TableName.nextPage()
lastPage	Displays the last page of records	TableName.lastPage()

To Enter Code to Add Navigation Buttons

The buttons used to navigate through the records are standard HTML <form> buttons, but are entered without a form. When a user clicks a button, the onClick event handler calls the associated built-in method. Table 12–32 shows the code to add the navigation buttons to the HTML Web page.

Table 12–32 Code for Adding Navigation Buttons

Line	Code
53	`<button type="button" onClick="inventoryStock.firstPage()">|< Start </button>  `
54	`<button type="button" onClick="inventoryStock.previousPage()">< Previous Items </button>  `
55	`<button type="button" onClick="inventoryStock.nextPage()"> Next Items > </button>  `
56	`<button type="button" onClick="inventoryStock.lastPage()"> Last Items >| </button>`

The inventoryStock object in each line associates the onClick event handlers for each button to the <table> tag, which will have an id attribute inventoryStock that will be entered in a later step.

Line 53 creates the Start button with the caption |< Start. The code < is an ASCII character reference that creates a less-than symbol (<), or angle bracket, on the button caption. The Start button calls the firstPage() method, which tells the Web page to display the first set of records in the table. The code,   , is an ASCII character reference that represents the two spaces that separate the buttons. Line 54 creates the Previous Items button with the caption, < Previous Items. The Previous Items button calls the previousPage() method, which tells the Web page to display the previous set of records in the table. Line 55 creates the Next Items button with the caption, Next Items >. The > code is an ASCII character reference that creates a greater-than symbol (>), or angle bracket, on the button caption. The Next Items button calls the nextPage() method, which tells the Web page to display the next set of records in the table. Line 56 creates the Last Items button with the caption, Last Items >|. The Last Items button calls the lastPage() method, which tells the Web page to display the last set of records in the table. Each button uses the ASCII character reference,   , to place spaces between the buttons.

The following step adds the navigation buttons to the HTML Web page.

- Click line 53.
- Enter the code shown in Table 12–32 on the previous page and do not press the ENTER key after line 56 (Figure 12–32).

```
31
32 table {
33     margin-left: auto;
34     margin-right: auto;
35     width: 60%;
36     border: 1px solid black;
37 }
38
39 td {
40     border: 1px solid black;
41     padding: 5px;
42 }
43
44 -->
45 </style>
46 </head>
47 <body>
48 <div class="div_format"><img border="0" src="chapter12-1banner.gif" alt="banner" /></div>
49 <p class="heading">Calumet Restaurant Supply Inventory </p>
50 <p class="div_format"><img src="browndivider.jpg" width="750" height="5" alt="divider" /></p>
51 </div>
52 <div class="div_format">
53   <button type="button" onClick="inventoryStock.firstPage()">|&lt; Start </button>  
54   <button type="button" onClick="inventoryStock.previousPage()">&lt; Previous Items </button>  
55   <button type="button" onClick="inventoryStock.nextPage()"> Next Items &gt; </button>  
56   <button type="button" onClick="inventoryStock.lastPage()"> Last Items &gt;| </button>
57 </div>
58
59 <div style="margin-left:20%;"><a href="chapter12-1homesolution.html">Home</a></div>
60 </body>
61
```

code for navigation buttons with built-in meth

do not press ENTER key

Figure 12–32

To Enter <table> Table Header and Row Tags

Table 12–33 shows the <table> tag and the attributes needed to indicate the width of the table, indicate the number of rows to be displayed, and bind the data source object. The code in Table 12–33 includes the table heading <thead> and the individual column heading names.

Table 12–33 Code for <table> and Table Header and Row Tags

Line	Code
59	<table datapagesize="4"id="inventoryStock" datasrc="#dsoTableList" >
60	<thead>
61	<tr>
62	<th>Item Id</th>

Table 12–33 Code for <table> and Table Header and Row Tags (continued)

Line	Code
63	<th>Description</th>
64	<th>In Stock</th>
65	<th>Cost</th>
66	</tr>
67	</thead>

Line 59 starts the table definition with the <table> tag and includes an id attribute to name the table, inventoryStock, which relates to the onClick event handler for the buttons and built-in functions. The datasrc attribute must match the name of the data source object defined in the <xml> element on line 3 and be preceded by a pound sign (#) to read: #dsoTableList. The datapagesize attribute sets the size of the page to 4, so the table will displayed four records or rows at a time. Line 60 starts the table header with the <thead> tag. The header is a single row indicated in line 61 with the <tr> tag. Lines 62 to 65 contain the text for the column headings with the <th> tags. Line 66 closes the row tag </tr> and line 67 closes the header with the </thead> tag. The border and cellpadding attributes for the table are defined in the embedded style sheet. The following step starts the HTML table.

- Click line 58, press the ENTER key once.
- On line 59, enter the code shown in Table 12–33 to create the table header and press the ENTER key once after line 67 (Figure 12–33).

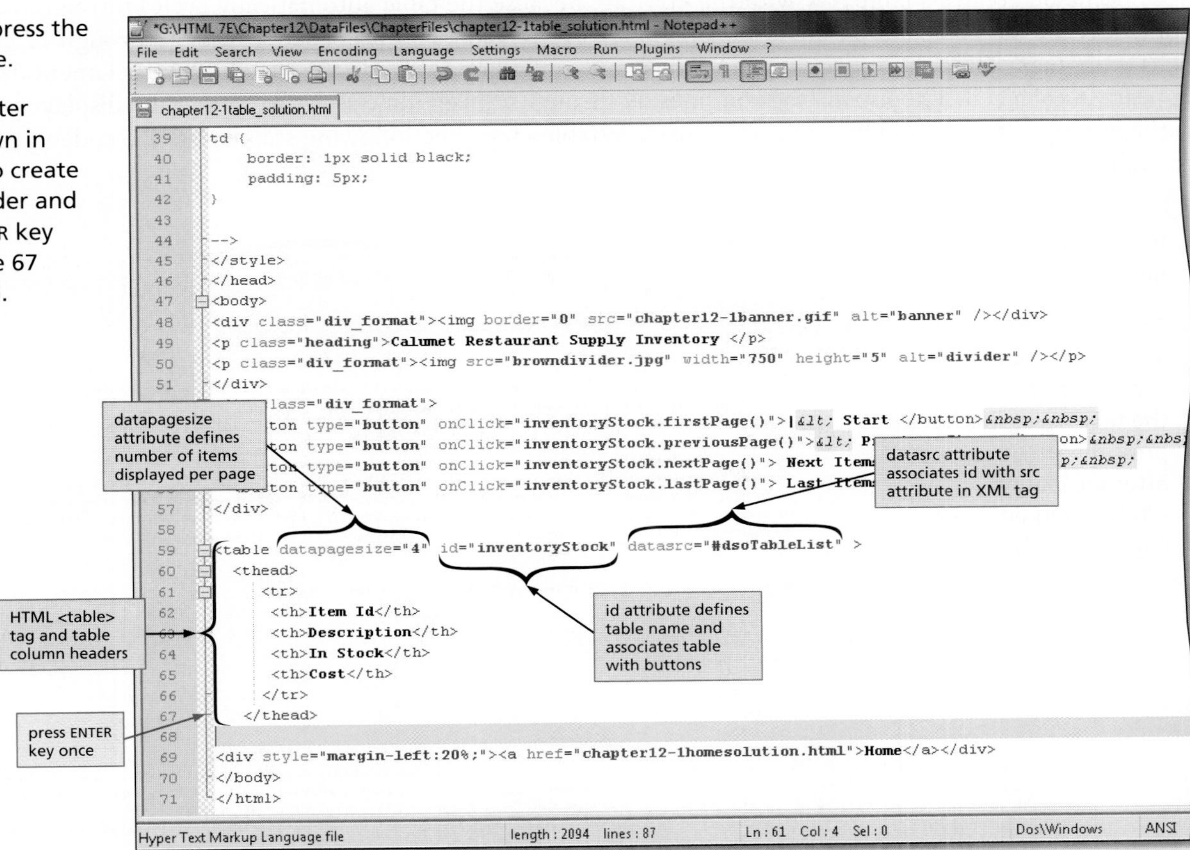

Figure 12–33

To Enter <tr> Tags and Attribute Values to Bind XML Elements to a Table

Table 12–34 shows the code to complete the table that will display each row of data. The table contains one row and five cells of data. The <span> tag and the datafld attribute identify the XML element value to be displayed in each cell. Inline styles format the contents of the cells.

Table 12–34 Code for <tr> Tags and Attributes to Bind the XML Elements to the HTML Table

Line	Code
68	`<tr>`
69	`<td><span datafld="item-id" style="font-family:arial; font-size: 10pt; font-weight:bold"></span></td>`
70	`<td><span datafld="item-description" style="font-family:arial; font-size: 10pt"></span></td>`
71	`<td><span datafld="item-boh" style="font-family:arial; font-size: 10pt"></span></td>`
72	`<td style="text-align:right"><span datafld="item-cost" style="font-family:arial; font-size: 10pt"></span></td>`
73	`</tr>`
74	`</table>`

Line 68 creates a table row with the <tr> tag. Because the table automatically cycles through the data and is controlled by the datapagesize attribute, only one HTML table row is needed. Lines 69 through 72 create table data cells (<td> tags) using the <span> tags and the datafld attribute to define the specific XML element data value that appears in each cell. The <span> tags on lines 69 through 72 use inline styles to format the displayed values. Line 73 is the closing </tr> tag and line 74 is the closing </table> tag. The following step enters the code to complete the table.

- If necessary, click line 68.
- Enter the code shown in Table 12–34 to bind the XML elements to the table rows. Do not press the ENTER key after the closing </table> tag on line 74 (Figure 12–34).

```
45  </style>
46  </head>
47  <body>
48  <div class="div_format"><img border="0" src="chapter12-1banner.gif" alt="banner" /></div>
49  <p class="heading">Calumet Restaurant Supply Inventory </p>
50  <p class="div_format"><img src="browndivider.jpg" width="750" height="5" alt="divider" /></p>
51  </div>
52  <div class="div_format">
53    <button type="button" onClick="inventoryStock.firstPage()">|&lt; Start </button>  
54    <button type="button" onClick="inventoryStock.previousPage()">&lt; Previous Items </button>  
55    <button type="button" onClick="inventoryStock.nextPage()"> Next Items &gt; </button>  
56    <button type="button" onClick="inventoryStock.lastPage()"> Last Items &gt;| </button>
57  </div>
58
59  <table datapagesize="4" id="inventoryStock" datasrc="#dsoTableList" >
60    <thead>
61      <tr>
62        <th>Item Id</th>
63        <th>Description</th>
64        <th>In Stock</th>
65        <th>Cost</th>
66      </tr>
67    </thead>
68    <tr>
69       <td><span datafld="item-id" style="font-family:arial; font-size: 10pt; font-weight:bold"></span></td>
70       <td><span datafld="item-description" style="font-family:arial; font-size: 10pt"></span></td>
71       <td><span datafld="item-boh" style="font-family:arial; font-size: 10pt"></span></td>
72       <td style="text-align:right"><span datafld="item-cost" style="font-family:arial; font-size: 10pt"
         ></span></td>
73    </tr>
74  </table>
75  <div style="margin-          href="chapter12-1homesolution.html">Home</a></div>
76  </body>
```


Figure 12–34

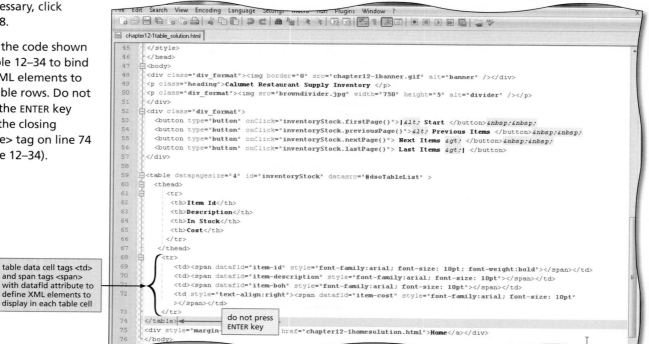

To Save the HTML File and Test the Web Page

With the Web page complete, you should save and test the HTML code.

1

- With the USB drive plugged into your computer, save the file. Close the chapter12-1table_solution.html file but leave Notepad++ open.
- Activate your browser. If necessary, maximize the window.
- Type `G:\Chapter12\ChapterFiles\chapter12-1table_solution.html` in the Address bar and then press the ENTER key.
- If a security message appears, click the 'Allow blocked content' button. (If you are running Internet Explorer 8 or lower, your security message may be different.)
- Click the Next Items button (Figure 12–35).
- Click the Start button and then click the Last Items button to scroll through the table.

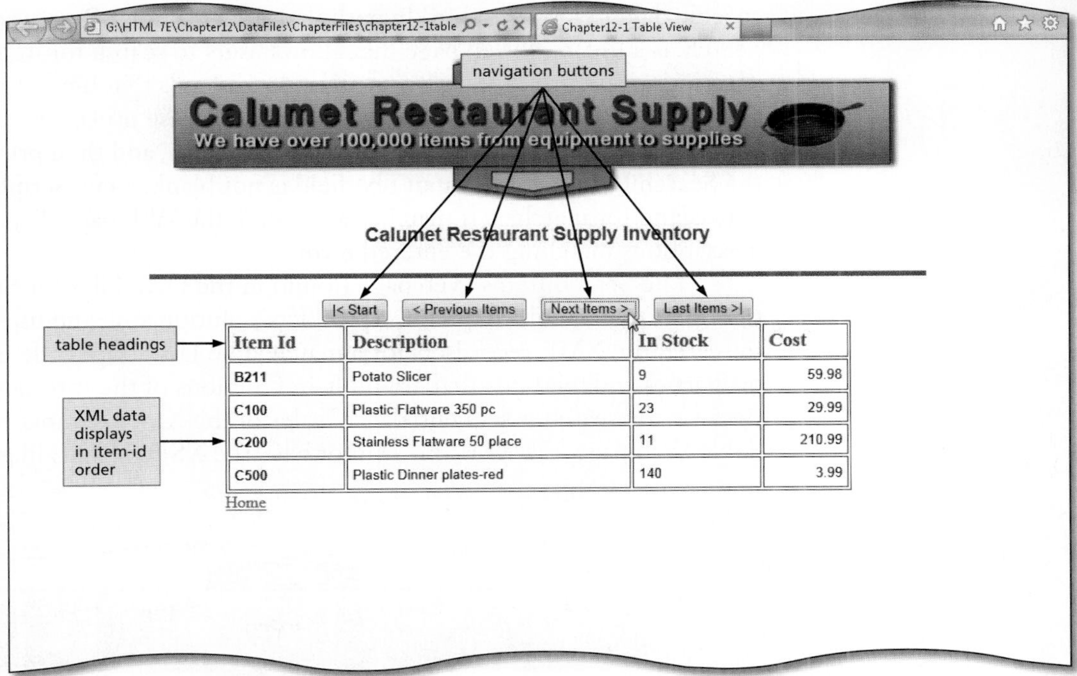

Figure 12–35

Courtesy of Evan-Amos, Wikimedia

Q&A

No JavaScript was actually entered into this HTML code. Where is the function that is associated with the buttons?

The firstPage(), nextPage(), previousPage(), and lastPage() functions are built into the Internet Explorer browser. These codes will not work with other browsers such as Firefox.

Plan Ahead

Creating an HTML document to search an XML document and display results.

The JavaScript code to search for product items by description has four key components that you will create:

- The HTML element <xml> to create a data island
- An input text box and Search command button
- A <div> tag with an id attribute to identify the output area on the Web page
- A JavaScript function to search through the recordset until it finds a match between the text box input value and the corresponding XML data element

After adding the four key elements, you will need to do the following:

- Bind the XML document to the HTML so the JavaScript user-defined function can find the data.
- Add a form text field for input.
- Add a button to activate the search.
- Determine the output display area and format.

Using JavaScript to Search an XML Document and Display Results on a Web Page

A common use for an XML data island is providing a mechanism for users to search for specific data items. The third hyperlink on the Calumet Restaurant Supply home page, Search, is a link to a Web page that allows users to search for items using any part of the description (Figure 12–36). By creating data islands that bind with a Web page, a user can view records without conflicting with other database processes. This Web page allows users to enter a description or part of a description, and then press the ENTER key or click the Search button. If the input text field is not blank, a JavaScript function searches the data island for matches. If matches are found, the Web page displays all the items with descriptions matching the entered term.

The Search Items Web page (found in the Data Files for Students) is bound to the XML document, chapter12-1products_solution.xml, and uses a JavaScript function to search the XML recordsets for a match. The JavaScript code uses data source object properties and methods that are built-in functions of the Internet Explorer browser. Because the search is sequential, the order of the XML is immaterial; however, as with the Table Web page, the XML file cannot have the XSD or XSL files bound to it.

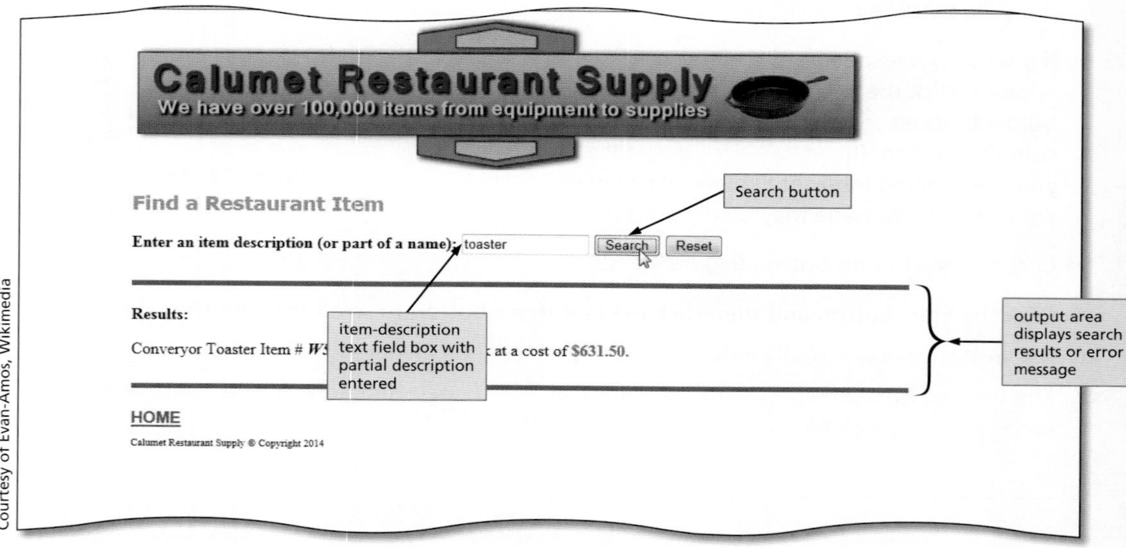

Figure 12–36

To Open an HTML Document and Save It with a New Name

The following steps open the HTML Web page that allows users to search an XML document and view the results, and save the document with a new name.

1. If necessary, click the Notepad++ button on the taskbar to activate the Notepad++ window.
2. With the USB drive plugged into your computer, open chapter12-1search-items.html, from the Chapter12\ChapterFiles folder.
3. Save the file as `chapter12-1search-items_solution.html`.

To Enter Code to Bind an XML Document with an HTML Web Page

To allow a user to search the XML document using the search function on this Web page, the XML document chapter12-1products_solution.xml must be bound to the HTML Web page by first linking the XML document to the HTML Web page and then binding the XML document with the HTML Web page. The following step enters the code that links the XML document, chapter12-1products_solution.xml, with the HTML Web page.

1

- With the chapter12search-items_solution.html Notepad++ window active, click line 3.
- Type `<xml id="dsoInventory" src="chapter12-1products_solution.xml"></xml>`, but do not press the ENTER key, to bind the XML document with the HTML code (Figure 12–37).

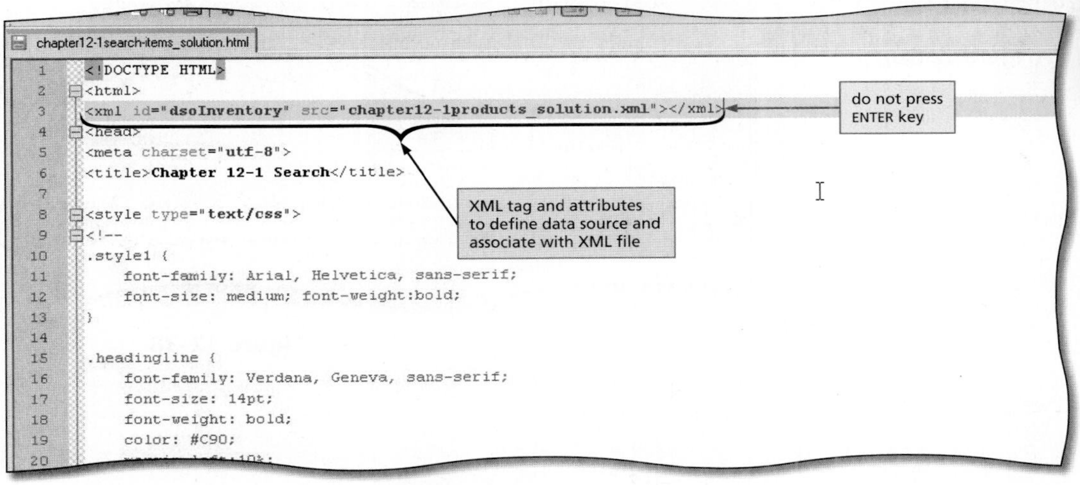

chapter12-1search-items_solution.html

```
1  <!DOCTYPE HTML>
2  <html>
3  <xml id="dsoInventory" src="chapter12-1products_solution.xml"></xml>
4  <head>
5  <meta charset="utf-8">
6  <title>Chapter 12-1 Search</title>
7
8  <style type="text/css">
9  <!--
10 .style1 {
11     font-family: Arial, Helvetica, sans-serif;
12     font-size: medium; font-weight:bold;
13 }
14
15 .headingline {
16     font-family: Verdana, Geneva, sans-serif;
17     font-size: 14pt;
18     font-weight: bold;
19     color: #C90;
```

do not press ENTER key

XML tag and attributes to define data source and associate with XML file

Figure 12–37

To Enter Code for the <input> and <button> Elements

The next step is to add the HTML <input> and <button> elements to create the input text box and Search and Reset command buttons. The code for the <input> and <button> element is shown in Table 12–35.

Table 12–35 Code for <input> and <button> Elements with onKeyPress and onClick Event Handlers

Line	Code
39	`<input type="text" id="SearchText" size="15" onKeyPress="keyPressed()"/>`
40	`<button type="button" onClick="findItem()">Search</button>`
41	`<button type="button" onClick="clearField()">Reset</button></p>`

Line 39 defines an <input> object. The type attribute defines the object as a text field. The id attribute names the text box as SearchText, which becomes an object that the user-defined JavaScript function uses to access the input characters. The size attribute sets the width of the text field to 15 characters. The onKeyPress event handler calls the keyPressed() user-defined function every time a user presses a key. The keyPressed() user-defined function calls the findItem() user-defined function if the ENTER key has been pressed.

Line 40 defines a button with a caption of Search. The onClick event handler calls the user-defined JavaScript function findItem() if the user clicks the Search button. Line 41 defines a button with a caption of Reset. This button is not a normal <form> Reset button and needs the onClick event handler that calls the user-defined JavaScript function clearField() when the user clicks the button. This function clears the text field and the output area of any listings or error messages.

The following step enters the code for the <input> and <button> elements to the Web page.

- Click line 39.
- Enter the code in Table 12–35 on the previous page. Do not press the ENTER key after line 41 (Figure 12–38).

```
33  <body>
34  <div style="margin-left:8%">
35    <span style="text-align:center"><img bor...2-1banner.gif" alt="banner" width="750" height="150"
      ></span>
36  </div>
37  <p class="headingline">Find a Restaurant Item </p>
38  <p class="prompt_text">Enter an item description (or part of a name):
39    <input type="text" id="SearchText" size="15" onKeyPress="keyPressed()">
40    <button type="button" onClick="findItem()">Search</button>
41    <button type="button" onClick="clearField()">Reset</button></p>
42  <p style="margin-left:10%">
43     <img border="0" src="browndivider.jpg" alt="divider" width="750" height="5">
44  </p>
45  <p class="prompt_text">R...
46
47  <p style="margin-left:10...
48     <img border="0" src="browndivider.jpg" alt="divider" width="750" height="5">
49  </p>
50  <p style="font-size: x-small; margin-left:10%"><span class="style1"><a href="chapter12-1homesolution.html">HOME</a>
    </span></p>
51  <p style="font-size: x-small; margin-left:10%">Calumet Restaurant Supply &copy; Copyright 2014</p>
52  </body>
53  </html>
```

id defines text field box for use as JavaScript object

defines button captions

do not press ENTER key

onKeyPress event handler called to test if ENTER key pressed

Figure 12–38

To Enter an HTML <div> Tag Container

The next step is to add the <div> tag container to define an output area of the Web page where search results will appear. Recall from Chapter 9 the use of the <div> tag container and the innerHTML property. To create the dynamic output area for the search results, the <div> tag uses the id attribute and value, SearchResult, to indicate that search results will be displayed in that area. The JavaScript user-defined function uses that id value to assign the search results to the output area of the Web page. An inline style attribute sets the left margin at a relative distance of 10% of the screen width, so the results are aligned with the input text field. The following step enters the <div> element to define the output area of the Web page.

- Click line 46.
- Type `<div id="SearchResult" style="margin-left:10%">` and press the ENTER key.
- On line 47, type `</div>` and do not press the ENTER key (Figure 12–39).

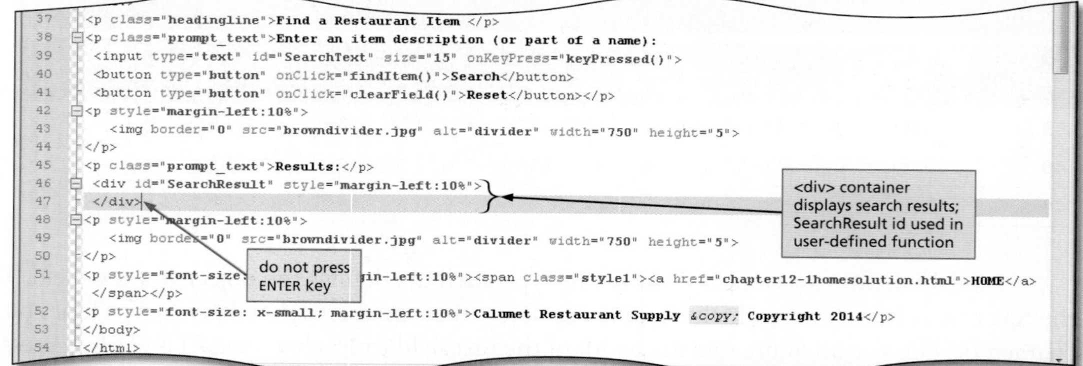

Figure 12–39

Q&A Why is the margin-left set to 10% and not a specific number of pixels?

By using a percent value, the left margin will always be 10% from the left regardless of the screen resolution. If it was set to a specific number of pixels, it might look too small or too large at different resolutions.

Plan Ahead

Writing the user-defined function findItem().

The user-defined function, findItem(), uses a combination of standard document object model (DOM) objects, properties, and methods and Internet Explorer's built-in XML parser methods to find inventory items by item description in the XML document. The findItem() function will accomplish the following activities to complete this action:

1. Convert the text field (search) input value character data to uppercase characters.
2. Validate that the input value is not blank or a noncharacter value.
3. Move to the first record in the XML document.
4. Compare each element in the XML document with the text box value until a match is found.
5. Construct an output text string with search results.

Creating the JavaScript User-Defined Functions, findItem() and keyPressed()

The next step is to create the JavaScript user-defined function that takes a target value from the input search text box and compares it with the <item-description> elements in the XML document, chapter12-1products_solution.xml.

With the XML document linked to the chapter12-1 search-items_solution.html Web page, the next step is to add the JavaScript user-defined functions, findItem() and keyPressed(), to the HTML document. The findItem() function is called when a user clicks the Submit button. The keyPressed() function is called with every key pressed by the user and tests if the user pressed the ENTER key on the keyboard by comparing the key to ASCII value 13, which represents the ENTER key. If the ENTER key was pressed, the findItem() function is called.

To Enter Code for the findItem() User-Defined Function

The code to begin the JavaScript section and create the findItem() user-defined function is shown in Table 12–36.

Table 12–36 Code to Begin the JavaScript Section and Create the findItem() Function

<table>
<tr><th>Line</th><th>Code</th></tr>
<tr><td>7</td><td><script type="text/javascript"></td></tr>
<tr><td>8</td><td><!--Hide from old browsers</td></tr>
<tr><td>9</td><td>function findItem() {</td></tr>
<tr><td>10</td><td>SearchString=SearchText.value.toUpperCase()</td></tr>
<tr><td>11</td><td>if ((SearchString=="") || (SearchString==" ")) {</td></tr>
<tr><td>12</td><td>SearchResult.innerHTML="<Please enter a valid description.>"</td></tr>
<tr><td>13</td><td>return</td></tr>
<tr><td>14</td><td>}</td></tr>
</table>

Lines 7 and 8 start the JavaScript <script> section. Line 9 defines the findItem() user-defined function. Line 10 converts the SearchText text field value to uppercase characters using the toUpperCase() method. Line 11 is a standard if statement to determine if the resulting SearchString value is blank or null. If the string is blank or null, the code on line 12 assigns a message to the contents to <div> area innerHTML property. The return statement on line 13 stops the search and displays the error message. The brace on line 14 closes the if statement.

The following step enters the statements to convert the text field to uppercase characters and test for blank or null values in the findItem() user-defined function.

- Click line 7.
- Enter the code shown in Table 12–36 on the previous page and then press the ENTER key after line 14 to enter the findItem() user-defined function (Figure 12–40).

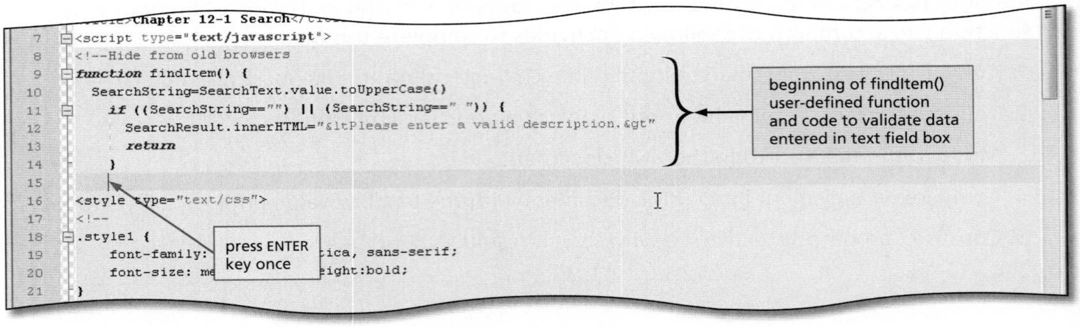

beginning of findItem() user-defined function and code to validate data entered in text field box

press ENTER key once

Figure 12–40

Searching the Recordset Values and Outputting Results

After testing that the SearchText text field input value is not blank or null, the findItem() user-defined function sequentially searches through the data in the linked XML document, chapter12-1products_solution.xml, to find a match for the text box input value. The search uses the data source object, dsoInventory, and Internet Explorer's built-in methods to move through the records in the XML document. If a match is found, the function creates a results message that incorporates specific XML elements in the HTML string. Table 12–37 shows the JavaScript code that sequentially searches the XML document and creates the results message to be displayed in the output area.

Table 12–37 Code for Searching the Recordset Values and Building the Output String

Line	Code
15	`dsoInventory.recordset.moveFirst()`
16	`var outputResult=""`
17	`while (!dsoInventory.recordset.EOF) {`
18	`itemString=dsoInventory.recordset("item-description").value.toUpperCase()`
19	`if (itemString.indexOf(SearchString)>=0)`
20	`outputResult+=dsoInventory.recordset("item-description")`
21	`+" Item # <span style='font-style:italic; font-weight:bold;'>" + dsoInventory.recordset("item-id")`
22	`+ ". We have </span> "`
23	`+ dsoInventory.recordset("item-boh")`
24	`+ " in stock at a cost of <span style='font-weight:bold; color:#cc0000;'>$"`
25	`+ dsoInventory.recordset("item-cost") + ".</span><p></p>"`
26	`dsoInventory.recordset.moveNext();`
27	`}`

Recall that a recordset is a collection of data records. The built-in moveFirst() method on line 15 positions an internal pointer to the first record in the recordset of the data source object, dsoInventory. Line 16 initializes an output variable, outputResult, to a null value. Line 17 starts a while processing loop. As you learned in Chapter 10, the while loop relies on a conditional statement to terminate. In this function, the while loop processes each record until the EOF property is true. **EOF** means end of file and signals that all XML document records have been read.

Line 18 assigns the values of the <item-description> element to the itemString variable of the current record. To determine if the value in the SearchString matches any part of the search text, the if statement in line 19 uses the indexOf() method to look for SearchString value in itemString. Recall from Chapter 10 that the indexOf() method returns the relative location of the value found. If the returned value is greater than or equal to 0, indicating a match was found, lines 20 through 25 construct an output value concatenating the various elements and descriptive text together. This method is used to allow this script to be changed easily and adapt to searching any text string.

The <p></p> tags at the end of line 25 ensure that each outputResult string will appear on a separate line in the output area of the Web page. To read each of the records in the recordset, line 26 uses the built-in moveNext() method to tell the function to read the next record in the XML document. Line 27 closes the while loop.

To Enter Code to Search the Recordset Values and Build the Output String

The following step enters the code to search the chapter12-1products_solution XML file for items using all or part of the description.

1

- If necessary, click line 15.
- Enter the code shown in Table 12–37 to search the recordset values and build the output string. Press the ENTER key after line 27 (Figure 12–41).

Q&A Why isn't there a bracket ({) after the if statement on line 19?

Normally, in JavaScript you cannot break statements in the middle of a line. The expression at line 20 is one exception because an expression statement can be broken at places like operands. Recall that if an if statement has only one statement after the condition, no brace is needed to set a block of code. In this case lines from 20 to 25 are treated as one JavaScript expression.

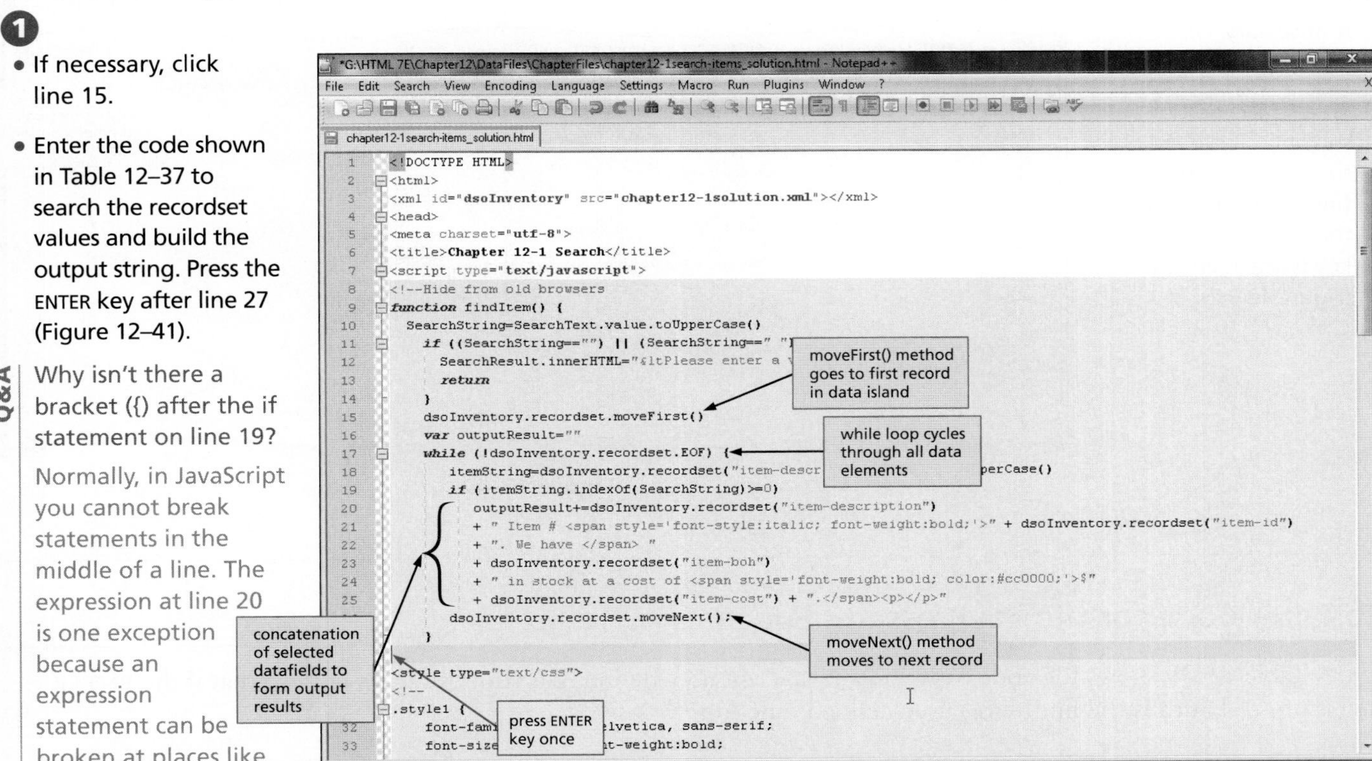

Figure 12–41

To Enter Code to Complete the findItem() Function

The next step is to test if the outputResult string has any content. If not, then a message to tell the users no results were found is assigned to the SearchResult.innerHTML object. Table 12–38 shows the code for building the no result found message.

Table 12–38 Completing the findItem() Function

Line	Code
28	`if (outputResult=="")`
29	`SearchResult.innerHTML="<Sorry, that description was not found, please modify and try again.>";`
30	`else`
31	`SearchResult.innerHTML=outputResult`
32	`}`

Line 28 tests the outputResult variable. If the outputResult is blank because no match was found on line 18, then line 29 assigns a message to the SearchResult.innerHTML property that no record was found. If a match is found, the else portion of the if...else statement on line 31 displays the outputResult results message constructed on lines 20 through 25 using the innerHTML property. Line 32 ends the user-defined function. The following step completes the findItem() function.

- If necessary, click line 28.
- Enter the code shown in Table 12–38 to complete the findItem() function and then press the ENTER key twice at line 32 (Figure 12–42).

```
19        if (itemString.indexOf(SearchString)>=0)
20          outputResult+=dsoInventory.recordset("item-description")
21          + " Item # <span style='font-style:italic; font-weight:bold;'>" + dsoInventory.recordset("item-id")
22          + ". We have </span> "
23          + dsoInventory.recordset("item-boh")
24          + " in stock at a cost of <span style='font-weight:bold; color:#cc0000;'>$"
25          + dsoInventory.recordset("item-cost") + ".</span><p></p>"
26        dsoInventory.recordset.moveNext();
27      }
28      if (outputResult=="")
29        SearchResult.innerHTML="&ltSorry, that description was not found, please modify and try again.&gt;";
30      else
31        SearchResult.innerHTML=outputResult
32  }
33
34
35  <style                s">
36  <!--
37  .style1 {
38      font-family: Arial, Helvetica, sans-serif;
39      font-size: medium; font-weight:bold;
40  }
```


Figure 12–42

To Enter Code for the keyPressed() Function

Table 12–39 shows the code to create a JavaScript user-defined function, keyPressed(), so that if the ENTER key is pressed, it calls the findItem() user-defined function.

Table 12–39 Code for the keyPressed() User-Defined Function

Line	Code
34	`function keyPressed(k) {`
35	`var hitEnter=event.keyCode`
36	`if (hitEnter==13) findItem()`
37	`}`

Line 34 declares the keyPressed() user-defined function and accepts a parameter value k, which represents the key pressed. Line 35 assigns the value of the keyCode property of the key pressed to a decimal value stored in the variable, hitEnter. The if statement on line 36 tests if the value of hitEnter is equal to an ASCII 13, which is the equivalent of the ENTER key. If hitEnter is equal to 13, meaning the ENTER key has been pressed, then the findItem() user-defined function is called. The keyPressed() function is called with every press of a key until the ENTER key is pressed. Line 37 closes the JavaScript function.

The following step enters the keyPressed() user-defined function.

- If necessary, click line 34.
- Enter the code shown in Table 12–39 to create the keyPressed() function. Press the ENTER key twice after line 37 (Figure 12–43).

```
23          + ". We have </span> "
24          + dsoInventory.recordset("item-boh")
25          + " in stock at a cost of <span style='font-weight:bold; color:#cc0000;'>$"
26          + dsoInventory.recordset("item-cost") + ".</span><p></p>"
26        dsoInventory.recordset.moveNext();
27      }
28      if (outputResult=="")
29          SearchResult.innerHTML="&ltSorry, that description was not found, please modify and try again.&gt;";
30      else
31          SearchResult.innerHTML=outputResult
32  }
33
34  function keyPressed(k) {
35      var hitEnter=event.keyCode
36      if (hitEnter==13) findItem()
37  }
38
39
40  <style t
41  <!--
```


Figure 12–43

To Enter Code for the clearField() Function

The Reset button does not automatically clear the input text field as in a normal HTML form, nor does it clear the output area of the <div> container. Table 12–40 shows the code to create a JavaScript user-defined function called clearField() that clears the input text field, clears the <div> container area, and sets the focus back in the text field.

Table 12–40 Code for the clearField() User-Defined Function

Line	Code
39	`function clearField() {`
40	`        SearchText.value = ""`
41	`        SearchResult.innerHTML = ""`
42	`        SearchText.focus()`
43	`}`
44	
45	`//-->`
46	`</script>`

Line 39 defines the clearField() user-defined function. Line 40 clears the SearchText text field. Line 41 uses the innerHTML to clear the SearchResult <div> container. Line 42 sets the focus and places the insertion point back in the SearchText text field for the next entry. Lines 45 and 46 close the HTML comment and the </script> section.

The following step enters the clearField() user-defined function.

1

- If necessary, click line 39.
- Enter the code shown in Table 12–40 on the previous page to create the clearField() function. Do not press the ENTER key after line 46 (Figure 12–44).

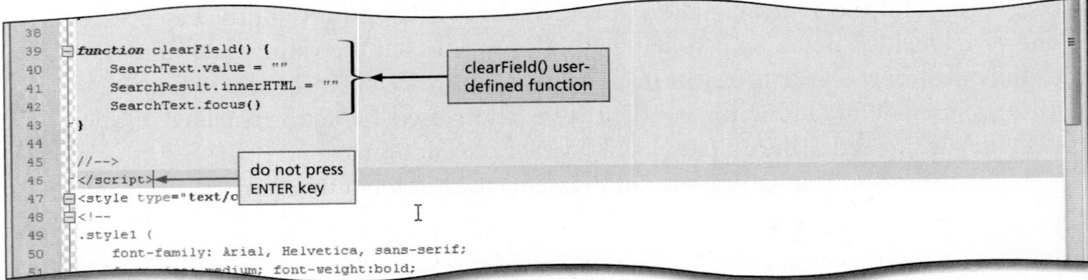

Figure 12–44

To Save and Test the HTML Document in the Browser

1

- Save your file.
- Activate the browser.
- Type `G:\Chapter12\ChapterFiles\chapter12-1search-items_solution.html` in the Address bar, and then press the ENTER key.
- If a security message appears, click the 'Allow blocked content' button. (If you are running Internet Explorer 8 or lower, your security message may be different.)

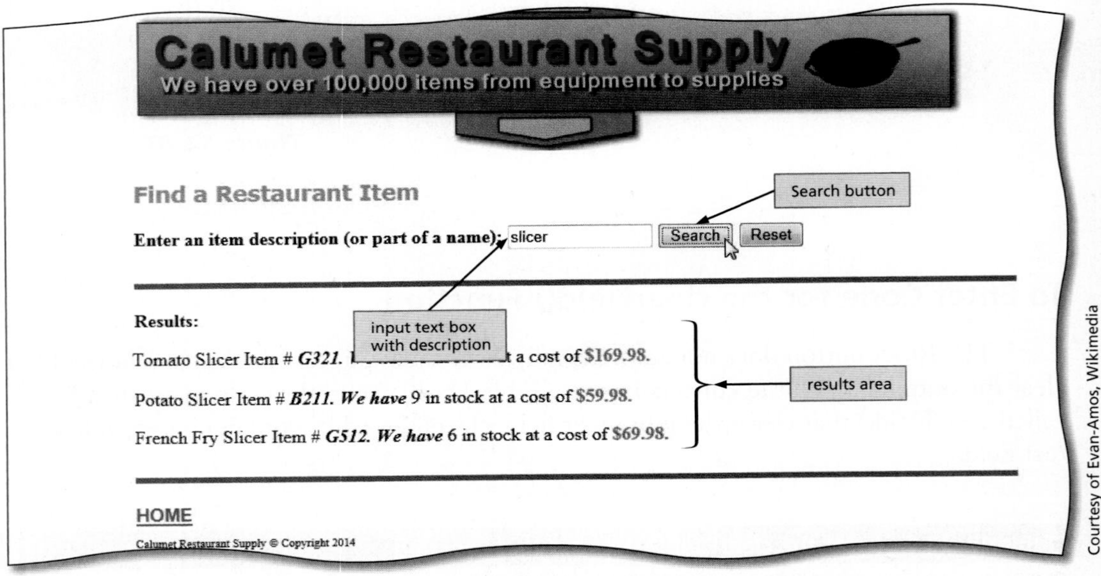

Figure 12–45

Courtesy of Evan-Amos, Wikimedia

- Enter the data values in the Description column in Table 12–41 in the input text box, and then click the Search button to test this Web page. Figure 12–45 shows how the lowercase word slicer entered for the description returns the three different types of slicers available.

Table 12–41 Search Test Data

Test Data Set	Description	Results Message
1	toaster	One conveyor toaster item should display.
2		<Please enter a valid description.>
3	oven	<Sorry, that description was not found, please modify and try again.>
4	slicer	A tomato, potato, and french fry slicer should display.

To Verify the Links on the Calumet Restaurant Supply Home page

The Calumet Restaurant Supply home page has already been created and is included in the Data Files for Students. A final test is necessary to verify that the links in the home page function correctly. The following step verifies that the links on the Calumet Restaurant Supply home page are correct.

1

- Click the Address bar. Type `G:\Chapter12\ChapterFiles\chapter12-1homesolution.html`, and then press the ENTER key.
- Click the List image hot spot link (Figure 12–46a).
- After viewing the Web page, click the Back button to return to the Calumet Restaurant Supply home page.
- Click the Table image hot spot link and then click the Next Items button twice (Figure 12–46b).
- After viewing the Web page, click the Back button or click the Home link to return to the Calumet Restaurant Supply home page.
- Click the Search image hot spot link.
- Type `stainless steel` in the search text field, and then click Search to search for items made with stainless steel (Figure 12–46c).

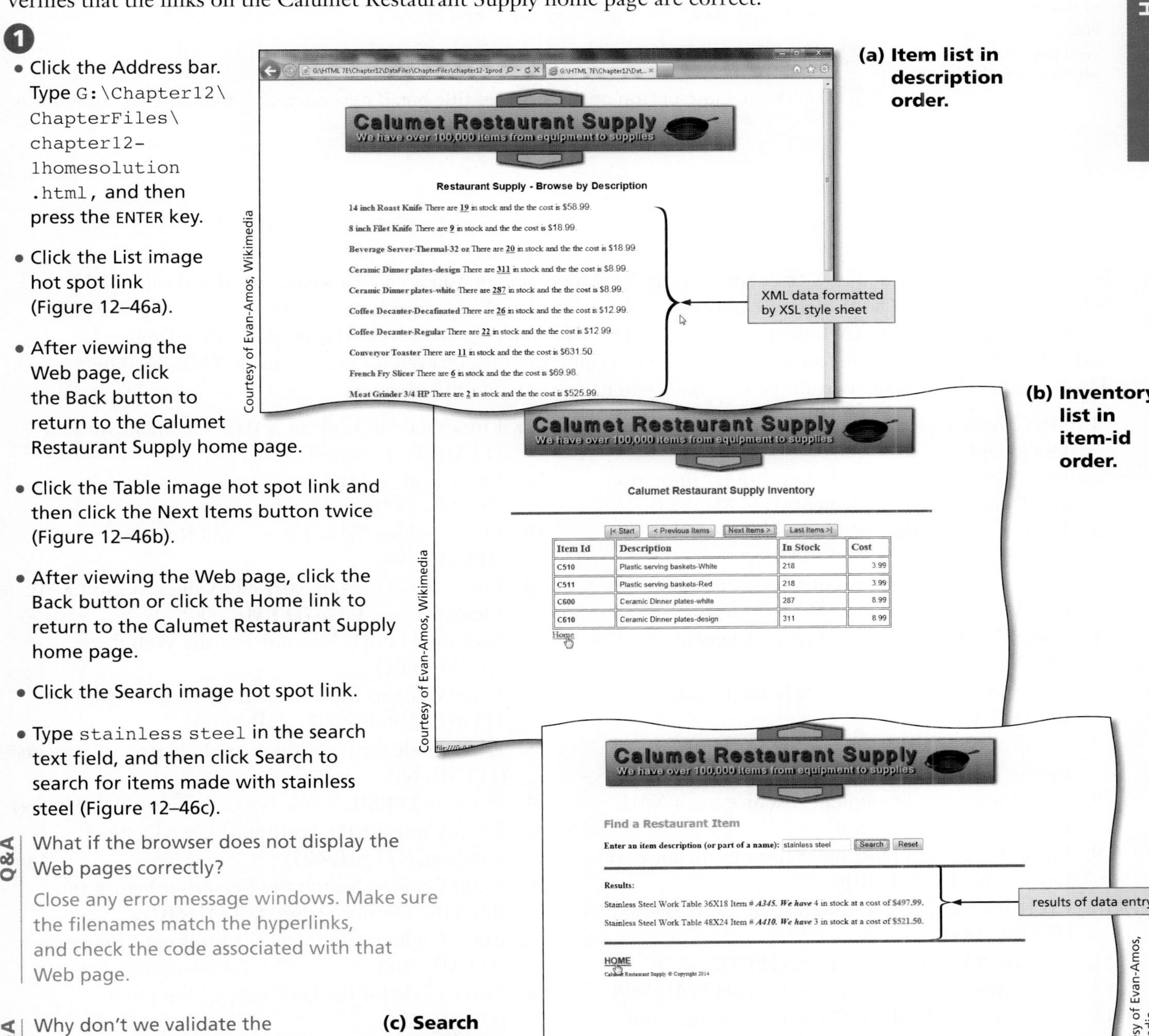

Figure 12–46

Q&A What if the browser does not display the Web pages correctly?

Close any error message windows. Make sure the filenames match the hyperlinks, and check the code associated with that Web page.

Q&A Why don't we validate the Web page at this point?

The <xml> tag is unique to Internet Explorer and therefore when you submit the HTML file to the w3.org validator, that tag will not validate. The validator also does not recognize many of the attributes associated with the <xml> tag, such as the datafld attribute in the <span> tag, resulting in numerous errors from the validator.

BTW **Quick Reference**
For more information on XML and XSL, see the XML Quick Reference (Appendix H) at the back of this book, or visit the Book Companion Site Web page for this book at www.cengagebrain.com.

To Quit Notepad++ and the Browser

After verifying that the links on the Calumet Restaurant Supply home page are correct and that the Web page is valid, close Notepad++ and your browser.

1. In Notepad++, click the File menu, then Close All.
2. Click the Close button on the Notepad++ title bar.
3. Click the Close button on the browser title bar. If necessary, click the Close all tabs button.

Chapter Summary

In Chapter 12, you learned how to create and use XML documents. You created a well-formed and valid XML Schema Definition and XML document instance. You created an XSL style sheet to format and display an XML document. By binding an XML document with an HTML Web page, you created Web pages that displayed XML data in a table and you learned to code a JavaScript function to search for records in an XML document. The items listed below include all the new skills you have learned in this chapter.

1. Start Notepad++ and Create a New XML Schema Document (HTML 570)
2. Enter the Code for the Prolog, Root, Annotation, and Documentation Elements (HTML 573)
3. Enter Code for the <products> Element (HTML 574)
4. Enter Code for the <complexType> Element (HTML 575)
5. Enter Code for the Child Group Elements (HTML 576)
6. Save and Validate an XML Schema Definition File (HTML 577)
7. Create a New XML Document and Enter the Prolog Code (HTML 579)
8. Start Entering a Document Instance in an XML Document (HTML 580)
9. Finish Entering a Document Instance in an XML Document (HTML 581)
10. Correct a Tag Error and Retest an XML Document (HTML 584)
11. Validate XML and XSD Files (HTML 585)
12. Start Creating an XSL Style Sheet (HTML 589)
13. Enter HTML Code to Display the Banner and Header Text in a Web Page (HTML 590)
14. Add XSL Style Sheet Tags (HTML 591)
15. Link an XSL Style Sheet to an XML Document (HTML 594)
16. Save and Test an XML Document Formatted Using an XSL Style Sheet (HTML 594)
17. Enter Code to Link an XML Document with an HTML Web Page (HTML 597)
18. Enter Code to Add Navigation Buttons (HTML 597)
19. Enter <table> Table Header and Row Tags (HTML 598)
20. Enter <tr> Tags and Attribute Values to Bind XML Elements to a Table (HTML 600)
21. Save the HTML File and Test the Web Page (HTML 601)
22. Enter Code to Bind an XML Document with an HTML Web Page (HTML 603)
23. Enter Code for the <input> and <button> Elements (HTML 603)
24. Enter an HTML <div> Tag Container (HTML 604)
25. Enter Code for the findItem() User-Defined Function (HTML 605)
26. Enter Code to Search the Recordset Values and Build the Output String (HTML 607)
27. Enter Code to Complete the findItem() Function (HTML 608)
28. Enter Code for the keyPressed() Function (HTML 608)
29. Enter Code for the clearField() Function (HTML 609)
30. Save and Test the HTML Document in the Browser (HTML 610)
31. Verify the Links on the Calumet Restaurant Supply home page (HTML 611)

Learn It Online

Test your knowledge of chapter content and key terms.

Instructions: To complete the following exercises, please visit www.cengagebrain.com. At the CengageBrain.com home page, search for *HTML5 and CSS, 7th Edition* using the search box at the top of the page. This will take you to the product page for this book. On the product page, click the Access Now button below the Study Tools heading. On the Book Companion Site Web page, select Chapter 12, and then click the link for the desired exercise.

Chapter Reinforcement TF, MC, and SA

A series of true/false, multiple choice, and short answer questions that test your knowledge of the chapter content.

Flash Cards

An interactive learning environment where you identify chapter key terms associated with displayed definitions.

Practice Test

A series of multiple choice questions that test your knowledge of chapter content and key terms.

Who Wants To Be a Computer Genius?

An interactive game that challenges your knowledge of chapter content in the style of a television quiz show.

Wheel of Terms

An interactive game that challenges your knowledge of chapter key terms in the style of the television show, *Wheel of Fortune*.

Crossword Puzzle Challenge

A crossword puzzle that challenges your knowledge of key terms presented in the chapter.

Apply Your Knowledge

Reinforce the skills and apply the concepts you learned in this chapter.

Instructions: Start Notepad++. Open the file apply12-1bigbox_emails.txt from the Chapter12\Apply folder of the Data Files for Students. See the inside back cover of this book for instructions on downloading the Data Files for Students, or contact your instructor for information about accessing the required files.

The text file contains a logical relation model the similar to the definition on page HTML 568. It is the data for three order confirmation e-mails sent to customers. You are to create an XML document, an associated XML Schema Definition file, and an XSL style sheet to display formatted data in a browser. Figure 12–47 shows the Big Box Business XML page as it would be displayed in a browser using the XSL style sheet that you will create and link to the XML data file.

Continued >

Apply Your Knowledge *continued*

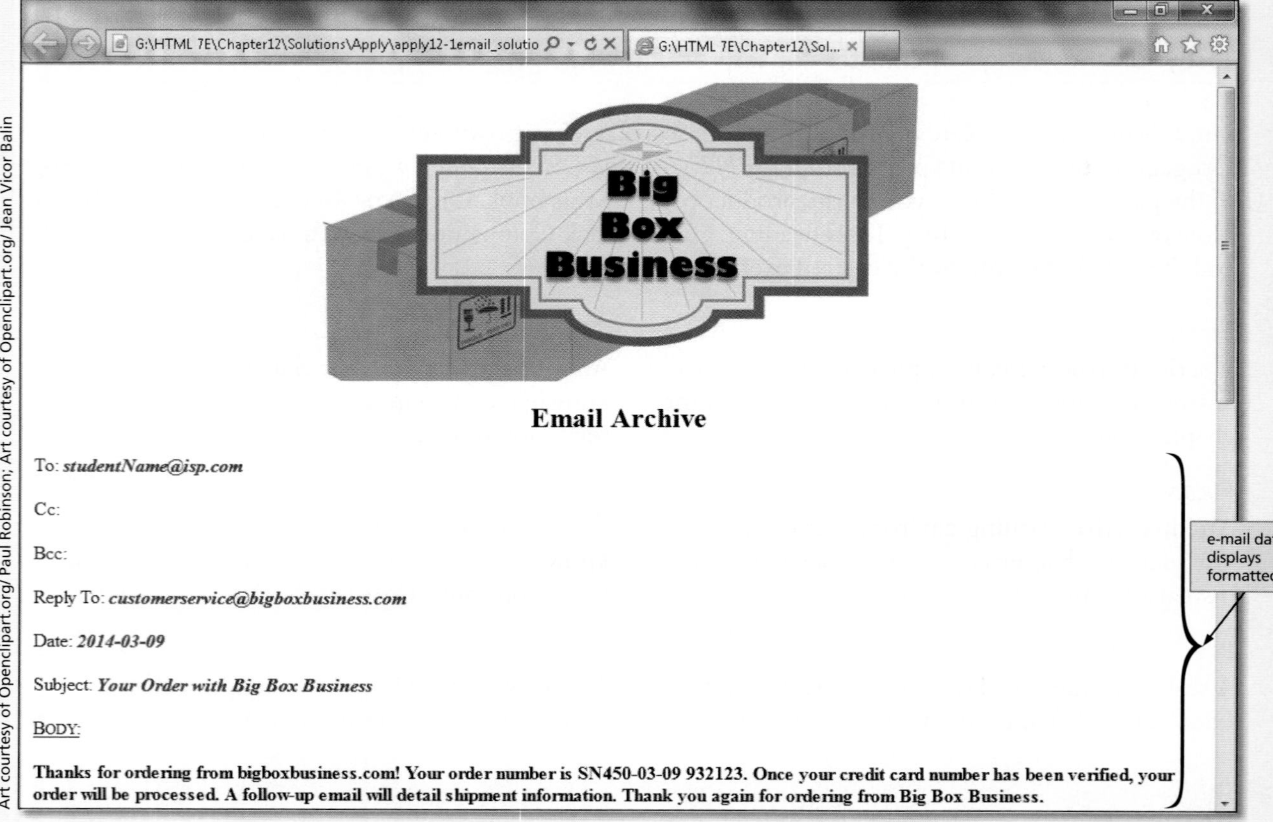

Figure 12–47

Perform the following tasks:

1. Start a new Notepad++ file. Using the code in Tables 12–11, 12–12, 12–14, and 12–15 on pages HTML 573 to HTML 576 as a guide, create the XML Schema Definition file for the Big Box Company e-mail data.
2. Save the XSD file in the Chapter12\Apply folder using the filename apply12-1email_schema_solution.xsd.
3. Start a new Notepad++ file. Save the XML document in the Chapter12\Apply folder using the filename apply12-1email_solution.xml.
4. Using the code in Tables 12–17 and 12–19 on pages HTML 579 and HTML 580 as a guide, enter the XML document instance elements using the item data in the apply12-1bigbox_emails.txt file. Save your XML file.
5. Start your browser. Navigate to your storage device and select the apply12-1email_solution.xml file. If the XML file does not display properly, check your code, save your file, activate the browser, and then refresh the Web page.
6. Start a new Notepad++ file and save it as apply12-1email_style_solution.xsl.

7. Using the code in Tables 12–23, 12–24, and 12–28 on pages HTML 589 to HTML 592 as a guide, create an XSL style sheet to display the e-mails as shown in Figure 12–47. For each of the defined fields, use a <span> tag with an inline style setting the font-famiy to Arial, Helvetica, sans-serif; the font-style to italic; the font-weight to bold; and the color to #000099. Use a <p> tag with an inline style to set the label, Body, text-decoration to underline and the font-variant to small caps. Use another <p> tag to place the body data on new line. Use a <span> tag with an inline style and set the font-famiy to Times, Times New Roman, serif, and the font-weight to bold. After the body of the e-mail, use a <p> tag and the <xsl:text> tag to insert a string of asterisks to separate the current e-mail message from the next one.
8. If necessary, activate your browser. In the Address bar, type www.corefiling.com/opensource/schemaValidate.html and then press the ENTER key to load the Web page as in Figure 12–21 on page HTML 585. Click the Browse button next to the XML Schema input text field. Navigate to your storage device and select the apply12-1email_schema_solution.xsd file.
9. Click the Browse button next to the XML Instance text field. Navigate to your storage device and select the apply12-1email_solution.xml file.
10. Click the Validate button. When the "Your results are ready" page displays, click the "Click here" link to see if your XML and XSD files are valid.
11. If an error occurs, check your code against the instructions in Steps 1 through 7 and then save and test the XML and XSD document files again.
12. Submit the XSD, XML, and XSL files in the format specified by your instructor.

Extend Your Knowledge

Extend the skills you learned in this chapter and experiment with new skills. You will need to search the Internet to complete the assignment.

Learning More about Displaying XML Data Islands

Instructions: Start Notepad++ and your browser. Open the file extend12-1menu.xml from the Chapter12\Extend folder of the Data Files for Students. See the inside back cover of this book for instructions on downloading the Data Files for Students, or contact your instructor for information about accessing the required files.

Two files are provided, extend12-1menu.xml, and extend12-1home.html, which is a simple Web page with four links: list breakfast items, list lunch items, list supper items and list items under $4. You are to create an XSL style sheet using the <xsl:if> tag to display the breakfast, lunch, and supper items only and link with the menu XML file. You will also create an XSL style sheet that uses the <xsl:choose> tag to display only items less than $4. Search the Internet for tutorials on the use of the <xsl:if> and <xsl:choose> tags.

Continued >

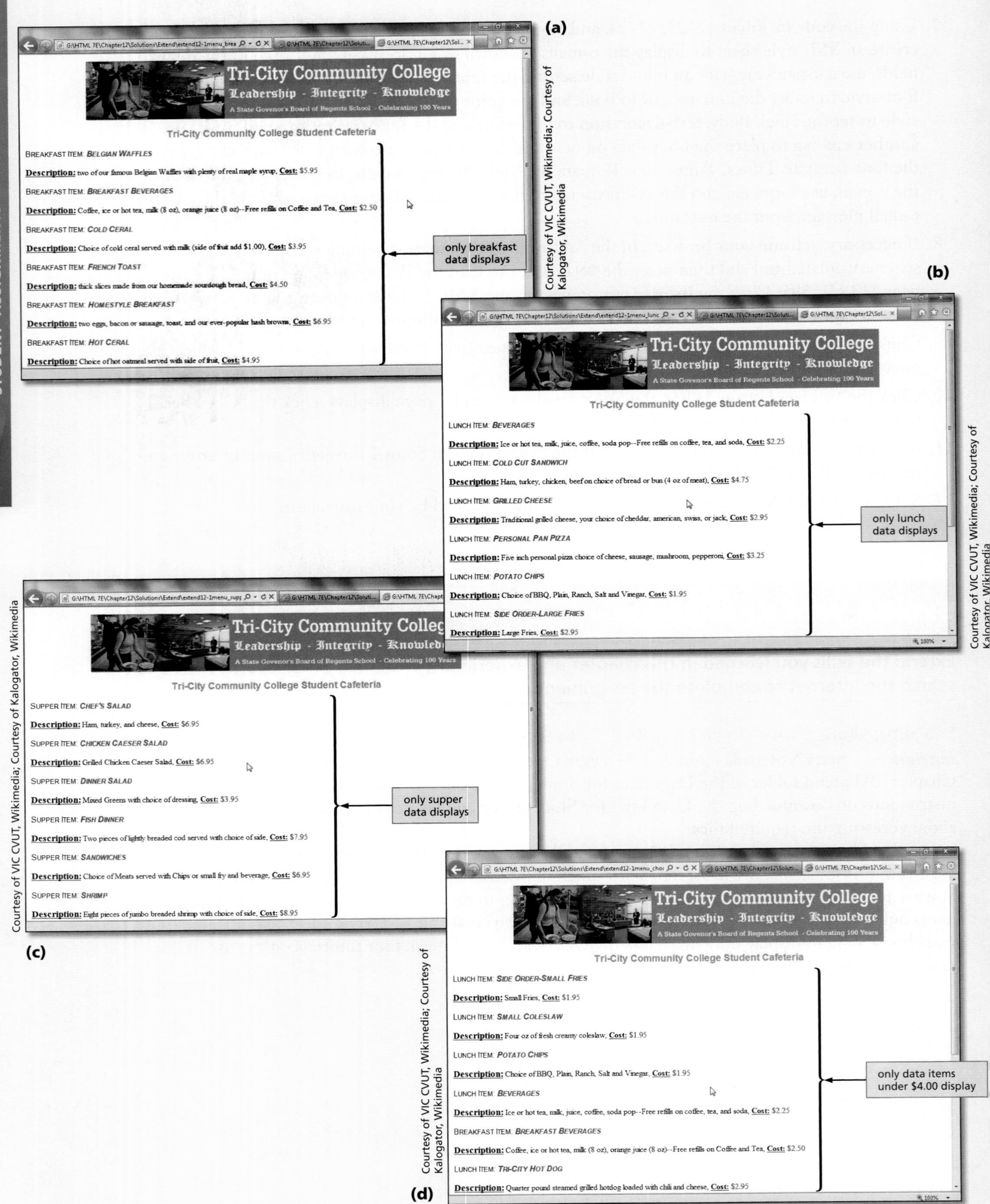
(a)
Tri-City Community College
Leadership - Integrity - Knowledge
A State Govenor's Board of Regents School - Celebrating 100 Years
Tri-City Community College Student Cafeteria
BREAKFAST ITEM: BELGIAN WAFFLES
Description: two of our famous Belgian Waffles with plenty of real maple syrup, Cost: $5.95
BREAKFAST ITEM: BREAKFAST BEVERAGES
Description: Coffee, ice or hot tea, milk (8 oz), orange juice (8 oz)--Free refills on Coffee and Tea, Cost: $2.50
BREAKFAST ITEM: COLD CERAL
Description: Choice of cold ceral served with milk (side of fruit add $1.00), Cost: $3.95
BREAKFAST ITEM: FRENCH TOAST
Description: thick slices made from our homemade sourdough bread, Cost: $4.50
BREAKFAST ITEM: HOMESTYLE BREAKFAST
Description: two eggs, bacon or sausage, toast, and our ever-popular hash browns, Cost: $6.95
BREAKFAST ITEM: HOT CERAL
Description: Choice of hot oatmeal served with side of fruit, Cost: $4.95
only breakfast data displays
Courtesy of VIC CVUT, Wikimedia; Courtesy of Kalogator, Wikimedia
(b)
LUNCH ITEM: BEVERAGES
Description: Ice or hot tea, milk, juice, coffee, soda pop--Free refills on coffee, tea, and soda, Cost: $2.25
LUNCH ITEM: COLD CUT SANDWICH
Description: Ham, turkey, chicken, beef on choice of bread or bun (4 oz of meat), Cost: $4.75
LUNCH ITEM: GRILLED CHEESE
Description: Traditional grilled cheese, your choice of cheddar, american, swiss, or jack, Cost: $2.95
LUNCH ITEM: PERSONAL PAN PIZZA
Description: Five inch personal pizza choice of cheese, sausage, mushroom, pepperoni, Cost: $3.25
LUNCH ITEM: POTATO CHIPS
Description: Choice of BBQ, Plain, Ranch, Salt and Vinegar, Cost: $1.95
LUNCH ITEM: SIDE ORDER-LARGE FRIES
Description: Large Fries, Cost: $2.95
only lunch data displays
Courtesy of VIC CVUT, Wikimedia; Courtesy of Kalogator, Wikimedia
(c)
SUPPER ITEM: CHEF'S SALAD
Description: Ham, turkey, and cheese, Cost: $6.95
SUPPER ITEM: CHICKEN CAESER SALAD
Description: Grilled Chicken Caeser Salad, Cost: $6.95
SUPPER ITEM: DINNER SALAD
Description: Mixed Greens with choice of dressing, Cost: $3.95
SUPPER ITEM: FISH DINNER
Description: Two pieces of lightly breaded cod served with choice of side, Cost: $7.95
SUPPER ITEM: SANDWICHES
Description: Choice of Meats served with Chips or small fry and beverage, Cost: $6.95
SUPPER ITEM: SHRIMP
Description: Eight pieces of jumbo breaded shrimp with choice of side, Cost: $8.95
only supper data displays
Courtesy of VIC CVUT, Wikimedia; Courtesy of Kalogator, Wikimedia
(d)
LUNCH ITEM: SIDE ORDER-SMALL FRIES
Description: Small Fries, Cost: $1.95
LUNCH ITEM: SMALL COLESLAW
Description: Four oz of fresh creamy coleslaw, Cost: $1.95
LUNCH ITEM: POTATO CHIPS
Description: Choice of BBQ, Plain, Ranch, Salt and Vinegar, Cost: $1.95
LUNCH ITEM: BEVERAGES
Description: Ice or hot tea, milk, juice, coffee, soda pop--Free refills on coffee, tea, and soda, Cost: $2.25
BREAKFAST ITEM: BREAKFAST BEVERAGES
Description: Coffee, ice or hot tea, milk (8 oz), orange juice (8 oz)--Free refills on Coffee and Tea, Cost: $2.50
LUNCH ITEM: TRI-CITY HOT DOG
Description: Quarter pound steamed grilled hotdog loaded with chili and cheese, Cost: $2.95
only data items under $4.00 display
Courtesy of VIC CVUT, Wikimedia; Courtesy of Kalogator, Wikimedia

Figure 12–48

Perform the following tasks:

1. Start a new Notepad++ document. Create an XSL style sheet that uses the <xsl:if> tag to display only the breakfast items <menu_type> sorted on the <name> element. Display the menu_type as Arial, Helvetica, sans-serif, make the font size 12pt and the font as small caps. Display the name in small caps, but italic, bold, and the color #834411. Display the description underlined, 14 point font size, and bold starting a new paragraph. Display the label Cost as bold and underline, but the price as normal, medium, and color #990000. Insert a "$" in front of the price. Save this XSL file as extend12-1menu_breakfast.xsl.
2. Open the extend12-1menu.xml file. Save it immediately as extend12-1menu_breakfast.xml. Using the code shown in Figure 12–27 on page HTML 594, add the code to link the breakfast XSL style sheet you just created to the XML document. Save the XML document.
3. With the extend12-1menu_breakfast.xsl style sheet open, save the file as extend12-1menu_lunch.xsl. Modify the <xsl:if> tag to display only the lunch <menu_type> items sorted on the <name> element. Save the modified XSL file. Select the extend12-1menu_breakfast.xml file and modify the XSL style sheet link code to bind the lunch XSL style sheet to the XML document. Save the XML document as extend12-1menu_lunch.xml.
4. With the extend12-1menu_lunch.xsl style sheet open, save the file as extend12-1menu_supper.xsl. Modify the <xsl:if> tag to display only the supper <menu_type> items sorted on the <name> element. Save the modified XSL file. Select the extend12-1menu_lunch.xml file and modify the XSL style sheet link code to bind the supper XSL style sheet to the XML document. Save the XML document as extend12-1menu_supper.xml.
5. With the extend12-1menu_supper.xsl style sheet open, save the file as extend12-1menu_choose.xsl. Change the <xsl:if> tag and use the <xsl:choose> tag to display only the items with a price less than $4. Change the <xsl:sort> to sort in price order. Save the modified XSL file. Select the extend12-1menu_supper.xml file and modify the XSL style sheet link code to bind the chosen XSL style sheet to the XML document. Save the XML document as extend12-1menu_choose.xml.
6. Start your browser. Enter G:\Chapter12\Extend\extend12-1home.html in the Address box to view the various XML documents in your browser. If any errors occur, check your code against the instructions in Steps 1 through 5 and then save and test the XML page again.
7. Submit the revised XML and XSL files and HTML Web page in the format specified by your instructor.

Make It Right

Analyze the XML code on a Web page and correct all errors.

Correcting Syntax Errors

Instructions: You will use the make12-1plant_list_error.xml, make12-1schema_error.xsd, and make12-1table_error.html files from the Chapter12\MakeItRight folder of the Data Files for Students. See the inside back cover of this book for instructions on downloading the Data Files for Students, or contact your instructor for information about accessing the required file.

The Stems Floral and Garden Supply XML and XSD files and Web pages have a total of five errors. When you attempt to display the XML data file, it will only display four instances because of an error in the fourth instance. The XSD file will not validate because of an error in the data types. The data will not display in the HTML table because of three errors. You are to identify the errors in all three files and correct them. The corrected Web page will show the list of floral items as shown in Figure 12–49.

Continued >

Make It Right *continued*

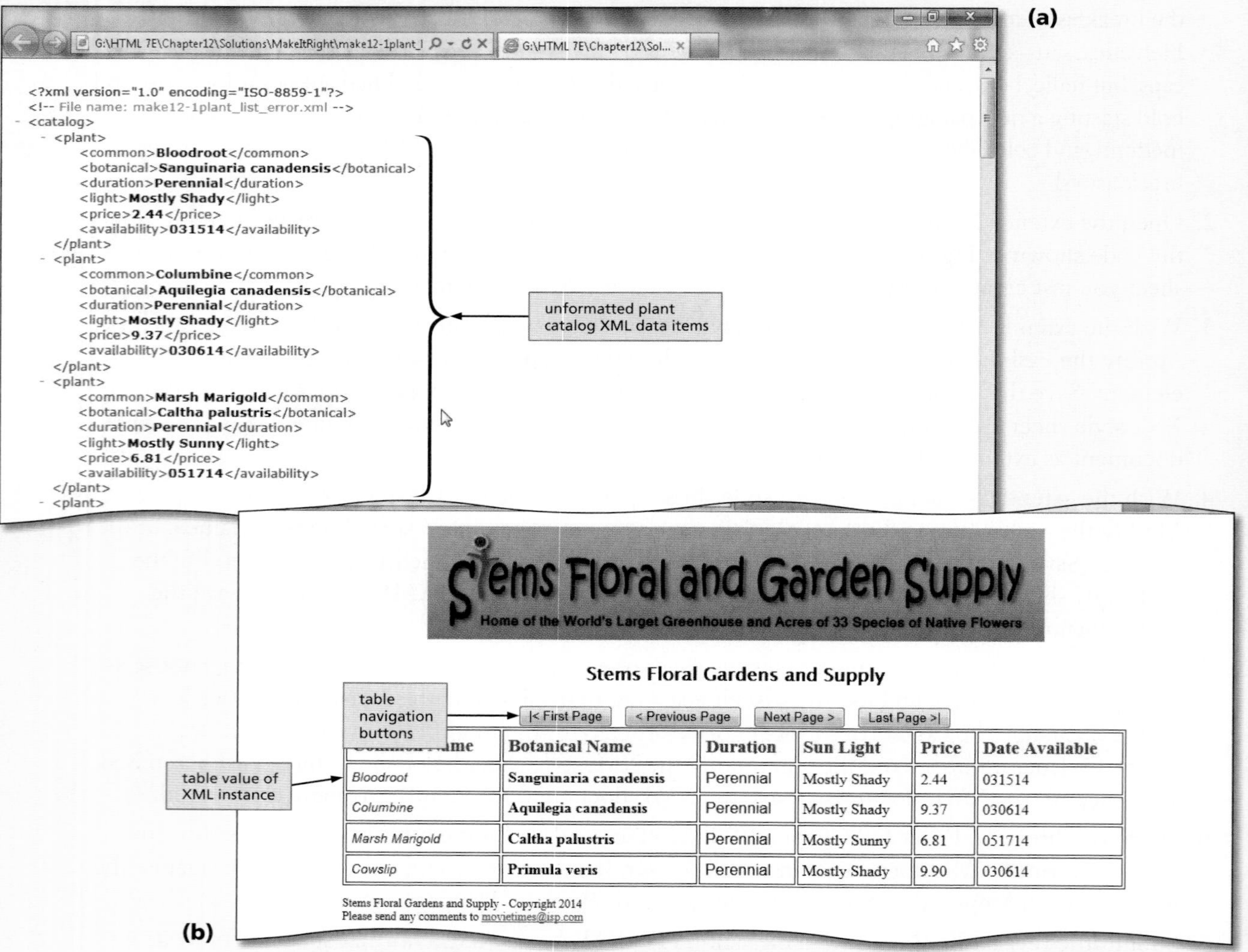

Figure 12–49

Perform the following tasks:

1. Open make12-1plant_list_error.xml in Notepad++ and save it as make12-1plant_list_solution.xml.
2. Activate the browser. Enter G:\Chapter12\MakeItRight\make12-1plant_list_solution.xml in the Address box to view the XML document in your browser. Make note of the last instance that displays.
3. Correct the error in Notepad++ and then save the XML file. Activate the browser and refresh the Web page. Make sure the XML file is error-free before continuing.
4. Open make12-1schema_error.xsd in Notepad++ and save it as make12-1schema_solution.xsd.
5. Activate your browser. Enter www.corefiling.com/opensource/schemaValidate.html in the Address box to view the CoreFiling XML Schema validator Web page in your browser.
6. Click the Browse button next to the XML Schema input text field. Navigate to your storage device and select the make12-1schema_error.xsd file (this file has the errors).
7. Click the Browse button next to the XML Instance text field. Navigate to your storage device and select the make12-1plant_list_solution.xml file (this is your corrected XML instance document).
8. Click the Validate button. When the "Your results are ready" page displays, click the "Click here" link to see an error message regarding the invalid XSD file. The list of errors will describe three errors in the XML file, but two of those errors relate to the XSD Schema file.

9. Correct the XML and XSD file errors, save the file as make12-1schema_solution.xsd, and revalidate the file using the CoreFiling Web page. Do not continue until both the XSD and XML documents are error-free.
10. Open the make12-1table_error.html file and save it as make12-1table_solution.html.
11. Activate your browser, and enter G:\Chapter12\MakeItRight\make12-1table_solution.html in the Address box to view the HTML table. Nothing displays because three errors exist in the file that relate to the src in the <xml> tag, the <table> tag datasrc attribute, and one of the datafld names.
12. Find and correct the errors and then save the make12-1table_solution.html file.
13. Activate the browser and click the Refresh button.
14. If an error still occurs, check the spelling of the data source name, save the file, and test again in the browser.
15. Submit the revised XML, HTML, and XSD files in the format specified by your instructor.

In the Lab

Design and/or create a Web page using the guidelines, concepts, and skills presented in this chapter. Labs are listed in order of increasing difficulty.

Lab 1: Displaying the Indiana Oil Company's Asset List

Instructions: You are one of the Web page developers for the Indiana Oil Company (InOCo). They have an intranet and use XML for displaying various database items. One such database is the list of assets for the Accounting and Finance Department. You have been assigned to create an XML file and XSL style sheet to display the data (Figure 12–50). You are given the company banner and a text file (lab12-1data.txt) with a relational model schema of the data. You will create a well-formed XML instance and a well-formed XSL style sheet.

Courtesy of Timpcrk87, Wikimedia; Art courtesy of Openclipart.org/ Kevin Cowtan

Figure 12–50

Continued >

In the Lab *continued*

Perform the following tasks:

1. Start a new Notepad++ file. Using the information and data in the lab12-1data.txt file, create a well-formed XML file. Save as lab12-1asset_solution.xml.
2. Using the code in Tables 12–11, 12–12, 12–14, and 12–15 on pages HTML 573 through HTML 576 as a guide, create an XML Schema Definition file and save it as lab12-1asset_solution.xsd. Note the format of the date in the XML instance document.
3. Start your browser. Enter www.corefiling.com/opensource/schemaValidate.html in the Address box to view the CoreFiling XML Schema validator Web page in your browser.
4. Browse to the lab12-1asset_solution.xsd and lab12-1asset_solution.xml files, click the Validate button, and then click the Click here link to see if any error messages display.
5. If errors exist, correct your XSD file, save it, and revalidate at the CoreFiling Web page. Do not continue until both the XSD and XML documents are error-free.
6. Start a new Notepad++ file and save immediately as lab12-1asset_solution.xsl. Use the code presented in Tables 12–24 and 12–28 as a guide to create an XSL style sheet to display the formatted contents of the lab12-1asset_solution.xml file.
7. Sort the items on asset_description.
8. Use a <span> tag to format a label, Asset ID:, as bold. Use a <span> tag to format the display content of asset_id as font-variant:small-caps, font-style:italic, font-weight:bold, and color:#834411.
9. Use an <xsl:text> tag to insert a label, Description:. Format the content of the asset_description with font-variant as normal, font-weight as bolder, and color as #000000. Follow the description with a comma and a space.
10. Insert a label, Location of asset:, followed by the content of asset_location formatted with an inline style. Format font-variant as normal, font-weight as medium, color as #000000, and text-decoration as underline. Follow the content with a comma and a space.
11. Place a label, Date asset acquired, and then format the contents of asset_date_acquired as font-variant:normal, the font-weight:medium, and the color:#000000. Follow the content with the text ", and date asset sold: ". Be sure to include the spaces.
12. Format the asset_date_sold with font-variant as small-caps, font-weight as bold, and color as #834411. Follow the date with a comma and a space, then the text "asset has a salvage value: ". Format the asset_salvage_value with font-variant as small-caps, font-weight as bold, and color as #834411.
13. Be sure to close any open tags.
14. Save the completed XSL file. Activate the lab12-1asset_solution.xml file. Add the <?xml> tag to link the XSL style sheet to the XML file. Save the XML file.
15. Test the completed XML file using your browser. If an error occurs, check your code from Steps 9 through 14, and then save and test again.
16. Submit the completed XML file, XSD file, and XSL file in the format specified by your instructor.

In the Lab

Lab 2: Creating the Indy Airline XML Data Island

Instructions: You are a summer intern for the IT Department of Indy Air, out of Indianapolis, IN. Management wants to develop a flight schedule database. The Webmaster, Evonn Woods, assigns you the task of converting the text file version of the flight schedule to an XML data island. She wants you to create two versions of the Web page that display the flights. One version is a table that displays all the flights in destination order, four at a time; the other Web page allows customers to search for flights by destination. The XML file and the HTML search page appear as shown in Figure 12–51.

(a)

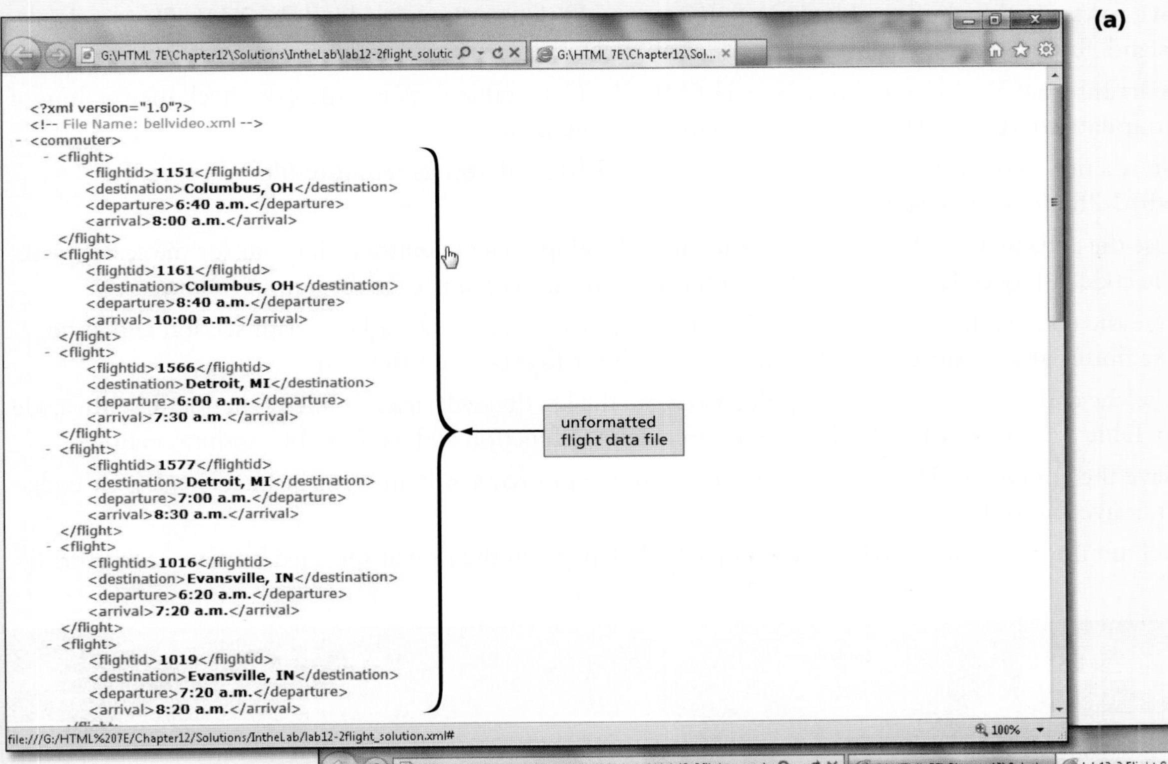

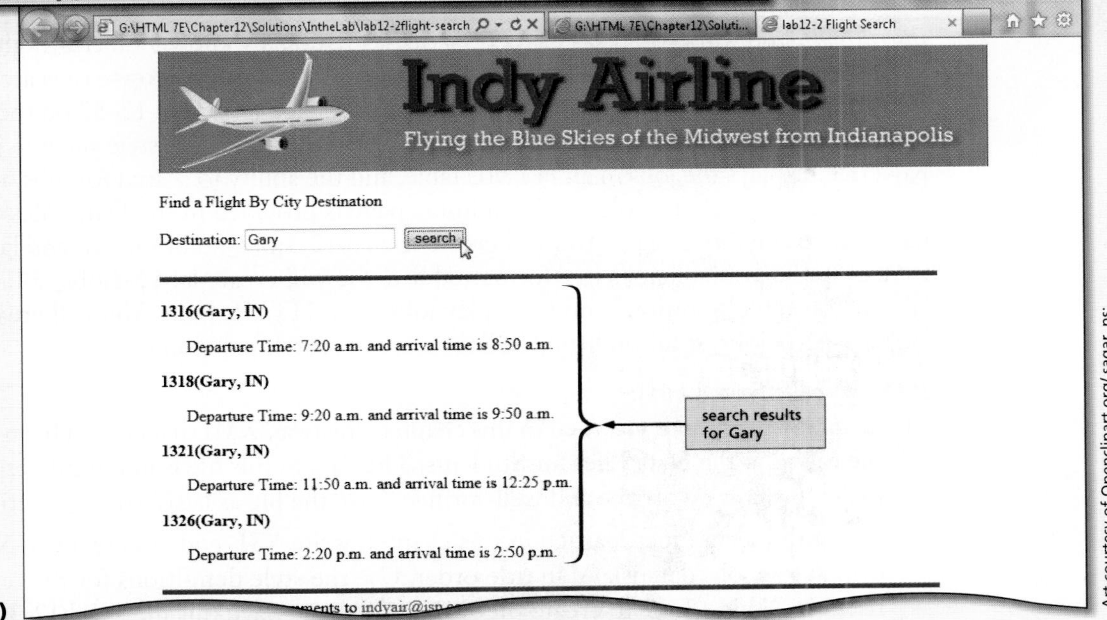

(b)

Figure 12–51

Art courtesy of Openclipart.org/ sagar_ns;

Continued >

In the Lab *continued*

Perform the following tasks:

1. Use Notepad++ to open the lab12-2flight_data.txt file from the Chapter12\IntheLab folder of the Data Files for Students.
2. Create an XML data file using this data and save the file as lab12-2flight_flight_solution.xml.
3. Start another new Notepad++ session, open the lab12-2flight-table.html file, and save it as lab12-2flight-table_solution.html.
4. Use the code presented in Figures 12–32 through 12–34 on pages HTML 598 through HTML 600 as a guide to write the HTML code to display the flights in a table. Set the attributes to display five rows at a time in the table. Do not forget to add the <xml> tag to bind the XML file as a data island. Save your HTML file.
5. Start Internet Explorer and test your HTML file. If the table does not display, check the spelling of your data source objects and datafld attributes in the table cells.
6. Start a new Notepad++ document, and open the lab12-2flight-search.html file, and save it as lab12-2flight-search_solution.html.
7. Use the code in Table 12–35 as a guide to enter the <input> and <button> elements for the search. Use the code in Figure 12–39 as a guide to enter the <div> tag container for the output results.
8. Use the code in Tables 12–36, 12–37, and 12–38 as a guide to start a JavaScript section and enter the findFlights() user-defined function to search for flights by destination.
9. Use the code in Table 12–39 as a guide to create the keyPressed() user-defined function. Use the code in Table 12–40 to create the clearField() user-defined function and to close the <script> section.
10. Save the completed HTML file and test it using your browser. If an error occurs, check your code and save and test again.
11. Submit the completed XML file and HTML Web pages in the format specified by your instructor.

In the Lab

Lab 3: Creating the Texas Career Services Web Site

Instructions: You work for Texas Career Services, a nationally known job clearinghouse. You recently converted the jobs data to an XML data island to allow clients to browse or search for currently available jobs. Your assignment is to create the Web pages depicted in Figure 12–52 on the next page. The Web pages include an XML instance document displayed using an XSL style sheet in job title order, a Web page that displays the jobs in an HTML table, and the ability to search for jobs by job title.

The lab12-3homesolution.html home page is provided in the Data Files for Students. This page has links to the three pages. You will create the lab12-3jobs_solution.xml and lab12-3jobs_solution.xsl to display the available jobs in a formatted list. You will create lab12-3jobs_solution.xml and lab12-3jobstable_solution.html to display jobs in an HTML table. You will create lab12-3searchjobs_solution.html to allow users to search position by title.

Perform the following tasks:

1. Using the techniques learned in this chapter, create an XML data island from the lab12-3jobs_data.txt file found in the Data Files for Students. The data in this file is in job title order. Test the XML file to make sure it is error-free and well-formed. Save the file as lab12-3jobs_solution.xml.
2. Using the techniques learned in this chapter, write XSL code to create an XSL style sheet that will display the jobs data island in title order. Use the style definitions for the text and element items listed in Table 12–42 to create the XSL style sheet. Save this file as lab12-3jobs_solution.xsl. In addition, add the proper XML processing statement to link the XSL style sheet to the lab12-3jobs_solution.xml file created in Step 1.

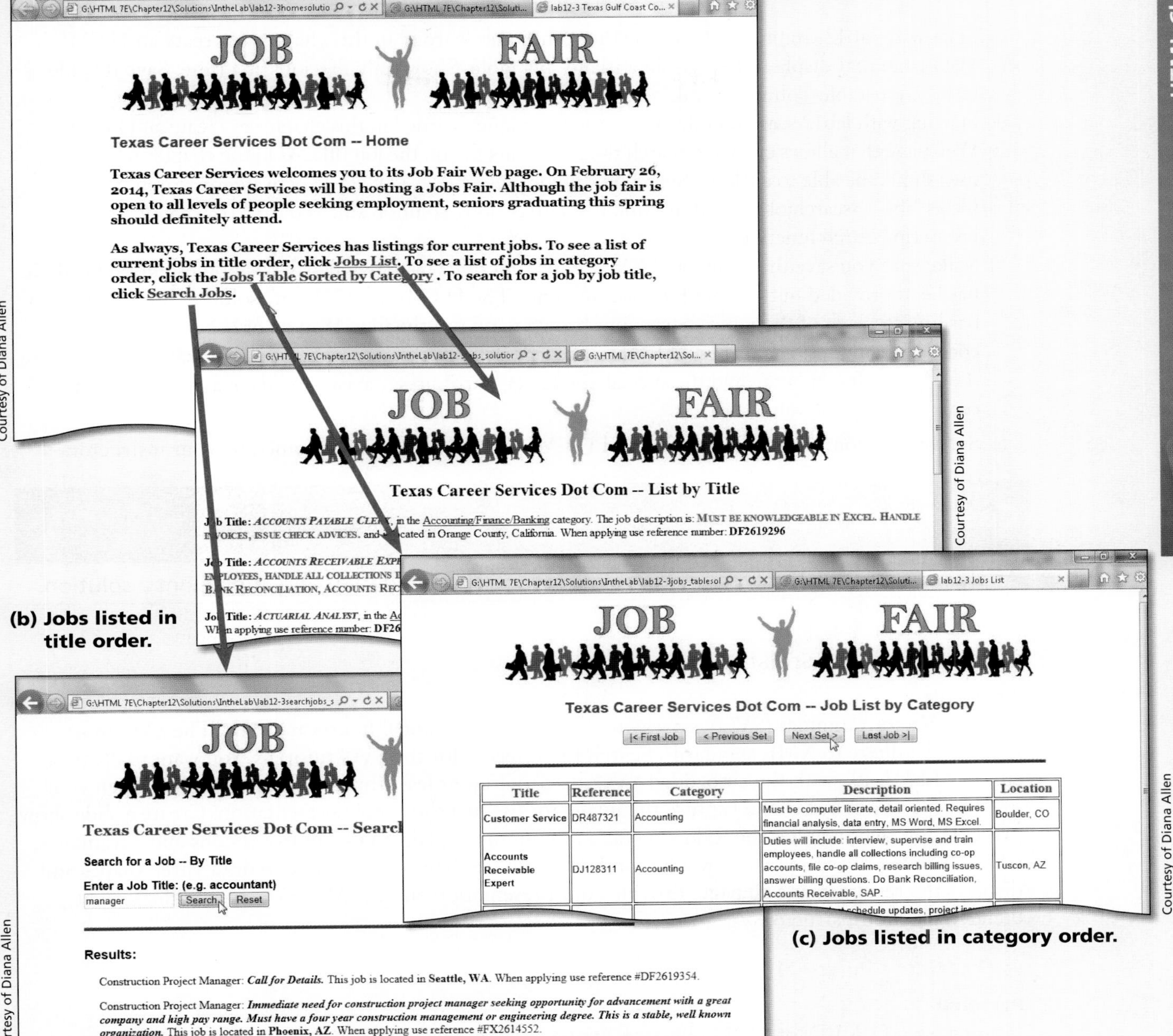

(a) home page.

(b) Jobs listed in title order.

(c) Jobs listed in category order.

(d) Search by job title.

Courtesy of Diana Allen

Figure 12–52

Table 12–42 Style Definitions

Text/Element Items	Style
Job Title:	font-weight:bolder
value-of select="title"	font-variant:small-caps; font-style:italic; font-weight:bold; color:#0000ff
value-of select="category"	font-variant:normal; font-weight:medium; color:#000000; text-decoration:underline
value-of select="description"	font-variant:small-caps; font-weight:bold; color:#834411
value-of select="location"	font-variant:normal; font-weight:medium; color:#000000
value-of select="reference"	font-variant:normal; font-weight:bolder; color:#000000

Continued >

In the Lab *continued*

3. Start with lab12-3table.html and use the techniques learned in this chapter to create an HTML Web page that displays the jobs data island in a table. Show only five jobs at a time. Save this file as lab12-3jobstable_solution.html.
4. Starting with lab12 searchjobs.html, use the techniques learned in this chapter to create an HTML Web page that allows clients to search the XML data file on the job title. As in the chapter project, the user should be able to click the Search button or press the ENTER key to activate the search. Save this file as lab12-3searchjobs_solution.html. Use lab12-3jobs_solution.xml as the XML data island for the JavaScript search function.
5. Make sure you save the completed XML, XSL, and HTML files. The lab12-3homesolution.html file has been provided in the Data Files for Students. The HTML lab12-3homesolution.html Web page has links to each of these files. Start your browser and test the files. If an error occurs, check your code, save, and test again. The HTML Web page will not validate at the validator.w3.org site because the Microsoft <xml> tag and the special <table> tag attributes (datasrc and datapagesize) are not recognized by the validator.
6. Submit the completed XML, XSL, and HTML files in the format specified by your instructor.

Cases and Places

Apply your creative thinking and problem solving skills to design and implement a solution.

1: Learning about Scalable Vector Graphics

Academic

Scalable Vector Graphics (SVG) is a way to draw two-dimensional figures in XML. The SVG must follow and adhere to XML standards. Search the Internet for the SVG tutorials. You want to create a simple HTML file with the embedded SVG code to draw at least three shapes with color. Open your HTML file in a browser and capture the image for use in a slide show presentation. Create a slide show presentation that includes the following (as a minimum): explain SVG and its versions and advantages, what is needed to create and view a file, and demonstrate the necessary code to draw three shapes and displays the results in a Web page. Provide your presentation and HTML/SVG files in the format dictated by your instructor.

2: Creating a Personal XML Database

Personal

Using your CD, DVD, or MP3 collection, create an XML file with at least six instances. Include an XSD Schema that describes your database. To display your database create either an XSL style sheet or an HTML Web page using an HTML table. In addition, create an HTML Web page to query your data island in Internet Explorer by artist name.

3: Creating a Schedule of Events XML Database

Professional

You are a newly hired intern at Redding Botanical Gardens. Your first task is to create an XML data island to display in an HTML table for the current month. The table should have seven columns, for each day of the week, and display only one week at a time. To see other weeks, the user will click the forward or backward buttons you create. Search the Internet for other botanical gardens to get ideas for events. Example events might be a weekend flower show, classes, field trips, fundraising activities, or other activities you can invent.

Appendix A

HTML Quick Reference

HTML Coding Standards

HTML is the original language used for publishing hypertext on the World Wide Web. It is a nonproprietary format based on Standard Generalized Markup Language (SGML). HTML documents can be created with a wide variety of tools, from simple text editors such as Notepad and Notepad++, to sophisticated WYSIWYG authoring tools such as Adobe Dreamweaver. Extensible Markup Language (XML) is a markup language that uses tags to describe the structure and content of a document, not just the format.

Extensible Hypertext Markup Language (XHTML) is a reformulation of HTML so it conforms to XML structure and content rules. By combining HTML and XML, XHTML provides the display features of HTML and the stricter coding standards required by XML.

HTML5 is the newest version of HTML. HTML5 is a very flexible language that does not have coding standards like the XHTML standards defined by the World Wide Web Consortium (W3C). For instance, with HTML5, you can combine lowercase, uppercase, or mixed-case lettering in your tags and attributes. Despite the HTML5 flexibility, this book adheres to good coding practices (other than the XHTML <!DOCTYPE> tag) that would make it easy to convert to XHTML standards if they should one day override HTML5. The coding practices to which the book adheres are shown in Table A–1. The projects in this book use the HTML5 <!DOCTYPE> tag and follow the standards outlined in Table A–1. This information is also shown in Table 1–3 in Chapter 1.

Table A–1 Coding Practices

Practice	Invalid Example	Valid Example
All tags and attributes must be written in lowercase	<IMG HEIGHT="346" />	<img height="346" />
All attribute values must be enclosed by single or double quotation marks	<img height=346 />	<img height="346" />
All tags must be closed, including tags such as img, hr, and br, which do not have end tags, but which must be closed as a matter of practice	 <hr> <p>This is another paragraph	 <hr /> <p>This is another paragraph</p>
All elements must be nested properly	<p><strong>This is a bold paragraph</p></strong>	<p><strong>This is a bold paragraph</strong></p>

HTML Tags and Attributes

HTML uses tags such as <h1> and <p> to structure text into headings, paragraphs, lists, hypertext links, and so on. Many HTML tags have attributes that can be defined in different ways to further structure the content of the Web page. Attributes are the parts of HTML elements that define them. Attributes provide additional information that a browser can use to determine things like how to display an element. As an example, the height and width attributes in the <img> tag describe the size of the image. **Global attributes** are those that can be used with most (there are exceptions) HTML tags. HTML4 had a number of global attributes, and HTML5 has added some new ones (as indicated below). Table A–2 lists the HTML5 global attributes. This is a comprehensive list of attributes that are common to all HTML5 elements (with some exceptions).

Table A–2 HTML5 Global Attributes

	Attribute	Value	Description
	accesskey	*character*	Specifies a shortcut key to access an element
	class	*classname*	Refers to a class specified in a style sheet
NEW	contenteditable	true false inherit	Specifies whether a user can edit the content of an element or not
NEW	contextmenu	*menu_id*	Specifies a context menu for an element; the value must be the id of a <menu> element
	dir	ltr rtl auto	Specifies the text direction for the content in an element
NEW	draggable	true false auto	Specifies whether a user is allowed to drag an element or not
NEW	dropzone	copy move link	Specifies what happens when dragged items/data are dropped in the element
NEW	hidden	hidden	Specifies that an element should be hidden
	id	*id*	Specifies a unique id for an element
	lang	*language_code*	Specifies the language of the element's content
NEW	spellcheck	true false	Specifies if the element must have its spelling and grammar checked
	style	*style_definitions*	Specifies an inline style for an element
	tabindex	*number*	Specifies the tab order of an element
	title	*text*	Specifies extra information about an element

As the W3C continually updates the HTML specifications, HTML tags are added to, deleted, and replaced by newer tags. Table A–3 lists HTML tags and their associated attributes. The list provides a brief description of each tag and its values. The default value for each attribute is indicated by bold text in the Description column. Certain tags and elements listed in Table A–3 are highlighted as follows:

NEW The NEW icon indicates tags or attributes that are new with HTML5 and validate successfully with the HTML5 DOCTYPE. Note that these tags may not work with all browsers.

* Deprecated tags are indicated by an asterisk. Those are tags that have been replaced by newer elements and validate successfully with the Transitional DOCTYPE.

** Two asterisks indicate tags and attributes not supported (or absent) in HTML5. Using these tags with an HTML5 DOCTYPE will result in validation errors. However, these tags will validate with the Transitional DOCTYPE. They remain in Table A–3 because you will encounter them in Web pages that you maintain.

Deprecated elements are still available for use, and most browsers still support them. Browsers will probably continue to support deprecated tags and attributes in the near future, but eventually these tags may become obsolete, so future support cannot be guaranteed. It is therefore best not to use deprecated tags.

For a comprehensive list of HTML tags and attributes, more thorough descriptions, examples of HTML tags, and XHTML coding standards, visit the W3C Web site at w3.org.

Table A–3 HTML Tags and Attributes

HTML Tag and Attributes	Description	
<!DOCTYPE>	Indicates the version of HTML used	
<!--Text here-->	Inserts comments that are ignored by browsers	
<a>....</a>	Anchor; creates a hyperlink or fragment identifier	
charset=*character set* **	Specifies the character encoding of the linked resource	
href=*URL*	Hyperlink reference that specifies the target URL	
media=*media_query*	Specifies what media/device the target URL is optimized for	NEW
id=*text*	Specifies an id for enclosed text, allowing it to be the target of a hyperlink	
rel=*relationship*	Indicates the relationship going from the current page to the target	
rev=*relationship* **	Indicates the relationship going from the target to the current page	
target=_blank, _self, _parent, _top, *framename*	Defines the name of the window or frame in which the linked resource will appear	
type=*MIME_type*	Specifies the MIME type of the target URL	NEW
<address>....</address>	Used for information such as authorship, e-mail addresses, or addresses; enclosed text appears italicized and indented in some browsers	
<area>....</area>	Creates a clickable area, or hotspot, on a client-side image map	
alt=*text*	Specifies an alternate text for the area	NEW
coords=*value1, value2*	Specifies the coordinates that define the edges of the hotspot; a comma-delimited list of values	
href=*URL*	Hyperlink reference that specifies the target URL	
hreflang=*language_code*	Specifies the language of the target URL	NEW
media=*media query*	Specifies what media/device the target URL is optimized for	NEW
nohref**	Indicates that no link is associated with the area	
shape=circle, poly, rect	Identifies the shape of the area	
target=_blank, _self, _parent, _top, *framename*	Defines the name of the window or frame in which the linked resource will appear	
type=*MIME_type*	Specifies the MIME type of the target URL	NEW
<article>...</article>	Defines an article	

NEW New with HTML5   * Deprecated tags   ** Not supported in HTML5

Table A–3 HTML Tags and Attributes *(continued)*

	HTML Tag and Attributes	Description
NEW	**<aside>...</aside>**	Defines content aside from the main page content
NEW	**<audio>...</audio>**	Defines sound content
	autoplay=autoplay	Specifies that the audio should start playing as soon as it is ready
	controls=controls	Specifies that playback controls should be displayed
	loop=loop	Specifies that the audio should start over again, when it is finished
	preload=auto, metadata, none	Specifies whether or not the audio should be loaded when the page loads
	src=*URL*	Specifies the URL of the audio to play
	<b>....</b>	Specifies text to appear in bold
	<base />	Identifies the base in all relative URLs in the document
	href=*URL*	Specifies the absolute URL used to resolve all relative URLs in the document
	target=_blank, _self, _parent, _top, *framename*	Defines the name for the default window (or frame*) in which the hyperlinked pages are displayed
	<big>....</big> **	Increases the size of the enclosed text to a type size bigger than the surrounding text; exact display size depends on the browser and default font
	<blockquote>....</blockquote>	Sets enclosed text to appear as a quotation, indented on the right and left
	cite=*URL*	Specifies the source of the quotation
	<body>....</body>	Defines the start and end of a Web page's content
	alink=*color* **	Defines the color of an active link
	background=*URL* **	Identifies the image to be used as a background
	bgcolor=*color* **	Sets the document's background color
	link=*color* **	Defines the color of links not yet visited
	vlink=*color* **	Defines the color of visited links
	** **	Inserts a line break
NEW	**<canvas>...</canvas>**	Defines graphics
	height=*pixels*	Specifies the height of the canvas
	width=*pixels*	Specifies the width of the canvas
	<caption>....</caption>	Creates a caption for a table
	align=*position* **	Sets caption position
	<center>....</center> **	Centers the enclosed text horizontally on the page
	<cite>....</cite>	Indicates that the enclosed text is a citation; text is usually displayed in italics
	<code>....</code>	Indicates that the enclosed text is a code sample from a program; text is usually displayed in fixed width font such as Courier
	<col>....</col>	Organizes columns in a table into column groups to share attribute values
	align=*position* **	Sets horizontal alignment of text within the column
	span=*number*	Sets the number of columns that span the <col> element
	valign=*position* **	Specifies vertical alignment of text within the column
	width=*pixels* **	Sets the width of each column in the column group
	<colgroup>....</colgroup>	Encloses a group of <col> tags and groups the columns to set properties
	align=*position* **	Specifies horizontal alignment of text within the column
	char=*character* **	Specifies a character on which to align column values (for example, a period is used to align monetary values)

NEW New with HTML5   * Deprecated tags   ** Not supported in HTML5

Table A–3 HTML Tags and Attributes *(continued)*

HTML Tag and Attributes	Description	
<colgroup>....</colgroup> *(continued)*		
charoff=*value* **	Specifies a number of characters to offset data aligned with the character specified in the char property	
span=*number*	Sets the number of columns the <col> element spans	
valign=*position* **	Specifies vertical alignment of text within the column	
width=*pixels* **	Sets the width of each column spanned by the colgroup statement	
<command>...</command>	Defines a command button	NEW
checked=checked	Defines if the command is checked or not; use only if type is radio or checkbox	
disabled=disabled	Defines if the command is available or not	
icon=*URL*	Defines the URL of an image to display as the command	
label=*name*	Defines a name for the command; the label is visible	
radiogroup=*groupname*	Defines the name of the radiogroup this command belongs to; use only if type is radio	
type=checkbox, command, radio	Defines the type of command; default value is command	
<datalist>...</datalist>	Defines a dropdown list	NEW
<dd>....</dd>	Indicates that the enclosed text is a definition in the definition list	
<details>...</details>	Defines details of an element	NEW
<div>....</div>	Defines block-level structure or division in the HTML document	
align=*position* **	Specifies alignment of the content block	
<dl>....</dl>	Creates a definition list	
<dt>....</dt>	Indicates that the enclosed text is a term in the definition list	
<em>....</em>	Indicates that the enclosed text should be emphasized; usually appears in italics	
<embed>...</embed>	Defines external interactive content or plugin	NEW
height=*pixels*	Specifies the height of the embedded content	
src=*URL*	Specifies the URL of the embedded content	
type=*MIME_type*	Specifies the MIME type of the embedded content	
width=*pixels*	Specifies the width of the embedded content	
<fieldset>....</fieldset>	Groups related form controls and labels	
disabled=disabled	Specifies that a fieldset should be disabled	
form=*form_id*	Specifies one or more forms that a fieldset belongs to	
name=*text*	Specifies the name of the fieldset	
<figcaption>...</figcaption>	Defines the caption of a figure element	NEW
<figure>...</figure>	Defines a group of media content, and their captions	NEW
<font>....</font> **	Defines the appearance of enclosed text	
color=*color* **	Sets the font color; can be a hexadecimal value (#rrggbb) or a word for a predefined color value	
face=*list* **	Identifies the font face; multiple entries should be separated by commas	
point-size=*value* **	Sets the point size of text for downloaded fonts	
size=*value* **	Sets the font size in absolute terms (1 through 7) or as a relative value	
weight=*value* **	Sets the weight of the font, ranging from 100 (lightest) to 900 (heaviest)	
<footer>...</footer>	Defines a footer for a section or page	NEW

NEW New with HTML5 * Deprecated tags ** Not supported in HTML5

	Table A–3 HTML Tags and Attributes *(continued)*	
	HTML Tag and Attributes	**Description**
	<form>....</form>	Marks the start and end of a Web page form
	action=*URL*	Specifies the URL of the application that will process the form; required attribute
NEW	autocomplete=on, off	Specifies whether or not the form should have autocomplete enabled
	enctype=*encoding*	Specifies how the form element values will be encoded
	method=get, post	Specifies the method used to pass form parameters (data) to the server
	name=*form_name*	Specifies the name for a form
NEW	novalidate=novalidate	If present the form should not be validated when submitted
	target=_blank, _self, _parent, _top, *framename*	Specifies the frame or window that displays the form's results
	<frame>....</frame> **	Delimits a frame within a frameset
	frameborder=*option* **	Specifies whether the frame border is displayed
	marginheight=*value* **	Adds *n* pixels of space above and below the frame contents
	marginwidth=*value* **	Adds *n* pixels of space to the left and the right of the frame contents
	name=*text* **	Specifies the name of the frame
	noresize **	Prevents the user from resizing the frame
	scrolling=*option* **	Adds scroll bars or not—always, never, or add when needed
	src=*URL* **	Defines the URL of the source document that is displayed in the frame
	<frameset>....</frameset> **	Defines a collection of frames in a frameset
	cols=*value1*, *value2*,... **	Defines the number and width of frames within a frameset
	frameborder=*option* **	Specifies whether the frame border is displayed
	rows= *value1*, *value2*,... **	Defines the number and height of frames within a frameset
	<head>....</head>	Delimits the start and end of the HTML document's head
NEW	**<header>...</header>**	Defines a header for a section or page
NEW	**<hgroup>...<hgroup>**	Defines information about a section in a document
	<h*n*>....</h*n*>	Defines a header level *n*, ranging from the largest (h1) to the smallest (h6)
	align=left, center, right **	Specifies the header alignment
	<hr />	Inserts a horizontal rule
	align=left, center, right **	Specifies the alignment of the horizontal rule
	noshade=noshade **	Specifies to not use 3D shading and to round the ends of the rule
	size=*value* **	Sets the thickness of the rule to a value in pixels
	width=*pixels, %* **	Sets the width of the rule to a value in pixels or a percentage of the page width; percentage is preferred
	<html>....</html>	Indicates the start and the end of the HTML document
NEW	manifest=*URL*	Specifies the URL of the document's cache manifest
	version=*data* **	Indicates the HTML version used; not usually used
	<i>....</i>	Sets enclosed text to appear in italics
	<iframe>....</iframe> *	Creates an inline frame, also called a floating frame or subwindow, within an HTML document
	height=*pixels*	Sets the frame height to a value in pixels
	marginheight=*value* **	Sets the margin between the contents of the frame and its top and bottom borders to a value in pixels
	marginwidth=*value* **	Sets the margin between the contents of the frame and its left and right borders to a value in pixels

NEW New with HTML5   * Deprecated tags   ** Not supported in HTML5

Table A–3 HTML Tags and Attributes *(continued)*

HTML Tag and Attributes	Description	
<iframe>....</iframe> * *(continued)*		
name=*text* *	Assigns a name to the current frame	
noresize *	Prevents the user from resizing the frame	
sandbox=*allow-option*	Specifies restrictions to the frame content	NEW
scrolling=*option* **	Adds scroll bars or not—always, never, or add when needed	
seamless=seamless	Specifies that the iframe should be seamlessly integrated	NEW
src=*URL* *	Defines the URL of the source document that is displayed in the frame	
srcdoc=*HTML_code*	Specifies the HTML of the document showing in the iframe	NEW
width=*pixels* *	Sets the frame width to a value in pixels	
<img>....</img>	Inserts an image into the current Web page	
align=*type* **	Defines image alignment in relation to the text or the page margin	
alt=*text*	Provides a text description of an image if the browser cannot display the image; should always be used	
border=*value* **	Sets the thickness of the border around the image to a value in pixels; value is 0 or 1; developers discouraged from using this	
height=*pixels*	Sets the height of the image to a value in pixels (not percentages); should always be used	
src=*URL*	Specifies the URL of the image to be displayed; required	
usemap=*#mapname*	Specifies the map of coordinates and links that defines the href within this image	
width=*pixels*	Sets the width of the image to a value in pixels (not percentages); should always be used	
<input>....</input>	Defines controls used in forms	
alt=*text*	Provides a short description of the control or image button; for browsers that do not support inline images	
autocomplete=on, off	Specifies whether or not the input field should have focus on page load	NEW
autofocus=autofocus	Specifies that the input field should have focus on page load	NEW
checked=checked	Sets radio buttons and check boxes to the checked state	
disabled=disabled	Disables the control	
form=*form_id*	Specifies one or more forms the input element belongs to	NEW
formaction=*URL*	Overrides the form's action attribute. Defines where to send the data when the form is submitted (for type="submit" and type="image")	NEW
formenctype=*encoding*	Overrides the form's enctype attribute. Defines how form data should be encoded before sending it to the server (for type="submit" and type="image")	NEW
formmethod=get, post	Overrides the form's method attribute. Defines the HTTP method for sending data to the action URL (for type="submit" and type="image")	NEW
formnovalidate= formnovalidate	Overrides the form's novalidate attribute. Defines that the input element should not be validated when submitted	NEW
formtarget=_blank, _self, _parent, _top, *framename*	Overrides the form's target attribute. Defines the target window to use when the form is submitted (for type="submit" and type="image")	NEW
height=*pixels, %*	The height of an input element (for type="image")	NEW
list=*datalist_id*	Refers to a datalist that contains predefined options for the input element	NEW
max=*number, date*	Specifies a maximum value for an input field	NEW
maxlength=*number*	Sets a value for the maximum number of characters allowed as input for a text or password control	

NEW New with HTML5   * Deprecated tags   ** Not supported in HTML5

Table A–3 HTML Tags and Attributes *(continued)*

	HTML Tag and Attributes	Description
	<input>....</input> *(continued)*	
	multiple=*multiple*	If present, the user is allowed more than one value
	name=*text*	Assigns a name to the control
NEW	pattern=*regexp_pattern*	Specifies a pattern or format for the input field's value
NEW	placeholder=*text*	Specifies a hint to help users fill out the input field
	readonly=readonly	Prevents changes to the control
NEW	required=required	Indicates that the input field's value is required in order to submit the form
	size=*number*	Sets the initial size of the control to a value in characters
NEW	step=*number*	Specifies the legal number intervals for the input field
	src=*URL*	Identifies the location of the image if the control is set to an image
	type=*type*	Defines the type of control
	value=*value*	Sets the initial value of the control
	<ins>....</ins>	Identifies and displays text as having been inserted in the document in relation to a previous version
	cite=*URL*	Specifies the URL of a document that has more information on the inserted text
	datetime=*datetime*	Date and time of a change
	<kbd>....</kbd>	Sets enclosed text to display as keyboard-like input
NEW	**<keygen>...</keygen>**	Defines a generated key in a form
	autofocus=autofocus	Makes the input field focused on page load
	challenge=challenge	Specifies that the value of the keygen is set to be challenged when submitted
	disabled=disabled	Disables the keytag field
	form=*form_id*	Defines one or more forms the input field belongs to
	keytype=rsa, dsa, ec	Specifies the security algorithm of the key (for example, rsa generates an RSA key)
	name=*text*	Defines a unique name for the input element; the name attribute is used to collect the field's value when submitted
	<label>....</label>	Creates a label for a form control
	for=*element_id*	Indicates the name or ID of the element to which the label is applied
	form=*form_id*	Specifies one or more forms the label field belongs to
	<legend>....</legend>	Assigns a caption to a fieldset element, as defined by the <fieldset> tags
	<li>....</li>	Defines the enclosed text as a list item in a list
	value=*value*	Inserts or restarts counting with value
	<link />	Establishes a link between the HTML document and another document, such as an external style sheet
	charset=*character set* **	Specifies the character encoding of the linked resource
	href=*URL*	Defines the URL of the linked document
	name=*text*	Names the current anchor so that it can be the destination for other links
	rel=*relationship*	Indicates the relationship going from the current page to the target
	rev=*relationship* **	Indicates the relationship going from the target to the current page
NEW	sizes=*heightxwidth, any*	Specifies sizes (height and width) of the linked resource
	target=*name* **	Defines the name of the frame into which the linked resource will appear
	type=*MIME_type*	Indicates the data or media type of the linked document (for example, text/css for linked style sheets)

NEW New with HTML5   * Deprecated tags   ** Not supported in HTML5

Table A–3 HTML Tags and Attributes *(continued)*

HTML Tag and Attributes	Description	
<map>....</map>	Specifies a client-side image map; must enclose <area> tags	
name=*text*	Assigns a name to the image map	
<mark>...</mark>	Defines marked text	NEW
<menu>...</menu>	Defines a list/menu of commands	
label=*menulabel*	Specifies a visible label for the menu	NEW
type=context, toolbar, list	Specifies which type of menu to display	NEW
<meta />	Provides additional data (metadata) about an HTML document	
charset=*character_set*	Specifies the character encoding for the HTML document	NEW
content=*text*	Specifies the value for the <meta> information; required	
http-equiv=content-type, default-style, refresh	Specifies the HTTP-equivalent name for metadata; tells the server to include that name and content in the HTTP header when the HTML document is sent to the client	
name=*text*	Assigns a name to metadata	
scheme=*text* **	Provides additional context for interpreting the information in the content attribute	
<meter>...</meter>	Defines measurement within a predefined range	NEW
form=*form_id*	Specifies which form this meter belongs to	
high=*number*	Specifies at which point the measurement's value is considered a high value	
low=*number*	Specifies at which point the measurement's value is considered a low value	
max=*number*	Specifies the maximum value; default value is 1.0	
min=*number*	Specifies the minimum value; default value is 0	
optimum=*number*	Specifies which measurement's value is the best value	
value=*number*	Required. Specifies the measurement's current or "measured" value	
<nav>...</nav>	Defines navigation links	NEW
<noframes>....</noframes> **	Defines content to be displayed in browsers that do not support frames	
<object>....</object>	Includes an external object in the HTML document such as an image, a Java applet, or other external object	
data=*URL*	Identifies the location of the object's data	
form=*form_id*	Specifies one or more forms the object belongs to	NEW
height=*pixels*	Sets the height of the object to a value in pixels	
name=*text*	Assigns a control name to the object for use in forms	
type=*MIME_type*	Specifies the content or media type of the object	
usemap=#*mapname*	Associates an image map as defined by the <map> element	
width=*pixels*	Sets the width of the object to a value in pixels	
<ol>....</ol>	Defines an ordered list that contains numbered list item elements (<li>)	
reversed=reversed	Specifies that the list order should be descending	NEW
start=*start*	Specifies the start value of an ordered list	
type=*option* **	Sets or resets the numbering format for the list	
<optgroup>...</optgroup>	Defines an option group	NEW
disabled=disabled	Specifies that an option group should be disabled	NEW
label=*text*	Specifies a label for the option group	NEW

NEW New with HTML5   * Deprecated tags   ** Not supported in HTML5

Table A–3 HTML Tags and Attributes *(continued)*

	HTML Tag and Attributes	Description
	<option>….</option>	Defines individual options in a selection list, as defined by the <select> element
	disabled=disabled	Disables the option items
	label=*text*	Provides a shorter label for the option than that specified in its content
	selected=selected	Sets the option to be the default or the selected option in a list
	value=*text*	Sets a value returned to the server when the user selects the option
NEW	**<output>…</output>**	Defines some types of output
	for=*element_id*	Specifies one or more elements the output field relates to
	form=*form_id*	Specifies one or more forms the output field belongs to
	name=*text*	Specifies a name for the object (to use when a form is submitted)
	<p>….</p>	Delimits a paragraph; automatically inserts a blank line between text
	align=*position* **	Aligns text within the paragraph
	<param>….</param>	Passes a parameter to an object or applet, as defined by the <object>
	name=*text*	Defines the name of the parameter required by an object
	type=*MIME_type* **	Specifies the content or media type of the object
	value=*data*	Sets the value of the parameter
	valuetype=data, ref, object **	Identifies the type of parameter used in the value attribute
	<pre>….</pre>	Preserves the original format of the enclosed text; keeps line breaks and spacing the same as the original
NEW	**<progress>…</progress>**	Defines progress of a task of any kind
	max=*number*	Defines the value of completion
	value=*number*	Defines the current value of the progress
	<q>….</q>	Sets enclosed text as a short quotation
	cite=*URL*	Specifies the source URL of the quote
NEW	**<rp>…</rp>**	Used in ruby annotations to define what to show if a browser does not support the ruby element
NEW	**<rt>…</rt>**	Defines explanation to ruby annotations
NEW	**<ruby>…</ruby>**	Defines ruby annotations, which are used for East Asian typography
	<s>…</s>	Defines text that is no longer correct, accurate, or relevant
	<samp>….</samp>	Sets enclosed text to appear as sample output from a computer program or script; usually appears in a monospace font
	<script>….</script>	Inserts a client-side script into an HTML document
NEW	async=async	Defines if the script should be executed asynchronously or not
	defer=defer	Indicates that the browser should defer executing the script
	src=*URL*	Identifies the location of an external script
	type=*MIME_type*	Specifies the MIME type of the script
NEW	**<section>…</section>**	Defines a section
	<select>….</select>	Defines a form control to create a multiple-choice menu or scrolling list; encloses a set of <option> tags to define one or more options
NEW	autofocus=autofocus	Makes the select field focused on page load
	disabled=disabled	Disables the selection list
	form=*form_id*	Defines one or more forms the select field belongs to
	multiple=multiple	Sets the list to allow multiple selections

NEW New with HTML5 * Deprecated tags ** Not supported in HTML5

Table A–3 HTML Tags and Attributes *(continued)*

HTML Tag and Attributes	Description	
<select>....</select> *(continued)*		
name=*text*	Assigns a name to the selection list	
size=*value*	Sets the number of visible options in the list	
<small>....</small>	Sets enclosed text to appear in a smaller typeface	
<source>...</source>	Defines media resources	NEW
media=*media_query*	Specifies what media/device the media resource is optimized for; default value: all	
src=*URL*	The URL of the media	
type=*MIME_type*	Specifies the MIME type of the media resource	
<span>....</span>	Creates a user-defined container to add inline structure to the HTML document	
<strike>....</strike> **	Sets enclosed text to appear with strong emphasis; usually displayed as bold text	
<strong>....</strong>	Sets enclosed text to appear with strong emphasis; usually displayed as bold text	
<style>....</style>	Encloses embedded style sheet rules for use in the HTML document	
media=*media_query*	Identifies the intended medium of the style	
scoped=*scoped*	If present, the styles should only apply to this element's parent element and its child elements	NEW
type=text/css	Specifies the MIME type of the style sheet	
_{....}	Sets enclosed text to appear in subscript	
<summary>...</summary>	Defines the header of a "detail" element	NEW
^{....}	Sets enclosed text to appear in superscript	
<table>....</table>	Marks the start and end of a table	
align=*position* **	Aligns the table text	
border=*value*	Specifies if the table cells have borders or not; the only values are "" and 1	
cellpadding=*pixels* **	Sets padding around each cell's contents to a value in pixels	
cellspacing=*pixels* **	Sets spacing between cells to a value in pixels	
frame=*option* **	Defines which parts of the outer border (frame) to display	
rules=*option* **	Specifies which inner borders are to appear between the table cells	
summary=*text* **	Provides a summary of the table's purpose and structure	
width=*pixels, %* **	Sets table width in pixels or a percentage of the window	
<tbody>....</tbody>	Defines a groups of rows in a table body	
align=*option* **	Aligns text	
char=*character* **	Specifies a character on which to align column values (for example, a period is used to align monetary values)	
charoff=*value* **	Specifies a number of characters to offset data aligned with the character specified in the char property	
valign=*position* **	Sets vertical alignment of cells in a group	
<td>....</td>	Defines a data cell in a table; contents are left-aligned and normal text by default	
abbr=*text* **	Provides an abbreviated version of the cell's contents that browsers can use if space is limited	
align=*position* **	Specifies horizontal alignment	

NEW New with HTML5   * Deprecated tags   ** Not supported in HTML5

Table A–3 HTML Tags and Attributes *(continued)*

	HTML Tag and Attributes	Description
	<td>....</td> *(continued)*	
	bgcolor=*color* **	Defines the background color for the cell
	char=*character* **	Specifies a character on which to align column values (for example, a period is used to align monetary values)
	charoff=*value* **	Specifies a number of characters to offset data aligned with the character specified in the char property
	colspan=*value*	Defines the number of adjacent columns spanned by the cell
	headers=*header_id*	Defines the list of header cells for the current cell
	rowspan=*value*	Defines the number of adjacent rows spanned by the cell
	scope=*option* **	Specifies cells for which the element defines header cells
	valign=*position* **	Sets vertical alignment of cells in the group
	width=*pixels, %* **	Sets the width of the table in either pixels or a percentage of the whole table width
	<textarea>....</textarea>	Creates a multiline text input area within a form
NEW	autofocus=autofocus	Specifies that the text area field should have focus on page load
	cols=*value*	Defines the number of columns in the text input area
	disabled=disabled	Disables the element
NEW	form=*form_id*	Specifies one or more forms the text area belongs to
NEW	maxlength=*number*	Specifies the maximum number of characters allowed in the text area
	name=*text*	Assigns a name to the text area
NEW	placeholder=*text*	Specifies a hint to help users fill out the input field
	readonly=readonly	Prevents the user from editing content in the text area
NEW	required=required	Indicates that the input field's value is required in order to submit the form
	rows=*value*	Defines the number of rows in the text input area
NEW	wrap=hard, soft	Specifies how the text in the text area is wrapped, and if it should be wrapped when submitted in a form
	<tfoot>....</tfoot>	Identifies and groups rows into a table footer
	align=*position* **	Specifies horizontal alignment
	char=*character* **	Specifies a character on which to align column values (for example, a period is used to align monetary values)
	charoff=*value* **	Specifies a number of characters to offset data aligned with the character specified in the char property
	valign=*position* **	Sets vertical alignment of cells in a group
	<th>....</th>	Defines a table header cell; contents are bold and center-aligned by default
	colspan=*value*	Defines the number of adjacent columns spanned by the cell
NEW	headers=*header_id*	Specifies one or more header cells a cell is related to
	rowspan=*value*	Defines the number of adjacent rows spanned by the cell
NEW	scope=col, colgroup, row, rowgroup	Specifies whther a header cell is a header for a column, row, or group of columns or rows
	width=*pixels, %* **	Sets the width of the table in either pixels or a percentage of the whole table width

NEW New with HTML5   * Deprecated tags   ** Not supported in HTML5

Table A–3 HTML Tags and Attributes *(continued)*

HTML Tag and Attributes	Description	
<thead>....</thead>	Identifies and groups rows into a table header	
align=*position* **	Specifies horizontal alignment	
char=*character* **	Specifies a character on which to align column values (for example, a period is used to align monetary values)	
charoff=*value* **	Specifies a number of characters to offset data aligned with the character specified in the char property	
valign=*position* **	Sets vertical alignment of cells in a group	
<time>...</time>	Defines a date/time	NEW
datetime=*datetime*	Specifies the date or time for the time element; this attribute is used if no date or time is specified in the element's content	
pubdate=pubdate	Specifies that the date and time in the <time> element is the publication date and time of the document (or the nearest ancestor article element)	
<title>....</title>	Defines the title for the HTML document; should always be used	
<tr>....</tr>	Defines a row of cells within a table	
align=*position* **	Specifies horizontal alignment	
bgcolor=*color* **	Defines the background color for the cell	
char=*character* **	Specifies a character on which to align column values (for example, a period is used to align monetary values)	
charoff=*value* **	Specifies a number of characters to offset data aligned with the character specified in the char property	
valign=*position* **	Sets vertical alignment of cells in a group	
<tt>....</tt> **	Formats the enclosed text in teletype- or computer-style monospace font	
<u>....</u> **	Sets enclosed text to appear with an underline	
<ul>....</ul>	Defines an unordered list that contains bulleted list item elements (<li>)	
type=circle, disc, square **	Sets or resets the bullet format for the list	
<var>....</var>	Indicates the enclosed text is a variable's name; used to mark up variables or program arguments	
<video>...</video>	Defines a video	NEW
autoplay=autoplay	If present, then the video will start playing as soon as it is ready	
controls=controls	If present, controls will be displayed, such as a play button	
height=*pixels*	Sets the height of the video player	
loop=loop	If present, the video will start over again, every time it is finished	
muted=muted	Specifies the default state of the the audio. Currently, only "muted" is allowed	
poster=*URL*	Specifies the URL of an image representing the video	
preload=auto, metadata, none	Specifies whether or not the video should be loaded when the page loads	
src=*URL*	The URL of the video to play	
width=*pixels*	Sets the width of the video player	
<wbr>...</wbr>	Defines a possible line break	NEW

NEW New with HTML5   * Deprecated tags   ** Not supported in HTML5

Appendix B

Browser-Safe Color Palette

Browser-Safe Colors

Three hardware components help deliver color to a computer user: the processor, the video card, and the monitor. Because of the wide variety of components that exist, the color quality that users see varies greatly. The software on a user's computer, specifically the Web browser, also affects the way that color is displayed on a monitor. It is very difficult, if not impossible, to plan for all possible color variations created by a Web browser. In the past, Web developers had to make sure that they used browser-safe colors. These browser-safe colors restricted the number of colors used on a Web page and minimized the impact of color variations. The trend for monitors today is to display "true color," which means that any of 16 million colors can be displayed on the monitor. Few people use 8-bit monitors anymore, so you generally do not have to limit yourself to browser-safe colors.

A total of 216 browser-safe colors appear the same on different monitors, operating systems, and browsers—including both Windows and Macintosh operating systems and Internet Explorer, Apple Safari, Google Chrome, and Mozilla Firefox browsers. When using color on your Web site, keep in mind that using only the 216 browser-safe colors can be very restrictive. On those 8-bit monitors, only the browser-safe colors will be displayed. If you decide to use a non-browser-safe color, the browser will try to create the color by combining (a process called dithering) any number of the 216 acceptable colors. The resulting color could be slightly different from the color you had intended.

For a complete list of the 216 browser-safe colors, see Table B–1 on the next page or visit the Book Companion Site Web page for this book at www.cengagebrain.com.

Note that you can use either the color name or the color number when identifying a particular color to use. For instance, you can use the number #000099 (see color sample on the following page) or the word "navy" to specify the same color. Also note that to comply with XHTML standards, color names such as "navy" or "silver" must be all lowercase letters and all colors, whether identified by name or number, should be enclosed within quotation marks. Although the book teaches HTML5, for which the XHTML standards do not apply, we still stress using lowercase letters and quotation marks.

Table B–1 Browser-Safe Colors

#ffffff	#ffffcc	#ffff99	#ffff66	#ffff33	#ffff00
#ffccff	#ffcccc	#ffcc99	#ffcc66	#ffcc33	#ffcc00
#ff99ff	#ff99cc	#ff9999	#ff9966	#ff9933	#ff9900
#ff66ff	#ff66cc	#ff6699	#ff6666	#ff6633	#ff6600
#ff33ff	#ff33cc	#ff3399	#ff3366	#ff3333	#ff3300
#ff00ff	#ff00cc	#ff0099	#ff0066	#ff0033	#ff0000
#ccffff	#ccffcc	#ccff99	#ccff66	#ccff33	#ccff00
#ccccff	#cccccc	#cccc99	#cccc66	#cccc33	#cccc00
#cc99ff	#cc99cc	#cc9999	#cc9966	#cc9933	#cc9900
#cc66ff	#cc66cc	#cc6699	#cc6666	#cc6633	#cc6600
#cc33ff	#cc33cc	#cc3399	#cc3366	#cc3333	#cc3300
#cc00ff	#cc00cc	#cc0099	#cc0066	#cc0033	#cc0000
#99ffff	#99ffcc	#99ff99	#99ff66	#99ff33	#99ff00
#99ccff	#99cccc	#99cc99	#99cc66	#99cc33	#99cc00
#9999ff	#9999cc	#999999	#999966	#999933	#999900
#9966ff	#9966cc	#996699	#996666	#996633	#996600
#9933ff	#9933cc	#993399	#993366	#993333	#993300
#9900ff	#9900cc	#990099	#990066	#990033	#990000
#66ffff	#66ffcc	#66ff99	#66ff66	#66ff33	#66ff00
#66ccff	#66cccc	#66cc99	#66cc66	#66cc33	#66cc00
#6699ff	#6699cc	#669999	#669966	#669933	#669900
#6666ff	#6666cc	#666699	#666666	#666633	#666600
#6633ff	#6633cc	#663399	#663366	#663333	#663300
#6600ff	#6600cc	#660099	#660066	#660033	#660000
#33ffff	#33ffcc	#33ff99	#33ff66	#33ff33	#33ff00
#33ccff	#33cccc	#33cc99	#33cc66	#33cc33	#33cc00
#3399ff	#3399cc	#339999	#339966	#339933	#339900
#3366ff	#3366cc	#336699	#336666	#336633	#336600
#3333ff	#3333cc	#333399	#333366	#333333	#333300
#3300ff	#3300cc	#330099	#330066	#330033	#330000
#00ffff	#00ffcc	#00ff99	#00ff66	#00ff33	#00ff00
#00ccff	#00cccc	#00cc99	#00cc66	#00cc33	#00cc00
#0099ff	#0099cc	#009999	#009966	#009933	#009900
#0066ff	#0066cc	#006699	#006666	#006633	#006600
#0033ff	#0033cc	#003399	#003366	#003333	#003300
#0000ff	#0000cc	#000099	#000066	#000033	#000000

Appendix C

Accessibility Standards and the Web

Making the Web Accessible

Nearly 15% of the world population has some sort of disability, a physical condition that limits the individual's ability to perform certain tasks. The U.S. Congress passed the Rehabilitation Act in 1973, which prohibits discrimination for those with disabilities. In 1998, Congress amended this act to reflect the latest changes in information technology. Section 508 requires that any electronic information developed, procured, maintained, or used by the federal government be accessible to people with disabilities. Disabilities that inhibit a person's ability to use the Web fall into four main categories: visual, hearing, motor, and cognitive. This amendment has had a profound effect on how Web pages are designed and developed.

Although Section 508 is specific to Web sites created and maintained by the federal government, all competent Web developers adhere to the Section 508 guidelines. It is important to include everyone as a potential user of your Web site, including those with disabilities. To ignore the needs of nearly 15% of our population is just poor practice. However, some portions of Section 508 are not supported by HTML5. For example, longdesc (§ 1194.22a) and frames (§ 1194.22i) are no longer supported by HTML5. A Web developer would not use those elements, which renders those Section 508 requirements null.

The World Wide Web Consortium (W3C) sponsors its own initiative, called the Web Accessibility Initiative (WAI), that develops guidelines and support materials for accessibility standards. These guidelines, known as the Web Content Accessibility Guidelines (WCAG), cover many of the same issues defined in the Section 508 rules and expand on them relative to superior Web site design.

Section 508 Guidelines Examples

The 13 parts of the Section 508 guidelines are as follows:

- Subpart A—General
  - 1194.1 Purpose.
  - 1194.2 Application.
  - 1194.3 General exceptions.
  - 1194.4 Definitions.
  - 1194.5 Equivalent facilitation.

- Subpart B—Technical Standards
  - 1194.21 Software applications and operating systems.
  - 1194.22 Web-based intranet and Internet information and applications. 16 rules.
  - 1194.23 Telecommunications products.
  - 1194.24 Video and multimedia products.
  - 1194.25 Self contained, closed products.
  - 1194.26 Desktop and portable computers.
- Subpart C—Functional Performance Criteria
  - 1194.31 Functional performance criteria.
- Subpart D—Information, Documentation, and Support
  - 1194.41 Information, documentation, and support.

Web developers should review these guidelines thoroughly. We focus on the specific guidelines for intranet and Internet development in the following sections.

Subsection **§ 1194.22** of Section 508, **Web-based intranet and Internet information and applications**, is the segment of the amendment that impacts Web design. There are 16 paragraphs within § 1194.22, which are lettered (a) through (p). These 16 paragraphs describe how each component of a Web site should be designed to ensure accessibility. The following is a list of the 16 paragraphs:

§ 1194.22 (a) A text equivalent for every non-text element shall be provided (e.g., via "alt", "longdesc", or in element content).

Graphical images that contain Web page content should include a text alternative. For good Web development practice, all images should include the alt attribute to describe that image, as shown in Chapter 2. As mentioned earlier, longdesc is not supported by HTML5.

§ 1194.22 (b) Equivalent alternatives for any multimedia presentation shall be synchronized with the presentation.

Audio clips should contain a transcript of the content; video clips need closed captioning.

§ 1194.22 (c) Web pages shall be designed so that all information conveyed with color is also available without color, for example from context or markup.

Although color is an important component of most Web pages, you need to consider those site visitors with forms of color blindness if the color contributes significantly to the Web site content.

§ 1194.22 (d) Documents shall be organized so they are readable without requiring an associated style sheet.

Style sheets have an important role in Web development. Some browsers, however, allow users to create their own customized style sheets, which could alter the style sheets that you have designated. When developing a Web site using style sheets, ensure that the site maintains its functionality, even if your specified style sheets have been turned off.

§ 1194.22 (e) Redundant text links shall be provided for each active region of a server-side image map.

and

§ 1194.22 (f) Client-side image maps shall be provided instead of server-side image maps except where the regions cannot be defined with an available geometric shape.

This means that it is preferable for the Web developer to use client-side image maps unless the map uses a shape that the client-side will not allow. If the Web developer chooses to use server-side image maps, the developer should provide text alternatives for each link on the image map.

§ 1194.22 (g) Row and column headers shall be identified for data tables.
and

§ 1194.22 (h) Markup shall be used to associate data cells and header cells for data tables that have two or more logical levels of row or column headers.

You should structure your tables so that they appear in a linear fashion. In other words, the table content should be displayed one cell at a time, working from left to right across each row before moving to the next row.

§ 1194.22 (i) Frames shall be titled with text that facilitates frame identification and navigation.

Although frames are not supported by HTML5, it is important to understand what the law requires. Nonvisual browsers open frame sites one frame at a time. It is therefore important that the Web developer gives a name to each frame, and that the name reflects the contents of that frame. You can use either the title or the id, but because nonvisual browsers differ in which attribute they use, the Web developer should use both attributes.

§ 1194.22 (j) Pages shall be designed to avoid causing the screen to flicker with a frequency greater than 2 Hz and lower than 55 Hz.

Animations on a Web page can be irritating to many people. However, they can also be quite harmful to people who have certain cognitive or visual disabilities or seizure disorders. You should therefore ensure that animations fall within the ranges stated, and you should limit the use of animations when possible. You also should make certain that necessary page content is available without the animations.

§ 1194.22 (k) A text-only page, with equivalent information or functionality, shall be provided to make a Web site comply with the provisions of this part, when compliance cannot be accomplished in any other way. The content of the text-only pages shall be updated whenever the primary page changes.

If you cannot comply with the other 15 guidelines, you should provide a text-only page to display the content of the page. You should also provide an easily accessible link to that text-only Web page.

§ 1194.22 (l) When pages utilize scripting languages to display content, or to create interface elements, the information provided by the script shall be identified with functional text that can be read by assistive technology.

Scripts are often used to create a more interesting and dynamic Web page. You should ensure that the functionality of the script is still available for any person using nonvisual browsers.

§ 1194.22 (m) When a Web page requires that an applet, plug-in, or other application be present on the client system to interpret page content, the page must provide a link to a plug-in or applet that complies with 1194.21 (a) through (l).

Any applet or plug-in that is used on your Web pages should also comply with Section 508. The Web developer should provide a link to the applet or plug-in that is compliant with Section 508.

§ 1194.22 (n) When electronic forms are designed to be completed on-line, the form shall allow people using assistive technology to access the information, field elements, and functionality required for completion and submission of the form, including all directions and cues.

Forms need to be accessible to anyone, including those using nonvisual browsers. You should therefore include value attributes or alternative text for buttons, input boxes, and text area boxes on any form included on your Web page.

§ 1194.22 (o) A method shall be provided that permits users to skip repetitive navigation links.

It can be helpful to provide text links at the very top of a Web page so that users of nonvisual browsers can quickly link to the content of the Web site. Some Web developers use a link that allows users to skip to the main content of the Web page immediately by using a transparent image.

§ 1194.22 (p) When a timed response is required, the user shall be alerted and given sufficient time to indicate that more time is required.

Users need to be given sufficient time to react to a time-out from inactivity by notifying users that the process will soon time out. The user should then be given a way to easily request additional time.

WAI Guidelines

The WAI identifies 12 guidelines for Web developers, known as Web Content Accessibility Guidelines (WCAG) 2.0. The Web Content Accessibility Guidelines (WCAG) documents explain how to make Web content more accessible to people with disabilities. Web **content** generally refers to the information in a Web page or Web application, including text, images, forms, sounds, and such. All Web developers should review the information at the official Web site at w3.org/WAI/intro/wcag.php for complete information on these guidelines, and should apply the guidelines to their Web page development.

The 12 WCAG 2.0 guidelines are organized under four principles: perceivable, operable, understandable, and robust. Anyone who wants to use the Web must have content that is:

Perceivable: Information and user interface components must be presentable to users in ways they can perceive. Users must be able to perceive the information being presented (it can't be invisible to all of their senses).

Operable: User interface components and navigation must be operable. Users must be able to operate the interface (the interface cannot require interaction that a user cannot perform).

Understandable: Information and the operation of the user interface must be understandable. Users must be able to understand the information as well as the operation of the user interface (the content or operation cannot be beyond their understanding).

Robust: Content must be robust enough that it can be interpreted reliably by a wide variety of user agents, including assistive technologies. Users must be able to access the content as technologies advance (as technologies and user agents evolve, the content should remain accessible).

If any of these are not true, users with disabilities will not be able to use the Web.

For each guideline, there are testable success criteria, which are at three levels: A, AA, and AAA. In order for a Web page to conform to WCAG 2.0, all of the following conformance requirements must be satisfied:

- **Level A:** For Level A conformance (the minimum level of conformance), the Web page satisfies all the Level A Success Criteria, or a conforming alternate version is provided.
- **Level AA:** For Level AA conformance, the Web page satisfies all the Level A and Level AA Success Criteria, or a Level AA conforming alternate version is provided.
- **Level AAA:** For Level AAA conformance, the Web page satisfies all the Level A, Level AA, and Level AAA Success Criteria, or a Level AAA conforming alternate version is provided.

Table C–1 contains a summary of the WCAG 2.0 guidelines and the corresponding level of conformance.

Table C–1

WCAG 2.0 Guidelines	Level
Principle 1: Perceivable—Information and user interface components must be presentable to users in ways they can perceive.	
Guideline 1.1 Text Alternatives: Provide text alternatives for any non-text content so that it can be changed into other forms people need, such as large print, braille, speech, symbols or simpler language.	
1.1.1 Nontext Content: All nontext content that is presented to the user has a text alternative that serves the equivalent purpose.	A
Guideline 1.2 Time Based Media: Provide alternatives for time-based media.	
1.2.1 Audio-only and Video-only (Prerecorded): An alternative for time-based media is provided that presents equivalent information for prerecorded audio-only or video-only content.	A
1.2.2 Captions (Prerecorded): Captions are provided for all prerecorded audio content in synchronized media, except when the media is a media alternative for text and is clearly labeled as such.	A
1.2.3 Audio Description or Media Alternative (Prerecorded): An alternative for time-based media or audio description of the prerecorded video content is provided for synchronized media, except when the media is a media alternative for text and is clearly labeled as such.	A
1.2.4 Captions (Live): Captions are provided for all live audio content in synchronized media.	AA
1.2.5 Audio Description (Prerecorded): Audio description is provided for all prerecorded video content in synchronized media.	AA
1.2.6 Sign Language (Prerecorded): Sign language interpretation is provided for all prerecorded audio content in synchronized media.	AAA
1.2.7 Extended Audio Description (Prerecorded): Where pauses in foreground audio are insufficient to allow audio descriptions to convey the sense of the video, extended audio description is provided for all prerecorded video content in synchronized media.	AAA

Table C–1 *(continued)*	
WCAG 2.0 Guidelines	**Level**
1.2.8 Media Alternative (Prerecorded): An alternative for time-based media is provided for all prerecorded synchronized media and for all prerecorded video-only media.	AAA
1.2.9 Audio-only (Live): An alternative for time-based media that presents equivalent information for live audio-only content is provided.	AAA
Guideline 1.3 Adaptable: Create content that can be presented in different ways (for example simpler layout) without losing information or structure.	
1.3.1 Info and Relationships: Information, structure, and relationships conveyed through presentation can be programmatically determined or are available in text.	A
1.3.2 Meaningful Sequence: When the sequence in which content is presented affects its meaning, a correct reading sequence can be programmatically determined.	A
1.3.3 Sensory Characteristics: Instructions provided for understanding and operating content do not rely solely on sensory characteristics of components such as shape, size, visual location, orientation, or sound.	A
Guideline 1.4 Distinguishable: Make it easier for users to see and hear content including separating foreground from background.	
1.4.1 Use of Color: Color is not used as the only visual means of conveying information, indicating an action, prompting a response, or distinguishing a visual element.	A
1.4.2 Audio Control: If any audio on a Web page plays automatically for more than 3 seconds, either a mechanism is available to pause or stop the audio, or a mechanism is available to control the audio volume independently from the overall system volume level.	A
1.4.3 Contrast (Minimum): The visual presentation of text and images of text has a contrast ratio of at least 4.5:1 (for specific exceptions, refer to w3.org/TR/WCAG).	AA
1.4.4 Resize text: Except for captions and images of text, text can be resized without assistive technology up to 200 percent without loss of content or functionality.	AA
1.4.5 Images of Text: If the technologies being used can achieve the visual presentation, text is used to convey information rather than images of (for specific exceptions, refer to w3.org/TR/WCAG).	AA
1.4.6 Contrast (Enhanced): The visual presentation of text and images of text has a contrast ratio of at least 7:1 (for specific exceptions, refer to w3.org/TR/WCAG).	AAA
1.4.7 Low or No Background Audio: For prerecorded audio-only content in which 1) the audio does not contain background sounds, 2) the background sounds can be turned off, or 3) the background sounds are at least 20 decibels lower than the foreground speech content.	AAA
1.4.8 Visual Presentation: For the visual presentation of blocks of text, a mechanism is available to manipulate the look of the page (e.g., background colors, text size) easily.	AAA
1.4.9 Images of Text (No Exception): Images of text are only used for pure decoration or where a particular presentation of text is essential to the information being conveyed.	AAA
Principle 2: Operable—User interface components and navigation must be operable.	
Guideline 2.1 Keyboard Accessible: Make all functionality available from the keyboard.	
2.1.1 Keyboard: All functionality of the content is operable through a keyboard interface without requiring specific timings for individual keystrokes, except where the underlying function requires input that depends on the path of the user's movement and not just the endpoints.	A
2.1.2 No Keyboard Trap: If keyboard focus can be moved to a component of the page using a keyboard interface, then focus can be moved away from that component using only a keyboard interface, and, if it requires more than unmodified arrow or tab keys or other standard exit methods, the user is advised of the method for moving focus away.	A
2.1.3 Keyboard (No Exception): All functionality of the content is operable through a keyboard interface without requiring specific timings for individual keystrokes.	AAA

Table C–1 *(continued)*

WCAG 2.0 Guidelines	Level
Guideline 2.2 Enough Time: Provide users enough time to read and use content.	
2.2.1 Timing Adjustable: The user should be able to easily change each time limit that is set by the content.	A
2.2.2 Pause, Stop, Hide: The user should be able to pause, stop, or hide moving, blinking, scrolling, or auto-updating information.	A
2.2.3 No Timing: Timing is not an essential part of the event or activity presented by the content, except for noninteractive synchronized media and real-time events.	AAA
2.2.4 Interruptions: Interruptions can be postponed or suppressed by the user, except interruptions involving an emergency.	AAA
2.2.5 Re-authenticating: When an authenticated session expires, the user can continue the activity without loss of data after re-authenticating.	AAA
Guideline 2.3 Seizures: Do not design content in a way that is known to cause seizures.	
2.3.1 Three Flashes or Below Threshold: Web pages do not contain anything that flashes more than three times in any one second period, or the flash is below the general flash and red flash thresholds.	A
2.3.2 Three Flashes: Web pages do not contain anything that flashes more than three times in any one second period.	AAA
Guideline 2.4 Navigable: Provide ways to help users navigate, find content, and determine where they are.	
2.4.1 Bypass Blocks: A mechanism is available to bypass blocks of content that are repeated on multiple Web pages.	A
2.4.2 Page Titled: Web pages have titles that describe topic or purpose.	A
2.4.3 Focus Order: If a Web page can be navigated sequentially and the navigation sequences affect meaning or operation, focusable components receive focus in an order that preserves meaning and operability.	A
2.4.4 Link Purpose (In Context): The purpose of each link can be determined from the link text alone or from the link text together with its programmatically determined link context, except where the purpose of the link would be ambiguous to users in general.	A
2.4.5 Multiple Ways: More than one way is available to locate a Web page within a set of Web pages except where the Web Page is the result of, or a step in, a process.	AA
2.4.6 Headings and Labels: Headings and labels describe topic or purpose.	AA
2.4.7 Focus Visible: Any keyboard operable user interface has a mode of operation where the keyboard focus indicator is visible.	AA
2.4.8 Location: Information about the user's location within a set of Web pages is available.	AAA
2.4.9 Link Purpose (Link Only): A mechanism is available to allow the purpose of each link to be identified from link text alone, except where the purpose of the link would be ambiguous to users in general.	AAA
2.4.10 Section Headings: Section headings are used to organize the content.	AAA
Principle 3: Understandable—Information and the operation of user interface must be understandable.	
Guideline 3.1 Readable: Make text content readable and understandable.	
3.1.1 Language of Page: The default human language of each Web page can be programmatically determined.	A
3.1.2 Language of Parts: The human language of each passage or phrase in the content can be programmatically determined except for proper names, technical terms, words of indeterminate language, and words or phrases that have become part of the vernacular of the immediately surrounding text.	AA

Table C–1 *(continued)*

WCAG 2.0 Guidelines	Level
3.1.3 Unusual Words: A mechanism is available for identifying specific definitions of words or phrases used in an unusual or restricted way, including idioms and jargon.	AAA
3.1.4 Abbreviations: A mechanism for identifying the expanded form or meaning of abbreviations is available.	AAA
3.1.5 Reading Level: When text requires reading ability more advanced than the lower secondary education level after removal of proper names and titles, supplemental content, or a version that does not require reading ability more advanced than the lower secondary education level, is available.	AAA
3.1.6 Pronunciation: A mechanism is available for identifying specific pronunciation of words where the meaning of the words, in context, is ambiguous without knowing the pronunciation.	AAA
Guideline 3.2 Predictable: Make Web pages appear and operate in predictable ways.	
3.2.1 On Focus: When any component receives focus, it does not initiate a change of context.	A
3.2.2 On Input: Changing the setting of any user interface component does not automatically cause a change of context unless the user has been advised of the behavior before using the component.	A
3.2.3 Consistent Navigation: Navigational mechanisms that are repeated on multiple Web pages within a set of Web pages occur in the same relative order each time they are repeated, unless a change is initiated by the user.	AA
3.2.4 Consistent Identification: Components that have the same functionality within a set of Web pages are identified consistently.	AA
3.2.5 Change on Request: Changes of context are initiated only by user request or a mechanism is available to turn off such changes.	AAA
Guideline 3.3 Input Assistance: Help users avoid and correct mistakes.	
3.3.1 Error Identification: If an input error is automatically detected, the item that is in error is identified and the error is described to the user in text.	A
3.3.2 Labels or Instructions: Labels or instructions are provided when content requires user input.	A
3.3.3 Error Suggestion: If an input error is automatically detected and suggestions for its correction are known, then the suggestions are provided to the user, unless it would jeopardize the security or purpose of the content.	AA
3.3.4 Error Prevention (Legal, Financial, Data): For Web pages that cause legal commitments or financial transactions for the user to occur, that modify or delete user-controllable data in data storage systems, or that submit user test responses, a mechanism is available for reviewing, confirming, and correcting information before finalizing the submission.	AA
3.3.5 Help: Context-sensitive help is available.	AAA
3.3.6 Error Prevention (All): For Web pages that require the user to submit information, a mechanism is available for reviewing, confirming, and correcting information before finalizing the submission.	AAA
Principle 4: Robust—Content must be robust enough that it can be interpreted reliably by a wide variety of user agents, including assistive technologies.	
Guideline 4.1 Compatible: Maximize compatibility with current and future user agents, including assistive technologies.	
4.1.1 Parsing: In content implemented using markup languages, elements have complete start and end tags, elements are nested according to their specifications, elements do not contain duplicate attributes, and any IDs are unique, except where the specifications allow these features.	A
4.1.2 Name, Role, Value: For all user interface components (including but not limited to: form elements, links, and components generated by scripts), the name and role can be programmatically determined; states, properties, and values that can be set by the user can be programmatically set; and notification of changes to these items is available to user agents, including assistive technologies.	A

Appendix D

CSS Properties and Values

This appendix provides a brief review of Cascading Style Sheets (CSS) concepts and terminology, and lists CSS level 1, 2, and 3 properties and values. The CSS3 properties and values are indicated with a NEW icon. CSS3 utilizes a modularized approach to style sheets, which allows CSS to be updated in a more timely and flexible manner. Many of the new properties are not supported by all browsers as of yet. As stated previously, CSS3, like HTML5, is a moving target. Browsers adapt new properties on an ongoing basis and will continue to do so.

CSS Concepts and Terminology

CSS supports three types of style sheets: inline, embedded (or internal), and external (or linked). A **style** is a rule that defines the appearance of an element on a Web page. Inline styles are used to change the appearance (or style) for individual elements, such as a heading or a paragraph. A **style sheet** is a series of rules that defines the style for a Web page or an entire Web site. The **style statement** changes that specific element, but does not affect other elements in the document. With an embedded style sheet, you add the style sheet within the <style></style> container between the <head></head> tags of the HTML document. An embedded, or internal, style sheet allows you to define the style for an entire Web page. With a linked, or external, style sheet, you create a text file that contains all of the styles that you want to apply, and save the text file with the file extension .css. You then add a link to this external style sheet on any Web page in the Web site in which you want to use those styles. External style sheets give you the most flexibility and are ideal to apply the same formats to all of the Web pages in a Web site. External style sheets also make it easy to change formats quickly across Web pages.

The part of the style statement that identifies the page element that you want to change is called the selector. In the example below, the selector is the h1 (heading size 1) element. The part of the style statement that identifies how the element(s) should appear is called the declaration. In this example, the declaration is everything between the curly brackets {color: red}. This includes the property named color and the value named red.

```
h1   {color: red;}
```

You could use the statement above in both an embedded and an external style sheet. With an external (linked) style sheet, you save the file with the selectors and declarations as a .css file. You then link that file into any Web page into which you want those styles to apply. To add the same style statement into an embedded style sheet, you have to put the selector and declaration within the <style></style> container as shown below. This code would be inserted within the <head></head> container.

```
<style type="text/css">
  h1   {color: red;}
</style>
```

These two style sheets (embedded and external) give you the most flexibility. For instance, if you want all h1 and h2 headings to be the color red, you would simply add the code below:

```
h1, h2      {color: red;}
```

You could also make the style change to the h1 heading as an inline style. You insert that code within the body of the Web page in the following format:

```
<h1 style="color: red">
```

Although inline styles can be very useful, understand that you would have to insert the same declaration for every h1 (or h2 or h3) heading within the Web page. That makes the inline style less flexible than the other style sheets.

As shown in Table D–1, the three style sheets supported by CSS control the appearance of a Web page at different levels. Each style sheet type also has a different level of precedence or priority in relationship to the others. An external style sheet, for example, is used to define styles for multiple pages in a Web site. An embedded style sheet is used to change the style of one Web page, but overrides or takes precedence over any styles defined in an external style sheet. An inline style sheet is used to control the style within an individual HTML tag and takes precedence over the styles defined in both embedded and external style sheets.

Table D–1 CSS Precedence

Type	Level and Precedence
Inline	• Changes the style within an individual HTML tag • Overrides embedded and external style sheets
Embedded	• Changes the style of one Web page • Overrides external style sheets
External	• Changes the style of multiple pages in a Web site

Because style sheets have different levels of precedence, all three types of style sheets can be used on a single Web page. For example, you may want some elements of a Web page to match the other Web pages in the Web site, but you also may want to vary the look of certain sections of that Web page. You can do this by using the three types of style sheets.

For a more comprehensive list of CSS properties and values, see the Web site of the World Wide Web Consortium (w3.org). In addition to an abundance of information about CSS levels 1 and 2, the W3C site also has extensive information about CSS3, from its history to its use with browsers today. The Web site also includes many online tutorials for learning CSS levels 1 and 2 as well as CSS3.

CSS Properties

Tables D–2 through D–30 show the property names, descriptions, and valid values for various categories of CSS properties. Properties shown with the NEW icon are new to CSS3. The NEW icon next to a table name indicates that all properties in the table are new with CSS3. Values listed in bold are the default.

Acceptable Units of Measure

Table D–2 Units of Measure

Property Name	Description	Values
color	A color is either a keyword or a numerical hexidecimal, RGB, RGBA, HSL, or HSLA color specification	[keyword] [#rrggbb]
length	Indicates both relative (em, ex, px) and absolute (in, cm, mm, pt, pc) lengths	em – relative to size of capital M of browser default font ex – relative to small x of browser default font px – represents one pixel, smallest unit of measure in – one inch cm – one centimeter mm – one millimeter pt – 1/72 of an inch pc – 1/12 of an inch
percentage	Values are always relative to another value	percentage of width or height of parent element; if only one value is given, the second is set to "auto"

Animation Properties

NEW

Table D–3 Animation Properties

Property Name	Description	Values
@keyframes	Specifies the animation	[animationname] [keyframes-selector] [css-styles]
animation	A shorthand property for all the animation properties below, except the animation-play-state property	
animation-delay	Specifies when the animation will start	[time]
animation-direction	Specifies whether or not the animation should play in reverse on alternate cycles	**normal** alternate
animation-duration	Specifies how many seconds or milliseconds an animation takes to complete one cycle	[time]
animation-iteration-count	Specifies the number of times an animation should be played	[n] infinite
animation-name	Specifies a name for the @keyframes animation	[keyframename] **none**
animation-play-state	Specifies whether the animation is running or paused	paused **running**
animation-timing-function	Specifies the speed curve of the animation	linear **ease** ease-in ease-out ease-in-out cubic-bezier

Background and Color Properties

Table D–4 Background and Color Properties

Property Name	Description	Values
background	The background property is a shorthand property for setting the individual background properties	
background-attachment	Sets the background image to fixed or scrolls with the page	**scroll** fixed inherit
NEW background-clip	Specifies the painting area of the background	
background-color	Sets the background color of an element	**transparent** [color]
background-image	Sets an image as the background	**none** [URL]
NEW background-origin	Specifies the positioning area of the background images	
background-position	Sets the starting position of a background image	[length] [percentage] bottom center left right top

Table D–4 Background and Color Properties *(Continued)*

Property Name	Description	Values	
background-repeat	Sets if/how a background image will be repeated	**repeat** repeat-x repeat-y no-repeat inherit	
background-size	Specifies the size of the background images		NEW

Border Properties

Table D–5 Border Properties

Property Name	Description	Values	
border	Set all the border properties in one declaration		
border-color	Shorthand property for setting the color of the four borders in one declaration; can have from one to four colors	[color] transparent	
border-bottom-color border-left-color border-right-color border-top-color	Sets the respective color of the top, right, bottom, and left borders individually	[color]	
border-image	A shorthand property for setting all the border-image-*n* properties		NEW
border-image-outset	Specifies the amount by which the border image area extends beyond the border box	[length] [number]	NEW
border-image-repeat	Specifies whether the image-border should be repeated, rounded, or stretched	**stretch** repeat round	NEW
border-image-slice	Specifies the inward offsets of the image-border	[number] [percentage] fill	NEW
border-image-source	Specifies an image to be used as a border	**none** [image]	NEW
border-image-width	Specifies the widths of the image-border	[number] [percentage] auto	NEW
border-radius	A shorthand property for setting all the four border-*n*-radius properties		NEW
border-bottom-left-radius border-bottom-right-radius border-top-left-radius border-top-right-radius	Sets the shape of the border of the bottom-left, bottom-right, top-left, and top-right corners individually	[percentage] [length]	NEW NEW NEW NEW
border-style	Shorthand property for setting the style of the four borders in one declaration; can have from one to four styles	**none** dashed dotted double groove inset outset ridge solid	

Table D–5 Border Properties *(Continued)*

Property Name	Description	Values
border-bottom-style border-left-style border-right-style border-top-style	Sets the respective style of the top, right, bottom, and left borders individually	**none** dashed dotted double groove inset outset ridge solid
border-width	Shorthand property for setting the width of the four borders in one declaration; can have from one to four values	**medium** [length] thick thin
border-bottom-width border-left-width border-right-width border-top-width	Sets the respective width of the top, right, bottom, and left borders individually	**medium** [length] thick thin
NEW box-decoration-break		
NEW box-shadow	Attaches one or more drop-shadows to the box	[h-shadow] [v-shadow] [blur] [spread] [color] inset

Box Properties

NEW **Table D-6 Box Properties**

Property Name	Description	Values
overflow-style	Specifies the preferred scrolling method for elements that overflow	**auto** scrollbar panner move marquee
overflow-x	Specifies whether or not to clip the left/right edges of the content, if it overflows the element's content area	**visible** hidden scroll auto no-display no-content
overflow-y	Specifies whether or not to clip the top/bottom edges of the content, if it overflows the element's content area	**visible** hidden scroll auto no-display no-content

Table D-6 Box Properties *(Continued)*

Property Name	Description	Values
rotation	Rotates an element around a given point defined by the rotation-point property	[angle]
rotation-point	Defines a point as an offset from the top-left border edge	left top left center left bottom right top right center right bottom center top center center center bottom

Classification Properties

Table D–7 Classification Properties

Property Name	Description	Values
display	Describes how/if an element is displayed on the canvas, which may be on a printed page, a computer monitor, etc.	**block** inline list-item none
white-space	Declares how white-space inside the element is handled: the 'normal' way (where white-space is collapsed), as *pre* (which behaves like the <pre> element in HTML) or as *nowrap* (where wrapping is done only through elements)	**normal** pre nowrap

Color Properties

Table D-8 Color Properties NEW

Property Name	Description	Values
color-profile	Permits the specification of a source color profile other than the default	
opacity	Sets the opacity level for an element	[value] inherit
rendering-intent	Permits the specification of a color profile rendering intent other than the default	

Content for Paged Media Properties

NEW

Table D-9 Paged Media Properties

Property Name	Description	Values
bookmark-label	Specifies the label of the bookmark	
bookmark-level	Specifies the level of the bookmark	
bookmark-target	Specifies the target of the bookmark link	
float-offset	Pushes floated elements in the opposite direction of the where they have been floated with float	
hyphenate-after	Specifies the minimum number of characters in a hyphenated word after the hyphenation character	
hyphenate-before	Specifies the minimum number of characters in a hyphenated word before the hyphenation character	
hyphenate-character	Specifies a string that is shown when a hyphenate-break occurs	
hyphenate-lines	Indicates the maximum number of successive hyphenated lines in an element	
hyphenate-resource	Specifies a comma-separated list of external resources that can help the browser determine hyphenation points	
hyphens	Sets how to split words to improve the layout of paragraphs	
image-resolution	Specifies the correct resolution of images	
marks	Adds crop and/or cross marks to the document	

Dimension Properties

NEW

Table D-10 Dimension Properties

Property Name	Description	Values
height	Sets the height of an element	**auto** [length] [percentage] inherit
max-height	Sets the maximum height of an element	**none** [length] [percentage] inherit
max-width	Sets the maximum width of an element	**none** [length] [percentage] inherit
min-height	Sets the minimum height of an element	[length] [percentage] inherit
min-width	Sets the minimum width of an element	[length] [percentage] inherit
width	Sets the width of an element	**auto** [length] [percentage] inherit

Flexible Box Properties

Table D-11 Flexible Box Properties NEW

Property Name	Description	Values
box-align	Specifies how to align the child elements of a box	start end center baseline **stretch**
box-direction	Specifies in which direction the children of a box are displayed	**normal** reverse inherit
box-flex	Specifies whether the children of a box is flexible or inflexible in size	[value]
box-flex-group	Assigns flexible elements to flex groups	[integer]
box-lines	Specifies whether columns will go onto a new line whenever it runs out of space in the parent box	**single** multiple
box-ordinal-group	Specifies the display order of the child elements of a box	[integer]
box-orient	Specifies whether the children of a box should be laid out horizontally or vertically	horizontal vertical **inline-axis** block-axis inherit
box-pack	Specifies the horizontal position in horizontal boxes and the vertical position in vertical boxes	**start** end center justify

Font Properties

Table D–12 Font Properties

Property Name	Description	Values
font	Shorthand property for setting font properties	
@font-face	A rule that allows Web sites to download and use fonts other than the "Web-safe" fonts NEW	
font-family	A prioritized list of font-family names and/or generic family names for an element	[family-name] cursive fantasy monospace sans-serif serif
font-size	Sets the size of a font	[length] [percentage] large larger **medium** small smaller x-large x-small xx-large xx-small inherit

Table D–12 Font Properties *(Continued)*

	Property Name	Description	Values
NEW	font-size-adjust	Preserves the readability of text when font fallback occurs	[number] **none** inherit
NEW	font-stretch	Selects a normal, condensed, or expanded face from a font family	
	font-style	Sets the style of a font	**normal** italic oblique
	font-variant	Displays text in a small-caps font or a normal font	**normal** small-caps
	font-weight	Sets the weight of a font	**normal** bold bolder lighter

Generated Content Properties

Table D-13 Generated Content Properties

	Property Name	Description	Values
	content	Used with the :before and :after pseudo-elements, to insert generated content	none normal counter attr [string] open-quote close-quote no-open-quote [URL] inherit
	counter-increment	Increments one or more counters	**none** [id number] inherit
	counter-reset	Creates or resets one or more counters	**none** [id number] inherit
NEW	crop	Allows a replaced element to be just a rectangular area of an object, instead of the whole object	
NEW	move-to	Causes an element to be removed from the flow and reinserted at a later point in the document	
NEW	page-policy	Determines which page-based occurrence of a given element is applied to a counter or string value	
	quotes	Sets the type of quotation marks for embedded quotations	none [string] inherit

Grid Properties

Table D-14 Grid Properties NEW

Property Name	Description	Values
grid-columns	Specifies the width of each column in a grid	[length] [percentage] **none** inherit
grid-rows	Specifies the height of each column in a grid	[length] [percentage] **none** inherit

Hyperlink Properties

Table D-15 Hyperlink Properties NEW

Property Name	Description	Values
target	A shorthand property for setting the target-name, target-new, and target-position properties	
target-name	Specifies where to open links (target destination)	**current** root parent new modal [name]
target-new	Specifies whether new destination links should open in a new window or in a new tab of an existing window	**window** tab none
target-position	Specifies where new destination links should be placed	**above** behind front back

Linebox Properties

Table D-16 Linebox Properties NEW

Property Name	Description	Values
alignment-adjust	Allows more precise alignment of elements	
alignment-baseline	Specifies how an inline-level element is aligned with respect to its parent	
baseline-shift	Allows repositioning of the dominant-baseline relative to the dominant-baseline	
dominant-baseline	Specifies a scaled-baseline-table	
drop-initial-after-adjust	Sets the alignment point of the drop initial for the primary connection point	
drop-initial-after-align	Sets which alignment line within the initial line box is used at the primary connection point with the initial letter box	

Table D-16 Linebox Properties *(Continued)*		
Property Name	**Description**	**Values**
drop-initial-before-adjust	Sets the alignment point of the drop initial for the secondary connection point	
drop-initial-before-align	Sets which alignment line within the initial line box is used at the secondary connection point with the initial letter box	
drop-initial-size	Controls the partial sinking of the initial letter	
drop-initial-value	Activates a drop-initial effect	
inline-box-align	Sets which line of a multiline inline block align with the previous and next inline elements within a line	
line-stacking	A shorthand property for setting the line-stacking-strategy, line-stacking-ruby, and line-stacking-shift properties	
line-stacking-ruby	Sets the line-stacking method for block elements containing ruby annotation elements	
line-stacking-shift	Sets the line-stacking method for block elements containing elements with base-shift	
line-stacking-strategy	Sets the line-stacking strategy for stacked line boxes within a containing block element	
text-height	Sets the block-progression dimension of the text content area of an inline box	

List Properties

Table D–17 List Properties		
Property Name	**Description**	**Values**
list-style	A shorthand property for setting list-style-image, list-style-position, and list-style-type in one declaration	
list-style-image	Sets an image as the list-item marker	**none** [URL]
list-style-position	Indents or extends a list-item marker with respect to the item's content	**outside** inside
list-style-type	Sets the type of list-item marker	**disc** circle square decimal lower-alpha lower-roman upper-alpha upper-roman

Margin and Padding Properties

Table D–18 Margin and Padding Properties

Property Name	Description	Values
margin	Shorthand property for setting margin properties	
margin-bottom margin-left margin-right margin-top	Sets the top, right, bottom, and left margin of an element individually	[length] [percentage] auto inherit
padding	Shorthand property for setting padding properties in one declaration	
padding-bottom padding-left padding-right padding-top	Sets the top, right, bottom, and left padding of an element individually	[length] [percentage] inherit

Marquee Properties

Table D-19 Marquee Properties NEW

Property Name	Description	Values
marquee-direction	Sets the direction of the moving content	
marquee-play-count	Sets how many times the content moves	
marquee-speed	Sets how fast the content scrolls	
marquee-style	Sets the style of the moving content	

Multicolumn Properties

Table D-20 Multicolumn Properties NEW

Property Name	Description	Values
column-count	Specifies the number of columns an element should be divided into	[number] **auto**
column-fill	Specifies how to fill columns	**balance** auto
column-gap	Specifies the gap between the columns	[length] **normal**
column-rule	A shorthand property for setting all the column-rule-*n* properties	
column-rule-color	Specifies the color of the rule between columns	[color]
column-rule-style	Specifies the style of the rule between columns	**none** hidden dotted dashed solid double groove ridge inset outset

Table D-20 Multicolumn Properties *(Continued)*		
Property Name	**Description**	**Values**
column-rule-width	Specifies the width of the rule between columns	thin **medium** thick [length]
column-span	Specifies how many columns an element should span across	**1** all
column-width	Specifies the width of the columns	**auto** [length]
columns	A shorthand property for setting column-width and column-count	

Paged Media Properties

NEW

Table D-21 Paged Media Properties		
Property Name	**Description**	**Values**
fit	Gives a hint for how to scale a replaced element if neither its width nor its height property is auto	
fit-position	Determines the alignment of the object inside the box	
image-orientation	Specifies a rotation in the right or clockwise direction that a user agent applies to an image	
page	Specifies a particular type of page where an element should be displayed	
size	Specifies the size and orientation of the containing box for page content	

Positioning Properties

Table D-22 Positioning Properties		
Property Name	**Description**	**Values**
bottom	Specifies the bottom position of a positioned element	**auto** [length] [percentage] inherit
clear	Specifies the sides of an element where other floating elements are not allowed	left right both **none** inherit
clip	Clips an absolutely positioned element	[shape] **auto** inherit

Table D-16 D-22 Positioning Properties *(Continued)*

Property Name	Description	Values
cursor	Specifies the type of cursor to be displayed	[URL] **auto** crosshair default e-resize help move n-resize ne-resize nw-resize pointer progress s-resize se-resize sw-resize text w-resize wait inherit
display	Specifies the type of box an element should generate	none block **inline** inline-block inline-table list-item run-in table table-caption table-cell table-column table-column-group table-footer-group table-header-group table-row table-row-group inherit
float	Specifies whether or not a box should float	left right **none** inherit
left	Specifies the left position of a positioned element	**auto** [length] [percentage] inherit
overflow	Specifies what happens if content overflows an element's box	**visible** hidden scroll auto inherit
position	Specifies the type of positioning method used for an element (static, relative, absolute, or fixed)	**static** absolute fixed relative inherit

Table D-22 Positioning Properties *(Continued)*

Property Name	Description	Values
right	Specifies the right position of a positioned element	**auto** [length] [percentage] inherit
top	Specifies the top position of a positioned element	**auto** [length] [percentage] inherit
visibility	Specifies whether or not an element is visible	**visible** hidden collapse inherit
z-index	Sets the stack order of a positioned element	**auto** [number] inherit

Print Properties

Table D-23 Print Properties

Property Name	Description	Values
orphans	Sets the minimum number of lines that must be left at the bottom of a page when a page break occurs inside an element	
page-break-after	Sets the page-breaking behavior after an element	**auto** always avoid left right inherit
page-break-before	Sets the page-breaking behavior before an element	**auto** always avoid left right inherit
page-break-inside	Sets the page-breaking behavior inside an element	**auto** avoid inherit
widows	Sets the minimum number of lines that must be left at the top of a page when a page break occurs inside an element	

Ruby Properties

Table D-24 Ruby Properties

NEW

Property Name	Description	Values
ruby-align	Controls the text alignment of the ruby text and ruby base contents relative to each other	
ruby-overhang	Determines whether, and on which side, ruby text is allowed to partially overhang any adjacent text in addition to its own base, when the ruby text is wider than the ruby base	
ruby-position	Controls the position of the ruby text with respect to its base	
ruby-span	Controls the spanning behavior of annotation elements	

Speech Properties

Table D-25 Speech Properties

NEW

Property Name	Description	Values
mark	A shorthand property for setting the mark-before and mark-after properties	
mark-after	Allows named markers to be attached to the audio stream	
mark-before	Allows named markers to be attached to the audio stream	
phonemes	Specifies a phonetic pronunciation for the text contained by the corresponding element	
rest	A shorthand property for setting the rest-before and rest-after properties	
rest-after	Specifies a rest or prosodic boundary to be observed after speaking an element's content	
rest-before	Specifies a rest or prosodic boundary to be observed before speaking an element's content	
voice-balance	Specifies the balance between left and right channels	
voice-duration	Specifies how long it should take to render the selected element's content	
voice-pitch	Specifies the average pitch (a frequency) of the speaking voice	
voice-pitch-range	Specifies variation in average pitch	
voice-rate	Controls the speaking rate	
voice-stress	Indicates the strength of emphasis to be applied	
voice-volume	Refers to the amplitude of the waveform output by the speech syntheses	

Table Properties

Table D-26 Table Properties

Property Name	Description	Values
border-collapse	Specifies whether or not table borders should be collapsed	collapse **separate** inherit
border-spacing	Specifies the distance between the borders of adjacent cells	[length] inherit
caption-side	Specifies the placement of a table caption	**top** bottom inherit
empty-cells	Specifies whether or not to display borders and background on empty cells in a table	hide **show** inherit
table-layout	Sets the layout algorithm to be used for a table	**auto** fixed inherit

Text Properties

Table D–27 Text Properties

	Property Name	Description	Values
	color	Sets the color of text	[color] inherit
	direction	Specifies the text direction/writing direction	**ltr** rtl inherit
NEW	hanging-punctuation	Specifies whether a punctuation character may be placed outside the line box	none first last allow-end force-end
	letter-spacing	Increases or decreases the space between characters	**normal** [length] inherit
	line-height	Sets the line height	**normal** [length] [number] [percentage] inherit
NEW	punctuation-trim	Specifies whether a punctuation character should be trimmed	none start end allow-end adjacent
	text-align	Specifies the horizontal alignment of text	left right center justify inherit

Table D–27 Text Properties (*Continued*)

Property Name	Description	Values	
text-align-last	Describes how the last line of a block or a line right before a forced line break is aligned when text-align is "justify"		NEW
text-decoration	Adds decoration to text	**none** blink line-through overline underline inherit	
text-indent	Indents the first line of text in an element	[length] [percentage] inherit	
text-justify	Specifies the justification method used when text-align is "justify"	**auto** interword interideograph intercluster distribute kashida none	
text-outline	Specifies a text outline	**none** [thickness] [blur] [color]	
text-overflow	Specifies what should happen when text overflows the containing element	**clip** ellipsis [string]	
text-shadow	Adds shadow to text	[h-shadow] [v-shadow] [blur] [color]	NEW
text-transform	Controls text capitalization	**none** capitalize lowercase uppercase inherit	
text-wrap	Specifies line breaking rules for text	**normal** none unrestricted suppress	NEW
vertical-align	Sets the vertical positioning of text	**baseline** [length] [percentage] bottom middle sub super text-bottom text-top top inherit	
white-space	Specifies how white-space inside an element is handled	**normal** nowrap pre preline prewrap inherit	

Table D–27 Text Properties (*Continued*)

Property Name	Description	Values
NEW word-break	Specifies the line breaking rules for non-CJK scripts	**normal** break-all hyphenate
word-spacing	Increases or decreases the space between words	**normal** [length] inherit
NEW word-wrap	Allows long, unbreakable words to be broken and wrap to the next line	**normal** break-word

2D/3D Transform Properties

NEW **Table D-28 2D/3D Transform Properties**

Property Name	Description	Values
backface-visibility	Defines whether or not an element should be visible when not facing the screen	**visible** hidden
perspective	Specifies the perspective on how 3D elements are viewed	
perspective-origin	Specifies the bottom position of 3D elements	[x-axis] [y-axis]
transform	Applies a 2D or 3D transformation to an element	
transform-origin	Allows you to change the position on transformed elements	[x-axis] [y-axis] [z-axis]
transform-style	Specifies how nested elements are rendered in 3D space	**flat** preserve-3d

Transition Properties

NEW **Table D-29 Transition Properties**

Property Name	Description	Values
transition	A shorthand property for setting the four transition properties	
transition-delay	Specifies when the transition effect will start	[time]
transition-duration	Specifies how many seconds or milliseconds a transition effect takes to complete	[time]
transition-property	Specifies the name of the CSS property the transition effect is for	none **all** property
transition-timing-function	Specifies the speed curve of the transition effect	linear **ease** ease-in ease-in-out ease-out cubic-bezier

User-Interface Properties

Table D-30 User-Interface Properties

NEW

Property Name	Description	Values
appearance	Allows you to make an element look like a standard user interface element	**normal** icon window button menu field
box-sizing	Allows you to define certain elements to fit an area in a certain way	**content-box** border-box inherit
icon	Provides the author with the ability to style an element with an iconic equivalent	**auto** [URL] Inherit
nav-down	Specifies where to navigate when using the arrow-down navigation key	**auto** [id] [target-name] inherit
nav-index	Specifies the tabbing order for an element	**auto** [number] inherit
nav-left	Specifies where to navigate when using the arrow-left navigation key	**auto** [id] [target-name] inherit
nav-right	Specifies where to navigate when using the arrow-right navigation key	**auto** [id] [target-name] inherit
nav-up	Specifies where to navigate when using the arrow-up navigation key	**auto** [id] [target-name] inherit
outline-offset	Offsets an outline, and draws it beyond the border edge	[length] inherit
resize	Specifies whether or not an element is resizable by the user	**none** both horizontal vertical

Appendix E
Publishing Web Pages to a Web Server

Publishing your Web site means transferring your files to a Web server (Web host) that will make your pages available 24/7 on the Web. Publishing involves two basic steps: choosing a Web host and uploading your Web site files (usually via FTP) to that host.

Choosing a Web Host

There are many options available for Web hosting, as detailed in the "Finding a Web Hosting Site" section of the Special Feature on "Attracting Visitors to Your Web Site." Common options are to use the ISP that you use to connect to the Internet or to use a Web hosting service.

Your Internet service provider (ISP) may provide space for its clients to host a Web site. If it does, you should contact the network system administrator or technical support staff at your ISP to determine if their Web server supports FTP, and to obtain necessary permissions to access the Web server. There are other options for hosting Web sites as well. You can search for free Web hosts using any browser and search engine. Whatever Web host you choose, you must secure a username and password in order to gain access to the host.

Uploading Files to the Host

Once you have chosen a Web host, you'll need a program to transfer your files to the Web server. The most common file transfer program is called FTP. **File Transfer Protocol (FTP)** is an Internet standard that allows computers to exchange files with other computers on the Internet. FTP was developed to promote file sharing across a variety of computers reliably and efficiently. FTP programs that run on personal computers are sometimes called FTP clients.

There are many FTP programs available for free on the Internet. Search for FTP using any search engine, and you will find a variety of programs. Read the documentation to ensure that the program works with your computer and operating system. Then download and install the FTP program of your choice.

Now you can use your FTP program to upload your Web pages to the server. Be sure to include all HTML files, CSS files, and any graphic files that make up your Web site. Table E–1 shows the steps to use FTP to upload your files. All of the necessary information (e.g., username) should be provided to you by the network administrator for the Web host. Specific keystrokes or mouse clicks to accomplish each step may vary among FTP clients.

Table E–1 Using FTP to Upload Your Web Files
1. Start your FTP program.
2. Type in the host name/address as provided by the network administrator.
3. Select the host type.
4. Enter your FTP user ID and password as provided by the network administrator.
5. You should see both a local system (your computer) as well as the remote system (the Web host) in the FTP dialog box.
6. Navigate your local drive to find the folders in which you stored your files; then locate the folders on the remote system.
7. Highlight the files that you want to upload and copy the files to the remote system.

Appendix F

Symbols and Characters Quick Reference

Using Symbols and Special Characters

There is a way to insert special characters into your HTML and XHTML code by using the entity character reference. Tables F–1 through F–3 contain the most commonly used character references, mathematical and technical character references, and arrow character references. Several projects in the book use these character references to enhance content on the Web pages that you create.

You can find a complete list of characters at unicode.org. You can also search the Web for many other unicode character map resources.

Table F–1 Most Commonly Used Character References

Symbol	Character Reference	Description
&	&	Ampersand
¦	¦	Broken vertical bar
¢	¢	Cent sign
©	©	Copyright sign
¤	¤	Currency sign
†	†	Dagger
‡	‡	Double dagger
€	€	Euro
>	>	Greater-than sign
«	«	Left-pointing double angle quotation mark
<	<	Less-than sign
—	—	Em dash
[Tab]		Nonbreaking space (can be used for tabbing on a Web page)
–	–	En dash
¬	¬	Not sign
¶	¶	Paragraph sign
£	£	Pound
"	"	Quotation mark = APL quote
®	®	Registered mark sign
»	»	Right-pointing double angle quotation mark
§	§	Section sign
™	™	Trademark sign
¥	¥	Yen

Table F–2 Mathematical and Technical Character References

Symbol	Character Reference	Description
∧	∧	Logical and
∠	∠	Angle
≈	≈	Almost equal to
∩	∩	Intersection
∪	∪	Union
°	°	Degree sign
÷	÷	Division sign
≡	≡	Identical to
∃	∃	There exists
ƒ	ƒ	Function
∀	∀	For all
½	½	Fraction one half
¼	¼	Fraction one quarter
¾	¾	Fraction three quarters
≥	≥	Greater-than or equal to
∞	∞	Infinity
∫	∫	Integral
∈	∈	Element of
≤	≤	Less-than or equal to
µ	µ	Micro sign
∇	∇	Backward difference
≠	≠	Not equal to
∋	∋	Contains as a member
∂	∂	Partial differential
⊥	⊥	Perpendicular
±	±	Plus-minus sign
∏	∏	n-ary product
∝	∝	Proportional to
√	√	Square root
~	∼	Tilde
∑	∑	n-ary summation
∴	∴	Therefore

Table F–3 Arrow Character References

Symbol	Character Reference	Description
↓	↓	Downward arrow
↔	↔	Left right arrow
←	←	Leftward arrow
→	→	Rightward arrow
↑	↑	Upward arrow

Appendix G

JavaScript Quick Reference

JavaScript Introduction

Webster's dictionary defines **script** in several ways: first, as a style of handwriting or font style, such as cursive; second, as a document; and third, as text for stage, film, or a radio or television show. A stage, movie, or television script also contains stage directions for actors. Computers, however, also use scripts, which are a set of instructions used by a program to perform a specific task or set of tasks. A **scripting language** follows a set of rules and has its own syntax. Scripting languages generally need to be interpreted by the program or utility using the script.

Scripting languages like JavaScript extend the power of HTML and allow Web pages to be interactive. Whereas HTML tells your browser how to display text and images, set up lists and option buttons, and establish hyperlinks, JavaScript brings Web pages to life by adding dynamic content and interactive elements. Using JavaScript, a Web page developer can add features such as:

- Scrolling messages
- Animation and dynamic images
- Pop-up windows
- Dynamic messages
- Data validation

JavaScript is a product resulting from a joint venture between Sun Microsystems and Netscape. Netscape developed a script language called LiveScript, and Sun Microsystems was trying to simplify its Java programming language. The cooperation of those two efforts brought about JavaScript. The first JavaScript standards were created and developed by the European Computer Manufacturers Association (ECMA) with edition 1 in 1997. The current edition of ECMAScript is edition 5, which was finalized in December of 2009.

JavaScript version 1.5 was based on ECMAScript edition 3. Disagreement among members, who include Yahoo!, Microsoft, Mozilla, and Google has led to the development of JavaScript extensions beyond version 1.5 based on individual browser engines. The Mozilla developer Web site lists JavaScript at version 1.8.5. The versions beyond 1.5 are browser specific, and contain objects, properties, and methods specific to that browser and browser version.

The following reference guide applies to the JavaScript model version 1.5, which is still in effect for all cross-browser applications. Later versions of JavaScript are browser-specific and are not detailed in this appendix. For more detailed information about JavaScript, see the Mozilla Developer Network Web site at developer.mozilla.org/en/JavaScript. For the complete ECMA standards documentation, you can download the PDF file at www.ecma-international.org/publications/files/ECMA-ST/Ecma-262.pdf.

Why Use JavaScript?

Using JavaScript enhances your Web page by adding interactivity to it. Users can receive instant feedback, without complicated Common Gateway Interference (**CGI**) scripts and languages. A CGI script is any program that runs on a Web server for the purpose of processing data. The Web page sends the data to the server that processes the data and may return a result to the Web page. Along with server-side scripts and programs, many Web sites use CGI for searching databases or processing purchase orders on a server.

The disadvantage of using CGI scripts is that they waste resources when the needed task can be processed on the user's computer. For example, with JavaScript you can validate a data-entry form, such as a purchase request, immediately on the user's computer. The need to send the data back to the server for validation is eliminated. The user receives feedback instantly and does not have to wait for a response during heavy Internet traffic times.

Reserved Words

Reserved words (also called **keywords**) are words with special meaning to a programming language. Most reserved words are used in program statements or in defining data. A reserved word cannot be used as a JavaScript variable, function, method, or object name. Table G–1 contains a list of ECMA specification and typical browser reserved words for JavaScript.

Table G–1 Reserved Words

abstract	double	in	throw
boolean	else	instanceof	throws
break	enum	int	transient
byte	export	label	true
case	extends	long	try
catch	false	native	typeof
char	final	new	var
class	finally	null	void
const	float	return	volatile
continue	for	short	while
debugger	function	super	with
default	goto	switch	
delete	if	synchronized	
do	import	this	

Some of the reserved words have special meaning to JavaScript; some are reserved for future use with JavaScript extensions. Table G-2 lists these future reserved words.

Table G–2 Future Reserved Words

implements	package	public
interface	private	static
let	protected	yield

Data Types

Data type refers to the category of data held by a variable. JavaScript variables are dynamically typed, which means they do not have to be declared as a specific type before using them in Web page. JavaScript supports several data types, including primitive data types (numbers, strings, and boolean values), compound types (objects and arrays), special types (null and undefined), regular expressions, and functions. Table G–3 summarizes the primitive and special data types.

Table G–3 Primitive and Special Data Types

Data Type	Form	Description	Example	Range
Boolean	True/False	Can represent yes or no, on or off, true or false	check_pt = true test_2 = false	true or false
Null	No value	Empty	val_hold = null	null
Numeric	Integer	Positive or negative numbers with no decimal places	count = 4	-2^{32} to 2^{32}
	Floating-point	Positive or negative numbers, with decimal places, or numbers written using exponential notation	accum = 4.678 amt = –67.126 distance = 2e11	Approximately +1.79769e308 to –1.7e308
	Special numbers	NaN Infinity (or MAX_VALUE or POSITIVE_INFINITY) –Infinity (or MIN_VALUE or NEGATIVE_INFINITY)	ValType = NaN highNum = Infinity highNegNum = –Infinity	NaN means Not a Number MAX_VALUE: +1.7976931348623157e308 MIN_VALUE: +5e-324
String	Text and nonnumeric characters	A set of continuous characters surrounded by quotation marks	productName = "Router" phone = "555-1212"	zero or more characters
Undefined	No value	A variable that has been declared but not yet assigned a value	var i	undefined

Variable Names

A **variable name** (also called an **identifier**) must begin with a letter, dollar sign ($), or underscore (_) and cannot be a reserved word shown in Table G–1 on the previous page. Variable names are case sensitive and may not contain a space. Variables can be declared with the var statement, where they can also be initialized.

Although the dollar sign ($) is a valid variable name character, most developers avoid using it because the dollar sign can also indicate machine-generated code to the interpreter. In addition, the number of characters in a variable is not subject to any specific limitation. Older browsers, however, do have a limitation of 255 characters for an entire statement.

A variable name cannot use a period because periods separate objects, properties, and methods. See Table G–4 on the next page for examples of valid and invalid variable names. In addition, you must remember that, in JavaScript, variable names are case sensitive. If you create a form and use mixed-case spelling, such as State, as a variable name, and later use the uppercase spelling, STATE, as a variable name, JavaScript will treat these spellings as two different variable names.

Table G–4 Valid and Invalid Variable Names

Valid Variable Names	Invalid Variable Names
cust_id	cust.id
Cust_Id	%Cust_Id
_cust_id	+cust_identifier
cust_id_number	Cust id number
CustIdNumber	9custIDNumber
Custid1	Cust ID
_case	case

Variables are declared the first time they are used by inserting the word **var**, then the variable name, followed by an equal sign (=), and then the value. For example, if you declare a variable named gpa by typing `var gpa`, this variable would be assigned no value. To assign a variable an initial value of zero, type `var gpa=0`. Current versions of Mozilla Firefox and Microsoft Internet Explorer indicate that a variable is **undefined** if the variable has not been assigned a value. In addition, a variable can have a **null** value.

Literals

While a variable is used to store data or values, a **literal** is a constant value that does not change. A literal is an actual number or text, rather than a calculated result or value input from a keyboard. If the literal is a number, it is called a numeric literal; if it is a character or text value, it is called a string literal.

A **string literal** is text enclosed in quotation marks. With string literals, you must place the text inside a pair of quotation marks. If numeric digits are enclosed within quotation marks, they will be treated as a string, not as a number. Think of the characters between quotation marks as a sequential group of characters, one after the other, forming a continuous string.

Escape Sequences in Strings

The **escape character** (\) indicates that the character that follows in a string has a special meaning. The escape character and its following character form an **escape sequence**. The escape sequences are summarized in Table G–5.

Table G–5 Escape Sequences

Escape Sequence	Meaning	Escape Sequence	Meaning
\'	Apostrophe or single quotation mark	\r	Carriage return
\"	Double quotation mark	\t	Horizontal tab
\\	Backslash	\v	vertical tab
\b	Backspace	*ddd*	Octal sequence (deprecated)
\f	Form feed	\x*dd*	Hexadecimal sequence
\n	New line	\u*dddd*	Unicode sequence

where *d* is a digit

Operators

Operators are symbols used to manipulate operands in an expression.

Operator Types

Table G–6 summarizes the JavaScript operator types.

Table G–6 Operator Types

<table>
<tr><th>Type</th><th>Operator</th><th>Name</th><th>Description</th><th>Example</th></tr>
<tr><td>Arithmetic</td><td>+</td><td>Addition</td><td>Adds two operands</td><td>rtn = amt + 5.6</td></tr>
<tr><td></td><td>–</td><td>Subtraction</td><td>Subtracts one operand from another</td><td>rtn = amt – disc</td></tr>
<tr><td></td><td>*</td><td>Multiplication</td><td>Multiplies one operand by another</td><td>rtn = amt * .5</td></tr>
<tr><td></td><td>/</td><td>Division</td><td>Divides one operand by another</td><td>rtn = amt / 4</td></tr>
<tr><td></td><td>%</td><td>Modulus</td><td>Returns the remainder of a division operation</td><td>rtn = amt % 3</td></tr>
<tr><td></td><td>++</td><td>Increment</td><td>Increases an operand by one</td><td>newAmt = ++oldAmt
newAmt = oldAmt++</td></tr>
<tr><td></td><td>– –</td><td>Decrement</td><td>Decreases an operand by one</td><td>newAmt = – –oldAmt
newAmt = oldAmt– –</td></tr>
<tr><td></td><td>–</td><td>Negation</td><td>Returns the opposite value of an operand</td><td>newAmt = –oldAmt</td></tr>
<tr><td>Assignment</td><td>=</td><td>Assigns</td><td>Assigns the value of the right operand to the left operand</td><td>discRate = 4</td></tr>
<tr><td></td><td>+=</td><td>Combines</td><td>Adds the value of the right operand to the value of the left operand and assigns a new value to the left operand</td><td>discRate += 13</td></tr>
<tr><td></td><td>– =</td><td>Subtracts</td><td>Subtracts the value of the right operand from the value of the left operand and assigns a new value to the left operand</td><td>discRate –= 3</td></tr>
<tr><td></td><td>*=</td><td>Multiplies</td><td>Multiplies the value of the right operand by the value of the left operand and assigns a new value to the left operand</td><td>discRate *= .2</td></tr>
<tr><td></td><td>/=</td><td>Divides</td><td>Divides the value of the left operand by the value of the right operand and assigns a new value to the left operand</td><td>discRate /= 10</td></tr>
<tr><td></td><td>%=</td><td>Modulus</td><td>Divides the value of the left operand by the value of the right operand and assigns the remainder (or zero) to the left operand</td><td>discRate %= 5</td></tr>
<tr><td>Bitwise</td><td>~</td><td>Complement</td><td>Performs a binary NOT</td><td>secur = ~rights</td></tr>
<tr><td></td><td><<</td><td>Shift left</td><td>Performs a binary shift left of the bits of an integer</td><td>Op = 15 << 1</td></tr>
<tr><td></td><td>>></td><td>Shift right</td><td>Performs a binary shift right of the bits of an integer</td><td>Op = 15 >> 1</td></tr>
<tr><td></td><td>>>></td><td>Shift right with zero extension</td><td>Performs a binary unsigned shift right on an integer</td><td>Op = 15 >>> 1</td></tr>
<tr><td></td><td>&</td><td>AND</td><td>Performs a bitwise AND on an integer</td><td>Op = 01111 & 11111</td></tr>
<tr><td></td><td>^</td><td>XOR</td><td>Performs a bitwise XOR on an integer</td><td>Op = 01111 ^ 11111</td></tr>
<tr><td></td><td>|</td><td>OR</td><td>Performs a bitwise OR on an integer</td><td>Op = 01111 | 11111</td></tr>
</table>

Table G–6 Operator Types (continued)

Type	Operator	Name	Description	Example
Comparison	==	Equal	Returns true if operands are equal	if (a == b) {
	!=	Not equal	Returns true if operands are not equal	if (a != b) {
	>	Greater than	Returns true if the left operand is greater than the right operand	if (a > b) {
	<	Less than	Returns true if the left operand is less than the right operand	if (a < b) {
	>=	Greater than or equal	Returns true if the left operand is greater than or equal to the right operand	if (a >= b) {
	<=	Less than or equal	Returns true if the left operand is less than or equal to the right operand	if (a <= b) {
	===	Equal (no type conversion done)	Returns true if operands are equal and their types are the same	if (a === b) {
	!==	Not equal (no type conversion done)	Returns true if operands are not equal or their types are the same	if (a !== b) {
	in	in	Returns true if the property is found as a property member of the object	(property in object)
	instanceof	instanceof	Returns true if the datatype matches the object	(datatype instanceof object)
Conditional	?:	If?then:else	Performs an inline if-then-else and assigns one of two possible values	Ret = (test == true) ? "It's true" : "It's false"
Expression Control	void	Return a void	Sets a variable to an undefined state	ret = void
Logical	&&	And	Returns true if both the left operand and the right operand return a value of true, otherwise it returns a value of false	if ((a < b) && (c > d)) {
	||	Or	Returns true if either the left operand or the right operand returns a value of true; if neither operand returns a value of true, then the expression containing the || (or) operator returns a value of false	if ((a < b) || (c > d)) {
	!	Not	Returns true if an expression is false and returns false if an expression is true	if (!(a < b)) {
Multiple Evaluation	,	Evaluate/Return right+	Evaluates two expressions and returns the second one	Ret = (x- -, z) * (y- -, q)
Object	new	New object	Creates a new object	CD = new Album
	delete	Remove an object property	Removes a single property of an object	delete CD
String	+	Concatenation	Combines two strings	lang = "Java" + "Script"
	+=	Concatenates	Concatenates the value of the right operand to the value of the left operand and assigns a new value to the left operand	Lang += "Script"
Type Identification	typeof	Return type	Returns the data type of the operand	ret = typeof(CD)

Order of Precedence

Unless parentheses/brackets/dots dictate otherwise, reading from left to right in an expression, all negation/increment/misc are performed first, then all multiply/divide/modulo, then all addition/subtraction, then all comparison, then all equality/identity, then all logical and, then all logical or, and then all assignment operators. The **order of precedence** is summarized in Table G–7.

Table G–7 Order Of Precedence

Operator	Symbol	Precedence
Parentheses/brackets/dot	( ) [ ] . new	highest
Increment/negate/misc	++ – – ! + – ~ delete typeof void	
Multiply/divide/modulo	* / %	
Addition/subtraction	+ –	
Shift	<< >> >>>	
Comparison	< <= > >= in instanceof	
Equality/Identity	== !=== !== != ===	
Bitwise AND	&	
Bitwise XOR	^	
Bitwise OR	|	
Logical and	&&	
Logical or	||	
Conditional	?:	
Assignment operators	= += –= *= /= %=	
Multiple evaluation	,	lowest

JavaScript Statements

Statements are used to write JavaScript instructions. Table G–8 summarizes the JavaScript statements.

Table G–8 JavaScript Statements

Statement	Description
;	Used to separate statements, when used as an empty statement returns normal.
block	A block of JavaScript statements delimited by a pair of braces { }.
break	Exits switch statements and loops. Transfers program control to the statement line following the switch statement or following the terminated loop.
comment	Notations that explain what a script does. Comments are ignored by the interpreter. Single-line comments begin with //. Multiple-line comments begin with /* and end with */.
const	Identifies a declared constant value.
continue	Halts execution of a block of statements in a while or for loop and continues execution of the loop with the next iteration.
do...while	Executes the block of statements in a loop until the test condition evaluates to false. Statements in a loop execute at least once.
debugger	Will cause a breakpoint to occur when code is run in a debugger, otherwise, it has no effect.
finally	Executes a block of statements after the try and catch block of statements execute. The finally block of statements executes whether or not an exception is thrown. A good use for the finally block of statements is to allow a graceful failure.
for	Creates a loop that consists of three optional expressions, enclosed in parentheses and separated by semicolons, followed by a block of statements executed in the loop. The test to terminate a loop is done before the block of statements in the loop executes.
for...in	Iterates a specified variable over all the properties of an object. For each distinct property, JavaScript executes the specified statements.
for...of	Iterates through object property line arrays and array-like objects (Gecko engine only).

Table G–8 JavaScript Statements (continued)	
Statement	**Description**
for each...in	Iterates a specified variable through object property line arrays and array-like objects (Gecko engine only).
function	Defines a new function. Acceptable parameters include strings, numbers, and objects. For example, function myfunc( ) {.
if...else	Executes one block of statements if the condition is true. Executes another block of statements if the condition is false.
label	Provides an identifier that can be used with break or continue to indicate where the program should continue execution.
let	Initializes a local variable in a block.
return	Causes the current function to halt and possibly returns a value to the caller. For example, return endingval.
switch	Allows a program to evaluate an expression and attempts to match the expression's value to a case label.
throw	Throws or sends an exception. The exception can be an expression or an object.
try...catch	Executes a block of statements to try, and the statements to execute if an error occurs. Implemented in Internet Explorer 5 and later.
var	Declares and possibly initializes new variables. For example, var retval.
while	Creates a loop that evaluates an expression, and if it is true, executes a block of statements. The loop then repeats, as long as the specified condition is true.
with	Establishes the default object for a block of statements.

Event Handlers

JavaScript makes HTML documents dynamic through events. An **event** is an action that a user makes, such as clicking a button. Usually, when an event occurs, JavaScript code executes. Event handler names always begin with "on." In standard HTML, event handler names are in mixed case; the first letter after the word "on" is in uppercase. In XML and XHTML, because all attributes must be in lowercase, they are spelled in all lowercase characters. Table G–9 summarizes the JavaScript event handlers.

Table G–9 Event Handlers			
Event Handler	**Triggered When**	**Handler For**	**Used in HTML Statement**
onabort	The loading of an image is interrupted	Image	<img>
onafterprint	After page has printed	Window (Internet Explorer only)	<body>
onbeforeprint	Fires just before a page is printed or examined for Print Preview	Window (Internet Explorer only)	<body>
onbeforeunload	Displays message just before a page is unloaded	Window	<iframe>
onblur	An element becomes inactive	Button, Checkbox, FileUpload, Layer, Password, Radio, Reset, Select, Submit, Text, Textarea, Window	<body> ... </body> <frameset> ... </frameset> <frame> ... </frame> <input type="text" /> <textarea> ... </textarea> <select> ... </select>
onchange	The value of an element changes	FileUpload, Select, Text, Textarea	<input type="text" /> <textarea> ... </textarea> <select> ... </select>

Table G–9 Event Handlers (continued)

Event Handler	Triggered When	Handler For	Used in HTML Statement
onclick	An element is clicked once	Button, Checkbox, Document, Link, Radio, Reset, Submit	<a> ... </a> <input type="submit" /> <input type="reset" /> <input type="radio" /> <input type="checkbox" /> <input type="text" />
onclose	Current window is being closed		Window elements
oncontextmenu	Right-click to fire context menu	Return of false prevents context menu from displaying	All elements
oncopy	Text is being copied to be placed on Clipboard	Return of false prevents text from being copied	<textarea> ... </textarea> <input type="text" /> <select> ... </select>
oncut	Text is being cut to be placed on Clipboard	Return of false disables cutting of text	<textarea> ... </textarea> <input type="text" /> <select> ... </select>
ondblclick	An element is double-clicked	Document, Link	<a> ... </a> <input type="submit" /> <input type="reset" /> <input type="radio" /> <input type="checkbox" /> <input type="text" />
ondragdrop	An object is dragged and dropped into a window	Window (may not be available on all platforms)	<body> ... </body>
onerror	An error occurs when loading a document or image	Image, Window	<img /> <body> ... </body>
onfocus	An element becomes active	Button, Checkbox, FileUpload, Layer, Password, Radio, Reset, Select, Submit, Text, Textarea, Window (may not be available on all platforms)	<body> ... </body> <input type="text" /> <textarea> ... </textarea> <select> ... </select>
onhashchange	Fires when the hash portion (anything after the #) of a URL is changed	Firefox 3.5 and Internet Explorer 8+ only in Window and Body elements	
onkeydown	A designated key is pressed	Document, Image, Link, Textarea	<body> ... </body> <img /> <a> ... </a> <textarea> ... </textarea>
onkeypress	A designated key is pressed and released	Document, Image, Link, Textarea	<body> ... </body> <img /> <a> ... </a> <textarea> ... </textarea>
onkeyup	A designated key is released	Document, Image, Link, Textarea	<body> ... </body> <img /> <a> ... </a> <textarea> ... </textarea>
onload	A document or image loads	Image, Layer, Window	<img /> <body> ... </body>

Table G–9 Event Handlers (continued)

Event Handler	Triggered When	Handler For	Used in HTML Statement
onmousedown	A mouse button is pressed	Button, Document, Link	<a> ... </a> <input type="submit" /> <input type="reset" /> <body> ... </body>
onmouseenter	For use when mouse first enters element and does not continue to fire for all inner elements, unlike onmouseover	(Internet Explorer only)	All elements
onmouseleave	For use when mouse leaves element	(Internet Explorer only)	All elements
onmousemove	The mouse moves	Not associated with any particular object because the mouse moves so frequently; must be specifically associated with a particular object	<body> ... </body>
onmouseout	The mouse moves off an element	Layer, Link	<a> ... </a> <area> ... </area>
onmouseover	The mouse moves over an element	Layer, Link	<a> ... </a> <area> ... </area>
onmouseup	A button is released	Button, Document, Link	<a> ... </a> <input type="submit" /> <input type="reset" /> <body> ... </body>
onmousewheel	User scrolls with mouse wheel (Internet Explorer 6+, Opera, Safari) Firefox uses DOMMouseScroll	wheelDelta property to determine direction and amount of scroll	All elements
onmove	A window or frame is moved	Window (Internet Explorer only)	<body> ... </body>
onoffline	Browser is working offline		Browser
ononline	Browser is working online		Browser
onpaste	When user attempts to paste from Clipboard	Return of false prevents paste	All <form> elements
onreset	A form resets	Form	<form> ... </form>
onresize	A window or frame is resized	Window	<body> ... </body>
onselect	A user selects a field in a form	Text, Textarea	<input type="text" /> <textarea> ... </textarea>
onsubmit	A user submits a form	Form	<form> ... </form>
onunload	A document unloads	Window	<body> ... </body>

Objects

This section lists the properties, methods, and events of the major JavaScript objects.

Date Object

The **Date object** is used to access the system time and date. The Date object methods are summarized in Table G–10.

Table G–10 Date Object

Method	Returns	Method	Sets
getDate()	Day of month of Date object	setDate()	Day of month of Date object
getDay()	Day of week of Date object	setFullYear()	Four-digit year of Date object
getFullYear()	Year of Date object (four-digit format)	setHours()	Hours of Date object
getHours()	Hour of Date object	setMilliseconds()	Milliseconds of Date object
getMilliseconds()	Milliseconds of Date object	setMinutes()	Minutes of Date object
getMinutes()	Minutes of Date object	setMonth()	Month of Date object
getMonth()	Month of Date object	setSeconds()	Seconds of Date object
getSeconds()	Seconds of Date object	setTime()	Time of Date object (as number of milliseconds since January 1, 1970)
getTime()	Time of Date object (as number of milliseconds since January 1, 1970)	setUTCDate()	Date of Date object in universal time
getTimezoneOffset()	Local time zone offset in minutes from the current date and GMT	setUTCFullYear()	Four-digit year of Date object in universal time
getUTCDate()	Date of Date object in universal time	setUTCHours()	Hours of Date object in universal time
getUTCDay()	Day of week of Date object in universal time	setUTCMilliseconds()	Milliseconds of Date object in universal time
getUTCFullYear()	Four-digit year of Date object in universal time	setUTCMinutes()	Minutes of Date object in universal time
getUTCHours()	Hours of Date object in universal time	setUTCMonth()	Month of Date object in universal time
getUTCMilliseconds()	Milliseconds of Date object in universal time	setUTCSeconds()	Seconds of Date object in universal time
getUTCMinutes()	Minutes of Date object in universal time		
getUTCMonth()	Month of Date object in universal time		
getUTCSeconds()	Seconds of Date object in universal time		
Method	**Converts**		
parse()	Parses a date into component pieces (in milliseconds)		
toDateString()	Returns a date as a string in current time zone		
toLocaleDateString()	Date as string value in current time zone		
toLocaleString()	Date object to string, set to the current time zone		
toLocaleTimeString()	Time as string value in current time zone		
toString()	Date object to string		

Table G–10 Date Object (continued)

Method	Converts
toTimeString()	Time as string value in current time zone
toUTCString()	Date object to string, set to universal time
UTC()	Converts a date to milliseconds (as number of milliseconds since January 1, 1970)
valueOf()	Date object to millisecond format

Document Object

The **Document object** represents the content of a browser's window. Table G–11 summarizes the Document object properties and methods. Note that all properties and methods may not work with all browsers, especially older versions. Nonstandard properties are not included in this list to avoid confusion.

Table G–11 Document Object

Property	Description
activeElement	Element that currently has focus
alinkColor	Color of an active link specified by the alink attribute of the <body> tag; recommend using style sheet in place of property (Deprecated)
all[]	Array referring to all HTML elements in a document (Deprecated)
anchors[]	Array referring to the document's anchors
applets[]	Array referring to the document's applets (Deprecated)
bgColor	Background color of the document as specified by the bgColor attribute of the <body> tag; recommend using style sheet in place of property (Deprecated)
body	Contains the content of the document
characterSet	Character set currently in use
cookie	Specifies a cookie for the current document
domain	Domain name of the server where the current document is located
embeds[]	Array referring to the document's ActiveX controls and plug-ins
fgColor	Foreground text color of the document as specified by the fgColor attribute of the <body> tag; recommend using style sheet in place of property (Deprecated)
forms[]	Array referring to multiple forms within a document
head	Contains content of head node of document
images[]	Array referring to the document's images
lastModified	Date the document was last modified
links[]	Array referring to the document's links
location	URL of the document
parentWindow	Refers to the document's window
plugins[]	Array referring to objects used in the document, synonym for embeds[] array
readyState	State of the document as it loads
referrer	URL of the document that provided a link to the current document
title	Title of the document as specified by the <title> ... </title> tag pair in the document's <head> section
URL	URL of the current document
vlinkColor	Color of the document's visited links as specified by the vlink attribute of the <body> tag (deprecated)

Table G–11 Document Object (continued)	
Method	**Converts**
close()	Notifies the Web browser you are finished writing to a window or frame and that the document should be displayed
createAttribute	Creates new attribute node
elementFromPoint()	Specifies which HTML element is at a point
getElementById()	Refers to an object by its specified id; id attribute values may be enclosed in single or double quotation marks
getElementsByName()	Refers to an object by its name value; name attribute values may be enclosed in single or double quotation marks
getElementsByTagName()	Refers to an object by its tag name; tag attribute values may be enclosed in single or double quotation marks
getSelection()	Returns selected text
open()	Opens a window, other than the current window, and is used to update its contents with the write() and writeln() methods
routeEvent()	Passes the captured events to the next event handler
write()	Creates new text on a Web page
writeln()	Creates new text on a Web page followed by a line break

Assigning Color to an Object

When assigning color to an object, like foreground or background, the color should follow the red, green, blue (rgb) color scheme. The color can be written as a standard color name, red, orange, green and so on; or the color can be represented by its hexadecimal value of r, g, b. The hexidecimal value of the color red would be written as #ff0000, where ff means full red, and 0000 means no green or blue. Color may also be written as an rgb() method, where green would be written as rgb(0,255,0).

Form Object

The **Form object** represents forms created with the <form> ... </form> tag pair. Table G–12 summarizes the Form object properties and methods.

Table G–12 Form Object	
Property	**Description**
action	URL to which a form's data will be submitted
autocomplete	Browser (Boolean values: on, off) can autocomplete form controls (new in HTML5)
elements[]	Array representing a form's elements
elements.length	Number of elements on a form
encoding	Format of data being submitted
method	Method in which a form's data will be submitted (GET or POST)
name	Name of a form (Deprecated: id property is preferred)
novalidate	Boolean value indicates that form should not be validated if submitted to server CGI (New in HTML5)
target	Window in which any results returned from the server are displayed
Method	**Function**
reset()	Clears any data entered into a form
submit()	Submits a form to a Web server

History Object

The **History object** keeps track of the pages that have been visited. Table G–13 summarizes the History object property and methods.

Table G–13 History Object

Property	Description
current	URL of the current document
length	Contains the specific number of documents that have been opened during the current browser session
next	URL of the next document in the history array
previous	URL of the previous document in the history array
Method	**Function**
back()	Equivalent to clicking a Web browser's Back button
forward()	Equivalent to clicking a Web browser's Forward button
go(n)	Opens a specific document in the history list indicated by n (n is an integer or a URL)
toString()	Returns history in a string format

Image Object

The **Image object** represents images created using the <img> tag. Table G–14 summarizes the Image object properties and events.

Table G–14 Image Object

Property	Description
border	Read-only property containing border width, in pixels, as specified by border attribute of <img> tag, including if an error occurs during loading
complete	Boolean value that returns true when an image is completely loaded
height	Read-only property containing height of image as specified by height attribute of <img> tag
hspace	Read-only property containing amount of horizontal space, in pixels, to left and right of image, as specified by hspace attribute of <img> tag
name	Name assigned to tag (results are unpredictable because name attribute is deprecated in HTML5)
src	URL of displayed image
vspace	Read-only property containing amount of vertical space, in pixels, above and below image, as specified by vspace attribute of <img> tag
width	Read-only property containing width of image as specified by width attribute of <img> tag
Event	**Description**
onabort	User cancels the loading of an image, usually by clicking the Stop button
onerror	Error occurs while loading image
onload	Image finishes loading

JSON Object

The **JSON object** (JavaScript Object Notation) provides the capability of inserting data in a script without using XML. Table G–15 shows two examples of how to represent JSON data, and Table G–16 summarizes JSON methods.

Table G–15 JSON Example	
Examples	**Rules**
{ "author": "Mark Twain", "title": "Tom Sawyer", "year": 1876 }	All string values must be in double quotation marks. The identifier (field name) must be in double quotation marks and followed by a colon. A value cannot be a function or property.
var jsonBooks={ "author": "Mark Twain", "title": "Tom Sawyer", "year": 1876 }	

Table G–16 JSON Methods	
Method	**Description**
stringify(object, [replacer, space])	Converts an object into a JSON string. Replacer and space are optional. Replacer is a user-defined function used to replace one value with another. Space is an integer used to place spaces in front of data elements.
parse(string [reviver])	Converts a JSON string into an object. Reviver is optional. Reviver is a user-defined function used to modify any data further.
toJSON()	Dictates how JSON.stringify will serialize data.

Math Object

The **Math object** provides the capability of performing calculations. Table G–17 summarizes the Math object properties and methods.

Table G–17 Math Object	
Property	**Description**
E	Base of a natural logarithm (approximately 2.718)
LN10	Natural logarithm of 10 (approximately 2.302)
LN2	Natural logarithm of 2 (approximately 0.693)
LOG2E	Base-2 logarithm of E (approximately 1.442)
LOG10E	Base-10 logarithm of E (approximately 0.434)
PI	Ratio of the circumference of a circle to its diameter (approximately 3.142)
SQRT1_2	Square root of 1/2 (approximately 0.707)
SQRT2	Square root of 2 (approximately 1.414)
Method	**Function**
abs(x)	Absolute value of x
acos(x)	Arccosine of x
asin(x)	Arcsine of x
atan(x)	Arctangent of x
atan2(y,x)	Arctangent of the quotient of its arguments
ceil(x)	Value of x rounded to the next highest integer
cos(x)	Cosine of x
exp(x)	Exponent of x
floor(x)	Value of x rounded to the next lowest integer
log(x)	Natural logarithm of x

Table G–17 Math Object (continued)

Property	Description
max(x,y)	Larger of two numbers
min(x,y)	Smaller of two numbers
pow(x,y)	Value of x raised to the y power
random()	Random number between 0.0 and 1.0
round(x)	Value of x rounded to the nearest integer
sin(x)	Sine of x
sqrt(x)	Square root of x
tan(x)	Tangent of x

Location Object

The **Location object** contains information about a Web page. Table G–18 summarizes the Location object properties and methods.

Table G–18 Location Object

Property	Description
hash	URL's anchor
host	Combination of URL's host name and port sections
hostname	URL's host name
href	Full URL address
pathname	URL's path
port	URL's port
protocol	URL's protocol
search	URL's search or query portion
Method	**Function**
reload()	Causes the page currently displayed in the Web browser to open again
replace()	Replaces the currently loaded URL with a different one

Navigator Object

The **Navigator object** is used to get information about the current Web browser. Table G–19 summarizes the Navigator object properties and methods.

Table G–19 Navigator Object

Property	Description
appName	Web browser name
appVersion	Web browser version
cookieEnabled	Boolean result to indicate if cookies are enabled
language	Language used by the Web browser
mimeTypes[]	Array containing MIME types supported by the client browser
online	Returns a Boolean indicating whether the browser is working online
oscpu	Returns a string that represents the current operating system
platform	Operating system in use
plugins[]	Array containing installed plugins

Table G–19 Navigator Object (continued)

Property	Description
userAgent	User agent
Method	**Function**
javaEnabled()	Determines whether Java is enabled in the current browser
plugins.refresh()	Enables newly installed plugins on the client
savePreferences()	Saves all user preferences

Window and Frame Objects

The **Window object** represents a browser's window or an individual frame within a window. Thus, every **Frame object** is a window object, and uses all the methods and properties of the Window object. Table G–20 summarizes the Window and Frame objects' properties, methods, and events. (*Note:* Frames are not supported by HTML5 and not recommended for users with accessibility needs; they should be avoided if possible. Frames are included in the event that you encounter older Web pages.)

Table G–20 Window and Frame Objects

Property	Description
closed	Boolean value to determine if window has been closed
defaultStatus	Default text that is written to the status bar
document	Reference to the Document object
frames[]	Array listing the Frame objects in the window
history	Reference to the History object
length	Number of frames in a window
location	Reference to the Location object
name	Name of a window
navigator	Points to the Navigator object for the browser
opener	Window object that opens another window
parent	Parent frame that contains the current frame
screen	Screen information where the browser is running
self	Self-reference to the Window object
status	Temporary text that is written to the status bar
top	Topmost Window object that contains the current frame
window	Self-reference to the Window object
Method	**Function**
alert()	Displays a message dialog box with an OK button
blur()	Removes the focus from the window
clearTimeout()	Cancels a set timeout
close()	Closes the window
confirm()	Displays a confirmation dialog box with OK and Cancel buttons
focus()	Makes the Window object the active window
moveBy(x,y)	The moveBy() method moves the window horizontally or vertically by the number of pixels; positive numbers move right and down, negative move in the opposite direction

Table G–20 Window and Frame Objects (continued)

Method	Function
moveTo(x,y)	The moveTo() method moves the window to the location specified by the numeric values
open()	Opens a new window
prompt()	Displays a dialog box prompting a user to enter information
setTimeout()	Executes a function after a specified number of milliseconds has elapsed
Event	**Triggered When**
onblur	Window becomes inactive
onerror	Error occurs when the window loads
onfocus	Window becomes active
onload	Document is completely loaded in the window
onresize	Window is resized
onunload	Current document in the window is unloaded

The Window object open() method has many possible parameters. Table G–21 shows the features and values for the open() method.

Table G–21 open() Method

Feature	Description	Written As
directories	New window shows extra buttons	"directories=yes"
location	Includes address bar	"location=yes"
menubar	Includes menu bar	"menubar=yes"
resizeable	Allows user to resize	"resizeable=yes"
scrollbars	Includes scroll bars	"scrollbars=yes"
status	Includes status bar	"status=yes"
titlebar	Removes title bar	"titlebar=no"
toolbar	Includes toolbar	"toolbar=yes"
width	States width in pixels	"width=220"
height	States height in pixels	"height=450"

Number Object

The **Number object** gives support for special constants that may be platform specific and exposes one conversion method. Table G–22 summarizes the Number object properties and methods.

Table G–22 Number Object

Property	Description
MAX_VALUE	Maximum numeric value
MIN_VALUE	Minimum numeric value
NaN	Not a number value
NEGATIVE_INFINITY	Value for negative infinity
POSITIVE_INFINITY	Value for positive infinity

Table G–22 Number Object (continued)

Method	Description
toExponential()	Returns a string representing the number in exponential notation
toFixed()	Returns a string representing the number in fixed-point notation
toLocaleString()	Returns a string representation of the number based on system setting
toPrecision()	Returns a string representing the number to a specified precision in fixed-point notation
toString()	Converts a numeric value to a string value

Function Object

The **Function object** gives the programmer access to information about specific functions. Table G–23 summarizes the Function object properties and methods.

Table G–23 Function Object

Property	Description
caller	Name of the function that called the current one
length	Number of arguments declared for the function
prototype	Prototype for a class of objects
Method	**Description**
apply()	Uses a function as a method for an object
call()	Allows you to call (execute) a method of another object in the context of a different object (the calling object)
toSource()	Returns a string representing the source code of the function; overrides the Object.toSource method
toString()	Converts a function to a string value

Screen Object

The **Screen object** gives platform-specific information about the user's screen. Table G–24 summarizes the Screen object properties.

Table G–24 Screen Object

Property	Description
availHeight	Available height of the screen
availLeft	First horizontal pixel available
availTop	First vertical pixel available
availWidth	Available width of the screen
colorDepth	Depth of the client browser's color palette
height	Height of the client screen
pixelDepth	Color resolution (in bits per pixel) of the client browser's screen
width	Width of the client screen

Boolean Object

The **Boolean object** converts other objects to Boolean values. A value of False is returned for values of undefined, null, 0, -0, false, NaN, or an empty string (""). All other values return a value of True. Table G–25 summarizes the methods for the Boolean object.

Table G–25 Boolean Object

Method	Function
toSource	Returns a string representing the source code of an object; you can use this value to create a new object. It overrides the Object.toSource method.
toString	Returns a string representing the specified object. It overrides the Object. toString method.

Array Object

An **array** is an ordered set of values associated with a single variable name. Table G–26 summarizes the properties and methods for the Array object.

Table G–26 Array Object

Property	Description
index	For an array created by a regular expression match, the zero-based index of the match in the string
input	For an array created by a regular expression match, reflects the original string against which the regular expression was matched
length	Reflects the number of elements in an array; can be changed to truncate or extend array
Method	**Function**
concat()	Joins two arrays and returns a new array
join()	Joins all elements of an array into a string
pop()	Removes the last element from an array and returns that element
push()	Adds one or more elements to the end of an array and returns the new length of the array
reverse()	Transposes the elements of an array; first array element becomes the last and the last becomes the first
shift()	Removes the first element from an array and returns that element
slice()	Extracts a section of an array and returns a new array
sort()	Sorts the elements of an array
splice()	Adds and/or removes elements from an array
toLocaleString()	Returns a string representing the array and its elements
toSource()	Returns an array literal representing the specified array; use this value to create a new array as it overrides the Object.toSource method
toString()	Returns a string representing the array and its elements; overrides the Object.toString method
unshift()	Adds one or more elements to the front of an array and returns the new length of the array

String Object

The **String object** represents a set of characters. Any object converted to the String object can use any of the string methods. Table G–27 summarizes the property and methods for the String object.

Table G–27 String Object

Property	Description
length	Specifies the length of the string
Method	**Function**
anchor()	Creates a hypertext target
big()	Displays text in a big font as if it were in a <big> ... </big> tag
blink()	Blinks text as if it were in a <blink> ... </blink> tag
bold()	Displays text as if it were in a <b> ... </b> tag
charAt()	Returns the character at the specified location (relative index)
charCodeAt()	Returns a number indicating the Unicode value of the character at the given location (relative index)
concat()	Combines the text of two strings
fixed()	Displays text in a fixed-pitch font as if it were in a <tt> ... </tt> tag
fontcolor()	Displays text in the specified color as if it were in a <font> ... </font> tag
fontsize()	Displays text in the specified font size as if it were in a <font> ... </font> tag
fromCharCode()	Creates a string by using the specified sequence of Unicode values
indexOf()	Returns the index within the calling String object of the first occurrence of the specified value, or –1 if not found
italics()	Displays a string to be italic as if it were in an <i> ... </i> tag
lastIndexOf()	Returns the index within the calling String object of the last occurrence of the specified value, or –1 if not found
link()	Creates an HTML hypertext link that requests another URL
match()	Matches a regular expression against a string
replace()	Matches a regular expression and a string, and replaces the matched substring with a new substring
search()	Searches for a match between a regular expression and a specified string
slice()	Returns a new string from an existing string
small()	Displays text in a small font as if it were in a <small> ... </small> tag
split()	Splits a String object into an array of substrings
strike()	Displays text as struck-out text as if it were in a <strike> ... </strike> tag
sub()	Displays text as a subscript as if it were in a _{...} tag
substr()	Returns the characters in a string starting at a specific location for a specific length
substring()	Returns a substring of a string
sup()	Displays text as a superscript as if it were in a ^{...} tag
toLowerCase()	Displays a string value converted to lowercase
toSource()	Returns the source of the instance created; overrides the Object.toSource method
toString()	Returns the object type or name of the constructor that created the object; overrides the Object.toString method
toUpperCase()	Displays a string value converted to uppercase

Regular Expression

A **Regular Expression** (RegExp) is used for pattern matching. The special characters used for the patterns are described in Table G–28.

Table G–28 RegExp

Character	Description
/	Every pattern must begin with a slash
\d	Match any digit
\s	Match any space, newline, tab, return
\w	Match any alphanumeric character
^	Beginning of a string
$	End of a string
?	First of all characters (?xy) means x or xy
*	Multiple of characters (*xy) means x or xy or xyy
+	Multiple of all characters (xy+) means xy, or xyy, or xyyy
[xx]	Used in brackets for alternatives; (Adobe CS[3456]) would return Adobe CS3, Adobe CS4, Adobe CS5, or Adobe CS6
[x–x]	Used in brackets for sequence; (JavaScript 1.[1–5]) means JavaScript 1.1 or JavaScript 1.2, etc.
[^x–x]	Used in brackets to match anything BUT the selected characters; ([^w–y]) means any letter but w through y
(x)	Subpattern
.	The dot means any character
{min, max}	The minimum or maximum number of sequences; (x{1,3}) means x or xx or xxx

Global Functions

Table G–29 summarizes the **global functions** that always are available in JavaScript.

Table G–29 Global Functions

Function	Description
decodeURI()	Decodes or replaces an escape sequence in the encoded URI with the character that it represents; cannot decode escape sequence not coded by encoded URI
decodeURIComponent()	Decodes or replaces each escape sequence in the encoded URIComponent() with the character that it represents
encodeURI()	Replaces all characters, except those with special meaning in a URI, with the appropriate UTF-8 escape sequences
encodeURIComponent()	Assumes that the URI is not complete, and does not treat reserved Component() characters as if they have special meaning and encodes them
escape()	Returns the hexadecimal code
eval()	Evaluates a string of JavaScript code without reference to a particular object
isFinite()	Evaluates an argument to determine whether it is a finite number
isNaN()	Evaluates an argument to determine if it is not a number
number()	Converts an object to a number
parseFloat()	Parses a string argument and returns a floating-point number
parseInt()	Parses a string argument and returns an integer
string()	Converts an object to a string
unescape()	Returns the ASCII string for the specified hexadecimal encoding value

Appendix H
XML Quick Reference

What Is XML?

Extensible Markup Language (XML) is a subset of the Standard Generalized Markup Language (SGML). The current version of XML is version 1.0, and the fifth edition is not a new version but an update of changes based on reported errors (www.w3.org/TR/xml/). XML allows developers to create their own document elements or tags. The World Wide Web Consortium (W3C, www.w3.org) develops the standards for XML and other Web languages.

An XML document consists of two main parts: the prolog and the document instance. The **prolog** contains processing instructions and any additional comments necessary to provide information about the document's content and structure. An XML prolog can include any of the following:

- XML declaration statements and comments
- Document type declaration with an optional Document Type Definition (DTD) to define elements, attributes, and logical relationships of data
- Optional link to either a CSS or XSL style sheet

The **document instance** contains the main content or elements of the XML document and provides a logical structure for the document.

Well-Formed and Valid XML Documents

XML documents must be well-formed to be processed by an application. A valid XML document is one that adheres to the rules and structure specified in a DTD or an XML Schema Definition (XSD). The element is the basic building block of any XML file. Table H–1 shows the syntax rules that define well-formed and valid XML documents. An XML document must be at least well-formed. Besides the Web site shown in Chapter 12, www.corefiling.com/opensource/schemaValidate.html, you can check the syntax of your XML document at www.w3schools.com/dom/dom_validate.asp or check for a valid DTD at www.xmlvalidation.com/. See the Web sites for instructions on how to use and validate XML documents.

Table H–1 Rules for Well-Formed and Valid XML Documents

Rule Number	Rules
1	Must contain at least one properly tagged element.
2	Must contain a unique start and end tag that includes the entire document.
3	All remaining tags must be nested properly and may not overlap.
4	XML tags are case sensitive.
5	An XML document must contain at least one root element and nest the child elements within the root.
6	All elements include a start and end tag.
7	Element attribute values must be enclosed in quotation marks.
8	Elements can be empty; empty elements must be formatted correctly to include a / (forward slash) before the end tag.
9	Only entity references may use < and & characters.

XML Processing Instructions

Table H–2 shows the basic form of the declarations, statements, and comments found in the prolog section of an XML document.

Table H–2 XML Instructions

Instruction	General Form	Example	Comment
XML declaration	<?xml version="#" [encoding="encoding" standalone="yes|no"]?>	<?xml version="1.0" standalone="yes"?>	Defines version, character encoding, and if DTD is required to parse XML document; standalone="yes" means no external markup documents impact the XML data processed by the parser
Document type declaration	<!DOCTYPE ROOT-ELEMENT PUBLIC/SYSTEM="URL-DTD.DTD">	<!DOCTYPE PHONELIST SYSTEM="PHONELIST.DTD">	PUBLIC indicates location of public DTD; SYSTEM indicates location of private DTD
Processing Instruction	<?target attribute="value" ?>	<?xml-stylesheet type="text/xsl" href="products.xsl"?>	Gives instruction to the application to access a document or file outside the application (in this example, a style sheet); can include one or more attributes
Comment	<!--Comments -->	<!-- File Name: products.xml -->	Provides a user or developer with information about the document; comments are ignored by application
Character Data Type (Unparsed)	<![CDATA [text]]>	<![CDATA [The <b> tag should always have an end </b> tag.]]	Special section of character data not interpreted as markup, as opposed to parsed character data (PCDATA), to which the XML syntax rules apply; CDATA sections often used to show XML or HTML syntax examples

XML Element and Attribute Rules

Elements must be bound by start and end tags or be an empty element. Elements may contain other elements, but they must be nested in the proper order. Table H–3 lists the syntax rules for creating valid XML elements. Table H–4 contains a list of element rules. Table H–5 shows examples of valid, invalid, and empty XML elements.

Table H–3 XML Element Syntax Rules

Rule Number	Rules
1	Must begin with a letter or an underscore
2	May contain letters, numbers, hyphens, periods, or underscores
3	May not contain spaces, commas, or symbols (@#$%^&*!)
4	May not begin with XML, which is reserved for future use
5	Names are case sensitive; start and end tags must use same case
6	Colons are acceptable only for declaring namespaces
7	Empty elements have no text or values, but may contain attributes

Table H–4 XML Element Rules

Symbol	Meaning
#PCDATA	Element contains parsed character data or text and conforms to XML constraints (CDATA attributes are nonparsed character data)
element name (by itself)	Element name may be used one time only
element name ?	Element is used either once or not at all
element name +	Element has a one-to-many (1:n) relationship
element name *	Element has a zero, or one-to-many (1:n) relationship
, (comma)	Used between elements to indicate order
| (bar)	Used between elements to indicate either/or
( )	Used to group related elements together; may be nested

Table H–5 Valid and Invalid Examples of XML Elements

Example	Comment
<FirstName></FirstName>	Valid
<Picture SRC="mypic.jpg" />	Valid empty element
<_Project></_Project>	Valid
<First-Name></First-Name>	Valid
<Hanger_41></Hanger_41>	Valid
<Java Script></Java Script>	Invalid (contains a space)
<xmlproject></xmlproject>	Invalid (may not begin with xml)
<Para></PARA>	Invalid (start and end tags use different case)
<45Degree></45Degree>	Invalid (starts with a numeral)

Element attributes describe additional information about the element. Attribute values must be enclosed in quotation marks (either single or double quotation marks are acceptable). Attribute names follow the same rules as elements. Table H–6 shows the reserved attributes.

Table H–6 Reserved Attributes

Attribute	Comment	Example
xml:lang="code"	where code indicates language of element body	<Greet xml:lang="en">Hey</Greet>
xml:space="action"	where action is either default or preserve; preserve means preserve white space, default means treat white space based on default settings	<Lines xml:space="preserve">This is one line </Lines>
xml:link="type"	where type is simple, extended, locator, group, or document	<a xml:link="simple" href=http://www.w3.org>W3C</A>

XML Schema Definition (XSD)

An **XML Schema Definition (XSD)** describes in more exact detail the structure of an XML document. Because the XML document can be used as a database, its structure must be defined. The XSD describes the fields, the data types, and the values that can be stored in a field. XSD files are external documents to the XML document instance and are linked to the XML file in the root <xml> tag.

The **Document Type Definition** (**DTD**) is a precursor to the XSD and defines the elements and attributes in an XML document. While the DTD was used to validate the structure of an XML file, it has been abandoned because the XSD provides more detail about the XML structure because it can define specific data types to enforce data validity. A DTD defines an XML document using one data type. In an XSD, you must define the content by its particular type of data. For example, a DTD cannot define a field as a date, whereas an XSD can. Moreover, a DTD cannot create and define complex data types in the same way an XSD can. In an XSD, an element defined as a date must conform to the format of a date.

An XML Schema Definition is an XML file in itself. It must conform to the same rules of any XML document to be valid and well-formed. An XSD file contains the primary components of simple type definitions, complex type definitions, attributes declarations, and elements. **Simple type** definitions do not contain child elements nor do they contain attributes. **Complex type** definitions contain other elements and attributes. **Attributes** are values that appear in start or empty elements. **Elements** define the contents of an XML file and the relationship to other elements.

The <schema> element is the root element of every XSD. The <schema> contains information to identify and associate the namespace to the schema definitions. The xmlns attribute points to the URI to define the namespace. A **namespace** is used to prevent confusion over multiple elements being used by different sources. These elements may have the same name but have data types. Table H–7 shows the general form of the <schema> root element of the XSD defining the namespace.

Table H–7 The Root <schema> Element

Root element:	<xs:schema xmlns:xs="http://www.w3.org/2001/XMLSchema" [targetNamespace="URI " xmlns="URI " elementFormDefault="qualified"] >
Comment:	The **xs** is the namespace. The **xmlns** is the XML namespace location and associates the xs to the schema of all schemas at the *www.w3.org* Web site. The most used namespaces are xs or xsd. The optional elements within brackets are **targetNamespace** that associates other namespace items with the designated URI. The **xmlns** defines the default namespace location and the **elementFormDefault** indicates that the definition must be namespace qualified.
Example	<xs:schema xmlns:xs="http://www.w3.org/2001/XMLSchema">

To define an XML element, the XSD <element> tag names the element and data type. Table H–8 shows the general form of the XSD <element> tag.

Table H–8 The <element> Tag Element

General form:	<xs:element name="field name" type="data type" />
Comment:	xs: is a namespace, to differentiate this element from any other element that may have the same name. The **name** is an attribute to define the field name; **type** is an attribute to state one of the valid data types. Simple elements may have an optional default or fix attributes to assign a default value to a field. The default value is assigned if no other value is assigned; the fixed value does not allow any other value to be assigned. Most developers use xs or xsd as a default namespace. This book uses xs.
Examples:	<xs:element name="qoh" type="xs:integer" default="0" />

Table H–9 defines the remaining XSD elements that define the structure of any XML document.

Table H–9 XSD Elements

Element Name	Description
all	Indicates child elements can appear in any order (see sequence)
annotation	Indicates the top-level element for schema comments
any	Allows extension of the XML document with elements not defined by the schema
anyAttribute	Allows extension of the XML document with attributes not defined by the schema
appInfo	Contained within an annotation element; holds information to be used by the application
attribute	Defines an attribute
attributeGroup	Defines an attribute group to be used in complex type definitions
choice	Within a group, choice, sequence, complexType, or restriction elements, only one of the elements may be present within the element
complexContent	Indicates whether mixed content is allowed; an element of xs:extension allows mixed, whereas xs:restriction does not allow mixed content
complexType	Defines a complex type element
documentation	Contained with the annotation for comments about the schema
element	Defines an element
extension	Extends an existing simpleType or complexType element
field	An XPath expression used by unique, key, or keyref
group	Defines a group of elements used in a complex type definition
import	References schemas for namespace for additional namespace definitions
include	Used to break large schemas into smaller parts
key	Indicates an attribute or element value as a key that must be unique
keyref	Defines constraints on specified key or unique element
list	Available only in a simple type element to specify a list of values to be used in content
notation	Allows the format of non-XML data
redefine	Redefines simple, complex types, and groups (see include)
restriction	Defines restrictions on a simpleType, simpleContent, or a complexContent to clarify domains (valid ranges)
schema	Defines the root element of a schema
selector	Selects a set of elements for an identity constraint (see key, unique, keyref)
sequence	Indicates that the child elements must appear in a sequence.
simpleContent	Used in complexType elements to define simple content such as text and attributes
simpleType	Defines a simple type and specifies the constraints and information about the values of attributes or text-only elements
union	Allows creation of simple type as a collection (union) of more than one type of data
unique	Indicates that an element or an attribute value must be unique within the document

Simple Types

A simple element is an XML element that does not contain any other elements or attributes. In the XSD, the <element> tag declares the name of the element and its data type. A sample simple XML element and its associated schema is shown in Table H–10.

Table H–10 Simple Type Element

Simple XML Element	XML Schema
an XML element that contain only text <first_name>Bill</first_name>	<xs:element name="first_name" type=" xs:string" />

The <element> tag in the XSD must have a data type. Table H–11 shows the most common data types.

Table H–11 XSD Data Types

Data Types	Description
AnyURI	A valid URI Internet address
Binary	A set of binary codes in groups of eight
Boolean	Binary logic of true or false, yes or no, on or off, or 1 or 0
Date	Represent the date as YYYY-MM-DD
Decimal	Data is any number that contains a decimal fraction
Integer	Data is any whole number not a fraction
String	Data is any set of characters

Data types can have constraints or facets. These values further define restrictions or validations for the data contained within an XML element beyond whether it is a string or a numeric value. For example, to specifically define acceptable values in an element, enumeration constraint is used to list acceptable values. Table H–12 shows the common constraints or facets.

Table H–12 Constraints or Facets

Data Type Constraints	Description
enumeration	A list of acceptable values
fractionDigits	Defines the maximum number of decimal places and value must be equal to or greater than zero
length	Explicitly states the number of characters or list items allowed and must be equal to or greater than zero
maxExclusive	The numeric values for the upper bound for a domain
maxInclusive	Defines the upper bounds for numeric values
maxLength	Defines the maximum number of characters or list items allowed and the value must be equal to or greater than zero
minExclusive	The numeric values for the lower bounds
minInclusive	Defines the lower bounds for numeric values
minLength	Defines the minimum number of characters or list items allowed and the value must be equal to or greater than zero
pattern	Defines the exact sequence of characters that are acceptable
totalDigits	Defines the number of digits allowed and must be greater than zero
whiteSpace	Defines line feeds, tabs, spaces, and carriage returns

Complex Types

A complex element is an XML element that contains other elements or attributes. In the XSD, the <element> tag declares the name of the element and its data type. A sample complex element and its associated schema is shown in Table H–13.

Table H–13 Complex Type Element

Complex XML Element	XML Schema
an XML element that contains child elements or attributes <schedule_item> <course_no>CSCI-C340</course_no> <course_title>Web programming</course_title> </schedule_item>	<xs:element name="schedule item"> <xs:complexType> <xs:sequence> <xs:element name="course_no" type="string" /> <xs:element name="course_title" type="string" /> </ xs:sequence> </ xs:complexType> </ xs:element>

XSL Style Sheets

Extensible Stylesheet Language (**XSL**), which is a language for expressing style sheets, incorporates three technologies:

- **XSL Transformations** (**XSLT**), a language for transforming XML documents into other types of documents.
- **XML Path Language** (**XPath**), a language used by XSLT to access or refer to parts of an XML document.
- **XSL Formatting Objects**, a language that defines XML formatting and display.

Table H–14 shows the XSLT elements specified by the W3C.

Table H–14 XSLT Elements

Element Name	Description
xsl:apply-imports	Applies template rule from an imported style sheet
xsl:apply-templates	Applies a template rule to the current element
xsl:attribute	Adds a new attribute to the current output element
xsl:attribute-set	Defines a named set of attributes
xsl:call-template	Provides a way to call a named template
xsl:choose	Provides a selection mechanism based on conditions
xsl:comment	Adds a comment node to the output
xsl:copy	Copies the current node to the output
xsl:copy-of	Creates a copy of the current node
xsl:decimal-format	Defines the characters and symbols to be used when converting numbers into strings in conjunction with the format-number() function

Table H–14 XSLT Elements (continued)

Element Name	Description
xsl:element	Adds a new element node to the output
xsl:fallback	Indicates code to execute if the processor does not support an XSLT element
xsl:for-each	Provides a mechanism to create a loop in the output stream
xsl:if	Provides a conditional branch mechanism based on a condition
xsl:import and xsl:include	Merges rules from different style sheets
xsl:key	Declares a named key that can be used in the style sheet with the key() function
xsl:message	Writes error message to the output
xsl:namespace-alias	Replaces namespaces in the style sheet with different namespaces in the output
xsl:number	Determines the integer position of the current node and formats a number
xsl:otherwise	Is part of the choose mechanism (see xsl:choose)
xsl:output	Defines the format of the output document
xsl:param	Declares a local or global parameter
xsl:preserve-space	Indicates elements to preserve white space
xsl:processing-instruction	Adds a processing statement or instruction to the output
xsl:sort	Reorders input before copying to output
xsl:strip-space	Indicates elements to remove white space
xsl:stylesheet	Defines the root element of the style sheet
xsl:template	Defines a template
xsl:text	Writes literal text or spaces to the output
xsl:transform	Defines the root element of a style sheet
xsl:value-of	Defines a node to insert into the output
xsl:variable	Defines constants
xsl:when	Is part of the choose mechanism (see xsl:choose)
xsl:with-param	Defines the value of a parameter to be passed into a template

Document Type Definition (DTD)

A **document type declaration** is a processing instruction that tells the processor where to locate the Document Type Definition. A Document Type Definition (DTD) defines the elements and attributes in an XML document. A DTD also defines the order in which the elements and attributes appear. The DTD can be embedded within a document type declaration, or linked as an external document. Using a DTD allows the developer to confirm that an XML document is valid, meaning it conforms to the specified structure in the DTD. The DTD, however, has been largely replaced by developers in favor of the more succinct definition of the XML Schema Definition. It is included here strictly for reference only.

The prolog can also contain a document type declaration that tells the processor where to locate the DTD. The DTD can be an external file or embedded within the XML document. The DTD has two elements that indicate a relationship between the parent (<Video>) and the child (<Movie>). Table H–15 shows the general form of a document type declaration identifying an embedded DTD.

Table H–15 General Form of a Document Type Declaration with an Embedded Document Type Definition

General form:

```
<!DOCTYPE Name
   [
   <!ELEMENT Parent Definition (Child Definition * | + | ?)>
     <!ELEMENT Child Definition (child element list)
     <!ELEMENT Child element Definition ANY|(#PCDATA)>
   ]
>
```

Comment: **!DOCTYPE** is a reserved word that indicates the start of a document type declaration. *Name* is any valid name of an element and defines the name of the embedded DTD. The square bracket on line 2 indicates the beginning of the DTD. **!ELEMENT** is a reserved word that defines the type of elements in the document. The child definition qualifiers are an asterisk (*), a plus sign (+), or a question mark (?). The asterisk means zero to many, the plus sign means one to many, and the question mark means zero or one only. *Definition* is one or more valid element definitions. Whereas ANY indicates that any type of data may be associated with the element, #PCDATA indicates that the element contains parsed character data, which is text data. The square bracket in line 6 ends the DTD, and the right angle bracket on line 7 ends the document type declaration.

```
<?xml version="1.0" encoding="UTF-8"?>
<!-- File Name: video_collection.xml -->
<!DOCTYPE Video
   [
   <!ELEMENT Video (Movie*)>
   <!ELEMENT Movie (Year, Title, Director, Type, Actor_Male, Actor_Female, Time, Rating)>
   <!ELEMENT Year (#PCDATA)>
      <!ELEMENT Title (#PCDATA)>
      <!ELEMENT Director (#PCDATA)>
      <!ELEMENT Type (#PCDATA)>
      <!ELEMENT Actor_Male (#PCDATA)>
      <!ELEMENT Actor_Female (#PCDATA)>
      <!ELEMENT Time (#PCDATA)>
      <!ELEMENT Rating (#PCDATA)>
   ]
>

<Video>
   <Movie>
      <Year>2000</Year>
      <Title>Cast Away</Title>
      <Director>Robert Zemeckis</Director>
      <Type>Adventure</Type>
      <Actor_Male>Tom Hanks</Actor_Male>
      <Actor_Female>Helen Hunt</Actor_Female>
      <Time>143</Time>
      <Rating>PG-13</Rating>
   </Movie>
</Video>
```

A Document Type Definition (DTD) is similar to a database schema and defines the elements and attributes in an XML document. A DTD indicates how elements of an XML document relate to each other. A DTD provides the grammar rules of a document. When an XML document adheres to a DTD, it is considered valid.

A DTD can include element declarations, attribute list declarations, entity declarations, and notation declarations. An **element declaration** defines the type of content contained in an element. Table H–16 describes the basic form of an element declaration.

Table H–16 General Form of an Element Declaration

General form:	<!ELEMENT element-name (rule)>
Comment:	**!ELEMENT** is the declaration; *element-name* is any valid XML element name (see rules in Table H–3 on page APP 74); *rule* is a keyword, such as ANY or #PCDATA. The ANY keyword means other valid tags and data can be displayed; #PCDATA means only parsed character data can be displayed.
Example:	<!ELEMENT SONG (Title, Singer)> <!ELEMENT Title (#PCDATA)> <!ELEMENT Singer (#PCDATA)>

Attribute List Declarations

A DTD can also contain an attribute list declaration. The items in the attribute list must correspond to any attributes declared within XML elements. Table H–17 shows the general form of an attribute list declaration.

Table H–17 General Form of an Attribute List Declaration

General form:	<!ATTLIST element-name attribute-name data-type default-value>
Comment:	The *element-name* is the name of the XML element. The *attribute-name* is the name of the attribute. The *data-type* is the data type of the attribute. The *default-value* is any default value of the attribute. In the example, width is an attribute of the txtBox element, with a CDATA (character data) type and default value of 10.
Example:	<!ATTLIST txtBox width CDATA "10">

The data type in an attribute list declaration can be one of 10 different kinds of data type attributes, as shown in Table H–18.

Table H–18 DTD Data Type Attributes

Type	Description
CDATA	Character data; can include any character string as well as special symbols for ampersand (&), less-than and greater-than symbols or angle brackets (< or >), or quotation marks (")
Enumerated	List of possible values for an attribute (such as cash/check/charge); only one can be used
ENTITY	Single entity; either external data or declared DTD entity
ENTITIES	Multiple entities; either external data or declared in DTD
ID	Unique element identifier for an attribute that distinguishes one element from others
IDREF	Identifies the value of a unique ID of another element
IDREFS	Identifies multiple values for an attribute, separated by white space
NMTOKEN	XML name token; restricts the attribute value to any valid XML name (letters, number, hyphens, underscores, and periods)
NMTOKENS	Allows the attribute value to include multiple XML names, separated by white space
NOTATION	Allows the attribute value to be a value specified in a DTD notation declaration

The default value in an attribute list declaration must match the data type. If a specific value is noted, the value must be enclosed within quotation marks. A default value consists of one of the four options shown in Table H–19.

Table H–19 DTD Data Type Attributes	
Modifier	**Description**
#DEFAULT value	Specific value set at the default attribute value
#FIXED "value"	Attribute value is fixed and must always take the default value assigned
#IMPLIED	Attribute value is optional; if used in an element type, no default value is supplied
#REQUIRED	Attribute value must be specified with the element

Entity Declarations

As just discussed, a DTD can also include **entity declarations**, which assign a name to a block of text or other characters that can be interpreted as markup language and substituted in a document. The replacement text must begin with an ampersand (&) and end with a semicolon (;). Entity declarations can be internal or external. Table H–20 shows the general form of an internal entity declaration. Table H–21 shows the predefined symbols that can be used in an entity declaration.

Table H–20 General Form of Internal Entity Declaration	
General form:	<!ENTITY name "&replacement;"> <ELEMENT>text "&replacement;"</ELEMENT>
Comment:	The attribute *name* is a valid element name and *replacement* is the entity characters to be substituted within the string. Circular references are not allowed.
Example:	<!ENTITY copyright "©"> <PUBLISHED>2014 Cengage Learning ©right;</PUBLISHED>

Table H–21 Predefined Entity Symbols		
Entity	**Symbol**	**Explanation**
&	&	Cannot be used in processing instructions
<	<	Use with attributes beginning with quotation marks
>	>	Use after]] in normal text and processing instructions
"	"	Use in attributes within double quotation marks
'	'	Use in attributes within single quotation marks
&#x*hex*;	[varied]	Where *hex* is replaced with a hexadecimal value for a character, such as A9 for the copyright symbol (©)

XML allows the use of external entities to refer to the contents of another file. An external entity exists at a specified location or URL. The content of the external file is inserted at the point of reference and parsed as part of the referring document. Table H–22 shows the general form of an external entity.

Table H–22 General Form of an External Entity	
General form:	<!ENTITY name PUBLIC/SYSTEM "URI/URL"> <ELEMENT>text "&replacement;" </ELEMENT>
Comment:	The attribute *name* is a valid element name; the *URI* or *URL* is an identifier that points to a file on that system or a public file available via URL. **ENTITY** must be declared first.
Example:	<!ENTITY stockquotes SYSTEM "www.cnbc.com/id/26272770/site/14081545/"> <finances> <dowjones>Dow Jones Industrial Averages</dowjones> &stockquotes; </finances>

Unparsed Entities and Notation Declarations

A **notation declaration** tells a processor that an entity refers to non-XML content that should not be parsed. Unparsed entities are used most frequently on XML elements that incorporate graphics into a document.

A notation also has to be declared in an entity. An unparsed entity is indicated by the NDATA keyword. Ampersands and semicolons are not used with unparsed data. Table H–23 shows an example.

Table H–23 Unparsed Entity Example
<!ENTITY imageA SYSTEM www.imaginary_site.org/myimage.gif NDATA GIF89a><image src="imageA" />

Index

Note

- Page numbers in bold type indicate definitions.
- Page numbers followed by "t" indicate tables.
- Page numbers followed by "BTW" indicate margin notes.
- Page numbers followed by "+t" or "+BTW" indicate discussions plus tables or margin notes.

Symbols

& (ampersand): entity symbol begin character, **APP** 83+t, 84
* (asterisk): child definition qualifier, APP 75t, 81t
@ page rule, HTML 348+BTW
\ (backslash): escape character, **APP** 54
: (colon): XML reserved character, HTML 566BTW
$ (dollar sign): variable name character, **APP** 53
// (double slash): comment symbol, HTML 418BTW
<!--...-->: comment codes, **HTML** 113, 115, 333, 418+BTW; **APP** 3t
!DOCTYPE reserved word, **APP** 81t
<!DOCTYPE> tag/statement, **HTML** 12, 39+BTW, 40t, 43, 397; **APP** 1, 3t
!ELEMENT reserved word, **APP** 81t
– (minus sign): collapse document level sign, **HTML** 584–585
(nonbreaking space), **HTML** 260
. (period)
  class name delimiter, **HTML** 127, 179BTW, 181
  method/property name delimiter, **HTML** 413
  as not a variable name character, **APP** 53
.. (periods): one directory level up symbol, **HTML** 109
| (pipe symbol): link separator, **HTML** 175
  coloring, **HTML** 338
+ (plus sign)
  child definition qualifier, **APP** 75t, 81t
  concatenation operator, **HTML** 427; APP 56t
  expand document level sign, **HTML** 584–585
+= (plus equal signs): concatenates operator, **APP** 56t
(pound sign)
  id selector symbol, **HTML** 540
  link target symbol, **HTML** 96, 135, 599
#PCDATA keyword, **APP** 75t, 81t, 82t
? (question mark): child definition qualifier, **APP** 75t, 81t
?: (question mark colon): conditional operator, **APP** 56t
"" (quotation marks)
  attribute value delimiters, **HTML** 568BTW
  null element (empty set), **HTML** 520
  string literal delimiters, **APP** 54
'' (quotation marks): attribute value delimiters, **HTML** 568BTW
® (registered trademark symbol), **HTML** 260, 261
; (semicolon)
  entity symbol end character, **APP** 83+t, 84
  statement terminator, **APP** 57t
/*...*/: comment symbols (JavaScript), **HTML** 418BTW
[] (square brackets): subscript delimiters, **HTML** 520
™ (trademark symbol), **HTML** 260
_ (underscore): XML tag name character, **HTML** 566BTW

Numbers

2D/3D transform properties, **APP** 44t

A

a selector (anchor/link element), **HTML** 93, 114, 126, 184
<a> tag (anchor tag), **HTML** 10t, 92, 93, 95, 96+BTW, 97, 103, 105, 106, 108–109, 123, 512–513+t; **APP** 3t
<a> tag attributes, **HTML** 103–104t; **APP** 3t
  id attribute, **HTML** 103t, 135; **APP** 3t
  subject and body attributes (e-mail links), **HTML** 106
  See also href attribute
</a> tag, **HTML** 104
absolute paths, **HTML 107**–109
absolute value (position property), **HTML** 337, 338t
Access documents: converting into Web pages, **HTML** 13
accessibility guidelines, **HTML** 22, 262BTW
  researching, **HTML** 32
  Section 508 guidelines, **HTML** 17BTW; **APP** 17, 17–20
  WCAG guidelines, **APP** 17, 2021, 2124t
accesskey attribute (global), **APP** 2t
Acrobat documents: converting into Web pages, **HTML** 13
action attribute (<form> tag), **HTML** 293–294; **APP** 6t
actions. *See* events
Active X controls (Internet Explorer), **HTML** 367–368, 372BTW
  validating and viewing Web pages using, **HTML** 377–378
ADA standards, **HTML** 394+BTW
  converting frames to, **HTML** 394–396, 401–404, 405, 406–407
add-ons. *See* plug-ins
<address> tag, **APP** 3t
addressing, relative, **HTML 422**+t
Adobe Photoshop, **HTML** 254BTW
Adobe Premiere Elements, **HTML** 366
advanced selection menus, **HTML** 301–302
AIFF format, **HTML** 368t
airline seating chart image maps, **HTML** 240
alert messages, **HTML** 475, 476t, 488
aligning text, **HTML** 126, 128, 129
  wrapping text around images, **HTML** 128–130, 132–133; stopping/clearing, **HTML** 134
alt attribute (<area> tag), **HTML** 263+t; **APP** 3t
alt attribute (<img> tag), **HTML** 65+t, 66, 258, 512t; **APP** 7t
alternate text for images, **HTML** 64, 66
  See also alt attribute (<img> tag)
alternate text for video clips, **HTML** 382
Americans with Disabilities Act standards. *See* ADA standards
ampersand (&): entity symbol begin character, **APP** 83+t, 84
analyzing Web page needs, **HTML** 36, 90, 158, 236, 286, 326, 363
analyzing Web sites, **HTML** 16
  for image map use, **HTML** 280
  questions regarding, **HTML** 15t
anchor element. *See* a selector
anchors, **HTML** 10t
  attributes. *See* <a> tag attributes
  creating, **HTML** 92–93
  See also a selector; <a> tag
animated inline images, **HTML 38**
animation (with JavaScript), **HTML** 531BTW
animation properties, **APP** 28t
<annotation> tag (XML), **HTML** 572+t, 573+t
ANY keyword, **APP** 81t, 82t
application documents: converting into Web pages, **HTML** 13
<area> tag, **HTML** 248, 263, 263–264+t; **APP** 3t
  inserting coordinates into, **HTML** 248
<area> tag attributes, **HTML** 248, 263+t; **APP** 3t
arguments (of methods), **HTML 413**, 414BTW
arithmetic operators, **APP** 55t
  precedence, **APP** 57t
ARPANET, **HTML** 3
array elements: referencing, **HTML** 520
array names, **HTML 519**
Array object: properties and methods, **APP** 70+t
arrays, **HTML 483**, **519**+BTW
  creating, **HTML** 519–520+t, 526+t
  referencing elements, **HTML** 520
  slide show image array, **HTML** 526+t
arrow character references, **APP** 50t
<article> tag, **HTML** 45; **APP** 3t
articles (independent content), **HTML** 45, 46t
<aside> tag, **HTML** 45; **APP** 4t
asides (side issues/tangential content), **HTML** 45, 46t
assigning colors, **HTML** 428+BTW
  to built-in objects, **APP** 63
assigning form input data values to text fields, **HTML** 472+t
assigning images to defined locations, **HTML** 514+t, 525
assignment operators, **APP** 55t
  precedence, **APP** 57t
asterisk (*): child definition qualifier, **APP** 75t, 81t
attracting visitors to Web sites, **HTML** 220–231
attribute list declarations in DTDs, **APP 82**–83+t
attribute selectors, **HTML** 540BTW
attribute value delimiters ("", ''), **HTML** 568BTW

attribute values
 global attribute values, **APP** 2t
 XHTML coding practices/standards, **HTML** 13t; **APP** 1t
attributes (of HTML elements). *See* HTML tag attributes
attributes (open() method), **HTML** 489+t
attributes (of XML elements), **HTML** 570; **APP** 75+t
attributes (of XSD elements), **HTML** 570; **APP 76**
attributes (of XSDs), **APP 76**
AU format, **HTML** 368t
audio clips, **HTML** 362, 363, 365
 adding (inserting), **HTML** 369–376; with the <audio> tag, **HTML** 373–374, 376, 386–387; multiple files on a Web page, **HTML** 387–388; with the <object> tag, **HTML** 370–373
 container for. *See* <audio> tag container
 finding, **HTML** 364, 366+BTW
 formats, **HTML** 368+t, 392
 vs. video clips, **HTML** 364
<audio> element. *See* <audio> tag container
<audio> tag attributes, **HTML** 373+t, 374; **APP** 4t
<audio> tag container (<audio> tag/element), **HTML** 366, 370, 373, 374; **APP** 4t
 adding (inserting) audio clips with, **HTML** 373–374, 376, 386–387
author (meta name), **HTML** 223–224+t
autoplay attribute (<audio> tag), **HTML** 373t, 374; **APP** 4t
autostart parameter (<object> tag), **HTML** 372t, 380
AVI format, **HTML** 369t

B

<b> tag, **HTML** 110, 111+t; **APP** 4t
Back button (on browsers), **HTML** 107, 125, 126, 131
background colors
 for image links, **HTML** 139
 for images, **HTML** 63
 in tables, **HTML** 161, 203
background properties, **HTML** 113t; **APP** 28–29t
background sound: adding, **HTML** 386–387
backgrounds, **HTML 37**
 properties, **HTML** 113t; **APP** 28–29t
 sound, **HTML** 386–387
 See also background colors
backslash (\): escape character, **APP** 54
banner images
 adding box shadows to, **HTML** 171–172
 adding/inserting, **HTML** 100–101; with box shadows, **HTML** 172–173
 centering, **HTML** 173, 590
 header text, **HTML** 590+t
<base /> tag, **APP** 4t
beginPos variable (scrollingMsg() function), **HTML** 459
 determining the value of, **HTML** 461–463
 incrementing, **HTML** 461+t
<big> tag, **APP** 4t
binding of data (data binding), **HTML** 596BTW
binding XML documents with Web pages, **HTML** 603
binding XML elements to tables, **HTML** 600
bitwise operators, **APP** 55t
 precedence, **APP** 57t
blank lines, **HTML** 10
 inserting, **HTML** 40t, 43, 46
block statement, **APP** 57t
<blockquote> tag, **HTML** 111t; **APP** 4t
Blu Wav Music Web page form, **HTML** 284–313
blur, **HTML** 475
body (of a Web page/HTML document), **HTML 37**, 39
 See also body selector (body element)
body attribute (e-mail link), **HTML** 106
body selector (body element), **HTML** 114, 184, 334
body text, **HTML** 44
 font setting, **HTML** 334
<body> tag, **HTML** 39, 40t, 44; **APP** 4t
bold tag. *See* <b> tag
bolder class, **HTML** 201
 adding, **HTML** 183, 206
bolding text
 with a bold tag, **HTML** 110, 111t
 with the bolder class, **HTML** 183, 206
 with an inline style, **HTML** 52–53
boldword class, **HTML** 268, 269
bookmarks (favorites), **HTML 37**+BTW
bookstore survey form, **HTML** 318–319
Boolean data types (JavaScript), **HTML 419**; **APP** 53+t
Boolean object: methods, **APP** 70+t
border colors for image links, **HTML** 92
 changing, **HTML** 93
border properties, **HTML** 113t; **APP** 29–30t
 table properties, **HTML** 162, 167, 168t; **APP** 42t
border spacing (around cells), **HTML** 162, 167, **198**, 199
 adding, **HTML** 200
border-collapse property, **HTML** 168t; **APP** 42t
border-spacing property, **HTML** 162, 167, 168t; **APP** 42t
borderless tables, **HTML** 156, 160, 162
 creating navigation bars with, **HTML** 174–176
borders, **HTML 343**
 image link border colors, **HTML** 92, 93
 for images, **HTML** 167BTW
 for tables. *See* table borders
 tables with, **HTML** 193; creating, **HTML** 194–195+t
 See also border properties
box model (Web page structure), **HTML 343**+BTW
box properties, **APP** 30–31t, 33t
 flexible box properties, **APP** 33t
 linebox properties, **APP** 35–36t
box shadows
 adding to banner images, **HTML** 171–172
 inserting banner images with, **HTML** 172–173
box-shadow property, **HTML** 162, 171–172+t; **APP** 30t
boxes (for Web page elements), **HTML** 338–339
 model (structure), **HTML 343**+BTW
 See also borders

 tag, **HTML** 10t, 40t, 134, 491+t; **APP** 4t
break statement, **APP** 57t
broad Web sites, **HTML** 19–20
browser window: maximizing, **HTML** 41, 58
browser window elements (on Web pages), **HTML** 37
 See also backgrounds; body; titles
browser-safe colors, **HTML** 67BTW; **APP** 15, 16t
browsers (Web browsers), **HTML 7**
 <audio> element support, **HTML** 373, 374
 Back button, **HTML** 107, 125, 126, 131
 displaying XML documents in, **HTML** 588, 590–593, 613–614
 Hide from old browsers comment, **HTML** 417, 418+BTW+t, 434
 HTML support, **HTML** 11
 plug-in support, **HTML** 381; <audio> element, **HTML** 373, 374; <video> element, **HTML** 382
 quitting/closing Notepad++ and, **HTML** 78, 142, 208, 271, 314, 351, 493, 612
 refreshing the view, **HTML** 72
 research project, **HTML** 451
 scroll bar color, **HTML** 428–429, 442, 443
 starting, **HTML** 58
 <video> element support, **HTML** 382
 viewing HTML code in, **HTML** 76–77
 viewing Web pages in, **HTML** 58, 59, 72, 120, 141, 178, 190, 195, 201, 207, 265, 270, 311, 341, 384, 405; using Active X controls, **HTML** 377–378
 Web site compatibility testing, **HTML** 24, 58BTW
 See also Internet Explorer
built-in data types (XML/XSD elements), **HTML** 571+t
built-in functions (JavaScript), **HTML** 471–472, 475+t
 global functions, **APP** 72+t
built-in objects (JavaScript), **HTML 412**–414+t
 coloring, **APP** 63
 Math object, **HTML** 413t, 480BTW; **APP** 65–66+t
 methods, **HTML 413**–414+t+BTW; **APP** 60–71+t. *See also specific methods*
 properties. *See* properties (of built-in objects)
 setting the focus on, **HTML** 472+t
 See also arrays; Date object; *and other specific objects*
bulleted lists (unordered lists), **HTML** 44, 46, 47, **49**
 creating, **HTML** 50, 51+t
 defining items, **HTML** 50
 defining styles, **HTML** 337–338
 positioning, **HTML** 337–338
 restyling, **HTML** 66, 70
 vs. tables, **HTML** 164
bullets, **HTML 44**
 changing types, **HTML** 51, 66; with inline styles, **HTML** 70

options, **HTML** 50; **APP** 36t
businesses (companies): Web site uses, **HTML** 5–6, 16
button images: changing, **HTML** 512, 514–515+t
<button> tag, **HTML** 304BTW
buttons (on forms)
creating, **HTML** 304BTW
disabling/enabling, **HTML** 496–498
event handlers associated with, **HTML** 466+t; **APP** 58–60t
navigation buttons, **HTML** 597–598
Search button, **HTML** 603–604+t
See also radio buttons (option buttons); Reset button; Submit button

C

CalcLoanAmt() function, **HTML** 468
calling, **HTML** 477
creating, **HTML** 472+t, 476, 479
calculating costs, **HTML** 499–501
calculating monthly payments, **HTML** 478–481, 504–505
calculating the number of days to a future date, **HTML** 417, 424–426+t
calling user-defined functions, **HTML** 414, 435–436
recursive calls, **HTML** 464, 527, 531
See also under specific functions
Calumet Restaurant Supply Web page, **HTML** 562–563, 565, 567–611
<canvas> tag, **APP** 4t
<caption> tag, **HTML** 201; **APP** 4t
caption-side property, **HTML** 168t; **APP** 42t
captions. *See* pop-up captions; table captions
cardinality (of XML elements), **HTML 574**
Caroline's Dance Studio Web site, **HTML** 394–395, 397–399
Cascading Style Sheets (CSS), **HTML** 2, **11**–12+BTW, 22, **61**, 327
advanced techniques, **HTML** 324–359
basic concepts/terminology, **HTML** 61–63; **APP** 25–27
current version (CSS3), **HTML** 11–12, 61; **APP** 25, 27
in the Document Object Model, **HTML** 12, 508
Web site resources, **HTML** 327BTW, 358
See also classes; properties (of Web page elements); style sheets (CSS); style statements; styles (for Web page elements)
case
for tags, **HTML** 13t, 44
for variable names, **APP** 53
CDATA. *See* character data
ceil() method, **HTML** 424–425+t, 519, 520t, 521
cells (in tables), **HTML 161**
data cells, **HTML 161**, 166, 167, 194, 195
heading cells. *See* table headers
spacing around, **HTML** 162. *See also* border spacing; padding
cellspacing attribute, **HTML** 162; **APP** 11t
<center> tag, **APP** 4t
centering images, **HTML** 63
banners, **HTML** 173, 590
centering tables, **HTML** 186
cents. *See* dollars and cents
CGI scripts, **HTML 294**; **APP 51**
form information processing with, **HTML** 292, 293–294+BTW
character data (CDATA), **APP** 74t
converting to numbers, **HTML** 471+t+BTW, 476t
character encoding, UTF-8, **HTML** 39, 223
character references (character entities), **HTML 260**+BTW; **APP** 49–50t
inserting special characters, **HTML** 260+BTW, 261
check boxes (on forms), **HTML** 287, 288+BTW, 289
adding, **HTML** 297–298
checkbox controls (on forms), **HTML** 287t, **288**
See also check boxes
child definition qualifiers (*, +, ?), **APP** 75t, 81t
child elements (in an XML document), **HTML 569**
defining, **HTML** 575+t
entering, **HTML** 576+t
parent elements and, **HTML** 574
circular map areas, **HTML** 247–248, 263–264
<cite> tag, **APP** 4t
class attribute (global), **APP** 2t
class name delimiter (.), **HTML** 127, 179BTW, 181
class selectors, **HTML** 540–543+BTW
classes (of Web page elements) (CSS), **HTML 126**–128
bolder class, **HTML** 183, 201, 206
defining/naming, **HTML** 127, 179BTW, 181
in external style sheets, **HTML** 179, 181, 268, 269
for menu/navigation bar elements, **HTML** 175, 179–180, 181, 186
pseudoclasses, **HTML** 114–**115**, 337+BTW
as selectors, **HTML** 540–543+BTW
stripe class, **HTML** 183, 198, 201
whitepipe class, **HTML** 338
wrapping text around images with, **HTML** 129–130, 132–133; stopping/clearing wrapping, **HTML** 134
classification properties, **APP** 31t
clearField() function, **HTML** 603+t, 609–610BTW
clearTimeout() method, **HTML** 529
clickable areas (on image maps). *See* hotspots
client-side image maps, **HTML 242**–243+BTW, 257, 258
closing Notepad++. *See* quitting Notepad++ and a browser
closing start tags, **HTML** 9–10+t, 13t, 40; **APP** 1t
closing XML files in Notepad++, **HTML** 595
<code> tag, **APP** 4t
coding
image maps, **HTML** 248, 263–264
JavaScript, **HTML** 417–418+BTW
tables, **HTML** 166–167
coding practices
HTML standards, **HTML** 10, 11; **APP** 1+t
JavaScript standards, **APP** 51
UTF-8 character encoding, **HTML** 39, 223
XHTML standards, **HTML** 11+BTW, 12, 13t; **APP** 1
<col> tag, **APP** 4t
<colgroup> tag, **APP** 4–5t
collapse document level sign (-), **HTML** 584–585
colon (:): XML reserved character, **HTML** 566BTW
color codes, common, **HTML** 67
color properties, **APP** 31t
background property, **APP** 28t
border properties, **APP** 29t
font property, **HTML** 110t
text property, **APP** 42t
units of measure property, **APP** 27t
coloring
built-in objects, **APP** 63
headings. *See* coloring headings
images, **HTML** 64
links, **HTML** 334
the pipe symbol (|), **HTML** 338
the scroll bar, **HTML** 428–429, 442, 443
coloring headings, **HTML** 66, 67
with embedded style sheets, **HTML** 116
with inline styles, **HTML** 69, 117
colors, **HTML** 67+BTW
assigning, **HTML** 428+BTW; to built-in objects, **APP** 63
background. *See* background colors
browser-safe colors, **HTML** 67BTW; **APP** 15, 16t
common color codes, **HTML** 67
finding, **HTML** 184
font color, **HTML** 110t
image link background colors, **HTML** 139
image link border colors, **HTML** 92, 93
text link. *See* text link colors
See also color properties; coloring
Colors group (Paint window), **HTML** 250
cols attribute (<textarea> tag), **HTML** 289; **APP** 12t
colspan attribute (<th>/<td> tag), **HTML** 167, **201**; **APP** 12t
column headers. *See* table headers
column spanning, **HTML** 165–166, 201+BTW, 203
columns (in tables), **HTML 161**
header columns. *See* table headers
spanning, **HTML** 165–166, 201+BTW, 203
<command> tag, **APP** 5t
commas: inserting in dollar values, **HTML** 484–486
comment codes (HTML) (<!--...-->), **HTML** 113; **APP** 3t
within JavaScript, **HTML** 417, 418+BTW+t, 434
within <style> tag container, **HTML** 115, 333
comment symbols (JavaScript) (//, /*...*/), **HTML** 418BTW; **APP** 57t
comments (HTML), **HTML** 113, 342
Hide from old browsers comment, **HTML** 417, 418+BTW+t, 434
See also comment codes (HTML)
comments (JavaScript), **HTML** 418BTW; **APP** 57t
comments (XML), **HTML** 578+t; **APP** 74t

commerce, electronic (e-commerce), HTML 5–6+BTW
companies. *See* businesses
comparison operators (conditional operators), HTML 462+t+BTW; APP 56t
precedence, APP 57t
compatibility testing (of Web sites on browsers), HTML 24, 58BTW
complex type XML/XSD elements, HTML 570, 571t, 574, 575; APP 79+t
entering, HTML 574t, 575t, 576+t
complex type XSDs, APP 76, 79
concatenates operator (+=), APP 56t
concatenating strings, HTML 427
concatenation operator (+), HTML 427; APP 56t
conditional operator (?:), APP 56t
precedence, APP 57t
conditional operators. *See* comparison operators
conditional statements (conditions)
in if statements, HTML 461–462+t
in loops, HTML 485+t
Conformance Checker, HTML5, HTML 72, 75
conformance levels (WCAG guidelines), APP 21
const statement, APP 57t
containers (tag sets), HTML 414, 540
for audio clips. *See* <audio> tag container; <object> tag container
for embedded style sheets. *See* <style> tag container
for headers: <header> tag container, HTML 45, 100–101; APP 6t. *See also* <head> tag container
for inline styles. *See* <span> tag container
for sections. *See* <div> tag container
for text emphasis (<strong> tag container), HTML 52–53, 111t; APP 11t
for video clips. *See* <embed> tag container; <object> tag container; <video> tag container
content (information) (on Web sites/pages)
content for paged media properties, APP 32t
defining/choosing, HTML 16, 36, 90, 158, 326, 363
dynamic. *See* dynamic text
entering/adding, HTML 45, 46–53
on forms. *See under* Web page forms
generated content properties, APP 34t
independent content (articles), HTML 45, 46t
observing and learning from, HTML 25
organizational standards, HTML 17t, 28t
sections for, HTML 45, 46t
structural elements, HTML 45, 46t. *See also* footers; headers; sections
tangential content (side issues/asides), HTML 45, 46t
testing, HTML 22
See also images; multimedia; text
content for paged media properties, APP 32t
content owners and authors: identifying, HTML 16
contenteditable attribute (global), APP 2t
contextmenu attribute (global), APP 2t
continue statement, APP 57t
control panel. *See* player control panel
controls. *See* fieldset controls; input controls
controls attribute (<audio> tag), HTML 373t, 374; APP 4t
controls attribute (<video> tag), HTML 381t, 382; APP 13t
converting
application documents into Web pages, HTML 13
character data to numbers, HTML 471+t+BTW, 476t
dates and times (Date object methods), APP 61–62t
frames to ADA standards, HTML 394–396, 401–404, 405, 406–407
milliseconds to days, HTML 424–425
numbers to strings, HTML 479, 487
paper forms to Web page forms, HTML 321
the system date to a string, HTML 420–421+t
coordinates (of hotspots), HTML 246–248, 252
determining (locating), HTML 249, 251–253, 263–264
inserting into <area> tags, HTML 248
coordinating headings with graphics, HTML 100
coords attribute (<area> tag), HTML 248, 263+t; APP 3t
copying embedded style sheets into Web pages, HTML 331
copying HTML code, HTML 138–139
to other Web pages, HTML 191; navigation bar code, HTML 402–404, 524–525, 530, 537–538
copying Web page structures, HTML 44, 98BTW
copyright message: displaying, HTML 432–433+t, 491+t, 521–522+t
copyRight() function, HTML 432–433+t, 491+t, 522–523+t
Corel VideoStudio Pro, HTML 366
cost calculator, HTML 499–501
countDown() function, HTML 427+t
Coupon Web page (pop-up window), HTML 533+t
coupon() function, HTML 533+t, 534+t
course evaluation form, HTML 315
course management, electronic, HTML 6, 16
credit card information, HTML 299+BTW
credit card payment calculator, HTML 504–505
CSS. *See* Cascading Style Sheets
CSS files (.css files), HTML 62; APP 25, 26
saving and printing, HTML 270
See also external style sheets
CSS style sheets. *See* style sheets (CSS)
CSS3, HTML 11–12, 61; APP 25, 27
currElement parameter (popupCaption() function), HTML 540–541
currency. *See* dollars and cents
cursor: setting, HTML 336
cursor property, APP 39t
custom data types (XML/XSD elements), HTML 571+t
customer survey form, HTML 317

D

data (on forms). *See* form input data
data (in XML documents). *See* XML data
data binding, HTML 596BTW
See also binding ...
data blocks, HTML 562BTW
data cells (in tables), HTML 161, 167
text in, HTML 161, 166, 194, 195
data collections (relations), HTML 568
logical designs. *See* schemas
data input controls (on forms), HTML 287+t, 288–289, 290
See also check boxes; radio buttons; Reset button; selection menus; Submit button; *and also* text input controls
data islands (XML), HTML 562+BTW, 565, 595, 602
creating, HTML 595BTW, 596, 621–622, 624
disadvantage, HTML 562BTW
displaying, HTML 604, 606–607+t, 615–617; in tables, HTML 595–601, 622–624
data source object (dso), HTML 596
See also data islands
data type attributes in DTD attribute list declarations, APP 82–83+t
data type constraints/facets (for XSD elements), APP 78+t
data types
in DTD attribute list declarations, APP 82–83+t
in JavaScript, HTML 419; APP 53+t
for XML/XSD elements, HTML 571+t; APP 78+t
data validation. *See* validating form input data
database management systems (DBMSs), HTML 564
databases. *See* data islands
<datalist> tag, APP 5t
datapagesize attribute (<table> tag), HTML 598t, 599
datasrc attribute (<table> tag), HTML 598t, 599
date data types (JavaScript), HTML 419
date last modified: displaying, HTML 17t, 432–433+t, 491–492+t, 521–522+t
Date object, HTML 420
creating an instance variable, HTML 420+t, 424
methods, HTML 420BTW; APP 61–62t
See also system date
dates
converting (Date object methods), APP 61–62t
document last modified date, HTML 17t, 432–433+t, 491–492+t, 521–522+t
future date: calculating the number of days to, HTML 417, 424–426+t
inserting in scripts, APP 64–65+t
system date: converting to a string, HTML 420–421+t; extracting, HTML 420–423+BTW
days
calculating the number to a future date, HTML 417, 424–426+t
converting milliseconds to, HTML 424–425

DBMSs (database management systems), **HTML** 564
<dd> tag, **HTML** 52+t; **APP** 5t
debugger statement, **APP** 57t
declarations
  document type declarations, **APP 80**, 80t
  in DTDs, **APP** 81–84
  of DTDs, **APP** 80, 81t
  namespace declarations, **HTML** 572+t; **APP** 76+t
  in style statements, **HTML 62**, **113**+BTW, 126; **APP** 25
  XML declarations, **HTML 568**, **578**, 579+t; **APP** 74t
declaring variables (JavaScript), **HTML** 419+t; **APP** 54
decode functions, **APP** 72t
deep Web sites, **HTML** 20–21
definition lists, **HTML 52**–53
  creating, **HTML** 52, 81–82
delete operator, **APP** 56t
deprecated attributes, **HTML 11**, 111BTW; **APP** 3
deprecated tags, **HTML 11**, 39, 110, 111BTW; **APP** 3
descriptions (meta names), **HTML** 221, 222, 223–224+t
  adding, **HTML** 222, 225
designing and developing Web sites, **HTML** 17–22, 29–31, 90, 159
  through observation, **HTML** 25
  questions regarding, **HTML** 15t
  using logs, **HTML** 25
<details> tag, **APP** 5t
digital images. *See* images
dimension properties, **APP** 32t
dir attribute (global), **APP** 2t
directory level up symbol (..), **HTML** 109
directory structure. *See* folder structure
disability law. *See* Section 508 (Rehabilitation Act)
display object (Web page forms), **HTML 457**
displayDateLast id attribute (<div> tag), **HTML** 491+t
<div> tag container (<div> tag), **HTML** 45, 63, 117, 139, 173, 334–335, 343, 414, 416, 534BTW; **APP** 5t
  converting from frames with, **HTML** 401–402
  defining an output area, **HTML** 604
  displaying a copyright message, **HTML** 432–433+t, 491+t
  displaying pop-up captions, **HTML** 540, 545, 549+t
  displaying the date last modified, **HTML** 432–433+t, 491–492+t
  form objects vs., **HTML** 459BTW
  positioning objects with, **HTML** 534–535+BTW+t
  vs. <span> tag, **HTML** 541BTW
dividing Web pages into sections, **HTML** 63, 139, 343
<dl> tag, **HTML** 52+t; **APP** 5t
do...while statement, **APP** 57t
!DOCTYPE reserved word, **APP** 81t
<!DOCTYPE> tag/statement, **HTML** 12, 39+BTW, 40t, 43, 397; **APP** 1, 3t
document header, **HTML** 39
document instance (in an XML document), **HTML 568**, **569**, 580; **APP 73**
  creating, **HTML** 580–582
document level collapse/expand signs (−, +), **HTML** 584–585
Document object: properties and methods, **APP** 62–63+t
Document Object Model (DOM), **HTML** 11BTW, 12, **508**+BTW, 510+BTW, 512BTW
document type declarations, **APP 80**, 80t
Document Type Definitions. *See* DTDs
documentation tags for XSDs, **HTML** 572+t, 573+t
<documentation> tag (XML), **HTML** 572+t, 573+t
documents. *See* application documents; HTML documents/files; XML documents/files
dollar sign ($): variable name character, **APP** 53
dollarFormat() function, **HTML** 482
  creating, **HTML** 483–487
dollars and cents (currency)
  formatting monthly payments as, **HTML** 482–487
  inserting commas in dollar values, **HTML** 484–486
  passing monthly payment values to functions, **HTML** 487
  reconstructing, **HTML** 486–487+t
  separating, **HTML** 483–484+t
DOM (Document Object Model), **HTML** 11BTW, 12, **508**+BTW, 510+BTW, 512BTW
domain (range of values), **HTML** 476BTW, **571**
domain names (for Web sites), **HTML** 222
  determining and checking availability, **HTML** 226
double period (..): one directory level up symbol, **HTML** 109
downButton() function, **HTML** 514, 515t
draggable attribute (global), **APP** 2t
dragging and dropping images, **HTML** 560
drawing area (Paint window), **HTML** 250
drawing shapes in XML documents, **HTML** 624
drop-down menus
  adding, **HTML** 333–341, 352–353
  on forms. *See* selection menus
  linking to URLs via, **HTML** 429–431
  select list selectedIndex property, **HTML** 429–430+BTW+t, 431
  submenus, **HTML** 333–334, 336–337
dropzone attribute (global), **APP** 2t
dso (data source object), **HTML 596**
  See also data islands
<dt> tag, **HTML** 52+t; **APP** 5t
DTDs (Document Type Definitions), **APP** 80, 81
  data type attributes, **APP** 82–83+t
  declarations in, **APP** 81–84
  declarations of, **APP** 80, 81t
  URL references to, **HTML** 39
  XSDs vs., **HTML** 570; **APP** 76
dynamic text (messages/greetings): displaying, **HTML** 414, 417, 420, 426–427, 442–443
dynamic Web page features. *See* floating images; image rollovers; pop-up captions; pop-up images; pop-up text; pop-up windows; scrolling messages; slide shows

E

e-commerce, **HTML 5**–6+BTW
e-mail addresses
  form information posting to, **HTML** 292, 294+BTW
  linking to, **HTML** 96BTW, 97, 105
  on Web pages, **HTML** 17t
  See also e-mail links
e-mail links, **HTML** 90, **96**–97, 103, 105BTW, 236
  adding, **HTML** 96BTW, 97, 105
  adding information to, **HTML** 106
ECMA standards (JavaScript), **APP** 51
editors for creating HTML documents, **HTML** 13–14, 24
element declarations in DTDs, **APP 81**–82+t
!ELEMENT reserved word, **APP** 81t
<element> tag (in XSDs), **HTML** 570+t, 580+t; **APP** 76+t, 77+t, 79+t
  data types, **HTML** 571+t; **APP** 78+t
em units/values, **HTML** 336t+BTW
<em> tag, **HTML** 111t; **APP** 5t
e-mail. *See* e-mail ..., *above*
<embed> element. *See* <embed> tag container
<embed> tag container (<embed> tag/ element), **HTML** 367, 381; **APP** 5t
embedded style sheets, **HTML 62**+t, 366; **APP** 25
  classes in, **HTML** 126–128
  container for. *See* <style> tag container
  copying into other Web pages, **HTML** 331
  creating (adding/using), **HTML** 62, 93, 112–116, 126–128, 159, 308–310, 327, 328, 331–341
  creating external style sheets from, **HTML** 331
  for navigation bars, **HTML** 332–341
  for pop-up captions, **HTML** 540–543+t, 548–549+t
  precedence, **HTML** 62+t, 112, 115, 330t; **APP** 26–27+t
  style statements for, **HTML** 112–113, 114; **APP** 25–26
  uses/utilizing, **HTML** 93, 112+BTW, 159, 179, 181, 330, 331
  wrapping text around images with, **HTML** 129–130, 132–133; stopping/clearing wrapping, **HTML** 134
empty HTML elements, **HTML** 9
empty set (null element) (""), **HTML** 520
empty-cells property, **HTML** 168t; **APP** 42t
encode functions, **APP** 72t
end tags, **HTML** 9–10+t, 13t, 40; **APP** 1t
English Literature Class Web site, **HTML** 362–363, 365, 367
entities, external (XML), **APP 83**+t
entities, unparsed (XML), **APP** 84
entity declarations in DTDs, **APP 83**–84+t
entity symbols, predefined, **APP** 83+t
EOF property, **HTML** 606t, 607
errors in HTML code, **HTML** 72–73
  common validation errors, **HTML** 118BTW
escape character (\), **APP** 54
escape sequences, **APP** 54+t
escape() function, **APP** 72t

eval() function/statement, **HTML** 538BTW; **APP** 72t
evaluating user surveys, **HTML** 27–28
evaluating Web sites, **HTML** 25, 29
event handlers, **HTML 414**, 434, 435+t, **465**; **APP** 58–60+t
  calling user-defined functions with, **HTML** 414, 435–436
  objects associated with, **HTML** 466+t; **APP** 58–60t
  See also mouse event handlers; *and specific* on... *event handlers*
event-driven programming, **HTML** 412BTW
event-driven programming languages, **HTML** 412
events (actions), **HTML** 414, 435, **465**; **APP 58**
  associating user-defined functions with, **HTML** 414, 435–436
evnt parameter (popupCaption() function), **HTML** 540–541
Excel documents: converting into Web pages, **HTML** 13
expand document level sign (+), **HTML** 584–585
exponentiation: pow() method, **HTML** 480+t
expression control operator, **APP** 56t
extended markup languages created using XML, **HTML** 565, 566t
Extensible Hypertext Markup Language. *See* XHTML
Extensible Markup Language. *See* XML
Extensible Stylesheet Language. *See* XSL
external entities (XML), **APP 83**+t
external multimedia files, **HTML** 366–367
external style sheets, **HTML 62**+t, 179–190; **APP** 25
  adding your name to, **HTML** 181BTW
  classes in, **HTML** 179, 181, 268, 269
  creating (adding/using), **HTML** 62, 93, 159, 179–180, 181–183+t, 269–271, 327, 328–329, 342–347, 353–354, 356–358; from embedded style sheets, **HTML** 331; for printing, **HTML** 348–349, 355–356
  linking to, **HTML** 180, 181, 187–188, 200, 204, 342, 346–347, 349
  for pop-up images, **HTML** 343–347
  for pop-up text, **HTML** 357–358, 358
  precedence, **HTML** 62+t, 112, 115, 330t; **APP** 26–27+t
  saving and printing CSS files, **HTML** 270
  style statements for, **HTML** 179–180, 184–186; **APP** 25–26
  testing, **HTML** 350
  uses, **HTML** 93, 112BTW, 159, 179, 181, 330
  validating, **HTML** 186BTW, 344BTW
extracting the system date, **HTML** 420–423+BTW
extranets, **HTML 5**+t+BTW

F

favorites (bookmarks), **HTML 37**+BTW
fieldset controls (on forms), **HTML 289**–290, **306**, 307
  adding, **HTML** 306–308
  grouping information with, **HTML** 284, 286, 289–290, 296, 306–310+BTW, 320–321
<fieldset> tag, **HTML** 284, 286, 289–290, 291t, 296, 306; **APP** 5t
<figcaption> tag, **APP** 5t
<figure> tag, **APP** 5t
File Transfer Protocol. *See* FTP
files. *See* CSS files; HTML documents/files; multimedia files; XML documents/files; XSDs (XML Schema Definitions)
films. *See* video clips
Final Cut Pro X, **HTML** 366
finally statement, **APP** 57t
finding
  colors, **HTML** 184
  graphics, **HTML** 63
  multimedia files, **HTML** 364, 366+BTW, 392
  tables, **HTML** 217
  Web servers (hosts), **HTML** 227+BTW; **APP** 47
  See also searching XML documents ...
findItem() function, **HTML** 603+t, 605–606+t, 608+t
fixed decimal value: setting, **HTML** 480+t
fixed value (position property), **HTML** 338t
Flash format, **HTML** 369t, 381
Flash Video format, **HTML** 369t
flexible box properties, **APP** 33t
float property, **HTML** 128–129, 133, 309; **APP** 39t
floating images, **HTML** 128–129
  displaying, **HTML** 529–535, 550–552, 559
  formatting, **HTML** 534
floatingImage() function, **HTML** 531+t
  calling, **HTML** 535
floor plan image maps, **HTML** 242
focus (on an object): setting, **HTML** 472+t
focus() method, **HTML** 472+t
folder structure, **HTML** 21, 36, 54, 107
  one directory level up symbol (..), **HTML** 109
  paths, **HTML** 107–109
font properties, **HTML** 110t+BTW, 113t, 334; **APP** 33–34t
<font> tag, **APP** 5t
font-family property, **HTML** 113, 334; **APP** 33t
fonts
  determining system font support, **HTML** 341
  specifying (setting), **HTML** 113, 114, 181, 184, 334
  specifying alternatives, **HTML** 114BTW
  specifying weight, **HTML** 341BTW
  See also font properties
footer messages, **HTML** 432–433, 491–492
<footer> tag container, **HTML** 45; **APP** 5t
  displaying a copyright message, **HTML** 521–522+t
  displaying the date last modified, **HTML** 521–522+t
footers, **HTML** 45, 46t
  adding, **HTML** 53+t, 521–522+t
  messages, **HTML** 432–433, 491–492
  restyling, **HTML** 66, 71
  See also <footer> tag container
for each...in statement, **APP** 58t
for statement (for loops), **HTML** 484, **485**+t; **APP** 57t
for...in statement, **APP** 57t
for...of statement, **APP** 57t
for-each element (in XSL style sheets), **HTML** 590–591+t+BTW
form input controls. *See* input controls
form input data
  assigning values to text fields, **HTML** 472+t
  converting character data to numbers, **HTML** 471+t+BTW
  determining whether numbers, **HTML** 471+t, 472BTW
  validating. *See* validating form input data
Form object: properties and methods, **APP** 63+t
form objects, **HTML** 459+BTW
  See also buttons; text fields
form tags, **HTML** 291+t
  attributes, **HTML** 291–292+t
  See also <form> tag; <input /> tag; <option> tag; <select> tag; <textarea> tag
<form> tag, **HTML** 291t, 293; **APP** 6t
<form> tag attributes, **HTML** 291t, 293–294; **APP** 6t
formatting
  floating images, **HTML** 534
  tables, **HTML** 159, 162–163, 167, 168
  text. *See* formatting text
  Web pages, **HTML** 45–46, 158, 327
  XML documents, **HTML** 565, 587–593, 613–615
  See also restyling
formatting text, **HTML** 44, 100, 101, 152
  bolding. *See* bolding text
  with embedded style sheets, **HTML** 126–128
  with external style sheets, **HTML** 179–180, 184
  font properties, **HTML** 110t+BTW, 113t, 334; **APP** 33–34t
  headings, **HTML** 110–111. *See also* coloring headings
  with inline styles, **HTML** 117, 143–144
  tags for, **HTML** 110–111+t
  See also spacing text
forms (for user input): converting paper forms to Web page forms, **HTML** 321
  See also Web page forms
four-frame structure, **HTML** 400–401
frame definition file, **HTML** 396–397+BTW
Frame object: properties and methods, **APP** 67–68+t
frame structure (layouts), **HTML** 396, 397, 399–401
<frame /> tag, **HTML** 396t, 397; **APP** 6t
<frame /> tag attributes, **HTML** 396t, 397; **APP** 6t
frames (on Web pages), **HTML 394**–407; **APP** 67
  converting to ADA standards, **HTML** 394–396, 401–404, 405, 406–407
  definition file, **HTML** 396–397+BTW
  problems with, **HTML** 394
  structure (layouts), **HTML** 396, 397, 399–401
  Web pages with: converting to ADA standards, **HTML** 394–396, 401–404, 405, 406–407; viewing, **HTML** 398–399; vs. without, **HTML** 394
frameset document type, **HTML 39**

<frameset> tag, **HTML** 396t, 397; **APP** 6t
framesets, **HTML** 397+BTW
FTP (File Transfer Protocol), **APP 47**
FTP programs (software), **HTML** 24; **APP** 47
  uploading files with, **APP** 48+t
Function object: properties and methods, **APP** 69+t
function statement, **APP** 58t
functionality (of Web sites)
  defining, **HTML** 16
  testing, **HTML** 22, 58BTW
functions (JavaScript): built-in functions, **HTML** 471–472, 475+t; global functions, **APP** 72+t
  See also user-defined functions
future date: calculating the number of days to, **HTML** 417, 424–426+t
future reserved words (JavaScript), **APP** 52+t

G

generated content properties, **APP** 34t
generic identifiers for XML tags, **HTML** 566BTW
geographical maps as image maps, **HTML** 239
get method (form information processing), **HTML** 294
getElementById() method, **HTML** 512BTW, 514+t, 525, 527
getElementsByTagName() method, **HTML** 428+t+BTW
getTime() method, **HTML** 424
GIF (Graphics Interchange Format) files, **HTML 64**+t, 65
Gift Shop Web page, **HTML** 508, 509, 529–535
global attributes, **APP 2**+t
global functions, **APP** 72+t
global variables (JavaScript), **HTML 419**
goals (for Web sites): identifying, **HTML** 16
Google: registering Web sites with, **HTML** 229
GPA Web page, **HTML** 505–506
graphical images. *See* images (graphics)
Graphics Interchange Format (GIF) files, **HTML 64**+t, 65
graphics tools/programs, **HTML** 65, 254BTW
  image map tools, **HTML** 254+t, 281
  See also Paint
greetings. *See* dynamic text
grid properties, **APP** 35t
group elements (in an XML document), **HTML** 575+t, 576
  defining, **HTML** 575+t
  entering, **HTML** 576+t
grouping information on forms, **HTML** 284, 286, 289–290, 296, 306–310+BTW, 320–321

H

<h1> through <h6> tags, **HTML** 40t, 46–47+BTW; **APP** 6t
hard drive: saving HTML files to, **HTML** 54
head (of a Web page/HTML document), **HTML** 39
<head> tag container, **HTML** 39, 40t, 43+t, 112, 180, 414, 416BTW, 417–418; **APP** 6t, 25, 26
header rows, **HTML** 163
  See also table headers
<header> tag container, **HTML** 45, 100–101+t; **APP** 6t
headers, **HTML** 39, 45, 46t
  banner header text, **HTML** 590+t
  of tables. *See* table headers
  See also head; <head> tag container; <header> tag container
headers attribute (<th>/<td> tag), **HTML** 167; **APP** 12t
heading cells. *See* table headers
headings, **HTML 38**, 46
  coloring, **HTML** 66, 67; with embedded style sheets, **HTML** 116; with inline styles, **HTML** 69, 117
  consistent use of, **HTML** 46–47+BTW
  coordinating with graphics, **HTML** 100
  entering, **HTML** 49
  formatting, **HTML** 110–111. *See also* ... coloring, *above*
  main headings, **HTML** 44, 46; banner images as, **HTML** 100–101
  organizational standard, **HTML** 17t, 28t
  planning, **HTML** 44, 100
  sizes, **HTML** 44, 46–47BTW
  in tables. *See* table headers
  tags. *See* <h1> through <h6> tags
  utilizing, **HTML** 44, 100
height attribute (<img> tag), **HTML** 64, 65+t, 258+BTW; **APP** 7t
height attribute (<object> tag), **HTML** 370, 380; **APP** 9t
height attribute (<video> tag), **HTML** 381t, 382; **APP** 13t
<hgroup> tag, **APP** 6t
Hickory Oaks Forest Preserve Web site, **HTML** 508–509, 511–518, 520–547
hidden attribute (global), **APP** 2t
Hide from old browsers comment, **HTML** 417, 418+BTW+t, 434
hierarchical Web site structure, **HTML** 18–19
History object: properties and methods, **APP** 64+t
home builder's Web site, **HTML** 279–280
home page (start page), **HTML 4**, **58**, 97
  copying navigation bar HTML code to, **HTML** 402–403
  creating, **HTML** 97–123, 255–267, 279–280
  formatting text on, **HTML** 101
  image map uses, **HTML** 279–280, 280
  Jared Adam's Adventure Travel Web site, **HTML** 326, 327, 330, 332, 333–339
  links back to, **HTML** 18, 19, 19–20, 93, 94, 124–125, 126; adding, **HTML** 139–140
  name options, **HTML** 54BTW
  Oceanside Hotel and Sports Club Web site, **HTML** 156, 157
  Underwater Tours by Eloise Web site, **HTML** 88, 89
Home tab (Paint window), **HTML** 250
homeLoanForm form, **HTML** 468
horizontal menu bars. *See* navigation bars
horizontal rules, **HTML 38**, 66, 68
  adding/inserting, **HTML** 40t, 68, 70–71
  organizational standard, **HTML** 17t, 28t
  styling, **HTML** 63
  in tables, **HTML** 210–211
hosts. *See* Web servers
hotspots (image map areas), **HTML 38**, 236, 237, 238, 242BTW
  choosing (selecting), **HTML** 243
  defining, **HTML** 247–248, 263–264
  sketching, **HTML** 244–245
  See also coordinates (of hotspots)
hover styles (for links), **HTML** 114–115, 344
hovering over links, **HTML** 91, 337
<hr /> tag, **HTML** 38, 40t; **APP** 6t
href attribute (<a> tag), **HTML** 93, 95, 96+BTW, 97, 103+t, 104, 105, 106, 108–109, 130, 135, 543, 544, 549+t; **APP** 3t
href attribute (<area> tag), **HTML** 263+t, 264; **APP** 3t
href attribute (<link /> tag), **HTML** 180, 187; **APP** 8t
.htm extension, **HTML** 54+BTW
HTML (Hypertext Markup Language), **HTML** 2, **8**–11; **APP** 1
  code. *See* HTML code
  coding practices, **HTML** 10, 11; **APP** 1+t
  current version. *See* HTML5
  in the Document Object Model, **HTML** 12, **508**+BTW, 510
  elements. *See* HTML elements
  platform independence, **HTML 8**
  quick reference, **APP** 1–13
  style sheet enhancement. *See* Cascading Style Sheets (CSS)
  styling limitation, **HTML** 11, 61
  supported versions, **HTML** 11
  tags. *See* HTML tags
  See also XHTML (Extensible Hypertext Markup Language)
HTML code (source code)
  comments. *See* comments (HTML)
  copying. *See* copying HTML code
  errors in, **HTML** 72–73; common validation errors, **HTML** 118BTW
  files. *See* HTML documents/files
  indenting, **HTML** 10, 51, 173, 176, 205
  practice standards, **HTML** 10+BTW, 11+BTW; **APP** 1+t
  printouts, **HTML** 77–78
  puffed up code, **HTML** 14
  starting the next line, **HTML** 43, 205
  validating. *See* validating HTML code/Web pages
  viewing, **HTML** 76–77
HTML documents/files
  converting application documents into, **HTML** 13
  date last modified, **HTML** 17t, 432–433+t, 491–492+t, 521–522+t
  defining, **HTML** 39–44+t
  elements. *See* HTML elements
  event handlers associated with, **HTML** 466+t; **APP** 58–60t
  naming, **HTML** 54
  opening, **HTML** 125, 199, 203, 293, 333, 375, 415, 457–458, 524, 529, 602

organization of. *See* folder structure
printing, **HTML** 77–78, 119, 140, 189, 201, 207, 225, 266–267, 312–313, 379, 385, 404, 439
saving. *See* saving HTML files/Web pages
tools for creating, **HTML** 13–14, 24; **APP** 1
types supported by W3C, **HTML** 39
uploading to Web servers. *See* publishing (Web pages/sites)
validating. *See* validating HTML code/Web pages
See also Web pages
HTML elements, **HTML 9**–10+t
attributes. *See* HTML tag attributes
nesting, **HTML** 13t
not supported by HTML5, **APP** 17
structural elements, **HTML** 45, 46t. *See also* footers; headers; sections
See also HTML tags; Web page elements
.html extension, **HTML** 54+BTW
HTML files. *See* HTML documents/files
HTML Goodies Web site, **HTML** 38BTW
HTML guides on Web page forms, **HTML** 287BTW
HTML object editors, **HTML 13**
HTML tag attributes, **HTML 8**, **9**; **APP** 2, 3–13t
deprecated attributes, **HTML 11**, 111BTW; **APP** 3
global attributes, **APP** 2+t
not supported by HTML5, **HTML** 162, 167
setting, **HTML** 161
standards resources, **HTML** 10BTW, 25BTW
XHTML coding practices, **HTML** 12, 13t; **APP** 1t
See also specific tag attributes
HTML tags, **HTML 8**–9, 113BTW; **APP** 2, 3–13t
attributes. *See* HTML tag attributes
basic tags, **HTML** 40t. *See also* initial tags
case, **HTML** 13t, 44
defining Web page structures with, **HTML** 39–44+t, 45, 98–99+t, 169–170+t, 255–256+t
deprecated tags, **HTML 11**, 39, 110, 111BTW; **APP** 3
end tags, **HTML** 9–10+t, 13t, 40; **APP** 1t
form. *See* form tags
initial. *See* initial tags
layout tags, **HTML** 45
logical style tags, **HTML 111**+BTW
nesting, **HTML** 13t; **APP** 1t
physical style tags, **HTML 111**+BTW
quick reference, **APP** 1–13
researching, **HTML** 72BTW, 86
resources on, **HTML** 10BTW, 25BTW, 39BTW, 78BTW; **APP** 3
semantic tags, **HTML 45**, 63
sets. *See* containers
start tags, **HTML** 9; closing, **HTML** 9–10+t, 13t, 40; **APP** 1t
for structural elements, **HTML** 45. *See also* initial tags
for tables, **HTML** 166–167+t, 167; **APP** 11, 12; attributes, **HTML** 167
text formatting tags, **HTML** 110–111+t
for Web page forms. *See* Web page form tags
XHTML coding practices, **HTML** 12, 13t; **APP** 1+t
See also specific tags
HTML text editors, **HTML 13**, 24
<html> tag, **HTML** 39, 40t, 43; **APP** 6t
HTML5, **HTML** 11, 12, 39; **APP** 1
attributes not supported by, **HTML** 162, 167
doctype tag/statement. *See* <!DOCTYPE> tag/statement
elements not supported by, **APP** 17
and frames, **HTML** 394
global attributes, **APP** 2+t
layout tags, **HTML** 45
and multimedia, **HTML** 366, 367, 368, 370
researching, **HTML** 32
structural elements, **HTML** 45, 46t. *See also* footers; headers; sections
XML and, **HTML** 565BTW
HTML5 Conformance Checker, **HTML** 72, 75
HTTP (Hypertext Transfer Protocol), **HTML 4**
hyperlink properties, **APP** 35t
hyperlinks. *See* links
hypertext links. *See* text links
Hypertext Markup Language. *See* HTML
Hypertext Transfer Protocol (HTTP), **HTML 4**

I

<i> tag, **HTML** 111t; **APP** 6t
ICANN (Internet Corporation for Assigned Names and Numbers), **HTML** 226
id attribute (<a> tag), **HTML** 103t, 135; **APP** 3t
id attribute (<div> tag), **HTML** 540, 549+t
displayDateLast, **HTML** 491+t
id attribute (global), **APP** 2t
id attribute (<img> tag), **HTML** 512+t, 514, 525, 526
id attribute (<input> tag), **HTML** 603+t
id selector, **HTML** 525, 534, 540–543+BTW
identifiers
generic identifiers for XML tags, **HTML** 566BTW
variable names, **HTML** 418–419+t; **APP** 53–54+t
identifying goals, users, and content owners and authors, **HTML** 16
identifying user tasks, **HTML** 16
if statements, **HTML** 469BTW, 607
entering, **HTML** 461–463+t
if ... else statement(s), **HTML** 469+BTW; **APP** 58t
inserting commas in dollar values, **HTML** 485–486
validating form input data, **HTML** 469–471, 474
if?then:else operator, **APP** 56t
<iframe> tag, **APP** 6–7t
image attributes. *See* <img> tag attributes
image borders: table borders as, **HTML** 167+BTW
image elements (on Web pages), **HTML** 38
See also horizontal rules
image link background colors, **HTML** 139
image link border colors, **HTML** 92
changing, **HTML** 93
image links, **HTML** 38
back to the home page, **HTML** 93, 94, 124–125; adding, **HTML** 139–140
background colors, **HTML** 139
border colors, **HTML** 92, 93
on image maps. *See* hotspots
navigation bars with, **HTML** 174–176, 186; in image maps, **HTML** 238–239, 277–279
thumbnail images as, **HTML** 130–131+BTW
image map navigation bars, **HTML** 238–239, 277–279
image map tools, **HTML** 254+t, 281
image maps, **HTML 38**, 234
client-side image maps, **HTML 242**–243+BTW, 257, 258
coding, **HTML** 248, 263–264
creating, **HTML** 243–255, 257–258, 263–264, 272–273, 274–275, 276–277, 279–280
hotspots. *See* hotspots
inserting images to use as, **HTML** 257–258
navigation bars in, **HTML** 238–239, 277–279
performance issues, **HTML** 237
planning, **HTML** 263
server-side image maps, **HTML 242**–243+BTW, 257
and text links, **HTML** 237, 238, 261BTW
types, **HTML** 242–243+BTW
uses, **HTML** 238–242+BTW, 281; on home pages, **HTML** 279–280, 280
Image object: properties and methods, **APP** 64+t
image objects
creating, **HTML** 512+t; and positioning, **HTML** 525–526+t, 534–535+t
image rollover functions
copying the HTML code to other Web pages, **HTML** 525, 530, 538
creating, **HTML** 514–517
image rollovers: navigation bars with, **HTML** 511–518, 558–559
images (graphics), **HTML** 36, **38**
adding/inserting, **HTML** 65–66, 100–101, 128–131, 172–173
alternate text for, **HTML** 64, 66. *See also* alt attribute
assigning to defined locations, **HTML** 514+t, 525
attributes. *See* <img> tag attributes
background color, **HTML** 63
banners. *See* banner images
borders, **HTML** 167BTW
as buttons, **HTML** 304BTW
centering, **HTML** 63, 173
choosing, **HTML** 236
coloring, **HTML** 64
coordinating headings with, **HTML** 100
determining height and width, **HTML** 173
dragging and dropping, **HTML** 560

event handlers associated with, **HTML** 466t; **APP** 58–59t
file types (formats), **HTML** 64–65+t
finding (sources), **HTML** 63
floating. *See* floating images
inline images, **HTML 38**. *See also* image maps
inserting to use as image maps, **HTML** 257–258
as maps. *See* image maps
as objects. *See* image objects
obtaining/downloading, **HTML** 128BTW
opening in Paint, **HTML** 251
optimizing, **HTML** 64BTW
organizing, **HTML** 54
overusing, **HTML** 65BTW
planning, **HTML** 63, 64, 100, 126, 168, 243, 249
pop-up images, **HTML** 343–347
positioning with tables, **HTML** 160, 212–213
random images, **HTML** 519–521, 556
researching, **HTML** 86
resizing, **HTML** 130BTW, 344
tag. *See* <img> tag
thumbnail images, **HTML** 130–131+BTW
uses, **HTML** 36, 64+t, 65
utilizing, **HTML** 100, 126, 168
wrapping text around, **HTML** 128–130, 132–133; stopping/clearing, **HTML** 134
<img> tag, **HTML** 38, 64, 65–66+t, 109, 129, 173, 512+t, 514; **APP** 7t
positioning objects with, **HTML** 525–526t, 534–535+t
<img> tag attributes, **HTML** 64, 65+t, 66, 109, 257–258+t+BTW, 512BTW; **APP** 7t
iMovie, **HTML** 366
implementing Web sites, **HTML** 24
question regarding, **HTML** 15t
in operator, **APP** 56t
indenting text, **HTML** 10, 51, 173, 176, 205
indexOf() method, **HTML** 420+t+BTW, 422–423+t, 606t, 607
individuals (persons): Web site uses, **HTML** 6–7, 16
information. *See* content
informational Web pages: creating, **HTML** 83–85
inherit value (position property), **HTML** 338t
inheritance (object inheritance), **HTML** 413BTW
initial tags (HTML), **HTML** 39, 43t
defining Web page structures with, **HTML** 39–44+t, 98–99+t, 169–170+t, 255–256+t
saving, **HTML** 44, 98BTW
inline images, **HTML 38**
See also image maps
inline styles, **HTML 62**+t, 63; **APP** 25
adding banner images with, **HTML** 100–101
adding horizontal rules with, **HTML** 68, 70–71
bolding text with, **HTML** 52–53
changing bullet types with, **HTML** 70
coloring headings with, **HTML** 69, 117
container for, **HTML** 117, 176
creating (adding/using), **HTML** 62, 63, 357
formatting text with, **HTML** 117, 143–144
precedence, **HTML** 62+t, 112, 115, 330t; **APP** 26–27+t
restyling bulleted lists with, **HTML** 70
restyling footers with, **HTML** 71
style statements for, **HTML** 63
uses, **HTML** 63, 93, 112+BTW, 159, 179, 181, 330
Web site resource, **HTML** 62BTW
wrapping text around images with, **HTML** 129
inline text, **HTML 540**
innerHTML property: displaying dynamic text, **HTML** 426–427+t, 491+t
input controls (on forms), **HTML** 284, 286, **287**–290+t, 293
event handlers associated with, **HTML** 466t; **APP** 58–60t
grouping, **HTML** 284, 286, 289–290, 296, 306–310+BTW, 320–321
planning, **HTML** 295–296
selecting, **HTML** 300
See also check boxes; password text boxes; radio buttons; Reset button; Search button; selection menus; Submit button; text fields; textarea fields
input data. *See* form input data
<input /> tag, **HTML** 287–289, 290, 291t; **APP** 7–8t
<input /> tag attributes, **HTML** 287–289, 290, 291t, 296, 603+t; **APP** 7–8t
<ins> tag, **APP** 8t
insertion point: placing in text fields, **HTML** 472+t
instance of operator, **APP** 56t
instructors: Web site uses, **HTML** 6, 16
interactive Web pages, **HTML** 12
interest rate: validating, **HTML** 475–476+t
internal entity declarations, **APP 83**+t
internal style sheets. *See* embedded style sheets
internationalization of Web sites, **HTML** 22
Internet, **HTML 2**–3, 5t
history resources, **HTML** 4BTW
services on, **HTML** 3. *See also* validation services
See also the Web (World Wide Web)
Internet backbone, **HTML 3**
Internet Corporation for Assigned Names and Numbers (ICANN), **HTML** 226
Internet Explorer features, **HTML** 428BTW, 510BTW, 562+BTW, 583BTW, 595, 596BTW, 602
See also Active X controls
Internet Service Providers. *See* ISPs
Internet sites. *See* Web sites
InterNIC service and Web site, **HTML** 226+BTW
intranets, **HTML 5**+t+BTW
isFinite() function, **APP** 72t
ismap attribute (<img> tag), **HTML** 257+t
isNaN function, **HTML** 468, 471+t, 472BTW; **APP** 72t
ISPs (Internet Service Providers), **HTML 3**
as Web site hosts, **HTML** 227; **APP** 47
italic tag. *See* <i> tag
iTunes, **HTML** 367

J

Jared Adam's Adventure Travel Web site, **HTML** 324–350, 359
Java applets, **HTML** 365BTW
JavaScript, **HTML** 410–452, 519BTW
advantages and disadvantages, **HTML** 412BTW
animation with, **HTML** 531BTW
built-in functions. *See* built-in functions
built-in objects. *See* built-in objects
calculating monthly payments, **HTML** 478–481, 504–505
calculating the number of days to a future date, **HTML** 417, 424–426+t
changing the scroll bar color, **HTML** 428–429, 442, 443
comments, **HTML** 418BTW; **APP** 57t
completing (ending), **HTML** 433–434, 465
correcting, **HTML** 444–445, 498–499, 552–553
creating image rollover functions, **HTML** 514–517
creating slide shows, **HTML** 524–528
creating Web pages using, **HTML** 446–452
data types, **HTML 419**; **APP 53**+t
displaying dynamic text, **HTML** 414, 417, 420, 426–427
displaying floating images, **HTML** 529–535, 550–552
displaying scrolling messages, **HTML** 457–467, 495–496
displaying the date last modified, **HTML** 432–433+t, 491–492+t, 521–522+t
in the Document Object Model, **HTML** 12, **508**+BTW, 510+BTW, 512BTW
escape sequences, **APP** 54+t
event handlers. *See* event handlers
extracting the system date, **HTML** 420–423+BTW
formatting monthly payments as currency, **HTML** 482–487
functions. *See* built-in functions; user-defined functions
generating random images, **HTML** 519–521
HTML comment codes within, **HTML** 417, 418+BTW+t, 434
linking to URLs, **HTML** 429–431
objects. *See* built-in objects
operators. *See* operators
origins, **APP** 51
project guidelines, **HTML** 412, 456
Quick Reference, **HTML** 493BTW; **APP** 51–72
reserved words, **HTML 419**; **APP 52**+t
searching XML documents and displaying results, **HTML** 601–610, 622–624
standards, **APP** 51
starting (<script> tag), **HTML** 417–418+t+BTW
statements, **APP 57**–58+t. *See also specific statements*
user-defined functions. *See* user-defined functions
uses, **APP** 51, 52
validating form input data, **HTML** 456, 468–477+BTW
variables. *See* variables

versions, **APP** 51
Web site resources, **HTML** 414BTW; **APP** 51
JavaScript Kit Web site, **HTML** 560
Joint Photographic Experts Group (JPEG) files, **HTML** **64**+t, 65
JPEG (Joint Photographic Experts Group) files, **HTML** **64**+t, 65
JSON object: properties and methods, **APP** 64–65+t

K

<kbd> tag, **APP** 8t
<keygen> tag, **APP** 8t
keyPressed() function, **HTML** 603+t, 605, 608–609+t
keywords (JavaScript). *See* reserved words
keywords (meta names), **HTML** 221, 222, 223–224+t
adding, **HTML** 222, 224

L

label statement, **APP** 58t
<label> tag, **APP** 8t
Lake Tahanna Tourism Web site, **HTML** 234–238, 243–248, 251–253, 255–271
lang attribute (global), **APP** 2t
lastModified property (document objects), **HTML** 432+t+BTW, 491t, 492
layout tags, **HTML** 45
Learn It Online exercises, **HTML** 26, 79, 142, 208, 272, 314, 351, 386, 440, 494, 548, 613
<legend> tag, **HTML** 284, 286, 291t, 306; **APP** 8t
legends, **HTML** 306, 307
restyling, **HTML** 308–310
length units/values, **HTML** 333BTW, 336t; **APP** 27t
let statement, **APP** 58t
<li> tag, **HTML** 40t, 50; **APP** 8t
line breaks, **HTML** 10t
inserting, **HTML** 40t
line-height property, **HTML** 335BTW; **APP** 42t
linear Web site structure, **HTML** 17–18
linebox properties, **APP** 35–36t
lines of text: spacing, **HTML** 335BTW
link element. *See* a selector
link properties (hyperlink properties), **APP** 35t
link separator (|), **HTML** 175
link target symbol (#), **HTML** 96, 135, 599
link targets
creating (setting), **HTML** 135, 136, 144–145, 147–148, 148–150
linking to, **HTML** 135, 137–138, 148, 150
<link /> tag, **HTML** 180, 187, 346; **APP** 8t
linked style sheets. *See* external style sheets
linked text colors. *See* text link colors
linking
to e-mail addresses, **HTML** 96BTW, 97, 105
to external style sheets, **HTML** 180, 181, 187–188, 200, 204, 342, 346–347, 349
to link targets, **HTML** 135, 137–138, 148, 150
to text: on a Web page on another Web site, **HTML** 94–95, 107; on a Web page on the same Web site, **HTML** 93–94, 103–104
to URLs, **HTML** 429–431
linking to Web pages, **HTML** 7–8, 90
on another site, **HTML** 94–95, 107
back to the home page, **HTML** 139–140
on the same page, **HTML** 93BTW, 96, 103, 123–124, 135–138
on the same site: another page, **HTML** 93–94, 103–104, 109; back to the home page, **HTML** 139–140; the same page, **HTML** 93BTW, 96, 103, 123–124, 135–138
linking XML documents to Web pages, **HTML** 596, 597, 603
linking XSL style sheets to XML documents, **HTML** 593–594
links (hyperlinks), **HTML** **7**–8, **38**
adding/using, **HTML** 91–97, 135–140, 147–153, 214–215. *See also* linking ...
back to the home page, **HTML** 18, 19, 19–20, 93, 94, 124–125, 126; adding, **HTML** 139–140
coloring, **HTML** 334
e-mail. *See* e-mail links
event handlers associated with, **HTML** 466+t; **APP** 58–60t
hover styles, **HTML** 114–115, 344
hovering over, **HTML** 91, 337
image. *See* image links
on image maps. *See* hotspots
planning, **HTML** 103, 126, 168
to pop-up captions, **HTML** 543–544, 549+t
properties, **APP** 35t
researching, **HTML** 91BTW
separator (|), **HTML** 175
states, **HTML** 114
styles, **HTML** 114–115, 184
targets. *See* link targets
testing, **HTML** 121–122, 179, 197, 266, 611
text. *See* text links
To top links, **HTML** 124, 126; adding, **HTML** 138
types, **HTML** 88, 103
utilizing, **HTML** 103, 126, 168
Web page elements as, **HTML** 88, 91
See also anchors; linking ...
list properties, **HTML** 113t; **APP** 36t
list styles, **HTML** 49BTW
list-style-type property, **HTML** 51; **APP** 36t
changing, **HTML** 70
lists, **HTML** **38**
bulleted. *See* bulleted lists (unordered lists)
definition lists, **HTML** **52**–53, 81–82
numbered lists (ordered lists), **HTML** 47, **50**
organizational standard, **HTML** 17t, 28t
properties, **HTML** 113t; **APP** 36t
styles, **HTML** 49BTW
types, **HTML** 47, 51
literals, **APP** **54**
Live Movie Maker (Windows), **HTML** 366
loadInfo() function, **HTML** 430–431+t
loan payment calculator, **HTML** 454–455, 468–488
calculating monthly payments, **HTML** 478–481
enhanced version, **HTML** 506
formatting monthly payments as currency, **HTML** 482–487
validating form input data, **HTML** 456, 468–477+BTW
loan years: converting and validating, **HTML** 476+t
local variables (JavaScript), **HTML** **419**
LocaleString() method, **HTML** 420–421+t
locating navigation bars, **HTML** 174BTW
Location object: properties and methods, **APP** 66+t
location property (windows), **HTML** 430+t
logical operators, **APP** 56t
precedence, **APP** 57t
logical style tags, **HTML** **111**+BTW
logos. *See* banner images
logs for Web sites, **HTML** 25
long file names: operating systems supporting, **HTML** 54
loop attribute (<audio> tag), **HTML** 373t, 374; **APP** 4t
loops, **HTML** **484**–486
for loops, **HTML** 484, **485**+t; **APP** 57t
while loops, **HTML** 484, **485**–486+t, 606t, 607; **APP** 58t

M

MAGIX Movie Edit Pro, **HTML** 366
main headings, **HTML** 44, 46
banner images as, **HTML** 100–101
maintaining Web sites, **HTML** 24–25
questions regarding, **HTML** 15t
<map> tag, **HTML** 248, 263, 263+t; **APP** 9t
margin properties, **HTML** 114t, 128–129, 133; **APP** 37t
margins (around borders), **HTML** **343**
<mark> tag, **APP** 9t
marketing Web sites, **HTML** 222, 228, 230
marquee properties, **APP** 37t
Math object, **HTML** 413t, 480BTW
properties and methods, **APP** 65–66+t
mathematical character references, **APP** 50t
maximizing windows, **HTML** 41, 58
maxlength attribute (<input /> tag), **HTML** 287, 296; **APP** 7t
measurement unit properties, **APP** 27t
measurement units/values, **HTML** 333BTW, 336t+BTW; **APP** 27t
Media Player. *See* Windows Media Player
media players, **HTML** **367**
menu bars. *See* navigation bars
menu class, **HTML** 175, 179–180, 181, 185, 186
styles, **HTML** 335
<menu> tag, **APP** 9t
menuicon class, **HTML** 175, 179–180, 181, 185, 186
menupipe class, **HTML** 175, 179–180, 181, 185, 186

menus. *See* drop-down menus; selection menus
messages
alert messages, **HTML** 475, 476t, 488
copyright message, **HTML** 432–433+t, 491+t, 521–522+t
date last modified, **HTML** 17t, 432–433+t, 491–492+t, 521–522+t
See also dynamic text; scrolling messages
meta names (metadata), **HTML** 221, 222, 223–224+t
adding, **HTML** 222, 224, 225
<meta /> tag, **HTML** 39, 40t, 43+t, 220, 223–224; **APP** 9t
<meter> tag, **APP** 9t
method attribute (<form> tag), **HTML** 294; **APP** 6t
methods (of built-in objects) (JavaScript), **HTML 413**–414+t+BTW; **APP** 60–71+t
See also specific methods
MIDI format, **HTML** 368t
Midwest Bridal Expo Web page, **HTML** 410–411, 420–439
milliseconds
calculating the number to a future date, **HTML** 424
converting to days, **HTML** 424–425
minus sign (-): collapse document level sign, **HTML** 584–585
modification dates on Web pages, **HTML** 17t
monitoring Web sites, **HTML** 25
monthly payments
calculating, **HTML** 478–481, 504–505
formatting as currency, **HTML** 482–487
passing values to functions, **HTML** 487
monthlyPmt() function, **HTML** 478, 479
calling, **HTML** 479
creating, **HTML** 480–481
mouse event handlers, **HTML** 466t, 514, 516–517+t, 534+t, 543, 544
mouse pointer hovering over links, **HTML** 91, 337
moveFirst() method, **HTML** 606+t
moveNext() method, **HTML** 606t, 607
Movie Edit Pro (MAGIX), **HTML** 366
moving. *See* positioning Web page elements
MP3 format, **HTML** 368t, 369t
MP4 format, **HTML** 368t, 369t
MPEG format, **HTML** 369t
multicolumn properties, **APP** 37–38t
multimedia, **HTML** 362–392, **364**
HTML5 and, **HTML** 366, 367, 368, 370
planning, **HTML** 364
uses, **HTML** 21–22, 364–365
See also multimedia files
multimedia files
creating, **HTML** 364, 366
embedded files, **HTML** 366
external files, **HTML** 366–367
finding, **HTML** 364, 366+BTW, 392
formats, **HTML** 364, 365, 368–369+t, 392
See also audio clips; video clips
multipage Web sites: planning and designing, **HTML** 159
multiple evaluation operator, **APP** 56t
precedence, **APP** 57t
music lessons survey form, **HTML** 319–320

N

name attribute (<img> tag), **HTML** 512BTW, 525; **APP** 7t
name attribute (<input /> tag), **HTML** 290, 296; **APP** 8t
namespace declarations, **HTML** 572+t; **APP** 76+t
namespaces (XML), **HTML** 570t; **APP 76**
defining, **HTML** 588
See also namespace declarations
naming
classes, **HTML** 127, 179BTW, 181
HTML documents/files, **HTML** 54
text fields, **HTML** 457
user-defined functions, **HTML** 417+t
variables, **HTML** 418–419+t; **APP** 53–54+t
Web page forms, **HTML** 457
Web pages, **HTML** 20, 36
XML tags, **HTML** 566BTW
See also domain names; meta names
naming system (in DOM), **HTML** 508BTW, 510BTW
Nature Center Web page, **HTML** 508, 509, 524–528
<nav> tag, **HTML** 45; **APP** 9t
navigation bars (menu bars)
copying the HTML code to other Web pages, **HTML** 402–404, 524–525, 530, 537–538
creating (adding), **HTML** 261–262; with embedded style sheets, **HTML** 332–341; with tables, **HTML** 174–176+t, 512–513+t
element classes, **HTML** 175, 179–180, 181, 186, 268, 269
with image links, **HTML** 174–176, 186; in image maps, **HTML** 238–239, 277–279
with image rollovers, **HTML** 511–518, 558–559
locating, **HTML** 174BTW
testing, **HTML** 517–518
with text links, **HTML** 261–262
navigation buttons (for displaying XML data), **HTML** 597–598
navigation section/structure, **HTML** 45, 46t
Navigator object: properties and methods, **APP** 66–67+t
navlist class, **HTML** 268, 269
nested if...else statements
inserting commas in dollar values, **HTML** 485–486
validating form input data, **HTML** 469–471, 474
nesting HTML elements, **HTML** 13t; **APP** 1t
Netscape: JavaScript origins, **APP** 51
networks, **HTML 3**
intranets/extranets, **HTML 5**+t+BTW
See also Internet
new command, **HTML** 519t
new operator, **APP** 56t
<noframes> tag, **APP** 9t
nonbreaking space ( ), **HTML** 260
normal text, **HTML 38**
notation declarations in DTDs, **APP 84**+t
Notepad, **HTML** 13, 14, 34
Notepad++, **HTML** 13, 14, 34
activating, **HTML** 60
adding to the Start menu/taskbar, **HTML** 41
closing XML files in, **HTML** 595
enabling word wrap in, **HTML** 42
quitting/closing, **HTML** 78, 142, 208, 271, 314, 351, 439, 493, 612
starting, **HTML** 40–41, 98, 169, 255, 293, 333, 375, 570
null data type (JavaScript), **APP** 53+t
null element (empty set) (“”), **HTML** 520
number bases: radix, **HTML** 471BTW
Number object: properties and methods, **APP** 68–69+t
number styles for numbered lists
changing, **HTML** 51
options, **APP** 36t
number() function, **APP** 72t
numbered lists (ordered lists), **HTML** 47, **50**
See also number styles for numbered lists
numbers (numeric literals), **APP** 54
converting character data to, **HTML** 471+t+BTW, 476t
converting to strings, **HTML** 479, 487
determining whether form input data are, **HTML** 471+t, 472BTW
fixed decimal value, **HTML** 480+t
rounding, **HTML** 424–425
See also calculating ...; dollars and cents (currency)
numeric data types (JavaScript), **HTML 419**; **APP** 53+t
numeric literals. *See* numbers

O

object editors, HTML, **HTML 13**
object element. *See* <object> tag container
object inheritance, **HTML** 413BTW
object instance variables, **HTML** 420+t, 424, **519**
object instances, **HTML** 420+t, 424, **519**
object operators, **APP** 56t
object parameters. *See* <object> tag parameters
<object> element. *See* <object> tag container
<object> tag attributes, **HTML** 370–371+t, 380; **APP** 9t
<object> tag container (<object> tag/element), **HTML** 366, 370–371, 381, 382; **APP** 9t
adding (inserting) audio clips with, **HTML** 370–373
adding (inserting) video clips with, **HTML** 380, 388
<object> tag parameters, **HTML** **372**–373+BTW+t, 380
object-based programming languages, **HTML** 412
object-oriented programming (OOP), **HTML** 412BTW
objects, **HTML** 12, **370**, 508BTW, 510
built-in. *See* built-in objects (JavaScript)
data source object (dso), **HTML 596**
event handlers associated with, **HTML** 466+t; **APP** 58–60t
form objects, **HTML** 459+BTW. *See also* buttons; text fields

image. *See* image objects
positioning with <div>/<span> tags, **HTML** 534BTW
See also Web page elements
observing and learning from users, **HTML** 22–23
observing and learning from Web sites, **HTML** 25
Oceanside Hotel and Sports Club Web site project, **HTML** 156–207, 274–275
Ogg format, **HTML** 368t, 369t
<ol> tag, **HTML** 50; **APP** 9t
on... event handlers. *See* event handlers; *and specific* on... *event handlers below*
onBlur event handler, **HTML** 466t, 468, 475; **APP** 58t
onChange event handler, **HTML** 436, 466t; **APP** 58t
OnChange events: associating user-defined functions with, **HTML** 436
onClick event handler, **HTML** 466+t, 534+t, 603+t; **APP** 59t
one directory level up symbol (..), **HTML** 109
onKeyPress event handler, **HTML** 466t, 603+t; **APP** 59t
online learning exercises. *See* Learn It Online exercises
onLoad event handler, **HTML** 435–436, 466+t, 489, 490, 522, 527, 535; **APP** 59t
onLoad events: associating user-defined functions with, **HTML** 435–436
onMouseDown event handler, **HTML** 466t, 514, 516–517+t; **APP** 60t
onMouseOut event handler, **HTML** 466t, 514, 516–517+t, 534+t, 543, 544; **APP** 60t
onMouseOver event handler, **HTML** 466t, 514, 516–517+t, 534+t, 543, 544; **APP** 60t
onMouseUp event handler, **HTML** 514, 516–517+t; **APP** 60t
OOP (object-oriented programming), **HTML** 412BTW
open() method, **HTML** 489+t, 490, 533
open() method attributes/parameters, **HTML** 489+t; **APP** 68+t
opening HTML documents/files, **HTML** 125, 199, 203, 293, 333, 375, 415, 457–458, 524, 529, 537, 602
opening images in Paint, **HTML** 251
opening XML documents/files, **HTML** 587
operable principle (WCAG), **APP** 20
operands (in if statement conditions), **HTML** 461BTW, 462BTW
operating systems: long file names support, **HTML** 54
operators (JavaScript), **APP** **55**–56+t
comparison operators (conditional operators), **HTML** 462+t+BTW; **APP** 56t
concatenation operator (+), **HTML** 427; **APP** 56t
precedence, **APP** **56**–57+t
<optgroup> tag, **HTML** 302BTW; **APP** 9t
optimizing images, **HTML** 64BTW
optimizing Web sites, **HTML** 224BTW, 228BTW
option buttons. *See* radio buttons
<option> tag, **HTML** 291t, 302BTW, 430; **APP** 10t
<option> tag attributes, **HTML** 292t, 301–302, 430; **APP** 10t
order forms, **HTML** 499–503
order of precedence of operators, **APP** **56**–57+t
ordered lists. *See* numbered lists
organization of files. *See* folder structure
organizational standards for Web pages, **HTML** 17+t, 28t
organizations: Web site uses, **HTML** 16
output area (of a Web page)
defining, **HTML** 604
displaying search results in, **HTML** 606–607+t
<output> tag, **APP** 10t
overButton() function, **HTML** 514, 515t
overusing images, **HTML** 65BTW

P

p selector (paragraph element), **HTML** 127, 184
<p> tag (paragraph tag), **HTML** 40t, 607; **APP** 10t
inserting blank lines, **HTML** 40t, 46
</p> tag, **HTML** 102
padding (around cells), **HTML** 162, 167, **198**, 199
adding, **HTML** 200
padding (around Web page elements), **HTML 343**
padding properties, **APP** 37t
shorthand statements, **HTML** 335–336+t
page box model, **HTML 348**
page length: organizational standard, **HTML** 17t, 28t
@page rule, **HTML 348**+BTW
page selector, **HTML** 348
paged media properties, **APP** 38t
content for paged media properties, **APP** 32t
Paint (program)
opening images in, **HTML** 251
starting, **HTML** 249–250
window elements, **HTML** 250
Paint button (Paint window), **HTML** 250
paint tools/programs, **HTML** 65, 254BTW
image map tools, **HTML** 254+t, 281
See also Paint
Paint window elements, **HTML** 250
paper forms (for user input): converting to Web page forms, **HTML** 321
paragraph element. *See* p selector
paragraphs
boxes surrounding, **HTML** 338–339
entering/adding, **HTML** 9–10, 48+t, 102, 176–177, 259
formatting beginning/middle/end paragraphs, **HTML** 127–128
organizational standard, **HTML** 17t, 28t
separating, **HTML** 46
styles, **HTML** 184, 338–339
See also p selector; <p> tag
<param> tag, **HTML** 370; **APP** 10t
parent elements (in an XML document), **HTML** 574
entering, **HTML** 574t
parsed character data (PCDATA), **APP** 74t, 81t
parseFloat() function, **HTML** 468, 471+t+BTW, 475; **APP** 72t
parseInt() function, **HTML** 468, 471+t+BTW; **APP** 72t
parsers (XML), **HTML** 566+BTW
passing monthly payment values to functions, **HTML** 487
password controls (on forms), **HTML** 287t, **288**
password text boxes (on forms), **HTML** **287**, 288
paths (of files): absolute and relative, **HTML** 107–109
pattern matching: Regular Expressions, **APP** 72+t
PCDATA (parsed character data), **APP** 74t, 81t
perceivable principle (WCAG), **APP** 20
period (.)
class name delimiter, **HTML** 127, 179BTW, 181
method/property name delimiter, **HTML** 413
as not a variable name character, **APP** 53
periods (..): one directory level up symbol, **HTML** 109
Perl, **HTML** 413BTW
personal data islands: creating, **HTML** 624
Personal Mortgage Insurance (PMI), **HTML** 506
personal Web pages: creating, **HTML** 85–86, 86, 451, 560
persons (individuals): Web site uses, **HTML** 6–7, 16
Photoshop (Adobe), **HTML** 254BTW
physical style tags, **HTML** **111**+BTW
pipe symbol (|): link separator, **HTML** 175
coloring, **HTML** 338
placeholders: assigning images to, **HTML** 514+t, 525
placing the insertion point in text fields, **HTML** 472+t
placing Web page elements. *See* positioning Web page elements
planning Web pages, **HTML** 36, 158, 255
browser scroll bar color, **HTML** 428
calculating monthly payments, **HTML** 478
converting frames to ADA standards, **HTML** 396
date last modified, **HTML** 432
dynamic text, **HTML** 414, 417, 420, 426
event handlers, **HTML** 434
findItem() function, **HTML** 605
floating images, **HTML** 529
formatting monthly payments as currency, **HTML** 482
forms: information processing options, **HTML** 292; input controls, **HTML** 295–296
guidelines, **HTML** 36, 90, 158–159, 221–222, 236, 286, 326–327, 363–364, 396, 412, 456, 510
headings, **HTML** 44, 100
image maps, **HTML** 263
image rollover functions, **HTML** 514
images (graphics), **HTML** 63, 64, 100, 126, 168, 243, 249, 529

inserting commas in dollar values, **HTML** 484
JavaScript projects, **HTML** 412, 456
links, **HTML** 103, 126, 168
multimedia, **HTML** 364
navigation bars, **HTML** 331, 511
pop-up captions, **HTML** 537
random image generators, **HTML** 519
slide shows, **HTML** 524
storage media, **HTML** 36, 54+BTW, 159
styles/style sheets, **HTML** 112, 181, 192, 267, 326, 330, 331
tables, **HTML** 165, 168, 199, 203, 595
testing, **HTML** 36, 121+BTW, 159, 327
text formatting, **HTML** 44, 100, 101, 152
video clips, **HTML** 380
visual enhancements, **HTML** 66
XML documents, **HTML** 564, 578, 580, 587; data searches, **HTML** 601
planning Web sites, **HTML** 16, 90, 236, 286, 326, 363
multipage sites, **HTML** 159
questions regarding, **HTML** 15t, 31
testing, **HTML** 364
platform independence of HTML, **HTML 8**
playcount parameter (<object> tag), **HTML** 372t, 380
player control panel
displaying, **HTML** 370, 373
views, **HTML** 370–371+t
plug-ins (add-ons), **HTML 367**–368+BTW
browser support for, **HTML** 381; <audio> element, **HTML** 373, 374; <video> element, **HTML** 382
support tags, **HTML** 370
plus equal signs (+=): concatenates operator, **APP** 56t
plus sign (+)
child definition qualifier, **APP** 75t, 81t
concatenation operator, **HTML** 427; **APP** 56t
expand document level sign, **HTML** 584–585
PMI (Personal Mortgage Insurance), **HTML** 506
PNG (Portable Network Graphics) files, **HTML 64**+t, 65
podcasts, **HTML 364**
pointing hand mouse pointer, **HTML** 91
polygonal map areas, **HTML** 247–248, 263–264
pop-up captions, **HTML 508**
displaying, **HTML** 537–545, 548–549+t, 553–555+t, 557, 559+t
embedded style sheet selectors for, **HTML** 540–543+t, 548–549+t
links to, **HTML** 543–544, 549+t
pop-up images: creating external style sheets for, **HTML** 343–347
pop-up text, **HTML** 358
creating external style sheets for, **HTML** 357–358
See also pop-up captions
pop-up windows, **HTML 488**
displaying, **HTML** 488–491+BTW, 533+t
popupCaption() function, **HTML** 537
calling, **HTML** 543–544
creating, **HTML** 538–540
parameters, **HTML** 540–541
popUpNotice() function, **HTML** 489
calling, **HTML** 490
creating, **HTML** 489–490+t
Portable Network Graphics (PNG) files, **HTML 64**+t, 65
position locator variable. *See* beginPos variable
position property values, **HTML** 337–338+t; **APP** 39t
positioning properties, **APP** 38–40t
position property values, **HTML** 337–338+t; **APP** 39t
positioning Web page elements, **HTML** 337–338, 510
navigation bars, **HTML** 174BTW
objects with <div>/<span> tags, **HTML** 534BTW
text and images with tables, **HTML** 160, 212–213
post method (form information processing), **HTML** 294
pound sign (#)
id selector symbol, **HTML** 540
link target symbol, **HTML** 96, 135, 599
pow() method, **HTML** 480+t
PowerPoint documents: converting into Web pages, **HTML** 13
<pre> tag, **HTML** 111t; **APP** 10t
precedence of operators, **APP 56**–57+t
precedence of styles/style sheets, **HTML** 62+t, 112, 115, 330+t; **APP** 26–27+t
predefined colors, **HTML** 67
predefined entity symbols, **APP** 83+t
preload attribute (<audio> tag), **HTML** 373t, 374; **APP** 4t
Premiere Elements (Adobe), **HTML** 366
primitive data types (JavaScript), **APP** 53+t
print properties, **APP** 40t
printing
CSS files, **HTML** 270
HTML documents/files, **HTML** 77–78, 119, 140, 189, 201, 207, 225, 266–267, 312–313, 379, 385, 404, 439
Web pages, **HTML** 77–78, 123, 141, 190, 195–196, 201, 207, 271, 348BTW, 379, 385; creating external style sheets for, **HTML** 348–349, 355–356
processing instructions (in an XML document), **HTML 568**, 572+t, 573+t; **APP** 74+t, 80
for an XSL stylesheet, **HTML** 593+t
products element (XML), **HTML** 574+t
programming languages, **HTML** 412
See also scripting languages
<progress> tag, **APP** 10t
prolog (of an XML document), **HTML** 568+BTW, 578; **APP 73**, 80
creating, **HTML** 578–579
display in Internet Explorer, **HTML** 583BTW
See also processing instructions
properties (of built-in objects) (JavaScript), **HTML 413**+t; **APP** 60–71+t
innerHTML property, **HTML** 426–427+t
lastModified property, **HTML** 432+t+BTW, 491t, 492
location property (windows), **HTML** 430+t
selectedIndex property, **HTML** 429–430+BTW+t, 431
properties (of Web page elements) (CSS), **HTML 62**–63; **APP** 27–45+t
2D/3D transform properties, **APP** 44t
animation properties, **APP** 28t
background properties, **HTML** 113t; **APP** 28–29t
border properties, **HTML** 113t; **APP** 29–30t
box properties, **APP** 30–31t, 33t
classification properties, **APP** 31t
color. *See* color properties
content for paged media properties, **APP** 32t
dimension properties, **APP** 32t
flexible box properties, **APP** 33t
font properties, **HTML** 110t+BTW, 113t, 334; **APP** 33–34t
generated content properties, **APP** 34t
grid properties, **APP** 35t
hyperlink properties, **APP** 35t
linebox properties, **APP** 35–36t
list properties, **HTML** 113t; **APP** 36t
main property options, **HTML** 113–114t
margin properties, **HTML** 114t, 128, 129; **APP** 37t
marquee properties, **APP** 37t
multicolumn properties, **APP** 37–38t
padding properties, **HTML** 335–336+t; **APP** 37t
paged media properties, **APP** 38t
positioning. *See* positioning properties
print properties, **APP** 40t
ruby properties, **APP** 41t
setting, **HTML** 161
shorthand properties, **HTML** 335–336+BTW+t
speech properties, **APP** 41t
table properties, **HTML** 168t; **APP** 42t
text. *See* text properties
transition properties, **APP** 44t
units of measure properties, **APP** 27t
user-interface properties, **APP** 45t
Web site resource, **APP** 27
See also specific properties
pseudoclasses in style statements, **HTML** 114–**115**, 337+BTW
publicizing Web sites, **HTML** 220–231
publishing (Web pages/sites), **HTML 4**, 24, 227–228; **APP** 47–48+t
puffed up HTML code, **HTML** 14

Q

<q> tag, **APP** 10t
question mark (?): child definition qualifier, **APP** 75t, 81t
question mark colon (?:): conditional operator, **APP** 56t
questionnaires. *See* user surveys
QuickTime format, **HTML** 369t
QuickTime Player, **HTML** 367
parameters, **HTML** 372–373+t, 380
quitting Notepad++ and a browser, **HTML** 78, 142, 208, 271, 314, 351, 439, 493, 547, 612

quotation marks ("")
attribute value delimiters, **HTML** 568BTW
null element (empty set), **HTML** 520
string literal delimiters, **APP** 54
quotation marks (''): attribute value delimiters, **HTML** 568BTW

R

radio buttons (option buttons) (on forms), **HTML** 287, **288**–289+BTW
adding, **HTML** 298–299
disabling/enabling, **HTML** 496–498
radio controls (on forms), **HTML** 287t, **288**
See also radio buttons
radix (number base), **HTML** 471BTW
random images: generating, **HTML** 519–521, 556
random() method, **HTML** 519, 520t, 521
RealAudio format, **HTML** 368t
RealVideo format, **HTML** 369t
recordsets (of XML data), **HTML** **596**
navigation buttons, **HTML** 597–598
searching and displaying results, **HTML** 606–607+t
rectangular map areas, **HTML** 247–248, 252, 263–264
recursion (of functions), **HTML** 464+BTW
recursive function calls, **HTML** 464, 527, 531
refreshing the view in a browser, **HTML** 72
registered trademark symbol ®, **HTML** 260, 261
registering Web sites with search engines, **HTML** 228–229
Regular Expressions, **APP** 72+t
Rehabilitation Act, **APP** 17
See also Section 508
rel attribute (<a> tag), **HTML** 103t; **APP** 3t
relational operators. *See* comparison operators (conditional operators)
relations (collections of data), **HTML** **568**
logical designs. *See* schemas
relative addressing, **HTML** **422**+t
relative paths, **HTML** **109**
relative value (position property), **HTML** 338t
reserved attributes (of XML elements), **APP** 75+t
reserved words (keywords) (JavaScript), **HTML** **419**; **APP** **52**+t
reserved words (keywords) (XML), **APP** 81t
Reset button (on forms), **HTML** 284, 287, **290**, 304
adding, **HTML** 304–305
creating, **HTML** 603–604+t
reset control (on forms), **HTML** 287t, **290**
See also Reset button
resizing images, **HTML** 130BTW, 344
restartFloat() function, **HTML** 532–533+t, 534+t
restaurant questionnaire form, **HTML** 316–317
restyling
bulleted lists, **HTML** 66, 70
footers, **HTML** 66, 71
legends, **HTML** 308–310
result tree, **HTML** **588**
return statement, **APP** 58t
rgb() method, **HTML** 428; **APP** 63
rndImage() function, **HTML** 520–521, 522–523
robust principle (WCAG), **APP** 21
Rock Climbing Fun Web page project, **HTML** 34–78
root element (of an XML document), **HTML** **568**, 569, 572+t, 573+t
display in Internet Explorer, **HTML** 583BTW
root element (of an XSD), **APP** 76+t
root element (stylesheet/transform element) (of an XSL style sheet), **HTML** 588+t+BTW
root location (of a file), **HTML** **107**
rounding numbers, **HTML** 424–425
row color, **HTML** 198, 199
adding, **HTML** 200
row headers (header rows), **HTML** 163
See also table headers
row spanning, **HTML** 165–166, 201–203+BTW, 204–206
rows (in tables), **HTML** **161**, 166
header rows, **HTML** 163. *See also* table headers
rules between, **HTML** 210–211
spanning, **HTML** 165–166, 201–203+BTW, 204–206
rows attribute (<textarea> tag), **HTML** 289; **APP** 12t
rowspan attribute (<th>/<td> tag), **HTML** 167, **201**; **APP** 12t
Roxio Creator, **HTML** 366
<rp> tag, **APP** 10t
<rt> tag, **APP** 10t
ruby properties, **APP** 41t
<ruby> tag, **APP** 10t
rules: in tables, **HTML** 210–211
See also horizontal rules

S

<s> tag, **APP** 10t
<samp> tag, **APP** 10t
Sample Photographs Web page, **HTML** 88, 89, 96, 123–125
See also second Web page
saving CSS files, **HTML** 270
saving HTML files/Web pages, **HTML** 54–57+BTW, 99–100, 117, 140, 170, 176–177, 192, 195, 201, 207, 225, 257, 265, 297, 311, 341, 436–437, 467, 477, 481, 488, 492, 523, 528, 535, 546, 601, 602, 610
saving initial tags, **HTML** 44, 98BTW
saving XML documents, **HTML** 587–588, 594
saving XSD files, **HTML** 577
Scalable Vector Graphics (SVG), **HTML** 624
schedules in tables, **HTML** 216–217, 217
schemas (<schema> element), **HTML** **568**, 572+t, 573+t; **APP** 76+t
definitions. *See* XSDs (XML Schema Definitions)
school bookstore survey form, **HTML** 318–319
schools: Web site uses, **HTML** 6, 16
Screen object: properties, **APP** 69+t
screen readers
alternate text for, **HTML** 64
and frames, **HTML** 394
<script> tag, **HTML** 417–418+t+BTW; **APP** 10t
</script> tag, **HTML** 433–434+t, 465
scripting languages, **HTML** 412, 413BTW; **APP 51**
in the Document Object Model, **HTML** 12, **508**+BTW, 510+BTW
See also JavaScript
scripts, **APP 51**
inserting dates in, **APP** 64–65+t
scroll bar (browsers): changing the color, **HTML** 428–429, 442, 443
scrollColor() function, **HTML** 428–429
scrolling messages, **HTML** **457**+BTW
displaying, **HTML** 457–467, 495–496
scrollingMsg() function, **HTML** 459
calling, **HTML** 466; for continuous display, **HTML** 464
creating, **HTML** 459–463
Search button (on forms): creating, **HTML** 603–604+t
search engine optimization (SEO), **HTML** 224BTW, 228BTW
search engines
optimizing Web sites for, **HTML** 224BTW, 228BTW
registering Web sites with, **HTML** 228–229
Search Items Web page, **HTML** 602–604
searching XML documents and displaying results, **HTML** 601–610, 622–624
seating chart image maps, **HTML** 240
second Web page
creating, **HTML** 151–152, 190–197
editing (improving), **HTML** 123–125
Section 508 (Rehabilitation Act), **APP** 17
guidelines on accessibility, **HTML** 17BTW; **APP** 17, 17–20
<section> tag, **HTML** 45; **APP** 10t
sections (of Web pages), **HTML** 45, 46t
dividing Web pages into, **HTML** 63, 139, 343
JavaScript sections, **HTML** 417–418+t
security of credit card information, **HTML** 299BTW
select controls (on forms), **HTML** 287t, **289**, 299
See also selection menus
select lists (drop-down menus): selectedIndex property, **HTML** 429–430+BTW+t, 431
<select> tag, **HTML** 291t, 302BTW; **APP** 10–11t
<select> tag attributes, **HTML** 292t, 301–302; **APP** 10–11t
selectedIndex property (select lists), **HTML** 429–430+BTW+t, 431
selection boxes (on forms), **HTML** 299
selection menus (drop-down menus on forms), **HTML** 287+t, 289, 299, 300
adding, **HTML** 299–300
advanced menus, **HTML** 301–302
submenus, **HTML** 302BTW
selectors (in style statements), **HTML** **62**, **113**+BTW, 126; **APP** 25
a selector, **HTML** 93, 114, 126, 184

attribute selectors, **HTML** 540BTW
body selector, **HTML** 114
class selectors, **HTML** 540–543+BTW
id selector, **HTML** 525, 534, 540–543+BTW
p selector, **HTML** 127, 184
page selector, **HTML** 348
for pop-up captions, **HTML** 540–543
pseudoclass applied to, **HTML** 114–**115**
See also classes
semantic tags, **HTML** **45**, 63
semicolon (;)
entity symbol end character, **APP** 83+t, 84
statement terminator, **APP** 57t
senior center Web page, **HTML** 276–277
SEO (search engine optimization), **HTML** 224BTW, 228BTW
separating dollars from cents, **HTML** 483–484+t
server-side image maps, **HTML** **242**–243+BTW, 257
servers. *See* Web servers (hosts)
services on the Internet, **HTML** 3
See also validation services
setTimeout() method, **HTML** 464, 527, 529, 531
SGML (Standard Generalized Markup Language), **HTML** 565BTW
shadows. *See* box shadows
shape attribute (<area> tag), **HTML** 263+t; **APP** 3t
shapes: drawing in XML documents, **HTML** 624
Shoreline State Bank Web page, **HTML** 454–493, 506
shorthand properties, **HTML** 335–336+BTW+t
side issues (asides/tangential content), **HTML** **45**, 46t
simple type XML/XSD elements, **HTML** **570**, 571t; **APP** 77+t
simple type XSDs, **APP** **76**, 77–78
size attribute (<input /> tag), **HTML** 287–288, 296, 603+t; **APP** 8t
sketching hotspots, **HTML** 244–245
sketching tables, **HTML** 165, 203
slide show image array, **HTML** 526+t
slide shows, **HTML** **524**
creating, **HTML** 365BTW, 524–528, 555–557, 559, 560
slideShow() function: creating, **HTML** 526–527+t
<small> tag, **HTML** 111t; **APP** 11t
sort element (in XSL style sheets), **HTML** 591+t+BTW
sounds: background, **HTML** 386–387
See also audio clips
source (XML document), **HTML** **588**
source code, **HTML** **76**
See also HTML code
source object, data (dso), **HTML** **596**
<source> elements
in <audio> element, **HTML** 374
in <video> element, **HTML** 380, 382
See also <source> tag
<source> tag, **HTML** 374; **APP** 11t
See also <source> elements
souvenir image maps, **HTML** 240–241
spacing around cells, **HTML** 162
See also border spacing; padding
spacing text, **HTML** 10
lines, **HTML** 335BTW
words, **HTML** 333BTW
See also blank lines; indenting text
<span> tag container (<span> tag), **HTML** 117, 176; **APP** 11t
vs. <div> tag, **HTML** 541BTW
positioning objects with, **HTML** 534BTW
spanning rows/columns in tables, **HTML** 165–166, 201–203+BTW, 204–206
special characters
inserting, **HTML** 260+BTW, 261
references/entities, **HTML** **260**+BTW; **APP** 49–50t
See also symbols; *and specific characters in Symbol section*
special data types (JavaScript), **APP** 53+t
speech properties, **APP** 41t
spellcheck attribute (global), **APP** 2t
split() method, **HTML** 482, 483–484+t
square brackets ([]): subscript delimiters, **HTML** 520
src attribute (<audio> tag), **HTML** 373t, 374; **APP** 4t
src attribute (<img> tag), **HTML** 65+t, 109, 258; **APP** 7t
src attribute (<video> tag), **HTML** 381t, 382; **APP** 13t
Standard Generalized Markup Language (SGML), **HTML** 565BTW
standards
Web page development standards (W3C), **HTML** 10BTW, 11+BTW
Web page organizational standards, **HTML** 10BTW, 11+BTW, 17+t, 28t
XML standards, **HTML** 565+t
See also accessibility guidelines; ADA standards; coding practices
Start menu: adding Notepad++ to, **HTML** 41
start page. *See* home page
start tags, **HTML** 9
closing, **HTML** 9–10+t, 13t, 40; **APP** 1t
starting
browsers, **HTML** 58
the next line of code, **HTML** 43, 205
Notepad++, **HTML** 40–41, 98, 169, 255, 293, 333, 375, 570
Paint, **HTML** 249–250
statement terminator (;), **APP** 57t
statements (JavaScript), **APP** **57**–58+t
See also specific statements
statements (XML), **APP** 74+t
static value (position property), **HTML** 338t
Status bar (Paint window), **HTML** 250
stock market club Web page, **HTML** 505
stopFloat() function, **HTML** 532+t, 534+t
storage media, **HTML** 36, 54+BTW, 159
See also USB flash drives
storing Web pages, **HTML** 36, 54+BTW, 412
stress testing Web sites, **HTML** 24
strict document type, **HTML** **39**
<strike> tag, **APP** 11t
string data types (JavaScript), **HTML** **419**; **APP** 53+t
string literals, **APP** **54**
String object: property and methods, **APP** 71+t
string operators, **APP** 56t
string() function, **APP** 72t
strings
concatenating, **HTML** 427
converting numbers to, **HTML** 479, 487
converting the system date to a string, **HTML** 420–421+t
escape sequences in, **APP** 54+t
length limit, **HTML** 426BTW
stripe class, **HTML** 198, 201
adding, **HTML** 183
<strong> tag container, **HTML** 52–53, 111+t; **APP** 11t
structural elements in HTML, **HTML** 45, 46t
See also footers; headers; sections
structures. *See* folder structure; Web page structures; Web site structures
style attribute (global), **APP** 2t
style sheets (CSS), **HTML** **11**, 62+t, 327, 510BTW; **APP** **25**
creating (adding/using), **HTML** 93, 326, 327–329, 330–349
in the Document Object Model, **HTML** 508+BTW, 510+BTW
one linked vs. a linked XSL style sheet, **HTML** 589
planning (utilizing), **HTML** 90, 112+BTW, 159, 181, 192, 267, 326, 330, 331
precedence, **HTML** 62+t, 112, 115, 330+t; **APP** 26–27+t
project files, **HTML** 330–331+t, 343–344
See also embedded style sheets; external style sheets
style sheets (XSL). *See* XSL style sheets
style statements (CSS), **HTML** **62**–63, 113BTW; **APP** **25**
classes in. *See* classes (of Web page elements)
for embedded style sheets, **HTML** 112–113, 114; **APP** 25–26
for external style sheets, **HTML** 179–180, 184–186; **APP** 25–26
for inline styles, **HTML** 63
pseudoclasses in, **HTML** 114–**115**, 337+BTW
style tags: text formatting tags, **HTML** 110–111+t
See also <style> tag container
<style> tag container, **HTML** 112–113, 114, 159, 335; **APP** 11t, 25, 26
comment codes within, **HTML** 115, 333
styles (for Web page elements) (CSS), **HTML** **11**, **61**, 110, 327; **APP** **25**
for bulleted lists, **HTML** 66, 70, 337–338
font properties, **HTML** 110t+BTW, 113t, 334; **APP** 33–34t
for links, **HTML** 114–115, 184
menu class styles, **HTML** 335
for paragraphs, **HTML** 184, 338–339
planning (utilizing), **HTML** 112+BTW, 159, 181, 192, 267
precedence, **HTML** 62+t, 112, 115, 330+t; **APP** 26–27+t
for tables, **HTML** 162, 167, 185, 186
See also inline styles; style sheets; style statements

stylesheet element (in XSL style sheets), **HTML** 588+t+BTW
<sub> tag, **HTML** 111t; **APP** 11t
subject attribute (e-mail link), **HTML** 106
submenus (of drop-down menus), **HTML** 333–334, 336–337
of selection menus (on forms), **HTML** 302BTW
Submit button (on forms), **HTML** 284, 287, **290**, 304
adding, **HTML** 304–305
submit control (on forms), **HTML** 287t, **290**
See also Submit button
subscript delimiters ([]), **HTML** 520
subscripts (of arrays), **HTML** **519**, 520
substr() method, **HTML** 421–423+t
substring() method, **HTML** 420+t, 422–423+t, 460, 491–492+t
<summary> tag, **APP** 11t
Sun Microsystems: JavaScript origins, **APP** 51
<sup> tag, **HTML** 111t; **APP** 11t
surveys. *See* user surveys
SVG (Scalable Vector Graphics), **HTML** 624
switch statement, **APP** 58t
symbols: predefined entity symbols, **APP** 83+t
See also special characters
system date
converting to a string, **HTML** 420–421+t
extracting, **HTML** 420–423+BTW
Systems Development Life Cycle for Web Development. *See* Web development life cycle

T

tabindex attribute (global), **APP** 2t
table attributes. *See* table tag attributes
table borders, **HTML** **163**
as image borders, **HTML** 167+BTW
table captions, **HTML** **163**, 201, 203
adding, **HTML** 204
styles, **HTML** 185, 186
table element methods, **HTML** 597+t
table elements, **HTML** 161, 162BTW
See also cells; columns; rows
table headers (heading cells), **HTML** **161**, **163**, 166
styles, **HTML** 185, 186
text in, **HTML** 161, 163, 194, 195
table properties, **HTML** 168t; **APP** 42t
border-spacing property, **HTML** 162, 167, 168t; **APP** 42t
table tag attributes, **HTML** 167
See also <table> tag attributes; <td> tag attributes; <th> tag attributes; <tr> tag attributes
table tags, **HTML** 166–167+t
See also <table> tag; <td> tag; <th> tag; <tr> tag
<table> tag, **HTML** 166–167+t, 167, 595, 598–599+t; **APP** 11t
<table> tag attributes, **HTML** 162, 167; **APP** 11t
table-layout property, **HTML** 168t; **APP** 42t
tables, **HTML** **159**–168
attributes. *See* table tag attributes
background colors, **HTML** 161, 203
binding XML elements to, **HTML** 600
borderless. *See* borderless tables
borders, **HTML** **163**, 167+BTW
with borders, **HTML** 193; creating, **HTML** 194–195+t
vs. bulleted lists, **HTML** 164
captions. *See* table captions
centering, **HTML** 186
coding, **HTML** 166–167
creating, **HTML** 164–167; with borders, **HTML** 194–195+t; with multiple images, **HTML** 212–213; with rules, **HTML** 210–211; tutorials online, **HTML** 165BTW
creating navigation bars with, **HTML** 174–176+t, 512–513+t
defining, **HTML** 598–599+t
determining if needed, **HTML** 164
displaying XML data in, **HTML** 595–601, 622–624
editing, **HTML** 209–210
element methods, **HTML** 597+t
elements, **HTML** 161, 162BTW. *See also* cells; columns; rows
features, **HTML** 163
finding, **HTML** 217
formatting, **HTML** 159, 162–163, 167, 168
headers. *See* table headers
planning, **HTML** 165, 168, 199, 203, 595
positioning text and images with, **HTML** 160, 212–213
rules in, **HTML** 210–211
schedules in, **HTML** 216–217, 217
sketching, **HTML** 165, 203
spanning rows/columns, **HTML** 165–166, 201–203+BTW, 204–206
styles, **HTML** 162, 167, 185, 186
tags. *See* table tags
text in, **HTML** 161, 194, 195
uses, **HTML** 160, 161BTW, 327
utilizing, **HTML** 168
width, **HTML** 186
tag attributes. *See* HTML tag attributes
tag sets. *See* containers
tags. *See* HTML tags; XML tags
tangential content (side issues/asides), **HTML** **45**, 46t
taskbar: adding Notepad++ to, **HTML** 41
<tbody> tag, **APP** 11t
<td> tag, **HTML** 166–167+t, 600+t; **APP** 11–12t
<td> tag attributes, **HTML** 162, 167, 201; **APP** 11–12t
teachers: Web site uses, **HTML** 6, 16
technical character references, **APP** 50t
template element (in XSL style sheets), **HTML** 588, 589t+BTW
templates (for XML documents), **HTML** **588**
testing
external style sheets, **HTML** 350
links, **HTML** 121–122, 179, 197, 266, 611
navigation bars, **HTML** 517–518
Web page forms, **HTML** 286
XML documents, **HTML** 583, 584–585, 594
See also testing Web pages; testing Web sites
testing Web pages, **HTML** 24, 90, 141, 190, 236, 266BTW, 271, 311–312, 437–438, 467, 477–478, 481, 488, 492–493, 517–518, 523, 528, 535–536, 546–547, 601, 610
planning, **HTML** 36, 121+BTW, 159, 327, 364
See also validating HTML code/Web pages
testing Web sites, **HTML** 22–24, 58BTW
planning, **HTML** 364
questions regarding, **HTML** 15t
text
aligning, **HTML** 126. *See also* ... wrapping around images, *below*
alternate. *See* alternate text ...
body text, **HTML** 44; font setting, **HTML** 334
bolding. *See* bolding text
controls. *See* text controls
dynamic. *See* dynamic text
elements, **HTML** 38. *See also* footers; headers; headings; lists; paragraphs
emphasis container (<strong> tag), **HTML** 52–53, 111t; **APP** 11t
formatting. *See* formatting text
indenting, **HTML** 10, 51, 173, 176, 205
inline text, **HTML** **540**
linking to: on a Web page on another Web site, **HTML** 94–95, 107; on a Web page on the same Web site, **HTML** 93–94, 103–104
links. *See* text links
pop-up. *See* pop-up text
positioning with tables, **HTML** 160, 212–213
properties. *See* text properties
spacing. *See* spacing text
in tables, **HTML** 161, 194, 195
Web page form use instructions, **HTML** 295
wrapping around images, **HTML** 128–130, 132–133; stopping/clearing, **HTML** 134
See also character data
text boxes. *See* text fields
text controls (on forms), **HTML** **287**–288+t
password controls, **HTML** 287t, **288**
textarea controls, **HTML** 287t, **289**
See also text fields (text boxes)
text editors, **HTML** **13**, 14, 77
HTML editors, **HTML** **13**, 24
Notepad, **HTML** 13, 14, 34
WordPad, **HTML** 40BTW
See also Notepad++
text element (in XSL style sheets), **HTML** 591
text elements (on Web pages), **HTML** 38
See also footers; headers; headings; lists; paragraphs
text fields (text boxes) (on forms), **HTML** **287**–288, 457
adding/creating, **HTML** 296–297, 302–303, 603–604+t; for scrolling messages, **HTML** 458–459+t
assigning form input data values to, **HTML** 472+t
disabling/enabling, **HTML** 496–498
event handlers associated with, **HTML** 466t; **APP** 58–60t

naming, **HTML** 457
password text boxes, **HTML 287**, 288
placing the insertion point in, **HTML** 472+t
See also textarea fields
text files. *See* CSS files
text formatting. *See* formatting text
text formatting tags, **HTML** 110–111+t
text input controls (on forms), **HTML 287**–288+t, 289
See also text fields
text link colors (linked text colors), **HTML** 91, 92, 114, 115
changing, **HTML** 93, 114
text links, **HTML** 38, 91
colors. *See* text link colors
and image maps, **HTML** 237, 238, 261BTW
navigation bars with, **HTML** 261–262
styles, **HTML** 114
To top links, **HTML** 124, 126, 138
to a Web page on another Web site, **HTML** 94–95, 107
to a Web page on the same site, **HTML** 93–94, 103–104
text properties, **HTML** 114t; **APP** 42–44t
line-height property, **HTML** 335BTW; **APP** 42t
word-spacing property, **HTML** 333BTW; **APP** 44t
text wrapping. *See* wrapping text around images
text-decoration property, **HTML** 93, 114, 126, 176, 334; **APP** 43t
textarea controls (on forms), **HTML** 287t, **289**
See also textarea fields
textarea fields (on forms), **HTML 287**, 289+BTW, 290, 303
adding, **HTML** 303–304
event handlers associated with, **HTML** 466t; **APP** 58–60t
<textarea> tag, **HTML** 289, 291t; **APP** 12t
<textarea> tag attributes, **HTML** 292t; **APP** 12t
<tfoot> tag, **APP** 12t
<th> tag, **HTML** 166–167+t, 598–599+t; **APP** 12t
<th> tag attributes, **HTML** 162, 167, 201; **APP** 12t
<thead> tag, **HTML** 598–599+t; **APP** 13t
three-frame structure, **HTML** 400
throw statement, **APP** 58t
thumbnail images, **HTML** 130–131+BTW
<time> tag, **APP** 13t
times: converting (Date object methods), **APP** 61–62t
title attribute (global), **APP** 2t
<title> tag, **HTML** 10t, 39, 40t, 44; **APP** 13t
titles (of Web pages/HTML documents), **HTML** 10t, **37**
organizational standard, **HTML** 17t, 28t
To top links, **HTML** 124, 126
adding, **HTML** 138
toFixed() method, **HTML** 480+t
toLocaleString() method, **HTML** 420–421+t
tools for creating HTML documents, **HTML** 13–14, 24; **APP** 1
Tools group (Paint window), **HTML** 250
toString() method, **HTML** 479, 487
tournament schedule Web page, **HTML** 211–212
<tr> tag, **HTML** 166–167+t, 598–599+t, 600+t; **APP** 13t
<tr> tag attributes, **HTML** 167; **APP** 13t
trademark symbol ™, **HTML** 260
Trails Web page, **HTML** 508, 509, 537–545
transform element (in XSL style sheets), **HTML** 588+t+BTW
transform properties, 2D/3D, **APP** 44t
transition properties, **APP** 44t
transitional document type, **HTML 39**
try...catch statement, **APP** 58t
<tt> tag, **APP** 13t
tutorials online for creating tables, **HTML** 165BTW
two-frame structure, **HTML** 399–400
2D/3D transform properties, **APP** 44t
type attribute (<a> tag), **HTML** 104t
type attribute (<input /> tag), **HTML** 287, 296; **APP** 8t
typeof operator, **APP** 56t

U

<u> tag, **APP** 13t
<ul> tag, **HTML** 40t, 50; **APP** 13t
undefined data type (JavaScript), **APP** 53+t
undefined variables (JavaScript), **HTML** 419BTW; **APP 54**
underlined text (for text links), **HTML** 38, 91, 114
disabling, **HTML** 93, 114
underscore (_): XML tag name character, **HTML** 566BTW
understandable principle (WCAG), **APP** 20
Underwater Tours by Eloise Web site project, **HTML** 88–141
unescape() function, **APP** 72t
Unicode Transformation Format (UTF), **HTML 39**, 223
Uniform Resource Locators (URLs), **HTML 7**
units of measure properties, **APP** 27t
unordered lists. *See* bulleted lists
unparsed entities (XML), **APP** 84
upButton() function, **HTML** 514, 515t
updating Web sites/Web pages, **HTML** 24
uploading HTML files to Web servers. *See* publishing (Web pages/sites)
URL parameter (<object> tag), **HTML** 372t, 373, 380
URLs (Uniform Resource Locators), **HTML 7**
DTD references, **HTML** 39
linking to, **HTML** 429–431
usability, **HTML 22**
usability surveys. *See* user surveys
usability testing, **HTML 22**–24
USB flash drives: saving HTML files to, **HTML** 54, 55–57, 100
usemap attribute (<img> tag), **HTML** 257+t, 258; **APP** 7t
user interfaces
design, **HTML** 18BTW
properties, **APP** 45t
user surveys (questionnaires), **HTML** 23
creating, **HTML** 32
evaluating, **HTML** 27–28
user tasks: identifying, **HTML** 16
user-defined functions (JavaScript), **HTML 414**
calling, **HTML** 414, 435–436; recursive calls, **HTML** 464, 527, 531. *See also under specific functions*
creating/adding, **HTML** 416–417, 440–442
linking to URLs via, **HTML** 430–431+t
naming, **HTML** 417+t
passing monthly payment values to, **HTML** 487
recursion, **HTML** 464+BTW
See also specific functions
user-interface properties, **APP** 45t
users (of Web sites)
identifying, **HTML** 16
identifying tasks, **HTML** 16
observing and learning from, **HTML** 22–23
Web site uses, **HTML** 5–7, 16
See also user interfaces; user surveys
UTF (Unicode Transformation Format), **HTML 39**, 223
UTF-8 character encoding, **HTML** 39, 223

V

vacation Web page, **HTML** 146
validating external style sheets, **HTML** 186BTW, 344BTW
validating form input data, **HTML** 456, 468–477+BTW
with built-in functions, **HTML** 471–472, 475+t
with nested if...else statements, **HTML** 469–471, 474
validating HTML code/Web pages, **HTML** 12, 22, 36, 72–75, 117–118, 140, 188, 190, 195, 201, 207, 225, 265, 311, 341, 384, 404, 439, 493
using Active X controls, **HTML** 377–378
<xml> tag and, **HTML** 596+BTW
validating XML files, **HTML** 585–586
validating XSD files, **HTML** 577–578, 585–586
validation errors, common, **HTML** 118BTW
validation services, **HTML** 72
W3C Markup Validation Service, **HTML** 72, 73, 73–75
validSalesAmt() function, **HTML** 468
calling, **HTML** 468, 475
creating, **HTML** 472–474+t
value attribute (<input /> tag), **HTML** 290; **APP** 8t
value-of element (in XSL style sheets), **HTML** 591+t+BTW
values: measurement units/values, **HTML** 333BTW, 336t+BTW; **APP** 27t
See also attribute values
var statement, **APP** 54, 58t
<var> tag, **APP** 13t
variables (JavaScript), **HTML** 418–419+t; **APP** 53–54
array names, **HTML 519**
beginPos variable, **HTML** 459, 461–463+t

declaring, **HTML** 419+t; **APP** 54
naming, **HTML** 418–419+t; **APP** 53–54+t
object instances, **HTML** 420+t, 424, **519**
undefined, **HTML** 419BTW; **APP 54**
VBScript, **HTML** 413BTW
video clips, **HTML** 362, 363, 365, 382
adding (inserting), **HTML** 380–383, 390–391; with the <object> tag, **HTML** 380, 388; with the <video> tag, **HTML** 380, 381–383
alternate text for, **HTML** 382
vs. audio clips, **HTML** 364
container for. *See* <video> tag container
creating, **HTML** 364, 366
file sizes, **HTML** 380BTW
finding, **HTML** 364, 366+BTW
formats, **HTML** 368, 369+t, 392
software options, **HTML** 366, 392
<video> element. *See* <video> tag container
<video> tag attributes, **HTML** 381–382+t; **APP** 13t
<video> tag container (<video> tag/ element), **HTML** 366, 370, 380, 381, 382; **APP** 13t
adding (inserting) video clips with, **HTML** 380, 381–383
VideoStudio Pro (Corel), **HTML** 366
viewing HTML code, **HTML** 76–77
viewing Web pages, **HTML** 58, 59, 72, 120, 141, 178, 190, 195, 201, 207, 265, 270, 311, 341, 384, 405
using Active X controls, **HTML** 377–378
viewing Web pages with frames, **HTML** 398–399
virtual Web hosting, **HTML** 227
viruses, **HTML** 63
visitors to Web sites
attracting, **HTML** 220–231
feedback from, **HTML** 303BTW
visual enhancements, **HTML** 66, 67–72
See also images (graphics)
visual parameters: classification properties, **APP** 31t

W

W3C (World Wide Web Consortium), **HTML** 4BTW
CSS information, **HTML** 327BTW
HTML document types supported, **HTML** 39
HTML updates, **APP** 2
WCAG guidelines, **APP** 17, 20–21, 21–24t
Web page development standards, **HTML** 10BTW, 11+BTW
W3C Markup Validation Service, **HTML** 72, 73, 73–75
WAI (Web Accessibility Initiative): WCAG guidelines, **APP** 17, 20–21, 21–24t
WAV format, **HTML** 368t
<wbr> tag, **APP** 13t
WCAG guidelines, **APP** 17, 20–21, 21–24t
on scrolling messages, **HTML** 457BTW
the Web (World Wide Web), **HTML** 3–4
accessibility. *See* accessibility guidelines
history resources, **HTML** 4BTW
See also browsers; Web development life cycle; Web development projects; Web pages; Web servers; Web sites
Web Accessibility Initiative (WAI): WCAG guidelines, **APP** 17, 20–21, 21–24t
Web browsers. *See* browsers
Web Content Accessibility Guidelines. *See* WCAG guidelines
Web development life cycle, **HTML 15**–25
phase questions, **HTML** 15+t
See also analyzing Web sites; designing and developing Web sites; implementing Web sites; maintaining Web sites; planning Web sites; testing Web sites
Web development projects
Blu Wav Music Web page form, **HTML** 284–313
Calumet Restaurant Supply Web page, **HTML** 562–563, 565, 567–611
Caroline's Dance Studio Web site, **HTML** 394–395, 397–399
English Literature Class Web site, **HTML** 362–363, 365, 367
guidelines, **HTML** 36, 90, 158–159, 221–222, 236, 286, 326–327, 363–364, 396, 412, 456, 510
Hickory Oaks Forest Preserve Web site, **HTML** 508–509, 511–518, 520–547
Jared Adam's Adventure Travel Web site, **HTML** 324–350, 359
Lake Tahanna Tourism Web site, **HTML** 234–238, 243–248, 251–253, 255–271
Midwest Bridal Expo Web page, **HTML** 410–411, 420–439
Oceanside Hotel and Sports Club Web site, **HTML** 156–207, 274–275
Rock Climbing Fun Web page, **HTML** 34–78
Shoreline State Bank Web page, **HTML** 454–493, 506
Underwater Tours by Eloise Web site, **HTML** 88–141
Web page elements, **HTML** 36, 37–38
box model for, **HTML 343**+BTW
as links, **HTML** 88, 91
organizational standards, **HTML** 17+t, 28t
positioning. *See* positioning Web page elements
properties. *See* properties (of Web page elements)
selections. *See* classes
structural elements, **HTML** 45, 46t. *See also* footers; headers; sections
styles. *See* styles
utilizing, **HTML** 168
See also backgrounds; body; head; images; links; objects; text; titles; *and also* HTML elements
Web page form tags, **HTML** 291+t
attributes, **HTML** 291–292+t
See also <fieldset> tag; <form> tag; <input /> tag; <legend> tag; <option> tag; <select> tag; <textarea> tag
Web page forms (for user input), **HTML** 284
adding: check boxes, **HTML** 297–298; fieldset controls, **HTML** 306–308; radio buttons, **HTML** 298–299; Reset button, **HTML** 304–305; selection menus, **HTML** 299–300; Submit button, **HTML** 304–305; text boxes, **HTML** 296–297, 302–303; textarea boxes, **HTML** 303–304
components, **HTML** 284, 287–292
converting paper forms to, **HTML** 321
correcting, **HTML** 317
cost calculator, **HTML** 499–501
creating, **HTML** 286, 292–305, 315–317, 318–320
credit card payment calculator, **HTML** 504–505
data. *See* form input data
editing (improving), **HTML** 321
event handlers associated with, **HTML** 466t; **APP** 60t
grouping information on, **HTML** 284, 286, 289–290, 296, 306–310+BTW, 320–321
HTML guides on, **HTML** 287BTW
information processing options, **HTML** 292, 293–294+BTW, 322. *See also ...* grouping information on, *above*
input data. *See* form input data
instructions for use, **HTML** 295
for loan payments. *See* loan payment calculator
naming, **HTML** 457
objects, **HTML** 459+BTW. *See also* buttons; text fields
order forms, **HTML** 499–503
organizing, **HTML** 286. *See also ...* grouping information on, *above*
Search Items Web page, **HTML** 602–604
tags. *See* Web page form tags
testing, **HTML** 286
validating. *See* validating form input data
Web page structures
box model, **HTML 343**+BTW
copying, **HTML** 44, 98BTW
defining, **HTML** 39–44+t, 45, 63, 98–99+t, 139, 169–170+t, 255–256+t, 334, 343
Web pages, **HTML 4**, **8**–9
analyzing needs for, **HTML** 36, 90, 158, 236, 286, 326, 363
binding XML documents with, **HTML** 603
coloring. *See* coloring; colors
content. *See* content (information)
converting application documents into, **HTML** 13
copying embedded style sheets into, **HTML** 331
copying HTML code to other pages, **HTML** 191; navigation bar code, **HTML** 402–404, 524–525, 530, 537–538
correcting, **HTML** 82, 146, 211–212, 275–276, 354, 388
creating, **HTML** 8–9, 83–86, 88–153, 159, 236; with embedded style sheets, **HTML** 112–116, 126–128; with external style sheets, **HTML** 179–190; guidelines, **HTML** 36, 90, 158–159, 221–222, 236, 286, 326–327, 363–364, 396, 412, 456, 510; a home page, **HTML** 97–123, 255–267, 279–280; with image maps, **HTML** 276–277, 279–280; with inline styles. *See* inline styles; with links, **HTML** 91–97, 135–140, 147–153, 214–215; overviews, **HTML** 34, 89, 158, 220, 236, 286, 326, 362, 394, 410, 456, 510, 564; for searching XML documents and displaying results, **HTML** 601–610, 622–624; a second Web page, **HTML** 151–152,

190–197; with tables, **HTML** 159–179; using JavaScript, **HTML** 446–452; Web site resource, **HTML** 38BTW. *See also* images; links; styles; tables; Web development life cycle; Web development projects
data elements separate from. *See* data islands
development standards (W3C), **HTML** 10BTW, 11+BTW
displaying XML data on, **HTML** 604, 606–607+t, 615–617
dividing into sections, **HTML** 63, 139, 343
dynamic features. *See* floating images; image rollovers; pop-up captions; pop-up images; pop-up text; pop-up windows; scrolling messages; slide shows
editing (improving), **HTML** 60–72, 80–81, 123–125+BTW. *See also* ... correcting, *above*
elements. *See* Web page elements
formatting, **HTML** 45–46, 158, 327
with frames: converting to ADA standards, **HTML** 394–396, 401–404, 405, 406–407; viewing, **HTML** 398–399; vs. without frames, **HTML** 394
frames on. *See* frames
home. *See* home page (start page)
images. *See* images
interactive pages, **HTML** 12
linking. *See* linking ...
linking XML documents to, **HTML** 596, 597, 603
links. *See* links (hyperlinks)
metadata. *See* meta names
multimedia on. *See* multimedia
naming, **HTML** 20, 36
organizational standards, **HTML** 17+t, 28t
output area. *See* output area
personal Web pages, **HTML** 85–86, 86, 451
planning. *See* planning Web pages
printing, **HTML** 77–78, 123, 141, 190, 195–196, 201, 207, 271, 348BTW, 379, 385; creating external style sheets for, **HTML** 348–349, 355–356
publishing, **HTML 4**, 24, 227–228; **APP** 47–48+t
saving. *See* saving HTML files/Web pages
saving structures, **HTML** 44, 98BTW
second. *See* second Web page
sections, **HTML** 45, 46t; dividing Web pages into, **HTML** 63, 139, 343
start. *See* home page (start page)
storage media, **HTML** 36, 54+BTW, 159
storing, **HTML** 36, 54+BTW, 412
structures. *See* Web page structures
styles. *See* styles
tables. *See* tables
testing. *See* testing Web pages
updating, **HTML** 24
validating. *See* validating HTML code/Web pages
viewing, **HTML** 58, 59, 72, 120, 141, 178, 190, 195, 201, 207, 265, 270, 311, 341, 384, 405; using Active X controls, **HTML** 377–378
See also HTML documents/files; Web sites
Web servers (hosts), **HTML 4**
finding/choosing, **HTML** 227+BTW; **APP** 47
publishing Web pages/sites to, **HTML 4**, 24, 227–228; **APP** 47–48+t
Web site structures, **HTML** 17–21
exercises, **HTML** 26
Web site resources, **HTML** 21BTW
See also Web page structures
Web sites, **HTML 4, 5**
accessibility. *See* accessibility guidelines
analyzing, **HTML** 16; for image map use, **HTML** 280; questions regarding, **HTML** 15t
attracting visitors to, **HTML** 220–231
broad Web sites, **HTML** 19–20
content. *See* content (information)
creating: guidelines, **HTML** 90, 221–222, 236, 510; prototype, **HTML** 153. *See also* ... designing and developing, *below*
deep Web sites, **HTML** 20–21
designing and developing, **HTML** 17–22, 29–31, 90, 159, 218; through observation, **HTML** 25; questions regarding, **HTML** 15t; using logs, **HTML** 25. *See also* Web development life cycle; Web development projects
domain names, **HTML** 222, 226
evaluating, **HTML** 25, 29
folder structure, **HTML** 21, 36, 54, 107; paths, **HTML** 107–109
functionality: defining, **HTML** 16; testing, **HTML** 22, 58BTW
hosts: finding/choosing, **HTML** 227+BTW; **APP** 47
implementing, **HTML** 24; question regarding, **HTML** 15t
logs, **HTML** 25
maintaining, **HTML** 24–25; questions regarding, **HTML** 15t
marketing, **HTML** 222, 228, 230
monitoring, **HTML** 25
multimedia on. *See* multimedia
observing and learning from, **HTML** 25
optimizing, **HTML** 224BTW, 228BTW
planning, **HTML** 16, 90, 236, 286, 326, 363; multipage sites, **HTML** 159; questions regarding, **HTML** 15t, 31
publicizing, **HTML** 220–231
publishing, **HTML 4**, 24, 227–228; **APP** 47–48+t
registering with search engines, **HTML** 228–229
structures. *See* Web site structures
testing, **HTML** 22–24+BTW, 58BTW; questions regarding, **HTML** 15t
types, **HTML** 5+t, 31
updating, **HTML** 24
user interface design, **HTML** 18BTW
uses, **HTML** 5–7, 16
visitor feedback on, **HTML** 303BTW
See also Web pages; *and specific Web sites*
webbed Web site structure, **HTML** 19
WebM format, **HTML** 369t
welcome messages. *See* dynamic text
well-formed XML documents, **HTML** **566**–567, 568BTW; **APP** 73
creating, **HTML** 568–586
"What's New" announcements, **HTML** 24
while statement (while loops), **HTML** 484, **485**–486+t, 606t, 607; **APP** 58t
whitepipe class, **HTML** 338
width attribute (<img> tag), **HTML** 64, 65+t, 258+BTW; **APP** 7t
width attribute (<object> tag), **HTML** 370–371+t, 380; **APP** 9t
width attribute (<video> tag), **HTML** 381t, 382; **APP** 13t
window elements (on Web pages), **HTML** 37
See also backgrounds; body; titles
Window object: properties and methods, **APP** 67–68+t
windows
event handlers associated with, **HTML** 466t; **APP** 58–60t
location property, **HTML** 430+t
maximizing, **HTML** 41, 58
See also window elements
Windows Live Movie Maker, **HTML** 366
Windows Media format, **HTML** 369t
Windows Media Player, **HTML** 367
control panel: displaying, **HTML** 370, 373; views, **HTML** 370–371+t
parameters, **HTML** 372+t
with statement, **APP** 58t
.wmv files, **HTML** 369t, 380
Word documents: converting into Web pages, **HTML** 13
word wrap, **HTML** **42**, 48
enabling in Notepad++, **HTML** 42
word-spacing property, **HTML** 333BTW; **APP** 44t
WordPad, **HTML** 40BTW
words: spacing, **HTML** 333BTW
World Wide Web. *See* the Web
World Wide Web Consortium. *See* W3C
wrapping text around images, **HTML** 128–130, 132–133
stopping/clearing, **HTML** 134
write() method, **HTML** 426
writeln() method, **HTML** 426+BTW
WYSIWYG editors, **HTML** **13**–14+BTW, 24

X

x-axis, **HTML** 246
XHTML (Extensible Hypertext Markup Language), **HTML** 11BTW, **12**, 565BTW; **APP** 1
coding practices, **HTML** 11+BTW, 12, 13t; **APP** 1
XML (Extensible Markup Language), **HTML** **12**, 562, **564**–565; **APP** 1, **73**
comments, **HTML** 578+t; **APP** 74t
and HTML5, **HTML** 565BTW
namespace declarations, **HTML** 572+t; **APP** 76+t
namespaces, **HTML** 570t; **APP** **76**
Quick Reference, **APP** 74–84
reserved words, **APP** 81t
standards, **HTML** 565+t
uses, **HTML** 565, 566t+BTW
XML data
displaying, **HTML** 604, 606–607+t, 615–617; in tables, **HTML** 595–601, 622–624
searching XML documents for and displaying, **HTML** 601–610, 622–624
See also data islands; recordsets
XML declarations, **HTML** **568**, **578**, 579+t; **APP** 74t

- XML documents/files, **APP** 73, 75
  - binding with Web pages, **HTML** 603
  - closing in Notepad++, **HTML** 595
  - correcting, **HTML** 584, 617–619
  - creating, **HTML** 562–563, 564, 565BTW, 568–586, 619–620
  - data in. *See* XML data
  - definitions. *See* DTDs (Document Type Definitions); XSDs (XML Schema Definitions)
  - designing, **HTML** 565
  - displaying in browsers, **HTML** 588, 590–593, 613–614
  - drawing shapes in, **HTML** 624
  - elements. *See* XML elements
  - formatting, **HTML** 565, 587–593, 613–615
  - instance. *See* document instance (in an XML document)
  - linking to Web pages, **HTML** 596, 597, 603
  - linking XSL style sheets to, **HTML** 593–594
  - opening, **HTML** 587
  - planning, **HTML** 564, 578, 580, 587; data searches, **HTML** 601
  - processing instructions. *See* processing instructions
  - prolog. *See* prolog
  - saving, **HTML** 587–588, 594
  - searching and displaying results, **HTML** 601–610, 622–624
  - syntax rules, **HTML** 566+t; **APP** 73t; for elements, **APP** 74t
  - templates, **HTML 588**
  - testing, **HTML** 583, 584–585, 594
  - validating, **HTML** 585–586
  - well-formed, **HTML 566**–567, 568BTW; **APP** 73
- XML elements, **HTML** 566BTW; **APP** 73, 75t
  - attributes, **HTML** 570; **APP** 75+t
  - binding to tables, **HTML** 600
  - cardinality, **HTML 574**
  - child elements, **HTML 569**; defining, **HTML** 575+t; entering, **HTML** 576+t; parent elements and, **HTML** 574
  - complex types, **HTML 570**, 571t, 574, 575; **APP** 79+t; entering, **HTML** 574t, 575t, 576+t
  - data types, **HTML** 571+t; **APP** 78+t
  - defining, **APP** 76+t
  - group elements, **HTML** 575+t, 576; defining, **HTML** 575+t; entering, **HTML** 576+t
  - parent elements, **HTML** 574; entering, **HTML** 574t
  - root element, **HTML 568**, 569, 572+t, 573+t
  - simple types, **HTML 570**, 571t; **APP** 77+t
  - syntax rules, **APP** 74t
  - usage rules, **APP** 75t
  - XSL style sheet elements vs., **HTML** 588
  - *See also* XML tags; XSD elements
- XML parsers, **HTML** 566+BTW
- XML Path Language (XPath), **APP 79**
- XML prefix, **HTML** 566BTW
- XML Schema Definitions. *See* XSDs
- XML tags, **HTML** 565, 570
  - naming, **HTML** 566BTW
  - XSD documentation tags, **HTML** 572+t, 573+t
  - *See also* <element> tag (in XSDs)
- <xml> tag/element, **HTML** 562+BTW, 596+t+BTW
- xmlns attribute (XSDs), **HTML** 572t; **APP** 76+t
- XPath (XML Path Language), **HTML** 587BTW; **APP 79**
- XSD elements, **HTML** 570+t; **APP 76**+t, 77t
  - attributes, **HTML** 570; **APP 76**
  - complex types, **HTML 570**, 571t, 574, 575; **APP** 79+t; entering, **HTML** 574t, 575t, 576+t
  - data types, **HTML** 571+t; **APP** 78+t
  - root element, **APP** 76+t
  - simple types, **HTML 570**, 571t; **APP** 77+t
  - *See also* <element> tag
- XSDs (XML Schema Definitions) (XSD files), **HTML** 568, **570**; **APP 75**–76
  - complex types, **APP 76**, 79
  - creating, **HTML** 570–573
  - documentation tags, **HTML** 572+t, 573+t
  - vs. DTDs, **HTML** 570; **APP** 76
  - elements. *See* XSD elements
  - saving, **HTML** 577
  - simple types, **APP 76**, 77–78
  - validating, **HTML** 577–578, 585–586
- XSL (Extensible Stylesheet Language), **HTML** 562, **565**, 587BTW; **APP 79**
- XSL Formatting Objects, **APP 79**
- XSL style sheet elements
  - for-each element, **HTML** 590–591+t+BTW
  - root (stylesheet/transform) element, **HTML** 588+t+BTW
  - sort element, **HTML** 591+t+BTW
  - stylesheet element, **HTML** 588+t+BTW
  - template element, **HTML** 588, 589t+BTW
  - text element, **HTML** 591
  - transform element, **HTML** 588+t+BTW
  - value-of element, **HTML** 591+t+BTW
  - vs. XML elements, **HTML** 588
- XSL style sheet tags, **HTML** 590–591+t
  - adding, **HTML** 591–592+t
- XSL style sheets, **HTML** 587BTW, 588; **APP** 79–80
  - creating, **HTML** 588–589, 615, 619–620
  - elements. *See* XSL style sheet elements
  - formatting XML documents using, **HTML** 565, 587–593
  - linking to XML documents, **HTML** 593–594
  - more than one linked, **HTML** 589
  - one linked vs. a linked CSS style sheet, **HTML** 589
  - processing instruction, **HTML** 593+t
  - tags. *See* XSL style sheet tags
- XSL stylesheet processing instruction, **HTML** 593+t
- XSLT (XSL Transformations), **HTML** 587BTW; **APP 79**
- XSLT elements, **APP** 79–80t

Y

- y-axis, **HTML** 246
- Yahoo!: registering Web sites with, **HTML** 229
- years for the loan: converting and validating, **HTML** 476+t